KT-409-123

Environmental Law

Environmental Law

Seventh Edition

Stuart Bell

Professor of Law
York Law School, University of York

Donald McGillivray

Senior Lecturer in Law
Kent Law School, University of Kent

OXFORD
UNIVERSITY PRESS

OXFORD
UNIVERSITY PRESS

Great Clarendon Street, Oxford OX2 6DP

Oxford University Press is a department of the University of Oxford.
It furthers the University's objective of excellence in research, scholarship,
and education by publishing worldwide in

Oxford New York

Auckland Cape Town Dar es Salaam Hong Kong Karachi
Kuala Lumpur Madrid Melbourne Mexico City Nairobi
New Delhi Shanghai Taipei Toronto

With offices in

Argentina Austria Brazil Chile Czech Republic France Greece
Guatemala Hungary Italy Japan Poland Portugal Singapore
South Korea Switzerland Thailand Turkey Ukraine Vietnam

Oxford is a registered trade mark of Oxford University Press
in the UK and in certain other countries

Published in the United States
by Oxford University Press Inc., New York

© Stuart Bell and Donald McGillivray 2008

The moral rights of the authors have been asserted

Crown copyright material is reproduced under Class Licence
Number C01P0000148 with the permission of OPSI
and the Queen's Printer for Scotland

Database right Oxford University Press (maker)

All rights reserved. No part of this publication may be reproduced,
stored in a retrieval system, or transmitted, in any form or by any means,
without the prior permission in writing of Oxford University Press,
or as expressly permitted by law, or under terms agreed with the appropriate
reprographics rights organization. Enquiries concerning reproduction
outside the scope of the above should be sent to the Rights Department,
Oxford University Press, at the address above

You must not circulate this book in any other binding or cover
and you must impose the same condition on any acquirer

British Library Cataloguing in Publication Data

Data available

Library of Congress Cataloging in Publication Data

Bell, Stuart, 1965-
    Environmental law / Stuart Bell, Donald McGillivray.—7th ed.
      p. cm.
    Includes index.
    ISBN 978–0–19–921102–9
  1. Environmental law—Great Britain—Cases.   I. McGillivray, Donald,
1967- II. Title.
    KD3372.B45 2008
    344.4104'6—dc22   2008012360

Typeset by Newgen Imaging Systems (P) Ltd, Chennai, India
Printed in Italy by L.E.G.O. S.p.A.

ISBN 978–0–19–921102–9

10 9 8 7 6 5 4

OUTLINE CONTENTS

Part I **Introductory themes** 1

1 What is environmental law? A brief introduction 3
2 History and challenges 17
3 Values, principles, and environmental law 41
4 Sources of environmental law 79
5 The administration of environmental law and policy 98

Part II **Integrated themes** 131

6 International law and environmental protection 133
7 The European Community and the environment 170
8 The regulation of environmental protection 222
9 Environmental crime 253
10 Public participation 293
11 Private law and environmental protection 329

Part III **Sectoral coverage** 371

12 Town and country planning 373
13 Environmental assessment 431
14 Environmental permitting and IPPC 476
15 Climate change and air quality 509
16 Contaminated land 547
17 Water pollution and water quality 579
18 Waste management 630
19 The conservation of nature 680
20 Landscape management 731

DETAILED CONTENTS

PREFACE TO THE SEVENTH EDITION   xvii
TABLE OF CASES   xxiii
TABLE OF STATUTES   xxxv
TABLE OF STATUTORY INSTRUMENTS   xliii
TABLE OF EUROPEAN LEGISLATION   xlix
TABLE OF CONVENTIONS AND AGREEMENTS   lv
LIST OF ABBREVIATIONS   lix

Part I **Introductory themes**   1

1 What is environmental law? A brief introduction   3

Why a book on environmental law?   3
What is 'environmental law'?   4
Some themes of the book   10
Policy and environmental law   11
Rights and environmental law   13
CHAPTER SUMMARY   15
QUESTIONS   15
FURTHER READING   16

2 History and challenges   17

Lessons from the past   17
The legacy of early controls   20
The modern age of environmental law   20
Second-generation environmental policy   29
Environmental law—reflections and future prospects   32
CHAPTER SUMMARY   39
QUESTIONS   40
FURTHER READING   40
WEB LINKS   40

3 Values, principles, and environmental law   41

Introduction   41
Values and environmental law   42
The law and balancing environmental values   47
Law and risk   47
Perspectives on environmental issues   49
Environmental principles   53

The Precautionary Principle 63

Human rights and environmental values 71

CHAPTER SUMMARY 73

QUESTIONS 74

FURTHER READING 75

4 Sources of environmental law 79

International environmental law 79

European Community (EC) law 80

Layers of law 82

National law 84

Environmental laws in practice 92

Case law 94

CHAPTER SUMMARY 96

QUESTIONS 96

FURTHER READING 97

5 The administration of environmental law and policy 98

Introduction 98

Scotland, Northern Ireland, Wales, and the regions 99

The 'British' style of administration—centralization and decentralization 101

Central government 103

Regulatory agencies 112

The Environment Agency 115

Other regulatory agencies 120

Local authorities 121

Non-government organizations (NGOs) 123

The courts 126

CHAPTER SUMMARY 127

QUESTIONS 128

FURTHER READING 128

WEB LINKS 129

Part II **Integrated themes** 131

6 International law and environmental protection 133

Why is international law important for environmental protection? 134

International law and the UK 134

International law and the EC 136

Nation states and global commons 137

Sources of international law—'hard law' 139

Sources of international law—'soft law' 143

International law and policy development 145

Institutional organizations and other actors   149
Dispute settlement and dispute settlement bodies   150
Making agreements more effective   154
International trade and the environment   158
Future directions in international environmental law and policy   164
CHAPTER SUMMARY   166
QUESTIONS   167
FURTHER READING   167
WEB LINKS   169

7 The European Community and the environment   170
Key developments in EC environmental law and policy   171
The EC and UK environmental law and policy   172
An introductory guide to EC law   173
EC environmental law and policy   183
The scope of EC environmental law   188
The range of environmental Directives   192
Environmental law—towards uniformity or flexibility?   194
Compliance by member States with EC law   204
EC environmental law and the UK   213
CHAPTER SUMMARY   218
QUESTIONS   218
FURTHER READING   219
WEB LINKS   221

8 The regulation of environmental protection   222
Introduction   222
Administrative regulation   223
Standards in environmental law   228
Regulatory approaches and tools   237
Market mechanisms, or the use of economic tools   239
The Polluter Pays Principle   244
Self-regulation as a tool for environmental protection   245
The role of criminal and civil law   248
Optimal environmental regulation   249
CHAPTER SUMMARY   249
QUESTIONS   250
FURTHER READING   250
WEB LINKS   252

9 Environmental crime   253
What is 'environmental crime'?   254
The lack of uniformity of environmental crime   258
The moral dimension of environmental crime   258

Strict liability   260
Defences   263
Individual and corporate offenders   264
Enforcement agencies   267
The enforcement of environmental law   272
The 'British' approach to environmental enforcement   275
Sanctions for environmental crime   281
Optimal enforcement   287
CHAPTER SUMMARY   288
QUESTIONS   289
FURTHER READING   290
WEB LINKS   292

10 Public participation   293
Introduction   294
Access to environmental information   296
Public participation in environmental decision making   311
Judicial review   313
The ombudsman   322
Other complaints mechanisms   323
An environmental court   323
CHAPTER SUMMARY   326
QUESTIONS   326
FURTHER READING   327
WEB LINKS   328

11 Private law and environmental protection   329
Private law and environmental liability   329
Human rights law   330
The law of tort and environmental protection   332
Other private law mechanisms   349
Civil law remedies   349
The utility of private law for environmental protection   352
The future of private law as an environmental protection mechanism   356
Private law, public regulation, and 'the public interest'   357
Statutory nuisance   360
The way ahead? Civil liability in statutes, compensation funds, and EC developments   360
CHAPTER SUMMARY   365
QUESTIONS   367
FURTHER READING   367
WEB LINKS   369

Part III Sectoral coverage	371

12 Town and country planning	**373**
The main features of town and country planning	373
Town and country planning as a tool of environmental policy	374
The scope of planning law	375
Town and country planning, and some themes of this book	376
The planning legislation	377
What is 'town and country planning'?	378
The objectives of planning and the environment	382
Planning authorities	384
Forward planning—development plans	385
Development control—the meaning of 'development'	393
Exemption from the need to apply for planning permission	396
'Development' activities for which planning permission is granted by statute	398
Special cases	400
Is planning permission required?	401
Applying for planning permission	401
Determining the planning application	403
Environmental considerations as material considerations	409
Planning conditions	411
Planning obligations and contributions	414
Planning appeals	420
Enforcing planning law	421
Powers in cases in which there is no breach of planning law	425
Planning, the environment, and risk	425
Future developments	426
CHAPTER SUMMARY	427
QUESTIONS	428
FURTHER READING	429
WEB LINKS	430

13 Environmental assessment	**431**
What is 'environmental assessment'?	431
Environmental assessment in international law and practice	433
Environmental impact assessment in the EC	439
Is the project subject to EIA?	441
Exemptions from EIA	455
The environmental statement	456
Determining EIA applications—considering environmental information	461
What if environmental effects have been considered without EIA?	464
EIA and national procedural rules	466

EIA—its impact on decision making   467
The Strategic Environmental Assessment Directive   468
Developing environmental assessment   472
CHAPTER SUMMARY   472
QUESTIONS   473
FURTHER READING   474
WEB LINKS   475

14 Environmental permitting and IPPC   476
Introduction—the development of integrated controls   477
Moves towards administrative integration—the environmental permitting regime 478
The scope of environmental permitting   479
Analysing the environmental permitting regime   496
Applying the environmental permitting requirements in practice—the
    IPPC Directive   497
How integrated is environmental permitting and IPPC?   503
Is IPPC a better way of approaching pollution?   504
CHAPTER SUMMARY   506
QUESTIONS   507
FURTHER READING   507
WEB LINKS   508

15 Climate change and air quality   509
Air and atmospheric pollution   509
International law, and air and atmospheric pollution   516
Climate change   519
Climate change compensation   532
Europe and air pollution policy   532
European law on air quality   533
Domestic air pollution and air quality law and policy   538
CHAPTER SUMMARY   541
QUESTIONS   543
FURTHER READING   543
WEB LINKS   545

16 Contaminated land   547
Introduction   548
Contaminated land and environmental liability   548
Current contamination vs historical contamination   549
What is 'contaminated land'?   554
The regulation of historically contaminated land   554
The statutory definition of contaminated land   555
The identification of contaminated land   558
Special sites   558

Remediation standards 559

The nature of remediation works 561

The duty to serve a remediation notice 561

Remediation notices 562

The allocation of liability—who is liable? 563

Allocation of liability—other stages 568

Registers 574

Contaminated land and the market 574

Part 2A in practice 575

CHAPTER SUMMARY 576

QUESTIONS 576

FURTHER READING 577

WEB LINKS 578

17 Water pollution and water quality 579

Water pollutants and their sources 579

The state of the water environment 581

The regulatory challenges 581

History of the water sector and controls on water quality 583

International law and water quality 586

The EC and water quality 589

Water Framework Directive 593

Water and sewerage financing 596

Drinking water quality 597

Standard setting, water quality, and consents for the discharge of trade or
    sewage effluent 598

Water quality objectives 605

Groundwater pollution 606

Water pollution offences 607

Sampling and enforcement powers 613

Enforcement policy and penalties 614

Access to information 615

Preventative and remedial powers, and diffuse pollution 616

Overlapping controls 621

Water pollution and private law controls 623

CHAPTER SUMMARY 626

QUESTIONS 627

FURTHER READING 627

WEB LINKS 629

18 Waste management 630

The nature and scale of the problem 631

The challenge of regulating waste management 632

The history of domestic waste law and policy 633

International law and waste management 635

European waste management law and policy 637

Domestic waste policy 642

What is 'waste'? 644

Waste authorities 654

Environmental permitting 656

Offences 657

Landfills 662

The duty of care 664

Economic instruments and waste management 667

Waste disposal, and town and country planning 671

Other overlapping controls 672

Civil liability for the unlawful disposal of waste 673

Future directions—integrated product policy 675

CHAPTER SUMMARY 675

QUESTIONS 677

FURTHER READING 677

WEB LINKS 679

19 The conservation of nature 680

Why conserve? 681

The history and development of controls 682

Types of legal protection and the conservation law toolbox 685

The nature conservation agencies 686

General biodiversity duties 688

Habitat conservation—national law 688

Habitat conservation—EC law 704

The protection of individual animals and plants 719

Integrative approaches 726

Future developments 727

CHAPTER SUMMARY 727

QUESTIONS 728

FURTHER READING 729

WEB LINKS 730

20 Landscape management 731

Introduction 731

Regulatory mechanisms 732

The international and EC dimensions 733

Town and country planning 734

Natural England 737

Landscape designations 737

Agriculture, landscape, and nature conservation   745

Agriculture, landscape, and environmental impact assessment   747

Trees, woodland, and hedgerows   748

CHAPTER SUMMARY   760

QUESTIONS   760

FURTHER READING   761

WEB LINKS   761

INDEX   763

Writing a preface for this book has always been a bit of a self-indulgent luxury. We use the opportunity to take a (prolonged) overview of the landscape of environmental law as well as setting out some justifications and explanations of coverage. We preface the preface with the continuing assertion that this book is written primarily to reflect the authors' interests and is not designed as a 'one size fits all' work. We receive all sorts of comments from users and reviewers—most, if not all, are constructive in any criticism. The underlying theme of these comments is, however, that 'you can't please all of the people all of the time'. We hope that the changes to this edition (including the removal of some 'old favourites' to the Online Resource Centre) please more people than they annoy!

Updating a text always seems to take longer, and involve more work, than anticipated. We have, however, drawn some comfort from the fact that the changes made for this edition have not been quite so extensive as for the 6th edition. Having said that, the legislators and the Courts always seem to conspire to make each edition a roller-coaster ride by introducing new material right at the last minute!

There have, of course, been a number of significant developments. In terms of legislation, the Natural Environment and Rural Communities Act 2006 has established Natural England and made a number of changes to the law on nature conservation. The Clean Neighbourhoods and Environment Act 2005 has also made a diverse set of changes to areas like waste management enforcement and to statutory nuisance. A number of areas of law have also been 'Aarhused'. Other legislative developments worth noting here are the Contaminated Land (England) Regulations 2006 and the Transfrontier Shipment of Waste Regulations 2007.

The devolved administrations have also passed a number of key enactments, with Scotland in particular taking a distinctive approach through e.g. the Water Environment (Controlled Activities) (Scotland) Regulations 2005, which introduce a tiered, risk-based approach to regulating harmful activities, and the Planning (Scotland) Act 2006. The former is quite a good example of an instance where a devolved administration is now taking the lead on environmental law reform, whereas (in the case of water pollution legislation at least) it tended historically to lag a little behind England.

There has also been some degree of updating of legislation, especially at the European level, for example with the new Waste Framework Directive and the consolidation of a number of key water quality directives including the Dangerous Substances in Water Directive, Groundwater Directive, and a new Bathing Water Directive.

The desire to simplify legislation, at least for the benefit of industry, has also given us the Environmental Permitting (England and Wales) Regulations 2007, which come into force on 6 April 2008 (it is interesting to reflect on why the start of the tax year is an appropriate date to select for enacting non-tax related environmental legislation). In one sense these Regulations are an attempt at streamlining the permissions process, especially for activities which require e.g. both waste and PPC permits (both are now just the 'environmental permit'). But from a legal point of view they are interesting, and potentially more radical, in other ways. For example, they institute a quite novel approach in the UK to implementing EC environmental law with far less attempt at transposing the provisions of directives and much greater use simply of requiring decision makers to ensure compliance with the terms of directives (we call this a 'conveyor belt' approach to transposition, an approach which recognizes the role that is now played by the European Court of Justice in developing an ever-increasing body of interpretive case law). Furthermore, the Regulations seem to be the opening shot in what is likely to be a wider drive towards national harmonization of more areas of the procedural aspects of environmental laws (determining applications, appeals, enforcement etc), and proposals to extend this common platform in the Permitting Regulations to other areas—such as water discharge consents—can be anticipated (and would underscore further the national view that the approach taken in the common platform of the Permitting Regulations provides a negotiating baseline of best practice for licensing and enforcement). The Regulations were introduced at a very late stage in the editing process. We have tried to accommodate the main changes but inevitably the detailed amendments to existing legislation may have been missed—we apologise for that but would point readers to the shiny new Online Resource Centre for continuing updates.

The courts have also handed down judgment in a number of important environmental law cases. On the scope of IPPC permits (now, environmental permits), for example, the House of Lords has shown just how indeterminative the law can be, for example in relation to whether sewage works needs IPPC permits (*United Utilities Water plc v. Environment Agency* [2007] UKHL 41).

In relation to waste, the ECJ has ruled on the scope of the Waste Framework Directive in relation to waters escaping from sewerage networks (Case C-252/05 *R (Thames Water Utilities Ltd) v. Bromley Magistrates Court* [2008] Env LR 3), while the Court of Appeal has ruled on the meaning of waste in relation to solvent recovery, preferring what it claims is a common sense approach to any failed search for logical consistency with the definition of waste (*OSS Group Ltd v. Environment Agency* [2008] Env LR 8), and on further Waste Framework Directive obligations (*R (Horner) v. Lancashire County Council and Castle Cement* [2007] EWCA Civ 784).

In the field of land use law, the European Court of Justice has reaffirmed its faith in the EIA Directive in its important ruling in relation to staged projects and environmental impact assessment (*R (Barker) v. Bromley LBC* [2007] Env LR 20), and continued its purposive approach to interpretation in the field of nature conservation, e.g. forcing various changes to national law on things like the assessment of development plans for conservation reasons (Case C-6/04 *Commission v UK* [2005] ECR I-9017) and in relation to scrutiny of alternatives to damaging development (Case C-239/04 *Commission v Portugal* [2006] ECR I-10183). Nationally the courts have confirmed the wide scope that is given to the nature conservation agencies to determine that land should be designated as an SSSI (*R. (on the application of) Western Power Distribution Investments Ltd) v. Countryside Council for Wales* [2007] Env LR 25, but have ruled that compensatory habitat need not be established before damaging development begins (*Humber Sea Terminals v. Secretary of State for Transport* [2006] Env LR 4).

In terms of liability law, the House of Lords has made its feeling known about who should pay for certain classes of contaminated land (*R (National Grid Gas plc, formerly Transco plc) v. Environment Agency* [2008] Env LR 4). There have also been notable decisions in relation to the relationship between statutory enforcement mechanisms and the scope for common law and human rights-based claims, which have put some important limits to the *Marcic* ruling (*Dobson v. Thames Water Utilities Ltd* [2007] EWHC 2021 (TCC); *Ministry of Defence v. Thames Water Utilities plc* [2007] Env LR 15). And at the interface of liability and enforcement, the European Court of Human Rights has, incrementally, pushed back the boundaries of the right to life (*Oneryildiz v. Turkey* (2005) 41 EHRR 20) and reaffirmed the role of Article 8 as a means of restraining abuses of domestic pollution laws (*Fadeyeva v. Russia* [2005] ECHR 376).

In a range of further areas the ECJ has made important rulings, often showing a sensitivity to environmental law claims, e.g. on the balance between internal trade and environmental protection (Case C-320/03 *Commission v. Austria* [2006] Env LR 31), the use of the penalty provisions under Article 228 of the EC Treaty (Case C-304/02 *Commission v. France* [2005]

ECR I-6263), the scope of European environmental criminal law (Case C-176/03 *Commission v. Council* [2006] Env LR 18; Case C-440/05 *Commission v. Council, 23 October* 2007) and on the scope for the EC asserting exclusive competence over international law in resolving disputes between member States (Case C-459/03 *Commission v. Ireland* [2006] Env LR 16). But it continues its refusal to deviate from its settled case law on access to justice to challenge Community decisions (Joined Cases T-236/04 and T-241/04 *European Environmental Bureau v. Commission* [2005] ECR II-4945). Last but not least, the World Trade Organisation continues to play an important role in ruling on environmentally-minded restrictions to global trade (e.g. in its *EC/Biotech* decision).

There is, however, a sense of writing during the lull before the storm. There is both a sense of anticipation, and of uncertainty, in key areas—as we write, Bills on Climate Change (setting national reduction targets), Planning Reform (speeding up consent for major infrastructure projects), Regulatory Enforcement and Sanctions (broadening the enforcement toolkit and promoting the use of non-criminal penalties), and Energy (which would allow licensing of carbon capture and storage) are all working their way through Parliament, and are expected onto the statute book in 2008. A Marine Bill merging nature conservation and resource use controls is also being worked on, and may get onto the statute book before the next edition of this work is published. Also expected (indeed, overdue) are regulations to implement the EC Environmental Liability Directive. Too late for much discussion, internationally the Bali Conference in late 2007 signalled a successor to the Kyoto Protocol, and general political agreement on the need for deep cuts in emissions, but no agreement as yet on the details. At European level, an ambitious climate change programme was unveiled in January 2008 which, amongst other things, signalled major revisions to directives on renewables and emissions trading, and a paving of the way for carbon capture and storage. And, of course, there is the Lisbon Treaty, which if ratified will lead to further changes to the scope and nature of EC environmental law.

Any significant developments in these areas will be tracked on our Online Resource Centre (www.oxfordtextbooks.co.uk/orc/bell7e), where we have also put two chapters (on Local Controls and on Discharges to Sewers) that have been removed from the printed text on the grounds that these would likely be of least interest to students. We may not please all teachers with these decisions but nevertheless we acknowledge that they remain important parts of the discipline as a whole. Most other chapters have been reduced in length to some extent.

Finally, we must mention the ever-increasing extent to which climate change is influencing the content of environmental law and therefore of this book. We have tried to expand coverage of the basic legal provisions at international, EC and national level, albeit still within an atmospheric pollution framework. This approach, of course, tends to underplay the magnitude of the topic. However, it is still an instructive way to teach key aspects of the subject from a law and policy point of view—for example, by appreciating how the UN Framework Convention on Climate Change and Kyoto Protocol are, imperfectly, modelled on the Ozone Treaty and Montreal Protocol that went before. Nevertheless, at a time when the 'Bible' of current awareness, the ENDS Report, now seems to cover energy and climate change more than all other topics combined, a consideration of the relationship between climate change law and environmental law is probably overdue.

A Note on Further Reading

Further readings are given at the end of specific chapters. It is worth stressing that we generally exclude anything that doesn't give a fairly up-to-date account of the law, unless it is worth mentioning for a particular historic or policy purpose. Readers wishing to trace back should start by consulting earlier editions of this book.

No study of environmental law would be terribly balanced if it relied only on a single accompanying text. In terms of other books that we think are a helpful complement, J. Holder and M. Lee (2007) *Environmental Protection: Text and Materials*, Cambridge: Cambridge University Press, is a sophisticated text that can be recommended especially for those approaching the subject at an advanced level. B. Richardson and S. Wood (eds) (2006), *Environmental Law for Sustainability*, Oxford: Hart, has a number of excellent extended introductory essays on things like risk, regulation and economic approaches, participation, and international law, which ought to be accessible for undergraduates. And D. Bodansky et al. (eds) (2007) *The Oxford Handbook of International Environmental Law*, Oxford: OUP, is a masterful collection of essays giving up-to-date snapshots on every conceivable topic.

In terms of journals, there is an expansive body of scholarship which, if you are pursuing environmental law in any depth, you will need to access. In the age of online bibliographic searches bringing up hundreds of references on a topic, it helps to have some sense of the strengths of various journals. In terms of journal articles, the UK-based *Journal of Environmental Law* and *Environmental Law Review* are probably the best, with the former tending to catch more of the good regulatory literature and also having a slightly more transnational, comparative, flavour. Both of these are available online, via Westlaw and LexisNexis. Of other journals—and there are many—*Environmental Law and Management* has more of a focus on current developments in the UK and EC but also contains articles (though it seems difficult to access online). Specialist journals on EC and international law, or on specific sectoral topics, are referred to at the end of the appropriate chapter.

The ENDS Report is an essential resource both for keeping up to date, and a highly useful archive that lets you track developments (it has an especially good online facility). It is the premier source of informed comment on environmental developments.

Environmental Law and Your University Education

There is no requirement that students of environmental law should necessarily be committed to 'the environment' any more than students of family law should value 'the family'. However, we hope that the reason that some of you, and your teachers, are using this book is because you are aware of environmental problems and are curious about how the law can be used to respond positively to these. For some environmental law students, this curiosity is systematically sucked out of you until, at the end of the semester or year, you are examined on the definition of waste, on advising the Environment Agency how to respond to a water pollution incident, or on comparing and contrasting command and control regulation with the use of economic tools (we hold our hands up here for including quite a few of these types of questions at the end of chapters). Thankfully, this is not the only way that environmental law can be taught, and there are other ways of learning about environmental law which are probably educationally preferable. For example, it is often said, with some justification, that environmental law is a complex subject, beset by layers of laws and other rules, and that the only way in which it can really be grasped, and appreciated, is through a detailed look at one or two issues or problems. We have some sympathy with this critique, and want to stress here that, by its structure, we don't wish this book to be seen as an endorsement of an approach to the study of environmental law on a 'its week 6 we must be doing air pollution' basis. With the study of environmental law, less is almost certainly more.

A second point is that environmental law should be law for the 'real world'. In this book we stress that this means, in part, that it has to engage with other disciplines, and a range of other non-legal approaches, which rightly have a contribution to make to solving environmental problems. However, there is another sense in which environmental law can be 'real world' law, which is that the study of environmental law can be combined with using the law to address real issues. Around the world, law students, during their degree programmes, are using the law to respond to environmental problems, and learning about the law, and about the scope for law to make a difference. There is in the USA, for example, a long tradition of environmental law clinics, and environmental law students have helped argue many vital, and precedent, cases over the years. There are, to be sure, important differences between US and UK law schools, but there is no reason in principle why learning environmental law by *doing* environmental law should not be undertaken in UK law schools. We hope that this book is as useful to students and teachers pursuing this way of learning about environmental law as it is to those on more traditional modules.

A final point is that, as university students, you are part of powerful institutions which have a major environmental impact—indeed, it is very likely that your university will be one of the largest employers in its county. Increasingly, the university sector is coming under the scope of environmental regulation (for example, emissions trading is likely to cover the university sector in the next few years). Even if not as part of your degree, there may be existing opportunities—or you could make these opportunities—to use your environmental law knowledge to challenge your university to improve its environmental performance, whether this is by pressing your university about its environmental policy (does it have one? how strong is it? could it be strengthened?), looking at an aspect of your university's environmental impact as part of a class project, or through campaigning. If you are seeking inspiration, try M. M'Gonigle and J. Starke (2006) *Planet U: Sustaining the World, Reinventing the University,* New Society Publishers.

Acknowledgements

Producing a new edition is always a difficult task. It has been made much easier with the support of the team at OUP. They have combined the right amount of encouragement, sympathy, patience and practical help which has allowed us to (almost always!) meet deadlines.

Stuart would like to thank the team at Eversheds—Sarah Taylor, John de Belin, Kirsty Gomersal, Louise Howarth, Angela Philip (along with many others) and John Kerr at Acquisition & Environmental who allow me to test the idea that environmental law is best seen as 'law in action'. There are also those at the newly created York Law School who remind me why I wanted to be an academic in the first place. In particular Louise Prendergast offers practical day-to-day support in so many different ways and Laurence Etherington has continued to act as a wise counsel. Finally, I want to take the slightly unusual step of paying tribute to my co-author (I have the benefit of making the final amendments to the text!). He is everything you would want in a co-author. Amongst many admirable characteristics he is loyal, hard-working, knowledgeable, full of insight, utterly dependable and great fun to work with. He is also incredibly self-effacing and humble. I constantly remind myself how very lucky I am to be able to write with him—thank you Don. As with past editions, my portion of this one is dedicated to Philippa, Nicholas, Oliver, Andrew and Thomas—thank you for your continuing love and support.

Don is grateful to Ian Bache, Bill Howarth and Huw Williams for information and advice, and especially to Mike Purdue who, as ever, has willingly kept him up to date, and on course, with developments in planning law. I am enormously fortunate to share my life with Jane, Sam, Gus, Roddy and Ben, and since the last edition also Sasha—this is especially for her, my beautiful daughter, and for her grandparents.

Stuart Bell
Donald McGillivray

TABLE OF CASES

AB v South West Water Services Ltd [1993] QB 507 . . . 352

ARCO Chemie Nederland Ltd v Minister van Volkshuivesting and EPON (Case C-418/97) [2003] Env LR 40 . . . 648, 652

Aannamaersbedrijf PK Kraaijveld BV v Gedeputeerde Staten van Zuid-Holland (C72/95) [1997] All E.R. (EC) 134; [1996] E.C.R. I-5403; [1997] 3 C.M.L.R. 1; [1997] Env. L.R. 265, ECJ . . . 81, 209, 447–50, 466

Adams v Advocate General for Scotland (2002) UKHRR 1189 . . . 317

Alconbury case See R v Secretary of State for the Environment, Transport and the Regions ex parte Holding and Barnes plc

Alderson v Secretary of State for the Environment (1984) 49 P & CR 307 . . . 411

Alford v Secretary of State for the Environment, Food and Rural Affairs; Sub Nom: Department for Environment, Food and Rural Affairs v Alford; Secretary of State for the Environment, Food and Rural Affairs v Alford [2005] EWHC 808 (Admin) . . . 748

Allen v Gulf Oil Refining Ltd [1981] AC 1001 . . . 339, 359, 364, 597

Alphacell Ltd v Woodward [1972] AC 824; [1972] 2 All ER 475 . . . 33, 45, 261, 609–12

Antonetto v Italy (2003) 36 EHRR 10 . . . 424

Arlington Securities Ltd v Secretary of State for the Environment (1989) 57 P & CR 407 . . . 408

Ashcroft v Cambro Waste Products Ltd [1981] 1 WLR 1349 . . . 659

Ashworth v United Kingdom, 20 January 2004, ECHR . . . 353

Associated Provincial Picture Houses v Wednesbury Corp. . . . 116, 458, 504

Associazone Agricoltori della Provincia di Rovigo v Commission (Case C-142/95P) [1996] ECR I-6669 . . . 59

Attorney-General v Cory Bros & Co. [1921] 1 AC 521 . . . 348

Attorney-General v PYA Quarries Ltd [1957] 2 QB 169 . . . 340

Attorney-General's Reference (No. 1 of 1994) [1995] 1 WLR 599 . . . 610

Attorney-General's Reference (No. 5 of 2000) [2002] Env LR 5 . . . 648

Australia v France ICJ Rep (1974) 253 . . . 138

Ballard v Tomlinson (1885) 29 ChD 115 . . . 624–5

Bamford v Turnley (1862) 122 ER 27 . . . 336–7, 363

Barnes v Irwell Valley Water Board [1930] 1 KB 21 . . . 343

Barnet LBC v Eastern Electricity Board [1973] 1 WLR 430 . . . 750

Baxter v Camden (No. 2) [2000] Env LR 112 . . . 333

Beef Hormones See EC Measures Concerning Meat and Meat Products

Begum v Tower Hamlets LBC [2003] UKHL 5 . . . 421, 694

Behring Fur Seals Arbitration (1898) 1 Moore's Int Arbitration Awards 755 . . . 145

Bell v Canterbury City Council [1989] 1 JEL 90 . . . 754–5

Bellew v Cement Ltd [1948] IR 61 . . . 332

Bellway Urban Renewal Southern v Gillespie [2003] Env LR 30 . . . 453–4

Berkeley v Secretary of State for the Environment, Transport and the Regions and Fulham Football Club (No. 1) [2001] Env LR 16 . . . 81, 97, 126, 212, 217, 313, 447, 451, 454, 456–7, 461, 465, 466–8

Berkeley v Secretary of State for the Environment, Transport and the Regions and Fulham Football Club (No. 3) [2002] Env LR 14 . . . 449–51

Bettati v Safety Hi-Tech Srl (Case C-341/95) [1998] ECR I-4355 . . . 67, 189

Blackburn v ARC Ltd [1998] Env LR 469 . . . 359, 623

Blackburn v Attorney-General [1971] 1 WLR 1037 . . . 134

Blackland Park Exploration Ltd v Environment Agency [2004] Env LR 33 . . . 663

Blake & Sons v Secretary of State for the Environment and Colchester BC [1998] Env LR 309 . . . 393

Bliss v Hall (1838) 4 Bing NC 183 . . . 338

Blue Circle Industries v Ministry of Defence [1998] 3 All ER 385; [1999] Env LR 22 . . . 334, 361, 554

Bluhme (Case C-67/97) [1998] ECR I-8033 . . . 201

Bovis Homes Ltd v New Forest DC [2002] EWHC 483 . . . 385

Bowden v South West Water Services Ltd [1999] Env LR 438, CA (reversing in part [1998] Env LR 445) . . . 211, 349, 625

Bown v Secretary of State for Transport [2004] Env LR 26 . . . 217, 706

Bradford MBC v Secretary of State for the Environment (1987) 53 P & CR 55 . . . 412

British Aggregates Association v HM Treasury [2002] CMLR 51 . . . 204

British Airports Authority v Secretary of State for Scotland [1980] JPL 260 . . . 413

British Columbia v Canadian Forest Products Ltd [2004] 2 SCR 74 . . . 367

British Telecommunications plc v Gloucester City Council [2001] EWHC 1001 . . . 447, 451, 453

Bruton v Clarke [1994] Water Law 145 . . . 617, 626

Bryant v Macklin [2005] EWCA Civ 762, CA (Civ Div) . . . 351

Budden and Albery v BP Oil [1980] JPL 586 . . . 359

Bullock v Secretary of State for the Environment (1980) 40 P & CR 246 . . . 751

Bund Naturschutz in Bayern v Freistaat Bayern (Case C-396/92) [1994] ECR I-3717 . . . 443, 714

Burdle v Secretary of State for the Environment [1972] 1 WLR 1207 . . . 395

Burgemeester en welthouders van Haarlemmerliede en Spaarnwoude v Gedeputeerde Staten van Noord-Holland (Case C-81/96) [1998] ECR I-3923 . . . 445

C v Imperial Design [2001] Env LR 33 . . . 674

CPC (UK) v National Rivers Authority [1995] Env LR 131 . . . 262, 610, 613

Cambridge Water Co. v Eastern Counties Leather plc [1994] 2 AC 264 . . . 33, 35, 126, 335, 343, 345–7, 352, 354, 356–7, 360–1, 367, 624

Cameron v Nature Conservancy Council 1991 SLT (Lands Tribunal) 85 . . . 701

Castle Cement v Environment Agency and Lowther [2001] Env LR 45 . . . 648, 650

Cemex UK Cement Ltd v Department for Environment, Food and Rural Affairs [2006] EWHC 3207 (Admin); [2007] Env. L.R. 21, QBD (Admin) . . . 526

Chasemore v Richards (1859) 7 HL Cas 349 . . . 624

Cheshire CC v Secretary of State for the Environment [1995] Env LR 316 . . . 413

Chile/EC (Swordfish) 40 ILM 475 (2001) . . . 136

Circular Facilities (London) Ltd v Sevenoaks DC [2005] EWHC 865 (Admin); [2005] Env. L.R. 35; [2005] J.P.L. 1624, QBD (Admin) . . . 565–6, 569

Clyde & Co. v Secretary of State for the Environment [1977] 1 WLR 926 . . . 407

Coal Contractors v Secretary of State for the Environment [1995] JPL 421 . . . 733

Collis Radio Ltd v Secretary of State for the Environment (1975) 29 P & CR 390 . . . 407

Comitato di Coordinamento per la Difesa della Cava v Regione Lombardia (Case C-236/92) [1994] ECR I-483; [1994] Env LR 281 . . . 209, 643

Commission v Austria (Case C-320/03)[2006] Env LR 31 . . . 203

Commission v Belgium (Case C-2/90) (Walloon Waste) [1992] ECR I-4431 . . . 189, 202–3

Commission v Belgium (Case C-133/94) [1996] ECR I-2323 . . . 448

Commission v Council (Case C-155/91) [1993] ECR I-939 . . . 187

Commission v Council (Case C-281/01) [2002] ECR I-12049 . . . 187

Commission v Council (Case C-94/03) [2006] Env LR 45 . . . 187

Commission v Council (Case C-176/03) [2006] Env LR 18 . . . 187, 205, 256

Commission v Council (Case C-440/05) [2007] . . . 188, 205, 256

Commission v Denmark (Case 302/86) (Danish Bottles) [1988] ECR 4607 . . . 174, 176, 180, 201–3, 219, 243

Commission v Denmark (Case C-246/99) . . . 202

Commission v France (Case C-166/97) [1999] Env LR 781 . . . 705

Commission v France (Case C-96/98) [2000] 2 CMLR 681 . . . 705

Commission v France (Case C-256/98) [2000] ECR I-2487 . . . 450

Commission v France (Case C-374/98) [2000] ECR I-10799 . . . 709

Commission v France (Case C-233/00) [2003] ECR I-6625 . . . 300

Commission v France (Case C-280/02) [2004] ECR I-8573 . . . 608

Commission v France (Case C-304/02) [2005] ENDS Report 367 (French Fishing case) . . . 206–8

Commission v Germany (Case C-131/88) [1991] ECR I-825 . . . 210

Commission v Germany (Case C-57/89) (Leybucht Dykes) [1991] ECR I-883 . . . 709, 714–5, 718

Commission v Germany (Case C-431/92) [1995] ECR I-2189 . . . 446, 465

Commission v Germany (Case C-184/97) [1999] ECR I-7837 . . . 206

Commission v Germany (Case C-71/99) [2001] ECR I-5811 . . . 707

Commission v Hellenic Republic (Case C-387/97) (Chania Waste) [2000] ECR I-3823 . . . 207–8

Commission v Hellenic Republic (Case C-103/00) [2002] ECR I-1147 . . . 722

Commission v Ireland (Case C-392/96) [1999] ECR I-5901 . . . 444

Commission v Ireland (Case C-117/00) [2002] ECR I-5335 . . . 710

Commission v Ireland (Case C-494/01) [2005] Env LR 36 . . . 206

Commission v Ireland (Case C-459/03) [2006] Env LR 16 . . . 154

Commission v Italy (Case 91/79) [1980] ECR 1099 . . . 183, 185

Commission v Italy (Case C-365/97) (San Rocco Valley) [2003] Env LR 1 . . . 179, 208–9

Commission v Italy (Case C-87/02) [2004] ECR I-0000 . . . 464

Commission v Netherlands (Case C-339/87) [1990] ECR I-851 . . . 705

Commission v Netherlands (Case C-3/96) [1999] Env LR 147 . . . 706, 714

Commission v Spain (Case C-92/96) [1998] ECR I-505 (Spanish Bathing Water I) . . . 181

Commission v Spain (Case C-355/90) (Santoña Marshes) [1993] ECR I-4221 . . . 705–6, 709, 714–5

Commission v Spain (Case C-278/01) (Spanish Bathing Water II) . . . 181, 207–8

Commission v United Kingdom (Case C-337/89) (UK Drinking Water I) [1992] ECR I-6103 . . . 178, 205, 215

Commission v United Kingdom (Case C-56/90) (UK Bathing Water I) [1993] ECR I-4109 . . . 178, 216, 591

Commission v United Kingdom (Case C-340/96) (UK Drinking Water II) [1999] ECR I-2023 . . . 215

Commission v United Kingdom (Case C-69/99) [2000] ECR I-10979 . . . 619

Commission v United Kingdom (Case C-434/01) [2003] ECR I-13239 . . . 725

Commission of the European Communities v Ireland (C282/02) [2005] E.C.R. I-4653; [2006] Env. L.R. 21, ECJ (2nd Chamber) . . . 590

Commission of the European Communities v Portugal (C239/04) [2007] Env. L.R. D4; [2006] E.C.R. IA-10183, ECJ . . . 712

Commission of the European Communities v Spain (C416/02) [2005] E.C.R. I-7487, ECJ . . . 646

Commission of the European Communities v Spain (C227/01) [2004] E.C.R. I-8253; [2005] Env. L.R. 20, ECJ . . . 443, 446

Commission of the European Communities v Spain (C221/04) [2006] E.C.R. I-4515; [2006] Env. L.R. D10, ECJ . . . 722

Commission of the European Communities v United Kingdom (C508/03) [2006] Q.B. 764; [2006] 3 W.L.R. 492; [2006] E.C.R. I-3969; [2007] Env. L.R. 1 . . . 446, 457

Commission of the European Communities v United Kingdom (C6/04) [2005] E.C.R. I-9017 . . . 711, 718, 722–3

Concordia Bus Finland (Case C-513/99) [2002] ECR I-7213 . . . 174, 204

Conwy County BC v Lloyd [2003] Env LR 264 . . . 759

Council for National Parks Ltd v Pembrokeshire Coast National Park Authority; Sub Nom: R. (on the application of Council for National Parks Ltd) v Pembrokeshire Coast National Park Authority [2005] EWCA Civ 888 . . . 406

Countryside Residential (North Thames) Ltd v Tugwell, *The Times*, 4 April 2000 . . . 342

Courage Ltd v Crehan (Case C-435/99) [2001] ECR I-6297 . . . 211

Crossley and Sons Ltd v Lightowler (1867) LR 2 Ch App 478 . . . 624

Daniel Davies and Co. v Southwark LBC [1994] JPL 1116 . . . 418

Dartmoor National Park Authority v Secretary of State for Transport, Local Government and the Regions [2003] EWHC 236 . . . 743

Delaware Mansions v Westminster City Council [2001] UKHL 55 . . . 752

Denmark v Commission (Case C-3/00) [2003] ECR I-2643 . . . 196

Dennis v Ministry of Defence [2003] Env LR 34 . . . 332, 334, 336, 338, 340, 350–1, 356–8

Deponiezweckverband Eiterköpfe v Land Rheinland-Pfalz (Case C-6/03) [2005] Env LR 37 . . . 196

Dilieto v Ealing BC [1998] 2 All ER 885 . . . 423

Dobson v Thames Water Utilities Ltd [2007] EWHC 2021 (TCC) . . . 338, 351, 597

Durham CC v Peter O'Connor Industrial Services Ltd [1993] Env LR 197 . . . 263–4, 660

Dyason v Secretary of State for the Environment and Chiltern DC [1998] JPL 778 . . . 421

EC–Measures Affecting Asbestos and Asbestos-Containing Products (2001) 40 ILM 497 . . . 161–3

EC–Measures Concerning Meat and Meat Products (Beef Hormones) WT/DS26/AB/R and WT/DS48/AB/R. 16 January 1998 . . . 142, 161

EC/Sardines (2002) AB-2002–3 . . . 152

EVN AG & Wienstrom GmbH v Austria/
Stadtwerke Klagenfurt AG [2004] 1 CMLR 22
. . . 204

Eastern Counties Leather plc v Eastern Counties
Leather Group Ltd [2003] Env LR 13 . . . 33, 572

Edinburgh City Council v Secretary of State for
Scotland [1998] JPL 224 . . . 405

Elliott v Islington LBC [1991] 1 EGLR 167 . . . 752

Empress Car Co. (Abertillery) Ltd v National
Rivers Authority [1998] Env LR 396 . . . 611–3, 615

Entick v Carrington (1765) 19 St Tr 1029 . . . 341

Envirocor Waste Holdings Ltd Secretary of State
for the Environment, ex parte Humberside CC
and British Cocoa Mills (Hull) Ltd [1996] Env
LR 49 . . . 425–6

Environment Agency v Biffa Waste Services Ltd
[2006] EWHC 1102; [2006] Env. L.R. 47, QBD
(Admin) . . . 612

Environment Agency v Brock plc [1998] Env LR
607 . . . 600, 612

Environment Agency v Melland [2002] Env LR 29
. . . 659

Environment Agency v Newcomb [2003] Env LR
12 . . . 278

Environment Agency v Short [1998] Env LR 300
. . . 660–1

Environment Agency Stanford [1999] Env LR 286
. . . 278

Esso Petroleum v Southport Corp. [1956] AC 218
. . . 341

Euro Tombesi (Case C-304/94) [1998] Env LR 59
. . . 647–8

European Environmental Bureau v Commission
(T-236/04, T-241/04) [2005] ECR II-4945 . . . 182

Express Dairies v Environment Agency [2005]
Env LR 7 . . . 261, 264, 608, 611

Express Ltd (t/a Express Dairies Distribution) v
Environment Agency [2003] Env LR 29 . . . 263,
608, 612

Fairchild v Glenhaven Funeral Services Ltd [2002]
UKHL 22 . . . 343

Fantask (Case C-188/95) [1998] All ER (EC) 1 . . .
212

Farley v Skinner [2001] UKHL 49 . . . 351

Fayrewood Fish Farms v Secretary of State for the
Environment [1984] JPL 267 . . . 394

First Secretary of State v Chichester DC [2004]
EWCA Civ 1248 . . . 408

Fisher v English Nature [2004] EWCA Civ 663;
[2005] Env LR 10, CA; affirming [2004] Env LR 7
. . . 126, 692–5

Fisheries Jurisdiction *See* Spain v Canada

Forestry Commission v Frost (1989) 154 JP 14 . . .
756

Francovich and Boniface v Italy (Case C-6 &
C-9/90) [1991] ECR I-5357 . . . 210–2, 625

Gabčikovo-Nagymaros case ('Danube Dam') 37
ILM (1998) 162, ICJ . . . 137–8, 151–2, 435

Gateshead MBC v Secretary of State for the
Environment [1995] Env LR 37; [1995] JPL 432
. . . 414, 425, 503–4

Gateway Professional Services (Management) Ltd
v Kingston upon Hull City Council [2004] Env
LR 42 . . . 665

Gaunt v Fynney (1872) 8 LR 8 . . . 335

Germany v United States (LaGrand) (2001) ICJ
Rep 516 . . . 154

Gertsen v Municipality of Toronto (1973) 41 DLR
(3d) 646 . . . 674

Gillingham BC v Medway (Chatham) Dock Co.
Ltd [1993] QB 343 . . . 340, 358

Goldfinch (Projects) Ltd v National Assembly for
Wales [2002] EWHC 1275 . . . 407

Goldman v Hargrave [1967] AC 645 . . . 344, 625

Good v Epping Forest DC [1994] JPL 372 . . . 416

Graham and Graham v Re-Chem International
Ltd [1996] Env LR 158 . . . 337, 343

Grampian Regional Council v Aberdeen DC
(1983) 47 P & CR 633 . . . 412

Green v Somerleton [2003] EWCA Civ 198 . . . 345

Griffin v South West Water Services Ltd [1995]
IRLR 15 . . . 210

Guerra v Italy (1998) 26 EHRR 357 . . . 298, 344

Hall & Co. Ltd v Shoreham-by-Sea UDC [1964] 1
WLR 240 . . . 412

Halsey v Esso Petroleum [1961] 2 All ER 145 . . . 356

Hamilton v Papakura DC and Watercare Ltd
[2002] UKPC 57 . . . 598

Harrison v Southwark and Vauxhall Water Co.
[1891] 2 Ch 409 . . . 334

Hartley v Minister of Housing and Local
Government [1970] 1 QB 413 . . . 397

Hatton v United Kingdom (2003) 37 EHRR 28 . . .
331, 335, 339, 353, 359, 408

Henry Boot Homes Ltd v Bassetlaw DC [2002]
EWCA Civ 983 . . . 401

Herbert v Lambeth LBC (1991) 90 LGR 310 . . . 241

Hopkins Developments Ltd v First Secretary of
State; Sub Nom: Hopkins Development Ltd
v First Secretary of State [2006] EWHC 2823
(Admin); [2007] Env. L.R. 14 . . . 414

Housieaux v Delegues du Conseil de la Region de Bruxelles-Capitale [2006] Env LR 2 . . . 300

Humber Sea Terminal Ltd v Secretary of State for Transport; Sub Nom: Humber Sea Terminals v Secretary of State for Transport [2005] EWHC 1289 (Admin); [2006] Env. L.R. 4 . . . 712

Hunter v Canary Wharf Ltd [1997] 2 WLR 684 . . . 35, 337, 347, 351, 356–7, 359–60, 749

IFAW v Commission [2004] ECR II-4135 . . . 299

Impress (Worcester) Ltd v Rees [1971] 2 All ER 357 . . . 611

Inter-Environnement Wallonie v Regione Wallone (Case C-126/96) [1996] Env LR 625 . . . 647, 648

Ireland v UK (MOX case) 41 ILM 405 . . . 66, 137, 153

JB & M Haulage Ltd v London Waste Regulation Authority [1993] Env LR 247 . . . 270

Jan de Nul (UK) Ltd v Axa Royale Belge SA [2002] EWCA Civ 209; affirming [2000] 2 Lloyd's Rep 790 . . . 336, 343, 352

Jégo-Quéré & Cie SA v Commission (Case C-263/02P) [2004] 2 CMLR 12, ECJ, reversing (Case T-177/01) [2002] ECR II-2365, CFI . . . 182–3

Jennings Motors Ltd v Secretary of State for the Environment [1982] QB 541 . . . 397

Jodie Phillips v First Secretary of State [2003] EWHC 2415 . . . 407–8, 425

John Young & Co. v Bankier Distillery Co. [1893] AC 691 . . . 624

Jones v Llanrwst UDC [1911] 1 Ch 393 . . . 341, 625

Kane v New Forest DC (No. 1) [2001] EWCA Civ 878 . . . 409

Kemikalienspektionen v Toolex Alpha AB (Case C-473/98) [2000] ECR I-5681 . . . 203

Kennaway v Thompson [1981] QB 88 . . . 350

Kensington and Chelsea RBC v Secretary of State for the Environment [1981] JPL 50 . . . 395

Kent CC v Batchelor (1976) 33 P & CR 185 . . . 751

Kent CC v Beaney [1993] Env LR 225 . . . 659

Kent CC v Queensborough Rolling Mill Co. Ltd (1990) 89 LGR 306 . . . 647

Kerr v Revelstoke Building Materials Ltd (1976) 71 DLR (3d) 134, Alta SC . . . 341

Khatun v United Kingdom (1 July 1998, unreported) . . . 331, 338, 359

Khorasandjian v Bush [1993] QB 727 . . . 337

Kincardine and Deeside DC v Forestry Commissioners [1993] Env LR 151 . . . 749

Korenburgerveen [2002] Milieu en Recht 3 (Netherlands) . . . 715

LCB v United Kingdom (1999) 27 EHRR 212 . . . 72

LMS International Ltd v Styrene Packaging & Insulation Ltd [2005] EWHC 2065 (TCC); [2006] T.C.L.R. 6, QBD (TCC) . . . 347

Ladbrokes Ltd v Secretary of State for the Environment [1981] JPL 427 . . . 412

Land Oberösterreich and Austria v Commission (Cases C-439/05 and C-454/05P) September 13, 2007, ECJ . . . 196

Landelijke Vereniging tot Behoud van de Waddenzee, Nederlandse Vereniging tot Bescherming van Vogels v Staatssecretaris van Landbouw, Natuurbeheer en Visserij (Case C-127/02) [2004] ECR I-7405 . . . 77, 189, 711

Lappel Bank See R v Secretary of State for the Environment, ex parte RSPB

League Against Cruel Sports v Scott [1985] 2 All ER 489 . . . 341

Leakey v National Trust [1980] QB 485 . . . 344

Leigh Land Reclamation Ltd v Walsall MBC (1991) 155 JP 547 . . . 633, 658

Levy v Environment Agency [2003] Env LR 11 . . . 226, 485

Lippiatt v South Gloucestershire CC [2000] QB 51, CA . . . 337

London Residuary Body v Lambeth LBC [1990] 1 WLR 744 . . . 91

López Ostra v Spain (1995) 20 EHRR 277 . . . 298, 331

Lough v First Secretary of State [2004] EWHC 23 . . . 424

Luxembourg v Linster (Case C-287/98) [2000] ECR I-6917 . . . 209, 455

McDonald v Associated Fuels Ltd [1954] 3 DLR 775 . . . 341

McGinley and Egan v United Kingdom (1999) 27 EHRR 1 . . . 298

McKenna v British Aluminium [2002] Env LR 30 . . . 135, 338, 343

McKinnon Industries v Walker [1951] 3 DLR 577 . . . 335

Maclaine Watson v Department of Trade and Industry [1989] 3 All ER 523 . . . 134

Maidstone BC v Mortimer [1980] 3 All ER 552 . . . 750

Maile v Wigan BC [2001] Env LR 11 . . . 304

Main v Swansea City Council (1984) 49 P & CR 26 . . . 402

Manchester Airport plc v Dutton [2000] QB 133 . . . 342

Marcic v Thames Water Utilities [2004] Env LR 25 . . . 126, 340, 345, 357, 596–7

Marquis of Granby v Bakewell UDC (1923) 87 JP 105 . . . 351

Mass Energy Ltd v Birmingham CC [1994] Env LR 298 . . . 319

Massachusetts v Environmental Protection Agency (2007) 127 S Ct 1438 . . . 511

Mayer Parry Recycling Ltd v Environment Agency [1999] Env LR 489 . . . 647–8

Mayor and Burgesses of Bromley LBC v Susanna [1998] Env LR D13, CA . . . 342

Mecklenburg v Kreis Pinneberg–Der Landrat [1998] ECR I-3809 . . . 299

Merlin v British Nuclear Fuels plc [1990] 2 QB 557 . . . 361

Meyrick Estate Management Ltd v Secretary of State for the Environment, Food and Rural Affairs [2007] EWCA Civ 53; [2007] Env. L.R. 26 . . . 740

Miller-Mead v Minister of Housing and Local Government [1963] 2 QB 196 . . . 423

Ministry of Defence v Thames Water Utilities Ltd; Sub Nom: Thames Water Utilities Ltd v Ministry of Defence [2006] EWCA Civ 1620; [2007] Env. L.R. 15; (2006) 150 S.J.L.B. 1608, CA (Civ Div); reversing [2006] EWHC 66 (TCC); [2006] Env. L.R. 37, QBD (TCC) . . . 596

Mitchell v Secretary of State for the Environment [1994] JPL 916 . . . 411

Molyneaux, ex parte [1986] 1 WLR 331 . . . 134

Monsanto v Tilly [2000] Env LR 313 . . . 342

MOX Plant Case See Ireland v United Kingdom

Murdoch v Glacier Metals Co. Ltd [1998] Env LR 732 . . . 144, 230, 359

National Rivers Authority v Alfred McAlpine Homes East Ltd [1994] 4 All ER 286; [1994] Env LR 198 . . . 45, 265, 613

National Rivers Authority v Biffa Waste [1996] Env LR 227 . . . 600

National Rivers Authority v Welsh Development Agency [1993] Env LR 407 . . . 610–1

National Rivers Authority v Wright Engineering Co. Ltd [1994] 4 All ER 281 . . . 611–2

National Rivers Authority v Yorkshire Water Services Ltd [1995] 1 AC 444 . . . 601, 609–10

Nederhoff v Dijkgraaf en Hoogheemraden van het Hoogheemraadschap Rijnland (C232/97) [1999] E.C.R. I-6385 . . . 599

Network Rail Infrastructure Ltd v CJ Morris (t/a Soundstar Studio) [2004] Env LR 41 . . . 335

New Zealand v France ICJ Rep (1974) 457 . . . 138

New Zealand v France (Nuclear Tests II) [1995] ICJ Rep 288 . . . 65, 143, 435

New Zealand v Japan; Australia v. Japan (2001) ILR 148 (the Southern Bluefish Tuna cases) . . . 66

Newbury DC v Secretary of State for the Environment [1981] AC 578 . . . 411, 413

Newport BC v Secretary of State for Wales and Browning Ferris Ltd [1998] Env LR 174 . . . 425

Newsum v Welsh Assembly [2005] Env LR 16, CA; [2004] EWHC 50 . . . 709, 724

Nicholls v Ely Beet Sugar Factory Ltd [1936] Ch 343 . . . 624

North Uist Fisheries Ltd v Secretary of State for Scotland 1992 SLT 333 . . . 697

Northavon DC v Secretary of State for the Environment (1980) 40 P & CR 332 . . . 395

OSS Group Ltd v Environment Agency [2008] Env LR 8 . . . 650–1

Oerlemans v Netherlands (1993) 15 EHRR 561 . . . 385, 694

Oneryildiz v Turkey (2005) 41 EHRR 20; 18 B.H.R.C. 145 . . . 298, 330, 344

Outokumpu (Case C-213/96) [1998] ECR I-1777 . . . 204

Overseas Tankship (UK) Ltd v Miller Steamship Co. (The Wagon Mound) (No. 2) [1967] 1 AC 617 . . . 340

Palin Granit Oy v Vehmassaion kansanterveystyon kuntayhtyman hallitus (Case C-9/00) [2002] Env LR 35 . . . 648–50

Parkwood Landfill v Customs & Excise Commissioners [2003] Env LR 19 . . . 668

People of the State of California (ex rel Lockyer) v. General Motors Corporation and ors No. C06–05755 (ND Cal 20 Sept, 2006) . . . 532

Pergau Dam Case See R v Secretary of State for Foreign and Commonwealth Affairs, ex parte World Development Movement Ltd

Perrin v Northampton BC [2006] EWHC 2331 (TCC); [2007] 1 All E.R. 929; [2006] B.L.R. 504; [2007] Env. L.R. 12 . . . 752

Pfizer Animal Health SA v Commission (Case T-13/99) [2002] ECR II-3305 . . . 67–8, 70, 180, 189

Phipps v Pears [1965] 1 QB 76 . . . 424

Pioneer Aggregates (UK) Ltd v Secretary of State for the Environment [1985] AC 132; [1984] 3 WLR 32 . . . 377, 397

Powell and Rayner v United Kingdom (1990) 12 EHRR 355 . . . 330–1

PreussenElektra AG v Schleswag AG (Case C-379/98) [2001] ECR I-2159 . . . 189, 203

Price v Cromack [1975] 1 WLR 988 . . . 610, 612

Pride of Derby and Derbyshire Angling Association Ltd v British Celanese [1953] Ch 149 . . . 351, 626

Procureur de la République v Association de Défense des Brûleurs d'Huiles Usagées (Case 240/83) [1985] ECR 531 . . . 185

Pye Ltd v West Oxfordshire DC [1982] JPL 577 . . . 407

Queensland v Commonwealth (1989) 167 CLR 232 . . . 733

R v Anglian Water Services Ltd [2004] Env LR 10 . . . 45, 271, 284–5, 615

R v Birmingham City Council, ex parte Ferrero Ltd [1993] 1 All ER 530 . . . 420

R v Bolton MBC, ex parte Kirkman [1998] Env LR 719 . . . 414, 643–4

R v British Coal Corp., ex parte Ibstock Building Products Ltd [1995] Env LR 277 . . . 304

R v Carrick DC, ex parte Shelley [1996] Env LR 273 . . . 561

R. v Cemex Cement Ltd [2007] EWCA Crim 1759; (2007) 151 S.J.L.B. 985; [2007] N.P.C. 100; [2008] Env. L.R. 6, CA (Crim Div) . . . 285, 615

R v Ceredigion CC, ex parte McKeown (1998) 2 PLR 1 . . . 318

R v City of London Corp., ex parte Allan (1980) 79 LGR 223 . . . 408

R v Cornwall CC, ex parte Hardy [2001] Env LR 25 . . . 453, 462–3

R v Croydon Justices, ex parte Dean [1993] QB 769 . . . 278

R v Daventry DC, ex parte Thornby Farms Ltd; R (on the application of Murray) v Derbyshire CC [2002] Env LR 28 . . . 410, 499, 500, 644

R v Department of Trade and Industry, ex parte Greenpeace [2000] Env LR 221 . . . 125, 319

R v Derbyshire CC, ex parte Murray [2001] Env LR 26 . . . 69

R v Derbyshire CC, ex parte Woods [1998] Env LR 277 . . . 407

R v DPP, ex parte C (1995) 1 Cr App 136 . . . 280

R v Dovermoss Ltd [1995] Env LR 258 . . . 600, 607

R v Durham CC, Sherburn Stone Co. Ltd & Secretary of State for the Environment, Transport and the Regions, ex parte Huddleston [2000] JPL 409 . . . 210

R v Environment Agency, ex parte Gibson [1999] Env LR 73 . . . 396

R v Environment Agency, ex parte Petrus Oils Ltd [1999] Env LR 732 . . . 320, 420, 494

R v Environment Agency, ex parte Sellars and Petty [1999] Env LR 73 . . . 644

R v Ettrick Trout Co. Ltd [1994] Env LR 165 . . . 320

R v Exeter City Council, ex parte JL Thomas and Co. Ltd [1991] 1 QB 471 . . . 358, 409

R v Falmouth and Truro Port HA, ex parte South West Water Ltd [2000] Env LR 658; [2000] NPC 36 . . . 320, 622

R v Garrett [1998] Env LR D2 . . . 283

R v Greenwich LBC [1996] 255 ENDS Rep 49 . . . 195

R v Hammersmith and Fulham LBC, ex parte Burkett See R (on the application of Burkett) v Hammersmith and Fulham LBC

R v Hertfordshire CC, ex parte Green Environmental Industries Ltd [2000] 2 WLR 373; [2000] 1 All ER 773 . . . 270, 614

R v Hillingdon LBC, ex parte Royco Homes Ltd [1974] 2 QB 720 . . . 411

R. v Inland Revenue Commissioners Ex p. National Federation of Self Employed and Small Businesses Ltd; Sub Nom: Inland Revenue Commissioners v National Federation of Self Employed and Small Businesses Ltd [1982] A.C. 617; [1981] 2 W.L.R. 722; [1981] 2 All E.R. 93; [1981] S.T.C. 260; 55 T.C. 133; (1981) 125 S.J. 325, HL . . . 314

R v Inspectorate of Pollution, ex parte Greenpeace Ltd (No. 2) [1994] 4 All ER 329 . . . 316

R v Jenner [1983] 1 WLR 873 . . . 423

R v Justices of Antrim (1906) 2 IR 298 . . . 608

R v Legal Area No. 8 (Northern), ex parte Sendall [1993] Env LR 167 . . . 320

R v Leicester CC, Hepworth Building Products Ltd and Onyx (UK) Ltd, ex parte Blackfordby and Boothcorpe Action Group Ltd [2001] Env LR 2 . . . 644

R v Leighton and Town and Country Refuse Collections Ltd [1997] Env LR 411 . . . 658

R v Leominster DC, ex parte Pothecary [1998] JPL 335 . . . 406

R v London Boroughs Transport Committee, ex parte Freight Transport Association Ltd [1991] 1 WLR 828 . . . 195

R v Mayor of London, ex parte Westminster City Council [2002] EWHC 2440 . . . 317

R v Metropolitan Police Commissioner, ex parte Blackburn (No. 3) [1973] 1 QB 241 . . . 280

R v Metropolitan Stipendiary Magistrate, ex parte London Waste Regulation Authority [1993] All ER 113 . . . 658

R v National Rivers Authority, ex parte Moreton [1996] Env LR 234 . . . 91, 92

R v Nature Conservancy Council, ex parte Bolton MBC [1995] Env LR 237 . . . 693

R v Nature Conservancy Council, ex parte London Brick Co. Ltd [1996] Env LR 1 . . . 692–3, 697

R v North Somerset DC, ex parte Garnett [1998] Env LR 91 . . . 317

R v North West Leicestershire DC, ex parte Moses [2000] JPL 733 . . . 315

R v North West Leicestershire DC and East Midlands International Airport Ltd, ex parte Moses (No. 2) [2000] Env LR 443 . . . 466

R v North Yorkshire CC, ex parte Brown [1998] Env LR 623 . . . 81, 440, 445

R v O'Brien and Enkel (2000) Env LR 156 . . . 283

R. v Parole Board Ex p. Watson [1996] 1 W.L.R. 906 . . . 486

R v Plymouth City Council, ex parte Plymouth and South Devon Co-operative Society Ltd (1993) 67 P & CR 78 . . . 417–8

R v Poole BC, ex parte Beebee [1991] JPL 643 . . . 313, 464, 699

R. v Rimmington; R. v Goldstein [2005] UKHL 63 . . . 341

R v Rochdale MBC, ex parte Milne [2001] Env LR 22 ('Tew II') . . . 451

R v St Edmundsbury BC, ex parte Walton [1999] JPL 805 . . . 451, 454

R v Secretary of State for the Environment, ex parte Friends of the Earth [1995] Env LR 11 . . . 215

R v Secretary of State for the Environment, ex parte Greenpeace Ltd [1994] Env LR 401 . . . 320, 445

R v Secretary of State for the Environment, ex parte Kingston upon Hull City Council [1996] Env LR 248 . . . 91–2, 217, 592

R v Secretary of State for the Environment, ex parte Rose Theatre Trust [1990] 1 All ER 754 . . . 316

R v Secretary of State for the Environment, ex parte RSPB (Case C-44/95) [1997] QB 206, ECJ . . . 59, 92, 705–6

R v Secretary of State for the Environment, ex parte RSPB [1997] Env LR 431, HL; [1997] JEL 168, CA . . . 176

R v Secretary of State for the Environment, ex parte West Wiltshire DC [1996] Env LR 312 . . . 414

R v Secretary of State for the Environment and Havering BC, ex parte PF Ahern (London) Ltd [1998] Env LR 189 . . . 397

R v Secretary of State for the Environment and Minister of Agriculture, Fisheries and Food, ex parte Standley and Metson (Case C-293/97) [1999] ECR I-2603; [1999] Env LR 801 . . . 183, 189, 200, 244, 619–20

R v Secretary of State for the Environment and Minister of Agriculture, Fisheries and Food, ex parte Watson [1999] Env LR 310 . . . 335

R v Secretary of State for the Environment and RJ Compton and Sons, ex parte West Wiltshire DC [1996] Env LR 312 . . . 487, 500

R v Secretary of State for the Environment, Transport and the Regions, ex parte Alliance against Birmingham Northern Relief Road (No. 1) [1999] Env LR 447 . . . 304

R v Secretary of State for the Environment, Transport and the Regions, ex parte First Corporate Shipping Ltd (Case C-371/98) [2001] ECR I-9235 . . . 59, 707, 709

R v Secretary of State for the Environment, Transport and the Regions, ex parte Holding and Barnes plc [2001] UKHL 23 ('Alconbury') . . . 380, 404

R v Secretary of State for the Environment, Transport and the Regions and Parcelforce, ex parte Marson [1998] JPL 869 . . . 463

R v Secretary of State for Foreign and Commonwealth Affairs, ex parte World Development Movement Ltd (Pergau Dam) [1995] 1 WLR 386; [1995] 1 All ER 611 . . . 316–7, 439

R v Secretary of State for the Home Department, ex parte Brind [1991] 1 AC 696 . . . 135

R v Secretary of State for Trade and Industry, ex parte Duddridge [1995] Env LR 151 . . . 69, 189, 214, 320

R v Secretary of State for Trade and Industry, ex parte Greenpeace (No. 1) [1998] Env LR 413 . . . 319

R v Secretary of State for Trade and Industry, ex parte Greenpeace (No. 2) [2000] Env LR 221 . . . 135, 217, 708

R v Secretary of State for Transport, ex parte Richmond upon Thames LBC (No. 1) [1994] 1 WLR 74 . . . 331

R v Secretary of State for Transport, ex parte Richmond upon Thames LBC (No. 2) [1995] 7 ELM 52 . . . 331

R v Secretary of State for Transport, ex parte Richmond upon Thames LBC (No. 3) [1995] 7 ELM 127 . . . 331

R v Secretary of State for Transport, ex parte Richmond upon Thames LBC (No. 4) [1996] 8 ELM 77 . . . 331

R v Secretary of State for Transport, ex parte Surrey CC, 1993, unreported November 1993 . . . 443

R v Sefton MBC, ex parte British Association of Shooting and Conservation Ltd [2001] Env LR 10 . . . 43

R v Sheffield City Council, ex parte Mansfield (1978) 37 P & CR 1 . . . 420

R. v Sissen [2001] 1 W.L.R. 902 . . . 283

R v Somerset CC, ex parte Dixon [1998] Env LR 111 . . . 317

R v Somerset CC, ex parte Fewings [1995] 1 WLR 1037 . . . 43

R v South Northamptonshire DC, ex parte Crest Homes plc [1995] JPL 200 . . . 418

R v South West Water Authority [1991] LMELR 65 . . . 598, 625

R v Swale BC, ex parte RSPB [1991] 1 PLR 6 . . . 81, 318, 443, 447, 450

R v Tandridge DC, ex parte Al Fayed [2000] Env LR D23, CA; [1999] 1 PLR 104 . . . 426

R v Warwickshire CC, ex parte Powergen plc [1997] JPL 843 . . . 415

R v Waveney DC, ex parte Bell [2001] Env LR 24 . . . 467

R v Westminster City Council, ex parte Monahan [1988] JPL 557 . . . 408

R v Wicks [1997] 2 All ER 801 . . . 423

R v Wirral MBC, ex parte Gray [1998] Env LR D13 . . . 450

R v Yorkshire Water Services Ltd [2002] Env LR 18 . . . 284, 597

R (on the application of Adlard) v Secretary of State for Transport, Local Government and the Regions [2002] EWCA Civ 735 . . . 403, 421, 466

R (on the application of Aggregate Industries Ltd) v English Nature [2003] Env LR 3 . . . 693–5

R (on the application of Amvac Chemical UK Ltd) v Secretary of State for the Environment, Food and Rural Affairs (2002) ACD 34 . . . 69

R (on the application of Barker) v Bromley LBC (C290/03); Sub Nom: Barker v Bromley LBC (C290/03) [2006] Q.B. 764; [2006] 3 W.L.R. 492; [2006] E.C.R. I-3949; [2007] Env. L.R. 2 . . . 446, 457, 467

R (on the application of Blewett) v Derbyshire CC [2005] Env LR 15 . . . 411, 414, 457–8, 644

R (on the application of Burkett) v Hammersmith and Fulham LBC [2002] UKHL 23; [2003] Env LR 6 . . . 318–9, 381, 454

R (on the application of Candlish) v Hastings BC [2005] EWHC 1539 (Admin) . . . 443

R (on the application of Catt) v Brighton and Hove City Council [2007] EWCA Civ 298; [2007] Env. L.R. 32 . . . 453–4

R (on the application of Corner House Research) v Secretary of State for Trade and Industry [2005] EWCA Civ 192 . . . 320–1

R (on the application of Council for National Parks Ltd) v Pembrokeshire Coast National Park Authority See Council for National Parks Ltd v Pembrokeshire Coast National Park Authority

R (on the application of Edwards) v Environment Agency [2004] Env LR 43 . . . 315

R (on the application of Edwards) v Environment Agency [2007] Env LR 9 . . . 310, 313, 322, 443, 483

R (on the application of England) v Tower Hamlets LBC (Permission to Appeal) [2006] EWCA Civ 1742, CA (Civ Div) . . . 443

R (on the application of Fernback) v Harrow BC [2002] Env LR 10 . . . 454–5

R (on the application of Friends of the Earth) v Environment Agency [2004] Env LR 31 . . . 637

R (on the application of Friends of the Earth) v Secretary of State for the Environment, Food and Rural Affairs [2002] Env LR 24 . . . 153

R (on the application of Gavin) v Haringey LBC [2003] EWHC 2591 . . . 403

R (on the application of Goodman) v Lewisham LBC [2003] Env LR 28 . . . 447, 454

R (on the application of Greenpeace) v Secretary of State for the Environment, Food and Rural Affairs [2003] Env LR 9 . . . 682

R (on the application of Gregan) v Environment Agency [2003] EWHC 3278 . . . 444

R (on the application of Grundy & Co. Excavations Ltd) v Halton Division Magistrates Court [2003] EWHC Admin 272 . . . 757

R (on the application of Hardy) v Pembrokeshire CC [2005] EWHC 1872; [2006] Env. L.R. 16, QBD (Admin) . . . 318

R (on the application of Horner) v Lancashire CC; Sub Nom: Horner v Lancashire CC [2007] EWCA Civ 784; [2005] EWHC 2273 (Admin) . . . 449, 644

R (on the application of JA Pye (Oxford) Ltd) v Oxford CC [2002] EWCA Civ 1116 . . . 389

R (on the application of Jones) v Mansfield DC [2003] EWHC 7 . . . 452, 458

R (on the application of Jones) v North Warwickshire BC [2001] EWCA Civ 315 . . . 407–8

R (on the application of Kathro) v Rhondda Cynon Taff BC [2002] Env LR 15 . . . 450, 464

R (on the application of Kent) v First Secretary of State; Sub Nom: Kent v First Secretary of State [2004] EWHC 2953 (Admin); [2005] Env. L.R. 30 . . . 458, 504

R (on the application of Lebus) v South Cambridgeshire DC [2003] Env LR 17 . . . 454, 465

R (on the application of Lewis) v Environmental Agency [2005] EWHC 1110 (Admin); [2006] Env. L.R. 10, QBD (Admin) . . . 607

R (on the application of Lichfield Securities Ltd) v Lichfield DC [2001] EWCA Civ 304 . . . 418

R (on the application of Lowther) v Durham CC [2002] Env LR 13 . . . 395–6

R (on the application of Malster) v Ipswich BC and Ipswich Town Football Club [2001] EWHC Admin 711 . . . 450, 452

R (on the application of Mayor and Citizens of the City of Westminster, Preece and Adamson) v Mayor of London [2002] EWHC 2440 . . . 210, 443

R (on the application of Medway Council) v Secretary of State for Transport [2002] EWHC 2516 . . . 712

R (on the application of Murray) v Derbyshire CC [2002] Env LR 28 . . . 217

R (on the application of National Grid Gas Plc (formerly Transco Plc)) v Environment Agency [2007] UKHL 30; [2007] 1 W.L.R. 1780; [2007] 3 All E.R. 877 . . . 565, 567

R (on the application of O'Dwyer) v Westminster City Council [2006] EWHC 3016, QBD (Admin) . . . 409

R (on the application of Orchard) v First Secretary of State [2004] Env LR 12 . . . 451

R (on the application of Philcox) v Epping Forest DC [2002] Env LR 2 . . . 422

R (on the application of Rackham) v Swaffham Magistrates Court and Environment Agency [2004] EWHC 17 . . . 652

R (on the application of Reprotech (Pebsham) Ltd) v East Sussex CC [2002] UKHL 8 . . . 377, 381

R (on the application of Rockware Glass Ltd) v Chester City Council; Sub Nom: R. (on the application of Rockware Glass Ltd) v Quinn Glass Ltd [2006] EWCA Civ 992; [2007] Env. L.R. 3 . . . 500

R (on the application of Thames Water Utilities Ltd) v Bromley Magistrates' Court (C-252/05); Sub Nom: Thames Water Utilities Ltd v Bromley Magistrates Court (C-252/05) [2007] 1 W.L.R. 1945; [2007] 3 C.M.L.R. 2; [2007] 20 E.G. 295 (C.S.); [2008] Env. L.R. 3; The Times, May 25, 2007, ECJ . . . 651

R (on the application of Vetterlein) v Hampshire CC [2002] Env LR 8 . . . 457

R (on the application of Wall) v Brighton and Hove City Council [2004] EWHC 2582 (Admin) . . . 404

R (on the application of Wells) v Secretary of State for Transport, Local Government and the Regions (Case C-201/02) [2004] Env LR 27 . . . 210, 212, 445–6, 467

R (on the application of) Western Power Distribution Investments Ltd) v. Countryside Council for Wales [2007] Env LR 25 . . . 53, 126, 693

Rainham Chemical Works Ltd v Belvedere Fish Guano Co. [1921] 2 AC 465 . . . 347

Read v Croydon Corp. [1938] 4 All ER 631 . . . 348, 598

Read v Lyons [1947] AC 156 . . . 346

Reay and Hope v British Nuclear Fuels Ltd [1994] 5 Med LR 1 . . . 343

Regan v Paul Properties Ltd [2006] EWCA Civ 1391 . . . 350

Richmond upon Thames LBC v Secretary of State for the Environment, Transport and the Regions (Tree Preservation Order) [2002] JPL 33 . . . 753

Rickards v Lothian [1913] AC 263 . . . 346

Robinson v East Riding of Yorkshire Council [2003] JPL 894 . . . 753

Robinson v Kilvert (1889) 41 Ch 88 . . . 334

Rookes v Barnard [1964] AC 1129 . . . 352

RSPB and The Wildfowl and Wetlands Trust v Secretary of State for Scotland (Islay Geese) [2001] Env LR 19 . . . 125, 710

RSPCA v Cundey [2002] Env LR 17 . . . 724

Rushmer v Polsue and Alfieri Ltd [1906] 1 Ch 234 . . . 333

Rylands v Fletcher (1868) LR 3 HL 330 . . . 329, 336, 343, 345–8, 353, 356–7, 365, 598, 625, 674

St Helen's Smelting Co. v Tipping (1865) 11 HL Cas 642 . . . 333, 356

Salvin v North Brancepath Coal Co. (1876) 9 Ch App 705 . . . 334

Sanders Clark v Grosvenor Mansions Co. Ltd [1900] 2 Ch 373 . . . 332

Saunders v United Kingdom (1997) 23 EHRR 313 . . . 614

Savage v Fairclough [2000] Env LR 183 . . . 609

Schulmans Incorporated Ltd v National Rivers Authority [1993] Env LR D1 . . . 612

Scott-Whitehead v National Coal Board (1987) P & CR 263 . . . 344

Scottish Power Generation Ltd v Scottish Environment Protection Agency (No.1) 2005 S.L.T. 98; [2005] Eu. L.R. 449; [2005] Env. L.R. 38; 2005 G.W.D. 1–1, OH . . . 650

Secretary of State for the Environment, Food and Rural Affairs v Feakins; Sub Nom: Department for Environment, Food and Rural Affairs v Feakins; Feakins v Department for Environment, Food and Rural Affairs [2005] EWCA Civ 1513; [2007] B.C.C. 54; [2006] Env. L.R. 44 . . . 339

Secretary of State for Transport v Fillingham [1997] Env LR 73 . . . 342

Secretary of State for Transport v Haughian [1997] Env LR 59, CA . . . 342

Seymour v Flamborough Parish Council, The Times, 3 January 1997 . . . 759

Shanks and McEwan (Teesside) Ltd v Environment Agency [1997] Env LR 305 . . . 266, 659

Sherras v De Rutzen [1895] 1 QB 918 . . . 259

Shrimp/Turtle See United States–Import Prohibition of Certain Shrimp and Shrimp Products

Smith v Secretary of State for the Environment, Transport and the Regions [2003] EWCA Civ 262 . . . 451

Southern Blue Fish Tuna Cases See New Zealand v Japan; Australia v Japan

Southern Water Authority v Nature Conservancy Council [1992] 1 WLR 775 . . . 118, 695

Southern Water Authority v Pegrum (1989) 153 JP 581 . . . 611

Southport Corp. v Esso Petroleum [1954] 2 QB 182 . . . 337

Spain v Canada (Fisheries Jurisdiction case) (1998) ICJ Rep 432 . . . 152

Spain v Council (Case C-36/98) [2001] ECR I-779 . . . 182

Staffordshire CC v Challinor [2007] EWCA Civ 864; [2007] N.P.C. 101, CA (Civ Div) . . . 422

Steeples v Derbyshire CC [1985] 1 WLR 256 . . . 400

Stichting Greenpeace Council v Commission (Case C-321/95P) [1998] ECR I-1651 . . . 182–3

Stirk v Bridgnorth DC [1997] JPL 51 . . . 392

Stringer v Minister of Housing and Local Government [1970] 1 WLR 1281 . . . 405, 407

Sturges v Bridgman (1879) 11 ChD 852 . . . 333, 338–9

Swan v Secretary of State for the Environment (No. 1) [1998] Env LR 545 . . . 467

Sweet v Secretary of State for the Environment and Nature Conservancy Council [1989] JEL 245 . . . 694, 696

T Mobile (UK) Ltd v First Secretary of State [2004] EWHC 1713 . . . 425

Tameside MBC v Secretary of State for the Environment [1984] JPL 180 . . . 407

Tameside MBC v Smith Brothers (Hyde) Ltd [1996] Env. L.R. D4, QBD . . . 414, 495

Tapecrown Ltd v First Secretary of State; Sub Nom: R. (on the application of Tapecrown Ltd) v First Secretary of State [2006] EWCA Civ 1744 . . . 422

Taylor Woodrow Property Management Ltd v National Rivers Authority (1994) 158 JP 1101 . . . 613

Tesco Supermarkets Ltd v Nattrass [1972] AC 153 . . . 265

Tesco Stores Ltd v Secretary of State for the Environment [1995] 1 WLR 759; [1995] JPL 581 . . . 405, 417–8

Thames Waste Management Ltd v Surrey CC [1997] Env LR 148 . . . 658

Thanet DC v Kent CC [1993] Env LR 391 . . . 652

Times Investments Ltd v Secretary of State for the Environment [1990] JPL 433 . . . 413

Trail Smelter Arbitration See United States v Canada

Trailer and Marina (Leven) Ltd v Secretary of State for the Environment, Food and Rural Affairs [2004] EWCA Civ 1580 upholding [2004] EWHC Admin 153 . . . 694, 701

Transco v Stockport MBC [2003] UKHL 61 . . . 346–8, 356

Trevett v Secretary of State for the Environment [2002] EWHC 2696 . . . 425

Tulk v Moxhay (1848) 41 ER 1143 . . . 349

Tuna/Dolphin (1992) 30 ILM 1598 . . . 159–60, 171, 162–3

Tuna/Dolphin II (1994) 33 ILM 839 . . . 159

Turner v Secretary of State for the Environment (1973) 28 P & CR 123 . . . 421

Unión de Pequeños Agricoltores (UPA) v Council (Case C-50/00P) [2002] ECR I-6677 . . . 176, 182–3

United Kingdom v Commission of the European Communities (T178/05) Sub Nom: Greenhouse Gas Emission Allowance, Re (T178/05) [2006] 1 C.M.L.R. 33; [2006] Env. L.R. 43, CFI (1st Chamber) . . . 526

United States v Canada ('Trail Smelter') 3 RIAA 1907 (1941) . . . 137, 139, 146, 516–7

United States–Gasoline (1996) 35 ILM 603 . . . 160

United States–Import Prohibition of Certain Shrimp and Shrimp Products (Shrimp/Turtle I) (1999) 38 ILM 121 . . . 150, 158, 160–3

United States–Import Prohibition of Certain Shrimp and Shrimp Products (Shrimp/Turtle II) (2001) . . . 161

United Utilities Water Plc v Environment Agency [2007] UKHL 41; [2007] 1 W.L.R. 2707; [2007] 43 E.G. 201 (C.S.); (2007) 104(42) L.S.G. 36; (2007) 151 S.J.L.B. 1366; [2007] N.P.C. 107; The Times, October 26, 2007, HL; affirming [2006] EWCA Civ 633 . . . 480, 673

Van de Walle v Région de Bruxelles-Capitale (Case C-1/03) [2005] Env LR 24 . . . 552, 651, 672

Van Rooij v Dagelijks Bestuur van het Waterschap de Dommel (C231/97) Sub Nom: Van Rooj v Dagelijks Bestuur van het Water Schap de Dommel (C231/97) [1999] E.C.R. I-6355 . . . 590, 599

Vessoso and Zanetti (Cases C-206 & C-207/88) [1990] ECR I-1461; I-1509 . . . 647

Wales v Thames Water Authority (1987) 1(3) Env Law 3 . . . 616

Wallington v Secretary of State for Wales (1990) 62 P & CR 150 . . . 395

Wandsworth LBC v Railtrack plc [2002] Env LR 9, CA; [2001] Env LR 441 . . . 345

Warren v Uttlesford DC [1997] JPL 1130 . . . 392

Waste Incineration Services Ltd v Dudley MBC [1993] Env LR 29 . . . 660

West Coast Wind Farms Ltd v Secretary of State for the Environment and North Devon DC [1996] JPL 767 . . . 409

West Sussex CC v Secretary of State for the Environment, Transport and the Regions [1999] PLCR 365 . . . 390

Westminster City Council v Great Portland Estates plc [1985] AC 661 . . . 378, 389, 392

Wheeler v JJ Saunders Ltd [1996] Ch 19 . . . 333, 358–60

Wilderness Society v Morton 463 F 2d 1262 (1972) . . . 439

William Sinclair Holdings Ltd v English Nature [2002] Env LR 4 . . . 694

Woodhouse v Walsall MBC [1994] Env LR 30 . . . 267

World Wildlife Fund-UK Ltd and RSPB v Secretary of State for Scotland [1999] Env LR 632 . . . 708

World Wildlife Fund (WWF) EA v Autonome Provinz Bozen (Case C-435/97) [1999] ECR I-5613; [2000] 1 CMLR 149 . . . 449, 453

Wychavon DC v National Rivers Authority [1993] 1 WLR 125 . . . 610–2

Wychavon DC v Secretary of State for the Environment [1994] Env LR 239 . . . 97

X (Minors) v Bedfordshire CC [1995] 2 AC 633 . . . 348

X and Y v Germany (1976) 5 Eur Com HR Dec & Rep . . . 338

Ynys Mon BC v Secretary of State for Wales [1993] JPL 225 . . . 402

TABLE OF STATUTES

Australia
Land and Environment Court Act 1979 . . . 323

Netherlands
Soil Protection Act 1987 . . . 560

Spain
Constitution 1978
  Art. 45 . . . 166

Turkey
Constitution 1982
  Art. 56 . . . 166

United Kingdom
Agriculture Act 1947 . . . 683
Agriculture Act 1986
  s. 18 . . . 746
Alkali Act 1863 . . . 19, 20, 512, 514
Alkali, &c, Works Regulation Act 1906 . . . 477,
  512
Ancient Monuments and Archaeological Areas
  Act 1979 . . . 316
Anti-Social Behaviour Act 2003 . . . 749, 752
  Pt VIII . . . 749

Building Act 1984
  s. 1 . . . 375

Channel Tunnel Act 1987 . . . 400
Civil Aviation Act 1982
  s. 76(1) . . . 339
Clean Air Act 1956 . . . 44, 124, 513–4
Clean Air Act 1968 . . . 513
Clean Air Act 1993 . . . 272, 540
  Pt I . . . 257
Clean Neighbourhood and Environment Act 2005
  . . . 4, 325, 573
  s. 37 . . . 270
  s. 104 . . . 573
Clean Rivers (Estuaries and Tidal Waters) Act
  1960 . . . 583
Climate Change and Sustainable Energy Act 2006
  . . . 531
Companies Act 1985

s. 741 . . . 267
Conservation of Seals Act 1970 . . . 719
Contracts (Rights of Third Parties) Act 1999 . . .
  349, 383, 416
Control of Pollution Act 1974 . . . 21–3, 111, 114,
  172, 267, 297, 301, 583, 601, 615, 623, 633, 634,
  671
  Pt I . . . 633
  s. 3(4) . . . 660
Control of Pollution (Amendment) Act 1989 . . .
  654, 666
  s. 1(1) . . . 666
  s. 5 . . . 270
  s. 5(1) . . . 666
  s. 5(2)(d) . . . 666
  s. 5A . . . 270
  s. 5B-C . . . 666
Countryside Act 1968 . . . 113, 738
  s. 11 . . . 737
  s. 15 . . . 247, 701
  s. 37 . . . 697
Countryside and Rights of Way Act 2000 . . . 23,
  25, 53, 118, 124, 272, 277, 353, 691–3, 695–704,
  717, 719, 725, 727, 738, 744, 759
  Pt III . . . 688
  s. 28M(1) . . . 701
  s. 28N . . . 702
  s. 28P(1) . . . 282
  s. 74 . . . 109
  s. 75(4) . . . 702
  s. 81 . . . 721
  s. 82 . . . 743
  s. 85 . . . 109, 743, 744
  s. 86 . . . 744
  s. 87(1) . . . 744
  s. 89 . . . 744
  s. 91 . . . 744
  Sch. 11, para. 9 . . . 701
  Sch. 11, para. 17 . . . 701
  Sch. 12, para. 1 . . . 721
  Sch. 13 . . . 744
Countryside (Scotland) Act 1967
  s. 66 . . . 737
Criminal Justice Act 1988

s. 24 . . . 614

Deposit of Poisonous Waste Act 1972 . . . 44, 111, 633

Deregulation and Contracting Out Act 1994 . . . 280

Electricity Act 1989 . . . 400
   s. 3A . . . 59
   Sch. 9 . . . 712
Energy Act 2004 . . . 102
   s. 129 . . . 34
Environment Act 1995 . . . 22–4, 28, 34, 83, 89, 102, 109–10, 113–4, 116, 122, 128, 280, 471, 536, 538–9, 584–5, 634, 642, 654, 739
   Pt III . . . 738
   s. 1(1) . . . 115
   ss. 4–7 . . . 604
   s. 4 . . . 59, 69, 116, 119
   s. 4(1) . . . 116
   s. 4 (3) . . . 117
   ss. 5–9 . . . 117
   s. 5 . . . 117, 119
   s. 6 . . . 117
   s. 7 . . . 117
   s. 7(1) . . . 117
   s. 7(1)(a) . . . 117
   s. 7(1)(b) . . . 117
   s. 7(2) . . . 117
   s. 8(1)–(4) . . . 118
   s. 9 . . . 118
   s. 11 . . . 115
   s. 37(7) . . . 120
   s. 37 (8) . . . 120
   s. 38 . . . 115
   s. 39 . . . 92, 119
   s. 40 . . . 108, 603
   s. 41 . . . 120, 602
   s. 42 . . . 120, 602
   s. 43 . . . 120
   s. 56(1) . . . 119
   s. 61 . . . 739
   s. 63 . . . 741
   s. 66 . . . 742
   s. 71 . . . 742
   s. 72 . . . 742
   s. 80 . . . 539
   s. 81 . . . 539
   s. 87 . . . 539

s. 91 . . . 539
s. 93 . . . 669
s. 97 . . . 758
s. 98 . . . 746
s. 108 . . . 270, 558, 613, 666
s. 108(1) . . . 270
s. 108(4) . . . 270
s. 108(4)(a) . . . 270
s. 108(4)(b) . . . 270
s. 108(5) . . . 270
s. 108(6) . . . 271
s. 108(8) . . . 270
s. 108(13) . . . 270
s. 109 . . . 666
s. 110 . . . 270
s. 111 . . . 613
s. 202 . . . 603
Sch. 7 . . . 741
Environmental Protection Act 1990 . . . 20, 22–4, 28, 82, 89, 101, 113–4, 172–3, 282, 301, 506, 584, 633–4, 645, 654, 658, 664
   Pt I . . . 112, 122, 320, 477–8, 487
   Pt II . . . 267, 634
   Pt IIA . . . 23, 46, 55, 90, 103, 122, 244, 304, 360, 365, 547, 549, 552, 555–9, 562–4, 566–8, 572–6, 617, 623, 651, 656, 672
   Pt III . . . 622
   Pt IV . . . 257
   s. 1 . . . 7
   s. 3(5) . . . 243
   s. 7(2) . . . 606
   s. 29 . . . 661
   s. 30 . . . 654
   s. 33 . . . 257, 550, 658, 662, 664–6, 674
   s. 33(1) . . . 657–8, 661, 673
   s. 33(1)(a) . . . 658, 665
   s. 33(1)(c) . . . 658–9, 661, 673
   s. 33(3) . . . 661
   s. 33(5) . . . 659
   s. 33(7) . . . 263
   s. 33(7)(a) . . . 660
   s. 33(8) . . . 659
   s. 33(9) . . . 659, 661
   s. 33B . . . 660
   s. 33C . . . 660
   s. 34 . . . 112, 648, 654, 664, 674
   s. 34(2) . . . 664
   s. 34(6) . . . 665
   s. 34(7) . . . 665

s. 34(10) . . . 665
s. 34A . . . 665
s. 39 . . . 47, 281
s. 43 . . . 281
s. 44A . . . 108, 642
s. 45 . . . 654
s. 46 . . . 654
s. 46(2) . . . 655
s. 47 . . . 654
s. 48 . . . 655
s. 49 . . . 654–5
s. 51 . . . 655
s. 52 . . . 242, 655
s. 52(3) . . . 655
s. 55 . . . 655
s. 59 . . . 241, 285, 550, 552, 661, 672
s. 59(3) . . . 661
s. 59(4) . . . 661
s. 59(5) . . . 661
s. 59(6) . . . 661
s. 59(7) . . . 662
s. 59(8) . . . 662
s. 59ZA . . . 550, 661
s. 61 . . . 89
s. 62 . . . 652, 674
s. 63(2) . . . 673–4
s. 71 . . . 270, 666
s. 73 . . . 362, 665
s. 73(6) . . . 362, 673–4
s. 75(4) . . . 652
s. 78 . . . 562
s. 78(2) . . . 555
s. 78(4) . . . 556
s, 78A . . . 567
s. 78A(2) . . . 554, 556
s. 78A(9) . . . 557
s. 78B(1) . . . 558
s. 78B(3) . . . 559
s. 78C(1)–(3) . . . 558
s. 78E . . . 561–2
s. 78E(1) . . . 562
s. 78E(4) . . . 561–2
s. 78F(2) . . . 563
s. 78F(4) . . . 566
s. 78G(4) . . . 559
s. 78H . . . 573
s. 78H(1) . . . 559

s. 78H(4) . . . 559
s. 78H(5)(b) . . . 562
s. 78H(5)(c) . . . 562
s. 78H(5)(d) . . . 562
s. 78H(5A) . . . 562
s. 78H(6) . . . 559, 562
s. 78H(7) . . . 559
s. 78J . . . 567
s. 78K . . . 563
s. 78K(3) . . . 567
s. 78K(4) . . . 567
s. 78L(1) . . . 573
s. 78M . . . 257, 573
s. 78M(3) . . . 574
s. 78M(4) . . . 574
s. 78N . . . 574
s. 78N(3)(a) . . . 562
s. 78N(3)(e) . . . 562
s. 78N(3)(f) . . . 562
s. 78P . . . 574
s. 78P(8) . . . 574
s. 78Q . . . 558
s. 78Q(4) . . . 559
s. 78R . . . 305, 574
s. 78R(2) . . . 555
s. 78R(3) . . . 574
s. 78X(2) . . . 558
s. 78X(3) . . . 567
s. 78YB . . . 562
s. 78YB(1) . . . 550, 672
s. 78YB(3) . . . 550, 672
ss. 80–81 . . . 551
s. 80 . . . 271
s. 80(4) . . . 257, 264, 551
s. 81 . . . 241
s. 122 . . . 306
s. 130 . . . 687
s. 131(4) . . . 692
s. 132(1)(a) . . . 692
s. 143 . . . 89, 575
s. 157 . . . 266, 267
Sch. 2A . . . 642

European Communities Act 1972 . . . 83, 85, 216, 441
s. 2(1) . . . 82
s. 2(2) . . . 85
s. 2(4) . . . 95
s. 3(1) . . . 95

Finance Act 1996 . . . 634, 667
  Pt III . . . 257
  s. 40 . . . 668
Finance Act 2000
  Pt II . . . 257
  s. 30 . . . 528
  Sch. 6 . . . 257, 528
Flamborough Enclosure Act 1765 . . . 759
Food and Environment Protection Act 1985 . . . 46, 480, 608
Forestry Act 1967 . . . 755, 757
  s. 1(3A) . . . 757
  s. 9(2) . . . 756
  s. 17 . . . 257
Forestry Act 1986 . . . 758
Freedom of Information Act 2000 . . . 296–7, 301–3
  s. 8 . . . 302
  ss. 21–44 . . . 302
  s. 39 . . . 302
  ss. 45–46 . . . 302
  ss. 50–56 . . . 302
  ss. 57–61 . . . 302
  s. 58(1) . . . 305
  s. 59 . . . 305
  Sch. 1 . . . 302–3

Government of Wales Act 1998 . . . 585
  s. 121 . . . 59
Government of Wales Act 2006 . . . 384
  s. 79 . . . 109
Gulf Oil Refining Act 1965 . . . 339

Health and Safety at Work etc. Act 1974 . . . 477
  s. 28 . . . 301
Household Waste Recycling Act 2003 . . . 85, 125, 656
Housing and Planning Act 1986 . . . 399
Housing, Town Planning etc. Act 1909 . . . 19, 377
Human Rights Act 1998 . . . 14, 72, 135, 298, 314, 317, 330–1, 337, 351, 359, 367, 380, 596
  s. 6 . . . 330
  s. 6(2) . . . 339

Law of Property Act 1925
  s. 84 . . . 416
    Legislative and Regulatory Reform Act 2006 . . . 615
Local Government (Access to Information) Act 1985 . . . 301, 404
Local Government Act 1972 . . . 742

Local Government Act 1992 . . . 121
Local Government Act 1999 . . . 404
  s. 15 . . . 656
Local Government Act 2000
  s. 4 . . . 59, 122–3, 388
Local Government, Planning and Land Act 1980 . . . 399

Merchant Shipping Act 1995 . . . 114, 361–2

National Parks and Access to the Countryside Act 1949 . . . 113, 688, 690, 738, 741, 743
  s. 5 . . . 738–9
  s. 5(1) . . . 741
  s. 5(2) . . . 740–1
  s. 5(2A) . . . 740
  s. 11A(1) . . . 739
  s. 11A(2) . . . 739, 742
  s. 15 . . . 689
  s. 21 . . . 689
National Parks (Scotland) Act 2000 . . . 741
  s. 11 . . . 742
  s. 12 . . . 742
  s. 14 . . . 742
National Trust Act 1907 . . . 124
National Trust Act 1937 . . . 124
National Trust Act 1939 . . . 124
National Trust Act 1953 . . . 124
National Trust Act 1971 . . . 124
Natural Environment and Rural Communities Act 2006 . . . 4, 113, 118, 701, 703, 737, 739–41
  Pt. V . . . 738
  s. 2 . . . 687, 737
  s. 5 . . . 739
  s. 7 . . . 115, 701, 738
  s. 8 . . . 115
  s. 12 . . . 726
  s. 40 . . . 688
  s. 41 . . . 727
  s. 99 . . . 740
  s. 105(1) . . . 689
  Sch. 11, para. 12 . . . 689
Natural Heritage (Scotland) Act 1991 . . . 114, 687
  s. 1(1) . . . 59
Nature Conservation (Scotland) Act 2004 . . . 114, 688, 719
Norfolk and Suffolk Broads Act 1988 . . . 384, 740
Nuclear Installations Act 1965 . . . 359, 361
  ss. 7–10 . . . 361

Petroleum Act 1987 . . . 46

Planning and Compensation Act 1991 . . . 386, 397, 405, 415, 423, 445, 742

s. 15 . . . 441

Planning and Compulsory Purchase Act 2004 . . . 59, 306, 378, 381–2, 384, 386, 389, 391–2, 398–9, 401, 403, 415–6, 419, 429, 671, 735

Pt 1 . . . 101, 112, 388, 390

Pt 4 . . . 390

s. 1 . . . 388

s. 1(1) . . . 388

s. 1 (2) . . . 388

s. 3(2) . . . 388

s. 4 . . . 391

s. 5(4) . . . 391

s. 6 . . . 391

s. 15(2) . . . 388

s. 19(2) . . . 388

s. 19(5) . . . 391

s. 23 . . . 389

s. 38(6) . . . 388, 392, 405–6

s. 39 . . . 390

s. 40 . . . 400

s. 44 . . . 403

s. 45 . . . 399

s. 46 . . . 247

s. 50 . . . 404

s. 53 . . . 402

s. 70(2) . . . 389

s. 113 . . . 392

Planning etc (Scotland) Act 2006 . . . 384

Police and Criminal Evidence Act 1984

s. 76 . . . 614

s. 82 . . . 614

Pollution Prevention and Control Act 1999 . . . 4, 23–4, 89, 113, 122, 216, 243, 584

s. 2 . . . 80

Sch. 1, para. 3 . . . 80, 606

Sch. 1, para. 20 . . . 86

Powers of Criminal Courts (Sentencing) Act 2000

s. 35 . . . 241

s. 130 . . . 241, 285

s. 131 . . . 241

Prosecution of Offenders Act 1985

s. 6(1) . . . 271

Protection of Animals (Amendment) Act 2000 . . . 271

Protection of Badgers Act 1992 . . . 719, 725

s. 6(c) . . . 725

Protection of Birds Act 1954 . . . 124

Protection of Wild Mammals (Scotland) Act 2002 . . . 317

Public Health Act 1875 . . . 18, 20, 512

Public Health Act 1936 . . . 622

s. 259(1)(a), (b) . . . 622

Public Health (Smoke Abatement) Act 1926 . . . 512

Radioactive Substances Act 1993 . . . 114, 445, 622

Regional Development Agencies Act 1998 . . . 101

s. 4(e) . . . 60

Regulatory Reform Act 2001 . . . 286

Rehabilitation of Offenders Act 1974 . . . 666

River Boards Act 1948 . . . 19, 583

Rivers Pollution Prevention Act 1876 . . . 18, 582–3, 585

Rivers (Prevention of Pollution) Act 1951 . . . 583

Rivers (Prevention of Pollution) Act 1961 . . . 301, 583

Road Traffic Reduction Act 1997 . . . 540

Road Traffic Reduction (National Targets) Act 1998 . . . 540

Road Traffic Regulation Act 1984 . . . 540

s. 1(g) . . . 540

Salmon and Freshwater Fisheries Act 1975

s. 4 . . . 607

Scotland Act 1998 . . . 585

ss. 28–30 . . . 99

s. 29 . . . 99

s. 35 . . . 100

Sea Birds Preservation Act 1869 . . . 44, 683

Sea Birds Preservation Act 1872 . . . 683

Sea Birds Preservation Act 1880 . . . 683

Supreme Court Act 1981

s. 31(3) . . . 314

s. 31(6) . . . 317

Sustainable and Secure Buildings Act 2004 . . . 375

Sustainable Energy Act 2003

s. 6 . . . 464

Territorial Sea Act 1987 . . . 600, 689

Theft Act 1968

s. 4(3) . . . 256, 719

Town and Country Planning Act 1947 . . . 377, 382, 385, 394, 427, 684

Town and Country Planning Act 1968 . . . 385

Town and Country Planning Act 1971 . . . 385

Town and Country Planning Act 1990 . . . 23, 89–90, 95, 113, 272, 377–8, 384, 390, 415, 422, 424, 756

Pt III . . . 397

s. 46 . . . 415, 416

s. 55 . . . 89, 394

s. 55(1) . . . 393

s. 55(2)(a)–(g) . . . 396

s. 55(2)(e) . . . 735, 749

s. 55(3)-(5) . . . 393

s. 55(3)(b) . . . 671

s. 55(4) . . . 394

s. 57(1) . . . 393

s. 59 . . . 398

s. 61A–C . . . 400

s. 63(2) . . . 401

s. 69 . . . 306, 404

s. 70(1) . . . 411

s. 70(2) . . . 392, 405, 416

s. 71(9) . . . 551

s. 71A . . . 441

s. 72 . . . 411

s. 73 . . . 401

s. 75 . . . 411

s. 76A . . . 403

s. 76B . . . 403

s. 77 . . . 403, 405

s. 78 . . . 405, 420

s. 78A . . . 404

s. 82 . . . 399

s. 87 . . . 399

s. 88 . . . 399

s. 90 . . . 400

s. 92 . . . 401

ss. 97–100 . . . 397

s. 97 . . . 397, 425

s. 102 . . . 397, 425

s. 106 . . . 415–6

s. 171A . . . 422

s. 171B(1) . . . 422

s. 171B(2) . . . 422

s. 171B(3) . . . 422

s. 174(2)(a)–(g) . . . 423

s. 182 . . . 423

s. 187A . . . 551

ss. 191–194 . . . 422

s. 192 . . . 401

s. 196A–C . . . 422

ss. 197–214 . . . 749

s. 197 . . . 749

s. 198 . . . 749

s. 198(6) . . . 752

s. 200 . . . 752

s. 201 . . . 751, 755

s. 202 . . . 750

s. 203 . . . 754

s. 206 . . . 753

s. 206(4) . . . 751

s. 207 . . . 754

s. 208 . . . 754

s. 209 . . . 754

s. 210(1) . . . 750

s. 210(4) . . . 750

s. 211 . . . 754

s. 212 . . . 754

s. 214A . . . 750

s. 215 . . . 551

s. 284 . . . 421

s. 287 . . . 392

s. 288 . . . 314, 318, 404, 421, 751

s. 289(4A) . . . 423

s. 289(4B) . . . 423

s. 289(5C) . . . 423

s. 303 . . . 402

s. 316 . . . 400

s. 320 . . . 420

s. 321 . . . 420

s. 331 . . . 266

s. 336 . . . 394, 735

Sch. 1 . . . 672

Town and Country Planning (Scotland) Act 1997 . . . 384

Trade Descriptions Act 1968

s. 1 . . . 309

Transport Act 2000 . . . 102, 540

Transport and Works Act 1992 . . . 379, 400

Utilities Act 2000

s. 5A . . . 464

s. 10 . . . 109

s. 14 . . . 109

s. 62 . . . 527

Waste and Emissions Trading Act 2003 . . . 243

Pt 1 . . . 206

s. 32 . . . 654–5

Waste Minimisation Act 1998 . . . 85

Water Act 1973 . . . 583

Water Act 1989 . . . 267, 584, 590

Water Act 2003 . . . 113, 556, 584

   Pt 1 . . . 579

   s. 40 . . . 109

   s. 57 . . . 597

   s. 86 . . . 557, 623

   s. 105(3) . . . 556

   s. 105(5) . . . 556

Water Environment and Water Services Act
(Scotland) 2003 . . . 585

Water Industry Act 1991 . . . 23, 113–4, 215, 357,
584, 596–7, 602

   s. 18 . . . 596

   s. 67 . . . 597

   s. 70 . . . 257, 348, 597, 625

   s. 118 . . . 503, 609

   s. 196 . . . 306

   s. 209(3)(b) . . . 348

Water Industry (Scotland) Act 2002 . . . 114

Water Resources Act 1963 . . . 583

Water Resources Act 1991 . . . 20, 23, 89, 113, 357,
480, 491, 584–5, 601, 607, 615, 622, 626, 659, 663,
673

   s. 24 . . . 257

   s. 40 . . . 606

   ss. 82–84 . . . 605–6

   s. 82 . . . 605

   s. 83 . . . 604–5, 615

   s. 84 . . . 604–6

   s. 85 . . . 90, 256–8, 265, 282, 503, 551, 599, 601,
607, 609, 611–3, 617, 622

   s. 85(1) . . . 44–5, 590, 607

   s. 85(3) . . . 608

   s. 85(5) . . . 608

   s. 85(6) . . . 263, 599, 607, 613

   s. 85(7) . . . 607

   s. 86 . . . 599

   s. 87 . . . 609

   s. 87(1) . . . 609

   s. 87(2) . . . 601, 609–10

   s. 88 . . . 263, 503, 608

   s. 89 . . . 263, 608

   s. 90B . . . 258, 617

   s. 91 . . . 603

   s. 92 . . . 69, 617

   s. 93 . . . 618

   s. 93(3) . . . 618

   s. 94 . . . 618

   s. 100(b) . . . 348, 623

   s. 104 . . . 600

   s. 161 . . . 69, 241, 361, 364, 616–7, 662

   ss. 161–161D . . . 551

   s. 161A . . . 258, 285, 364, 549, 651

   s. 161A-D . . . 616

   s. 189 . . . 306

   s. 190 . . . 306, 615

   s. 191 . . . 306

   s. 191B(11) . . . 305

   s. 206 . . . 600

   s. 207 . . . 108

   s. 216 . . . 271

   s. 217 . . . 266

   s. 217(1) . . . 613

   s. 217(3) . . . 261, 611

   s. 221 . . . 599

   Sch. 10 . . . 600

   Sch. 10, para. 2(5) . . . 600

   Sch. 10, para. 5 . . . 603

   Sch. 10, para. 7 . . . 602

   Sch. 10, para. 9 . . . 602

Water (Scotland) Act 1980 . . . 114

Wild Mammals (Protection) Act 1996 . . . 719, 725

Wildlife and Countryside Act 1981 . . . 11, 23, 25,
27, 85, 113, 124, 680, 685, 690–2, 694, 699, 701,
703, 719, 720–2, 724–6

   Pt I . . . 258, 719, 722, 725

   Pt II . . . 258, 688

   s. 1(1) . . . 720

   s. 1(2) . . . 720

   s. 1(5) . . . 721

   s. 1A(a) . . . 724

   s. 2(2) . . . 724

   s. 4 . . . 724

   s. 4(2)(c) . . . 725

   s. 5 . . . 720–1

   s. 6 . . . 720

   s. 9(1) . . . 721

   s. 9(2) . . . 721

   s. 9(4) . . . 721

   s. 9(4A) . . . 721

   s. 10 . . . 722

   s. 10(3)(c) . . . 725

   s. 10(4) . . . 724

   s. 11(1 . . . 721

   s. 11(2) . . . 721

s. 13 . . . 721
s. 13(2) . . . 725
s. 14 . . . 685
s. 16 . . . 722–3
s. 27 . . . 723
s. 28 . . . 53, 692, 694
s. 28(1) . . . 692–3
s. 28(4) . . . 692
s. 28(4A) . . . 692
s. 28(5) . . . 692–3
s. 28(7) . . . 264, 693
s. 28(8) . . . 699
s. 28(8)(b) . . . 263
s. 28B . . . 694
s. 28E . . . 696
s. 28J . . . 697
s. 28K . . . 698
s. 28M . . . 697
s. 28N . . . 702
s. 28P(1) . . . 696
s. 28P(4) . . . 698
s. 28P(9) . . . 696
s. 29 . . . 696, 703

s. 34 . . . 688
s. 35 . . . 689
s. 36 . . . 689
s. 37 . . . 689
s. 39 . . . 738
s. 39(5) . . . 738
s. 41(3) . . . 736
s. 42 . . . 744
s. 70B . . . 692
Sch. 1 . . . 721, 725
Sch. 2, Pt II . . . 724
Sch. 5 . . . 721, 724–5
Sch. 6 . . . 721
Sch. 8 . . . 721
Sch. 9 . . . 685
Sch. 12 . . . 689
Wildlife and Countryside (Amendment) Act 1985
s. 4 . . . 757

United States of America

Comprehensive Environmental Response
  Compensation and Liability Act 1981 . . . 577
Endangered Species Act 1973 . . . 713
National Environmental Protection Act 1969 . . . 468

Action Programmes for Nitrate Vulnerable Zones (England and Wales) Regulations 1998 (SI 1998/1202) . . . 619

Air Quality (England) Regulations 2000 (SI 2000/928) . . . 539

Air Quality Standards Regulations 2007 (SI 2007/64) . . . 230, 238

Air Quality Standards Regulations 2007 (SI 2007/64) . . . 83, 87, 539

   reg. 6 . . . 540

   reg. 7 . . . 540

   reg. 10 . . . 540

   regs. 24–25 . . . 540

   Sch. 1 . . . 540

   Sch. 2 . . . 540

Anti-Pollution Works Regulations 1999 (SI 1999/1006) . . . 616

Bathing Waters (Classification) Regulations 1991 (SI 1991/1157) . . . 732

Civil Procedure Rules (SI 1998/3132)

   Pt. 54 . . . 318

   r. 54.5 . . . 317

   r.54.5(1)(b) . . . 318

Clean Air (Arrestment Plant) (Exemption) Regulations 1969 (SI 1969/1262) . . . 434

Common Agricultural Policy Single Payment and Support Schemes Regulations 2005 (SI 2005/219) . . . 746

Conservation (Natural Habitats etc.) (Amendment) Regulations 2000 (SI 2000/192) . . . 715

Conservation (Natural Habitats etc.) (Amendment) (England & Wales) Regulations 2006

   Sch. 1 . . . 716

Conservation (Natural Habitats etc.) Regulations 1994 (SI 1994/2716) . . . 86–7, 113, 214, 449, 715–9, 721–2, 725–6

   reg. 3(2) . . . 717

   reg. 11 . . . 715

   reg. 12 . . . 715

   reg. 13 . . . 715

   reg. 14 . . . 723

   reg. 15 . . . 723

   reg. 39 . . . 722

   reg. 44 . . . 724–5

   reg. 44(2)(c) . . . 724

   reg. 48 . . . 717

   reg. 49 . . . 717

   reg. 50 . . . 718

   reg. 53 . . . 717

   Sch. 2 . . . 721

   Sch. 4 . . . 721

Conservation (Natural Habitats etc.) (Amendment) Regulations 2007 (SI 2007/1843)

   reg. 5(55) . . . 711

   reg. 13 . . . 722

   Sch. 1 . . . 711

Contaminated Land (England) Regulations 2000 (SI 2000/227) . . . 86

Contaminated Land (England) Regulations 2006 (SI 2006/1380) . . . 305, 555

   reg. 2 . . . 573

   reg. 4 . . . 562

   reg. 7 . . . 573

   reg. 9(1) . . . 573

   reg. 12 . . . 573

   Sch. 1 . . . 558

   Sch. 3 . . . 574

Control of Major Accident Hazards Regulation 1999 (SI 1999/743) . . . 257

Control of Pesticides Regulations 1986 (SI 1986/1510) . . . 257

Control of Pollution (Anglers' Lead Weights) Regulations 1986 (SI 1986/1992) . . . 44

Control of Pollution (Applications, Appeals and Registers) Regulations 1996 (SI 1996/2971) . . . 306, 600, 603, 616

Control of Pollution (Oil Storage) (England) Regulations 2001 (SI 2001/2954) . . . 618

Control of Pollution (Radioactive Waste) Regulations 1989 (SI 1989/1158) . . . 622

Control of Pollution (Silage, Slurry and Agricultural Fuel Oil) (Amendment) Regulations 1999 (SI 1999/547) . . . 617

Control of Pollution (Silage, Slurry and Agricultural Fuel Oil) Regulations 1991 (SI 1991/324) . . . 617

Control of Trade in Endangered Species
(Enforcement) Regulations 1997 (SI 1997/1372)
. . . 258

Controlled Waste (Registration of Carriers and
Seizure of Vehicles) (Amendment) Regulations
1998 (SI 1998/605) . . . 666

Controlled Waste (Registration of Carriers
and Seizure of Vehicles) Regulations 1991 (SI
1991/1624) . . . 666

reg. 2 . . . 666

reg. 3 . . . 666

reg. 4 . . . 666

reg. 4(9) . . . 666

reg. 5 . . . 666

reg. 10 . . . 666

Sch. 1 . . . 666

Controlled Waste Regulations 1992 (SI 1992/588)

reg. 7(1) . . . 658

reg. 7A . . . 652

reg. 17(1) . . . 480

Development Commission (Transfer of Functions
and Miscellaneous Provisions) Order 1999 (SI
1999/416) . . . 737

Drinking Water (Undertakings) (England and
Wales) Regulations 2000 (SI 2000/1297) . . . 215

End-of-Life Vehicles (Producer Responsibility)
Regulations 2005 (SI 2005/263) . . . 669

reg. 7 . . . 670

regs. 10–12 . . . 670

reg. 18 . . . 670

Energy Information (Washing Machines)
Regulations (SI 1996/600) . . . 310

Energy Performance of Buildings (Certificates
and Inspections) (England and Wales)
Regulations (SI 2007/991) . . . 310

Environmental Assessment of Plans and
Programmes Regulations 2004 (SI 2004/1633)
. . . 391, 469

Environmental Impact Assessment (Agriculture)
(England) (No.2) Regulations 2006 (SI
2006/2522) . . . 748

Environmental Impact Assessment (Uncultivated
Land and Semi-Natural Areas) (England)
Regulations 2001 (SI 2001/3966) . . . 747

Environmental Impact Assessment (Forestry)
(England and Wales) Regulations 1999 (SI
1999/2228) . . . 749

Environmental Information Regulations 2004 (SI
2004/3391) . . . 296–7, 301–5

reg. 1 . . . 303

regs. 5–7 . . . 303

reg. 9 . . . 303

reg.10 . . . 485

reg. 11 . . . 304

reg. 12(6) . . . 304

reg. 14 . . . 303

reg. 18 . . . 305

Environmental Permitting (England and Wales)
Regulations 2007 (SI 2007/ 3538) . . . 83, 87, 122,
231, 306, 478, 497, 500, 506–7, 598, 607, 634,
639–40, 643–5, 651, 654, 656, 660, 662–3, 673

reg. 2 . . . 479, 646, 656

reg. 4 . . . 479–80

reg. 5 . . . 480, 488

reg. 5(2) . . . 481

reg. 7 . . . 481, 488

reg. 7(b) . . . 481

reg. 8 . . . 479

reg. 9 . . . 479

reg. 12 . . . 482, 488

reg. 13 . . . 481, 485

reg. 15 . . . 492

reg. 16 . . . 492

reg. 17 . . . 480, 482

reg. 18 . . . 607

reg. 19 . . . 607

reg. 20 . . . 493

reg. 21 . . . 491

regs. 22–23 . . . 493

reg. 22 . . . 493

reg. 24 . . . 492

reg. 25 . . . 492

reg. 25(6) . . . 491

reg. 26 . . . 491

reg. 27(3) . . . 491

reg. 31 . . . 495

regs. 31(8) . . . 495

reg. 31(9) . . . 494–5

reg. 32 . . . 481

reg. 32(1) . . . 481

reg. 32(2) . . . 481

reg. 33 . . . 108, 481

reg. 34 . . . 226, 488, 492–3

reg. 35(d) . . . 641, 662

reg. 36 . . . 494, 550

reg. 37 . . . 493–4, 550

reg. 38 . . . 257, 494

reg. 39 . . . 282

reg. 40 . . . 495, 660

reg. 41 . . . 660

reg. 42 . . . 495, 550, 659

reg. 44 . . . 495

reg. 46 . . . 485

regs. 47–56 . . . 485

reg. 47(3) . . . 485

reg. 48 . . . 305, 485

reg. 49 . . . 485

reg. 52(1) . . . 485

reg. 52(3) . . . 485

reg. 53 . . . 495

reg. 53(3) . . . 485

reg. 58 . . . 503

reg. 59 . . . 483

reg. 61 . . . 108

reg. 62 . . . 482–3

reg. 65 . . . 120

reg. 68 . . . 658

reg. 69(1) . . . 482

reg. 69(2) . . . 482

reg. 70 . . . 482

reg. 72(1)(c) . . . 482

Sch. 1 . . . 479–80, 647

Sch. 1, Pt.5 . . . 662

Sch. 2 . . . 227, 488, 654

Sch. 2, para. 3 . . . 481

Sch. 3 . . . 480–1, 488, 656

Sch. 3, para.4 . . . 608

Sch. 4 . . . 503

Sch. 5 . . . 482–3, 492

Sch. 5, para. 1 . . . 483

Sch. 5, para. 2 . . . 482

Sch. 5, para. 4(1) . . . 482

Sch. 5, para. 5(2) . . . 484

Sch. 5, para. 5(5) . . . 484

Sch. 5, para.13 . . . 246, 486

Sch. 5, para.14 . . . 492

Sch. 5, para. 15(2) . . . 482

Sch. 5, para. 16 . . . 482

Sch. 6 . . . 495

Sch. 6, para. 5 . . . 495

Sch. 7 . . . 479, 503, 606

Sch. 9 . . . 479, 488, 642, 657

Sch. 9, para.2 . . . 672

Sch. 9, para.3 . . . 643

Sch. 9, para.4 . . . 643

Sch. 10 . . . 479, 489, 641, 662

Sch. 11 . . . 479, 489

Sch. 12 . . . 479, 489

Sch. 13 . . . 479, 489

Sch. 14 . . . 479, 489

Sch. 15 . . . 479, 490

Sch. 16 . . . 479, 490

Sch. 17 . . . 479, 490

Sch. 18 . . . 479, 490

Sch. 20 . . . 488, 642

Sch. 20, para.3 . . . 643

Sch. 20, para.4 . . . 643

Environmental Protection (Duty of Care) Regulations 1991 (SI 1991/2839) . . . 663–4

Environmental Protection (Restriction on Use of Lead Shot) (England) Regulations 1999 (SI 1999/2170) . . . 44

Freedom of Information (Additional Public Authorities) Order 2002 (SI 2002/2623) . . . 303

General Development Procedure Order 1995 (SI 1995/419 . . . 622

Genetically Modified Organisms (Deliberate Release) Regulations 2002 (SI 2002/2443) . . . 306

Greenhouse Gas Emissions Trading Scheme Regulations 2005 (SI 2005/925) . . . 96, 526, 530

Groundwater Regulations 1998 (SI 1998/2746) . . . 606, 618, 620, 651, 673

reg. 18 . . . 480

Hazardous Waste (England and Wales) Regulations 2005 (SI 2005/894) . . . 640, 652

reg. 6 . . . 652

reg. 12(2) . . . 652

reg. 19 . . . 652

reg. 20 . . . 653

reg. 21 . . . 653

reg. 22 . . . 653

reg. 23 . . . 653

regs. 35–38 . . . 653

regs. 47, 48 . . . 653

regs. 49–51 . . . 653

reg. 53 . . . 653

reg. 54 . . . 653

reg. 65 . . . 653

reg. 66 . . . 653

Hedgerows Regulations 1997 (SI 1997/1160) . . . 749, 758

reg. 6(1)(j) . . . 759

Highways (Traffic Calming) Regulations 1999 (SI 1999/1026) . . . 540

Landfill Tax Regulations 1996 (SI 1996/1527) . . . 667–8

Landfill (England and Wales) Regulations 2002 (SI 2002/1559) . . . 231, 634, 662–3

reg. 8(2) . . . 243

Landfill Tax (Qualifying Materials) Order 1996 (SI 1996/1528) . . . 86, 667

Landfill Tax (Contaminated Land) Order 1996 (SI 1996/1529) . . . 667

List of Wastes (England) Regulations 2005 (SI 2005/895) . . . 90, 640, 652

Local Government (Best Value) Performance Indicators and Performance Standards (England) Order 2007 (SI 2007/585) . . . 656

Motor Vehicles (Type Approval) (Great Britain) Regulations 1994 (SI 1994/981) . . . 541

National Emissions Ceiling Regulations 2002 (SI 2002/3118) . . . 83, 535

Offshore Marine Conservation (Natural Habitats etc.) Regulations 2007 (SI 2007/1842) . . . 708, 718

Offshore Petroleum Activities (Conservation of Habitats) Regulations 2001 (SI 2001/1754) . . . 708

Planning (Northern Ireland) (Amendment) Order 2003 (SI 2003/430 (N18)) . . . 384

Planning (Northern Ireland) Order 1991 (SI 1991/1220 (N.I. 11)) . . . 384

Pollution Prevention and Control (England and Wales) Regulations 2000 (SI 2000/1973) . . . 86, 550

Sch. 1, Pt I . . . 529

Producer Responsibility Obligations (Packaging Waste) Regulations 2007 (SI 2007/871) . . . 669

reg. 4 . . . 669

reg. 4(5) . . . 669

regs. 6–7 . . . 669

reg. 6 . . . 669

regs. 14–18 . . . 669

regs. 20–22 . . . 669

Sch. 2 . . . 669

Sch. 3, Pt. 1 . . . 669

Sch. 4 . . . 669

Protection of Water against Agricultural and Nitrate Pollution (England and Wales) Regulations 1996 (SI 1996/888) . . . 619

Protection of Water against Agricultural and Nitrate Pollution (England and Wales) (Admendment) Regulations 2006 (SI 2006/1289) . . . 619

Road Vehicles (Construction and Use) Regulations 2003 (SI 2003/2695) . . . 541

Statutory Nuisance (Appeals) Regulations 1995 (SI 1995/2644) . . . 86

Town and Country Planning (Appeals) (Written Representations) (England) Regulations 2000 (SI 2000/1628) . . . 420

Town and Country Planning (Assessment of Environmental Effects) Regulations 1988 (SI 1988/1199) . . . 441

Town and Country Planning (Determination by Inspectors) (Inquiries Procedure) Rules 2000 (SI 2000/1625) . . . 420

Town and Country Planning (Environmental Impact Assessment) (Amendment) Regulations 2006 (SI 2006/3295) . . . 441

Town and Country Planning (Environmental Impact Assessment) (England and Wales) Regulations 1999 (SI 1999/293) . . . 85, 398, 441, 445–6, 448, 452, 456–7, 465, 473, 744

reg. 2(1) . . . 456–7, 461

reg. 3 . . . 462

reg. 3(2) . . . 461

reg. 4(4) . . . 455

reg. 4(4)(a)(ii) . . . 455

reg. 4(6) . . . 463

reg. 4(7) . . . 454

reg. 4(8) . . . 450

reg. 4(9) . . . 454

reg. 5(1) . . . 454

reg. 5(6) . . . 454

reg. 7 . . . 456

reg. 10 . . . 459

reg. 11 . . . 459

reg. 12 . . . 459

reg. 13 . . . 459

reg. 17 . . . 461

reg. 18 . . . 461

reg. 19 . . . 456, 462

reg. 21 . . . 463

reg. 27 . . . 439

reg. 28 . . . 439

reg. 30 . . . 461

reg. 32 . . . 461

Sch. 1 . . . 443, 446–7, 454

Sch. 2 . . . 443, 447–8, 450–1, 453–4, 463, 469

Sch. 3 . . . 448

Sch. 4, Pt. I . . . 457

Sch. 4, Pt. II . . . 456

Town and Country Planning (General Development Procedure) (England) (Amendment) Order 2002 (SI 2002/828) . . . 418

Town and Country Planning (General Development Procedure) Order 1995 (SI 1995/419) . . . 306, 378, 398, 401

art. 3 . . . 401

art. 4 . . . 398, 401

arts. 6–8 . . . 402

art. 10 . . . 402, 699

art. 10(3) . . . 403

art. 12 . . . 672

art. 20 . . . 404

art. 22 . . . 404

art. 25 . . . 404, 418

Town and Country Planning (General Development Procedure) (England) (Amendment) Order (SI SI 2003/2047) . . . 404

Town and Country Planning (General Permitted Development) Order 1995 (SI 1995/418) . . . 89, 378, 398, 445, 735–6

art. 1(5) . . . 736

art. 4 . . . 400, 736

Sch. 1 . . . 398

Sch. 2 . . . 735

Sch. 2, para.6 . . . 735–6

Sch. 2, para.7 . . . 735–6

Town and Country Planning General Regulations 1992 (SI 1992/1492) . . . 400

Town and Country Planning (Initial Regional Spatial Strategy) (England) Regulations 2004 (SI 2004/2206) . . . 386

Town and Country Planning (Inquiries Procedure) (England) Rules 2000 (SI 2000/1624) . . . 420

Town and Country Planning (Local Development) (England) Regulations 2004 (SI 2004/2204) . . . 389

Town and Country Planning (Regional Planning) (England) Regulations 2004 (SI 2004/2203) . . . 386

Town and Country Planning (Simplified Planning Zones) Regulations 1992 (SI 1992/2414) . . . 399

Town and Country Planning (Tree Preservation Order) (Amendment) Regulations 1988 (SI 1988/963) . . . 755

Town and Country Planning (Tree Preservation Order) Regulations 1969 (SI 1969/17) . . . 754–5

Town and Country Planning (Trees) Regulations 1999 (SI 1999/1892) . . . 751, 755

reg. 8 . . . 754

reg. 9 . . . 753

Sch. 751

Town and Country Planning (Use Classes) (Amendment) Order 1995 (SI 1995/297) . . . 396

Town and Country Planning (Use Classes) Order 1987 (SI 1987/764) . . . 86, 89, 378, 396

Town and Country Planning (Windscale and Calder Works) Special Development Order 1978 (SI 1978/523) . . . 399

Transfrontier Shipment of Waste Regulations 1994 (SI 1994/121) . . . 637

Transfrontier Shipment of Waste Regulations 2007 (SI 2007/1711) . . . 636

Urban Waste Water Treatment (England and Wales) Regulations 1994 (SI 1994/2841) . . . 87, 592, 673

Waste Electrical and Electronic Equipment Regulations 2006 (SI 2006/3289) . . . 670

regs. 8–9 . . . 670

reg. 8 . . . 670

reg. 10 . . . 670

reg. 12 . . . 670

reg. 15 . . . 670

Sch. 1 . . . 670

Sch. 2 . . . 670

Sch. 4 . . . 670

Sch. 5 . . . 670

Water Environment (Controlled Activities) (Scotland) Regulations 2005 (SI 2005/348) . . . 585, 604

Waste (Household Waste Duty of Care) (England and Wales) Regulations 2005, SI 2005/2900 . . . 31

Waste Management (England and Wales) Regulations 2006 (SI 2006/937) . . . 607

Waste Management Licensing (Amendment) (Scotland) Regulations 2003 (SI 2003/171) . . . 100

Waste Management Licensing Regulations 1994 (SI 1994/1056) . . . 87, 552, 606, 634, 643, 667

reg. 20 . . . 667

Sch. 4, Pt.II . . . 646

Sch. 5 . . . 667

Water and Sewerage (Conservation, Access and Recreation) (Code of Practice) Order 2000 (SI 2000/477) . . . 118

Water Environment (Controlled Activities) (Scotland)Amendment Regulations 2007 (SSI 2007/219) . . . 605

Water Environment (Water Framework Directive) (England and Wales) Regulations 2003 (SI 2003/3242) . . . 596

Water (Northern Ireland) Order 1999 (SI 1999/662) (NI 6) . . . 586

Water (Prevention of Pollution) (Code of Practice) Order 1998 (SI 1998/3084) . . . 609

Water Protection Zone (River Dee Catchment) Designation Order 1999 (SI 1999/915) . . . 618

Water Protection Zone (River Dee Catchment) (Procedural and Other Provisions) Regulations 1999 (SI 1999/916) . . . 618

Water Resources (Licences) Regulations 1965 (SI 1965/534) . . . 306

Water Supply (Water Quality) Regulations 2000 (Amendment) Regulations 2007 (SI 2007/2734) . . . 598

Water Supply (Water Quality) Regulations 2000 (SI 2000/3184) . . . 114, 230, 597

TABLE OF EUROPEAN LEGISLATION

Treaties

Accession Treaty 2003 . . . 200

EC Treaty (Treaty of Rome) . . . 28, 68, 154, 171, 173, 177–8, 182, 184–5, 187, 197, 214, 218–9, 256

Art. 2 . . . 58, 183, 186

Art. 3 . . . 183, 186

Art. 5 . . . 197

Art. 6 . . . 56, 58, 73, 105, 174, 186, 189, 190, 203–4, 219, 225

Art. 10 . . . 95, 204–5, 466–7, 714

Art. 28 . . . 176, 201, 203

Art. 29 . . . 201

Art. 30 . . . 201, 203

Art. 93 . . . 181

Art. 94 . . . 183, 185, 188

Art. 95 . . . 181, 185, 187–8, 195, 197–8, 201

Art. 95(3) . . . 202

Art. 95(4) . . . 188, 195–6

Art. 95(5) . . . 188, 195–6

Art. 95(6) . . . 195

Art. 95(10) . . . 198

Art. 133 . . . 187

Art. 141 . . . 178

Arts 174–176 . . . 185, 188

Art. 174 . . . 198

Art. 174(1) . . . 73, 188, 190

Art. 174(2) . . . 67, 137, 188, 191, 202, 619

Art. 174(3) . . . 190

Art. 174(4) . . . 187, 190

Art. 175 . . . 181, 187–8, 190, 194, 201, 214

Art. 175(1) . . . 190

Art. 175(4) . . . 190

Art. 175(5) . . . 181, 190, 199

Art. 176 . . . 188, 196

Art. 207 . . . 299

Art. 226 . . . 207–8

Art. 228 . . . 181, 206–8, 216

Art. 230 . . . 182–3

Art. 230(4) . . . 175

Art. 234 . . . 175, 183, 209, 216

Art. 249 . . . 204, 206

Art. 251 . . . 181

Art. 253 . . . 198

Art. 255 . . . 299

Art. 308 . . . 185, 194

Euratom Treaty . . . 173

EU Reform Treaty (Wisbon Treaty) . . . 172, 174

Maastricht Treaty . . . 171, 173, 181, 186, 202, 207

Moon Treaty
Art 7 . . . 7

Ozone Treaty 1985 . . . 21, 157

Single European Act 1987 . . . 21, 26, 171, 173, 185–6, 188, 195–7

Treaty of Amsterdam . . . 28, 171, 173, 186, 195–6, 720

Declaration No. 24 . . . 720

Protocol 33 . . . 720

Treaty of Lisbon (Reform Treaty) 2007 . . . 186–7

Treaty of Nice . . . 174, 182

Decisions

Decision 93/98/EEC . . . 636

Decision 94/3/EC European Waste Catalogue . . . 639

Decision 98/3 . . . 46

Decision 2000/479/EC . . . 537–8

Decision 2000/532/EC European List of Wastes . . . 640, 646

Decision 2002/358/EC
Annex B . . . 523

Decision 2005/166 . . . 524

Decision 2007/2 . . . 523

Council Framework Decision on Environmental Criminal Law 2003/80 . . . 187

Commission Decision 2004/470/EC . . . 510

Commission Decision 2006/944/EC . . . 524

Directives

Directive 67/548 (Labelling Dangerous Produce) . . . 171, 184

Directive 70/157 (Sound Levels from Motor Vehicles) . . . 195

Directive 70/220 (Emissions from Vehicles) . . . 192, 536

Directive 73/404 (Detergents) . . . 589

Directive 75/439 (Waste Oils) . . . 185, 642

Directive 75/440 (Surface Water for Drinking) . . . 591

Directive 75/442 (Waste Framework Directive) . . . 633–4, 636, 639–40, 642–3, 645, 648–51, 657, 668, 672–3

    Art. 1(a) . . . 646, 650

    Art. 2 . . . 639

    Arts. 3–7 . . . 642

    Art. 4 . . . 209, 643

    Art. 5 . . . 643

    Art. 7 . . . 642

    Annex I . . . 646

    Annex IIA . . . 647, 657

    Annex IIB . . . 647, 657

Directive 76/160 (Bathing Waters) . . . 208, 216, 591, 595, 625

Directive 76/403 (Disposal of PCBs) . . . 193

Directive 76/464 (Dangerous Substances in Water) . . . 236, 498, 589–90, 594, 599

Directive 76/769 (Marketing and Use of Pesticides . . . 232

Directive 78/109 (Titanium Dioxide Waste) . . . 68

Directive 78/170 (Energy Efficiency of Boilers) . . . 232

Directive 78/176 (Titanium Dioxide Industry) . . . 193, 589, 642

Directive 78/319 (Toxic Waste) . . . 193

Directive 79/409 (Wild Birds) . . . 26, 176, 185, 194, 704–5, 707, 709, 714–5, 720, 724, 745

    Art. 1 . . . 705

    Art. 2 . . . 705

    Art. 3 . . . 705

    Art. 4 . . . 705

    Art. 4(1) . . . 710

    Art. 4(2) . . . 710

    Art. 4(4) . . . 709

    Art. 5 . . . 710

    Annex I . . . 705–6

Directive 79/831 (Classification, Packaging and Labelling of Dangerous Substances) . . . 193

Directive 79/923 (Shellfish Waters) . . . 211, 349, 625

Directive 80/68 (Groundwater) . . . 590, 593, 606, 673

    List I . . . 590, 673

    List II . . . 590, 673

Directive 80/778 (Drinking Water) . . . 192, 211, 215, 619

Directive 82/501 (Major Accident Hazards, 'Seveso I') . . . 193

Directive 83/129 (Seal Skins) . . . 720

Directive 83/513 (Cadmium) . . . 193

Directive 84/156 (Mercury) . . . 193

Directive 84/360 (Emissions from Industrial Plants) . . . 193, 533

Directive 84/491 (Lindane) . . . 193

Directive 84/631/EC (Shipment of Hazardous Waste) . . . 202

Directive 85/337 (Environmental Impact Assessment) . . . 26–7, 81, 181, 193, 199, 209–10, 216–7, 400, 433, 439–43, 446, 449–50, 452–5, 457–9, 462, 464–73, 478, 496, 711, 734, 748

    recital (1) . . . 457

    Art.1(2) . . . 80

    Art. 1(4) . . . 455

    Art. 1(5) . . . 455

    Art. 2 . . . 449

    Art. 2(1) . . . 440, 447

    Art. 2(3) . . . 447, 455

    Art. 4 . . . 447, 449

    Art. 7 . . . 439

    Annex I . . . 442–3, 445–7

    Annex II . . . 442, 444–5, 448–9, 747

    Annex III . . . 448

Directive 86/188 (Noise in the Workplace) . . . 193

Directive 86/278 (Sewage Sludge) . . . 193

Directive 86/280 . . . 590

Directive 87/217 (Asbestos) . . . 193, 479

    Art. 3 . . . 490

    Art. 4(1) . . . 490

    Art. 5 . . . 490

    Art. 6(1) . . . 490

    Art. 6(2) . . . 490

    Art. 8 . . . 490

    Annex . . . 490

Directive 88/76 (Emissions from Vehicles) . . . 192

Directive 88/77 (Vans and Heavy Duty Vehicles) . . . 536

Directive 89/369 (Municipal Waste) . . . 640

Directive 89/428 (Titanium Dioxide Industry) . . . 193

Directive 89/548 (Emissions from Vehicles) . . . 192

Directive 90/219 (Contained Use of Genetically Modified Organisms) . . . 173, 194

Directive 90/220 . . . 68

Directive 90/313 (Access to Environmental Information) . . . 299–301

Directive 91/156 (Waste Framework Directive (Amendment)) . . . 187, 639

Directive 91/157 (Batteries and Accumulators) . . . 638, 642

Directive 91/271 (Urban Waste Water Treatment) . . . 37, 91, 193, 199, 214, 217, 587, 592–3, 601–2, 619, 621, 625, 673

   Art. 4 . . . 231

   Art. 14 . . . 27

Directive 91/414 (Pesticides) . . . 68

Directive 91/441 (Emissions from Vehicles) . . . 192

Directive 91/676 (Agricultural Nitrates) . . . 68, 183, 192, 200, 208, 244, 593, 608, 619, 627, 745

Directive 91/689 (Hazardous Waste) . . . 193, 638, 640, 642, 652

   Art. 1(4) . . . 639

Directive 92/43 (Habitats) . . . 87, 125, 135, 179, 194, 214, 217, 319, 400, 419, 450, 462, 473, 623, 700, 704–6, 708, 711–2, 715, 717–8, 721, 723–4, 734, 745

   Art. 2(3) . . . 707

   Art. 4 . . . 53

   Art. 5 . . . 707, 715

   Art. 6 . . . 433, 470, 474, 709, 712, 714

   Art. 6(1) . . . 710

   Art. 6(2)-(4) . . . 714

   Art. 6(2) . . . 710–11, 715

   Art. 6(3) . . . 710–11

   Art. 6(4) . . . 710–11, 714, 716–7

   Art. 7 . . . 470

   Art. 10 . . . 704

   Art. 11 . . . 704

   Arts. 12–16 . . . 719

   Art. 12(1)(d) . . . 721

   Art. 16 . . . 725

   Annex I . . . 688, 705, 710

   Annex II . . . 705

   Annex III . . . 706

Directive 92/75 (Energy Label) . . . 310

Directive 92/112/EEC (Titanium Dioxide) . . . 479

   Art. 4 . . . 490

   Art. 6 . . . 490

   Arts. 9–11 . . . 490

   Annex . . . 490

Directive 94/62 (Packaging and Packaging Waste) . . . 193, 197, 202, 641–2, 669

Directive 94/63 (Volatile Organic Compounds) . . . 193, 479, 533

   Art. 3(1) . . . 490

   Art. 4(1)-(3) . . . 490

Art. 6(1) . . . 490

Annex I . . . 490

Annex II . . . 490

Annex III . . . 490

Annex IV . . . 490

Directive 94/67 (Hazardous waste) . . . 640

Directive 95/12 (Washing Machines) . . . 310

Directive 96/59 (Waste PCBs and PCTs) . . . 638, 642

Directive 96/61 (Integrated Pollution Prevention and Control) . . . 26, 125, 173, 176, 193, 198–9, 214, 216, 478, 497–8, 506, 533, 535, 673

   Art. 15(3) . . . 176, 537

   Art. 18 . . . 498

   Annex I . . . 537

Directive 96/62 (Ambient Air Quality Assessment and Management Framework) . . . 26, 83, 192, 534, 539, 543

Directive 97/11 . . . 439–41, 445–7, 459–60, 463, 503

Directive 98/69 (Auto Oil) . . . 181, 534

Directive 98/70 (Content of Petrol and Diesel Fuels) . . . 193, 536

Directive 98/83 (Drinking Water Quality) . . . 178, 211–2, 215, 582, 591, 593, 597

Directive 1999/13 (Volatile Organic Compounds) . . . 83, 193, 479, 534

   Art. 4(4) . . . 489

   Art. 5 . . . 489

   Art. 7(2) . . . 489

   Art. 8(1)-(4) . . . 489

   Art. 9 . . . 489

   Art. 10 . . . 489

Directive 1999/30 (Limits for NOx, SO2, PM10 and Pb) . . . 83, 192

Directive 1999/31 (Landfill) . . . 193, 199, 236, 479, 632, 638, 642, 656–7, 662, 669

   Art. 1 . . . 489

   Art. 2 . . . 641

   Art. 4 . . . 489, 641

   Art. 5 . . . 227, 641

   Art. 5(2) . . . 663

   Art. 5(3) . . . 489, 662

   Art. 5(4) . . . 489

   Art. 6 . . . 227, 489, 641, 662

   Art. 6(a) . . . 663

   Art. 7 . . . 489

   Art. 8 . . . 489

   Art. 9 . . . 489

   Art. 10 . . . 489, 641

Art. 11(1) . . . 489

Art. 12 . . . 489

Art. 13 . . . 489, 663

Art. 14 . . . 489, 662

Annex I . . . 641, 662

Annex II . . . 663

Annex III . . . 662

Directive 1999/32 (Sulphur Content of Fuels) . . . 534

Directive 1999/51 (PCPs) . . . 198

Directive 1999/52 (Private Cars) . . . 536

Directive 1999/86 (Heavy Duty Vehicles) . . . 534

Directive 2000/14 (Noise from Outdoor Equipment) . . . 193

Directive 2000/53 (End of Life Vehicles) . . . 30, 193, 205, 232, 235, 479, 553, 633, 641, 657, 669, 670

Art. 6(1) . . . 489

Art. 6(3) . . . 489

Annex I . . . 489

Directive 2000/60 (Water Framework) . . . 26, 30, 31, 181, 192, 197, 208–9, 214, 225, 230, 236–7, 244, 363, 557, 584–91, 593, 595–6, 606, 620, 622–3, 626–7

Directive 2000/69 (Limits for Benzene and Carbon Monoxide) . . . 83, 192

Directive 2000/76 (Incineration of Waste) . . . 83, 193, 479, 500, 534, 638, 640, 657

Art. 1 . . . 640

Art. 4 . . . 587, 640

Art. 4(2)–(5) . . . 489

Art. 5 . . . 489, 640

Art. 6 . . . 489

Art. 7(1)–(4) . . . 489

Art. 8(1)–(7) . . . 489

Art. 9 . . . 489

Art. 10 . . . 489

Art. 11 . . . 489

Art. 12(2) . . . 489

Art. 13 . . . 489

Art. 16(1) . . . 587

Annex II . . . 489, 640

Annex IV . . . 489

Annex V . . . 489, 640

Annex VI . . . 489

Directive 2001/18 (Deliberate Release of Genetically Modified Organisms) . . . 69, 194, 196

Art. 23 . . . 198

Directive 2001/42 (Strategic Environmental Assessment) . . . 192–3, 199, 391, 433, 440, 469, 471–3

Art. 2(a) . . . 470

Art. 3.2 . . . 470

Art. 3.2(a) . . . 470

Art. 3.2(b) . . . 470

Art. 3.3 . . . 470

Art. 3.4 . . . 470

Art. 3.5 . . . 470

Art. 3.8 . . . 470

Art. 3.9 . . . 470

Directive 2001/77 (Renewable Energy Sources) . . . 194, 199, 201, 524

Directive 2001/80 (Emissions from Large Combustion Plants) . . . 83, 193, 199, 479, 527, 534–5

Art. 4(1)–(4) . . . 490

Art. 5(1) . . . 490

Arts. 6–10 . . . 490

Arts. 12–14 . . . 490

Annexes III-VIII(A) . . . 490

Directive 2001/81 (National Emissions Ceilings) . . . 83, 232, 527, 534–5

Directive 2002/3 (Limits for Ozone) . . . 83, 192

Directive 2002/49 (Monitoring and Mapping Noise) . . . 193

Directive 2002/91 (Energy Performance of Buildings) . . . 310, 525

Directive 2002/95 (Hazardous Substances in Electrical and Electronic Equipment) . . . 188, 193, 197–8, 670

Directive 2002/96 (Waste Electrical and Electronic Equipment) . . . 188, 193, 198–200, 205, 232, 479, 553, 641, 657, 670

Art.6(1) . . . 489

Art.6(3) . . . 489

Art.6(4) . . . 489

Annex III . . . 489

Directive 2003/4 (Freedom of Access to Information on the Environment) . . . 194, 211, 300–2, 310

Art. 1 . . . 301

Art. 2 . . . 301

Art. 3 . . . 301

Art. 4(1) . . . 301

Art. 4(2) . . . 301

Art. 5 . . . 301

Art. 6 . . . 301

Art. 7 . . . 301

Directive 2003/17 . . . 536

Directive 2003/30 (Promoting Biofuels) . . . 194, 524

Directive 2003/35 (Public Participation in relation to Plans and Programmes required under the EIA and IPPC Directives) . . . 194, 311, 441

Directive 2003/87 (Greenhouse Gas Emissions Trading Scheme) . . . 96, 194, 205, 523–5, 530

Art. 4 . . . 526

Art. 6 . . . 526

Art. 7 . . . 526

Art. 8 . . . 526

Art. 9 . . . 526

Annex I . . . 525, 526

Annex II . . . 525

Directive 2003/96 (Taxation of Energy Products and Electricity) . . . 181, 191, 194

Directive 2004/8/EC . . . 524

Directive 2004/12 . . . 669

Directive 2004/35 (Environmental Liability) . . . 194, 242, 249, 360, 363–5

Art. 17 . . . 553

Directive 2004/101/EC . . . 524, 527

Directive 2004/107/EC . . . 535

Directive 2004/156/EC . . . 524

Directive 2005/20 . . . 669

Directive 2006/7/EC (Bathing Waters) . . . 192, 214, 591, 593, 596

Directive 2006/11/EC (Dangerous Substances in Water) . . . 192–3, 498, 589–91, 593, 599, 604

Directive 2006/12/EC (Waste Framework Directive) . . . 26, 81, 179, 193, 211, 414, 479, 481, 552, 607, 638–9

Art.1(1)(a) . . . 80, 90

Art. 3(1) . . . 488

Art.4 . . . 217, 410, 488

Art.5 . . . 488

Art.9(1) . . . 488

Art.10 . . . 488

Art.11 . . . 488

Art.13 . . . 488

Art.14 . . . 488

Directive 2006/32/EC (Energy Efficiency and Services) . . . 525

Directive 2006/44/EC (Freshwater Fish Waters) . . . 192, 591, 593

Directive 2006/113/EC (Shellfish Waters) . . . 192, 591, 593

Directive 2006/118/EC (Groundwater) . . . 192, 595, 622

Directive 2007/589/EC . . . 524

Directive 2008/1/EC (Integrated pollution prevention and control) . . . 69, 82–3, 94, 231, 236–7, 479, 498, 503, 505–6, 638, 656, 662

Art. 1 . . . 498

Art. 2(12) . . . 501

Art. 3 . . . 488, 498–9

Art. 3(1)(f) . . . 502

Arts. 4–9 . . . 498

Art. 6(1) . . . 488

Art. 9 . . . 488, 499

Art. 9(1) . . . 500

Art. 9(8) . . . 499

Art. 10 . . . 488, 500

Art. 11 . . . 488

Art. 12 . . . 488

Art. 13 . . . 488

Art. 14 . . . 488

Art. 15 . . . 505

Art. 15(1) . . . 488

Art. 16 . . . 498, 505

Art. 16(3) . . . 226

Art. 19(1) . . . 498

Annex I . . . 498, 505

Annex II . . . 488

Annex III . . . 488, 499

Annex IV . . . 488, 501

Annex V . . . 488

Directive 2008/ /EC (Air Quality and Cleaner Air for Europe) . . . 192, 533

Regulations

Regulation 348/81 (Whale Products) . . . 720

Regulation 797/85 (Agricultural Structures) . . . 746

Regulation 1210/90 (European Environment Agency) . . . 176, 194

Regulation 3254/91 (Animal Pelts) . . . 720

Regulation 880/92 (Eco-Labelling) . . . 194, 247, 310

Regulation 1973/92 (Financial Instrument for the Environment (LIFE)) . . . 194

Regulation 1836/93 (Eco-Management and Audit Systems (EMAS)) . . . 144, 194, 246, 308

Regulation 3093/94 (Substances that Deplete the Ozone Layer) . . . 189

Regulation 338/97 (Trade in Endangered Species) . . . 194, 258

Regulation 2821/98 . . . 68

Regulation 1257/99 (Rural Development) . . . 194, 747

Regulation 1980/2000 (Eco-Labelling Scheme) . . . 232, 309

Regulation 2037/2000 (Phasing Out Ozone-Depleting Substances) . . . 193, 523

Regulation 1049/2001 (Public Access to European Parliament, Council and Commission Documents (Transparency Regulation)) . . . 299

Art. 2(1) . . . 299

Regulation 1641/2003 (EEA Transparency) . . . 299

Regulation 1782/2003 (Agricultural Support) . . . 242, 745

Regulation 1882/2003 . . . 669

Regulation 1946/2003 (Transboundary Movement of Genetically Modified Organisms) . . . 194

Regulation 1698/2005 (Rural Development) . . . 747

Art. 4(1)(b) . . . 747

Art. 17 . . . 747

Regulation 166/2006 . . . 538

Regulation 1907/2006 (Chemicals and their Safe Use) . . . 232

Regulation 1367/2006 (Aarhus and EC Institutions) . . . 192

Regulation (EC) 1907/2006 (Registration, Evaluation, Authorisation and Restriction of Chemicals) . . . 56, 193

Regulation 1013/2006/EC (Waste Shipments) . . . 193, 635–6

TABLE OF CONVENTIONS AND AGREEMENTS

Aarhus Convention on Access to Information, Public Participation and Decision-Making in Environmental Matters 1998 . . . 22, 135, 141, 148–9, 155, 165, 192, 213, 294, 298, 300–2

preamble . . . 295

Arts. 6–9 . . . 311

Art. 9(2) . . . 313

Art. 9(4) . . . 320

Aarhus Protocol on Heavy Metals 1999 . . . 83

Aarhus Protocol on Persistent Organic Pollutants 1998 . . . 83

Agreement on the Application of Sanitary and Phytosanitary Measures (SPS) . . . 161

Agreement on the Conservation of African-Eurasian Migratory Waterbirds 1995 . . . 155

Agreement on Technical Barriers to Trade (TBT) . . . 161

Antarctic Environmental Protocol 1991 . . . 442

Basel Convention on the Control of Transboundary Movements of Hazardous Waste and their Disposal 1989 . . . 141, 163, 635, 636

Berne Convention on the Conservation of European Wildlife and Natural Habitats 1979 . . . 140, 723

Bonn Convention on the Conservation of Migratory Species of Wild Animals 1979 . . . 139–40, 154

Bremen Declaration on the Protection of the North Sea 1984 . . . 64

Cartagena Biosafety Protocol . . . 136, 140, 157, 161, 165, 187, 190

Art. 11 . . . 65

Civil Liability Convention and 1992 . . . 141

Convention on Biological Diversity (biodiversity) 1992 . . . 65, 140–1, 147, 149, 155, 157, 187, 437, 682, 688, 720, 726

preamble . . . 65, 681

Art. 2 . . . 681

Art. 6 . . . 726

Art. 10 . . . 726

Art. 14 . . . 435

Art. 14(1) . . . 436

Protocol on Biosafety . . . 148

Convention on Civil Liability for Oil Pollution Damage 1992 . . . 587

Convention on International Trade in Endangered Species (CITES) . . . 137, 140, 142, 149–50, 156–7, 163, 685, 720

Annex I . . . 80

Appendix III . . . 681

Convention on Long-Range Transboundary Air Pollution 1979 (LRTAP) . . . 140

Convention for the Protection of Birds Useful to Agriculture 1902 . . . 139

Convention on the Protection of the Environment through Criminal Law 1998 . . . 141

Council of Europe European Landscape Convention 2004 . . . 734

Espoo Transboundary EIA Convention 1991 . . . 141, 437–9, 447, 733

Appendix III . . . 437

European Convention on Human Rights and Fundamental Freedoms 1950 . . . 14, 36, 72–4, 135, 298, 330, 332

Art. 2 . . . 298, 330

Art. 6 . . . 318, 381, 385, 421, 424, 694

Art. 7 . . . 651–2

Art. 8 . . . 298, 330–1, 338, 345, 359, 408

Art. 10 . . . 72

Art. 11 . . . 72

Art. 14 . . . 334

First Protocol, Art. 1 . . . 424, 694

European Landscape Convention 2000 . . . 141

Fourth North Sea Declaration 1995 . . . 136

GATT/WTO Agreement . . . 136, 149, 159, 161–3

Art. III(4) . . . 162

Art. XI . . . 159

Art. XX . . . 159–60, 162

Art. XX(b) . . . 159–60, 162

Art. XX(g) . . . 159–60

preamble . . . 28

Geneva Convention on Long-Range Transboundary Air Pollution 1979 . . . 83, 517–9

Art. 2, . . . 517

Art. 6 . . . 517

First Protocol . . . 518

Second Protocol . . . 518

Geneva Protocol on Volatile Organic Compounds 1991 . . . 83, 518

Gothenburg Protocol to Abate Acidification, Eutrophication and Ground-level Ozone 1999 . . . 83

HNS Convention . . . 361

Helsinki Convention on the Protection of the Baltic Sea 1992

Art. 3(2) . . . 65

Helsinki Protocol on Reduction of Sulphur Emissions 1985 . . . 83

ICJ Statute

Art. 38 . . . 139

Art. 59 . . . 143

Johannesburg Declaration on Sustainable Development 2002 . . . 143, 148

Kiev Protocol to the Espoo Convention 2003 . . . 434, 437, 469

Kiev Protocol on Pollutant Release and Transfer Registers 2004 . . . 298

Kiev Strategic Environmental Assessment Protocol 2004 . . . 141

Kyoto Protocol 1997 . . . 79, 137, 140, 142, 156–7, 163, 234, 520–5, 531, 539

Art. 4 . . . 137

Art. 17 . . . 96

Liability and Compensation for Hazardous and Noxious Substances at Sea Convention 1996 . . . 141

Liability and Compensation Protocol to the Basle Hazardous Waste Convention 1999 . . . 141

London Convention on the Prevention of Marine Pollution by Dumping of Wastes and Other Matter 1972 . . . 522

Lugano Environmental Civil Liability Convention 1993 . . . 141

MARPOL International Convention for the Prevention of Pollution from Ships 1973 . . . 141, 156, 165, 587

Monitoring and Evaluation Protocol 1984 . . . 83

Montreal Amendment on Ozone Depletion 1990 . . . 140, 163

Montreal Protocol on Ozone Depletion 1987 . . . 138, 140, 155, 227, 514–5, 519

Oil Pollution Fund Convention 1992 . . . 141, 242

Oslo Protocol on Further Reduction of Sulphur Emissions 1994 . . . 83, 518

OSPAR Convention for the Protection of the Marine Environment of the North East Atlantic (Paris)1998 . . . 27, 64, 139, 141, 153–5, 587–8, 635

Art. 2(1)(a) . . . 140

Art. 2(2)(b) . . . 140

Persistent Organic Pollutants Convention 2001 . . . 155

Persistent Organic Pollutants Protocol 1998 . . . 148

Ramsar Convention on Wetlands of International Importance 1971 . . . 140, 155, 687

Rio Convention on Biodiversity . . . 62

Rio Convention on Climate Change . . . 62

Rio Earth Summit . . . 135

Agenda 21 . . . 57, 147–9, 151, 298, 434, 758

para. 39.10 . . . 151

Rio Declaration on the Environment and Development 1992 . . . 54, 73, 143, 147–8, 164, 435

Principle 1 . . . 147

Principle 2 . . . 55, 148, 438

Principle 3 . . . 148

Principle 7 . . . 147

Principle 10 . . . 56, 147, 165, 294

Principle 12 . . . 160

Principle 13 . . . 165

Principle 15 . . . 147

Principle 16 . . . 147

Principle 17 . . . 147, 434

Principle 18 . . . 147

Principle 19 . . . 147

Rome Statute of the International Criminal Court

Art. 8 . . . 166

Rotterdam Prior Informed Consent to Trade Convention 1998 . . . 141, 187

Sofia Protocol on Nitrogen Oxides 1988 . . . 83, 518

Southern Blue Fish Tuna Treaty . . . 66

Stockholm Convention on Persistent Organic Pollutants . . . 141

Stockholm Declaration on the Human Environment . . . 143

Principle 1 . . . 147

Principle 21 . . . 146–7, 438

Principle 24 . . . 146

Transboundary Watercourses Convention 1992
. . . 733

UN Convention on the Law of the Sea 1982
(UNCLOS) . . . 141, 635

Arts. 192–194 . . . 635

Art. 206 . . . 436, 588

Art. 207 . . . 588

Art. 208 . . . 588

Art. 210 . . . 588

UNESCO World Heritage Convention 1972 . . .
140, 150, 523

UN Framework Convention on Climate Change
(UNFCCC, or the Climate Change Treaty) . . .
32, 65, 79, 140, 142, 147, 155–7, 165, 520, 525

Art. 2 . . . 520

Art. 3 . . . 143, 520

Art.3(3) . . . 65

Art. 4 . . . 520–1

Art. 4(1) . . . 520

Art. 4(1)(f) . . . 435

Art. 4(2) . . . 520

Art. 4(2)(a) . . . 520

Art. 4(2)(b) . . . 520

Art. 6 . . . 298, 521

Art. 12 . . . 521

Art. 17 . . . 521

Annex I . . . 520, 521

Universal Declaration of Human Rights . . .
148

Vienna Convention on the Law of Treaties 1969
. . . 140

Vienna Convention on the Protection of the
Ozone Layer 1985 . . . 140, 149, 155–6, 518,
523

Whaling Convention 1946 . . . 136, 150, 155

World Charter for Nature 1982 . . . 682

World Heritage Convention 1972 . . . 733, 734

AEBC	Agriculture and Environment Biotechnology Commission
ACBE	Advisory Committee on Business and the Environment
ACEA	European Automobile Manufacturers Association
AONB	Area of Outstanding Natural Beauty
AQMA	Air Quality Management Area
AQS	air quality standard
AWE	Atomic Weapons Establishment
BAT	best available techniques
BATNEEC	best available techniques not entailing excessive cost
BATRRT	best available treatment recovery and recycling techniques
BERR	Department for Business, Enterprise and Regulatory Reform
BOD	biochemical oxygen demand
BPEO	best practicable environmental option
BPM	best practicable means
BREF	BAT Reference Document
BSE	Bovine spongiform encephalopathy
CAFE	Clean Air for Europe
CAP	Common Agricultural Policy
CBI	Confederation of British Industry
CCL	Climate Change Levy
CCS	Carbon capture and storage
CCW	Countryside Council for Wales
CERCLA	Comprehensive Environmental Response Compensation and Liability Act 1981
CFC	chlorofluorocarbon
CICS	Common Incident Classification Scheme
CITES	Convention on the International Trade in Endangered Species
COD	chemical oxygen demand
COPFS	Crown Office and Procurator Fiscal Service
COP	Conference of the Parties
CoPA	Control of Pollution Act 1974
COPFS	Crown Office and Procurator Fiscal Service
CPRE	Campaign to Protect Rural England
CROWA	Countryside and Rights of Way Act
DEFRA	Department for Environment, Food and Rural Affairs
DETR	Department of the Environment, Transport, and the Regions
DTLR	Department of Transport, Local Government and the Regions
DOE	Department of the Environment
DTI	Department of Trade and Industry
DWI	Drinking Water Inspectorate
EAP	Environmental Action Programme
EC	European Community
ECB	European Central Bank
ECCP	European Climate Change Programme
ECHR	European Convention on Human Rights
ECtHR	European Court of Human Rights

ECJ	European Court of Justice
ECSC	European Coal and Steel Commission
EEC	European Economic Community
EEZ	exclusive economic zone
EHS	Environmental and Heritage Service
EIA	Environmental Impact Assessment
EIONET	European Environment Information and Observation Network
ELS	Entry Level Scheme
ELV	Emission limit value
ELV	End-of-Life Vehicle
EMAS	Eco-Management and Audit Scheme
EMEP	Programme for Monitoring and Evaluation of Long-Range Transmission of Air Pollutants in Europe
EMS	European Monetary System
EPAC	Environment Protection Advisory Committee
EPA	Environmental Protection Act
EPAC	Environment Protection Advisory Agency
EPER	European Pollutant Emission Register
E-PRTR	European Pollutant Release and Transfer Register
EQS	Environmental Quality Standard
ES	Environmental Statement
ESA	Environmentally Sensitive Area
ESS	Environmental Stewardship Scheme
EU	European Union
Euratom	European Atomic Energy Community
FOI	Freedom of Information
FTSE	Financial Times and the London Stock Exchange
GATS	General Agreement on Trade in Services
GATT	General Agreement on Tariffs and Trade
GBRs	General Binding Rules
GDPO	Town and Country Planning (General Development Procedure) Order
GEF	Global Environment Facility
GGI	Greening Government Initiative
GIA	Grant in Aid
GM	genetically modified
GMO	genetically modified organism
GPDO	Town and Country Planning (General Permitted Development) Order
GQA	General Quality Assessment
HCFC	Hydrochloroflourocarbon
HFC	hydrofluorocarbon
HMIP	Her Majesty's Inspectorate of Pollution
HMRC	HM Revenue & Customs
ICJ	International Court of Justice
ILC	International Law Commission
IMPEL	European Union Network for Implementation and Enforcement of Environmental Law
IPC	integrated pollution control
IPCC	Intergovernmental Panel on Climate Change
IPPC	integrated pollution prevention and control
ISO	International Organization for Standardization
ITLOS	International Tribunal on the Law of the Sea

IUCN	International Union for the Conservation of Nature
JNCC	Joint Nature Conservation Committee
JPL	Journal of Planning and Environment Law
LCPD	Large Combustion Plants Directive
LDO	Local Development Order
LEAP	Local Environment Agency Plan
LOSC	Law of the Sea Convention
LTCS	Landfill Tax Credit Scheme
LTP	Local Transport Plan
MARAD	The US Maritime administration
MARPOL	The International Convention for the Prevention of Pollution from Ships (1973)
MBC	Metropolitan Borough Council
MNR	Marine nature reserve
MOD	Ministry of Defence
MOX	Mixed Oxide Plant
MWDF	Minerals and Waste Development Framework
NCC	Nature Conservancy Council
NDPB	Non-departmental public body
NERC	Natural Environment and Rural Communities Act 2006
NGO	Non-governmental organization
NIMBY	Not in my back yard
NNR	National Nature Reserve
NPACA	National Parks and Access to the Countryside Act 1949
NRA	National Rivers Authority
NVZ	Nitrate Vulnerable Zone
ODPM	Office of the Deputy Prime Minister
OECD	Organisation for Economic Co-operation and Development
OELS	Organic Entry Level Scheme
Ofwat	Water Services Regulation Authority
OSPAR	The Convention for the Protection of the Marine Environment of the North-East Atlantic (1992)
PCO	Protective costs order
PCP	pentachlorophenol
PCPA	Planning and Compulsory Purchase Act 2004
PERN	packaging waste export recovery note
PFC	perfluorocarbon
POP	Persistent Organic Pollutant
PPC	Pollution Prevention and Control
PPCA	Pollution Prevention and Control Act 1999
PPG	Planning Policy Guidance Note
PPS	Planning Policy Statement
PRN	packaging recovery note
PSA	Public Service Agreement
RCEP	Royal Commission on Environmental Pollution
RDC	Rural Development Commission
REACH	Registration, Evaluation, Authorisation and Restriction of Chemicals
RPG	Regional Planning Guidance
RSPB	Royal Society for the Protection of Birds
RSPCA	Royal Society for the Prevention of Cruelty to Animals
RSS	Regional Spatial Strategy

SAC	special area of conservation
SBT	Southern Bluefish Tuna Treaty
SEA	strategic environmental assessment
SEPA	Scottish Environment Protection Agency
SLF	substitute liquid fuel
SNH	Scottish Natural Heritage
SPA	special protection area
SPL	significant pollutant linkage
SPS	Agreement on the Application of Sanitary and Phytosanitary Measures
SPZ	simplified planning zone
SSSI	Site of Special Scientific Interest
TBT	Agreement on Technical Barriers to Trade
TCPA	Town and Country Planning Act 1990
TED	turtle excluder device
THORP	Thermal Oxide Reprocessing Plant
TPO	Tree Preservation Order
TPR	Town Planning Review
UNCLOS	UN Convention on the Law of the Sea
UNECE	United Nations Economic Commission for Europe
UNEP	United Nations Environment Programme
UNESCO	UN Educational, Scientific and Cultural Organization
UNFCCC	UN Framework Convention on Climate Change
VOC	volatile organic compound
WCA	Wildlife and Countryside Act 1981
WEEE	Waste Electrical and Electronic Equipment Directive
WHO	World Health Organization
WHS	World Heritage Site
WMO	World Meteorological Organization
WIA	Water Industry Act 1991
WRA	Water Resources Act 1991
WTO	World Trade Organization
WWF	World Wide Fund for Nature

PART I

Introductory themes

1 What is environmental law? A brief introduction

→ **Overview**

This introductory chapter deals with the difficult issue of defining 'environmental law' for the purposes of this book. It covers the definition of certain key terms and provides an outline of some of the underlying themes that will be found in many chapters. It is designed for use at the very beginning of a course of study to help to establish a context for future study. The notes and questions at the end of the chapter are designed to provoke thought about the way in which law, policy, and rights might affect everyday environmental issues and problems.

After studying this chapter, you should be able to:

✔ understand basic definitions of 'the environment' and 'law';

✔ appreciate some of the difficulties of defining 'environmental law';

✔ understand the basic outline of some of the key themes of this book and the subject;

✔ understand the basic interrelationship between environmental law and policy;

✔ understand some of the different meanings of 'rights' within environmental law.

Why a book on environmental law?

Before we launch into a description of the subject, it is perhaps pertinent to start with a few points of justification. Why have a book on environmental law? Without wanting to prejudge some of the matters that will be dealt with in other chapters, we would like to propose some starting points—opinions that justify why we think the subject is important and why you should study it.

- **The environment is important**
  There is a general recognition that the environment is important and that efforts should be made to protect it. It is clear that the general topic is one of the big issues—perhaps *the* biggest contemporary issue—that we face. Issues such as climate change and rising waste production require significant responses. Environmental considerations have become central to policymaking and decision making across a wide range of issues, and it is increasingly perceived that environmental considerations are integral to all aspects of life.

- **Protecting the environment presents a big challenge**
  It is a big challenge in political terms, because protection of the environment is high on most people's priorities in the twenty-first century. It is big in terms of the size of the problems faced and the solutions required: climate change, the protection of the marine environment, acid rain, deforestation, and toxic waste are all global issues that require an appropriately global response. It is big in terms of the range of problems and issues: air pollution; water pollution; noise pollution; the safe management of waste; radioactivity;

pesticides; countryside protection; conservation of wildlife—the list is virtually endless. Finally, it is big in terms of the knowledge and skills required to understand a particular issue. Law is only one element in what is a major cross-disciplinary topic. Lawyers need some understanding of the scientific, political, social, and economic processes involved in environmental degradation. Equally, all those whose activities and interests relate to the environment need to acquire an understanding of the structure and content of environmental law, because it has a large and increasing role to play in environmental protection.

- **Law is central to the management of the environment**
  This remains the case despite the increasing use of voluntary approaches and market mechanisms, such as taxes, subsidies, and instruments that affect the behaviour of consumers. To some extent, the centrality of environmental law as a tool to manage the environment merely reflects the regrouping or re-categorization of matters that have always been there. Of course, this depends on the tricky question of the exact scope and definition of 'environmental law', which the rest of this chapter seeks to answer.

- **Environmental protection laws are vast in numbers and complexity**
  The last twenty or so years have seen a dramatic increase in the number and complexity of laws seeking to protect the environment. Numerous EC Directives have been agreed and there are major pieces of domestic legislation—such as the Pollution Prevention and Control Act 1999, the Clean Neighbourhoods and Environment Act 2005, and the Natural Environment and Rural Communities Act 2006. There is also a large amount of secondary legislation, and an even larger amount of policy and guidance.

- **Environmental disputes and cases with an environmental element are becoming more frequent**
  It is increasingly the case that the public views the results of 'environmental' decisions as unsatisfactory—in other words, that there is a perception that policies and decision-making procedures are failing both the public and the environment. This has led to the increasing use of law by environmental groups as an alternative to direct action, and to pressure on the planning system as local residents protect their own personal and property interests against unwelcome developments.

What is 'environmental law'?

In identifying the subject matter of this book, it is first necessary to consider whether there is any identifiable subject that could be termed 'environmental law'. It might seem to be a defensive or unnecessary starting point, but it could be argued that the boundaries of the subject are not particularly well defined[1] or that the subject is not necessarily distinctive. This potential lack of doctrinal certainty has, in the UK at least, led to a number of attempts to 'justify' the existence of a coherent subject known as 'environmental law' as a discrete legal subject area.[2] A major aim of this book is, therefore, to illustrate the proposition that there has developed such a thing as environmental law and, while not seeking to straitjacket the boundaries of the subject, to provide an outline of a number of key components that form the substantive heart of the subject.

Most lawyers are brought up on the idea that there are a number of core, or basic, subjects that are essentially about techniques and in which a set of central organizing principles can be distilled from the law. Criminal law, public law, contract law, torts, equity, and land law would be good examples. The traditional view would then be that, alongside those basic

---

1 See Z. Plater (1999) 23 Harv Envtl L Rev 359, and R. Lazarus (1999) 23 Harv Envtl L Rev 327.
2 See, e.g., C. Reid (1998) 4 Jur Rev 236.

subjects, there are as many areas of law as there are areas of life, in each of which the techniques of the basic subjects are used: for example, the law relating to intellectual property rights or the law relating to housing. But, over a period of time, there is no doubt that these topic-related areas build up their own principles and reasoning processes—for example, through the application and interpretation of subject-specific laws and policy in decision making, and through cases in the courts. A good example of this process would be the development of the principles of family law over the last fifty years.

We would argue that environmental law has its own conceptual apparatus, in the sense that there is a set of principles and concepts that can be said to exist across the range of subjects covered. For example, the Polluter Pays Principle has a status as a principle, or tool, of good environmental management and has an exclusive link to environmental law. Clearly, this and other environmental principles—for example, the Precautionary and Preventative Principle—provide a theoretical context in which to view the detail of environmental law. Although there continues to be a valid debate about the extent to which these principles have gained universal acceptance as principles with meaningful legal effect, there can be little doubt that they have played a key role in establishing environmental law as an identifiable discipline in its own right.

In addition to these underlying principles, we would also argue that there is a core grouping of topics that might comprise substantive environmental *laws*. While there may be disagreement over the exact nature of the 'core' topics, we would suggest that there is an inclusive definition that would include most of the topics included in this book. For example, most courses (or textbooks) on environmental law will consider different aspects of pollution control (air, water, land contamination). In addition, there will be certain topics, such as European environmental law or planning law, which have a general application across different parts of the 'core'. These are so integral that they must form part of the core itself.

There are, however, other topics that might be said to lie on the periphery of the subject. That is not to say that such topics are unimportant; indeed, some of them are at the forefront of modern concerns about the environment. These include topics such as natural resource depletion, deforestation, international trade, transport, genetically modified organisms (GMOs), agriculture, pesticides, and energy production. This list, which is by no means exhaustive, illustrates the fact that there are difficult decisions to make about drawing the boundaries of the subject. Clearly, all of these topics raise environmental issues and all have a legal dimension in some respects. Nevertheless, there is a danger that, in drawing the boundaries too wide, the subject may become 'the environment and the law' rather than 'environmental law'. While there is nothing inherently wrong in taking a broad definition of the subject, a lack of focus and precision can hinder the development of the law and the institutions that administer it. For example, the fact that the definition of environmental law was unclear had been put forward as a potential reason for rejecting the idea of an environmental court.[3]

This discussion explains the division of the book into three parts. Part I of the book looks at those general issues that cut across all issues of environmental protection, but which are, in practice, an essential part of any understanding of the law. The discussion in this part should also provide a form of vocabulary to help with an understanding of the context of the specific laws and practices that are dealt with in Parts II and III. Part I thus covers perspectives on the environment and how the law overlaps with environmental issues, the nature of the regulatory systems adopted for environmental protection, the sources of environmental law, the institutions and agencies involved in environmental protection, the process of setting environmental standards and the different types of standard that may be adopted, and the role of the EC and international law.

3 See the speech of Lord Bach in the House of Lords at **www.publications.parliament.uk/pa/ld199900/ldhansrd/ vo001009/text/01009-26.htm**.

In Part II, we examine certain issues that also play a role in addressing environmental problems, but which are impossible to explain in terms of environmental media, pollutants, or targets. The law on town and country planning is an example: it clearly has a central role in protecting against threats to amenity and is, in other ways, an important part of the law on environmental protection. For example, hazardous or undesirable developments can be prevented or controlled by the imposition of conditions, making the need for planning permission an essential part of most systems of pollution control. But it also has a role in organizing economic development, which is outside environmental law in its strict sense. We also look at the role of public participation in environmental law, the role of private law, and environmental crime, including the important question of how environmental laws are actually enforced.

In Part III, the specific laws relating to particular environmental issues are treated on a chapter-by-chapter basis. There is, however, a significant problem of organization here: should the law be divided up according to the medium in which the environmental threat manifests itself—for example, air, water, land, etc.—or should it be divided according to the identity of the polluter—for example, cars, factories, power stations, etc.? Should it be divided according to the nature of the pollutant—for example, radiation, chemicals, pesticides, chlorofluorocarbons (CFCs), etc.? Or might it even be divided according to the nature of the target that is being protected—for example, people, animals, ecosystems, and the atmosphere? There is no single answer. The laws are not designed on any one of these four axes, but on all four at once. The best that can be done is to select groupings of laws that more or less hang together in a way that makes sense to someone faced with a problem. It must then be remembered that, in reality, all of these things interrelate, so that a problem on the disposal of waste to land cannot be considered without some consideration of the law on incineration, or discharges to water, or recycling.

We intend to concentrate on those laws and practices that relate primarily to the protection of the whole or part of the environment, as opposed to those in relation to which the true objective is the protection of public health, or individual people, such as workers or consumers. Obviously, it is not possible to consign some areas of law with certainty to one category or another, and, as a result, the exact dividing line between what is and what is not included is rather artificial. But a line has to be drawn somewhere and we have tried to select those topics that form the core of the subject. Accordingly, we cover the law and practice on the protection of air, water, and land against pollution, laws relating to development, and the conservation of biodiversity and landscape features.

Such things as consumer protection laws, product liability laws, health and safety legislation, and animal protection laws are not covered, although they can often be relevant to solving environmental problems. There are also a number of areas of what is undeniably environmental law that are omitted on grounds of space: the growing package of legislation on the protection of the cultural heritage is omitted; little will be said about radioactivity, in relation to which the law is very complex indeed, and in which area there is a large overlap between the environmental and human protection parts of the law. Other topics on the periphery have also been omitted. To counter any objections to such omissions, we have tried, where possible, to use examples from these areas as illustrations of more general points.

The importance of definitions

Part of the uncertainty about the definition of environmental law is that many of the ideas that are central to the subject are contested—that is, certain terms have no generally agreed, objective definition. This may be a result of a clash between the subjective and objective, or the distinction between 'facts' and values. As we shall see, certain terms such as 'environment' and 'pollution' are often used to describe particular sets of 'facts'—for example, to describe our surroundings in terms of environmental media. This should be distinguished

Not an anthropocentric approach.

from interpretations of such terms that reflect particular values or judgments. For example, what may be a wilderness environment worthy of protection from any human influence to one person may be the source of natural resources worthy of exploitation to another, or the home of indigenous peoples who have helped to sustain and manage biodiversity for many centuries to another. When defining things by reference to values, we automatically view things in the way in which we think they should be viewed. Of course, this influences our response to what we think should be done in terms of environmental policies and laws.

But we cannot ignore definitions, because they mark out what is worthy of protection. In some cases, a definition may be stretched and developed to accommodate new challenges. For example, there are treaties protecting the moon and other celestial bodies from 'harmful contamination'.[4] Definitions also make a difference because, as Dryzek puts it, '*language matters...the way we construct, interpret, discuss and analyse environmental problems has all kinds of consequences*'.[5] For good or bad, environmental law provides us with part of the language with which to discuss—and hopefully solve—environmental problems.

Although there are many definitions that are contested, the challenge of defining the boundaries of environmental law is fundamentally interlinked with the two central concepts of what we mean by 'the environment' and what we mean by 'law'. As we shall see, these two concepts are capable of many different meanings, all of which have some substance, but which would be distinctive enough to lead to very different formulations of the boundaries of the subject.

'Environment(al)'

The definition of 'the environment' is a central, but problematic, term in environmental law. It is generally considered to be a phrase that has no singular definition because it is a relational concept.[6] Its normal meaning relates to 'surroundings', but that is obviously a concept that is relative to whatever is the object that is surrounded. Used in that sense, environmental law might include virtually anything; indeed, as Einstein is said to have remarked: '*The environment is everything that isn't me*.'[7] Certainly in the context of environmental *law*, however, 'the environment' can be given a rather more specific meaning—although still a very vague and general one—and may be treated as covering the physical surroundings that are common to all of us, including air, space, waters, land, plants, and wildlife. Thus the environment is defined by reference to physical, non-human, environmental media, including land, water, air, flora and fauna, and so on. In this context, the environment is given some scientific significance. Some specific definitions are set out in Box 1.1.

BOX 1.1 **Definitions of 'the environment'**

...all, or any, of the following media, namely, the air, water and land; and the medium of air includes the air within buildings and the air within other natural or man-made structures above or below ground.

(Environmental Protection Act 1990, s. 1)

---

4 For example, Art. 7 of the Agreement Governing the Activities of States on the Moon and Other Celestial Bodies 1979 (the Moon Treaty).

5 J. S. Dryzek (2005) *The Politics of the Earth: Environmental Discourses*, 2nd edn, Oxford: Oxford University Press, p. 10.

6 J. Barry (1999) *Environment and Social Theory*, London: Routledge, pp. 11–13.

7 Even this, however, does not present the full picture, because Einstein himself and any individual is part of the 'environment'.

...surroundings in which an organisation operates, including air, water, land, natural resources, flora, fauna, humans and their interrelation. Surroundings in this context extend from within the organisation to the global system.

(Environmental Management Standard ISO 14001)

...the combination of elements whose complex interrelationships make up the settings, the surroundings and the conditions of life of the individual and of society, as they are or as they are felt. *Vague.*

(European Commission[8])

In this more specific sense, the idea of 'the environment' is relatively recent and, in terms of policy and lawmaking, the notion of 'the environment' as being something worthy of protection and enhancement through public controls dates only to the 1960s.[9] The idea of protecting something for its contribution to biodiversity is something that is linked to recent times. Historically, private law mechanisms such as the law of nuisance and trespass controlled activities that were environmentally harmful, but only in the context of interferences with the rights of ownership of property.

These definitions are helpful in establishing the operating parameters for environmental law, but only take us so far. In order to define the environment, we must know the subject to which it relates. For example, there are different layers to the environment—international, European, national (English, Scottish, etc.), and local—for example, areas of outstanding natural beauty (AONBs), sites of special scientific interest (SSSIs)—but these are legal constructs. Delineating the boundaries of 'the environment' in this way makes no sense to flora and fauna; migrating birds do not choose to winter in 'England' or in a particular nature reserve.

Social and cultural influences also play a part in defining the environment: someone living in a mining town may consider large slag heaps to be part of their environment; a city dweller will think about parks, open spaces, and buildings; a country dweller may consider the environment to be stone walls, ploughed fields, and woodland.

One final thought is that the environment also needs to be considered by reference to time. In thinking about the laws that protect our environment today, we need to be aware that the environment of future generations may also need to be taken into account.

'Law'

This book is not intended to be merely a description of the various rules and regulations, although obviously that is a part of any useful book on the law—such a description would give little clue to what happens in practice. Whether, and how, the law is enforced is just as important as what the law is. Indeed, given the discretionary nature of many of the powers and duties imposed on environmental decision makers, it is unreal to draw a hard-and-fast distinction between what the law is and how it is used. This book will therefore seek to emphasize policy as much as law, and practice as much as principle.

Law in practice is also affected by the values and culture of those who make the rules, those who set the standards by which those rules operate, those who implement and enforce the rules and standards, and those whose activities are controlled by those rules and standards. In environmental law and policy, this extends to us all, and the impact of these values can be

---

8 First Environmental Action Programme 1973–76; see A. Gilpin (1996) *Dictionary of Environment and Sustainable Development*, Chichester: Wiley.

9 Although previously legislation and policies were introduced to deal with aspects of society that might have involved aspects of environmental protection, see Dryzek (2005) pp. 4–5 and see Chapter 2 below.

stretched further to include non-human interests and the interests of future generations. The word 'values' covers the things that are important to us and the priority that we give to those things. There is therefore a direct connection between that which we consider to be a priority, and the laws and policies that are introduced to control, promote, or otherwise regulate the area concerned. We therefore cover the role that values play in environmental law and policy, and the various perspectives on environmental issues or decisions.

The terms 'rules' and 'law' are often used interchangeably in many parts of the book. That is because environmental 'law' arguably comes from different sources, many of which would not necessarily fall within the definition of statutes or regulations. Thus there are guidance notes, circulars, official policy documents, and codes of practice that all have a marked effect upon the way in which the law operates in practice. For example, the Environment Agency or the Department of the Environment, Food and Rural Affairs (DEFRA) may publish some guidance on the interpretation of a vague statutory phrase, such as the meaning of 'waste'. Although there may be arguments over whether the guidance is 'correct', it can only be overturned by a legal challenge. Unless a challenge is made, this interpretation may become the new rule for practical purposes. In other situations, the statutory scheme may require either policy or technical guidance to flesh out the general definitions. Thus decisions on whether to grant planning permission for out-of-town retail development are closely controlled by a series of rules dressed up as policy in planning policy statements (PPSs). In the area of pollution control, there are many technical guidance notes that set process or other standards, which act as rules that guide decision makers—or, more properly, structure their discretion—in granting authorizations, consents, or permissions. Understanding the role of these rules and, in particular, the legal effect that is created when such rules exist is crucial to any understanding of the way in which environmental law works in practice.

There are some other general limitations on the subject matter of the book in addition to those mentioned above: it is not about all of those laws that 'relate to' the environment, because that too could cover virtually anything. Instead, we intend to concentrate on those laws and practices that have as their object or effect the *protection* of the environment. Those things that merely have an indirect impact on the state of the environment—such as general tax levels, grants, and incentives—are thus excluded from full coverage, although their relevance is referred to in passing and they may frequently be of crucial importance to the policymaker.

As the understanding of the global nature of environmental impacts grows, there is an increasing recognition that principles and rules need to be agreed in the international arena if there is to be a concerted effort to address common issues. Thus the role played by international agreements and principles in influencing and moulding our domestic law is covered in outline. We do not, however, attempt to deal with truly international problems in any detail, leaving such coverage to specialized works to which we refer in the Further Reading at the end of each chapter.

The crucial relevance of European Community (EC) law must be emphasized. We adopt the attitude that EC law *is* domestic law, in the sense that it cannot be ignored, even though it does not always give rise to enforceable obligations and remedies. Therefore, EC controls are integrated into each part of the book where relevant. In addition, there is a separate chapter on the basic constitutional rules of the EC and on the history, philosophy, and current direction of its environmental policy. It is hard to overestimate the central importance of EC law and policy to UK environmental law. This importance is often masked by the fact that, in the environmental field, EC law tends to require some form of transposition and implementation in this country before it is formally recognized. Once implemented, the EC derivation of the rule is then frequently forgotten, because the domestic law is cited as the applicable law.

Some themes of the book

This description of the scope of the book highlights a number of important themes. One is that there is a great deal of interaction between rules that have as their main objective the protection of the environment and those that aim to protect people. Just as in nature conservation it has become accepted in the last thirty years that there is no use in protecting individual animals or species unless you also protect their habitats, in all matters, we now accept that the protection of human beings involves protection of their environment. The converse is also true, in that many rules originally aimed at protection of people end up protecting the environment. For example, standards in relation to radioactivity are often set with the protection of humans in mind, but have an important impact on environmental levels of radiation; similarly, the presence or absence of laws on cruelty to animals has a significant impact on nature conservation, even though that is not their primary motive.

A related theme is that rules are simply the tools of the trade of lawmakers, environmental protection agencies, and environmentalists. A rule that has as its objective one goal is frequently of enormous use in an entirely different way. For example, the law of private nuisance owes its existence and shape to the objective of protecting property rights, but it still has an important, although often unpredictable, part to play in regulating environmental standards in the interests of the community. This is one of the major themes of this book: there is often more than one way of tackling a problem and the environmental lawyer must be seen as a problem solver who chooses the most appropriate tool for the particular problem encountered. Often, this will involve using a combination of different tools. As an example, many rules of property law may be used to further environmental ends: the Royal Society for the Protection of Birds (RSPB) follows a policy of buying land for nature reserve purposes on the principle that the exercise of ownership rights will often provide a better method of protection than many statutory designations or protections. This is not to say that the whole of property law must somehow be annexed as a part of environmental law, but that environmental lawyers should make use of any piece of law that has a relevance to the problem in hand.

A further issue relates to the nature of law. It is often stated that law is not constructive, that it does not build houses or plant trees—but we regard this as an inaccurate notion. There is no doubt that many laws do lay down straightforward negative rules restricting specified forms of behaviour, but many laws lay down rights as well as wrongs. Much of environmental law consists of setting out a framework for behaviour—who should make decisions, how they should make them, what procedures must be followed. In promoting good environmental decision making, such law is clearly not only negative; there is also the practical point that the regulatory agencies spend a far greater proportion of their time providing positive advice on how to reach the standards they set than they do on enforcing those standards through legal threats and remedies.

This distinction between negative and positive tools links to a division in the subject matter of environmental law: it is common to equate environmental protection with pollution control, but, while pollution control undoubtedly represents a major part of environmental law, there are many other issues, such as the conservation of biological diversity and landscape, which also make up the subject. These issues often require slightly different legal mechanisms. Indeed, the evidence of a growing maturity of environmental law can be seen in the use of a more extensive range of these positive tools. The producer responsibility legislation that sets out targets for the recycling and recovery of specific waste streams—for example, packaging and electrical equipment—along with take-back requirements for end-of-life products (with the implicit incentive to reduce the amount of waste produced) is a good example of the use of positive legal rules to bring about environmental improvement.

Another theme of the book is that it is a central function of environmental law to assist in dispute resolution. Disputes about the environment are distinctive, although care must be taken here to differentiate what is different about environmental *issues* and what is different about environmental *disputes*.

Many legal subjects involve the adjudication of disputes, which are characterized as involving a relatively small number of parties (typically two) seeking answers to yes–no questions. Environmental disputes, meanwhile, can involve many parties and are often multifaceted or 'polycentric'. In these cases, substantive legal control (as opposed to procedures that lay down a framework for the resolution of disputes) is of little use. The determination of many environmental disputes involves the balancing of difficult policy questions. In this sense, there is no 'right' answer (certainly, there is no answer that satisfies every interested party) and the interconnection of interests cannot be accommodated fully within the legal system or any dispute resolution mechanism. Typically, therefore, environmental decisions are made 'in the public interest' or 'on balance weighing various considerations'. Environmental law—or, more accurately, the decisions made within the procedural and substantive framework of environmental law—has to incorporate the ideas of 'balancing competing interests' and attaching 'weight' to different factors as a fundamental element of the subject.

In addition, environmental disputes often have overlapping or interrelated causes. Consider, for example, the question of flooding from overflowing sewers: is the problem caused by the water undertakers' underinvestment in satisfactory infrastructure or by the water regulator's refusal to allow water prices to rise to pay for the sewerage improvement, or by developers building houses where there is inadequate sewerage provision, or by planning authorities granting planning permission for hard impermeable surfaces, such as car parks, by which rain water cannot be absorbed, or by the increase in rainfall brought about by climate change? Of course, each of these explanations has multiple causes and so the complexity of the problem increases.

This last point raises a further feature of environmental disputes—their complexity. The facts are often in dispute, which typically leads to complex scientific and economic arguments about what is 'safe' or whether the cost of doing something would outweigh the benefits. Furthermore, the issues often involve a complex interplay between public, private, and criminal law, with parties desiring remedies across those different areas of law.

This links to the final and perhaps most important theme, which is that environmental law provides remedies. To many people, this is the most central aspect of law, because they need to know what they can do about a situation. One of the interesting developments of recent years has been the search for adequate remedies for environmental problems. Legal tools have been accepted as legitimate devices for helping to solve environmental problems. Law plays an often underrated, but enormously important, role, alongside scientific, technological, social, and economic solutions, in helping to combat environmental degradation. In this role, many novel legal concepts have been developed.

Policy and environmental law

Environmental law is a political discipline. The extent to which it is 'political' in a narrow sense—that is, party political—has, in recent years, reduced. In the past, however, major differences could be discerned as to the correct policy to apply. These differences did not normally relate to the ends to be achieved, but to the methods to be adopted in doing so and the costs to be incurred. A clear example was the controversy provoked by the passage of the Wildlife and Countryside Act 1981 over whether voluntary or compulsory controls should be adopted in relation to the protection of important natural sites (see Chapter 19). A further example relates to the whole history of town and country planning in the 1980s, when the very dramatic changes to planning policy led to disagreement and dispute. These are clear examples of the application of 'Thatcherism' to the environment, as a government with a deep suspicion of planning and regulation sought to grapple with a system based on coherent planning for the future. There are, however, others that relate to such things as privatization and deregulation. In the twenty-first century, there has been a greater degree of consensus on environmental policy choices,[10] although the rhetoric can seem a little opportunistic at times.

Environmental law is also political in the wide sense, in that it involves the making of policy decisions about the best way in which to achieve certain objectives. This is emphasized in this book by looking at law as being about techniques or tools for solving problems. It is not only lawyers and environmentalists who have a choice of tools with which to achieve a particular objective; legislators and policymakers also have a range of tools available to them. The law is one tool, alongside such things as fiscal policy, education, research, and voluntary solutions. There are different types of legal mechanism that may be used, such as the setting of environmental quality objectives, or of strict limits on emissions, or controls attached to processes or products. These various possibilities are discussed in detail in Chapter 8, but it ought to be recognized that, in order to combat complex problems of pollution and environmental harm, a combination of methods is often required.

It is impossible to say that the UK always adopts one method rather than another, but it is clear that the tendency has been to adopt flexible mechanisms of control, where what is permitted is judged by reference to its effect on the receiving environment. As a result, the UK approach to pollution control has tended to be fairly pragmatic, involving the use of a great deal of discretion. This discretion is normally exercised by specialist regulatory agencies, although local authorities also have very significant environmental protection functions. An important point is that this discretion is exercised on grounds that are not restricted to environmental factors. Traditionally, there has been a close connection in UK environmental regulation between social, political, and economic factors, and decisions on environmental protection.

This emphasis on taking into account a wide range of factors before making a decision links to a fundamental point about the way in which 'pollution' and 'environmental harm' are defined. Once again, it is difficult to formulate precise definitions, but a general guide would be to say that they cover situations in which there is an excess of something above that which is desirable. There is no doubt that they are relative concepts: one person's waste is another's raw material. This relativity also applies to other forms of environmental harm. For example, a rock concert for some is a noise nuisance for others and what would be thought as intrusive development in one locality will blend in in another.

The level of pollution is also relative. For example, because of the self-cleansing properties of the environment (at least, for certain polluting substances), it may well be said to be less polluting to discharge into a large fast-flowing river than into a small sluggish one, and higher levels of pollution from industrial sources may be better tolerated in one area than in another because of the corresponding advantages of the economic prosperity that the industries bring. It is nonsensical to talk of getting rid of pollution: pollution and the harm caused thereby are, to a certain extent, necessary risks, because they accompany activities that most of us are unwilling to do without. Certain polluting processes are beneficial to our existence, so to prohibit them entirely would, arguably, cause more harm than good. Reducing pollution comes at a price and the more levels are reduced the greater the cost.

In addition, there are limits to what can be achieved through technological means and, even if great reductions can be made, there are questions about how activities would be monitored and enforced. Accordingly, it only makes sense to consider how to reduce pollution and the levels that are acceptable. This involves economic, political, social, and cultural

---

10 For example, in relation to areas that had previously been seen as 'party political', such as nuclear energy and the expansion of London's airports.

criteria, as well as those that are scientific and environmental. It is therefore important to understand that, in implementing environmental protection policies, regulatory agencies are effectively carrying out a political balancing process. As Hawkins puts it: '*The power to define and enforce consents is ultimately a power to put people out of business, to deter the introduction of new business or to drive away a going concern.*'[11]

Rights and environmental law

In recent years, the language of 'rights' and environmental law has emerged as a potential counterpoint to the discretionary, flexible basis of much of environmental law and decision making. Many of the typical characteristics of domestic environmental law appear to be weak, because of the inherent substantive flexibility and discretion, and the reliance on the pragmatic approach of acceptability. One is left with an impression that there is little definite substance. Therefore, the talk of 'rights', with its inherent certainty and enforceability, appears to be much more attractive. If an individual or group of people has a 'right' to a 'clean' environment (whatever that might mean), that right can be relied upon as against a political decision to allow a development (for example, a road) that interferes with those 'rights'. Accordingly, the right can override a decision made in the public interest, in relation to which various factors are balanced such as economic and social considerations in order to determine what is 'acceptable'.[12]

As with many other of the key terms discussed in this chapter, the phrase 'rights' and its interpretation needs some explanation. The language of rights is very common—but what does the phrase mean in the context of environmental protection? The need for clarity comes from the manner in which the word is used. One might see reference to a 'right' to pollute or trade in pollution credits, a right to be heard at an inquiry, a right to bring a judicial review action, a right of access to environmental information, a right to a healthy environment, a right to clean air or water, and a right to participate in environmental decision making. Clearly, all of these things cannot possibly invoke the same right: moral rights must be distinguished from legal rights, procedural rights from substantive rights, derivative rights from 'first-order' rights, and so on. The term 'rights' is used in a number of different contexts, both in this book and more generally.

In general, the term 'right' is used to convey something that is a permanent entitlement normally protected by objective rules. In this sense, a legal right can be differentiated from a moral right, which may be a claim for a right where the basis of the right is disputed, but which proponents may argue is valid for its own sake (compare and contrast, for example, the rights of a child with animal rights). In practice, moral rights and legal rights may be mutually supportive—that is, a right that is disputed may become valid, because it is protected by rules (for example, animal rights in the context of animal welfare legislation).

There are two broad strands of rights that might be used as a means of protecting the environment. The first is the concept of legal rights for the natural environment, such as trees, rivers, animals, plants, and geological features.[13] The basic argument for the creation of such rights is that this would be one of the natural consequences of human development. Historically, we have recognized the role that law, through the granting of rights, has had

11 K. Hawkins (1984) *Environment and Enforcement*, Oxford: Oxford University Press, p. 24.

12 The phrase 'rights as trumps' conveys this overriding power. See, e.g., J. Rawls (1993) *Political Liberalism*, New York: Columbia University Press, p. 6. For Dworkin's idea of rights as trumps, see his book (1978) *Taking Rights Seriously*, Cambridge, Mass: Harvard University Press, ch. 4, and his article 'Rights as trumps' in J. Waldron (ed.) (1984) *Theories of Rights*, Oxford: Oxford University Press, pp. 153–67.

13 For a discussion of the creation of this sort of right and generally, see C. Stone (1996) *Should Trees Have Standing? And Other Essays on Law, Morals and the Environment*, New York: Oceana Publishing, ch. 1.

to play in the granting of autonomy to people—for example, women and children—and the control that people have over things—for example, rights of ownership of real property, ideas, and even other people, in the form of slaves. Given our understanding of the importance of, and the need to protect, the environment, it would be one way in which law can recognize the significance of environmental protection for its own sake.

The notion that the environment should be granted rights of its own is, however, not without objection. One of the main criticisms is that it is simply unnecessary to grant the environment rights, because the questions involved in protecting animals, plants, and geological features are essentially moral questions, which cannot necessarily be addressed through the creation of new rights. For example, we might agree that it would be wrong to take a hammer to the statue of the Venus de Milo, but we would not consider that the best way of protecting the Venus de Milo would be to grant legal rights to all statues.[14] In the same way, while we all may agree that we have a preference that biodiversity is protected or even enhanced, this is not the same as saying that rare species should be granted rights. Thus, while the idea of this type of such 'environmental right' is the subject of philosophical debate, the concrete examples of the granting of such rights are few and far between.[15]

The second strand of 'rights' as a means of protecting the environment is more anthropocentric in nature—that is, it is used to protect human interests—although, in many cases, environmental protection can be 'derived' from the basic right. Thus a right to bring a nuisance action may help to prevent pollution of the environment as well as protecting private property rights. In this book, the term 'rights' is typically used in this anthropocentric fashion.

In general, the term is used in three broad ways.

- **Private rights**
  These tend to be based upon the protection of property interests, such as the right to take action against nuisances to prevent unreasonable interference with the enjoyment of land or the right to prevent a trespass.

- **Public law rights**
  These tend to be procedural in nature, including the right to participate in decision making, the right to information, the right to be heard at an inquiry, or the right to bring a judicial review action or a private prosecution.

- **Substantive legal rights**
  These include, for example, some of the rights under the European Convention on Human Rights, such as a right to life, the right to respect for home life, and the right to property.

Much of the recent activity surrounding 'rights' has been the adoption of procedural, public law rights, either generally, or specifically in relation to environmental decision making—most notably, rights based on international law agreements.[16] Despite their procedural nature, these rights may have substantive consequences: for example, in blocking development. In terms of substantive rights, the European Court of Human Rights has not generally taken an expansionist view of human rights as a tool for environmental protection,[17] using the idea of a 'margin of appreciation' to apply its own balancing of political, environmental,

14 See J. Merrills (1998) 'Environmental protection and human rights: conceptual aspects' in A. Boyle and M. Anderson (eds) *Human Rights Approaches to Environmental Protection*, Oxford: Clarendon Press, p. 34.

15 For arguments in relation to the creation of 'ecocentric' environmental rights from existing laws, see C. Miller (1998) *Environmental Rights*, London: Routledge, esp. ch. 9.

16 Respectively, see, in particular, the incorporation of the European Convention on Human Rights by the Human Rights Act 1998, and the UN/ECE Convention on Access to Environmental Information, Public Participation in Decision Making and Access to Justice in Environmental Matters (the Aarhus Convention).

17 Compared, e.g., to the Indian Supreme Court, which has actively used constitutional provisions such as the right to life to develop environmental law—see A. Dias (1994) 6(2) JEL 243.

and economic considerations as against individual rights. Much of the Court's reticence to develop the law in this way is linked to the difficult nature of environmental disputes (see p. 11), and the existence of specialist regulatory regimes and regulatory bodies entrusted to make environmental decisions (see p. 485).

CHAPTER SUMMARY

1   Environmental law is a significant subject because law is central to managing the environment, which is considered to be an important and challenging issue.

2   The boundaries of environmental law are not very well defined, although there are certain 'core' principles and topics that would form an inclusive definition to most of which most people would probably agree.

3   Defining certain key terms in environmental law is difficult, because they can have a factual and value-based meaning. Thus great care needs to be taken when using concepts such as 'environment' and 'pollution' in order to make this fact–value distinction.

4   Environmental law originates from a range of sources. Law in practice is different from law on the page. Such things as the way in which the law is enforced make a huge difference to its effectiveness.

5   There are various important underlying themes in this book. Laws are tools that can be used to protect the environment and selecting the right tool for the right task is critical; laws that protect humans can also be used to protect the environment. The law is not only restrictive in nature: it can be used as a positive tool to encourage environmental improvement and to assist in the resolution of complex environmental disputes. In addition, environmental law provides remedies.

6   Environmental law is a political discipline: it involves the making of policy decisions about the best way in which to achieve acceptable environmental objectives.

7   Although the term 'rights' can have a number of meanings, in this book, it is generally used to cover public law rights, private law rights, and substantive legal rights.

QUESTIONS

1   Consider the following examples. In each case, what interests are involved, what issues of policy arise, what rights (if any) are being infringed, and is there any issue about the conception of the environment?

   a A proposal to ban people entering a national park to prevent damage to sensitive ecosystems and landscapes.

   b The use of a new chemical that is linked to harm to fish and to impacts on human fertility.

   c Empty bottles of spring water left behind by students after a lecture.

   d A non-native bird that, because of climate change, is now found in the south of England and is having a negative impact on (although not yet endangering) the robin.

   e The transportation of waste from a wealthy part of the country to an incinerator sited in an area of relative poverty.

   f Giving contraception to an expanding seal population that is having a detrimental impact upon fish stocks.

   g Culling badgers living in a sett under Stonehenge. (Would your answer differ if rats were doing the damage?)

h A proposal to develop a large offshore wind farm, which may have an adverse effect on migratory birds. (How would your answer differ if it were being built near to a successful seaside resort?)

i The UK has agreed to reduce its emissions to combat climate change, but UK industry has increased its emissions in the last ten years.

j The imposition of a tax of £100 on 'no-frills' airline tickets to counter the effects of air transport on climate change.

k An application to extend a waste landfill into a locally important nature conservation site if there is a risk that, when the waste breaks down, it will pollute nearby drinking water supplies within the next hundred years.

l Revoking a power station's licence to abstract water because of fears that low flows will damage an endangered mayfly's habitat.

2 How far should society go in conferring rights on the environment? Do groups have rights that are different from the rights of individuals who make up the group?

3 Look at three websites of bodies operating in the environmental field. (You might try the websites of the Environment Agency, Friends of the Earth, and the Chemical Industries Association.) How would you characterize their concepts of the environment? To what extent do these groups seem to be pressing for changes to policy? Or to law? What role do environmental rights seem to play?

4 What would you include within your definition of 'environmental law'? How might this differ in ten, fifty, and a hundred years' time?

 FURTHER READING

Environmental law is quite a difficult subject to access for the complete beginner. You may want a gentle introduction and to read around the subject to get a feel for the language. Some of the best introductions can be found in Routledge's *Introductions to the Environment* series—in particular, the environment and society texts (eds D. Pepper and P. O'Keefe). These include: D. Wilkinson (2002) *Environment and Law*, London: Routledge; J. Barry (1999) *Environment and Social Theory*, London: Routledge; T. Doyle and D. McEachern (2001) *Environment and Politics*, London: Routledge. Another helpful introduction that helps 'set the scene' for later discussions is J. Dryzek (2005) *The Politics of the Earth: Environmental Discourses*, 2nd edn, Oxford: Oxford University Press.

On the difficult question of the definition of 'environmental law', have a look at Z. Plater, 'Environmental law and three economies: navigating a sprawling field of study, practice, and societal governance in which everything is connected to everything else' (1999) 23 Harv Envtl L Rev 359 and R. Lazarus, 'Environmental scholarship and the Harvard difference' (1999) 23 Harv Envtl L Rev 327. For a British perspective, see C. Reid, 'Environmental law: sifting through the rubbish' (1998) Jur Rev 236.

For a discussion on the creation of environmental rights, see C. Stone (1996) *Should Trees Have Standing? And Other Essays on Law, Morals and the Environment*, New York: Oceana, ch. 1. Further readings on environmental rights are given at the end of Chapter 3.

The best way to get an insight into what is happening in the 'real world' of environmental law is to visit the web pages of environmental organizations such as Greenpeace—**www.greenpeace.org.uk**—which tends to concentrate on global issues and Friends of the Earth—**www.foe.org.uk**—which is more localized. These provide up-to-the-minute information on the most significant (or media-friendly, depending upon your viewpoint) topics of the moment. In recent years, there have been some interesting books attempting to counter what some see as excessive 'green pessimism'. Three good examples of the genre are R. North (1995) *Life on a Modern Planet: A Manifesto for Progress*, Manchester: Manchester University Press, J. Simon (1998) *Ultimate Resource 2*, Princeton, NJ: Princeton University Press, and B. Lomborg (2001) *The Skeptical Environmentalist*, Cambridge: Cambridge University Press.

2   History and challenges

Overview

What we now call 'environmental law' has tended to develop incrementally—and often haphaz-ardly—rather than by revolutionary leaps. This means that some of its shape and content is still influenced by what has gone before. But in regulating polluting industries and dealing with envir-onmental problems, challenges have been thrown up and (in theory) lessons learnt that must be appreciated. This chapter builds on Chapter 1 by considering, through a broad lens, the origins and evolution of environmental law and policy. It then moves on to look at some of the key challenges for the future, and at possible trends in environmental law and in the costs of complying—and of not complying—with environmental law.

At the end of this chapter, you should be able to:

✔ understand in outline the origins, development, and main features of UK environmental law;

✔ appreciate some of the main difficulties in making environmental laws that work;

✔ appreciate possible future directions in environmental policy and some of the legal challenges that these raise.

Lessons from the past

Not surprisingly for such a densely populated country, environmental controls have a long history, going back to medieval statutes on small-scale pollution and the development of pri-vate law principles to deal with threats to communal assets, such as water. Of course, until recently, few would have thought of these laws as part of something called 'environmental law', because their main focus was on the protection of private and common property. The adequacy of the private law in particular fell far short of an effective protection regime, even for affected individuals (see Box 2.1).

[handwritten margin note: Roots of Env. law found in]

> BOX 2.1 **Royal Commission on the Pollution of Rivers**, Third Report, *The Rivers Aire and Calder* (1867) Cmnd 3850, pp. li–liii
>
> So far as river abuses affect only private rights, each individual is left to protect himself by putting the law in motion. An aggrieved individual has the option of bringing an action for damages…or an injunction. Either course is necessarily invidious, expensive and doubtful in its result.…The plaintiff may prove that he has suffered injury from the pollution of the river and that the defend-ant has polluted the river above him; but that is not enough. The plaintiff has also to prove that what he has suffered has been caused wholly or in part by the special act of the defendant, which

[handwritten margin note: Causation link same as torts.]

[margin handwritten note: human base.]

> is always difficult—often impossible.... Several instances have come before us where a manufacturer, sued for polluting running water, has brought the litigation to a close, not by ceasing to foul the river, but by simply removing the discharge into the river to a point below the works of the complainant.... In the neighbourhood of large towns it has come to be thought that a river foul with sewage is inevitable; inhabitants are reluctant to come forward as witnesses to denounce that to which they have become long familiar.... In the case of sewage pollution it is not usually difficult to trace the offender home.... For the principal offenders are the governing bodies of the large towns. These do not prosecute one another for the reason that each is guilty of the same offence towards his neighbour, and they are rarely prosecuted by private persons because few are willing to bear the expense and odium of acting as public prosecutors.... The expense of such litigation generally far exceeds the value of the personal interest of any individual in the stoppage of the nuisance. Accordingly, whatever the inconvenience to the public, the nuisance continues unabated. Rich and poor alike submit to it as a sort of destiny...

Or, as a later Royal Commission put it:

> In such centres the interests of the community are largely bound up with the interests of the manufacturer and that to demand from manufacturers costly schemes of purification might injure the community without any corresponding improvement in the character of the river which is already materially, if not hopelessly impaired...
>
> (1914–16, Cmnd 7819, p. 3)

Britain's position as the cradle of the Industrial Revolution led to the very early development of public controls specifically related to environmental protection. The most significant provisions were developed in response to public health problems, such as typhoid and cholera, in the mid-nineteenth century, which were traced to the state of the urban environment and the drinking of contaminated water. Although the legal response was initially to give permissive powers to local bodies, mandatory duties on local sanitary authorities were eventually provided for in 1872 and the legislation consolidated in the landmark Public Health Act 1875.

[margin handwritten note]

Although the early public health laws were largely successful in removing sewage from the centres of industrial towns, this was often achieved by encouraging the dumping of untreated wastes into convenient watercourses. Water pollution controls were therefore needed and followed in the Rivers Pollution Prevention Act 1876. This Act gives a flavour of the traditional approach to pollution control through the use of criminal offences and a practical reliance on the 'best practicable means' of pollution control. But it also shows a reluctance to use criminal law enforcement for environmental protection or to allow individuals to enforce the law (see Box 2.2).

BOX 2.2 The Rivers Pollution Prevention Act 1876

Under this Act—the first general water pollution prevention statute in the UK—all forms of river pollution were prohibited, but enforcement action against the manufacturing and mining sectors was only possible in very limited situations.

- Only a sanitary authority could bring proceedings and then only with the consent of the local government board (LGB).
- In deciding whether to grant consent, the LGB was to have regard to '*the industrial interests involved in the case and to the circumstances and requirements of the locality*'.

[margin handwritten note: Utilitarian approach of balance good / bad]

- Consent to prosecution was not to be granted in cases in which the district in question was '*the seat of any manufacturing industry*' unless the LGB was satisfied, '*after due enquiry*', that there were reasonably practicable and available means for rendering the polluting liquid harmless *and* that proceedings would not inflict material injury on the interests of industry.
- Two months' notice had to be given before proceedings were brought.

'The extraordinary character of these legislative provisions scarcely requires emphasis: there can hardly have been a more blatant attempt by Parliament to obstruct the enforcement of a law which by the same enactment it created.'

(Richardson, Ogus and Burrows (1983) *Policing Pollution*, Oxford: Clarendon, p. 41)

Good Utilitarian confusion quote.

Britain is a forerunner of the development.

Britain also introduced some of the earliest provisions on town planning. The first legislation to cover this subject was the Housing, Town Planning etc. Act 1909, which again derived from public health pressures and which vested controls in local authorities, at this stage on a non-obligatory basis. Obligatory town and country planning controls were introduced on a nationwide scale in 1947—again, early in world terms.

Most public health and environmental protection was therefore carried out at a local level by a vast array of local boards and, at a later stage, local authorities (although, in the case of water pollution, a river catchment approach to regulation began with the River Boards Act 1948, which removed some of the incoherence caused by more than one local authority having responsibility for discharges to a river). Britain can, however, boast what is normally considered the world's first national public pollution control agency, the Alkali Inspectorate, which was established by the Alkali Act 1863 to control atmospheric emissions primarily from the caustic soda industry (see Box 2.3). But national, centralized control of problems (such as through the Alkali Inspectorate) was very much the exception in this period of development and most of the early provisions reflected a tendency—which, to a lesser extent, is still apparent—to regulate only the most dangerous or sensitive matters at a central level.

BOX 2.3 The Alkali Act 1863

Although this Act controlled certain noxious fumes from alkali works, it did not prohibit the emission of smoke into the atmosphere, which brought about problems of lower level pollution along with the production of smog; nor could the imposition of individualized emission standards for alkali works take into account the cumulative effect of a large concentration of such operations. Because the Act had set only a reduction for acidic emissions in terms of a percentage for each plant, the overall concentration of such emissions rose as the number of factories increased. Finally, in an echo of the adverse consequences for the water environment of early public health legislation, one effect of the early Alkali Acts and the controls over atmospheric emissions is reputed to have been an immediate worsening of water quality as industries chose liquid discharge as a replacement method for the disposal of their wastes.

In addition to these public controls, the law of nuisance was developed (especially in the nineteenth century) as a means of providing private redress for environmental harm, although on a very selective basis (see Box 2.1 and, further, Chapter 11).

Britain also had some of the earliest voluntary bodies concerned with environmental protection. The National Smoke Abatement Society campaigned for higher fines for polluters under the Public Health Act and a number of bodies were particularly concerned with the protection of nature. In the absence of laws protecting important wildlife habitats, these bodies began to use ordinary private property laws to acquire nature reserves. With the exception of miscellaneous Acts protecting sea birds from slaughter and ancient hunting laws designed to maintain numbers of quarry species, there was little legislation in this area.

In these formative years, lawmaking tended to be ad hoc in the extreme. This is self-evident with case law, which, by its very nature (as Box 2.1 illustrates), must react to the facts of cases brought. But legislative changes were also reactive, piecemeal, and short-sighted, with Parliament tending to legislate for problems on an individual basis, in isolation from other areas. The Alkali Act 1863 illustrates many of the difficulties (see Box 2.3).

A century later, controls on smog—introduced after the serious London smog in 1952 killed nearly four thousand people—led indirectly to the policy of dispersing emissions via taller chimney stacks. This reduced emissions nationally, but exported the problem of acid rain to Scandinavia.

These early pollution Acts also show clearly how the concern of the law was not with what we would now call pollution of 'the environment', but with the human consequences of, for example, poor air and water quality, or insanitary housing conditions. The objective of these early Acts was improvements to human health and improving environmental quality was merely the means to this end.

The legacy of early controls

One effect of this long, and unplanned, history is that modern Britain has inherited a far less coherent system of pollution control than that of many other countries, with individual pieces of legislation dealing with what are perceived to be individual problems. The same historical factors also explain the relatively large number of agencies dealing with environmental matters, although changes in institutional responsibility have significantly improved matters in this respect (see below).

A further point to note here is the continuing relevance of what might seem to be some very dated legislative provisions. For example, although changes were made in the Environmental Protection Act 1990, we still have laws on statutory nuisances (which have also been adopted as a loose model for the regulation of historically contaminated land) that retain the essential shape that they were given in the Public Health Act 1875 and key provisions of the Water Resources Act 1991 on water pollution offences use key terms that date from the Victorian era. The courts have been forced to consider the extent to which the continuing relevance of their historical context should prevail over the fact that these provisions are now contained in statutes that have environmental protection as their main aim.

The modern age of environmental law

It is consequently hard to differentiate sharply between consecutive phases or 'ages' of environmental law, because some of the features of very early controls remain today. Nevertheless, by the early 1970s, it was clear that the developments begun in the late stages of the nineteenth century had gained momentum, and there was widespread recognition that the state had to take a more active role in the control of pollution and protection of the environment. A very clear measure of this was the creation, in 1970, of the Department of the Environment (previously, environmental affairs had formed part of other Ministerial portfolios, such as housing and town planning). Globally, 1970 was also the year of the first Earth Day, which represented recognition of increasing global environmental concerns.

There are a number of possible explanations for this shift. They stretch from the theoretical—for example, that private law failed either to reflect the external costs of pollution or to protect the interests of future generations by conserving resources, and the changes in public consciousness emerging in a post-industrial era—to the pragmatic and political—for example, impending membership of the European Community or the growth in environmental regulation in other developed countries, which required some form of governmental response. Whatever the reason, the beginning of the modern age of environmental law was characterized by the passing of environmental 'laws' or statutory frameworks in relation to aspects of environmental protection. Typically, these environmental statutes were based upon a model that has become known as 'command and control', whereby centralized environmental standards are set and policed by a combination of government and regulatory agencies. This growth in the number of environmental laws over the last forty years reflects the readiness with which the UK government adopted this type of environmental regulation.

BOX 2.4 **Landmarks in the modern history of environmental law and policy (1962–2007)**

1962 Publication of Rachel Carson's *Silent Spring* (a book on the effect of pesticides on the natural environment), which raises wide-reaching questions about the human impact on the environment.

1968 Apollo 8 sends back the first pictures of the Earth from space, which are seen by many as showing both the Earth's beauty and fragility. Coincides with a period of growing concerns about possible human impacts on the environment. The late 1960s marks the start of a first wave of modern environmental concern.[1]

1969 Greenpeace and Friends of the Earth founded.

1970 UK Department of the Environment established. Earth Day celebrated globally—first mass global citizen action on environmental issues.

1972 UN (Stockholm) Conference on the Human Environment. First major global gathering to address environmental issues. Neo-Malthusian dimension to environmentalism seen in the publication of the Club of Rome's *Limits to Growth*.

1973 As a direct result of the Stockholm Conference, the first EEC Environmental Action Programme is adopted, marking the emergence of the European Community as an important actor in the development of environmental policy and a major source of environmental law.

1974 Control of Pollution Act enacted. First piece of legislation not simply targeted at single environmental media or industrial processes, but far short of integrated control. The Organisation for Economic Co-operation and Development (OECD) reports into making the 'polluter pay'.

1985 Ozone Treaty agreed. Subsequent discovery of hole in ozone layer over Antarctica.

1987 The Brundtland Report (*Our Common Future*) is published by the UN. Seen as a seminal report on the linkages between developmental and environmental problems, and on the advancement of technological solutions, it popularizes the term 'sustainable development'. The Single European Act formally embeds environmental policy within the EC.

---

1 For key developments in the USA during the 1960s, see 'Environmentalism 1960–86', available online at **history. sandiego.edu/gen/nature/environ5.html.**

1988 Intergovernmental Panel on Climate Change (IPCC) established. Mrs Thatcher's 'Green' speech stresses environmental stewardship.

1989 National Rivers Authority established as the first regulatory body in this area without conflicting operational duties. Marks a shift in attitudes generally towards environmental crime.

1990 The Environmental Protection Act establishes a system of integrated pollution control for the most polluting industrial processes.

1992 The (Rio) UN Conference on the Environment and Development marks the high point of this second wave of environmental concern. Major treaties on climate change and biodiversity signed.

1995 The Environment Act establishes (in England and Wales) a national Environment Agency, subject to sustainable development duties. The Agency becomes the largest of its kind in the world.

2001 The Aarhus Convention comes into force—a key landmark in environmental citizenship establishing rights in relation to public participation, environmental information, and access to justice.

2007 IPCC and Al Gore win the Nobel Peace Prize for raising awareness of climate change. Concern about climate change reaches unprecedented levels for an environmental problem.

There has also been a shift in the emphasis of the law to reflect newer environmental concerns. Many problems were simply not perceived as such in the 1960s, or were subordinated to other more pressing matters, such as the raising of living standards or the provision of full employment. The emphasis at that stage was on health and safety matters—a point well illustrated by the placing of the Alkali and Clean Air Inspectorate within the Health and Safety Executive when it was established in 1974. Land use was also emphasized; indeed, it could be argued that the very fact that Britain had (and still has) what is probably the world's most comprehensive system of land use planning led to the concentration of controls at that stage, rather than to encouraging the development of adequate continuing pollution controls.

By comparison, the focus of the laws that have been enacted in the last thirty years or so has been on the control of pollution, with the environment increasingly being regarded as worthy of protection in its own right. This does not mean that the environment has been accorded 'rights' (as the definitions of 'pollution' and 'the environment' in the Environmental Protection Act (EPA) 1990 illustrates, (see p. 7), but it is undeniable that pollution control laws have moved on from narrow, public health-based concerns to encompass a much wider range of adverse changes to the natural environment. There has also been a growing concern, and legal responses, to global and transfrontier problems, especially climate change, the control of hazardous substances and processes, the minimization and management of waste, the conservation of natural resources, and the protection of ecosystems. In short, current concerns tend to reflect the need to control the almost inevitable by-products of the modern, technological, post-industrial, information age.

Features of the modern age

Legislative consolidation and direction

The process of producing a coherent body of environmental law began with the Control of Pollution Act (CoPA) 1974. This put most of the law on water pollution and waste disposal in one place, but a measure of the sectoral approach of the time is that it had little to say about air pollution.

Although CoPA 1974 is now virtually fully replaced by later legislation in England and Wales, the emergence of a more coherent statute book has certainly moved forward some distance. In terms of legislation, the law is becoming more concentrated in a smaller number of Acts (see Box 2.5). One of the important features of this process is that the development and direction of the statutory controls is more planned than before. The main Acts referred to below are all government-sponsored Acts, illustrating an increasing tendency to plan and interlink legislation properly (the government White Paper (1990) *This Common Inheritance*, Cm 1200, underlined this commitment to a planned development of environmental policy). By contrast, many environmental measures in the past resulted from single issue campaigns, or from private members' bills.

BOX 2.5 The main environmental statutes

Environmental Protection Act (EPA) 1990—contains the main bulk of provisions on air pollution from stationary sources, waste management and disposal, litter, the environmental impact of genetically modified organisms (GMOs), noise, and the statutory control of environmental nuisances.

Town and Country Planning Act (TCPA) 1990—consolidated most of the relevant statutory law on town and country planning, and tree protection (major changes to the planning of development have been made by the Planning and Compulsory Purchase Act 2004).

Pollution Prevention and Control Act (PPCA) 1999—provides for a permitting system to control industrial processes in an integrated way (which is fleshed out in Regulations).

Water Resources Act (WRA) 1991—contains much of the law on water pollution and water resources (the latter significantly revised by the Water Act 2003).

Water Industry Act (WIA) 1991—matters relating to water supply and sewerage, including economic regulation of the water and sewerage companies.

Wildlife and Countryside Act (WCA) 1981—includes much of the relevant law on nature conservation in Pts I and II (significantly amended by the Countryside and Rights of Way Act 2000).

Environment Act 1995—introduced new legal provisions in relation to liability for contaminated land (as Pt IIA of EPA 1990). Also created the Environment Agency, which took over functions related to waste regulation, water pollution and water resources, radioactive substances, and most aspects of integrated pollution control, although without any major changes in the substance of the law.

None of these Acts is a full code in relation to the relevant subject matter. There are numerous individual issues dealt with by separate pieces of legislation, such as on radioactivity or on pesticides. There are other issues in relation to which the controls are still spread among a large number of Acts, such as in relation to landscape protection. In addition, much of the detailed law in any area is actually provided in statutory instruments and a wide range of other documents made under the relevant Acts. This is especially true of much of the vast body of law with its origins in EC environmental Directives.

National strategies

Alongside this more planned approach has been, in recent years, the introduction of a more strategic approach to many environmental issues. In a response to the traditional reactive mode of policy and rulemaking, a wide array of national strategies has been adopted. This is partly because of the need to flesh out the policy framework in the sustainable development strategy, partly to indicate the manner of achieving certain goals or targets that have been set down either nationally or internationally, and partly because of the history of inadequate policymaking in many areas of environmental policy. Thus we have—or, in some cases, will have—strategies on sustainable development, waste management, air quality, chemicals, climate change, soil protection, sustainable distribution, sustainable construction, and sustainable communities. On the one hand, while these can provide a helpful framework for future action and specific targets at which we can aim, there is a danger that the overuse of such strategies can be used to present mere 'aspirations' that can be manipulated or dropped if progress in meeting the targets is slow. On the other hand, recent legislation on strategic environmental assessment should give the public a greater say in the process by which some of these strategic plans are adopted (see p. 468).

Institutional coherence

There is also an increasing institutional coherence. Her Majesty's Inspectorate of Pollution was established in 1987 to bring together a number of sectoral inspectorates. The National Rivers Authority was established in 1989 as a national body (in England and Wales) regulating water pollution and the wider water environment. In 1996, the creation of the Environment Agency brought the main pollution control functions—that is, integrated pollution control, waste management, and the regulation of water pollution—under one administrative body for the first time. (Specialist conservation agencies such as the former Nature Conservancy Council have historically remained separated from the pollution control authorities, although the extent to which nature and landscape conservation have been linked institutionally has tended to fluctuate.)

A different aspect of developments in relation to institutional responsibilities has been the policy of splitting production from regulation (or differentiating the 'poachers' from the 'gamekeepers'). As early as the Victorian period, the reluctance of bodies that were themselves polluters to prosecute others for doing so was recognized (see Box 2.1). In recent years, this policy has been realized by the creation of the National Rivers Authority; prior to that, the regulation of water pollution was the responsibility of the regional water authorities, which were also responsible for causing pollution from sewage works that they operated. Another example is the enforced separation of waste regulation functions from waste disposal functions in EPA 1990, a process that was taken further in the Environment Act 1995 (see p. 654).

Integrative laws

EPA 1990 gave HM Inspectorate of Pollution integrated powers over the most hazardous industrial processes, meaning that, for the first time, discharges to air, water, and land were regulated in a unified way. This was intended to overcome some of problems of a sectoral approach (which have a long history—see Box 2.3). Central to this new approach to integrated pollution control was that the Best Available Techniques Not Entailing Excessive Cost (BATNEEC) had to be used for controlling releases and that these had to take the environment as a whole, having regard to the best practicable environmental option (BPEO) available in respect of the substances that were to be released. This approach has been taken further under the Pollution Prevention and Control Act 1999—which takes integration a step further by looking at *inputs*, such as energy consumption and resource use, as well as polluting releases—but the vast majority of polluters remain subject to separate legal controls contained in separate statutes and regulations.

Administrative centralization

A final change, which may be seen from the examples, is that environmental protection is becoming increasingly centralized (see further p. 101), both in terms of where standards are set, and which bodies implement and enforce these. This must, however, be seen against the perspective that, as already stated, the system inherited was particularly decentralized.

There are many reasons for this centralization:

- the increasing complexity of environmental risks, which create technological and scientific demands on regulators;

- years of central government antipathy towards local government;

- the growth in emphasis on uniform and integrated planning of solutions to problems;

- the increase in institutional coherence;

- the impact of EC membership.

Changing styles of regulation

The development of regulatory approaches and current policy is considered in detail in Chapter 8; here, we cover only some of the main developments that have taken place.

Command and control remains the central pillar of pollution control legislation, and more prescriptive approaches have also been introduced in other areas, such as the protection of important wildlife sites, in relation to which the law previously took a more voluntaristic approach—see the changes to the Wildlife and Countryside Act made by the Countryside and Rights of Way Act 2000 (p. 688). But other legal techniques have been used to try to influence decision making and behaviour. These have ranged from procedural laws (such as those requiring that significant environmental impacts of certain major development projects are assessed before consent is given) and information-based provisions (rules opening up access to environmental information, or eco-labels), to the use of economic instruments (such as taxes on disposing of waste in landfills and greenhouse gas emissions trading).

This use of a broader range of instruments reflects a third phase in the growth of sources of environmental law: traditional public law, command-and-control legislation is combined with different regulatory approaches to secure the most effective forms of control over environmental pollution. This blend of instruments has been termed 'smart regulation'.[2] Underlying this search for the optimal mix of controls is the idea that regulation should work with the market wherever possible.

This search for flexibility in the selection of the instruments is illustrated by climate change policy (see Box 2.6).

BOX 2.6 Flexibility and climate change

Consultation papers on the climate change programme considered a range of instruments, including voluntary agreements to reduce energy consumption, a direct tax on the use of energy, emissions trading schemes, growth in renewable energy, and emission controls under the implementation of the Integrated Pollution Prevention and Control (IPPC) Directive (96/61/EC).

In addition, the Kyoto Protocol (which contains the latest agreed programme for the reduction of emissions that contribute to climate change) has other innovative mechanisms for achieving compliance with cuts in emissions of greenhouse gases including:

- *emissions trading*, whereby an industrialized country can buy or sell emission 'credits' to or from other countries;

---

2 See N. Gunningham and P. Grabosky (1998) *Smart Regulation: Designing Environmental Policy*, Oxford: Clarendon Press.

- the use of the so-called *clean development mechanism*, whereby industrialized countries can earn cuts in their own targets by investing in greenhouse gas reduction projects in developing countries.

These 'flexibility mechanisms' are not without criticism, but they reflect an increasing concern that policies should be as adaptable as possible in order to meet the specified goals and targets.

The blending of different types of instrument means that, if one mechanism is less effective, another mechanism may reduce the gap between aspiration and the achievement of the policy objective (see further Chapters 8 and 9).

Enforcement

Access to information is important in ensuring that there is adequate enforcement of environmental legislation. Leaving enforcement to specialized regulators has historically given rise to potential conflicts, such as when the enforcing body has itself been a polluter (see p. 267). The rise of specialist regulators has avoided this problem, but the closeness of the ongoing relationship between the regulator and the regulated can be a concern, and there are good reasons why other actors, such as environmental non-government organizations (NGOs), should be able to bring enforcement proceedings or, at the very least, to bring potential breaches of the law to the notice of enforcement bodies such as the European Commission. There is also the elusive search for the most effective or optimal enforcement and, in recent years, there have been moves to broaden the enforcement toolkit away from relying on the ordinary criminal law. This includes putting more emphasis on using the enforcement process as a way of cleaning up environmental harm.

The rise of EC environmental law

A most important factor in all of these changes has been the influence of the European Community (EC). The EC has a well-developed environmental policy and has passed numerous pieces of environmental law since it adopted its first Environmental Action Programme in 1973, some of which pre-date explicit reference to the environment in the EC Treaty, which did not occur until the Single European Act 1987. Some of these have been implemented through the framework of national statute law described above, while others have (or will be) given effect to by secondary legislation.

BOX 2.7 **Some key EC Directives**

- Directive 2006/12/EC on waste (the Waste Framework Directive)
- Directive 2000/60/EC establishing a framework for Community action in the field of water policy (the Water Framework Directive)
- Directive 96/62/EC on ambient air quality (a revised directive will be passed in 2008)
- Directive 96/61/EC concerning integrated pollution prevention and control (the IPPC Directive)
- Directives 79/409/EEC on the conservation of wild birds (the Birds Directive) and 92/43/EEC on the conservation of natural habitats and of wild fauna and flora (the Habitats Directive)
- Directive 85/337/EEC on the assessment of the effects of certain public and private projects on the environment (the Environmental Impact Assessment, or EIA, Directive)

At a general level, membership of the EC has led to the consideration and adoption of new methods of control, and to the need to confront environmental issues in an organized way at central government level. More specifically, EC legislation and pressure has led to many actual and proposed changes in the law (often after UK resistance), for example, on sulphur dioxide emissions, nature conservation, and reductions in emissions from vehicles. Some of these, such as the introduction of a ban on dumping sewage sludge at sea, also illustrate the way in which international law has played a part in the evolution of UK environmental law in the modern era (see Box 2.8). Because of concerns that it should not get too involved in the substance of individual decisions about things such as development consents, the EC has played an important role in the rise of procedural environmental laws such as the Environmental Impact Assessment (EIA) Directive (85/337/EEC).

BOX 2.8 Marine disposal of sewage sludge

1990	The Third International North Sea Conference (attended by the Environment Ministers of the eight North Sea states and the EC) reached a political agreement to phase out the disposal of sludge by dumping from ships, or discharge from pipelines, by the end of 1998. Such agreements are, in law, strictly non-binding.
1990	The provisions of the ban are repeated in Decision 90/1 of the Oslo and Paris Commissions (the predecessors of what is now the Commission of the OSPAR North Atlantic Convention). In theory, Decisions are 'binding', but there is no legal enforcement mechanism.
1991	The ban is provided for in Art. 14 of the EC Urban Waste Water Treatment Directive (91/271/EEC).
1996–97	The UK continues to dump around one quarter of its sewage sludge—264,000 tonnes—at sea.
Dec 1998	Sludge ban under EC law effective. All UK dumping ceased.

Other changes have been more indirect: for example, the Wildlife and Countryside Act 1981 was necessary to comply with EC Directive 79/409/EEC on Wild Birds and the opportunity was taken to modify other areas of the law at the same time. Without the EC obligation, there must be some doubt whether any legislation would have been brought forward at that time—and even greater doubt as to whether it would have been persevered with in the light of the widespread opposition to the government's original proposals, which were significantly altered as the Bill passed through Parliament.

Internationalization

A feature of the modern age of environmental law has been the international dimension of many problems. High-profile issues—such as global warming, depletion of the ozone layer, and the global conservation of biological diversity—have galvanized interest in environmental issues and an increasing amount of legislation gives effect to international obligations, either directly or via EC law. Major conferences at Stockholm in 1972 and at Rio de Janeiro in 1992, in particular, played important roles in spurring the global community into action. There is little doubt that the future agenda will increasingly be set on the international stage.

Sustainable development and environmental integration

In the last twenty years, a central concept has been 'sustainable development'—an idea that was originally developed by the World Commission on Environment and Development (the Brundtland Commission) in its report, *Our Common Future*, in 1987. We can think of sustainable development as a bridge between the emergence and development of a body of environmental law, from the Victorian era onwards, to some of the future developments and challenges that are considered later in this chapter.

There are three key strands to *Our Common Future*. First, it defined sustainable development in general terms as '*development that meets the needs of the present without compromising the ability of future generations to meet their own needs*', thus suggesting that global resources (including environmental resources) should be measured, with the objective of ensuring that they are not depleted over time. Clearly, this idea requires some further development itself—in particular in relation to how one goes about measuring intangible global assets and whether it is permissible to substitute one type of asset for another.

Secondly, its central concern was the increasing globalization of various crises (environmental, developmental, energy, etc.) and the connections between them, with the report noting: '*They are all one.*' It therefore went much further than the steps towards policy and legal integration of the kind that we have seen took place with EPA 1990, because it stressed that real progress would only be made if the connections between, for example, environmental protection and energy consumption could be made.

Thirdly, although sustainable development represents a commitment to economic growth, growth can be positive if it is steered in the right direction. For example, because all pollution is a waste of something (energy, raw materials, etc.) to the polluter, then businesses ought to be able to reduce pollution and, at the same time, increase profits. In other words, environmental policy should work with the market and shift from simply penalizing polluters towards trying to make them internalize the external costs of their pollution, or spreading good advice on how to cut down on waste in its various forms. This is one aspect of what is known as 'ecological modernization' (see p. 62).

As a matter of UK law, the term 'sustainable development' first appeared in the Environment Act 1995. The Act requires the Agency, in discharging its functions to protect or enhance the environment, taken as a whole, to make a contribution towards attaining the objective of achieving sustainable development required of it by Ministers (see p. 116). It now appears across a wide range of Acts and policy guidance, and, since the changes made by the 1997 Amsterdam Treaty, is mentioned in the EC Treaty, which expressly links integrating environmental protection into all other EC policy areas with reference to sustainable development. The European Court of Justice has used this duty to justify some quite far-reaching relaxations to the basic free movement laws in the interests of environmental protection (see pp. 203–04). It also has legal status in international law, including international trade law—for example, the Preamble to the WTO Agreement refers to the '*optimal use* [of resources] ... *in accordance with the objective of sustainable development*'.

BOX 2.9 Sustainable development—solution or sham?

The leading environmental lawyer Stephen Tromans has written that:

> The principle of 'sustainability' has now become a totem to which all must bow, a debased currency appropriated by politicians more concerned with the next election result than any supposed long term consequences. Or it is seen as a useful profit line for advice by consultants, who then self-interestedly promote it. To doubt it has become heresy. A decision to expand Stansted airport can be justified as the 'sustainable' option....Ah, you may say, but 'sustainability' is simply shorthand for the relevant criteria in each case, and everyone understands it as such. To some extent that may be a fair point, but the response is that it would be better to justify or repudiate

a proposed course of action on the relevant explicit grounds rather than under the spurious rigour of portmanteau 'sustainability' criteria.

(UK Environmental Law Association e-journal, March 2004, p. 10, available online at **www.ukela.org**)

Second-generation environmental policy

In the light of EC membership and the pressure now brought to bear by the whole international community on environmental issues, it is difficult to disentangle UK policies from those that are global and regional. It is also difficult to predict the future in this area, because—as the US rejection of the Kyoto Protocol on climate change shows—environmental policy continues to be a highly political area.

There is, nonetheless, a clear shift of emphasis away from controlling the impact of pollution towards, in effect, trying to design pollution—and other environmental harms, such as adverse consequences on nature—out of industrial and other processes. Put differently, there is a change of focus away from tackling the most apparent symptoms of environmental problems towards tackling their source. This evolution is often referred to as modern environmental policy entering its 'second generation'. Some examples of this shift can be seen in Table 2.1.

Table 2.1 Shifting policy concerns	
First generation	**Second generation**
Waste disposal and management	Waste minimization and elimination
Environmental quality standards	Eliminating hazardous substances
Controlling stationary, point-source pollution (e.g. chimneys)	Controlling the effects of pollutants from diffuse and mobile sources (e.g. climate change)
Focus on polluting industries	Shared responsibility for environmental problems between government, producers, and consumers
Environmental regulation (top-down, mainly via command-and-control regulation)	Environmental governance (more diffuse, greater role for public participation in the regulatory system, more attention to third-party interests, and greater emphasis on reflexive self-regulation)

One feature of this shift is that activities that were once considered 'good' are now seen more negatively. For example, maximizing waste disposal once had an overriding public health value, but is now problematic, in terms of waste management objectives such as reducing waste going to landfill.

Preventing environmental harm

So the emphasis is shifting away from the more traditional, reactive methods of solving environmental problems towards the prevention of harm. There are different aspects to this: for example, harm can be prevented by setting stringent discharge or emissions limits, including bans on certain substances entering the natural environment (an example of this is the Water Framework Directive (2000/60/EC), which requires the 'cessation' of discharges of priority hazardous substances—see Box 17.2). Although this looks like traditional command-and-control regulation, the innovation is the underlying assumption that no safe level can be set for certain dangerous substances in an environmental medium. In the case of these water pollutants, the main reason for seeking their elimination is that they bioaccumulate—that is, they accumulate the higher up the marine food chain one goes—and are not dispersed in the environment in the way that some pollutants can be. But as a policy shift, elimination is still quite a radical step.

Alternatively, harm can be prevented not only by looking at the production process, but also by trying to 'design out' various harms to which such products might give rise. This is the approach taken, for example, with old vehicles, the disposal of which gives rise to various environmental problems. Under Directive 2000/53/EC on so-called 'end-of-life vehicles', producers are required to set up collection systems, and to ensure that a minimum percentage of each vehicle is recycled and reused. This puts the burden on lessening the wider impact of the product (and the associated costs) firmly on the producer, who is clearly best placed to know what materials, etc. have been used (see p. 669).

Looking at the whole life cycle of products is also the approach that is now being taken to waste reduction more generally. For many years, both law and policy have put waste minimization at the top of the hierarchy of controls without any noticeable impact (indeed, the amount of waste being generated has continued to rise). One way in which to tackle this is to shift the focus away from the question of what we should do with waste to the pre-emptive question of how we can generate less waste. This approach, shifting attention towards the product and away from the waste that it generates, is at the heart of recent moves by the EC to introduce an integrated product policy (see p. 675).

Compensating and offsetting

A different approach is the idea that the law should allow impacts created by harmful processes or activities to be reduced other than at the point at which the harm-causing activity occurs. Examples might include providing compensatory habitat to replace habitat lost to development, or carbon offsetting schemes. A wider issue in this area is the idea that environmental harms should be addressed at the least cost (both to those who pollute and to society more widely).

There are now a range of legal tools that work along these lines: for example, developed states may, under the Kyoto Protocol's Clean Development Mechanism (CDM—see p. 521), combat global warming by financing projects in the developing world that will reduce greenhouse gas emissions or soak them up via natural sinks such as forests. Some of the key challenges in relation to this are in monitoring—for example, whether the new habitat actually compensates for what was lost, which means taking a long view of responsibility—and ensuring that these measures are genuinely additional to what would have happened anyway. The idea that the law should focus more on compensating those harmed, including the environment itself through clean-up and restoration, is also a theme of current reforms to enforcement.

Setting environmental targets

First-generation environmental law and policy was, as we have said, often about curbing the worst excesses of industrialization as these affected humans (for example, preventing the spread of disease or environmental blight) and only latterly encompasses other adverse changes. There are some signs that the new era will also judge the legality of activities against a notional environment free from human activity. Indeed, this is the approach taken in the

2000 EC Water Framework Directive (2000/60/EC). Although the main obligation is to aim to achieve 'good status' of water (meaning good chemical and ecological status), its higher aspiration is that high ecological status is established where (among other things):

there are no, or only very minor, anthropogenic alterations to the values of the physico-chemical and hydromorphological elements for the surface water body type from those normally associated with that type under undisturbed conditions.[3]

Although not without its analytical difficulties and although there are strong doubts about how much effort will be expended to achieve high ecological status, this is a move from (negatively) controlling pollution to (positively) setting and achieving environmental quality objectives. Moreover, these objectives are not based on the environment being the conduit for any harm to humans: environmental quality is clearly being regarded as an end in itself.

Tackling diffuse pollution

There are various aspects to tackling diffuse pollution. There may be no environmental gain if emissions from one factory are controlled, but more factories are constructed (see Box 2.3), and laws making car engines quieter have barely kept pace with the rapid rise in the number of cars on the road. There are also problems in curbing pollution from diffuse sources rather than from more readily identifiable sources (such as factory chimneys or discharge pipes). The entry of nitrates causes water quality problems, but these tend to leach unseen from agricultural land or fall as deposits of nitric acid originating from vehicle exhausts. It is difficult to use traditional command-and-control techniques to tackle problems like this, which often stem from the aggregate of numerous activities that, in themselves, seem fairly innocuous, and more imaginative solutions need to be found.

Sharing responsibility

The EC has championed the notion of 'shared responsibility', meaning that the responsibility for environmental problems is shared between government, producers, and consumers. By suggesting that producers and consumers should be empowered to make decisions that have an impact on environmental performance, this notion heralds the development of a wider range of legal and policy responses to environmental problems.

There is another dimension to the idea of shared responsibility, which is that important environmental policy issues are not only the concern of a remote group of individuals or companies with the label of 'polluters' (and whose changed behaviour would make everything all right), but that environmental protection is a matter for everyone and involves everyone making informed decisions about their own lifestyles.

Although some general pollution offences can be committed by anyone, the law has not always imposed the same responsibilities on individuals as it has on companies. Traditionally, for example, householders have generally been exempt from waste management licensing, although they are now under a duty of care to ensure that waste is only passed onto an authorized person.[4] Or, in practice, individuals may not feel the force of the law in the way that companies may: for example, anyone pouring paint down a drain is unlikely to be prosecuted, either because the individual amount of the pollution loading is fairly minimal or, more likely, because the law is simply not designed to identify, regulate, and punish individuals in this situation. It is easier and more effective to regulate the solvent factory, but when the low-hanging regulatory fruit has been picked and additional improvements are being sought, then this might only be possible by regulating individual behaviour more closely

3 Ibid., Annex V, s. 1.2.
4 Waste (Household Waste Duty of Care) (England and Wales) Regulations 2005, SI 2005/2900—see p. 664.

(for example, with by-laws that provide offences for not separating domestic waste or for incentive charging for domestic waste collection). The more that the law regulates individual behaviour rather than tries to steer it, the more that conflicts will arise between environmental protection and other values, such as individual liberty.[5]

A final point in this area is that the law must strike the right balance between those whose behaviour might be changed to address an environmental problem and this is a long-standing concern. For example, Britain's ageing industrial base creates difficulties when new, improved controls and standards are introduced. Fairness requires that existing producers are given some time to adapt to new standards, yet there is, at the same time, a problem of unfairness if controls are introduced so as to produce an inequality between new and existing producers. Another example is that all the new EC member States have derogations that allow them to postpone the deadlines for complying with key environmental Directives for several years (see Box 7.5).

Environmental governance

At a simple level, 'governance' is a term used to distinguish forms of decision making that are less top-down than have been traditional approaches under which the legislature makes the rules with little public input, described by one commentator as the 'vote, shut up, and obey' approach.[6] Central to governance is widening public participation in decision making. Involving a wider community of interest is said to provide for greater legitimation of the decision-making process (important when law enforcement is in the hands of specialist, unelected bodies such as the Environment Agency) and to lead to a better quality of decision making, by involving key actors in the rule-making process and improving the feedback processes that allow regulators to better the existing ways of doing things.

Environmental law—reflections and future prospects

The uncertainties about how environmental policy will develop are magnified when it comes to forecasting the further evolution of environmental law. For example, the obligations entered into under the United Nations Framework Convention on Climate Change (UNFCCC, or the Climate Change Treaty) provided targets without identifying the specific legal (or otherwise) instruments that would have to be used. Even where the direction of policy is fairly clear, there remains, then, the added uncertainty of knowing which way (and to what extent) law will be used to reach these goals.

The starting point, however, is to repeat the proposition that environmental law has not been developed as a self-contained discipline, but has simply borrowed concepts from other areas of law. One result is undoubtedly a degree of incoherence, but another is that the objective of the protection of the environment is not always best served by the legal mechanisms available, because these other areas were not developed with the particular problems of environmental protection in mind. For example, the private law concentrates on the protection of private interests and has difficulties when it comes to protecting common or public interests in the unowned environment. No damages are payable for harm to the environment as such and only those with personal or property rights may bring an action (thus excluding animals, trees, rivers, etc.). No value is placed on the environment itself and environmental protection is simply an incidental by-product of the protection of other interests (see Case 2.1). As Lord Scarman observed:[7]

---

5 D. Wilkinson (2002) *Environment and Law*, London: Routledge, pp. 262–63.
6 P. Selznick (1992) *The Moral Commonwealth*, Berkeley, Calif: University of California Press, p. 314.
7 (1974) *English Law: The New Dimension*, London: Stevens and Sons, p. 69.

for "environment" a traditional lawyer reads "property": English law reduces environmental problems to questions of property.... The judicial development of the law, vigorous and imaginative though it has been, has been found wanting.

CASE 2.1 *Cambridge Water Co. v. Eastern Counties Leather plc* [1994] 2 AC 264

Over many years, solvents had been spilt at a tannery, ending up in an aquifer from which Cambridge Water Company (CWC) had the right to abstract water. The contamination took the water below EC drinking water quality standards. The most cost-effective action for CWC was to sink another bore-hole at a cost of £1m. CWC eventually lost its case in the House of Lords (see p. 335). Even had it won, however, the groundwater would have remained contaminated. The legal interest at stake was the public law right to abstract the water; as a matter of common law principle, there were no property rights in the groundwater. Whether CWC won or lost, the aquifer would remain contaminated.

Note that the National Rivers Authority (now the Environment Agency) did, in fact, require the aquifer to be cleaned up—showing the reach of public regulation beyond private law disputes—which resulted in an indemnity dispute (*Eastern Counties Leather plc v. Eastern Counties Leather Group Ltd* [2003] Env LR 13; see also Case 11.3).

There have been some steps to use private liability mechanisms to combat particular environmental problems—for example, liability funds to pay for the clean-up after major oil spills, which can also be used to pay for restoration of the natural environment (at least if spending money would be more appropriate than simply letting nature restore itself over time—see p. 362). Recently, there have also been some limited steps to use civil liability as a supporting mechanism to bolster other environmental regimes such as those protecting important species and habitats, but, again, the response has been partial and we still remain some way from having general laws that would, in effect, allow bodies such as environmental NGOs to sue for damages when some aspect of the unowned environment has been harmed (see p. 364).

Public law does recognize the public interest, but difficulties arise out of a lack of acceptance of the idea that the environment has some independent status or value, as distinct from rights conferred on individuals and communities. Even the criminal law struggles with environmental 'crimes', because it has often been pointed out in the courts that many of the offences created are not criminal in the 'true' sense (see the acceptance by the House of Lords, in *Alphacell Ltd v. Woodward* [1972] AC 824, that water pollution offences are in the category of '*acts which in the public interest are prohibited under a penalty*').[8] Finally, the structure of the judicial system (with its emphasis on adversarial and backward-looking, two-party litigation, and with its procedural rules, which are not user-friendly to those wishing to bring environmental cases and which fail to give the public interest a separate voice)[9] is not particularly well suited to consideration of most typical environmental disputes, for a variety of reasons.

These reasons are considered in more detail in Chapters 1 and 3, but include that:

- they have multiple causes;
- they give rise to complex, scientific arguments;

---

8 But note that one consequence of this is that the offences themselves are interpreted more strictly in favour of the prosecution than they would be if they were 'true crimes', in relation to which greater protections are given to the defendant—see further Box 3.2 and p. 258.

9 There now appears to be greater scope to bring amicus curiae (friend of the court) briefs, but some concern at how much court time is given to counsel to argue these.

- they involve a complex interplay between public, private, and criminal law;

- they require the balancing of difficult political or policy questions.

With these current defects in mind, the following thoughts can be put forward about the evolution of environmental law.

One criticism of command-and-control laws has always been that the sanctions that may be imposed may be inappropriate. Consideration is now being given to the 'decriminalization' of whole areas of environmental law, so that a distinction could be drawn between, on the one hand, infringements that are properly characterized as administrative in nature and, on the other, truly criminal breaches, such as blatant cases of environmental vandalism.[10] One advantage of this may be to encourage stiffer penalties for those in the second category, linked to any economic gains made from polluting. In turn, this is linked with the idea of improving the effectiveness of sentencing for environmental crimes. Although there have been attempts to introduce consistent sentencing principles that would encourage judges to impose higher fines, particularly in relation to wealthy defendants, these will only magnify the problems associated with conflating true environmental crime with routine administrative breaches. Neither is acceptable, but sentencing for the former should be based upon the need to sanction and deter, while in the case of the latter, it should be aimed at ensuring that any environmental harm is rectified and prevented in future. Politically, 'decriminalization' may be difficult to sell, but, in relation to new obligations, there are already examples of the use of civil penalties (for example, in relation to the renewable transport fuel obligation under the Energy Act 2004, s. 129), and it may be easier to introduce if the penalties available are broadened out to include things such as profit orders and adverse publicity orders, and if these are actually used.

There is, perhaps, a growing realization that the different areas of law—public law; private law; criminal law—merely provide, in the environmental context, a set of different tools with which to achieve a specified objective—in this case, the protection of the environment. For example, in relation to contaminated land leading to groundwater contamination, someone has to 'pay' for the contamination, either by cleaning it up or by living with the consequences (see Box 2.10). The interesting thing about the solution provided in the Environment Act 1995 is that it combines the various tools in quite a sophisticated fashion, and produces a situation in which the public interest is protected by a combination of mechanisms that borrow from public, private, and criminal law (see further Chapter 8).

BOX 2.10 Paying for contaminated land

There are essentially four possible parties who might 'pay' for historically contaminated land:

- the polluter might be made liable—that is, the Polluter Pays Principle;

- the current owner or occupier might be liable;

- the state might pay—that is, through some public clean-up mechanism—meaning that the public would pay through some form of taxation;

- the loss might lie where it falls—that is, a *Polluted* Pays Principle—meaning that the environment, the local community, the fishery owners, the water companies, etc., would effectively 'pay'.

For a policymaker, the issue is how to come up with a solution that is effective, efficient, and fair, while the tools that are available include, but are not limited to, legal mechanisms.

---

10 Regulatory Enforcement and Sanctions Bill, Cm 7083. 15 May 2007—see p. 286.

This raises the question of whether the development of the law is a matter for the courts or for Parliament. In *Cambridge Water Co. v. Eastern Counties Leather plc* [1994] 2 AC 264 (see Case 2.1), Lord Goff stated in respect of environmental protection:

given that so much well-informed and carefully structured legislation is now being put in place for this purpose, there is less need for the courts to develop a common law principle to achieve the same end, and indeed it may well be undesirable that they should do so.[11]

This can be interpreted as a reflection of the fact that Parliament is able to create a coherent and structured system, rather than one developed on an ad hoc, case-by-case basis. But it also reflects the point that Parliament has a greater democratic legitimacy than the courts when it comes to allocating responsibility for environmental harm.

In the same passage, Lord Goff also stated: '*As a general rule, it is more appropriate for strict liability in respect of operations of high risk to be imposed by Parliament, than by the courts.*'[12] This raises a different point about the nature of the liability that should be imposed. At present, there is a clear division between those (such as the government and most industrial organizations) who see the imposition of strict liability as unfair and punitive, and who therefore wish to retain a fault-based system as far as possible, and those (including the EC Commission) who see strict liability as the most efficient and effective method of allocating responsibility for environmental harm. This issue is likely to remain a controversial one for many years (see further pp. 363–65).

So what does current experience tell us about the way in which the approach of the UK courts may develop in future? While acknowledging the dangers of generalization, it is possible to detect different approaches to different types of case. In the civil or common law cases, the courts appear to be keen to restrict the extension of liability for environmental harm unless there are clearly identifiable parameters within which future decisions can be made. In *Cambridge Water* and in *Hunter v. Canary Wharf Ltd* [1997] 2 WLR 684, the House of Lords refused to extend common law principles to accommodate the concept of environmental damage or damage to those who did not have any property interests, respectively. There may be some change to this to accommodate human rights concerns (see p. 358), but the basic point remains that the courts are always likely to defer to Parliament and decisions of specialist regulators when it comes to setting environmental standards.

Administrative challenges to environmental decisions have also been dealt with in a very narrow fashion by the courts. Although the courts have not rejected every challenge, it is uncommon for environmental decisions to be overturned. (In a recent study, the decision was overturned in only four out of 55 environmental judicial review cases.)[13] Although this often reflects the essentially discretionary nature of the decision-making process in many environmental matters, it also suggests that, in the main, the courts have been very cautious when it comes to developing new ideas on environmental protection.

In contrast, the cause of environmental protection has tended to fare rather better in cases in which administrative discretion is less at issue. This comes through most clearly from decisions on the balancing of freedom of trade and national measures restricting this for environmental reasons. When bodies such as the European Court of Justice and also the Appellate Body of the World Trade Organization (in effect, the World Trade Court) have had to rule on this, the cause of environmental protection has tended to fare rather well.

In relation to criminal cases, the courts have increasingly adopted a purposive approach to construing statutes. For example, in the case of water pollution offences, the extent to which successive courts have been willing to find that a party has 'caused' pollution has been very

11 At 305.
12 Ibid.
13 R. Macrory and M. Woods (2003) *Modernising Environmental Justice: Regulation and the Role of an Environmental Tribunal*, London: University College London.

wide. This purposive approach appears to stem from the judicial desire to provide law that is effective in terms of environmental protection.

There is another area in which the courts have proved active. In more recent years, there has been an increased willingness to develop judicial review mechanisms to provide for openness in decision making and accountability to the public for decisions made in its name. For example, the courts now accept a very wide role for environmental and other public interest groups in litigation, and the value of meaningful public participation in decision making has been recognized in international treaties such as the Aarhus Convention (see Chapter 10) and at the highest level judicially (see p. 465). This can be seen to be part of a wider process of recognizing the contested nature of environmental decision making (see Box 2.11).

BOX 2.11 Values and environmental standards

Setting environmental standards is an exercise in practical judgement. Judgement is reached by a process of deliberation which seeks ways of meeting a multiplicity of constraints and viewpoints... Better ways need to be developed for articulating people's values and taking them into account from the earliest stage in what have been hitherto relatively technocratic procedures.

(Royal Commission on Environmental Pollution, *Setting Environmental Standards*, 21st Report (1998) Cm 4053, paras 8.31 and 8.37)

Despite the negative points that have emerged, however, there will certainly be a continuing increase in environmental litigation. The increased formality of many areas of environmental policy increases the possibility of a successful public law challenge; practising lawyers are increasingly aware of the possibilities thrown up by legal action; environmental interest groups have learnt the usefulness of the legal process in making political points, as well as in winning cases; EC law, and now the European Convention on Human Rights throw up a whole new area of litigation arising out of the doctrines of claims about EC rights and of Convention rights. All manner of legal claims are now being brought in relation to areas such as airport expansion, the dismantling of old ships, discharges from Sellafield, oil exploration, the redevelopment of football stadia, the import of mahogany from Brazil, which would, even a few years ago, have been very unlikely.

Finally, whatever happens in relation to these major issues, there will continue to be some fine-tuning of the mechanisms that already exist. One of the defects of the law has been its piecemeal development and it is clear that measures that have proved successful in one area are likely to be adopted in others.

The threat of environmental law

The basic premise in this chapter is that, albeit slowly and often in a piecemeal way, laws have responded to particular environmental problems that, in turn, have been addressed—some more successfully than others.[14] But laws can also hinder our efforts to tackle environmental problems: property laws allow landowners too much control over features of environmental interest on their land and company laws have sheltered directors from individual responsibility for pollution caused by their companies. Today, it may be that we need to add environmental laws to the list of laws that might prevent us from addressing environmental problems adequately. This is not meant in any narrow sense—that the laws we have do not go far or

---

14 This is not the only way in which developments occur; see B. Pontin (2007) 19(2) JEL 173 (noting a cyclical development in integrated pollution control, or IPC).

fast enough—but rather that today's *environmental* laws may be used to block what some see as essential to greater levels of environmental protection. An example is the use of environmental impact assessment (EIA) laws to challenge the London congestion charge (see p. 343). This is a concern that is voiced in particular in relation to climate change. Objections are raised to renewable energy projects, such as wind farms or tidal barrages, on the basis of their breaching environmental laws (for example, on nature conservation) and, although not all agree on its value in combating climate change, attempts to build a new generation of nuclear power stations will come under immense scrutiny, in the main because of its compatibility with modern environmental laws. A major challenge is to ensure that environmental laws are part of the solution to environmental problems—and not the problem itself.

The costs of compliance

Whatever the exact direction that the law takes, one thing is clear about the future: the cost of compliance with the law is going to rise sharply, both for polluters and for society in general. This is mainly because regulatory standards are getting stricter and are being enforced more rigorously. But there are other factors, such as a heightened perception of the true environmental cost of many activities (which is further increased when explicit links are drawn with the introduction of environmental taxes) and the greatly increased pressure that is being brought to bear by the public, environmental groups, and green consumers and investors. The cost of sewage disposal illustrates the point (see Box 2.12).

BOX 2.12   The demise of 'flush and forget'

Disposal to the sewers has traditionally been a fairly cheap and efficient way of disposing of wastes—but the introduction of integrated pollution control meant that increased controls were applied to discharges of prescribed substances to the sewers. The costs of sewage treatment have also been increasing because of changes relating to the disposal of such wastes by sewage works: for example, the standards set for discharges to controlled waters are being tightened as the Environment Agency reviews existing consents, in the light of the need to meet the requirements of the Urban Waste Water Treatment Directive (91/271/EEC).

The cost of disposal of sewage sludge is rising fast. Not only has the cheap option of dumping sewage sludge in the sea been phased out (see Box 2.8), but the cost of disposal on land has risen significantly. Incineration is another possibility for disposal of sludge, but that too is coming under increasingly tight regulation (not to mention public opposition). The privatized nature of the sewerage undertakers emphasizes the need to take these factors into account, and undertakers are imposing tighter conditions and levying higher charges on discharges.

All of this is feeding back up through the chain, putting pressure on the producers to reduce the polluting nature of their effluent.

There are other aspects to the cost of compliance. It may be that, in the future, certain operators will be required to have insurance covering the costs of cleaning up and restoring the environment in the event of a damaging incident (much in the way that all drivers must have compulsory third-party insurance). There is also the issue of environmental subsidies and other incentives that governments might give to promote things such as clean technologies and zero-carbon energy generation. In a European—and increasingly globalized—context, these will come under scrutiny for the possible effects that they may have on the freedom of trade. But it may be asked whether, without some form of subsidy, green technologies will really be able to compete with technologies that may, themselves, have been heavily subsidized to begin with.

The costs of non-compliance

Apart from the direct cost to business of complying with stricter regulatory controls, the potential liabilities for non-compliance are also increasing. These liabilities fall into six general categories.

- **Criminal liabilities**
  The number of criminal offences for non-compliance with environmental legislation is immense and increasing, and the regulatory agencies have shown an increased willingness to resort to prosecution. Private prosecution is also a possibility. Fines will be the usual penalty, although, in a number of cases, sentences of imprisonment have been imposed (there is normally a potential personal liability for directors and senior managers). Maximum fine levels have risen, as have actual levels of fines imposed.

- **Administrative sanctions**
  In most regulatory systems, there is a range of options available to the regulator, including variation, suspension, or revocation of a licence. Because these steps may lead to the closure of a plant, they are obviously of great importance. One aim of the Regulatory Enforcement and Sanctions Bill[15] is to strengthen, and make more coherent, the suite of sanctioning powers held by regulators.

- **Other administrative penalties**
  If member States do not meet their obligations under EC environmental law, they can be fined. In some areas, individual local authorities can be penalized if they fail to make the appropriate contribution to meeting these obligations—for example, to targets for diverting waste from landfill. Ultimately, therefore, it is local residents who will pay for non-compliance, through higher Council Tax bills.

- **Clean-up costs**
  In most environmental legislation, there is a power to clean up after a pollution incident and recover the cost from the polluter, or (in some cases) the occupier. These costs often exceed the levels of fine that can be imposed.

- **Civil liability**
  Private law actions can be a valuable supplement to administrative regulation and, while liability may often be difficult to establish, the size of claims may be very high indeed. Increasing attention is being given to the use of civil liability in relation to climate change.

- **Adverse publicity**
  In practice, the publicity attracted as a result of infringements of the law may be as costly as any direct costs.

In the light of all of these risks—not to mention the increased costs of waste disposal and of complying with stricter standards—some of the most significant recent developments in the environmental field relate to management issues. For example, there is an international standard for environmental management systems (ISO 14001). Although this scheme is voluntary, in the sense that there is no compulsion to join, there are pressures from within industry—that is, within the supply chain—and from outside—for example, from the

15 Cm 7083, 15 May 2007—see p. 286.

public, insurers, and financial institutions—which mean that, in practice, environmental management systems need to be adopted.

CHAPTER SUMMARY

1 The history of environmental law is the history of the state using statutory law to address some of the weaknesses of private law controls.

2 The central failings of private law (such as nuisance law) were that it protected private property rights rather poorly and largely failed in furthering broader environmental protection interests.

3 Much of what we now call 'environmental law' has its origins in statutory public health-based controls from the Victorian and Edwardian era. This legacy is important—public health control is an important dimension to many environmental statutes—but it provides a narrow, anthropocentric basis for the emergence of modern environmental law.

4 Early legal controls, which were often ad hoc and lacking coherence, tended to be formulated in a way that gave public bodies—which were usually local, rather than centralized, authorities—considerable discretion in enforcing them.

5 Modern environmental law—that is, that dating from the 1960s to the present—departs from this earlier body of law in several ways.

6 A key development is the rise both of the European Community and of international agreements in setting environmental standards and making environmental laws.

7 In part, because of this, there is a trend towards environmental standards being set centrally as a matter of law, rather than locally as an exercise of administrative discretion, and towards greater formalism and legalism generally. There is a greater resort to law to challenge environmental decisions (which is not to say that the courts are necessarily any more likely to find in favour of such challengers).

8 A national (and powerful) Environment Agency has been created to implement and enforce key statutes on water, waste, seriously contaminated land, and industrial processes.

9 There have been moves towards regulating the more polluting processes on an integrated basis and, on a broader scale, ever-increasing attention is being given to integrating environmental concerns into other areas of policymaking (for example, agriculture, transport, and energy).

10 In terms of policy development, there is a shift beyond fighting some of the 'easier battles' of tackling pollution from identifiable sources towards trying to combat pollution from diffuse sources, and trying to design waste and pollution out of industrial processes. This usually involves trying to find the right blend of legal and non-legal tools, rather than any single solution.

11 Increasing attention is being paid to the contribution that individuals make to environmental problems, but also to their role in improving environmental decision making. These can be taken together as a concern with the 'green citizen'.

12 The costs of both complying and not complying with environmental law are each likely to rise.

13 Environmental laws may be used to frustrate (depending on one's values) environmentally desirable actions.

Q QUESTIONS

1 What should the objectives of environmental law be (for example, how far should we go to try to recreate an undisturbed environment)?

2 Catalogue the steps that have been taken to integrate the environment into decision making and to consider the environment in an integrated way. Do these go far enough?

3 What are the main challenges that environmental law will have to face in the immediate future? What lessons from history can help in addressing these?

4 To what extent does English law recognize the public interest in environmental protection?

5 Look at the EC's Restriction on Hazardous Substances Directive 2002/95/EC and its companion Waste Electrical and Electronic Equipment Directive 2002/96/EC (there is some comment on these on p. 670). Critically analyse these in the context of modern approaches and challenges to environmental law.

FURTHER READING

There are several good books on the history of environmental problems. A. Markham (1994) *A Brief History of Pollution*, London: Earthscan, is a short volume that gives an engaging overview, while, more comprehensively, C. Ponting (1991) *A Green History of the World*, London: Sinclair-Stevenson, contains what can seem an almost unremitting stream of salient historical evidence (and also reminds us that what we now call environmental problems did not begin with the Victorians). A. Wohl (1984) *Endangered Lives: Public Health in Victorian Britain*, London: Methuen, is the definitive history in this field. C. Rose (1990) *The Dirty Man of Europe: The Great British Pollution Scandal*, London: Simon and Schuster, is written by a leading campaigner of the 1980s who coined the term 'The Dirty Man of Europe' to describe the UK (particularly because of its reticence to introduce controls on sulphur emissions). D. Vogel (1986) *National Styles of Regulation*, Ithaca, NY: Cornell University Press, stretches back to the nineteenth century to try to explain the (then) shape of UK environmental policy.

Further reading on the history of controls can be found within, and at the end of, the chapters in Part III of the book, while the regulatory issues introduced in this chapter are explored in more depth in Chapter 8.

G. Winter, 'Perspectives for environmental law: entering the fourth phase' (1989) 1 J Env Law 38 remains a thought-provoking contribution and charts what the author sees as the shift from use, to exploitation, to management, to new solutions respecting environmental uncertainties. Published in the very first issue of the *Journal of Environmental Law*, it is interesting to read this article and to reflect on how far we have come since then, and in which direction. A good source for thinking about current challenges is D. Osborn, 'From pollution control to sustainable development: lucid law for fuzzy objectives' (1999) 1 Env L Rev 79, which argues that modern environmental laws must *tend towards* solutions that are integrative and that pursue sustainable development, rather than try to tackle single environmental problems with single, simplistic, legal solutions, but that the role of law in doing so—and in making sure that everyone plays by the book—is no less important for that. R. Lazarus (2004) *The Making of Environmental Law*, Chicago, Ill: University of Chicago Press, focuses on the USA, but, in doing so, offers the most sophisticated general survey of how modern environmental law has developed.

@ WEB LINKS

See the Online Resource Centre for links to a range of relevant historical and contemporary documents.

Values, principles, and environmental law

→ Overview

In this chapter, we consider the interaction between values and environmental law, which involves some reflection on differing attitudes to the environment. We then examine some of the ways in which these values are translated into political principles, such as the goal of sustainable development or the Precautionary Principle; we go on to consider the question of whether these principles are capable of being rules or law in the sense that they create legally enforceable rights and duties. Finally, we consider the role of human rights and environmental protection.

At the end of this chapter, you should be able to:

✔ identify some of the different approaches to environmental decision making and some of the considerations that are taken into account during that process;

✔ understand in outline the interaction between values and law, and the way in which differing environmental perspectives have an impact upon decision making and dispute resolution;

✔ understand in outline the role of the main environmental principles and their translation into legal principles;

✔ understand in outline the role that rights—especially human rights—play in environmental law and policy.

Introduction

One of the defining characteristics of environmental problems is their complexity, in the sense that there are often many interconnected, variable elements to the problem. There are, for example, strong links between the burning of fossil fuels, emissions from transport, deforestation, depletion of the ozone layer, and climate change. Trying to 'solve' environmental problems means addressing different aspects of the problem that, in turn, give rise to their own challenges. For example, a partial solution to climate change might be to reduce the amount of energy produced from fossil fuels, which might be achieved by increasing the use of wind or nuclear energy. But, unfortunately, these solutions have their own connected problems, including visual impact, interference with nature conservation interests, capacity—that is, low energy output requiring huge wind farms—and nuclear waste disposal and the associated risks. Other solutions might involve the creation of more forests as 'carbon sinks' or reducing car use; these too have corresponding disadvantages, such as the loss of agricultural land and the loss of individual autonomy.

This complexity of environmental problems has the consequence that there are many ways of looking at, thinking about, and even talking about the same problem. Just as an optical illusion can look like two different things at the same time, so perspectives on the same environmental problems can vary. To some, wind farms are a sustainable alternative energy source;[1] to others, they are an *'ineffective source of electricity . . . an example of green tokenism, which does nothing to meet any environmental objectives'*.[2] Whether or not these alternatives are more or less attractive depends largely upon the values that are attached to the different variables.[3]

Environmental law may provide some assistance in resolving these sorts of tensions through pollution control or planning legislation, which sets down a framework for making decisions. There is, however, no necessary connection between this framework and the decisions on what pollutants to ban, at what level to set an acceptable legal emission standard, or in relation to an individual application for planning permission or pollution control authorization. This gap between the procedural framework and the substantive decision is where environmental values play a critical role.

Values and environmental law

What do we mean by 'values'? In its 21st Report, the Royal Commission on Environmental Pollution (RCEP) suggested that values are *'beliefs, either individual or social, about what is important in life and thus about the ends or objectives which should govern and shape public policies'*.[4] The Commission went further and identified certain factors that may influence individuals' attitudes to the environment. These included such things as the environment as a vital resource for humans, the richness of biodiversity, and the cultural, historical, or social significance of the environment. For example, an industrial landscape may be an important part of the local environment, as might be such natural features as the 'Seven Oaks' of the eponymous Kentish town.

Taking the broad definition adopted by the RCEP, we can characterize 'environmental values' as what people believe to be important about the environment and thus what should be the priorities for environmental policy and ultimately environmental law. At the outset, however, it is important to distinguish between, on the one hand, 'opinions and attitudes' and, on the other, the wider, deeper sort of values that are held by groups and sections of society as a whole. Individual 'values' can be sincerely held opinions that fluctuate or are mutually inconsistent; at their worst, they are little more than consumer-type preferences for a favourite brand of chocolate bar or washing powder. Representative values held by groups and sections of society should be the product of debate, participation, and, where possible, the attainment of consensus, and should therefore be much more likely to be consistent and to underpin rational rule and decision making.

The definition of values adopted for the purposes of this chapter therefore distinguishes 'environmental values' from a different categorization of environmental ethics. The latter is not covered in detail. Partly, this is because the subject has been covered more than adequately elsewhere;[5] more importantly, perhaps, the aim of this chapter is to place values as part of a matrix, which includes strongly held moral and ethical positions, and environmental principles, such as sustainable development and the Precautionary Principle. It also includes formal law and other rules, and the values contained in these, which can be environmental values—for example, the need to take into account the interests of future

---

1 See **www.yes2wind.com**, a site set up by Friends of the Earth, Greenpeace, and WWF to advocate for more wind energy projects.

2 See **www.countryguardian.net**, the website of a UK conservation group campaigning against 'the construction of wind turbines in environmentally sensitive areas'.

3 See, generally, J. Holder and M. Lee (2007) *Environmental Protection, Law and Policy*, 2nd edn, Cambridge: Cambridge University Press, ch.17, and below at p. 732 and Box 3.2.

4 (1998) *Setting Environmental Standards*, Cm 4053.

5 For example, see J. Alder and D. Wilkinson (1999) *Environmental Law and Ethics*, London: Macmillan Press.

generations or legal values, such as legal certainty and respect for the 'rule of law'. There is, therefore, no deep analysis of underlying ethical issues, nor is there much detailed discussion of so-called 'normative ethics'—that is, the questions of what is right and wrong or of what the law should be as opposed to what it is.

These normative questions are not irrelevant; neither are these aspects of environmental ethics unimportant. There is, however, no necessary connection between normative environmental ethics and the way in which people behave in practice, just as most murderers probably believe murder is wrong. There are many people who subscribe to the idea that environmental protection is important and that certain things are 'right' or 'wrong', but that view makes no impact on the way in which they live their lives. Alternatively, there are others who follow what we might term 'green' lifestyles, such as those who do not own a car and who recycle their waste, but do not adopt this stance from an environmentalist perspective.

Also, the domestic courts appear not to be interested in the concept of normative environmental ethics. This is true of both administrative and public law, but also in relation to judge-made law, such as the common law tort of nuisance. Although many of the participants in the environmental disputes that end up in the courts are concerned with the fundamental issues of what is 'right' and 'wrong', the judiciary tends to refocus attention on legalistic interpretation of rules, deference to Parliament's capacity and authority to decide complicated questions of what is in the public interest, and the exercise of lawful administrative powers.[6] By contrast, values have had a limited impact upon the way in which the courts view, for example, environmental offences (see Chapter 9).

The interaction between values and law

Although there is no *direct* connection between environmental values and the way in which law is made and functions on a practical level, there are many ways in which values play a indirect part in the operation of an environmental regulatory system.

Triggering the formulation of new policy and law

Environmental laws are often made as a consequence of political aims and goals, and the setting of scientific standards (see p. 224). The ignition of the policy 'fuse', however, can be brought about by shifts in environmental values, in the sense that new priorities are identified and action called for. These may be general shifts in public opinion, or specific interest groups may generate them.

BOX 3.1 Examples of changing values triggering new legislation

The history of environmental law features a number of examples of legislation responding to public concern over a single issue or particular event.[7] The following examples reflect the way in which shifts in values can bring something to the forefront of environmental policy and consequently result in changes in environmental law.

Public Health Act 1848—triggered by the Chadwick report into sanitary living conditions.

---

6 See *R v. Somerset County Council, ex parte Fewings and ors* [1995] 1 WLR 1037, in which the Court of Appeal overturned a decision to ban hunting on county council land on the moral ground of animal cruelty. The Court held that such a consideration was irrelevant and unlawful. Cf *R v. Sefton Metropolitan Borough Council, ex parte British Association of Shooting and Conservation Ltd* [2001] Env LR 10, in which the banning of shooting wildfowl was lawful, because it was on the legal ground that it was 'for the benefit of the area'.

7 For more examples in the field of nature conservation, see D. Evans (1997) *A History of Nature Conservation in Britain*, London: Routledge.

Sea Birds Preservation Act 1869—introduced a close season for hunting 33 species of bird in response to wholesale slaughter of sea birds whose feathers were used in hat making.

Clean Air Act 1956—followed a public outcry after smog descended on London, which was caused by the burning of poor quality coal in the capital's homes and power stations. It is estimated that four thousand people lost their lives as a result of the pollution.

Deposit of Poisonous Waste Act 1972—containers of cyanide waste were dumped at a derelict brick kiln near Nuneaton. A public outcry and newspaper articles outlining the dubious activities of 'cowboy' waste operators triggered legislative intervention. The severity of the outcry was reflected in the fact that the legislation only took a month to pass through Parliament.

Control of Pollution (Anglers' Lead Weights) Regulations 1986[8] and the **Environmental Protection (Restriction on Use of Lead Shot) (England) Regulations 1999**[9]—banned the supply and import of lead weights used in angling because of a public concern over harm to wildlife caused by poisoning.

These shifts in values have tended to be narrowly focused and have resulted in piecemeal, reactive legislation. For this reason, they should be distinguished from more fundamental changes in the way in which we view the environment. The general public is now much more aware of the need for environmental protection at individual, local, regional, national, and international levels. This means that, although issues-based values continue to be important, there are shifts in the general way of looking at environmental issues—particularly in relation to the future impacts of current pollution levels and the pursuit of the goal of sustainable development.

Influencing the interpretation and enforcement of environmental laws

The day-to-day interpretation of environmental law shifts slowly to reflect changing public values. Judicial attitudes can reflect these shifts. Sometimes, it is difficult to distinguish between causes and effects, particularly when new laws establish new rights or approaches. For example, the influence of European law has had an impact upon the way in which domestic environmental law is interpreted; this, in turn, affects the way in which the public and the legal profession use law to protect the environment. We can take other more general examples, such as the Precautionary Principle, biodiversity damage, or sustainable development, and see how concepts that were unknown thirty years ago have had a significant impact on the way in which laws are interpreted and made today.

BOX 3.2 Changes in judicial attitudes to environmental protection

If we consider a relatively straightforward pollution control provision designed to protect water from pollution (now contained in the Water Resources Act 1991, s. 85(1)), we can compare and contrast judicial attitudes underlying the interpretation of similar provisions over a period of thirty years during which environmental values have shifted.

The first extract reflects the notion that the nature of pollution control offences were seen to be 'technical' in nature with no moral blame:

---

8 SI 1986/1992, as amended.
9 SI 1999/2170, as amended.

> This Act is, in my opinion, one of those Acts…which…deals with acts which are not criminal in any real sense, but are acts which in the public interest are prohibited under a penalty.
>
> (*Alphacell Ltd v. Woodward* [1972] 2 All ER 475 *per* Viscount Dilhorne)

Within twenty years, the judicial view had shifted to considering water pollution to be a clearly criminal activity. The breach of the analogous provision was considered clearly to be 'criminal', with greater emphasis being placed on the importance of environmental protection:

> The object of the relevant words of s. 85(1) and the crime created thereby is the keeping of streams free from pollution for the benefit of mankind generally and the world's flora and fauna.
>
> (*National Rivers Authority v. Alfred McAlpine Homes East Ltd* [1994] 4 All ER 286 *per* Morland J)

More recently, this view has been reinforced:

> The environment in which we live is a precious heritage and it is incumbent on the present generation to preserve it for the future. Rivers and watercourses are an important part of the environment and there is an increasing awareness of the necessity to preserve them from pollution.
>
> (*R v. Anglian Water* [2004] Env LR 10 *per* Scott Baker LJ)

Of course, it is possible to read too much into such extracts taken in isolation, particularly when the rhetoric in the latter two was not necessarily matched by effective criminal sanctions (see p. 284). These cases do, however, tend to illustrate a much wider picture of the way in which the courts reflect changing public attitudes to the environment. Other examples can be seen in the shifting judicial attitudes to public participation in the environmental assessment process (see p. 465) and the purposive approaches that have been taken to waste management offences (see p. 644) and nature conservation provisions (see Chapter 19).

Influencing individual decision making

The 'British approach' to environmental law is heavily dominated by discretionary decision making based upon political factors (see p. 91). It is possible to identify the impact that shifting values have upon the way in which new policies are given weight in the context of individual decision making. As we shall see, the principle of sustainable development and the Precautionary Principle are particularly difficult to transform into legal rules. In the context of policy formulation and individual decision making, however, the principles can be fleshed out and applied in a practical manner with practical consequences. For example, the policy of developing 'brownfield' sites and the consequent effect on planning applications for such developments reflects an understanding and acceptance of the need to use resources effectively and sustainably. We can also see the effect of the public perception of environmental risks and associated values in the sequence of planning cases, which suggest that, even in cases in which such perceptions of risk are 'unsubstantiated', they may still be taken into account when making development decisions.

Influencing the regulated

Changing public values can affect those who are regulated. For example, regulated companies may change their behaviour in response to shifting consumer values even when their activities are officially sanctioned and supported at the highest level.

BOX 3.3 **Influencing the regulated—the *Brent Spar* saga**

One of the clearest examples of shifting values affecting the regulated is the *Brent Spar* saga.[10] Between 1991 and 1993, Shell considered various options for the disposal of the *Brent Spar*, one of its defunct storage and loading buoys, before finally deciding to sink the rig in deep Atlantic waters. In December 1994, the UK government approved the disposal plan under the Petroleum Act 1987 and the Food and Environment Protection Act 1985. During 1995, Greenpeace encouraged direct action in the form of a boycott of Shell petrol stations across Europe. In the light of this protest and despite support from the UK government, Shell abandoned its planned disposal route. Shell towed the *Brent Spar* to Norway while it considered other disposal options. In 1999, the *Brent Spar* was dismantled and recycled as part of a new ferry terminal in Norway.

Although it is not unusual for public campaigns to be launched against companies on environmental issues, the *Brent Spar* saga is notable because it took place against a background of active government support within the existing framework of legislation and policy. In addition, there was reasonable evidence that the planned sea disposal was, in fact, the best practicable environmental option. While this may have been true for the isolated example of the *Brent Spar*, there were serious misgivings about the knock-on effects on future disposals of oil rigs, which led to the Greenpeace protests and shift in public opinion.

In 1998, the majority of European countries, including the member States of the EC, agreed to ban all disposals of offshore installations, subject to certain derogations, under OSPAR Decision 98/3.

Shifts in values can have a more general impact on the regulated. There is an increasing reliance upon self-regulatory or voluntary instruments in environmental regulation. These include such things as corporate environmental reporting or the introduction of accredited systems of environmental management. There are various explanations for the growth of the 'privatization' of environmental regulation, but at least part of the reason is that there has been a commercial recognition of the importance of environmental values as weighed against the accumulation of profit. It could be argued that certain unrelated factors such as the cost of environmental compliance, with a consequent need for cost reduction and risk minimization, and the maintenance of a competitive industrial advantage have been particularly influential. The impact of changing public perceptions of environmental values has, however, also been significant, leading to, among other things, the promotion of 'green advertising'.[11]

Assisting with the legitimacy of environmental laws

Just as values provide a trigger for new environmental laws, they also ensure that laws are considered to be legitimate by those who are regulated and by the general public. For example, one of the reasons for the many delays in the introduction of the contaminated land regime under Pt 2A of the Environmental Protection Act (EPA) 1990 was the perceived unfairness of a system of law that introduced retrospective strict liability.[12] In areas in which environmental legislation does not reflect contemporary values, it becomes difficult to police, because the regulated feel justified in ignoring 'unfair' requirements.

---

10 For a more detailed analysis, see G. Jordan (1998) 76 Pub Adm 716.

11 F. Jarvis (1999) 'Save as you spend: consumer protection of the environment and local social cohesion' in J. Holder and D. McGillivray (eds) *Locality and Identity: Environmental Issues in Law and Society*, Aldershot: Dartmouth.

12 S. Bell and L. Etherington (1999) 2 Nott LJ 48.

The law and balancing environmental values

There is a general consensus that environmental protection is an important matter—indeed, one of the justifications for introducing a system of comprehensive environmental regulation was that it was, and is, in the public interest to protect the environment. Thus, everyone from the judiciary, to regulators, to interested industrial parties stress that environmental protection should be at the heart of our activities. To put it another way, it is very rare to hear the contrary view—namely, that it is desirable to destroy the environment. This general consensus, however, masks fundamental differences in the choices that different people might make and the emphasis that they might place upon the importance of the environment as weighed against other factors.

Environmental law is controversial, and thus interesting, because it deals with questions of changing values and, therefore, differing priorities. The key question is: 'How does the law interact with the process of change?' A spectrum of views on the importance of environmental protection, might range from one end at which environmental interests are paramount and all other considerations overridden, to the other end at which environmental interests are inconsequential and do not play a part in any aspect of life. Of course, simplistic views such as these tend to caricature the problems involved in regulating for environmental protection. For example, should the law make owners clean up contaminated land notwithstanding the fact that they were not responsible for the original pollution? What if the owner was a company and it had to make workers redundant to balance the books? What if it was to be made bankrupt? These are very specific questions, but there are other more general concerns, such as how we should use resources today so that they can be used by future generations.

Each of these issues magnifies the problem of establishing a legal framework of rules that can assist in the balancing of competing interests. They also raise the question of whether the law should have anything to do with these issues at all. Some might argue that law is unsuited to dealing with political balancing acts in which competing interests need to be 'traded off' with one another. We would argue that law promotes the consistency, transparency, and accountability of decision making and controls the discretion of the decision maker. There are, however, other things that the law might do, such as increase the legitimacy of some of the environmental principles discussed below.

Law and risk

One of the factors that is placed into the balance of environmental decision making is the nature and extent of risk to the environment and human health. In this context, the term 'risk' covers the probability of an event causing harm to the environment or to human health in relation to the magnitude of that event occurring. For example, a 0.1 per cent chance of a methane gas explosion that will blow up a town may be considered to be 'riskier' than a 50 per cent chance of a discharge that may pollute an already contaminated watercourse.

One of the characteristics of many of the hottest debates about environmental issues has been the role of risk and the perception of that risk. If we think of climate change, the *Brent Spar* fiasco, or the controversy over the potential hazards posed by genetically modified (GM) crops and foods, we can see that the disagreement and doubts over the long-term implications of associated risks have only helped to obscure the decision-making process. The problem of risk is not, however, confined to individual issues, but permeates the whole of environmental regulation, whether by way of analysing the costs and benefits of taking action against pollution as the Environment Agency is required by law to do,[13] in assessing whether it is appropriate to clean up a contaminated site, or in determining the appropriate

---

13 Under EPA 1990, s. 39, and see p. 119.

strategy to reduce the threat of climate change. It is hard enough to decide upon individual priorities or policy goals in cases in which the issues are clear, without the additional complexity of factoring in short- or long-term risks that are the subject of scientific and non-scientific debate.

The problem of risk is often linked to the relationship between science and environmental law. Science plays a role in the identification and assessment of environmental risks. The science of environmental hazards is often uncertain, largely as a consequence of the complex nature of environmental problems, and scientists have therefore developed methods of risk assessment to bridge the gap between this scientific uncertainty and the need for an objective framework for decision making. While there are quantitative methods for assessing risks, such as ranking hazards in relation to the size of risk, the objectivity and reliability of these methods in providing *all* of the answers is flawed for a number of reasons.

- Certain assumptions are made when undertaking a scientific risk assessment. These may be in terms of the nature of the hazard, the aggregation of different events, the existence of alternatives, or anticipating future trends as against present knowledge. These assumptions are often determined by reference to subjective and unscientific criteria.

- As a consequence of the differing assumptions that underpin risk assessment, the final conclusions can be variable. For example, a risk assessment carried out on the potential effects of accidental releases of ammonia resulted in 11 different risk estimates, ranging from 1 in 400, to 1 in 10 million.[14]

- A scientific risk assessment fails to take into account the public perception of risk, which is not necessarily based upon objective criteria.[15]

There are different ways of approaching the question of defining and assessing environmental risks, which tend to reflect the different perspectives that people take on environmental issues. These approaches influence the way in which decisions are made about regulating environmental risks (for example, banning a pollutant) or making an individual decision in which risks are involved (for example, to grant permission for an incinerator). Thus the decision or rule maker may be influenced differently depending upon whether risk is measured economically (through balancing costs and benefits), scientifically (by examining a statistical basis of probabilities based upon past experiences or by assessing the incidence of hazards across large numbers of people), or psychologically (by taking into account people's perceptions of, for example, voluntary risks such as those associated with smoking, which are seen as more acceptable than imposed risks, such as those associated with the granting of planning permission for a landfill site in the locality).

Environmental risks can be addressed in a number of ways, from increasing the accuracy and independence of 'expert' analysis (for example, with the creation of a 'Risk Commission'),[16] to improving public participation in rule and decision making. Ultimately, however, the problem of how to deal with environmental risks is concerned with underlying issues, such as priorities for regulatory action, the trade-off between environmental protection, including human health as against other goals, and the acceptance of priorities for action by the general public.

---

14 S. Contini, A. Amendola, and I. Ziomas (1991) *Benchmark Exercise on Major Hazard Analysis*, EUR 13386, EN 1991, Luxembourg: Commission of the European Communities.

15 Royal Commission on Environmental Pollution 21st Report (1998) *Setting Environmental Standards*, Cm 4053.

16 As an attempt at this, see (in the private sphere) **www.rsariskcommission.org/default.aspa** and (publicly) the Risk and Regulation Advisory Council, established in early 2008. Both of these seem to have an 'over-regulation' emphasis.

Perspectives on environmental issues

We have seen how values underpin many aspects of environmental law, but values on their own can only progress matters so far. In the case of many of the difficulties that environmental law and policy seek to resolve, the underlying values may not be controversial. Collective or public values, such as the needs to protect human health, to use our resources wisely, or to provide food, warmth, and accommodation, would not raise much debate. Problems arise, however, when competing values need to be prioritized.

When it comes to rule making, for example, there may be benefits from banning a pollutant that has a causal link with disease or is degrading our environment. But what if the ban means the closure of factories in a number of depressed areas, which puts people out of work, lowers the quality of life for many others, and has an overall detrimental effect on the national economy? What if scientists could 'prove' that the effects of the pollutant would only be revealed over a 250-year period or that it would only result in one death per 100,000 residents per year?

These practical problems highlight a number of theoretical issues: how do we compare costs and benefits that appear to be so different? What weight should we give to environmental interests over other considerations? How do we assess what we should forfeit today in order to do justice to future generations? What sort of information should assist in the decision as to whether or not regulatory intervention is required? Of course, these issues are magnified when they are put into the context of individual decision making. In these circumstances, the subjectivity of the participants in the decision-making process makes the choices much starker—although there is often some confusion between individual attitudes and collective values perhaps best illustrated by the so-called 'NIMBY' ('not in my backyard') argument.

These issues are complex without any obvious solution. In seeking some way out of the problem of making environmental rules and decisions, we have to examine some of the different approaches that may be taken. In doing so, there is no suggestion that these perspectives are strictly drawn or exclusive. Indeed, people may adopt different perspectives in relation to different issues. There is, however, some value in trying to disassemble some of the justifications for making (or not making) rules or decisions. These perspectives provide some way of trying to balance competing values, and explain how and why opposing arguments are put forward to support individual positions. By 'perspective', we imply an overview of values rather than a particular view on a particular issue. In general, when rules or decisions are made, many different perspectives often influence them; the significance lies in the weight that is attached to each perspective, or perhaps the perspective that can best justify the end result that the maker of the decision or rule desires.

Environmental perspectives

An environmentalist perspective can be characterized as placing greatest weight—and, at its extreme, to the exclusion of other balancing factors—on the need to protect the environment and, if there is no conflict with such protection, human health. Thus, an 'environmentalist' would presume that environmental protection was paramount and outweighed considerations such as cost, or scientific arguments that any associated risks were small. It is worth noting that, in the context of examples in which environmental protection is to be balanced against 'quality of life' issues and societal inequalities, this crude representation of views masks more sophisticated arguments.

There is a spectrum of views that might fall within the category of what we have termed 'environmentalist' perspectives. The spectrum can be linked to basic viewpoints associated with environmental ethics. The critical distinction between these viewpoints is the extent to which they give the environment moral worth in its own right—that is, what we might term an 'ecocentric' perspective—as opposed to placing it within the sphere of human interests, such that the environment has a value only within the context of its relationship to humans—that is, what we might term an 'anthropocentric' perspective.[17]

Economic perspectives

The economic perspective of environmental issues and values is concerned with making rational decisions on the basis of an analysis of the costs and benefits of individual options. In this sense, some argue that it allows more representative forms of decision making, because there can be an acknowledgement of intensity of people's preferences. For example, an economic approach examines the *extent* to which people value a habitat, not simply whether a development of that habitat should be allowed to go ahead. Accordingly, it would be concerned with only taking action if it were economically efficient, such that the benefits accruing from the action outweigh the costs of doing so. Thus, an economist aims to identify underlying measures of value, including attaching worth to such intangibles as a human life and the environment. On a theoretical level, this sort of valuation is fraught with difficulties. For the purposes of this discussion, however, economic techniques are simply a basis for decision or rule making—that is, one way of determining whether or not a particular decision will generate the maximum benefit to the most people.

Valuation of intangibles such as the environment can be based upon the preferences that people have, which can be established by examining people's behaviour and analysing the choices that they make. For example, the reduction in house prices of properties surrounding a polluted area or the increase in prices in areas in which the environment is desirable may form the basis of such a valuation—termed 'hedonistic pricing'. Even in the case of a human life, it is possible to determine, on an objective level at least (sometimes referred to as a 'statistical life'), what someone might be willing to pay to avoid the risk of death. For example, someone might be willing to pay £1,000 to avoid a 1 in 10,000 chance of death. From the economic perspective, this would make a statistical life worth £10,000,000.[18]

It is not possible to value everything on the basis of explicit preferences, particularly in the case of things such as the unowned environment, which are unrelated to human life or property. For example, in the case of a remote wilderness, it is unlikely that there are any objective measures of what people would be willing to pay to preserve it. In these circumstances, economists use 'contingent values', established by carrying out a survey of people in relation to the amount of money that they would be willing to pay to conserve some environmental feature, or the amount they would want to *be* paid as compensation for its loss.

BOX 3.4 'Costing the Earth'

Some economists have attempted to estimate the value of the global ecosystem by reference to the 'services' that it provides.[19] Such services include the supply of raw materials, food production, climate regulation, the purification of air and water, the mitigation of floods, pest control, and the generation of fertile soils. The value of such intangibles as recreational and cultural services,

---

17 See B. Norton (1984)(6) Environmental Ethics 131.

18 See further F. Ackerman and L. Heinzerling (2004) *Priceless*, New York: New Press.

19 See R. Costanza, R. d'Arge, R. de Groot, S. Farber, M. Grasso, B. Hannon, K. Limburg, S. Naeem, R. V. O'Neill, J. Paruelo, R. G. Raskin, P. Sutton, and M. van den Belt (1997) 387 Nature 253 and the summary of the response in Anon (1998) 395 Nature 430.

including holidays, ecotourism, and artistic or spiritual uses of the environment, were included. In 1997, the average value of these services was estimated at $33tn.

The process of 'costing the Earth' was controversial: the methodology was criticized for being too 'broad-brush'. For example, assumptions had been made about the uniformity of the value of ecosystems across the world—such as the suggestion that a hectare of grassland in the USA provided the same services as a similar area in Africa. Some economists argued that it was not possible to place a value on aggregated resources on a 'willingness to pay' basis. While it may be possible for people to put a price on an area of woodland or even of wilderness, it was not credible to ask people to put a value on the loss of *every* ecosystem.

In response to this and other criticisms, it was argued that the justification for the valuation was as much political as it was economic. The claim was that the value of ecosystem services had been largely ignored. Because the estimated value of the services was larger than global gross national product, it was actually much more important to human welfare than had been previously assumed and, therefore, the value of ecosystem services deserved much more atten-tion than it had previously been given. The failure to put a monetary value on these services had distorted global pricing mechanisms and certain commodities that depended more on ecosystem services, such as water supply, would demand higher prices if the true value of ecosystems services were to be factored in.

Although the valuation methodology may have been open to criticism, the exercise was import-ant because it raised the general issue of how to take into account the value of ecosystem services both generally and in relation to individual projects.

Social and cultural perspectives

Taking social and cultural perspectives into account in decision making has been rela-tively late in coming, but is gaining currency. In contrast to economic perspectives, this approach questions whether it even makes sense, for example, to ask people how much they are willing to *pay* for environmental assets; instead, it argues that values are not static, in the sense of being beliefs *from* which we argue, but rather are things *towards* which we reason. Deliberative techniques involve stakeholder—in its widest sense including those from whom an interest in the environment is a 'stake'—consultation in order to arrive at a common understanding of the different factors that can lead to decisions that are acceptable to all. This is easier said than done, but involves the construction of ways of decision making that involve some form of collective deliberation about what things we value and why, rather than asking for individual preferences in surveys.

A socially and culturally informed perspective would also question attitudes to natural scientific assessments of risk. This might be as a result of their failing to take local attitudes or 'lay' knowledge seriously enough—for example, by having too much confidence that 'labora-tory' assumptions apply to the real world in which regulation takes place. It might also be for the wider reason that, inevitably, risk is constructed culturally—that is, that our attitudes to risk and, therefore, also to precaution are related, at an individual level, to how risk-seeking or risk-averse we are, and to broader issues about how much trust we place in regulators and in 'official' knowledge. Our attitudes to risk are also affected by wider public perceptions, formed by numerous factors, about how fragile the environment is.

From this perspective, therefore, cost–benefit and other economic approaches to habitat conservation will be rejected for wrongly equating natural resources with consumer goods. Instead, more discursive valuation techniques will be preferred. There are already some signs of this: the Environment Agency now requires the use of deliberative valuation techniques, involving small groups discussing which criteria they think are important, when drawing up Local Environment Agency Plans (LEAPs).

Scientific perspectives

Broadly, a scientific perspective or a natural science approach embodies what we might call a 'technocratic' approach to environmental regulation—that is, it both suggests that a range of environmental issues and disputes can be resolved 'scientifically', and provides a means for reaching 'objective', conclusive opinions about such matters. Arguably, much UK pollution control law has, at least ostensibly, been framed along such lines—in particular, standards relating to public health, such as drinking water standards or air quality. The approach has also been seen in something of an elitist 'we know best' attitude by regulators towards things such as the granting of environmental licences.[20]

To operate successfully, such a 'top-down' approach requires a considerable degree of public trust in science and in scientists acting for regulatory bodies and governments. Events such as the BSE crisis have led to something of a crisis of confidence, however, and levels of public trust in scientific evidence—especially in evidence produced by government—is low compared with the trust placed in research seen as being more 'independent'—for example, that produced by respected environmental pressure groups. Faith in official science has also been one of the reasons behind the traditionally secretive nature of decision making, because a technocratic approach has little reason for public involvement other than, perhaps, to rubber-stamp decisions already taken. But it must be recognized that those who are sceptical of the role of science in decision making still tend to rely upon scientific evidence to *reveal* environmental problems: most of climate change policy, for example, is based upon scientific evidence of the causes and effects.

BOX 3.5 Different perspectives in practice

These differing perspectives can usefully be illustrated by thinking about how decisions would be reached about a local green space threatened with a mixed use development including housing, retail, and light industrial uses.

- **The ecological/environmental perspective**
  An ecological perspective would view the destruction of the habitat in purely ecological terms. The ecocentrist would view the benefits of the provision of the new development as an irrelevant factor; indeed, the status of the habitat—whether it was protected or 'special' in any way—would also be irrelevant. The guiding principle would be that humans have no right to interfere with nature.

  The anthropocentrist perspective might, however, involve different considerations. For example, although the habitat would be considered to be of great importance, there would be some justifications for its destruction should the overall contribution to human welfare be substantial—for example, if it were to be towards the building of a much-needed hospital—or if the environmental importance of the site were to be limited—that is, if it were to be of little ecological significance.

- **The economic perspective**
  An economist would undertake a valuation of the development after deducting construction costs. This valuation would represent what a buyer would be willing to pay. There is an

---

20 See p. 502.

assumption that this valuation reflects, in the absence of any value that might be attached to the habitat, what the development is 'worth'. If the habitat were to have no direct connection to local people, in the sense that it could not be valued by its use alone, an economist would undertake a survey to determine what an accurate contingent valuation might be. If that survey were to show that local residents would be willing to pay (or be paid) more than the value of the development, the development would be refused. Of course, much depends upon how widely the survey sample is drawn.

- **The cultural/social perspective**
A social perspective would concentrate on 'capturing' the importance of the green space, along with other considerations, through stakeholder consultation and public participation. The site may be thought to be important because local people use it for recreational purposes, because it is the 'focal point' of the village, or because it has historical connections with a famous Civil War battle. Alternatively, the development might provide jobs and low-cost housing for young families in the area who would otherwise be forced to move away. In cases of dispute, alternative dispute resolution (ADR) mechanisms would be used to rationalize differences and to try to achieve a consensus—or the nearest to a consensus—that could reasonably be achieved.

A social or cultural approach would also hesitate before accepting any quantitative valuation of harm to a species or habitat. It would almost certainly find problematic the idea of 'translocating' habitat elsewhere, because the value of the habitat is not only its contribution to national or global biodiversity, but also includes its meaning and importance for (usually) local people.

- **The scientific perspective**
A scientific, or 'technocratic', approach would concentrate entirely upon the nature conservation interest of the site. This is exemplified in the approach to the designation of sites of special scientific interest and to the designation of 'European sites' under EC law, in relation to which only scientific criteria can be taken into account.[21] This would be a matter for technical judgment, which would not involve the public, political, or economic considerations.[22] Thus, if the area is home to a number of rare species, designation may be made regardless of the benefits or otherwise of the development.

By contrast, the planning system that decides whether development will be permitted is more open to participation, and is less technocratic, in the sense that decisions are taken at both local and national levels by elected politicians. In contrast to other perspectives, therefore, a scientific or technocratic approach would only form part of the overall assessment of whether economic development could outweigh the nature conservation interests.

Environmental principles

As a response to some of the problems of approaching environmental law or decisions from any one particular perspective, attempts have been made to formulate general concepts and principles that can accommodate at least some of the features of these various perspectives. The difficulty in doing this is that there has to be flexibility in the manner in which the

---

21 See Wildlife and Countryside Act 1981, s. 28 (as amended by the Countryside and Rights of Way Act 2000); e.g., EC Habitats Directive 92/43, Art. 4—see respectively pp. 692 and 705.

22 An approach confirmed, in relation to sites of special scientific interest, in *R (on the application of) Western Power Distribution Investments Ltd) v. Countryside Council for Wales* [2007] Env LR 25 and see p. 693.

principle can be interpreted—and this flexibility can create problems of certainty and precision. By their very nature, such principles need to be applied across sweeping expanses of environmental law and policy, and also beyond the environmental field. Thus, a dynamic relationship exists within these principles—which underpin environmental laws at all levels—between the formulation of the law, and its implementation and enforcement.

The most common substantive principles associated with environmental law and policy are those relating to sustainable development, the Precautionary Principle, the Preventative Principle, and the Polluter Pays Principle. We focus here on sustainable development and the Precautionary Principle, because these are the most developed as matters of law and policy within international, European, and domestic law.[23] Other general underpinning approaches, particularly of a procedural nature, also have an impact. This would include the procedural principles associated with environmental assessment. Finally, there are certain subsidiary principles, including the Self-Sufficiency, Public Participation, and Substitution Principles. Many of these are found as constituents of the overarching principle of sustainable development and are found in the 1992 Rio Declaration on the Environment and Development; others tend to be used in specific contexts. Because principles are general guides to action rather than detailed rules, there are different versions found in different legislation and policy.

Some care should be taken with the definitions of principles set out in Box 3.6, because they are not the *only* definitions of these principles and they are often incomplete. For example, the Polluter Pays Principle says nothing about the crucial definitions of the 'polluter' or what 'pollution' is; what is important is the background purpose of the principle. What is it trying to promote? Whether it promotes this background purpose or not is heavily dependent upon the weight that is attached to it as a guiding principle. In this sense, principles do not operate in an all-or-nothing fashion; they indicate desired objectives, but leave the fulfilment of those objectives to individual law and decision makers.

A further point that can be made about the interrelationship of these principles is that they are not necessarily mutually supportive. For example, there may be a tension between the local management of environmental problems and what might be perceived to be the 'best' solution to the problem. Thus, in the case of waste management, local disposal and management may bring home the costs of waste—therefore linking to the Polluter Pays Principle—and may also meet the aims of the Self-Sufficiency Principle. This may, however, be antagonistic towards what could be viewed as being the 'best' solution in terms of promoting sustainable development, which might involve exporting the waste for reuse or recycling in developing countries.

A final point is that some of these principles are more fragile than others, in the sense that their status as principles can alter because of changes in policy. On the one hand, some of these principles are now so well established that their status as binding norms of international law is discussed (if not always agreed upon). On the other hand, an excellent example is provided by the Proximity Principle, which, for many years, was a central principle of EC waste management policy and under which waste was to be dealt with as close to the point of production as possible. Although the definition of this principle was fairly unproblematic, it is no longer found in EU waste law. The reasons for this are probably because, first, so much waste management—for example, of hazardous waste—is now undertaken in specialized, centralized operations, and secondly, because of the general difficulties in managing waste locally. That this principle is no longer found, at least in the EC waste context, is a good example of the extent to which these are widely regarded as *policy* principles rather than as binding legal principles.

---

23 The Polluter Pays Principle is discussed on p. 244.

BOX 3.6 Environmental principles—a summary

- **Sustainable development**

  …development that meets the needs of the present without compromising the ability of future generations to meet their own needs.

  (Report of the 1987 World Commission on Environment and Development, *Our Common Future*, known as the Brundtland Report)

  Of all environmental principles, sustainable development has the most contested definition—that is, it means different things to different people. The focus of sustainable development under the Brundtland definition is on improving the quality of life for humans without increasing the use of natural resources beyond the capacity of the environment to supply them indefinitely.

- **The Precautionary Principle**

  Where there are threats of serious or irreversible damage, lack of full scientific certainty shall not be used as a reason for postponing cost-effective measures to prevent environmental degradation.

  (European Commission (2000) Com (2000) 1 on the Precautionary Principle)

  The basis of the principle is that science cannot predict absolutely how, when, or why adverse impacts will occur, or what their effect may be on humans or ecosystems. In the absence of proof, there is often enough information to identify a serious risk that some impacts are likely to lead to unacceptably high costs, which should be avoided. Where reasonable evidence exists, actions to avoid these impacts are necessary. In this sense, the Precautionary Principle is about being 'safe rather than sorry'.

- **The Polluter Pays Principle**

  The Polluter should bear the expenses of carrying out…pollution prevention and control measures…to ensure that the environment is in an acceptable state. In other words, the cost of these measures should be reflected in the cost of goods and services which cause pollution in production and/or consumption.

  (1974 OECD Recommendation on the Implementation of the Polluter Pays Principle, C(74)223)

  The basis of the Polluter Pays Principle is that those responsible for pollution meet the costs of its consequences. This is also contested, but might include retrospective liability for historic pollution—for example, under the clean-up provisions of Pt 2A of the Environmental Protection Act 1990—or paying for pollution prevention measures and wider responsibility on the producers of waste.

- **The Preventative Principle**

  States have…the responsibility to ensure that activities within their jurisdiction or control do not cause damage to the environment of other States or of areas beyond the limits of national jurisdiction.

  (1992 Rio Declaration on the Environment and Development, Principle 2)

  The Preventative Principle is often linked to the Precautionary Principle. This principle promotes the prevention of environmental harm as an alternative to remedying harm already caused. A good example of the Preventative Principle is the use of the Best Available Techniques (BAT) to prevent pollution under the integrated pollution prevention and control regime.

- **The Integration Principle**

Environmental protection requirements must be integrated into the definition and implementation of [all areas of policy] in particular with a view to promoting sustainable development.

(EC Treaty, Art. 6)

The Integration Principle seeks to apply environmental considerations across all policy areas. The aim is to avoid otherwise contradictory policy objectives that result from a failure fail to take into account environmental protection or resource conservation goals. An example would be the failure to consider the environmental consequences of liberalizing air travel or road-building programmes designed to meet priority transport objectives.

- **The Public Participation Principle**

Environmental issues are best handled with the participation of all concerned citizens, at the relevant level. At the national level, each individual shall have appropriate access to information concerning the environment that is held by public authorities, including information on hazardous materials and activities in their communities, and the opportunity to participate in decision-making processes. States shall facilitate and encourage public awareness and participation by making information widely available. Effective access to judicial and administrative proceedings, including redress and remedy, shall be provided.

(1992 Rio Declaration on the Environment and Development, Principle 10)

The Participation Principle seeks to encourage widespread and informed public participation in decision making through the three 'pillars' of participation in decision making, access to information on the environment, and access to justice.

- **The Substitution Principle**

Chemicals that are of concern should be substituted with safer chemicals, or with materials or safer technologies not entailing the use of such chemicals, especially where safer alternatives already exist, taking account of socio-economic aspects in the choice of the best substitute.

(Commission White Paper on Strategy for a New Chemicals Policy, COM (2001) 88)

The Substitution Principle is an emerging principle that encourages the replacement of dangerous substances or processes by other, less harmful, substances or processes. The principle lies at the heart of the European Chemicals Strategy. The principle is an extension of the Precautionary Principle in the sense that it promotes technology-driven changes rather than waiting for the proof of harm. A good example of the Substitution Principle in action can be found in the EC REACH Regulation on chemicals and their safe use. Amongst more general measures, the Regulation provides for the progressive substitution of the most dangerous chemicals when suitable alternatives have been identified. [24]

Sustainable development

The concept of sustainable development is central to the recent and future development of environmental law and policy. The idea of 'sustainability', which indicates the state of something being sustainable in the long term, has always been considered as part of the system of land-use planning within the UK, in the sense that the long-term implications of resource depletion and other environmental factors have always been material considerations when determining planning applications. The precise principle of 'sustainable development' that

24 See Regulation (EC) 1907/2006 on the Registration, Evaluation, Authorisation and Restriction of Chemicals (REACH).

has gained credibility within international law is, however, both relatively new and uncertain, although its all-pervasive characteristics can be found explicitly in many environmental policy documents in relation to different topic areas.[25]

What is meant by the phrase 'sustainable development'? Although the idea can be traced back at least to 1972 and the United Nations Stockholm Conference on the Human Environment, the common definition that is used most often comes from the Brundtland Commission's 1987 Report, *Our Common Future*, in which it was suggested that the phrase covered '*development that meets the needs of the present without compromising the ability of future generations to meet their own needs*'.

This definition is, however, vague, and requires further elaboration. First, the primary objective of the principle is to meet current and future *human* needs and aspirations; there is also the issue of what is meant by 'needs and aspirations'. The emphasis is clearly anthropocentric, although, under the Brundtland Commission's definition, the environment is considered to be an integral part of human well-being. Secondly, there is an underlying objective of fairness in the manner of development that applies as between different sectors of the current generation—such as 'poor' and 'rich' nations, and classes of society—and as between current and future generations—termed 'intergenerational equity'. Thus, future generations have the same rights to develop as do we and preventing such development would be unfair. Finally, there is an inherent assumption that we can identify the impact of current activity in terms of resource depletion and the ability of the environment to absorb pollution. Any doubts over the nature of the risks involved will inevitably cloud the decisions that need to be made to achieve the goal of sustainable development.

Although sustainable development is found in a number of legal instruments, the most coherent attempts to flesh out the bare bones of the Brundtland Commission's definition of sustainable development can be found in policy documents, although, even here, there is a great deal of 'woolliness' as befits the breadth of the matters covered under the principle. Most of the significant policy work is aimed at providing meaningful goals and objectives against which the pursuit of sustainable development can be benchmarked.

Sustainable development as a legal and policy instrument

The goal of sustainable development has been translated into some form of legal obligation in a number of international, European, and domestic sources of law, although the nature of the legal effects of the obligation is the subject of some debate. The transposition of the goal of sustainable development into legal forms—perhaps a legal principle—is becoming increasingly common and is set to continue. The implementation of the principle is perhaps more problematic.

International law

In international law, sustainable development as a *legal* concept has tended to be found mostly in 'soft law' documents—that is, in documents that are not directly binding and which have more of a policy feel to them. The most important document here is Agenda 21, signed at the 1992 Rio Earth Summit, which is essentially a lengthy blueprint for realizing sustainable development. This pays particular attention to action at the local level and picks up many of the recommendations made in the Brundtland Report about greater public involvement in decision making through, for example, access to environmental information. There are signs that at least some of the judges of the International Court of Justice (ICJ) are beginning to recognize the procedural dimension to issues of sustainable development and to recognize sustainable development as a *principle* rather than only as a *concept*.

---

25 For general coverage of the development of the principle in international law, see L. Rajamani (2003) 12 RECIEL 23.

CASE 3.1 *Case concerning the Gabčíkovo-Nagymaros Project (Hungary/Slovakia)* 37 ILM (1998) 162 *(Danube Dam)*

The principle of sustainable development was first recognized explicitly in a judgment of the International Court of Justice (ICJ) in a case concerning an international treaty on the construction of a dam and associated development on the River Danube between Bratislava and Budapest, Hungary.[26] Some years after the development was commenced, Hungary suspended, and later abandoned, work in response to criticisms of the environmental impacts of the project. The issue that was brought before the ICJ was whether Hungary was entitled to abandon the project. Among other points, Hungary argued that new 'environmental norms', such as the principle of sustainable development, had emerged since the signing of the original treaty, which had radically transformed the nature of its obligations.

The ICJ rejected that argument, finding that the developing 'environmental norms' were foreseeable at the time that the treaty was agreed. For the first time, the ICJ referred to the need to balance economic development and environmental protection. In a strong separate opinion, Vice President Weeramantry discussed the role of sustainable development in international law in the context of legal instruments and the historical background, concluding that:

> The principle of sustainable development is ... a part of modern international law by reason not only of its inescapable logical necessity, but also by reason of its wide and general acceptance by the global community.

In spite of clear recognition by the ICJ and beyond agreement on basic procedural requirements of the kind referred to in the Rio Declaration in relation to public participation in its broadest sense, there is little sign yet of anything resembling an international legal consensus on what sustainable development might mean substantively. This lack of progress on the principle of sustainable development was characterized by the World Summit on Sustainable Development held in Johannesburg in 2002. In contrast to the Rio Conference, no conventions or statements of principle were adopted and the Declaration on Sustainable Development issued at the conclusion of the conference was aspirational in intent, rather than binding.[27]

European law and policy

Perhaps most significantly, the principle has been made a fundamental *justification* for the existence of the EC, with the incorporation of sustainable development into Art. 2 of the EC Treaty, which states that the Community '*shall have as* [one of its tasks] ... *to promote throughout the Community harmonious, balanced and sustainable development of economic activities*'. This justification applies across all policy areas and legislation, and is not necessarily restricted to environmental considerations. It is backed up by the principle explicitly requiring the integration of environmental protection requirements into other policy areas '*in particular with a view to promoting sustainable development*'.[28]

The European Court of Justice (ECJ) has neither explicitly interpreted nor fleshed out the concept of sustainable development, although it is possible to identify judgments that implicitly incorporate some of the more important aspects of sustainable development, including

---

26 Also discussed at p. 151.

27 I. von Frantzius (2003) Environmental Politics 467; for an alternative view, see M. Pallemaerts (2003) 12 RECIEL 1.

28 The Integration Principle found in Art. 6 EC—see p. 189.

the recognition of the need to value environmental resources in decision making and the balancing of environmental considerations as against other issues.[29]

European policy on sustainable development can be found in the Sixth Environmental Action Programme, *Environment 2010: Our Future, Our Choice*,[30] and in the EU Strategy for Sustainable Development.[31] Both the Action Programme and the Strategy are frameworks within which detailed objectives are to be set. The two documents set a number of priority areas for action, including climate change, nature and biodiversity, public health, natural resources, and waste management. Clearer objectives are set in several 'thematic strategies', which address the headline issues in more detail. These objectives are, however, general and are not intended to be legally binding.[32]

UK law and policy

The transformation and integration of the principle of sustainable development into formal rules within the UK reflects the European experience, in the sense that it is relatively recent and is taking place within an overarching administrative and institutional framework, rather than through changes to substantive environmental laws. Although 'sustainable' was introduced in s. 1(1) of the Natural Heritage (Scotland) Act 1991 as something that Scottish Natural Heritage must have '*regard to the desirability of securing*', the initial step of incorporating sustainable development in UK law was taken with the introduction of the Environment Agency's principal aim under s. 4 of the Environment Act 1995. This requires the Agency, in discharging its functions so to protect or enhance the environment, taken as a whole, to make the contribution towards attaining the objective of achieving sustainable development.

The 1999 White Paper on Sustainable Development contained a government commitment to consider incorporating the sustainable development principle as a legal goal for any newly created public body.[33] Sustainable development is accordingly more than simply a policy instrument and the increasing incorporation of the duty to 'meet' or 'achieve' sustainable development objectives is evidenced in different statutes.

BOX 3.7 Examples of the application of sustainable development in UK legislation[34]

Every local authority must prepare a strategy…for promoting or improving the economic, social and environmental well-being of their area and contributing to the achievement of sustainable development in the United Kingdom.

(Local Government Act 2000, s. 4)

The [Welsh] Assembly shall make a scheme setting out how it proposes, in the exercise of its functions, to promote sustainable development.

(Government of Wales Act 1998, s. 121)

---

29 For example, in relation to the irrelevance of economic considerations in determining have been judged to be irrelevant: see *R v. Secretary of State for the Environment, ex parte RSPB* [1997] QB 206, *R v. Secretary of State for the Environment, Transport and the Regions, ex parte First Corporate Shipping* [2001] ECR I-9235, and further Case 19.1 and Case 19.2.

30 COM (2001) 31.

31 COM (2001) 264.

32 See Case C-142/95P *Associazone Agricoltori della Provincia di Rovigo and ors v. Commission* [1996] ECR I-6669.

33 UK Government (1999) *A Better Quality of Life: A Strategy for Sustainable Development for the United Kingdom*, Cm 4345.

34 Other examples include s. 3A of the Electricity Act 1989 and s. 39 of the Planning and Compulsory Purchase Act 2004, which requires planning authorities to exercise their functions in relation to regional spatial strategies (RSSs), with the objective of contributing to the achievement of sustainable development.

> A regional development agency shall…contribute to the achievement of sustainable development in the United Kingdom where it is relevant to its area to do so.
>
> (Regional Development Agencies Act 1998, s. 4(e))
>
> These legal instruments are of interest, because they demonstrate a formal commitment to the sustainable development principle, but there are a number of factors affecting the practical implementation of the legal duty. First, and perhaps most significantly, there is no specific definition of the phrase 'sustainable development'. Even if the Brundtland Commission definition were to be adopted as a suitable definition by default, there would still be a number of ambiguities that would make precise legal interpretation impossible.
>
> Secondly, the wording of the relevant sections is too wide to create a legally enforceable duty, even if a suitably consistent definition of the principle could be agreed.
>
> Thirdly, the content and objectives of the duty are, in some of the cases, controlled centrally by way of a requirement to 'have regard to' guidance set by central government.
>
> Finally, the different Acts have slightly different impacts on the activities of the statutory bodies concerned. The wording of the different statutory provisions have different effects: some impose specific obligations, whereas others are much more flexible without any obvious legal effect. Whether there is any practical distinction in terms of the consequences for environmental law or decision making is perhaps more difficult to anticipate.

Although there are a number of examples of statutory requirements to 'achieve' or 'contribute to' sustainable development, the principle is too loose a concept to be developed by the courts. (This fits in nicely with the discretionary, policy-based approach of other aspects of environmental decision making.) This is not to say that the principle will have no practical impact, because the aims and objectives of administrative bodies do play an integral part in influencing the setting of policies and the making of individual decisions.

As in the case of legal instruments, domestic policy is following the same path as European measures (although, unusually perhaps, the use of specific measures of sustainable development is slightly more advanced). The main policies on sustainable development can be found in the 2005 Sustainable Development Strategy, *Securing the Future: Delivering UK Sustainable Development Strategy*. The Strategy provides a broad framework for the whole of the UK, with devolved countries producing different strategies within the five principles agreed at the national level. These five principles are:

- living within environmental limits;
- ensuring a strong, healthy and just society;
- achieving a sustainable economy;
- promoting good governance;
- using sound science responsibly.

The Strategy also sets out shared priority areas for UK action:

- sustainable consumption and production;
- climate change and energy;
- natural resource protection and environmental enhancement;
- sustainable communities.

There has been slight tinkering with the various headline indicators of sustainable development, but the 2005 Strategy is broadly the same as that of 1999, with greater emphasis on the decentralization of sustainable development to regional government and local authorities.

This document is, however, only part of a broad incorporation of the sustainable development principle within all areas of administration. At a national level, the Sustainable Development Commission is responsible for monitoring progress on sustainable development and for building consensus on action to accelerate its achievement. In addition the Sustainable Development in Government initiative is intended to monitor the achievement of sustainable development across all government activities (see further Box 5.2). At regional and local levels, the regional sustainable development frameworks are to be prepared for eight English regions, while local Agenda 21 strategies are to be prepared by all local authorities.

Achieving sustainable development in practice

Anyone reading the above discussion of the burgeoning legal and policy instruments might consider that there has been a great deal of progress towards a practical, workable definition of sustainable development. This would, however, mask some of the fundamental problems underlying the principle. In particular, the feasibility of sustainable development is dependent on the manner in which some of these problems are addressed.

'Weak' vs 'strong' versions of sustainable development

Although not without criticism, a distinction is often made between 'strong' and 'weak' versions of sustainable development. The distinction is really as much about matters of emphasis as it is about matters of principle. Thus, a 'strong' approach to sustainability emphasizes the extent to which natural assets are irreplaceable, in the sense that their loss cannot be adequately replaced by compensatory benefits. In contrast, 'weak' sustainability would accept that natural assets may be consumed or sacrificed if the overall benefit would be positive—that is, if the total stock of resources passed on to future generations would not be diminished. 'Resources' here, however, would include non-environmental resources, such as human knowledge and creativity; this would mean that there should not be too much concern about losing any individual environmental resource, as long as there is sufficient ingenuity—or sufficient investment to ensure that there will be sufficient ingenuity—to ensure that something equivalent or better will emerge in time.

On one view, strong sustainability is morally abhorrent, because it privileges environmental 'assets' above all others, suggesting that we should devote whatever it takes to save a species even if this means that individual humans starve.[35] Further, weak sustainability is seen as no different from the types of trade-off that have been made for centuries in the interests of raising human standards of living and, in this sense, is simply 'business as usual'. Many environmental economists and philosophers agree that, presented in these terms, weak sustainability is something of an empty concept.[36] But others stress, for example, that environmental and human resources are not completely interchangeable: no matter how skilful we become, we will still need to live off a base of natural resources.[37] A difficulty is, therefore, knowing which resources future generations will need and value, or rather maintaining a sufficient *diversity* of resources.

The definition of 'needs'

The 'needs' of future generations are central to the Brundtland definition of sustainable development. 'Needs' are distinguishable from preferences. Beyond those things that form the very minimum necessary for survival—food; clean air and water; shelter; a tolerable

---

35 W. Beckerman (2002) *A Poverty of Reason*, Oakland, Calif: The Independent Institute, p. 2.

36 M. Jacobs (1999) 'Sustainable development as a contested concept' in A. Dobson (ed.) *Fairness and Futurity. Essays on Environmental Sustainability and Social Justice*, Oxford: Oxford University Press.

37 See H. Daly (1995) 4 Environmental Values 49.

climate—there is considerable debate about what we really 'need', even among present generations.[38] Even thinking about some of these basic needs shows some of the problems involved. For example, humans are not dependent on any single food source in the way that giant pandas require bamboo shoots, nor do we need to make our homes out of any particular raw material. We cannot therefore say that the sources of even our most common foodstuffs must be conserved, even for present generations (although we might make an argument that a sufficient *diversity* of seeds, genetic material, etc., should be conserved to guard against the impacts of climate change and other unknowns).

The problem is also compounded when we engage in judging what the needs of those several generations hence will be, because, apart from the basics necessary for survival, the things that have been valued over the centuries have, of course, changed. Even if things have been treasured as 'necessary' in the past and present, this is no guarantee that future generations will 'need', or even value, them. While we might conceivably find agreement across the generations in relation to what humans need, it is difficult to say objectively that anything particular must be conserved or preserved to satisfy such needs. Indeed, it has even been argued that, in seeking to prioritize the unknown needs of future generations, we ignore the known needs of the current generation.[39]

Ultimately, there is some connection between one's view of sustainability, in strong or weak terms, and the question of needs, because those with more optimistic views of human ingenuity to 'fix' environmentally related problems will be more sanguine about exploiting resources today in the confidence that future generations will be able to satisfy their needs through a lesser abundance of natural resources. There is also the thorny question of the 'right to develop' (central to the Rio Declaration) and thus the liberty of present generations to destroy the natural environment in the interests of development.[40]

The role of technology

Central to weak and strong sustainability, and to the question of needs, is the role of technology. There are various strands to this, including how much faith to place in technological progress as against the conservation of natural resources, and whether we can say that developing countries 'need' technology from the developed world to give practical effect to their right to develop. Central to the two Rio Conventions on Climate Change and on Biodiversity is the idea that there should be a transfer of technology to developing countries—either 'clean technology' to reduce greenhouse gas emissions or pharmaceutical-type technology to allow for the commercial exploitation, and thus, it is argued, sustainable use, of biological diversity.

This approach marks something of a shift from earlier 'waves' of environmentalism, which have generally been sceptical of technical 'fixes' to what have been seen as deeper-seated problems with the structuring of societies and economies. But the Brundtland Report stressed that it did not consider capitalism as necessarily destructive of the environment and therefore advocated solutions from within the existing economic framework. In a climate in which support for alternative models of organization is practically non-existent, it is perhaps inevitable that there is growing backing for fine-tuning the current model, and reliance on more effective technology and its more efficient use are central to what has been termed 'ecological modernization'.[41] This is the idea that environmental resources can be more efficiently managed to produce the same, or higher, levels of goods and services, leading to so-called 'win–win' results from which both the economy and the environment benefit.

---

38 M. Redclift (1993) Environmental Values 3.

39 W. Beckerman and J. Pasek (2001) *Justice, Posterity and the Environment*, Oxford: Oxford University Press.

40 UN Commission on Human Rights Resolution 2003/71, 'Human rights and the environment as part ofsustainable development', para. 1.

41 See, e.g., M. Hajer (1996) *The Politics of Environmental Discourse: Ecological Modernisation and the Policy Process*, Oxford: Clarendon Press.

(Because social issues are generally included within sustainable development, however, we really need to find virtuous circles leading to 'win–win–win' solutions.)

This has obvious relevance to issues such as waste management or climate change, and, in some senses, is obviously furthered by making polluters pay for the 'external' costs imposed on society caused by their activities, such as air pollution, which does not infringe on private rights. But a 'more from less' approach might also mean more efficient use of space and therefore less pressure on land of conservation interest. A growing body of what we might call the 'literature of hope' therefore argues that there is a path to sustainability that does not involve adopting a strong environmentalist perspective (as defined above).

The assessment of fairness and intergenerational equity

Finally, there are considerable difficulties in deciding what is 'fair' to future generations. As discussed above, the background to this question will include factors such as faith in human creativity and what 'needs' are, which, in practice, tend to be highly subjective. There is also the problem that there would never be a consensus on values, even if values were not to shift over time.

One influential attempt to guide decisions about future generations is given by Brown Weiss.[42] She argues for three principles to underpin intergenerational equity:

- '*conservation of options*'—conserving biodiversity contributes to the robustness of ecosystems;
- '*conservation of quality*'—handing on environmental quality, at local and global levels, without worsening its state;
- '*conservation of access*'—equitable rights of access to what past generations have handed on, while keeping open equitable access for future generations.

A virtue of this approach is that it tries not to second-guess what future generations will want or value: for example, conserving options does not require any particular species to be saved from extinction. But difficulties remain: for example, how is environmental quality to be measured? How are the trade-offs between the principles to be handled if, for example, improving conservation of access within the present generation means that someone else's environmental quality is necessarily reduced? And why should one generation not decide to sacrifice a measure of environmental quality in the interests of future generations? As issues such as climate change testify, there are no easy answers to deciding who, within the current generation, should have to bear burdens for past greenhouse gas emissions, or whether these burdens—or at least changes—should be sufficient to allow developing countries to continue increasing their emissions to further their chosen development path.

The Precautionary Principle

Although there are a number of different interpretations of the Precautionary Principle, it generally describes an approach to the protection of the environment or human health that is based around taking precautions even if there is no clear evidence of harm or risk of harm from an activity or substance. For example, the Precautionary Principle suggests that we should ban a pollutant that is suspected of causing serious harm even in circumstances under which there is no conclusive scientific proof of a clear link between the substance and the harm.[43] In other words, although scientific evidence is never final (in the sense that it is

42 E. Brown Weiss (1991) 'Intergenerational equity: a legal framework for global environmental change' in E. Brown Weiss (ed.) *Environmental Change and International Law*, Tokyo: United Nations University. For an opposing view, see Beckerman and Pasek (2001).

43 Although the specific definition is contested. One author lists 19 different variations, see P. Sandin (1999) 5 Human and Ecological Risk Assessment 889.

only conclusive to the extent that it is based on premises that have not yet been overturned), there comes a point at which we have to rely upon 'instinct' and take action regardless.

The Precautionary Principle is often associated with areas of high public controversy and concern in relation to which there are unknown—or, in some cases, arguably unknowable—risks to the environment or human health. Obvious examples that have been mentioned elsewhere in this book include the BSE crisis, the planting of GM crops, or the link between mobile phone masts and diseases such as cancer. The Precautionary Principle is often used in the debates about such issues to support the notion that scientific analysis of risks should form the core of environmental rules and decisions, notwithstanding the fact that such analysis may be uncertain. Alternatively, the principle could be used to support an argument that there are limits to the extent that science can inform the debate and that, ultimately, rules and decisions have to be made having regard to other considerations, such as the public perception of the risk and the potential for harm.

These mutually inconsistent views underline the fact that the principle is necessarily subject to interpretations of concepts such as the significance of risks and the acceptability of scientific evidence as 'proof'. Ultimately, the use of the Precautionary Principle is subject to the same limitations, restricting the resolution of any debate about environmental values. In other words, the principle provides a framework for any discussion about how to 'trade off' the risk of environmental harm as against other considerations, but it does not necessarily provide any 'right' answer. In this sense, it is merely another ingredient that goes into the melting pot of environmental rule and decision making, along with other relevant considerations such as the public perception of risk, the benefit of the proposed activity, the notion of the 'public interest', and the protection of individual rights.

The Precautionary Principle and law

The Precautionary Principle in international law

The formal origin of the Precautionary Principle can be traced back to Germany in the 1970s with the *Vorsorgeprinzip*. Translated as the 'Foresight' Principle, this broad principle is a philosophical approach to risk prevention, involving concepts of good environmental management in taking protective measures against specific environmental hazards in order to avoid or reduce environmental risks.[44] This approach was subsequently adopted in various international agreements. For example, a number of North Sea Ministerial conferences, including the 1984 Bremen Declaration on the Protection of the North Sea, were based on the Precautionary Principle. A similar approach has been taken in relation to the reductions of radioactive and other hazardous substances under the 1992 Oslo–Paris (OSPAR) Convention. In addition, the principle has been adopted in an increasing number of international conventions from the 1980s onwards.

BOX 3.8 **Examples of the Precautionary Principle in international law**

States…must not wait for proof of harmful effects before taking action…

(1984 Bremen Ministerial Declaration of the International Conference on the Protection of the North Sea)

The Contracting Parties shall apply the precautionary principle, i.e., to take preventive measures when there is reason to assume that substances or energy introduced, directly or indirectly, into the marine environment may create hazards to human health, harm living resources and marine

---

44 See S. Boehmer-Christiansen (1994) 'The Precautionary Principle in Germany: enabling government' in T. O'Riordan and J. Cameron (eds) *Interpreting the Precautionary Principle*, London: Earthscan.

ecosystems, damage amenities or interfere with other legitimate uses of the sea even when there is no conclusive evidence of a causal relationship between inputs and their alleged effects.

(1992 Helsinki Convention on the Protection of the Baltic Sea, Art. 3(2))

The Parties should take precautionary measures to anticipate, prevent or minimize the causes of climate change and mitigate its adverse effects. Where there are threats of serious or irreversible damage, lack of full scientific certainty should not be used as a reason for postponing such measures...

(1992 Framework Convention on Climate Change, Art. 3(3))

...where there is a threat of significant reduction or loss of biological diversity, lack of full scientific certainty should not be used as a reason for postponing measures to avoid or minimize such a threat.

(1992 Convention on Biological Diversity, Preamble)

Lack of scientific certainty due to insufficient relevant scientific information and knowledge regarding the extent of the potential adverse effects of a living modified organism on the conservation and sustainable use of biological diversity in the Party of import, taking also into account risks to human health, shall not prevent that Party from taking a decision, as appropriate, with regard to the import of that living modified organism intended for direct use as food or feed, or for processing, in order to avoid or minimise such potential adverse effects.

(2000 Cartagena Protocol on Biosafety, Art. 11)

A number of important international conventions have incorporated the principle, including the Conventions on Climate Change and on Biological Diversity (and the associated Protocol on Biosafety, which is concerned with the handling and use of genetically modified organisms, or GMOs). As can be seen in Box 3.8, however, each convention tends to contain a slightly different formulation of the principle, which makes it difficult to identify an interpretation with which all states can be said to agree implicitly as a matter of binding international law.

Like sustainable development, precaution has found only limited judicial support so far in international law, this despite many commentators arguing that it has reached the status of a principle of customary international law.[45] In a case challenging the right of France to carry out nuclear tests in the South Pacific, Judge Weeramantry's opinion suggested that the Precautionary Principle—which was '*gaining increasing support as part of the international law of the environment*'—should be used where there was insufficient material before the Court to justify action, even if this meant acting ahead of '*full scientific evidence*'.[46] This opinion was, however, a dissent and it is worth comparing the case with more recent examples of international disputes in which the Precautionary Principle has featured.

CASE 3.2 *EC Measures Concerning Meat and Meat Products (Hormones)* WT/DS26/AB/R and WT/DS48/AB/R, 16 January 1998

The USA and Canada brought a dispute settlement case before the World Trade Organization (WTO) against the EC, which, in 1989, had banned the import of beef fed with growth hormones on the grounds that it was not safe for human consumption. The EC argued that its import ban was justified in the light of the Precautionary Principle, which it presented as a binding rule of international

45 See, e.g., O. McIntyre and T. Mosedale (1997) 9 JEL 221.
46 *New Zealand v. France* [1995] ICJ Rep 288.

customary law. The USA and Canada denied that the principle already had such a status (although Canada did admit that it was an emerging principle.) The WTO found that the EC import ban violated WTO law, but, in doing so, found that the role of the Precautionary Principle in international law was uncertain.

In spite of the judgment, the EC has continued to impose its ban and was forced by the WTO to compensate Canada and the USA for lost trade.

CASE 3.3 *New Zealand v. Japan; Australia v. Japan* (2001) ILR 148 (the *Southern Bluefish Tuna* cases)

Australia and New Zealand brought a claim against Japan for breaching obligations under the Southern Bluefish Tuna (SBT) Treaty. The Treaty had been agreed in order to address the decline in numbers of SBT brought about by overfishing. Japan had subsequently commenced an Experimental Fishing Programme, which was intended to assess the numbers of fish. This involved breaching the agreed fishing quotas under the Treaty. Australia and New Zealand sought a provisional measure that the parties to the Treaty '*act consistently with the Precautionary Principle*' in fishing for SBT. The International Tribunal for the Law of the Sea (ITLOS) ordered the parties to observe the fishing quotas and to '*act with prudence and caution to ensure that effective conservation measures are taken to prevent serious harm to the* [SBT] *stock*'.

On the basis of the arguments put to the Tribunal, however, Judge Laing rejected the notion that the Precautionary Principle was an established norm of customary international law. He was keen to distinguish the precautionary *approach* taken by the Tribunal and the application of the Precautionary *Principle*. In doing so, he stated that adopting an approach, rather than a principle, was more flexible and highlighted the problems of making '*premature pronouncements about desirable normative structures*' in cases of risk and scientific uncertainty.

CASE 3.4 *Ireland v. United Kingdom* (2002) 41 ILM 405 (the *MOX Plant* case)

Ireland sought to prevent continuing operations at the mixed oxide (MOX) plant at Sellafield in the UK. One of Ireland's arguments was that the Precautionary Principle required the UK to demonstrate that no harm would arise from the operation of the plant. The UK countered that there was no evidence of serious harm and that therefore the Precautionary Principle did not apply.

The Tribunal did not agree with Ireland's arguments. Judge Wolfram's opinion stated that whether the Precautionary Principle was a part of international customary law was still '*a matter for discussion*'. The only aspect of the principle upon which there was agreement was that it reversed the burden of proof so that those undertaking a risky activity had to prove that it would not result in any harm. Judge Wolfram went further, stating that, even if the principle were a part of customary international law, the matter should not be resolved by a Tribunal assessing 'provisional measures' (effectively, an injunction hearing); in contrast to the *Southern Bluefin Tuna* cases, in which there was agreement on the nature of the problem and the potential harm caused—that is, low levels of fish and overfishing—there was disagreement about the nature of the potential harm from the MOX plant. This question could only be assessed against full evidence.

While both the International Tribunal for the Law of the Sea (ITLOS) and the World Trade Organization Appellate Body acknowledged the idea of the Precautionary Principle, they rejected its use as a norm of customary international law and failed to arrive at any concrete conclusions about its application. Partly, this is because, as Box 3.8 illustrates, there is no consistent application of the principle in international conventions (there are differing obligations and formulations of the principle) and partly because, as a *principle*, it is, by nature, incapable of being prescribed as anything other than a general guide to action. As the cases illustrate, the application of the principle depends largely on evidence about the nature of the risk and the correct 'trigger' point or standard at which it is invoked.

European law and the Precautionary Principle

The requirement to take account of the Precautionary Principle in European law and policy is now enshrined in Art. 174(2) of the EC Treaty. But what is the practical effect of this provision? It was assumed that the general nature of the wording of Art. 174(2) was such that the Precautionary Principle (and others) did not have binding legal effect.[47] The ECJ hinted that, in extreme cases, it might be prepared to find that EC legislation had not taken the Precautionary Principle into account, but this would probably require complete oversight or wilful disregard.

CASE 3.5 **Case C-341/95 *Bettati v. Safety Hi-Tech Srl* [1998] ECR I-4355**

The manufacturer of a hydrochlorofluorocarbon (HCFC) sought to overturn the ban under Regulation 3093/94 on substances that deplete the ozone layer on the basis that the Regulation did not accord with (among others) the Precautionary Principle set out in EC Treaty, Art. 130R(2) (now Art. 174(2)). The European Court of Justice (ECJ) was prepared to consider the compatibility of the Regulation with (among other principles) the Precautionary Principle. It considered that there was a need to strike a balance between certain objectives, such as the Precautionary Principle, and the complexity of actually implementing those objectives. Thus, some discretion would be given to the Council of Ministers as lawmakers and the ECJ would only overturn laws in which the principles had clearly been ignored.[48]

Although the *Bettati* decision (see Case 3.5) established the role of the principle in lawmaking, it did little to define what the principle might mean in European law. The lack of clarity was highlighted in the *Beef Hormones* litigation[49] and, in response, the first attempt at a detailed explanation of the Precautionary Principle came in the shape of a communication from the European Commission,[50] which set out its guidelines on using the Precautionary Principle.

The document sets out the risk-based context of the Precautionary Principle, emphasizing the relationship between the principle and the management of risks that might impinge upon the environment, and human, animal, or plant health. The communication also makes it clear that the principle is not to be invoked defensively as a '*disguised form of protectionism*'. This reflects the fact that it has been invoked as a justification of what might more appropriately be called a 'trade ban' in relation to the French and German ban on British beef—although this might be contrasted with the EC's own use of precaution in relation to beef hormones.

---

47 See, e.g., J. Holder (1997) 'Safe science? The Precautionary Principle in UK environmental law' in J. Holder (ed.) *The Impact of EC Environmental Law in the United Kingdom*, Chichester: John Wiley.

48 See further M. Doherty (1999) 11 JEL 378.

49 Case T-13/99 *Pfizer v. European Commission* [2002] ECR II-3305 and Box 3.6.

50 COM (2000) 1.

In particular, the policy makes it clear that identifying an 'acceptable' level of risk is an essentially political decision, which must take into account such things as proportionality in the context of the steps taken and the risks involved, an analysis of the costs and benefits associated with the measure—including non-economic considerations such as public acceptability of other options—and their effectiveness and consistency in relation to the measures taken in similar areas. Some assistance with the 'fleshing out' of the Precautionary Principle has come with the ECJ's judgment in the *Pfizer* case (see Case 3.6), which addressed, for the first time, the nature and application of the principle.

CASE 3.6 **Case T-13/99 *Pfizer v. European Commission* [2002] ECR II-3305**

Following scientific advice given to the European Commission, EC Regulation 2821/98 banned the use of four antibiotics as additives in animal foodstuffs on the grounds that there was a risk of increasing resistance to the antibiotics in animals and that such resistance could be transmitted to humans through consumption. The sole manufacturer of one of the banned antibiotics, Pfizer, sought to challenge the Regulation primarily on the ground that there had been an unlawful application of the Precautionary Principle. Pfizer argued that a scientific assessment of risk was a condition precedent of the application of the Precautionary Principle and that no proper assessment had been carried out. In the alternative, if a risk assessment had been carried out, Pfizer argued for a much higher standard of proof than had been accepted by the European Commission—that is, that before banning, any risks identified were probable rather than hypothetical.

The Court of First Instance disagreed with Pfizer's interpretation of the Precautionary Principle, noting that the application of the principle could not be based purely on a hypothetical risk, but was acceptable in situations in which a risk existed even if the risk could not be fully demonstrated completely. Accordingly, the Court found that the Commission and other Community institutions had acted lawfully when they had relied upon the scientific advice given to them.[51]

While the decision in *Pfizer* was an important step towards defining the parameters of the application of the Precautionary Principle, it leaves a lot of issues undetermined. In particular, there is the problem of the trigger point for the application of the principle. It is clear that it applies in cases in which there is more than 'zero' risk; what was not made clear in the judgment was the point at which uncertainty would demand a precautionary response.

In comparison with the principle of sustainable development, however, the Precautionary Principle is explicitly or implicitly incorporated into a number of different substantive European laws. For example, the Nitrates Directive (91/676/EEC) creates a system of nitrate vulnerable zones (NVZs) in which farming activities are restricted notwithstanding that pollution and the risk of environmental harm may have come from a different source. Thus, even where if is no evidence of pollution from individual farms, activities are restricted on those farms, based upon the need to take precaution in areas that are vulnerable to nitrate pollution. The establishment of various environmental quality standards implicitly adopting the precautionary approach in relation to substances that are liable or likely to cause harm provides a further example.[52] As the dates of these Directives show, precautionary measures were being taken before precaution found its way into the EC Treaty. The classic example of this is Directive 90/220/EEC—perhaps the most explicitly precautionary EC measure—which

---

51 See W. Th. Douma (2003) 15 JEL 372.

52 For example, in relation to the Titanium Dioxide Waste Directive 78/109/EEC and the Pesticides Directive 91/414/EEC.

restricted the deliberate release of GMOs despite the (then) complete lack of evidence about possible harmful impacts.[53]

UK law and the Precautionary Principle

One of the first detailed references to the Precautionary Principle in the UK can be found in the 1990 government White Paper, *This Common Inheritance*. This put forward a 'weak' form of the Precautionary Principle on the basis that there would be action taken against 'significant risks' even in cases of scientific uncertainty if the 'balance of costs and benefits' justified it. Although this was a firm policy commitment to the *idea* of the Precautionary Principle, the practical significance of this statement was little more than an acceptance of the growing international and European recognition of the principle. This approach was followed in the guidance to the Environment Agency under s. 4 of the Environment Act 1995 and in weak policy responses to such episodes as the BSE crisis, *Brent Spar*, and the debate over GMOs.[54]

Even this weak form of the Precautionary Principle has not been incorporated directly into domestic legislation. Thus, there is no overarching statutory duty, or aspiration, to achieve the Precautionary Principle (unlike that of sustainable development). There have, however, been a number of domestic cases that have discussed the application of the Precautionary Principle. The general thrust of these decisions is that, while the principle may be an integral part of international, European, and domestic law,[55] it has no legal force and should be viewed as a policy objective.[56] Even in cases in which the courts have been willing to consider the substantive application of the Precautionary Principle, the lack of any settled, specific, or identifiable mechanism of risk assessment as part of the principle was fatal.[57]

CASE 3.7 *R v. Secretary of State for Trade and Industry, ex parte Duddridge* [1995] Env LR 151

Three children living in close proximity to newly laid power lines sought a judicial review of the Secretary of State's failure to protect them from non-ionizing radiation emitted from the lines. The applicants argued that the Secretary of State was obliged, under the Precautionary Principle, to make regulations specifying maximum thresholds for such radiation. In dismissing the application, Smith LJ acknowledged the existence of the Precautionary Principle in EC and international law, but concluded that there was no direct obligation to apply the principle within member States, and that neither should the principle be applied as a matter of '*common sense*'.

Although there are no explicit references to the Precautionary Principle in domestic law, there are other rules that involve aspects of it. For example, the Water Resources Act 1991, s. 92, gives the Secretary of State power to make regulations in order to take precautions against water pollution.[58] Other examples include the powers to serve works notices to prevent water pollution under s. 161 of the Water Resources Act 1991 and the concept of the Best Available Techniques (BAT) process standard adopted under Directive 2008/1/EC on integrated pollution prevention and control (IPPC) to prevent unacceptable environmental impacts.

---

53 See, now, Directive 2001/18/EC.

54 For example, see p. 46.

55 See *R v. Derbyshire County Council, ex parte Murray* [2001] Env LR 26.

56 See *R v. Secretary of State for Trade and Industry, ex parte Duddridge* [1995] Env LR 151.

57 See *R (Amvac Chemical UK Ltd) v. Secretary of State for Environment, Food and Rural Affairs and ors* (2002) ACD 34.

58 These powers are better thought of as being preventative, but the element of taking precautions against pollution still exists—see p. 617.

The Precautionary Principle has had some impact on individual decision making. There have been a number of decisions based around the need to take precaution, particularly in relation to drinking water supplies.[59] In general terms, however, there is relatively scant mention of precaution in things such as planning policy statements (PPSs) compared with the now-ritual mention of sustainable development. Otherwise, at best, we find modestly precautionary policies such as giving 'draft' sites for protection under EC habitat conservation law the same level of protection as fully designated areas.[60] And whether precaution is wholly compatible with moves to speed up things such as planning decisions might be questioned.

Applying the Precautionary Principle in practice

The practical application of the Precautionary Principle is afflicted with similar issues as those besetting sustainable development. First, there is the problem of 'weak' and 'strong' versions of the principle. In the case of the former, the requirement to take precaution is modified by balancing the costs and benefits of taking action, mirroring current EC and UK approaches to the principle. At its extreme, the 'strong' version of the principle would prohibit any action, resulting in significant or irreversible environmental harm, regardless of the cost of doing so.[61] Both versions of the principle raise theoretical concerns. Under the weak version, on the one hand, there are difficulties in assessing the costs and benefits of uncertain risks that may need to be extrapolated over a long period of time. On the other hand, a 'strong' interpretation of the principle can be criticized on the basis that there is no such thing as a zero-risk activity and that a strong interpretation of the Precautionary Principle could result in a prohibition on beneficial activities simply on the basis that the understanding of the risks was uncertain. This is impractical and stifles the development of progressive technologies. Moreover, a strong interpretation assumes that there is no cost in doing nothing; in some circumstances, it is argued, *not* doing something may actually be more harmful than doing it.

The second problem with the practical application of the Precautionary Principle is the reliance upon 'sound science' in the assessment of risks.[62] Of course, there can never be 'certain' or 'exact' science, but this reliance does suggest a privileging of science over other forms of knowledge or constructions of belief, and therefore a certain rationality and unresponsiveness to shifts in public opinion. The *Pfizer* decision emphasizes that it is the wider scientific process that is important, as much as the end result—but it also continues the approach to decision making that assumes that assessing risks and then agreeing responses to risk (either legally or politically) are completely separate. Many now question whether this can ever be the case. As Jasanoff observes:

Studies of scientific advising leave in tatters the notion that it is possible, in practice, to restrict the advisory process to technical issues or that the subjective values of scientists are irrelevant to decision-making. The negotiated and constructed model of scientific knowledge, which closely captures the realities of regulatory science, rules out the possibility of drawing sharp boundaries between facts and values or claims and context.[63]

59 For example, the dismissal of a planning application for a landfill site in Hampshire: see (1998) ENDS Report 280, 15.

60 Although it is somewhat difficult to say that the level of protection actually given to such sites is precautionary—see, generally, p. 708.

61 See, generally, C. Sunstein (2005) *Laws of Fear: Beyond the Precautionary Principle*, Cambridge: Cambridge University Press.

62 See, e.g., the Sustainable Development Strategy of the Department for Environment, Food and Rural Affairs (DEFRA) (2002) *Foundations for our Future*.

63 S. Jasanoff (1990) *The Fifth Branch: Science Advisers as Policymakers*, Cambridge Mass: Harvard University Press, p. 231.

The third problem with the Precautionary Principle is that it does not determine what kinds of standards should be used. Inserting precaution into the EC Treaty, for example, has not resolved the tension between environmental quality standards and process controls, even if resolving this were desirable. Indeed, for countries such as Germany, precaution implied the use of the best pollution abatement techniques—that is, process controls—while the UK's response was to emphasize 'sound science' and cost–benefit, on which the traditional 'British' preference for quality standards was based.

Finally, and perhaps most importantly, the Precautionary Principle does not fit easily into the institutional and administrative framework that so happily accommodates the principle of sustainable development. Precaution is not an aspiration that cuts across departmental boundaries, which can be the subject of 'indicators' and fleshed out policy documents; rather, many see it as a response to the public mistrust of scientific 'objectivity' and a recognition that there will be circumstances under which there is a policy gap between that which a decision maker 'knows' about a risk (or can be told by science) and that with which the public are concerned. Thus, the Precautionary Principle fills that gap and provides the decision maker with a flexible principle that assists with the balance, or trade-off, between different options involving environmental risks—and this may be little more than a further justification for decisions that would have been reached anyway. At its worst, by suggesting a clear divide between the certain and uncertain, the Precautionary Principle may, paradoxically, give strength to the idea of certainty in some situations.

Another way of looking at the principle is as a practical 'tool' of environmental management that is interpreted and applied differently depending upon context. Doing so means that it is possible to 'open up' the principle so that it can be viewed in something other than monolithic or totemic terms. This naturally accords with the notion of a principle, as opposed to a rule, and would avoid the contested nature of the Precautionary Principle as falling definitively somewhere on the spectrum of 'strong' and 'weak' interpretations. On this interpretation, context matters, because, depending upon whether the principle is being used as a 'sword'—that is, to challenge a decision in relation to which the risks are alleged to be too great—or a 'shield'—that is, to protect a decision that attaches too much weight to residual risks—is critical to how decision makers and courts give effect to the principle. In other words, the 'tipping point' is relative to what is being challenged and a flexible, contextual interpretation permits the principle to be given an active effect without undermining its general application.[64] This would accord with the view that there is no point in trying to reach conclusions about whether the courts are applying the Precautionary Principle in a coherent and consistent fashion, because—at least in the EC context, in which it is a principle of European environmental law rather than a rule of EC law—it is applied to different administrative decision-making processes, such as EC member States acting unilaterally, or acting pursuant to an EC regime, or by the EC legislator itself.[65]

Human rights and environmental values

It may seem surprising to conclude a chapter on environmental *values* and environmental *law* with discussion of something that might not appear directly concerned with either. But, as we have already commented, environmental regulation does not take place in a vacuum, but rather within its own 'matrix' of values, practices, and moral standpoints relating to our interaction with the natural environment. Beyond this, however, environmental law also exists in a wider context of generally held values that underpin modern, liberal-democratic societies. These include things such as respect for individual rights and for private property,

64 See V. Hayvaert (2006) 31 Eur LR 185.
65 See E. Fisher (2006) 69 MLR 288.

respect for procedural fairness in decision making, and respect for the 'rule of law', which generally fall under the rubric of human rights law. We outline some of the more important provisions of human rights legislation and case law elsewhere (see pp. 330–32), and generally touch on relevant human rights issues throughout this book; the purpose of this section is therefore to consider the impact that the increasing attention given to human rights will have, and how the various perspectives described above are furthered or constrained when human rights enter the equation.

The idea that individuals *should* enjoy various general rights and freedoms has a long heritage, but only relatively recently have these values been laid down in binding legal texts. In a European context, the most important is the 1950 European Convention on Human Rights and Fundamental Freedoms (known as the European Convention on Human Rights, or ECHR). This was a response both to the aftermath of the Second World War and to the onset of the Cold War, and sought to embed a number of civil rights and freedoms in law. The Convention provides for various degrees of protection for the interests it covers: for example, while freedom from torture is protected absolutely, in relation to most other interests, the member State has a 'margin of appreciation' to decide whether a stated exception should apply, such as whether the right to privacy and the protection of home life can be outweighed by economic interests, as long as these are 'necessary in a democratic society'.

Under the Human Rights Act 1998, UK courts and public bodies are bound to act in accordance with the Convention. There is one exception to this, which is that the Convention right to an individual remedy is not transposed. Instead, there are in effect 'collective' remedies, in the sense that legislation can be declared incompatible with the Convention and fast-tracked through Parliament for reform. (In practice, this has meant that there are certain individual remedies.) The ECJ has already accepted that the ECHR provides one of the general principles of law that it must uphold.

The European Convention on Human Rights and the environment

In broad terms, European human rights law operates at three levels in relation to the environment.

(a) At a general level, it clearly gives great symbolic weight to the idea that human rights are deserving of protection and that they are actually protected—although there is considerable debate on this latter point.[66] Alongside trade freedom, human rights are one of the major 'narratives' of our times. For the vast majority of people, human rights will tend to outweigh environmental rights or interests.

(b) The European Court of Human Rights (ECtHR) has interpreted some civil and political rights to protect against environmental harms. For example, the Court has, in fairly extreme cases, creatively interpreted the right to respect for home life (Art. 8) to provide a remedy against extreme pollution.[67]

(c) Human rights law may have a more indirect impact in the environmental sphere. For example, the Convention provides for various qualified freedoms, such as freedom of expression (Art. 10) and the right to assemble peacefully (Art. 11).

To the extent that changes to environmental law or policy are argued for through public protest rather than lobbying, depending on various factors, human rights law may justify

---

66 See A. Boyle (1996) 'The role of international human rights law in the protection of the environment' in A. Boyle and M. Anderson (eds) *Human Rights Approaches to Environmental Protection*, Oxford: Clarendon Press.

67 Although it is also notable that those who have suffered more serious injury, unconnected with property, have been less successful: see, e.g., *LCB v. UK* (1999) 27 EHRR 212.

such protest or, conversely, may restrict it by the use of one of the exceptions on which the Convention allows governments to rely.

The 'pros' and 'cons' of environmental rights

Because the ECHR mostly protects civil and political freedoms, it is rather light on protections for other interests. In particular, the Convention—and human rights law generally—has yet to protect, or further genuinely, collective rights such as rights relating to environmental quality or resources. One reason for this is the extent to which broad questions of public interest and often a complex balancing of various factors are involved. Alternatively, as with European law, a rights-based approach to environmental law has been shunned in the EC Treaty in favour of integrating environmental protection into other policy sectors and reference to '*protecting the quality of the environment*'.[68] Although the ECJ sometimes speaks the language of 'rights', what is really at stake is compliance by the member States with specific, existing, legal obligations (see Chapter 7).

The 1992 Rio Declaration consciously avoids reference to environmental rights, although it does speak of national 'rights' to exploit the environment and the right to develop. Elsewhere in international law, however, we can see a gradual coming together of various 'strands', including sustainable development and human rights, indicating the extent to which rights *within* generations (or 'intragenerational rights') are seen as indivisible from the pursuit of sustainability. For example, Art. 4 of the 1995 Draft International Covenant on Environment and Development of the IUCN (the World Conservation Union) provides that '*Peace, development, environmental protection and respect for human rights and fundamental freedoms are interdependent*'.

It is, however, notable that most modern constitutions make some reference to environmental rights, usually by enshrining a very general right to a 'clean' or 'decent' environment.[69] Although often this gives little hard legal edge to the right, attempts to flesh out a human 'right to environment' have been made. This is the approach taken in parts of the 1994 Ksentini Report—a report made by the UN Special Rapporteur on Human Rights and the Environment (see Chapter 6). This report identifies various substantive rights and freedoms, such as freedom from pollution and environmental degradation, and the right to the highest attainable standard of health free from environmental harm, qualified by exceptions similar to those found in the ECHR. It should be apparent from what has been said above, however, that whether these are anything more than policy aspirations or a symbolic gesture is questionable. While they may guide decision makers in a general sense, courts are reluctant to require potentially vast sums of money to be spent on environmental improvement works to uphold such rights, not least because this might involve protecting the 'first right to get to court' at the expense of other, perhaps more worthy, improvement schemes.[70]

CHAPTER SUMMARY

1   The complexity and interconnection of environmental problems mean that it is possible to take different perspectives on how they should be addressed.

2   Environmental law does not necessarily resolve these different perspectives, but it does set down a framework for making decisions. Law also promotes the consistency, transparency, and accountability of decision making, and controls the discretion of the decision maker.

---

68 Articles 6 and 174(1) EC.

69 See, generally, A. Boyle and M. Anderson (eds) (1996) *Human Rights Approaches to Environmental Protection*, Oxford: Clarendon Press.

70 See, e.g., W. Howarth (2003) 14(5) Journal of Water Law 235.

3   There is, however, a gap between the procedural framework for making law and decisions, and the substantive decisions themselves—that is, what laws and decisions to make. Part of this gap is 'filled in' by collective values that are held about the environment.

4   Environmental values can be defined as 'what people believe to be important about the environment, and thus what should be the priorities for environmental policy and ultimately environmental law'.

5   Environmental values affect environmental law in a number of ways, including acting as a trigger for new policy and laws, promoting new interpretation of existing laws, influencing those who are regulated by environmental laws, and reinforcing the legitimacy of environmental law.

6   Problems arise, however, when competing values need to be prioritized. Different perspectives on environmental problems provide some way of trying to balance competing values, and explain how and why opposing arguments are put forward to support individual positions. Thus competing values can be prioritized by reference to environmental, economic, social, and scientific criteria.

7   Another way of addressing the problem of prioritizing environmental values is through the use of environmental principles such as the Polluter Pays, Precautionary, and Preventative Principles.

8   Environmental principles are guides to action, rather than rules, and, although they have been incorporated to a greater or lesser extent in law at all levels, the courts have generally declined to elaborate on this general guiding role.

9   The sustainable development principle is overarching, in the sense that it includes many aspects of other environmental principles. It is referred to in many legal and policy documents, although its meaning is contested and its application is largely aspirational.

10 The Precautionary Principle attempts to fill the gap between states of certainty and uncertainty—in cases in which a threat of environmental harm can be ascertained, but the possibility of the occurrence of the risk of that harm remains uncertain. It has been incorporated into laws at international and European levels. Although its meaning is contested, the European Court of Justice has attempted to flesh out its practical meaning.

11 Human rights law can also underpin decision making on environmental matters. The European Court of Human Rights has interpreted some of the civil and political rights contained in the European Convention on Human Rights to protect against environmental harms.

Q QUESTIONS

1   How do different values and perspectives on environmental issues contribute to environmental decision making?

2   In what ways do you think a truly ecocentric approach would affect environmental law and policy in the UK? What are the barriers to such an approach?

3   What are the arguments for and against putting a value on the environment?

4   How do environmental principles play a role in environmental law and decision making? What are the problems of using the principles in practice? How might environmental principles be made more effective?

5   Look at the latest sustainable development policy adopted by the UK government (available online at **http://www.sustainable-development.gov.uk/publications/uk-strategy/index.htm**). In what ways has the UK government established benchmark indicators of sustainable development? How accurate and helpful do you think these indicators are?

6   How are risk and precaution addressed in environmental law and decision making? Why do you think the courts are so reluctant to 'flesh out' the Precautionary Principle?

7   Consider the different issues in the first of the questions at the end of Chapter 1. How might the different perspectives and environmental principles outlined in this chapter affect your consideration of those issues?

 FURTHER READING

This chapter has ranged across a number of topics that stray into other areas of environmental ethics, economics, politics, and social theory. Bear in mind, therefore, that this list is very selective.

General

J. Alder and D. Wilkinson (1999) *Environmental Law and Ethics*, London: Macmillan, is an outstanding text that covers environmental ethics within the legal and policy context of environmental law. An extremely interesting portrayal of different ways of looking at environmental issues can be found in J. Ruhl, 'The case of the Speluncean polluters: six themes of environmental law, policy, and ethics' (1997) 27 Env Law 343, which takes a mythical case before a Supreme Court and presents different judicial perspectives in a manner that is immediately accessible without being simplistic—highly recommended for raising the interest of the disinterested and uninterested student!

Another good introduction to the idea of different perspectives on the environment can be found in J. Dryzek (2005) *The Politics of the Earth: Environmental Discourses*, 2nd edn, Oxford: Oxford University Press, which contains a fuller and deeper analysis of the range of perspectives (or discourses) than we have covered here (for example, the administrative, or bureaucratic, perspective).

Environmental perspectives

For a consideration of some of the issues surrounding the environmentalist perspective, have a look at C. Stone (1996) *Should Trees Have Standing? And Other Essays on Law, Morals and the Environment*, New York: Oceana, D. Wilkinson (1999) 'Using environmental ethics to create ecological law' in J. Holder and D. McGillivray (eds) *Locality and Identity: Environmental Issues in Law and Society*, Aldershot: Ashgate, and J. Holder, 'New age: rediscovering natural law' (2000) 53 CLP 151, particularly 165–71. These all contain good ways of rethinking law in a more ecocentric fashion.

Economic perspectives

A classic critique of the economic perspective can be found in M. Sagoff (1988) *The Economy of the Earth*, Cambridge: Cambridge University Press. His thesis is forcefully presented in a clear and readable fashion. Sagoff developed these arguments in (2004) *Price, Principle and the Environment*, Cambridge: Cambridge University Press, which suggests that economic valuation fails on a number of fundamental counts and that the best way of balancing competing interests is through principles that are elucidated through deliberative political processes.

In similar vein (although with different conclusions), D. Farber (1999) *Eco Pragmatism*, Chicago, Ill: University of Chicago Press, and L. Tribe 'Ways not to think about plastic trees: new foundations for environmental law' (1974) 83 Yale LJ 1315 consider the rights and wrongs of valuing nature. In particular, C. Sunstein (2002) *Risk and Reason*, Cambridge: Cambridge University Press, argues for the 'cost–benefit state' and claims that environmental laws have the capacity of killing more people then they protect. This last text prompts one word of warning: most of these originate from the USA and therefore come from a tradition where formal cost–benefit analysis is much more developed than it is in the UK.

For further reading on how decisions about conservation and development might be framed, we recommend F. Ackerman and L. Heinzerling (2004) *Priceless*, New York: New Press, P. Macnaghten and J. Urry (1998) *Contested Natures*, London: Sage, and C. Harrison, J. Burgess, and J. Clark (1999) 'Capturing values for nature' in J. Holder and D. McGillivray (eds) *Locality and Identity: Environmental Issues in Law and Society*, Aldershot: Ashgate, as good counterpoints to the economic approaches referred to above. There is also a specialist journal—*Environmental Values* (quarterly; White Horse Press)—within which much of the debate on values and sustainability is conducted.

Participatory approaches

The idea that participatory approaches are the best way of resolving different perspectives on the environment is gathering pace. For a discussion of the main themes, see M. Lee and C. Abbot, 'The usual suspects? Public participation under the Aarhus Convention' (2003) 66 MLR 80 and J. Steele 'Participation and deliberation in environmental law: exploring a problem-solving approach' (2001) 21 OJLS 415.

   Further reading on this issue is found at the end of Chapter 10.

Scientific perspectives

There is a plethora of material dealing with the perception of risk (including environmental risk). For an entertaining and illuminating examination of the topic, see J. Adams (1994) *Risk*, London: UCL Press, complete with idiosyncratic diagrams of angels and fish. A more difficult book (but one that is definitive in the area) is U. Beck (1992) *Risk Society*, London: Sage, which suggests that environmental impacts and the associated risks are part of a fundamental shift in society. Also have a look at J. Steele (2004) *Risks and Legal Theory*, Oxford: Hart, especially pt III on environmental risk generally. While not necessarily an easy read, it is thought provoking and well considered.

   D. Winickoff, S. Jasanoff, L. Busch, R. Grove-White, and B. Wynne, 'Adjudicating the GM food wars: science, risk and democracy in world trade law' (2005) 20 Yale J Intl L 81 considers the competing approaches to risk regulation on either side of the Atlantic and makes a well-argued case for taking values and public participation into account in determining what is 'sound science'. In many ways, the first part of the article is an excellent (and accessible) primer on how to think about the role of science in risk from a social science perspective, but as importantly, the article as a whole nicely considers how, in the authors' view, having regard to local cultural sensitivities in relation to matters of risk need not clash unduly with other objectives such as trade liberalization.

Environmental principles

Comprehensive coverage of the form and function of environmental principles can be found in N. de Sadeleer (2002) *Environmental Principles: From Political Slogans to Legal Rules*, Oxford: Oxford University Press. This is a heavyweight work that covers not only the substantive issues, but also a deeper analysis of the role of principles in the shift from rules-based 'modernist' law to principles-based 'postmodernist' law. Another (shorter) general introduction to the area can be found in M. Doherty, 'The status of the principles of EC environmental law' (1999) 11 JEL 379.

Sustainable development

For those wanting a general introduction to sustainable development, A. Dobson (2000) *Green Political Thought*, London: Routledge, gives a clear overview. For more detail, see A. Dobson (1999) *Fairness and Futurity: Essays on Environmental Sustainability and Social Justice*, Oxford: Oxford University Press. On the relationship between law and sustainable development, see M. Jacobs (1999) 'Sustainable development as a contested concept' in A. Dobson (ed) *Fairness and Futurity: Essays on Environmental Sustainability and Social Justice*, Oxford: Oxford University Press. For an up-to-date critique. see A. Ross-Robertson, 'Is the environment getting squeezed out of sustainable development?' [2003] Pub L 249, as well as S. Hendry, 'Worth the paper that it's written on? An analysis of statutory duty in modern environmental law' [2005] JPL 1145, which provides a study of various statutory duties in relation to sustainable development.

   One of the best-known critics of sustainable development is Wilfred Beckerman, a former member of the Royal Commission on Environmental Pollution. As an introduction to his work, see 'Sustainable development: is it a useful concept?' (1994) 3 Environmental Values 191, and a response from H. E. Daly, 'On Wilfred Beckerman's critique of sustainable development' (1995) 4 Environmental Values 49. A more comprehensive critique of sustainable development and the Precautionary Principle can be found in Beckerman

(2002) *A Poverty of Reason: Sustainable Development and Economic Growth*, Oakland, Calif: Independent Institute, well worth reading if only for a balanced counterpoint to the mainstream support for sustainable development.

A. Boyle and D. Freestone (eds) (2001) *International Law and Sustainable Development*, Oxford: Oxford University Press, covers the main legal developments of sustainable development in international law.

The Precautionary Principle

There are huge amounts of literature on this topic. As a starting point, try P. Harremoës, D. Gee, M. MacGarvin, A. Stirling, J. Keys, B. Wynne, and S. Guedes Vaz (eds) (2001) *The Precautionary Principle in the 20th Century: Late Lessons from Early Warnings*, London: Earthscan. This presents 14 detailed accounts of the application of the Precautionary Principle in relation to various hazards. It also reflects on the lessons learned and how they might inform the development of the principle. For an alternative view, see J. Morris (ed.) (2000) *Rethinking Risk and the Precautionary Principle*, London: Butterworth Heinemann, a collection of essays that are highly critical of the Precautionary Principle as a *'meaningless soundbite that can be used to justify just about any policy, including quite contradictory policies'*.

You will have no problem identifying any number of good books and articles on law and the Precautionary Principle. Try any of: R. Harding and E. Fisher (eds) (1999) *Perspectives on the Precautionary Principle*, Sydney: Federation Press; T. O'Riordan and J. Cameron (eds) (2000) *Reinterpreting the Precautionary Principle*, London: Cameron May; D. Freestone and E. Hey (eds) (1995) *The Precautionary Principle and International Law: The Challenge of Implementation*, The Hague: Kluwer. All three of these provide comprehensive collections of essays on different aspects of the Precautionary Principle.

Shorter articles on the topic include: O. McIntyre and T. Mosedale, 'The Precautionary Principle as a norm of customary international law' (1997) 9 JEL 221; M.-C. Cordonnier Segger and M. Gehring, 'The WTO and precaution: sustainable development implications of the WTO *Asbestos* dispute' (2003) 15(3) JEL 289; E. Fisher 'Is the Precautionary Principle justiciable?' (2001) 13 JEL 315. There is a useful note by E. Stokes in (2005) 7(3) Env L Rev 206 on what is known as the *Waddenzee* case (Case C-127/02 *Landelijke Vereniging tot Behoud van de Waddenzee, Nederlandse Vereniging tot Bescherming van Vogels v. Staatssecretaris van Landbouw, Natuurbeheer en Visserij* [2004] ECR I-7405). The argument put forward is that the European courts have been stretching the margins of precaution, from applying to scientifically established risk to being used in relation to unquantifiable uncertainties that cannot be ruled out.

Also on precaution in a European context, Cass Sunstein's 2005 book *Laws of Fear: Beyond the Precautionary Principle*, Cambridge: Cambridge University Press, is worth reading. Instead of adopting the Precautionary Principle, Sunstein advances three causes: a narrow 'anti-catastrophe principle', whereby regulators would have to identify the worst cases and eliminate the worst of these—that is, to focus on the most serious risks; close attention to costs and benefits; what he terms 'libertarian paternalism', which amounts to getting people to take more seriously the genuine risks that they currently ignore and to reduce their fear of trivial or non-existent risks (in effect, a kind of enforced rationalism). For a fierce attack on this book, however, see E. Fisher's review in (2006) 69 MLR 288. Fisher argues that Sunstein *'mischaracterises the precautionary principle, . . . mischaracterises the problems that it addresses; and . . . mischaracterises the context it applies in'*.

Rights

On rights issues, an excellent introduction is C. Miller (1998) *Environmental Rights: Critical Perspectives*, London: Routledge, which critically probes the value of thinking about environmental protection (both generally and in particular areas, such as air quality or nature conservation) through rights (on the creation of 'ecocentric' environmental rights from existing laws, see especially ch. 9). Equally good as a way in—although with much more of an international and comparative perspective—is A. Boyle and M. Anderson (eds) (1996) *Human Rights Approaches to Environmental Protection*, Oxford: Oxford University Press. The opening chapter of this fine set of essays neatly locates environmental rights in the context of the evolution of rights more generally and the chapter by Merrills is highly recommended. K. Morrow, 'The rights question: the initial impact of the Human Rights Act on domestic law relating to the environment' [2005] JPL 1010 provides a general overview of recent case law on human rights. For a provocative debate on the reconceptualization of environmental law in an ecocentric context, see C. Cullinan (2003) *Wild Law*, Dartington: Green Books, with a series of discursive articles discussing the pros and cons of the 'wild law' approach currently freely available online at **www.lawtext.com/lawtextweb/default. jsp?PageID=2&PublicationID=6.**

4 Sources of environmental law

 Overview

As a result of the range and nature of environmental problems, environmental law emerges at international, European, and national levels. This is partly because the complex, interconnected nature of environmental problems requires a range of solutions at all of these levels, but it is also because each source of law can fulfil different purposes. Each source possesses its own characteristics and functions. The general focus of this chapter is national law, but we also introduce international and European sources. We also examine some of the key characteristics of environmental laws that help to explain both the form and function of UK environmental law.

There is a large degree of overlap between this chapter and others in this book. You might find it useful to read the sections on lawmaking in Chapters 6 and 7 on international and European law, and to reflect on the role of private law in environmental protection as covered in Chapter 11. When considering the courts as a source of law, you may want to refer to the material on the calls for an environmental court in Chapter 10, which deals with public participation. We also consider briefly the role that overarching principles and rules play in environmental protection.

At the end of this chapter, you should be able to:

✔ understand where environmental law comes from, at international, regional, and national levels;

✔ appreciate some of the interrelationships between different sources of environmental law;

✔ identify some of the basic characteristics of different sources of environmental law;

✔ identify some of the key features of environmental legislation;

✔ appreciate the status and force of different forms of law for decision makers.

International environmental law

International law governs relations between states and, accordingly, international *environmental* law seeks to address environmental concerns that are applicable across different states or of general global application. By definition, such problems are likely to be complex and difficult to solve. Thus international environmental law is characterized by negotiation and the need to gain a consensus from across as large a number of countries as possible. International environmental law is often aspirational in nature, laying down broad frameworks for action. Unlike EC law, it has no direct effect on domestic law or on individuals, but it will often have an indirect effect—for example, by publicizing a particular issue, by laying down generally accepted standards, or by imposing political pressure on states to change their laws or practices. In this way, the Climate Change Convention and the Kyoto Protocol have had an important impact on UK law and policy in relation to greenhouse gas emissions.

Many pieces of legislation include powers for governments to introduce changes into domestic law in order to comply with international obligations.[1]

For the most part, international environmental law consists of broad conventions agreed by signatory states. Conventions can be precise and specific in terms of the obligations they create.[2] More typically, however, conventions are developed in an incremental way, moving from broad agreements on the nature of a problem to more specific measures. There may be an initial agreement over a framework that will promote an understanding of a particular environmental problem through general obligations to exchange information, share research, and take 'appropriate measures' to address the problem. The convention will then be fleshed out by further, more specific, obligations under further agreements called protocols. The important point is that, however precise the obligation, such law is not ultimately binding, except in a political sense, because of the lack of sanctions available for non-compliance.

This approach reflects the pragmatic nature of much of international environmental law. The negotiation process lets countries begin to thrash out a controversial problem even before there is full agreement on the exact nature of the problem or, indeed, on whether there is a problem at all. Such an approach can accommodate countries that are unconvinced of the need for action, because it is better to participate and influence the shape of the agreement than to be 'on the outside'. High levels of participation lend legitimacy to the issue and this, in turn, can lead to pressure to take the subject seriously by participating in a convention or risk international isolation.

European Community (EC) law

The European Community (EC) is a very important source of environmental law. Post-enlargement, the EC includes 27 member States working jointly through common institutions such as the European Parliament, the European Commission, the European Central Bank (ECB), the Council of Ministers, and the European Court of Justice (ECJ). The EC is often referred to as the European Union (or EU). Strictly speaking, the European Union includes not only the European Community, but also the other two European pillars of the European integration process—namely, the Justice and Home Affairs Policy and the Common Foreign and Security Policy. In practice, the two are synonymous.

In contrast to domestic law, EC environmental law is often purposive in character, although the purposes are combined with very specific standards in relation to environmental quality and emission levels. This purposive approach is the product of the influence of civil law countries. In such countries, the law is found in codes that lay down general principles.[3] These principles are given effect by the national courts, which take a purposive approach in trying to apply the law. This is reflected in the extensive recitals that accompany EC legislation, which explain the basis for the Directives. Another reason for the purposive approach is that clarity is needed when drafting in many different languages. There is often a danger that misunderstandings will arise unless the differences can be smoothed out by reference to the general purposes of the legislation. The wording of the substantive provisions of environmental Directives may be unclear; certain key phrases will be open to interpretation.[4] The purposive approach in EC law suggests that the recitals help to define the

---

1 For example, the Pollution Prevention and Control Act 1999, s. 2 and Sch. 1, para. 3, enable the Secretary of State to make regulations for the purpose of implementing EC or international obligations.

2 For example, the Convention on International Trade in Endangered Species lists certain categories of protected species—species in danger of becoming extinct are listed in Annex I—with corresponding obligations in relation to each category.

3 For a discussion in the context of waste regulation, see B. Lange (1999) 11(1) JEL 63.

4 For example, the definition of 'project' in Art. 1(2) of the Environmental Assessment Directive 85/337/EEC (see p. 443) and the definition of 'waste' in Art. 1(1)(a) of the Waste Framework Directive 2006/12/EC (see p. 645).

statutory provisions. This is in contrast to the UK approach, which has traditionally been based upon a literal approach to the plain meaning of words.

BOX 4.1 **Purposive and literal interpretations of environmental law**

The distinction between the literal and purposive approaches has been noted particularly in relation to the interpretation of the Environmental Impact Assessment (EIA) Directive.[5] The contrast is greatest when comparing cases decided in the early 1990s, at which time the European case law in the area was relatively underdeveloped, with cases from the mid-1990s, at which time the European Court of Justice (ECJ) took a strong purposive line in interpreting some key provisions of the Directive.

In 1993, Alder argued that English law was *'inadequate to secure the aims'* of the EIA Directive and that English legal culture was hostile to purposive regulation. In relation to literalism, he commented:

> A…characteristic of English legal culture is a semantic and literalistic approach to drafting and interpreting legal rules. It would be an oversimplification to contrast this automatically with a purposive approach because some approaches may well be advanced by semantic techniques. However in the context of European law the semantic approach is especially likely to clash with the policies of the European Community because their policies are implemented by draftsmen schooled in the more open textured and purposive methods used by continental lawyers.[6]

Although this was true in the early 1990s, the position has changed somewhat, given the weight of purposive case law that has emanated from the ECJ, particularly in relation to the interpretation of the EIA Directive.

Examples of this shift in judicial approach can be seen in relation to many different aspects of EIA, from the definition of 'consent',[7] to the question of whether a project should be subject to EIA at all. In the latter situation, the English courts originally treated the question as a matter of fact and degree for the planning authority to determine.[8] Subsequently, the ECJ took a purposive approach to this question. In Case C-72/95 *Aanemersbedriff P K Kraaijeveld BV v. Gedeputeerde Staten van Zuid-Holland* [1996] ECR I-5403, the ECJ held that the *'wide scope and broad purpose of the Directive'* should not be undermined by granting unlimited discretion to member States to determine whether all projects of a certain type would, or would not, have 'significant effects' (see p. 447). This purposive approach was then adopted in subsequent cases in England, notably by the House of Lords in *Berkeley v. Secretary of State for the Environment, Transport and the Regions and Fulham Football Club* [2001] Env LR 16.[9]

Purposive approaches have also been adopted in relation to substantive issues such as the definition of waste (see p. 645 and Case 14.3). In particular, the semantic difficulties of agreeing on a consistent definition of the word 'discard' across different member States and different situations has seen both the ECJ and the domestic courts relying on the overall purposes of the Waste Framework Directive (2006/12/EC) in determining whether or not something is waste. The case law on the subject illustrates the advantages and disadvantages of taking a purposive approach.

---

5 Directive 85/337/EEC (as amended from 1999 by Directive 97/11/EC).
6 J. Alder (1993) 5 JEL 217.
7 See *R v. North Yorkshire County Council, ex parte Brown* [1998] Env LR 623 and Case 13.2.
8 See *R v. Swale Borough Council, ex parte RSPB* [1991] 1 PLR 6.
9 See W. Upton (2001) 13(1) JEL 89 and Case 13.7.

> On the positive side, the test is coherent and easily stated, because the Preamble to the Directive spells out the underlying purposes of the legislation; on the negative side, the purposes of the legislation may themselves be vague and difficult to pin down when applied to specific situations.[10]

Membership of the EC has clearly involved a distinct loss of sovereignty for member States and, in the UK, this is given constitutional force by the European Communities Act 1972. Section 2(1) of that Act provides that EC legislation is recognized as law in the UK—although by no means all EC environmental legislation is directly effective, in the sense that it can be relied upon by individuals before it is implemented by domestic measures. For example, although EC regulations are effective as law without any further intervention or action on the part of the member States, EC Directives are only 'binding as to the result to be achieved' in that they lay down objectives, but leave the member States some discretion as to how to achieve them. Thus a distinction is drawn between the requirement to transpose a Directive—that is, to translate it into national law—and the fulfilment of the obligations created. The amount of discretion varies greatly. Problems arise when member States exceed the discretion by failing to implement EC law. This might arise from a failure to implement certain substantive or procedural provisions of a Directive.

In addition to the concept of EC law as UK law, there are rules and principles that can be applied to the institutions of the EC—that is, EC law as it affects internal bodies. Thus such things as the Precautionary Principle and the need to integrate environmental considerations into all areas of EC policy apply to the Commission when it is formulating legislative proposals, and to the European Parliament and Council of Ministers when they are debating and making European environmental laws. EC law is explained in greater detail in Chapter 7, but an important point to establish here is that, as with domestic law, EC environmental law consists of far more than legal rules. It is as necessary to understand the policies, principles, and future direction of EC law as it is to understand its current legal content.

Layers of law

Although international law, EC law, and domestic law are described as separate sources of law, they are increasingly interdependent. Domestic or EC legislation often implements obligations under international environmental law. But the relationship is not only 'top-down': the EC plays an important part in negotiating international agreements on behalf of its member States and the UK plays an important part in setting the agenda on certain environmental issues in the EC. A good example of the latter point is the way in which the UK was a leader in the development of the Integrated Prevention Pollution and Control (IPPC) Directive (2008/1/EC), based largely on experience with integrated pollution control (IPC) introduced under the Environmental Protection Act 1990.[11]

The interaction of domestic, European, and international sources of environmental law produces a 'layering' effect, which sees laws that address particular problems overlapping. To illustrate this, Box 4.2 sets out the layering of various sources of law on air pollution. It illustrates the division between conventions and protocols in international law, framework and daughter Directives in EC law, and primary statutes and secondary legislation in national law. This table is, however, only schematic and is not a comprehensive description of all of the relevant laws on air pollution. For example, it might feature a further layer below the UK, which describes laws in the devolved countries, or it might describe technical or policy documents at all levels. It does, however, highlight a number of points.

10 See p. 645.
11 See p. 477.

BOX 4.2 Layers of law—air pollution

International	1979 Geneva Convention on Long-range Transboundary Pollution						
	1984 Monitoring and Evaluation Protocol	1985 Helsinki Protocol on reductions of sulphur emissions	1988 Sofia Protocol on nitrogen oxides	1991 Geneva Protocol on volatile organic compounds	1994 Oslo Protocol on further reduction of sulphur emissions	1998 Aarhus Protocol on heavy metals	1999 Gothenburg Protocol to abate acidification, eutrophication and ground-level ozone
		1998 Aarhus Protocol on persistent organic pollutants (POPs)					
EC	Framework Directive 1996/62/EC on ambient air quality assessment and management		Directive 2008/1/EC on integrated pollution prevention and control (IPPC)	Directive 1999/13/EC on volatile organic compounds	Directive 2000/76/EC on the incineration of waste	Directive 2001/80/EC on large combustion plants	Directive 2001/81/EC on national emission ceilings
	Directive 1999/30/EC on limits for NOx, SO₂, PM₁₀, Pb	Directive 2000/69/EC on limits for benzene and carbon monoxide	Directive 2002/3/EC on limits for ozone				
UK	European Communities Act 1972		Environment Act 1995			Environmental Permitting (England and Wales) Regulations 2007[15]	
	Air Quality Standards Regulations 2007[12]	National Emissions Ceiling Regulations 2002[13]	Air Quality Standards Regulations 2007[14]				
			National Air Quality Strategy 2007		Technical guidance documents		

12 SI 2007/64.
13 SI 2002/3118.
14 SI 2007/64.
15 SI 2007/3538.

- There are layers within layers—namely, broad frameworks that have the details fleshed out in other legislation.

- Not all topics will be layered in the same way. Although the law on any particular environmental issue can come from a variety of sources, there are certain issues, such as transboundary pollution, which require international solutions. Other areas are more appropriately dealt with at regional or national levels.

- There is no 'conveyor belt' system by means of which environmental law is transferred from one layer to another. Because international and European obligations are often framed in very broad terms, a range of measures may be adopted at a national level. They may not be directly linked to any European or international measures even though they have the function of meeting the obligations laid down elsewhere.

National law

In the UK, the term 'environmental law' is commonly used to mean that branch of public law which contains statutes that cover pollution control and wider environmental issues. This only provides part of the picture, however, because there are other mechanisms for the control or influence of activities that cause environmental harm that are not governed by statute. These might be voluntary in nature or based upon the use of the market. As the nature of environmental issues becomes more complex and the diversity of ways of addressing those issues increases, so the sources of environmental law expand, and the traditional boundaries and divisions of legal mechanisms blur.[16]

As examples of this diversity, consider the following.

- **Instruments that are hybrids of the public and private law**
  This would include environmental agreements made under statutory powers by public bodies with private individuals or groups.[17]

- **Instruments that impose self-regulatory requirements**
  An example of this would be the existence of compliance schemes under the producer responsibility legislation for the recovery and recycling of packaging waste. The Regulations exempt all companies who would otherwise have had to comply with the producer responsibility obligations if they are members of a compliance scheme that is registered for the purposes of the Regulations. The compliance scheme takes on collective responsibility for meeting its members' obligations under the legislation. Thus the regulation of the activities is delegated to a small number of self-regulated organizations.[18]

- **Instruments that are based upon increasing public information about polluting activities**
  These include not only rights of access to information on specific emissions and activities regulated under licences that are held on public registers, but also more sophisticated information, such as inventories of general and aggregated pollution levels, product labelling, and possible requirements to include environmental information in companies' annual reports.[19]

---

16 As to the development of environmental laws, see Chapter 2.
17 For example, management agreements in nature conservation—see p. 700.
18 See p. 669.
19 See p. 247.

- **Economic instruments that can cover a range of measures**
  These might range from the direct taxation of polluting substances[20] and the creation of a market in the pollution credits,[21] to fees and charges for licences that reflect the level of environmental risk or harm caused by an authorized activity.[22]

This use of a broader range of instruments reflects a growth of sources of environmental law, in which traditional public law, 'command and control' legislation is combined with different regulatory approaches to secure the most effective forms of control over environmental pollution.[23]

UK environmental legislation

Although the boundaries between different types of legislation and rules are often blurred in practice, the source of domestic environmental legislation can be broken down into three main categories.

Primary legislation

Acts of Parliament—also known as statutes, or enactments—provide the basic framework for most domestic environmental law. Although they are subject to full parliamentary scrutiny, their general nature means that there is often little controversy concerning the substantive provisions of environmental statutes, because they do not contain anything of sufficient certainty to give rise to party political disputes, although there are notable exceptions to this (the primary example being the Wildlife and Countryside Act 1981). Another notable feature of environmental statutes is that legislation on single environmental issues is often promoted in the form of private members' Bills, reflecting the individual interests of MPs and the effective lobbying of non-government organizations (NGOs).[24]

There is little direct public participation such as public consultation in the creation of environmental statutes. The main justification for this is that Parliament has representative accountability through the electorate and is therefore presumed to pass laws on behalf of everyone. In addition, both Houses of Parliament scrutinize new legislation in standing committees and debates. In reality, this scrutiny is often no more than passing consideration, because of pressure on parliamentary time and, commonly, the numerical strength of the incumbent government.

Although there has been a consolidation of the administration of environmental protection over recent years, environmental legislation still extends over a relatively large area. The main environmental legislation is outlined in Box 2.5, but this is by no means a comprehensive list. It is increasingly common to have narrower statutes that focus on perhaps one or two main issues rather than the broad coverage of these Acts.

There is another more general statute that might be said to be a primary source of environmental law. The European Communities Act 1972, s. 2(2), gives powers for the passing of secondary legislation that is necessary to comply with EC law. One of the main disadvantages of this power is that it only permits bare implementation measures. Thus any secondary legislation must accord exactly with the European obligations—no more and no less.[25]

---

20 For example, the Landfill Tax: see p. 667.

21 For example, the emissions trading scheme—see pp. 525–29.

22 For example, see p. 240.

23 N. Gunningham and P. Grabosky (1998) *Smart Regulation: Designing Environmental Policy*, Oxford: Clarendon Press.

24 Examples of private members' Bills on environmental issues that have reached the statute book in recent years include the Waste Minimisation Act 1998 and the Household Waste Recycling Act 2003.

25 Many important pieces of environmental legislation have been passed under the powers of the European Communities Act, including the Town and Country Planning (Assessment of Environmental Effects) (England and

Secondary legislation

The second main source of environmental law stems from the first: beneath the tier of primary legislation there is a range of detailed secondary legislation that is used to flesh out much of the detail of environmental law. This is commonly made by the appropriate Secretary of State under the delegated authority of Parliament. Typically, it is known as regulations, or statutory instruments, although, in relation to environmental laws, there are other types of secondary legislation.[26] This tier of legislation is entirely dependent upon the powers that have been granted within the primary statute. In environmental law, there has been some controversy about the breadth of some of the powers that have been granted by primary statutes. There appears to have been a desire to broaden the scope of the power to make secondary legislation in order to give more and more flexibility to the rule makers.[27]

This controversy illustrates some of the concerns about using secondary legislation for many of the elements of environmental laws. Unlike primary legislation, there is little parliamentary scrutiny of detailed secondary legislation. Many environmental regulations are passed under a negative resolution procedure that, in practice, consists of laying the statutory instrument before both Houses of Parliament for a specified period in advance of its coming into force. Some more controversial aspects of secondary legislation are subject to the alternative affirmative procedure, which ensures that there are debates in both Houses before the legislation is passed.

One of the main reasons for the lack of parliamentary scrutiny is that environmental secondary legislation tends to be highly technical and the lack of any sufficient expertise would make such scrutiny less than effective. Another is that environmental secondary legislation is commonly sent out for public consultation, which enables a broad range of technical views to be taken into account prior to finalizing the details. In these circumstances, the lower levels of parliamentary scrutiny can be justified, because there is a broader public scrutiny involved in the lawmaking process.

It is impossible to provide any comprehensive list of environmental secondary legislation, but there are certain categories that can be identified.

(a) **Procedural**

Certain aspects of environmental regulation are too detailed and complex to be placed in primary legislation. Procedures for applications for licences and for appealing against refusals or enforcement action can often be found in secondary legislation. In addition, provisions on other procedural matters, such as registers of information on emissions, are left to delegated powers.[28]

(b) **Detailed categories**

Primary legislation may set down general definitions that can be more properly defined in technical secondary legislation.[29]

Wales) Regulations 1999, SI 1999/293, and the Conservation (Natural Habitats etc.) Regulations 1994, SI 1994/2716. This power has been supplemented with a wider power to transpose and modify environmental obligations under EC law under the Pollution Prevention and Control Act 1999, Sch. 1, para. 20.

26 For example, the Town and Country Planning (Use Classes) Order 1987, SI 1987/764.

27 The Pollution Prevention and Control Bill featured a particularly wide power allowing the Secretary of State to pass regulations in respect of a series of statutory purposes relating to environmental pollution. This would have given a virtually unlimited scope to control any activity that gave rise to pollution without any parliamentary scrutiny. This power was subsequently amended after objections were lodged in the House of Lords: see House of Commons Research Paper 99/58 (1999) *Pollution Prevention and Control Bill*, pp. 49–62.

28 For examples, see the Contaminated Land (England) Regulations 2000, SI 2000/227, and the Statutory Nuisance (Appeals) Regulations 1995, SI 1995/2644.

29 For example, categories of installations controlled under PPC (see Pollution Prevention and Control (England and Wales) Regulations 2000, SI 2000/1973) exempt categories of waste that qualify for the lower rate of landfill tax (see the Landfill Tax (Qualifying Materials) Order 1996, SI 1996/1528) can be found in secondary legislation.

(c) Standards

It is common for the many different types of standard that play an important role in environmental regulation to be set out in secondary legislation.[30]

(d) Transposing European obligations

Certain European obligations have been transposed directly into secondary legislation. The justification for using secondary legislation is that there should be little political controversy over the transposition of measures that have been agreed at a European level. Thus these regulations are direct translations of the corresponding European measures.[31]

Tertiary legislation, guidance, and other 'rules'

Although secondary legislation provides the bulk of the technical details of environmental law, it is still not particularly user-friendly, nor does it set out a comprehensive set of definitions. There is an increasing reliance on other rules and guidance to explain the practical workings of environmental laws, and to provide a structure for statutory discretion. There are so many different types of this source of law that it is impossible to identify any meaningful classification, other than by looking at the purpose behind the guidance or rule, as follows.

(a) As an aid to the interpretation of statutory provisions

Because the main statutory provisions in primary and secondary legislation can be complex and technical, there is often a need to flesh out definitions and to provide an interpretation of such provisions in non-legalistic language.[32]

(b) As a more flexible form of informal guidance or rule

There are some areas that do not lend themselves to the traditional sources of environmental law. These include matters that cannot easily be reduced to simple rules, perhaps because there is a need for a little more flexibility and less legal rigidity in the use of language. An example is the code of practice on the duty of care, which provides detailed guidance on the type of conduct that might be considered to be reasonable when handling materials throughout the waste management chain (see p. 664). Another example is the statutory guidance in the contaminated land regime (see p. 554). Both of these examples set out principles and rules in a prose style that enables a wider range of issues to be discussed and balanced than would be the case if they were set out in formal legislation. In addition, broad strategic documents are more easily framed in informal documents than in formal legislation, because they set out general policies, strategies and programmes that are to be used in meeting statutory or non-statutory environmental quality targets. Examples include the national strategies on waste and air quality.[33]

(c) As statements of regulatory agency policy and practice

Regulatory agencies will often publish policy documents that set out their aims and policies on particular areas. The Environment Agency has policy and practice documents relating to a number of areas, including the protection of groundwater and of floodplains.[34] These documents are used in liaison with other agencies—primarily, the

---

30 Examples include the Air Quality Standards Regulations 2007, SI 2007/64, and the Urban Waste Water Treatment (England and Wales) Regulations 1994, SI 1994/2841.

31 Examples include the Conservation (Natural Habitats etc.) Regulations 1994, SI 1994/2716 (transposing the Habitats Directive 92/43/EC) and the Environmental Permitting (England and Wales) Regulations 2007, SI 2007/3538 transposing a range of Directives.

32 An example is the definition of 'waste', which is defined in the primary statute in a few lines, fleshed out in different ways in the Waste Management Licensing Regulations 1994, SI 1994/1056, but explained in simpler terms in the Department of the Environment Circular 11/94.

33 See p. 539.

34 See p. 413.

planning authorities—in carrying out overlapping functions and in exercising decision-making powers, such as in determining planning applications.

(d) As a way of structuring discretion, and promoting consistency and transparency in decision making

In areas in which environmental agencies implement and enforce wide discretionary statutory powers, there is often guidance that aims to direct them in the exercise of those powers. Documents such as the Environment Agency's Enforcement and Prosecution Policy set out objective principles that guide individual officers as to when and how enforcement action should be taken when environmental laws are breached (see p. 278). This should ensure that there is a degree of consistency and uniformity in enforcement practices across the country, and thereby increase the transparency and fairness of the otherwise unstructured use of enforcement powers.

(e) As rules and guidance on procedural or other technical matters

Although secondary legislation often sets out the formal legislative requirements for procedural or other technical matters, it does not deal with many of the practical issues that can arise on a day-to-day basis. Thus there is a need to provide information and practical guidance in non-legalistic language. Examples of this can be found in general guidance issued by the Secretary of State and the Environment Agency in relation to the Best Available Techniques (BAT) process standard under pollution prevention and control (PPC) legislation (see p. 500).

These types of tertiary rules and guidance have become a common method of supplementing formal primary and secondary legislation as a source of environmental law. In areas of policy rather than law, the use of circulars and other guidance documents is relatively well established. While there is a very significant degree of overlap between law and policy, the range of tertiary rules in modern environmental law goes much further than mere policy documents providing assistance with decision making. The use of technical guidance and documents that interpret general statutory concepts is one of the ways in which environmental laws operate in the real world (although the use of such documents is not without its own set of difficulties).

The level of formality of such rules differs. Some—such as the code of practice on the duty of care or the statutory guidance on contaminated land—have their origins in primary or secondary legislation (and so might be referred to as 'sub-delegated' legislation); others appear somewhat spontaneously and do not have any formal basis. The key problem with the use of tertiary rules is, however, that there is a great deal of uncertainty and confusion about the extent to which such rules have legal effect. For example, if an interpretive guidance document sets out a detailed interpretation of a general statutory definition—such as the government's interpretation of the definition of waste in Circular 11/94 or the Environment Agency's view on the definition of packaging[35]—does that interpretation have any legal force?

Theoretically, at least, such interpretations or rules do not have any determinative status as law. Indeed, it is common for such guidance documents to make it clear that the individual interpretation is no substitute for a court's view. This theory unfortunately ignores the fact that, in practice, the interpretation often supplants the general definition in the minds of the regulator and the regulated. Moreover, if the interpretation is ever challenged in court, there is a great temptation for a judge to 'adopt' the official interpretation over any other.

Generally speaking, tertiary rules will have a persuasive status, either as material considerations that cannot be ignored, but which are not prescriptive, or as presumptive starting points for a decision maker or regulatory agency, such as guidance notes in relation to IPPC,

---

35 See p. 669.

within which the process standard set out is presumed to represent BAT, but other circumstances could give rise to alternatives. The one exception to this general rule is in the case of the National Waste Strategy, which has been held to carry special weight in the decision-making process (see p. 642).

Characteristics of UK environmental legislation

Environmental legislation covers a wide range of areas, which means that the substance of the legislation is often very different. There are, however, some characteristics that might be said to be common to all.

Complex tiers of rules

Much of the detail of environmental statutes is left to be worked out in various forms of delegated legislation. This is particularly true of some of the main pieces of legislation in environmental law—the Environmental Protection Act (EPA) 1990, the Water Resources Act 1991, the Environment Act 1995, the Town and Country Planning Act (TCPA) 1990, and the Pollution Prevention and Control Act 1999. In each case, the statute only provides a limited description of what the law is. For example, the central TCPA 1990 definition of what requires planning permission owes just as much to statutory instruments—the Town and Country Planning (General Permitted Development) Order 1995[36] and the Town and Country Planning (Use Classes) Order 1987[37]—as to the general definition laid down in s. 55 of the Act.

There is no typical type of delegated legislation within UK environmental law, and detailed laws come under names such as regulations, rules, orders, and schemes. The upshot of all of these different types of legislation and other rules is that it is often difficult to find out about the law on a particular issue in anything other than a very general manner. For example, if one were to want to find out about the rules that govern an application for a PPC permit, the basic information about application procedures would have to be supplemented with technical guidance on specific industrial sectors and general guidance on such things as monitoring requirements. The complexity and interaction of these many tiers of rules can obscure the effects of the law in that the informal rules and guidance can have greater practical significance than the primary or secondary legislation.

Delayed commencement

Legislation often requires implementation by statutory instrument before it comes into force. EPA 1990 included a provision for most of it to be brought into force by commencement order. This led to the provisions on waste management licensing not being brought into force until May 1994. Other key provisions on contaminated land registers (s. 143) and closed landfill sites (s. 61) were repealed before they ever came into force. It seems contrary to the rule of law that the decision on whether, and how far, to implement enacted legislation should be left entirely to the discretion of the Secretary of State, but that is the position and the same approach is adopted in most major pieces of environmental legislation. Apart from the suspicion that such delays are used for political purposes, this gradualist approach obscures what the law is and brings it into disrepute by creating uncertainty for the public, regulatory bodies, and industry alike.

Definitions

Definitions are often left unclear in the legislation. Normally, this is to preserve flexibility in the application of the law. For example, until the enactment of EPA 1990, the central

36 SI 1995/418.
37 SI 1987/764.

concept in the law on air pollution was that of 'best practicable means' (BPM). This phrase was never statutorily defined. Instead, it was explained in relation to different processes in BPM Notes published by Her Majesty's Inspectorate of Pollution (HMIP) and its predecessors. Even these were not comprehensive, because an important feature of BPM was that it allowed flexibility to cater for local and individual circumstances. Interestingly, the BPM Notes were often drawn up in consultation with interested parties, including representatives of the industry concerned.

A similar process can be seen in TCPA 1990, in which fundamental concepts such as 'development' and 'material change of use' have deliberately been left as open as possible in the legislation. In this case, they have been further defined by the courts in numerous cases, but the original flexibility has been retained by the courts' insistence that the application of the law to the facts of any individual case is a matter for the relevant decision maker—the so-called 'fact and degree' test.

If anything, this approach is becoming more common. Under the contaminated land regime in Pt 2A of EPA 1990, the fundamental question of whether land is 'contaminated' owes as much to guidance issued by the Secretary of State that local authorities must follow as it does to the partial definition set out in the Act. What should be determined as a matter of law is thus relegated to a matter of administrative discretion. This process illustrates the broader idea of centralization, along with a clear shift in power away from Parliament and the courts towards the executive government (see p. 101).

Purposive and listing approaches

One of the consequences of having to balance such wide definitions against the technical nature of much of environmental law is that there are two typical approaches to drafting legislative concepts. First—and probably most commonly—is the approach outlined above, under which the rule maker balances flexibility and certainty by creating complex tiers of rules. Characteristically, this will involve a broad definition within primary legislation, followed by lists of a more technical nature in secondary regulations. Examples of this can be found in the formation of exemptions from the legislative system in many areas of environmental legislation.[38] The primary statute empowers the rule maker to create classes of exempt activities and these are set down in detailed secondary legislation.

The main alternative to this approach is to set down a purposive definition that stands alone without any need for further clarification: the purpose of the definition is self-explanatory. An example of this can be found in Water Resources Act 1991, s. 85, which makes it an offence to cause the entry of 'polluting' matter into controlled waters. The key phrase 'polluting' is not defined in the Act (see p. 607).

Some environmental laws combine both of these approaches. For example, the definition of waste relies both on a general purposive definition—'*any substance or object... which the holder discards*'[39]—and general descriptions of categories of wastes, recovery, and disposal operations '*in the categories set out in Annex I*',[40] and extremely detailed classifications of waste found in the European Waste Catalogue.[41]

Interestingly in this context, European law sets out the specific purposes of legislation in recitals that form part of Directives. Because more and more European law is being transposed into domestic law by means of straight translation—also referred to as 'copy out'—and the doctrine of indirect effects—namely, that national laws should be interpreted so as to comply with EC law—the courts are interpreting national environmental laws in accordance with the underlying purposes.

---

38 For example, from the need for planning permission (see p. 398) or exempt waste operations (see p. 479).
39 Waste Framework Directive 2006/12/EC, Art. 1(1)(a).
40 Ibid.
41 See List of Wastes (England) Regulations 2005, SI 2005/895.

Discretions

Wide discretions are frequently given in the legislation. This is a particularly clear feature of UK environmental law. The amount of discretion is great at all of the stages of regulatory decision making. Parliament rarely sets firm policies and standards in legislation, allowing for these to be defined in delegated legislation or through administrative guidance. There are many examples, ranging from the discretion given to the Secretary of State on the form of delegated legislation, through discretion as to whether an area should be designated for special protection[42] and discretion on the setting of standards,[43] to discretion over the enforcement of the law.[44] In all areas of environmental law, it is hard to get away from discretionary decision making.

At the standard-setting and consent-setting levels, the discretion is usually given to the relevant regulatory body. For example, the Environment Agency has discretion over the setting of standards for discharges to water and in the definition of BAT in relation to PPC.[45] A similar wide discretion can be seen at the enforcement stage. There are few statutes that lay down duties to enforce the legislation or which set out statutory factors to take into account, and usually the decision whether to take action is taken by the regulatory body, on the basis of practical and political factors that are not mentioned in the legislation. Because many of the most important remedies are administrative remedies that are unavailable to individuals, this discretion is of enormous practical importance.

Judicial interference is frequently limited by the width of discretions given in legislation. This is best illustrated in the town and country planning legislation, within which there is a clear policy of judicial non-intervention in decisions about the weight to be attached to material considerations.[46] As a result of all of these factors and also because of the general UK preference for variable, rather than uniform, standards, the UK system of environmental control has become characterized by flexibility and lack of uniformity.

Although there is a wide discretion granted to decision makers, however, this is not completely unfettered and the courts have intervened in cases, which demonstrates that the exercise of discretion can be challenged over and above the level of individual decisions. Thus, there have been a number of cases in which both the ECJ and the High Court have rejected discretionary decisions that have been based upon incorrect criteria. In particular, this has been the case when dealing with the relative importance of economic considerations over environmental factors.

CASE 4.1 *R v. Secretary of State for the Environment, ex parte Kingston upon Hull City Council* [1996] Env LR 248

The Secretary of State established the outer limits of the Humber and Severn estuaries for the purposes of the EC Urban Waste Water Directive (91/271/EEC). In doing so, he relied upon the extra cost of treating waste waters within the designated area. The Court held that, although member States had a discretion in deciding how to establish limits, the cost of treatment was not a relevant consideration; what was required was a genuine and rational assessment of what constituted the estuary, having regard to the purpose of the Directive and all other relevant considerations.

The *Kingston upon Hull* decision can be contrasted with the decision in *R v. National Rivers Authority, ex parte Moreton* [1996] Env LR 234, in which it was held that the NRA was entitled to take into

---

42 For example, as a site of special scientific interest—see p. 690.

43 For example, in the permitted level of a pollutant discharged or emitted—see p. 230.

44 For example, to prosecute—see p. 272.

45 See pp. 600 and 499.

46 For example, see *London Residuary Body v. Lambeth London Borough Council* [1990] 1 WLR 744 and further Case 12.4 on the *Tesco* case.

account economic considerations—the investment budget of the water company—in addition to the achievement of water quality standards when deciding whether or not to grant a discharge consent (perhaps illustrating the distinction between the exercise of general discretion in *Kingston upon Hull* compared to individual decision-making discretion in *Moreton*).

Other examples of the limits of discretion in relation to establishing boundaries can be seen in various nature conservation cases.[47]

Although discretion still plays a central role in domestic legislation, two important trends must be pointed out at this stage. These are the increases in both the structuring of discretion and in the role played by central government. In the past, it has been normal for environmental legislation to grant regulatory agencies and bodies a large amount of discretion, often in the form of a subjective power, which is then controlled by the courts. More recently, the agencies have themselves structured the exercise of their discretion, through such things as internal agency guidelines and strategies, and have thus made the whole system more formalized (an example is the adoption by the Environment Agency of a formal policy on prosecution and other enforcement action). This gives the courts a greater potential role in environmental decisions. But the effect is arguably limited by the other trend, which is that ever-greater powers are being given to central government to dictate the sorts of considerations that must be taken into account in any exercise of a discretion. This process is seen very clearly in the Environment Act 1995. As a specific example, s. 39 imposes a requirement that the Environment Agency take into account the likely costs and benefits before making decisions; more generally, the whole way in which the Agency operates is effectively decided by guidance and directions issued by central government.

These features of environmental legislation help to explain some of the essential characteristics of the 'British approach' to environmental protection, such as flexibility and pragmatism. The width of the discretions given also militates against uniformity in either the definition or the application of the law.

Environmental laws in practice

As much of the above discussion illustrates, the reading of environmental statutes may provide us with a source of environmental law, but it does not necessarily represent how such laws work in the real world. One of the key characteristics of environmental law is that it is—or rather, should be—law in action, rather than law for lawyers. It involves the solving of practical problems, so everything that is likely to have an impact on the solution of a problem should be understood, including tertiary rules such as guidance and evidence of practice. The sources of environmental law are forward-looking, in the sense that they often provide frameworks for future action.[48] Thus, it is often desirable to know what the law is going to be as well as what it is. It may also be argued that the sources of law should include the actual practice of agencies with responsibilities in the environmental field; an argument that is at its strongest when dealing with enforcement. This makes it desirable that as much as possible about the practice and policy actually relied upon by decision makers is published officially, an aim that is still not yet met in practice.

Thus there is often a gap between published law and policy, and what actually happens in the real world. This gap illustrates that making environmental law is not the end of the process. The manner in which laws are transformed from the legislative page into effective action depends upon how they are implemented and enforced. Inadequate implementation leads to

---

47 *R v. Secretary of State for the Environment, ex parte RSPB* [1997] QB 206 and further Case 19.1.

48 For example, the structured implementation of the IPPC Directive, see Chapter 14.

regulatory failure. There are many factors that may influence how laws are implemented: legislation may be too vague or complex to be put into practice, or it may be unrealistic in terms of timescale for compliance or the requirements that it imposes on the regulated. Even in cases in which legislation is clear, simple, and not excessively onerous, there is no guarantee that the rules or standards will be imposed in practice. Administrative arrangements may mean that different regulatory bodies find it difficult to coordinate and cooperate on implementation, or may adopt different approaches on overlapping issues. Financial or resource constraints may mean that there are not enough suitably qualified regulators to issue licences, or to supervise regulated activities. Scientific limitations may mean that it is difficult to monitor some emissions accurately, or there may be alternative measurement methods that produce inconsistent results.

The inadequate implementation of environmental regulation can be contrasted with another aspect of the gap between sources of law and effective environmental regulation— namely, the proper enforcement of those laws. While there may be an overlap in these issues—for example, the lack of sufficient regulators—the enforcement of environmental law is more influenced by the exercise of discretion by regulators in taking a cooperative stance with those who are in breach. There are a variety of reasons why such an approach is adopted and these are covered more fully in Chapter 9.

Gradualism and the reliance on scientific evidence

Environmental law in practice has to be interpreted within a very practical context. Gradualism and the role of scientific evidence are two key components of that context. Historically, this has been explained as:

The philosophy of gradualism is that pollution controls should be strengthened gradually as economic circumstances, the goodwill of producers and scientific abilities allow. This links very strongly with the related idea that decisions should be taken on the basis of a reliable scientific base, although it should be recognised that science does not necessarily produce facts in the environmental sphere, but estimates of risks or probabilities. There is accordingly always a political factor involved in whether to accept a risk or not.[49]

One major effect of these two ideas has been that environmental controls have tended to be reactive, rather than anticipatory. They have rarely been concerned with laying down a framework in advance, leading to the fragmentation of the system and to its lack of uniformity. A more specific effect is that time is normally given for changes to be made in order to give industry time to adjust capital programmes and work methods.[50] As mentioned above, the delayed implementation of many environmental statutes also reflects this gradualistic approach. At the EC level, this approach is also reflected in the timescale allowed for the implementation of Directives, which is normally at least two years and is often five years. A final example is that the British have frequently rejected the use of 'technology-forcing' rules. These represent the setting of a rule that is stricter than currently achievable, although with a timescale for its achievement. The theory is that producers will thus be forced to adapt their current technology to meet the requirements. This concept is much used in the USA, but, in the UK, the potential cost to industry and benchmarking against best practice at national or international level is more frequently used to argue for a gradual change.[51]

49 Department of the Environment (1975) *Environmental Standards: The UK Practice*, Pollution Paper No. 11, HMSO.

50 This is best seen in the use of process standards such as Best Practicable Means (BPM) and the practicability of the upgrading of existing processes in the IPPC system—see p. 482.

51 See D. Vogel (2003) *National Styles of Business Regulation*, Washington, DC: Beard Books, p. 76.

The importance of context

In establishing environmental controls, importance is nearly always attached to economic and other factors. This flexibility is evidenced by the:

tendency in setting standards…to use scientific principles and all relevant and reliable evidence, then to try and progressively reduce emissions in a way that is consistent with economic and technological feasibility and with what at any one time is thought to be an acceptable ultimate objective.[52]

It is difficult to separate the reasons for this policy from its effects. One primary reason undoubtedly relates to the definition of pollution and the objectives of environmental controls.[53]

Pollution has been defined as a relative concept, in the sense that there is no absolute rule about what amounts to pollution. The same applies to other forms of environmental change, such as urban or agricultural development. It is not possible to eradicate pollution; it is possible only to reduce it. It follows that, at some stage, a choice has to be made about what is, and what is not, permissible. This is ultimately a political question and involves a balancing of various factors. There are, however, two possible objectives of pollution control: one is to aim to reduce pollution to 'acceptable' levels; the other is to aim to reduce pollution as far as possible. In the UK, the first approach is implicitly adopted in relation to most substances. This explains the inevitability of a political balancing process and also the preference for variable environmental quality standards. The second approach tends to lead to a reduction in discretion and to greater reliance on uniform standards, because if one producer can reduce to a particular level, others should be able to do so as well.

Taking a contextual approach means that there is always going to be a trade-off between environmental protection and other factors, such as cost. This is fundamental to most UK environmental controls. For example, the use of BAT within the IPPC Directive (2008/1/EC) is balanced by the idea of 'proportionality', which means that costs to the operator are balanced against the benefits to the environment when determining what process should be adopted.

This philosophy of balancing environmental protection with material welfare is apparent in most areas of the law. It explains the wide discretions given to decision makers, the emphasis on decisions being taken by reference to local factors, and the practice of defining some concepts after consultation with the industry involved. The emphasis on balance also explains such fundamental features of UK law as the preference for flexible environmental standards rather than uniform ones, and the flexible and cooperative enforcement strategies that are employed by regulatory agencies.

Case law

In the UK, most of the formal sources of environmental law are statutory. Compared with subjects such as contract or tort, there is very little judge-made law and most of what there is consists of the interpretation of statutory provisions. Having said that, case law—that is, the decisions made by judges in the courts—comprises a growing source of law. On a very general level, substantive environmental cases come before the courts in three main ways.

1. If there is a dispute about a statutory definition in primary or secondary legislation, a court can be asked to interpret the statutory phrase. In these cases, the court's interpretation of the definition becomes the law.[54]

---

52 Department of the Environment (1975).

53 See p. 12.

54 In this context, it is also important to note the role and influence of the ECJ, which is discussed further in Chapter 7.

2. There are common law disputes that have an environmental flavour. These include actions in nuisance, negligence, and trespass (see Chapter 11). In these cases, the courts are developing principles that have a long history in order to address modern environmental disputes.

3. Because most of the sources of environmental law are statutory, cases arise when the powers granted to government and regulatory agencies are used unlawfully or statutory procedures ignored and the courts are asked to judicially review the exercise of the power (see Chapter 10).

In addition to the domestic cases, ECJ decisions exert an increasing influence over the interpretation of domestic law. Theoretically, this was always the case, because domestic courts are bound not only to accept the authority of the ECJ on the interpretation of European law,[55] but also to ensure that the objectives of Directives are to be achieved.[56] In practice, however, the courts have struggled to move away from a discretionary-based approach to the implementation of European law.

Administrative appeals and decision making

In addition to judicial decisions, there is a range of quasi-judicial decisions that can provide a source of law in its widest sense—that is, in the same way that tertiary rules form a source of law. In a subject that is heavily dominated by policy, it is clear that the relevant Secretary of State, in his role as ultimate arbiter on questions of policy in the system of administrative appeals, can set precedents in terms of the manner in which central rules or guidance are to be interpreted, both generally and on a case-by-case basis. Although such administrative decisions are not binding upon other decision makers, they can effectively dictate the decision-making processes of the regulatory agencies to whom such powers have been devolved. An example of this can be found in the way in which decisions in planning appeals have been used to reinforce changing planning policies over the last twenty years.[57]

The system of environmental appeals addresses questions of law,[58] fact,[59] policy,[60] scientific and technical issues,[61] or any combination of these. In this way, such appeals are concerned with the substantive—as opposed to procedural—'rights and wrongs' of environmental decision making, with all of the consequential impact that this has on public participation, the provision of adequate and objective evidence, and the clarity and transparency of the decision itself.

In many ways, the 'battleground' of environmental decision making lies within the context of the administrative appeals system. Although the courts have supervisory powers under the judicial review process, this is not concerned with the substantive decision, but with the manner in which the decision was made. One of the main problems with this approach is that there can be a tendency for administrative appeals to be viewed by the public as being more concerned with going through the correct procedures than with debating and adjudicating on the substantive issues at hand, because the appeals process is concerned primarily with applying central policy within an individual set of facts, rather than with debating whether that policy is, in itself, acceptable.[62]

55 European Communities Act 1972, ss. 2(4) and 3(1).

56 See Art. 10 EC and the doctrine of useful effect—see Chapter 7.

57 See p. 420.

58 For example, whether or not something is 'development' within the meaning of the Town and Country Planning Act 1990.

59 For example, whether a planning use was commenced more than ten years ago.

60 For example, whether a particular development should be situated outside a town centre in contravention of central government guidance.

61 For example, whether a particular process option represents BAT.

62 For example, whether an incinerator is acceptable at a particular location, rather than whether we should be using waste minimization techniques to ensure that there is no need for further incinerators.

CHAPTER SUMMARY

1 International law generally consists of agreements between countries on the approach to be taken in relation to international environmental problems. By nature, it is broad in application and general in terms of the obligations imposed.

2 EC law is a very significant source of environmental law. Many areas of UK environmental law have their origins in EC law, particularly in relation to environmental quality and emission standards. Although EC regulations do not need transposing into national law, there is a requirement to transpose and implement the obligations in the case of Directives.

3 Different sources of law are interrelated to one another through the 'layering' of different obligations. Thus, international obligations may be transposed through European and/or domestic legislation. The relationship is not only 'top-down', because the EC plays an important part in negotiating international agreements on behalf of its member States and the UK plays an important part in setting the agenda on certain environmental issues in the EC.

4 Modern environmental law is characterized by the development of a mixed regulation approach, whereby a range of different instruments are used to address environmental problems, including economic instruments such as taxes, greater access to environmental information, public participation, and voluntary agreements.

5 Primary legislation in UK environmental law is dominated by broad framework Acts that need fleshing out in detailed secondary legislation, and in technical and policy guidance.

6 UK environmental law can be characterized as having many tiers, delayed commencement, and wide discretionary definitions, which promotes flexibility and pragmatism.

7 Although rules and decision making may be clear, there is no guarantee that these standards are imposed in practice. There is a gap between the sources of law and what happens in the real world. This gap is caused by inadequacies in implementation and enforcement.

8 Compared to other subjects such as contract or tort, environmental law has relatively little judge-made law. What there is consists mostly of statutory interpretation of environmental legislation.

9 Historically, the UK judiciary has been conservative in its interpretation of environmental statutes, preferring to take a non-interventionist approach to largely discretionary decisions made by regulatory bodies. In recent years, the decisions of the European Court of Justice and a greater understanding of the purposive approach of European law has seen a shift in emphasis.

10 Decisions that are determined by regulators and on administrative appeal can take into account a range of factors, including issues of fact, law, and policy. The UK judicial tradition is that the courts should not intervene in policy decisions unless it is so extreme as to be irrational or if procedural injustices have occurred.

QUESTIONS

1 Look at the following. Try to classify each document as a 'source of law'. What, if any, relationship does each of these documents have with each other? What does this tell you about the 'layering' of environmental law?

   a Article 17 of the Kyoto Protocol (available online at **unfccc.int/resource/docs/convkp/kpeng.html**).

   b EC Directive 2003/87/EC on greenhouse gas emissions trading (available online at **europa.eu.int/comm/environment/climat/emission/implementation_en.htm**).

   c The Greenhouse Gas Emissions Trading Scheme Regulations 2005, SI 2005/925 (available online at **www.opsi.gov.uk/si/si2005/20050925.htm**).

d The Approved Phase II National Allocation Plan 2008–12 (available online at **www.defra.gov.uk/ environment/climatechange/trading/eu/phase2/pdf/nap-phase2.pdf**).

e DEFRA, *Climate Change: The UK Programme 2006*, ch. 4, paras 29–38 (available online at **www. defra.gov.uk/environment/climatechange/uk/ukccp/index.htm**).

2 What factors affect the level from which environmental law originates? What justifications are there for legislating at the international, European, and national levels?

3 Compare and contrast the decisions in *Wychavon District Council v. Secretary of State for the Environment* [1994] Env LR 239 and *Berkeley v. Secretary of State for the Environment* [2001] Env LR 16. How do these two judgments show how the judiciary has changed its attitude to the interpretation of European environmental legislation?

FURTHER READING

Much of the specific reading on the different sources of law will be found at the end of the relevant chapters dealing with European law, international law, and the regulation of environmental protection. For a general introduction and a historical account of different sources of law, have a look at D. Robinson (1998) 'Regulatory evolution in pollution control' in T. Jewell and J. Steele (eds) *Law in Environmental Decision Making*, Oxford: Clarendon Press. This gives a clear picture of the development of new types of law. The relationship between EC and UK sources of law is explored in ch. 3 of C. Hilson (2000) *Regulating Pollution: A UK and EC Perspective*, Oxford: Hart Publishing. It provides a good overview of the justifications for legislating at different levels both generally, in federal/devolved countries, and more particularly, in the UK and EC. A. Gouldson and J. Murphy (1998) *Regulatory Realities*, London: Earthscan, provides an interesting comparative study of the implementation of industrial environmental regulation. In particular, ch. 1 examines the role of implementation and some of the barriers that prevent perfect implementation.

Two articles that give some historical perspective on the way in which English courts used to approach questions of European law, particularly in relation to environmental assessment, are J. Alder, 'Environmental impact assessment: the inadequacies of English Law' (1993) 5 JEL 203 and A. Ward 'The right to an effective remedy in European Community law and environmental protection: a case study of United Kingdom judicial decisions concerning the Environmental Assessment Directive' (1993) 5 JEL 221. For a more up-to-date perspective, have a look at W. Upton, 'The EIA process and the directly enforceable rights of citizens' (2001) 13 JEL 98. More detailed reading on EIA can also be found at the end of Chapters 7 and 13.

5 The administration of environmental law and policy

 Overview

This chapter covers those institutions that are involved in the administration of environmental law and policy. As such, it links in with many other different chapters in this book. Most obviously, it links in with the chapters in Part III that deal with specific sectoral topics, in the sense that it explains who is responsible for what in terms of the day-to-day running of different regulatory systems. We will concentrate almost exclusively on UK structures and institutions, because European and international administrative arrangements are considered elsewhere. In addition, the position and powers of local authorities are considered in detail in the Online Resource Centre. An underlying theme of this chapter is the way in which administrative structures are used to encourage the integration of environmental law and policy both internally—for example, through the creation of the Environment Agency as a single regulatory agency—and externally—for example, through various methods of scrutinizing environmental policy across government departments.

At the end of this chapter, you should be able to:

✔ identify and understand the role of the main regulatory bodies involved in environmental protection in the UK;

✔ understand the general functions of these bodies;

✔ identify and understand some of the general statutory aims and objectives of these bodies;

✔ appreciate the role played by a range of different bodies (governmental, non-governmental, and judicial) in the lawmaking process;

✔ appreciate the main similarities and differences in the institutional structures in the devolved administrations.

Introduction

The administration of environmental law and policy is carried out by a diversity of bodies. By 'administration', we mean responsibility for making, implementing, and enforcing environmental law and policy. This includes central government departments, regulatory agencies such as the Environment Agency, and a range of quasi-governmental bodies. Their functions range from rule and policymaking, through implementation, by way of decision making, to enforcement and the imposition of sanctions. In addition, there are many non-government organizations (NGOs) that play a role in environmental administration in various ways such as influencing policy through direct and indirect means, such as lobbying or public campaigns to raise issues. Finally, the courts have a partial role to play in the enforcement of environmental law and also in supervising the actions of other administrative bodies.

Any attempt to identify who does what in environmental law and policy runs into the same definitional problems that we faced in Chapter 1. The large number of bodies with responsibilities, duties, and powers in relation to the protection of the environment reflects some of the difficulties in drawing up boundaries for a subject that could cover every aspect of political, social, economic, and legal life. Coordinating diverse policy areas such as transport, energy, agriculture, and trade and industry, which all have direct links to environmental protection, presents very real difficulties. There is an increasing understanding that the decisions and actions of many bodies that do not necessarily have any direct interest in the environment can have an indirect environmental consequence, and one distinctive feature of environmental problems is their interdependence. Governments have to address ideas and concerns that do not necessarily fit neatly into nicely delineated administrative structures. Even within areas with a clear link to the environment, there has been a tendency to consider pollution as a series of discrete problems requiring fragmented responses, typically involving separate regulatory systems with different administrative arrangements.

In recent years, the integration of environmental law and policy has been offered as a solution to this problem. 'Integration' is used here in two senses[1]—namely, to reflect external and internal changes. External integration addresses the problem of coordination across different departments by promoting the consideration of environmental issues across all policy areas.[2] Internal integration addresses the problem of fragmentation among diverse regulatory agencies by drawing together regulatory responsibilities for different environmental emissions and impacts within one single authority and/or within one single permit.[3]

Scotland, Northern Ireland, Wales, and the regions

Because there are separate legal systems in Scotland and Northern Ireland, there have always been slightly different administrative and regulatory arrangements in these two countries. These differences, in so far as the system of environmental regulation is concerned, are more structural and procedural than substantive (reflecting the fact that many new laws are the result of EC or international influences, which apply to the UK as a whole), although some minor differences do occur. These differences are, however, quite often rarely more than cosmetic, for a number of reasons.

- **The devolution of primary lawmaking powers is not comprehensive.**
  While the Scottish and Northern Ireland assemblies have the powers to pass primary legislation in certain areas including the environment,[4] Wales has only the power to pass secondary legislation.

- **The power to pass any new environmental legislation is constrained by the need to comply with EC law or international obligations.**[5]
  Because the UK is a member State of the EC, it has the responsibility to ensure that there is overall compliance with any obligations imposed in each country. Historically, this has led to problems of non-implementation and non-transposition of Directives—particularly in relation to Northern Ireland.[6] There are powers available to UK authorities in cases in which there has been any failure to give effect to EC law in each country, whether that

---

1 'Integration' can be used in other ways: see J. Steele and T. Jewell (1998) 'Law in environmental decision making' in T. Jewell and J. Steele (eds) *Law in Environmental Decision Making*, Oxford: Clarendon Press, p. 3.

2 The integration of environmental issues at the European level is discussed in A. Weale and A. Williams (1992) 1(4) Environmental Politics 45.

3 See further Chapters 14 on Environmental Permitting and 13 on environmental impact assessment (EIA).

4 For example, the Scotland Act 1998, ss. 28–30.

5 Ibid., s. 29.

6 See S. Turner (2006) 18(1) JEL 55 and (2006) 18(2) JEL 245.

is the country passing incompatible legislation or that which is failing to transpose EC measures.[7]

- **Because the obligations fall upon the UK as a whole, they are negotiated on behalf of the UK and none of the devolved assemblies has a formal say in the formation of those laws or policies.[8]**
  Thus the uniformity of obligations as between different countries of the UK will continue. It should be noted, however, that EC law and policy is becoming more sensitive to regional environmental differences, which could mean that, in future, the nature of the obligations may vary in emphasis.

- **Some areas—notably, tax-raising powers—do not fall within the remit of national governments.[9]**
  Other areas, including transport, energy, and consumer protection, have been transferred to a greater or lesser extent.

In the light of the above restrictions, there is little opportunity to create major differences in environmental law in each country. That is not to say, however, that different styles of environmental regulation are not adopted. In particular, there are some opportunities, within the constraints mentioned above, to construct and scrutinize environmental legislation from the very different cultural perspectives of each country. There is also scope to alter the terms of secondary legislation to take into account national concerns. For example, such things as statutory exemptions from pollution control licensing vary from country to country (see Box 5.1 below). Over time, the aggregation of these minor differences could result in distinct bodies of law with national characteristics.

BOX 5.1 **Scotland and waste exemptions**

A good example of the impact that regionalized and local issues can have on post-devolution law-making can be seen in the case of the outcry over the land spreading of waste in the small village of Blairingone in Kinrosshire, Scotland, in 1997. The practice of spreading certain wastes on agricultural land has been exempt from waste management controls in cases in which the spreading is for the purpose of 'agricultural benefit', land reclamation, and construction (see Case 14.2).

In Blairingone, sewage, blood, and guts from abattoirs were spread on fields for a number of years, despite protests from local communities who experienced certain health problems, including increased incidences of throat infections and blisters among young children. A local action group petitioned the Scottish Parliament—a procedure that enables the public to petition elected representatives over matters of public concern. The Scottish Parliament is the only assembly in the UK with such a procedure. Following a highly critical public report on the matter, the Parliament introduced Regulations that established a system of registration for previously exempt spreading operations, coupled with increased monitoring and enforcement powers.[10]

By contrast, in England and Wales, the land spreading of industrial wastes was heavily criticized by the Royal Commission on Environmental Pollution (RCEP) in 1996.[11] Several years after Scotland took action, the controls over the exempt waste activities have been tightened in England

---

7 Scotland Act 1998, s. 35.
8 G. Little (2000) 12 JEL 155, 171.
9 Ibid., 158–65.
10 Waste Management Licensing (Amendment)(Scotland) Regulations 2003, SSI 2003/171.
11 RCEP Nineteenth Report (1996) *Sustainable Use of Soil*, Cm 3165.

and Wales so as to address the problems of excessive spreading of waste materials in the name of agricultural improvement or ecological benefit.[12]

Each country in the UK has its own priorities and problems in relation to environmental issues. For example, nature conservation sites cover a greater proportion of land in Scotland than they do in England and Wales, and different policy approaches to the management of such sites are already being pursued. In addition, rural issues, such as the environmental impact of agriculture and forestry, will have a greater significance in Scotland than, for example, pressure to release green-belt land for housing or economic development.

This variation of national legislation—albeit at the margins—raises questions of uniformity and consistency in the application and implementation of national and international obligations in the UK. The dangers of inconsistency of application can be seen in the debate over the separation of nature conservation responsibilities under the Environmental Protection Act (EPA) 1990 (see p. 687). It is not inconceivable that an increase in distinct national approaches to other environmental issues could give rise to inequalities across the UK (although it could be argued that these existed under arrangements within which policy and rule making were more centralized).

The changes in lawmaking powers are part of a wider attempt to decentralize certain aspects of government and can be viewed in tandem with other attempts to regionalize facets of environmental policymaking. The Regional Development Agencies Act 1998 created English regional development agencies to match similar agencies in Scotland (Scottish Enterprise) and Wales (the Welsh Development Agency). While these bodies are not directly concerned with environmental protection policies, they have a remit to consider economic and social issues in a regional setting, which will have inevitable consequences for the pursuit of sustainable development. More recently, the role of regional planning has been elevated by the emergence of regional spatial strategies (RSSs) under Pt I of the Planning and Compulsory Purchase Act 2004 (see p. 388).

The substantive and procedural differences are such that trying to accommodate coverage of each jurisdiction in a book of this type is impossible. There are some brief details of the administrative arrangements below, but the majority of this book will cover the law and administration of environmental protection in England.

The 'British' style of administration—centralization and decentralization

A simple description of the various bodies with responsibility for administering environmental law would not necessarily give any indication as to *how* the law is administered. The style of administration is a key element of the 'British' approach to environmental protection (see p. 237). In structural terms, the most significant characteristic is decentralization.

The structure of the administration of environmental law in the UK is largely decentralized in three main ways:

- through the creation of a diverse range of administrative bodies;

- through significant use of delegation to those bodies;

- through geographical decentralization to local and regional bodies.

12 The whole issue of the nature of 'exempt waste activities' is under detailed consideration as a consequence of the introduction of the system of environmental permitting, see further Ch.14.

Although the creation of the Environment Agency unified a variety of pollution control functions, the UK still has a large number of autonomous, or semi-autonomous, environmental agencies. These and other Non-Departmental Public Bodies (NDPB) set up by central government[13] and local authorities have wide-ranging environmental protection powers in relation to such things as air pollution, contaminated land, noise control, town and country planning, and environmental health.

Traditionally, there has also been decentralization within central government. For many years, the nominal responsibility for environmental policy has been located with the Department of the Environment (and its variants). This has obscured the fact that many decisions and policies that have important environmental effects have been made by other departments, including the Department of Trade and Industry,[14] and the Department for Transport.[15] At various times, some of these areas have been considered within the same department,[16] but, generally, the responsibilities for environmental matters have been spread widely.

This diversity has been compounded by the tendency to have separate bodies in Wales and Scotland, which has been increased with the re-emphasis of regional policymaking and devolution. It is also important to bear in mind the role of the Treasury as the decision maker in terms of budgets for many of the environmental agencies. Various attempts have been made to integrate environmental considerations into all government departments through initiatives such as the introduction of the Environmental Audit Committee (see p. 106). Even within single government departments that deal with environmental matters, decision making is often delegated. For example, most environmental appeals—nominally dealt with by the relevant Secretary of State—are normally dealt with by the Planning Inspectorate.

Historically, this decentralization of power resulted in a rather incoherent environmental policy, with very little uniformity across the country. Even such a central function as the monitoring of the environment was carried out in an uncoordinated way, but, over the last thirty years, there has been an increasing trend towards coherence through the creation of centralized bodies. For example, the regulation of water pollution was organized on a regional basis until 1989, when the National Rivers Authority (NRA) was established as a national body covering England and Wales. Her Majesty's Inspectorate of Pollution (HMIP) was created in 1987 to draw together a number of inspectorates that were, at that time, operating separately within the Department of the Environment and the Health and Safety Executive. Both of these institutional changes clearly fostered uniformity in decision making. The Environment Act 1995 created the Environment Agency for England and Wales and the Scottish Environment Protection Agency for Scotland, thus continuing the process of producing a more coherent and uniform institutional structure.

Decisions are also commonly made locally. Local authorities have wide powers of decision making in relation to planning decisions, for example, while many of the inspectorates and other agencies operate on a regional basis, granting some discretion to local decision makers. There is a philosophy underpinning this, of course: the UK approach to environmental regulation is geared pragmatically towards the protection of the receiving environment, so it is sensible that decisions are taken by people or bodies with a knowledge of local conditions, whether environmental, social, or economic.

Although the decentralization of administrative bodies is a key characteristic, a further important change has been the *centralization* of certain policy decisions. This has been most marked in relation to matters that involve a conflict between central and local government.

---

13 Including the Health and Safety Executive and Natural England.

14 Now the Department of Business Enterprise and Regulatory Reform, e.g., on energy projects such as power stations and transmission lines under the Energy Act 2004.

15 For example, on emissions from vehicles and the routes of new roads under the Transport Act 2000.

16 For example, in the late 1990s under the Department of the Environment, Transport and the Regions (DETR).

For example, in the town and country planning system, increased intervention in local decisions by central government was the major issue of the 1980s. It was manifested mainly through hard-hitting and directory circulars, which were applied on appeal so as to alter the policy context of most planning decisions, although there were also changes to the law and in institutional structure designed to reduce local control, through such creations as urban development corporations.

Centralization is also a reality in relation to pollution control. For example, local authorities have lost a significant amount of discretion in relation to air pollution, in addition to a reduction of the numbers of installations controlled as a result of the implementation of the pollution prevention and control (PPC) system, while the Environment Agency has taken over the waste regulation functions previously carried out by local authorities. Even in an area in which local authorities have been given new powers—such as in the regulation of historic contamination under Pt 2A of EPA 1990—they are obliged to act in accordance with central guidance or are subject to technical advice from the Environment Agency.

Centralization may also be seen at work in the control of public spending. Local authorities have been severely limited for many years in their ability to make capital expenditure decisions. For bodies such as the nature conservation bodies that rely almost entirely on government grant, the position is even clearer.

Finally, there is a very significant element of centralization involved in the relationship between the UK and the EC. Not only is EC decision making essentially secret, but also there is little formal input by local or regional bodies in the UK. The crucial point, however, is that EC law is binding on member States. The requirement to conform with it, coupled with the policy goal of harmonization throughout the EC, means that power can be taken away from local and non-governmental bodies, and given instead to central bodies.[17]

Central government

The main policy and rule-making powers in environmental matters lie with central government. Table 5.1 sets out the main central government departments and their areas of responsibility.

Central government plays a part in environmental matters in many ways. Historically, the responsibility for many important environmental functions, such as pollution control and planning, lay with one major department. There has been a Department of the Environment since 1970, although, prior to that, other departments, such as that for Housing and Local Government, had dealt with relevant areas such as town and country planning. Since 1970, the responsibility for the environment has been shared with a number of additional responsibilities, which have included policy areas such as local government and transport. Currently, the Department of the Environment, Food and Rural Affairs (DEFRA) is responsible for many environmental policy areas. As the name suggests, it is also responsible for food safety, fisheries, and rural affairs (such as agricultural policy). There are, however, some substantial environmental policy areas that fall outside DEFRA's remit: perhaps most significantly, the Department of Communities and Local Government has responsibility for all town and country planning law and policy, including environmental assessment.

As noted above, one of the characteristics of central government is the fragmentation of responsibilities that have environmental implications across a number of departments. Government departments, such as the Departments of Business Enterprise and Regulatory Reform, Transport, and the Treasury, all have key responsibilities for activities and issues that have environmental implications, from the building of new power stations, to that of new

17 In this context, the principle of subsidiarity has a centralizing nature when circumstances dictate that it is needed: see J. Golub (1996) Political Studies 686.

roads, airports, and other major infrastructure projects. Other departments have responsibilities for residual matters. For example, the Home Office is responsible for neighbourhood nuisances and licensing, and the Foreign and Commonwealth Office plays an important role in the negotiation of environmental treaties. All of these departments exercise enormous influence in their own fields. In some areas, coordination is facilitated through joint departmental responsibility, with a 'lead department' being responsible for legislation and issuing policy.[18] As discussed above, the Executive bodies in Scotland, Wales, and Northern Ireland exercise an increasing control within their own geographical areas.

Table 5.1 Central government—administrative responsibilities for environmental protection

Government department	Main areas of responsibility for environmental matters	Other areas of responsibility

Department of Environment, Food and Rural Affairs (DEFRA)	• Access to environmental information
	• Agriculture
	• Climate Change Programme
	• Contaminated land
	• Forestry
	• Landscape protection (including national parks)
	• Nature conservation
	• Noise
	• Pollution control:
	  – air quality and pollution;
	  – water quality and pollution:
	  – water supply;
	  – water resources;
	  – drinking water;
	  – sewerage;
	  – coastal and marine environment;
	  – integrated PPC;
	  – waste management.
	• Radioactivity:
	  – licensing;
	  – radioactive waste management.
	• Sustainable development
		• Animal health and welfare
		• Farming
		• Fisheries policy
		• Food and drink
		• Horticulture (plants and seeds including genetically modified—or GM—crops)
		• Rural affairs (including hunting)
		• Zoos

Department of Communities and Local Government (DCLG)	• Town and country planning • Environmental assessment	• Devolution • Housing • Local government and the regions • Regeneration • Urban policy

18 An example is producer responsibility, which is coordinated jointly by DEFRA and BERR.

TABLE 5.1 (Continued)

Government department	Main areas of responsibility for environmental matters	Other areas of responsibility

Department for Business, Enterprise and Regulatory Reform (BERR)	• Waste management:
	  – producer responsibility:
	  – packaging waste;
	  – waste electrical and electronic equipment;
	  – restriction on hazardous substances;
	  – end-of-life vehicles;
	  – batteries;
	  – waste tyres.
	• Energy production and transmission, including renewable energy
		• Company law (including corporate social responsibility)
		• Competition (including world trade)
		• Consumer protection policy (including product labelling)
		• Oil and gas industries

Department for Transport (DfT)	• Transport, including infrastructure projects such as road building, new airports, and new ports	• Local transport (including buses, taxis, and cycle provision) • Motor vehicles (including emissions and other product standards) • Railways • Roads (including road safety and traffic management) • Vehicles
Treasury	• Environmental taxes, such as the landfill tax, Climate Change Levy, and Aggregates Levy • Provides central funding for certain environmental regulators	• Overseas debt relief

This fragmentation of responsibilities has significant consequences in terms of the potential for integrated solutions across different departmental areas. For example, an integrated transport policy will have implications for localized air quality, climate change (road traffic is a significant source of greenhouse gases), planning policy (in terms of areas for new development, traffic generation, and demand), nature conservation, public health, and resource depletion.

This wide diversity of departments also raises difficult questions of coordination and how environmental considerations are taken into account in practice. For some departments, it is clear that there will be direct or indirect conflict between the main responsibility and the need to give weight to environmental considerations. In other circumstances, departments may not consider the environmental implications of new policies or decisions, because they may not be immediately obvious.

Accordingly, the idea of external integration promotes the incorporation of environmental considerations across all policy areas. This can be through legal means,[19] but, in the UK, a looser policy approach has been taken under what was initially called the 'Greening

19 For example, Art. 6 EC explicitly requires external integration—see further p. 189.

Government Initiative' (GGI). GGI was originally launched in 1990 when a Minister in each government department was made responsible for considering the environmental implications of its policies and programmes, and for the introduction of some form of wider environmental appraisal of policies.[20] In 2001, GGI was 'rebranded' as 'Sustainable Development in Government' (SDiG), reflecting the shift from considerations of environmental impacts to broader issues, such as economic and social impacts. SDiG is a collective name for a number of bodies and initiatives, but is represented at Cabinet level by the Sub-Committee on Energy and the Environment (EE). In addition, the House of Commons' Environmental Audit Select Committee acts as a 'watchdog' over central government departments and their attempts to broaden the base of environmental appraisal, in the same way as the Parliamentary Accounts Committee checks public spending. The Committee produces regular reports, covering such things as annual reviews of progress, the Budget, and the Climate Change Programme. The Audit Committee has drawn unfavourable comparisons between the relative unimportance of this initiative as compared with other cross-departmental policy measures.

BOX 5.2 'Sustainable Development in Government'

The integration of environmental considerations across different government departments presents a difficult challenge. Attempts to do so in England have raised the question of whether 'Sustainable Development in Government' (SDiG) is an effective method of external integration. The Environmental Audit Select Committee has been a strong critic of 'greening government' and has identified the government as being poor at providing adequate leadership on many cross-departmental environmental issues.[21] The complexity of external integration should not be underestimated, however, and cross-departmental initiatives at least provide some form of institutional structure that should enable environmental issues to be integrated into the wider policy arena over time. Perhaps most importantly, the Environmental Audit Committee is pursuing departments and policies that are not obviously environmental, but which have a clear environmental impact, while providing accountability and transparency for sustainable development in government as a whole.[22]

The Department of the Environment, Food, and Rural Affairs (DEFRA)

A significant proportion of control of environmental matters falls to the Department of the Environment, Food and Rural Affairs. As the name suggests, the department is also responsible for food policy and certain countryside issues. Control is mainly manifested at the level of policy, but, because environmental law is essentially about the taking of discretionary, political decisions, this means that DEFRA has an enormous impact, even if this is not always apparent from a bare statement of the law.

A number of important qualifications must, however, be made about the role of DEFRA. Firstly, it could be argued that DEFRA is not a particularly strong department within central government. The direct predecessor of DEFRA, the Department of the Environment, Transport and the Regions, had a much more significant portfolio of responsibilities, incorporating town and country planning, transport, and regional policy. The separation of these

---

20 HM Government (1990) *This Common Inheritance*, Cm. 1200.

21 House of Commons Environmental Audit Select Committee Sixth Report (1998–99) *The Greening Government Initiative*; see also A. Ross (2000) 12 JEL 175.

22 Ibid.

functions from environmental protection could hardly be argued to have been a progressive step.[23] Indeed, the incorporation of one of the weakest governmental departments, the Ministry of Agriculture, Fisheries and Food, into DEFRA has been argued to be a downgrading of the political significance of environmental responsibilities.[24] Even in relation to environmental matters, DEFRA is not necessarily strong. For example, as certain controversies have shown, other government departments often carry greater weight in interdepartmental disputes.[25]

Secondly, DEFRA has few operational powers relating to environmental protection and those that it has are often delegated to others. Thirdly, DEFRA has a very wide portfolio and is not concerned simply with environmental *protection*. Some of these areas—for example, the regulation of the economic and competition aspects of the water industry—not only take priority over environmental protection, but also are often in direct conflict with environmental aims.

BOX 5.3 How government works—air travel and the environment

The diffusion of responsibilities with environmental implications across different government departments can lead to a lack of coordination on important issues. In some cases, environmental policies can be overridden by the policy initiatives of other, arguably stronger, departments in related areas.

When the Department of Transport (DoT) was amalgamated with the Department of the Environment (DoE) in 1997, to form the Department of the Environment, Transport, and the Regions (DETR), it was taken as a sign of the importance of the integration of these two policy areas. The subsequent 'divorce' of these two departments in 2001 has seen an increasing divergence of views on such issues as the impact of future transport policies on agreed reduction targets for greenhouse gases.

This should not, however, be viewed as a simple row between two government departments. Following a recommendation from the Royal Commission on Environmental Pollution (RCEP), the 2003 Energy White Paper (produced by the Department of Trade and Industry) contained an aim to reduce greenhouse gas emissions by some 60 per cent by 2050.[26] This was to be achieved through a variety of mechanisms, but largely through reductions in greenhouse gas emissions across different industry sectors under pollution control regulation. The Department for Transport then published proposals to liberalize and expand provision for air travel. These proposals suggested that the aviation sector would increase greenhouse gas emissions by a factor of three during the same period.[27] In order to meet the general reduction target, the increase from aviation sources would mean that other industrial sectors would have to reduce emissions by more than 50 per cent.

The Department for Transport's aviation policy was heavily criticized by a number of independent environmental bodies, including RCEP,[28] the Sustainable Development Commission,[29] and the

---

23 'Restructure in haste, repent at leisure' and 'Whitehall restructuring sidelines environment' (2001) ENDS Report 317, 2–4.

24 Environment, Food and Rural Affairs Select Committee Tenth Report (2001–02) *The Role of DEFRA*, paras 9–10.

25 See the debate on Air Transport and Box 5.3.

26 Department of Trade and Industry White Paper (2003) *Our Energy Future: Creating a Low Carbon Economy*.

27 Department for Transport (2004) *The Future of Air Transport*.

28 RCEP Twenty-Second Report (2000) *Energy: The Changing Climate*; RCEP Special Report (2002) *The Environmental Effects of Civil Aircraft in Flight*.

29 Sustainable Development Commission (2004) *Missed Opportunity: Summary Critique of the Air Transport White Paper*.

House of Commons Environmental Audit Committee,[30] on the grounds that it made it unlikely that the significant environmental policy aim of long-term greenhouse gas reduction would be achieved.

DEFRA exercises its powers largely through the role of the Secretary of State, who has very wide legislative and quasi-legislative powers that stem from the framework nature of the main environmental protection legislation and also from the need to update legislation in the light of EC requirements. Other very wide discretionary powers are also granted: for example, the decision to give the Environment Agency a specific or general 'direction' is virtually an unfettered discretion given to the Secretary of State. In relation to individual functions, they include directions that:

- require the exercise of any function in relation to environmental permits;[31]

- require the Agency to take specific enforcement action in relation to environmental permits;[32]

- require the Agency (among other things) to carry out surveys of waste arising in relation to the National Waste Strategy;[33]

- are made in the interests of national security or to mitigate the effects of a civil emergency.[34]

Section 40 of the Environment Act 1995 gives the Secretary of State a further general power to issue any directions of a specific or general character. This power is exercisable under the Secretary of State's discretion and represents a formidable tool to centralize certain aspects of the Agency's activities.

There are also very wide powers in relation to appeals against decisions made by the regulatory bodies. This is most obvious in the planning area, but an appeal to the Secretary of State is a common feature of many of the regulatory systems covered in this book. This reflects the political—that is, policy-based—nature of much of this area of law. For example, it is significant that the Planning Inspectorate has always been kept within the Department of Communities and Local Government (and its predecessors), which is responsible for planning policy, rather than being moved to the Ministry of Justice (and its predecessors), which is responsible for the tribunals and courts. This reflects the fact that the important feature of its decisions is that they are based on policy, rather than on any notion of judicial fairness, despite the increasing formality of environmental appeal procedures.

DEFRA may impose its policies in a number of ways. One is by changing the law (a feature of the UK administrative system is that the government is rarely defeated in Parliament); another is through exercising powers granted under the legislation. This may include the making of directions, the power to approve actions of regulatory bodies, the power to make appointments to the various regulatory bodies, or the power to hear appeals. Interference has been at its clearest in town planning, in relation to which there is the greatest opportunity to disagree over matters of policy. A third method is by the manipulation of available resources: DEFRA and the Treasury have complete responsibility for the budgets of

---

30 House of Commons Environmental Audit Committee Ninth Report (Session 2002–03) *Budget Report and Aviation*; House of Commons Environmental Audit Committee Third Report (Session 2003–04) *Pre-Budget Report: Aviation Follow-Up*.

31 See Environmental Permitting (England and Wales) Regulations 2007, SI 2007/3538, reg. 33.

32 See ibid., reg. 61.

33 EPA 1990, s. 44A.

34 Water Resources Act 1991, s. 207.

a number of the regulatory agencies.[35] One avenue for future development in this area is the way in which regulatory agencies are being encouraged to acquire some financial independence by charging for parts of their work. This theme has been developed strongly in the Environment Act 1995, with a range of revenue-raising measures.[36] Given the importance of independent regulatory agencies in environmental law, it is also significant that DEFRA is the channel through which parliamentary accountability of a number of these agencies, such as the Environment Agency and Natural England, is provided.

General environmental duties

There are further areas in which central government plays a part in environmental matters. There are bodies that are bound to take into account environmental considerations in relation to the exercise of their functions. This can apply to executive bodies,[37] government Ministers and departments, local authorities, regulators, and operational bodies, such as utility companies. For example, a number of pieces of legislation now include general requirements to take the environment into account, either through the pursuit of the general goal of sustainable development, or through more specific requirements to have regard to the desirability of conserving and enhancing such things as biodiversity or landscape.[38]

In the utilities sector, the Secretary of State is under an obligation to provide environmental guidance to regulators, with the aim of trying to ensure that, in fulfilling the primary statutory duties such as promoting competition and protecting consumers, utilities operators are also obliged to take into account the environmental costs of operations.[39] Although these general duties can be so vague as to be meaningless—other than in cases in which the duty has been completely ignored—they do provide certain formal requirements that can have a positive, longer-term effect upon the policy- and rule-making process. They also provide a benchmark against which policies, decisions, and performance can be measured.

Scrutiny of central government—the parliamentary select committees

Given the wide discretion to make law and policy that is given to central government departments, there is a need to have some accountability mechanisms for their day-to-day activities. Parliamentary select committees may be said to perform these functions. In the area of environmental law and policy, the select committee plays an important role in helping to inform the public debate outside Parliament, and therefore in increasing the accountability of, and accessibility to, the policy and rule makers in DEFRA and elsewhere (particularly in otherwise unaccountable regulatory agencies, such as the Environment Agency). In the House of Lords, the European Communities Sub-committee has been especially important in analysing the potential impact of proposed EC legislation.

In the House of Commons, the select committees are organized so as to mirror government departments. Thus, there is a House of Commons Select Committee on the Environment, Food and Rural Affairs. This body has had a large impact on the direction of environmental policy in the recent past, arguably constituting the loudest parliamentary voice for a greater role for environmental regulation. The issues considered by the Environment Select Committee reflect the remit of the government department and therefore include areas

35 Most notably. the Environment Agency and Natural England.
36 See p. 120.
37 For example, the Welsh Assembly: see Government of Wales Act 2006, s. 79.
38 See further p. 117 and the Countryside and Rights of Way Act (CROWA) 2000, ss. 74 and 85.
39 See Utilities Act 2000, ss. 10 (gas) and 14 (electricity), and the Water Act 2003, s. 40.

outside the traditional boundaries of environmental protection (including such things as food safety and rural affairs).

The range of topics covered by the select committees includes most of the main areas of environmental policy and administration. Along with the evidence given to the committee, they make interesting reading and give a good introduction to many of the practical issues surrounding controversial topics. Most reports contain recommendations for changes in law, policy, and practice, and the government responds to each of these in a special report.[40] Because the select committee structure generally mirrors that of government departments, there are other select committees that have reported on environmental issues. Naturally, these vary according to the different departmental responsibilities, but, historically, the Office of the Deputy Prime Minister (ODPM), Trade and Industry,[41] and Transport Select Committees have all regularly considered important issues with environmental significance.

As mentioned above (see Box 5.3), the House of Commons Environmental Audit Committee, launched as part of GGI, has played an active role in scrutinizing various environmental issues. The primary responsibility of the Environmental Audit Committee is to oversee the implementation of the external integration of environmental policies. Thus it is concerned not so much with the performance of DEFRA, or associated legislation and policies, but with the manner in which environmental policies are taken into account across other government departments. Over time, there has been an increasing amount of overlap between the DEFRA Select Committee and the Environmental Audit Committee, with a number of reports being published on similar topics.[42]

There is little doubt that the reports of these inquiries—all of which have been unanimous on a cross-party basis—have an influence on government policy and legislation. The Committee is not, however, necessarily expert in any of the areas upon which it reports. It relies heavily on expert advisers and the witnesses who give evidence (normally representatives of interested parties such as DEFRA, the Environment Agency, NGOs, and relevant industry sectors). Accordingly, the Committee's views are shaped by what is a relatively select group of witnesses. This can have two consequences: first, there is little attempt to elicit wider views or public values that would promote greater public participation; secondly, some of the conclusions can be based on erroneous or incomplete information. Having said this, however, the Committee has acted as the 'ignition point' for many changes in environmental law, policy, and practice over the last twenty years.[43]

The Royal Commission on Environmental Pollution (RCEP)

The Royal Commission on Environmental Pollution (RCEP) is a rather rare beast: an independent-standing Royal Commission with its own secretariat. It was established in 1970 with a wide remit to advise government on '*matters concerning the pollution of the environment*'. It is a multidisciplinary body made up of individual experts from various fields who consider the legal, economic, technical, and social aspects of environmental issues. Beyond this very general framework, the Commission is not restricted in its choice of topics to study.

---

40 See, generally, **www.parliament.uk/parliamentary_committees/environment_food_and_rural_affairs.cfm**. Recent topics include: *The Work of the Role of DEFRA* (2002), the Future of Waste Management (2003), the Water Framework Directive (2003), the Environment Agency (2006), waste policy and the Landfill Directive and the implementation of the Environmental Liability Directive (2007).

41 See, e.g., ODPM Select Committee Fourth Report (Session 2003–04) *Planning, Competitiveness and Productivity* and DTI Select Committee First Report (Session 2001–01) *End-of-Life Vehicles Directive*.

42 For example, Environmental Audit Committee Fourth Report (Session 2002–03) *Waste: An Audit*; DEFRA Select Committee Ninth Report (Session 2002–03) *The Future of Waste Management*.

43 For example, the introduction of the controls over the clean-up of historically contaminated land in the Environment Act 1995 owes a lot to the Select Committee's inquiry and report—see p. 553.

The Commission takes a leading role in the development of environmental law and policy, by providing a forum for discussion on controversial or emerging issues. The RCEP process in producing reports is much more deliberative than that of the select committees. It can take up to two years to investigate a particular issue, and the Commission seeks a wide range of views through oral and written evidence, and by holding public meetings and site visits.

At the end of 2002, the Commission published its first special report. These special reports have had a much narrower focus than the general reports. As such, they are compiled over a shorter period and normally address a particular short-term need for policy advice and recommendation. For example, the First Special Report on Aviation was compiled quickly prior to the publication of the White Paper on Air Transport.[44]

The RCEP's reports have enormous authority in relation to the subject matter discussed and exert a significant influence on the direction of future policy, although by no means all of the Commission's recommendations are implemented. The Commission has been a particularly strong supporter of public participation in environmental decision making, including the widening of access to environmental information and the investigation of the public's perception of environmental risk. It has also been at the forefront of promoting a number of fundamental concepts in environmental law and policy, and can claim to have popularized such ideas as best practicable environmental option (BPEO) and integrated pollution control (IPC).

Table 5.2 Reports of the Royal Commission on Environmental Pollution

Number, title, and year of report	Subject matter covered
First Report (1971) Cmnd 4585	A 'scene-setting' report, looking at the nature of the challenges to the environment.
	Included a contemporary state-of-the-environment review, with priorities for future action to tackle pollution.
Second Report (1972) *Three Issues in Industrial Pollution*, Cmnd 4894	The 'three issues' were secrecy (which was to become a recurring theme), hazardous chemicals, and controls over industrial waste disposal. (The latter predated the introduction of the first controls over waste disposal in the Deposit of Poisonous Waste Act 1972 and the Control of Pollution Act 1974.)
Fourth Report (1974) *Pollution Control: Progress and Problems*, Cmnd 5780	An overview of the substance and administrative structures of environmental law and policy in the UK.
	Along with the government's response in Pollution Paper No 4, represents a historical picture of many aspects of the 'British' approach to pollution control.
Fifth Report (1976) *Air Pollution Control: An Integrated Approach*, Cmnd 6371	Introduced the concept of best practicable environmental option (BPEO) as a means of integrating pollution controls.
Tenth Report (1984) *Tackling Pollution: Experience and Prospects*, Cmnd 9149	Published to mark the ten-year anniversary of the Fourth Report.
	Featured a wide-ranging review of environmental law and policy.
	Focused on the impact of European environmental law and policy.
	Further coverage of access to environmental information and BPEO.

44 See Box 5.3.

Table 5.2 (Continued)	
Number, title, and year of report	**Subject matter covered**
Eleventh Report (1985) *Managing Waste: The Duty of Care*, Cmnd. 9675	Damning critique of the problems involved in the waste chain, from the production of waste, to its final disposal. Introduced the concept of the duty of care now found in s. 34, EPA 1990.
Twelfth Report (1988) *Best Practicable Environmental Option*, Cm 310	Further development of the concept of BPEO first covered in the Fifth, Tenth, and Eleventh Reports. Influential in the setting up of the system of integrated pollution control (IPC) found in Pt I of EPA 1990.
Twenty-First Report (1998) *Setting Environmental Standards*, Cm 4053	Broad-ranging discussion of environmental standards and the role that values and the public, and its perception of risk, have to play in the setting of standards.
Twenty-Third Report (2002) *Environmental Planning*, Cm 5459	Discusses the role of town and country planning in environmental protection. Revisits the enhancement of public participation methods in decision making and policymaking. Discusses the idea of spatial strategies now found in Pt I of the Planning and Compulsory Purchase Act 2004.
Twenty-Sixth Report (2007) *The Urban Environment*, Cm 7009	Examines the environment within urban areas and the wider environmental impacts of towns and cities, and considers the relationship between the urban environment, and human health and well-being.

Other advisory bodies

In addition to the RCEP, central government has established a number of other non-departmental public bodies (NDPBs) that play an increasingly important role in the implementation of environmental law and policy. There are over fifty NDPBs listed on the pages of the DEFRA website, ranging from the Advisory Committee on Business and the Environment (ACBE), to the Pesticides Residue Committee and the Zoos Forum. They are non-statutory, in the sense that they are set up by government without explicit statutory authority. In most cases, they are 'sponsored' by a government department, which selects members, and provides staff and funding. These bodies provide assistance to the government on a wide range of technical matters, including expert advice on scientific matters[45] or other areas,[46] a forum for the exchange of views,[47] or a conduit for best practice.[48]

Regulatory agencies

The day-to-day implementation and enforcement of environmental law and policy lies in the hands of a variety of regulatory bodies. The main bodies and their duties are outlined in Table 5.3.

45 For example, the Air Quality Expert Group.
46 For example, the Advisory Committee on Packaging.
47 Referred to as a 'stakeholder group', e.g., the Hazardous Waste Forum.
48 For example, the Advisory Committee on Business and the Environment.

Table 5.3 Who does what in environmental law and policy?

England and Wales

Agency	Primary responsibilities	Key legislation	Other comments
Environment Agency	• Pollution control • Industrial regulation (PPC—Pt A installations) • Water resource management (abstraction licensing) • Waste management (including the National Waste Strategy) • Producer responsibility (Packaging waste, end-of-life vehicles, WEEE) • Historically contaminated land (special sites)	• Environment Act 1995 • Pollution, Prevention and Control Act 1999 • Water Resources Act 1991 • Environmental Protection Act 1990	Other general water-related functions include: the supervision and administration of flood defences, fisheries regulation, and navigation, harbour, and conservancy duties.
Natural England	• Nature conservation • Species and habitats protection • Protection of geological features • Landscape protection and rural affairs	• National Parks and Access to the Countryside Act 1949 • Countryside Act 1968 • Wildlife and Countryside Act 1981 • Conservation (Natural Habitats, etc.) Regulations 1994[49] • Countryside and Rights of Way Act 2000 • Natural Environment and Rural Communities Act 2006	Merger of English Nature and Countryside Agency, following the Haskins Review. Countryside Council for Wales carries out similar functions in Wales.
Water and sewerage undertakers	• Water supply • Sewers • Regulation of trade effluent discharges	• Water Resources Act 1991 • Water Industry Act 1991 • Water Act 2003	Private companies created subject to regulation on economic issues, water pricing, and competition from the Water Services Regulation Authority.
Local authorities	• Town and country planning • Air quality and management • Historically contaminated land (non-special sites) • Statutory nuisance • Noise control	• Town and Country Planning Act 1990 • Environmental Protection Act 1990 • Environment Act 1995	

49 SI 1994/2716.

Table 5.3 (Continued)

Agency	Primary responsibilities	Key legislation	Other comments
Maritime and Coastguard Agency	• Marine pollution from ships and offshore installations	• The Merchant Shipping Act 1995	There is an overlap with the Environment Agency in cases of estuarine oil pollution.
Drinking Water Inspectorate	• Monitoring and enforcing drinking water quality	• Water Industry Act 1991	Enforces standards under the Water Supply (Water Quality) Regulations 2000.[50]
Nuclear Installations Inspectorate	• Licensing nuclear sites • Storage and accumulation of radioactive waste at licensed nuclear sites	• Radioactive Substances Act 1993	

Scotland

Agency	Primary responsibilities	Key legislation	Other comments
Scottish Environment Protection Agency	• Pollution control	• Environment Act 1995 • Environmental Protection Act 1990 • Control of Pollution Act 1974	Note that unlike the Environment Agency, SEPA has no general water-related functions.
Scottish Water	• Water supply • Treatment of sewage and trade effluent	• Water Industry (Scotland) Act 2002	Performs the same functions as those of the water and sewerage undertakers in England and Wales.
Scottish Natural Heritage (SNH)	• Conservation and enhancement of habitats, species, and landscapes	• Natural Heritage (Scotland) Act 1991 • Nature Conservation (Scotland) Act 2004	Broadly, SNH replicates Natural England in Scotland.
Drinking Water Quality Regulator	• Monitors and enforces drinking water quality	• Water (Scotland) Act 1980 • Water Industry (Scotland) Act 2002	

In England and Wales, primary control over pollution is carried out by a single body—the Environment Agency—although, as explained below, the administrative arrangements are far from simple and there is a degree of overlap in institutional responsibilities. Indeed, even within the Agency itself, there are different sections carrying out separate functions and the true integration of the pollution control functions is perhaps clearer in theory than it is in practice.

For many years prior to the creation of the Environment Agency, the number of different agencies involved in environmental protection reflected the fragmented nature of policy and

---

50 SI 2000/3184.

law enforcement in this area. The creation of the Agency, in April 1996, saw the amalgamation of three of the four main regulatory agencies at the time:

- the National Rivers Authority, in relation to water quality and other operational functions;
- the Waste Regulation Authorities, in relation to the regulation of waste management;
- HMIP, primarily in relation to controls over emissions from industrial processes.

The creation of the Agency was accompanied by a recentralization of many regulatory powers, certainly within England and Wales, with national strategies on waste and air quality, for example, and centralized guidance on such things as PPC and contaminated land. While individual decisions continue to be made on a case-by-case basis, reflecting individual conditions, there has been a shift away from local control, probably on the basis of improving the quality and consistency of decision making. A side effect of this recentralization has been the consequential loss of accountability. A distinction needs to be drawn between those bodies with and those without electoral accountability. The Environment Agency is a creature of statute, with no direct public accountability. In the light of the wide discretionary powers that the Agency exercises, and the policy and rules for which it is responsible, this remains a central issue.

As mentioned above, the institutional arrangements in Northern Ireland and Scotland are different from those in England and Wales. During the parliamentary debates on the Environment Bill, there were strong arguments put forward in favour of creating separate agencies for England and Wales. This was rejected on the basis that there were geographical—for example, river catchments—and institutional—for example, NRA personnel—overlaps that suggested that integrated management across national boundaries was to be preferred. Provisions were made, however, to ensure that creating one place on the Environment Agency Board for Welsh interests and setting up an Advisory Committee for Wales furthered the Welsh national interest (Environment Act 1995, s. 11).

The Environment Agency

The structure of the Agency

The Environment Agency is an independent corporate body (Environment Act 1995, s. 1(1)) and does not have Crown immunity, although partial immunity can be granted in cases in which the Agency exercises its functions under an agreement to carry out a Ministerial function (s. 38). In order to assist with the carrying out of its functions, the Agency is under a duty to establish an environment protection advisory committee (EPAC), made up of people with a 'significant interest' in the Agency's functions. An EPAC is established for each Agency region. Once established, the Agency is under a duty to consult the committee and consider any representations made by it.

Agency role and functions

The name of the Agency is misleading: it does not have control over all environmental regulation. The Drinking Water Inspectorate is not included; nor are any direct functions relating to nature conservation or landscape protection, although there are a number of general duties relating to sites that are of nature conservation interest.[51] These omissions—when coupled with the areas of environmental regulation that remain with local authorities—mean that the Environment Agency is effectively a pollution control authority with a large number of water-related functions—such as land drainage and flood defence—and the interesting side effect that the number of staff in these areas outnumber those in pollution control.

---

51 Ibid., ss. 7 and 8, and see also general duties on the Agency under the NERC Act 2006—see p. 688.

Having said that, the Agency is one of the largest environmental regulators in the world and its responsibilities range from issuing fishing licences, to regulating the disposal of hazardous waste. It was formed from over eighty predecessor bodies with different styles and roles. This broad diversity of functions can create some tension between those responsibilities that might be considered to be mutually antagonistic, such as conserving salmon fisheries and issuing rod licences, or potentially harmful to biodiversity or the environment, such as constructing sea and flood defences. These tensions raise questions about the nature and role of the Agency.

In order to provide some coherence to these differing functions, the Agency is subject to a complicated framework of aims, duties, and objectives. These aims and duties are also designed to underpin the policy decisions of the Agency, but do not unduly fetter that discretion. The duties are expressed in a variety of ways, with the Agency being required to 'have regard to' some duties, whereas others have to be 'taken into account'. When it comes to individual decision making, the Agency has a wide discretion and the weight that attaches to each duty will be variable. Therefore, it would be difficult to challenge legally any decision made by the Agency on the basis that it had failed to carry out the duty unless the Agency had acted unreasonably in the *Wednesbury* sense.

It is important to bear in mind that the aim, objectives, and duties are not framed in a statutory vacuum. In addition to the general matters set out in the Environment Act 1995, there is an increasing range of specific statutory objectives that are set out in relation to individual functions of the Agency. Many of these have been imposed as a result of the need to meet EC legislation, which favours the use of such specific targets. For example, the Agency must seek to achieve water or air quality objectives when exercising its functions in determining authorizations and consents, and, in doing so, it must place those objectives above the general aims and duties.

The principal aim, other duties, and objectives of the Agency

Section 4 of the Environment Act 1995 defines the principal aim for the Agency.[52] This is a broad obligation and its legal significance is somewhat uncertain. A number of factors, set out in s. 4, are designed to influence the implementation of the duty in practice.

BOX 5.4 The principal aim and objectives of the Environment Agency

Section 4(1) of the Environment Act 1995 provides:

> It shall be the principal aim of the Agency (subject to and in accordance with the provisions of this Act or any other enactment and taking into account any likely costs) in discharging its functions so to protect or enhance the environment, taken as a whole, as to make the contribution towards attaining the objective of achieving sustainable development...

First, the Agency must take into account the likely costs of achieving the principal aim. This ensures that environmental considerations are not paramount when pursuing the aim of sustainable development and that the costs of the pursuit of the principal aim are proportionate. This emphasizes the fact that protecting the environment is not the same as seeking sustainable development. The former puts the environment as a central and singular pursuit, which takes precedence over other considerations. The latter involves balancing a range of factors, including costs.

52 See Box 5.4.

Secondly, the principal aim is to be pursued in relation to the conservation and enhancement of the environment 'taken as a whole'. This ensures that policy and decision making is not overburdened by detailed consideration of impacts on individual environmental media.

Thirdly, the principal aim has to be viewed in relation to all of the other objectives that apply to the Agency—surprisingly, there are no other statutory 'aims'—which rather raises a question relating the use of the word 'principal'. The 'principal' aim will only take precedence over other statutory objectives in cases in which there is a direct conflict between the two: thus, in situations in which the Agency is making a decision to act and it cannot meet both objectives, the principal aim will take precedence. Confusingly, however, the aim is stated to be 'subject to' other provisions of the Act, which would include the other objectives. This confusion over the hierarchy of the principal aim and the other statutory objectives underlines the difficulty of introducing a principal aim that does not actually create any legally enforceable rights. It rather defeats the purpose of a 'principal aim' when it is subject to the myriad of other statutory objectives and functions.

Finally, the Agency must have regard to guidance issued by the Secretary of State when discharging its functions (s. 4(3)).[53]

In addition to the principal aim of the Environment Agency, a range of other duties and objectives is set out in ss. 5–9 of the Environment Act 1995.

- Section 5 provides that the Agency's pollution control powers shall be exercised for the purpose of preventing, minimizing, remedying, or mitigating the effects of pollution of the environment.

- Section 6 places the Agency under a duty generally to promote the conservation and enhancement of the amenities of inland and coastal waters, the use of such waters for recreational purposes, and the conservation of water-dependent flora and fauna. This duty is not particularly onerous, requiring action only when the Agency considers that it is desirable to do so.

- Section 7 provides that the Agency—and the relevant Secretaries of State—when formulating or considering any proposals, is to *have regard to* the desirability of conserving and enhancing natural beauty, and the conservation of flora, fauna, and geological or physiographical features (s. 7(1)(b)). In relation to non-pollution control powers and functions, this duty is raised so that the Agency is required to *further* conservation etc. (s. 7(1)(a)). This distinction reflects the fact that the Agency cannot be said to be furthering environmental conservation when it is issuing consents, authorizations, or licences for activities that, by definition, will be polluting. The meaning of 'proposals' is undefined and therefore would appear to apply to any context, from individual determinations for discharge consents, to general matters, such as river basin management plans or general policy formulation.

In addition, the Agency must have regard to a range of matters, including the desirability of protecting heritage sites or public access to areas of natural beauty, the effect of proposals on the beauty of any area, and the effect on the economic and social well-being of rural communities (s. 7(1) and (2)).

There are specific duties in relation to notification and consultation in the case of any land of a special conservation interest that may be affected by any works carried out by the Agency or by any authorization that it is considering. If land of special interest has been previously notified to the Environment Agency by Natural England or by the Countryside Council for Wales (CCW), the Agency is under a duty to consult with either of those bodies before

53 See Department of the Environment, MAFF, and the Welsh Office (1996) *The Environment Agency and Sustainable Development*, and see p. 59.

carrying out or authorizing works, operations, or activities that are likely to destroy or damage the features of special interest or importance (s. 8(1)–(4)).[54]

The Secretary of State has the power to issue codes of practice under s. 9 of the Environment Act 1995 to assist the Environment Agency in carrying out any of the duties referred to above. This power has been exercised in the issue of the Water and Sewerage (Conservation, Access and Recreation) (Code of Practice) Order 2000[55] and the Code of Practice on Conservation, Access and Recreation, which gives practical guidance to the Agency (and water and sewerage undertakers) relating to their environmental and recreational duties. Another example is the Code of Practice on Environmental Procedures for Flood Defence Operating Authorities. Contravention of a code does not give rise to any criminal offence or civil right of action, but will be taken into account by relevant bodies in deciding whether to use any powers available to them.

BOX 5.5 The practical significance of the duties of the Environment Agency

All of these different duties and obligations can be confusing. Under any type of analysis—legal, philosophical, or even semantic—the complexities of the principal aim and the other duties obscure the nature of the legal obligations that are created. Do they actually make any difference in practice? It is difficult to identify the impact of these duties in relation to individual decision making, because they are all factors that will be thrown into the balance. It is more helpful to consider how the duties would have affected past decisions and actions, in relation to which environmental damage has been caused by regulatory agencies carrying out operational functions that are now undertaken by the Environment Agency.

Consider the situation in which a landowner wants to drain some land in order to mitigate the effects of sea flooding. The site is designated as a site of special scientific interest (SSSI) for its ecological importance. The landowner enters into an agreement with the Agency to undertake land drainage works. Regardless of other statutory controls (including the need for planning permission, environmental assessment, or other procedures) that may or may not apply, the Agency would be under an obligation to consult with Natural England prior to undertaking the works. In addition, the Code of Practice on Environmental Procedures for Flood Defence Operating Authorities emphasizes the importance of the minimization of environmental impacts and the need to avoid damage to sensitive wildlife features. These practical steps are underpinned by the general duties to further the conservation of flora and fauna when undertaking operational functions.

While none of these safeguards guarantee that the works would not be undertaken, they mean that such work would be much more difficult to carry out without due regard to the consequences and the anticipation of mitigation of severe environmental effects. In *Southern Water Authority v. Nature Conservancy Council*,[56] a water authority carried out land drainage works on a Site of Special Scientific Interest. Southern Water was aware of the site's ecological importance, because it owned land in a different part of the SSSI. The House of Lords described the works that would now be undertaken by the Environment Agency as 'ecological vandalism'—and such vandalism should now be unthinkable.

---

54 There are further duties under CROWA 2000 and under NERC 2006, discussed in Chapter 19.
55 SI 2000/477.
56 [1992] WLR 775—see further p. 695.

Thus, although there is a great deal of uncertainty over the nature of the legal obligation created by the aims and duties, they are still of importance in internal decision making within the Agency, as political levers for environmentally sensitive decisions, and for shaping and developing Environment Agency culture.

The cost–benefit duty

In addition to these general duties and obligations, there is an explicit duty upon the Agency to take into account the costs and benefits of exercising its powers (Environment Act 1995, s. 39). 'Costs' are defined as environmental, as well as personal, costs (s. 56(1)) and, although 'benefits' are surprisingly (given the mutual relationship between the phrases) not defined, the term would arguably include environmental benefits in addition to any personal benefits.

There are two important restrictions on the application of the duty.

1. It does not apply if it would be unreasonable in the circumstances of a particular case. The clearest example of this would be if emergency action were to be required by the Agency.

2. The duty does not affect the exercise of other mandatory obligations, such as complying with environmental quality objectives. In such circumstances, the decision-making discretion of the Agency is constrained within the pursuit of the specific objective, and the costs and the benefits become less relevant. The general cost–benefit duty does, however, apply if the Agency can select from a range of potential options when seeking to achieve these objectives, and if the costs and benefits of each of those options can be considered when selecting which is the most appropriate.

Thus, taking account of costs and benefits does not necessarily mean that the Agency has to demonstrate that the costs outweigh the benefits (or vice versa), or even that, once it has carried out such an appraisal, it must act in accordance with the conclusions. A requirement to take account of costs and benefits arguably does no more than raise an evidential presumption that they will be considered. In classic administrative fashion, it does not prescribe the weight that should be attached to such costs or benefits and, therefore, any decision based on such an analysis will be difficult to challenge.

The Secretary of State has issued non-statutory guidance on the cost–benefit duty as part of the explanatory document that accompanies the statutory guidance on the principal aim of the Agency.[57] The guidance emphasizes the importance of carrying out environmental appraisals before exercising decision-making powers. In addition, the guidance points out the difficulties in quantifying environmental costs, benefits, and places, and sets out a number of factors that may be relevant in reaching a decision. Arguably, the most important section of the guidance stresses the fact that, in many situations, the application of the duty will require the exercise of judgment by the Agency—a judgment that is likely to be unchallengeable in the courts.

In addition to this general duty under s. 39, the Agency has to consider the costs associated with other duties. Thus there is a duty to consider 'any likely costs' when seeking to achieve its principal aim under s. 4, and the Agency must set out the costs and benefits for exercising its options under the pollution control functions in s. 5.

Financial arrangements

The Environment Agency derives its funding from three main sources.

- A good proportion is grant-in-aid, received directly from DEFRA. This emphasizes the difficult nature of the Agency's relationship with its primary funder: while it is not part of

---

57 Department of the Environment, MAFF, and WO (1996). There is also an Environment Agency Policy Note (1999) *Sustainable Development: Taking Accounts of Costs and Benefits*.

central government, it does rely upon DEFRA to fund key resources, such as staffing, and research and development.

- A second income stream funding operational flood defence schemes comes from levies raised on local authorities.

- The final significant proportion of funding is recovered through operating receipts—that is, money generated from charging schemes and licence fees related to pollution control systems.

Sections 41 and 42 of the Environment Act 1995 provide the power to introduce charging schemes for all forms of environmental licensing. The Agency can exercise this power itself, unlike some of the previous powers to raise fees and charges that were exercisable by the Secretary of State.[58] To ensure that the schemes are subject to proper scrutiny, each must be published in draft and approved by the Secretary of State and the Treasury before it can come into operation. Furthermore, the scheme must be made by statutory instrument and can be annulled by either House of Parliament. At present, all charges are levied on a fixed basis, with variations for certain classes of licence, although, in theory, there are no restrictions on the amount that can be charged, nor on any differentials in charging to reflect the administrative burden of each individual application.

In addition to this specific power, the Agency has general powers to charge for any services provided in connection with environmental licences under s. 37(7) and (8).[59] This would cover any advice or assistance provided to applicants when preparing applications. The use of this power would enable the Agency to introduce charging rates that more accurately reflect the administrative burden, without necessarily complicating the existing charging schemes.

Other regulatory agencies

Although the Environment Agency has primary responsibility for the majority of powers in relation to pollution control, there remain a number of other bodies with direct responsibility for specific aspects of pollution control and wider areas of environmental protection. In particular, local authorities play an important role in regulating the clean-up of historically contaminated land, statutory nuisances, noise, air quality (including smoke control and other atmospheric emissions), and planning. In addition, the privatized water companies act as sewerage undertakers, controlling discharges to sewers. There is a good deal of overlap in these areas that covers both substantive law and administration. An outline of these overlaps is given in each of the relevant chapters in Part II.

Sewerage undertakers

In relation to discharges to sewers, the licensing body is the privatized sewerage undertaker, which grants what are called 'trade effluent consents'. This is an unusual example of a private body undertaking an environmental regulation function, although it is arguable that a sewerage undertaker is, in reality, doing little different from a private waste disposal contractor in providing a method of waste disposal through privately owned facilities. The Water Services Regulation Authority (OFWAT), the main functions of which relate to the regulatory control of the privatized water industry, hears appeals against trade effluent consent decisions.

Countryside bodies

One of the positive aspects of the creation of DEFRA was the integration of rural affairs into a department that deals with wider environmental concerns. DEFRA deals with agricultural

---

58 For example, environmental permitting under the Environmental Permitting (England and Wales) Regulations 2007, SI 2007/3538. Note that this power is separate from the power to charge for the permit itself—see Reg. 65.

59 There are further incidental powers under the Environment Act 1995, s. 43.

policy and other related matters; there are, however, other independent agencies within the government that are responsible for specific matters. In England, Natural England has responsibilities for nature conservation, and for recreation, landscape, and amenity. The Countryside Council for Wales (CCW) and Scottish Natural Heritage (SNH) perform similar functions.

Local authorities

There has been a great deal of restructuring in local authorities in England over recent years. In 1986, the abolition of the metropolitan county councils led to the creation of two separate structures for local government in England (with slight variations in the case of London). As a result of further local government reorganization under the Local Government Act 1992, there are now three main types of local authority.

- **Single-tier London boroughs and metropolitan districts**
  In metropolitan areas, there is a one-tier system—the metropolitan district councils. These obviously have responsibility for all matters, although joint boards of the councils run some functions—namely, police, fire, and transport.

- **Non-metropolitan areas**
  In non-metropolitan areas, there is a two-tier system of county and district councils. In constitutional terms, these two tiers are equal, but they have differing responsibilities. County councils have responsibility for the police, fire services, personal social services, transport, highways, education, libraries, and development control in certain prescribed 'county matters', including waste disposal and minerals development. District councils have responsibility for housing, general development control, recreation, environmental, and public health. This split causes problems for the public, which often finds it difficult to identify which tier is responsible for any particular matter. The problem is particularly acute in the environmental sphere, because of the overlapping powers of the two tiers (for example, in relation to town planning). This confusion was cited as one of the factors that led to the reorganization of local government and the introduction of unitary authorities.

- **Unitary authorities**
  This third class of local authority was created after a review of local government considered a large number of proposals to introduce more single-tier authorities to replicate the powers of the metropolitan district councils.

All local authorities undertake a wide variety of tasks in relation to environmental protection.[60] In outline, there are six main areas to consider:

Town and country planning

The local authority is normally the local planning authority. This means that it is responsible for the making of development plans and for the control of development. The powers also incorporate responsibility for related matters, such as tree preservation orders (TPOs), listed building protection, conservation areas, hazardous substances consents, the control of derelict land, and the protection of the countryside. As explained above, planning functions are split between county and district councils, with county councils being responsible for minerals and waste disposal matters, while district councils have responsibility for other development control decisions and smaller scale development planning in local plans. In

---

60 These are considered in detail in the Online Resource Centre.

national parks, the planning function is undertaken by special planning authorities, with representation from the various local authorities whose area falls within the national park.

Public health matters

Local authorities have always had responsibility for a very wide range of matters under the Public Health Acts. In particular, this involves duties in relation to the control of statutory nuisances, the law on which was remodelled in EPA 1990, Pt III. Authorities also have responsibilities for monitoring the quality of private water supplies.

The control of noise

Local authorities have primary responsibility for the control of noise from premises. In the past, these provisions had been separate from those relating to statutory nuisance, but, in EPA 1990, the two sets of powers were treated together.

Air pollution

Local authorities have long had responsibility for the control of smoke, dust, grit, and fumes under the Clean Air Acts and related legislation. In EPA 1990, Pt I, they were given more complete powers to control air pollution from plants that are not the responsibility of the Environment Agency under IPC. This general split was maintained under the Pollution Prevention and Control Act 1999 and the Environmental Permitting (England and Wales) Regulations 2007 (SI 2007/3538). In addition to these specific controls over emissions, the Environment Act 1995 gave local authorities greater responsibilities for establishing strategic control over air quality matters. This includes a duty to review air quality in an area in order to assess compliance with air quality standards, a duty to designate air quality management areas where those standards are not being met, and a duty to prepare an action plan to address the problems of air quality.

Waste collection and disposal

Responsibilities for waste collection and the arrangements for the disposal of waste remain with local authorities under the waste collection and waste disposal authorities. Local authorities also play an important role in ensuring that waste reduction—that is, that they are responsible for meeting landfill reduction quotas—and recycling targets can be achieved, because they control a large proportion of the waste arising at the place of production.

Contaminated land

Under Pt 2A, EPA 1990, local authorities are responsible for the inspection and identification of land within their area that is contaminated land and for taking action against the person responsible for the contamination, or the owner/occupier of the land. These responsibilities are shared, in some respects, with the Environment Agency, which is given corresponding powers and duties in respect of sites that are more heavily contaminated, known as 'special sites'.

General duties and sustainable development

In addition to these areas, it is clear that local and regional policies on such things as transport provision, recreation, and strategic planning, specifically, and all of an authority's functions, generally, all have a part to play in the protection of the environment and the pursuit of sustainability. Section 4 of the Local Government Act 2000 places on all local authorities, including county and district councils, a duty to prepare 'community strategies' for promoting or improving the economic, social, and environmental well-being of their areas, and for contributing to the achievement of sustainable development in the UK. It also gives authorities broad new powers to improve and promote local well-being as a means of helping them to implement those strategies. Section 4 of the Act also requires local authorities in England to have regard to any guidance issued by the Secretary of State in preparing their community strategies.[61]

Non-government organizations (NGOs)

'NGO' is a convenient label for a wide diversity of bodies ranging from huge membership groups with an international agenda, such as Greenpeace and Friends of the Earth, to national groups, such as the National Trust and the Royal Society for the Protection of Birds (RSPB), as well as even smaller groups, such as the National Federation of Badger Groups or the local wildlife trusts. The defining characteristic of these groups is that the group exists to promote an environmental cause that is not only linked to the interest of its members. Thus the term 'public interest groups' has been used to distinguish these organizations from groups with a specified local agenda—often to stop local development proposals—which have been characterized as NIMBY ('not in my back yard') groups.

The UK has a long tradition of non-government organizations (NGOs) being involved in different aspects of environmental law and policy. A number of NGOs have their origin in the nineteenth century. In the early stages, three main groups formed, focusing on nature conservation (the RSPB in 1889), the countryside (the Commons, Open Spaces and Footpaths Preservation Society in 1865), and animal welfare (the Royal Society for the Prevention of Cruelty to Animals (RSPCA) in 1824). An increase in the interest in environmental issues has been reflected by the dramatic growth in membership of environmental NGOs since the 1970s, with membership of some groups such as the RSPB and Friends of the Earth increasing by a factor of 10. Table 5.4 sets out a few of the main environmental NGOs in the UK, along with the relevant main areas of interest.

Table 5.4 Environmental non-government organizations (NGOs)

NGO	Comments
Campaign to Protect Rural England	Founded in 1926. Focus on rural aspects of town and country planning, agriculture, and transport. Membership c. 59,000.
Earth First!	Not a group as such, but a *'convenient banner for people who share similar philosophies to work under'*. Uses radical direct action, including occupation and sabotage (see Box 19.4). Particularly active in relation to protests against road building.
Friends of the Earth	Founded in 1969. Largest international environmental NGO. Campaigns across a wide range of environmental issues. Particularly effective at securing changes in law.

61 ODPM (2001) *Preparing Community Strategies: Government Guidance to Local Authorities.*

Table 5.4 (Continued)

NGO	Comments
Greenpeace	Founded in 1971.
	221,000 members in the UK as part of 2.8 million members worldwide.
	Runs campaigns on genetically modified organisms (GMOs), nuclear power, ancient forests, chemicals, climate change, and whaling.
Environmental Protection UK	Founded in 1899 as the Coal Smoke Abatement Society.
	Latterly, the National Society for Clean Air and Environmental Protection.
	Largely responsible for the introduction of the Clean Air Acts in the 1950s.
	Particular interest in air quality and noise.
	Membership includes public and private sector organizations and companies.
	Focus on training and education.
National Trust	Founded in 1895, with over 3 million members.
	Owns 250,000 hectares of land and around 650 miles of protected coastline.
	An incorporated body governed by powers in various National Trusts Acts from 1907 to 1971.
Royal Society for the Protection of Birds	Founded in 1889.
	Over a million members.
	As its name suggests, primary aim is to protect bird species and habitats.
	Owns or manages over 180 nature reserves, which provide homes to 80 per cent of the UK's rarest birds.
	Plays a prominent role in investigating wildlife crime.
	Responsible for the introduction of many pieces of legislation, including the Protection of Birds Act 1954.
Royal Society of Wildlife Trusts	Previously known as the Royal Society of Nature Conservation.
	Founded in 1912 to protect wild animals and their habitat across the UK.
	Owns or manages 2,560 nature reserves.
	Made up of 47 independent local wildlife trusts.
	Membership more than 560,000.
The Open Spaces Society	Founded in 1865, making it the oldest conservation group.
	Its aim is to create and conserve common land, village greens, open spaces, and rights of public access, in town and country, in England and Wales.
Campaign for Better Transport	Formerly, Transport 2000.
	Lobbies and briefs government on issues relating to transport and the environment.
	Representative sits on the Commission for Integrated Transport.
Wildlife and Countryside Link	Founded in 1980.
	Represents a coordinating body for many wildlife organizations.
	Members include the RSPB, wildlife trusts, the Ramblers Association, Greenpeace, and Friends of the Earth.
	Influential in shaping the Wildlife and Countryside and Act 1981 and the Countryside and Rights of Way Act 2000.

Table 5.4 (Continued)	
NGO	**Comments**
WWF-UK	Founded in 1961 to promote the conservation of rare and endangered species. Over 330,000 members. In addition to campaigning internationally, also involved in the enforcement of international wildlife laws.[62]

Environmental NGOs play a variety of roles in the administration of environmental law and policy. For many groups, there is a direct role as owners or stewards of land that is protected. For example, local wildlife trusts own or manage over 2,500 nature reserves. The primary role of NGOs is, however, to undertake activities that are designed to influence decision makers, and to secure favourable changes to environmental law and policy. They do this through a variety of mechanisms. At a local level, such groups may participate in the development plan process or as consultees on planning applications. Nationally, they participate in the policymaking process through such things as giving evidence to select committees and the RCEP, and lobbying government departments and relevant agencies.

NGOs also seek to have a direct influence on environmental law by campaigning for new legislation. The government has a large degree of control over the parliamentary timetable and therefore any NGO that wants to introduce new legislation must either persuade the government to adopt its ideas or use the private member's Bill procedure. This procedure allocates time for parliamentary debate for Bills introduced by MPs. The places are decided by a ballot with only 20 successful places allocated annually. Large numbers of MPs apply for places in the ballot without any specific Bill in mind. If allocated a high place in the Ballot, they will be targeted by NGOs with suggestions for Bills and draft clauses. The procedure can only be used for relatively uncontroversial proposals, because the government effectively has a veto over any Bill by controlling the amount of parliamentary time available. As a consequence, the success rate for environmental Bills is not particularly high, although some do get passed. A recent example of a successful private member's Bill on the environment was the Household Waste Recycling Act 2003, which was drafted and promoted by Friends of the Earth, and steered through Parliament by Joan Ruddock MP.

NGOs also play a role in the implementation and enforcement of environmental law. This might be through the setting of environmental standards[63] or through the use of private prosecutions. NGOs have also developed a leading role in challenging government and regulatory agencies through the use of judicial review actions. In doing so, they have clarified the rules on those who are able to bring such actions,[64] and brought about changes to the law in such areas as the incorrect implementation of the Habitats Directive (92/43/EEC) in relation to marine habitats[65] and the unlawful shooting of protected birds.[66]

---

62 See Box 6.3.

63 For example, the role that NGOs play in the Integrated Pollution Prevention and Control Directive (IPPC) Information Exchange—see Box 14.2.

64 The law on standing—see p. 314.

65 See R v. Department of Trade and Industry, ex parte Greenpeace [2000] Env LR 221.

66 See RSPB and The Wildfowl and Wetlands Trust v. Secretary of State for Scotland [2001] Env LR 19.

The courts

Although traditionally seen as separate from Parliament and therefore unconcerned with questions of policy, do the courts play a role in the administration of environmental law?

The High Court supervises the exercise of statutory powers and duties by many of the other regulatory bodies in this chapter through the adjudication of judicial review actions (see Chapter 10). In exercising this supervisory function, the courts have often emphasized that they are not concerned with the merits of any decision made as a result of exercising a particular power or fulfilling a duty, but with whether the proper procedures have been complied with. Thus, in cases in which a regulatory body, such as a local planning authority, is determining whether to grant planning permission based upon different policy considerations—for example, job creation weighed as against environmental harm—a court will intervene if the procedures for environmental assessment have not been followed, but not on the grounds that it was wrong to give greater weight to employment over the environment.[67] A court is also reluctant to intervene in cases in which a regulatory agency has exercised its powers to make an expert determination. For example, a court would not interfere with Natural England's determination that land was of special scientific interest unless it could be shown that it had ignored some statutory procedural requirement.[68]

The courts also fulfil an appellate function (for example, magistrates courts hear appeals in relation to statutory nuisance abatement notices), determine civil disputes with an environmental flavour (for example, in relation to environmental nuisances), and try cases involving environmental crimes.

The effectiveness of the courts' role in environmental cases has been the subject of a number of criticisms and proposals over recent years. The background to the calls for a separate form of environmental tribunal is covered further in Chapter 10. In terms of the administration of environmental law and policy, some of the general criticisms reflect some of the problems outlined above in relation to the internal and external integration of environmental considerations across different areas of decision making and government departments. There are convincing arguments put forward that the courts are not necessarily effective when dealing with environmental disputes, and a new structure and set of procedures—probably involving some sort of environmental tribunal or court—may well address these issues.

The courts and environmental cases

Although the courts have been at the forefront of the development of some of the key issues in environmental law—such as the definition of waste, the fulfilment of the idea of environmental assessment, and the identity of the 'polluter' in relation to water pollution—some judges have questioned whether the development of the law is a matter for the courts or for Parliament. The House of Lords has made it clear that, because more and more new legislation is addressing environmental problems in a structured fashion, it is unnecessary—and perhaps even undesirable—for the courts to develop private law principles to address the same issues.[69] For example, the House of Lords chose to defer to a statutory scheme of compensation for damage from overflowing sewers rather than to develop the law of nuisance.[70]

---

67 See *Berkeley v. Secretary of State for the Environment, Transport and the Regions* [2001] Env LR 16 and Case 13.7.

68 See *Fisher v. English Nature* [2004] EWCA Civ 663; *R (Western Power Distribution Investments Ltd) v. Countryside Council for Wales* [2007] Env LR 25.

69 See *Cambridge Water Co. v. Eastern Counties Leather plc* [1994] 2 AC 264 and Case 11.3.

70 See *Marcic v. Thames Water* [2004] Env LR 25 and Case 11.7.

This can be interpreted as a reflection of the fact that Parliament is able to create a coherent and structured system, rather than one developed on an ad hoc, case-by-case basis—but it also reflects the point that Parliament has a greater democratic legitimacy than the courts when it comes to allocating responsibility for environmental harm, particularly when it comes to questions of the allocation of resources, such as expenditure on environmental improvements.[71]

CHAPTER SUMMARY

1   There are numerous bodies that are responsible for the administration of environmental law and policy. One of the major challenges of recent years has been to integrate environmental considerations across these different bodies.

2   Integration can be achieved externally, by promoting the consideration of environmental issues across all policy areas, or internally, by drawing together regulatory responsibility for different environmental emissions within one single authority.

3   Devolution has shifted responsibility for much of environmental law and policy to the national executives in Scotland, Wales, and Northern Ireland. Although there are distinctive environmental laws in each country, the general framework of environmental law is the same, because European and international law is so influential.

4   Within central government, the Department of the Environment, Food and Rural Affairs (DEFRA) is responsible for many, but not all, environmental issues. Other departments with significant environmental responsibilities include the Department of Communities and Local Government, the Department of Business Enterprise and Regulatory Reform, and the Department for Transport.

5   Various bodies, such as parliamentary select committees, play an important role in scrutinizing the activities of central government departments and regulatory agencies. Along with the Royal Commission on Environmental Pollution (RCEP), they are also catalysts for the creation of new laws and policies.

6   The Environment Agency is the primary environmental regulator in England and Wales. It is effectively a pollution control authority, with a large number of water-related functions, such as land drainage and flood defence. The Agency is subject to a complicated framework of aims, duties, and objectives, which underpin all of its activities. The Agency provides a good example of the internal integration of environmental law, because it is responsible for many different pollution control functions that had previously been regulated by different agencies.

7   Other main environmental regulators include nature conservation and countryside bodies (Natural England, Scottish Natural Heritage, and Countryside Council for Wales), the private water and sewerage industry (the public body Scottish Water in Scotland), and the local authorities (main responsibilities include: town and country planning, statutory nuisances, and contaminated land).

8   Non-governmental organizations (NGOs) play an important role in the administration of environmental law through participation in law and policymaking, implementation, and enforcement.

9   The courts play an important role in the enforcement of environmental law. They supervise the exercise of administrative powers through judicial review, sanction offenders for pollution offences, and adjudicate on environmental disputes. The courts tend to be conservative and have been reluctant to expand their role in developing law as a mechanism for environmental protection.

---

71 R. Lee [2005] J Law & Soc 111; W. Howarth (2002) 14 JEL 353 makes the same point in a critical comment on the Court of Appeal's judgment.

Q QUESTIONS

1   In what ways has the administration of environmental law become more integrated over the last ten years? In what ways has it become more fragmented?

2   What are the advantages and disadvantages of devolution in terms of the administration of environmental law and policy in the UK?

3   What responsibilities does the Environment Agency have? How does the Environment Act 1995 seek to balance some of the competing responsibilities?

4   What role do NGOs play in the administration of environmental law and policy?

FURTHER READING

The idea of administrative integration and the creation of the Environment Agency are covered in some depth in J. Steele and T. Jewell (1998) 'Law in environmental decision making' in T. Jewell and J. Steele (eds) *Law in Environmental Decision Making*, Oxford: Clarendon Press. These themes are further developed in an article by the same authors, 'UK regulatory reform and the pursuit of "sustainable development": the Environment Act 1995' [1996] 8 JEL 283, which also gives a deeper analysis of the duties and powers of the Agency under the Environment Act 1995. There is an interesting analysis of the work of the Environment Agency, and the criticisms of its role and performance, in D. Bell and T. Gray, 'The ambiguous role of the Environment Agency in England and Wales' (2002) 11(3) Environmental Politics 76.

A good overview of the issues raised by devolution can be found in a collection of essays from the 1999 UKELA Conference on Devolution and the Environment in N. Faris and S. Turner (eds) (1997) *Public Law and the Environment: New Directions*, Upper Basildon: UKELA. Another introduction to the topic can be found in R. Macrory (1999) 'The environment and constitutional change' in R. Hazell (ed.) *Constitutional Futures: A History of the Next Ten Years*, Oxford: Oxford University Press.

More detail on specific countries can be found in general texts. Northern Ireland is covered, generally, in S. Turner and K. Morrow (1997) *Northern Ireland Environmental Law*, Dublin: Gill and Macmillan. On more recent developments, see S. Turner, 'Transforming environmental governance in Northern Ireland: Part One—The process of policy renewal' (2006) 18 JEL 55 and 'Transforming environmental governance in Northern Ireland: Part Two—The case of environmental regulation' (2006) 18 JEL 245, and B. Jack, 'Environmental governance in Northern Ireland: returning to the drawing board' (2007) Env LR 1. Scotland, generally, is dealt with in C. Reid (1997) *Environmental Law in Scotland*, 2nd edn, Edinburgh: W. Green, and comprehensively in M. Poustie (2007) 'The laws of Scotland' in *Stair Memorial Encyclopaedia*, London: Lexis Nexis-Butterworths. Useful articles on devolution in Scotland and Wales are G. Little, 'Scottish devolution and environmental law' (2000) 12 JEL 155 and V. Jenkins, 'Environmental law in Wales' (2005) 17 JEL 207.

The role of the Environmental Audit Committee and the general approach to scrutinizing government activities is covered in A. Ross, 'Greening government: tales from the new sustainability watchdog' (2000) 12 JEL 175, and K. Hollingsworth, 'Environmental monitoring of government: the case for an environmental auditor' (2000) 20 LS 241. A. Ross, 'The UK approach to delivering sustainable development in government: a case study in joined-up working' (2005) 17 JEL 27 explores some of the difficulties, both in terms of the vital need for Prime Ministerial support, and in trying to 'join up' government on the basis of unclear and inconsistent objectives.

NGOs

There are some general texts dealing with environmental NGOs, although the best are a little dated. These are P. Lowe and J. Goyder (1983) *Environmental Groups in Politics*, London: Allen and Unwin, and G. Jordan and W. Maloney (1997) *The Protest Business*, Manchester: Manchester University Press. The long history of nature conservation NGOs, and the significant impact that they have had on law and policy, is chronicled in D. Evans (1997) *A History of Nature Conservation in Britain*, 2nd edn, London: Routledge.

@ **WEB LINKS**

Most of the web links for this chapter are self-explanatory and can be sourced from the central government web portal **www.open.gov.uk**. The Department for Environment, Food and Rural Affairs (DEFRA) web page **www.defra.gov.uk** is also a good link to many other related sites, including the various executive and non-departmental public bodies. A degree of perseverance and patience is needed with the Environment Agency's website **www.environment-agency.gov.uk** and the judicious use of the search facility is the best way of navigating around. The Select Committees' pages of the Houses of Parliament website **www. parliament.uk** gives access to the evidence, reports and any government response on many areas of environmental law and policy. Details of the work of the Royal Commission on Environmental Pollution (RCEP) can be accessed at **www.rcep.org.uk**. Unfortunately, there is only full access to the text of the most recent reports.

PART II

Integrated themes

6

International law and environmental protection

→ **Overview**

International law, and hence international environmental law, is rather different from the other areas of law discussed in this book. Most obviously, there is no single body with the power to make and enforce law—against states, companies, or individuals—effectively. This has often resulted in international 'law' being regarded as something rather closer to international relations. This view (and, to some degree, the reality behind it) is receding—but this feature of international law means that the gap between law and policy here is not as great as that evident in national or European law.

Another key feature of international law is that, in the UK, it does not have a direct impact on domestic law or on individuals. Treaties need to be given effect to through national legislation and are concerned with the action of states, not individuals within states—with some notable exceptions, such as the law on war crimes. In this sense, international law is quite different from national law and, to the extent that it gives individuals remedies, European law.

This chapter describes the development, scope, and application of international environmental law, which has expanded significantly since the late 1960s. The focus is on international treaties relating to environmental protection. Fuller discussion of how the key international environmental treaties work is left to Part III.

In general, this chapter is restricted to discussing public, rather than private, international law—that is, the law between states, rather than the conflict of legal systems. The latter is, of course, relevant in environmental law—for example, in determining which court should hear pollution-related claims against transnational corporations. Such cases raise the issue of whether different standards can be employed by such companies working in developing countries (which covers similar ground to wider questions about international environmental law and sustainable development), but are not directly addressed here.

At the end of this chapter, you should be able to:

✔ understand what international environmental law is and how it is made;

✔ appreciate the interaction between international law, European law, and UK national law;

✔ assess the development of international environmental law and policy;

✔ understand the potential conflicts between environmental standards and the rules of international free trade, and appreciate how these are currently resolved;

✔ form a view on likely developments in international environmental law.

Why is international law important for environmental protection?

International law is important for environmental protection, and for the issues covered in the rest of this book, in the following central ways.

- Transboundary and global problems require international—or, at the very least, bilateral—solutions, and international legal regulation of some kind will be either necessary or desirable.

- International agreements may generate standards that are adopted in national law or by regional groupings such as the European Community (EC), or which guide decision making in areas such as the interface between international trade and the environment.

- The international arena is important for the development of principles of environmental law, such as sustainable development or the Precautionary Principle (see further Chapter 3). Indeed, such principles often develop precisely because their origins are in agreements that are not legally binding.

- Because of its nature, recent developments in international law have focused on how an attention to procedures and on positive inducements to comply, rather than on negative 'command and control'-style enforcement mechanisms, can be used to secure compliance. Although born of necessity, there is again much for national and EC law to learn from this experience.

- Perhaps negatively, the development of environmental law at all levels may be subject to restrictions originating in international law: for example, import restrictions that are deemed to be incompatible with the rules regulating international trade.

International law and the UK

The relationship between international law and the UK has two dimensions: the first is the extent to which international law affects rights, duties, and policymaking at national level; the second is the contribution of the UK to developments in international environmental law and policy.

The direct application of international environmental law

In the UK, international agreements only become part of national law once they are given effect to by Parliament, usually through legislation. Moreover, both the making of treaties (*Blackburn v. Attorney-General* [1971] 1 WLR 1037) and their implementation (*Ex parte Molyneaux* [1986] 1 WLR 331) are seen by the courts as a matter solely for government:

Treaties…are not self-executing. Quite simply, a treaty is not part of English law unless and until it has been incorporated into the law by legislation.

(*Maclaine Watson v. Department of Trade and Industry* [1989] 3 All ER 523 *per* Lord Oliver at 545)

This is the case even if the treaty has been ratified, because, in the UK, ratification is a matter for central government, not Parliament. Following devolution, the power to ratify treaties remains with the UK government, as a matter of foreign affairs.

All of this means that international agreements have what might be called 'high-level' rather than 'low-level' effect—that is, they create obligations that bind the UK in its international relations, rather than obligations of the kind on which individuals can rely or have duties under. There are exceptions—for example, the direct application of human rights law—but international environmental law is mainly concerned with getting states to take action to influence non-state actors, rather than imposing burdens directly on polluters themselves. In the UK, international agreements cannot be used as the basis for an action by groups or individuals against the state or a public body (in the way that EC Directives may be), nor are they, in themselves, a direct source of rights and duties in legal actions between individuals.

The indirect application of international environmental law

Even if a treaty is not 'self-executing', courts will prefer interpretations of statutes that conform with international treaties to which the UK is a party to those that do not. This does not necessarily mean that, in all cases of discretion, there is a presumption in favour of the convention (*R v. Secretary of State for the Home Department, ex parte Brind* [1991] 1 AC 696). But if national legislation is introduced to give effect to a treaty or treaty obligation, then the treaty *can* be used as an aid to interpreting the national law and it is presumed that Parliament did not intend to legislate contrary to the UK's international commitments. In *R v. Secretary of State for Trade and Industry, ex parte Greenpeace (No. 2)* [2000] Env LR 221, the High Court held that the Habitats Directive (92/43/EEC) should have been applied beyond territorial waters. Although, in this case, it was EC legislation that was being interpreted, the Court looked for an interpretation of the Directive that seemed most consistent not only with other provisions of EC law, but also with a range of international agreements on marine conservation.

In some cases, the relationship between the treaty and implementing legislation will be spelt out more precisely. For example, the Human Rights Act 1998, which 'incorporates' the European Convention on Human Rights (ECHR), makes it clear that the English courts must take account of previous decisions of the European Court of Human Rights (ECtHR) when interpreting the Act. This is important because of the limited steps that the ECtHR has already taken to interpret the Convention in a creative way to give incidental protection to the environment (see p. 71). Rights under the Convention may also challenge some of the traditional common law rules on environmental protection. An example of this is *McKenna v. British Aluminium* [2002] Env LR 30, in which the High Court thought that the rules relating to who can bring a private law action in nuisance might need to be modified so that the human rights of these people were adequately protected (see p. 338).

The impact on policy

Developments in international law are often reflected in policy developments at national level. The government's 1994 *Sustainable Development: The UK Strategy*, Cm 2426, came as a response to Agenda 21, the soft-law[1] document agreed at the 1992 UN Conference on Environment and Development (the Rio Earth Summit), and national policy in many areas reflects commitments originally made at Rio. These agreements, however, tend to contain general principles that give a considerable degree of latitude to governments in their implementation.

The UK government has arguably used this latitude to translate soft international law into soft policy commitments—for example, in relation to improving access to environmental justice (and only with the legally binding 1998 Aarhus Convention, which specifically covers this and related areas, have there been moves to put this on a firmer international law footing—see Chapter 10). There has been a long-standing, pragmatic reluctance to sign up to international treaty obligations that appear incapable of being met in practice. (As an

---

1 We define 'soft law' below, p. 143.

example, the 1995 Fourth North Sea Declaration contained agreement on reducing hazardous substances in the marine environment, but a footnote stated that '*The UK shares the ideal of these aims, but does not accept that they are currently practicable*'.)

The UK and the development of international environmental law

As far as the role of the UK in developing international law is concerned, the record has tended to be patchy at best[2] and it is difficult to identify key environmental treaties in relation to which the UK has taken a lead in the negotiations. Very often, however, it is now the EC as a bloc that negotiates, which makes it difficult to assess the particular stance taken by the UK (although it appears to be one of the more progressive member States in relation to climate change). The UK's role has often appeared to be negative—that is, an attempt to weaken the wording of commitments—although there are, of course, examples of positive involvement. For example, although the UK was initially sceptical of the Cartagena Protocol to the Convention on Biological Diversity, which regulates the international movement of living modified organisms, it eventually came to be one of the member States within pushing for it most strongly. The UK has tended to show most leadership in relation to treaties such as the 1946 Whaling Convention, an area in relation to which the UK no longer has any economic interests.

In recent years, however, the attitude of the UK towards the making of international environmental agreements appears to have softened somewhat, although there is often a certain dragging of heels when it comes to the details, such as with radioactive discharges at sea (see further Case 6.7).

International law and the EC

In some cases, treaties may be open to signature by 'regional economic integration organizations', a term covering the EC, which has signed all of the most recent multilateral environmental agreements. The basic procedure is that the Commission does the negotiating, while the Council signs any treaty: a unanimous vote in the Council may be needed if the treaty deals with issues that require unanimity within the EC. (On voting procedures in relation to the EC adopting international environmental agreements, see p. 137, and also p. 187.)

This should not hide the often hotly contested division of competence between the EC and the member States as regards external matters. International trade and marine fisheries conservation are areas of exclusive Community competence, which means that it is the Community that negotiates any agreements in these areas—such as the General Agreement on Tariffs and Trade (GATT)/World Trade Organization (WTO) Agreement. When the EC is a party to a convention in an area of its exclusive competence, then it may take cases, or be taken, before the relevant international court or tribunal. For example, in *Chile/EC (Swordfish)* 40 ILM 475 (2001), Chile and the EC agreed to submit a dispute about conserving swordfish stocks to the International Tribunal for the Law of the Sea (ITLOS); see also Cases 6.8 and 6.9. Beyond these fields, there is a considerable amount of scope for disagreement about the proper balance of competence in the environmental field. At a time when there are pulls both towards globalization and devolution, we might even question what 'exclusive competence', either for the EC or for the member States, actually means. (On using the European Court of Justice (ECJ) rather than an international tribunal to settle disputes, see Case 6.7.)

2 See R. Churchill (1991) 'International environmental law and the UK' in R. Churchill, L. Warren, and J. Gibson (eds) *Law, Policy and the Environment*, Oxford: Blackwell.

If both the EC and the member States are parties to a treaty, there needs to be some way of deciding on voting rights under the treaty and on coordinating their obligations. In relation to the former, the normal position is that the EC votes as a bloc, so if unanimity is required and this cannot be achieved, the EC may have to abstain. There are concerns that this means that the will of those states forming a majority within the EC on a particular issue may not be counted. One example is the Convention on the International Trade in Endangered Species (CITES), under which the trade in ivory by certain countries was blocked where the EC was united, but allowed where it could not agree a unanimous position. (There are obvious transparency problems here as well, if the position of the EC is left to last-minute negotiations conducted behind closed doors.) On coordinating obligations, a unique example of how this is done is under the 1997 Kyoto Climate Change Protocol. Both the UK and the EC are parties to this, which requires specified reductions of emissions. Under Art. 4 of the Protocol, the member States can 'bubble' their reductions, so that the EC decides which states take heavier and lighter loads depending on things such as their state of economic development (see Box 15.3).

Although EC environmental law is said to flow from developments in international law—specifically, the 1972 Stockholm Conference (see p. 146)—the unique nature of the EC has made it a testing ground for international environmental cooperation. For example, the balancing of trade and environmental concerns in the EC is often held up as a model for integration; the insertion of environmental policy principles in the EC Treaty (now contained in Art. 174(2)) also means that their legal status can be explored within the EC, but contributes to the development of similar principles in international environmental law. In this way, there is a clear synergy between EC and international law and policy.

Nation states and global commons

Because international law is the law of nation states, different considerations apply depending on whether we are concerned with activities that:

- take place within a state and affect only the environment of that state—such as most contamination of land or harm to non-migratory species. Although other states might claim to be injured by non-compliance, in practice, claims are not brought unless there is some direct cross-border problem;

- have an impact as between states, neighbouring or otherwise—for example, transboundary air pollution or pollution of an international river by an upstream state—see the *Trail Smelter* arbitration (Case 6.4), and the *Gabčíkovo* (Case 6.5) and *MOX* cases (Case 6.7);

- affect the 'global commons'—that is, all natural resources beyond the territory of any individual state.

The term 'global commons' includes things such as the atmosphere and the ozone layer. It also includes the oceans and deep seabed beyond the 200-nautical-mile limit of states' 'exclusive economic zones' (EEZs)—although this does not apply to a state's continental shelf if it goes beyond this limit—and space.

The global commons should not be confused with resources that might be said to form a global 'common heritage'. The vast majority of known species, for example, live within or between national borders, which helps to explain why the 1992 Biodiversity Convention refers only to the conservation of biodiversity (by definition, a global resource) as a matter of 'common concern' and makes explicit reference to principles of national sovereignty over natural resources. The concept of 'common heritage' developed, from the 1960s onwards, alongside demands for a new international economic order and focused on the equitable sharing of benefits arising from the use of resources such as the moon, the Antarctic, and the deep seabed. Other than these examples, however, such calls have gone largely unanswered and there is a preference for other ways of dealing with global interest in environmental matters—for example, through 'fair' sharing of the costs of clean technology and differentiated responsibilities among the developed and developing worlds for addressing problems such as climate change (see p. 520).

Finally, the idea of nations owing obligations to all members of the international community—that is, obligations said to be owed *erga omnes*—ought to be especially relevant to international environmental law. In practice, it has not been much relied upon (although, in the *Gabčikovo* case—see Case 6.5—Judge Weeramantry, in a separate opinion, argued that sustainable development and taking a precautious approach should have the same status, *erga omnes*, as international human rights).

CASE 6.1 *Australia v. France* ICJ Rep (1974) 253; *New Zealand v. France* (1974) ICJ Rep 457 (the first *Nuclear Tests* cases)

In 1974, Australia and New Zealand tried to stop French atmospheric nuclear testing in the South Pacific. An unsuccessful attempt was made in the International Court of Justice to argue that they could bring the claim because France owed a general obligation to all states to be free from nuclear tests generally or that France was in violation of the freedom of the high seas. Nevertheless, there were judges in the minority prepared to accept that the right to bring an action of behalf of the international community (an *actio popularis*) might exist and who linked the right to bring such an action with the substantive nature of such *erga omnes* obligations.

Although a matter of dispute, there are those who would argue for the right of a state to bring such an action in relation not only to the global commons, but also to matters of common concern. But as the example of international trade law shows, the difficulty is for states to avoid unilaterally imposing national standards beyond their borders and to try to identify appropriate rules of international law that might apply. In treaty law, however, there are now examples of any state being able to enforce a treaty obligation without having to show that it has suffered material damage from the alleged failure. The non-compliance and dispute-settlement mechanisms under the 1987 Montreal Protocol on Ozone Depletion, discussed below, are an example.

A tragedy of the commons?

A frequent justification for environmental regulation is to prevent damage to areas that are beyond effective individual control and in relation to which traditional property rights do not apply (the idea of environmental 'externalities' is discussed in more depth on p. 239). This is a particular problem in international law, especially for the 'global commons'. Of course, there are some examples from international relations in which it is always in all countries' interests to cooperate—for example, it makes no sense for one state to go it alone when it comes to running international postal services. But in environmental regulation, there may be situations in which individual states have an incentive not to cooperate, even though mutual cooperation would ultimately benefit the state concerned (the so-called 'prisoner's dilemma'). This can be seen, for example, in the difficulties in reaching effective agreement about climate change or overfishing.

A variant of this argument is Hardin's 'Tragedy of the Commons' thesis.[3] Hardin's main argument is that common or open-access resources will always be prone to overexploitation.

---

3 (1968) 162 Science 1243.

His preferred solution is to 'privatize' common resources wherever possible. Failing this, regulation—'mutual coercion, mutually agreed upon'—is required. The former solution can be seen in, for example, the 1982 Law of the Sea Convention, which greatly extended the reach of states' EEZs to 200 nautical miles, effectively 'privatizing' as much as 90 per cent of the known living resources of the seas.

As the failure to stem the decline in world fisheries demonstrates, however, such moves may not be enough, in themselves, to counter unsustainable resource use and, at a national level, the thesis is subject to various theoretical and empirical criticisms. The principal of these is that individuals and groups do not always (or necessarily) act in possessively individualistic ways; whether states always act as rational individual actors at the international level is also subject to debate, but various factors appear to influence the extent to which states come together to reach international agreements (discussed in more detail at p. 154). Hardin's thesis does, however, point to a role for law and legal institutions in providing the necessary framework for states to have confidence that all parties are honouring the agreements into which they enter.

The global commons is only one area requiring international environmental regulation. Resources shared between states may also be subject to 'commons'-type problems, as evidenced by the historic use of the North Sea as little more than an international dumping ground for its riparian states, not least the UK. Shared resources, however, also include things such as migratory species, some of which were the subject of early international 'conservation' law (for example, the 1902 Convention for the Protection of Birds Useful to Agriculture) and which now receive a measure of protection for less directly economic reasons (the 1979 Bonn Convention on the Conservation of Migratory Species of Wild Animals). Finally, activities in one state may impact negatively on another state, for example, through transboundary pollution—see the *Trail Smelter* case (Case 6.4).[4]

What is becoming discernible, however, is the way in which the linkages between globalization and continued economic development, and the natural environment on which that development depends, are becoming better understood. Notably, the emergence of truly global issues requiring regulation is perhaps the most important development of recent years. These include issues that affect everyone and which require common solutions (global warming, ozone layer protection, etc.). But they also include the range of concerns about the linkage between the global economy and environmental degradation that lies at the heart of theories of sustainable development (see p. 56). These include both the 'environmental shadow' cast by developed economies on less-developed regions, and the relationship between poverty and environmental damage.

Sources of international law—'hard law'

The sources of international law are generally divided into 'hard' and 'soft' law. 'Hard law', which takes the various forms listed below (and is recognized by Art. 38 of the ICJ Statute), is binding in the sense that any legal rule or principle binds a state only in its relations with *other states*. It is not necessarily of any relevance in deciding legal disputes between individuals and the state, such as a judicial review action, or as between individuals, such as in nuisance law.

By way of example, the 1992 Convention for the Protection of the Marine Environment of the North East Atlantic (the Oslo–Paris, or OSPAR, Convention) requires states to take '*all possible steps to prevent and eliminate pollution*' and, in doing so, to apply the Polluter Pays

---

4 For a fuller discussion, see C. Stone (1993) *The Gnat is Older than Man*, Princeton: Princeton University Press, chs 2–4.

Principle.[5] These provisions matter, if at all, only as between the parties to the Convention. They do not create general obligations of the kind on which individuals can rely; nor can they be used as the basis for an action against the state or a public body, in the way that EC Directives sometimes can be.

The same can be said of any rules of customary international environmental law. If it were decided that the UK was bound by the Precautionary Principle as customary law, this would not directly assist an individual in bringing a legal argument based on precaution, although it might add weight generally to precautionary arguments or be helpful in reaching a precautionary interpretation of an ambiguous legal text.

Treaties (or conventions, or agreements)

Treaties are the pre-eminent form of international law. The basic rules are laid down in the Vienna Convention on the Law of Treaties 1969, the fundamental principle of which is that states may only be bound with their consent, which is only fully given once the convention has been ratified. The various terms—'treaties'; 'conventions'; 'agreements'—all mean the same thing. A 'protocol' also has the same legal force, although it is a sub-agreement to a treaty, generally used to flesh out or amend the treaty.

In 2001, it was estimated that there were over five hundred international agreements related to the environment. Important international agreements—especially those that are referred to in this chapter and elsewhere in this book—have been made in the following areas.[6]

- **Nature conservation**
  1971 Ramsar Wetlands Convention
  1973 Convention on International Trade in Endangered Species (CITES)
  1979 Berne Convention on the Conservation of European Wildlife and Natural Habitats
  1979 Bonn Convention on Migratory Species of Wild Animals

- **Biodiversity conservation**
  1992 Convention on Biological Diversity
  2000 Cartagena Biosafety Protocol

- **Natural and cultural heritage**
  1972 UNESCO World Heritage Convention

- **Climate change**
  1992 Framework Convention on Climate Change
  1997 Kyoto Protocol

- **Protecting the ozone layer**
  1985 Vienna Convention for the Protection of the Ozone Layer
  1987 Montreal Protocol
  1990 Montreal Amendments

- **Air pollution**
  1979 Convention on Long-Range Transboundary Air Pollution (LRTAP) and a number of protocols made under this on emissions of sulphur dioxide (1994), nitrous oxides (1988), volatile organic compounds (1991), persistent organic pollutants (1998), and heavy metals (1998)

---

5 Respectively, see Arts 2(1)(a) and 2(2)b of the OSPAR Convention.

6 We use the shorter, common name of a treaty (e.g. the 1971 Ramsar Wetlands Convention) rather than the lengthier, formal name (Convention on Wetlands of International Importance especially as Waterfowl Habitat). As this example shows, often, a convention is known by the name of the place at which it was agreed. If a common acronym or abbreviation is used, this is also given.

- **Toxics**
  1989 Basel Transboundary Waste Shipment Convention
  1998 Rotterdam Prior Informed Consent to Trade Convention
  2001 Stockholm Convention on Persistent Organic Pollutants

- **The global marine environment**
  1982 UN Convention on the Law of the Sea (UNCLOS)

- **Regional seas**
  For example, 1992 Marine Environment Convention (OSPAR)

- **Pollution from shipping**
  1973 MARPOL Convention

- **Landscape**
  2000 European Landscape Convention

Most of these treaties contain provisions both about environmental standards (of varying degrees of strictness) and about the main mechanisms used to reach them.

Other treaties, of varying importance, focus more on procedural aspects or seek to provide a general underpinning to international environmental law—for example, on the following areas.

- **Environmental assessment**
  1991 Espoo Transboundary EIA Convention
  2004 Kiev Strategic Environmental Assessment Protocol

- **The rights of civil society**
  1998 Aarhus Convention on Access to Information, Public Participation and Decision-Making and Access to Justice in Environmental Matters

- **Environmental civil liability**
  1992 Civil Liability Convention and 1992 Oil Pollution Fund Convention, and Liability and Compensation for Hazardous and Noxious Substances at Sea Convention 1996 (adopted under MARPOL)
  1993 Lugano Environmental Civil Liability Convention
  1999 Liability and Compensation Protocol to the Basel Hazardous Waste Convention

- **Environmental criminal liability**
  1998 Convention on the Protection of the Environment Through Criminal Law

Treaties generally come into force a specified number of days after a certain number of states have ratified, although, sometimes, a formula is used to ensure that enough key states have ratified (see the example of the climate change regime, below). There are several factors that determine how quickly a treaty comes into force, most important of which are the strictness and clarity of the obligations under it. Thus, on the one hand, the 1992 Convention on Biological Diversity entered into force within 18 months, partly because of the generality of its provisions; on the other hand, the 1982 United Nations Law of the Sea Convention took 12 years to come into force, largely because details about mining the resources of the deep-sea bed were not satisfactorily agreed until the end of this period. Some treaties may never come into force.

Ratification usually requires the approval of the legislature. This can delay treaties from coming into force or from binding key states: the lobbying of the genetic and pharmaceutical industries, for example, has meant that the USA has yet to ratify the Convention on Biological Diversity. But it does mean that treaties will only bind a state once the body responsible for enacting legislation to make the treaty work gives its approval. This is an important consideration in practice where (as in the USA) the executive and legislature may be controlled by different groupings; it may also be relevant if a convention is agreed by a government that then loses power in an election.

Of course, the success—or at least, the workability—of a treaty will usually depend on whether key states are parties and have ratified (see Box 6.1).

BOX 6.1 Bringing the Kyoto Protocol into force

The 1997 Kyoto Protocol to the 1992 UN Climate Change Convention specifies a formula that is designed to ensure that a core of carbon-emitting developed world states have agreed to its provisions. For the Protocol to come into force, at least 55 parties to the Convention had to ratify it *and* these 55 parties had to include 'Annex I' parties—that is, all Organisation for Economic Co-operation and Development (OECD) states and certain states from the former Soviet Bloc (which accounted for at least 55 per cent of the total carbon dioxide emissions of Annex I parties in 1990).

By July 2004, 124 parties had ratified or acceded to the Protocol, including the EC. But the Protocol had not entered into force, because these states only accounted for just over 44 per cent of emissions and key polluting states, including Russia and the USA, had yet to ratify.

In late 2004, seemingly as part of a deal to allow it entry to the WTO, the former ratified, which brought the Protocol into force in February 2005. In the USA, meanwhile, the Bush Administration made it clear that it would not sign. Despite the absence of the world's major greenhouse gas emitter, the parties to the Protocol have taken steps to bring the Protocol to life.

There are some treaties, however, which may extend, in practice, to non-parties (see the discussion of CITES in Box 6.4).

Custom

Customary international law is created by implicit, rather than explicit, agreement, and needs both the practice of states and a conviction that they consider themselves legally bound to act in certain ways. There are problems in ascertaining exactly what a state does and problems of identifying customs in the wider global community, but the uncertainty of custom does offer the potential for flexibility and the scope for creative argument to develop principles of customary international environmental law.

In this sense, flexibility offers possibilities for the development of principles in a way that vagueness elsewhere cannot (for example, in more developed areas of law and policy). Many international law scholars, for example, claim that a number of the central principles of environmental law—such as the Precautionary and Preventive Principles—are now established international customary law, at least for those states that are a party to a sufficient number of the many texts that now make reference to them. But the precise scope and content of, for example, the precautionary principles laid down in various treaties and 'soft law' documents is rarely duplicated, so there is a problem in identifying what it is *exactly* to which states can be said to have implicitly agreed—for example, the degree of risk needed to trigger the principle's application (see the WTO *Beef Hormones* case on p. 161 and also Case 3.2). It also presupposes that such principles have meanings that can be transferred from one legal context to another—and some might dispute whether this is the case. For example, arguably, the Precautionary Principle means different things depending on whether it is being used to challenge a failure of a rule maker to make a rule or a decision that is argued to be overly precautionary.[7]

---

7 See, e.g., V. Hayvaert (2006) 31 Eur LR 185, and p. 71.

Generally recognized principles of law

Generally recognized principles of law are of limited scope and are used where no treaty provision or custom can be. They are mostly used to identify basic principles of procedure on which to decide particular issues—for example, the admissibility of evidence. They should not be confused with the 'principles' of international environmental law, which are contained either in treaties or which may be distilled from treaties, or principles inferable from customary international law (see above).

Judicial decisions and the work of international jurists

Judicial decisions include not only decisions of the International Court of Justice (ICJ) and the various international tribunals that exist, but also those of regional bodies (for example, the ECJ) and national courts. Previous decisions of the ICJ are binding only between the parties and only as to the case under consideration (Art. 59, ICJ Statute), hence their subsidiary nature. They do not create precedents, although, in practice, they function in a not-too-dissimilar way.

The dearth of previous case law may help to explain why academic writing is often referred to in international law, although this also reflects a closer relationship between legal academics and the ICJ. The work of jurists is often referred to if relatively new ground is being covered. A good example of this is the second *Nuclear Tests* case (*New Zealand v. France* [1995] ICJ Rep 288), in which the dissenting opinion of Judge Weeramantry referred to academic opinion about the requirements of the sustainable development principle.

Sources of international law—'soft law'

The hallmarks of 'soft law' are that it is not binding in form, is often neither clear nor specific in content, and is not readily enforceable in character. Examples include the following.

Declarations

Three key documents in international environmental law are the 1972 Stockholm Declaration of the UN Conference on the Human Environment, the 1992 Rio Declaration on Environment and Development, and the 2002 Johannesburg Declaration on Sustainable Development (see p. 146). Such declarations perform a number of functions:

- they consolidate and restate what are already rules of customary international law—for example, national sovereignty over natural resources;

- they contribute towards moving principles forward to the status of custom;

- they reflect the agreed aspirations of the international community.

The five Declarations of the North Sea Conferences, which fall into this last category, have had a marked impact on EC and UK policy on, for example, stopping the dumping of industrial waste and sewage sludge at sea.

Principles

As well as hard, binding obligations (however vaguely expressed), treaties may also contain what are essentially principles. Examples include Art. 3 of the 1992 Framework Convention on Climate Change, which sets out a list of principles intended to guide the parties in implementing the treaty. These include principles relating to duties owed to future generations and to the '*common but differentiated responsibilities and respective capabilities*' of the parties (see p. 156). Elaborating specific principles in the treaty itself, as opposed to its Preamble, is increasingly common.

Recommendations

Towards the 'softer' end of the spectrum, recommendations may embody the germs of principles, or even of treaties. Good examples are the many recommendations of the Organisation for Economic Co-operation and Development (OECD), which relate directly to the development of environmental policy—for example, on the Polluter Pays Principle (1974) and on the use of economic instruments in environmental policy (1991).

Standards

International standards can be a useful way in which to encourage environmentally beneficial changes in behaviour and have varying degrees of legal force.

1. Binding standards may, in practice, be based on international standards—for example, EC drinking water quality standards are influenced by World Health Organization standards.

2. Some non-legislative international standards provide the benchmark against which international trade restrictions are judged—for example, the *Codex Alimentarius* in relation to certain food standards under the WTO agreements.

3. Some international standards may be accorded the status of binding law. The EC Regulation on Environmental Management and Auditing Systems, for example, allows for participation through compliance with specified national, European, and international standards, such as ISO 14001 (see p. 246).

An example of the use of international standards in the English courts is the *Glacier Metal* case (Case 6.2).

CASE 6.2 *Murdoch v. Glacier Metal Co. Ltd* [1998] Env LR 732

The claimants brought a civil action arguing that they were exposed to noise levels that exceeded World Health Organization (WHO) standards. Although these are numeric, they are still 'soft law' standards. Standards such as these can play a part in deciding whether there is an actionable nuisance. Here, however, the mere fact that noise exceeded WHO levels was not sufficient to found a claim of nuisance; in all of the circumstances, the noise from the metal company was judged to be reasonable. A crucial factor was that the complainants lived on a noisy road—that is, the locality of the area was already noisy. Indeed, it is worth noting here that the majority of the UK population live in areas that exceed WHO noise guidelines[8] (see Case 8.1).

The adoption of soft law over binding treaty law has several theoretical advantages:

- domestic treaty ratification processes can be avoided;

- it provides an autonomous form of lawmaking for international organizations;

- it is more easily amended or replaced than treaties;

---

8 See the Noise Incidence Study available online at **www.defra.gov.uk/environment/noise/research/index.htm**.

- it provides immediate evidence of consensus;

- it is easier to reach agreement on its content *because* of its non-binding character.

Soft law instruments may codify existing law, interpret or amplify treaties and other existing legal rules, act as a step in the process of concluding binding agreements, and serve as evidence of the obligations that states feel they are under. They are an important part of the repetition and interplay with multilateral treaties and state practice.

There is, however, some work that questions some of these basic assumptions. For example, in his study of the North Sea Declarations,[9] Pallemaerts argues that soft law has been mainly used not as a precursor and supplement to hard law, but as a substitute for it, satisfying symbolic needs, rather than effecting real change in an instrumental way. Obviously, if commitments are too soft, they may be virtually meaningless. Arguably, the 1992 Non-Binding Authoritative Statement of Principles on Forests (see p. 147) served only to highlight the absence of any measure of consensus in this area at the time, although, equally, there are global private forest product certification schemes that, while limited in some respects, nevertheless have a number of positive aspects in linking producers and consumers.

International law and policy development

The development of international environmental law can be traced back at least to the nineteenth century and the adoption of a number of bilateral treaties concerning fishing stocks. Thereafter, other bilateral and regional treaties were adopted, but tended to cover things such as species conservation. Although some bilateral treaties sought to regulate transboundary pollution, on the whole, developments in treaty law were, as Sands notes, '*ad hoc, sporadic and limited in scope*'.[10] Enforcement issues, in particular, received scant attention and many conventions were little more than 'sleeping treaties', existing only on paper because of the absence of any effective institutional and enforcement arrangements (see p. 155). There was little development of customary international environmental law.

The approach of international law generally to environmental problems is well illustrated by two international arbitrations (see Cases 6.3 and 6.4).

CASE 6.3 *Behring Fur Seals Arbitration* (1898) 1 Moore's Int Arbitration Awards 755

Fur seals were born on US territory, but then migrated beyond the (then) three-nautical-mile limit of US territorial waters, where British sealing ships killed them. The USA alleged that the seals were being overexploited. The panel found that the USA had no right of '*protection or property*' in the seals, despite the importance of their conservation for local US citizens and the threat of their extinction. The radical argument that the USA was acting '*for the benefit of mankind*'—that is, an *erga omnes* or perhaps even 'common heritage' argument—was also rejected. The outcome of the dispute was, however, a series of provisions, binding on the two parties, to regulate seal fishing in the area. These provisions displayed many of the features of modern conservation treaties: closed seasons; limited means of killing or taking, etc. But the decision did not bind the other states sealing in the area, which continued unrestricted until a treaty binding all relevant states was agreed in 1911.

The second decision of note was in the *Trail Smelter* arbitration.

9 M. Pallemaerts (2003) *Toxics and Transnational Law*, Oxford: Hart.

10 P. Sands (2003) *Principles of International Environmental Law*, 2nd edn, Cambridge: Cambridge University Press, p. 27.

CASE 6.4 *USA v. Canada* (1941) 3 RIAA 1907 (the *Trail Smelter* case)

Sulphur emissions from a factory in Canada damaged crops, trees, and pastures in the US State of Washington. The issue was not the right to exploit natural resources on Canadian territory, but rather whether the manner of doing so was limited because of neighbouring states' interests. The tribunal held that:

> No state has the right to use or permit the use of its territory in such a manner as to cause injury by fumes in or to the territory of another of the properties or persons therein, when the case is of serious consequence and the injury is established by clear and convincing evidence.

For further comment on this dispute, see Case 15.2.

From these beginnings, an extensive body of international treaty law has emerged, together with the more tentative emergence of new norms of customary international environmental law. Various landmarks deserve special mention.

The Stockholm Conference

The United Nations Conference on the Human Environment held in Stockholm in 1972 was the first occasion on which the international community of states united to discuss international environmental issues more generally and more coherently. Although no treaty was signed, the conference adopted an Action Plan of 109 Recommendations and a Declaration of 26 Principles. It also adopted a resolution on institutional and financial arrangements that led, among other things, to the establishment of the United Nations Environment Programme (UNEP) (see p. 149).

For some, the Stockholm Declaration is the foundation of modern international environmental law. Its principles, however, are largely aspirational, rather than mandatory—that is, expressed as 'should' rather than 'shall'—and few impose clear duties on states. The key principles in the Declaration are:

- '*the sovereign right* [of States] *to exploit their own resources pursuant to their own environmental policies, and the responsibility to ensure that activities within their jurisdiction or control do not cause damage to the environment of other States or of areas beyond the limits of national jurisdiction*' (Principle 21);

- a requirement (although not a duty) for international cooperation to '*effectively control, prevent, reduce and eliminate adverse environmental effects resulting from activities conducted in all spheres, in such a way that due account is taken of the sovereignty and interests of all States*' (Principle 24).

Perhaps more importantly, the Stockholm Conference marked the beginning of a rapid increase in the number of international environmental agreements concluded. Over 60 per cent of all international environmental agreements post-date Stockholm.

The Brundtland Report

Although a strictly non-legal text, the report of the World Commission on Environment and Development (1987) *Our Common Future*, known as the 'Brundtland Report', was pivotal in changing the direction of international environmental law. Its central concern was the increasing globalization of various crises—environmental; developmental; energy, etc.— and the connections between them. As it memorably summarized: '*They are all one.*' Most memorable is the Report's stress on sustainable development, defined as '*development that meets the needs of the present without compromising the ability of future generations to meet their own needs*' (see Chapter 3). But the report provided little solid guidance on the exact components of what such a duty to future generations might entail. (On Brundtland, see further Chapter 2.)

The Rio Conference

The UN Conference on Environment and Development held in Rio in 1992 provided an opportunity to put flesh on the bones of sustainable development in international law and to address the concern, noted in the Brundtland Report, of the 'sectoral' and 'piecemeal' nature of international environmental law. The legal texts to emerge from Rio were important in developing international environmental law—but they fell some way short of providing the radical change in direction some had envisaged.

The legal texts that emerged were:

- the Rio Declaration (see below);

- the Convention on Biological Diversity (see Chapter 19, especially p. 681);

- the Framework Convention on Climate Change (see p. 520);

- Agenda 21 (an 800-page global action plan on development and the environment);

- in the absence of agreement on a global forest convention, a 'non-legally binding authoritative statement' of principles in this area.

In terms of the general development of customary international environmental law, however, the Rio Declaration is central. Agreed to by all 176 states attending, it is a key soft law document and an important text in relation to the consolidation of a number of principles of customary international environmental law (see Box 6.2).

BOX 6.2 **Key regulatory principles in the Rio Declaration**	
Principle 7	Common, but differentiated, responsibilities
Principle 10	Fostering public awareness and participation in environmental decision making
Principle 15	The precautionary approach
Principle 16	The Polluter Pays Principle
Principle 17	Environmental impact assessment (EIA)
Principles 18 and 19	Risk communication

Although the Preamble states that it is reaffirming and building upon the Stockholm Declaration, important principles are conspicuously modified (Principle 21, Stockholm) or even weakened. Thus, Principle 1 of Stockholm, which refers to the '*fundamental right to...an environment of a quality that permits a life of dignity and well-being*' becomes, in Principle 1 of Rio: '*Human beings are at the centre of concerns for sustainable development. They are entitled to a healthy and productive life in harmony with nature.*' Interestingly, the Brundtland Commission had mandated an expert group, from North and South, to elaborate a set of general principles that could be submitted to the UN General Assembly with a view to their forming the basis of a universal declaration.[11] Ultimately, the Commission failed to give its endorsement to this work, which might have underpinned a more ecological 'Earth Charter' akin to the Universal Declaration of Human Rights, as advocated by some states.

The effect of the Rio Declaration, therefore, was something of a mixed bag in relation to the development of international environmental law and legal principles. Specifically, the double-edged quality of the explicit incorporation of developmental concerns (see Principles 2 and 3) might be seen either as an important accommodation of developing world interests or as allowing generally for 'business as usual'. Similarly, the lack of development of common heritage concepts might be viewed differently according to whether the focus is the global commons or biodiversity, and depending on whether one adopts a 'northern' or 'southern' perspective.

Post-Rio

Developments up to, and beyond, Rio suggest a maturing of international environmental law, although numerous problems remain. In relation to treaty law, many issues continued to be dealt with sectorally—for example, ozone depletion and biodiversity conservation; elsewhere, specific processes or products have come under international regulation—for example, the agreement of a 1998 Protocol on Persistent Organic Pollutants to the 1979 Convention on Long-Range Transboundary Air Pollution. A range of different types of agreement are now found, from bilateral, sub-regional, and regional agreements, to global conventions, and there has been no let-up in the number of agreements reached.

Sadly, sudden shocks, rather than creeping crises—that is, Chernobyl or the 'ozone hole' discovery, rather than global warming forecasts and concerns about biodiversity—tend to help to secure agreement. This illustrates the continuing nature of international law as, in general, reactive rather than proactive. But the Biosafety Protocol, negotiated under the Convention on Biological Diversity, can be seen as the first example of a truly precautionary international environmental agreement, because it deals with threats to biodiversity—relating to the import and export of living modified organisms—in relation to which the nature of the threat is at best theoretical (see Box 3.8).

As with developments in the EC, there has been a perceptible shift in recent years from simply promulgating substantive new agreements towards putting effort into making existing agreements more effective and achieving higher levels of compliance.[12] Particular mention should be made in this context of the 1998 UN/ECE Convention on Access to Information, Public Participation and Decision-Making and Access to Justice in Environmental Matters (the Aarhus Convention). This Convention has not only led to a strengthening of EC law, but it has also proved to be a catalyst for giving wider civil society participatory rights in other conventions (for example, the Biosafety Protocol). Implementation and compliance issues, and other future developments, are discussed in more depth below.

Finally, mention should be made of the Johannesburg Summit—the World Summit on Sustainable Development—in 2002. This was a ten-year follow-up to the Rio Conference, but the main focus of the Summit was on the alleviation of poverty. No statement of principle or conventions were adopted and the Johannesburg Declaration on Sustainable Development did not propose any specific action. A plan of implementation was adopted, and this does contain certain targets and timetables, but, as with Agenda 21—which it confirms and, to a limited extent, takes a step further—the commitments are generally soft, mostly requiring

---

11 See R. Munro and J. Lammers (eds) (1987) *Environmental Protection and Sustainable Development: Legal Principles and Recommendations*, London: Graham and Trotman.

12 See, e.g., Part I of the Programme for the Development and Periodic Review of Environmental Law for the First Decade of the Twenty First Century, adopted by the UNEP Governing Council in 2001.

states only to 'encourage', 'aim', and 'promote' certain objectives. This is not to say that these ambitions have no real-world effect and much attention has been given, for example, to the aspiration to halve by 2015 the number of people without access to clean drinking water or significantly to reduce the decline in biodiversity by 2010. These are not enforceable in any traditional legal sense, but do have some degree of political and policy 'bite'.

Institutional organizations and other actors

A feature of international environmental law is the wide range of bodies involved either in the development of treaties or their enforcement. This is because, unlike international trade law, for example, there is no main or 'umbrella' convention governing the area in the way that GATT regulates these aspects of international trade; nor is there a body similar to the WTO when it comes to compliance (international trade and the environment is discussed more fully below).

The key players in international law remain individual states (including within this definition the EC, which may speak for all 27 member States—see p. 136). Treaties are often advocated by individual states that are keen to see regulation in an area of particular importance to them or, conversely, are opposed by states, usually for economic reasons, and, of course, there can be no international law without the agreement of states.

A slightly less reactive and piecemeal approach to treaty making ought to be a responsibility of the United Nations Environment Programme (UNEP), which was established following the Stockholm Conference. Based in Nairobi, UNEP is now the only UN body charged exclusively with international environmental matters and has played an important role in the development of international environmental law, not least through its promotion of numerous regional seas treaties, the 1985 Vienna 'Ozone' Convention, and the 1992 Biodiversity Convention. But, in general terms, UNEP has been a weak institution, which is somewhat underfunded and of relatively low visibility.

Although not a specialist environmental body, the International Law Commission (ILC) plays an important role in the drafting of treaties, and in the development of customary international law and general principles, although its work is not specific to the environmental area.

Another institution that deserves special mention is the International Union for the Conservation of Nature (IUCN), established in 1948, which has a unique mix of governmental and non-governmental members, and a quasi-institutional status. The IUCN was an influential force behind the Convention on the International Trade in Endangered Species (CITES) treaty and the driving force behind the influential 1982 World Charter for Nature, both of which have played an important role in bringing nature conservation to international legal attention.

Increasingly, non-government organizations (NGOs) representing environmental and other interests are also involved in the negotiating of international agreements. Usually, this is at the fringes, although some conventions have started life as texts drafted by NGOs. A notable development was that NGOs were formally involved in the negotiation of the 1998 Aarhus Convention not only as observers and, perhaps because of its subject matter, have important rights under it, including the right to nominate candidates for election to the Convention's Implementation Committee. Unquestionably, environmental NGOs have played an important role in shaping the general political climate that has spawned increased activity in this area in the last thirty years.

Like negotiation, enforcement is usually handled on a treaty-by-treaty basis and treaties tend to establish their own 'executive' organizations, such as the CITES Secretariat or the OSPAR Commission. Some soft-law documents also do this: the UN Commission on Sustainable Development is charged with implementing Agenda 21. This proliferation of organizations (and of treaties) may frustrate attempts to establish policy coherence in this area, as well as make policy and legal integration more difficult. Environmental NGOs therefore also have an increasingly important role in relation to compliance. Formerly, this tended to be limited to their 'observer status' at the meetings of parties to conventions such as CITES and the 1946 Whaling Convention, with some scope for bringing implementation problems to wider attention.[13] In some cases, their role now extends more directly to enforcement matters (see Box 6.3).

BOX 6.3 TRAFFIC and CITES

TRAFFIC is a wildlife trade-monitoring network jointly established by the WWF (formerly the World Wildlife Fund) and the IUCN (the World Conservation Union). Over time, it has moved from an informal monitoring role to a point at which it now has a formal role in policing the international trade in certain elephant species under the Convention on International Trade in Endangered Species of Wild Fauna and Flora (CITES). Its compliance function is supported by its being an international organization that is not tied to any particular state, meaning that it can take an ecoregional approach: we can question whether rich, northern states would be equally comfortable with the involvement of formal NGOs in monitoring their compliance with treaty obligations.

In the *Shrimp/Turtle* case (see Case 6.9), it was notable that environmental NGOs were allowed (as a matter of discretion, rather than as of right) to make unsolicited representations to the WTO. This might be seen as a first step towards their greater involvement in world trade rule making, although this whole issue is highly controversial.[14]

Finally, the role of bodies with primarily economic remits should not be overlooked. This is seen below, in relation to the role of the WTO, but other bodies are also important. The lending policy of the World Bank, for example, is crucial in relation to a wide range of development projects (we discuss this in relation to the Bank's internal requirements relating to environmental impact assessment in Box 13.2) and the Bank plays an important role more widely in financing measures to implement multilateral environmental treaties, through funds such as the Global Environment Facility and Prototype Carbon Fund. The OECD has also played a significant role, for example, in promoting the use of economic instruments and in advancing the Polluter Pays Principle. The integration of environmental objectives into economic and other policy areas is likely to increase the number of bodies that pursue (or ought to pursue) environmental issues, especially if, institutionally, international environmental law remains as fragmented as it is.

Dispute settlement and dispute settlement bodies

There are a number of reasons why resolving disputes before international courts and tribunals is problematic:

- generally, only states may be parties (but see below);
- both states must accept the jurisdiction of the court or tribunal—but, even then, taking a case is often seen as politically unfriendly and international diplomacy is usually preferred;

---

13 For example, the World Heritage Committee of the UNESCO World Heritage Convention encourages private individuals and NGOs to contact it regarding threats to listed world heritage sites.

14 For an analysis, see R. Howse (2003) 9 ELJ 496.

- diplomatic solutions—for example, mediation or negotiation—are less risky, because the likelihood of accepting a politically unacceptable decision is reduced;

- very few disputes are exclusively, or even primarily, legal disputes. For the more powerful states, the temptation is not to submit to rules that mean that their advantages, and non-legal issues, are left at the door of the court or tribunal, and are not exploited politically.

All of these mean that non-legal routes are generally preferred, but if international disputes need to be resolved formally, they tend to be settled by arbitration. That said, some commentators have perceived a greater role for adjudication since the mid 1990s: '[T]*he adjudicative function has assumed increasing importance in interpreting and applying—and even developing—the rules of international law in the field of the environment*.'[15] This is more a reflection on how little 'environmental jurisprudence' there has been until recent years, however, than a comment on any vast expansion in environmentally related disputes being decided by courts and tribunals.

It is also worth noting that, increasingly, consultation provisions are built into treaties by which other states may be affected by actual or risky activities beyond their boundaries[16]—that is, a preventive approach to dispute resolution has increasingly been adopted.

The International Court of Justice (ICJ)

Very little resort is made to the ICJ, a UN body consisting of 15 judges elected by the General Assembly and the Security Council, and less than a third of UN members (of which the UK is one) have accepted its compulsory jurisdiction. The ICJ's caseload has not been substantial, amounting to roughly three decisions per year. In addition to hearing disputes between states, however, the Court can also be asked to deliver Advisory Opinions by specialist UN agencies. A notable example was the request by the UN General Assembly in relation to the *Legality of the Threat or Use of Nuclear Weapons* 35 ILM 809 and 1343 (1996), in which states' responsibilities not to cause environmental damage beyond their territories or to the global commons were explicitly recognized by the ICJ:

The existence of the general obligations of States to ensure that activities within their jurisdictions and control respect the environment of other States or of areas beyond national control is now part of the corpus of international law relating to the environment.[17]

Although an Environmental Chamber of the ICJ was established in 1993, it has yet to hear any cases and the full ICJ has only ever given judgment in one contested environmental 'case': the *Gabčíkovo-Nagymaros* case (see Case 6.5).[18] Because the mechanisms available in international law have been under-utilized in the environmental sphere, the extent to which they are appropriate for resolving international environmental disputes remains, perhaps at best, unclear.

CASE 6.5 **The *Gabčíkovo-Nagymaros* case (1998) 37 ILM 162 (the *Danube Dam* case)**

In 1977, Hungary and Czechoslovakia agreed, by treaty, to dam a section of the River Danube to facilitate economic development. This meant that, over a significant stretch of the river, most of the

---

15 Sands (2003) p. 13.

16 See, generally, para. 39.10 of Agenda 21.

17 At [29].

18 There is a dispute currently before the ICJ between Argentina and Uruguay concerning the impact of pulp mills on the River Uruguay, a shared resource—it is worth checking the website of the ICJ and the Online Resource Centre for developments.

Danube would be diverted into a vast artificial waterway. The treaty contained some very rudimentary provisions to protect the environment. In 1989, Hungary abandoned construction work following concerns about the project's environmental impact. In 1991, the Czech government proceeded to a provisional solution involving construction work entirely on Czech territory and, in 1992, the Danube was diverted, leading to considerable environmental damage. Hungary then terminated the treaty. The two countries eventually agreed to take their dispute to the International Court of Justice (see *Case concerning the Gabčíkovo-Nagymaros Project (Hungary/Slovakia)* (1998) 37 ILM 162).

The central question was whether the situation was sufficiently serious to justify Hungary's actions. As a matter of the rules on treaties, the Court accepted that concerns about its natural environment could justify this, but then found that the environmental damage was neither sufficiently serious nor immediate. The ICJ also found that the Czech action in 1991 was disproportionate, violating the principle that shared watercourses should be utilized 'equitably'; on the other hand, neither could Hungary lawfully terminate as it had done, because the 1977 treaty provided, in theory, a means of adjusting the obligations of the parties to new conditions.

The Court therefore emphasized the extent to which relations between the two countries continued to be governed primarily by terms agreed to between the parties. But the Court did decide that, in implementing the treaty, the parties had to give effect to new norms of international environmental law, not only in relation to new activities, but also retrospectively, and that they had, in the light of sustainable development, to 'look afresh' at the environmental consequences of the project with a view to reconciling economic development and environmental protection. The Court did not elaborate further on how this was to be done (perhaps because the Court lacked a specialist knowledge of the available techniques), although the separate opinion of Vice President Weeramantry argued for a duty of 'continuous' environmental impact assessment—that is, one that requires the continual assessment of environmental impact in the light of modern knowledge. The Court also held that the parties had to find a 'satisfactory solution' to the volume of water being released into the old bed of the Danube, a strong reading of which suggests that the obligation on the parties is not only procedural.

In some ways, the judgment is unsatisfactory: for example, it did not discuss the principles that should be used when calculating environmental damage. Taking a wider perspective, it is not clear that the problem was limited to the two parties (the area affected is Europe's last inland delta and is, arguably, of much wider importance).[19] It is clear, however, that the Court sees some legal substance to the concept of sustainable development, even if this is couched in terms of requiring states to ask the correct questions about whether environmental protection is being integrated in decision making and how this is being done (for example, by ensuring that there are processes in place, such as impact assessment, with which to do so).

It is worth considering, since both states now belong to the European Union, whether the ICJ has any continuing jurisdiction over this case (see the discussion in Case 6.7).

A telling example of the limits of the ICJ's jurisdiction is the *Fisheries Jurisdiction* case (Case 6.6).

CASE 6.6 *Spain v. Canada* (1998) ICJ Rep 432 (the *Fisheries Jurisdiction case*)

This case was brought after Canada had used force to stop a Spanish trawler (the *Estai*) from fishing in an area that was important for Canadian fisheries interests, but which lay beyond the 200-mile limit

---

19 A useful consideration here is the role that amicus briefs might play. For example, the Appellate Body of the WTO has given itself a discretion to accept these, not only from NGOs, but also from other states not directly affected (see, e.g., *EC/Sardines* (2002) AB-2002-3 and see also p. 150).

of its exclusive economic zone. In 1994, Canada amended its coastal fisheries law to allow it to board such vessels if they were violating a law that was ostensibly aimed at preventing overfishing. Canada was aware of the possible inconsistencies of this national law with the international law of the sea. Hence, two days before its coastal fisheries law was amended, Canada effectively refused to let the International Court of Justice hear cases involving Canadian fisheries conservation matters such as that at stake. This was sufficient for the ICJ to decide that it had no right to hear the complaint, even though Canada's actions were otherwise, at best, of dubious legality.

(b) Other international courts and tribunals

In addition to the ICJ, there are other international courts and tribunals that may hear environmental cases. These include the Appellate Body of the World Trade Organization (see p. 158) and the International Tribunal for the Law of the Sea (ITLOS). As with cases that might be decided by the ICJ, however, in general, it is the interests of nation states, rather than individuals, that are at stake and there are few opportunities for individuals to raise actions in these international fora. The right for individuals to take cases to the ECtHR is a notable exception (see p. 135); another is the right of individuals under the Aarhus Convention to submit complaints about non-compliance. These complaints are heard by a review body made up of members nominated not only by state parties, but also by accredited NGOs, and, although its decisions are not legally enforceable in any traditional sense—that is, there is no direct sanction—the review body's findings may act as a trigger to bring states into compliance.

Some problems of litigating international environmental disputes, especially in a European context, emerge clearly from the dispute between Ireland and the UK over the mixed oxide (MOX) plant at Sellafield (see Case 6.7).

CASE 6.7 **The *Sellafield* (or *MOX*) cases**

There is a dispute between Ireland and the UK about the operation of a mixed oxide (MOX) plant at Sellafield. There are concerns about discharges into the Irish Sea, and about the movement of nuclear materials to and from the plant. This has led to distinct legal disputes involving Ireland and the UK.[20] Together, they illustrate how international law might be relied on in an interstate environmental dispute and how international environmental law intersects with other 'layers' of law, such as EC law.

First, Ireland pursued a case under the UN Law of the Sea Convention (LOSC), on the basis, among other things, that the UK had not carried out a proper environmental impact assessment before the plant was authorized. In November 2001, provisional measures were sought, essentially requesting something similar to a pre-emptive injunction to stop the plant from commencing operation. The International Tribunal for the Law of the Sea (ITLOS) decided that the situation was not sufficiently serious for this, but did require the parties to cooperate by exchanging information, monitoring risks, and preventing pollution. There was, however, disagreement among the judges on the importance of the environmental impact assessment in deciding how risky the operation of the plant would be.

Ireland also pursued a case against the UK under the Oslo–Paris (OSPAR) Treaty over access to information about the economic justification for the plant. Ultimately, the Arbitration Tribunal decided in favour of the UK, although it did decide that the obligation on states under OSPAR to make information available was not only an obligation on competent authorities within each party to do so. This is

---

20 See also the domestic challenge that the plant was not 'justified' under Euratom law: *R (Friends of the Earth) v. Secretary of State for the Environment, Food and Rural Affairs* [2002] Env LR 24.

important because it shows how international environmental law can create obligations both within and between states. But which body has jurisdiction to hear these disputes?

Both Ireland and the UK are parties to the OSPAR Convention, and member States of the EC Treaty and the Treaty establishing the European Atomic Energy Community (Euratom). For matters covered by the latter, member States must resolve any disputes through European law. The Tribunal decided that it had jurisdiction, but, in 2003, proceedings in the subsequent Arbitration Tribunal were suspended pending clarification on jurisdictional issues relating to EC competence. In Case C-459/03 *European Commission v. Ireland* [2006] Env LR 16, the European Court of Justice (ECJ) held that, because, when it ratified the LOSC, the EC had formally asserted its exclusive competence over pollution prevention provisions to the extent that the LOSC clashed with its own rules, Ireland was in breach of the EC Treaty because it had not had the consent of the EC Commission before it started the arbitration proceedings.

It is not clear that this means that all international law disputes involving two or more EC member States must be resolved through the ECJ, and there is at least one recent example in which a dispute has been decided by international arbitration and not through that Court.[21] The practical point seems to be whether the EC will, in fact, assert its competence and then, if the member States use alternative tribunals, object.

This range of tribunals raises concerns about their ability to decide cases with an environmental dimension and the equally important question of which body is most appropriate to decide any particular dispute. This has implications for the development of a coherent body of international environmental law, although, in practice, problems have not yet arisen. Indeed, there is some evidence that competition between these various tribunals may stimulate useful reforms. For example, the ICJ has held that its pre-judgment provisional measure orders create binding obligations on the parties (*Germany v. USA (LaGrand)* (2001) ICJ Rep 516), which could be important in cases in which there is the threat of serious irreversible environmental harm (in this sense, the very essence of provisional measures can be seen as precautionary), and it may have been that this decision was reached because bodies such as ITLOS already have this power. There is also an argument that specialist tribunals such as ITLOS will have greater confidence to take a purposive approach to deciding disputes, which might lead to a more responsive body of case law (a similar line of reasoning is put forward for the establishment of environmental courts in the UK—see p. 323).

Making agreements more effective

As noted above, international law cannot be 'enforced' in the same way as domestic law or even EC law. The limited role for the courts in resolving international environmental disputes is also clear. This has meant a focus on other means of securing compliance with international agreements, especially positive inducements rather than negative sanctions. Note also that few states ever have individual incentives to initiate action for non-compliance.

But states are often reluctant to delegate enforcement matters to bodies such as treaty secretariats. The following conclusions may be drawn as to what makes for a more 'successful' treaty (and see also Box 6.4).

Who is a party?

Attention should be paid to which states will be party to any treaty or any agreements made under treaties. A good, and perhaps unique, example is the 1979 Bonn Convention on

21 See P. Cardwell and D. French (2007) 19 JEL 121.

Migratory Species, which provides for AGREEMENTS (*sic*) open to accession by all states across whose borders species migrate regardless of whether they are parties to the convention (see, for example, the 1995 AGREEMENT on the Conservation of African-Eurasian Migratory Waterbirds). These 'sub-treaties' allow states to benefit from positive conservation measures without signing up to the negative restrictions imposed in relation to species that the convention lists as endangered.

The nexus between states and treaties can, of course, be controversial. Currently, there are concerns about the extent to which Japanese influence is leading certain non-whaling states to become parties to the 1946 Whaling Convention, voting to loosen restrictions on whaling. But this simply reverses a previous practice of the UK in using the same strategy the other way round.

Implementation and monitoring

Much attention is now paid to implementation and monitoring provisions, both at an institutional level and in relation to procedures. For example, the establishment of an active treaty secretariat, regular meetings of the parties, and sometimes provision for NGO involvement are now common. NGOs have built up considerable adeptness in gathering information about non-compliance with treaties, and in passing this on either to secretariats and/or to other sympathetic states. In some treaties—for example, the Aarhus Convention—this role is now formalized.

More generally, success is likely to correlate with the extent to which information about compliance and non-compliance is collected and disseminated to the actors concerned. This task may be given to a specialist body, such as the Subsidiary Body for Implementation established under the Climate Change Convention. Adverse reports about implementation may, in themselves, be sufficient to edge a party into compliance. Although the parties usually gather information, there are examples of the possibility of on-site monitoring responsibilities. The 1971 Ramsar Wetlands Convention, for example, allows for monitoring at the request of the host state authorities, which may prevent allegations of 'free-riding'. The functions of the Commission established under the 1992 OSPAR Convention include requiring the assessment of compliance and, where appropriate, enable it to call for necessary compliance measures. Nevertheless, there is still a general problem of ensuring adequate monitoring, even when there are treaty arrangements under which developed countries pay for monitoring in developing countries.

Positive assistance

Effectively designed institutions are also better able to administer the financial aspects of treaties, which, in this context, mean things such as financing, technology transfer, and so on. Unlike the EC, where the basic starting point is that the cost of implementing environmental policy should be borne by the member States and that the polluter should pay (subject to certain relaxations of this principle to alleviate particular national difficulties), there is no such starting point in international law. Giving positive assistance is therefore an acceptable, pragmatic, and increasingly central aspect of environmental treaties.

The use of positive assistance for developing states began with the London Amendments (1990) to the Montreal Protocol to the 1985 Vienna Ozone Treaty, establishing the Global Environment Facility (GEF), which is also used for the 1992 Climate Change Convention, the 1992 Biodiversity Convention, and the 2001 Persistent Organic Pollutants Convention. Financial aid has been given for the agreed incremental costs of compliance with control measures (under the 1990 London Amendments), and the agreed full costs of compliance with reporting and full incremental costs to secure compliance (for example, the Climate Change Convention and the POP Convention). Multilateral development banks, such as the

World Bank, now acknowledge the need to incorporate environmental considerations into their lending policy (see Box 13.2).

In this context, the increasing attention to taking the 'common but differentiated responsibilities' of parties seriously should be noted. An example of this is the Climate Change Convention, under which no new commitments are to be imposed on developing countries. Some would see the 'flexible implementation' provisions of the 1997 Kyoto Protocol (such as the Clean Development Mechanism, which allows industrialized parties that invest in emissions reduction projects in developing country parties to use accruing reductions to offset a part of their emissions reduction commitments—see p. 521) as also falling within this general principle. Technical assistance and education provisions are also found in some treaties.

Cross-checking non-compliance

One possible approach is to design agreements that reduce the practical possibilities for non-compliance. For example, the requirements in the 1973 International Convention for the Prevention of Pollution from Ships (MARPOL) to install pollution-prevention equipment would have to be violated by several parties—builders; classifiers; insurers; port authorities—for the rules to be evaded. Similarly, by requiring both import and export permits for species deemed most endangered, the CITES Treaty reduces the scope for individual parties to evade their obligations.

Involving non-state actors

In light of the considerable difficulties of interstate actions, increasing attention is being paid to the possibility of enforcement-type measures by non-state actors—that is, government and non-governmental organizations, and individual legal persons (for an example, see Box 6.3). As far as individual and group *rights* are concerned, however, even the limited mechanisms provided for in EC law (see p. 209) have yet to be replicated in international environmental treaty law more generally, although there are signs that non-state bodies are beginning to play a greater role more generally in relation to compliance.

BOX 6.4 Securing compliance—the Ozone, CITES, and Biological Diversity Treaties compared

Comparing these three treaties illustrates some general points about reaching effective international environmental agreements. The relative success of the Ozone Treaty regime is usually said to be due to:

- the very small number of parties (those states producing ozone-depleting chemicals) from which it was necessary to get agreement;

- a scientific consensus over the causes of the problem;

- the fact that no single state could be sure that it might lose if it did not cooperate (as some states might think is the case in relation to global warming);

- the relatively low costs involved in addressing the problem (including no availability of alternatives).

The initial use in 1985 of a Framework Convention (the Vienna Convention for the Protection of the Ozone Layer), fleshed out by later Protocols, also helped to facilitate compliance, as did a similar process in relation to the UN Framework Convention on Climate Change (UNFCCC), which allowed the parties to move from 'soft' standards to more binding targets for emissions reductions under the 1997 Kyoto Protocol. In relation to climate change, however, even with the use of independent international scientific assessment (the IPCC), there is arguably less agreement on the underlying science and, by contrast with the Ozone Treaty, a relative lack of interest from industry in tackling the problem.

The 1973 Convention on International Trade in Endangered Species of Wild Fauna and Flora (CITES) is also widely regarded as one of the more successful treaties. Despite a large membership, the Convention pays close attention to procedural issues, establishing a funded and effective Secretariat, and requiring—and, in practice, helping—states to establish national management and scientific authorities. The import-permitting requirement applies even to parties outside the Convention, which must comply with this provision on export, providing less incentive for non-participation.

By contrast, the 1992 Biological Diversity Convention is something of a qualified disappointment. The vagueness of the language used in many of its central provisions—often hedged with phrases such as 'as far as possible and as appropriate'—testifies to the considerable difficulties in trying to reconcile north–south tensions between environmental and development goals. Moreover, the Convention is essentially based on a route to biodiversity conservation through realizing the commercial value of biodiversity—for example, for pharmaceuticals—which may be optimistic. It has, however, spawned a Protocol on the movement of living modified organisms—the Cartagena Biosafety Protocol—which sets out specific rules on their import.

It seems likely that, for the short term, the emphasis will be on the implementation of existing treaties and improving compliance, especially with framework conventions such as those on climate change (see Box 6.5) and biodiversity, rather than on the negotiation of new treaties. In this context, the developing of procedural rights under international law is an important development (see p. 165).

BOX 6.5 **Compliance and the Kyoto Protocol**[22]

In March 2006, the parties to the Kyoto Protocol established a Compliance Committee. This Committee comprises two parts: an enforcement branch, with the power to determine consequences for parties that encounter problems with meeting their commitments, and a facilitative branch, which is designed to provide advice and assistance to parties in order to promote compliance.

Parties to the Protocol provide the UN Framework Convention on Climate Change (UNFCCC) Secretariat with annual reports of their greenhouse gas emissions, which then undergo a review process. The Secretariat also monitors the international carbon emission trading market and receives annual accounting reports from parties on carbon allowances acquired or transferred to another party, or resulting from project-level emission reductions. Compliance is then determined by comparing emissions to allowances.

22 Further details are available online at **unfccc.int/kyoto_protocol/compliance/items/2875.php** and the relevant text (Decision 27/CMP1, *Procedures and Mechanisms Relating to Compliance under the Kyoto Protocol*) is available online at **unfccc.int/resource/docs/2005/cmp1/eng/08a03.pdf#page=92**.

The 'teeth' of the new procedure (in section XV of Decision 27/CMP.1) aim to steer parties into compliance through a range of incentives and disincentives, cross-checks, and informational strategies. Thus there is provision requiring non-compliant states to submit plans (including an analysis of the causes of non-compliance), measures that the Party intends to implement in order to remedy the non-compliance, a timetable for implementing enabling the assessment of progress, and regular reports thereafter. In addition, a non-compliant state may lose its entitlement to use joint implementation, clean development, and emissions trading mechanisms. There is also provision for a state, if it fails to meet its reduction targets, to lose 1.3 times this loss from the next round of emissions reductions commitments—that is, in the period from 2012.

International trade and the environment

A potent mechanism for making international agreements effective is the prospect of trade restrictions being imposed against non-compliant states and some treaties (as discussed below) provide for this. Trade controls are, however, often used by one state against another when the import of goods is banned or restricted, often on ostensibly environmental grounds. This may happen either if there is an absence of agreed international rules or if the importing state goes beyond the restrictions allowed for under existing international rules.

National measures may hinder free international trade in one of two main ways:

- by regulating the quality of the goods themselves (product standards);

- by imposing restrictions on the manner in which goods are produced (process and production methods).

Process controls may be concerned with the polluting impact on a neighbouring state, or the way in which a national or global resource is exploited. Thus, restrictions may be enacted to protect the environment of the importing state, the exporting state, or the global commons. Regulating the extent to which measures enacted for environmental protection reasons may unlawfully hinder international trade is therefore important to environmental law at all levels—international, EC, and national—and to sustainable development.

The regulation of international trade rests primarily with bodies connected to the WTO. The WTO has a Committee on Trade and the Environment that must *'identify the relationship between trade measures and environmental measures in order to promote sustainable development'*[23] and make appropriate recommendations. To date, however, it has been singularly unsuccessful in doing so. This is partly because of concerns of the developing world about trade protectionism on environmental grounds, but there are also ever greater differences of opinion within the developed world—most notably, between the USA and the European Union on the application of the Precautionary Principle. As a result, rule making has, in effect, been left to the Appellate Body of the WTO, which is effectively becoming an international court of sustainable development, because it is taking the lead in deciding, under the WTO regime, where the balance between global trade freedom and environmental protection lies. This has raised understandable concerns among environmentalists and others, and is in contrast to the position in the EC, for example, where the ECJ decides both trade and environment cases, and cases combining both issues (although the Appellate Body has indicated that trade rules ought to defer to specialist rules laid down in environmental treaties—see the *Shrimp/Turtle* case in Case 6.9).

23 (1994) Decision on Trade and Environment, see **www.wto.org/english/tratop_e/envir_e/issu5_e.htm**.

This section focuses on three leading cases—one decided before, and two after, GATT 1994 and the WTO agreement that governs this area, the Preamble to which now qualifies emphasis on the 'full use of the resources of the world' with their:

optimal use…in accordance with the objective of sustainable development, seeking both to protect and preserve the environment and to enhance the means for doing so in a manner consistent with the respective needs and concerns at different levels of economic development.

CASE 6.8 *United States Restrictions on Imports of Tuna* (1992) 30 ILM 1598 *(Tuna/Dolphin I)*

This dispute centred around import restrictions imposed by the USA because of concerns about the incidental effect on dolphin populations of Mexican (and other) tuna-fishing methods. The panel upheld the complaint of Mexico that this violated the 'national treatment' provision, in Art. III of the General Agreement on Tariffs and Trade (GATT), which requires that all 'like products' receive similar treatment in international trade law, regardless of how they are produced. (Imported and domestic tuna had to be compared as *products*.)

The issue was then whether the US action amounted to a 'quantitative restriction' under Art. XI of GATT 1994—that is, to an obstacle in practice to a level playing field for international trade. This had to be determined in light of various exceptions in Art. XX. This provides that, as long as measures do not unjustly or arbitrarily discriminate between countries within which the same conditions apply, or act as a disguised restriction on international trade, parties to the GATT may adopt measures including those that:

(a) are necessary to protect human, animal, or plant life or health (under Art. XX(b));

(b) relate to the conservation of exhaustible natural resources if such measures are made effective in conjunction with restrictions on domestic production or consumption (under Art. XX(g)).

The panel held that these exceptions only applied to activities within the national jurisdiction of the country adopting the measure. By impacting on activities in international waters, the US action was unlawful. The objective of the GATT—reducing trade restrictions and barriers—would be 'eviscerated' if the USA could dictate conservation measures to Mexico as a condition of Mexican access to US markets. Even if the USA could take action beyond its borders, it had not shown that doing so would be necessary. There were other means by which the USA might pursue its conservation objectives—for example, through financial incentives or through negotiating international agreements.

In a further, related dispute, brought by the EC against the USA,[24] a GATT panel again found that US action, adopted following the initial dispute, fell foul of the GATT. Less restrictively, however, it did hold that there could be circumstances under which a country could employ trade restrictions to influence environmental policies beyond its territory if this was necessary to protect a global resource pursuant to an international environmental agreement, and if there was a direct causal connection between the measure and the environmental objective pursued.

As a footnote, in 1992, the USA, Mexico, and eight other nations—together responsible for 99 per cent of the tuna catch in the disputed area—did, in fact, sign an international accord to phase out, by 1994, the use of 'dolphin-unfriendly' nets. This reduced incidental dolphin mortalities such that the US embargo was lifted, something that it was not, as a matter of law, required to do, because Mexico did not ask the GATT Council to adopt the panel report. Would this have happened without the unlawful unilateral action of the USA to begin with? (In this context, note that the USA had been trying for twenty years to reach an international agreement on this issue.)

---

24 *Tuna/Dolphin II* (1994) 33 ILM 839.

Being pre-WTO, *Tuna/Dolphin* is now only of historic interest legally—but the disputes raised important questions about the interplay between trade freedom and environmental protection. For example, should it be unlawful unilaterally to block the import of products because they have been produced through relatively high-energy means, contributing to global warming? How does the distinction between product and process restrictions allow for effect to be given to the Polluter Pays Principle?

To understand current WTO law on trade and the environment, two key post-1994 disputes are examined in Case 6.9: *Shrimp/Turtle I* and *Shrimp/Turtle II*.

CASE 6.9 *United States Import Prohibition of Certain Shrimp and Shrimp Products* (1999) 38 ILM 121 (*Shrimp/Turtle I*)

The USA required any state exporting shrimp to the USA to show that its harvesting methods did not endanger sea turtles, or were, at least, regulated and no less damaging to sea turtle conservation than standards actually achieved in the USA. *Shrimp/Turtle* confirms that a two-stage test will be used in relation to Art. XX of the General Agreement on Tariffs and Trade (GATT) 1994:

1. provisional justification if the measure correctly comes within one of the exceptions;

2. further appraisal of these measures under the introductory clauses of Art. XX.

In relation to the first point, the US measures were acceptable under Art. XX(g). The view of a previous panel—that 'exhaustible natural resources' were not to be limited to non-renewable resources such as minerals, but extended to any finite resource and therefore covered living resources—was reaffirmed. But it appears that the turtle species in question were 'exhaustible' because of their recognized endangered status, not because action was required to prevent endangering them.[25]

Nevertheless, the remaining requirements to come within Art. XX(g) were fulfilled: the measure 'related to conservation' in light of an assessment of its primary aim, having regard both to its purpose and effect, and because it was sufficiently 'even-handed' as between imported and domestic shrimp. Because it satisfied that Article, the Appellate Body did not need to consider also whether it was 'necessary' under Art. XX(b). The US measures were therefore substantively acceptable—but they were an '*arbitrary or unjustified discrimination between countries where the same conditions prevail*'.

As to unjustified discrimination, four points were central.

1. In practice, the US rules forced importing states to adopt US policy without any flexibility of approach—that is, the USA only looked to see whether importing states required the fitting of 'turtle excluder devices' (TEDs), as required in the USA, rather than authorizing comparable measures. (Using its own inspectors to certify was hardly helpful and raises the question of whether something closer to 'mutual recognition' would have been preferable.)

2. The USA also banned the import of shrimp caught by boats using TEDs if they did so in the waters of otherwise non-compliant states.

3. The USA had failed to engage the importing states in serious negotiations for an international treaty on sea turtle conservation before imposing trade sanctions. This was in violation of several important statements emphasizing multilateralism, including Principle 12 of the Rio Declaration.

4. The USA had provided different levels of support through technology transfer to different countries, affecting the ability of all states to comply on equal terms.

---

25 In *US-Gasoline* (1996) 35 ILM 603, clean air was held to be an exhaustible natural resource.

The measures were also 'arbitrary' because of their informality, lack of transparency, and absence of procedural protections—for example, the absence of appeal or review rights.

What comes through clearly from *Shrimp/Turtle* is the evident tension between the interests of nation states and a 'common heritage' approach. 'Go it alone' approaches are strongly rejected, the Appellate Body encouraging the negotiation of multilateral agreements in the interests of opening up international decision making to those affected.[26] This is consistent with what the World Trade Organization (WTO) calls its preference for a 'rules-based' approach to free trade (see below).

This does not mean, however, that international agreements must, in fact, be concluded. This was one of the arguments put forward by Malaysia in a subsequent challenge to the legality of Revised Guidelines issued by the USA relating to its national conservation laws, which required importing states—if they did not use TEDs—to enforce the use of 'comparably effective' regulatory programmes. In *Shrimp/Turtle II*,[27] the Appellate Body thought that this would go too far, because, in practice, it would give a veto to individual states, and found that the USA had been engaged in sufficiently, and comparably, good faith efforts to negotiate international agreements with the countries concerned. The second challenge raised by Malaysia was that the Guidelines were insufficiently flexible and still unilaterally imposed US standards on exporters. This claim was also rejected because, on their face, the Guidelines did allow other countries' sea turtle conservation programmes to be considered when certification was being sought. This part of the judgment is seen as being aimed at relieving importing states of the burden of having to consider the conditions in all exporting states before imposing a trade restriction (a concern that had arisen following the first decision in *Shrimp/Turtle*).

Trade–environment disputes are not covered only by GATT 1994; also worth mentioning are the General Agreement on Trade in Services (GATS), which might be relevant to the greening of the financial services market, and two codes dating from 1994—the Agreement on Technical Barriers to Trade (the TBT Agreement) and the Agreement on the Application of Sanitary and Phytosanitary Measures (the SPS Agreement). The latter relates to additives, toxins, etc. in food, drinks, and animal feed, and is less relevant to environmental protection as discussed in this book; subject to the Cartagena Biosafety Protocol, however, it is relevant to disputes about trade in products containing genetically modified organisms (GMOs) and was central to the EC–Biotech dispute (*EC-Approval and Marketing of Biotech Products* (2006)[28]).

It is also worth noting that disputes involving the SPS Agreement may shed light on some of the principles of environmental law, as both the *Beef Hormones* (1997)[29] and *Biotech* disputes have done by rejecting the Precautionary Principle as a general principle of international law, although, in *Beef Hormones*, the WTO accepted that it could be an interpretive principle in risk assessment—for example, by allowing states to be guided not only by majority scientific opinion, but also by the views of qualified scientists reaching different conclusions—an approach subsequently taken in relation to GATT in the *Asbestos* case (see Case 6.10). The TBT Agreement is more directly relevant to trade–environment disputes, because it applies to product standards and process-and-production methods, and includes,

---

26 The dispute also deals rather unconvincingly with the question of jurisdictional limits to nation states' legitimate interests, doing little more than stating on the basis of flimsy reference to 'sustainable development', rather than positively arguing towards the connection in law between the turtle populations involved and the USA (although comparing the approach here with *Tuna/Dolphin* suggests a relaxation of the 'territorial nexus' issue).

27 *US/Shrimp* (2001) WT/DS58/AB/RW, 22 October 2001.

28 WT/DS291 (United States), WT/DS292 (Canada), and WT/DS293 (Argentina), a very lengthy decision summarized at (2007) JEL 413.

29 On *Beef Hormones*, see p. 65.

for example, provisions on packaging rules, eco-labels, and other regulatory controls. But there is, as yet, little 'case law' from the WTO on this code.

The *Asbestos* case (Case 6.10) raises important issues about the interpretation of GATT and its relationship with the TBT Agreement. Although, for technical reasons, it did not have to decide on the latter, it seems that both agreements operate concurrently to any dispute. This means that, even in cases in which the TBT Agreement is involved, the general GATT rules will still have a role to play (further discussion of the TBT Agreement is outside the scope of this analysis).

CASE 6.10 *EC—Measures Affecting Asbestos and Asbestos-Containing Products* (2001) 40 ILM 497 (*EC Asbestos*)

Asbestos is a known carcinogen. France banned the import of asbestos and construction products containing asbestos, because of health concerns; Canada challenged the French law. In the ensuing case, the Appellate Body upheld the import ban.

On whether, for the purposes of Art. III(4) of the General Agreement on Tariffs and Trade (GATT), the banned asbestos products were 'like' alternative construction products, the Appellate Body essentially noted that, because the two products were physically different, Canada had a higher hurdle to overcome in showing that they were 'like' because they were competing for the same share of the market. Because of the health risks from the products containing asbestos fibres, however, this burden had not been discharged. This is an important development, because it shows a certain sensitivity to the *effect* of products when judging whether one product is 'like' another. (The earlier panel, rather outrageously, had held that products such as asbestos that are known killers are 'like' those that are not.) The Appellate Body also went on to note that, even if two products were 'like' each other, this does not mean that they must be treated the same by national regulations. There must still be some form of 'less favourable treatment'—that is, trade protectionism—as between domestic and imported products. This might be used to argue that differences in process and production methods could be relied upon as a ground for restricting imports—contrary to the *Tuna/Dolphin* decision—as long as imported products are not treated any less favourably than domestic ones.

As to Art. XX, if there is a scientifically proven risk to health, then '*WTO members have the right to determine the level of protection of health that they consider appropriate*'. They can do this either because of the degree of seriousness of the risk (which can be a qualitative judgement about what is acceptable in the importing country) or because of the likelihood of it occurring. In effect, the greater the product of these two factors—quality and quantity—the more that the importing state's actions will be 'necessary' for the purposes of Art. XX(b). The Appellate Body therefore took a less restrictive view of what this test requires than it had previously and, by weighing the harm against the impact of the trade restriction, took an approach that is similar to that of the European Court of Justice to trade/environment cases in which the proportionality of the restrictions is an important factor (see p. 197). A measure will be necessary if no GATT-consistent alternative is reasonably available and provided that it entails the least degree of inconsistency with other GATT provisions.

The *Asbestos* decision clearly shifts the emphasis of the Appellate Body away from a very pro-trade position and it might be seen partly as a response to criticisms of the World Trade Organization system that flared into riots at Seattle in 1999. It is therefore seen in broadly positive terms from an environmental perspective. (Indeed, note that, in *Shrimp/Turtle*, the USA made no attempt to argue that shrimp caught with or without TEDs were not 'like products'.) But some care needs to be taken in assessing just how far-reaching the decision is: in accepting that health concerns could mean that products with the same end use were not 'like products', the Appellate Body emphasized that they would not be seen as alike by *consumers* of the products. This is some way from saying that *any* different effect that a product has will justify treating it as not 'like' a product that has the same end use and, in particular, it does not necessarily mean that, if harm to the environment is caused by making a product in one country but not another, the latter will be able to block its import.

The Appellate Body is still picking its way carefully and cautiously through issues of high political sensitivity. As one commentator has put it: *'The case does not clarify; it restrains the strongest form of free trade impulse, in favour of ambiguity and political peace.'*[30]

Assessment and future developments

Given the number of important multilateral environmental agreements that now exist, a key issue is where the balance will be struck between these and GATT/WTO. Some, for example, would like to see GATT amended to insert a defence that action was taken pursuant to treaties such as CITES, the Basel Convention on Hazardous Wastes, the Montreal Ozone Protocol, or the Kyoto Protocol, all of which provide for enforcement through trade restrictions. The basic rule of international law, however, is that the treaty that is later in time prevails and all of those mentioned pre-date the 1994 GATT/WTO. There is a practical answer to this: it is unlikely that two parties to such an agreement will raise a dispute over GATT incompatibility; from a legal perspective, however, it is clear from cases such as *Shrimp/Turtle* that the Appellate Body is keen that states seek to resolve their differences through genuine multilateral agreements, which suggests that it would look favourably at a specialist environmental treaty over the general provisions of the GATT. There appears to be some acceptance of this as a matter of political reality. For example, the Cartagena Biosafety Protocol expressly takes precedence over the rules of international trade, even though the pro-GMO trade 'Miami' group of states resisted this.

From the *Asbestos* case, it is clear that the resolution of trade–environment disputes is in a state of flux and many key questions remain undecided. For example, it is not clear how the increasing use of packaging and labelling requirements will be viewed.[31] Future disputes about what are 'like' products can consequently be expected.

What does seem clear is that global trade rules have a much greater real-world impact than do environmental treaties. As the Executive Director of UNEP has said:

International governance structures, and the rules that flow from them, must have the capacity to shape national policy. While international trade policy is rather effective in this regard, the impact of international environmental agreements is often less evident.[32]

Indeed, although the details of GATT law are important, as Vogel points out, the debate *'reflects a more profound clash of culture and world views between the trade community and environmentalists'*.[33] This clash is based, in part, upon competing views of whether security through free trade, or environmental security, is the more fragile. But it is also based on disagreement over the extent to which unilateral action contributes either to the progressive ratcheting up of international standards or to a deregulatory 'race to the bottom', raising difficult questions concerning sustainable development. It should be noted that, in *Tuna/ Dolphin*, however, the greatest reduction in dolphin deaths occurred before the import ban, by which time there was no evidence that the dolphin populations affected were endangered. Trade restrictions may serve only to depress the commercial value of natural resources in other states, driving up the number of units—of tropical hardwood trees; of endangered

30 S. Dillon (2002) *International Trade and Economic Law and the EU*, Oxford: Hart, p. 157.

31 Which throw up their own problems: see H. Ward (1997) 6 RECIEL 139.

32 UN Doc E/CN.17/2002/PC.2/7 (19 December 2001), para. 153.

33 D. Vogel (1995) *Trading Up: Consumer and Environmental Regulation in a Global Economy*, Cambridge, Mass: Harvard University Press, p. 134.

species—that must be sold to maintain revenues and driving down the incentives of national governments to invest in measures—for example, anti-poaching measures or habitat conservation—to conserve the resource.

Whatever the *actual* rules and resolution of disputes, however, there is a general feeling that international trade law has a 'chilling effect' on the setting of environmental and other standards, both within the EC and within individual nation states. On the one hand, there is, perhaps, an understandable caution about adopting laws on the basis of how the Appellate Body might be likely, in the future, to decide the issue and a focus instead on how it would be decided according to a cautious reading of the present, limited, body of 'case law'. On the other hand, it may also suit some rule makers to be able to point to international trade rules as a reason for regulatory inaction in tackling a problem.

For the immediate future, however, states are likely to prefer the speed and certainty provided by the WTO to dispute resolution under multilateral environmental agreements, which typically lack these features.[34] This has important implications for the development of customary principles of international law, which may become biased towards free trade concerns until such time as there is a greater shift in thinking in the WTO towards realizing the effective integration of environmental protection into global trade rules.[35]

Future directions in international environmental law and policy

In addition to greater attention to matters of compliance, it is arguable that a mix of approaches will colour the future of international environmental law. Increased attention is likely to be paid to individuals and to organizations, rather than to the traditional 'state-centric', intergovernmental approach of international law—although not necessarily through granting substantive, individual, environmental rights.

Rights-based approaches—substantive rights

Although clearly rejected at Rio in 1992, there have been some attempts to advance a substantive environmental human right, most notably in a report by a UN Sub-Commission on Prevention of Discrimination and Protection of Minorities on the relationship between human rights and the environment.[36] Finding that over sixty national constitutions contained some form of environmental rights protection, the report concluded that there had been *'a shift from environmental law to the right to a healthy and decent environment'*, comprising substantive rights to life, health, and development. This, it claimed, was rather more than a 'greening' of international human rights law, and the report proposed the adoption of principles of human rights and the environment, which would be enforceable by human rights organizations.

As the Johannesburg Summit shows, however, there is little willingness within the international community to sign up to a rights-based approach and the principles are making no progress in the UN system. There are probably several reasons for this, including the large number of international environmental treaties that now exist and the general turn

---

34 See J. Cameron (1998) 'Dispute settlement and conflicting trade and environment regimes' in A. Fijalkowski and J. Cameron (eds) *Trade and the Environment: Bridging the Gap*, London: Earthscan.

35 An excellent analysis of how the deregulatory WTO might nevertheless accommodate environmental protection norms in the way that the EC has done is contained in J. Scott (2004) EJIL 307.

36 F. Z. Ksentini (1994) *Human Rights and the Environment*, UN Doc. E/CN.4/Sub.2/1994/9, 6 July (the Ksentini Report).

away from substantive, towards procedural, rights. There is a similar lack of enthusiasm for granting specific rights to future generations (for example, enforceable by a global trustee).

This vacuum might be filled by other means. Although an individual right to sustainable development is unlikely to emerge, with a preference for operationalizing sustainable development in procedural ways, it is possible that existing rights—such as the right to life—might be reinterpreted creatively. This is the approach taken in the Ksentini Report[37] and has been taken most notably by the Indian courts.[38]

Procedural rights

There is a definite shift towards establishing and protecting procedural rights in international environmental law. This can be seen, for example, in Principle 10 of the Rio Declaration, which notes that environmental problems are best handled with the participation of all concerned citizens, at the relevant level. Specifically, at national level, individuals should have access to publicly held environmental information and the opportunity to participate in decision-making processes, while states should foster public awareness and participation by making information widely available, and should provide effective access to judicial and administrative proceedings. More specific elaboration of procedural rights is contained in the 1998 UN/ECE Aarhus Convention on Access to Information, Public Participation in Decision Making and Access to Justice in Environmental Matters (discussed in more detail at p. 294). References to 'the public concerned' include references to NGOs promoting environmental protection, which are deemed to have a sufficient interest in environmental decision making.

This leads to a slightly different point about procedural rights, which is that, as individuals and companies increasingly become the subject of international environmental law, then pressure may build to accommodate their interests at all levels of lawmaking and dispute resolution (see, for existing accommodation, the acceptance of amicus briefs by the WTO, at p. 150). As Sands notes of the emissions trading regimes established under the 1992 Climate Change Convention (see p. 521):

If these instruments create rights and obligations for the private sector, then why should they be content to be excluded from the legislative process or subject to traditional intergovernmental dispute settlement processes?[39]

Liability rules

There are existing examples of international treaties providing for liability rules in the event of damage to the environment. The best-known examples, relied on most often in practice, are the conventions agreed under the MARPOL Treaty on marine pollution, which provide for strict liability and compensation funds—financed by shippers—for the movement of oil (see p. 361). Principle 13 of the Rio Declaration requires states to cooperate in agreeing further liability rules, and, more recently, liability provisions have been agreed for the marine movement of other hazardous and noxious substances, and for the transboundary movement of hazardous wastes (although the latter have been criticized because a compensation fund is not established). There is also the prospect of liability and compensation rules being agreed in other specialist areas (for example, under the 2000 Biosafety Protocol).

---

37 Ibid.

38 For an excellent summary, see M. Anderson (1996) 'Environmental protection in India' in A. Boyle and M. Anderson (eds) *Human Rights Approaches to Environmental Protection*, Oxford: Clarendon Press.

39 P. Sands (2001) 33 NYU J Intl L & Pol 527.

There is some enthusiasm for internationally agreed liability rules, although, at the moment, their application tends to be limited to particularly hazardous activities in relation to which compensation funds are seen as necessary to alleviate public fears. From an international law perspective, what is interesting is that they shift the focus away from the liability of the state onto individual operators and (in the case of compensation funds) industrial sectors. There is, therefore, a role for state responsibility only in cases in which private parties are not liable—for example, if liability is fault-based and they have not been at fault—or if the amount of damage exceeds the amount payable under the compensation fund. They can therefore be seen as a mechanism for promoting compliance with international agreements.

Duty-centred approaches

A range of duty-centred approaches now exists. In national law, many constitutions include provisions requiring either individuals or the state (or both) to protect the environment. The 1978 Spanish Constitution, for example, provides that '*Everyone has the right to enjoy an environment suitable for the development of the person as well as the duty to preserve it*' (Art. 45), while some texts also require states or citizens to 'improve' the environment (for example, the 1982 Turkish Constitution, Art. 56). Perhaps the starkest example of legislating for individual responsibility is contained in the 1998 Rome Statute of the International Criminal Court, Art. 8, which provides for an international war crime against the environment.

Institutional reform

The creation of some kind of global environmental agency has been mooted since before the Stockholm Conference. There is an argument that the present diversity of environmental treaty regimes and of global institutions is problematic. As Charnovitz has said: '*If an organization chart of world environmental governance existed, its incoherence would be exhibit A for reformers.*'[40] Various reforms have been suggested to tackle this, including grouping treaties under general 'umbrellas'—for example, the marine environment or biodiversity—in order to streamline some of the administration, and to make negotiating amendments and new treaties easier. In 2005, the UN decided to '*agree to explore the possibility of a more coherent institutional framework*'.[41] But the development of environmental treaties—and of treaty law generally—has probably been helped, rather than hindered, by being negotiated on an issue-by-issue basis and there is little enthusiasm for a global body to deal with all environmental treaties in the way that the WTO deals with the main trade conventions.

CHAPTER SUMMARY

1 Many environmental problems cannot be resolved at national level and require some form of regulation at the transboundary, regional, or global levels.

2 International environmental law is comprised mainly of treaties and customary law, although other sources are also called upon. Although few international disputes ever reach courts or tribunals, the judgments in these also make up international law. Taking these sources together, international law often has an emergent quality, which can make it difficult to state with certainty what it requires.

3 Public international law is mainly about the rights and duties of states and—in the environmental sphere, at least—has not been greatly concerned with the rights of individuals within states. But the

---

40 (2002) 27 Colum J Envtl L 323 at 340.
41 **www.un.org/summit2005**.

limits to this approach are beginning to appear, not least because some international law obligations now effectively 'bite' on individuals and companies.

4   In the UK, international treaties only have direct legal force once an Act of Parliament gives effect to them, although they can also be used to interpret other legislation.

5   The main tension in international environmental law is between the sovereign right of states to use their own natural resources, and to choose their own levels of environmental protection and development objectives, and their duties not to cause harm to other states or to the global commons.

6   There are hundreds of international environmental agreements. Enforcing them is difficult, because there is not usually an enforcement body with the power to impose effective sanctions. This means that a range of other methods are often used to try to induce compliance.

7   Most states belong to the World Trade Organization (WTO) and the rules of international trade can affect how the UK or the EC regulates for environmental protection. The central concern in this area is striking an appropriate balance between the interests of states to trade freely, and to maintain control over questions of environmental and natural resource protection.

Q QUESTIONS

1   How sovereign are nation states when it comes to actions that *will* be harmful to the environment? What about in relation to actions that *may* be harmful to the environment?

2   How are environmental interests (as you define these) represented in international law?

3   What application does the Polluter Pays Principle have in international environmental law?

4   Should environmentalists be concerned about international trade law? Consider, for example, the following and what further information you would need.

  a   State A imposes a product-based energy tax to imported products.

  b   State B imposes a process-based energy tax to imported products.

  c   State C imposes a tax based on the recycled content of bottles.

  d   State D imposes a ban on fur from animals caught in the wild, but allows the import and marketing of fur from animals reared in fur farms.

  e   State E requires all natural products circulating in its market to be labelled with information about the impact on biodiversity of their production.

5   You are instructed by an NGO to draft an international treaty on conserving ancient woodlands. Prepare a short paper on the main legal and policy issues that will need to be addressed.

FURTHER READING

There are two excellent texts on international environmental law: P. Birnie and A. Boyle (2002) *International Law and the Environment*, 2nd edn, Oxford: Oxford University Press, and P. Sands (2003) *Principles of International Environmental Law*, 2nd edn, Cambridge: Cambridge University Press. The former is a little more doctrinal, while the latter is slightly more comprehensive, especially on the tools of international environmental law, and contains very useful bibliographic sources (in much more depth than we can provide here). A rather more forthright approach is taken in V. Nanda and G. Pring (2003) *International Environmental Law and Policy for the 21st Century*, Ardsley, NY: New York Transnational. P. Sands (2005) *Lawless World: America and the Making and Breaking of Global Rules*, London: Penguin, takes a critical look at international relations and the rule of law, and features (for present purposes) especially interesting chapters on trade and on climate change. Primary jurisprudential materials are contained in

C. Robb (ed.) (1999–2007) *International Environmental Law Reports*, Cambridge: Cambridge University Press, the five volumes of which cover *Early Decisions* (1999), *Trade and Environment* (2001), *Human Rights and Environment* (2001), *National Courts* (2005), and *International Tribunals* (2007).

In terms of up-to-date and reflective comment across the whole range of topics that fall within this chapter and beyond, the magnum opus is now D. Bodansky, J. Brunnée, and E. Hey (eds) (2007) *The Oxford Handbook of International Environmental Law*, Oxford: Oxford University Press, which covers a huge range of topics and is a further reading list in its own right. Further edited collections that contain valuable contributions include: A. Boyle and D. Freestone (eds) (1999) *International Law and Sustainable Development*, Oxford: Oxford University Press; R. Hurrell and D. Kingsbury (eds) (1992) *The International Politics of the Environment*, Oxford: Clarendon Press (placing international law in its wider context); on compliance, J. Cameron, J. Werksman, and P. Roderick (eds) (1996) *Improving Compliance with International Environmental Law*, London: Earthscan (which combines general discussion and examples, many about climate change); J. Werksman (ed.) (1996) *Greening International Institutions*, London: Earthscan. J. Vogler (1995) *The Global Commons: A Regime Analysis*, Chichester: John Wiley, is a good account of this particular aspect to international law and contains a very clear summary of the argument surrounding the 'tragedy of the commons' thesis.

In terms of journal articles, the following selection covers a good range of issues in international environmental law: A. Boyle, 'Globalising environmental liability: the interplay of national and international law' (2005) 17 JEL 3, which covers liability rules in an international context (not covered here); D. French 'A reappraisal of sovereignty in the light of global environmental concerns' (2001) 21 Leg Stud 376 examines the tension between the control of states over their own resources and their obligations not to cause environmental harm; I. Cheyne, 'The Precautionary Principle in EC and WTO law' (2006) 8(4) Env LR 257; P. Sands, 'Litigating environmental disputes' (2007) 37(2–3) EP&L 66; C. Sunstein, 'Of Montreal and Kyoto: a tale of two Protocols' (2007) Harv Env LR 1.

On the work of the International Court of Justice, there is a symposium on the *Gabčíkovo-Nagymaros* case in J. Brunnée and E. Hey (eds) (1997) *Yearbook of International Environmental Law*, Oxford: Oxford University Press. R. Clark and M. Sann (eds) (1996) *The Case Against the Bomb*, Camden, NJ: Rutgers University School of Law at Camden, provides a first-hand account of the ICJ's *Nuclear Weapons* Advisory Opinion and is an excellent way in to understanding the working of the ICJ. The *MOX* dispute, which is central to understanding the relationship between EC and international law, is discussed in R. Churchill and J. Scott, 'The MOX plant litigation: the first half-life' (2004) 53(3) ICLQ 643, and N. Lauranos (2005) EELR 213.

The role of national courts in implementation is researched in a British Institute of International and Comparative Law study of 12 countries (including the UK), the results of which are published as M. Anderson and P. Galizzi (eds) (2002) *International Environmental Law in National Courts*, London: BIICL.

On international trade and the environment, good starting points are the relevant chapters in Birnie and Boyle, and in Sands (see above). S. Charnovitz, 'The WTO's environmental progress' (2007) 10 JIEL 685 considers the extent to which environmental concerns are becoming increasingly important within the WTO. If you are really ambitious, you might want to tackle the *EU/Biotech* dispute (see p. 161) in some depth. Helpful works written before the decision are J. Peel, R. Nelson, and L Godden (2005) 'GMO trade wars: the submissions in the US–EC *Biotech* dispute in the WTO', available online at **www.law.nyu.edu/weilerj/ spring05/globalization/Jackie_Peel.pdf**, and D. Winickoff, S. Jasanoff, L. Busch, R. Grove-White, and B Wynne, 'Adjudicating the GM food wars: science, risk and democracy in world trade law' (2005) 20 Yale J Intl L 81 (the latter is based on an amicus ('friend of the court') brief to the WTO by a group of very eminent risk scholars). On the final decision (which runs to a thousand pages and needs some filleting before you get into it), see D. Prevost, 'Opening Pandora's box: the Panel's findings in the EC-Biotech Products dispute' (2007) 34 Legal Issues of European integration 67. For a comprehensive overview and analysis of this whole area see N. Bernascovi–Osterwalder et al. (2006) *Environment and Trade: A Guide to WTO Jurisprudence*, London: Earthscan.

For keeping up to date, the *Review of European Community and International Environmental Law* (RECIEL) and *Environmental Policy and Law* (EP&L) are regular and informative; the former having themed issues. The *Yearbook of International Environmental Law* (published annually; Oxford: Oxford University Press) contains both sectoral and country reports (including the implementation of international environmental law), recent primary materials, and a useful bibliography, as well as lengthy articles. *International Legal Materials* (ILM) provides most of the major treaties and decisions, although the Internet is now the main way of keeping up to date.

@ **WEB LINKS**

There is, as yet, no single portal for international environmental law, although the Electronic Information System for International Law, **www.eisil.org**, produced by the American Society of International Law, contains links to most of the key conventions and many of the secretariats. Every international organization, and most international agreements, have their own websites. These are an invaluable way of becoming familiar with how international law regimes (treaties and soft law, and the relevant institutions) operate. The fastest way to access these is via general search engines such as **www.google.com**. The Internet is also the primary way of accessing judicial material, such as judgments of the International Court of Justice (**www.icj-cij.org**), the International Tribunal for the Law of the Sea (**www.itlos.org**), and World Trade Organization decisions (**www.wto.org** and see also **www.worldtradelaw.net**). Finally, **www.wcl. american.edu/environment/iel** contains a neat set of links to accompany J. Salzman, D. Zaelke and D. Hunter (2006) *International Environmental Law and Policy*, 3rd edn, New York: Foundation Press, which is also recommended.

7

The European Community and the environment

→ Overview

Notwithstanding its economic basis, the European Community (EC) has long been a major source of UK environmental protection law. It also has a central and profound influence on the direction of environmental policy, both at a Community level and within each member State. As a result, every subject covered by this book is affected, either directly or indirectly, by the activities of the EC.

After a brief overview of how the EC shapes UK environmental law and policy, we begin by providing an introductory guide to EC law, outlining the key institutions of the EC, the different sources of EC law, and how EC law is made. We then look at the more substantive elements of EC law as they affect environmental protection, starting with the policy and constitutional bases for EC environmental law, and giving a flavour of the scope of EC environmental legislation, before considering the scope for national standards to exceed those set at EC level or to disrupt trade between the member States. We then look at the challenge of making EC environmental law work and conclude with some thoughts on the impact of the EC on UK environmental law, policy, and practice.

Alongside this chapter, you may also find it useful to read those sections of Chapter 8 that outline some of the key historical differences between the UK and other prominent member States in terms of approach to environmental regulation; you may also find it useful to access the key Articles of the EC Treaty (see Web Links at the end of this chapter). Most of the environmental laws mentioned in this chapter are covered in much greater depth in the relevant chapters of this book.

At the end of this chapter, you should be able to:

✔ understand how the EC is organized and the roles of the main institutions;

✔ identify the main sources of EC environmental law, and assess the legal bases and policy justifications for EC environmental law;

✔ appreciate the range of EC environmental legislation and the degree of flexibility given to member States in setting standards;

✔ assess the extent to which the member States may set standards above those in EC environmental laws, which may potentially hinder other objectives of the EC, such as trade freedom;

✔ evaluate the particular challenges of securing compliance with EC environmental laws, including the role of the European Court of Justice;

✔ appreciate the impact of the EC on national environmental law and policy, and assess the role played by national courts.

Key developments in EC environmental law and policy

What might be considered the defining moments in the development of European Community (EC) environmental law and policy are shown in Table 7.1. But as well as these landmark moments, it is also important to appreciate the incremental developments that are difficult to capture in a table like this. For example, over the years, the European Court of Justice (ECJ) has progressively strengthened EC law and the scope to make it effective at national level. These developments are especially important for environmental law.

Table 7.1 The development of EC environmental law and policy

Year	Development
1957	European Economic Community (Treaty of Rome). No mention of the environment.
1967	First 'environmental' Common Market Directive (on labelling dangerous products).
1972	UN Stockholm Conference. Seen as the catalyst for the first Environmental Action Programme.
1973	First Environmental Action Programme. (UK joins the EEC.)
1973–86	Expansion of EC environmental law in water, waste, and, latterly, air pollution.
1980	Common market measures can lawfully pursue environmental objectives (ECJ).
1985	Environmental protection is 'one of the Community's essential objectives' (ECJ).
1987	Single European Act. Environmental Title inserted into EC Treaty. Increased emphasis on implementation following the high-profile 'Seveso' pollution incident.
1987–93	Rapid expansion of environmental laws, mostly to complete the single market.
1988	Environmental protection is a 'mandatory requirement' of the EC (ECJ).
1989	Separate Environment Directorate General in the EC Commission.
1990	European Environment Agency agreed to (begins work in 1993).
1992	Seminal Fifth Environmental Action Programme, stressing 'shared responsibility' and greater flexibility in rule making.
1993	Maastricht Treaty adds the Precautionary Principle to the Environmental Title.
1997	Amsterdam Treaty. Promoting sustainable development becomes an objective of the EC. EC Treaty also requires environmental protection to be integrated across other policies.
1998	'Cardiff process' begins, furthering environmental policy integration.
2001	EC Sustainable Development Strategy.

Table 7.1 (Continued)	
Year	Development
2004	Start of enlargement of EC into central and eastern Europe.
2005	Popular rejection of EU Constitution in French and Dutch referenda.
2006	Renewed Sustainable Development Strategy.
2007	Political agreement on EU Reform Treaty.

The EC and UK environmental law and policy

There are four main ways in which the EC plays a role in shaping UK environmental law and policy.

1 Some pieces of EC legislation lay down rules and standards that are directly enforceable in member States without any need for further implementation. In these cases, EC law *is* UK law.

2 Other pieces of EC legislation are addressed to member States and require changes in UK law or administrative practice. This is normally the situation in relation to environmental legislation, because of the predominant use of Directives, which are not necessarily directly effective within member States. UK law is therefore not the same as EC law until the EC law has been implemented. In such cases, the precise role of the EC in initiating the change is often forgotten, because the domestic legislation resulting from the EC requirements will constitute the law that is applied in practice. An important point to note is that EC law and UK law often differ in such circumstances, because EC law frequently consists of aims and goals, and of procedural frameworks, rather than precise legal rules, and allows for discretion in the member States as to how and (sometimes) when to implement it.

3 The third role is somewhat wider and rests upon the constitutional position that the UK occupies as a member State of the EC. The EC not only passes environmental laws, but also has an environmental policy. This policy, and the general economic and environmental principles that underpin it, exert an important influence on UK policymaking, and on UK attitudes towards environmental law and its enforcement. The direction in which environmental protection will go therefore depends as much on wider European attitudes (and the changing nature of the EC itself as new member States join) as it does on ingrained British ideas, although, of course, British ideas will, in turn, help to mould the general EC view and to affect the attitudes of the other member States (see Box 7.1).

BOX 7.1 **The impact of EC environmental law and policy on UK law**

Comparing the two most wide-ranging pollution control statutes enacted in the last thirty years illustrates the expanding influence of the EC on UK environmental law. The Control of Pollution Act 1974 (enacted a year after the UK joined the EEC) was driven entirely by UK concerns and priorities, whereas the Environmental Protection Act 1990 was heavily influenced—and in some places driven—by EC law. Several sections of the latter Act specifically implemented EC environmental

Directives—for example, on genetically modified organisms (GMOs)—or were drafted with current or proposed EC laws in mind—for example, on waste—and much of the Act was drafted to take full account of Directives on, for example, air and water pollution. This was the case, for example, with integrated pollution control (IPC), which the 1990 Act introduced as a specifically national measure.

But the case of IPC also shows how UK environmental law and policy may, in turn, shape EC law: in 1996, the EC adopted Directive 96/61/EC on integrated pollution prevention and control (IPPC), which drew heavily on the UK's IPC law. This is just one example of how the UK has become less a 'taker', and more a 'shaper', of EC environmental policy and law (see also p. 82 and, on IPPC, Chapter 14).

4 Finally, the economic policies of the EC have a profound effect on the direction of both EC and domestic environmental law. Environmental protection cannot be isolated from economic policy and the substantial completion of the single internal market by the end of 1992 had significant spin-off effects—none of which had previously been formally assessed and most of which were negative—on the environment. Indeed, many 'green' commentators would argue that the EC's chosen development path, which continues to emphasize economic growth and economies of scale in industrial and agricultural production, remains antithetical to the achievement of the aims of a clean environment and the conservation of natural resources.

An introductory guide to EC law

The nature of the EC

The EC is more than a free trade agreement between (now) 27 European member States. It has institutions and lawmaking powers of its own, making it a form of federal entity in which the member States have restricted their sovereign rights, albeit within limited fields (although, for political reasons, the extent of this is often denied).

The activities over which the EC has powers are set out in the treaties that establish the EC, which are effectively the EC's constitution. In the past, there have been three treaties and three linked Communities: the European Economic Community (EEC), the European Coal and Steel Community (ECSC), and the European Atomic Energy Community (Euratom). It has been the EEC, established by the Treaty of Rome 1957, which has been the central Community and to which environmental policy relates.[1] The Treaty of Rome was amended by the Single European Act 1986, which first introduced references to the environment. All of the treaties were further amended by the 1992 'Maastricht' Treaty on European Union, which came into force on 1 November 1993 and altered the name of the EEC Treaty to the EC Treaty. In this book, all references to Treaty Articles are to the EC Treaty, as amended. Only aspects relating to the EC, which—together with foreign and defence matters, and justice and home affairs—forms one of three 'pillars' of the European Union (EU) are considered here, so references are to EC laws rather than those of the wider EU (although debates and developments within the EU obviously have a profound effect on the shape and direction of environmental policy).

Further amendments to the EC Treaty were made under the Treaty of Amsterdam, which came into force on 1 May 1999. The Amsterdam Treaty renumbered the EC Treaty. References

---

1 The Euratom Treaty does not have an environmental title or policy, and so formally, at least, remains directed at promoting nuclear energy, rather than at dealing with issues such as the disposal of hazardous nuclear waste.

below are generally to the new Articles, even when what we are referring to is pre-1999 (these are given in the form 'Art. 6 EC', meaning Art. 6 of the EC Treaty, and so on). Because the Treaty has generally been added to over time, rather than rewritten, this should not be too misleading. The Treaty of Nice put in place many of the necessary changes to allow for the accession of 12 new member States from 2004 (known as 'enlargement'), but did not make any significant changes to the Treaty Articles relating to the environment.

At the time of writing, the Lisbon Treaty, or European Reform Treaty (not unlike the previous European Constitution, which was never ratified) has been agreed, but the Treaty needs to be ratified by all member States before coming into force.

The institutions of the EC

The four main EC institutions[2] are the Commission, the Council of Ministers, the Parliament, and the European Court of Justice (ECJ). Each has powers and duties specified in the Treaty, and an obligation to further the aims of the EC.

(a) The Commission

The Commission is the executive of the EC. Currently, it consists of 27 independent members appointed by the member States (one from each member State), serviced by officials. The Commission has responsibility for implementing EC policies, including responsibility for enforcing EC law, in which role it has certain investigatory powers (although its powers in relation to the environmental areas are nothing like as extensive as they are in relation to, for example, competition policy).

It is the Commission that draws up the environmental action programmes and drafts proposed EC legislation. (Commission documents are given a reference in the form of 'COM(date)(number)' and, on occasion, we use this as a shorthand for a legislative proposal or Commission report.) By means of information agreements with the member States, the Commission is informed of proposals for domestic legislation and these often give rise to a Commission proposal for a common policy across the EC. There are also some situations in which the Commission, in effect, makes substantive decisions—for example, in giving its opinion whether damaging development may go ahead on very important wildlife sites (see p. 714).

The ambivalent nature of the Commission must be appreciated. On the one hand, it is often the driving force behind new environmental policies; on the other, it is responsible for enforcing the economic aims of the EC (see its position in the *Danish Bottles* case—Case 7.4—and the *Concordia Bus Finland* case—Box 7.7).

Internally, the Commission is divided into a number of Directorates General. The Environment Directorate General (DG Env), which became a separate directorate in 1989, mainly deals with environmental matters, but, because environmental policies should form a component of the EC's other policies, there are Commission officials in other Directorates— such as that for Energy and Transport (DG Transport)—who also deal with environmental issues.

(b) The Council of Ministers

The Council of Ministers (the Council) is a political body made up of one representative of each member State. The identity of this representative alters according to the nature of the business. Thus, environment ministers normally agree environmental measures, transport

---

2 Other institutions, of less significance here, include the Court of Auditors (which has occasionally produced quite critical reports on how environmental damage is, in effect, subsidized by the EC) and the Committee of the Regions and the Economic and Social Council, each of which, in relation to the environment, has played only a limited advisory role.

ministers normally agree transport measures, and so on. As a body, it has a duty to ensure the attainment of the Treaty objectives, but, clearly, national interests play a central role in the Council's decisions.

As a result, the Council's voting procedures are crucial. There are some differences in the procedures to be adopted for different matters: some pieces of legislation have to be passed unanimously by the Council, acting on a proposal from the Commission, and after consultation with Parliament and the Economic and Social Committee; most environmental legislation can now be passed by a qualified majority of the Council—a system of weighted voting in which member States can be outvoted (see p. 181)—although, in practice, there is often unanimity.

(c) The European Parliament

The European Parliament has members directly elected from each member State (the UK has 78 MEPs out of 785) and now has a significant role in the making of new legislation (see below). For many years, the Parliament has been a significant mouthpiece of concern over environmental issues and, for a long time, could claim that it had never considered a Commission proposal to be too environmentally protective (although whether it can still claim this is debatable).[3] It has generally opposed the use of 'soft law' rules of environmental law, but, in terms of its ability to affect the content of environmental legislation, its powers have tended to be limited.

(d) The European Court of Justice (ECJ)

The ECJ consists of judges appointed by common agreement of the member States. In most cases, it is assisted by Advocates-General, one of whom makes reasoned submissions to the Court in each case. It has supreme authority on matters of EC law—that is, it has ultimate power to interpret the meaning of the treaties and of any legislation made by the other institutions. The Court can thus, if asked, review the legitimacy of the actions of the other institutions, provide answers on matters of EC law to member States' courts, and declare whether member States are implementing EC law properly (and, if they are not, impose penalty payments).

The ECJ is widely considered to be a force for good when it comes to environmental law: it tends to interpret EC environmental Directives purposively, as much according to the spirit of their environmental objectives as to the letter of the law, and is particularly vigilant (and creative) in striving to ensure that EC law is properly implemented in the member States.[4] It has generally been sympathetic on issues such as the extent to which environmental protection measures unlawfully limit the free movement of goods, and active in developing and applying key principles of environmental law and policy, such as the Integration and Precautionary Principles.

Article 234 EC plays a major role here. Under Art. 234, any court or tribunal in a member State can refer any matter of EC law to the ECJ for its interpretation of the law. This procedure aims to ensure uniformity between member States in their application of the law and also provides a method of obtaining an authoritative ruling. Because the Court is the ultimate arbiter of any law having an EC input, Art. 234 references should be made in cases in which there is any doubt as to the meaning of EC law or the compatibility of domestic law with it. But many contentious issues of the interpretation of EC environmental law have often been resolved by national judges, without a reference, and these judges have often taken a less purposive interpretation than that which the ECJ has eventually taken (see Box 7.2).

---

3 See, e.g., (2006) 'MEPs weaken Air Quality Directive', ENDS Report, 28 September.
4 See Box 4.1. One exception to this has been the Court's interpretation of Art. 230(4) EC—see Box 7.3.

BOX 7.2 Referring environmental cases to the European Court of Justice

In practice, national courts effectively have a discretion whether to make a reference. This is because they can deem an issue of European law to be sufficiently clear that a reference is not needed. In this sense, the European Court of Justice (ECJ) is not a top court to which litigants have a right to appeal (like the European Court of Human Rights, which exists to uphold and interpret the European Convention on Human Rights and with which the ECJ should not be confused). So whether the ECJ gets to rule on a contested area of EC environmental law depends, in part, on the willingness of national judges to refer cases.

In the past, UK courts have seemed reluctant to refer environmental law cases (see p. 216). A clear example is the Court of Appeal's decision in the *Lappel Bank* case,[5] in which, although the judges were fundamentally split on whether economic factors could be taken into account in designating important bird habitats under Directive 79/409/EEC on wild birds, they declined to make a reference, although the House of Lords later rectified this absurdity by referring the case.[6]

While there have been a small number of references in recent years, there is still a reluctance to refer cases. It is hard to tell whether this is because of a general lack of familiarity with EC law, an undue confidence in the judges' ability to determine tricky points of EC law, or hostility to procedural measures that go against the grain of national decision-making procedures—but whether a reference will be made, and from which court, remains something of a lottery.

Regardless, if the aim is to have an environmental law issue ruled on by the ECJ, the best way forward is probably to bring the matter to the attention of the European Commission, which can take a case against the member State to the ECJ (see p. 206). In practice, environmental campaigning organizations will often use a twin-track approach, bringing a case in the national courts *and* notifying the Commission.

The Court gives one agreed judgment. These are often very brief and formal, and, for the full reasoning, the opinion of the Advocate-General must be read (although, on rare occasions, the Court and the Advocate-General do not agree).[7]

(e) The European Environment Agency

Although not formally an EC institution, the European Environment Agency—provided for in Regulation 1210/90 and established in October 1993—plays an important role. Based in Copenhagen, the Agency has the role of gathering information and data on the state of the European environment. A general report on the state of the environment must be published every three years, and the four reports published in 1995, 1998, 2003, and 2007 provide a valuable account of pressures on the European environment (see p. 299). A notable development is the European Pollutant Emission Register (EPER), based on monitoring of the Integrated Pollution Prevention and Control Directive (96/61/EC).[8]

The Agency has not been given any inspection or enforcement powers in relation to environmental legislation. Despite determined efforts by the European Parliament in the 1990s to see this happen, it is unlikely that such a role will emerge, because of the enormity and complexity of the task, and the political unpopularity that it would probably generate. Instead,

---

5 *R v. Secretary of State for the Environment, ex parte RSPB* [1997] JEL 168 (CA).

6 [1997] Env LR 431 (HL) and see Case 19.1.

7 Notable examples of disagreement in cases with environmental implications are the *Danish Bottles* case (Case 7.4), in which the Advocate-General considered both schemes to breach Art. 28, and the *UPA* case—(Case 7.3).

8 Article 15(3). EPER is available online at **www.eper.cec.eu.int**. It is being integrated into the European Pollutant Release and Transfer Register (E-PRTR)—see Chapter 15.

bodies such as IMPEL (an implementation network set up by the Commission, consisting of representatives from the member States) develop best practice and benchmarking standards for monitoring implementation.[9] Hence, alongside greater enforcement by the Commission (see p. 206), the EC is trying to improve compliance within the member States rather than to create an EC body to police environmental legislation.

Sources of EC environmental law

EC environmental law is contained in:

- the treaties;
- legislation passed by the institutions (regulations, Directives);
- international treaties to which the EC is a party;
- the judgments and principles of the ECJ.

To understand the relevance of these sources, an explanation of the concept of the supremacy of EC law is required. The doctrine of the supremacy of EC law is that, if there is a conflict between EC law and national law, EC law prevails, even if the national law is later in time. National courts should thus apply EC law rather than national law that does not comply with EC law.

This is, however, intimately linked with the related notions of 'direct effect' and 'useful effect'. A law has direct effect if it gives rise to rights and obligations that can be enforced by individuals and companies before national courts. If an EC law is directly effective, the doctrine of supremacy means that the non-conforming national law can simply be ignored. Not all EC law is directly effective in this sense: for any provision to be directly effective, it must be sufficiently clear and precise to form a cause of action. It must also be unconditional and must not require further definition at the discretion of the member State. There are also limitations on direct effect related to the source of the EC law: treaty Articles and regulations are capable of having direct effect, as long as they fulfil the above tests; for Directives, the Treaty suggested that they would not be capable of having direct effect—but the ECJ has indulged in some significant judicial creativity and has decided that Directives may have direct effect if the action is against the state or an emanation of the state, but not if it is against a private body (see p. 209).

In recent years, there has been a greater focus by the ECJ on the concept of 'useful effect'. This has also been driven by the Court's concern that EC law should not be a 'dead letter', but the focus is more on ensuring that member States should not avoid their obligations under EC law than it is on protecting individual rights (and, as a result, it is a particularly important development when it comes to environmental Directives, which often do not set out to grant individuals rights, but seek to improve environmental quality generally). Even if a Directive is not directly effective, therefore, there are legal limits on how member States exercise their discretion in implementing them and an individual may be able to bring a case arguing that this discretion has been exceeded. An example of this is given in Case 7.2. Again, this is discussed in more detail below.

(a) Treaty provisions

The provisions of the EC Treaty lay down the objectives of the EC, the powers of its institutions, and the decision-making procedures, as well as certain substantive legal requirements. They are of enormous importance in actions before the ECJ relating to the legality of

---

9 On which, see the Parliament and Council Recommendation on Minimum Criteria for Environmental Inspections 2001/331/EC.

EC actions. The Treaty is the source of the environmental principles and provides the basic default rules on, for example, where the balance between the free movement of goods and the environment should be struck. Some Treaty provisions are directly effective—for example, Art. 141 on equal pay—but this is not the case for the Articles concerned with the environment, because of their policy orientation.

(b) Regulations

Regulations are legislative acts of general application. They are normally directly effective, as long as they are sufficiently precise, but there are few regulations in the environmental sphere, other than those relating to the process of giving effect to international treaties (for example, on reducing ozone-depleting substances), agriculture and fisheries policies, administrative matters (such as setting up the European Environment Agency), and the eco-auditing and eco-labelling schemes.

(c) Directives

Directives are addressed to member States and are 'binding as to the result to be achieved'. This is discussed in more detail at p. 204, but a brief overview of what is required to comply with Directives is given here.

A member State's duty to implement EC environmental Directives is clearly central to their importance and enforceability. In the EC's early years, however, it was often thought that Directives imposed little more on member States than to make honest efforts to give effect to them. This was partly because, in the late 1970s and early 1980s, the Commission's attention tended to be focused more on adopting new legislation than on its implementation. In the UK, a further explanatory factor was probably the degree to which environmental laws generally tended to be seen as a framework for discretionary enforcement action rather than as binding standards. The ECJ has, however, given Directives greater weight (see Case 7.1).

CASE 7.1 Complying with environmental quality standards

The European Court of Justice (ECJ) has made it clear that *'binding as to the result to be achieved'* means what it says. A leading environmental case is the first *UK Drinking Water* case (Case C-337/89 *Commission v. UK* [1992] ECR I-6103; see also p. 215). This involved an alleged breach of the 1980 Drinking Water Directive (98/83/EC) by exceeding the maximum allowable concentration of nitrate in drinking water in various areas. In its defence, the UK argued that it was sufficient to take all practicable steps to achieve the water quality requirements, but the ECJ rejected this and held that practical compliance is an absolute obligation. The only get-out for the UK would have been if it had fallen within one of the specific derogations contained in the Directive (which, in this case, it did not).

The same approach was taken in Case C-56/90 *Commission v. UK* [1993] ECR I-4109, a case concerning the quality of bathing waters at Blackpool and Southport beaches. The ECJ held that it was not enough for the UK to take all necessary steps to achieve compliance; what was required was compliance with the quality standards in the Directive. Because it did not fall within any of the recognized exceptions in the Directive, the UK was in breach of its obligations.

The strength of the compliance duty in the latter case is undoubtedly more onerous, because the state has far less control over the factors that influence bathing water quality. Both of these cases show how the UK government was trying to maintain its traditionally pragmatic approach to environmental policy, at a time by which the legal outcome of these cases was, as a matter of law, not really in doubt.

EC environmental law (which has numerous Directives laying down practical compliance targets) would be of little value if the ECJ did not take this strict approach. But to avoid unnecessary and unexpected costs on the member States, one consequence is that environmental Directives often lack detail, contain vague commitments, and may contain quite wider-ranging derogations aimed at softening the impact on those member States that might be particularly hard hit. Environmental Directives are, in essence, often framework Directives and the less specific a Directive, the more difficult it is, in practice, to say that a member State has not complied with it. The leading case on these more general obligations is the *San Rocco Valley* case (Case 7.2).

CASE 7.2 Case C-365/97 *Commission v. Italy* [2003] Env LR 1 (the *San Rocco Valley* case)

In the San Rocco valley area of Italy, there had been a failure, over many years, to tackle unlawful waste tipping, which led to human health risks and damage to a watercourse. Under the Waste Framework Directive (2006/12/EC), member States must ensure that waste is disposed of without endangering human health or harming the environment. This is a general obligation, rather than a specific emission control or environmental quality standard, and, while not every inconsistent situation would breach the Directive, the factors here—a persistent breach resulting in significant environmental damage without any remedial intervention by the authorities—meant that Italy had exceeded the limits of its discretion.

The judgment opens up to judicial scrutiny some of the more general duties on member States, but it suggests that, with such provisions, it is not the severity of the resulting harm, but the adequacy of the response that governs whether the Directive has been properly implemented. (For an interesting comparison, see Case 11.1 for the view of the European Court of Human Rights.) This makes it very difficult to argue that such a Directive has not been properly complied with at the stage at which, for example, an environmental licence is applied for.

Directives are well suited to environmental measures, because they leave the choice of how to implement them to the member States, each of which will have different methods for setting environmental laws. Most EC environmental legislation is in the form of Directives. In this book, we generally refer to Directives by their common names—for example, the 'Habitats Directive'—rather than by the often lengthy titles that they are given formally—that is, Council Directive 92/43/EEC of 21 May 1992 on the conservation of natural habitats and of wild fauna and flora.

Implementation is required within a specified time period (often two years). This will be achieved by the member State changing its domestic law, and it will be in breach if it has not *fully and correctly* implemented the Directive within the time limit. In the UK, once the Directive is transposed, the domestic rule will constitute the relevant law, unless there has been partial or incomplete transposition.

A distinction must be drawn here between formal and actual compliance. Changing the law to comply with EC law constitutes formal compliance—but this is no guarantee that the law is complied with in practice, because, for example, a regulatory agency may exercise its discretion not to enforce the law or may interpret a legal term in a way that contravenes EC law. In enforcing environmental Directives generally, however, the Commission's lack of an inspection function, and lack of resources for monitoring developments in the member States and bringing actions before the ECJ is a significant constraint.

(d) Decisions, recommendations, and opinions

Decisions are binding on the individual or group to whom they are addressed, and may also be directly effective. They are rare in environmental law, being limited mainly to matters of monitoring and information gathering, such as monitoring greenhouse gas emissions. The institutions may also issue recommendations and opinions. These are not binding and only have a persuasive effect, and are seldom used in the environmental area (although a recent example can be seen in relation to the controversial issue of minimum criteria for environmental inspection—see p. 177). Historically, they have made little impact.

(e) Court decisions

The decisions of the ECJ give rise to law and this has been a particularly fertile area. The Court has borrowed and developed general principles of law from the jurisprudence of the member States, such as the principles of natural justice, proportionality, certainty, equality, and the protection of legitimate expectations and fundamental rights. In particular, proportionality is also a general standard against which all EC law is to be judged (see Box 7.3).

In practice, however, member States often tend to be forced to act by judgment in a Commission action against them, or a reference from their national courts. Decisions involving other member States often take much longer to influence decision making.

BOX 7.3 **Proportionality and EC environmental law**

Proportionality is a central concept in EC law. It entails that laws must be appropriate, must not go beyond what is necessary to achieve the desired objectives, and must take the least trade restrictive form. At national level, it is one of the key criteria against which proposals for new regulation, and their enforcement, are to be judged (see pp. 119 and 279), but only at the level of policy. Proportionality is also central to deciding whether certain human rights have been breached—for example, the right to property (see p. 71).

In relation to EC environmental law, proportionality is used by the European Court of Justice (ECJ) in:

- judging the validity of EC legislation (although EC lawmakers are given a wide discretion in relation to areas of social policy such as environmental regulation—see the *Standley* case, p. 619);

- balancing trade freedom and environmental protection—as applied in the *Danish Bottles* case (Case 7.4);

- assessing whether a member State may maintain or introduce national legislation providing stricter environmental protection than under certain EC environmental Directives (see p. 195)

- determining the appropriate level of 'fine' against a member State for not complying with its ruling (see p. 207).

Assessing proportionality tends to be a matter of judgment, but the court in Case T-13/99 *Pfizer Animal Health SA v. Council* [2002] ECR II-3305—a case about the validity of a precautionary ban on antibiotics in animal feed (see Case 3.6)—held that 'a *cost/benefit analysis is a particular expression of the principle of proportionality in cases involving risk management*'. It is not clear, however, how far the European courts will go in specifying the assessment methods that decision makers must use, but cases such as *Pfizer* indicate that the courts will give in-depth scrutiny to the basis of any scientific decisions.

Proportionality also plays a role in enforcing EC environmental law. Although the Court has not allowed proportionality to be used when it comes to the implementation of Directives, it has accepted that proportionality is relevant to any fine payable by a member State under Art. 228 EC. These propositions can be seen, respectively, in the first[10] and second[11] *Spanish Bathing Water* cases. Finally, a national implementing law can be challenged if it does not specify sanctions that are proportionate (see p. 205).

Making EC environmental law

The making of EC environmental legislation involves either unanimity or, more usually now, qualified majority voting, subject to some form of involvement of the Parliament.

(a) The role of the Council and the Parliament

For legislation adopted under either Arts 95 or 175 EC—the main bases in the Treaty for environmental legislation (see p. 185)—the 'codecision procedure' is used. The procedure is contained in Art. 251 and gives a strengthened role in the legislative process to the Parliament, although this is still quite negative in character. For example, as mentioned above, the Parliament still has no right to initiate new proposals. One feature of this procedure is the resolution of disputes, on matters of detail, by a conciliation committee made up of representatives of the Parliament and Council. This conciliation procedure has been invoked on a number of occasions in the environmental area: for example, in relation to the first 'Auto-Oil' Directive (98/69/EC) and the Water Framework Directive (2000/60/EC).

One important consequence of the greater involvement of the Parliament is that decision making is rather more open than it used to be, which goes some way towards tackling the problems of secrecy and lack of democratic accountability that are inherent in EC legislative procedures, although, by their nature, conciliation committees involve last-minute deals and lack transparency.

(b) Unanimity or majority voting?

Under the system of qualified majority voting, the number of votes in the Council is weighted roughly according to population (the UK has 29 votes in the Council out of 345). Its extension has restricted the number of areas in which unanimity among all member States is needed and therefore the scope for one unsupportive member State to veto a proposal. For example, the UK government opposed the ban on leaded fuel as from 2000, but this was nevertheless legislated for.

Another reason is that the system encourages the member States to reach a compromise position within the Council. The combined effect may enable some proposed Directives to avoid the fate of, for example, Directive 85/337/EEC on environmental impact assessment (EIA), which was delayed for many years by the opposition of one or two member States. This does not, however, mean that Directives will always be agreed swiftly, even with qualified majority voting, because there are also complex political considerations to take into account—although less-developed member States may now be bought off by concessions based on Art. 175(5) (see p. 190). The increasing involvement of the European Parliament is also relevant to whether a compromise position can be reached.

Since the Maastricht Treaty, most environmental legislation is subject to qualified majority voting. The only exceptions, in relation to which unanimity is still required, are those primarily of a fiscal nature,[12] measures relating to town and country planning or land use (unless they are concerned with waste management), measures concerning the quantitative

---

10 Case C-92/96 *Commission v. Spain* [1998] ECR I-505.

11 Case C-278/01 *Commission v. Spain* [2004] Env LR D3—see p. 207.

12 Notably, the Energy Tax Directive 2003/96/EC was adopted under Art. 93 EC.

management of water resources,[13] and measures affecting national policies on energy supply (for example, any proposal restricting the use of coal on environmental grounds).

Challenging EC legislation

The validity of regulations, Directives and decisions can be challenged within two months under Art. 230. This Article sets out grounds that are slightly wider than the UK's ultra vires rules. As a judicial review action, it also requires the applicant to have standing. Member States, the Commission, the Council, and Parliament have standing, but a private litigant must show direct and individual concern. Such a requirement virtually restricts individuals to challenging decisions addressed to them specifically, making direct challenges to environment measures highly problematic (see Case 7.3).

CASE 7.3 Article 230 EC and environmental protection challenges

In Case C-321/95P *Stichting Greenpeace Council and ors v. Commission* [1998] ECR I-1651, a decision by the Commission to allocate regional development funding to Spain for the construction of two power stations in the Canary Islands was challenged by Greenpeace, as well as by concerned local residents individually. The European Court of Justice (ECJ) held that none of the applicants was individually concerned for the purposes of Art. 230 EC and was unmoved by the argument that, in areas such as environmental protection in relation to which interests are often common and shared, there will never be a closed class of applicants satisfying the test of individual concern.

In Case C-50/00P *Unión de Pequeños Agricultores v. Council* [2002] ECR I-6677, Advocate General Jacobs saw no particular reason why 'individual concern' should be interpreted as requiring applicants to differentiate themselves from all other parties subject to the measure being challenged, and favoured an approach that would look at whether the measure has, or is liable to have, a substantial adverse effect on the applicant's interests. He said that this approach would remove the anomaly—seen in environmental cases such as *Greenpeace*—that the greater the number of persons affected, the less likely it is that effective judicial review is available. The ECJ, however, took a more conservative approach and restated the orthodox interpretation of individual concern, ruling that any change to this approach would have to be made by amending the EC Treaty. Why a test relating to differential impact rather than the degree of impact should be the only legally correct interpretation of individual concern is, however, debatable.

Finally, note that the Advocate General's harm-based test would have given standing to environmental organizations to challenge legislation,[14] whereas the test proposed by the Court of First Instance in Case T-177/01 *Jégo-Quéré & Cie SA v. Commission* [2002] ECR II-2365—another reformist case decided just prior to the ECJ ruling in the *UPA* case—was based on there being adverse *legal* effects (and while environmental interest groups serve a valuable role, their *legal* interests are unlikely to be affected by EC environmental law). The ECJ also overturned this decision,[15] again restating the orthodox position, and has continued to do so in subsequent cases.[16]

---

13 'Quantitative' was inserted by the Treaty of Nice, but this merely clarifies the interpretation given in Case C-36/98 *Spain v. Council* [2001] ECR I-779.

14 See the discussion of contrasting approaches to judicial review at national level on p. 313.

15 Case C-263/02 P [2004] 2 CMLR 12.

16 For a comprehensive refusal to extend the rules on standing, see, e.g., Joined Cases T-236/04 and T-241/04 *European Environmental Bureau v. Commission* [2005] ECR II-4945.

One way in which to get around this is to challenge the validity of EC law in national litigation. If the challenge has merit, then it may be (see p. 176) that the matter will be referred to the ECJ under Art. 234 EC and that the Court will then rule on the question of validity. An example of this is the *Standley* case,[17] in which, in the English courts, farmers challenged certain provisions of the 1991 Agricultural Nitrates Directive (91/676/EEC) as being incompatible with various principles of EC environmental policy. The High Court referred the case to the ECJ, which ultimately upheld the Directive against the challenge, among other things, that it unfairly discriminated against farmers (who are not the only contributors to this particularly challenging environmental problem). In the *Greenpeace*, *UPA*, and *Jégo Quéré* cases (discussed in Case 7.3), the availability of an Art. 234 reference was stressed by the ECJ in reaching its restrictive interpretation of Art. 230, but relying on this way to challenge EC law is subject to the vagaries of national courts' referring cases to the ECJ. The Court's ruling that, together, Arts 230 and 234 provide a complete system of legal remedies for challenging, directly and indirectly, the legality of EC action seems unduly optimistic and a relatively rare example of the Court not being receptive to environmental interests.

EC environmental law and policy

The rationale for EC environmental law and policy—the Common Market

The fundamental basis of the EC has always been economic. The primary aims were originally set out in Arts 2 and 3 of the Treaty of Rome, which established the EEC in 1957. These are the creation of a 'common market'—that is, a fully integrated single internal market within the boundaries of the member States—in 'goods, persons, services and capital', together with the progressive harmonization of the economic policies of the member States. In order to achieve these primary aims, internal barriers to trade and competition need to be dismantled, so that there are no internal frontiers to hamper the free movement of goods, persons, services, and capital, and no discrimination between people or firms on the grounds of nationality. This policy may be referred to as the provision of an economic, level playing field across the EC. In which respects the playing field should be level, however, is controversial (see Box 7.4).

BOX 7.4 Economic 'level playing fields' and beyond

In Case 91/79 *Commission v. Italy* [1980] ECR 1099, the Court was clear that environmental matters could fall within Art. 94—that is, within trade harmonization Directives:

> Provisions which are made necessary by considerations relating to the environment and health may be a burden on the undertakings to which they apply, and if there is no harmonization of national provisions on the matter, competition may be appreciably distorted.

But which provisions, exactly, are necessary in an EC context? Minimum standards for products that circulate in the internal market are more easily justified than similar standards relating to how such products are manufactured. If production processes do not give rise to adverse environmental effects in another member State why should they be regulated under EC environmental law? Indeed, it is only *because* there are various differences in market conditions—relating to things such as climate, the availability of natural resources, infrastructure, and social and fiscal

---

17 Case C-293/97 *R v. Secretary of State for the Environment and Minister of Agriculture, Fisheries and Food, ex parte Standley* [1999] ECR I-2603, see p. 619.

regimes—that there is any trade between states. So why should the EC try to level the economic playing field for manufacturers, etc., whose products do not lead to negative environmental effects (negative externalities or spillovers) beyond their borders?

One answer is that not doing so would lead to negative *economic* spillovers between member States, which might make the EC, as a whole, less productive and, in so far as environmental protection must be paid for, make regulating national environments that much harder economically.[18] Another explanation is that, in reality, the long-term effects of certain pollutants are not easily confined within national borders and that there is a danger in underestimating these physical spillovers (this is especially true of the more persistent, bioaccumulative pollutants). For example, the former British policy of discharging sewage effluent into coastal waters was justified on the grounds that the pollution would be diluted, but it has now been shown that many of the more polluting substances remain in the marine environment and give rise to problems for neighbouring states.

Perhaps the best explanation, however, is that the EC has never been only a free trade area: the Common Market always had a political objective—a peaceful and integrated Europe—and, even in its early years, the notion of a 'common market' was being stretched, by EC legislation and by the ECJ, to accommodate this agenda in a range of policy areas, including the environment.

It is clear that there is a fundamental conflict between some of the economic aims of the EC and the protection of the environment. This problem has been tackled by the creation of an environmental policy.

The EC's environmental policy

There was no mention of the environment in the original Treaty of Rome. To some extent, this was because the primary aims of the EEC were, as explained above, economic, but it was mainly because the potential environmental impact of the expansionist, growth-related economic policies adopted at the time was not perceived. By the early 1970s, however, the need for some form of policy on the protection of the environment was accepted. There were two reasons for this: one was the acceptance of the interrelationship between economic growth and environmental degradation; the other was that the environment was then emerging as a significant political issue. Environmental protection thus fits into the activities of the EC in two overlapping ways: first, as an adjunct to economic policy; secondly, as a positive end in itself.

In October 1972, declaring that '*economic expansion is not an end in itself*',[19] the heads of state of the member States accordingly requested the Commission to draw up an EC environmental policy. The Commission responded by formulating the first Action Programme on the Environment. (This has been followed by further Action Programmes in 1977, 1982, 1987, 1992, and 2002.) This was the effective beginning of what is now a very wide-ranging environmental strategy—but it was not the beginning of EC involvement in environmental matters. As long ago as 1967, Directive 67/548/EEC provided specifically for the classification, packaging, and labelling of dangerous substances. This was justified as necessary to achieve the Common Market, but environmental protection considerations were also influential.[20] Over two hundred items of new environmental legislation (and the same

18 See, J. Scott (1998) *EC Environmental Law*, London: Longman, pp. 12–15, for a good general discussion of this issue.

19 Paris Summit, October 1972. For the text, see Cmnd 5109.

20 Arguably, it was not until the sixth amendment to this Directive in 1979, which provided for pre-market control of hazardous chemicals, that a primarily environmental objective to this regime emerged.

number of amending laws) have now been agreed as part of this policy—both as an adjunct to the EC's economic and other policies, but also as primarily environmental measures—and these range across the whole spectrum of matters covered by this book.

It must also be noted that, since 2001, the EU has had a Sustainable Development Strategy. As with the Cardiff process begun in 1998 (see below), the Strategy emphasized the importance of integrating environmental protection requirements into other areas of EU policy, effectively placing the promotion of environmental protection alongside economic growth and social cohesion (by decoupling economic growth from negative environmental impacts) as the key aims of the EU. Opinion differs on whether this marks a genuine shift in attitudes, perhaps elevating sustainable development (and with it, environmental protection) as an underpinning rationale for the legitimacy of the EU, or whether it is merely window dressing, aiming for a degree of environmental integration for which, in key policy areas of the EU such as industry, transport, and agriculture, there is still insufficient political will. A Renewed Strategy was adopted in 2006 and has four 'key objectives' (of which environmental protection is one). The Strategy, however, has to be seen alongside the so-called 'Lisbon agenda for growth and jobs' of 2001, under which the member States agreed to push for economic expansion (to keep pace with economies such as India and China), and it is clear that, when the 2006 Strategy speaks of things such as 'sustainable consumption', it is not steering a course away from capitalistic consumerism.

The constitutional basis of EC environmental policy and law

The constitutional basis for environmental law and policy must be considered in two distinct phases: before and after the Single European Act 1986. The history of the development of the EC's environmental policy will be considered first, because it is a good illustration of the way in which the institutions have, in practice, widened the scope of what the EC deals with as a result of a generous reading of the Treaty.

(a) Before the Single European Act 1986

Before 1986, the legal justification for the policy was not entirely clear. In practice, two Articles of the Treaty—Arts 94 and 308 (the former relating to the harmonization of national laws in order to further the establishment of the Common Market; the latter relating to the EC's general and residual powers)—were used as justification. The majority of Directives, especially those relating to pollution control and common standards, tended to be justified on the basis of Art. 94, while those in which the content was almost purely environmental, such as Directive 79/409/EEC on Wild Birds, were justified on the basis of Art. 308. It was not unusual for both Articles to be cited, just in case of a challenge.

In cases that did come to the ECJ, the environmental policy was supported, which is not surprising, because it had been formulated with the agreement of all of the member States—see, for example, Case 91/79 *Commission v. Italy* [1980] ECR 1099 (Case 7.2). Most notably, in Case 240/83 *Procureur de la République v. Association de Défense des Brûleurs d'Huiles Usagées* [1985] ECR 531, on the legitimacy of Directive 75/439/EEC on Waste Oils, the Court stated that environmental protection was '*one of the Community's essential objectives*' and, as such, it justified some restrictions on the operation of the Common Market. In a sense, this amounted to a rewriting of the Treaty by the ECJ as a matter of political reality.

(b) The Single European Act 1986

In 1986, the Single European Act (SEA) 1986 went some way towards reflecting the reality of the situation by amending the Treaty to add a whole new title relating to the protection of the environment. By adding what are now Arts 174–176, SEA 1986 introduced explicit lawmaking powers in relation to environmental matters, making reliance on Art. 308 redundant. In addition, it added Art. 95, which has been of great importance for the development of environmental policy, even though it is primarily aimed at speeding up the completion of the single internal market. To some extent, these changes regularized the existing de facto position, but they also established some clearer constitutional rules than there had been in the past on the extent of the lawmaking powers and on how decisions were to be made. These required, for example, that differing environmental conditions across the Community, and potential costs and benefits of action or inaction, should be taken into account, but policy principles, such as the Polluter Pays Principle and that damage should be prevented and rectified at source, were also added by SEA 1986.

For some, however, the insertion of an environmental title was more about structuring and perhaps even *restricting* the competence of the Community, through procedural provisions such as requiring available scientific and technical data to be taken account of, than it was about regularizing and strengthening the role of the Community in the field of the environment by giving it an explicit legal base.[21] Regardless, these concerns failed to check the rapid growth in environmental legislation following SEA 1986.

(c) The Treaty on European Union 1992 (the 'Maastricht Treaty')

The Maastricht Treaty continued the process of integrating environmental matters into the heart of the EC's activities by making further amendments to the Articles mentioned above. It also recognized, for the first time, that the development of *'a policy in the sphere of the environment'* is one of the EC's main activities (see Art. 3) and replaced Art. 2, which sets out the objectives of the EC, with a new version that included the tasks of promoting throughout the Community *'a harmonious and balanced development of economic activities'*, and *'sustainable and non-inflationary growth respecting the environment'*. The Treaty thus acknowledged that there is a balance to be struck between economic and environmental factors, although the balance remained firmly with the former.

(d) Treaty of Amsterdam 1997

Further amendments to the Treaty came into force in 1999 that continued the development of European environmental policy. A new main goal of *'promoting a harmonious and balanced and sustainable development of economic activities'*, together with *'a high level of protection and improvement of the quality of the environment'* was included in Art. 2, and therefore applies to all policies and all institutions, not only to Commission initiatives. These goals are reinforced by Art. 6, which provides that *'environmental protection requirements must be integrated into the definition and implementation of Community policies and activities . . . in particular with a view to promoting sustainable development'*.

Although a version of this objective previously appeared in the environmental title, its elevation to the start of the Treaty is of considerable symbolic, legal, and policy importance.[22] It has led, under what is known as the 'Cardiff Process', to the publication by the Commission of a number of policy documents exploring the integration of the environment into Community policy generally, or in specific sectors such as energy and agriculture, but, as yet, there has been little radically integrative legislation.[23] It is notable that neither Art. 2 nor Art. 6 seeks to define sustainable development.

(e) The Treaty of Lisbon 2007

In 2004, political agreement was reached on a draft EU Constitution. In the early stages of negotiating the Constitution, it seemed that the environment was either completely off the radar screen, or was being consciously downgraded (for example, there were initially moves to define 'sustainable development' as being primarily about economic growth and social

---

21 The main proponent of this view is J. Golub (1996) 44 Political Studies 686.
22 For examples of the ECJ using Art. 6 EC, see pp. 203–04.
23 For a review, see COM(2004)394.

justice, and to exclude mention of environmental protection). The draft Constitution has now been superseded by a Reform Treaty (the Treaty of Lisbon 2007). This was agreed to too late for comment here—and has yet to be ratified—, but if ratified the Online Resource Centre will feature analysis.

Which Article?

It is clear from the above that EC law must have an explicit treaty basis. This is known as 'attribution'—that is, that any legislation must be attributed to one or more articles of the Treaty. If there is no legal basis for an EC environmental Regulation or Directive, or if the incorrect basis has been given, then the ECJ can annul the law.

The basic rule is that the Court will look for the 'centre of gravity' of the legislative measure. This approach was first taken in a case concerning the correct legal basis of the first amending Waste Framework Directive (91/156/EC)—Case C-155/91 *Commission v. Council* [1993] ECR I-939. In this case, it was decided that the principal objective of the Directive—the protection of the environment—was the crucial factor and not any ancillary effect on the functioning of the internal market. It is notable that this decision followed the conclusion of the Maastricht negotiations, which sanctioned the general use of qualified majority voting under Art. 175. In other words, as between Arts 95 and 175, there was now no need to prioritize the former because of the greater role for the Parliament, as had been the case before then. Hence, most environmental Directives are now based on Art. 175, although it remains possible to adopt harmonization Directives that have some environmental elements under Art. 95, as product-related Directives tend to be (see below).

There continue to be disputes between the institutions, however, about the correct legal base for measures relating to the environment. In Opinion 2/00 *Cartagena Protocol on Biosafety* [2001] ECR I-9713, for example, the ECJ was asked to rule on the correct legal base for adopting the Protocol (a subsidiary agreement made under the 1992 UN Convention on Biological Diversity). The Commission sought a dual legal base in Arts 174(4) and 133 regarding the EC's external trade policy (under which the EC has exclusive competence and negotiates on behalf of all of the member States), whereas the Council sought a single legal basis in the Environmental Title, the environment being a matter of shared competence between the EC and the member States. Voting procedure was not at stake, because both bases required qualified majority voting. The Court held that the Protocol was primarily an environmental protection measure—for example, it governed the interstate movement of living modified organisms even if this was not for commercial reasons—and so the view of the Council was upheld.

An example going the other way is Case C-281/01 *Commission v. Council* [2002] ECR I-12049. This case concerned the EC's 'buying into' the USA of the 'Energy Star' energy-saving labelling on office equipment such as computer monitors. Because the programme is voluntary and does not itself require greater energy efficiency, the Court held that it was primarily related to external trade and therefore should be based on the EC's common commercial policy (under which the Community's competence is exclusive), rather than on Art. 175 (a conclusion premised on voluntary labelling provisions being a trade barrier). In cases in which no overriding centre of gravity can be discerned and no legislative institution is prejudiced, then, a dual legal base is appropriate (see, for example, Case C-94/03 *Commission v. Council* [2006] Env LR 45—implementing the Rotterdam Convention on Prior Informed Consent regarding certain chemicals should be based on both Arts 133 and 175). There are Directives that base some of their provisions on Art. 95 and some that base their provisions on Art. 175.

There can also be disputes about whether a measure should be enacted under the EC Treaty or under another European treaty. In Case C-176/03 *Commission v. Council* [2006] Env LR 18, the ECJ ruled that the 2003 Framework Decision on Environmental Criminal Law, which had somewhat controversially been proposed under the Justice and Home Affairs 'pillar' of the EU Treaty, should properly have been enacted under Art. 175 EC, because it related to criminal law sanctions in support of environmental protection.[24]

Higher national standards

The rules allowing member States to adopt national standards going beyond those contained in EC environmental Directives is another reason why a legal base may be important. A good illustration of this is the adoption, under Art. 175, of Directive 2002/96/EC on waste electrical and electronic equipment (WEEE), and the simultaneous adoption, under Art. 95, of Directive 2002/95/EC, which restricts the use of certain hazardous substances in electrical and electronic equipment. These two Directives were originally contained in a single legislative proposal based on Art. 175, but they were split so that it would be more difficult for member States to maintain further bans or restrictions of dangerous substances in electrical and electronic equipment going beyond Directive 2002/95/EC except under the stricter conditions of Art. 95(4) and (5).

The scope of EC environmental law

Harmonizing legislation

A unified internal market depends upon trade and competition not being distorted by member States applying different rules and standards. The EC has therefore tried to harmonize laws in all of the member States so that a producer in one country does not have an unfair advantage over one in another. Initially used to harmonize *product* standards, this soon extended to *process* standards (see Box 7.4).

Under Art. 95, SEA 1986 introduced qualified majority voting for many proposals of this nature. As a safeguard, it also required as an objective that, if action is taken under Art. 95 concerning health, safety, environmental, or consumer protection, a high level of protection should be taken for those standards. In addition, member States may derogate from the common standards in certain limited ways under Art. 95(4) and (5) (see p. 195), and (10).

'Environmental' legislation—objectives, principles, and policy

Articles 174–176, however, provide a specific justification for environmental protection laws, even in cases in which there is no direct link to the economic aims of the EC. Article 175 provides the mechanics by setting out the voting procedures in the Council (see below). In contrast with Arts 94 and 95, either Directives or regulations are possible, although few environmental regulations have been made. A further contrast is that, while Art. 95 generally requires uniform baseline standards (subject to the scope for member States to derogate from these under Art. 95(4) and (5)), that is not always required under these Articles, because the motivating force behind them is the improvement of environmental standards rather than the realizing of the internal market. Accordingly, Art. 176 specifically allows member States to employ stricter measures than those agreed under Art. 175, as long as they are compatible with the rest of the Treaty (see p. 196).

Article 174(1) includes as *objectives* of the EC's environmental activities the preservation, protection, and improvement of the quality of the environment, the protection of human health, and the prudent and rational utilization of resources. Article 174(2) uniquely sets out the central *principles*[25] of EC environmental policy, which should be taken into account

---

24 See also Case C-440/05 *Commission v. Council* [2007] not yet reported (annulling the framework decision regarding criminal enforcement of ship source pollution).

25 On principles, generally, see Chapter 3.

when framing policy and legislation:

(a) preventative action should be preferred to remedial measures;

(b) environmental damage should be rectified at source;

(c) the Polluter Pays Principle;

(d) the Precautionary Principle.

A high level of environmental protection must also be aimed at, while the principle that environmental policies should form a component of the EC's other policies is now a general principle of the EC Treaty (Art. 6).

The principles are essentially policy principles, the purpose of which is to guide the form and content of EC environmental legislation. As noted, they must be taken into account—at best, this means that, if legislation has been adopted that completely fails to have regard to a principle, it might be annulled. This was the approach of the ECJ when it was asked to review the compatibility of the Ozone Regulation 3093/94 with the Precautionary Principle (Case C-341/95 *Bettati v. Safety Hi-Tech SRL* [1998] ECR I-4435 and see Case 3.5). In cases in which environmental principles have been cited, the Court has tended to use them to justify a decision reached—or at least reachable—on other grounds.[26] A good example is Case C-2/90 *Commission v. Belgium* [1992] ECR I-4431, in which the Court used the principle of rectification at source to justify upholding a ban on waste imports into the Walloon region of Belgium in the face of arguments that this infringed the right (see Case 7.5). There have been some recent cases, however, in which principles have been invoked in a way that suggests a reordering of the relative importance of trade and environmental interests within the Community (see the *PreussenElektra* and *Concordia Bus Finland* cases—Case 7.6 and Box 7.7, respectively), or to interpret secondary legislation (see the *Waddenzee* case on p. 77).

A difficulty, however, is that the meaning of the principles is far from settled. It was not clear whether the approach of the ECJ in the *Safety Hi-Tech* case was to avoid difficulties by deciding that only if the principle has not been considered will legislation be reviewable, or whether it also allows arguments based on fundamental misconceptions of the principles. Later cases such as *Pfizer* (see Case 3.6), however, show that the Court has been prepared to engage with the interpretation of environmental principles (in that case, the degree of risk needed to trigger the Precautionary Principle needing to be more than just a hypothetical risk).[27]

It is important to note that the principles are not directly enforceable obligations: they cannot be relied on in the abstract by, for example, an individual claiming that a polluter has not 'paid' for some aspect of pollution—by a claimant in a private nuisance case arguing that a polluter should pay for environmental pollution in relation to which there is no national law remedy—or that all regulatory action should be precautionary (see *R v. Secretary of State for Trade and Industry, ex parte Duddridge* [1995] Env LR 151, see Case 3.8). It can only be said with any certainty that they can be used to uphold or challenge EC law or, in exceptional cases such as *Walloon Waste* (Case 7.5), justify national measures or guide interpretation.[28] Case C-293/97 *R v. Secretary of State for Environment and ors, ex parte Standley and Metson* [1999] ECR I-2603 (discussed at p. 619) provides a good example of how the ECJ deals with challenges to EC environmental law that are based on alleged breach of environmental principles (in that case, the Polluter Pays Principle).

---

26 M. Doherty (2000) Env LR 251.

27 A decision that is consistent with, and perhaps influenced by, the jurisprudence of the World Trade Organization—see J. Scott (2003) Colum J Eur L 213, 228.

28 On their ambiguous status vis-à-vis the member States, see J. Scott and E. Vos (2002) 'The juridification of uncertainty' in C. Joerges and R. Dehousse (eds) *Good Governance in Europe's Integrated Market*, Oxford: Oxford University Press.

Under Art. 174(3) EC, the EC institutions are required to *take account of* available scientific and technical data, environmental conditions in the various regions of the EC, and the balanced development of those regions when preparing any proposals. In addition, some form of cost–benefit analysis should be performed before environmental measures are agreed. These requirements are in accord with the 'British' approach to pollution (see p. 223) and the UK government lobbied for their inclusion. The cost–benefit analysis obligation is given further practical effect by the Commission now undertaking regulatory impact assessments of its major legislative and policy proposals (for comment on this, see p. 472)

The international dimension is covered by Art. 174(4). Many pollution, conservation, and environmental matters, such as climate change, the protection of migratory species, or the pollution of the North Sea, are international in scope. A supranational body such as the EC is well placed to tackle them by having a common internal environmental policy with agreed standards; it may also act by putting forward a common platform in dealings with the rest of the world.[29] Article 174(4) specifically permits the negotiation and conclusion of international agreements, a power that justifies the EC's independent involvement in international treaties (although it appears from the *Cartagena Biosafety Protocol Opinion* [2001] ECR I-9713 that, notwithstanding Art. 174(4), Art. 175(1) is the correct legal basis for any measures imposing obligations on the Community). Promoting international cooperation is also an objective of the EC (Art. 174(1)).

The basic principle is that the member States bear the costs of implementing EC environmental laws (Art. 175(4)). But Art. 175(5) provides that, if a measure agreed under Art. 175 involves disproportionate costs for a particular member State, the Council may allow for temporary derogations and/or for financial support to meet those costs out of the special Cohesion Fund. This provision was inserted at Maastricht to buy off complaints from a number of the less-developed member States that the burden of EC environmental policy fell unfairly on them, because it hindered their industrial and economic development. They perceived this to be unfair, because the other member States have arguably reached their current level of development only by taking advantage of the absence in the past of the standards now imposed by modern environmental laws.[30]

Environmental Action Programmes and other policy drivers

A range of factors influences the scope of the future content of EC environmental policy. First, there are Environmental Action Programmes (EAPs). There have been six EAPs produced, the last published in 2002, and they have played an important role in shaping the content of EC environmental law. For example, the first two Programmes were reactive in nature, and concentrated on pollution control and on remedial measures, whereas the Third and Fourth EAPs began to emphasize preventive measures, such as product standards, and the design of industrial plant and processes. They also paid increasing attention to structural, or 'horizontal', measures that laid down procedures or ancillary administrative matters, such as environmental impact assessment (EIA) and freedom of access to environmental information, which could more easily be enacted under Art. 175.

The Fifth EAP, published in 1992, marked the shift towards greater emphasis on sustainable development, switching it away from grouping environmental controls by reference to environmental media, such as air, water, or land, to looking horizontally at all of the environmental implications of various sectors of the economy, especially industry, transport, agriculture, energy, and tourism.[31] The Fifth EAP also stressed the notion of 'shared responsibility'

---

29 In the draft Constitution, fostering global sustainable development becomes an explicit objective of the EU's external policies.

30 On derogations under Art. 175(5), see p. 199.

31 See also the integration duty, elevated in Art. 6 at around the same time.

between government, industry, and consumers for solving environmental problems (the first 'producer responsibility' Directives date from this period, recognizing that the 'polluter' is as much the manufacturer as the user). The Programme also marked a shift of emphasis from using legislation and regulation to solve problems towards a greater use of financial and other market mechanisms. It also suggested a more inventive use of legal instruments, including civil liability and voluntary mechanisms, the provision of more information on the state of the environment, a greater role for NGOs, and scrutiny of the financial sector's contribution towards sustainable development (see, generally, Chapter 8), although, in practice, there remains a preference for traditional command-style law.

The Sixth EAP covers the period 2002–12. In many ways, it continues the general approach taken in the previous EAP, emphasizing that environmental laws should work with the market, use a range of regulatory tools, and be better enforced. It identifies four priority environmental areas that need to be tackled:

- climate change;

- nature and biodiversity;

- environment and health, and quality of life;

- natural resources and waste.

Continuing the emphasis on integration, it also envisaged thematic strategies, seen as a way of tackling key environmental issues requiring a holistic approach because of their complexity, because of the diversity of actors concerned, and because no singular or traditional approach to regulation will be effective. Thematic strategies have been developed for soil protection, the marine environment, pesticides, air pollution, the urban environment, the sustainable use and management of resources, and waste recycling. In effect, these strategies are mini-EAPs. While some of the fruits of these strategies will be EC laws, there is an emphasis on non-legal means (based on the premise that the EC is already tackling those targets that are easiest to 'hit' with legislation).

Although not a themed area for action, the period of the Sixth EAP is seeing some degree of 'post-regulatory', procedural law being emphasized, such as measures to give effect to the provisions of the Aarhus Convention. It may also see further emphasis both on the rights of individuals and groups, and—deepening the notion of shared responsibility—on the responsibilities owed by these actors. Economic instruments are again stressed. But, as the Commission itself recognized in 1999, developments in this area at EC level have been stifled in large part by the need for unanimity among the member States when environmental measures of a fiscal nature are agreed (see Art. 175(2) EC). This has so far proved fatal to proposals for carbon taxes, not least because of UK hostility (although see now Directive 2003/96/EC). Even in areas in relation to which unanimity is not required, however, progress has been slow: attempts to adopt an EC-wide civil liability regime dragged on for many years before finally being adopted in 2004 (see p. 303). Examples of 'working with the market' include the EC greenhouse gas emissions trading scheme and tradable permit schemes may be explored further (although there seems little enthusiasm for them). Securing better compliance with EC environmental law, an enduring theme of recent action programmes, is said to be a 'strategic priority'.

It must be stressed that EAPs are guides to policy development and that EC environmental laws have been adopted that have not been heralded by such programmes (and that some suggested measures have not been adopted). The fate of the thematic strategies is a good example. In 2005, the Enterprise and Industry Commissioner announced a deregulation initiative,[32] with a particular focus on laws that could not be justified on economic grounds,

---

32 COM(2005) 535.

suggesting that only in obvious 'win–win' areas such as energy efficiency should there be environmental regulation. One aspect of this was an attempt to block the thematic strategies. Although not blocked, some of the strategies—such as the air quality strategy—seem to have been extensively watered down; this might suggest that the fight against 'over regulation' had an effect.

This links to another key driver of environmental policy: since 2001, the EU has had a Sustainable Development Strategy (see above) and this undoubtedly plays a role in guiding the content of policy.

Finally, although the EC Directive on strategic environmental assessment (2001/42/EC) does not directly apply to the Community's own plans and programmes, for some years, the Commission has undertaken regulatory impact assessment of major initiatives (see p. 472) and, under Regulation 1367/2006 (which applies the Aarhus Convention to the EC's own institutions), there is now a requirement to assess strategically things such as EAPs—a duty that entails public participation.

The range of environmental Directives

It is neither possible (nor terribly helpful) in the space available to list all EC Directives that relate to the environment. What follows instead is a selective list that is intended to illustrate the major areas of EC involvement, together with some indication of legislation in the pipe-line. Greater detail on individual Directives is given in the relevant chapters of Part III of this book and in Haigh (looseleaf, updated) *Manual of Environmental Policy: The EC and Britain*, London: Longman, which explains each Directive and its implementation in turn.

Important EC Directives have been made in relation to the following areas. In some cases, such as in relation to the use and production of CFCs or emissions from vehicles, no number is given simply because the amount of legislation is very great.[33]

- **Setting quality standards for water**
  Drinking Water 80/778/EEC
  Bathing Waters 2006/7/EC
  Freshwater Fish Waters 2006/44/EC
  Shellfish Waters 2006/113/EC
  Agricultural Nitrates 91/676/EEC

- **Setting emission standards for discharges to water**
  Dangerous Substances in Water 2006/11/EC
  Groundwater 2006/118/EC

- **Holistic management of the water environment, including quality and emission standards**
  Water Framework 2000/60/EC

- **Setting quality standards for air**
  Ambient Air Quality Assessment and Management 96/62/EC and its daughter Directives, covering: limit values for sulphur dioxide, nitrogen dioxide, particulate matter and lead (1999/30/EC); benzene and carbon monoxide (2000/69/EC) and ozone (2002/3/EC) (to be replaced in 2008 by a Directive on Air Quality and Cleaner Air for Europe)

- **Setting emission standards for emissions to the atmosphere**
  Various Directives on Emissions from Vehicles such as 70/220/EEC, 88/76/EEC, 89/548/EEC, and 91/441/EEC

---

33 Only Directives currently in force are mentioned, quite a number of which replace earlier Directives.

Emissions from Industrial Plants 84/360/EEC
Emissions from Large Combustion Plants 2001/80/EC
Waste Incineration 2000/76/EC
Volatile Organic Compounds 94/63/EC and 99/13/EC

- **Setting noise standards**
  Noise in the Workplace 86/188/EEC
  Noise from Outdoor Equipment 2000/14/EC
  Monitoring and mapping noise 2002/49/EC

- **Controlling emissions of dangerous pollutants**
  Dangerous Substances in Water 2006/11/EC
  Toxic Waste 78/319/EEC, as amended by 91/689/EEC
  Mercury 84/156/EEC
  Lindane 84/491/EEC
  Cadmium 83/513/EEC
  Disposal of PCBs 76/403/EEC
  Various Directives and regulations on ozone-depleting substances, lead, and pesticides

- **Controlling the disposal, management and reduction of waste**
  Framework Directive on Waste 2006/12/EC
  Toxic Waste 78/319 as amended by 91/689/EEC
  Sewage Sludge 86/278/EEC
  Urban Waste Water Treatment 91/271/EEC
  Landfill 99/31/EC

- **Setting product standards**
  Noise from Outdoor Equipment 2000/14/EC
  Emissions from Vehicles; Classification, Packaging and Labelling of Dangerous Substances 79/831/EEC
  Content of Petrol and Diesel Fuels 98/70/EC
  Hazardous Substances in Electrical and Electronic Equipment 2002/95/EEC
  Phasing out Ozone-Depleting Substances Regulation 2037/2000/EC
  Chemicals ('REACH') Regulation 1907/2006/EC

- **Promoting waste reduction among producers**
  Packaging and Packaging Waste 94/62/EC
  End-of-Life Vehicles 2000/53/EC
  Waste Electronic and Electrical Equipment 2002/96/EC

- **Controlling the storage and use of hazardous materials**
  Major Accident Hazards 82/501/EEC and 96/82/EC (the 'Seveso' I and II Directives)
  Asbestos 87/217/EEC

- **Controlling dangerous activities**
  Waste Shipments 1013/2006/EC

- **Setting standards for the operation of certain industries**
  Emissions from Industrial Plants 84/360/EEC
  Titanium Dioxide Industry 78/176/EEC and 89/428/EEC
  Emissions from Large Combustion Plants 2001/80/EC
  Integrated Pollution Prevention and Control 96/61/EC

- **Procedures for the planning of development**
  Environmental Impact Assessment 85/337/EEC
  Strategic Environmental Assessment 2001/42/EC

- **Protecting wildlife**
  Wild Birds 79/409/EEC
  Habitats 92/43/EEC
  Trade in Endangered Species Regulation 338/97/EC

- **Protecting the countryside**
  Rural Development Regulation 1257/99/EEC

- **Genetically modified organisms (GMOs)**
  Contained Use 90/219/EEC
  Deliberate Release 2001/18/EC
  Transboundary Movement Regulation 1946/2003/EC

- **Promoting energy efficiency and combating climate change**
  Promoting Electricity from Renewable Energy Sources 2001/77/EC
  Energy Performance of Buildings 2002/91/EC
  Establishing a Greenhouse Gas Emissions Trading Scheme 2003/87/EC
  Taxation of Energy Products and Electricity 2003/96/EC
  Promoting Biofuels 2003/30/EC

There are also important Directives and regulations on an ever-widening range of ancillary matters:

- Regulation 1210/90/EEC established the European Environment Agency (see p. 176);

- Directive 2003/4/EC on freedom of access to information on the environment, and Directive 2003/35/EC on public participation in relation to plans and programmes required under the EIA and IPPC Directives both form part of the essential process of sharing responsibility for environmental improvement between regulators, industry, and the public;

- the Environmental Liability Directive 2004/35/EC and steps being taken to harmonize the use of criminal law sanctions are measures designed to improve compliance with existing laws;

- Regulation 880/92/EEC on Eco-Labelling and Regulation 1836/93/EC on Eco-Management and Audit further emphasize the role that voluntary initiatives by business will play in future policy;

- lastly, there is the Financial Instrument for the Environment (LIFE)—originally contained within Regulation 1973/92/EEC—which provides financial support for environmental matters, especially on the promotion of sustainable development and nature conservation.

There are, of course, many areas of environmental policy in relation to which there has been little, or no, legislation from the EC. Examples relevant to this book include the use of energy and other taxes, town and country planning, and landscape and soil conservation. There are various reasons for this inaction. Using the examples just mentioned, in relation to energy taxes, there has been strong opposition by certain member States—especially the UK—to taxes set at EC level (at which unanimity is required), while measures aimed directly at spatial planning or conserving landscape features solely on aesthetic grounds would probably be seen as in conflict with the principle of subsidiarity, discussed below.

Environmental law—towards uniformity or flexibility?

As explained above, there is now a considerable body of EC environmental law, some of which has its origins in economic integration and some which has been adopted as more explicitly 'environmental' measures (under Arts 308 or 175). In one sense, all of this legislation aims at harmonizing practice across the Community, although the desirability of setting uniform standards is somewhat greater when it comes to measures passed to complete the internal market—that is, under Art. 95—especially product standards. Nevertheless, all of this legislation is essentially *minimum harmonization* legislation: it sets baseline standards that should not be breached. With both types of legislation, however, member States have some scope to set stricter standards at national level.

Three issues arise:

- how far a member State may go beyond EC environmental standards (the answer to which depends on whether the EC measure relates primarily to the internal market or to the environment);

- more generally, whether Directives tend towards uniform standards or impose different standards on different member States—that is, how much flexibility there is *in the Directive itself*;

- what the future holds.

Before considering these issues, it is worth noting that the *context* within which an environmental Directive operates is important. A good example can be seen in relation to Directives that regulate sound levels from motor vehicles under Directive 70/157/EEC, as amended. Member States may not refuse to grant EC or national type-approval to vehicles or exhaust systems, or to restrict their free movement, if the requirements of this Directive are met. But in *R v. London Boroughs Transport Committee, ex parte Freight Transport Association Ltd* [1991] 1 WLR 828, the House of Lords held that a distinction was to be made between controlling the free circulation of vehicles manufactured in accordance with the Directive and legitimate traffic control measures, and allowed the latter (see also *R v. London Borough of Greenwich* (1996) 255 ENDS Report 49). These cases illustrate that the *type* of harmonization has to be considered: a Directive that fully harmonizes one area of control may not do so in relation to other related areas.

Higher national standards

Internal market legislation

For 'internal market' legislation, under Art. 95(4), national provisions may be stricter than the Directive if the national provision is justified by the need to protect the environment. This exception was intended to cover the situation in which a Directive[34] was agreed under Art. 95 despite the opposition of a member State (and, for this reason, is called the 'environmental guarantee'). It was central to the political balance agreed in SEA 1986, because it provided a palliative to qualified majority voting. Following the Amsterdam Treaty, the Treaty now explicitly differentiates between national rules that are 'maintained' (Art. 95(4)) and those that are subsequently 'introduced' (Art. 95(5)). In both cases, whether a member State voted against the harmonizing measure is irrelevant.

In both cases, the Commission must decide whether to approve or reject the national provisions, having verified whether or not they are a means of arbitrary discrimination, or a disguised restriction on internal trade, or an obstacle to the internal market (Art. 95(6)). Because any national measures, existing or new, will potentially have some effect on the internal market, the Commission must, in effect, judge whether the derogation is *proportionate* to the aim of protecting the environment. If it does not do so within six months, the national measures are deemed to be approved.

---

34 The derogation provision also applies to harmonization measures emanating from the Commission through the comitology (committee) procedure, e.g., various scientific committees.

The ECJ has held that a member State may maintain stricter national provisions if its risk assessment differs from that of the Commission and if the area in question is one in relation to which divergent assessments of risk can be made, because of levels of scientific uncertainty, and if it can show that its national measures do, in fact, lead to greater protection and are not disproportionate. Although it gave this ruling in a case about food additives (Case C-3/00 *Denmark v. Commission* [2003] ECR I-2643), it would seem equally applicable to many areas of environmental regulation—although, in the *Denmark* case, the Commission's risk assessment was, in fact, held to be flawed (which might suggest that, in cases in which there are divergent views about the conclusions to be drawn from competing risk assessments that gave due weight to all relevant information, the Court might not be so generous towards the member State).

Because national laws introduced after a harmonization measure are potentially more disruptive to harmonization, however, under Art. 95(5) a member State may *introduce* further national provisions only in the light of new scientific evidence relating specifically to a problem arising in that member State after the harmonizing law was passed and which is notified to the Commission. Prior to 1999, the Commission interpreted this as meaning a country's specific objective needs—for example, relating to its geography or demography—although it did so fairly generously. In the *Denmark* case, the Court held that, under Art. 95(4), there did not have to be a problem related to a particular member State or new scientific evidence, although these would be relevant when the Commission made its decision whether or not to allow the derogation (in fact, Denmark was able to derogate without showing that either of these applied). These factors, then, go to deciding whether the member State's actions are proportionate under Art. 95(4), although, as the Advocate-General cautioned in the *Denmark* case, the fact that no specific problem relating to a member State needs to be proven when national provisions are being *maintained* has the potential effect of allowing member States a permanent opt-out of harmonizing measures.

Since 1999, member States have increasingly resorted to derogations from harmonization measures. In Joined Cases C-439/05 and C-454/05P *Land Oberösterreich and Austria v. Commission*, ECJ, 13 September 2007, the issue was whether Austrian authorities could introduce a ban on the use of GMOs in their region, notwithstanding that this was already governed by Directive 2001/18/EC. The Austrian authorities sought to argue that the region was characterized by small farms and had an important organic sector, but the ECJ did not accept that these amounted either to new evidence or evidence of problems particular to the area under Art. 95(5), partly because Austria had not put forward any evidence that unusual ecosystems would be harmed. It is likely that a strong case will need to be made to show that the conditions in Art. 95(5) are met.

Environmental legislation

Stricter protective measures may be maintained *or* introduced under Art. 176, as long as they are notified to the Commission and 'compatible with the Treaty' (which seems to mean that they should not give rise to unlawful trade distortions). This provision dates back to SEA 1986, and was included to allay fears from, in particular, Germany and Denmark (states traditionally seen as environmental 'leaders') at the possible impact of the enlargement of the EC, at that time, to include Spain and Portugal (states that did not have strong environmental protection regimes). Member States therefore have much greater freedom to go beyond the minimum standards laid down in environmental legislation and, arguably, a 'two-speed environmental Europe' has already emerged.[35]

The ECJ has held that the national measures do not have to pass any proportionality test (Case C-6/03 *Deponiezweckverband Eiterköpfe v. Land Rheinland-Pfalz* [2005] Env LR 37). So, more protective action by the member State can, in principle, aim at *any* greater level of

35 M. Soverski (2004) 13 RECIEL 127, 133.

environmental protection, as long as it is otherwise Treaty-compatible, but a member State cannot impose national measures that use a different type of regulatory tool (for example, a product ban, instead of a quality standard), because this would not be a stricter standard, but a different standard.

Subsidiarity, proportionality, and flexibility

What does the Treaty require when it comes to agreeing the content of Directives? The starting point is the general principle of 'subsidiarity', first introduced specifically to the Environmental Title by SEA 1986 and now contained in Art. 5 EC. This states that:

In areas which do not fall within its exclusive competence, the Community shall take action, in accordance with the principle of subsidiarity, only if and in so far as the objectives of the proposed action cannot be sufficiently achieved by the Member States and can therefore, by reason of the scale or effects of the proposed action, be better achieved by the Community. Any action by the Community shall not go beyond what is necessary to achieve the objectives of this Treaty.

In part, this is a competency clause, but it also relates to the amount of discretion given to member States in EC environmental legislation.

Following the Maastricht negotiations, the concept was much discussed. The Edinburgh Summit in December 1992, for example, resolved that the Community should only legislate to the extent necessary, that framework Directives should be preferred (see below), and that voluntary codes should be used where appropriate. The threat posed by subsidiarity was shown by the UK government's action in bringing forward a list of Directives that it wished to see amended and a further list of proposals that it wished to see discontinued. The first category included the various Directives on air quality standards, drinking water, bathing waters, and hazardous waste, while the second included the proposed Directives on landfill, packaging waste, and ecological quality of water, as well as proposals for strategic environmental assessment (SEA). This pressure has largely been resisted, although not without some drift towards more flexible legislation. A good illustration is the Water Framework Directive (2000/60/EC), considered at p. 593.

Alongside subsidiarity must be considered the concept of 'proportionality'. This relates to the intensity of EC legislation ('scale or effects'), although the concepts of subsidiarity and proportionality are closely linked (and are the joint subject of a Protocol to the Amsterdam Treaty).

Internal market legislation

As noted above, Directives adopted under Art. 95 aim to secure the functioning of the internal market subject to the important exceptions provided by the 'environmental guarantee'. Generally, this means that Directives will apply uniformly to all of the member States. Invariably, this is the case with Directives that govern the use of harmful substances in products—for example, Directive 2002/95/EC restricting the use of certain hazardous substances in electrical and electronic equipment—but there are examples of Directives, agreed under Art. 95, which have not been concerned with the make-up of products and in relation to which a more flexible approach has been taken. The Packaging Waste Directive (94/62/EC), for example, requires member States to establish national systems to provide for the collection and recovery of packaging. It then provides for recovery and recycling targets, although member States may set higher targets if they wish. In addition, three member States (Portugal, Greece, and Ireland) were allowed to meet lower targets, as long as they eventually came into line by 2005. It is clear that these differences were agreed as a political expedient, but it is hard to see how this fits in with the normal requirements of uniformity under Art. 95 (unless one is pragmatic about the legal base for the Directive, which, if it were adopted now, would probably be split between those aspects relating to packaging and those relating to packaging waste—see the example of Directives 2002/95/EC and 2002/96/EC at p. 188).

Partly, this is because Art. 95(10) enables harmonizing legislation to include *provisional* safeguarding measures if, for example, these are needed to deal with exceptional threats of limited duration. Examples include Art. 23 of Directive 2001/18/EC on the deliberate release into the environment of GMOs[36] under which a member State may suspend or terminate the placing on the market of a product containing a GMO, if this is done because of new or additional scientific information about risk to health or the environment. But the time periods for such temporary derogations and their justification can, in practice, be rather generous (see Box 7.5).

BOX 7.5 Derogations and internal market environmental legislation

Directive 99/51/EC on phencyclidines (PCPs) amended an earlier Directive from 1991. The revised Directive allows five member States, including the UK, to continue to apply the less strict provisions of the 1991 Directive until 2008, on the grounds that, as *'oceanic maritime Member States'*, there are technical reasons why they need to make certain uses of PCPs. As Krämer remarks, this is odd because of strong evidence in 1999 of less dangerous alternatives to PCPs and because other member States *not* granted the derogation, such as Greece, are also clearly maritime nations. He questions most forcefully why a national measure seeking more protective environmental provisions needs to be taken over the procedural hurdles of Art. 95 EC, while a derogation from a strict Community standard that allows less stringent standards to be applied nationally *'may be explained in three or four words'*.[37]

Environmental legislation

The background to this—especially the various policy principles—has been described above (see p. 189). In particular, Art. 174 provides that Community policy should be based on the principle that environmental damage should, as a priority, be rectified at source. But it also provides that, in preparing its environmental policy, the Community must take account of environmental conditions in, and balanced development of, the various regions of the Community. Arguably, the former points to a preference for emission standards, while the latter suggests a preference for target standards.

In general terms, the EC appears to be resolving this contradiction by a subtle mixture of approaches that may require Best Available Techniques (BAT) and similar types of standard to be used for things such as industrial emissions, but then tempering this by requiring these standards to be set having regard to regional differences. A good example of this is the Integrated Pollution Prevention and Control Directive (96/61/EC) under which emissions must be controlled with regard to firms' *'geographic location and local environmental conditions'*. Thus, while all regulated firms have to use BAT to minimize pollution, regional differences will play a part in determining what is 'best' for any installation (see p. 501).

A slightly different example of taking regional differences into account is the 'bubbling' of the EC's greenhouse gas emission reduction targets. Thus, the Community's target of reducing its emissions by 8 per cent by 2008–12 (compared to 1990 levels) is imposed unequally on member States, so that some states must reduce emissions—for example, the UK must

---

36 Adopted under Art. 95 EC. The use of this legal base might be questioned.

37 L. Krämer (2002) *Casebook on EU Environmental Law*, Oxford: Hart, p. 42, noting the differing standards when it comes to the duty to give reasons for adopting EC legislation (Art. 253 EC).

make a 12.5 per cent cut—while others can increase their emissions—for example, Greece is allowed a 25 per cent increase—which is a good illustration, in EC law, of the international law concept of 'common but differentiated responsibilities'.

Aside from this substantive differentiation, the other feature of environmental legislation has been an increasing use of procedural and reflexive techniques. This has taken two forms. One is that member States are increasingly required to adhere to specific procedures when implementing environmental Directives (an example of this is Directive 96/61/EC, which sets out quite detailed procedures for determining what the BAT for any particular sector will be—see p. 502). The other is the use of Directives that either comprise essentially procedural obligations (such as the Directives on Environmental Impact Assessment 85/337/EEC and Strategic Environmental Assessment 2001/42/EC) or try to stimulate improved environmental performance within the member States without specifically laying down binding targets (an example being the Renewable Energy Sources Directive 2001/77/EC, which lays down non-binding 'indicative' targets for the proportion of electricity generated from renewables and requires member States to publish reports on their performance).

In contrast to internal market laws, Art. 175(5) allows disproportionate costs to be alleviated by temporary derogations and/or financial support from the Cohesion Fund. It is worth noting that there is a move away from resorting to reliance on derogations (which must generally be granted by the Commission) towards setting out different targets in Directives (see, for example, the different national targets effectively provided for in the Landfill Directive 99/31/EC and further below). The latter may be preferable politically, because the member States can exercise more influence on the Council than on the Commission, but temporary derogations are still used: an example is the Waste Electronic and Electrical Equipment (WEEE) Directive (2002/96/EC), which sets specific collection and recovery targets, but under which Greece and Ireland were granted derogations for up to two years because of, positively, the low level of consumption of this kind of equipment and, negatively, their poor recycling facilities. Derogations have been used in particular to facilitate enlarging the EC eastwards (see Box 7.6).

BOX 7.6 Enlargement and the future of environmental law and policy

Even in an EC of 15 member States, environmental laws had to be sufficiently flexible to take geographic differences, and sometimes pragmatic abilities to comply, into account. From 2004, enlargement has brought 12 new member States into the EC, diversifying further the European environment, the strength of its national economies, and its institutional capacity to secure environmental protection.

The accession treaties require that all legislation apply fully to the new member States, but—as with previous enlargements—derogations regarding practical compliance have been given for specific Directives. These are normally time-limited, but there are differing degrees of derogation. For example, every accession country has been granted an extension—in some cases, of up to a decade—within which to comply with key provisions of the Urban Waste Water Treatment Directive (91/271/EC) and derogations in relation to the Large Combustion Plants Directive (2001/80/EC) are quite widespread, reflecting the difficulties that the new member States have in improving emission controls at existing power stations. In some cases, however, derogations have been granted that merely require 'all efforts' to be made: for example, for Estonia in relation to certain sulphur dioxide emissions, because of its use of oil shale for burning.

What is perhaps most notable about this is not that quite lengthy and, in some cases, seemingly unenforceable derogations have been agreed, but that there are so few.[38] It is highly unlikely that they mark the full extent to which the accession countries were complying with existing EC environmental law when they joined the EC; all existing member States are normally breaching one or more Directives at any given time. The reality is that it will take several years before the Commission can seek meaningful sanctions against the new member States—penalty payments imposed by the European Court of Justice—because the institutional apparatus to monitor practical non-compliance is underdeveloped. This period of delay will, in practice, serve as a form of derogation and each accession treaty protects only against very long-tail, or very expensive, economic risks.

New directions

For some time, the Community has been moving away from a model of regulation based on adopting legislation laying down binding legal obligations that try to harmonize laws across the Community. This has been a general trend, but it is particularly important for environmental protection law. Partly, this has been because of perceived shortcomings in old-style, command-and-control legislation as neither flexible enough, nor responsive enough, to the complex demands of environmental regulation (and which will become ever more difficult as the EU expands). But it has also been in response to some of the problems that the EC has faced in terms of its legitimacy—the perception that EC rule making is too remote from those it affects, and does not sufficiently engage with key stakeholders and the wider public (which, in an area such as environmental law, with a wide array of private and public interests, is a particular problem). For these reasons, there has been a shift of focus towards environmental *governance*.

There are three related features to this development (which, it must be stressed, is already taking shape). The first is a move away from exclusively 'top-down' environmental lawmaking to encompass decision-making processes that try to involve both state and non-state actors. In the environmental field, an existing example is the 'Auto-Oil' initiative, which brought together the Commission, vehicle manufacturers, and the oil industry in trying to tackle a problem (air pollution) that could not be addressed coherently without, in effect, the problem being 'shared' by these two sectors. (It is notable that this initiative resulted in traditional regulatory standards being adopted and that it has, in fact, been widely criticized—see Box 15.6.)

The second is a consequence of moving away from a focus on harmonization (especially substantive harmonization) and can be seen from the approach of the ECJ in the *Standley* case, in which the member States were given a considerable degree of discretion in how to implement the Agricultural Nitrates Directive (91/676/EEC) when it came to designating areas for protection (see p. 619).

The third is that there is an emphasis on using different regulatory techniques that seem to fit better with this approach. Thus, in place of binding standards set at EC level, there is much greater emphasis on trying to stimulate improved environmental performance within the member States. This is through such learning strategies as benchmarking and sharing best practice, but there is likely to be some legal force behind this approach—for example, legislation will set out, procedurally, the terms by which information is generated, and will require

---

38 The Council can grant new member States temporary derogations from legislation adopted between November 2002 and April 2003, the date of the Accession Treaty, and all of the new states have been granted derogations from the Directive on Waste Electrical Equipment adopted during this period.

that reports are published and reviewed by the Commission. The Renewable Energy Sources Directive (2001/77/EC) (p. 199) illustrates how this approach is already taken.

In short, therefore, there are various pressures to move away from legislative harmonization (and even, as in the case of the environment, away from minimum harmonization). At the level of policy, the 'Cardiff process' can be seen as a far-reaching example of this approach (see p. 186). In time, it is possible that this new approach will also be widely adopted in place of relying on traditional legal approaches such as the use of the standard-setting Directives that have tended to predominate in environmental law, especially in those areas in which issues about subsidiarity are more keenly felt. But the evidence so far is that 'new governance' approaches are used much less frequently than the rhetoric surrounding them would suggest.[39]

There are contrasting views on what is going on here. One view sees these developments in generally positive terms, emphasizing the need to give member States—and key actors—greater freedom to pursue environmental protection in ways that they consider to be the most appropriate, albeit against a backdrop of transparency, and structured evaluation and coordination. Another view, however, sees these developments in a more negative light, because substantive legal standards can, at least in principle, be enforced either through traditional legal means or, indirectly, by pressure groups raising awareness of non-compliance. On this view, headlines reporting that a member State has breached EC law by failing to submit an evaluative report on how it is combating pollution simply carry less force than similar publicity that the member State is polluting.

Internal trade and environmental protection

The tensions between uniformity and flexibility, or between harmonization and national interests, are also seen in the extent to which, in the absence of the EC having adopted legislation under Arts 95 or 175, environmental considerations may override the free movement of goods within the EC. Thus Art. 30 EC permits national laws effectively to restrict imports under Art. 28 (or exports, under Art. 29) if there is a genuine need to protect, among other things, human, plant, or animal health, or national treasures. ('Animal health' has been defined to include wider biodiversity conservation concerns—an important extension from its narrower agricultural origins: Case C-67/97 *Bluhme* [1998] ECR I-8033.)

The very important decision of the ECJ in the *Danish Bottles* case amplifies this point into a more general rule (Case 7.4).

CASE 7.4 Case 302/86 *Commission v. Denmark* [1988] ECR 4607 (*Danish Bottles*)

This case arose from a Commission challenge to Danish laws that required beer and soft drink containers to be returnable. The Commission argued that they were a form of disguised discrimination against foreign manufacturers and hence an impediment to free trade under Art. 28 EC. The European Court of Justice (ECJ) held, in clear terms, that it was permissible to use environmental protection to justify such discrimination. This was because the protection of the environment is, said the Court for the first time, one of the EC's 'mandatory requirements'. It can therefore justify an interference with the operation of the Common Market (even though environmental protection is not mentioned in Art. 30). In other words, the ECJ developed EC law by elevating the importance of environmental values.

It went on to hold, however, that such a derogation from the internal market must be proportionate to the end to be achieved. Because a returnability requirement was clearly more environment-friendly than one of recycling, this requirement was acceptable. But a further licensing requirement,

---

39 K. Holzinger, C. Knill, and A. Schäfer (2006) 12(3) Eur LJ 403.

whereby only a limited number of container shapes was permitted, was disproportionate and thus illegal in EC law. Denmark argued that this limitation was needed to make facilities for cleaning bottles, etc., less complex and therefore more efficient, but these shapes coincided with the shapes of bottles used by Danish producers.

This decision has an obvious impact on the ability of member States to pass environmental legislation that is stricter than that of other member States and which thus interferes with the internal market. But it also has an impact on the attitude of the Commission, because, in order to re-establish the internal market, it will seek to lay down common standards by proposing EC legislation. There is an incentive to move towards common standards based on the stricter environmental protection legislation of the non-conforming state, using Art. 95(3) as a justification. Indeed, to some extent, the Community has done this with the Packaging and Packaging Waste Directive (94/62/EC).[40]

Some extension of the *Danish Bottles* principle can be seen in the *Walloon Waste* case (Case 7.5).

CASE 7.5 **Case C-2/90 *Commission v. Belgium* [1992] ECR I-4431 (*Walloon Waste*)**

This case concerned what was effectively a ban on waste imports imposed by the Walloon Regional Executive. The European Court of Justice (ECJ) decided that waste constituted goods for the purposes of the Treaty and thus there was a clear infringement of the provisions on free movement of goods. It decided, however, that the ban was justified on environmental grounds. In so doing, it held that wastes are goods of a special character. Accordingly, the general principle set out in Art. 174(2) EC, that pollution should be rectified at source, was called into play to suggest that wastes should be disposed of as close to their place of origin as possible. This enabled the Court to avoid the otherwise inevitable conclusion that the ban was discriminatory and is an important example of how these general principles can be used so as to have an impact on the development of the law.

A further interesting feature of the case was the rather bizarre (but logical) result that the ban was legal as far as it applied to ordinary wastes, but not as far as hazardous wastes were concerned, because Directive 84/631/EC had already laid down an exhaustive system for the transfrontier shipment of hazardous waste. Therefore, the ban on hazardous waste was illegal because it contravened the provisions of the Directive (to which Belgium had obviously agreed).

Some attempt to formalize these decisions was made by the Maastricht Treaty, which added a new paragraph to Art. 174(2). This allows Directives seeking to harmonize EC laws to include a safeguard clause permitting a member State to take *provisional* measures for environmental reasons. This does not appear to alter anything decided by *Danish Bottles*, but the Article does add a further requirement that such measures are subject to inspection by the Commission.

A further important factor is whether, in the interests of environmental protection, laws may directly discriminate in favour of a country's own nationals, but nevertheless be lawful if the restrictions are for environmental protection reasons. In the *Walloon Waste* case, the Court clearly tried to avoid having to answer this, but later cases make it fairly clear that this can be justified (see Case 7.6).

---

40 In Case C-246/99 *Commission v. Denmark*, the Commission challenged the Danish drinks packaging regime (which included a ban on metal packaging), but the national law was repealed and the case was therefore dropped before reaching the ECJ. Some indication of the trade, environment, and harmonization issues involved, however, is given in the Advocate-General's opinion (which broadly favoured the Commission).

CASE 7.6 Case C-379/98 *PreussenElektra AG v. Schleswag AG* [2001] ECR I-2159

PreussenElektra operated a large number of conventional and nuclear power stations, and an electricity grid; Schleswag was the regional electricity distributor. Under German law, electricity suppliers must purchase electricity from renewables if this has been put on the German market. The price is determined by a complex formula intended to make renewables competitive, but the end result is that the supplier may have to pay more overall for its electricity. Above a certain threshold, the supplier can pass on the extra costs to the grid operator. Because of a vast increase in wind energy, PreussenElektra saw its monthly costs rise dramatically. The European Court of Justice decided that these rules did not contravene the rules on the free movement of goods (even though they clearly favoured green energy generated within Germany and therefore discriminated against green energy supplied by importers).

This is not a case like *Danish Bottles*, because the Court decided that there was no impediment to free trade—that is, that there was no breach of Art. 28 EC—so the Court did not approach this case as one in which a barrier to free trade had to be justified under Art. 30 EC using the 'mandatory requirement' of environmental protection. This was because of the environmental aims of the laws—which included meeting the EC's climate change obligations—as well as the specific characteristics of the EC electricity market—which had not been fully liberalized, so producers and suppliers did not operate in a completely free market. The Court accepted that, as things stood, once electricity was put into the grid it was impossible to trace its origin and this was a reason for favouring German producers by a guaranteed price. The Court also referred to the integration duty in Art. 6 EC to emphasize the need for an 'environmentally conscious' internal market.

Together with a number of disputes that have been settled without resort to the Court—which also shed light on how the balance between trade and environmental protection is being struck[41]—the case law indicates that a member State may adopt measures that disrupt the free movement of goods if such action:

- is not already covered by EC legislation that fully regulates the area in question (as seen in the *Walloon Waste* case, but, for a more recent leading case, see Case C-473/98 *Kemikalieinspektionen v. Toolex Alpha AB* [2000] ECR I-5681, in which, in essence, it was held that a framework Directive does not fully regulate an area in which, for example, an environmentally harmful substance is not yet the subject of a daughter Directive);

- does not arbitrarily discriminate between national producers and traders, and those in other member States (although note that, in the *Danish Bottles* case, the Court implicitly accepted that the returnability requirement did not discriminate against importers, even though the cost either of transporting glass to and from Denmark, or setting up a deposit-and-return scheme there, would have been high);

- is proportional (see *Danish Bottles* and see Box 7.3)—the ECJ generally takes a generous view of the proportionality of national measures in cases in which environmental protection is genuinely being pursued, although it will examine whether alternative, less restrictive, means might be used and whether alternatives have adequately been studied.[42]

Other aspects of the market beyond the free circulation of goods are also becoming more responsive to environmental interests and national environmental protection requirements

---

41 The best overview is L. Krämer (2003) *EC Environmental Law*, London: Sweet and Maxwell, pp. 96–111.

42 F. Jacobs (2006) 18 JEL 185; see also Case C-320/03 *Commission v. Austria* [2006] Env LR 31, a case about a ban on large lorry movements (note, in particular, that the Advocate-General argued that the national measures, although they contained exceptions for local traffic, were not thereby 'discriminatory').

are spreading to areas such as state aids (see *British Aggregates Association and ors v. HM Treasury* [2002] CMLR 51, an unsuccessful challenge to the aggregates levy as being in breach of EC rules on, among other things, state aids) and taxes (Case C-213/96 *Outokumpu* [1998] ECR I-1777). The ECJ's decisions in relation to the 'greening' of public procurement contracts are indicative of a generally sympathetic approach (see Box 7.7).

BOX 7.7 EC public procurement law and the environment

Public procurement rules promote effective competition for things such as public works contracts. The size of the EU public procurement market—around 11 per cent of the EU's gross domestic product—means that steering it towards environmentally preferable goods, services, or works can make a direct and major contribution to environmental protection, and can indirectly facilitate the development of greener products generally. EC public procurement rules aim at ensuring that tendering processes do not discriminate in favour of domestic contractors; contracts must be awarded on the basis of the lowest price or on the basis of what is 'economically most advantageous'. As with the tension between the free movement of goods and environmental protection, there is a balance to be struck between allowing member States to favour environmentally preferable products and the risk that they will use this to pursue a protectionist purchasing policy. 'Economically most advantageous' can include things such as running costs and can therefore include criteria such energy efficiency—but can it relate to factors that are aimed primarily at environmental protection?

In Case C-513/99 *Concordia Bus Finland* [2002] ECR I-7213, the issue was the legality of Helsinki's system of awarding points to tenderers whose bus fleets met specified air and noise pollution levels. On a restrictive interpretation of the rules (interestingly, supported by the Commission), there would not be any 'economic advantage'. But the European Court of Justice (ECJ) gave a generous interpretation to this phrase, ruling that it could include factors that were not purely economic, as long as there were certain safeguards—for example, that the criteria were transparent and linked to the subject matter of the contract. They must also be objectively quantifiable, so a tender that, without elaboration, favours bids that are 'environmentally friendly' or which 'promote sustainable development' is unlikely to be lawful.[43]

It also seems that criteria protecting not only the immediate locality, but also the global environment, would also be permissible—for example, a requirement that electricity is supplied from renewable energy sources (Case C-448/01 *EVN AG and Wienstrom Gmbh v. Austria/Stadtwerke Klagenfurt AG* [2004] 1 CMLR 22). The *Concordia Bus Finland* case is also notable for invoking Art. 6 EC concerning environmental integration to support its conclusion.

Compliance by member States with EC law

Articles 249 and 10 of the EC Treaty make clear that abiding by EC law entails a positive and a negative obligation: implementation of relevant Directives and not doing anything contrary to EC law. Because environmental law consists mainly of Directives, compliance will be discussed in their terms.

In terms of Art. 249 EC, '*A directive shall be binding, as to the result to be achieved, upon each Member State to which it is addressed, but shall leave to the national authorities the*

---

43 See further P. Kunzlik (2003) 15 JEL 175.

choice of form and method'. Article 10, meanwhile, states that member states must:

take all appropriate measures, whether general or particular, to ensure fulfilment of the obligations arising out of this Treaty or resulting from action taken by institutions of the Community … [and] abstain from any measure which could jeopardise the attainment of the objectives of the Treaty.

In order to comply with a Directive, a member State must implement it fully and within the time limit. Any incompatible law must be repealed. It is irrelevant whether other states have also failed to comply.

It thus appears that there are a number of ways in which there may be non-compliance with a Directive:

- a failure to transpose any, or all, of the Directive within the time allowed—that is, the 'communication duty' (the case law is clear that there is no real excuse for this, because the member State will have agreed the time limit in the first place);

- implementing by adopting an incorrect interpretation of the Directive—that is, the 'conformity duty' (the ECJ being the ultimate arbiter of this point);

- inadequate implementation in practice—that is, the 'application duty'.

A key issue is how much discretion member States have in selecting the method of implementing a Directive. The ECJ has made it clear that mere changes in administrative practices are not sufficient, because they do not provide binding guarantees that the legal requirements of the Directive will be complied with (thus forcing a change of approach by the UK, which, in the early years of EC environmental law, relied heavily on this approach). This is particularly relevant to broadening the range of tools away from traditional forms of regulation, such as licensing and criminal penalties, and towards the use of economic instruments (key themes of the Fifth and Sixth EAPs). For example, a member State may not use agreements to implement a Directive, because an agreement is usually only enforceable by either of the contracting parties and does not therefore sufficiently guarantee the protection of rights (although there is an exception to this rule if the Directive expressly provides for this, as with certain provisions of the End-of-Life Vehicles Directive 2000/53/EC and the WEEE Directive 2002/96/EC).

In this context, note that determining the penalties for breaching laws that implement EC environmental Directives is generally a matter for the discretion of the member States. Indeed, the ECJ does not require criminal sanctions to be used, as long as the sanction is effective, proportionate, and dissuasive (although, interestingly, the Greenhouse Gas Emissions Trading Directive (2003/87/EC) prescribes fixed sanctions that the member States have to impose if certain emission limits are breached). It has, however, recognized that the Commission may propose criminal law measures if these are deemed necessary to combat serious environmental crime (Case C-176/03 *Commission v. Council* [2006] Env LR 18).[44]

The last type of non-compliance arises in cases in which a member State has passed all of the legislation required to implement a Directive, but if there is no compliance in fact. For example, it might arise if a member State fails to enforce the provisions of a law, if standards laid down in a Directive are not adhered to in practice, or if there is a failure to establish a protected area. As noted above, in the first *UK Drinking Water* case, the ECJ effectively equated non-compliance in fact with non-compliance in law (see Case 7.1).

This is not to say, however, that a breach of a Directive will always be easy to identify. For example, many Directives require member States to designate protected areas for nature conservation or pollution control reasons. A complaint might be lodged with the Commission that a particular area has not been designated and that this is in breach of a Directive. In

44 But see, now, the restrictions following Case C-440/05 *Commission v. Council* [2007] not yet reported.

practice, however, the Commission rarely pursues infringement actions unless the failure to designate the area is a fairly clear-cut breach or if it forms part of a failure to designate sufficient areas more generally (although a recent case gives the Commission greater scope to pursue actions based on general non-compliance—see Case 7.7).

A further point is that, if a Directive sets an environmental objective—for example, an environmental quality standard or a limit value—and also requires member States to implement pollution reduction programmes, then it must still comply with the latter even if it has complied with the former. In other words, establishing the pollution reduction programme is also 'the result to be achieved' for the purposes of Art. 249 (Case C-184/97 *Commission v. Germany* [1999] ECR I-7837).

CASE 7.7 Case C-494/01 *Commission v. Ireland* [2005] Env LR 36

In this case, the Commission pursued Ireland both because of 12 instances of allowing waste to be dumped without a permit and because of the '*general and persistent nature of the deficiencies which characterise the actual application of the* [Waste Framework] *Directive in Ireland, of which the specific situations mentioned in those complaints simply constitute examples*'. Ireland argued that this more general charge was too vague to defend, but the European Court of Justice upheld the allegation, noting that the specific instances must, in practice, have evidenced the absence of an effective permitting system, which would mean that a range of obligations under the Directive would continue to be breached and could only be tackled by systemic measures. The formula used by the ECJ is that, while no presumptions can be made, once the Commission has presented some credible evidence of a breach, it is for the member State to challenge this.

This is an important case because it expressly recognizes the difficulties that the Commission, without investigative powers of its own, faces in trying to ensure that environmental law is implemented properly. The decision also increases the practical leverage of the Commission in terms of using its follow-up powers under Art. 228 EC to penalize non-compliance with any judgment of the ECJ (see below). Once the glare of the Commission is upon them, individual cases of non-compliance in an area such as small-scale waste dumping can probably be rectified fairly easily. But the size of any potential payment and the likelihood of it being imposed will be greatly increased if, beyond individual breaches, more systemic (and undoubtedly long-term) breaches can be alleged, as the *France Fisheries* case shows (see p. 207).

In an increasingly decentralized country such as the UK, one issue is that the national government may not necessarily be the body that was actually responsible for non-compliance and may not, in some cases, even be in a very strong position to rectify matters. Nevertheless, the national government will be held responsible as a matter of EC law. In practice, if it gets to the stage of the member State being fined for non-compliance, it will almost certainly recoup the penalty from the budget of the region responsible, as is the stated policy in the UK. Indeed, an example of where this is automatically provided for is Pt I of the Waste and Emissions Trading Act 2003, which deals with waste sent to landfills. If a waste disposal authority exceeds its landfill allowance, a penalty is payable to the Secretary of State (and a higher penalty is payable if the waste disposal authority's actions mean that a target date for staged compliance under the Directive is missed or if there is slippage from a target already met).

Non-compliance—enforcement by the Commission

If a member State does not implement a Directive properly or maintains in force a law that is contrary to EC law, there are only a limited number of options. The main responsibility for ensuring compliance rests with the Commission, which has a discretion to start infringement proceedings. Its current policy is to start these automatically in cases in which any failure to comply is alleged. Although its stated policy is to focus on formal non-compliance, in practice, the Commission tends to pursue more cases in which non-compliance in practice is at stake,[45] doubtless because these tend to be the higher-profile cases, and the kinds of cases that are brought to their attention by aggrieved individuals and pressure groups (either directly or via a petition to the European Parliament).

These infringement proceedings have various stages. The Commission will write to the state informally, asking it to explain its position. If a satisfactory answer is not received, a formal letter will be sent and the state's observations will be formally required. If the Commission is still not satisfied that the matter can be settled, it will issue a 'Reasoned Opinion', explaining what it thinks are the main features of the non-compliance. Most cases are resolved at these preliminary stages and there are obvious parallels with the graded procedures adopted in practice by most regulatory agencies when dealing with breaches of domestic environmental law.

Under Art. 226, the Commission is generally thought to have an absolute discretion to bring the member State before the ECJ. An individual has no standing to bring infringement proceedings or to compel the Commission to do so, but is limited to drawing an alleged non-compliance to the attention of the Commission. While the Community has been pursuing non-implementation of EC environmental law with greater rigour than previously, there is strong evidence pointing to a continuing culture, at least within the upper echelons of the Commission, which remains hostile to what is deemed to be over-zealous enforcement.

The ECJ is the ultimate arbiter of whether there has been compliance in law and will give a decision on whether the state is in breach of EC law, but, in the past, it simply had declaratory powers. Nevertheless, states normally comply as a matter of political necessity; otherwise, the Commission or another member State can reinstitute the infringement proceedings (again, this is rare).

Penalty payments

The Maastricht Treaty changed matters considerably. Under Art. 228, the Commission may now issue a Reasoned Opinion if it considers that a member State has not complied with a judgment of the Court. If the member State then continues to fail to comply, the Commission can bring the case back before the Court, seeking payment of a 'lump sum or penalty payment'.

To date, there have been three cases decided by the ECJ on this, all of them 'environmental'. The first was Case C-387/97 *Commission v. Hellenic Republic* [2000] ECR I-3823, a follow-up to breaching a Court ruling on unlawfully dumping waste (the *Chania Waste* case). The second case, Case 278/01 *Commission v. Spain* [2004] Env LR D3, concerned non-implementation of a Court ruling about the Bathing Water Directive (the *Spanish Bathing Water* case), and the third—and perhaps most important—case involved continuing breaches of EC fisheries law (Case C-304/02 *Commission v. France* [2005] ENDS Report 367, 50—the *French Fishing* case). From these cases, a number of points can be made.

1 The Court may impose *both* a lump sum and a daily penalty payment (*French Fishing*). The penalty payment aims to bring the member State into compliance, while the lump sum is a more general deterrent and reflects harm to other interests—for example, those of countries who *have* been complying. The lump sum is broadly equivalent to a fine for breach of an injunction.

2 There is little guidance on how much lump sums should be. In *French Fishing*, it was €20m, and the Court justified this on the grounds of the length of non-compliance (the original

45 See E. Hatton (2003) 15(3) JEL 273.

judgment was in 1991) and the harm to other states (fisheries being a common EC policy area). But the Commission did not seek a lump sum (the Court imposed one itself), so the Court did not really have to say what was reasonable. Inevitably, there will be several years before the Art. 228 action is heard (the shortest length of time was five years in *Spanish Bathing Waters*), which may mean that any lump sum will be very hefty. Further guidance, from either the Commission or the Court, is likely.

3 There is Commission guidance on the level of penalty payments—that is, daily fines approved by the Court. This will depend on the seriousness and duration of the violation, and the need for a 'dissuasive' effect. In addition to these factors, there is a degree of weighting that is applied, taking into account the member State's ability to pay, based on gross domestic product (GDP) and votes in the Council. The penalty in *French Fishing* was a massive €316,500 per day.

4 Instead of a daily 'fine', the penalty payment might have to be based on another period of time. Because compliance with the Bathing Waters Directive (76/160/EEC) is assessed annually, for example, the Spanish fine also had to be determined on this basis (otherwise a penalty might have been paid for a compliant period). In *French Fishing*, payment was required on a six-monthly basis, because this would give the Commission time in which to assess whether France was complying.

5 Other factors can also come into play. In *Spanish Bathing Waters*, for example, the fine was based on the percentage of bathing areas not complying with the Directive's mandatory values.[46] On this basis, penalty payments might decrease the closer that the member State gets to full compliance (or increase, if things were to get worse). The duration coefficient was also reduced, because the works needed to remedy the breach (for example, a new treatment plant) had to be properly tendered for under EC law.

6 When will the fine stop? In *Chania Waste*, the Commission closed the case when the unauthorized landfill was fenced off and another temporary landfill began operation, and after Greece had paid about £5m. But the illegally disposed of waste had not been removed and a better view may be that it would only be at the point at which the environmental impairment ceases that the breach has been remedied (for support of this view, see Case C-365/97 *Commission v. Italy* [1999] ECR I-7773). In other areas, the Commission might come under political pressure to close a case in which a member State had not reached full compliance, but had reached a level of compliance similar to that of other states. When the Commission closes the case is absolutely central to whether the environmental harm has been remedied, but following its case law on Art. 226, the ECJ is unlikely to permit any legal challenge to the exercise of this discretion.

It is likely that the possibility of Art. 228 proceedings greatly concentrate the minds of national decision makers (and their treasuries). There have certainly been cases in which the threat of a fine has had the desired effect of bringing a member State into compliance. The Commission has also explored the possibility of withholding EC funds provided for environmental matters in the event of non-compliance and there is some evidence that this form of cross-compliance may be effective. For example, compliance with the 1991 Agricultural Nitrates Directive (91/676/EEC) is now a precondition for granting aid under the EC's agri-environmental programmes and the Commission appears to be enthusiastic about the effectiveness of this approach.[47] It should also be stressed that EC environmental law is chronically under-enforced, which tempers the strictness of the duty to comply in practice.

46 In fact, because of an error in calculating the degree of non-compliance, the fine was never paid: see L. Krämer (2006) 18 JEL 407, 412.

47 Fourth Report of the HC Select Committee on Environment, Food and Rural Affairs (Session 2002–03) *The Water Framework Directive* (evidence from DG Environment).

Non-compliance—individual remedies

In addition to these formal infringement procedures, the ECJ has used the concept of the supremacy of Community law to develop various strands of case law that relate to the question of compliance with EC law. Two of these—the doctrine of direct effect and the concept of useful effect—have already been mentioned above (p. 177). But it is worth looking at these and other types of remedy in more detail, because, when these judicial developments are all taken together, they ensure that a lot of pressure can be exerted on member States to implement Directives properly and in full.

(a) Direct effect

The doctrine of direct effect is of great importance, because directly effective EC laws can be relied upon in the courts of member States without the need for implementation: any incompatible national law can simply be ignored. If a national court is unwilling to accept that a Directive is directly effective, the applicant may ask it to refer the question to the ECJ under the Art. 234 procedure.

But the doctrine has its limitations. Because the obligations must be sufficiently clear and precise, there are difficulties with Directives that seem to impose more general obligations to achieve results. For example, in Case C-236/92 *Comitato di Coordinamento per la Difesa della Cava v. Regione Lombardia* [1994] ECR I-483, the ECJ found that Art. 4 of the then Waste Framework Directive (75/442/EEC) did not have direct effect. This was because the Court held that it only laid down a general objective to be pursued and general measures by which to do so, rather than anything more concrete and binding (but see the *San Rocco Valley* case—Case 7.2).

(b) Useful effect

By contrast with direct effect, the concept of 'useful effect' means that a provision of a Directive might be imprecise, but it could nevertheless be clear that, in implementing it, a member State has gone beyond the bounds of its discretion. It is therefore the legality of the state's actions (or omissions) that are increasingly the focus: member States have *duties* to give proper effect to Directives within their legal systems and these must be capable of being enforced through the courts.

This approach has been developed by the ECJ in particular in cases relating to the Environmental Impact Assessment (EIA) Directive (85/337/EEC) and how much discretion member States have not to require EIA. The landmark case here is Case C-72/96 *Aanemersbedriff PK Kraaijeveld BV v. Gedeputeerde Staaten van Zuid-Holland* [1996] ECR I-5403, but the approach has been fully confirmed most recently in Case C-287/98 *Luxembourg v. Linster* [2000] ECR I-6917 (see p. 455).

(c) Direct effect and useful effect compared

It is clear that direct effect and useful effect are related, in so far as they both derive from a concern of the ECJ that member States should not be able to evade the implementation of EC law. The main difference can be stated as follows: with direct effect, the *degree* to which a member State has not properly implemented a Directive is irrelevant, whereas it is central to the useful effect approach (as the *San Rocco Valley* case—Case 7.2—illustrates).

A related point is that the useful effect route can be used when the obligations in a Directive are vague, which is not the case with direct effect, which requires that the obligation is sufficiently clear and precise. For example, under the Water Framework Directive (2000/60/EC), the main obligation relating to ecological water quality is 'good status', which the member State must 'aim to achieve'. There is a lack of precision about both what is being required and whether it amounts to a binding legal standard (see p. 593), but, if a body such as the Environment Agency were to be clearly exceeding its discretion by giving too lenient an interpretation to 'good status' and making no efforts to achieve this, then its actions may be reviewable.

A further point is that, unlike state liability claims (see below), it is still not clear whether individual rights need to be breached for a Directive to have direct effect. There is a line of authority that suggests that they do, but much of this comes out of actions brought by the Commission for non-compliance—for example, Case C-131/88 *Commission v. Germany* [1991] ECR I-825—and does not address the question directly. That said, most Directives setting standards can be interpreted as conferring implied rights on individuals. It is clear, however, that individual rights play little role when it comes to considering the useful effect of a Directive (because it is based much more on the duties of the member States).

(d) Vertical and horizontal effect

A potential drawback of direct effect and useful effect is that they only apply 'vertically' against central government or other 'emanations of the state', including public bodies such as the Environment Agency or local planning authorities, and not against another private body or person (which is known as 'horizontal effect'). One reason for this distinction is that the state itself cannot plead a failure to implement the Directive properly as a defence—a form of the estoppel principle. An 'emanation of the state' is to be decided according to the function that a body performs, and not its precise legal ownership and structure. Hence, bodies to which the state gives a public function—such as the privatized water and sewerage companies—will be treated as emanations of the state, at least as far as their 'public' functions are concerned. In *Griffin v. South West Water Services Ltd* [1995] IRLR 15, it was decided, in the context of employment law, that a privatized water company is an emanation of the state.

Does a challenge by one individual against a public authority—for example, a planning authority—which has the practical effect of adversely affecting another private party—for example, a developer—fall foul of the rule prohibiting Directives having horizontal effect? English case law has held that it does not[48] and this approach has been confirmed by the ECJ in Case C-201/02 *R (Wells) v. Secretary of State for Transport, Local Government and the Regions* [2004] Env LR 27, a reference about the EIA Directive (85/337/EEC) and quarrying. The Court held that the obligation to carry out an EIA did not amount to 'inverse direct effect', even though a consequence of challenging the permission that had been granted was that mining operations had to be halted. 'Adverse repercussions' on individuals could be tolerated and the motive for the challenge—as here, to deprive an individual of the benefit of a planning decision—was irrelevant.

Related to this is the question of whether direct effect is a doctrine that can be relied on by another public body. In *R (Mayor and Citizens of the City of Westminster, Preece and Adamson) v. The Mayor of London* [2002] EWHC 2440, although the issue did not need to be decided, the High Court held that a local authority could not challenge an allegedly wrongful implementation of the EIA Directive in relation to the London congestion charge, because direct effect is a remedy that is only available to individuals. This is somewhat restrictive, because the local authority could reasonably claim to be acting on behalf of its residents (and paying the costs of doing so), although there are obviously cases in which a public body will not be acting in a directly representative capacity—for example, if a public body such as the Environment Agency were to try to argue that the unimplemented terms of a Directive should apply against another public authority, such as a local planning authority.

(e) State liability

The decision of the ECJ in Cases C-6 and 9/90 *Francovich and Boniface v. Italy* [1991] ECR I-5357 developed a judicial damages remedy for certain breaches of EC law by member States.

---

48 *R v. Durham County Council, Sherburn Stone Company Ltd and Secretary of State for Environment, Transport and the Regions, ex parte Huddleston* [2000] JPL 409.

As developed in later cases, the state liability principle applies if:

(i) the rule of law is intended to confer rights on the individuals concerned;

(ii) the breach is sufficiently serious;

(iii) there is a direct causal link between the breach of the obligation resting on the state and the damage sustained by the injured parties.

The development in the case law has arisen in relation to the second requirement. While *Francovich* was a case of failure to implement a Directive, in later cases, the Court has held that there may be liability for incorrect transposition if the member State has 'manifestly and gravely disregarded' the limits of its discretion (effectively, a fault-based standard). What will constitute this includes, for example, persisting with a breach in the face of a contrary ECJ ruling or other settled case law. It will also depend on the breadth of discretion given to the state. (In this respect, contrast the very prescriptive Drinking Water Directive with, for example, the Waste Framework Directive.) Complete failure to implement a Directive, or failure to take any measures to achieve the objectives of the Directive, will always be a serious breach. In the case of environmental Directives, it is interesting to consider what degree of non-implementation in practice (for example, through non-enforcement of the law) would amount to a sufficiently serious breach.

Requirements (i) and (iii) also raise difficulties in an environmental context. While it is clear that Directives such as the Drinking Water Directive (98/83/EC) or the Environmental Information Directive (2003/4/EC) give rights to individuals, in many cases, the Directive is primarily directed towards protection of the environment. As noted above, however, most Directives laying down standards can be interpreted as conferring implied rights on individuals. In addition, economic harmonization Directives may confer individual rights. This was the view of the Court of Appeal in *Bowden v. South West Water Services Ltd* [1999] Env LR 438, which held that it was at least arguable that a shell fisherman had a state liability claim when his economic interests were harmed following alleged failures in the implementation of the Shellfish Waters Directive (79/923/EEC). But similar claims made under the Bathing Water and Urban Waste Water Treatment Directives were struck out, because the claims were for losses of income from the claimant's business. The Court did, however, keep the door open to a potential claim under the other Directives by holding merely that the claimant was not directly affected as a bather or by waste water. The causation issue is also tricky, because, in most situations, the harm will be caused by an operational failure rather than by the government's faulty implementation.

In its favour, the action is against the state and the liability of individual polluters need not be shown. But the absence to date of any successful environmental actions under *Francovich* suggests that it is of limited practical importance.

A final point is that the ECJ has held that, in some situations, there is an obligation owed between *individuals* to compensate for breaches of EC law. The Court has been careful to limit this so far to breaches of competition law (Case C-435/99 *Courage Ltd v. Crehan* [2001] ECR I-6297), but whether it will remain restricted in this way remains to be seen.[49]

(f) National procedural rules and remedies

The final area worth mentioning is the extent to which national procedural rules (such as the rules on standing, the time within legal challenges must be brought to the courts, or the remedies available to the courts) must be set aside to give effect to EC law. The basic principle is that procedural matters are for the member States to decide and will not be interfered with, as long as they do not make it impossible or excessively difficult, in practice, to obtain a

---

49 Expanding private liability in the environmental field would require the Court to go beyond the specific, although highly restrained, steps taken politically regarding environmental (civil) liability—see p. 363.

remedy (Case C-188/95 *Fantask* [1998] All ER (EC) 1). But there is something of a balance to be struck between making EC law effective and respecting very different national procedural rules. This is particularly problematic in cases in which discretionary remedies are being sought, as with judicial review applications. As noted below (p. 217), the House of Lords suggested in the *Berkeley* case that, in cases in which EC obligations are concerned, the courts have little room for discretion, but later cases have stressed that there may be reasons why an applicant for judicial review should not succeed if this would place too great a burden on, for example, a developer whose planning permission is challenged several years after it was granted. The important point is that, even if the breach of EC law is clear, this does not necessarily mean that an applicant must succeed.

The *Wells* case, mentioned above, however, places an important restriction on the member State's discretion in cases of non-compliance. In making good any harm caused by the failure to carry out its legal obligations, the national courts have to determine whether it is possible under domestic law to remedy the breach administratively—for example, by revoking or suspending a planning permission if an environmental assessment has not been conducted. It is clear that, before *Wells*, the UK courts did not seriously consider, in cases of non-compliance, revoking environmental licences such as planning permissions (in relation to which compensation must be paid) and certainly did not consider that they had an obligation to do so. In addition, however, the ECJ went on to say that the national courts had to consider '*alternatively, if the individual so agreed, whether it was possible for the latter to claim compensation for the harm suffered*'.[50]

It is not exactly clear what the Court means by this, but it may have had in mind a situation in which a development or industrial installation has been constructed (or construction has already begun), and in which, from an economic point of view, the efficient solution is to compensate the person bringing the legal challenge and not require demolition. Potentially, this accommodates both the rights of the applicant and the wider public interest. Quite how compensation to an environmental group challenging a decision should be calculated, however, remains obscure. Also, any compensation would be paid by the public authority responsible for authorizing the development and not to the developer, because requiring the latter to pay would clearly violate the basic rules of direct effect about horizontality and there seems to be no mechanism for clawing back the compensation from the party who stands to gain from receiving a benefit to which, as a matter of law, they may not be entitled. Another difficulty is knowing what the Court means when it says that the remedy must be 'agreed' to by the applicant. Presumably, whether an applicant agrees to be compensated depends on whether the court is minded to revoke the authorization, which suggests that courts should first ask the applicant whether they would be satisfied with compensation.

These various developments set in motion by the ECJ to improve compliance with EC law give rise to a range of propositions. For example, if a consumer were to become ill as a result of drinking water from the public supply that did not comply with the standards laid down in the Drinking Water Directive (98/83/EC), it would seem that there is a claim either directly in tort, or by relying on the direct effect of the Directive, or under the *Francovich* doctrine (as a breach of statutory duty), even if the water did comply with national standards. A more far-reaching example might be if an environmental group were to wish to challenge the non-implementation of a Directive (or even a failure to enforce it, because the two are, arguably, the same thing in practice). In addition to making a complaint to the Commission, it could seek a declaration claiming that directly effective standards were not being enforced or that a national authority had exceeded the limits of its discretion, and argue that any obstructive rules on delay should not be used to deny it access to the courts. It might even carry out a clean-up operation and claim its expenses under *Francovich*, even though such a claim would be bound to fail if only national laws were used.

---

50 R (*Wells*) v. *Secretary of State for Transport, Local Government and the Regions* [2004] Env LR 27, [69].

Non-compliance—new approaches and future prospects

The need to improve the enforcement of existing legislation has been an aim of the Commission for several years. Currently, around five hundred complaints are made to the Commission every year and it is remarkable that over a third of all complaints received and infringement cases taken by the Commission relate to environmental legislation. Over half of these cases relate to bad application of EC environmental law in practice, although it is unlikely that general 'under-enforcement' by member States is sufficiently caught.

Improving compliance with existing EC environmental law is a 'strategic priority' in the Sixth EAP, and several points may be made about how this is being addressed and what the future may hold. First, the Commission's work on implementation has led to a wider focus on the nature of the whole 'regulatory chain'—that is, *the whole process through which legislation is designed, drafted, adopted, implemented and enforced until its effectiveness is assessed*.[51] This has led to a greater concern with trying to 'design in' implementation, before problems arise. There may be dialogue between DG Environment and member States prior to the transposition deadlines and interpretive guidance on particularly tricky or sensitive issues is increasingly being produced.

Secondly, there is a desire to use new tools and to engage more actors. There have already been modest steps taken in relation to civil liability (see p. 363) and steps to enhance the use of criminal liability (see p. 256), both of which can be seen as ways of empowering national actors in implementing and enforcing environmental Directives. In addition to traditional infringement actions and the greater use of cross-compliance mechanisms, the Commission has also suggested using 'naming, shaming and praising'. There is also a European Forum of Judges for the Environment. Perhaps most notably, various steps are being taken to improve access to justice in environmental matters (through implementing this 'pillar' of the Aarhus Convention—see COM(2003) 624). If enacted, these would grant legal standing to individuals and groups in cases in which there is a suspected infringement of environmental law, and could have profound effects in terms of shifting the emphasis away from remedies based on directly effective obligations or individual rights.

Thirdly, and perhaps running contrary to the last point, there is the wider issue of how the search for 'new forms of governance' will impact on implementation and enforcement. If environmental policy and law become more concerned with ensuring active cooperation between the member States, and resort less to traditional regulation through setting environmental standards, then it may be more difficult to determine whether there has been non-compliance. This may, again, put an onus on the courts to devise novel approaches to ensuring this new-style legislation is effective, bearing in mind the interests that it is ultimately trying to protect.

EC environmental law and the UK

There is little doubt that the EC's environmental policy, and the various Directives and regulations adopted in pursuance of it, have had an important influence on UK environmental law. They have led directly to new legislation, to new standards being adopted, to significant changes in government policy, and also to a general reassessment of the whole 'British' approach to controlling pollution and conserving nature.

---

51 Communication from the European Commission (1996) *Implementing Community Environmental Law*, COM(96) 500 final.

Legislation

By definition, environmental Directives must be transposed into legislation. Usually this is achieved through regulations intended to transpose a specific Directive—for example, the Conservation (Natural Habitats etc.) Regulations 1994,[52] implementing the 1992 Habitats Directive (92/43/EEC)—but, sometimes, transposition is via an Act of Parliament. Sometimes, the very fact that a Directive has to be given effect to has stimulated additional—and, very occasionally, more stringent—legislation.

New standards have been adopted for a wide range of things, such as air quality, emissions from cars, and bathing waters. Industrial processes are heavily controlled via a range of EC environmental laws. And many products are restricted within, or even banned from, the internal market because of environmental concerns.

In the making of legislation, the move away from unanimous voting to qualified majority voting has undoubtedly forced the UK to agree to some measures that it might not have otherwise, although probably fewer than might be expected. Although the influence has not all been in one direction, it is notable that nearly all of the measures to which the UK objected to in the early 1990s on subsidiarity grounds (for example, on landfill) have now been adopted. One explanation for this, of course, is that EC environmental legislation is becoming more flexible in the style of the characteristically 'British' approach. Important examples include the Directives on IPPC (96/61/EC) and the Water Framework Directive (2000/60/EC).

There has been far less direct impact in relation to establishing environmental principles as *legislative* principles. The environmental principles in the EC Treaty are essentially policy principles and are not directly enforceable, and, while they may be having an indirect effect on national policy formulation, there is little sign that they are yet crystallizing into legislative principles of the kind that have direct application in the national courts. The classic example of this remains *R v. Secretary of State for Trade and Industry, ex parte Duddridge* [1995] Env LR 151, in which the Divisional Court refused to apply the Precautionary Principle, listed in Art. 175 of the Treaty, as a matter of English law. The Court held that the principle did not impose any immediate obligations on member States.

Policy

The impact on policy can be seen clearly in the case of the privatization of the water industry. The (then) government originally intended to privatize the whole industry, including the regulatory aspects, but was forced to create a public regulatory agency (in the form of the National Rivers Authority), because a private regulator would not fulfil the requirement for a 'competent authority' to have responsibility for overseeing the Directives on water pollution. A different example is that Directives on Urban Waste Water Treatment (91/271/EEC) and on Bathing Waters (now, 2006/7/EC), in particular, have led to important changes in capital spending programmes in the water industry (the full extent of which would almost certainly never have been undertaken as a purely national measure). It is also arguable that the partial shift in UK policy from basing controls on the impact on the receiving environment to using concepts based on BAT has been strongly influenced by the EC.

The existence of formal EC standards has also been of great importance for environmental groups, who now have something with which to compare UK practice when publicizing alleged deficiencies in environmental performance (and it should be noted that environmental pressure groups have been actively courted by DG Environment to help in

---

52 SI 1994/2716.

combating non-implementation).[53] These lobbying groups have also been able to influence the development of environmental policy at the EC level directly, as well as at national level, which is an important aspect of the system of multilevel governance that now characterizes the EU. Balanced against this, however, it is important to mention that national governments can act as 'gatekeepers' in protecting national interests and maintaining national policy styles, in the face of European-level developments.

A good illustration of the impact of EC environmental law can be seen in the national experience of implementing the Drinking Water Directive (98/83/EC; see Box 7.8).

CASE 7.8 **The *UK Drinking Water* cases**

In the first *UK Drinking Water* case (Case C-337/89 *Commission v. UK* [1992] ECR I-6103), the European Court of Justice decided that there had been a failure to implement the Drinking Water Directive (80/778/EC) by, among other things, failing to comply with the maximum admissible concentration of nitrate in some supply zones. As noted above (see Case 7.1), this part of the decision held the duty to comply with maximum admissible concentrations to be absolute, thus effectively treating non-compliance in practice in the same way as formal non-compliance, and opening the way for future infringement proceedings based on a failure to enforce EC standards properly in practice. In Britain, this is important because of the way in which much of the practical implementation of the law is delegated to independent agencies and quangos.

When it later transpired that certain water companies were supplying water that was in breach of the pesticide standards set out in the Directive, the Secretary of State had accepted undertakings from them about their plans to remedy the situation, rather than making an enforcement order. This was challenged in *R v. Secretary of State for the Environment, ex parte Friends of the Earth* [1995] Env LR 11, but the Court of Appeal accepted that, while the *primary* duty imposed by the Directive on the government was absolute, this then gave rise to a *secondary* duty to comply with the judgment. This secondary duty, said the Court, is not absolute in the same way, but is capable of being qualified by practical considerations.

Subsequently, the Commission took further infringement proceedings against the UK, alleging that the use of these undertakings—which, in practice, are drafted by the water companies and then agreed with government—breached the Directive. The UK government argued that the undertakings were a reasonable and legitimate response to remedying the problem after it was recognized that the deadline for complying with the Directive had been breached. But in the second *UK Drinking Water* case, the ECJ supported the Commission (Case C-340/96 *Commission v. UK* [1999] ECR I-2023). This decision was not really surprising, because the Water Industry Act 1991, under which the undertakings are made, does not specify the kinds of things to be covered in the compliance programme, nor indeed the speed with which compliance should be attained. But it does show the rather different approaches taken by the ECJ and the national courts. For the latter, in *Ex parte Friends of the Earth*, there was an obvious reluctance to interfere with the undertakings that had been accepted by government; for the ECJ, however, the undertakings were clearly incompatible with its established case law on implementation and the need for effective EC legislation.

As a postscript, following the second infringement case, the Drinking Water (Undertakings) (England and Wales) Regulations 2000[54] were enacted. These are an explicit response to the ECJ's judgment and, in effect, require undertakings to be entered into only for the shortest possible period, and only

---

53 For a deeper analysis of the impact on policy, see A. Jordan (2002) *The Europeanisation of British Environmental Policy*, London: Palgrave.
54 SI 2000/1297.

if no reasonable alternatives exist. It is unlikely that they really bring national law into compliance with EC law, but they are probably the least worse option politically (and seem to have headed off any action by the Commission under Art. 228 EC). They are, in any case, a further example of formalism in response to EC law.

Transposing Directives

Two related issues arise in relation to transposing Directives into national law. First, the practice now is for implementing regulations to repeat the wording of the relevant environmental Directive and to make little attempt to 'translate' what are often unclear terms into the sort of precise language that is normal in UK legislation.[55] (So-called 'gold-plating' enacting, implementing measures that go beyond the minimum required by a Directive, is expressly contrary to government policy unless there are exceptional reasons.)[56] The result is that the meaning of the regulations remains unclear and fuller enlightenment must await either administrative guidance (which gives undesirably wide powers to the administration and is, in any case, not conclusive), or a decision by the courts (normally, this would involve a judicial review action, with all of the difficulties and expense that entails, or a ruling from the ECJ in infringement proceedings against a member State). Such a roundabout method of discovering the scope of the law is most undesirable.

The second issue is that regulations to transpose Directives are usually enacted under the European Communities Act 1972, which means that matters not covered by the Directive cannot be legislated on at the same time (see, for example, the environmental assessment of projects not covered under Directive 85/337/EC, discussed at p. 441). Given the limitations on parliamentary time, this may have the practical effect of restricting the passage of environmental legislation in some situations. One way to avoid this difficulty is to enact framework statutes that allow for both EC and national measures to be passed. This is the case with the Pollution Prevention and Control Act 1999, which, although criticized for the breadth that it gives to the Minister to make regulations, allows for regulations to be made that go beyond simply transposing the IPPC Directive (96/61/EC).

The approach of the courts

In its earliest editions, this book was critical of the UK courts' negative attitude towards EC environmental law. This was for a variety of reasons: a tendency to interpret Directives and implementing legislation restrictively, a phobia of referring cases to the ECJ under Art. 234 EC, and a tendency to find some procedural reason why, even if, for example, a Directive was found to be directly effective, the applicant should not succeed. All of these are nicely illustrated by the attitude of the courts to the Environmental Assessment Directive (85/337/ EEC), discussed in more detail in Chapter 13.

By contrast, the ECJ has been willing, on a number of occasions, to interpret the somewhat vague provisions of environmental Directives as laying down clear objective criteria to ensure that their provisions are given effect to in the member States. For example, in Case C-56/90 *Commission v. United Kingdom* [1993] ECR I-4109, the Court stated that the criteria for designation as a traditional bathing water were objectively clear from Directive 76/160/ EEC, despite the rather vague language used in the Directive. The drinking water litigation mentioned in Case 7.8 is a good example of the extent to which the performance of the UK

---

55 National Audit Office (Session 2005–06) *Lost in Translation*, HC 26.
56 Cabinet Office Regulatory Impact Unit (2003) *Better Policymaking: A Guide to Regulatory Impact Assessment*.

courts in interpreting EC environmental law tended to compare unfavourably with the more robust approach to interpretation of the law taken by the ECJ.

There have, of course, been examples of the courts taking a purposive approach to interpreting EC environmental law and its implementing legislation. An excellent example is *R v. Secretary of State for the Environment, ex parte Kingston upon Hull City Council* [1996] Env LR 248, in which two local authorities successfully challenged the Secretary of State's unduly restrictive decisions as to the designation of zones for reduced levels of sewage treatment under the Urban Waste Water Treatment Directive (91/271/EEC). The High Court rejected the Secretary of State's contention that the cost of designation was a material factor in determining what an 'estuary' was, because this could frustrate the underlying purpose of the Directive. This case was also notable because the Court looked to giving effect to the Directive and no challenge appears to have been made to the action on the grounds that individual rights were not affected.

More recently, the case law has required us to re-evaluate whether the general approach of the national courts towards environmental law seems appropriate. Three cases illustrate a change in attitudes.

- In *R v. Secretary of State for Trade and Industry, ex parte Greenpeace (No. 2)* [2000] Env LR 221, the High Court held that the Habitats Directive (92/43/EEC) should have been applied beyond territorial waters and that any delay in bringing the proceedings was outweighed by the environmental public interest at stake—a decision that was clearly unwelcome to the government, because of possible constraints on the expansion of UK oil exploration (see p. 708).

- In *R (Murray) v. Derbyshire County Council* [2002] Env LR 28, the Court of Appeal held that the waste management objectives in Art. 4 of the Waste Framework Directive could not be reduced to mere 'material considerations' in deciding whether to grant planning permission, because this would mean that a decision maker could give them no weight (see p. 644).

- In *Berkeley v. Secretary of State for the Environment, Transport and the Regions* [2001] Env LR 16, the House of Lords held that, for the purposes of the EIA Directive (85/337/EEC), the failure of the developer to prepare a proper environmental statement (instead of a 'paper chase') was fatal to planning permission being granted (see Box 13.3).

Berkeley is perhaps the most important of these cases. It gave a highly purposive interpretation to the Directive, emphasizing the rights of the public to be involved in the decision-making process in a meaningful way. But the House of Lords also said that, when it came to errors of EC law, the courts had little room for discretion. This seemed to suggest that rules of EC environmental law should not be avoided either because of some procedural obstacle, or because of any adverse impact on other important social and legal interests (such as the rights of developers to develop their land and to do so with relative certainty about what the relevant rules are).

But later cases have emphasized that these remarks were made in relation to a case in which, by the time it reached the House of Lords, the developer no longer had an interest in developing the site, and that the courts must take into account factors such as the public interest in the development and possible losses to developers when deciding whether, as a matter of their discretion, to grant relief (*Bown v. Secretary of State for Transport* [2004] Env LR 26). For this reason, it may be that the *Berkeley* case will turn out to be, if not a false dawn, then a high-water mark in relation to the discretion that the courts have to give effect to Directives in cases in which competing economic interests are at stake.

✥ CHAPTER SUMMARY

1   Notwithstanding its economic origins, the EC has had a profound impact on the development of environmental law and policy in the UK over the last forty years.

2   EC law is found in the EC Treaty, in regulations and Directives, in international treaties to which the EC is a party, and in judgments and principles of the European Court of Justice.

3   EC law can be directly applicable, but, usually, Directives are used. Directives are addressed to the member States and not to individuals. They must be transposed into national law, which gives the member States some scope for discretion in their implementation. The overriding obligation on member States is, however, to ensure that Directives are 'binding as to their result' and to give effect to EC law generally.

4   The UK government has, at least in the past, taken a minimalist approach to implementing EC environmental law. This has been echoed by the courts, which, until recently, have often seen EC environmental law as an irritant to national laws rather than given effect to it in a purposive way. This is now changing.

5   EC legislation is generally made by the Council and the European Parliament acting together on a proposal from the European Commission. The European Court of Justice's interpretation of the Treaty has made it very difficult for this legislation to be directly challenged by environmental organizations.

6   EC environmental law and policy has developed from being an adjunct to its economic policy (helping in making a level economic playing field in Europe) to a self-standing policy area with its own legal basis in the EC Treaty. EC laws have been made on most of the areas covered in this book, although there are exceptions in areas such as contaminated land, and town and country planning, which are still seen as primarily domestic concerns.

7   This legal basis is built around broad objectives, principles, and policy criteria. These help to shape the scope of EC environmental law, but only in fairly extreme cases can these factors be used to challenge the validity of EC environmental laws.

8   Although some early laws had quite precise legal objectives, there has been a trend towards laws that are more flexible, which take into account national economic and environmental factors, and towards allowing member States to go further than the level of environmental protection set out in EC legislation.

9   The EC has a developed jurisprudence on balancing trade freedom and environmental protection. In general terms, the ECJ has been sympathetic to genuine environmental protection claims raised by member States.

10   Non-compliance has been the Achilles' heel of EC environmental law. Greater attention is now paid to this, including the scope for member States to be fined and greater scope for individuals to bring cases before their national courts.

Q QUESTIONS

1   The EC has passed legislation on wild bird conservation, the quality of bathing waters, and lawnmower noise. As a matter of law and of policy, in each case do you think it should have done so?

2   Developing the issues raised in the previous question and applying them to issues of contemporary salience, consider the arguments for and against the EC having competence to adopt laws on the energy efficiency of (i) products, (ii) industrial processes, and (iii) buildings. If it does so, how should it act? (Consider the appropriate legal base, and the issues of proportionality, subsidiarity, and flexibility). As a follow-up, you might take a critical look at what legislation has, in fact, been adopted in these areas so far (see Web Links for sources).

3   The EC Treaty does not prohibit pollution, whereas it does prohibit, with exceptions, things such as unlawful barriers to trade. Do you agree with the proposal that, to mirror the Treaty's basic provisions on trade, '*Subject to imperative reasons of overriding public interest, significantly impairing the environment or human health shall be prohibited*'? Could the Integration Principle in Art. 6 EC achieve the same objective?

4   Is making EC environmental law more responsive to different national circumstances consistent with its greater integration? What are the challenges?

5   Denmark introduces a national law prohibiting the operation of wind turbines that create noise levels above 50 decibels (50dB). Wind turbines are manufactured in France that make 60dB of noise (an increase of 10dB is the equivalent of a doubling in loudness). There is no EC Directive on noise levels from wind turbines. Is this an unlawful barrier to the free movement of goods in the EC? Would it make a difference if there were a Directive on wind turbines that required that they could only be sold with a noise-rating label?

6   Read the *Danish Bottles* case (see Case 7.4) in full. On the law as it now stands and the values that seem to be reflected by recent decisions of the European Court of Justice, imagine that the Court is rehearing this case. What arguments would you make for extending the scope of Denmark's power to require that drinks can only be marketed in containers of a particular type or shape?

7   What are the advantages and disadvantages of relying on the Commission to enforce EC environmental law? Is individual redress through the national courts a better option?

FURTHER READING

EC environmental law—general

A very readable introduction to the subject is J. Scott (1998) *EC Environmental Law*, London: Longmans, a text, the strength of which in discussing enduring issues such as the arguments for and against EC intervention remains, notwithstanding its datedness on the law. It is nicely complemented by M. Lee (2004) *EU Environmental Law*, Oxford: Hart, which is especially strong on analysing sustainable development, and on assessing both traditional and new legal tools in the EU context. More comprehensive coverage is given in the two leading general texts: J. Jans and H. Vedder (2007) *European Environmental Law*, 3rd edn, Groningen: Europa, and L. Krämer (2007) *EC Environmental Law*, 6th edn, London: Sweet and Maxwell. In researching an issue, try to read both to get a balanced view.

Many of the leading articles, capturing the development of EC environmental law, are gathered together in L. Krämer (ed.) (2003) *European Environmental Law*, London: Ashgate. This might usefully be supplemented by reading on the two key legal developments since then, the draft Constitution/Reform Treaty process, and enlargement. On these, see, respectively, J. Jans (ed.) (2003) *The European Convention and the Future of European Environmental Law*, Groningen: Europa, and M. Soverski (2004) 13 RECIEL 127 (the latter being an excellent analysis, linking enlargement with changing trends in policy approaches). R Macrory (ed.) (2005) *Reflections on 30 Years of EU Environmental Law: A High Level of Protection?*, Groningen: Europa, and M. Onida (ed.) (2005) *Legal Essays in Honour of Ludwig Krämer*, Groningen: Europa, mark the retirement from the European Commission of its most ardent environmental law champion. Together, they provide a wide range of essays on enduring and topical issues, and on sectoral achievements. Krämer's (2002) *Casebook on EC Environmental Law*, Oxford: Hart, analyses 50 recent leading cases and sets them in context, and is highly recommended.

Principles

R. Macrory, I. Havercroft, and R. Purdy (2004) *Principles of European Environmental Law*, Groningen: Europa, gives a good overview (and see also the further sources on principles cited in Chapter 3—especially de Sadeleer). Two particularly cutting-edge analyses of EC environmental law principles are V. Heyvaert,

'Facing the consequences of the Precautionary Principle in European Community law' (2006) 31(2) Eur LR 185 (contrasting cases in which the challenge has been based on under-precaution with those based on over-precaution) and E. Fisher, 'Opening Pandora's Box: contextualising the Precautionary Principle in the European Union', available online at **papers.ssrn.com/Abstract=956952**. (Both of these are well worth reading even if your particular interest is not precaution.)

Internal trade and the environmental

F. Jacobs, 'The role of the European Court of Justice in the protection of the environment' (2006) 18 JEL 185, written by the Advocate-General in a number of leading trade and environment cases, is especially good on how the Court has promoted environmental values, particularly as against trade freedom and concerns about discrimination between States.

Implementation and enforcement

C. Hilson (2004) 'Legality review of member State discretion under Directives' in T. Tridimas and P. Nebbia (eds) *European Union Law for the Twenty-First Century: Volume 1*, Oxford: Hart (which uses a number of examples from environmental Directives to question the limits of member States' discretion in implementation). E Hatton, 'The implementation of EU environmental law' (2003) 15(3) JEL 273 shows how, despite official pronouncements, the Commission still favours responding to high-profile complaints rather than more systematically following up non-implementation (which might have greater environmental value). M. Hedemann-Robinson (2006) *Enforcement of European Union Environmental Law: Legal Issues and Challenges*, London: Routledge-Cavendish is a comprehensive and thoughtful analysis that benefits from the author's first-hand experience of the Commission. L. Krämer, 'Statistics on environmental judgments by the EC Court of Justice' (2006) 18 JEL 407 stresses some of the shortcomings in enforcement, especially the great length of time that most cases take, and is a good antidote to the Commission's annual implementation and enforcement guide (available via the Commission's website).

Further valuable sources

M. Lee, 'Sustainable development in the EU: the Renewed Sustainable Development Strategy 2006' (2007) 9(2) Env L Rev 41 covers this in more detail than we can give here. The European Environmental Bureau (EEB) has published a special report that offers a helpful overview of *Your Rights Under the Environmental Legislation of the EU* (2004), including particular details on Aarhus issues (available online at **www.eeb.org/activities/General/Special-Report-on-Your-Rights-2004-Eng.pdf**).

EC environmental policy

For a single chapter overview, J. Connolly and G. Smith (2003) *Politics and the Environment*, 2nd edn, London: Routledge, is recommended. The best introductory text is J. McCormick (2001) *Environmental Policy in the European Union*, London: Palgrave, but it is now dated. See also C. Knill and D. Liefferink (2007) *Environmental Politics in the European Union: Policymaking, Implementation and Patterns of Multilevel Governance*, Manchester: Manchester University Press. A. Jordan (ed.) (2005) *Environmental Policy in the European Union*, 2nd edn, London: Earthscan, gathers together the leading journal articles (especially recommended is the editor's article on 'The implementation of EU environmental policy: a policy problem without a political solution?; also found in (1999) 17 Environment and Planning C: Government and Policy 69). W. Grant, D. Matthews, and P. Newell (2000) *The Effectiveness of European Union Environmental Policy*, London: Macmillan, considers this issue in detail, with case studies on air and water pollution, and on climate change. An excellent introduction to how national policy style evolved in response to EC membership is P. Lowe and S. Ward (eds) (1998) *British Environmental Policy and Europe*, London: Routledge, while A. Jordan (2007) 'Environmental policy' in I. Bache and A. Jordan (eds) *The Europeanization of British Politics*, Basingstoke: Palgrave Macmillan, looks at the interpenetration of the EU into national policymaking and vice versa. K. Holzinger, C. Knill, and A. Schäfer, 'Rhetoric or reality? New governance in EU environmental policy' (2006) 12(3) ELJ 403 is a detailed empirical study that calls into question some of the claims that the EU is undergoing a transition to the use of second-generation policy tools.

Keeping up to date, N. Haigh (looseleaf, updated) *Manual of Environmental Policy: The EC and Britain*, Leeds: Maney Publishing, is a library acquisition, but is updated fairly regularly (and is now available online). It spans law and policy, and analyses the history and scope of most environmental Directives, and how they are implemented at national level. Other ways of keeping up to date are obviously through specialist journals: the *European Environmental Law Review* (EELR; monthly; The Hague: Kluwer) combines news and articles, as does the *Review of EC and International Environmental Law* (tri-annually; Oxford: Blackwell), which has excellent coverage of case law. The annually published *Yearbook of European Environmental Law* (Oxford: Oxford University Press) also has a useful annual survey, but its real strength is the quality of its articles.

Finally, on whether, from a British perspective, the EU has been a force for good environmentally, read A. Jordan (2006) *The Environmental Case for Europe: Britain's European Environmental Policy*, CSERGE Working Paper EDM 06–11, available online at **www.uea.ac.uk/env/cserge/pub/wp/edm/edm_2006_11. pdf**. Against this, you might read D. Wood (1999) 'Challenging the ethos of the European Union: a green perspective on European Union policies and programmes for rural development and the environment' in J. Holder and D. McGillivray (eds) *Locality and Identity: Environmental Issues in Law and Society*, Aldershot: Ashgate, which examines how any claim by the EU to a strong environmental policy has to be set in the context of the EU being a leading proponent of global capitalism and economic growth, which tend to pull not only the EU, but the world economy, in an anti-environmental direction.

@ WEB LINKS

Some aspects of EC decision making are still comparatively secretive, but there is now much greater access to accessible information. Much of this can be found on the central website of the EU **europa.eu.int/eur-lex/en/index.html**, which links to legislation, case law, and preparatory documents. A better starting point for further information and research, however, is the website of DG Environment **europa.eu.int/comm/ environment/index_en.htm**, which groups information by sector and also includes the Sixth Environmental Action Programme, and the annual survey on implementation and enforcement. A site that combines legal texts with helpful dossiers and extensive links is the European Environmental Law Homepage **www.eel.nl**. As well as the ENDS Report, for keeping up to date, there is **www.euractiv.com**, which performs a similar service and which also has good links to previous documents, reports, etc., on any particular topic (making it a valuable research tool).

8 The regulation of environmental protection

 Overview

This chapter provides an introduction to the system of environmental regulation by building upon Chapter 4, in which we examined sources of environmental law. In practice, environmental law is made up of more than mere rules that forbid pollution. The process of environmental regulation begins before laws are made, when policies are established that can be translated into laws. Once in place, laws have to be given practical effect through the establishment of environmental standards, and systems of administrative decision making and enforcement. Thus, the system of environmental regulation involves many different aspects, including the setting, application, enforcement, and ongoing review of environmental standards. This means that this chapter is merely an introductory, but nonetheless significant, building block.

Many of the ideas explored will be returned to in different contexts in later chapters and you may find yourself re-reading different elements—for example, in relation to environmental standards and the way in which they are used in the environmental permitting system. In addition, bear in mind that some of the material in later chapters, including that on environmental crime and public participation, supplements the material in this chapter. Finally, parts of this chapter cover themes that underscore many of the remaining chapters and environmental law as a whole—for example, the impacts of discretion and gradualism—and should be reflected on within many different contexts.

Before reading this chapter, it might be helpful to have considered the material on the history and challenges of environmental law (Chapter 2) and European environmental law (Chapter 7).

At the end of this chapter, you should be able to:

✔ identify and understand in outline the system for addressing environmental problems by controlling activities through regulation by public bodies;

✔ identify and understand the main types of environmental standards used in environmental regulation;

✔ appreciate the different types of environmental standard and how they relate to one another;

✔ identify in outline the characteristics that might be classed as the 'British' approach to environmental regulation;

✔ understand in outline the idea of addressing environmental problems through the use of economic or market mechanisms and other means, such as self-regulation.

Introduction

The diversification of environmental law has increased dramatically over the last thirty years, reflecting not only the growth in the complexity of laws and regulatory systems generally, but also the continuing development of the understanding of how to address environmental problems through legal means. In addition to the diversity of domestic sources of law, there is an increasing 'layering' of laws, with different instruments having differing legal effects at international, European, national, and even regional levels.

Despite this proliferation of legal mechanisms and, in particular, the current vogue for suggesting economic or fiscal mechanisms for combating environmental problems, the system of regulation by public bodies remains the primary tool for environmental protection in this country. Whatever the political rhetoric, the use of taxation and subsidies will always be secondary to regulation in its widest sense.

What does 'regulation' mean in this sense? At one level, all the word means is the use of rules to control activities. This could be through mandatory regulation—often referred to, in very broad terms, as 'command and control' regulation, characterized by the imperative 'you must' and the prohibitive 'you must not'. Under this definition, these could include criminal law rules, civil law rules, or private non-legal rules operated by a body such as a trade association, or maybe even the 'rules' of the market. The word 'regulation' is used here in a general fashion, as shorthand for administrative or bureaucratic regulation—that is, the application of rules and procedures by public bodies so as to achieve a measure of control over activities carried on by individuals and firms.

This definition does not, however, encompass all aspects of environmental regulation. For example, European regulatory systems and self-regulatory mechanisms are not included.[1] Other means of controlling activities, such as criminal or civil law and the use of the market, will be considered later in this chapter, but because these are often subsidiary to administrative regulation, it is this that will be explained first.

Administrative regulation

Administrative regulation is far more than simply the setting of rules on what can and cannot be done. It denotes a coherent *system* of control in which the regulating body sets a framework for activities on an ongoing basis, with a view to conditioning and policing behaviour, as well as laying down straight rules. The advantages of such a system include the ability to provide uniformity, rationality, and fairness between those who are regulated. Some form of public accountability is also produced by having a public body responsible for regulation. In particular, one advantage over the criminal law is that a coherent link can be made with other policies, so as to balance all relevant factors. This is often seen as an important part of the 'British' approach to regulation: that it involves an explicit balancing of environmental factors with such things as economic and social considerations.

British regulatory systems can be said to exhibit a pragmatic and flexible approach: the same mechanism is not used for each situation. In some cases, the reason for this is simply that it is recognized that a control mechanism that works for one problem is unlikely to work for a different one. This is a good illustration of the use of law as a tool or a technique to help to solve particular problems. In other cases, there are historical reasons, because one of the features of having a long history of environmental control is that the administrative structures have built up piecemeal and in response to problems as they arise (see Chapter 2). For example, many controls have, in the past, been given to local authorities purely because they happened to be dealing with similar matters already, or because there was no other relevant body around at the time.

---

1 See further C. Hilson (2000) *Regulating Pollution: A UK and EC Perspective*, Oxford: Hart, pp. 1–2; A. Ogus (1994) *Regulation: Legal Form and Economic Theory*, Oxford: Clarendon Press, p. 1.

The processes of regulatory decision making

Before looking at the main features of regulation in this country, it is necessary to summarize the main processes or stages in regulatory decision making. These are set out in Box 8.1.

BOX 8.1 The regulatory process—a summary

The main stages of the environmental regulatory system include:

- establishing general policies on the environment;
- setting standards or specific policies in relation to the environmental issue concerned;
- applying these standards and policies to individual situations, normally through some sort of licensing system;
- enforcing standards and permissions through administrative and criminal sanctions;
- providing information about the environment and the regulatory process itself;
- using mechanisms to monitor and improve the regulatory system.

The establishment of general policies

The decision about *which* environmental problems to regulate and *how* to do so is determined within the process of environmental policymaking. This process has been characterized as having three stages.[2]

(a) The first is the 'ignition stage', at which governments are stimulated to address a problem, either through public opinion or particular events, or environmental conditions.[3] While shifts in environmental values play a part, it is not easy to identify any common trigger for the policymaking process, although there has been a shift from the historical reaction to particular events or catastrophes, towards a broader awareness of environmental issues from government, environmental groups, and the general public.[4]

(b) The second is the examination of the problem, and an assessment of the issues and risks involved, and of potential solutions.

(c) Finally, decisions have to be made about *whether* to regulate and these are essentially subjective decisions made on the basis of information gathered during the second stage. It is only at this third stage that the manner of regulation is considered in any depth.

The process of establishing general policies is not really part of the regulatory system, but a necessary precondition for any system of environmental control. Having said that, one of the most obvious features of the UK political system is the absence of a formal national 'policy for the environment'.[5] Even in areas in relation to which there are local or sectoral plans,

---

2 E. Ashby (1978) *Reconciling Man with the Environment*, Oxford: Oxford University Press.

3 Royal Commission on Environmental Pollution 21st Report (1998) *Setting Environmental Standards*, Cm 4053, paras 1.33–1.34.

4 Also see the role of the Driving Forces-Pressures-State-Impacts-Responses (DPSIR) framework, which allows policymakers to understand the causal relationships between different aspects of environmental problems and thereby identify possible responses: see further European Environment Agency (1999) *Environmental Indicators: Typology and Overview*, Technical Report No. 25.

5 R. Garner (2000) *Environmental Politics: Britain, Europe and the Global Environment*, 2nd edn, London: MacMillan, p. 152; S. Young (1993) *The Politics of the Environment*, Manchester: Baseline Books, p. 65.

there is often no national plan, or, if there is, it is made up of somewhat imprecise and flexible policies laid down in a variety of documents.

A good illustration of the flexible nature of policymaking in the UK is provided by the town and country planning system, within which the 'national plan' is to be found scattered among numerous circulars, planning policy statements (PPSs), Ministerial decisions, White Papers, and other assorted policy statements. There is some evidence that the position is altering, with moves towards national sectoral strategies in waste and air quality. EC law has been the trigger for many of these changes, with a number of Directives requiring coherent 'plans and programmes' for addressing certain environmental problems.[6]

Given the essentially political nature of much of environmental law, the general tenor of the policies tends to be decided by central government. The presumption in favour of development in town planning is one example, but general decisions on energy and transport policy—such as the favouring of road transport over rail, or the expansion of the wind energy programme—are others. Certain political philosophies may also be imposed by central government: good examples are the principle of voluntariness in relation to controlling agricultural activities, or the policy of privatization. But because of the decentralized nature of much of pollution control, some general policies are effectively decided by bodies other than the elected central government. Other policies stem from general assumptions about the nature of the regulatory system itself—namely, the characteristics that define the 'British' approach to environmental regulation.

A final factor is that the shape of many policies is now decided, or at least affected, by the EC. Arguably, some of the most significant impacts on the environment in the next few years will follow from various broad policy initiatives at the EC level, not least the continuing process under Art. 6 EC of integrating environmental policy into other, more general, areas of EC policy (see p. 189).

The setting of standards or specific policies in relation to the environmental issue concerned

The implementation of regulation requires more than only rules telling people what shall, or shall not, happen. Any system of control must have some objectives or standards that are set for it, otherwise it runs the risk of ceasing to be rational, uniform, or fair. These may be fairly explicit objectives, such as air quality standards with specific maximum concentrations for a range of pollutants, or they may be far more vague, such as a water quality objective to the effect that a river should be capable of supporting fish. These standards ensure that those that are regulated understand what they need to do to comply with regulation, but, more importantly, they guide those who regulate in determining how to achieve the overall objectives of the regulation and enforce the rules effectively.

In the past, reliance has usually been placed on rather vague standards, such as the test of nuisance at common law (see Chapter 11), or the idea that Best Practicable Means (BPM) should be used to reduce gaseous emissions to the atmosphere. In addition, standards were often set in an informal manner, as used to happen with non-statutory water quality objectives. More specific and more formal standards are becoming the norm rather than the exception, a good example being the use of the Best Available Techniques (BAT) standard to prevent pollution from industrial installations controlled under the environmental permitting regime and pollution prevention and control (PPC) Directive, which is fleshed out with technical guidance on the manner in which the standard may be achieved. There is often overlap between this stage and stage (a) above, because, in determining the policy to adopt in relation to a particular environmental problem, it is often necessary to consider what specific standard should be adopted and/or what objectives should be set.

---

6 For example, river basin management plans under the Water Framework Directive—see p. 593.

The application of these standards and policies to individual situations

This is often seen as the central part of the regulatory process. There are numerous examples in relation to which a permission, authorization, consent, or licence is required from a public body. Different pieces of legislation use different words, but they all mean essentially the same thing. Whether one is granted, and the nature of any conditions attached, will normally be a discretionary decision, but one that is made by reference to the general standards established at stage (b). The application of standards may also be seen in such processes as court actions for nuisance and the specific application of whether BPM or BAT are being used. The application of standards and policies is essentially a discretionary decision made by the expert regulator, which is difficult to challenge in the courts unless there has been a procedural error.[7]

The enforcement of standards and permissions

In practice, one of the most important areas of environmental law is whether the legal instruments that are available are used, because there is often considerable discretion given to the regulatory body. 'Enforcement' covers a far wider range of matters than the single question of whether or not to prosecute for breaches of the law. In any regulatory system, there is normally a whole range of administrative and other remedies available in addition to prosecution. The question of which remedy to use is also tied up with how the regulator should proceed. There is a wealth of evidence to show that informal methods of enforcement are often preferred and that regulators normally adopt a 'compliance strategy' towards enforcement, rather than a 'sanctioning strategy' (see Chapter 10). Questions of inspection and monitoring also arise as part of the enforcement process.

The provision of information about the environment and the regulatory process

A theme that runs through the regulatory process concerns the openness of the system. This includes such questions as the production of official information on the state of the environment, the availability of public registers, and the publication of information about how the regulatory system itself works. The UK's traditionally secretive administrative processes have become more open and the emphasis has shifted in recent years towards ensuring that the use of information is effective in encouraging public participation in the regulatory process. This is most obvious in relation to stage (c), but is also apparent in other stages of the regulatory process, enabling participation in the policymaking and standard-setting stage through increased consultation and the availability of more environmental information for enforcement purposes (see Chapter 10).

The use of feedback mechanisms to monitor and improve decision making

The final stage of the regulatory process links back into the first. An efficient regulatory system needs to be responsive to practical operational experience, and to changes in scientific and public opinion. Thus, monitoring and the review of the operation of existing regulation is now an integral part of many environmental laws. These iterative mechanisms work both generally in terms of pieces of legislation—particularly, European Directives[8]—and in relation to specific requirements to keep up to date with advances in pollution abatement technologies, or to review permits at certain periods,[9] or in response to newly identified problems (for example, variation of discharge consents to meet new environmental quality requirements). Finally, there are other methods of monitoring the operation of

---

7 See *Levy v. Environment Agency* [2003] Env LR 11.

8 For example, IPPC Directive 2008/1/EC, Art. 16(3).

9 For example, the review of environmental permits under the Environmental Permitting (England and Wales) Regulations 2007 (SI 2007/3538) Reg. 34.

environmental laws through informal mechanisms in which public bodies scrutinize the effectiveness of environmental law and policy.[10]

Anticipatory, continuing, and adaptive controls

Regulatory mechanisms may be divided into two general types: anticipatory controls and continuing controls.

Anticipatory controls

Anticipatory controls are measures imposed on an activity at its commencement in order to forestall potential environmental problems. Usually, the objective is to prevent the activity unless certain requirements or conditions are met. The category includes a wide range of licensing-type controls, under which permission of some sort is required before an activity may be started or carried on. These are normally complemented by a combination of criminal and administrative sanctions if the activity starts without permission, or if the permission is contravened.

BOX 8.2 The range of anticipatory controls

The range of possible anticipatory controls is quite wide and includes:

- an outright ban or prohibition—of course, there is no *necessity* for a public regulatory body to be involved here, but someone will need to police the ban;[11]
- a prohibition on an activity unless a particular body is notified in advance;[12]
- a prohibition on an activity unless it is registered, registration being something that cannot normally be refused by the registering body;[13]
- a prohibition on an activity until a licence, permission, authorization, or consent is obtained, should the granting of the permission be at the discretion of the regulating body.

There are two distinct categories of permission or consent. Some are one-off permissions that, once granted, create what are, in effect, permanent rights, because it is difficult to vary or revoke them. A good example is the granting of planning permission, in relation to which revocation entails the payment of compensation. Others provide for variation or revocation in the light of future circumstances. Most pollution control consents fall into this category, examples being the requirement to obtain an authorization or permit from the Environment Agency prior to operating a prescribed installation, or a consent for a discharge to controlled waters.

Continuing controls

Continuing controls are measures by which the carrying out of an activity is controlled on a continuing basis. Typically, they relate to the way in which an activity is carried on, so

---

10 For example, the parliamentary select committees and organizations such as the Royal Commission on Environmental Pollution (RCEP)—see p. 110.

11 For example, the ban on the use of CFCs in products under the 1987 Montreal Protocol on Substances that Deplete the Ozone Layer, or the ban on the dumping of tyres in landfills under the EC Landfill Directive (1999/31/EC), Arts 5 and 6.

12 For example see the registration requirements in relation to exempt waste operations under the Environmental Permitting (England and Wales) Regulations 2007, SI 2007/3538, Sch. 2.

13 For example, there is a requirement that carriers of controlled waste register with the Environment Agency—see p. 666.

another way of referring to them would be as *operational* controls. An obvious example is the ongoing duty to comply with the terms and conditions of a consent, licence, authorization, or permission granted by a pollution control authority, which will normally be combined with a range of other regulatory controls relating to monitoring and enforcement.

The distinction between anticipatory controls and continuing controls is thus that one relates to *whether* an activity should be carried on in the first place, while the other relates to *how* it is carried on once it has started.

Of course, anticipatory and continuing controls are mutually supportive and most regulatory systems combine the two types of mechanism. Anticipatory controls still require some monitoring to ensure that the prohibited activity is not being carried on; conversely, most continuing controls rest on the need for some initial permission before an activity may be started—indeed, the threat of withdrawal of the initial permission may well constitute the strongest inducement to comply with continuing regulatory requirements. For example, planning permission is required before a new activity is started, but that permission will often include conditions that require some adherence to defined standards over a period of time, such as permitted working hours or noise limits. Similarly, consents, permits, and licences obtained from pollution control authorities normally combine the initial need for a consent with an ability to vary the requirements as the situation changes. This mutually supportive position is reinforced by the fact that many activities are subject to the requirements of more than one regulatory system.[14]

Finally, a further category of controls can be identified, which combines anticipatory and continuing controls, and which is termed 'adaptive management'.[15] This has its origins in theories of ecological management, which stress the uncertainty of the consequences of intervening in natural processes and hence the need to continually keep impacts under review, and, where necessary, to look afresh at the initial regulatory authorization. There are examples of quasi-adaptive controls already in use: for example, planning permission can be given, in effect, on a trial basis (usually for three or five years) if the impacts of a development are uncertain. This approach avoids giving the developer full planning permission, which, if revoked, would require compensation to be paid. Another example might be the use of field trials of growing genetically modified (GM) crops.

There are, of course, some activities in relation to which it would probably not be appropriate to use this kind of approach. It is unlikely to be much use in authorizing the construction of a nuclear power station, for example, because there would be far too much uncertainty for the investors. But it has been argued that more use should be made of an adaptive, 'learning by doing' approach. Ideas such as this are, for example, behind calls to include more post-development monitoring within the laws on environmental impact assessment (EIA), which, arguably, place too much emphasis on the value of the certainty of reaching a decision on whether to go ahead and hence on trying to predict in advance what the likely impacts might be (see p. 460). Many impacts—for example, on habitats and species—might be rather uncertain and, if the developer is not required to respond to these—at least, over a reasonable period of time after authorization is granted—then the cost of these will be borne by the public.

Standards in environmental law

Most environmental controls rely on some form of measurable standard. This standard may be used as a guideline—that is, as an objective—or it may be used as a means of defining what an individual or firm may do. Indeed, one of the distinctive features of environmental

14 See the overlap between planning and pollution control on p. 503, although, historically, this multifaceted approach has also applied to different areas of pollution control.

15 From .C. Holling (ed.) (1978) *Adaptive Environmental Assessment and Management*, Chichester: John Wiley.

regulation is that the regulatory body often has responsibility for defining the standard, as well as for enforcing its application.

Types of standard

There are a number of different types of standard, but a crude division can be made into those that are set by reference to the *target* being protected and those that are set by reference to the *source* of the pollution. Source-related standards may be further divided into emission standards, process standards, and product standards. There are other factors that have a significant impact on the nature of a standard, such as whether it is centrally or locally set, uniform or flexible, precise or imprecise.

The following summary is not intended to be an exhaustive list of the various types of standard (from the list of variables above, it will be obvious that the number of potential types is high), but is an attempt to introduce a basic vocabulary of terms. It also aims to illustrate some of the more common methods used, together with some thoughts on their relative strengths and weaknesses. In a sense, these are the tools available to the legislator in deciding how a regulatory system is to work.

Environmental quality standards

Some standards—known as 'target standards', 'environmental quality standards', or 'ambient environmental standards'—concentrate on the effect on a particular target. In many cases, the protected target may be human and the standard is accordingly set by reference to the effect on that human (for example, the control of noise levels from machinery). However, since this is a book about environmental protection, it will mainly concentrate on situations in which the protected target is the environment, or part of it.[16] The phrases 'target standards' and 'environmental quality standards' will therefore be treated as interchangeable.

The effect on the target may be measured in different ways. It may relate to a biological effect, thus channelling all information directly into a consideration of the actual impact of a pollutant (for example, a standard requiring that a discharge to water is not harmful to fish or aquatic animals); alternatively, it may relate to the exposure of the target, from which certain biological or other effects may be presumed. In the environmental field, however, it will more usually relate simply to some measurable quality of the receiving environment, such as the level of a particular pollutant.

An environmental quality standard can therefore be defined as a standard under which conformity is measured by reference to the effect of a pollutant on the receiving environment. It is unusual for the selected target to be the whole environment. More commonly, a particular medium will be chosen as the reference point, such as air or water. In order to retain flexibility, there will frequently also be a geographical limitation: the standard may thus be set by reference to a particular river or area,[17] or may be even more specific, such as when air quality or noise levels are fixed within a factory, or any other enclosed area.

---

16 The controls over noise are the main exception, because they are mainly directed at humans. These controls are covered in the Online Resource Centre. The impact of noise on ecosystems is, however, a factor—see, e.g., p. 722.

17 For example, in relation to broad areas such as river catchments or basins, see p. 594, and smaller areas such as water protection zones, see p. 618.

BOX 8.3 Examples of environmental quality standards

- Air quality standards for the maximum or minimum concentration of any specified substance in air.[18]
- Water quality standards for the concentration of specified pollutants in water.[19]
- The nuisance test at common law, under which property owners are entitled to the enjoyment of their property without unreasonable interference from neighbours (see p. 332).

It will be clear that these standards may be set by reference to any number of parameters. For example, a water quality standard could be set specifically for the maximum concentration of a specific substance, or a whole range of parameters may be used. The Water Framework Directive (2000/60/EC) utilizes both approaches: on the one hand, setting standards for particularly hazardous, listed substances and, on the other, setting general standards, such as that surface waters should aim to be of 'good ecological status', which is defined according to a range of criteria (see p. 594). It will also be clear that the standard can be precise or imprecise—the nuisance standard is a good example of an imprecise standard.

CASE 8.1 Imprecise and precise standards—*Murdoch v. Glacier Metals* [1998] Env LR 732

Different types of environmental quality standard can overlap. In this case, the imprecise standard of nuisance law overlapped with precise standards found in international guidelines on acceptable noise levels.

The claimants argued that noise from a local factory was a nuisance. They brought evidence to show that measured noise levels breached the maximum noise levels for night time recommended by the World Health Organization (WHO). The Court held that, notwithstanding the breach of WHO guidelines, the noise was not a nuisance because the interference was not unreasonable. The claimants lived on a noisy road and none of the neighbours had complained.

Imprecise standards have the advantage of being variably applicable taking into account different situations. Thus, in another situation, it might be the case that noise levels below the WHO recommended standard would be an actionable nuisance, because, for example, background noise levels were very low or because the characteristics of the noise were unreasonable—for example, low humming or unexpected noises.

Emission standards

An emission standard—sometimes referred to as an 'emission limit value' (ELV)—can be defined as a standard under which conformity is measured by reference to what is emitted, rather than its effect on the receiving environment. Emission standards thus tend to concentrate on wastes produced. Emission standards can be specified in terms of specified levels, concentration, mass of substances, or percentage reduction requirements.

---

18 For example, the Air Quality Standards Regulations 2007, SI 2007/64, set mandatory standards for sulphur dioxide, nitrogen dioxide, lead, carbon monoxide, benzene, 1.3 butadiene, and small particles (PM10).

19 For example, see the Water Supply (Water Quality) Regulations 2000, SI 2000/3184, which set quality parameters for water supplied in England for drinking, washing, cooking, and food preparation and production.

BOX 8.4 Examples of emission standards

- The maximum content of a particular substance in a liquid discharge from a pipe to a sewer or 'controlled waters'.[20]
- The noise level measured as it emanates from a piece of machinery.[21]
- The maximum content of a particular substance in an emission from a chimney or exhaust pipe.[22]

Process standards

Process standards—sometimes also referred to as 'technical prescriptions', 'performance standards', or 'specification standards'—may be imposed on a process either by stipulating precisely the process that must be carried on, or by setting performance requirements that the process must reach. In the latter case, there would be a choice as to how to reach these requirements. These standards may relate to the whole of the process or, alternatively, to a part of it, such as the way in which a product is made or the way in which effluent is treated. They may include requirements about the technology that is used, the raw materials, or operational factors, such as whether the process is being carried out properly.

BOX 8.5 Examples of process standards

- A requirement that a particular pre-treatment plant for effluent be used.[23]
- A requirement that the Best Available Techniques (BAT) are used to prevent environmental harm (although the general requirement is often, in practice, translated into a set of emission standards in order to achieve environmental quality standards).[24]
- Conditions attached to the operation of a landfill site.[25]

It is clear that current practice is to emphasize the use of process standards and this is illustrated by their use in the PPC legislation. They are a good means of preventing harm to the environment arising in the first place.

Product standards

Product standards may be defined as those that control the characteristics of an item that is being produced. This may be done with the aim of protecting against damage that the product may cause while it is being used, or when it is disposed of, or even during its manufacture.

---

20 Typically set as a condition of a discharge consent or PPC permit.

21 Set by reference to condition of a consent or authorization. This can be contrasted with a blanket product standard, which limits the noise as a design and product certification issue.

22 Typically set as a condition of a PPC permit or, in the case of vehicle exhausts, general rules on emissions.

23 For example, a requirement for secondary treatment of urban waste water under the Urban Waste Water Treatment Directive 91/271/EEC, Art. 4.

24 For example, under the IPPC Directive 2008/1/EC and Environmental Permitting (England and Wales) Regulations 2007, SI 2007/3538.

25 For example, in relation to operational conditions on landfill sites found in the Landfill (England and Wales) Regulations 2002, SI 2002/1559.

BOX 8.6 **Examples of product standards**

- A requirement that a class of products are designed and constructed so that they may be recovered and recycled at the point of disposal.[26]

- A requirement that products meet energy efficiency levels—for example, the energy efficiency of boilers.[27]

- It may even be thought that requirements on the labelling of goods are a type of product standard, because the labels set down systems of conformity that relay information to the consumer about the product specification.[28]

Use standards

Another form of standard that is closely related to product standards is a standard that relates to the use of a product. As the name suggests, while product standards are primarily concerned with characteristics or concentrations, use standards relate to the marketing or use of the product. Examples include the restrictions on the use and marketing of new chemical substances,[29] pesticides,[30] and, perhaps most controversially, genetically modified organisms (GMOs).[31] These standards are concerned with the measurement of any risk associated with the consequences of the use of such products, rather than with any restrictions on the product itself.

The interrelationship of standards

Of course, these five types of standard are not exclusive of each other. An emission standard will often be set so as to achieve an environmental quality standard; product standards for a car will include many matters relating to the emissions from it, such as lead, carbon dioxide, or noise; a process standard may be set by reference to the meeting of certain emission standards or environmental quality standards. In addition, the cumulative effect of these emissions will have an impact on the attainment, or otherwise, of any environmental quality standard.

BOX 8.7 **An example of different types of standard—lead in the environment**

In relation to one particular toxic pollutant—lead—environmental concentrations may be controlled in a number of ways:

- environmental quality standards may be set, stating that levels of lead should not rise above a certain level in the air, in water, or in the soil;

---

26 For example, in relation to certain producer responsibility legislation in respect of motor vehicles—see the End-of-Life Vehicles Directive 2000/53/EC—and in relation to electrical equipment—see the Waste Electronic and Electrical Equipment Directive 2002/96/EC.

27 See Directive 78/170/EEC.

28 For example, under the EC eco-labelling scheme, Regulation 1980/2000/EC.

29 The REACH regime under the EC Regulation on Chemicals and their Safe Use (EC 1907/2006).

30 Marketing and Use of Pesticides Directive (76/769/EEC) (as amended).

31 EC Directive 2001/18/EC on the release and marketing of GMOs.

- emissions of lead may be controlled, so that any emission, whether into air or water, or on to land, should not include more than a specified concentration of lead, to be set in some form of permission or consent;

- processes may be regulated to reduce the use of lead or to reduce, by good design, possible emissions and escapes of lead into the environment;

- products likely to include lead may be regulated, either to ban its use—for example, lead fishing weights—or to limit the use of lead—for example, setting maximum amounts of lead in drinking water or in petrol.

Other characteristics of standards

As stated earlier, a number of other matters are also important in relation to the nature of a standard. The standard may be a precise one—such as one set by reference to a quantifiable maximum or minimum (often a numerical value)—or, it may be an imprecise one—such as a requirement that BPM or BAT are used—or it may be one applying the common law test of nuisance.

The standard may be a uniform one across a country or whole regions such as the EC, or it may vary from area to area. Indeed, it may even be set on an individual basis. Certain matters demand uniform standards. For example, uniformity is normally desirable for emissions from mobile sources such as cars, otherwise problems are caused at boundaries. For similar reasons, most product standards are set on a uniform basis. It is strongly argued by some that uniformity creates equality—a particularly important consideration in the context of the EC and the single internal market. Limit values, as used by the EC in a number of Directives, create a special form of uniformity. They require that a certain standard is reached, but allow member States to impose more stringent standards if circumstances require.[32]

The standard may be set centrally or locally. This distinction tends to reflect the same division as that between uniform and individualized standards, because centrally set standards will usually be uniform, while locally set ones will vary with the discretion given to the decision maker. In this context, it must be remembered that historically, few standards in Britain were set by legislation. In recent years, this has changed to some extent, with statutory standards set in relation to air, water, and technical requirements for the landfill of waste.

Strengths and weaknesses of different types of standard

Obviously, it is not possible to cover all types of standard, but it is possible to see the relative strengths and weaknesses of the more commonly used examples.

Environmental quality standards

By concentrating on what it is that requires protection, environmental quality standards are able to deal with inputs to the environment from all sources and via all potential pathways, while the other mechanisms, used on their own, tend to permit an accumulation of any particular pollutant. For the same reason, these standards can also cater for potentially harmful combinations of substances on the environment. They can thus enable a policymaker to identify areas in which work is needed and to channel resources effectively. They can also be tailored for particular circumstances—for example, by being more stringent in sensitive areas than in others.

---

32 On the scope to go further than EC-set standards, see p. 188.

There are, however, a number of limitations to environmental quality standards. They require constant monitoring of the environment, which may prove to be impractical or expensive. Enforcement also poses difficulties, because failure to reach a standard may indicate the existence of a problem, but does not necessarily specify the cause or how to remedy it. For example, in order to clean up a river that is chronically contaminated with organic wastes, a regulator would first have to identify the causes of the pollution, and then find some method of restricting inputs that was fair and enforceable. A further problem of environmental quality standards is that they may give no incentive to polluters to improve their performance in areas in which the standard is already being met. Finally, environmental quality standards are difficult to use for very large areas of the environment, such as the wider marine environment, partly because of uncertainties over what the 'right' standard should be and partly because of the problems of monitoring compliance with such a standard over a large area.

The very nature of environmental quality standards is that they tend to be set as *objectives* rather than as legal requirements, except in those situations in which there is a limited number of sources and targets, such as enclosed work environments. This use as objectives makes them useful at the strategic and planning stages of the regulatory process. For example, development plans often set environmental quality standards, even if they are frequently very imprecise, such as a policy that developments liable to cause a nuisance should not be permitted in a defined area.

Emission standards

By contrast, the strength of emission standards is that they are relatively easy to control and monitor by sampling at the point of emission. Enforcement is also easier, because of the simplicity of the causation requirements when there is a point of discharge. In addition, an emission standard may be tightened progressively to encourage a discharger to improve the process, while still retaining choice as to how this is done.

A main drawback of emission standards relates to the difficulty of controlling diffuse—or 'non-point'—emissions (such as fertilizer or pesticide run-off) by these means.[33] There is also the difficulty (shared with process standards and product standards) of organizing a system that can cope with an accumulation of similar emissions in one area, such as car exhausts within cities or similar industrial concerns in a single water catchment area. But this second difficulty is not an insoluble problem: it may be tackled by setting very strict local emission standards, by linking them explicitly to an environmental quality standard, or by applying the 'bubble' approach. Under the bubble approach, all emissions in a particular region, country, or other area are aggregated and a total amount of emissions for that area is specified. This aggregated amount is then usually shared out among different countries or sources.[34]

Process standards

Process standards are obviously limited to where there exists a process to control and thus tend to apply mainly to the manufacturing industry. Their main strength is that they may be set so as to prevent a problem arising in the first place. They may also help to pool resources for research at a central level. There is a potential disincentive for producers to find more effective ways of reducing pollution, unless the standards are made progressively stricter, or are periodically altered, or are set at levels that force the producer to develop the technology so as to reach the standard—that is, so-called 'technology-forcing' rules.

---

33 For discussion of diffuse water pollution, see p. 620.

34 A good example of this approach can be found in the allocation of the EU's apportionment of greenhouse gas reductions under the Kyoto Protocol—see p. 523.

Product standards

Product standards are similarly limited to areas in which there is a product, and have similar strengths and weaknesses to those of process standards. As stated above, both categories also have difficulty in catering for the cumulative effect of pollutants on their own. Increasingly, however, product standards are being used to make producers responsible for the whole life cycle of a product, from 'cradle to grave'. This has two advantages: first, it brings home the full environmental cost of the product; secondly, by requiring the use of the non-hazardous and recyclable materials, it reduces overall environmental impacts caused by the use and disposal of (mostly) consumer products.

But product standards do nothing in relation to the *use* of a product. For example, the EC End-of-Life Vehicles Directive (2000/53/EC) may address the design of cars and the way in which they should be recovered or recycled, but it does not seek to control fuel consumption, which probably causes greater environmental harm than product inputs or unsuitability for recycling.

Locally set and centrally set standards—the UK vs the EC

It has often been noted that the UK and the rest of the EC do not seem to see eye to eye on pollution control.[35] This is sometimes translated into a conflict between a British preference for locally set and variable—that is, non-uniform—emission standards, set by reference to local environmental quality, and an EC preference for centrally set, uniform emission standards.[36] These two types of standard provide an excellent opportunity for a case study on their relative strengths and weaknesses.

Locally set and variable emission standards set by reference to local environmental quality

Each of the features of this combination of ideas merits some mention. Referring everything to environmental quality can be said to target controls where they are needed—at the protection of the environment. In this way, the impact of non-point emissions and background levels of pollution may be taken into account, as well as discharges from pipes and chimneys. The fact that neither the emission standards nor the environmental quality standards are uniform provides flexibility. This enables more sensitive areas to be protected more strictly, or polluters who are seen as more useful to the community to be treated more leniently. In all cases, a great deal of discretion is granted to decision makers. It is also argued that, because standards can be varied to take account of local circumstances, the mechanism is economically efficient. For example, greater pollutant loads might be permitted in remote, unpopulated areas, or where the self-cleansing properties of the local environment are greater.

Centrally set, uniform emission standards

These have obvious advantages. Uniform standards are easily imposed, easily implemented, and easily monitored. They are fair between polluters, because all are treated the same, and they avoid difficult problems about allocating the right to pollute among different polluters. As a result, they may be relatively cheap for the regulator to operate, because they involve less administrative discretion than variable standards. They also fit in well with the economic principles of the EC's single market.

On the other hand, they can be said not to allow local conditions to be taken into account, because there is no flexibility, although this can be provided in terms of discretionary application of the standard, particularly at the enforcement stage. Uniform emission standards

---

35 G. Lubbe-Wolff (2001) 13 JEL 79.

36 It has been argued that these differences have been exaggerated: see N. Haigh (1990) *EEC Environmental Policy and Britain*, 2nd edn, London: Longman, and further below.

cannot address the situation in which there is a number of polluters in one area, because there is no jurisdiction to reduce the emission standard to fit local conditions. They are also sometimes said to lead to the possibility of a uniformly polluted country if there is one relevant discharge in every area. (These last two criticisms are rather too general, because good use of preventive controls would help in both cases.)

Do the UK and the EC still differ?

It is not difficult to think of reasons why the UK may differ from other member States within the EC. As an island, mainland Britain has no frontiers. Thus, the argument about fairness has never had the impact that it has in France and Germany, which share the Rhine as a border, and where the inequality of one factory being allowed to discharge more than another on the other bank is obvious. Other factors stem from the 'British' approach to pollution control—namely, a tradition of discretionary, local decision making and a system based on pragmatism, in which the effects on the environment are balanced with social, economic, and political factors.

But the main argument for the British position probably stems from self-interest: with its rainy climate, fast-running streams, ample coastline, and relative remoteness, the UK can claim a comparative advantage when it comes to pollution. Put very crudely, the same discharge may be thought to cause less pollution in the UK than in other countries, because of its lesser effect on the environment. When it comes to setting standards, it is certainly possible to argue against the application of stringent uniform standards across the EC if they have no justification in terms of environmental protection in the British context, even if they provide that protection elsewhere.

In recent years, at the EC level, the historic debate over the application of uniform emissions standards as compared to more general standards based upon individual and local circumstances have resulted in an uneasy compromise between the two approaches. For example, the Water Framework Directive (2000/60/EC) takes a 'combined approach' to standard setting, which requires both emission standards to control emissions from individual point sources, along with broad overriding requirements to achieve 'good' water quality status to limit the cumulative impact of such emissions. The IPPC Directive (2008/1/EC) relies largely upon application of broad process standards imposed in the light of local circumstances, rather than specifying emission limit values (ELVs). In this sense, the more flexible approach promoted by the UK is winning the day.[37] There is a degree of scepticism from some countries—notably, Germany—as to whether such an approach will result in consistency of environmental improvement.[38] It is also worth noting that, although the trend may be towards flexibility, there are some significant examples of the imposition of centrally set, prescriptive, uniform standards, such as those found in the Landfill Directive (99/31/EC) in relation to operation and technical requirements at landfill sites.[39]

In summary, therefore, although there are identifiable differences in approach to pollution control standards across different European countries,[40] these cannot be characterized as a simple EC–UK dispute in terms of environmental regulation at the European level. The British influence over Directives is evidenced historically[41] and, more recently, in the adoption of flexible standards over more specific emission limits in both the Water Framework Directive and the IPPC Directive.[42] These reflect a seemingly growing preference for the

37 See further p. 504.
38 Lubbe-Wolff (2001).
39 See further p. 662.
40 Lubbe-Wolff (2001).
41 For example, the final form of Directive 76/464/EEC on dangerous substances in water was largely influenced by the British approach to standard setting.
42 M. Doppelhammer [2000] EELR 199.

flexibility and individualized approach that is consistent with 'British' styles of environmental regulation.

In another example, deregulation has become increasingly common in the European context, particularly in recent years, through the doctrine of subsidiarity and consolidating framework legislation.[43] The idea that the detailed setting of standards should be delegated from the European level to member States can be seen clearly in a number of recent Directives, including the IPPC Directive and the Water Framework Directive, in which flexibility and the tailoring of regulatory solutions to individual circumstances at member-State level are at the heart of the regulatory system. The imposition of uniform Europe-wide standards are only to be used as a fallback position; in cases in which market distortions are present, or for persistent, bioaccumulative pollutants in relation to which an ambient approach is inappropriate.

Regulatory approaches and tools

A key part of the regulatory process is the way in which the coherent system of rules is applied in the 'real world'. There are certain characteristics that dominate UK environmental regulation, as compared to other approaches, and these all help to explain the way in which environmental law operates on a practical level. These characteristics answer basic questions about: what types of rule and standard are employed; how they are set and by whom; how they are enforced and by whom; and what role the public plays in these processes.

In 1986, Vogel identified a number of characteristics of the 'British' style. He found the UK's regulatory style to be characterized by flexibility and informality, and summarized the system as involving:

An absence of statutory standards, minimal use of prosecution, a flexible enforcement strategy, considerable administrative discretion, decentralized implementation, close co-operation between regulators and the regulated, and restrictions on the ability of non-industry constituents to participate in the regulatory process.[44]

At the risk of producing an unmanageable list, other points might be added to these, such as delegation of decision making to autonomous quasi-governmental—and non-governmental—bodies, extensive use of industrial self-regulation, a limited availability of legislative and judicial scrutiny of regulators, a gradualist approach to change, reliance on scientific knowledge for decision making, and habitual reference to economic factors before decisions are made.

Vogel compared this approach with that of the USA, which he characterized as rule-oriented, normally employing rigid and uniform standards, and making little use of industrial self-regulation. In addition, less use is made there of administrative discretion, prosecution is much more common, there is great executive and judicial scrutiny of regulators, and technology-forcing rules are favoured—all of which lead to conflict between regulator and regulated, and to an adversarial mentality.

Of course, many of these differences are not unique to environmental regulation in the two countries, but are a matter of general political culture. They probably stem from different attitudes towards regulation engendered by different population densities and degrees of cultural homogeneity. In the UK, the need for a balancing process is all too clear, while, in the USA, the 'frontier mentality' is understandably more prevalent.

---

43 Deregulation can also be applied in the context of removing market barriers to allow free movement of goods such as waste and recycled bottles: see further C. Hilson (2000) pp. 22–6.

44 D. Vogel (1986) *National Styles of Regulation*, Ithaca, NY: Cornell University Press.

At this point, a warning should be given. Since the 1960s, the situation in the USA has changed dramatically and what Vogel describes in the 1980s is quite different from what happened before.[45] Similarly, the 'British' approach has been undergoing a process of change over the last twenty years. The informal and flexible basis remains, but the approach has undoubtedly got more open, more centralized, more legalistic, and more contentious, especially in the last ten years or so. The changes in legislation have been substantial, but there have also been more disguised internal changes of practice by regulators. As a result, Vogel's analysis is now somewhat outdated.

One crucial factor in this change is the attitude of the EC. The 'British' approach has tended to conflict with that adopted by other member States and has had to be modified to fit in with that. This is, however, a 'two-way street', and other member States have also had to modify their own approaches in transposing and implementing Directives that reflect British modes of regulation.[46] At the same time, the increased profile of environmental issues—particularly international ones requiring common responses—has led to some changes of style out of political necessity. A further factor that has influenced the change away from the traditional 'British' approach has been the changing political landscape within a period of radical change in the regulation of environmental protection. The major policy features over the last twenty to thirty years have included the rejection of long-term planning in favour of market forces, the deregulation of unnecessary bureaucratic controls, the privatization of public services, the imposition of strict spending controls on public bodies, the general weakening of local authority power, and the use of voluntary controls allowing choice wherever possible.

The implications of the 'British' approach also vary at the different stages of the regulatory process identified earlier, with the result that, for example, general policymaking remains mainly a central function, rather than being particularly decentralized (although many of these general policies are now, in practice, agreed at international or EC level).

As with standard setting, a number of things appear to be changing in relation to the traditional British approach to regulation. In particular, there is an increasing tendency for standards to be set centrally (which often goes hand-in-hand with more uniform standards) and a further tendency for them to be set out more explicitly, in legislative instruments or formal policy documents.

A number of examples might be used to illustrate the point. Perhaps the clearest relates to the way in which EC standards are imposed through Directives, thus effectively replacing local discretion with central prescription, but there are also examples from domestic legislation. In relation to air pollution, there has been a major change over recent years, with the setting of statutory air quality objectives by the Secretary of State. Under the Air Quality (England) Regulations 2007,[47] local authorities are under a duty to undertake an assessment of air quality in their areas and to take action where the statutory objectives are not being met (see p. 539). This covers, among other things, powers in relation to setting pollution control conditions, and clearly entails the whole process becoming more open and predictable. It should be noted, however, that this shift towards centralism and formalism does not necessarily imply that local air quality management areas will be set uniformly, nor that individual pollution control conditions will be set in a blanket fashion: there will continue to be a considerable measure of local differentiation and local input in the setting of emission limits. It is, however, the *shift* from secretive, flexible, subjective, and individualistic approaches, towards more open, formal, objective, and collective forms of decision making that is significant.

---

45 For an updated view, see R. Kagan (2001) *Adversarial Legalism: The American Way of Law*, Cambridge, Mass: Harvard University Press.

46 See further J. Zottl (2000) 12 JEL 281, Lubbe-Wolff (2001), and J. Simila (2002) 14 JEL 143.

47 SI 2007/64.

As well as centralizing decisions and reducing discretions, this new formalism also increases the potential role of the courts. It has already been noted how the courts have played a lesser role in the development of environmental policy in this country than that in, for example, Germany or the USA (see p. 94). This is probably because of the wider discretions provided in the legislation, which are often unchallengeable. But the development of more explicit standards, coupled with clear operational duties imposed on the regulatory agencies, also means that a greater number of decisions may potentially be challenged through judicial review. An example is the duty imposed on local authorities to manage air quality in their areas referred to above: it is quite possible that this might be used in the future to compel an authority to adopt a certain course of action.

The likelihood of the courts playing an increasing role in the development of environmental law is further increased by developments in relation to judicial review and EC law. For example, the concept of the supremacy of EC law has been used to develop various doctrines, with the aim of ensuring not only that legislation is passed to implement EC Directives, but also that the laws that are passed are implemented and enforced in practice.

Of course, much of this discussion is only of real relevance to regulatory systems. If, as may be the case in the future, market mechanisms are preferred to regulation, they may represent a force moving in the opposite direction. One of the potential results of deregulation and a shift towards the use of market mechanisms is a decentralization of decisions from government to consumers and industry.

There is another general change that can be identified—that is, a discernible shift away from reliance on flexible standards based on the impact on the receiving environment towards standards based on the use of BAT. This is seen at its clearest in relation to systems of PPC, under which the conditions attached to permits are set by reference to BAT, but it is also an inevitable by-product of a more centralized and formal system. It also follows from the increased involvement of lenders, insurers, and other stakeholders in decisions on environmental management, because they are likely to insist on the use of BAT as a protection against liability or the loss of their stake.[48]

Market mechanisms, or the use of economic tools

The rather general phrases 'market mechanisms', or 'the use of economic tools', are meant to encompass all approaches that seek to use prices, or economic incentives and deterrents, to achieve environmental objectives. The production of goods and services involves not only costs to the producer, but also so-called social costs, which are 'allocated' to society as a whole. These include the costs of pollution and the depletion of natural resources. Regulatory instruments seek to control activities in order to minimize social costs; economic instruments seek to identify these social costs, and to include them in the prices of goods and services, so that the market has a more accurate idea of the full cost of the product or service. For example, pricing systems might signal the true environmental costs of products to consumers, thereby making 'environment-friendly' items cheaper than those that pollute or waste natural resources.

The general characteristic of all economic instruments is that they function through their impact on market signals. Economic instruments are often contrasted with command-and-control regulation, but, in truth, command-and-control and economic instruments supplement and complement each other, often through the implementation of statutory objectives. For example, the Climate Change Programme requires the reduction of greenhouse gas emissions. Some of these reductions can be met through regulation—by means of tightening conditions of PPC permits—and by market-oriented approaches, involving the use of

48 See L. Bergkamp (2003) 12 (3) RECIEL 269 and J. Lipton (1998) 6(6) Int ILR 198.

tradable quotas to allocate the emissions that are allowed in the most economically efficient manner.

In a sense, therefore, these economic tools or instruments are the exact opposite of using the free market, because they normally involve an interference or intervention in the free market for the purpose of environmental protection. They do, however, involve the use of the market, in the sense that they are normally designed to allow consumers and industry to make choices about their actions. By way of contrast, many people would argue that most—although certainly not all—regulatory systems tend to operate so as to remove choice. There is thus a potential confusion in referring simply to 'using the market' for environmental protection ends, because that runs together the policy of allowing an unrestricted free market to allocate resources, based on the assumption that this is somehow more efficient, and the separate policy of intervention in the market for protective purposes.

The Organisation for Economic Co-operation and Development (OECD) has identified five general categories of economic instrument used in environmental protection: charges; subsidies; deposit or refund schemes; the creation of a market in pollution credits; enforcement incentives.[49] There are other classes of instrument that have been categorized as economic, including property rights, liability instruments, and performance bonds. The use of economic instruments in the UK is increasing, having been developed from a basic system of using charging mechanisms and subsidies, to the adoption of more complex and sophisticated measures, such as trading schemes. It also becomes clear that some of the mechanisms are self-standing, while others—such as most charging schemes—require a regulatory framework and proper policing, so must be seen as additional to, rather than separate from, regulatory systems.

Types of economic instrument

A selection of economic tools or instruments is considered below.

Charges for the administrative cost of operating the regulatory system

Charging for the administrative costs of operating the regulatory system now goes under the title of 'cost recovery charging' and has been adopted in relation to a number of regulatory activities. The idea is to recover the regulatory costs that are incurred in granting applications or consents, or in such things as inspecting, monitoring, or policing those consents. The current policy is not to charge for the general costs of operating the whole regulatory system, but to limit the charge to the amount that can be referable to each consent or discharge.

In the interests of administrative simplicity, the charges are normally arranged in bands, rather than being worked out individually. For example, in relation to water pollution, there is a scheme of charging for applications for consent. This is intended to recoup the costs of administering the application procedures for discharge consents. There are also annual charges to recover the cost to the Environment Agency of policing any discharges to controlled waters. These are set so as to recoup the costs associated with inspecting and monitoring discharges, not the full cost of monitoring water quality, which will still be paid for by the taxpayer. Similar schemes operate in relation to applications and permits under the Environmental Permitting regime covering industrial installations and waste management operations.

Cost recovery charging systems may be progressive and thus have a beneficial environmental effect. For example, the charging schemes referred to involve higher charges for discharges that cost more to monitor and these are often those that cause more pollution.

---

49 OECD (1993) *Taxation and the Environment: Complementary Policies.* These are expanded upon in Annex A of the 1990 White Paper, *This Common Inheritance*, Cm 1200.

There has always been a rather different system of charging for discharges to sewers.[50] This involves a rate for domestic consumers, which is normally linked to property value, and a variable rate for trade dischargers, linked to the volume and strength of the discharge, as measured by chemical oxygen demand (COD). This produces a relatively unsophisticated method of charging for the cost of sewage treatment according to the demands made upon the system by the discharge. An incidental effect of concentrating on volume is, however, to reduce the level of water used and the level of waste, and thus to encourage both conservation of resources and recycling.

Charges reflecting the full environmental cost of an activity

The system of charging for sewage discharges shows the potential for use of charging systems that aim to charge for the full environmental cost of an activity. Such systems may be seen as true environmental or pollution taxes. While such taxes are a relatively simple way in which to reflect the environmental cost of an activity or discharge, there are distinct problems with the idea. One is obtaining sufficient information about the discharge or process to make the taxes work properly. This would seem to demand a strong regulatory structure to police the system, although self-monitoring methods may have a large part to play in this respect. Another is the problem of obtaining accurate information about environmental effects on which to base the tax levels. In reality, the levels that are set often indicate that taxes are aimed more at raising revenue than they are at reflecting the full environmental cost of an activity.[51]

Charges to finance environmental or pollution control measures

Some economic instruments work within a regulatory system by directly linking costs to the prevention, abatement, or clean-up of pollution. A number of examples may be given here. Under s. 161 of the Water Resources Act 1991, the Environment Agency may pass costs incurred in preventing or remedying water pollution back to the person who caused it. The Agency may also recover costs incurred in cleaning up unlawful deposits of waste from the occupier or the person who made the deposit.[52] In relation to statutory nuisances, there are similar abatement and cost-recovery powers available to local authorities.[53]

Fines levied in court for offences may also be seen as a form of environmental charge. Indeed, given the nature of environmental offences and the limited moral blame often attached to them, many people treat fines as administrative penalties rather than as true criminal sanctions.[54] The typically low level of fines means that their economic effect is limited, although levels are rising steadily. There is, however, no direct connection between the penalty and the environmental damage caused—primarily because there is no way of ensuring that fines are actually used for environmental benefit. One interesting development in this respect is that a compensation order may be made, in cases in which a statutory nuisance has caused damage, although there is a statutory limit of £5,000 on the sum that may be awarded.[55]

Civil law remedies may also be seen as achieving the same objectives. Many statutes now include civil liability for damage to people or their property, and the creation of a remedy

---

50 Charges are either levied through the trade effluent consent system or under private trade effluent agreement: see further the Online Resource Centre, and W. Howarth and D. McGillivray (2001) *Water Pollution and Water Quality Law*, Crayford: Shaw and Sons, p. 660.

51 N. Gunningham and P. Grabosky (1998) *Smart Regulation: Designing Environmental Policy*, Oxford: Clarendon Press, p. 76.

52 EPA 1990, s. 59.

53 EPA 1990, s. 81.

54 See further Chapter 9, and A. Ogus and C. Abbot (2002) 14 JEL 283, and P. De Prez (2000) 12 JEL 65.

55 See Powers of the Criminal Courts (Sentencing) Act 2000, ss. 130, 131, and *Herbert v. Lambeth London Borough Council* (1991) 90 LGR 310.

of breach of statutory duty may act as a potent method of reallocating costs. For example, the 1992 Oil Pollution Compensation Fund provides for the payment of reasonable costs towards environmental reinstatement.[56] The drawback at present is that there are few civil actions that recognize fully the costs involved in environmental damage. The law has never developed any concept of 'environmental rights', with the result that the only possible civil law claimants are people with private rights. Put more simply, animals, birds, and plants do not yet have civil law rights (although the Directive on Environmental Liability 2004/35/EC may have a limited impact here—see p. 363).

Charges levied on polluting materials or processes

Instead of a charge being levied on the results of pollution, it might be levied on a process or a product. The best example is the landfill tax, whereby a tax is levied on every tonne of waste disposed of in landfill sites—with lower rates and exemptions available for certain classes of waste. It is interesting to note that landfill operators are able to obtain rebates from the tax by setting up environmental trusts that promote sustainable waste management practices. This use of tax income is something of a breakthrough, because, although it has been appreciated for some time that taxes could be used to combat pollution and contamination problems, little has previously been achieved.

The Treasury has, however, always vigorously opposed any attempt to earmark taxes and charges for specific spending purposes—a process known as 'hypothecation'—and, without that, a subsidiary aim of environmental taxes—that is, that they should be linked directly to environmental spending—will not be achieved. For example, the proceeds from the landfill tax could be used to fund the clean-up of 'orphaned' closed landfill sites—that is, those for which the original operator cannot be found or does not have the resources to afford the clean-up—although the environmental trust funds may also be used in the same way. An alternative is that a charge may be reduced for relatively environment-friendly activities. The most obvious example was the reduced tax payable on unleaded petrol compared with that payable on leaded petrol, which led to a significant rise in the use of unleaded fuel. A further example is the use of waste recycling credits for authorities or others who retain waste for the purpose of recycling it, so that a recycler of waste may receive a credit equivalent to the savings made by a waste collection authority from not having to dispose of the waste.[57]

Subsidies, grants, and linked payments

Subsidies and grants are commonly used for environmental ends, although their use within the EC is restricted by the rules on illegal state aids. For example, subsidies are available for the construction of facilities for the improvement of the treatment of agricultural water and silage effluent—both particularly potent, and common, causes of pollution. Care has to be taken that the subsidies achieve the result intended. Some subsidies on forestry and agriculture, for example, have been accused of having detrimental environmental effects, because of their inability to select between beneficial and non-beneficial projects.[58]

Linked payments for environmentally beneficial activities may also be seen in this category. Historically, the prevailing policy in relation to countryside protection was one of voluntariness, whereby farmers and landowners were compensated for agreeing to forgo certain advantages, based on property rights, in the interests of the environment.[59] Nowadays, the dominant approach is to require positive environmental protection measures, such as creating or safeguarding habitat, either through negotiated management agreements or

---

56 See p. 361 (although, sometimes, the most reasonable and cost-effective response to oil pollution incidents is to let nature restore itself rather than to spend excessive sums in trying to remove all traces of oil pollution from the sea).

57 EPA 1990, s. 52; see p. 655.

58 C. Reid (1996) 8 ELM 59.

59 See EC Regulation 1782/2003.

schemes, or through general support payment regimes.[60] Also worth mentioning here is the technique of cross-compliance, whereby agricultural support payments are made conditional on compliance with environmental laws (and reduced or withdrawn in the event of these being breached—see p. 745).

The creation of a market in pollution credits

A further instrument is the use of tradable quotas, or 'emissions trading', which is a method of creating a market in the right to pollute. For example, a total for emissions of a specified substance may be set for a particular area. Firms may then bid for the right to take up a part of that total. Prospective or new polluters would have to buy the rights of existing holders if there were no spare capacity. By restricting the available emissions, prices would be driven up, providing an incentive to reduce emissions or to develop alternatives.

The idea is most developed in the USA,[61] but the groundwork for its use in the UK is laid in the Environmental Protection Act (EPA) 1990, s. 3(5), which allows the Secretary of State to establish total emissions of any substance either nationally or for a limited area, and to allocate quotas, with power to reduce progressively the total allowed. This provision has been supplemented with a power to introduce emissions trading schemes under the Pollution Prevention and Control Act 1999 and the Waste and Emissions Trading Act 2003. This power can cover all emissions, including releases to water and land, although the first target has been carbon dioxide emissions in order to meet internationally agreed reduction targets that have been set to combat climate change (see p. 527).

Deposit and refund schemes

Although deposit and refund schemes are clearly severe interferences with a free market, it is also clear that they may have an enormous impact on the amount of waste produced. Traditionally, in the UK, voluntary mechanisms have been preferred over instruments imposed by law. By way of example, the UK government intervened in the *Danish Bottles* case in the European Court of Justice (ECJ), supporting the EC Commission's argument that a Danish law requiring drinks containers to be returnable was contrary to the free market principles of the EC. The ECJ upheld most of the Danish scheme, despite its clear anticompetitive effect, on the grounds that the aim of environmental protection justified some interference with the operation of the single market within the EC.[62]

Future uses of economic instruments

The above summary is not intended to be an exhaustive list of those market mechanisms that might be tried, or even of those that are already in use, but to give an idea of the types of instrument that may be available. Other examples include the use of performance bonds, which require a deposit that is refunded on completion of a task such as the clean-up of a contaminated site or the maintenance of aftercare conditions.[63]

As stated before, there is little doubt that market-related instruments will increasingly be used in the future. Indeed, they might currently be said to be the '*hottest growth industry in environmental law*'.[64] One reason for this is that market mechanisms have a degree of political acceptability that crosses party-political, ideological boundaries. There is a strong link

---

60 See, on nature conservation management agreements, p. 700, and on general agri-environmental payments, p. 745.

61 See, generally, R. Kosobud (ed.) (2000) *Emissions Trading: Environmental Policy's New Approach*, New York: John Wiley.

62 Case C-302/86 *Commission v. Denmark* [1988] ECR 4607, discussed at Case 7.4.

63 Landfill (England and Wales) Regulations 2002, SI 2002/1559, reg. 8(2).

64 E. Orts (1995) 89 NW UL Rev 1227.

with the principle of choice—the idea that people should be given a choice of how to act, as long as their actions do not breach some generally accepted limits. This idea is seen most strongly in the realm of town and country planning, in which the importance attached to market forces is made explicit in much of central government policy advice. The principle is also seen in relation to such things as the preference for voluntary methods of protection in the countryside and pollution control systems, which set objectives, while leaving producers to work out for themselves how to achieve them. For example, the adoption of the BAT standard in PPC theoretically allows operators to minimize pollution by using the most economically efficient method (see p. 505). There is also a strong link with the related policy of deregulation discussed in Chapter 5. Among other things, this policy amounts to a rejection of imposed restrictions in favour of agreed ones and a removal of unnecessary state powers.

Within the EC, the Commission has also suggested a shift in EC environmental policy towards the greater use of economic instruments rather than the administrative regulation approach.[65] Although the Commission's proposals have seen little positive action, it is clear that European initiatives are likely to become more prevalent in the coming years, with the introduction of the EC emissions trading system and full cost-recovery charging for water use—although not for pollution—under the Water Framework Directive (2000/60/EC).

The Polluter Pays Principle

The EC can claim another important contribution to the development of economic instruments: its environmental policy has always included the adoption of the 'Polluter Pays Principle', although it was probably the OECD that first popularized the idea in the early 1970s.[66] The principle basically means that the producer of goods or other items should be responsible for the costs of preventing or dealing with any pollution that the process causes.[67] This includes environmental costs, as well as direct costs to people or property. It also covers costs incurred in avoiding pollution and not only those related to remedying any damage. There is a very strong link between the principle and the idea that prevention is better than cure. It will also be clear from the foregoing discussion that these costs should include the full environmental costs, not only those that are immediately tangible.

The relevance of this principle to the discussion of economic instruments is obvious, because a producer will have to pass on any costs in the price of goods to the ultimate consumer. But this is only a principle: it has no legal force and there is no agreed definition that has anything approaching the precision of a statute. On the contrary, there has frequently been dispute over its exact scope, especially over the limits on payments for damage caused.

Even when the question of payment is relatively settled, there is a further issue as to the identity of the polluter. There are many examples of the difficulty of identifying the 'polluter', including the Contaminated Land Regime in EPA 1990, Pt 2A (see further Box 16.5), and under the Agricultural Nitrates Directive 91/676/EEC (*R v. Secretary of State for the Environment and Minister of Agriculture, Fisheries and Food, ex parte Standley* [1999] Env LR 801—see p. 619). In any case in which certain polluters are targeted or excluded for administrative or other purposes, the principle is watered down to 'some polluters pay', which weakens its legitimacy and application. Like other environmental principles, it is essentially a guide to desirable courses of action, but it is fairly clear that it has rarely been fully satisfied in either EC or UK environmental legislation.

65 See, e.g., European Commission, Fifth Environmental Action Programme (1992) *Towards Sustainability*, and COM 97(9) on environmental taxes and charges in the single market.

66 OECD (1972) *Environment and Economics: Guiding Principles Concerning International Economic Aspects of Environmental Policies*, and (1974) *The Implementation of the Polluter Pays Principle*.

67 See, for a discussion of this principle in different contexts, N. de Sadeleer (2002) *Environmental Principles: From Political Slogans to Legal Rules*, Oxford: Oxford University Press.

As a result, the principle has sometimes seemed to be all things to all people and has even been used to justify views with which it has little connection—for example, the suggestion that producers may pollute as long as they pay for it, which is a complete misunderstanding of the principle's true meaning and the potential abuse of such an imprecise phrase should be appreciated.

Self-regulation as a tool for environmental protection

One of the consequences of the deregulatory move away from direct methods of regulation has been the upsurge in interest in developing effective mechanisms based upon voluntary action. Such action can be termed 'self-regulation'.[68] This term can have quite precise definitions—for example, in relation to a group that is responsible for the action of its members without any form of governmental or regulatory supervision. For the purposes of this discussion, the common identifying factor is that self-regulatory mechanisms are underpinned by voluntary action, rather than by compulsion. The triggers for such action may be diverse, including the threat of compulsory action, commercial benefit (such as cost savings or green marketing initiatives), or even a shift in values that attaches greater importance to environmental protection.[69]

These examples indicate that there are factors other than legal factors that can be influential in changing behaviour. Thus, economic benefits that accrue from increasing sales of so-called 'environmentally friendly' goods or the social benefits, such as employee satisfaction or enhanced public image, which result from environmental improvement can act as regulatory controls. Moreover, these triggers suggest that there are very few occasions on which actions are purely 'voluntary'. Indeed, there is a broad spectrum of mechanisms that can fall within this definition of self-regulation, ranging from the purely voluntary—in the sense that there is no form of compulsion at all—through to mechanisms that use a mixture of direct regulation and self-regulation.[70]

The strengths of self-regulatory mechanisms are clear, in that they are quick, flexible, non-interventionist, and therefore more acceptable to the companies that are regulated. Perhaps most importantly, they encourage a sense of environmental responsibility within the regulated companies, which should promote environmental improvement not as a reaction to legislation, but as part of corporate development generally. The disadvantages include that the voluntary nature of the mechanisms often means that there are no explicit enforcement mechanisms; there are also problems of so-called 'free-riders'—that is, of companies that do not adopt self-regulation and therefore possibly gain an advantage over competitors, while employing lower environmental standards. Additionally, there is a lack of transparency and accountability, and there is the problem of standards being set that are at the lower end of what is achievable, rather than the setting of goals that might not be attained.[71]

Given that the range of mechanisms is wide and the suggested definition of self-regulation imprecise, it is possible to set out only a selection of self-regulatory mechanisms below.

Management standards

Theoretically, management standards might have been included in the list of environmental standards that were discussed earlier in this chapter, or within the discussion of economic

---

68 See further S. Gaines and C. Kimber (2001) 13(2) JEL 157.

69 See Box 3.3.

70 See, e.g., the position of compliance schemes in relation to the producer responsibility legislation or the relationship between the links in the waste management chain under the duty of care—see Chapter 18.

71 See Gunningham and Grabosky (1998) p. 50.

instruments above, because they can have a direct economic impact. It is, however, argu-ably most appropriate to consider such standards within the context of self-regulatory tools, because they are voluntary and there are no specific legal sanctions for either failing to adopt the standards or to comply with them once adopted. At its widest, the term 'environmental management standards' (EMSs) can be said to cover such things as the technical compe-tence and financial security of a regulated operator. This would include the 'technical envir-onmental permitting' in relation to competence.[72] The more common use of management standards, however, relates generally to the use of systems of management that measure environmental performance and provide benchmarks against which the improvement of a company can be measured.

The systems are backed by a certification procedure, which provides a method of for-mal and objective verification for the system. The first EMS was introduced as a British standard—BS7750—in 1994 and the general requirements of this standard have provided the framework for others that have been adopted more widely. BS7750 was to influence the establishment of other EMSs, including an international standard ISO 14001, which, in turn, triggered the withdrawal of BS7750 in 1997, and the EC Eco-Management and Audit Scheme (EMAS) under EC Regulation 1836/93/EC.

These standards are based on a quality management approach, with the result that no specific levels of environmental performance are stipulated in the EMS itself, other than a general commitment to comply with all applicable environmental legislation; the setting of environmental objectives is a subjective matter for the company itself. These objectives are measured against a publicly produced environmental policy, which includes the minimum commitment of compliance with all legal standards while improving environmental per-formance. This commitment required the company to understand the environmental effects created by the business, to set both broad and detailed goals for environmental perform-ance with specific targets, to set up an active programme for managing the environmental performance that was designed to achieve these goals and targets, and to set up a system for auditing the EMS. Adherence to the requirements of the EMS is verified on an annual basis by accredited independent verifiers. The ISO standard commits companies to a goal of 'pollution prevention' rather than to environmental improvement, while the EMAS scheme also requires companies to establish procedures to protect the environment and to commit themselves to continuous environmental improvement.

The most significant difference between EMAS and ISO 14001 is that EMAS requires a company to publish a report setting out its environmental performance every three years and to have that report verified by an independent body that has been accredited for that purpose. The aim of such a report is to enable stakeholders, such as members of the public, to assess whether the company is meeting the requirements of the EMAS standard.

The uptake of the standards has been steady rather than spectacular, with an emphasis on those industries that have come under contractual pressures from customers, particularly in the global marketplace. Although the standards for the measurement of environmental per-formance can ensure that there is a degree of transparency and objectivity of assessment, it might be argued that the use of EMSs as a trigger for environmental improvement has been less successful. One of the main defects in the system is the subjective nature of the setting of improvement goals: it is perfectly possible for a company that achieves compliance with legal requirements to set very low targets and still achieve certification. On this level, an EMS is little more than an objective statement of keeping within the law. This defect, coupled with general antipathy towards the adoption of the standards, means that the use and effective-ness of EMS is still in some doubt.[73]

---

72 Environmental Permitting (England and Wales) Regulations 2007, SI 2007/3538, Sch. 5, para. 13.

73 See (2000) ENDS Report 311, 27–9, and (2002) ENDS Report 327, 31–3.

Information-based mechanisms

Although there are legal requirements to make certain environmental information available to the public through the systems of pollution control registers, there are other voluntary mechanisms whereby environmental information is made available to the public on wider issues. Companies have, for example, incorporated environmental information into annual reports.[74] Corporate environmental reporting has been patchily adopted by UK companies, with a wide variety of both quality and quantity of information, and an emphasis on industrial sectors that carry out particularly sensitive environmental operations.[75] Another interesting use of information is through the Environment Agency's 'name and shame' strategy whereby information on environmental performance—more typically, environmental failings—are disseminated publicly through annual reports, which identify the worst polluters by reference to industry sectors and numbers of pollution offences. This is made available not only to the general public, but also to institutional investors and other commercially interested parties, such as insurers and trade customers.[76]

Other information-based mechanisms include eco-labelling or certification processes that give consumers information about the environmental impacts of goods and products.[77] This scheme has had only limited success, because it has proved to be administratively cumbersome, with the consequence that relatively small numbers of products have been considered and the market credibility of the scheme has been undermined. Criteria are developed by the European Commission to enable the environmental impact of a product to be analysed by taking into account the whole of its life cycle. Product groups that have been covered under the scheme include light bulbs, paints, personal computers, footwear, textiles, and washing machines.

The Regulation was originally implemented in the UK through the establishment of an Eco-Labelling Board in November 1992. This Board was, however, abolished in 1999 as part of a move towards an integrated products policy that places eco-labelling in a curtailed role in reducing the environmental impacts of consumer products.[78] Although the Europe-wide system continues to operate, the prospects for a national eco-labelling scheme appear to diminish. There is likely to be greater emphasis placed upon the top of the supply chain—that is, the manufacturers of products—providing information on the environmental impacts, rather than the provision of general labelling criteria.[79]

Private agreements

The use of private agreements in environmental regulation ranges from the formal statutory mechanisms found in planning legislation[80] and nature conservation legislation,[81] to the more informal agreements that have been negotiated between government or the regulator and individual companies or industry sectors.[82] Although the uptake of these more informal agreements has traditionally been more prevalent in other countries,[83] the UK has started

---

74 See Gunningham and Grabosky (1998) p. 62.

75 For example, mining—see (2002) ENDS Report 327, 28–30.

76 See Box 9.14.

77 See EC Regulation 880/92/EEC, as revised and extended by Regulation 1980/00/EC, which introduced eco-labelling, and see L. Krämer (2000) YEEL 123.

78 See p. 675.

79 See p. 308.

80 Planning and Compulsory Purchase Act 2004, s. 46.

81 Countryside Act 1968, s. 15.

82 See Box 15.6.

83 Particularly the USA and the Netherlands—see Stewart (2001) 29 Cap UL Rev 21.

to adopt this mechanism with an increasing frequency.[84] The nature of these agreements differs widely, and is dependent upon the parties[85] to the agreement and what is required (for example, general or specific targets for reducing pollution). At a European level, the European Commission has produced guidelines on the use of such agreements between public authorities and industry.[86]

There are many criticisms of such voluntary agreements. Many of these reflect the criticisms of self-regulatory mechanisms generally, such as a lack of transparency or accountability, no public participation, and a lack of satisfactory enforcement mechanisms.[87] Most of these stem from the fact that the status of many of these agreements is uncertain, given that they are neither private contracts, nor agreements made under statutory powers. It would appear that the role of these agreements is to provide a further mechanism that is complementary to direct regulation. They allow government or regulators to set targets and goals that go beyond that which could be required under the legislative scheme.

Whether private agreements are actually used in this way is a matter of debate. Experience has shown that such agreements have been used to set targets that, at best, are the same as those that would have been imposed under direct regulation.[88]

The role of criminal and civil law

This chapter has provided an outline of the main regulatory techniques used to address environmental problems. As such, most of the techniques used are administered or policed by public bodies. This is by no means a comprehensive list, both in terms of the types of regulatory instrument used and the range of *legal* techniques used as a part of, or subsidiary to, the regulatory system. As far as the latter is concerned, both the criminal and civil—or private—law have a role to play as legal techniques to be used for environmental protection.

The criminal law can be used either to provide direct criminal sanctions for environmental harm, or in a subsidiary and complementary role within a regulatory system. It tends to be of greater influence when used in the second way. This is because the main purpose of the criminal law is to punish clearly identified wrongs. Yet, in relation to many environmental matters, it is often impossible to identify wrong without reference to other factors. For example, it is clearly desirable to have industry and many other activities that may cause pollution. The question is not a simple one of whether to have them, but a more difficult one of how much pollution is acceptable. That requires a balancing of the various factors involved against what is reasonable—a discretionary, political process, for which the regulatory system is well suited. But the criminal law is rather inadequate for such a balancing process and thus tends to be used mainly to deal either with clear acts of environmental vandalism, or to support the regulatory system once it has decided what is, and what is not, acceptable.[89]

As pointed out in the section on charges, the civil law can be seen as a form of market mechanism, so it is worth making a few general comments about civil liability in this chapter. There is little doubt that the last few years have seen a great increase in interest in the use that

---

84 For example, in relation to the Climate Change Levy, whereby energy-intensive sectors have been offered tax reductions on the basis that they enter into voluntary agreements to improve energy efficiency agreements: See B. Richardson and K. Chanwai (2003) 15(1) JEL 39.

85 For example, the European Commission, national governments, regional bodies, or regulatory agencies, on the one side, and industry sectors or individual operators, on the other.

86 Communication from the Commission to the Council and the European Parliament on Environmental Agreements, COM(96) 561.

87 See p. 536.

88 See Box 15.6 on voluntary agreements and the car sector.

89 See Box 9.1 and further Chapter 9.

can be made of civil law mechanisms—by policymakers, as well as by lawyers.[90] This interest has been heightened by the development of an EC-wide system of civil liability that was the subject of intense negotiations for over ten years, beginning in 1993. The long delay and relative weakness of the final version of the Directive on Environmental Liability (2004/35/EC) reflect the fundamental controversies surrounding rules that attempt to merge different approaches to environmental liability across member States (see p. 363).

The imposition of civil liability has other effects as well as simply sorting out the question of liability for specific incidents: it acts as an incentive to act in a particular way, because of the high possible risks. In so doing, it fulfils the Precautionary Principle and fits in well with the current EC emphasis on shared responsibility, because producers will act so as to reduce and manage risks themselves. It thus acts as a stimulus to integrate risk management principles into all levels of business decision making, because there is little doubt that the threat of civil action—at least for personal injury or property damage—is a potent one, especially in an age when insurance against such risks is hard to obtain.

Optimal environmental regulation

In concluding this chapter, it should be pointed out that no single regulatory instrument can be successful on its own. Historically, the means of addressing environmental problems was through the use of legal regulation—typically, a system of consents or permits, backed by criminal sanctions for breach. As our understanding of the complexity of the environment, and of the causes of pollution and degradation, has increased, so the range of regulatory instruments or tools has broadened. Traditional 'command and control' has its supporters,[91] but regulation cannot properly address every issue[92]—and the same could be said of other types of regulatory instrument. For example, economic instruments have been criticized for failing to address moral concerns.[93] Other instruments are palpably inefficient or ineffective on their own.

The key to using the 'tools' in the environmental lawyer's 'toolbox' is to combine different instruments so that the strength of certain types of tool complements the weaknesses of others, and vice versa. This is not to say that all instruments must be used in every situation. Indeed, this 'kitchen sink' or 'smorgasbordism' approach to selecting regulatory instruments and environmental standards has been argued to be 'seriously sub-optimal' and inefficient.[94] Optimal environmental regulation depends largely on combining those instruments that work well together to address particular environmental problems. This is a much broader question than simply: 'Which tool(s) will work best?' It involves understanding what the problem is, what standards to apply, who will be affected, which institutions will administer any new controls, and what hurdles might prevent the efficient and effective implementation of any regulatory system that is finally adopted.

CHAPTER SUMMARY

1   Administrative regulation is the most common method of addressing environmental problems in the UK. Administrative regulation is the application of rules and procedures by public bodies, so as to achieve a measure of control over activities carried on by individuals and firms.

90 For example, see the collection of essays in J. Lowry and R. Edmunds (eds) (2000) *Environmental Protection and the Common Law*, Oxford: Hart.

91 For example, see H. Latin (1985) 37 Stan LR 1267 and W. Wagner (2000) U Ill L Rev 83.

92 A. Alm (1992) EPA Journal, 18 May.

93 M. Sagoff (1988) *The Economy of the Earth*, Cambridge: Cambridge University Press, esp. ch. 9.

94 See R. Hahn (1993) 102 Yale LJ 1719, and Gunningham and Grabosky (1998) p. 389.

2   The system of making regulations to address environmental problems involves a number of stages, such as deciding what policies to adopt, what standards should apply, applying those standards through some form of consent, enforcing those standards, providing public information about the system, and monitoring and improving the system in the light of experience.

3   There are different types of standard that are used in environmental regulation. Generally, these can be divided into those that apply to the receiving environment (target standards) and those that apply to emissions (source standards).

4   Other standards can be used including process, product, and use standards. Each standard has advantages and disadvantages.

5   Traditionally, the UK has used target standards, although European Directives based upon emissions standards have meant that different approaches have been adopted in recent years.

6   UK regulatory systems can be said to exhibit a pragmatic and flexible approach, involving an explicit balancing of environmental factors with such things as economic and social considerations.

7   Other characteristics that can be used to describe the UK approach to environmental regulation include the use of discretion to set and enforce standards, gradualism and reliance on scientific evidence, and the decentralization of much decision making.

8   There is an increasing use of instruments other than administrative regulation. These include the use of economic instruments and self-regulation. The challenge is to find the correct blend of instruments that will provide the most effective results.

Q   QUESTIONS

1   What types of standard are used in environmental regulation?

2   Compare and contrast the different types of environmental standard in terms of the following.

   a Enforceability.

   b Cost.

   c Administrative simplicity.

   d Fairness.

   e Effectiveness.

3   What are the advantages and disadvantages of different methods of regulating environmental problems?

4   A private company has been developed a new chemical substance, 'terranium'. It is thought to be harmful to humans, plants, and animals at certain concentrations. How might an environmental regulatory system operate in order to control the risks associated with terranium? What standards might be applied and what regulatory instruments used? What further information about terranium would you want to know?

5   In what circumstances might voluntary mechanisms be more effective than compulsory regulation?

6   Give some examples of the use of economic instruments in UK environmental regulation. What role do economic instruments play in conjunction with other regulatory instruments? Are they effective?

FURTHER READING

Because the range of reading on regulation generally and on environmental regulation specifically is vast, the selection of further reading depends largely upon the nature of any further research. An excellent starting point for any deeper reading is N. Gunningham and P. Grabosky (1998) *Smart Regulation: Designing*

Environmental Policy, Oxford: Clarendon Press. For a historical perspective, see J. McLoughlin and E. Bellinger (1993) *Environmental Pollution Control: An Introduction to Principles and Practice of Administration*, London: Graham and Trotman, which is a very readable (if a little dated) account that combines legal and adminis-trative insights, and D. Robinson (1998) 'Regulatory evolution in pollution control' in T. Jewell and J. Steele (eds) *Law in Environmental Decision Making*, Oxford: Clarendon Press, which traces the different phases of regulatory evolution with an analysis of the reasons for those changes.

On the specific issue of the various types of standard that are available (and much more on environmen-tal decision making in general), see the 21st Report of the Royal Commission on Environmental Pollution (1998) *Setting Environmental Standards*, Cm 4053. R. Macrory, 'Regulating in a risky environment' (2001) CLP 619 provides an analysis of command-and-control regulation in comparison to newer forms of regu-latory instrument. A study of the different types of regulatory technique, with a comparison in terms of specific benchmarks such as accountability, efficiency, and effectiveness, can be found in C. Hilson (2000) *Regulating Pollution: A UK and EC Perspective*, Oxford: Hart.

The nature and role of environmental standards are discussed in G. Lubbe-Wolff, 'Efficient environmen-tal legislation: on different philosophies of pollution control in Europe' (2001) 13 JEL 79, and there is an analysis of the true nature of the apparent conflict between the UK and Europe in relation to the use of standards in N. Haigh (1990) *EEC Environmental Policy and Britain*, 2nd edn, London: Longman. A broader examination of the political background to the changing relationship between the UK and Europe can be found in P. Lowe and S. Ward (eds) (1998) *Britain Environmental Policy and Europe: Politics and Policy in Transition*, London: Routledge. Also on this, see R. Wurzel (2002) *Environmental Policymaking in Britain, Germany and the European Union*, Manchester, Manchester University Press, which challenges the notion that the UK prefers, or preferred, quality standards, and Germany, emission standards.

On the 'British approach' to pollution control, see D. Vogel (1986) *National Styles of Regulation*, Ithaca, NY: Cornell University Press, which, despite its age, still provides a thought-provoking comparison between UK and US approaches. This book claims to be '*an examination of British environmental policy as seen through the eyes of a student of American politics*', and consists of a comparison of approaches to environ-mental regulation in the UK and the USA. More recent coverage can be found in R. Kagan and L. Axelrad (eds) (2000) *Regulatory Encounters*, Berkeley, Calif: University of California Press. In particular, the first part of this book contains comparative studies of the regulatory styles in the USA, UK, and other countries, by examining the different approaches to waste and contaminated land regulation. Although it is tempting to think of regulation as being a two-way relationship between polluter and regulator, the reality is more com-plex. R. Kagan, N. Gunningham and D. Thornton (2002) *Explaining Corporate Environmental Performance: How Does Regulation Matter?*, UC Berkeley School of Law Public Law and Legal Theory Research Paper No. 78, is an empirical study of pulp and paper mills in various (English-speaking) countries and looks at the impact of regulation versus other influences on corporate behaviour. The empirical literature on enforce-ment mentioned at the end of Chapter 9 should also be mentioned here (because, in theory, compliance is a proxy for effectiveness).

In terms of newer approaches to regulation, a good introduction to various aspects of self-regulation can be found in S. Gaines and C. Kimber, 'Redirecting self-regulation' (2001) 13 JEL 157, which argues for a redir-ecting of self-regulation within the context of the private, as opposed to public, law contexts. A more the-oretical (and perhaps more difficult) article on the fundamentals of self-regulation can be found in E. Orts, 'Reflexive environmental law' (1995) 89(4) NW UL 1227. The use of environmental agreements are cov-ered in E. Orts and K. Deketelaere (2000) *Environmental Contracts: Comparative Approaches to Regulatory Innovation in the United States and Europe*, The Hague: Kluwer Law International, J. Verschuuren, 'EC envir-onmental law and self-regulation in the member States: in search of a legislative framework' (2000) 1 Yearbook of European Environmental Law 103, and A. Ross and J. Rowan-Robinson, 'Behind closed doors: the use of agreements in the UK to protect the environment' (1999) Env LR 82. There is an interesting study of the implementation and effect of the use of environmental management systems in A. Gouldson and J. Murphy (1998) *Regulatory Realities*, London: Earthscan, particularly in ch. 4. On the scope for adaptive approaches alongside other tools, especially for responding to uncertainty, a good overview is J. Jones

'Regulatory design for scientific uncertainty' (2007) JEL 347. There is a fair degree of overlap between adaptive regulation and so-called 'new governance' approaches to regulation, on which a good starting place is J. Scott and D. Trubek, 'Mind the gap: law and new approaches to governance in the European Union' (2002) 8 ELJ 1.

An interested reader would find many illuminating parallels with other areas of regulation that are described in general texts on regulatory theory, of which the most accessible and relevant include: B. Morgan and K. Yeung (2007) *Introduction to Law and Regulation: Text and Materials*, Cambridge: Cambridge University Press (which is good on the range of regulatory tools and on the interface with areas such as rights); R. Baldwin and M. Cave (1999) *Understanding Regulation*, Oxford: Oxford University Press, which has excellent chapters on standard setting, regulating risks, and regulatory enforcement; R. Baldwin, C. Scott, and C. Hood (eds) (1999) *A Reader on Regulation*, Oxford: Oxford University Press; A. Ogus (1994) *Regulation: Legal Form and Economic Theory*, Oxford: Oxford University Press. The last of these provides clear description of the use of different types of standard, and is a nice bridge into other texts that examine the relationship between economics and environmental law. Although there are many such texts, the starting point should be D. Pearce, A. Markandya, and E. Barbier (1989) *Blueprint for a Green Economy*, London: Earthscan, which has a number of sequels, the latest of which is D. Pearce and E. Barbier (2000) *Blueprint for a Sustainable Economy*, London: Earthscan. These provide an interesting study in how economic theory has developed over the last twenty years. Another useful study is T. O'Riordan (1996) *Eco-Taxation*, London: Earthscan.

For a justification of economic instruments over command-and-control regulation, see B. Ackerman and R. Stewart, 'Reforming environmental law: the democratic case for market incentives' (1988) Colum J Envtl L 171 and, more recently, R. Stewart (2000) 'Economic incentives for environmental protection: opportunities and obstacles' in R. Revesz, P. Sands, and R. Stewart (eds) *Environmental Law: The Economy and Sustainable Development*, Cambridge: Cambridge University Press. A counterpoint to these is D Driesen (2006) 'Economic instruments for sustainable development' in B. Richardson and S. Wood (eds) *Environmental Law for Sustainability*, Oxford: Hart, which argues in particular that traditional economic tools do not work well in providing for transformative technological innovation, which Driesen sees as central in working towards sustainable development.

Finally, B. Richardson (ed.) (2002) *Environmental Regulation Through Financial Organisations*, The Hague: Kluwer, goes beyond the range of economic instruments discussed here.

@ WEB LINKS

There are not very many good websites that capture the general nature of the fundamentals of environmental regulation. For an examination of regulatory approaches in context, have a look at the government's Better Regulation Task Force's report on *Producer Responsibility*, available online at **www.brtf.gov.uk**. This report looks at the regulatory process in relation to end-of-life vehicles and waste electronic and electrical equipment. For the latest thinking on regulatory tools at the European level, the Sixth Environmental Action Programme is available at **europa.eu.int/comm/environment/newprg/**. The Organisation for Economic Co-operation and Development (OECD) has a number of interesting resources. The Organisation has been a leading advocate for the role of economic instruments, as well as regulatory reform. There is a lot of material of a specific environmental nature, as well as more general information, to be found at **www.oecd.org**. Domestically, the Royal Commission on Environmental Pollution (RCEP) is one of the best sources of information on environmental regulation and can be found at **www.rcep.org.uk**. In addition to the excellent introduction to environmental standards found in the 21st Report, the other reports are an excellent way of looking at many different contemporary environmental challenges, and with discussion and assessment of the various possible regulatory responses. The main weakness of the site is that the majority of reports are summarized, with only the most recent to be found in full.

9 Environmental crime

Overview

This chapter is concerned with environmental crime and the enforcement of environmental law. The chapter starts with some consideration of the difficult definition of 'environmental crime', including the distinction between moral and legal meanings of the term. We then consider some of the basic framework of environmental crime, which helps to explain some of the approaches to the enforcement of environmental regulation. For example, the fact that many environmental crimes are strict liability offences explains why the rate of successful prosecutions is high (at around 95 per cent), but it may also provide an explanation as to why some consider the sanctions that are imposed by the courts to be too low.

The largest part of this chapter describes the enforcement practices adopted by regulatory agencies in England and Wales. There is a vast discrepancy between the number of potential offences committed and the number of prosecutions, which is explained by the 'cooperative approach' adopted by enforcement agencies. The reasons for this approach are discussed, along with alternative approaches. Because the majority of environmental crime is policed by the Environment Agency, there is greater emphasis placed upon the laws, policies, and practices that relate to the Agency's activities, as opposed to those of other environmental regulators, such as Natural England, local authorities, or HM Customs and Excise (in relation to the landfill tax).

At the end of this chapter, you should be able to:

✔ appreciate some of the difficulties in defining 'environmental crime';

✔ appreciate a basic outline of the legal characteristics of environmental crimes, including the nature of, justification for, and consequences of strict liability;

✔ identify and understand the law on corporate and individual liability for environmental offences;

✔ identify the main regulatory agencies with responsibilities for enforcing environmental crime and understand the main factors that influence the way in which they operate;

✔ appreciate the main issues involved in enforcing environmental law, including the characteristics that underpin the 'British' approach to enforcement;

✔ identify and distinguish the different approaches that might be taken when enforcing environmental law;

✔ identify in outline the main sanctions for environmental crimes;

✔ appreciate and evaluate the current dissatisfaction with the existing structures, processes, and outcomes of the enforcement of environmental regulation.

What is 'environmental crime'?

Various writers have attempted to define what is meant by an 'environmental crime' (see Box 9.1). As with other key terms in environmental law, these definitions tend to reflect different perspectives. Some writers consider that environmental crime should cover activities that may be lawful or licensed, but which cause significant environmental harm.[1] For example, activities such as peat extraction at nationally important nature conservation sites under the benefit of long-standing planning permissions might be considered to be 'criminal' in the eyes of many conservationists (see Box 19.4). Other influential perspectives could be spatial—that is, looking at crimes across international boundaries, as compared to more localized amenity offences[2]—or might relate to race or social justice—that is, to the inequalities of the causes and effects of environmental harm as between the developed and developing world, and between rich corporations and poorer sections of society.[3] These general notions of environmental crime convey a sense of judgment about what is 'wrong' about certain activities, but take us no further.

The definitions set out in Box 9.1 reflect different perspectives on environmental crime, from moral and philosophical, to legal and local amenity-led perspectives. Each of these perspectives characterize environmental crime differently from a broad interpretation incorporating the notion of environmental harm that may be lawful as a crime, to more legalistic definitions that place law at the centre of defining what is 'right' and 'wrong'.

BOX 9.1 Definitions of environmental crime

An environmental crime is an act committed with the intent to harm or with a potential to cause harm to ecological and/or biological systems and for the purpose of securing business or personal advantage.

(M. Clifford (1998) *Environmental Crime: Enforcement, Policy and Social Responsibility*, Gaithersburg: Aspen, p. 26)

An environmental crime is an unauthorised act or omission that violates the law and is therefore subject to criminal prosecution and criminal sanction. This offence harms or endangers people's physical safety or health as well as the environment itself. It serves the interests of either organizations—typically corporations—or individuals.

(Y. Situ and D. Emmons (2000) *Environmental Crime: The Criminal Justice System's Role in Protecting the Environment*, Thousand Oaks, Calif: Sage, p. 3)

Environmental crime includes littering, abandoned vehicles, graffiti, fly posting, dog fouling, fly-tipping, dumped business waste, vandalism, abandoned shopping trolleys and noise nuisance.

(*Tackling Environmental Crime Together*, available online at **www.together.gov.uk**)

Environmental crime includes all offences either created by statute or developed under the common law that relate to the environment.

(Sixth Report of the Environmental Audit Committee (Session 2003–04) *Environmental Crime*)

---

1 See M. Halsey (1997) Current Issues in Criminology 217.
2 For example, illegal transfrontier shipments of waste as compared to local fly-tipping.
3 See, e.g., in relation to the literature on environmental justice, R. Bullard (1993) Yale J Intl L 319.

The definition of environmental crime matters because it helps to frame many of the key aspects of criminal liability for environmental harm:

- whether an activity is viewed as a technical regulatory breach or as a 'crime against the environment';

- whether liability for environmental crime should be strict and, if so, what the justification is for this;

- the extent to which offenders should be viewed as truly criminal;

- the attitudes that should be taken towards enforcing the law;

- the sanctions that should be imposed for breach.

Legal approaches to defining environmental crime

The most obvious way for lawyers to define environmental crime is to include only those actions or omissions that directly or indirectly damage the environment and which are prohibited by law. This has the advantage of being value-free and objective. This approach includes both direct polluting acts (for example, depositing waste without a licence) and indirect omissions (for example, failing to pay landfill tax). But taking a legalistic, positivist approach to defining environmental crime still leaves a number of issues.

First, the problematic and uncertain definition of environmental law raises questions of where the outer boundaries of environmental crime are located. For example, compare and contrast the third and fourth definitions in Box 9.1. The fourth definition relies on a common understanding of what statutes 'relate to the environment'. Whereas this might not be an issue in relation to core topics such as pollution control and wildlife crime, there are other areas in which there is uncertainty. The third definition refers to the local environment, and includes such things as vandalism and graffiti, which might otherwise be classified as 'criminal damage'. While the definitions in Box 9.1 are not mutually exclusive, they illustrate that a legal approach can elicit broad and narrow definitions of 'environmental crime'.

Secondly, and following on from the first problem, a legal definition of environmental crime is uncertain, because there is such a wide range of activities and offenders to which the phrase could be applied. Under a broad definition, environmental crimes can be committed by the careless driver, the fly-tipping 'man in a white van', organized criminal gangs, the egg collector, and the global corporation. As we can see from the definitions in Box 9.1, typical offences might include littering, antisocial behaviour (such as noise nuisances), trade in endangered species, and major incidents of oil pollution. Thus, while it may be possible to characterize particular groups of offences by reference to particular criteria, these would not necessarily be applicable across all possible environmental offences. For example, the typical characteristics of pollution control offences may not be the equivalent of typical 'wildlife crimes' or landfill tax evasion.[4]

Thirdly, taking a legalistic approach to defining environmental crime has jurisdictional and geographical limitations. While there are some international agreements that require signatories to impose standard criminal sanctions,[5] there is no guarantee that an environmental crime in one country will be a crime in another. This is particularly the case in civil law countries, where the distinction between administrative offences and truly criminal offences is significant.[6]

---

4 For examples of typical characteristics of pollution control offences, see P. De Prez (2000) 12 JEL 65 at 66.

5 Examples include illegal waste transport and trade in endangered species.

6 H-U. Paeffgen (1991) 13 JEL 247.

BOX 9.2 Europe and the definition of 'Environmental Crime'

In relation to the EC, the issue of deciding who has the authority to determine whether environmentally harmful conduct should be subject to criminal sanctions is particularly topical and is the subject of a long-running dispute between the European Commission and the member States. In Case C-176/03 *Commission v. Council* [2006] Env LR 18, the ECJ effectively determined that the Commission had the right to define environmental crimes and sanctions. In doing so, the Court chose to distinguish environmental crimes—with their essential regulatory, economic, and social dimensions—from more traditional crimes. The Court held that the EC Treaty gave the Commission the power to lay down common criminal rules for environmental crimes and sanctions, which it could use if it could show that there was a need to do so. The Court stated:

> As a general rule, neither criminal law nor the rules of criminal procedure fall within the Community's competence...However, the last-mentioned finding does not prevent the Community legislature, when the application of effective, proportionate and dissuasive criminal penalties by the competent national authorities is an essential measure for combating serious environmental offences, from taking measures which relate to the criminal law of the Member States which it considers necessary in order to ensure that the rules which it lays down on environmental protection are fully effective.

This decision was followed by a Commission proposal for a Directive on environmental crime (see COM (2007)51 final). The rationale behind the proposed Directive is seemingly to provide consistency between different member States' regimes for environmental crime. The Directive would make no wholesale changes to domestic legislation, although the treatment of 'serious' offences committed intentionally or with serious negligence could raise some definitional issues. These 'serious offences' must be punishable by a maximum of at least five years' imprisonment and fines for companies of at least €750,000. In addition, the role of alternative sanctions, including restorative and administrative penalties, is also included. All of this is, of course, subject to the approval of Parliament and ultimately the Council—which leads to the very conflict upon which the ECJ adjudicated in the original case.[7]

For the purposes of this chapter, we adopt a fairly broad legal definition of 'environmental crime' based around the offences set out in the main environmental statutes outlined in Chapter 2. Box 9.3 sets out some of the main classes of environmental crime. Some are straightforward offences in and of themselves;[8] in other cases, these might be general acts, such as causing the entry of polluting matter into controlled waters,[9] or they might be specified activities that require a permit or authorization before being undertaken. In many of these latter offences, acting in accordance with a regulatory permit or licence will normally act as a defence.

Box 9.3 covers only the main groupings of environmental offences, but it conveys the breadth of topics that might be considered to be mainstream environmental offences. There are many other environmental regulatory offences,[10] as well as other non-regulatory criminal offences.[11]

---

7 Another very important case in this area is Case C-440/05 *Commission v. Council*, ECJ (Grand Chamber), 23 October 2007, a decision concerning EC criminal offences for ship-source pollution (although not directly relevant to the Environment title of the EC Treaty). For analysis, see the Online Resource Centre.

8 For example, supplying unwholesome drinking water—see p. 597.

9 Water Resources Act 1991, s. 85.

10 For example, under planning legislation—see p. 423.

11 For example, public nuisance is a common law offence, as well as a tort, and the uprooting of wild plants for sale or commercial purposes can be theft under s. 4(3) of the Theft Act 1968.

BOX 9.3 Typical environmental crimes[12]

Subject of offence	Nature of offence	Statutory provisions	Enforcement body
Air pollution	Emissions of dark smoke	Clean Air Act 1993, Pt I	Local authorities
Contaminated land	Failing to comply with a remediation notice	Environmental Protection Act 1990, s. 78M	Environment Agency and local authority
Drinking water quality	Supplying water unfit for human consumption	Water Industry Act 1991, s. 70	Secretary of State Drinking Water Inspectorate
Environmental taxes	Avoiding landfill tax Avoiding Climate Change Levy	Finance Act 1996, Pt III Finance Act 2000, Pt II and Sch. 6	HM Customs and Excise
Forestry	Illegal felling of trees	Forestry Act 1967, s. 17	Forestry Commission
Genetically modified organisms (GMOs)	Unauthorized release of GMOs	Environmental Protection Act 1990, Pt IV	Secretary of State Health and Safety Executive
Hazardous substances and major accident hazard sites	Offences relating to the storage, notification, and emergency planning at major accident hazards	Control of Major Accident Hazards Regulations 1999[13]	Health and Safety Executive and Environment Agency
Environmental Permitting	Environmental Permitting (e.g. operating without required permit)	Environmental Permitting (England and Wales) Regulations 2007[14] (reg. 38)	Environment Agency and local authorities
Pesticides	Misuse of pesticides	Control of Pesticides Regulations 1986[15]	DEFRA
Statutory nuisances	Failing to comply with an abatement notice	Environmental Protection Act 1990, s. 80(4)	Local authorities
Waste management	Illegal waste disposal/treatment	Environmental Protection Act 1990, s. 33	Environment Agency
Water abstraction	Abstracting water without a licence	Water Resources Act 1991, s. 24	Environment Agency
Water pollution	Causing or knowingly permitting entry of polluting matter into controlled waters	Water Resources Act 1991, s. 85	Environment Agency

12 Adapted from C. DuPont and P. Zakkow (2003) *Trends in Environmental Sentencing in England and Wales*, London: DEFRA.

13 SI 1999/743.

14 SI 2007/3538.

15 SI 1986/1510.

Subject of offence	Nature of offence	Statutory provisions	Enforcement body
Subject of offence	Nature of offence	Statutory provisions	Enforcement body
Wildlife crime	Controls on trade and possession of wild animals and plants	Wildlife and Countryside Act 1981, Pt I	Police
	Protection of habitats	Wildlife and Countryside Act 1981, Pt 11	Natural England Police
	Trade in endangered species	EC Regulation 338/97 Control of Trade in Endangered Species (Enforcement) Regulations 1997[16]	Secretary of State HM Customs and Excise Police

The lack of uniformity of environmental crime

In keeping with the growth of the subject as a whole, the development of environmental criminal law has been fragmented and inconsistent.[17] One of the consequences of this is that there are many disparities between the laws that seek to address different types of environmental crime. This can be seen in the many different ways in which environmental crime is constructed within statutes. Slight differences between the strictness of liability or defences can be detected between different offences,[18] and such differences are not insignificant. For example, on the one hand, one of the historic weaknesses of nature conservation legislation has been the relative narrowness of both the rules and enforcement options. On the other hand, the offence of causing the pollution of controlled waters under the Water Resources Act 1991, s. 85, is comparatively wide, covering a broad range of potential polluters.[19] Moreover, there is a range of other enforcement mechanisms that can be selected to try to deal with any water pollution that has been caused.[20] These examples illustrate how, at one extreme, an officer working for Natural England has relatively few enforcement options available to deal with damage to a site of special scientific interest (SSSI)—indeed, he or she may not be able to do anything at all—whereas the Environment Agency officer has the ability to select from an assortment of formal enforcement powers and possibly even from a list of potential polluters.

The moral dimension of environmental crime

Perhaps the fundamental problem in defining environmental crime by reference to legal criteria is that relatively few activities that harm the environment are crimes in and of themselves. Clearly, any definition that characterizes environmental crime as being 'activities that

---

16 SI.1997/1372, as amended.

17 W. Wilson (1998) *Making Environmental Laws Work*, Oxford: Hart, p. 110.

18 For example, the absence of a due diligence defence in water pollution—see p. 608.

19 The breadth of potential polluters stems from a liberal interpretation of the concept of 'causing' as found in s. 85—see p. 609.

20 For example, the Water Resources Act allows for the service of an enforcement notice under s. 90B or a works notice under s. 161A.

caused harm to the environment' would ignore the fact that many such activities are perfectly lawful. Criminal law is normally reserved for the punishment of socially unacceptable behaviour; harm to the environment is, in many situations, considered to be acceptable. For example, we are prepared to allow certain industrial activities that cause significant pollution, as long as those activities are controlled under licence or authorization, because it is an inherent consequence of many industrial activities that provide us with significant benefits. This is the rationale for having a system of regulation that defines the framework for determining whether such benefits outweigh the harm caused. The criminal law is not suited to such a balancing process and thus is used mainly to address clearly unacceptable behaviour or to reinforce the regulatory system.

The nature and extent of the environmental harm caused by these various crimes may be contested. There are many types of activity that cause harm to the environment, but which would not necessarily be classed as an *environmental* crime. Consider, for example, the offence of driving a car with exhaust emissions that exceed the legal limit. The emissions may cause harm when aggregated with many other vehicles, but should their release be classified as an environmental crime? Whether this is an environmental crime depends largely upon whether a broad or narrow definition of the term is adopted.

This uncertainty contributes to the moral ambivalence surrounding regulatory offences in general and in certain aspects of environmental crime in particular. The central question is whether environmental crime should be distinguished from 'real' crimes, such as murder or theft. These latter offences are viewed as being acts that are 'evil in themselves', whereas environmental crime is not thought to be inherently immoral (indeed, it is considered to be acceptable in some circumstances), but rather as made unlawful only by statute. This is not merely a theoretical consideration: the extent to which pollution or other environmental harm is viewed as a 'crime' by operators, regulators, and the general public is a factor that influences such things as whether to enforce and how to sanction or punish offenders. Thus, the moral opprobrium that attaches to environmental crime influences the exercise of discretion in taking enforcement action—that is, which power to exercise or whether to prosecute—and in sanctioning pollution by taking into account mitigating factors when sentencing.

Historically, the commission of environmental crimes by industrial operators was viewed as purely regulatory in nature and therefore 'not criminal in any real sense'.[21] It was thought that pollution was a natural consequence of industrial activity and the operators made a positive contribution to the local and regional economy. Arguably, attitudes to environmental harm, generally, and environmental crime, more specifically, have shifted over the years.[22] This has led to calls to distinguish between routine cases of environmental harm that result from general activities and environmental crimes that have been wilfully committed with a view to personal or business advantage. In the former case, it has been argued that civil penalties administered through civil or administrative means, such as standardized 'fines' for breaches of licence conditions, would be more appropriate, leaving criminal sanctions only for the worst type of offences.[23]

Other factors have played a part in the ambiguous nature of the moral dimension of environmental crime. Traditionally, those who have polluted have been of high status in society and those affected by pollution of low status. Pollution was more commonplace in working-class areas of high industrial activity. For example, one of the reasons that the 'west end' of cities tends to be more affluent than the 'east end' is partly connected to the historical transmission of pollutants from the west to the east either by prevailing winds or via rivers. Many

---

21 *Sherras v. De Rutzen* [1895] 1 QB 918.

22 See Box 3.2.

23 M. Woods and R. Macrory (2003) *Environmental Civil Penalties: A More Proportionate Response to Regulatory Breach*, London: University College London.

of those living in the area would have been working in the factory that was polluting the area; the pollution was often seen as a way of life, rather than as a matter for complaint.[24]

The changes in fundamental attitudes to the environment have started to have an impact upon attitudes to environmental crime. Underlying these changes is a basic shift in the way in which environmental problems are perceived, not only by the public, but also by the enforcement agencies and even by the general category of 'polluters'. The acknowledgement that environmental protection is important in its own right has undermined previous assumptions about the benefits of activities that cause environmental harm.

As environmental issues have become more important in the public eye, there is a desire to ensure that environmental standards are maintained and environmental damage minimized. Moreover, when public interest in the environment and the understanding of the consequences of environmental harm increases, there is an equivalent escalation in the amount of moral opprobrium that attaches to environmental offences. The publicity that is given to pollution incidents and other notorious examples of environmental damage tends to amplify the view that such harm and pollution is caused by something more than mere administrative difficulties, and should be dealt with severely. Given this increase in the public perception of the importance of environmental interests, it is not inevitable that environmental crime will always be viewed as being somehow a 'lesser' offence than 'real' crimes, such as burglary or assault. Indeed, some writers have argued for the idea that environmental crimes might 'swap places' with traditional crimes in the criminal justice system.[25]

Strict liability

Many of the common environmental offences impose strict liability. Thus, to establish an offence, the only thing that needs to be proved is the act or omission that forms part of the offence and there is no need to prove any negligence or fault on the part of the defendant or operator. There is a link between the moral dimension of environmental crime and the imposition of strict liability. The moral foundation of 'real' criminal law is that a crime requires both an unlawful act and the requisite mental responsibility or fault. The use of strict liability can be justified by reference to both trivial offences, through ease of prosecution, *and* serious offences, by acting as a deterrent and through the Polluter Pays Principle.

As a precursor to the following discussion of the arguments for the use of strict liability for environmental crimes, it is important to inject a note of realism. Although the absence of fault is irrelevant to the commission of many environment crimes, in practice, fault and blame are considered throughout the criminal process. First, enforcing authorities exercise a discretion when deciding whether and how to enforce, and they are often reluctant to use the ultimate sanction of prosecution unless moral blame is towards the top end of the scale—that is, in cases of criminal negligence or actual intent on behalf of the offender.

Secondly, evidence of fault and blame is gathered and presented by enforcing authorities in order to establish the blameworthiness of defendants so that courts can exercise sentencing discretion properly.

Finally, the courts use that sentencing discretion to differentiate between offences that are characterized as having high levels of culpability and those in relation to which the strictness of the liability catches otherwise blameless defendants.

24 See J. Brenner (1974) JLS 403 and J. Mclaren (1983) JLS 155.
25 See D. Nelken (1990) MLR 834.

Arguments for the use of strict liability

There are thought to be four main arguments for the use of strict liability[26]—that the imposition of strict liability:

- promotes the public interest goal inherent in environmental legislation;

- acts as a deterrent, which improves the quality of environmental risk prevention measures;

- increases the ease of prosecution, which increases the deterrent effect;

- accords with the Polluter Pays Principle.

The public interest goal

Environmental regulation is primarily aimed at preventing environmental harm, on the basis that this is in the public interest. Imposing strict liability for environmental crime ensures that this public interest goal is achieved by divorcing questions of blame or fault from the consequences of actions that cause environmental harm. Thus the emphasis is upon the prevention and minimization of harm, rather than on the motivation of a particular offender. The courts have implicitly emphasized the public interest goal inherent in environmental legislation by interpreting criminal liability for environmental crime in a broad fashion.[27]

Deterrence and risk management

Strict liability encourages those to whom the law applies to be extra-cautious in their attempts to comply with environmental regulation. The imposition of strict liability acts as a deterrent, which ensures that a broad approach is taken to environmental risk avoidance. The courts have emphasized this in adopting a expansive interpretation of criminal conduct in environmental cases. This can be found in cases such as *Alphacell v. Woodward* [1972] AC 824 (see Case 17.4), in which the House of Lords emphasized the need to do 'everything possible' to prevent pollution—as opposed to merely taking reasonable steps.[28] This approach has included imposing criminal liability for failing to conduct an assessment of the risks associated with *other people's* conduct (see Case 9.1). In such circumstances, it is clear that there will be an incentive to conduct operations going far beyond what is reasonable, to taking extreme steps to prevent pollution.

CASE 9.1 *Express Dairies v. Environment Agency* [2005] Env LR 7

The defendant, Express Dairies (ED), owned a dairy depot at which it allowed one of its customers to take delivery of cream from an outside supplier. During the transfer, the cream escaped into the surface drains and consequently into the nearby river. ED was found guilty of an offence under s. 217(3) of the Water Resources Act 1991 in that its customer had caused the entry of polluting matter into controlled waters and the offence was committed as a result of ED's default. The alleged default was that ED had failed to undertake an assessment of the risks associated with transferring cream in the yard.

ED appealed against the conviction arguing that there was no statutory requirement to undertake such a risk assessment. The High Court held that, in order to establish criminal liability under these

---

26 For a broader discussion of the difficult question of the precise definition of 'strict liability' and more generally, see A. Simester (ed.) (2005) *Appraising Strict Liability*, Oxford: Oxford University Press.

27 For example, the broad interpretation of 'causing' in relation to water pollution offences—see p. 608.

28 See Case 17.4.

provisions, all that had to be shown was that the offence committed by ED's customer was due to an act or default of ED. Land owners like ED, who allowed risky operations on their land, were under an obligation to carry out a risk assessment and to address the matters raised in that assessment. Only in those circumstances could they then argue that they were not in default.

The counter to this argument is that, instead of acting as a deterrent, it actually undermines the moral force of identifying and distinguishing environmental crimes as serious offences. There are some cases (see, for example, Case 9.2) in which the defendant's conduct can hardly be said to be criminal in any true sense of the word. Branding such actions as 'crimes' devalues the use of criminal law to address serious cases of environmental harm. According to this argument, criminal sanctions should only be used to address the worst examples of environmental harm. In prosecuting and punishing seemingly trivial breaches of the law, regulatory agencies may discourage people from taking a stringent approach to compliance, on the basis that they might as well be 'hung for a sheep as a lamb'.

Although fault is often taken into account when deciding whether to prosecute, there will be cases in which no significant fault can be found, but in which the environmental harm caused is so significant that prosecutions will still be brought.

CASE 9.2 *CPC (UK) v. National River Authority* [1995] Env LR 131

Piping at the defendant's factory had fractured, causing cleaning liquid to enter the drainage system and be discharged into the nearby river. The fracturing of the pipe had been caused by a failure to stick two sections together properly. A subcontractor had undertaken this work before the defendant had purchased the factory. It was accepted that the defendant could not have known or foreseen the crack in the pipe work. The defendant was found to have 'caused' the pollution.

The Court of Appeal upheld the conviction, finding that the fact that the defect was latent and that the defendant could not have foreseen the problem was irrelevant, because liability was strict.

A general counter to the deterrence argument in favour of strict liability is that, given the relatively long history of criminal regulation of environmental harm, there is no objective evidence to suggest that imposing strict liability makes any difference to compliance rates. There may be a number of reasons for this, including low sentences or the low rate of prosecution, but these are inextricably linked to the imposition of strict liability in the first place. Thus we have a 'chicken and egg' argument: is it strict liability or the responses to the harshness of strict liability, such as lenient sentences and low prosecution rates, which lead to ineffective deterrence?

Efficiency and ease of prosecution

A third reason for imposing strict liability presents a different aspect of this deterrence factor. The imposition of strict liability makes it easier for prosecutors to prove their case:[29] all that is needed is to establish the criminal act and the added complication of fault or blame can be ignored. Thus, when prosecutions are brought, they rarely fail. This 'freedom to prosecute' acts as a deterrent in various ways to those who would otherwise wish to fight cases on the basis that an offence had been accidental or that reasonable steps had been taken to avoid the commission of the offence. The imposition of strict liability also promotes flexibility in enforcement, in the sense that enforcement agencies are able to target particular offences or classes of offenders, in relation to which or whom non-compliance may be a problem, in

---

29 C. Abbot (2004) 16(2) ELM 67.

order to emphasize the deterrence factor. Of course, this also raises the question of whether this selective approach would be a fair or efficient approach to environmental enforcement.

The Polluter Pays Principle

The final argument in favour of imposing strict liability is that it accords with one interpretation of the Polluter Pays Principle, in the sense that the punishments imposed by criminal courts for environmental crime represent a 'payment': sometimes in the shape of a fine; in other situations, through compensation or even non-monetary sanctions, such as imprisonment.

Defences

Although there are many arguments in favour of imposing strict liability for environmental crimes, there is still a basic objection that criminalizing innocent or accidental actions is somewhat problematic. The true position is that there are very few environmental crimes that impose absolute strict liability—that is, for which there are no defences—because most offences balance the potential unfairness of such liability with certain statutory defences.[30]

The courts have tended to construe these defences narrowly in order to protect the underlying aims of environmental legislation. For example, in *Durham County Council v. Peter O'Connor Industrial Services* [1993] Env LR 197, the Court specifically rejected the notion that taking 'reasonable care' to avoid the commission of an offence would amount to 'due diligence', because this would negate the strictness of criminal liability for environmental crime. In that case, the Court suggested that, for due diligence to be established, all that could be done to ensure compliance should be done, even if that involved checking every transfer of waste from a site.

Examples of typical defences include the following.

- **Acting in accordance with a statutory consent**
  Typically, this will include complying with the conditions of such things as discharge consents.[31] Breaching conditions of a consent or authorization is generally an additional or alternative offence.[32]

- **Emergency situations**
  This defence is normally subject to a requirement to minimize harm and to report to the enforcement agency within a reasonable period.[33] Environmental harm caused in response to an emergency situation—such as water pollution from firefighting run-off—can still amount to an offence, because the emergency does not necessarily break the chain of causation.[34]

- **Exercising due diligence in carrying out operations**
  This would include explicit defences[35] and implicit due diligence requirements in relation to the use of Best Practicable Means (BPM) or Best Available Techniques (BAT).[36]

---

30 This is strongly linked to the historic use of use of criminal liability with broad defences for environmental crimes.

31 See, e.g., the Water Resources Act 1991, s. 88.

32 For example, ibid., s. 85(6).

33 See, e.g., in relation to: waste—EPA 1990, s. 33(7); nature conservation—Wildlife and Countryside Act 1981, s. 28(8)(b); water pollution—Water Resources Act 1991, s. 89.

34 This does not apply in cases in which the emergency arises in extraordinary conditions: see *Express Ltd (t/a Express Dairies Distribution) v. Environment Agency* [2003] Env LR 29.

35 For example, EPA 1990, s. 33(7), in relation to waste management.

36 For example, the requirement for BAT under the IPPC Directive—see Chapter 14.

Whether or not the due diligence defence can be made out is a question of fact in every case. The question arises of whether due diligence applies to actions taken by a company or by the employee. For example, would it fulfil the requirement to exercise due diligence if a very large company in delegating responsibility to individual sites were to provide rigorous training and supervision on the steps to take to prevent pollution, but if an individual employee were to ignore these steps? The *Durham County Council* case suggests that it will be the company that will be held responsible for the failures of its employees. Thus it would be harder to prove that a large undertaking has exercised sufficient due diligence to amount to a defence, because higher standards will be expected.[37] Greater resources are expected to be available to maintain standards in a large company. The 'due diligence' must relate to conduct aimed at preventing the offence, not to putting matters right afterwards. The burden of proving due diligence is on the defendant.

- **Having a 'reasonable excuse'**
  The test of whether something is a reasonable excuse is normally objective—that is, would a reasonable person consider that the excuse was consistent with a reasonable standard of conduct?[38]

Individual and corporate offenders

A diverse range of individuals and corporate bodies carry out the activities that lead to breaches of environmental law, from solo fly-tippers, to huge multinational corporations. The most significant acts of environmental harm through breaches of pollution control legislation tend to be caused by companies, simply because of the scale of the industrial operations. There are, however, important exceptions to this general rule in areas, such as wildlife crime, pollution from agricultural sources, and fly-tipping waste. Indeed, figures suggest that individuals are responsible for the majority of environmental crimes as a whole.[39] These figures are, however, slightly misleading, because they exclude local authority prosecutions, but include a significant proportion of individual wildlife offences (for example, egg collecting and animal cruelty) and from some sectors in which individual offenders are far more prevalent (for example, agriculture).

Offender type	Year			
	1999	**2000**	**2001**	**2002**
Corporate	359	625	732	880
Individual	487	965	1020	922
Total	846	1590	1752	1802

BOX 9.4 **Individual vs corporate offenders**[40]

37 A point that was reinforced by the decision in *Express Ltd v. Environment Agency* [2005] Env LR 7.

38 See, e.g., the Wildlife and Countryside Act 1981, s. 28(7), and, in relation to statutory nuisances, e.g., EPA 1990, s. 80(4).

39 See also Environment Agency evidence to House of Commons Audit Committee on Corporate Crime, 2004 HC 1135-I, in which it was estimated that the 38–40 per cent of all prosecutions were brought against registered companies.

40 Adapted from DuPont and Zakkow (2003).

This distinction between individual and corporate offenders raises a number of issues. First, it is often much easier to classify environmental offences as 'white collar' or business crimes, and therefore as being morally neutral, in which the defendant is a major corporation. In circumstances under which it is an individual who is responsible for the commission of an offence, however, there is likely to be criminal intent or negligence. On the one hand, then, in cases in which individuals are found to have committed an environmental crime, it will normally be easier for prosecutors to establish blameworthiness, which would lead to a prosecution. On the other hand, the number of prosecutions of corporate offenders does not correlate with corporate non-compliance with environmental law. In other words, although there may be fewer corporate defendants, the offences for which they are being prosecuted will tend to be at the serious end of the spectrum of environmental harm and there will be many more companies who are in breach, but not prosecuted.

Secondly, the structure of large companies means that it is often difficult to identify the root cause of many pollution incidents. Arguably, this has the effect of obscuring the blameworthiness of offending companies, because they seek to 'trivialize' their conduct by reference to factors outside their control.[41] This, however, obscures the fact that, in large organizations, management deficiencies are often to blame and truly innocent offenders are rare.

Finally, the prosecution of corporate offenders can be justified by the existence of the deterrence factor of the bad publicity associated with the prosecution for environmental crimes, and the development of a 'name and shame' policy for such offenders. This justification does not exist to the same extent for individual offenders.

Corporate liability

The nature of liability of companies for environmental crime is not necessarily straightforward. Some offences apply directly to companies—for example, where offences relate to the breach of licence conditions and the licence is held in the name of the company. In other situations, however, it is the acts or omissions of individual employees that will incur criminal liability. This raises the central question of corporate criminal liability—namely, in what circumstances can a company be held to account for the acts of its employees?

It had been thought that such corporate liability would only be established in cases in which the employees responsible were of sufficient seniority to act as the 'controlling mind' of the company.[42] The problem is that many pollution incidents are the responsibility of operational staff who are far removed from the 'controlling mind'. The courts have held that the actions of employees will create corporate criminal liability if it is clear that the relevant statutory purposes would be defeated if a company could not be prosecuted for the acts of its employees.

CASE 9.3 *National Rivers Authority v. Alfred McAlpine Homes East Ltd* [1994] Env LR 198

The defendant (AMHE) caused water pollution during construction works. At the trial, AMHE was acquitted on the basis that the prosecution had failed to demonstrate that the employees that had caused the pollution were of sufficiently senior standing within the company to bind the company by their actions. On appeal, the Court found AMHE to be liable. In particular, Morland J expanded on the purposive approach to vicarious liability—namely, that the offence under s. 85 of the Water Resources Act 1991 was designed to prevent water pollution. In order to make the legislation effective, there was a necessary implication that companies should be liable for the acts or omissions of *all*

---

41 P. DePrez (2000) 12 JEL 11.
42 See *Tesco Supermarkets Ltd v. Nattrass* [1972] AC 153.

of their employees as opposed to simply the senior employees who were 'controlling minds'. Morland J reinforced this by referring to the idea that companies were, in fact, best placed to control activities of even very junior employees through such things as training and supervision.

CASE 9.4 *Shanks and McEwan (Teesside) Ltd v. Environment Agency* [1997] Env LR 305

The defendant waste company (SM) was prosecuted for 'knowingly causing' the deposit of waste in breach of licence conditions. The relevant facts were that the supervisor of a landfill site, while complying with the requirements of the waste management licence on the delivery of some waste, had failed to complete a necessary waste disposal form when he redirected it to a containment bund rather than to the anticipated storage tank. At the trial, SM argued that it did not have the requisite knowledge of the deposit, because it had only been in the knowledge of the supervisor. SM was convicted on the basis that the site supervisor was part of the 'controlling mind' of the company.

On appeal, the Court held that the only knowledge that was required was general knowledge that waste was deposited as opposed to specific knowledge of the breach of condition. On this basis, either the supervisor's knowledge could be attributed to the company or the company had the general knowledge of waste deposits at the site because it was a landfill site. Thus, the purposes of this particular waste offence—that is, to prevent the unlawful disposal of waste—could be met either by saying that the 'controlling minds' of the company knew that waste was deposited at its landfill sites or that the supervisor's knowledge of specific deposits could be attributed to the company.

To underline the flexibility of the purposive approach, the decisions in Cases 9.3 and 9.4 can be contrasted with the approach to corporate liability taken in other areas, in which a company can only be held criminally liable for the acts of those who possess the 'controlling mind' of the company.[43]

Directors' liability

Generally, in the UK, when companies commit environmental offences, prosecutions are brought against that company rather than against any individual who might have responsibility within that company. This is in contrast to the practice in many civil law countries, where the doctrine of corporate liability is not particularly well developed and where it is far more common for individual managers of companies to be prosecuted.[44] The 'British' approach is not, however, restricted by law. Under many environmental statutes, directors and managers can be prosecuted individually in certain circumstances, and the trend in such prosecutions is upwards. For example, in 2006, 29 company directors were fined for environmental offences, up from 11 in 2003.[45]

Any director, manager, secretary, or other similar officer of a corporate body can be prosecuted personally if the offence is committed with their consent or connivance, or is attributable to their neglect.[46] (Note that these sections do not apply if the allegation is against an

---

43 Ibid.

44 C. Wells (2001) *Corporations and Criminal Responsibility*, 2nd edn, Oxford: Oxford University Press, pp. 138–40.

45 Environment Agency (2006) *Spotlight on Business: Environmental Performance in 2006*, and equivalent report from 2003.

46 See, e.g., EPA 1990, s. 157, Water Resources Act 1991, s. 217, and the Town and Country Planning Act 1990, s. 331.

2. There is the challenge of implementation deficit. That the easiest problems have been tackled means that we are now facing more fundamental concerns, which can only be addressed through concerted effort by the different stakeholders, including the general public. The emphasis on 'shared responsibility' as a means of addressing environmental problems reflects this view. For example, the shift from waste disposal regulation to waste reduction targets is primarily a shift from controlling industry to promoting shared responsibility.

3. Much has been made of the development of the 'risk society', with its reduced role for scientific experts and the breakdown of trust in the technocratic basis of decision making. One of the ways of solving environmental problems in the risk society is through the development of deliberative and participative techniques.

4. Sustainable development, with its focus on fairness and justice, has public participation at its heart.

The *benefits* of public participation in environmental matters are considered in Box 10.1.

BOX 10.1 The benefits of public participation

Lee and Abbot[2] identify a number of the potential benefits of promoting public participation.

- **Improving the quality of decisions**
  The Preamble to the Aarhus Convention emphasizes the role that public participation has to play in improving environmental decisions. It states that *'improved access and public participation in decision-making enhance the quality and the implementation of decisions'*. This can be done through such things as the input of specific expertise held by members of the public, or through the elicitation of social and cultural values.

- **Environmental problem solving**
  One of the ways in which competing values can be resolved is through techniques of deliberation—that is, 'bottom-up' discussions in which all sides of an issue are debated in an attempt to reach a consensus on an issue.

- **Promoting environmental citizenship**
  Environmental citizenship is loosely based upon the notion that individuals should take some responsibility for their own interaction with the environment. In promoting such citizenship, participation in environmental matters is critical. Engaging the public to play an active role in environmental policymaking and raising awareness of environmental issues are central to promoting environmental citizenship.

- **Improving procedural legitimacy**
  Increased involvement in decisions, access to good quality environmental information, and *ex post* review mechanisms through such things as judicial review increases the accountability of the decision maker and makes the process more legitimate in the eyes of the public.

- **Eliciting values**
  In Chapter 3, we discussed the role that different values play in the environmental decision-making process. Promoting public participation in decision making and widening access to environmental information is the best way of eliciting such values.

---

2 M. Lee and C. Abbot (2003) 66 MLR 80.

Access to environmental information

There has been a steady increase in openness and access to environmental information over recent years. The reasons for this growing emphasis on access are many and varied, with European legislation and international initiatives playing a significant part in the process. In addition, there has been a relaxation of secrecy in relation to all information held by public bodies. This has been formalized in the Freedom of Information Act (FOI) 2000, which promotes a general right of access to information held by public bodies. This is supplemented by greater powers of access in relation to environmental information in the Environmental Information Regulations 2004.[3]

Increasing access to environmental information allows for competing interests to be balanced, in the sense that the public interest suggests that access to information on the consequences of industrial activities, permits all relevant factors to be taken into account as part of the decision-making process. This has led the Royal Commission on Environmental Pollution (RCEP) to talk of a general public 'right' to environmental information: '...the public must be considered to have a right, analogous to a beneficial interest, in the condition of the air and water and to be able to obtain information on how far they are being degraded.'[4]

In addition, there is a clear link here between the provision of environmental information and the achievement of the goal of sustainable development. This link is made in two places. First, the provision of environmental information can influence the behaviour and decisions of private individuals or companies. Making information available on a wider scale can be the catalyst in changes in behaviour or can increase the effectiveness of other instruments. For example, publishing information on energy efficiency and associated environmental benefits can be used in conjunction with grants and subsidies to encourage people to reduce their consumption of energy by installing energy-efficient boilers or by turning the heating down. Secondly, information can help us to understand the consequences of our current actions in terms of the legacy that is being passed on to future generations.

Other justifications for widening access to information are summarized in Box 10.2.

BOX 10.2 Rationales for access to environmental information

- **Monitoring the effectiveness of regulation**
  One of the ways in which the effectiveness of a regulatory system can be monitored is to produce 'benchmarks' for performance, such as gathering and publishing data on waste going to landfill and recycling rates. This legitimates the introduction of new laws, ensures that existing laws are actually meeting the aims for which they were designed and ensures that ineffective laws are replaced.

- **Improving the enforcement of environmental law**
  Without adequate information, public rights to enforce environmental laws have little value. This includes basic information on the identity of polluters, where they are polluting, and how much is being emitted. To assess levels of compliance, either generally or in relation to an individual authorization, the public require access not only to information concerning the details of an authorization or consent, but also to monitoring data.

---

3 SI 2004/3391.

4 Royal Commission on Environmental Pollution Tenth Report (1984) *Tackling Pollution: Experience and Prospects*, Cmnd 9149.

- **Environmental information as a self-standing regulatory instrument**
  Environmental information can be used as a stand-alone mechanism to regulate behaviour and to complement other regulatory instruments. The use of eco-labelling to provide consumers with information that enables them to make informed purchasing decisions is an example of this.

- **Informing the public about environmental risks**
  A lack of information can increase the perception of risks associated with an activity—whether in relation to human health or to the environment. Greater disclosure of information enables informed debate about environmental risks and the manner in which they might be addressed, by allowing the widest possible range of interpretations of raw data, as opposed to relying upon assertions and interpretations of interested parties. Arguably, in practice, greater access merely enables the views of different interested parties to be placed in the balance.[5]

Although there are many arguments in favour of greater access to environmental information, the development of the legislation that has brought about this access was the subject of a vigorous debate, with opposition coming mainly from those to whom the information relates—namely, industry and governmental organizations. These objections are reflected in some of the exemptions from disclosure that are found in FOI 2000 and the 2004 Regulations.

One of the main objections to full public disclosure of environmental information has traditionally been that such disclosure would detrimentally affect the viability of business by breaching commercial confidentiality. Concern stemmed from the belief that industrial competitors would be able to use the data released to gain access to commercially confidential information. In rejecting these objections, the RCEP suggested that industry's refusal to disclose information on the basis of commercial confidentiality was often a 'reflex action', which did not reflect the commercial risk involved, and that the emphasis that was given to such confidentiality was '*disproportionate and misconceived*'.[6] Notwithstanding this rejection of the argument against greater disclosure, most legislative schemes that promote greater access to environmental information have provisions that exclude commercially confidential information.

Another objection to greater disclosure was that openness would lead to mischief making and an unacceptable level of interference by activists. In 1984, the Confederation of British Industry (CBI) referred to the access to information provisions of the Control of Pollution Act 1974 as a 'busybody's charter'.[7] Other predicted consequences of greater disclosure put forward by MPs included the disappearance of the chemicals industry from the UK and '*an endless stream of prosecutions*'.[8] During the passage of the Environmental Protection Bill through Parliament, one MP alleged that greater access to information and broader rights of prosecution would '*allow the "green nutters" to get on parade and have a field day of litigation against industry on entirely inconsequential grounds*'.[9] With hindsight, these predictions appear to have been unduly alarmist. Although environmental interest groups have used the information,[10] this has not been for the purpose of taking unreasonable enforcement action against industry.[11]

---

5 See P. Wald, 'Negotiations of environmental disputes: a new role for the courts' (1985) 10 Col J Env L 1.

6 See RCEP Seventh Report (1979) *Agriculture and Pollution*, Cmnd 7644, and Tenth Report (1984).

7 See RCEP Tenth Report (1984).

8 See a parliamentary question from T. Devlin MP, 171 HC Debate, 30 April 1990, Col. 761.

9 See Hansard Debates, 2 May 1990.

10 For example, Friends of the Earth's now-defunct 'Factory Watch' campaign, which aimed to make pollution information more available to the general public: see **www.foe.co.uk/factorywatch/index.html**.

11 See the discussions of private prosecutions at p. 271.

International approaches to access to information

The importance of a right of access to environmental information at all levels is emphasized by the weight that greater disclosure is given in international law. In particular, the role of information in meeting the goal of sustainable development is acknowledged in Agenda 21, the policy blueprint agreed at the 1992 Rio Earth Summit, which stresses the importance of ensuring that all stakeholders in the environment have access to relevant environmental information relating to products or activities that have an environmental impact. This general commitment to greater access is specifically implemented in various international conventions, including the Climate Change Convention, under which the exchange of public information on climate change is considered to be a precondition to the successful implementation of its other substantive provisions (Art. 6).

The need to ensure greater consistency and transparency of public access to environmental information within international law is evidenced by the inclusion of access to information provisions in the Aarhus Convention. The relevant provisions of the Convention are now largely mirrored in current EC and domestic legislation. The Kiev Protocol on Pollutant Release and Transfer Registers was signed in 2003 and makes provision for aggregated pollutant inventories, which again are found in European and domestic legislation.[12]

One other matter that should be considered within the international context is the effect of the incorporation of the European Convention on Human Rights (ECHR) into domestic legislation by way of the Human Rights Act 1998. In particular, the European Court of Human Rights (ECtHR) has interpreted certain Articles of the Convention—in particular, the right to privacy, home and family life under Art. 8—in a way that should mean that statutory provisions on access to information might have a much wider application than has previously been the case.

For example, in *Guerra v. Italy* (1998) 26 EHRR 357, the ECtHR held that public authorities were under a positive obligation to supply information about the risks involved in living in close proximity to an environmentally sensitive use so that residents could assess the risks from the factory. On a broad interpretation, it would not be possible for an authority to reject a request on the basis that it did not have the information.[13]

The ECtHR has also held that Art. 2 (the right to life) can give rise to positive obligations to inform people about severe risks. In *Oneryildiz v. Turkey* (2005) 41 EHRR 20, methane exploded at a rubbish tip, killing many members of a family living at the site. The risk to life meant that the state had a positive duty to inform those that might be affected—that is, the duty was not simply one of informing those who requested information about the risk.

Access to information held by European institutions

A distinction needs to be made between access to environmental information at member-State level and access to information about the decision-making process operated by European bodies, and, in particular, the European Commission and Council. Historically, the processes of decision making within the European Commission and the Council were shrouded in secrecy. For example, documents relating to infringement proceedings, such as letters of formal notice and reasoned opinions issued by the European Commission against member States, were secret. This meant that important information about possible breaches of European law were kept from the general public. Moves towards greater openness were formalized with a Code of Conduct on Public Access to Commission and Council Documents.

---

12 See Chapter 14.
13 See also *McGinley and Egan v. UK* (1999) 27 EHRR 1 and *Lopez Ostra v. Spain* (1995) 20 EHRR 277.

Article 255 of the EC Treaty gave a constitutional right to documents held by the European Parliament, Council, and Commission.[14]

This general right was fleshed out by Regulation 1049/2001/EC on public access to European Parliament, Council and Commission documents (the so-called 'Transparency Regulation'). This Regulation provides access to all information held by the main—but by no means all—European institutions.[15] The Regulation provides a general right of access to information for EU citizens, including corporate entities.[16] There are certain exceptions: in particular, if disclosure would undermine matters such as public security or defence matters (in relation to which non-disclosure is absolute), or matters such as commercial interests (in relation to which an overriding public interest disclosure test applies). Any information relating to 'third parties', such as member States and other non-Community bodies, is subject to a duty to consult to determine whether an exception applies, unless it is 'clear' whether or not the information is exempt.[17]

One final source of European information comes from the European Environment Agency. One of the reasons for the setting up of the Agency was to provide member States and the European public with objective and reliable information on the state of the environment within the EC. The Agency has adopted the Transparency Regulation in relation to its own documents (see Regulation 1641/2003) and it produces periodic reports on the state of the European environment, which are available online at **www.eea.eu.int**. The Agency is closely involved with the European Environment Information and Observation Network (EIONET), which connects national environmental information organizations within member States and includes some countries outside the EC, and with other organizations, such as the European Free Trade Association.

European legislation on access to environmental information

The disclosure of environmental information at member State level has been a significant part of EC environmental policy since the drawing up of the First Environmental Action Programme (EAP) in 1973. Although a wide range of environmental Directives had provisions for access to individual elements of environmental information, the first general legislative measure was adopted during the course of the Fourth EAP. Directive 90/313/EEC on the freedom of access to information on the environment was a broad framework measure that was intended to facilitate general access rights, but which did not impose any requirements in terms of practical arrangements for access, leaving that to the discretion of the member States. The Directive was interpreted in a broad manner, with the European Court of Justice (ECJ) taking a purposive approach to its provisions.

In Case C-321/96 *Mecklenburg v. Kreis Pinneberg—Der Landrat* [1998] ECR I-3809, a member of the public asked his local authority for a copy of a document that set out the countryside protection authority's views on a local road project. The authority refused on the basis that the information fell outside the terms of the Directive, in that it was not 'information relating to the environment'. The ECJ held that the concept of 'information relating to the environment' was broad and included documents that could be influential in determining the outcome of the decision-making process in relation to the road project. On the question of whether the information was exempt, the ECJ took the view that exemptions should be viewed narrowly and in accordance with the aims of the Directive.

---

14 See also Art. 207 EC covering access to documents held by the Council that relate to lawmaking activities.

15 Bodies not covered include the European Central Bank and the European Investment Bank.

16 Article 2(1). The European Ombudsman has a policing role in relation to access to information and can make orders relating to specific documents—see the draft recommendation made in relation to a complaint from Friends of the Earth available online at **www.euro-ombudsman.eu.int/recommen/en/000271.htm**.

17 This has been held to mean that member State secrecy overrides valid public interest grounds in disclosure: see, e.g., Case T-168/02 *IFAW v. Commission* [2004] ECR II-4135, a case concerning nature conservation damage.

Notwithstanding this purposive interpretation, the Directive was defective in a number of aspects (see Box 10.3). In the light of these defects and the need to implement the Aarhus Convention, the 1990 Directive was replaced in 2003.[18]

BOX 10.3 The defects of Directive 90/313/EC on the freedom of access to information on the environment

---

- **Scope of application**
  The Directive applied to information held by public bodies with 'responsibilities for the environment'. This vague definition led to disputes about whether the provisions of the Directive applied to bodies such as the privatized utilities whose primary functions were arguably neither public nor environmental.

- **Definition of 'environmental information'**
  Although the definition of 'environmental information' in the Directive was broad, it was unclear in relation to certain categories of information. This included information relating to impacts upon human health or economic data used to justify the viability for a particular project.

- **Broad exemptions**
  The general right of access was tempered by wide categories of exempt information with discretionary rights of refusal. In determining whether to grant access, there was no weight to be given to the public interest. These broad exemptions made it too easy for authorities to reject applications for disclosure even in cases in which there were no adverse impacts on legitimate interests protected under the exemptions.

- **Ineffective right to challenge decisions**
  In cases in which applications for information had been rejected, the Directive only provided for challenge by way of judicial or administrative review. In many member States—including the UK—this was a cumbersome and expensive route of challenge.

- **Excessive charges**
  In practice, many public authorities demanded unreasonably high charges for supplying information. In some cases, people were charged and subsequently told that they were not entitled to the information.

- **Long time limits**
  The Directive required authorities to 'respond' to requests for access within two months. This led to delays, because some authorities simply replied to the request within the time limit without actually making the information available within the two-month period.[19]

- **Reactive nature of the general scheme of access**
  The Directive was far too reactive in nature, imposing obligations to grant access to information purely on request. There was neither a general requirement to disseminate information, nor to provide aggregated information in the shape of reports on the state of the environment.

---

18 See further COM(2000) 400 Final and R. Hallo (ed.) (1996) *The Implementation and Implications of Directive 90/313*, The Hague: Kluwer.

19 See Case C-233/00 *Commission v. France* [2003] ECR I-6625 and Case C-186/04 *Housieaux v. Delegues du Conseil de la Region de Bruxelles-Capitale* [2006] Env LR 2.

Directive 2003/4/EC on public access to environmental information was designed to address many of the defects of the 1990 Directive. In addition, it formed one of the key instruments that would enable the ratification of the Aarhus Convention. In many ways, the revised Directive was developed in parallel with the access to information provisions of the Convention, which were drafted in light of the experience with the 1990 Directive. Thus there is a marked similarity in the two regimes.

The Directive applies to 'environmental information' held by any 'public authority'. Environmental information is defined very broadly to include not only the state of the environment, releases to the environment, and policies and plans relating to the environment, but also cost–benefit analyses, and the state of human health and safety *'inasmuch as they are affected by the state of the environment'* (Art. 1). The definition of 'public authority' has also been extended to include those bodies performing 'public administrative functions' and 'specific duties, activities or services' in relation to the environment (Art. 2). Thus private companies with public duties are clearly covered.

The obligation to provide environmental information must be met as soon as possible or within one month (Art. 3). In cases of complex information, the period can be extended to two months. There are general exemptions in relation to cases in which a request is vague or otherwise unreasonable (Art. 4(1)). In addition, there is a list of exempt categories, including information that is commercially confidential, concerned with national defence or security matters, concerned with the 'course of justice', or supplied voluntarily. In these cases, the authorities are obliged to consider whether disclosure would 'adversely affect' the protected interest in question (Art. 4(2)). In all cases, there is a general 'public interest' test whereby the authority is obliged to consider whether it would be in the public interest to disclose the information. Any charges imposed for access have to be 'reasonable' and contained in a published schedule (Art. 5). In cases of refusal, an applicant should have access to an 'expeditious' appeals procedure, which must be free or inexpensive (Art. 6). Finally, the Directive provides a positive obligation upon member States to disseminate environmental information including: legislation at international, national, and local levels; policies, plans, and programmes; 'state of the environment' reports (Art. 7).

Access to environmental information in the UK

The UK's approach to access to environmental information can be characterized as having three identifiable phases. The first—that is, the period up until about 1974—was based upon a presumption against disclosure. Examples can be found in many different statutes, including the Rivers (Prevention of Pollution) Act 1961 and the Health and Safety at Work Act 1974, s. 28.

The second phase lasted from the 1980s until the early 1990s and can be characterized as the time during which pollution control registers were introduced. These related to discharges to water—under the Control of Pollution Act (CoPA) 1974—and waste management operations and industrial activities—under the Environmental Protection Act (EPA) 1990—as well as better access to planning information under the Local Government (Access to Information) Act 1985.

Under the third phase, there have been moves towards the broadening of the classes of available information subject only to restricted classes of exemptions in FOI 2000 and the Environmental Information Regulations 2004.[20]

The basic practical distinction between these last two approaches is in the nature of the access. In the case of public registers, public authorities hold the information specifically for the purpose of public access. In the case of broader access, the information is disclosed only if a request is made, although the provision of information on registers is included within

---

20 SI 2004/3391.

this. Although these approaches characterize the approach to disclosure of pollution control information, there are other more sophisticated information instruments that are discussed further below.

The Freedom of Information Act (FOI) 2000

The two main statutory schemes under FOI 2000 and the 2004 Regulations operate in a complementary fashion, with the minimum of overlaps. FOI 2000 provides a general right to access information from public authorities, subject only to a list of exempt information. Environmental information is one of the two exceptions to the universal application of the FOI, the other being in relation to information on individuals under data protection legislation. Environmental information is exempt from the Act and any access is governed by the 2004 Regulations (Freedom of Information Act 2000, s. 39).

Subject to the exemptions in the Act, any person who makes a request to a public authority for information must be informed whether the public authority holds that information and, if so, be given access to the information. The request for information must be in writing, including the name and address of the person seeking the information, along with a description of the information required (s. 8). The Act applies to all 'public authorities'. Unlike previous legislation, the Act provides a comprehensive list of bodies to whom the duty to facilitate access applies (Sch. 1). It covers central and local government bodies, regulators, and privatized utilities.

There are 23 exemptions to the general right of access under FOI 2000 (ss. 21–44). Most of the exemptions have to be considered in two stages. First, there must be a decision on whether any exemption applies to all, or part, of the information requested. If it does, the second consideration is whether the public interest in maintaining the exemption outweighs the public interest in disclosing the information. These are known as the 'qualified' exemptions.

There are also a number of 'absolute' exemptions to which the public interest test does not apply. The exemption for environmental information under s. 39 is qualified. Thus, there is a residual role for FOI 2000 in relation to environmental information that is exempt from disclosure under the 2004 Regulations and in relation to which the public interest in disclosing the information is not outweighed by the public interest in maintaining the exemption under s. 39 of the Act—but it has been suggested that the circumstances under which disclosure would be granted under FOI 2000, when it had been refused under the 2004 Regulations, would be few and far between.[21] The other potential application of the FOI is to information that may not fall completely within the definition of 'environmental information' for the purposes of the 2004 Regulations. In such circumstances, information can be sought under both regimes.

Two codes of practice relating to access and the management of records govern the application of the Act (FOI 2000, ss. 45–46). Enforcement of the Act lies with the Information Commissioner, who has powers to instruct public authorities to disclose information (ss. 50–56). There is also a right of appeal to the Information Tribunal (ss. 57–61).

The Environmental Information Regulations 2004

The Environmental Information Regulations 2004 transpose and implement the provisions of Directive 2003/4/EC and, accordingly, pave the way for the ratification of the information provisions of the Aarhus Convention. Under the 2004 Regulations, 'public authorities' are under a duty to make 'environmental information' available to every person who requests it. The phrase 'environmental information' is defined widely in accordance with the Directive definition (see Box 10.4).

---

21 P. Coppel [2005] JPL 14.

BOX 10.4 'Environmental information'

Regulation 1 of the Environmental Information Regulations 2004 defines 'environmental information' as including:

(a) the state of the elements of the environment, such as air and atmosphere, water, soil, land, landscape and natural sites including wetlands, coastal and marine areas, biological diversity and its components, including genetically modified organisms, and the interaction among these elements;

(b) factors, such as substances, energy, noise, radiation or waste, including radioactive waste, emissions, discharges and other releases into the environment, affecting or likely to affect the elements of the environment referred to in (a);

(c) measures (including administrative measures), such as policies, legislation, plans, programmes, environmental agreements, and activities affecting or likely to affect the elements and factors referred to in (a) and (b) as well as measures or activities designed to protect those elements;

(d) reports on the implementation of environmental legislation;

(e) cost–benefit and other economic analyses and assumptions used within the framework of the measures and activities referred to in (c);

(f) the state of human health and safety, including the contamination of the food chain, where relevant, conditions of human life, cultural sites and built structures inasmuch as they are or may be affected by the state of the elements of the environment referred to in (a) or, through those elements, by any of the matters referred to in (b) and (c);

...

The Regulations apply to all 'public authorities'. Broadly speaking, these are the same as the authorities listed in Sch. 1 of FOI 2000. The definition is extended slightly to cover the requirements of the Directive, to include bodies with specific duties in relation to the environment. Authorities such as the Department of the Environment, Food and Rural Affairs (DEFRA), local authorities, and the Environment Agency are clearly covered, as are a broad range of other regulatory agencies, such as Natural England. The definition has, however, extended the requirements of disclosure to privatized utilities. It is also notable that the classes of public authority covered under FOI 2000 and the 2004 Regulations has been extended on a number of occasions since 2000.[22]

When a request for information is made, it must be answered within 20 working days of receipt of the request, which can be extended to a maximum of 40 working days if the request is 'complex and voluminous'. There are no formal requirements and requests can be verbal or written, electronic or hardcopy. Any response, however, must be in writing (regs 5–7). Public authorities have a responsibility to provide 'advice and assistance' to applicants (reg. 9). Thus, if a request were considered to be 'too general', an authority would be obliged to contact an applicant as soon as possible to try to determine specifically the exact nature of the information required.

In cases in which the public authority refuses to disclose all, or part, of the information requested, it must issue a refusal notice in writing, stating the exception under which the information falls, with reasons for any decision that the exception should be applied (reg. 14). In cases in which the confirmation of the mere existence of certain sensitive information

---

22 See, e.g., the Freedom of Information (Additional Public Authorities) Order 2002, SI 2002/2623.

may prejudice one of the protected exceptions, the authority may issue a decision that neither denies nor confirms that the requested information is held (reg. 12(6)).

There are various exceptions to the duty to disclose. The first is if the request is vague, manifestly unreasonable, or not held by the authority. The second is if the information relates to personal data, internal communications, or is incomplete. A good example of this type of information was seen in the *Maile* case (see Case 10.1).

CASE 10.1 **Incomplete information—*Maile v. Wigan Borough Council* [2001] Env LR 11**

The applicant lived in Wigan and made a request to his local authority to see a database detailing potentially contaminated sites that was being prepared in the light of the implementation of the contaminated land regime under Pt 2A of the Environmental Protection Act 1990. The local authority refused, saying that the information was incomplete. The court held that there was no requirement to disclose. Although, under the predecessor Regulations to the 2004 Regulations, local authorities were under a general duty to disclose environmental information to those persons requesting it, this duty did not apply if the information was still in the course of completion or was otherwise exempt as confidential. The database was considered to be 'speculative', and it was considered that its disclosure would cause 'unnecessary alarm' and 'despondency among local citizens'.

The third exemption arises when disclosure would adversely affect one of the identified categories of protected information. If information falls within one of these categories, it must also be shown that, in all of the circumstances of the case, the public interest in maintaining the exception outweighs the public interest in disclosing the information.

BOX 10.5 **Classes of exempt information**

A public authority may refuse to disclose information if its disclosure would adversely affect:

- international relations, defence, national security, or public safety;[23]
- the course of justice, the ability of a person to receive a fair trial, or the ability of a public authority to conduct an inquiry of a criminal or disciplinary nature;
- intellectual property rights;
- the confidentiality of the proceedings of that or any other public authority, if such confidentiality is provided by law;
- commercially confidential information, if such confidentiality is provided by law to protect a legitimate economic interest;[24]
- voluntarily supplied information;
- the protection of the environment to which the information relates.

The authority is obliged to tell the applicant of the right to appeal the decision, first to the authority and then, if not satisfied, to the Information Commissioner.

If the application for information is refused, an applicant has various rights of appeal. Initially, there is a right to ask the public authority itself to reconsider its decision (reg. 11). Following that,

---

23 See, e.g., *R v. British Coal Corporation, ex parte Ibstock Building Products Ltd* [1995] Env LR 277.

24 See, e.g., *R v. Secretary of State for the Environment, Transport and the Regions, ex parte Alliance against Birmingham Northern Relief Road (No. 1)* [1999] Env LR 447.

there are consequent rights to appeal to the Information Commissioner (reg. 18), the Information Tribunal (FOI 2000, s. 58(1)), and to the High Court (on a question of law) (s. 59).

Public registers

Although the general right of access to environmental information under the 2004 Regulations represents a significant development in the UK, the traditional format of disclosure of pollution control information is through the system of statutory public registers. Although the statutory provisions vary, depending upon the area of concern, there are common features in most of the pollution control registers. In these cases, the common features include the following.

- **The availability of information**

  Generally, information must be available at all reasonable times for inspection by the public free of charge. Copies of any document can be taken on payment of a reasonable charge. The registers are held at the principal offices of the relevant local authority or the regional office of the Environment Agency (in relation to the location of the operation that is the subject of the authorization or permissions).

- **The nature of the information**

  The information on registers covers: applications; details of permissions, authorizations, etc. including the name and address of the operator; particulars of any enforcement action or criminal actions; appeals; information provided by the operator in order to comply with conditions. This normally includes self-monitoring data and spot samples of environmental releases. Records can generally be kept in any form (for example, electronically).

- **Exemptions**

  There are exemptions for certain classes of information, the disclosure of which would affect national security or commercial confidentiality. Commercial confidentiality is defined by reference to whether disclosure would prejudice to an unreasonable degree the commercial interests of the person concerned.[25] If information is excluded from the register on the ground of commercial confidentiality, there is a statement in the register that indicates the existence of the information.

- **Rights of appeal**

  The preliminary determination of whether a particular piece of information is commercially confidential lies with the regulatory body (usually the Environment Agency). There is a right of appeal against that determination to the Secretary of State within 21 days of provisional notification and, until the appeal is finally decided, the information is kept off the register.

BOX 10.6 **The main environmental registers**			
Subject matter of register	**Type of information**	**Relevant legislation**	**Agency responsible for keeping information**
Contaminated land	Notices identifying land as contaminated, remediation notices, appeals, remediation statements	EPA 1990, s. 78R The Contaminated Land (England) Regulations 2006[26]	Environment Agency (in relation to special sites) Local authorities

25 See, e.g., Environmental Permitting (England and Wales) Regulations 2007, SI 2007/3538, reg. 48, and Water Resources Act 1991, s. 191B(11).

26 SI 2006/1380.

Subject matter of register	Type of information	Relevant legislation	Agency responsible for keeping information
Genetically modified organisms (GMOs)	Particulars of environmental impact assessments, applications, prohibitions, consents granted	EPA 1990, s. 122 Genetically Modified Organisms (Deliberate Release) Regulations 2002[27]	DEFRA
Industrial processes	Installations subject to environmental permitting	Environmental Permitting (England and Wales) Regulations 2007[28]	Environment Agency Local authorities
Planning	Environmental statements, planning applications, planning permissions, enforcement applications for planning permission	Town and Country Planning Act 1990, s. 69 Planning and Compulsory Purchase Act 2004 The Town and Country Planning (General Development Procedure) Order 1995[29]	Local authorities
Trade effluent	Consents for discharges of liquid waste to sewerage works, directions for discharges, agreements, notices	Water Industry Act 1991, s. 196	Sewerage undertaker
Waste management	Details of environmental permits, including enforcement and conditions	Environmental Permitting (England and Wales) Regulations 2007	Environment Agency
Water resources—abstraction licences	Abstraction licences and enforcement	Water Resources Act 1991, s. 189 Water Resources (Licences) Regulations 1965[30]	Environment Agency
Water pollution—discharge consents	Details of consents, compliance with conditions and enforcement	WRA 1991, ss. 190 and 191 The Control of Pollution (Applications, Appeals and Registers) Regulations 1996[31]	Environment Agency

27 SI 2002/2443.   28 SI 2007/3538.   29 SI 1995/419.
30 SI 1965/534.   31 SI 1996/2971.

Different classes of environmental information

There is an increasing recognition that the use of information can be an integral part of an environmental regulatory system in more sophisticated ways than through the provision of pollution data on public registers. There are, therefore, a number of broad, overlapping instruments that might be classified as 'information-based'. Although such classifications are crude, in the sense that they tend to be 'soft' and ill defined (often as a consequence of their voluntary nature), they paint a picture of how information can slot into various aspects of the regulatory system.

Environmental reporting

In addition to mandatory disclosure of information in the form of statutory public registers, many companies have developed a system of voluntary disclosure of environmental information, through the provision of annual corporate environmental reports. Research indicates that 89 per cent of the FTSE All Share Index (570 companies) publishes some environmental information as part of its annual reporting process.[32] Significantly, however, many of these are criticized as lacking any depth or objective value, with only 24 per cent of companies reporting quantitative data. One of the fundamental difficulties with corporate reporting is that there is no standard format for disclosure and that the quality of the information can vary. The reports range from little more than one-line references to the environment, to detailed assessments of environmental impacts.

Elements of a report might include:

- a discussion of the environmental issues that are relevant to the business;

- legislative compliance and the result of any environmental audits of the business;

- information on releases to the environment (whether or not they are included on a public register);

- energy efficiency and other resource conservation issues;

- local issues;

- the setting of key performance indicators and targets for future environmental performance;

- a comparative analysis of performance within the relevant industrial sector;

- the achievement of sustainable development targets.

Many of these issues are covered in a rudimentary manner, with more sophisticated analysis being dependent upon the development of environmental accounting that might place some of the matters covered into a corporate and financial context, such as by allocating a financial cost to the environmental impacts disclosed.

Environmental reporting has developed apace since the early 1990s. Part of the reason for this development has been external pressure from stakeholders, such as investors, environmental interest groups, and the general public—although it should be emphasized that internal corporate environmental responsibility, and the competitive advantage to be gained from demonstrating environmental compliance and improvement (in relation to corporate clients), have also had their parts to play. There are moves to formalize both the content of a, and the requirement to, report. The International Standards Organization (ISO) has published guidance on developing indicators of environmental performance.[33]

---

32 Environment Agency (2004) *Environmental Disclosures.*
33 See ISO 14031.

Real benefits can result from the process of voluntary disclosure. The most obvious benefit is that the public and other stakeholders have access to information about a company's operations that might not otherwise be disclosed. This might involve previously undisclosed qualitative (for example, types of waste arisings) and quantitative (for example, aggregated waste arisings) environmental information. In addition, the information will generally be in a format that can be easily communicated to, and accessed by, the public, including via the Internet.

The second main benefit is internal to the company compiling the report: the preparation of an environmental report means that a company must be aware of, and address, the environmental impacts that it creates. This preparatory work can assist the company in identifying areas in which environmental performance can be improved and/or cost savings made.

The third benefit is that the publication of reports can set standards within an industry sector that others must follow. This might be on a simplistic level, such as the 'name and shame' policy adopted by government to isolate those companies that are not preparing environmental reports, or it might be more sophisticated, in the sense that the presentation of comparative environmental performance indicators could set the standard within the industry sector.

In addition to this voluntary form of corporate environmental reporting, there is a more formalized system of disclosing the environmental impacts of a business through the environmental management standard (EMS) adopted under the EC Regulation on Eco-management and Audit Scheme (EMAS).[34] As part of the accreditation process, a business must publish a publicly available document outlining its environmental policy and targets for improvement. This written statement is subject to external and independent verification, but there are potential weaknesses in its role as a source of dependable environmental information.

Environmental information to the consumer

Environmental information on products can assist consumer choice by facilitating a better assessment of the environmental impacts or costs that are involved in their production and thereby, on a theoretical level at least, internalize some of the external environmental costs. Arguably, there is a legitimate debate about the extent to which the consumption of consumer goods can 'benefit' the environment.[35] The disclosure of information can, in conjunction with other instruments such as product standards or economic instruments, help with the process of 'market transformation', whereby there is an increase in the proportion of products that have lower environmental impacts, while decreasing the proportion of products that bring about greater environmental harm.[36] For example, a label might indicate the energy consumption of domestic central heating boilers. Additionally, there might be a ban on boilers with an energy-efficiency rating below a certain standard. Finally, a financial grant might be made available to assist people who want to replace any boiler of over ten years old with a new boiler that comes with a designated eco-label that indicates high levels of energy efficiency. The effect of these combined measures—the first and last of which are information instruments—would be to ensure that more energy efficient boilers were placed on the market.

The nature of this information can range from informal advertising information, often referred to as 'green claims', through more formal sectoral product certification schemes, such as timber products manufactured from sustainable managed timber certified by the Forest Stewardship Council or the Marine Stewardship Council certifying sustainable

---

34 Regulation 1836/93/EC.

35 See WorldWatch Institute (2004) *State of the World 2004: Special Focus—The Consumer Society,* Washington, DC: WorldWatch Institute.

36 See Department of the Environment, Transport and the Regions (1998) *Consumer Products and the Environment*, Consultation Paper.

fisheries, to official national eco-labelling schemes regulated by national authorities across a range of products, with specific criteria for each product grouping. Other matters that might be covered include information on the safe use, reuse, recycling, and disposal of products.

(a) Green claims

Once manufacturers recognized that environmental issues were a factor in purchasing decisions, they developed a range of green claims for their products, which included meaningless and objectively immeasurable claims—for example, 'environmentally friendly'—or statements that expressed a truism—for example, 'CFC free' in products after the implementation of the ban on CFCs. These sorts of claim undermine the primary purpose of disclosure of this type of information to consumers, which is to differentiate objectively between different products. Although there are some safeguards against claims that are factually incorrect,[37] statements that are empty of meaning, or axiomatic, fall outside existing statutory control. The governmental response to this problem has been to rely on self-regulation by producing the Green Claims Code, a voluntary code of practice with all of the weaknesses that such self-regulatory systems possess.[38]

(b) Eco-labelling

One way of addressing some of the weaknesses of these green claims is to ensure that there is a consistent, objective, and identifiable symbol that can indicate to the consumer that a product has been assessed and approved against a set of approved criteria. The European eco-labelling scheme[39] was designed to provide such a label in the shape of a characteristic blue and green flower. The scheme was launched across member States in July 1993, and applied first in the UK to eco-labels on dishwashers and to washing machines later that year.

The system of approval can be divided into three distinct phases.

- The European Commission classifies a product group after consulting and negotiating with interested parties, including consumer groups, environmental interest groups, and industry. Once the group is classified, the criteria for the award are established—once again, after consultation with stakeholders. The criteria for approval vary depending upon product groups, but are generally associated with such things as raw materials consumption, in addition to a broader life cycle assessment.

- The manufacturer applies to the national competent body for approval. In the UK, DEFRA deals with these applications.

- The third and final phase of the eco-labelling process is the revision of the product group criteria, which, once again, is carried out by the European Commission.

But the eco-labelling scheme has not been an overwhelming success either in terms of the quantity of the product groups that have been classified, or the level of consumer or market interest. The scheme is perceived to be overcomplicated, prescriptive in its criteria, and too rigid.[40]

(c) Other forms of product certification

There are other product certification schemes that have had greater levels of acceptance and success than the eco-label. For example, at the European level, there is an 'energy label' under

---

37 This would be a criminal offence under the Trade Descriptions Act 1968, s. 1.

38 The Code takes into account the international standard on environmental claims, ISO 14021. Other guidance can be found in DEFRA (2003) *Green Claims: Practical Guidance* and online at **www.defra.gov.uk/environment/ consumerprod/glc/claims.htm**.

39 Regulation 1980/2000.

40 See, e.g., the consultation responses to DETR (1999) *Consumer Products and the Environment*.

Directive 92/75/EEC, with subsequent daughter Directives for particular appliances.[41] The development of energy ratings for buildings is another example of product certification in relation to an atypical 'product'—namely, houses.[42] This scheme, implemented in the UK through the home information pack, is interesting in that it applies not only to new products, but also to products on reuse.[43] At national level, there are a number of sectoral labels, such as those in the timber and fishing industries referred to above or a scheme designed to show the volatile organic compound (VOC) content in paints promoted by the British Coating Federation.

The main problem with this proliferation of schemes is that they tend to undermine the credibility and power of centralized labelling schemes, with the inevitable consequences for the process of 'market transformation'.

Access to environmental information in the UK—an assessment

The broadening of access to environmental information over the last twenty years has not been without its criticisms.[44] Many of the problems encountered with the 1992 Regulations have been addressed by means of the clarifications found in the 2003 Directive and the transposing Regulations. The refining of certain definitions, and the extension of the scope and application of the Regulations in the light of experience, has facilitated greater access—indeed, some have argued that the pendulum has swung too far.[45] In addition, the provision of information when requested is only part of the justification for more liberal access to information regimes: in many cases, the information will require technical interpretation or may be presented in such a way that it is given a favourable slant.[46]

Similarly, although the system of public registers provides an easy source of information about polluting activities, empirical evidence suggests that they are underused by members of the general public.[47] There are a number of potential reasons for this, which are primarily connected to the accessibility of the registers themselves, and to the quality and comprehensiveness of the information found on the registers. For example, raw monitoring data, of the sort that is found in the registers, often shows the results of single samples without providing 'non-experts' with a clear picture of overall levels of compliance. In most cases, there is no information relating to general environmental quality standards or the cumulative effects of releases into the environment.

The provisions within the Regulations that are designed to promote the wider active dissemination of environmental information may assist in this regard. There have been a number of attempts to make pollution control information more accessible and user-friendly, specifically via the Internet. In particular, the Environment Agency's 'What's in your backyard?' website[48] sets out environmental data in a national, regional, and local context, and with general aggregated sources. The greater availability of general information about the environment is part of a general shift away from the mere production of environmental data on pollution, towards a broader communication of the implications of activities in terms

---

41 See, e.g., washing machines under Directive 95/12/EC and the Energy Information (Washing Machines) Regulations 1996, SI 1996/600.

42 See Directive 2002/91/EC on the energy performance of buildings, Art. 7.

43 See Energy Performance of Buildings (Certificates and Inspections) (England and Wales) Regulations 2007, SI 2007/991.

44 See, e.g., H. Jenn (1993) WL 163.

45 See 'An insult to open government and democracy' Observer, 20 May 2007, discussing the failed bid to exclude the House of Commons from FOI legislation.

46 M. Lee and C. Abbot (2003) 66 MLR 93. Also see *Edwards v. Environment Agency* [2007] Env LR 9, which is a good illustration of the difficulties of accessing technical information as part of the application process for a PPC permit.

47 See, e.g., T. Burton (1989) 1 JEL 192 and J. Rowan-Robinson , A. Ross, W. Walton, and J. Rothnie (1996) 8 JEL 19.

48 See www.environment-agency.gov.uk.

that people can understand. This is reflected in the moves towards active dissemination of information and the development of aggregated pollutant inventories.

Although access to such information can communicate on a much wider basis, it still has its limitations, in the sense that it does little to capture the social or cultural aspects of environmental values. For example, aggregated indicators may suggest that the loss of natural habitats has fallen on a year-by-year basis, but this might conceal the fact that, in one village, a particularly important green space that has cultural significance has been lost to development. This example merely illustrates that there will be some aspects of environmental protection that only gain significance when viewed within the local context and which, as such, are difficult to capture as general information.

Public participation in environmental decision making

There is a long history of public involvement in environmental decision making. Typically, participation in the planning system through local consultation on planning applications, and more general participation in development planning, provided plenty of opportunities for the public to comment on development proposals and more strategic issues. Somewhat paradoxically, however, it has been argued that, notwithstanding this long history of public involvement in the planning system, environmental regulation has been 'closed to public influence'.[49] This is because, in stark contrast to the planning system, most pollution control regimes had rudimentary notification and consultation processes, and nature conservation decisions were almost entirely determined by experts without recourse to the general public. The reasons for this are largely concerned with the technical nature of such decisions. Other factors included the close relationship between industry and the regulators, the lack of transparency in decision making, and the large degree of discretion to set environmental standards.

This process of change has been relatively swift, with increased participation in pollution control regimes and planning, through the introduction of formal environmental impact assessment (EIA) and the need to implement the requirements of Arts 6–9 of the Aarhus Convention. This has led to the EC adopting Directive 2003/35/EC on public participation in certain environmental plans and programmes. The Directive provides for the public to have 'early and effective opportunities' to participate in the preparation and review of plans and programmes made under six existing EC Directives, dealing with nitrates, waste, hazardous waste, packaging, batteries, and air-quality management.

The increased emphasis upon participation in decision making was taken up by the RCEP in its 21st Report (1998) *Setting Environment Standards* (Cm 4053), which called (at para. 9) for *'a more rigorous and wide-ranging exploration of people's values'* at the *'earliest stage'* in what had been *'hitherto relatively technocratic procedures'*. The RCEP called for more deliberative techniques in which the public played a significant role in setting strategies, rather than its consultation on already drafted proposals (para. 7.22).

Types of public participation

On a very general level, public participation consists of attempts to influence law, policies, and individual decisions made by governmental or regulatory bodies. This involves many different things, but it includes being able to have access to, understand, evaluate, formulate, and comment upon proposals, plans, and programmes. It can take the form of:

- pluralistic participation, within which representative bodies—such as non-government organizations (NGOs) or industry associations—speak on behalf of individuals;

---

49 J. Steele (2001) OJLS 418.

- stakeholder participation, within which proposals that have already been formulated are transmitted to interested parties to comment upon and refine;

- deliberative participation, which consists of 'agreeing the ground rules'—that is, involving the public in determining what general policies and strategies should be adopted—before moving to the stage of specific proposals.

In addition, participation can have differing degrees of legal force. For example, in EIA, public participation is a mandatory substantive requirement that is a precondition of the grant of planning permission. In many other situations, participation is facilitated through a procedural 'right' to be consulted or heard at an inquiry. In other circumstances, consultation takes place voluntarily in an attempt to use 'best practice' or to elicit values to settle issues of environmental risk.

BOX 10.7 Participation and environmental risk—the Agriculture and Biotechnology Commission

In 1999, in response to the growing public uncertainty about genetically modified crops and foods, the government reviewed the advisory and regulatory framework for biotechnology. The conclusions were that opinions on the topic were deeply divided and that more effort was needed to involve the public in the debate about what should be done. Consequently, the Agriculture and Biotechnology Commission (ABEC) was formed.

The Commission's membership was deliberately taken from people with a wide range of views on the topic, with a view to seeking expert opinion from all sides of the debate. It includes industry representatives, green activists, media personalities, and a philosopher. Its role is to advise the government on how to address the issues associated with genetically modified (GM) crops and foods, and, in doing so, it is obliged to consider ethical and social issues in addition to the more usual scientific considerations.

The Commission produced three annual reports, but its main role in promoting public participation was the national debate on GM foods run in the summer of 2003. Entitled 'GM Nation?', this involved a series of workshops to frame the debate, followed by over six hundred meetings held across the country involving thousands of people. The headline results of the exercise were that:

- people are generally uneasy about GM;
- the more people engage in GM issues, the harder their attitudes and more intense their concerns;
- there is little support for early commercialization of GM;
- there is widespread mistrust of government and multinational companies;
- there is a broad desire to know more and for further research to be done;
- developing countries have special interests;
- the debate was welcomed and valued.

After an independent review ABEC was wound up in 2005.

That such efforts were expended upon seeking to elicit views from the wider public, and the extent to which the evidence was put in an objective and comprehensive manner, were unique in environmental regulation. Perhaps the results were unsurprising, but the process was remarkable.

One of the central challenges of public participation is seeking to ensure that the *quality* of the participation is sufficient to engage the public actively and that proper opportunity is given to respond to any consultation exercise. In particular, the judiciary consistently ignored the importance of public participation as a fundamental rationale for undertaking an EIA. A number of early cases tended to view public participation as the 'icing on the cake' of what was merely an information-gathering exercise. Thus, in *R v. Poole Borough Council, ex parte Beebee* [1991] JPL 643, the absence of an environmental statement and any public participation that would have produced it was considered to be superfluous, because the necessary information was already before the planning authority.

This approach seemed to fly in the face of the original EIA Directive, which was to provide a procedural framework so as to guarantee that the environmental impact of a project was a part of the public debate and informed the resulting decisions. In *Berkeley v. Secretary of State for the Environment* [2001] Env LR 16 (known as *Berkeley (No. 1)*), the House of Lords considered the role of public participation in the EIA process. The Lords emphasized that an important part of the environmental assessment procedure was to provide the public with all of the relevant information in a rational and digestible form, then to facilitate public comment on that information. Thus it was the *process* of consultation that was important, even if the result was informed by the public's 'misguided or wrongheaded views'. The process was designed to give the public an opportunity to express its opinion.[50]

Access to environmental justice

The final aspect of facilitating public participation in environmental law is ensuring that there is adequate access to a means of enforcing environmental law or in seeking redress in resolving environmental disputes. This can have different aspects, including the right to bring private prosecutions or to bring private law actions with an environmental element. Under the Aarhus Convention, this is referred to as 'access to justice in environmental matters'.[51] Article 9(2) of the Convention provides that anyone who has a *sufficient interest* shall be able to *challenge the substantive or procedural legality of any decision, act or omission*. In the absence of third-party rights to appeal in relation to administrative appeals, the main 'right' to challenge the legality of administrative decisions in the UK courts comes through the mechanism of judicial review.

Thus, the focus of this section is mainly on procedural matters—that is, a right to bring a judicial review—and the structural and institutional issue—that is, the establishment of an environmental court—rather than the quality of substantive decisions provided by the legal system. In this context, it should be noted that 'justice' is probably not the most appropriate word with which to describe the objective of environmental law; arguably, at least, that objective should be more accurately characterized as ensuring that the environment is properly protected. Whether environmental law meets that objective is a substantive question that should be addressed separately from whether procedures, structures, and institutions function efficiently.

Judicial review

The process of judicial review is one way of making public bodies accountable to the courts and ensuring that they only act within the powers given to them by Parliament. Accordingly, judicial review addresses the legality, and not the merits, of a decision. The legality of a decision comprises two different aspects. Procedural legality ensures that people have a right to a

50 This notion of procedural fairness has been adopted in *Edwards v. Environment Agency* [2007] Env LR 9.
51 See, in the EC context, the proposal for an implementing Directive COM(2003) 624.

fair hearing and that there should be no bias or perception of bias in a decision-making process. In circumstances under which there is procedural illegality, a court will overturn the decision, but send the issue back to the original decision maker to be redetermined.

Where there is substantive illegality, however, courts overturn decisions that are illegal either because they are unfair, unreasonable, or unlawful. The exact grounds of judicial review are not necessarily clearly defined. For example, the edges between unreasonableness, irrelevancy, and disproportionality are blurred. A right to challenge an illegal decision in this sense should not be confused with any statutory right of appeal, which may give rise to a reconsideration of the merits of a case, rather than consideration of questions of law. Indeed, theoretically, a court exercising its power of judicial review is not entitled to substitute its own decision for that of the administrative body.

This general right to challenge administrative decisions is supplemented, in certain cases, by specific statutory rights to challenge decisions.[52] Although there are procedural distinctions between the two types of challenge—in particular, there are often much stricter time limits—the substantive issues remain broadly the same. It is important to note, however, that the statutory challenge is often an exclusive power that prevents any further challenge under general judicial review proceedings.

There is also the increasingly important issue of the overlap of judicial review with the right to seek a remedy under the Human Rights Act 1998. Human rights arguments have merged with arguments over illegality in judicial review actions.[53] Concepts such as proportionality have also emerged, taken from European law to extend notions of illegality further. These points merely emphasize the fluid nature of judicial review and the extent to which grounds of challenge emerge over time.

In examining judicial review as a tool for enhancing access to justice in environmental matters, there are a number of factors that must be taken into account. There are certain legal hurdles that must be overcome before bringing a claim and, in order to bring a judicial review, a claimant must have:

- standing—that is, a 'sufficient interest' in the subject matter of the decision being challenged;

- commenced proceeding promptly;

- no other avenue of redress.

Standing

In order to bring a claim for judicial review, an applicant must show a 'sufficient interest' in the decision or power to which the application relates.[54] In many cases, a sufficient interest is created directly through the holding of a relevant pollution control licence or authorization to which the application relates.

The basis of the law on standing is contained in *Inland Revenue Commissioners v. National Federation of Self Employed and Small Businesses Ltd* [1982] AC 617, in which Lord Wilberforce said that the decision as to who had a 'sufficient interest' had to be considered with the known merits of a case:

It will be necessary to consider the powers or the duties of those against whom the relief is asked, the position of the applicant in relation to those powers or duties, and to the breach of those duties said to have

---

52 For example, s. 288 of the Town and Country Planning Act 1990 makes provision for High Court challenges to decisions of the Secretary of State on points of law.

53 It has been found that human rights arguments are invoked in almost 50 per cent of all judicial review cases—see Public Law Project (2003) *The Impact of the Human Rights Act on Judicial Review: An Empirical Research Study*, London: Public Law Project.

54 Supreme Court Act 1981, s. 31(3).

been committed. In other words, the question of sufficient interest cannot, in such cases, be considered in the abstract, or as an isolated point: it must be taken together with the legal and factual context.[55]

More generally, it is clear that somebody with a private interest in land affected by an administrative decision would have 'sufficient interest' or standing. This can be expanded to include those who are living in proximity to an area that is affected by a decision, although there would appear to be some limitations.

CASE 10.2 **Proximity and standing—*R (Edwards) v. Environment Agency* [2004] Env LR 43 and *R v. North West Leicestershire District Council, ex parte Moses* [2000] JPL 733**

In *R (Edwards) v. Environment Agency*, the claimant had lived in Rugby all of his life, although he was temporarily homeless. He sought to challenge the grant of an IPPC permit by the Environment Agency to a local cement company. The claimant had played no part in the consultation process, although he had attended meetings of a local campaign group. The Agency argued that, because he was not an active participant in the consultation process, he did not have a 'sufficient interest' in the application. In addition, it was argued that he had been put forward as the claimant purely on the ground that he could secure funding from the Legal Services Commission to bring the action. The Court held that the claimant had standing even if he was temporarily homeless, because, as an inhabitant of Rugby, he would be affected by any adverse impact on the environment from the cement works. The arguments about funding were also rejected.

In contrast, in *R v. North West Leicestershire District Council, ex parte Moses*, an applicant sought to challenge various decisions to extend the runway at East Midlands International Airport. At the time of the decision and when she had applied for judicial review, she had lived close to the end of the runway. Since that time, she had moved some six miles away from the airport. The Court held that, since moving, the applicant no longer had a 'sufficient interest' in the proceedings. The Court considered that, had she lived six miles away at the time of the decision, she would have had no more interest in the decision than if she had lived in the 'Orkney or Shetland Islands'. This decision reflects a relatively limited view of the nature of the possible environmental impacts from the extension of a runway. It could equally be argued that a resident six miles away could be affected by indirect impacts such as an increase in noise or road transport associated with an expanding airport. It should be noted that, on appeal to the Court of Appeal, the decision was made on different grounds.

It is, however, more difficult to show that a person has the necessary standing by virtue of an interest in the environment as a whole, because it is not generally accepted that there are 'environmental rights' available to the public at large. This raises the question of representational, or public interest, standing. In the planning system, many actions have been brought by local interest groups in which sufficient interest can be demonstrated by objecting to proposals or giving evidence at a local inquiry, and an analogy can be drawn in relation to groups bringing challenges in connection with local environmental issues, such as environmental permits, statutory nuisances, or local air quality. The position of general environmental interest groups, such as Friends of the Earth or Greenpeace, is more problematic, because there is no necessary geographic connection with the matter being challenged. Representative bodies bring a significant number of judicial review actions, with a good percentage being brought by environmental NGOs.

---

55 At 630.

The courts have taken an increasingly liberal approach to standing for representational bodies.[56]

BOX 10.8 Estimated number of public interest court cases brought by environmental NGOs, citizen groupings, or individuals 1995–2001[57]

Category of applicant	Total number of cases
Established environmental NGOs (e.g. Greenpeace, Friends of the Earth)	25
Ad hoc identifiable grouping (e.g. the Crystal Palace Campaign)	20
Ad hoc collection of individuals (e.g. representing village residents)	21
Individual applicants reflecting a community concern (e.g. parents)	34
Individual applicants defending public interests (e.g. on radio masts)	8
Other (e.g. complaints engaging public environmental interest)	2

BOX 10.9 Representational standing

In *R v. Secretary of State for the Environment, ex parte Rose Theatre Trust* [1990] 1 QB 504, a group of objectors to the redevelopment of the Rose Theatre banded together to form a Trust Company to challenge the decision not to list the site of the Theatre as protected under the Ancient Monuments and Archaeological Areas Act 1979. The Court rejected the application for judicial review, on the basis that the Trust did not have standing to bring the action. Schiemann J found that the mere assertion of an interest was not, in itself, sufficient to demonstrate sufficient interest even if made by 'thousands of people'. He stated:

> it would be absurd if two people, neither of whom had standing could, by an appropriately worded memorandum, incorporate themselves into a company which thereby obtained standing.[58]

This low point on representational standing was doubted in *R v. Inspectorate of Pollution, ex parte Greenpeace Ltd (No. 2)* [1994] 4 All ER 329, in which Greenpeace challenged the decision to allow the thermal oxide reprocessing plant (THORP) at Sellafield to commence operations. Pointing to Greenpeace's genuine interest in the issues raised, and to its expertise and resources, Otton J decided that the group had sufficient interest, although he did note that it also had many members in the region who might be affected.

In *R v. Secretary of State for Foreign and Commonwealth Affairs, ex parte World Development Movement Ltd* [1995] 1 WLR 386 (the *Pergau Dam* case), the court, if anything, went even further in allowing a pure public interest claim to proceed, because there were clearly no local residents

---

56 M. Sheridan (2005) 'United Kingdom report' in N. de Sadeleer, G. Roller, and M. Dross (eds) *Access to Justice in Environmental Matters and the Role of NGOs: Empirical Findings and Legal Appraisal*, Groeningen: Europa Law.

57 Ibid.

58 At 521.

involved. In particular, it was emphasized that, if the applicants were not granted standing, then a clear illegality would not be subject to challenge.

Although general environmental interest groups have become increasingly accepted as having standing in judicial review actions, there is still a degree of uncertainty and there have been cases in which the courts have required a special interest in the subject matter of the challenge.[59] In *R v. Somerset County Council, ex parte Dixon* [1998] Env LR 111, the decision in *Pergau Dam* was, however, reaffirmed and the law on standing continued to be liberalized. In that case, the answer to the question of who had sufficient interest in the subject matter of the challenge was wide enough to include anyone who was neither a busybody nor a troublemaker. Public law challenges were concerned with the abuse of power, not the protection of private rights, and therefore the classes of those who sought to draw attention to those abuses must include anyone who had a genuine interest in the subject matter of the challenge irrespective of any private law interest.

There is a degree of contradiction in some of these cases, which have strikingly similar facts with very different results. While these differences emphasize the discretionary nature of judicial review proceedings, they also illustrate that there is little precedent value in previous decisions.

Challenges brought under the Human Rights Act 1998 are slightly different. Because an assertion of rights is linked to the individual, it is only a person who is a 'victim' of the rights abuse who can claim standing. A person who cannot show that he or she is personally affected by the law to a greater extent than any other person may not claim to be a victim. Thus there are no rights to bring a representative action for human rights breaches. For example, in *Adams v. Advocate General for Scotland* (2002) UKHRR 1189, the Countryside Alliance and the Masters of the Foxhounds Association sought to challenge the ban on fox-hunting under the Protection of Wild Mammals (Scotland) Act 2002. The Court held that, as representative bodies, they did not have sufficient standing, because some of the members of the group lived outside Scotland and would not have been affected by the ban. Similarly, in *R v. Mayor of London, ex parte Westminster City Council* [2002] EWHC 2440, a challenge to the London congestion charge on the grounds of an inadequate EIA and breaches of human rights failed because Westminster City Council did not fall within the definition of a 'victim' for the purposes of the Human Rights Act 1998.

It should be noted that there is one exception to all of this: the Attorney-General, as guardian of the public interest, always has standing. An applicant without 'sufficient interest' could therefore ask the Attorney-General to bring an action on his or her behalf. This is called a 'relator' action. The shadow applicant pays the costs, but manages to sidestep the rules on standing. The Attorney-General does, however, have an unchallengeable discretion whether to bring an action in this manner.

Delay

The second procedural hurdle for any application for judicial review is that the application must be made 'promptly'. Under CPR Rule 54.5, and the Supreme Court Act 1981, s. 31(6), a court must refuse an application for permission or grant of relief in cases in which there has been a lack of promptness, unless there are good reasons for extending the time or if it is unlikely that the persons affected by the grant of the relief would suffer hardship or prejudice.

There are three aspects to the issue of delay. The first relates to the time limit that is laid down for particular applications to be made. For example, challenges to planning decisions

---

59 For example, see *R v. North Somerset District Council, ex parte Garnett* [1998] Env LR 91.

made by the Secretary of State must be brought within six weeks from the Secretary of State's decision,[60] whereas applications made under CPR Part 54 must be brought within three months of the decision that is being challenged. The courts recognized the overlap between these two time limits by the adoption of an informal rule that applications should be made within the six-week period if they were to be considered 'prompt'.[61] Thus applications that have not been made 'promptly', but which fall within the longer three-month time period, can be dismissed[62] and applications made outside the period can be permitted if there are good reasons to do so.

This practice was criticized by the House of Lords in *R v. Hammersmith London Borough Council, ex parte Burkett* [2003] Env LR 6, in which the Lords emphasized the need to consider the three-month time limit and all of the circumstances of the case (see Case 10.3).

CASE 10.3 **Time limits and delay—*R v. Hammersmith London Borough Council, ex parte Burkett* [2003] Env LR 6**[63]

In this case, the applicant sought a judicial review of a decision to grant planning permission for a mixed-use development of Imperial Wharf in London. The local planning authority had resolved to grant the permission, subject to a call-in by the Secretary of State. The Secretary of State declined to call in the application and so outline permission was granted some eight months after the original resolution to grant permission. B had applied for judicial review, over a month before the final grant of permission, on the grounds that the environmental impact assessment carried out had been inadequate. The application was refused at first instance and at the Court of Appeal on the grounds of delay. Time was taken to run from the date of the resolution to grant permission if the grounds for objection to the application had not changed.

The House of Lords, however, rejected the idea that there was a six-week time limit for challenges to planning decisions, stating that this could not be displaced by a 'judicial policy decision'. The Lords also clarified the point that time only started to run when the planning permission was granted and not at the time of the resolution to grant. The rationale for the Lords' decision appears to have been a desire to ensure a clear, definable time limit upon which potential claimants can rely when determining whether and when to challenge a decision. This ties in with the need to ensure compatibility with Art. 6 of the European Convention on Human Rights. A settled time limit is much more likely to result in a fair trial than is relying upon potentially uncertain discretionary judgments. In addition, there are added practical advantages in a specific time limit, including giving flexibility to promote negotiated settlements prior to the deadline rather than applicants being forced to issue proceedings in order to avoid arguments about delay.

The second aspect of delay is the issue of when the time for challenge starts to run. Clearly, the decision-making process can have a number of stages, from informal resolution, to conditional and full permission. In addition, it may become clear—early on in the decision-making process—that an error of law has been made. CPR Rule 54.5(1)(b) makes it clear that time starts to run from the date on which grounds for the application first rose, which is not necessarily the same as the date on which any final decision is made. If an application

---

60 Town and Country Planning Act 1990, s. 288.

61 *R v. Ceredigion County Council, ex parte McKeown* (1998) 2 PLR 1.

62 *R v. Swale Borough Council, ex parte RSPB* [1991] 1 PLR 6, in which an application for leave was made ten weeks after the decision, but was dismissed for lack of 'promptness'.

63 Also see *R (Hardy and ors) v. Pembrokeshire County Council and ors* [2005] EWHC 1872 (Admin) and [2006] EWCA Civ 240.

is made too early, there is a risk that it will be premature or too late and that it will not have been made promptly.

A lot of the uncertainty in relation to planning cases was removed by the decision of the House of Lords in *Burkett*, in which the Lords held that the trigger date was the grant of planning permission, but in other areas, the question is not necessarily as clear-cut. A good example can be found in *R v. Secretary of State for Trade and Industry, ex parte Greenpeace Ltd* [1998] Env LR 413, in which Greenpeace sought to challenge the grant of licences to explore for North Sea oil, on the ground that the decision-making process was contrary to the requirements of the Habitats Directive 92/43/EEC (some of the areas subject to the licences were the habitat of a protected species under the Directive). Greenpeace sought to challenge the decision to grant licences that was made in April 1997. The court dismissed the application, on the basis that any application should have been made much earlier—before November 1995—when it was probable that licences would be granted in breach of the Directive.

The third aspect of delay is the question of extending the time for bringing an application beyond the need for 'promptness'. Generally, the courts have taken a strict line over the question of delay in environmental cases. The speed or otherwise of an application would appear to depend largely upon whether an affected third party would have suffered prejudice. This might include such things as its spending large sums of money after being granted permission or a licence to do something,[64] or doing other things in reliance on the grant of permission, such as commencing development. The applicant can minimize the extent of this prejudice by putting the affected third party on notice of potential proceedings.

Notwithstanding the decision of the House of Lords in *Burkett*, the ground of delay still allows the courts some discretion to determine applications for judicial review in accordance with general principles such as fairness, good administration, and prejudice. This discretion can also, however, be used to override any unfairness, if it is in the public interest to do so. This would include cases in which there have been clear and serious breaches of European legislation. In *R v. Secretary of State for Trade and Industry, ex parte Greenpeace (No. 2)* [2000] Env LR 221, in which Greenpeace brought a second challenge to the grant of oil exploration licences, Maurice Kay J considered that the application for judicial review had not been made 'promptly', thus mirroring the first challenge discussed above. He went on, however, to find that the implementation of the Habitats Directive had been incomplete within UK law—in particular, in relation to offshore habitats—and that the failure to implement the Directive was more important than any prejudice that would have been caused by the delay in making the application.

Judicial review and other avenues of challenge

Although judicial review remains one way of challenging a decision that has been made unlawfully, there are, in some cases, alternative remedies for aggrieved parties by way of a statutory right to administrative appeal. When considering the appropriate avenue of challenge, the courts consider all of the circumstances of the case, with the most important factor being the extent to which a statutory appeal process would provide an adequate alternative remedy to seeking a judicial review. If an adequate alternative remedy were available, any application for permission to seek a judicial review would normally be refused. The adequacy of the statutory right of appeal as an alternative remedy is dependent upon a number of variables, including: comparative speed, expense, and finality of the alternative procedure; the need and scope for fact finding; the desirability of an

---

64 See, e.g., *R v. Secretary of State for Trade and Industry, ex parte Greenpeace Ltd* [1998] Env LR 413 and *Mass Energy Ltd v. Birmingham City Council* [1994] Env LR 298.

authoritative ruling on any point of law arising; the apparent strength of the applicant's challenge.[65]

In circumstances under which a collateral challenge is brought—that is, as an incidental challenge to the main proceedings—the courts have dismissed such challenges as being an abuse of process if the decision that is being challenged was made many years before and the period for statutory challenge had passed.[66]

The usefulness of judicial review

How useful is judicial review as a mechanism for promoting public participation, and for controlling the activities and decision making of environmental bodies? As seen above, there are various procedural hurdles that must be overcome before an application for permission to bring a judicial review action will be granted, such as having standing, bringing any application 'promptly', and ensuring that there are no alternative adequate remedies available. The main problem here is not with the hurdles themselves, but that the determination of whether an applicant succeeds in 'jumping the hurdles' is largely discretionary and rests with the particular judge hearing the case. Although the basic principles of standing and delay are laid down, the manner in which these principles are applied within the factual context of an individual application can vary, depending upon the way in which a judge views the purposes of the procedural hurdles. Different judges can approach similar issues in entirely different ways. This discretion naturally leads to a degree of uncertainty as to whether an applicant might succeed, which, in turn, reduces the likelihood that an action will be taken.

In addition to these procedural hurdles, there is the difficult question of funding the cost of a judicial review action. Because most environmental actions tend to be brought on a representative basis either from local groups or interested parties, there is little direct financial interest in the outcome of an application, although there is a notable exception in the planning arena, in which commercial developers feature largely. The costs of litigation can be high, particularly when considering that legal aid is seldom available in judicial review cases,[67] although there are notable exceptions, including particular cases in which children have been selected as applicants.[68]

An extra pressure upon applicants is the fact that costs in judicial review proceedings normally follow the event, meaning that if an applicant loses (either at the full hearing or at the stage of seeking permission), he or she is normally obliged to pay the costs of the other side (again, there are notable exceptions to this rule—in particular, see *R v. Secretary of State for the Environment, ex parte Greenpeace Ltd* [1994] Env LR 401, in which there was no award of costs against the applicant because the application was considered to be brought 'in the public interest'). In practice, this rule has acted as a disincentive to those bringing proceedings and anecdotal evidence suggests that the potential for significant costs orders have been used as a tactic by some as a means of putting pressure on applicants to withdraw proceedings.[69] This potentially punitive approach to costs does not sit easily with the Aarhus Convention's requirement that access to justice should not be 'prohibitively expensive'.[70] The decision of the Court of Appeal in the *Corner House* case (see Case 10.4) has alleviated the

---

65 See *R v. Falmouth and Truro Port Health Authority, ex parte South West Water Ltd* [2000] NPC 36 and see also *R v. Environment Agency, ex parte Petrus Oils Ltd* [1999] Env LR 732, in which the court found that there was an adequate alternative remedy available to challenge the service of a revocation notice under Pt 1 of EPA 1990.

66 *R v. Ettrick Trout Company Ltd* [1994] Env LR 165.

67 See *R v. Legal Aid Area No. 8 (Northern), ex parte Sendall* [1993] Env LR 167.

68 See, e.g., *R v. Secretary of State for Trade and Industry, ex parte Duddridge* [1995] Env LR 151.

69 R. McCracken and G. Jones [2003] JPL 802.

70 Article 9(4).

problem to some extent, especially in cases in which there is a true public interest point to be tested.

CASE 10.4 **Balancing out the costs 'gamble'—Protective Costs Orders—***R (Corner House Research Ltd) v. Secretary of State for Trade and Industry* [2005] EWCA Civ 192

Although not strictly an environmental case, the Court of Appeal clarified the use of so-called protective costs orders (PCOs) in cases such as environmental challenges in which the public interest may be in issue. PCOs can be sought by applicants prior to a full hearing. If granted, the PCO will ensure that, even if an applicant loses, he or she will either not have to pay the other party's costs or will, at worst, have any costs award capped at a reasonable level. The Court held that applicants in public interest litigation, such as environmental judicial review, should be able to present a case using a reasonably competent advocate without being exposed to the serious financial risks that would deter it from advancing a case of general public importance at all.

Five further principles were identified for granting PCOs:

- that the issues raised are of general public importance;
- that the public interest requires that those issues should be resolved;
- that the applicant has no private interest in the outcome of the case;
- that it is fair and just to make the order, having regard to the financial resources of the parties and to the amount of costs that are likely to be involved;
- that the applicant would probably discontinue the proceedings if the order were not made.

In addition, there was the general proposition that the presence of pro bono advisers acting on behalf of the applicant would make it more likely that a PCO would be awarded. In other cases, it was likely that any costs award against the unsuccessful applicants would be capped and that, even if the applicant were to be successful, they would not recover more than the capped amount from the other side in relation to their own costs.

Note that this is not necessarily a broad approach: in particular, individual applicants with a personal interest in an application—such as land owners in cases in which the value of the land would be materially affected or in which an expensive, but experienced, team of lawyers was being used—would probably be precluded from seeking a comprehensive PCO. The ruling does, however, restore the balance a little in favour of public-interest litigants and prevents potential respondents racking up significant costs solely as a tactic to deter potential challengers.[71]

Although the procedural issues and the costs of taking action represent significant factors in deciding whether to pursue a judicial review action, other factors also play a part in reducing the effectiveness of judicial review. First, for many individuals or interest groups, a three-month time limit represents a very short period during which to receive notice of any decision, understand the implications, take legal advice, raise funds, and possibly negotiate with the body making the decision. In many circumstances, a potentially valid claim will not be brought, because the uncertainties of bringing a claim may be unresolved within the three-month period.

Secondly, the remedies that are available may be unsatisfactory or unsuitable. For example, any attempt to prevent an unlawful operation from taking place would need to be dealt with by way of interim injunction, which prevents any further action until a full hearing. Such

---

71 R. Stein and J. Beagent (2005) 17 JEL 413.

an injunction must be supported by an applicant giving an undertaking in damages, which would mean that, if the applicant were to be unsuccessful at the full hearing, they would be obliged to pay for any loss of profit resulting from the halting of the activity in question. In the case of certain projects, this can amount to considerable sums of money.

Thirdly, when an application for judicial review is heard, there is no consideration of the merits of a case. Thus, when a decision is quashed or a duty is enforced, it does not necessarily mean that the final decision of the administrative body will be to the liking of the person seeking judicial review. A good example of this is in the case of the judicial review of planning decisions. If an inspector, on appeal, makes an unlawful decision, the resulting decision may be challenged. The inspector's decision in those circumstances could be overturned by the High Court, but the final decision would be referred back to a fresh inspector, who could very well arrive at the same decision as the first inspector, even though taking into account the representations made.

Furthermore, in cases in which individuals with 'sufficient interest' apply for judicial review of a decision, they have to be able to show that they have suffered prejudice.[72] Therefore, although the court is not entitled to make a judgment on the merits of the individual case, it may be that the substance of the point raised by the interested party shows an unlawful act, but that, on the facts of the individual case, the applicant did not suffer any prejudice from the decision itself.

The ombudsman

There may be instances in which, although there is no abuse of the statutory power that would render a decision reviewable, there is some maladministration that could give rise to a public complaint. In such cases, a complaint can be made to the ombudsman in control of those activities. In the case of central government activities, the investigating ombudsman is the Parliamentary Commissioner for Administration, whereas in the case of complaints against a local authority, the matter is dealt with by the Commissioner for Local Administration. The governing factor in such complaints is whether or not the authority concerned has acted within appropriate standards of administrative conduct, rather than whether or not it has acted lawfully.

Complaints to the ombudsman normally go through either a local councillor or an MP, depending upon the level of authority concerned, although they need not do so in all cases. The nature of the ombudsman remedy is both singular and advisory. Therefore, an aggrieved party who has other rights of action, whether under the common law or by means of judicial review, must pursue that particular avenue, as long as it is realistic to do so. In addition, an ombudsman has no statutory power to impose an award of damages, or to alter the legal position, such as by quashing a decision. Normally, the ombudsman will make a recommendation for compensation that, although having no statutory backing, the statutory body concerned accepts in over 95 per cent of cases.

The role of the ombudsman should not be underestimated. The incidence of complaints to the ombudsman has risen in recent years, because it is a quick, cheap, and often-effective mechanism for channelling complaints about public authorities. It is a mechanism that the public are happy to utilize, because of its informal nature and simple procedure. It is perhaps worthwhile to point out that the stages of a complaint are relatively straightforward and provide an adequate opportunity for the proper presentation of grievances. It is also important that the ombudsman has significant investigatory powers: these will have an impact on the practices of the public bodies over which jurisdiction is exercised.

---

72 See *Edwards v. Environment Agency (No. 2)* [2007] Env LR 9.

Other complaints mechanisms

In the case of the privatized utilities, the regulators act as a controlling influence through various means, such as the amendment of undertakers' licences and more informal mechanisms (such as threats of action in the case of continuous underperformance). The effectiveness of the ombudsman in dealing with maladministration in central and local government, and the alternative avenues of redress in relation to the utilities, can be contrasted with the gaping accountability hole in relation to other important bodies with environmental responsibilities, such as the Environment Agency, Natural England, and the regional development agencies. In cases of public bodies such as these, incompetence, unfairness, or otherwise unsatisfactory performance can only be dealt with by way of internal complaints procedures.

An environmental court

There is a relatively long history of criticism of the existing arrangements for access to justice in environmental matters in the UK. A number of commentators, including senior judges and academics, have led the call to establish a specialist environmental court or tribunal. A specialist court would not be unique by any means, because such courts have existed in Australia for many years.[73] New South Wales has a Land and Environment Court that was established as long ago as 1980 as a court of record.[74] The Court consists of judges and technical assessors, and deals with criminal prosecutions, civil enforcement, appeals, and judicial reviews in relation to a range of planning and environmental legislation.[75] Proceedings are open to *any* person, and there is great flexibility in terms of procedures and remedies.

Similarly, South Australia has an Environmental Resources and Development Court, which effectively started work in 1994. This is also a court of record, chaired by a judge and sitting with two lay members, whose qualifications will vary according to the nature of the case. It deals with criminal prosecutions and civil enforcement, as well as appeals under a range of planning and environmental legislation. The procedures and powers are very flexible, and include a mandatory pre-trial conference and that decisions are made to equitably reflect the substantial merits of the case.[76]

Returning to the UK, the first main proponent of a specialist court was Sir Harry Woolf (who was to become the country's most senior judge), who suggested the creation of a special tribunal with general responsibility for overseeing and enforcing environmental law. It was to be a 'one-stop shop', combining services carried out by courts, tribunals, and inspectors. Woolf's suggestion was for an environmental division of the High Court, rather than changing basic pre-existing structures (see Box 10.10).

73 Environmental courts in other jurisdictions are outlined in M. Grant (2000) *Environmental Court Project: Final Report*, London: DETR.

74 Under the Land and Environment Court Act 1979—see P. Stein (1994) 'A specialist environmental court: an Australian experience' in D. Robinson and J. Dunkley (eds) *Public Interest Perspectives in Environmental Law*, Chichester: Wiley Chancery, and see P. Stein, 'Specialist environmental courts: the Land and Environmental Court of New South Wales, Australia' (2002) Env LR 5.

75 For a summary see P. Ryan (2002) 14 JEL 301.

76 W. Upton (1994) 1 Env Law 12.

BOX 10.10 **Woolf's proposals**[77]

Woolf suggested that a specialist tribunal should have:

- discretion to determine its own simple and user-friendly procedures;
- power to appoint specialist members;
- inquisitorial-type fact-finding powers (similar to the planning inquiry system);
- an informal and multidisciplinary approach;
- power to make ancillary enforcement decisions—for example, on compensation, punishment, and public law remedies;
- discretion to determine issues about standing, representation, and costs;
- an appeal structure with an appeal on a point of law to the Court of Appeal.

Robert Carnwath, another soon-to-be High Court judge, pursued these arguments, proposing an Environmental Division of the High Court, probably supplemented by a second-tier tribunal or court operating at a lower level. Alternatively, he suggested a unified tribunal answering to the 'needs of customers', to which the adjudicatory and sanctioning roles of planning and environmental law could be entrusted. He suggested combining the Planning Inspectorate with a High Court Environment Division, with a two-tier structure for appeals and review.[78]

Both Woolf and Carnwath point out the advantage that such a tribunal would offer in ensuring the consistent development of principles in a manner that is often incapable of achievement in the courts as presently constituted, because environmental issues come before too many different courts and judges in too many different forms. Carnwath also added that a specialist court could have an important impact on the development of EC and international environmental law. Both Woolf and Carnwath put a high value on any suggested court being allowed to develop in an evolutionary manner, and proposed leaving a number of matters to be developed by the court itself.

Taking a slightly different tack, McAuslan proposed an environmental court or tribunal that would '*help us forward into the new era of a more conscious and deliberate balancing of development and environmental protection, and a more knowledgeable weighing of risks, liabilities, and rights*'.[79] On the surface, his court would be similar in structure to that of Woolf. In substance, however, McAuslan proposed a model that went beyond traditional adjudicatory or dispute resolution types of court, to one that was 'investigative', taking a 'pro-active role', and serving as an advisory body to all other courts on scientific and technical matters.[80]

The debate moved on in 1999, with official recognition of the need to examine the role of an environmental court. The (then) Department of the Environment, Transport and the Regions (DETR) commissioned a report from Professor Malcolm Grant, in which he identified both a number of fundamental characteristics of an environmental court or tribunal, and a number of alternative models for an environmental court in England and Wales. He, too, favoured a two-tier judicial model, with the lower tier dealing with merit-based decisions that were reviewable by the second tier on questions of law.[81]

77 See Sir Harry Woolf (1992) 3 JEL 1.
78 R. Carnwath (1992) 4 JPL 799.
79 P. McAuslan (1991) JEL 195.
80 Adopting the suggestions of Trubatch [1985] 10 Col J Env L 255.
81 Grant (2000).

These proposals were considered, but rejected, by the government in the House of Lords.[82] More modest proposals for reform have been made subsequently by the RCEP and in a report from University College London (UCL) commissioned by DEFRA.[83] These consist of extending the current tribunal system to deal with a wide range of environmental matters, including such things as statutory nuisance and contaminated land appeals.[84]

All of these different proposals represent two different perspectives on the structural problems associated with access to justice in environmental matters. The vast majority of commentators—Woolf, Carnwath, Grant, the RCEP, and UCL—see the issue as primarily a practical–professional problem, within which the central dilemma is how to provide properly for cases that have an environmental element in the light of the perception that the significant features of environmental cases mean that they often sit uneasily in current legal structures. The uncharitable perspective is that this could be characterized as starting from the understanding that the system does not work from the practising lawyer's point of view. More charitably, it could be said that the system does not work properly from the claimant's point of view.

McAuslan sees the issue as being more concerned with participation and deliberation. An environmental court should be concerned with taking complex policy decisions and therefore his proposal reflects the need for principled decision making for decisions with an environmental element. This is what enables him to move beyond the traditional models of adjudication and dispute resolution, to a model that involves the court seeking different views in arriving at decisions on how to manage the environment.

Experience with the Land and Environment Court in Australia suggest that there have been 'unrealistic expectations', 'misunderstanding about the Court's role', 'unmet expectations' concerning how different interests would be balanced, and 'perceptions of Court bias' in favour of developers.[85] Largely, this is because the adequacy of any specialist court may be judged by some in terms of its ability to enhance environmental protection. These reactions reflect the fact that a specialist environmental court is not the same thing as an ecocentric, or even anthropocentric, environmental court. McAuslan gets the closest to such a model, but his underlying principles reflect the need to have principled and rational decision making, and not environmental concerns. The difficulty is that any court that makes 'environmental' decisions runs the risk of breaching the borderline between judicial and political functions.

At first sight, it is quite easy to establish a case that the current legal system does not work too well when confronted by environmental disputes, and that a new structure and set of procedures—probably involving some sort of environmental court or tribunal—would work better. Existing proposals reflect the views of professional lawyers concerned with the efficient operation of the legal system and therefore fail to capture either the need to facilitate true public participation (as opposed to the public represented by professional lawyers) or to address the question of whether environmental law is effective (in terms of protecting the environment). Ultimately, however, if the question is addressed from an environmental perspective, it becomes clear that the substance of the law is the problem, not the procedures or structure (although, of course, the two are related). This raises a paradoxical question: if the substance of environmental law were more effective in protecting the environment, would there be any need to have a separate environmental court?

---

82 617, HL Debate, 9 October 2000, cols 86–100.

83 See RCEP 23rd Report (2002) *Environmental Planning*, Cm 5459, and R. Macrory and M. Woods (2003) *Modernising Environmental Justice: Regulation and the Role of an Environmental Tribunal*, London: University College London.

84 In relation to contaminated land appeals, the current Clean Neighbourhood and Environment Act 2005 transfers these powers to the Secretary of State.

85 See P. Ryan (2002) 14 JEL 301.

CHAPTER SUMMARY

1   Public participation in environmental law takes a number of different forms. It generally consists of access to information about the environment, participation in environmental decisions and the making of plans and programmes, and access to justice in environmental matters.

2   Public participation in environmental law has increased in importance over the last twenty years. This is evidenced by the agreement of the Aarhus Convention, and the European and national legislation that implements the provisions of the Directive.

3   The arguments in favour of public participation are relatively uncontroversial. It brings many benefits, including the improvement of environmental decisions, helping to resolve difficult environmental disputes, improving procedural legitimacy, and promoting environmental citizenship.

4   Access to environmental information has been widened in recent years through the adoption of a general right to such information under the Environmental Information Regulation 2004. These Regulations provide a general right to access 'environmental information' held by public bodies.

5   In addition to a general right of access to environmental information, there are a number of public pollution control registers that contain information on releases to the environment and other important licensing information.

6   Other types of environmental information are available, and these include information to the consumer under such things as the eco-labelling scheme and company information released in annual reports.

7   Public participation in environmental decision making takes many forms. The general trend is to improve both the quantity and quality of public participation, and the use of deliberative systems to do so has been used in controversial areas such as genetically modified (GM) food and crops.

8   The courts have emphasized the importance of ensuring that the quality of public participation is safeguarded through the use of procedural mechanisms such as environmental impact assessment.

9   The public has a right of access to justice in relation to environmental matters primarily through the route of judicial review.

10   In order to bring a judicial review action, an applicant must show that they have standing, have commenced the application promptly, and have no other avenue of redress.

11   The courts have been interpreted fairly liberally the question of who has standing. This includes groups who represent particular environmental interests.

12   Applications have to be made within three months of the date on which the grounds for the application first arose. In many, but not all, cases, this will be the date of the grant of permission or authorization.

13   The effectiveness of judicial review is reduced by the uncertainty surrounding the rules on standing, delay, and costs.

14   The current court structure in the UK has been criticized as inadequate by many commentators. Various proposals have been made to replace the current system. Early proposals were mostly based around a two-tier division of the High Court. Later reform proposals have focused on replacing magistrates' powers with a specialist tribunal.

QUESTIONS

1   What is meant by 'public participation' in environmental law? Why are there moves to increase public participation? What problems might exist with involving the public more in environmental decision making?

2   What types of environmental information exist and how might they be accessed?

3   Consider whether a request for information would have to be acceded to in relation to each of the following.

   a   The electricity bills sent by an electricity provider to its customer, a prominent environmental campaigner, setting out household energy consumption.

   b   The exact location of the nesting sites of corncrakes in Scotland.

   c   The details of discussions between the UK government and other countries in relation to the processing and disposal of nuclear waste, some of which comes from military sources.

4   Bert comes to see you, wanting to challenge a decision of the Environment Agency to grant an environmental permit for a landfill site. What would you need to know before advising him whether he has a chance of challenging the decision? Would it make any difference if it were a national campaigning group asking the same question?

5   What are the arguments for and against the establishment of a specialist environmental court?

FURTHER READING

General reading

The best starting point is M. Lee and C. Abbot, 'The usual suspects? Public participation under the Aarhus Convention' (2003) 66 MLR 80, which gives a first-rate overview of the issues from both practical and theoretical viewpoints. J. Steele, 'Participation and deliberation in environmental law: exploring a problem-solving approach' (2001) 21 OJLS 415 is more theoretical, but thought provoking (and argues that participation does make for better decisions). In similar vein, K. Getliffe, 'Proceduralisation and the Aarhus Convention: does increased participation in the decision-making process lead to more effective EU environmental law?' [2002] Env LR 101 considers the basic rationales for increasing public participation. The impact of Aarhus on European institutions is considered in V. Rodenhoff 'The Aarhus Convention and its implications for the "institution" of the European Community' (2002) RECIEL 343.

Access to environmental information

If you are interested in the topic of access to information generally, have a look at H. Brooke (2004) *Your Right to Know: How to Use the Freedom of Information Act and Other Access Laws*, London: Pluto Press, which is a great guide to using the Act to get hold of information that you want. It is also backed up by a good web page (see Web Links below). For a more 'legal' guide to the area, see P. Coppel, 'Environmental information: the new regime' [2005] JPL 12, which provides a comprehensive guide to the operative provisions of the Regulations and the related role of the Freedom of Information Act 2000. The Royal Commission on Environmental Pollution has long campaigned for free access to environmental information. See, in particular, its Fifth Report (1975) *Air Pollution Control: An Integrated Approach*, Cmnd 6371, and its Tenth Report (1984) *Tackling Pollution: Experience and Prospects*, Cmnd 9149. The latter gives a good introductory account of the arguments for and against disclosure.

A general discussion of the issues can be found in C. Kimber (1998) 'Understanding access to environmental information: the European experience' in T. Jewell and J. Steele (eds) *Law in Environmental Decision Making*, Oxford: Oxford University Press. For an empirical study on the effectiveness of access to information, see J. Rowan-Robinson, A. Ross, W. Walton, and J. Rothnie, 'Public access to environmental information: a means to what end?' [1996] 8 JEL 19. Consumer-based information is considered in R. Gertz, 'Access to environmental information and the German Blue Angel: lessons to be learned' (2004) EELR 268.

Public participation

The starting point for any discussion of public participation in environmental law should be P. McAuslan (1980) *The Ideologies of Planning Law*, Oxford: Pergamon Press. The general thrust of the book is that planning law is a product of the tension between three competing 'ideologies' aimed at promoting private property, the public interest, and public participation. Although now out of date, it provides a good background and historical introduction to many of the issues. Deliberative theory is discussed in J. Bohman and W. Rehg (1997) *Deliberative Democracy: Essays on Reason and Politics*, Cambridge, Mass: MIT Press. The impact of Aarhus on planning is considered in P. Stookes and J. Razzaque, 'Community participation: UK planning reforms and international obligations' (2002) JPL 786, and J. Thompson, 'Involving people, changing lives: Community participation in the development process' (2004) JPL Occ Pap 32, 58.

An environmental court

Interesting to read (if you can get hold of a copy) is M. Grant (ed.) (1993) *Environmental Litigation: Towards an Environmental Court?*, London: UKELA, which, far from being a historical document, demonstrates that, although the arguments may have become more sophisticated, the principles of the debate have moved on little over the last decade. Other articles include: Sir Harry Woolf, 'Are the judiciary environmentally myopic?' (1992) 4 JEL 1; R. Carnwath, 'Environmental enforcement: the need for a specialist court' [1992] JPL 799; P. McAuslan, 'The role of courts and other judicial-type bodies in environmental management' (1991) 2 JEL 195; G. McLeod (1995) 'Do we need an environmental court in Britain?' in D. Robinson and J. Dunkley (eds) *Public Interest Perspectives in Environmental Law*, London: Wiley Chancery; M. Grant (2000) *Environmental Court Project: Final Report*, London: DETR; R. Macrory and M. Woods (2003) *Modernising Environmental Justice: Regulation and the Role of an Environmental Tribunal*, London: UCL; The Environmental Justice Project (2004) *Environmental Justice*; the 23rd Report of the Royal Commission on Environmental Pollution (2002) *Environmental Planning*, Cm 5459.

@ **WEB LINKS**

Comprehensive coverage of the Aarhus Convention can be found at **www.unece.org/env/pp/**. This includes the text of the Convention. as well as subsequent developments in its implementation. On a European level, **europa.eu.int/comm/environment/aarhus/** contains the texts of the relevant Directives and other literature relating to the three 'pillars' of public participation. The starting point for Internet sources on freedom of information is the Information Commissioner's office at **www.informationcommissioner.gov.uk**.

11 Private law and environmental protection

 Overview

The realm of public and administrative law does not solely govern the development of environmental law. Although the spread of regulatory control has accelerated within the last sixty years, traditionally—at least, at first glance—private law has attempted to serve a similar function in controlling environmental damage. As we describe below, however, the similarity is often superficial: the essential characteristic of private law is to regulate relationships between individuals (as opposed to the public law, which governs the activities of public bodies such as the Environment Agency and regulates the relationship between the state and individuals) by the balancing of individual interests, such as competing uses of land, rather than environmental protection.

In this chapter, we look in more detail at the torts—or civil wrongs—traditionally relied on in environmental litigation—private and public nuisance; trespass; negligence; the rule in *Rylands v. Fletcher*—as well as various instances of statutory civil liability. We preface this with some introductory remarks about the functions of civil liability as a tool for environmental protection.

Alongside this chapter, you may find it useful to revisit the remarks in Chapter 2 about the role of the courts in developing environmental law and, in particular, the outline discussion there of the potential for civil liability to act as an environmental protection mechanism.

At the end of this chapter, you will be able to:

✔ discuss the main ways in which private litigation might be used to further environmental protection and the available remedies;

✔ appreciate the relationship between these claims and public regulation;

✔ evaluate the main strengths and weakness of private law, compared to public environmental regulation;

✔ appreciate some of the main alternative models of private liability.

Private law and environmental liability

In looking at each of the various private law liability provisions considered below, it is useful to have in mind the range of overlapping (and sometimes competing) functions that they might serve: *Reasons*

- to compensate for harm suffered (and whether this should be to people and their property, or more widely to compensate 'the environment' in some way);

- to prevent harm (to people, property, or the environment);

- to internalize costs to producers—that is, liability as a market mechanism;

- to provide an incentive to improve environmental performance;

- to express social condemnation of environmentally harmful behaviour;

- to raise awareness of environmental problems—that is, an ombudsman function.

Potential limitations

Related to these are three further issues. The first is concerned with who has the right to bring any claim: who can sue? Should claims be restricted to cases in which individual rights have been affected or should claims also be allowed for damage to public goods or to the unowned environment?

foreseeability

The second issue relates to the strictness of liability. For example, is strict liability—that is, liability without having to prove fault—used? Does it matter whether the defendant could have foreseen that harm would be caused? Does it matter whether the defendant had the resources to prevent the harm occurring? *avoidability*

Thirdly, how is a value to be placed on the environment? In the interests of certainty, the defendant (or pollution fund) must know for what they are liable and how much this may cost them. There are various possibilities and the valuation of damages might be based on:

how should priorities be measured?

- the effect on the market price of the environmental asset—for example, the drop in value of land that has been polluted; *economics*

- the cost of *full* environmental restoration or remediation; *repercussions.*

- the cost of providing for the *reasonable costs* of restoration or remediation.

An important aspect of how the environment is to be valued, therefore, is how wide we cast the net when calculating damage—for example, how we quantify things such as the loss of ecological services.

Human rights law

Before looking at the individual torts, we must consider the role that the Human Rights Act (HRA) 1998 plays in relation to private law claims. This puts the cart before the horse historically, but it is important that potential breaches of human rights law are not thought of only as separate legal actions that might be taken on top of tort claims; human rights law can also influence the substance of tort law claims—that is, what can be sued for and by whom.

must consider future repercussions of an act.

This is because, while tort law is about relationships between legal persons—individuals, companies, etc.—the courts are public bodies under the Human Rights Act 1998, s. 6. They are therefore bound to act in a way that is compatible with the rights protected by the European Convention on Human Rights (ECHR). The judges therefore ought to develop the common law in a way that is consistent with, or at least avoids clashing with, Convention rights. Indeed, we could go further and say that the common law torts must develop in a way that, as a *minimum*, protects human rights—that is, that the Human Rights Act provides a floor of protection rather than a ceiling.

This matters because the European Court of Human Rights (ECtHR) has held that forms of environmental pollution may fall within the scope of the right to respect for private life and the home provided for in Art. 8 ECHR.[1] For example, in *Powell and Rayner v. United Kingdom* (1990) 12 EHRR 355, a case about noise from Heathrow airport, the court held that the rights of Mr Rayner, who owned land just over a mile away from a major runway, were clearly at stake because of the noise levels (although the Court ultimately found that running the airport was a modern economic necessity that justified the breach).

---

1 Article 8 is not the only basis in the Convention for claims originating in environmental-type harm—see, e.g., the use of Art. 2 (right to life) in *Oneryildiz v. Turkey* (2005) 41 EHRR 20 (fatal methane explosion at rubbish tip).

Art 8 successful

In *López Ostra v. Spain* (1995) 20 EHRR 277, however, a claim under Art. 8 succeeded in relation to exceptionally severe pollution coming from a factory 12 metres away from the applicant's home.

The current tensions within the ECtHR about human rights based on poor levels of environmental protection can be seen in *Hatton v. United Kingdom* (see Case 11.1).

CASE 11.1 *Hatton v. United Kingdom* (2003) 37 EHRR 28

Residents living near to Heathrow Airport brought an action before the European Court of Human Rights (ECtHR), alleging that noise from aircraft landing at night significantly disturbed their sleep and that this violated their rights under Art. 8 of the European Convention on Human Rights to respect for their home life. Under a statute, private law claims in the national courts had not been possible (see the coverage of noise on the Online Resource Centre).[2]

Initially, the claim—which was different from that in *Powell and Rayner* because it focused on a limited number of night flights rather than noise generally—was successful and modest damages were awarded (although the cost of compensating everyone similarly affected was estimated at around £2bn). The UK government appealed. The Grand Chamber held that, while there may have been a breach of Art. 8, this was justified because of the economic necessity of the flights. Although in extreme cases, environmental pollution could be in breach of the Convention, here, the degree of harm suffered was not severe and the Court deferred to the UK's assessment of the economic importance of the flights. Unlike in *López Ostra*, there was in this case no suggestion of any 'domestic irregularity', in the sense that Mrs López Ostra had clearly been let down by a culpable failure on the part of the regulatory authorities.[3] A strong dissenting judgment thought this approach to be too conservative and argued that the rights in the Convention should be interpreted in a way that would expand protection in environmental pollution cases.

It is also worth mentioning that the majority in this case were fairly unsympathetic to the applicants' situations and that this probably played a part in the decision that was reached.[4] Expanding on this point, it is hard to believe that the applicants in *Hatton* were the persons most affected by noise from Heathrow, but it is often the nature of litigation like this to be brought by those most willing and able to voice their concerns. This also raises more general issues as to whether individual litigation is able to pursue what are often, by their nature, collective interests.

Under HRA 1998, the courts must have regard to judgments and opinions of the ECtHR or the Commission respectively. Therefore, what has been a rather limited approach by these bodies so far to the use of human rights law for environmental protection may, in fact, hinder the national use of Convention rights for this purpose. The 1998 Act does not provide for a new tort of 'breach of the Convention' on which one individual can rely against another. But the courts must consider whether, for example, a claimant receives 'just satisfaction' if his or her human rights have been breached. If national law does not provide a sufficient remedy,

---

2 Although public law actions had been taken to the regulatory decisions authorizing increases in night noise: see *R v. Secretary of State for Transport, ex parte Richmond upon Thames London Borough* [1994] 1 WLR 74; *(No. 2)* [1995] 7 ELM 52; *(No. 3)* [1995] 7 ELM 127; *(No. 4)* [1996] 8 ELM 77.

3 This moves environmental human rights claims away from, in effect, being based on strict liability—in which the central question is simply whether rights have been violated—towards using a notion of fault. For a comparable approach in national law to upholding private rights in cases in which there has been regulatory tardiness, see *Wheeler v. JJ Saunders* [1996] Ch 19 on p. 358.

4 In *Khatun v. UK* (see p. 359), the applicants' case was weakened because they did not suffer health problems from the dust and the interference was for a limited time only.

then additional remedies may have to be given for the breach of Convention rights. There is no reason, however, why these must be remedies in tort law.

The law of tort and environmental protection

This book does not attempt to give a comprehensive account of the law of tort, which is more than adequately covered in specialist texts. The various torts and their general principles are, however, outlined below, along with illustrations of their usefulness in protecting environmental interests.

Private nuisance

The law of nuisance is concerned with the unlawful interference with a person's use or enjoyment of land, or of some right over or in connection with that land. This definition illustrates one of the primary distinctions between nuisance and other torts, in that the protection afforded is directed towards protecting proprietary interests rather than the control of an individual's conduct. The generality of the definition also means that private nuisance can take an infinite variety of forms (unlike statutory nuisance, which is restricted to quite a narrow range of nuisances—see p. 360 and the Online Resource Centre).

Protecting property rights can have the incidental effect of providing a general benefit to the wider community by achieving improvements in environmental quality. But there have been occasions on which the effect upon the community has been a negative one. In *Bellew v. Cement Ltd* [1948] IR 61, an interim injunction was granted to restrain the noisy blasting at a quarry. This remained effective for several months. The effect of this stoppage upon the supply of cement in Ireland was devastating, because 80 per cent of the cement used in Ireland was created by materials from the quarry and there was then a national housing shortage. Thus the court upheld the protection of the private right involved at the expense of employment and construction. Whether such strict protection would be given if a similar case arose today may, however, be doubted, as Case 11.2 shows.

CASE 11.2 *Dennis v. Ministry of Defence* [2003] Env LR 34

The claimants lived in a mansion on a large estate located near a base used for training RAF Harrier jets. Noise levels from the aircraft were found to be 'particularly fearsome', making dogs cower and, in some cases, reducing visiting children to tears. The claimants sued in private nuisance, alleging significant economic losses because of their inability to use their estate for commercial purposes such as hosting conferences, as well as losses because of damage to their enjoyment of their land. The Ministry of Defence argued that the national interest at stake meant that no nuisance arose, but the High Court rejected this approach and held that there was an actionable nuisance—but the Court refused to grant an injunction and instead awarded significant damages.

The basis for a claim in nuisance is founded upon a balancing exercise centred around the question of reasonableness. As was stated in *Sanders-Clark v. Grosvenor Mansions Co. Ltd* [1900] 2 Ch 373, 375:

the court must consider whether the defendant is using his property reasonably or not. If he is using it reasonably, there is nothing which at law can be considered a nuisance; but if he is not using it reasonably...then the [claimant] is entitled to relief.

Thus, in attempting to assess liability in a nuisance claim, a balance is made between the reasonableness of the defendant's activity and its impact upon the claimant's proprietary rights. Some disturbances, however, would seem to be incapable of being a nuisance—the everyday sounds of domestic life travelling between thin walls separating neighbours cannot be a nuisance, for example, because both parties would be committing it (*Baxter v. Camden (No. 2)* [2000] Env LR 112).

Balancing factors in private nuisance

In assessing where to strike the balance, a court will take into account a number of specific factors, including the locality of the nuisance, the nature, duration, and extent of the nuisance, the use that the claimant makes of his or her land, and the defendant's conduct. But any public benefit accruing from the defendant's actions is unlikely to be taken into account in deciding whether there is a nuisance.

(a) The locality doctrine

The locality doctrine is usually traced to the decision in *St Helen's Smelting Co. v. Tipping* (1865) 11 HL Cas 642. In the mid-nineteenth century, St Helens was the centre of the alkali industry. The average life expectancy was well under the age of 25 and it had built up a reputation as one of the dirtiest towns in Britain. The physical impact of the works had left most vegetation in the area dead and adversely affected the health of cattle. Mr Tipping brought a claim in private nuisance against a copper smelting works. The court drew the distinction between actual physical damage to property and a nuisance that would only cause 'personal discomfort'. In the latter situation, the locality of the nuisance would be a material factor in assessing the balancing exercise. As Thesiger LJ famously stated in the case of *Sturges v. Bridgman* (1879) 11 ChD 852: '*What would be a nuisance in Belgrave Square would not necessarily be so in Bermondsey.*' Or, as one commentator put it: '*Those who suffer most from the ravages of pollution are the least worthy of protection.*'[5]

Although there is a distinction drawn between actual damage done to property and interference with the enjoyment of property, in practice, there is often an overlap. It has been alleged that the economic effect of nuisance can be just as detrimental as physical damage to an interest in land. If, for example, a house is situated next to a pig farm, the smells emanating from that may well make the house less attractive to potential buyers, but, under the locality doctrine, it could be argued that, in an agricultural area, an owner has to expect such farmyard smells.[6]

Even in the most heavily industrialized areas, however, there is not an absolute freedom to produce polluting materials. An illustration was given in *Rushmer v. Polsue and Alfieri Ltd* [1906] 1 Ch 234, in which Cozens-Hardy LJ said:

It does not follow that because I live, say, in the manufacturing part of Sheffield I cannot complain if a steam-hammer is introduced next door, and so worked as to render sleep at night almost impossible, although previously to its introduction my house was a reasonably comfortable abode, having regard to the local standard; and it would be no answer to say that the steam-hammer is of the most modern approved pattern and is reasonably worked. In short, if a substantial addition is found as a fact in any particular case, it is no answer to say that the neighbourhood is noisy, and that the defendant's machinery is of first-class character.[7]

In that case, an injunction was granted against a printing press being operated in Fleet Street, even though there were many other printing presses in the area and others also operated at night. The same approach can be seen in relation to the noise disturbance from RAF aircraft

---

5 J. McLaren (1972) 10 Osgoode Hall LJ 505.
6 See, however, *Wheeler v. JJ Saunders Ltd* [1996] Ch 19 (see p. 358).
7 At 250.

in *Dennis v. MOD* (see Case 11.2). In that case, the judge noted in passing that if the next generation of fighter plane, projected to be twice as noisy, were to operate from the base, then this would be analogous to the steam hammer in *Rushmer*—that is, even in an already noisy environment, it could form the basis of a new claim in nuisance.

An important issue is what, precisely, judges do in locality cases. In some cases, for example, difficult questions may arise about the boundaries of the locality or the intensity of the activities carried on there. What judges may end up doing, therefore, may be as much about prescribing what activities can reasonably take place in any location as it is about reaching an objective judgment about the state of the area.

Finally, it may be that the locality rule is incompatible with human rights law. Under Art. 14 of the ECHR, other Convention rights must be enjoyed without discrimination. This may mean that judging the reasonableness of a polluting activity differentially according to whether it interferes with a 'run-down' or 'high-class' location will be discriminatory. Having said that, the justification tests still have to be applied—as does the judicially constructed test of 'domestic irregularity'—and the circumstances in which amenity damage will be so excessive as to be a human rights violation requiring an action in tort will be rare.

(b) The nature, duration, and intensity of the nuisance

Not every interference with property will be actionable in nuisance (contrast trespass, discussed below). There must be some appreciable harm, even in cases of property damage. This rule applies more generally to all nuisance claims, and the courts will look, among other things, to the nature, duration, and intensity (or seriousness) of the activity complained of.

For a nuisance to be actionable, it must be something that is more than temporary. Isolated incidents can give rise to a nuisance only if the use that gives rise to the risk of that isolated nuisance is, of itself, a continuing use. For example, a factory that produces fumes does not necessarily have to produce those fumes continuously for there to be a nuisance and isolated incidents occurring regularly can mean that the use of the land is a nuisance. The more isolated the occurrence, however, the less the likelihood that the use being carried out is a nuisance. A one-off incident, such as an act of demolition, would probably give rise to a nuisance only if there were actual physical damage or if unreasonable methods were used—for example, if, for no good reason, work was carried out at night (*Harrison v. Southwark and Vauxhall Water Co.* [1891] 2 Ch 409). Again, judicial thinking in this area seems to have been affected by taking a realistic balance of the number and type of occurrences as against the utility involved in the operation itself. Factors such as the duration of a nuisance may also be relevant to deciding which remedy is to be awarded if a nuisance is established.[8]

It is unlikely that the view that a nuisance must be capable of being sensed would now be upheld. In cases relating to the meaning of 'damage', it was once the law that damage could not be established by scientific evidence alone.[9] But this Victorian view was really aimed at filtering out trivial claims and is of doubtful authority today[10] when, for example, alterations to the genetic make-up of crops by genetically modified (GM) contamination might be regarded as property damage.

(c) The claimant's use of his or her land

The test for assessing a nuisance has two elements. Not only must the use of land that is complained of be unreasonable, but also the use of the land to which the nuisance applies must be a reasonable use. If a potential claimant is particularly sensitive to one type of nuisance, then it will not be actionable unless that nuisance would have affected a 'reasonable' person.[11]

---

8 See discussion of *Dennis v. MOD* in Case 11.2.

9 *Salvin v. North Brancepath Coal Co.* (1874) 9 Ch App 705.

10 Support for this shift can be seen in *Blue Circle Industries v. Ministry of Defence* [1998] 3 All ER 385, a case on radiation contamination (see p. 361).

11 *Robinson v. Kilvert* (1889) 41 ChD 88.

The effect of this rule is perhaps not as wide as first imagined. The principle only applies when the unreasonableness of the conduct is specifically the result of the hypersensitivity of the claimant. If there is an independent claim brought because of the inherent unreasonableness of the nuisance, then action can still be taken. In the Canadian case of *McKinnon Industries Ltd v. Walker* [1951] 3 DLR 577, the defendants operated a motorcar plant that emitted poisonous gases. The claimant grew orchids for sale and the gases killed off his stock. He brought an action in nuisance. The defendants argued that the growing of orchids was a hypersensitive activity and that, therefore, any damage suffered was not as a result of the unreasonable use of land. The court disagreed and held that the nuisance was independent of the special sensitivity of the claimant.

Thus, in pollution cases, there will be very few occasions on which this particular factor will be taken into account. Normally, the type of pollution complained of will itself be a cause of action that can cancel out any arguments put forward about hypersensitivity. There are signs, however, that the courts are moving away from assessing hypersensitivity, and subsuming this into the more general question of whether the relationship between the claimant and the defendant gives rise to reasonably foreseeable losses, considered in the next section.[12] If this approach is followed, then, for example, in the case of possible contamination of organic crops by GM pollen, the issue would not be whether organic crops are unduly sensitive to particular kinds of contamination (which the judge in *R v. Secretary of State for the Environment and Ministry of Agriculture, Fisheries and Food, ex parte Watson* [1999] Env LR 310 suggested might be the case), but whether the GM farmer could reasonably foresee that harm might be caused (and in the case of things such as crops grown to published standards, this may not be too heavy a burden).

Doing away entirely with the hypersensitive claimant does, however, pose some problems of its own. In relation to a large-scale noise disturbance, for example, it might be reasonably foreseeable that, over a wide area, there will be complaints. The device of the hypersensitive claimant allows unmeritous claims to be weeded out,[13] especially if the claimant is not the person most affected by the noise (there are clear echoes of this influencing the judgment in the *Hatton* case, above).

(d) Fault

The defendant's conduct will be a relevant consideration in those nuisance cases in which the activity complained of has ceased. (Questions of fault, of course, do not arise in cases in which the activity complained of is ongoing and an injunction is being sought, because the harm being caused is known about.) There are various factors that go to make up fault, including the foreseeability of the damage caused and the cost of taking preventive action. But the view that liability in nuisance is 'strict'—if it were ever true—receded with the decision of the House of Lords in the *Cambridge Water Co.* case (see Case 11.3).

CASE 11.3 *Cambridge Water Co. v. Eastern Counties Leather plc* [1994] 2 AC 264

Eastern Counties Leather had, for several years, used particular solvents. Until 1976, the way in which the solvent was delivered meant that there were often spillages. The solvent eventually found its way into underground strata and then into an aquifer, from which the Cambridge Water Company abstracted water. In 1982, the water company began testing for the solvent in the water, because

---

12 See the judgment of Buxton LJ in *Network Rail Infrastructure Ltd v. CJ Morris (t/a Soundstar Studio)* [2004] Env LR 41.

13 In *Gaunt v. Fynney* (1872) 8 LR 8, Lord Selborne LC said that '*a nervous or anxious or prepossessed listener hears sounds which would otherwise have passed unnoticed, and exaggerates into some new significance, originating within himself, sounds which at other times have been passively heard and not regarded*'.

new EC drinking water standards, which included parameters for the solvent, were to come into force in 1985. The tests found high levels of solvent, traceable back to the leather works. The cheapest option for the water company was to close down the borehole and open a new source of supply. The water company sued the leather works in nuisance (and also negligence and under *Rylands v. Fletcher*, discussed below).

The House of Lords held that liability depended on the foreseeability of the relevant type of damage occurring—that is, the pollution of groundwater above the levels laid down in the Directive. In the only full judgment, Lord Goff argued that, in relation to foreseeability, it would be unjust if liability for property damage under nuisance were to be stricter than liability for personal injury under negligence, at least in relation to the remoteness of damages. Liability is still 'strict', in the sense that there is no need to prove that the defendant has been careless.[14] The water company's claim in nuisance was therefore unsuccessful. The costs incurred by the water company only arose because of the changes to the drinking water quality regulations and the spillages had ceased before these came into force. (An interesting issue to consider is that the Directive is based on World Health Organization standards that date from 1970.)

It would seem that both the particular type of damage and the 'pollution pathway' must be foreseeable, although Lord Goff's reference in this case to what the 'reasonable supervisor' and the actual staff at the leather company knew at the time seems to take an unduly subjective, and restrictive, approach as to what it is that reasonable foreseeability requires. While the costs of preventing such a spill will not be a relevant factor—and, to that extent also, liability remains strict—investing in 'state of the art' pollution prevention technology and management systems may mean that liability is avoided because either the type of environmental damage caused or the way in which it is caused is unforeseen at the time. In this sense, adherence to current regulatory standards—for example, an industrial process using Best Available Techniques (BAT)—are likely to be directly relevant to whether there is liability in private law. In cases in which the damage and its cause might be revealed not because of regulatory controls, but if voluntary measures were followed—for example, should a firm be seeking accreditation under the Eco-Management and Audit Scheme (EMAS; see p. 308)— the position is less clear and seems inevitably to slide into questions of whether it would be reasonable for any particular industrial activity not to take such steps.

(e) Public benefit

Because nuisance is said to be about reasonable 'give and take' as between neighbours, this might be thought to imply that the greater the public benefit deriving from the neighbouring land use, the less likely that this will be an actionable nuisance (on the grounds that the affected neighbour, being a part of the general public, also benefits). In the absence of explicit statutory authority for doing so, however, the courts have been reluctant to allow private rights to be trumped by the public interest. In *Bamford v. Turnley* (1862) 3 B and S 62, a case about what would now be called local air pollution from brick burning, Bramwell B said that '*whenever a thing is for the public benefit, properly understood, the loss to the individuals of the public who lose will bear compensation out of the gains of those who gain*'.[15]

More recently, in *Dennis v. MOD* (see Case 11.2), Buckley J noted that the greater the public interests involved, the greater the interference might be (something that was clear in *Dennis* itself). Hence, there was an obvious danger if the public interest was considered when deciding whether a nuisance exists, because, in the case of serious nuisances caused by activities

---

14 See also *Jan de Nul (UK) Ltd v. Royale Belge* [2000] 2 Lloyd's Rep 790 (liability even though those responsible '*had taken all reasonable precautions to avoid such damage*').

15 At 85.

of great public importance, the sheer weight of the public benefit would, in effect, make it impossible to find in favour of the claimant. The judge therefore concluded, in a strong echo of *Bamford v. Turnley*, that '*public interest should be considered and that selected individuals should not bear the cost of the public benefit*'.[16] Notably, Buckley J thought that this approach had to be taken '*if the common law in this area is to be consistent with the developing jurisprudence of human rights*'.

Who can sue (and be sued) in private nuisance?

Anyone who, by their use of land,[17] creates a nuisance, or anyone who occupies land from which a nuisance emanates and who continues or adopts the nuisance, may be liable. Occupiers will be responsible for the acts of their employees and even for acts of trespassers, and, although the basic rule is that tenants are responsible for their own nuisances, landlords may be liable in a number of situations. Importantly, a polluter may be sued even though it is only one of many contributing to the pollution. In *Graham and Graham v. Re-Chem International Ltd* [1996] Env LR 158, although the claimants were ultimately unsuccessful, it was accepted that the defendant's dioxin emissions only had to amount to a 'material contribution' (a concept from the law of negligence—see below) to the damage to the claimant's cattle complained of.

The problem that has troubled the courts in recent years is who can bring a nuisance action. The issue was settled by the decision of the House of Lords in *Hunter v. Canary Wharf Ltd* (see Case 11.4).

CASE 11.4 *Hunter v. Canary Wharf Ltd* [1997] 2 WLR 684

In two separate actions, over five hundred residents in London's Docklands brought actions against the developers of Canary Wharf and the London Docklands Development Corporation for nuisance arising out of interference with television signals from Canary Wharf Tower and damage from dust emissions from road construction, respectively. The Court of Appeal had held that nuisance did not only protect property rights, but also anyone with a 'substantial link' with the enjoyment of the property as a home. This reflected the view that the old ideas of nuisance did not adequately protect those without legal interests in land, such as the specific interests of children or spouses.[18] But the House of Lords (by a majority of four–one) rejected this approach, calculating the potential damages according to damage to the property interests. Damages, had they been awarded, would not have been dependent on the number of residents affected.

In doing so, the House of Lords strongly restated the view that the right to sue in private nuisance can only be exercised by those with rights to the land affected, usually freehold owners or tenants in possession. In nailing down nuisance as an adjunct to property rights, the opportunity to develop it in a way that might offer greater protection of wider environmental interests was lost.

Whether this approach provides sufficient protection of the human rights of those, like children, who do not have rights in the land may need to be reconsidered in the light of HRA 1998. Some of the claimants in *Hunter v. Canary Wharf* took their case to the European

---

16 At [47].

17 In *Southport Corp. v. Esso Petroleum* [1954] 2 QB 182, obiter remarks in the Court of Appeal and House of Lords took opposing views on whether land of the defendant must be used (in that case, a tanker discharged oil at sea that washed ashore). In *Lippiatt v. South Gloucestershire Council* [2000] QB 51 (CA), the Court held that the council was liable for the nuisance-causing acts of licensees, because the nuisance was 'launched' from their land and it was relatively easy to remove them.

18 *Khorasandjian v. Bush* [1993] QB 727.

Commission of Human Rights. In *Khatun v. United Kingdom* (1 July 1998, unreported), the alleged breach of Art. 8 ECHR was ultimately unsuccessful (see p. 359). But the Commission did find that the right protected under Art. 8 applied to *all* of the applicants, whether they were property owners or merely occupiers. This got around one of the major obstacles to the claim re-erected by the House of Lords.

In *McKenna v. British Aluminium* [2002] Env LR 30, the High Court refused to strike out, as unarguable, an action brought, among others, by a number of children about alleged emissions and noise from the defendant's factory. The judge held that this would be inappropriate, because there was a 'real possibility' that a court might modify the common law rule about who can sue in private nuisance to make the common law comply with Art. 8. In *Dennis* (Case 11.2), however, damages were calculated on the basis of the property being a family home and the damages in nuisance were therefore the same as the damages awarded for the human rights claim. This is one way around the problem relating to standing.[19]

Notably, the ECHR does use a 'victim' test—meaning that there must be some legal person affected—and the ECtHR has rejected claims based only on protecting general ecological interests; there is no 'right to nature' (*X and Y v. Federal Republic of Germany* (1976) 5 Eur Com HR Dec & Rep). So the ECHR is a long way from granting, for example, an environmental pressure group a legal right to sue for damage to a natural habitat.

Defences to a claim for nuisance

There are a number of defences that attempt to restrict the scope of the law of nuisance. In practice, however, they are either so difficult to prove as to be useless, or of dubious merit.

(a) The defence of prescription

In principle, a right to pollute can be acquired as an easement through 20 years' continuous use. But there are so many caveats that the practical use of the defence is very restricted. For example, the right to pollute must be exercised openly, continuously, and not with any specific permission of the person against whom it is so acquired. It must also be the result of a lawful act, so a discharge in breach of a consent would not suffice. For example, in the case of *Sturges v. Bridgman* (1879) 11 ChD 852, the defendant, a confectioner, had used a noisy pestle and mortar in his premises without complaint for more than twenty years. But a doctor residing at the back of the site built a new consulting room close to the defendant's operational area and the noise became a problem. The Court of Appeal held that the defendant in this case had not acquired a right to pollute by prescription. The nuisance had begun only after the consulting room had been constructed, because previously the activities complained of did not give rise to any interference. Thus, the period of 20 years did not start to run until the consulting rooms were built.

Prescription was also raised in *Dennis v. MOD* (Case 11.2) because the Harrier jets had been flying from the RAF base since 1969. But the claim was rejected on the grounds, first, that the noise levels fluctuated too much and that therefore any prescriptive claim would be too imprecise, and, secondly, that Mr Dennis's repeated complaints over the years meant that he had not signalled his permission to the noise.

(b) No defence to say that the claimant came to the nuisance

In *Bliss v. Hall* (1838) 4 Bing NC 183, the defendant operated a business as a tallow chandler. This business had been operated for at least three years when the claimant moved in nearby. Unfortunately, the defendant's business created highly toxic fumes that were blown over the claimant's land. The defendant argued that, because he had been on the site before the claimant, the claimant should have realized the state of the premises nearby and should therefore not be able to bring a claim in nuisance. Tindal CJ said:

---

19 See also *Dobson v. Thames Water Utilities Ltd* [2007] EWHC 2021 (TCC), [236].

The [claimant] came to the house he occupies with all the rights which the common law affords, and one of them is the right to wholesome air. Unless the Defendant shows a prescriptive right to carry on his business in the particular area the [claimant] is entitled to judgment.[20]

When this principle is combined with the principle contained in *Sturges v. Bridgman*, it is clear that, whenever an individual moves into an area, there could be the creation of a new 'nuisance history', which negates the prescriptive rights principle because of the need to allow a further 20 years before a prescriptive right attaches. This might happen if there is a new development or change to an existing use.

In practical terms, the principle that it is no defence for a defendant to allege that the claimant has come to the nuisance is very important. For example, many factories and sewage works initially built on the outskirts of towns are now surrounded by housing. These potentially antagonistic uses can give rise to conflict. Industrialists may feel aggrieved that they have been carrying out polluting activities for a large number of years without complaint and that anyone who moved into the area would fully know of any problems. This principle may once have played an important role in facilitating the expansion of towns and cities that would otherwise have been hindered by factories without any legal reason to curb their pollution. This has led some to suggest that the advent of modern environmental regulation should kill the principle off.[21]

(c) Statutory authority

There may be occasions on which nuisances are caused by statutory or non-statutory bodies under express statutory authority. Where a body can point to such authority, then this will amount to a defence if an action is brought against them for any reasonably consequential nuisance.[22] This was the reason that there was no litigation in relation to noise disturbance from Heathrow, because private law claims relating to noise from civil aviation flying at a reasonable height are excluded by statute.[23]

Although most statutory obligations are expressly contained within the body of the statute itself, it is also clear that a defendant could claim the defence of statutory authority in cases in which there is a clear implication that such activities have been authorized by an Act.

CASE 11.5 *Allen v. Gulf Oil Refining Ltd* [1981] AC 1001

The Gulf Oil Refining Act 1965 (a private Act of Parliament) gave the defendants power to acquire land for an oil refinery at Milford Haven. The oil refinery emitted smells, noise, and vibration, and a local resident brought a claim against Gulf Oil in nuisance. The claimant argued that, although the Act gave the defendant the power to acquire land for constructing the refinery, it did not give any guidelines about the refinery's operation. So, when the defendant tried to rely on the defence of statutory authority, it was argued that, because the Act did not specifically allow for the operating of the plant in a manner that gave rise to a nuisance, the defence was unavailable. The House of Lords held that the statute implicitly gave the defendant an immunity to every act inevitably flowing from the construction of the refinery. The only possible exception to this would be if the nuisance complained of were to be of a greater degree than was necessary or if such activities were carried out negligently.

---

20 At 186.

21 T. Weir (2002) *Tort Law*, Oxford: Oxford University Press, p. 151.

22 B. Pontin [2001] 13 ELM 305 notes that, under s. 6(2) of the Human Rights Act 1998, there is a duty to respect the will of Parliament, meaning that there will be no national remedy, only the possibility of success in the ECtHR.

23 Section 76(1), Civil Aviation Act 1982. See comment on *Hatton v. UK* in Case 11.1. There is a decision that holds that statutory authority provides a defence to a private law action (in this case, trespass) even if the statutory authority violates EC law: *Feakins v. DEFRA* [2006] Env LR 44.

It should be pointed out that, if private rights are interfered with, it is often the case that statutes themselves provide for compensation. For example, in cases in which a new road is being built, statutory compensation is payable if there is injurious affection to the enjoyment of property that is the direct result of the works carried out. There are, however, situations in which the interference with private rights is not compensated, or in which, as in *Marcic v. Thames Water Utilities plc* [2004] Env LR 25 (see Case 11.7), statute provides for what might be considered an unsatisfactory enforcement mechanism.

Also, the statutory authority defence can be traced back to an era during which nuisance liability was stricter, in terms of the foreseeability test, than it is now. When this is coupled with the *Dennis* case and the possibility of taking public interest expressly into account, this may have knock-on consequences in terms of the courts' approaching statutory authority arguments less favourably to defendants.

More general issues relating to where private rights clash with public interests are discussed at p. 357.

Public nuisance

Although seemingly a close relative of private nuisance, the law relating to public nuisances contains some similar elements, but as many distinguishing features. Public nuisance is primarily a crime involving nuisance affecting a section of the general public, although the law developed over time so that anyone suffering 'special damage' beyond that suffered by the public generally has a claim in tort. This need only be a different degree, rather than type, of harm and may include purely economic losses. But in those environmental cases in which all suffer equally, there would appear to be no remedy in tort under public nuisance. Injunctions can be sought either by the Attorney-General or by local authorities, although individuals can take a claim with the Attorney-General's permission (a 'relator' action).

Attorney-General v. PYA Quarries Ltd [1957] 2 QB 169 shows the width of the class of persons that must be affected. The defendant company operated a quarry. During operations, it carried out various blasting activities. These caused vibration and noise over a wide area. In attempting to lay down guidelines, Denning LJ declined to specify what numbers would be required to show that a particular nuisance was public rather than private. But he did say:

I prefer to look to the reason of the thing and to say that a public nuisance is a nuisance which is so widespread in its range or so indiscriminate in its effect that it would not be reasonable to expect one person to take proceedings...to put a stop to it, but that it should be taken on the responsibility of the community at large.[24]

If the need to show an effect over a section of the public is set aside, there is a good degree of overlap with the factors that are taken into account when deciding whether or not there is a private nuisance—although one important difference is that public nuisance is, in principle, capable of protecting interests other than land rights[25] and it appears, as well, that the defendant's actions need not take place on land.[26]

An example of a claim in public nuisance is *Gillingham Borough Council v. Medway (Chatham) Dock Co. Ltd* [1993] QB 343 (see p. 358). Some would argue that, nowadays, public nuisance is something of an incongruous hybrid, relied on only in those cases in which the deficiencies of other torts have been exposed. For others, its strength lies in its potential elasticity, and it may represent the basis for developing an environmental tort action unconnected to land and capable of protecting wider community interests,[27] although the House of

24 At 191.

25 Although the situations in which it is typically pleaded tend to involve land interests.

26 *Overseas Tankship (UK) Ltd v. Miller Steamship Co. (Wagon Mound No. 2)* [1967] 1 AC 617.

27 J. Wightman (1998) MLR 870; in a similar vein, see D. Cooper (2003) 11 S&LS 5.

Lords has indicated that—as a crime, at any rate—it should not be used in cases in which the activity is regulated by a more specific offence (*R v. Rimmington* [2005] UKHL 63). The lack of connection to the claimant's or defendant's land is perhaps one reason why public nuisance has been the tort of choice in the USA for the first private law climate change cases.

Trespass

Trespass is the direct interference with personal or proprietary rights without lawful excuse. Trespass is actionable per se (*Entick v. Carrington* (1765) 19 St Tr 1029, 1066)—that is, it does not require proof of damage. This is well illustrated in the use of trespass law by the League Against Cruel Sports to hamper deer hunting in *League Against Cruel Sports v. Scott* [1985] 2 All ER 489. The League, which bought parcels of land on Exmoor, was successful in its action even though the hunt was not deliberately directed across its land. Simply walking over another's land without permission is sufficient basis under trespass for an injunction, even though no damage to property has been caused. By contrast, nuisance requires something consequential to the act complained of. For example, depositing waste on someone else's land will be a trespass, even if the waste can be removed without contaminating the soil or causing injury or disease. If, however, the waste is on other land, but causing loss of amenity because of smells or is spreading disease, then the most likely private law remedy will be an action in nuisance, because the harm is a consequence of the deposit, not the deposit itself. Trespass and private nuisance actions are mutually exclusive—that is, the same harm cannot be both direct and indirect).

The need to show direct interference has been a problem in environmental disputes, as two cases illustrate. In *Esso Petroleum v. Southport Corporation* [1956] AC 218, an oil tanker stranded in an estuary jettisoned oil to lighten the ship and to try to refloat. The oil drifted ashore and polluted the claimants' foreshore. The claimants (the Corporation) claimed for the costs of cleaning up the beach. Although trespass was not argued, two judges in the House of Lords thought that it would have failed, because the pollution was not inevitable.[28] This might be compared with a case such as *Jones v. Llanrwst Urban District Council* [1911] 1 Ch 393, in which the court did find that there was trespass when sewage was accidentally released and polluted the banks of a river downstream. In this case, the interference was held to be direct, because of the natural flow of the river. By contrast, in the *Esso Petroleum* case, there was no inevitability about the deposit of oil on the foreshore, which depended on the action of the wind, waves, and tide.

Because of the requirement of directness, trespass to the *person* has not been properly developed in pollution cases—although, in theory, making someone inhale toxic fumes could give rise to an action. If this requirement of directness is followed, it will be almost impossible to bring an action in trespass for airborne pollution unless the pollutant is deposited directly over the claimant's property. In the Canadian case of *Kerr et al v. Revelstoke Building Materials Ltd* (1976) 71 DLR (3d) 134 (Alta SC), for example, the claimants could claim for damages to them and their livestock because the offending cropduster had passed directly over their farm. Had the plane only sprayed over its own property and the chemicals been blown over onto the claimants' land, there would be no action in trespass—although, arguably, a nuisance action might have been taken. For these reasons, a tort law challenge to the spread of pollen from GM crops would probably have to be taken under nuisance law, either if the pollen were blown in the wind or, most likely, if it were brought on to the claimant's land by bees.

Trespass must also be intentional or negligent: *McDonald v. Associated Fuels Ltd* [1954] 3 DLR 775 illustrates this. Sawdust fuel was being supplied to the claimant's house. To deliver

---

28 But the matter is not clear-cut. In the Court of Appeal, Denning LJ also thought it was consequential, but Morris LJ treated it as direct.

it, the defendant company parked its truck and blew the sawdust into a bin inside the house by means of a blower unit. Unfortunately, the intake mechanism for the sawdust was too close to the truck's exhaust system, and both the sawdust and carbon monoxide fumes blew into the house. The occupants were overcome, one breaking a hip on collapsing. It is clear in this case that the trespass itself—that is, the entrance of the carbon monoxide directly into the house—was not intentional, but that the act that caused the trespass was.

Further points can be made about trespass law. Both illustrate the point that, unlike the other torts considered here, trespass cases can be initiated in order to *frustrate* action intended to further environmental protection. Two points can be seen in the case of *Monsanto v. Tilly* (Case 11.6).

CASE 11.6 *Monsanto v. Tilly* [2000] Env LR 313

Members of the campaigning group GenetiX snowball took direct action to destroy genetically modified crops at trial farm sites. One issue was whether Monsanto—by entering into an agreement with the farmer, but not actually owning or occupying the site—had sufficient interest to bring a trespass claim. The Court of Appeal held that it did (although, in another case, it has held that a developer that only had a right of access onto land to carry out surveys did not have a right of possession to maintain a trespass claim against a protester).[29]

A second issue was whether the trespass was necessary because, so the protesters alleged, destroying the crops was to protect third parties or the general public from harm. It is always difficult to rely on this line of defence and the Court of Appeal took a rather dim view of it, deciding that the protesters were really after publicity (they had arranged in advance for the press to be there and, in the event, pulled up very few plants). In any event, central government had responsibility for ensuring that the trials were carried out safely, so it would be difficult to justify third-party intervention of this kind.

This case, and the wider protest of which it was part, is discussed by Donson,[30] who looks at how business may resort to law and, in particular, to tort law (especially defamation, but also torts such as nuisance), to restrict protest and free speech. She illustrates how tort can also be used *against* those who campaign on things such as the environment.

In similar vein, environmental protestors have, on a number of recent occasions, unsuccessfully tried to defend possession proceedings in trespass actions, on the grounds that their action has been justified in some way as upholding environmental law.[31] Examples include efforts to require, as a matter of EC law, environmental impact assessment of the Newbury bypass[32] and the conservation of a protected species found on the site.[33]

Negligence

The law of negligence is a particularly large area of tort law and this book does not try to outline any more than its rudimentary features. The degree of coverage is also related to the general lack of utility of the law of negligence in environmental protection.

---

29 *Countryside Residential (North Thames) Ltd v. Tugwell* (2000) The Times, 4 April; see also *Manchester Airport plc v. Dutton* [2000] QB 133 (CA).

30 F. Donson (2000) *Legal Intimidation*, London: Free Association Press.

31 S. Tromans and J. Thomann [2003] JPL 1367.

32 *Secretary of State for Transport v. Haughian* [1997] Env LR 59 (CA); for another failed case regarding the EIA Directive, see *Mayor and Burgesses of the London Borough of Bromley v. Susanna* [1998] Env LR D13 (CA).

33 *Secretary of State for Transport v. Fillingham* [1997] Env LR 73.

The three main principles of negligence are that the claimant must establish that:

(a) a duty of care is owed by the defendant to the claimant;

(b) the defendant has breached that duty;

(c) there has been foreseeable damage to the claimant resulting from the breach.

There is no need to show a property interest and so anyone who suffers damage from an act of negligence can bring a claim. Damage here, however, generally means actual damage to property or physical injury (although this might include the costs of assessing whether there has been damage—see *Jan de Nul (UK) Ltd v. AXA Royale Belge SA* [2002] EWCA Civ 209, p. 352). In relation to claims for distress, annoyance, inconvenience, and physical symptoms short of personal injury—as might be the case, for example, with noise pollution—therefore, the torts of nuisance and *Rylands v. Fletcher* would probably have to be used (in so far as the damage can be tied to a sufficient interest in land).[34]

A key drawback of negligence is that it is a fault-based system: to succeed, there has to be some fault of the defendant. Compared with nuisance, for example, what is at issue is not the reasonableness of the use of the land, but the reasonableness of the defendant's actions— that is, whether the defendant has acted carelessly. In nuisance, as *Graham and Graham v. Re-Chem* [1996] Env LR 158 (see p. 337) shows, it is no defence to argue that state-of-the-art technology is being used. But in negligence, this is likely to be a critical factor and compliance with current regulatory standards will be sufficient to avoid liability. Negligence therefore tends to be relied on only in cases in which other common law remedies are not available. It is also necessary to foresee the type of harm that will result from an activity. In the *Cambridge Water Co.* case (see Case 11.3), therefore, the claim in negligence was dismissed at first instance because, at the time of the spillages, the reasonable supervisor could not have foreseen the changes to the drinking water regulations (and possibly also the pollution pathway). The House of Lords confirmed that it would not be sufficient to show that 'pollution' could have been foreseen, because that is too wide a category of damages.

But compared with trespass, for example, negligence (as with nuisance) requires proof that the defendant has caused damage to the claimant. Particularly in the so-called 'toxic tort' cases, this may be difficult, time-consuming, and expensive. *Graham and Graham* and the *Sellafield Leukaemia* litigation[35] are both prime examples of the evidential and technical difficulties involved in proving a case, the latter a salutary reminder of the problems of relying on epidemiological evidence.[36] Claimants may also be in a quandary because of the rules on the time limits for bringing cases. Waiting for certain proof of actual damage runs the risk that the court may say that the damage actually began beyond the limitation period.

Negligence is frequently used in everyday legal life, but overwhelmingly in relation to things like car accidents—that is, in cases in which individuals make mistakes. Pollution tends not to arise in this way, but results instead from lax regulation or systematic operational failures. Its general lack of use, or relevance, to environmental law should therefore not be surprising.

There are also cases in which a failure to warn about environmental damage has been found to be negligent. In *Barnes v. Irwell Valley Water Board* [1930] 1 KB 21, there was held

---

34 *McKenna v. British Aluminium* [2002] Env LR 30.

35 *Reay and Hope v. BNFL* [1994] 5 Med LR 1, discussed in J. Holder (1994) 47 CLP 287. On causation and foreseeability, see also J. Steele and N. Wikeley [1997] MLR 265.

36 The decision in *Fairchild v. Glenhaven Funeral Services Ltd* [2002] UKHL 22 makes 'environmental' negligence actions slightly easier to bring, because in cases such as those relating to exposure to asbestos, for example, in which it may be impossible to identify when the fatal inhalation took place (for example, if an employee has worked for a number of different employers over the years), the House of Lords has now held that damages can be apportioned among defendants, essentially according to the likelihood that the disease was contracted when the employee worked for them.

to be a common law duty of care on a water company to warn consumers of potentially unwholesome water and damages in negligence were recoverable. The application of this principle in relation to regulatory authorities can be seen in *Scott-Whitehead v. National Coal Board* (1987) P&CR 263. The defendants discharged a chlorine solution into a river. Because the river was in drought, there was insufficient water to dilute the strength of the pollutant. The claimant farmer abstracted water downstream, causing damage to his crops. The second defendant, the regional water authority, was held liable for failing to warn the farmer of the potential danger from the condition of the water that it knew was being abstracted. Extending the principle in this case, it would be possible to bring an action against an environmental regulator in negligence if it could be shown that a failure to warn materially contributed to damage. But there appear to be no reported decisions in which this has happened and any such argument would now have to overcome the general judicial reluctance to impose private law duties on public bodies, or find that these bodies have been at fault, especially in cases in which they are exercising their discretion and there are resource implications of imposing such a duty. In a fairly extreme case, the failure to warn of an environmental risk has been held to be a violation of the human rights to home life[37] and to the right to life itself.[38] In the latter case, the risk to life meant that the state had a positive duty to inform those that might be affected—that is, the duty was not simply one of informing those who requested informstion about the risk.

Natural nuisances

Nuisances can arise other than by the clash of everyday uses of land. First, a deliberate act by one landowner, bringing a hazardous substance onto his land, may lead to damage if there is an escape (considered in the following section). Secondly, there are situations in which a hazard arises *naturally*, but which, if it goes unchecked, might damage neighbouring land. As we will see, the main difference between how nuisance law applies at these two ends of the spectrum relates to the degree of fault—that is, negligence—that must be shown before the landowner is liable.

In *Leakey v. National Trust* [1980] QB 485, a case involving a landslip, the general principle was established that *'ownership of land carries with it a duty to do whatever is reasonable in all the circumstances to prevent hazards on the land, however these arise, from causing damage to a neighbour'*. In cases like this, in which the hazard comes about without direct human intervention,[39] landowners have what is referred to a 'measured duty of care' imposed on them. The essence of this is that, although any claim will be similar to an ordinary private nuisance action, what it is 'reasonable' to expect a landowner to do will depend on whether they:

(a) knew of the risk;

(b) had the means to prevent it happening;

(c) failed to do so in a reasonable time (*Goldman v. Hargrave* [1967] AC 645).

In this sense, it is like nuisance, but with a strong twist of negligence, in that there must be a pre-existing duty to take care, and the courts look to whether the defendant failed to meet the standard of care appropriate to the circumstances. Whether the defendant can be said to be careless will therefore depend, in part, on its resources. In this sense, therefore, any claim is different from a private nuisance action because, in private nuisance, it is immaterial

---

37 *Guerra v. Italy* (1998) 26 EHRR 357.

38 *Oneryildiz v. Turkey* (2004) 18 BHRC 145.

39 Lord Wilberforce in *Goldman v. Hargrave* [1967] 1 AC 645 refers to hazards 'whether natural or man-made', but subsequent cases have all been about the former.

whether the defendant was careless and the resources of the defendant are not a relevant factor.[40] This concession reflects both the fact that the defendant has not consciously created something that is potentially harmful and that the impact on neighbours of a naturally occurring hazard may be beyond the means of the defendant to prevent.

Liability under this principle has been established in several recent cases, including damage caused by pigeons fouling the road—and pedestrians—beneath a railway bridge in London,[41] and it has also been held to apply to naturally occurring flooding.[42] One important limitation to this principle, however, emerged in *Marcic v. Thames Water Utilities plc* (Case 11.7), a case that is also important on human rights grounds.

CASE 11.7 *Marcic v. Thames Water Utilities plc* [2004] Env LR 25

Mr Marcic suffered from repeated incidents of sewage flooding. The sewage flooded his garden and lapped at his back step, but never flooded his house. Thames, the sewerage undertaker, prioritized renovation work to combat internal flooding. The cause of the flooding was the overloading of the sewer network, which, although originally adequate, now had too many properties discharging into it. (Under statute, new properties are essentially given a right to connect to the existing sewerage network.) Following water privatization, a statutory scheme applies under which companies submit investment plans to the industry's economic regulator, who determines which projects to finance (see p. 596). The claimant sued in nuisance and for a breach of human rights under Art. 8 of the European Convention on Human Rights.

Overturning the Court of Appeal, the House of Lords rejected both claims. Although Thames had a natural hazard—sewage generated in the local area—on its land, it had not acted unreasonably. Because of its funding formula, it was a special kind of occupier of land whose ability to prevent or minimize the flooding had to be recognized. The statutory scheme under which it operated was also fatal to the human rights claim, because the Lords considered that Parliament had provided a statutory remedy, through enforcement orders, which the economic regulator can serve on sewerage companies if he or she feels that they should do more to protect the interests of their customers from things such as sewage flooding. So, the issue was whether this *statutory* scheme was human rights compliant; the Lords held that it did strike the right balance between the different interests involved—that is, as between the interests of those affected by flooding and all customers who ultimately pay for improvements through their bills. Had the House of Lords found in favour of Mr Marcic, it was estimated that the cost to Thames alone would have been in the region of £1bn (three times its gross annual profits).

Unnatural nuisances—the rule in *Rylands v. Fletcher*

The principle known as 'the rule in *Rylands v. Fletcher*' was first established in the case of that name ((1868) LR 3 HL 330). The defendant constructed a reservoir on his land, but the contractors failed to detect and block off mine shafts so that, when the reservoir filled up, water entered the shafts and flooded the claimant's mine. The problem was that there could be no action in negligence as the law then stood (there was no relationship between the contractor and the mine owner) and, because it was an isolated escape, a nuisance action was thought

---

40 Note that judges may find ways of taking them into account as, for example, when assessing the extent to which environmental damage was foreseeable: see *Cambridge Water* (Case 11.3).

41 *Wandsworth London Borough Council v. Railtrack plc* [2001] Env LR 441.

42 *Green v. Somerleton* [2003] EWCA Civ 198.

to be precluded. In the lower court ((1866) LR 1 Ex. 265), Blackburn J first expounded the principle:

> that the person who for his own purposes brings onto his land and collects and keeps there anything likely to do mischief if it escapes, must keep it at his peril, and, if he does not do so, is prima facie answerable for all the damage which is the natural consequence of its escape.[43]

Non-natural use or extraordinary use

In the House of Lords, however, the qualification was added that there would only be an action in cases in which there was a 'non-natural use' being made of the defendant's land. Originally, this may have meant that there would have been no liability if the water (in *Rylands*) had been a natural lake or naturally flooded area rather than an artificial reservoir. But, in time, it came to mean that the use had to be '*some special use bringing with it increased danger to others and must not merely be the ordinary use of land or such a use as is proper for the general benefit of the community*' (*Rickards v. Lothian* [1913] AC 263, 280). Over the years, this was applied to numerous activities, so that 'natural' became synonymous with anything for the general public benefit, no matter how *un*natural. The high point was perhaps reached in *Read v. Lyons* [1947] AC 156, in which the manufacture of high explosive shells was held by the House of Lords not to be a dangerous operation imposing on the manufacturer an absolute liability.

This decision may well have been influenced by the ongoing war effort at the time of the accident. But what is more important is that the House of Lords explicitly refused to extend the doctrine into a general theory of strict liability for ultra-hazardous activities, which, of course, would have had profound implications for the development of environmentally hazardous technologies. The House of Lords again took this approach in *Cambridge Water Co. v. Eastern Counties Leather* (see Case 11.3) and has done so again in *Transco v. Stockport Metropolitan Borough Council* (Case 11.8).

CASE 11.8 *Transco v. Stockport Metropolitan Borough Council* [2003] UKHL 61

Water was supplied to a block of flats owned by the council. Due to an undetected leak, a large volume of water collected under the flats, from where it leaked into an old railway embankment. The embankment collapsed, leaving a gas pipe in the embankment exposed and unsupported, and the gas supplier incurred costs making the pipe (which seems not to have been damaged itself) safe. The supplier sued under the rule in *Rylands v. Fletcher*. The House of Lords thought that the rule in *Rylands* had a continuing justification, but rejected the claim, essentially because it held that there was nothing extraordinarily risky about the council's use of its land. Although, as *Rylands* itself showed, large volumes of water can give rise to extraordinary risks, the water here, although contained in a larger than normal pipe, was not deliberately accumulated, but was piped into the block under normal mains pressure.

In *Transco*, then, what the House of Lords seems[44] to stress (whether it chose to call it 'non-natural use' or not) was that the defendant's use must, in the circumstances, be an extraordinary use of land giving rise to some extraordinary degree of risk. Whether something is extraordinary will depend on the time and place. But it is clear that, in the words of Lord Hoffmann, there is a '*high threshold for a claimant to surmount*'.[45] The House also played

---

43 At 279.
44 Five full judgments were given, each taking a slightly different approach.
45 At [49].

down, contrary to parts of Lord Goff's speech in *Cambridge Water*, any relationship between 'natural use' and the 'reasonable user' test in nuisance. Industrial activities can be out of the ordinary, but not 'unreasonable'—for example, because they operate properly under regulation (as, for example, the Eastern Counties Leather tannery did). In *LMS International Ltd and ors v. Styrene Packaging and Insulation Ltd and ors* [2005] EWHC 2065 (TCC), however, it was unsuccessfully argued by the defendants that, because they were carrying out an ordinary industrial process on an industrial estate, their activities were 'non-natural'.

The issue of the 'naturalness' of the activity is not unrelated to its dangerousness—that is, whether it will do 'mischief' if it escapes. Over the years, the rule has been applied in relation to water, fire, gases, electricity, oil, chemicals, colliery spoil, and poisonous vegetation. In *Transco*, differing approaches were taken in the House of Lords as to whether the 'mischief' test was a test to be applied separately, or rolled into the 'non-natural use of land' test. Given that the focus is on the degree of risk, it probably makes little difference: if something creates an extraordinary risk if it escapes, then the thing that escapes is likely to be dangerous (even if it is only dangerous because of the volume in which it escapes, as with water).

Other features of the use of the rule

It is now clear, following *Transco*, that the claimant must have an interest in land to invoke the rule. This really only confirms a point that was fairly clear following the decisions of the House of Lords in *Cambridge Water,* which held that the rule in *Rylands* is really only an aspect of nuisance law, and in *Hunter v. Canary Wharf* (see Case 11.4), which restricted the right to sue in nuisance in this way. It also means that the rule cannot be used to claim for personal injury.[46] So, as with nuisance, there must be something that passes—or, as in the case of *Rylands*, escapes—from the defendant's land to the claimant's land.

Two further, related, points can be made here. The first relates to whether there has been 'an escape'. This might not always be clear-cut. Indeed, in *Transco*, there was disagreement between the judges on this point: Lord Hoffmann thought that there had been an escape, because damage to the land supporting the pipe was analogous to damage to the pipe itself; Lord Scott held that there had not, because the actual damage had been to the council's land and the gas pipe had not actually been damaged). Secondly, while the effect of the escape must be felt beyond the defendant's land, it need not be the substance accumulated that escapes. This can be seen in *Rainham Chemical Works Ltd v. Belvedere Fish Guano Co.* [1921] 2 AC 465, in which a munitions factory exploded. The claim did not fail only because it was the bits of the factory, rather than the dangerous substance stored, that escaped. What is clear is that the balancing act between relaxing 'non-natural use' and now stipulating the reasonable foreseeability of the damage allows the courts to continue to pay attention to the costs of preventing damage arising.

Defences

There are a number of defences to an action brought under the *Rylands* rule. As with nuisance, the defence of statutory authority may be argued. It may also be argued that the escape was an 'act of God' or of a third party, such as a vandal[47] (a further limitation on seeing the rule in *Rylands* as a strict liability tort), although in the nature of especially risky activities

---

46 Which sits uneasily with reference in some of the judgments in *Transco* to justifying the retention of the rule in *Rylands*, because of the need for a rule to cover the human consequences of disastrous escapes from land. The effect of *Transco* is that the rule in *Rylands* might compensate people for their property losses, but not for their loss of life. This is an inevitable, although potentially appalling, consequence of tying *Rylands* to interests in land and one that is in tension with the notion—expressed most clearly in Lord Hoffmann's opinion—that the rule in *Rylands* is primarily about allocating the costs of dangerous activities (hence the irrelevance of whether the escape was reasonably foreseeable).

47 In contrast to the position with criminal liability for causing pollution, see p. 260.

it must be the case that greater foresight and consideration is required than in other situations in which this defence can be argued. (If it were not covered by specific legislation, nuclear installations would be a prime example.) In *Transco*, Lord Hoffmann, in noting the emergence of various statutory liability regimes for things such as pollution from waste and by radioactive matter (see p. 360) left open the question of whether these kinds of statutory provisions create an exhaustive code of liability that would exclude the rule in *Rylands*, and was also wary of applying the rule in situations in which liability might be excluded, by statute, for more risky activities (in a case such as *Transco*, if the escape had been from the water company's high pressure main, liability would have been excluded under statute—see s. 209(3)(b), Water Industry Act 1991).

A final point here is that Lord Bingham's opinion in *Transco* casts doubt on whether there is any longer a defence of 'common benefit' or 'public benefit'. Any such defence would, in practice, extend the principle from one of risk sharing to one of risk imposing. Whether any benefit to the particular claimant from the harmful activity provides a defence, however, remains unclear—although, in the past, if gas, electricity, or water supplies have caused damage to the claimant's property, no liability has been imposed on the basis that the potential claimant has, in effect, consented to the risk.[48]

The protection of riparian rights

There is a separate action for interference with the rights of owners of riparian land. Although this action has some similarities with private nuisance, it is, in practice, used far more frequently owing to the strength of riparian owners' natural rights to water. For further explanation, see p. 623.

Breach of statutory duty

In cases in which there is a breach of a statutory provision, so that a claimant suffers a loss, there may be a remedy in damages. Although there does not have to be any finding of negligence by the defendant, the tort is little used, because the courts have held that a claim will succeed only if it can be shown that Parliament intended the claimant to have a civil remedy. Sometimes, it is clear that Parliament specifically *excludes* this possibility, as is the case under the Water Resources Act 1991 (see s. 100(b)). Otherwise, if this is not spelt out in the statute, then it must be inferred and, if the statute involves general public law duties, then the broader the exercise of discretion involved, the less likely will be a right of claim for breach of statutory duty.[49] Also, the statute must give rights to a limited class of persons rather than to the general public, which makes its application in relation to general pollution control legislation difficult. It is used most frequently in relation to industrial safety legislation, but one example of its use in an environmental context was following the incident at Camelford in 1988 when 20 tonnes of aluminium sulphate wrongly ended up in the public water supply. The water authority eventually ended up settling the case out of court, on the basis of a breach of its statutory water supply duties.[50] (The Camelford incident is one reason why there is now a specific offence of supplying water that is unfit for human consumption under the Water Industry Act 1991, s. 70)

The common view is that if the statute provides for criminal enforcement, then this rules out civil claims. This is said to be because the criminal sanctions show that the interests of those affected are being taken seriously, although this would also support the view that this is precisely why civil claims for damages should also be available. Breach of statutory duty

---

48 See *Attorney-General v. Cory Brothers & Co.* [1921] 1 AC 521.
49 *X (Minors) v. Bedfordshire County Council* [1995] 2 AC 633.
50 See also *Read v. Croydon Corporation* [1938] 4 All ER 631, discussed at p. 598.

was argued before the High Court in *Bowden v. South West Water Services Ltd* [1998] Env LR 445 and rejected, because the judge thought that the three EC water Directives concerned were all too general in their application. But the overturning of this decision in relation to the Directive on shellfish waters (79/923/EEC) for the purposes of a state liability claim under the *Francovich* principle—that is, because the Directive was for the direct benefit of a limited class of shellfishermen—might suggest that a similar view could be taken in relation to breach of statutory duty (see the Court of Appeal decision at [1999] Env LR 438). Ultimately, however, the point remains that legislation intended to protect general environmental interests and which gives public authorities some discretion in implementation, such as in determining a licence, is unlikely to lead to a successful claim for breach of statutory duty.

Other private law mechanisms

Although the most common application of private law remedies as used for environmental protection is that of the law of tort, there are other private law mechanisms that may be useful in this context. Centrally, the law relating to property ownership shows both advantages and disadvantages for environmental protection. Using property law to exclude others from encroaching or trespassing on land has often been relied on by voluntary organizations such as the Royal Society for the Protection of Birds (RSPB) to protect habitats, or by bodies such as the National Trust to protect cherished landscape features. The reverse of this is that, as a matter of property law, owners are, in principle, allowed to interfere with their land in any way they wish. So, as a matter of private law, wild plants can be uprooted and land contaminated as long as neighbouring landowners are not affected.

Similarly, restrictive freehold covenants may regulate future land development (see *Tulk v. Moxhay* (1848) 41 ER 1143). This may help to prevent damaging development, but preservation and 'doing nothing' are not always compatible with enlightened environmental protection, and, in any case, their use is ultimately subject to statutory control.

Another example is planning obligations (see p. 414), which, unlike freehold covenants, can provide both for negative restrictions and for positive environmental benefits. Although such obligations are the creation of statute, developers and local planning authorities are given considerable width to enter into them. When they do so, they are contacts between the developer and the planning authority, and agreements entered into after the Contracts (Rights of Third Parties) Act 1999 came into force might be enforceable by local residents for whose benefits the agreements are undoubtedly made.

More recognizably, contractual agreements are also used in the form of management agreements, such as those entered into between the Nature Conservancy Council and landowners (see p. 691). These types of management agreement are not as wide-ranging as freehold or leasehold covenants, because they are not necessarily binding on third parties (unless, of course, statute makes them so). There is some use of private agreements between industrial organizations (such as the Chemical Industries Association) and government, but, so far, these are limited. Contracts will have to be used where, under an environmental management system (EMS), for example, the whole of the supply chain must operate to certain standards.

Civil law remedies

The use of the common law as a mechanism for environmental protection would be useless unless there were effective remedies once a cause of claim had been established. The two main types of remedy that can be sought are preventive and compensatory remedies. An injunction allows for actions creating environmental problems to be stopped by order of the court; monetary damages act as compensation for any damage suffered, but can also pay for any clean-up costs involved in rectifying the damage.

Common law remedies have both positive and negative features when it comes to protecting the environment. On the positive side, the courts tend to treat remedies as following directly from the right that has been infringed—that is, they do not engage in a further balancing exercise between the claimant's rights and the defendant's (or wider social) interests. This is seen most clearly in relation to the preference for granting injunctions rather than awarding damages. Negatively, remedies are available to benefit claimants' rights, not environmental interests. So, for example, damages need not be spent on restoring the environment.

Injunctions

The granting of an injunction is a discretionary remedy that can either prohibit or restrict a defendant from carrying on an environmentally damaging activity. Normally, either the activity complained of has to be continuing at the date of claim, or there has to be a threat that the activity will continue. Although injunctions are discretionary, however, the general principle in the two torts in which continuing damage is likely—nuisance and trespass—is that claimants can expect to obtain an injunction unless the activity complained of is not of sufficient gravity or duration to justify stopping the defendant's actions. This long-standing principle was affirmed in *Kennaway v. Thompson* [1981] QB 88, a complaint about noise from powerboat racing. The Court of Appeal decided to award the claimant an injunction restricting the times at which the boats raced and the noise they made, notwithstanding the public interest in the sport. The importance of this decision is that it confirms that a party that causes a nuisance or trespass cannot simply 'buy off' the rights of those affected by paying an award of damages.

In *Dennis v. MOD* (see Case 11.2), however, the exceptional public necessity in training RAF fighter pilots was held to justify an award of damages rather than an injunction.[51] The judge also thought it was relevant that the Harrier jets had been flying at the base for over thirty years and the probability that most jet fighter training at the site would (partly because of the increased noise generated by the next generation of jets) cease after about a further nine years. This indicates that even nuisances that will continue many years into the future may not be stopped if, looking at the wider picture, this would be unduly harsh.

This and other cases illustrate a possible trend that plays down the right to an injunction, while at the same time stresses the importance that those who suffer harm to their land interests should be compensated. In other words, the less that a court feels it must award an injunction, the more likely it may be to hold that there has been a nuisance and then compensate for the loss this causes.[52] In the case of multiparty claims, of course, it is debatable whether courts could ever properly assess the right amount of damages payable if damages were ever to be preferred to injunctions on economic efficiency grounds.

There are situations in which it is possible to obtain an injunction before the occurrence of the event causing injury or damage. Such anticipatory injunctions do not require proof of environmental damage at all, but there must be sufficient proof of imminent damage and it must be demonstrated that, if the activity were to continue, the damage accruing would be significant enough to make it difficult to rectify. Such injunctions are seldom granted.

Injunctions are rarely specific in nature: the court merely sets the standard for the defendant to meet and this standard can be achieved in any way possible. For example, it may be

---

51 Strictly, in *Dennis*, a declaration against the MOD was sought rather than an injunction (because of issues peculiar to seeking injunctions against the Crown), but the MOD agreed that it would 'act appropriately in the face of such a declaration'.

52 Although see *Regan v. Paul Properties Ltd* [2006] EWCA Civ 1391 (blocking of light by development; injunction granted requiring building to be reduced in height).

met either by closing down a particular plant that is causing environmental difficulties or by fitting new arrestment equipment. To give defendants time to make such changes, injunctions are often 'suspended' for a certain period before being enforceable.[53]

Damages

Unlike an injunction, a claimant can *demand* that the court award damages. The aim of such damages is to place the claimant as far as possible in the position in which they would have been had the wrongful act not occurred. This could be calculated in two ways: on the basis of the cost of clean-up operations necessary to restore the property to its previous state, or on the basis of the difference between the value of the property as it was after the pollution had affected it and before. The approach of the courts now, however, is to calculate damages according to the latter method. So, in cases in which there has been no physical damage, damages will be based on lost capital values—usually the difference in possible rental value during the period of the nuisance (see *Hunter v. Canary Wharf*). This means that damages will not depend on the number of people affected, in line with the idea that nuisance is a *land* tort.

Damages might, however, also be awarded for loss of amenity—that is, interference with the enjoyment of the use of land—on top of capital losses, although the courts try to restrict such awards to relatively modest sums.[54] This type of loss is similarly calculated on the (somewhat artificial) basis of loss of amenity to the land, rather than of people living on the land. This approach might be capable of absorbing the impact of HRA 1998,[55] but, in another case, it has been held that 'just satisfaction' for the purposes of human rights law may require that damages for things such as mental distress might also be needed (not least if a large number of people, but not their land values, are affected).[56] In other words, human rights law has begun to fill the damages 'gap' between nuisance and negligence, which might mean in future that, even in a non-human rights claim, the courts will give damages for these kinds of losses.

If there is actual damage, however, this will have to be compensated. An example of this is *Marquis of Granby v. Bakewell Urban District Council* (1923) 87 JP 105. The defendant operated a gas works that discharged poisonous effluent into a river over which the claimant had fishing rights, killing numerous fish. The claimant received compensation equalling the costs of restocking the river, in addition to the loss of a large amount of the food supply for other stocks. The court also took into account the effects of the pollution on higher quality areas of the river and considered that the damages would be higher where environmental pollution was greater. But, in some cases, compensatory damages must have regard to what is fair both to the claimant and the plaintiff. For example, in *Bryant v. Macklin* [2005] EWCA Civ 762, the claimant's mature trees were damaged by the acts of a neighbour. The court would not award the full cost of replacement (which, at £400,000, would have been as much as the value of the claimant's house), but nor did it give the claimant only the drop in value of his land. The court based its award on what a reasonable claimant of unlimited funds would have spent in replacing the trees, taking into account the value of the property. The wider environmental point is that, at no point does the court consider any ecological value that might be lost and bases its decision on damages simply with regard to the owners' property rights.

---

53 An example is *Pride of Derby and Derbyshire Angling Association Ltd v. British Celanese* [1953] Ch 149, see p. 626.

54 *Farley v. Skinner* [2001] UKHL 49, a case about aircraft noise; for an example of an award outside these guidelines, because of the exceptional level of interference, see *Dennis v. MOD* (Case 11.2).

55 See ibid., [91].

56 *Dobson v. Thames Water Utilities Ltd* [2007] EWHC 2021 (TCC).

A positive development in the area of damages comes from *Jan de Nul (UK) Ltd v. AXA Royale Belge SA* [2002] EWCA Civ 209. A wildlife trust was awarded £100,000 of costs incurred in conducting surveys to assess whether, following dredging operations, silt had caused any long-term damage to a nature reserve that it owned. This was notwithstanding that the survey did not find any such damage. It was important, however, that there had actually been physical interference with the land and that any clean-up would have cost more, which allowed the court to decide that the survey was a reasonable response. This case should not therefore be taken as deciding that any precautionary expenditure can be claimed when, in fact, no damage has been caused. For example, it is doubtful whether the costs of a private medical examination would be a reasonable response from someone who had been living in the vicinity of a release of hazardous substances into the air.

Damages for all *future* loss are only available in lieu of an injunction. This remedy is used only sparingly because of the ready availability of the more usual injunction procedure.

Lastly, punitive damages—that is, damages going beyond mere compensation—can be awarded in specific instances. The basis of such an award is to deter the defendant and others from committing torts that may result in financial benefit to the person responsible. The scope for these damages is, however, limited to cases in which there has been oppressive, arbitrary, or unconstitutional action by servants of the government, or in which the defendant's conduct was calculated to make a profit that would exceed the damages payable (*Rookes v. Barnard* [1964] AC 1129). Thus a claim for punitive damages in public nuisance after the public water supply at Camelford was polluted was rejected on the ground that public nuisance fell outside the above categories.[57] The very limited extent to which punitive damages are payable in English tort law is an obstacle to its usefulness in protecting environmental interests. Even if a polluter compensates for losses it has caused, this only puts it on a par with other firms who have not caused such losses. Similarly, gains to the polluter are unlikely to be taken into account unless (exceptionally) punitive damages are awarded. Both of these factors inhibit tort from influencing potentially polluting behaviour.

The utility of private law for environmental protection

As the brief analysis above of the various private law mechanisms makes clear, there are a number of general limitations on the use of private law (especially tort law) to protect environmental interests. There is also the key issue of the affordability of private law claims and other practical difficulties in its use.[58]

(a) Private law acts only as a protector of private interests

Both the land torts and the contractual mechanisms considered above aim to protect private interests rather than the more nebulous concept of environmental 'rights' or 'interests'. This has two important consequences. First, the level of environmental protection that flows from these mechanisms will be determined according to private rather than public interests. *Cambridge Water Co. v. Eastern Counties Leather* (see Case 11.3) is a paradigm example, in which the damages sought by the water company would, had it been successful, have paid for the relocation of its borehole to an unpolluted site. Whichever way the case was decided, the land and groundwater remained contaminated (and, as Case 11.3 shows, there *was* considered to be a public interest in clean-up). Private law will only lead to the remediation of such sites if this is the most reasonable (which usually means the cheapest) way for the claimant

---

57 *AB v. South West Water Services Ltd* [1993] QB 507. For criticism, see P. Cane (1993) 5 JEL 149.

58 For detailed criticism from a broadly law-and-economics perspective of most of the following points, see D. Howarth, (2002) Washburn LJ 469.

to be compensated. A similar point can be seen in *Hatton v. United Kingdom* (see Case 11.1), in which the ECtHR held that it was reasonable to take into account the affected individuals' ability to leave the area without undue hardship. Again, any indirect environmental benefit from litigation is absent.[59] Another negative example is the possibility that an easement to pollute a river might be acquired. It is arguable whether such a claim could ever be in the interests of the environment.

Secondly, the right to bring a claim is generally restricted in some way. For example, private nuisance and *Rylands* claims are restricted in this way. Although there are narrow rights for groups to take action in public nuisance, private law mechanisms serve narrowly drawn private interests—essentially, interests relating to the ownership or possession of land. Even in cases in which a private right can be argued, the substance of the right may do little to improve the environment of those who would stand to benefit the most from such improvements, as the operation of the locality rule in private nuisance shows.

In both cases, effective environmental protection requires wider public interests to be taken into account, including both wider ecological interests and the interests of non-land owners, and perhaps also of future generations. It is true, of course, that the exercise of private rights may coincide with the protection of wider ecological interests. But English private law seems a long way off accepting the idea that, for example, there should be scope to bring a claim on behalf of wild plants and animals, rather as children bring claims through a guardian in family law proceedings.

(b) Private rights are based on imprecise or unduly absolute standards

As we have seen in Chapter 8, environmental regulation increasingly involves the setting both of specific target standards and then specifically worded licences to try to meet these standards. Often, both of these will be expressed as quantitative limits. One advantage of these is that they make enforcement easier, because the detection of breaches can be accurately monitored and proper assessments made of any discharge. There is, of course, a range of more qualitative standards that are used. The BAT standard in pollution prevention and control (PPC) permits is perhaps the best example, but even with BAT there is quite detailed guidance given to operators as to what standards will be required. The effective regulation of many industrial processes can only be dealt with through quantitative standards and scientific monitoring.

Private law mechanisms meet neither criteria. Generally, the common law is based upon standards that are either unduly tightly drawn or necessarily imprecise. Both have their drawbacks. For example, trespass law does not require any proof of damage and therefore provides a fairly absolute protection of property rights. While this level of protection does have its environmental advantages—for example, in conserving nature conservation sites— the more general problem is that trespass law does not allow for the kind of balancing that might be needed in other contexts and, arguably, over-regulates in some situations, which may not be in the wider public interest. It also has the drawback that the absolute protection afforded to landowners' interests might be judged by some to prevent a wider experience of nature (although, to some extent, this has been rectified by the Countryside and Rights of Way Act 2000, which establishes a limited 'right to roam').

In the case of imprecise standards, as we see clearly in nuisance law, the law tries to balance competing private interests, looking to the reasonableness of the activities rather than restricting conduct to specified levels. What is reasonable depends on the circumstances of each case. While this may be necessary in order to deal with disputes over matters as subjective as some noise nuisances, it makes the outcome of a nuisance claim highly uncertain, especially if it involves amenity damage. Although the context-specificness of nuisance law

---

59 Another illustration of this is *Ashworth and ors v. United Kingdom*, ECtHR, 20 January 2004.

is admired by theoretical economists—who point to its advantages over generalized rules that may over- or under-regulate—inevitably, this uncertainty discourages arguable cases from being brought by private litigants.[60]

Problems of proof

Environmental regulation typically involves the setting of standards that, if exceeded, lead to a punishable breach. Standards may either be breached without damage to the environment—as with 'technical' breaches of process standards—or because some quantitative standard has not been met. The key point is that there will usually be some monitoring on the site recording the breach; only rarely does the regulator have to take samples from the environment and try to establish where the pollutant came from. This, however, is often what has to be done in environmental tort claims. For instance, airborne deposits could have originated from a site many miles from the area of the damage; seeking to show that the damage emanates from a particular site in these circumstances is particularly difficult. In heavily industrialized areas, the problem is even more acute.

The common law does go some way towards solving this problem. As we have seen, it will be enough in negligence and nuisance to show that the defendant 'materially contributed' to the damage caused, even if his or her own contribution was insignificant if viewed in isolation (see p. 337). This is an important rule, especially in those situations in which it would be impossible to pin down the exact contribution of any one polluter, as with nitrate run-off. Nevertheless, it has its limits. First, it is not enough to show that the damage is of the kind generally associated with operators like the defendant, as *Cambridge Water Co v. Eastern Counties Leather* (Case 11.3) illustrates.

Secondly, there are practical and evidential limits: there must be evidence linking the defendant's operations with the damage caused, and proving causation is often technically difficult and very costly.

Thirdly, and rather obviously, the rule is of no practical use in cases in which environmental damage has a vast number of small contributors—for example, low-level ozone pollution from motor vehicles. All of these problems arise, therefore, not because it may be difficult to show that an activity is genuinely causing harm—a problem common to private and public environmental law controls—but because, in private law, the nature of the burden of proving causation is individualized. In contrast, statutory regulation can shift the focus on to a polluting sector and lead to improvements by imposing tighter controls across the board—for example, on a particularly polluting sector of industry.

Private law as a fault-based system

Although trespass gives rise to strict liability, in other circumstances, the bringing of a claim under common law either requires some carelessness on behalf of the person creating the damage (negligence), or at least foreseeability of the damage caused (nuisance). But most pollution loading and isolated pollution spills do not occur because of deliberate actions by careless and unthinking individuals. Most pollution incidents arise because of a number of circumstances that would not normally be foreseeable, but which give rise to damage. In the interests of doing justice to defendants, the common law does not always seek to redress any damage caused by such accidents and corrective justice becomes a secondary consideration. Clearly, this is contrary to the general thrust of the Polluter Pays Principle.

---

60 Uncertainty of outcome is a barrier to most litigation: see H. Genn (1999) *Paths to Justice*, Oxford: Hart.

Reactive controls

Private law controls are generally reactive[61] and compensatory, rather than preventive. It is only very rarely that private law can be used to prevent environmental damage, although it is possible in limited situations to seek anticipatory injunctions. While the general priority given to injunctions over damages in nuisance law is beneficial, private law does not offer continuing controls that might gradually improve standards over time. Nor does it provide an appropriate mechanism for dealing with uncertain risks, because tort law does not really have the capacity to impose safety margins. Putting all these points somewhat differently, we doubt whether the prospect of being sued in nuisance ever really influences the behaviour of polluting industries in the way that meeting an environmental regulator does.

An environmental injustice?

Despite many negative features, the common law torts contain a range of general principles that ought, in theory, to have gone much further in protecting both human and wider environmental interests. Instead, the need for environmental regulation was recognized at a relatively early stage of industrialization. In large part, this was because of an underutilization of the common law, for a number of connected social, political, and economic reasons.

Resort to the law in the nineteenth century was always a rich person's prerogative. Taking a claim to law was both lengthy and, ultimately, outside the reach of the vast majority of the population. Lack of access to technical knowledge and resources followed inevitably from poverty, and made monitoring almost impossible. Even today, the costs of private litigation are prohibitive for many potential claimants and present the biggest hurdle in bringing environmental law claims.[62]

Also, as we have seen, bringing a claim in nuisance required a proprietary interest. In the mid-nineteenth century it has been estimated that only around 15 per cent of the population were owner/occupiers. Thus, the vast majority of the population would have had great difficulty in even founding a claim. When coupled with the level of damages—notoriously low for interference with the enjoyment of land—there were considerable obstacles to taking legal action.

Moreover, what has subsequently been identified as a complex system of power relationships ensured that, in the social context, there was tremendous pressure not to 'cause trouble'. Few workers would wish to proceed against their bosses and it was clear that there was a certain degree of class solidarity among the industrialists themselves. The perceived economic benefits to the local community were inevitably to the fore in the minds of the local authorities, which were most reluctant to use their powers to prosecute for public nuisances and which, indeed, were often responsible for much pollution themselves. Moreover, many factory owners bought up large areas of land surrounding their own sites and constructed low-cost, high-density housing for their workers. This, coupled with the impact of industry on surrounding land prices, effectively meant that a factory owner could purchase the right to pollute the surrounding area very cheaply. (Of course, the landowner would be most likely to have lived upwind of the prevailing westerly winds—one factor behind the association of affluence with the 'west end' of a town or city.)

61 Even public regulation, of course, is often reactive in the sense of being a political or administrative response to perceived problems: see Chapters 2 and 8.
62 Genn (1999); WWF, Environmental Law Foundation, and Leigh Day and Co. (2004) *Environmental Justice?*, available online at **www.wwf.org.uk/filelibrary/pdf/envirojustice.pdf**.

Furthermore, the relative expense of bringing private law actions is well illustrated by the Third Report of the Royal Commission on the Pollution of Rivers in 1867:

[Bringing a common law claim] is an expensive remedy. For the same money which is spent over a hard fought litigation against a single manufacturer, a Conservancy Board armed with proper powers, might for years keep safe from all abuse, a long extensive river with hundreds of manufacturers situated on its banks.

St Helens Smelting Co. v. Tipping (see p. 333) illustrates some of these points well. Mr Tipping was an enormously rich cotton magnate who owned 1,300 acres of land. He could afford to risk the backlash of industrialists because of the well-documented conflict between the cotton and chemical industries.[63] The damages received in his case and also in other nuisance cases were appallingly low (although Tipping also got an injunction and the copper works had to relocate). In one case—*Halsey v. Esso Petroleum* [1961] 2 All ER 145—the claimant received only £200 damages following five years of noise, dirt, and commotion from the neighbouring oil storage depot. This raises another problem with nuisance claims—namely, that the effect of the locality rule means that any damages that are awarded may be small, reducing the incentive to complain.

The future of private law as an environmental protection mechanism

Following *Cambridge Water Co. v. Eastern Counties Leather* (see Case 11.3), *Hunter v. Canary Wharf* (see Case 11.4), and now *Transco v. Stockport Metropolitan Borough Council* (see Case 11.8), it is clear that the House of Lords, at least, is reluctant to see significant development of the common law as a mechanism for environmental protection. In *Cambridge Water*, it stated explicitly that the rule in *Rylands* should not be developed further into a more specific strict liability common law rule about the control of hazardous substances.[64] But this was wrapped up in more general language about private law and environmental regulation:

given that so much well-informed and carefully structured legislation is now being put in place for [the escape of hazardous substances], there is less need for the courts to develop a common law principle to achieve the same end, and indeed it may well be undesirable that they do so.[65]

The approach taken by the House of Lords in *Hunter*, putting private nuisance law back to its original position of protecting only property rights holders, shows a similar cautiousness. As Lord Hoffmann said, '*the development of the common law should be rational and coherent. It should not distort its principles and create anomalies as an expedient to fill a gap*'.[66]

The distinction which the House of Lords in *Hunter* was eager to make—between damage to land and damage to persons—can, however, be conceived of too simply. Consider, for example, interference with the use of a public footpath across private land. There may be no reason for the landowner to litigate to prevent or remedy any damage to the right of way if there is no damage to his or her agricultural interests. But those who use the footpath are left without a private law remedy, which calls into question the 'privateness' of private law.[67] There may, therefore, be an argument that the connection between nuisance and property

---

63 *Dennis v. MOD* (Case 11.2) is a more recent example of 'rich claimant/deep pocket defendant'.

64 [1993] Env LR 105, 125. See also Lord Bingham in *Transco v. Stockport Metropolitan Borough Council* [2003] UKHL 61, adopting this reasoning.

65 [1993] Env LR 105, 126.

66 [1997] Env LR 488, 518.

67 J. Wightman (1998) MLR 870.

rights is justified in so far as the holder of the right acts in his or her own interests. But if this feature is absent and the litigant (perhaps an environmental organization or conservation trust) acts in a custodial manner in pursuit of wider 'public' interests, the justification for the strict nexus with land loses force.

The more general point, however, is whether the judges should take such a conservative approach to the development of the common law as they have done recently. It is no answer to say that regulation is to be preferred, whether this is through contaminated land legislation at national or EC level (*Cambridge Water*) or town and country planning law (*Hunter*, discussed more fully below). Indeed, it is trite to say so and the general advantages of regulation over private law mechanisms have been explored above. It is, however, worth reflecting on the extent to which, when Parliament acts, it does not always do so in a way that enhances the protection of individual rights or environmental interests. For example, the scheme for making enforcement orders under the Water Industry Act 1991 might be said unduly to insulate water and sewerage companies—not known for having difficulties in generating considerable profits—from compensating those who, like Mr Marcic (Case 11.7), suffered because of their inaction. A second issue here is the extent to which public law controls are actually used by public regulators: for example, the enforcement orders under the Water Industry Act 1991, so relied on by the House of Lords in *Marcic*, have never been used by the regulator.

The key point is that both private and public law controls must coexist, even if this is through either:

(a) principles of private law that make statutory authority a defence to a claim in private nuisance, trespass or (most probably) the rule in *Rylands*;

(b) statutory rules that determine the extent to which compliance with an environmental licence may be a defence to a common law claim.[68]

If private law is to maintain the position that most commentators claim for it—that of a subsidiary control when considered alongside public regulation—then it must, at a minimum, be sustained in this function. The obvious danger that we have seen in this chapter is that, although there have been some important 'victories' in recent years (*Dennis* being one—see Case 11.2), the conservative orientation of the higher courts is frustrating the ability of the common law to keep pace, *even in its subsidiary role*, with developments in public regulation. Human rights law may force through some welcome developments—for example, in relation to the rights to bring nuisance actions and the kinds of damages for which claimants can sue—but in other respects there appears to be a degree of ossification. One example that looks particularly outmoded is the right to claim in public nuisance when no particularized damage has been suffered; having to defer to public authorities to mount such actions has rightly been criticized as looking out of place alongside developments in the law of standing to bring public law challenges in environmental cases.[69]

Private law, public regulation, and 'the public interest'

There is often a conflict between private law and public regulation, in the sense that an activity may be lawful under one regime, but not under the other. Private law rights can clash with many regulatory controls, although most of the case law has been about planning law. Many uses of land that give rise to nuisances, for example, have the benefit of planning permission. In granting a planning application, it must be assumed that the local planning authority has

---

68 See, e.g., s. 100(b), Water Resources Act 1991, see p. 148.

69 K. Stanton and C. Willmore (2000) 'Tort and environmental protection' in J. Lowry and R. Edmunds (eds) *Environmental Protection and the Common Law*, Oxford: Hart.

balanced the impact of the development upon private interests (for example, neighbours) with any competing public interests and concluded that the public interests in allowing the development to proceed should prevail. But two problems remain:

- what weight do planning authorities have to give to private rights in the decision-making process?

- how does the grant of the planning permission—or other environmental licence—affect such private rights?

On the first point, a planning permission can be granted that makes a nuisance action by the new owner/occupiers likely (*R v. Exeter City Council, ex parte JL Thomas and Co. Ltd* [1991] 1 QB 471; see also p. 409). A public law challenge to such a planning permission will have to do something more than simply argue that private rights will be interfered with. Although environmental impact relating to land use will be a 'material consideration' to which the planning authority is to have regard, the courts have given considerable discretion to planning authorities to decide how much weight to give such considerations (including no weight at all).

In relation to the impact of the grant of planning permission, recent case law has now confined the scope of the controversial ruling in *Gillingham Borough Council v. Medway (Chatham) Dock Co. Ltd* [1993] QB 343. The local authority granted planning permission for dock development, but later took a public nuisance action following complaints about noise and vibration caused by lorries going to and from the port, especially at night. There were two readings of Buckley J's judgment refusing to grant an injunction restricting lorry movements at night. A broad reading was that planning permission was equivalent to the defence of statutory authority (see p. 339). This raised concerns that any activities engaged in under a planning permission could not lead to liability in nuisance, meaning that private rights would be extinguished without any redress or compensation contrary to established principles of English law.

But it is the narrow reading of the judgment that has prevailed. On this view, planning permission does not act as a *defence* to a claim in nuisance; instead, Buckley J's decision went to the heart of the *definition* of a nuisance and the locality doctrine in particular. The question was whether the planning permission had so changed the nature of the area that the locality became a commercial area, making the lorry movements a reasonable user of the locality. The Court of Appeal upheld this narrower view in *Wheeler v. JJ Saunders Ltd* [1996] Ch 19. In this case, planning permission was granted for pig-weaning units to be built close to the claimant's land. The claimant successfully complained of smell nuisance that followed once the development was implemented. The Court essentially laid down three rules.

1. The *Gillingham* case only decided that 'strategic' planning decisions, affected by considerations of public interest, could legalize certain nuisances by changing the nature of the locality. This might have been the case with the major port development at the Chatham Dockyard, but it was not the case with lesser developments such as pig units. (Quite where the dividing line is was not elaborated upon.)

2. The *Gillingham* decision is restricted to those situations in which the effects of the development make a specific change in the nature of the locality. Building pig units in the countryside is not such a radical change.[70]

3. The Court clarified that it is *actual* development, rather than development plans, that matters. This was sensible, not least because many developments earmarked in plans never materialize.

---

70 Nor, it would seem, did operating the RAF base in *Dennis* change the location, which remained 'essentially rural' (see Case 11.2).

The basic approach taken in *Wheeler* was later upheld by the Court of Appeal in *Hunter*, and approved of in some of the speeches in the House of Lords in that case.

What is perhaps most important about the law in this area is the way in which it highlights a certain amount of unease among the judiciary about the overlap between the exercise of rights conferred by public law powers and private law remedies. As Gibson LJ said in *Wheeler* '*The Court should be slow to acquiesce in the extinction of private rights without compensation as a result of administrative decisions which cannot be appealed and are difficult to challenge.*'[71] Certainly, traditional compensation concepts apply rather uneasily in relation to concepts such as environmental harm. The value of keeping open the private law claim may therefore lie more with the way in which its existence may influence decision making by public bodies, providing a means of keeping regulatory systems open and accountable. Indeed, this appears to have influenced the judges in *Wheeler*, who were clearly troubled by what they thought to be an injudicious grant of planning consent, seemingly obtained on the basis of inaccurate and incomplete information, and with little, or no, regard to the claimant's interests. On this line of thinking, protecting private rights furthers, rather than restricts, public interests.

The relationship between private law and public regulation is not confined to questions involving planning permissions, and can arise in relation to other environmental licences. In *Blackburn v. ARC Ltd* [1998] Env LR 469 (a nuisance case), a waste management licence was held not to change the locality surrounding a landfill site. Contrast this with *Budden and Albery v. BP Oil* [1980] JPL 586, in which a claim in negligence was brought against two oil companies based on their use of lead in petrol, even though the companies had adhered to regulatory standards. For the court, allowing the claim would mean that valid regulations prescribing the lead content in petrol would effectively be replaced by a lower, judicially determined, standard. The case illustrates the way that, especially in negligence cases, statutory standards may dictate common law standards. But the 'balancing act' quality to nuisance law and the fact that decisions are made according to local circumstances provides for rather more flexibility. Thus in *Murdoch v. Glacier Metal Co. Ltd* [1998] Env LR 732, a claim about noise levels exceeding World Health Organization standards failed, in part because of the already noisy area—alongside a main road—in which the claimants lived (Cases 6.2 and 8.1).

As to the impact of HRA 1998 here, in cases in which legislation is involved (such as under the Nuclear Installations Act 1965, or if a private law right comes up against a public law authorization such as a planning permission or environmental licence), the courts must 'read and give effect to' this legislation to make it compatible with ECHR if it is at all possible to do so. This might mean, for example, some relaxations to the strict approach to statutory authority authorizing a nuisance taken in *Allen v. Gulf Oil* (see Case 11.5), although it is likely that the limits that the courts have already placed on such rights, so that those rights cannot be used to authorize any interference that is more than necessary or which is negligent, will go a long way to showing that a proper balance has been struck.

It is also worth mentioning that, in *Khatun v. United Kingdom* (the follow-up to *Hunter v. Canary Wharf*) the European Commission on Human Rights ultimately rejected the claim that Art. 8 ECHR had been breached because of the regard that must be had to the fair balance to be struck between the competing interests of the individual and of the community as a whole. In this context, the UK had shown that the development was 'necessary'—that is, that the interference corresponded to a pressing social need and was proportionate to the aim pursued (namely, economic redevelopment). In a sense, the economic justification for the development legitimated what the planning permission alone could not do.

A final point is that the *Hatton* case (Case 11.1) suggests that there must be some sort of regulatory failure before there can be a breach of Art. 8. This might suggest that any development—for example, with a valid planning permission—cannot breach Art. 8 rights. It is

---

71 [1996] Ch 19, 35.

questionable whether the logic of this conclusion should, or will, be followed through (or it may be that, in cases similar to *Wheeler v. Saunders*, there will be much more scrutiny of the decision-making process).

Statutory nuisance

The law of statutory nuisance represents a bridge between the private law of nuisance and the more characteristic statutory mechanisms considered in Part III of this book. Like the various torts considered above, however, statutory nuisance really provides indirect protection for the environment, having developed as a public health mechanism. It covers various activities if they are either prejudicial to health, or a nuisance (and because it only covers listed activities, its scope can only really be extended if Parliament increases the range of activities covered, as it occasionally does). Nevertheless, there are many ways in which statutory nuisance can be used to combat environmental concerns, such as air pollution or the deposit of sewage on beaches, and it is often used to deal with complaints about unacceptable noise levels.

Local authorities are under a duty to inspect their areas periodically for statutory nuisances and, if they are satisfied that a statutory nuisance exists, then they must serve an abatement notice. (This is the basic model that has been used for some modern environmental laws—most notably, contaminated land.) The mandatory character of these provisions is notable, although, in some situations, trades and businesses have a defence if they can show that they are using Best Practicable Means (BPM) to abate the nuisance. Also, in practice, local authorities may have limited resources to inspect their areas. Instead of using judicial review, however, affected individuals may go directly to the magistrates' court and ask the court to serve an order requiring the nuisance to be abated. Statutory nuisance can therefore provide a quick and easy remedy to abate nuisances with which private law is too slow or too expensive to deal. Because its primary purpose is abating nuisances, however, the amount of damages that can be awarded are limited, so any loss beyond these basic levels will have to be sued for via some other route.

Statutory nuisance is one of a number of mechanisms that can be used at the local level by local authorities to tackle environmental problems. Others include noise controls, local air pollution controls, and controls on traffic. There is no particular coherence to these, but they can be an invaluable part of the environmental lawyer's toolbox. (All of these controls are covered in detail in the Online Resource Centre.)

The way ahead? Civil liability in statutes, compensation funds, and EC developments

One of the obvious limitations of private law controls such as nuisance law is that they are essentially aimed at protecting individual rights, or rights relating to property. As cases such as *Cambridge Water* and *Hunter* show, many judges are clearly reluctant to develop these mechanisms so that they are *directly* concerned with environmental protection. But there are already some statutory regimes that try to overcome the inadequacies of ordinary private law in relation to problematic areas such as pollution from international oil spills.

What links many of these statutory regimes (and the EC's Environmental Liability Directive 2004/35/EC) is the extent to which they might be directly concerned with environmental protection or remediation, and not only the protection of people and property. In this sense, these regimes can be said to follow on from measures such as those contained in Pt IIA of the Environmental Protection Act (EPA) 1990 relating to contaminated land, or the Water Resources Act 1991, s. 161, which allows for the clean-up of polluted water. In practice, both might *indirectly* benefit other property owners (who will avoid having to pay for the cost of clean-up) and directly affect the person paying for the cost of clean-up in a way that, for them, is probably indistinguishable from compensating another private party (the person whose brownfield site is cleaned up benefits from the other party by seeing an increase in the value of his or her land). Their central concern, however, is with the quality of the environment in its own right, which can be cleaned up, for example, so that ecosystems are restored.

The purpose of the following sections is to explore the possibilities of statutory civil liability regimes, which would obviously meet the objection made by Lord Goff in the *Cambridge Water* case that it is not for the courts to develop the common law in areas in which rule and decision making is complex and involves many stakeholders. Readers are invited to draw their own conclusions as to the merits of statutory civil liability as against, for example, regulatory clean-up regimes.

Statutory civil liability

In addition to the common law, there are a number of statutes that impose liability by means of private law remedies, rather than the more usual public law methods.

(a) The Nuclear Installations Act 1965

The law of tort does not adequately deal with the individual problems of nuclear installations. As the Chernobyl incident demonstrated, the damage caused by nuclear actions can be widespread and not confined to a specific period of time. There are also difficulties of proving a causal link between the injury caused and exposure to radiation. Many diseases that are caused by radiation also occur naturally and trying to establish whether or not there is an epidemiological link is frequently fraught with difficulties. To avoid these difficulties, the Nuclear Installations Act 1965 introduced absolute civil liability for all damage caused from certain occurrences (ss. 7–10).

Not all loss from nuclear damage is covered under the Act. Economic loss can only be recovered if there is specific physical harm caused to the land. This has been held not to include the loss in value of a house in the area of the Sellafield nuclear installation resulting from radioactive contamination, because there was no physical harm (*Merlin v. British Nuclear Fuels plc* [1990] 2 QB 557), but as including the diminution in value of land neighbouring the Atomic Weapons Establishment (AWE) at Aldermaston, which had been contaminated by radiation, but then remediated, but which could not be sold because of the blight (*Blue Circle Industries v. Ministry of Defence* [1998] 3 All ER 385). The court distinguished the damage in *Merlin* from the contamination at the AWE by linking the economic loss in the *Blue Circle* case to the actual physical harm caused by the radioactive contamination, which is somewhat unconvincing. It is probably better to see *Blue Circle* as simply taking a less restrictive approach to damage (or, has been suggested, as the courts protecting business interests more than those of householders).[72]

(b) The Merchant Shipping Act 1995

In the wake of numerous oil disasters in the mid- to late 1960s, international concern led to the introduction of legislation to compensate for damage from oil. This is now consolidated in the Merchant Shipping Act 1995,[73] which applies to spills from both tankers and other ships. The Act imposes strict liability on owners of ships in relation to physical damage to

---

72 M. Day (2001) 3 Env LR 163, 164.

73 The Act also makes provision for the eventual transposition of the 1996 International Convention on Liability and Compensation for Damage in Connection with the Carriage of Hazardous and Noxious Substances by Sea (the HNS Convention).

property and personal injury from oil pollution (ss. 153 and 154). The major innovation is that the financing of the majority of losses stemming from the Act is covered by a compulsory insurance scheme, although there is a further international fund for compensation that pays out when the shipowner cannot afford to. This fund paid out compensation following both the *Braer* (1993) and *Sea Empress* (1996) oil spills off the UK coast.

BOX 11.1 Marine oil pollution compensation

The basic principle for accidental or intentional oil spillages from ships is that, if oil is discharged or escapes from a tanker, the registered owner is liable for:

(a) *'any damage caused . . . by* contamination *resulting from the discharge or escape'*; and

(b) the cost of any reasonable pollution prevention or reduction measures taken.

Claims for preventing marine contamination may also be made, but the Merchant Shipping Act 1995 limits claims for environmental impairment to 'reasonable reinstatement costs'—that is, it rules out general claims about loss of environmental services or amenity unless reasonable costs have been incurred in making the situation better. This avoids having to calculate, in money terms, the 'damage' suffered by the environment. So, following the *Braer* spill in 1993, claims relating to health risks, general anxiety suffered by the affected community, and environmental amenity were rejected. In relation to pure environmental damage, the international fund will only pay out—as it did following the *Sea Empress* spill in 1996—in cases in which, for example, charities have incurred the cost of cleaning oiled birds or bodies such as the Environment Agency have incurred costs.

Because reinstatement costs must be reasonable, compensation might be payable following a minor spill, but it will not be payable after a major spill with devastating ecological consequences (because, in the latter case, reinstatement may simply be impossible or the cost of reinstating may be disproportionately expensive). Unlike some areas of environmental law, this scheme does not look to maintaining ecological coherence by requiring damage to one site to be compensated—ecologically—by improvements to other areas (see, for example, p. 712). Also, awards are made based on the lower of the diminution of market value or the cost of repairs—that is, the basic principle behind cars being 'written off' following accidents, under which the repair costs would exceed their value. So if an important habitat is badly damaged by a spill, then, if the land has a low market value (as land protected by conservation designations often will have, because developing the land will be difficult), it is likely that damage will simply not be repaired. Again, there will be an uncompensated loss of ecological services. For various reasons, therefore, some aspects of environmental damage go uncompensated.

(c) The Environmental Protection Act 1990, s. 73

Section 73(6) of EPA 1990 imposes civil liability for the unlawful deposit of waste (see p. 673).

Compensation funds

The above are all examples in which 'the state' has established specific rules to cover particular kinds of damage, although, in each case, liability is still imposed on an individual—or, in the case of marine oil pollution, collective risk pool—basis. Another approach would be for the state itself to provide compensation for losses. This has traditionally occurred in cases in which there has been thought to be a wider public interest—for example, in culling infected livestock to prevent the spread of disease—but it is a technique that can also be applied in other contexts. Reintroducing endangered species into an area might, for example, lead to economic losses for some landowners. So, for example, to increase otter numbers in one region of Austria, a damage compensation scheme for fishpond owners was established and finances made available to prevent damage arising. These measures enabled the damage to be kept at a level considered acceptable to the fishpond owners. Steps such as these are a creative use of compensation and recognize the argument made in *Bamford v. Turnley* (1862) 122 ER 27 (see p. 337) that individuals should not be made to bear the cost of securing the public interest.

EC developments

A final consideration is the adoption of an EC Directive on Environmental Liability (2004/35/EC). This is more of a public law measure than a private system of redress, but it might impact on the general development of private law liability. The key features of the Directive are as follows.

- Personal injury, damage to private property, and economic loss are not covered. There will be liability for 'environmental damage', justified because the unowned environment fares badly under the civil liability regimes of most EC member States. The Directive does not cover things such as noise pollution, etc., even though noise control is the subject of numerous EC Directives. Environmental damage is restricted to:
  - damage to species and habitats protected under EC conservation legislation (see Chapter 19);
  - (only if the member State chooses) sites and species designated under national conservation law such as sites of special scientific interest (SSSIs);
  - damage to waters protected by the EC Water Framework Directive (2000/60/EC—see p. 593);
  - soil contamination.

- This is a narrow view of environmental damage that does not even cover all of the areas protected under EC law, such as nitrate vulnerable zones (NVZs), and falls short of what we already have at national level under the contaminated land regime, which extends to more general ecosystem damage (see Chapter 16). It also privileges what might be termed 'nature conservation biodiversity' over agricultural biodiversity—for example, an organic farm fearing contamination from neighbouring GM crops will not be protected if it lies outside a protected area.

- For environmental damage generally, only certain activities that must be regulated under EC environmental law—for example, processes subject to integrated pollution prevention and control (IPPC)—are covered, although here liability is in principle strict (but see below). If the polluter has been at fault or negligent, however, any operational activity causing damage to species and habitats is covered.

- This approach is notable for differentiating between strict and fault-based liability not on the normal grounds that the former is a more appropriate way to internalize the costs of hazardous new technologies or processes, but rather because its aim is to improve enforcement of EC environmental law and to give polluters incentives to comply with environmental Directives. Damage to 'national' biodiversity interests is more a matter for member State discretion, in which to impose strict liability might exceed normal national liability rules.

- In two key situations, the strictness of liability may, if the member State, decides, be limited:
  - if the damage is authorized under a permit issued to comply with the listed EC environmental laws that the Directive covers;
  - if state-of-the-art scientific and technical knowledge meant that, at the time of the damaging act, environmental damage was not thought likely.

- These are not complete defences, but their consequence is that the operator may not have to pay the costs of remedial action unless it is shown that they were at fault (echoing, respectively, the approach in *Allen v. Gulf Oil*, and the rules on reasonable foreseeability of damage).

- Many provisions of the Directive bear a strong resemblance to the kinds of statutory pollution prevention and clean-up powers introduced in the UK in the 1990s,[74] although there are important differences. Operators must prevent pollution arising if it is imminent, or must control and remediate pollution if it has already occurred—the key differences from most existing national clean-up or abatement provisions being that the duty to do so is not triggered by the serving of any notice, and that neither is the duty to remediate couched in terms of what is reasonably practicable. Prevention and remediation duties are backed by powers for competent authorities (such as the Environment Agency or Natural England) to require action or undertake it themselves.[75] In either case, it is the polluter who must pay.

- There are detailed provisions about what exactly 'remediation of environmental damage' means. These include, among other things, interim ecological compensation and, if there will not be a full ecological recovery of the area damaged, long-term replacement by equivalent natural resources. There is an inevitable vagueness to a lot of what this means, although some criteria are given and, in making polluters pay for losses during the period when ecosystems are being restored, the polluter ought to be paying something more closely resembling the full costs—including environmental costs—of pollution.

- A key difference between national rules on pollution prevention and clean-up is that the Directive gives affected individuals, or bodies such as environmental non-government organizations (NGOs), the right to press the regulatory authorities to take action. The regulator must give its reasons for either choosing (or declining) to act and the NGO has the right to question the basis of the regulator's decision (either in a court or another competent, independent, and impartial body). This is weaker than earlier drafts of the Directive, which envisaged that NGOs would have standing to bring actions directly if the state had failed to act or to act promptly (akin to what, in the USA, are called 'citizen suits'). Earlier drafts also granted to NGOs, in urgent cases, the right to ask a court to issue an injunction or be reimbursed for reasonable costs spent in preventing environmental damage. This has also been removed, with the emphasis now being firmly on the regulator acting and imposing liability.

- The emphasis is on remediation of environmental damage: damages awarded will have to be applied to environmental restoration, and to compensatory schemes to cover interim damage and in cases in which restoration is not possible.

- Liability applies only to future damage—that is, to damage caused by an emission, event, or occurrence after the due date for transposition of the Directive (30 April 2007). To avoid

74 See, e.g., Water Resources Act 1991, ss. 161 and 161A, discussed at p. 616.
75 Importantly, in cases in which the operator cannot be identified ('orphan damage'), or will not act, or is not required to bear the costs, the regulatory body only has a power, not a duty, to act itself.

claims relating to latent damage, the Directive does not cover damage caused by an emission, event, or incident that takes place subsequent to this date, but which stems from a specific activity that took place and finished before this date. So, if an oil drum is dumped on a site before 2007, but only starts leaking in 2008, it seems that this is not covered by the Directive. Any damage arising more than 30 years after the damage-causing activity is not covered, again emphasizing that this is not a measure aimed at dealing with historically contaminated land.

- Although supported by some member States, provisions requiring compulsory insurance against environmental damage were not included in the Directive (to which issue the EC is to return in a few years' time).

These proposals may result in improved protection for the unowned environment, but the impact on statutory clean-up regimes, such as the newly implemented regime for contaminated land under Pt 2A of the Environment Act 1990, will be slight. Depending on how any restriction against imposing retrospective liability is interpreted, there would simply be no duplication with the provisions for historic pollution contained in Pt 2A (see further Chapter 16). Note also that the Directive does not cover liabilities arising from the nuclear sector or those that are covered under international oil pollution conventions; nor does it cover diffuse pollution unless it is possible to establish a causal link between the damage and the activities of an individual operator.

In essence, the Directive is neither environmental (in any holistic sense), nor does it provide for civil liability. It is little more than an administrative adjunct to EC environmental legislation. This in itself is not a bad thing, but a negative view would be to ask whether the tortuous process of agreeing the Directive—which took over ten years—in order to create a limited liability regime was really worth the effort, or whether it would have been preferable to focus more on ensuring that breaches of EC environmental law are better monitored and punished, and that fines or administrative penalties are used to pay for environmental clean-up. A more positive view, however, might stress that it has opened the door to what environmental liability laws might do in terms of, for example, ecological losses and the role of NGOs, which might, in the future, be picked up by national courts developing national civil law actions and remedies.

Draft Regulations were published in February 2008 with a view to implementation by December 2008. These indicate that (at least in England and Wales) a reluctance to go beyond the minimum required by the Directive—that is, that there will be little 'gold plating' (see p. 216). However, the present intention is that the Regulations will not be limited to damage to species and habitats protected under EC conservation law but will also extend to all species and habitats within an SSSI for which the SSSI has been notified. We will analyse the implementing regulations in the Online Resource Centre when they emerge.

CHAPTER SUMMARY

1 There is no overarching principle behind the 'environmental' torts (or torts generally). Private law protects private rights, in the case of tort law, by imposing obligations on certain parties not to act in some way that is broadly unreasonable.

2 The main torts that might be used to pursue environmentally related interests are private and public nuisance, trespass, negligence, and the rule in *Rylands v. Fletcher*. These are separate torts[76] with their own particular history and rules.

---

76 Although it has been suggested that the rule in *Rylands* is not a tort based on breaching a duty not to do something harmful, but simply a mechanism for allocating the costs of dangerous behaviour: N. McBride and R. Bagshaw (2005) *Tort Law*, 2nd edn, London: Longman, p. 32.

3   With the exception of negligence and public nuisance, the torts mentioned protect interests in land—that is, the interests of landowners and those possessing land.

4   The main tort used in environmental cases is private nuisance. This imposes a duty of 'good neighbourliness' between landowners. Whether this is breached depends on a matrix of factors, including the locality, the nature, the duration and extent of the nuisance, and the use of the claimant's land. It does not require fault, in the sense of having to show that the defendant acted carelessly.

5   Trespass provides a strict level of protection for property rights against direct interference, but this is of limited use in the context of pollution (which is often spread in an indirect way—for example, noise or fumes) and may also be used to stifle environmental protest.

6   For isolated escapes of dangerous substances from land, the rule in *Rylands v. Fletcher* applies. But the courts have severely limited its practical application by setting a very high hurdle to overcome in showing that an activity is of sufficiently extraordinary risk for the rule to apply. Most such activities will probably be regulated anyway.

7   The main remedies in tort law are injunctions (for continuing harms) and money damages. If available, injunctions should provide a strong degree of protection of property rights and this may have indirect benefits for wider environmental interests.

8   If a polluting activity is judged to be in the public interest, it may still be a nuisance, but damages, rather than an injunction, might be awarded. Whether compensation adequately protects the environment, or makes the polluter pay, is debatable.

9   In some situations, tort law claims must defer to what Parliament has decided; in other cases in which environmental licences have been granted for a polluting activity, the courts are reluctant to see private law claims trumped by regulatory permissions.

10 In recent years, the courts have demonstrated a conservative attitude to developing tort law to fill gaps created by environmental regulation, preferring to leave matters to Parliament. This may make it increasingly difficult for tort to play an important subsidiary role alongside public law controls.

11 Most commentators consider private law to be an inferior environmental protection mechanism compared to public regulation.

12 Environmental litigators must also think about whether there has been any breach of human rights. The European Convention on Human Rights does not expressly secure the right to live in a decent environment free from pollution, or which contains adequate natural resources, but a few of the Articles of the Convention are now interpreted to protect interests associated with living free from harmful levels of environmental interference (for example, noise). If human rights have been violated, then the court may be asked for remedies in addition to that which tort law can provide.

13 There is a very high threshold to establish a human rights violation in environmental cases and rights violations may be justified on the basis of the wider public interest. Unless the interference is extreme, or wholly unjustified, or has fallen outside of normal regulatory controls, a violation of human rights leading to a claim for damages is highly unlikely.

14 Some consider that tort law is essentially a mechanism for providing corrective, compensatory justice—that is, for righting wrongs.[77] Tort law may also act as a mild deterrent to harmful behaviour, and strategic claims can raise awareness of environmental problems and influencing public policy. But while a tort claim can advance an alternative vision of what 'the public interest' requires, there is little real world evidence to support either of these propositions. While tort law sometimes protects the environment, it is not clear that it should pursue this—or any other—instrumental function. The criticisms of tort made in this chapter are made with this in mind.

77 E. Weinrib (1995) *The Idea of Private Law*, Cambridge: Cambridge University Press. Similarly, see p. Cane (2001) 13 JEL 3 (arguing that environmental torts are not so special that they should be treated differently as torts).

Q QUESTIONS

1   What private law claims might arise from the following and what further information would you need?

   a Genetically modified (GM) crops are grown on land neighbouring an organic farm.

   b A public water supply is contaminated by spills of diesel from a garage forecourt.

   c Road traffic noise.

   d Skyglow—that is, too much artificial lighting of the sky, preventing sight of the stars.

2   Does tort law make polluters pay? Does it deter environmental pollution? Should it do so?

3   What values underpin tort law? Could these ever be the basis of a body of private law that better protected the natural environment?

4   'I do not accept that there is anything so peculiar about "environmental damages" as to disqualify them from consideration by the Court. The legislatures may choose to bring in a statutory regime to address environmental loss ... That said, there is no reason to neglect the potential of the common law, if developed in a principled and incremental fashion, to assist in the realization of the fundamental value of environmental protection.' (British Columbia v. Canadian Forest Products Ltd [2004] 2 SCR 74, a Canadian Supreme Court case). How is this approach to the development of the common law of tort different to that taken by Lord Goff in the Cambridge Water case (Case 11.3)? Which approach is preferable?

5   Despite fierce local opposition, the Environment Agency and the local planning authority grant the necessary consents for a waste incinerator. After the incinerator begins operation, there are continued fears about its impact on health, including concerns that the plant is being run by 'cowboys' who only got planning permission because of very generous community benefits that they offered to the planning authority. There are also concerns about off-site effects of the incinerator on rare orchids on a nearby nature reserve. Advise the owner of the nature reserve.

6   In 1982, an RAF base was built with all of the necessary permissions required at the time. The landing strip is used both by military jets and, on occasion, as an 'overspill' runway by charter airlines when the regional airport is closed due to bad weather. Depending on the prevailing wind, high levels of noise emanate from the base, affecting residents over a wide area. What private law claims and claims under the Human Rights Act 1998 might be made by the following?

   a Amy, who has lived in the area since 1969 and who complains that a recent increase in the number of flights has seen the value of her property fall by 20 per cent.

   b Ben and Bella, who, since 2000, have lived with a number of foster children in a rented cottage near the perimeter. Their sleep is disturbed, and they are becoming physically ill and mentally fatigued.

   c The local parish council, which is concerned about the impact of the noise on local wildlife.

📖 FURTHER READING

General tort texts

If you want to explore English tort law further, then an excellent introductory text is S. Hedley (2006) Tort, 5th edn, Oxford: Oxford University Press. Alongside this, we also recommend M. Lee, 'What is private nuisance?' (2003) 119 LQR 298, which is an excellent analysis of the way in which the law in this area is developing—especially the way in which nuisance is dividing into fault-based, strict liability and 'ordinary' liability (a division that we hope is reflected in this chapter).

The function of tort

Although not a traditional textbook, J. Conaghan and W. Mansell (1998) The Wrongs of Tort, 2nd edn, London: Pluto, discusses the economic and doctrinal underpinnings to tort law, and has an excellent critique of the limitations of tort law for environmental protection. Against this, look at J. Wightman, 'Nuisance: the environmental tort?' (1998) 61 MLR 870, a particularly good analysis not only of *Hunter v. Canary Wharf*, but of private nuisance generally. A stronger defence of nuisance law over regulation from a critically economistic perspective is D. Campbell, 'Of coase and corn: a (sort of) defence of private nuisance' (2000) MLR 197. For some, tort law is just a compensation mechanism that, in an age of regulation, should not be relied on to provide socially good things such as environmental protection: P. Cane, 'Are environmental harms special?' (2001) 13 JEL 3 argues this in a very readable fashion.

Socio-legal and historical issues

Leading journal articles on the common law and the environment from a broadly socio-legal perspective include: J. McLaren, 'Nuisance law and the industrial revolution: some lessons from social history' (1983) OJLS 155; J. Brenner, 'Nuisance law and the Industrial Revolution' (1974) J Leg Stud 403; A. Ogus and G. Richardson, 'Economics and the environment: a study of private nuisance' (1977) CLJ 284; B. Pontin, 'Tort law and Victorian government growth: the historiographical significance of tort in the shadow of chemical pollution and factory safety regulation' (1998) OJLS 661. B. Pontin, 'Integrated pollution control in Victorian Britain: rethinking progress within the history of environmental law' (2007) 19 JEL 173 shows how, even in the nineteenth century, attempts were made to make tort more of an effective tool against pollution and that this was being argued for by regulators (which may require some rethink of the traditional historical accounts provided by writers such as McLaren and Brenner). H. Marlow Green, 'Common law, property rights and the environment: a comparative analysis of historical developments in the United States and England and a model for the future' (1997) 30 Cornell Intl LJ 541 examines how the US state of Oregon gave an expansive interpretation to what is direct harm, allowing it to decide more actions under trespass and hence under stricter liability, and the advantages of this from an environmental protection point of view.

Private law and public regulation

A good starting point in relation to this subject is a strong set of essays assessing the contribution of private law collected together in J. Lowry and R. Edmunds (eds) (2000) *Environmental Protection and the Common Law*, Oxford: Hart Publishing. The interface between private law and public regulation raises legal issues such as the effect of a regulatory licence on a private law claim. But it also raises wider questions about the relative merits of private and public law controls. Discussion of both aspects is contained in J. Steele, 'Private law and the environment: nuisance in context' (1995) 15 Leg Stud 236 and 'Remedies and remediation: foundational issues in environmental liability' (1995) MLR 615. D. McGillivray and J. Wightman (1997) 'Private rights, public interests and the environment' in T. Hayward and J. O'Neill (eds) *Justice, Property and the Environment*, Aldershot: Ashgate, explores the scope for private law to defend alternative, unofficial conceptions of the public interest, a theme developed in M. Stallworthy, 'Environmental liability and the impact of statutory authority' (2003) 15 JEL 3, which also explores the idea of holding regulators liable in civil law for environmental damage caused by their failure to regulate strictly enough (something that earlier versions of the EC Liability Directive proposed). M. Lee, 'Tort, regulation and environmental liability' (2002) 22 Leg Stud 33 provides a detailed analysis of the public law–private law relationship in the context of the Environmental Liability Directive.

Human rights, property rights, and the environment

Many sources in this area were written before the Grand Chamber judgment in *Hatton v. UK* in 2003. For a critical view of this decision, see D. Hart and M. Wheeler, 'Night flights and Strasbourg's retreat from environmental rights' (2003) JEL 100, and for more detailed analysis on this case and on *Marcic*, an accessible analysis is given in A. Layard, 'Human rights in the balance: *Hatton* and *Marcic*' (2004) Env LR 196. On more domestic issues, see B. Pontin, 'Beyond nuisance: enforcing the right to a healthy environment within the framework of the Human Rights Act 1998' (2002) ELM 305 and M. Wilde, '*Locus standi* in environmental torts and the potential influence of human rights jurisprudence' (2003) Review of EC and International Environmental Law 284.

Finally, because many of the torts that relate to the environment are property-based, it is fruitful to think more deeply about property and the environment, and an innovative discussion on this theme (with important conclusions to be drawn for environmental regulation) is S. Coyle and K. Morrow (2004) *The Philosophical Foundations of Environmental Law: Property, Rights and Nature*, Oxford: Hart.

Contemporary topic areas

C. Rodgers, 'Liability for the release of GMOs into the environment' (2003) CLJ 371 looks at the range of possible tort actions to this area, including comment on the (then) draft EC Civil Liability directive. In contrast to Rodgers, D. Howarth, 'Civil liability for GM farming: unanswered questions' (2004) ELLR 137 wonders whether the use of civil liability was dismissed too readily. Also worth reading is the report of the Royal Commission on Environmental Pollution (2005) *Crop Spraying and the Effects on Health of Residents and Bystanders*, ch. 4 of which is short and accessible, and considers the potential application of civil liability rules and the difficulty of using any particular legal action to address this problem—for example, the limitations of private nuisance if property rights are not affected (as would be the case with bystanders).

The EC Liability Directive

V. Fogelman, 'The Environmental Liability Directive and its impacts on English environmental law' [2006] JPL 1443 gives a comprehensive account of the Directive and how it differs from existing national approaches. The Sixth Report of the House of Commons Environment, Food and Rural Affairs Committee (2007) *Implementation of the Environmental Liability Directive, 2006–7*, HC 694, covers the key areas in which there is discretion in implementation (and is highly criticial of government for not proposing to go beyond the bare minimum requirements). One of the key features of the Liability Directive is damages for ecological losses; on this see E. Brams, 'Liability for Damage to Public National Resources under the 2004 EC Environmental Liability Directive' (2005) Env L Rev 90.

Tort and climate change

This is an area of growing academic and practical interest. There is a special issue on 'Climate change liability and the allocation of risks' (2007) 26A(1) Stan Envtl LJ that is useful. P. Cullet, 'Liability and redress for human-induced global warming: towards an international regime' (2007) 26A(1) Stan Envtl LJ 99 provides a good general overview.

International liability rules

The general international environmental law texts mentioned at the end of Chapter 7 all cover this area. A. Boyle, 'Globalising environmental liability: the interplay of national and international law' (2005) 17 JEL 3 is a particularly valuable source for keeping abreast of recent thinking. R. S. J. Tol and R. Verheyen, 'State responsibility and compensation for climate change damages' (2004) 32 Energy Policy 1109 links these areas.

WEB LINKS

There are few websites of direct relevance to this chapter, although **www.iopcfund.org** gives a good insight into how the oil pollution funds work, and **www.climatelaw.org** is a good source on current developments in climate change litigation (not only liability actions). To track developments in implementing the EC Environmental Liability Directive, see **www.defra.gov.uk/environment/liability.** Judgments in the cases mentioned can be found via the web sources mentioned in the Online Resources Centre.

PART III

Sectoral coverage

12 Town and country planning

→ *Overview*

The UK system of town and country planning is undoubtedly one of the most sophisticated systems of land use control in the world. It is exceptional in incorporating controls over the use of land as well as over the design and form of the built environment. Accordingly, it plays a central role in environmental law, because of its enormous importance in relation to locational issues, as well as determining how much of any particular activity (such as house-building) is allowed in any place and the intensity of such development. It is, as stated earlier (see Chapter 8), perhaps the pre-eminent example in this country of a proactive, anticipatory system of control—but 'town and country planning' is not only about environmental protection. It has a wider role in organizing economic development, but in balancing economic, political, social, and environmental factors to do with development in a democratic context it ought to be a key mechanism for making development more sustainable.

well done.

but is sustainability the key focus ↳ politics

Specific aspects of planning law relevant to other chapters within Part III of the book are summarized at the appropriate place, although some thoughts are offered here on the general nature of the relationship between town and country planning and environmental protection. There is also a good deal of overlap between the coverage in this chapter and the next, which focuses on environmental assessment. A final introductory point is that this chapter deals with town and country planning law, rather than the role of planning-type mechanisms in general. The law now requires various plans relating to the environment, such as the national strategies for air and waste, and river catchment plans for water quality regulation, while there are also non-statutory plans, such as local transport plans, and informal plans, such as local Environment Agency plans.

not specific but encompasses wide areas of influence.

At the end of this chapter, you will be able to:

✔ identify and understand the main features and scope of the town and country planning system;

✔ appreciate the contribution of planning controls alongside specialist environmental protection regimes;

✔ evaluate the strengths and weaknesses of planning law in furthering environmental protection.

The main features of town and country planning

Because the town and country planning system is not a specialist environmental protection regime, but has wider objectives, it is helpful to set out its main features first.

1. Development is planned and controlled by taking a wide range of factors—social, economic, and environmental—into account. But environmental concerns are becoming increasingly prominent.

Nationally & locally produced development plans

2. Individual planning decisions are taken within a framework set by the development plan. Development plans are permissive—that is, they do not guarantee what is going to happen, or themselves authorize development, but act as guides to future development.

3. All 'development', which includes changes of use as well as physical development, requires planning permission from the local planning authority.

4. Planning permission is deemed to be granted for certain minor developments. Certain changes of use are also excluded from being 'development', where old and new activities have similar land use impacts. In this latter case, planning permission is simply not required.

5. Applications for planning permission involve consultation with other public bodies and some limited public involvement.

6. The local planning authority decides whether to grant permission or refuse it, taking as its starting point the development plan, but also recognizing central government policies and any other material considerations. Each application must be considered on its merits.

7. If permission is granted, it may (and invariably will) be subject to conditions; some permissions will also be accompanied by planning obligations, under which developers pay for some of the associated infrastructure and environmental costs of the development.

8. The applicant may appeal to the Secretary of State against any refusal or conditions. This is a complete rehearing of the whole matter, including the policy issues, enabling the Secretary of State to exercise a stranglehold on policy by having the final say on it.

9. There is no right of appeal for third parties and no right to appeal against a grant of planning permission.

10. There is a further right of appeal from the decision of the Secretary of State to the High Court on what are essentially the same grounds as those for judicial review. The courts thus exercise a supervisory jurisdiction over the procedures and the decisions taken, but the courts will not intervene on grounds of fact or policy.

11. It is not an offence to develop without permission, but rather an offence to fail to comply with an enforcement notice. Enforcement is discretionary.

12. Planning permission effectively gives a right to develop. Unlike most systems of pollution control, there is no power to vary a planning permission in the future (unless compensation is paid).

13. The role of law and the courts is primarily procedural and supervisory: ensuring that decisions have been reached correctly, rather than interfering with matters of planning policy or judgment.

Town and country planning as a tool of environmental policy

There are three main areas that have relevance to environmental law.

- **The system of development plans**
  This ensures that environmental protection is considered at the level of policymaking. These plans set the basic ground rules for action on the environment in any particular area, although they must be read in conjunction with central government policy guidance.

- **The development control process**
  Planning permission is required from the local planning authority for acts of development. This ensures a strict anticipatory control over many activities before they start and normally involves liaison with the specialist environmental regulatory agencies.

- **The power to impose conditions, and enter into agreements, relating to environmental protection on a grant of planning permission**
  These are capable of creating some form of continuing control over activities.

BOX 12.1 | Planning vs building controls

Planning controls are essentially locational, whereas traditionally building control regulations have been to do with ensuring health and safety features of new buildings and building work. But building regulations can now be made for a wide range of environmental reasons, including (specifically) furthering fuel and power conservation, and preventing water wastage or contamination, and (more generally) furthering the protection or enhancement of the environment, or facilitating sustainable development (under s. 1, Building Act 1984, as amended by the Sustainable and Secure Buildings Act 2004). These are only permissive and how far they will, in fact, contribute to these ends depends upon how strict building standards are made. Historically, UK standards on things such as insulation have tended to fall some way short of those in comparable countries, but there is an increasing emphasis on building controls as a means of addressing climate change (see e.g., DEFRA (2008) **Code for Sustainable Homes**, p. 6).

The scope of planning law

The impact of planning control is, in many ways, incomplete or inadequate. Planning permission is not required for all environmentally harmful activities: it is not required, for example, for mobile pollutants—such as cars—or offshore activities—such as tidal power schemes (because it governs the development of *land,* which means land out to the mean low-water mark)—or in relation to most agricultural activities. There are difficulties if some form of continuing control is required, because of the limitations on planning conditions, or if positive management is required, because it is mainly a preventive system. The system also tends to get circumvented in various ways in cases in which nationally important development is desired by central government.

Planning as a negotiative process

Modern town planning is best seen as a negotiative process, and consultation between the prospective developer and the local planning authority in advance of the application is the norm. The local planning authority and the developer often have a community of interest in carrying out a particular development: the developer gets its proposal granted and the local authority obtains the revitalization of the economy of an area, or the creation of jobs, or some other economic benefit. (Indeed, developments by local authorities and developers in partnership with each other are now quite common.) In addition, arrangements between developers and local authorities in which 'planning gain' is bargained for are increasingly used to supplement the regulatory controls.

Planning law and environmental protection

In 1976, the Royal Commission on Environmental Pollution (RCEP) commented: '*Our concern is not that pollution is not always given top priority; it is that it is often dealt with inadequately, and sometimes forgotten altogether in the planning process.*'[1] In general terms, the town and country planning system was, for a variety of institutional and other reasons, relatively *under*used for environmental protection (for example, in relation to imposing planning conditions),[2] although, through its relative openness and participatory nature, and a number of high-profile public inquiries, planning law has helped to shape the way in which environmental harm is conceptualized and has provided valuable opportunities for public expressions of environmental concern.[3] Now, although planning remains a political process, the concern is not so much that environmental considerations are ignored, but that '*a much more comprehensive approach is needed, and ... new environmental objectives must be integrated into the planning process*'.[4]

The planning system is of central importance in many areas of environmental law, especially when used in conjunction with other regulatory controls. This is seen clearly in relation to waste disposal: planning permission for a waste disposal site is required before a waste management licence can be granted. In other areas, planning control is arguably of greatest importance when the enforcement of pollution control is inadequate, because non-enforcement at the operational end puts increased pressure on initial siting and design issues. But planning controls may also 'trump' specialist environmental or conservation regimes: one example is when acting under a planning permission amounts to a reasonable excuse to damaging a site of special scientific interest (SSSI; see p. 698).

Town and country planning, and some themes of this book

The town and country planning system illustrates a number of the major themes of this book: it is a good example of a sophisticated, anticipatory, regulatory mechanism and it emphasizes prevention of harm. That also means that the predominant method of control is through negative, restrictive measures, rather than through positive mechanisms. Local decision making dominates, although there has been some shift of power towards central government in recent years (see p. 380). It is a highly discretionary system, in which decisions are made on a case-by-case basis. And it is a democratic system in which ultimate political control rests with elected members rather than with officers (on appeal responsibility rests with an elected Secretary of State)—although, in practice, most decisions are actually taken by officers. It is a fairly open and public system, but with inevitable trade-offs between speed and participation. Enforcement is underemphasized, being almost exclusively the responsibility of the local planning authority, and dependent on political and tactical factors, as well as on adequate resources (which, in practice, are often not available). But the most important point is that it is a highly political system of decision making. Local planning authorities and the Secretary of State make discretionary decisions by balancing economic, political, environmental, and social factors. It is therefore just as important to understand the prevailing policy in relation to a particular issue as it is to understand the relevant law.

1 Fifth Report of the Royal Commission on Environmental Pollution (1976) *Air Pollution Control: An Integrated Approach*, Cmnd 6371.
2 C. Wood (1989) *Planning Pollution Prevention*, London: Butterworths.
3 R. Grove-White (1991) 18 JLS 32.
4 RCEP 23rd Report (2002) *Environmental Planning*, Cm 5459.

The role of the law and the courts requires some explanation here. The planning system is one in which the law generally exercises a supervisory, or review, function. It is there to define the various concepts used in the planning system (such as what development is, or what types of condition are legitimate), to ensure that the correct procedures are used and to ensure that discretionary decisions are taken in the proper manner. The law is therefore ultimately about procedures—that is, about ensuring that decisions are made correctly rather than that the correct decisions are made.

[handwritten margin note: like J.R. + some env. enforcement wouldn't be possible because they might require moral judgement]

The planning legislation

As Lord Scarman stated in *Pioneer Aggregates (UK) Ltd v. Secretary of State for the Environment* [1985] AC 132: '*Planning control is the creature of statute . . . Parliament has provided a comprehensive code of planning control.*' Although private law rights can be used for rudimentary development planning and control (see Box 12.2), statutory planning law is not based on common law foundations in the way that, for example, the law of statutory nuisance is. This means that it is a largely self-contained code as far as interpreting planning legislation is concerned.[5]

BOX 12.2 The shortcomings of private law for planning

Land development is controlled using private law in one of two main ways.

1. Nuisance law (a common law land tort) may be used. This prohibits unlawful interference with a person's use or enjoyment of land—for example, nuisance law can, in theory, control smoke or noise emanating from another property. But nuisance is about actual interference and is not an effective anticipatory control; nor—because the courts have generally restricted its scope to damage caused by emanations—is it effective in regulating development that does not emit anything harmful, or in protecting things such as wildlife or landscapes. *[handwritten margin note: Midland Bank ✓]*

2. A restrictive covenant can be imposed by an owner on the sale of land, preventing all subsequent owners (not only the purchaser) from developing the land contrary to the covenant. This is a useful anticipatory device and can regulate future changes to land uses, but relies on the preferences of individual sellers of land at the time of the sale and is not an effective technique for regulating competing modern uses.

Modern planning legislation is generally traced back to the Housing, Town Planning etc. Act 1909. The notable features of this Act, with its focus on the urban environment and discretion to implement, characterized much early planning legislation. It was not until the Town and Country Planning Act 1947 that a uniform and mandatory countrywide system of development control—Lord Scarman's 'comprehensive code'—was introduced. One of the most remarkable things about planning is that, while there have been numerous detailed additions and amendments to the law, the basic structure of much of this system (apart from that relating to development plans) has remained unchanged since then, although the way in which it is operates has, in practice, changed quite radically. *[handwritten margin note: Uniformity.]*

The legislation was consolidated in the Town and Country Planning Act (TCPA) 1990. Important changes were made under the Planning and Compensation Act 1991, but inserted

---

5 A point that the courts have had occasion to stress in recent years—see, e.g., *R (Reprotech (Pershan) Ltd) v. East Sussex County Council* [2002] UKHL 8, see p. 381.

into the 1990 Act as amendments or additions. The Planning and Compulsory Purchase Act (PCPA) 2004 makes further important changes to the law; some of these amend the 1990 Act, but some important changes, especially to development planning, have not been consolidated. At the time of writing, a Planning Reform Bill has been introduced into Parliament, which, again, may make significant changes (see p. 426).

Unless otherwise stated, therefore, wherever a section number is given in this chapter without reference to a particular Act, it refers to the 1990 Act. Frequent reference will also be made to subordinate legislation, which fleshes out much of the detail of the law. Central here are:

- the Town and Country Planning (General Permitted Development) Order 1995;[6]
- the Town and Country Planning (General Development Procedure) Order 1995;[7]
- the Town and Country Planning (Use Classes Order) 1987.[8]

The first two relate to the grant of automatic planning permission for a wide range of activities, while under the last, a significant number of changes in the use of land are declared not to be 'development' and so fall outside the planning system altogether.

What is 'town and country planning'?

Town planning has been described simply as 'how much of what is put where'. As befits a political system, the question of what planning covers has, over the years, largely been left to those who make planning decisions. The result has been an expansion of the idea—beyond straightforward amenity, public health, and land use issues, towards taking into account the economic and social impact of decisions.

This widening of the scope of planning has received the support of the courts. In exercising their supervisory jurisdiction, they have often had to ask the question 'what is planning?' in order to decide whether a power has been used legitimately. In doing so, they have proved willing to decide that most things are within the scope of planning. The most commonly used legal test is that given by Lord Scarman in *Westminster City Council v. Great Portland Estates plc* [1985] AC 661, who suggested that town planning covers anything that '*relates to the character of the use of land*'.

This general formulation, however, hides fundamental divisions over the legitimate role and scope of planning (see Box 12.3). Until the 1970s, town and country planning was a relatively uncontroversial topic in party-political terms, with the exception of the questions of compensation for refusal of permission and taxation of profits resulting from a grant of permission (betterment). There was a degree of consensus over of what planning should consist and over the preferred policies. The role of the state itself as a major developer was accepted.

BOX 12.3 McAuslan's ideologies of planning law

1 Law exists to protect private property and its institutions (traditional common law approach)

2 Law exists and should be used to advance the public interest, if necessary against 1 (orthodox public administration and planning approach)

---

6 SI 1995/418.
7 SI 1995/419.
8 SI 1987/764.

3 Law exists and should be used to advance the cause of public participation against both 1 and 2 (radical or populist approach)

(P. McAuslan (1980) *The Ideologies of Planning Law*, Oxford: Pergamon Press, pp. 3–6)

In the 1980s, the extent to which socio-economic issues should be a legitimate part of planning became contested. Some saw planning as one means by which a particular form of social development might be produced; others wished to see planning restricted as much as possible on the grounds that it interfered unduly with the free market. The second view was effectively the one that was espoused by the Conservative governments of the 1980s, with their firm beliefs in deregulation, a minimalist approach to restrictions on commercial activity, the power of the market as a distributor of resources, and the consequent need for speed and certainty in any system of control. This deregulatory approach included changes to the law: for example, removing the need for planning permission in many situations, fast-tracking development control in designated areas, and centralizing decision making for certain major infrastructure projects under the Transport and Works Act 1992. But it also included important changes to government policy guidance, which emphasized the interests of developers in being granted planning permission and the need to speed up the process of dealing with planning applications. Many of these changes indicated a significant move away from upholding participation as an important objective of the planning system in its own right—a strong theme of the late 1960s and early 1970s (McAuslan's third ideology)—and from the more general notion that planning is, above all, a process through which decisions are made, rather than anything with an absolutely definitive subject matter.

The centrality of planning policy and the Secretary of State

The deregulatory agenda operated both at a procedural and substantive level. There has always been some sort of presumption in favour of granting permission and the statistics on planning permission show that, of the large numbers of applications made each year, approximately 90 per cent are granted. The difference is that, in the 1980s, this presumption changed in substance from the basic public law requirement that reasons be given for a decision affecting someone's right to develop, to a *policy* in favour of development that may have a great weight attached to it by the decision maker. This is only one example of the increased importance attached to planning policy in the system, notwithstanding the retention of the basic legal structure of the system outlined above.

Increasingly, change was effected by administrative means, particularly by the concerted application of strong central government policy, often on appeal. For example, Circular 14/85 stated that:

There is always a presumption in favour of allowing applications for development, having regard to all material considerations, unless that development would cause demonstrable harm to interests of acknowledged importance.

Circular 1/85, meanwhile, emphasized that conditions should not be attached unless they could be justified on clear grounds.

Naturally, on appeal, the Secretary of State also took this pro-development approach in applying his own policies. Often, these would carry so much weight that local planning authorities ignored them at their peril, knowing that developers could exercise their right to appeal. These explicitly directory circulars grew to have far greater importance than local policies, such as development plans. The appeals process was used to support this shift in power from local to central government, and the number of appeals—and of successful appeals—rose significantly. A similar story was apparent in relation to appeals against enforcement notices.

In keeping with the policy of doctrinal neutrality on the content of planning policies, the courts did not interfere with these changes, except to preserve the rationality of the decision-making process by insisting that adequate reasons were given for decisions. But the planning system has always been pro-development to some extent. This stems from the prominence of property-based ideas within it and is evident in, for example, third parties and objectors[9] not being given the same rights to appeal against the grant of planning permission as those given to developers when permission is refused. The result is that permission will be granted if *either* the local planning authority or the Secretary of State is in favour of it.

Centralization and decentralization

In the 1980s, the planning system became far more centralized, in two main senses: more decisions were taken at a central level and central policy pervaded every decision even at a local level. One effect was to shift power from local government to central government; another was to increase the areas of conflict between the two levels. But, interestingly, at the same time, the system became in a way *less* centralized. This was because the changes in policy were designed to increase the role of the market at the expense of the state and to make the system more developer-led. The system moved away from the direct promotion of wider social, economic, and environmental objectives; reflecting the shift from public to private development, it became more concerned with resolving a myriad of competing land uses in the wider public interest.

it is not in the private sectors interest to make provisions for environment.

The 1990s also saw a mix of centralizing and decentralizing tendencies. The Secretary of State no longer had to approve all development plans and a presumption in favour of development in accordance with such plans was introduced. But the activity of land use planning became even less contentious politically. There were no longer the same debates about the purposes of planning as there had been up to the 1980s and so there was less need to impose government policy on appeal. But the importance of central government rose, because planning policy contained ever more prescriptive 'guidance'—more in the form of rules for local authorities to follow, than of best practice to be commended. Increasingly, this prescriptive guidance shaped development plans, although, in terms of content, the emphasis was on facilitating private development.

In the light of evidence that suggests that, in areas of discretion, the main influence on the formulation of local planning officers' judgment is overwhelmingly central government guidance and sometimes even less formalized expressions of policy,[10] this can be seen as a further centralizing step. In the 1990s, the focus also shifted to the propriety of the planning system[11] and government guidance effectively put an onus on elected members to justify decisions taken against the advice of officers' written reports.

The role of the courts

A major challenge to the non-interventionist approach of the courts came with the Human Rights Act (HRA) 1998, which, for a short period, threatened to upset the traditional approach to planning. In the seminal litigation in *R v. Secretary of State for the Environment, Transport and the Regions, ex parte Holding and Barnes plc and ors* [2001] UKHL 23 (generally known as the *Alconbury* case), which related to cases where the decision maker was the

---

9 The negative language of 'objectors' is revealing in itself: see A. Davies (2001) 72 TPR 193.

10 An example is the persuasive role of the Energy White Paper in relation to wind farm development: see Toke (2005) 33(12) Energy Policy 1527, discussed in Case 12.3.

11 The 1997 Third Report of the Nolan Committee on Standards in Public Life (Cm 3702) received more complaints about planning than any other activity of local government.

[handwritten margin notes: "→ no accountability.", "To right to fair trial @ risk?"]

Secretary of State,[12] the Divisional Court had originally objected to the Secretary of State being '*the judge in his own cause where his policy is in play*' so that, to comply with Art. 6 of the European Convention on Human Rights (the right to a fair trial, sometimes expressed as including the right to a court), '*he cannot be both policy maker and decision-taker*'.[13] The House of Lords nonetheless upheld the distinction between the legality of a planning judgment and the merits of a decision, and thought it was misconceived to look on the Secretary of State's role as that of a judge: to have done so would obviously have disturbed the whole scheme of the planning legislation.

The House of Lords has, however, stressed the public law nature of planning (and hence the rejection, for example, of private law concepts such as estoppel entering planning law,[14] or the privileging of developer interests in relation to raising challenges to planning decisions).[15] In some ways, this is simply a continuation of the idea that planning is a comprehensive statutory code, but the decision in *R (Burkett) v. Hammersmith and Fulham London Borough Council* [2002] UKHL 23 (see Case 10.3)—that the time for bringing a challenge to a planning permission runs not from the date that the planning authority resolves to grant permission, but from the date that the permission is actually granted—is especially significant, because it represents the courts making a clear choice about the importance of public participation in planning (in effect, elevating McAuslan's third ideology at the expense of the first and second ideologies). According to Lord Slynn:

[handwritten margin note: "social"]

> I realise that this [decision] may cause some difficulties in practice, both for local authorities and for developers, but for the grant not to be capable of challenge, because the resolution has not been challenged in time, seems to me wrongly to restrict the right of the citizen to protect his interests.[16]

Finally, making planning decisions has become a much more legalistic process. This is especially so in relation to environmental protection, in which area there is an increasing range of legal obligations, some of which arise from EC Directives, which must be considered and given due weight in planning decisions (see p. 409). One consequence is that decision makers, especially on appeal, no longer simply take policy guidance and legal obligations into account and apply them; increasingly, these sources are *interpreted* in the light of previous decisions and cases. This process of juridification may be seen as a valuable safeguard in ensuring that decisions are reached consistently and in accordance with the 'real meaning' of legal obligations. Alternatively, it may be seen as a threat to the speed and flexibility of response that the modern property market claims to require.

The Planning and Compulsory Purchase Act 2004

[handwritten margin note: "PCPA 2004"]

Further change to the planning system came with the Planning and Compulsory Purchase Act (PCPA) 2004. Some indication of the importance of this reform is that its preceding Green Paper[17] received a record number of (mostly highly critical) responses. The Act contains a number of potentially centralizing measures—for example, in relation to development planning (see p. 386). PCPA 2004 was one plank of a planning reform programme that is seeing the revisions of all existing government policy guidance. In some ways, it may be the revisions to policy guidance that will be the most important development, because the stated

12 Either because the application was 'called in', or an appeal was 'recovered', or for other reasons that meant that the Secretary of State was the decision maker.

13 [2001] HRLR 2, [86].

14 *R (Reprotech (Pebsham) Ltd) v. East Sussex County Council* [2002] UKHL 8 (a consequence of this was that a decision that converting waste to electricity was ancillary to an existing waste management use was overturned).

15 *R (Burkett) v. Hammersmith and Fulham London Borough Council* [2002] UKHL 23.

16 At [5].

17 *Planning: Delivering a Fundamental Change* (2001).

intention is to simplify this so that guidance concentrates on issues of principle. Another view of the PCPA 2004, however, is that it was the first serious attempt to legislate on contentious issues such as fast-tracking controversial major infrastructure projects and that the legislative process at the time must be seen in this light.

A main aspiration behind the reforms was the shift from a negative process—a set of constraints to development that developers have to overcome if they are to get planning permission—to positive management, which seeks more active engagement with key stakeholders and the public. This shift can be seen in regional spatial strategies (RSSs), which replace county-level structure plans. The strategies are not restricted to laying down a framework for how land is used and developed, but are intended to have a wider function of coordinating development control with forward-looking mechanisms such as transport plans, environmental quality plans, and so on. Hence, only certain parts of the spatial strategy will be 'the development plan', with the result, as one commentator has described it, of land use planning 'nesting' within spatial strategies.[18]

But it is also clear that there will be no return to the post-war vision of the planned national economy, that the private sector will remain the most important driving force behind development, and that—as with its predecessors—the present Labour Government does not see its role as directing development towards less prosperous regions and away from economic hotspots concerned about the impact of new development on the environment. The market economy must 'go ahead at full speed on all engines'.[19]

Whatever the objectives behind the 2004 Act, the tensions between speed and participation, predictability and flexibility, are probably an inescapable feature of planning (as they are with most other regulatory systems).[20] The more streamlined that various parts of the process are made, the more that decisions may be challenged through the courts, because stakeholders (and particularly objectors) feel that their views have not been heard or adequately taken into account.[21]

The objectives of planning and the environment

A comparison between the parliamentary debates preceding the 1947 and 2004 Acts shows that concern with social objectives has been replaced by an increasing emphasis on environmental protection and sustainable development. In its 23rd Report (2002) *Environmental Planning*, the RCEP proposed that the town and country planning system be given a statutory purpose '*to facilitate the achievement of legitimate economic and social goals while ensuring that the quality of the environment is safeguarded and, wherever appropriate, enhanced*' (para. 8.33). This was not accepted and, instead, the 2004 Act provides a loosely worded statutory sustainability objective for the making of development plans, while making no mention of sustainable development in relation to development control. There is however much more attention, especially in policy guidance, on the approach of planning towards the environment (see Box 12.4)

18 M. Tewdwr-Jones [2004] JPL 560.

19 Government Office for the South East, Regional Planning Guidance for the South East of England: Public Examination May–June 1999—Report of the Panel, para. 4.9 (government representation).

20 Whether, in fact, planning acts as a drag on competitiveness may be more myth than reality: see HC ODPM: Housing, Planning, Local Government and the Regions Committee Fourth Report (2002–03) *Planning, Competitiveness and Productivity.*

21 For example, the more flexibility is given to decision makers to relax planning controls at local level—and the 2004 Act allows local planning authorities to make local development orders, in effect a form of local permitted development rights—the more that those with neighbouring land lose certainty about the amenity of their area.

BOX 12.4 Planning law and environmental harm

Consider the following, from the latest general policy guidance on the aims of the planning system:

Planning authorities should seek to enhance the environment as part of development proposals. Significant adverse impacts on the environment should be avoided and alternative options which might reduce or eliminate those impacts pursued. Where adverse impacts are unavoidable, planning authorities and developers should consider possible mitigation measures. Where adequate mitigation measures are not possible, compensatory measures may be appropriate. In line with the UK sustainable development strategy, environmental costs should fall on those who impose them—the "polluter pays" principle.

(Planning Policy Statement 1 (2005) *Delivering Sustainable Development*, para. 19)

Although this takes a preventive approach, it still envisages that, ultimately, some harm may be unavoidable. Moreover, saying that something 'should' happen is a weaker obligation than saying that it 'shall'. Also, it is unclear who should pay for environmental harm—modern development is often a partnership between local authorities and developers (sometimes, planning authorities will underwrite developers' costs) and therefore both parties might be said to 'impose' environmental costs. Like the Polluter Pays Principle generally (see p. 244), it is vague about how these should be paid for, and about the balance between the costs of preventing and mitigating environmental harm and those associated with negative environmental impact.

By contrast, the policy guidance on nature conservation states—at least in one section—that, if significant harm cannot be prevented, mitigated, or compensated, then development should not be allowed. Elsewhere in the same guidance, however, there is reference to harm being acceptable if the benefits from the development outweigh the environmental damage (see PPS9 (2005) *Biodiversity and Geological Conservation*, paras 1(vi) and 8). This cannot be a distinction between significant and 'insignificant' harms, because the latter relates to impacts on Sites of Special Scientific Interest (SSSIs), the key national protective designation. It does seem difficult to pin down, from these examples, what the objective of planning should be.

Consider, as well, the issue of design in planning. This is no longer seen as a secondary consideration, not least because reducing environmental impacts from development has to start on the drawing board and not be bolted on as an afterthought. Hence:

Planning policies should promote high quality inclusive design in the layout of new developments and individual buildings in terms of function and impact, not just for the short term but over the lifetime of the development. Design which fails to take the opportunities available for improving the character and quality of an area should not be accepted...

(Planning Policy Statement 1 (2005) *Delivering Sustainable Development*, para. iv)

Putting these examples together, we can ask whether the purpose of planning is to:

(a) reduce harm, but allow trade-offs with, for example, economic development?

(b) to prevent harm?

(c) to pursue better environmental quality?

The *legal* answer seems to be that a decision maker can, in principle, probably choose any of these approaches. There is no rule of law that says, for example, that planning permission cannot be refused because no harm (in the sense of a decrease in environmental quality) will arise; this might once have been the inclination of the courts, but it is now widely accepted that the right to develop land is not a right held solely by the landowner, but is one that is, in effect, shared between the landowner and the state. The 2006 Barker Review of Planning (see p. 426) is notable in this context because it advocates that, at least for changes of use, planning permission should not be refused in cases in which there is no harm.

[handwritten: What constitutes harm?]

Planning authorities

Most decisions on planning applications are taken by local authorities, which, in this context, are generically called 'local planning authorities'. There are three main types of local planning authority that deal with most applications: district authorities; single-tier London boroughs and metropolitan districts; unitary authorities.

Different rules apply to national parks, in relation to which the national park authority takes development control decisions. In the Broads, the similarly constituted Broads Authority takes all decisions (Norfolk and Suffolk Broads Act 1988). In relation to what are termed 'county matters', such as minerals developments and waste disposal applications, the relevant local authority is the county council. County planning authorities are responsible both for making decisions on planning applications and for preparing plans relating to these county matters.

Decisions on planning applications take as their starting point the development plan for the area. Development plans have a regional and a local element. Under PCPA 2004, with the exception of waste and minerals matters, the regional level replaces the county level, county council structure plans being replaced by RSSs. Keeping RSSs up to date is the responsibility of regional planning bodies, which (in the unlikely event that the English regions ever decide to establish them) will be the elected regional assemblies, but which, for the foreseeable future, are an uneasy mix of elected members acting as delegates from local and county-level planning authorities—at least 60 per cent of the regional planning body must comprise such members—and unelected members.

The Greater London Authority is not a local planning authority, although it plays a strategic role in relation to development because it must develop a 'spatial development strategy' (see p. 387).

[handwritten: Look into this.]

Wales, Scotland, and Northern Ireland

Planning in Wales remains subject to the TCPA 1990. The Government of Wales Act 2006 enables the National Assembly of Wales to pass primary legislation in the field of town and country planning. Since devolution, however, powers in relation to delegated legislation and powers of the Secretary of State have been exercised by the Assembly, but this has not led to major divergences with England, although—given the extent to which planning law and policy depends on decisions made at this level—there has been considerable scope for this.

In Scotland, planning legislation was consolidated in the Town and Country Planning (Scotland) Act 1997, which is broadly similar to the TCPA 1990, but is undergoing change under the Planning etc. (Scotland) Act 2006, which is modernizing planning law along similar—but by no means identical—lines to the law in England under PCPA 2004. Planning cases decided by the House of Lords that have their origins in the Scottish courts are therefore usually equally important elsewhere in the UK, because analogous terms are being interpreted.

Town and country planning matters in Northern Ireland are also governed by legislation that mirrors TCPA 1990. This is largely contained in the Planning (Northern Ireland) Order 1991. An important amending order from 2003—SI 2003/430 (NI8)—brings certain key aspects of the law into line with the rest of the UK—for example, the legal presumption in favour of the development plan.

Because there is only limited EC involvement in planning law, there is considerable scope for the devolved legislatures to develop law and policy in their own direction.

Forward planning—development plans

Development plans guide or influence development in the areas that they cover. In this country, development plans lay down policies, aims, objectives, and goals, rather than prescribe what is going to happen in an area. They have no immediate effect other than as a statement of what the local planning authority considers is desirable (see Box 12.5), but they do have a great and growing importance in the decision whether or not to grant planning permission.

[handwritten marginalia: GOOD DEF OF Development Plans.]

BOX 12.5 Development plans vs zoning ordinances *[handwritten: Not in UK.]*

In 'zoning' law, plans are *presumptive*. *[handwritten: OF OPORTUNITY]* If an area of land is zoned for an activity and a developer wishes to develop land in accordance with the plan, then the development is authorized (and vice versa). The main area for legal argument is therefore whether the proposed activity conforms to the plan policies. Zoning schemes were used in the UK prior to the Town and Country Planning Act 1947, and are still used in the USA and in many European countries (for example, the Netherlands). This approach usually gives greater weight to the interests of landowners and an advantage is said to lie in greater certainty for developers. *[handwritten: industrial zones.]*

In the UK, development plans are *permissive*. Plans are the starting point for deciding whether a proposed development will be authorized, but developers must submit a planning application within which all of the material factors are considered. One consequence is that designating land in a plan will not generally engage rights under Art. 6 of the European Convention on Human Rights (see, for example, *Bovis Homes Ltd v. New Forest District Council* [2002] EWHC 483).[22] There are, however, some instances in which a zoning-type approach is taken in the UK: examples include enterprise zones, simplified planning zones, and local development orders, the essence of which is that desired commercial development should be fast-tracked in certain areas (see p. 398). But experience suggests that these are of limited value, because developers will usually have to engage the planning authority in negotiations anyway, regardless of whether, in principle, the development can proceed. *[handwritten: Greater Control.]* *[handwritten: The Docklands? & will be regulated anyway.]*

The system of development plans has been one area within planning law in which there seems to have been a constant state of change. There are two main reasons for this. The first is that, while the need for some form of forward planning has been recognized since 1947, adopting plans and keeping them up to date has always been a complex and drawn-out affair (made the more so by the recognition, in the late 1960s, of the need for greater public involvement in plan making—see the changes introduced by the Town and Country Planning Act 1971). Various changes were made over the years to address this problem, the main one being the introduction of a two-tier system of structure plans and local plans by the Town and Country Planning Act 1968.

---

22 Although it might do, if it were a protective designation that de facto prevented development: *Oerlemans v. Netherlands* (1993) 15 EHRR 561. The contingent nature of development plans has also been considered in relation to the issue of the 'locality' in nuisance claims—see p. 358.

The second reason for upheaval is less technical and more political, particularly because government in the 1980s was unconvinced by the need for strong forward planning and anti-pathetic to the power of local authorities. Nevertheless, to give a greater degree of certainty to *developers'* forward plans, the Planning and Compensation Act 1991 strengthened the status of the development plan in decision making (see p. 405) and, in line with this, actually extended the scope of development plans. For example, local plans were required to cover the *whole* of the area of a local planning authority (something that few had done in the past). With this shift, came an increase in the practical and legal importance of plans, and a resulting slow-down in the speed of their adoption.

Development planning and the 2004 Act

This permanent revolution has continued with the Planning and Compulsory Purchase Act 2004. The provisions of the 2004 Act relating to development plans and, in particular, the replacement of structure plans with RSSs, are perhaps its most ambitious.

As explained above, prior to 2004, there were two tiers of plan—structure plans and local plans—collectively referred to as 'the development plan' (in metropolitan areas; in Wales, unitary development plans combined both functions). There was *no* national plan, the nearest equivalent being central government policy set out in planning policy guidance (PPG) notes and government circulars. Nor were there formal regional plans, although groupings of local planning authorities did produce general regional strategies and there was formal regional planning guidance issued by central government, often based on advice from these regional groupings. This was taken a stage further in planning guidance issued in 2000 (PPG 11), which anticipated a strengthened role for regional planning guidance (RPG) and long-term RSSs, in line with government policy (now, it seems, abandoned) of establishing regional governance structures (regional assemblies). At around the same time, informal spatial strategies began to be adopted in Scotland, Wales, and Northern Ireland, while in London, the first formal legal recognition of wider spatial planning was provided in the duty on the Mayor to adopt a spatial development strategy (see below).

The 2004 Act, at least for England and Wales, formalizes and strengthens the role of RSSs by making them the 'upper tier' of development planning, to replace structure plans. Until the new RSSs are adopted (and, by early 2008, none had been), existing regional planning guidance is used.[23] In place of local plans, the 'lower tier' of the development plan is now not one document, but a number of discrete local development documents, made under a local development scheme prepared by the local planning authority, including minerals and waste development plan documents adopted by county councils (or, as the case may be, unitary authorities). There was a three-year transitional period (to September 2007) during which the existing local plan still applied. There has been slow progress on adopting local development frameworks and this period has had to be extended.[24] The local development documents should provide the framework for delivering the spatial strategy for the area.

As with other areas of the 2004 Act, its provisions relating to development plans require a good deal of fleshing out by regulations (on procedural matters) and guidance.[25]

23 In England, see the Town and Country Planning (Initial Regional Spatial Strategy) (England) Regulations 2004, SI 2004/2206.

24 In individual cases, by Ministerial letter.

25 In England, see the Town and Country Planning (Regional Planning) (England) Regulations 2004, SI 2004/2203, and PPS 11, *Regional Spatial Strategies*, and PPS 12, *Local Development Frameworks*.

Table 12.1 The development plan

Development plans (England)

	Upper tier	Lower tier (the local development framework)			Documents *not* forming part of 'the development plan'	
	Regional spatial strategy*	Local development plan documents (forming part of 'the development plan')				
		Local development plan documents (general)	Minerals development plan documents	Waste development plan documents	Supplementary planning documents	Statement of community involvement
Plan-making body	Regional planning body	Local planning authority—district council or unitary district authority (UDA)	County council or UDA	County council or UDA	District or county council or UDA	District council or UDA

Development plans (Wales)

Local development plan (all Welsh authorities are unitary, combining general local planning, waste, and minerals functions).

Provision is made for a Welsh spatial plan, but this is not, as yet, formally the upper tier.

Development plans (London)

Spatial development strategy	Local development plan documents (all London boroughs are unitary authorities)

* RPGs replaced structure plans, which will, in turn, be replaced by RSSs adopted by regional assemblies. Progress on adopting RSSs and LDFs has been slow.

Regional spatial strategies (RSSs)

RSSs are provided for in Pt I of the 2004 Act. Each region must have a spatial strategy that *'must set out the Secretary of State's policies (however expressed) in relation to the development and use of land within the region'* (s. 1(1) and (2)).

Two related points arise concerning this seemingly straightforward provision. The first is the enormous width given to the Secretary of State to determine what matters may be covered by an RSS (and, it would seem, how he can do so). With structure plans, a range of matters—physical; economic; demographic; transport-related—had to be kept under review while, latterly, there were statutory duties to include policies in respect of the conservation of the natural beauty and amenity of the land, the improvement of the physical environment, and the management of traffic. By contrast, a regional planning body is subject to a much more general duty to keep under review matters that may be expected to affect development in its region and the planning of that development (s. 3(2)). The Act itself contains nothing specifically requiring environmental matters to be included in the RSS; it is only guidance that requires that, among other things, 'priorities for the environment', transport and waste management 'should be taken into account' (PPS11, para. 1.3). The RSS is not, however, merely to be a negative framework within which decisions on individual planning applications are made (which was a criticism of structure plans); spatial strategies are intended to direct development planning towards the *positive management of development* in an integrated, long-term fashion.

The reason for the width discussed above is the second point that can be made about s. 1, which is the obvious centrality of the Secretary of State. RSSs are to be vehicles for giving effect to national policy. They stem from national policy guidance, issued mainly by the Secretary of State responsible for planning matters (currently, in England, the Secretary of State for Communities and Local Government). There is simply no need to circumscribe in law the general subject matter of RSSs. Instead of confining the discretion of county councils over the scope of structure plans, for reasons explained below, Pt I of the Act envisages that disputes over the content of RSSs are as likely to come between government departments (to be thrashed out as matters of politics rather than law).

Local development documents

Local plans have always been more detailed, consisting of written policies and specific land use allocations by reference to a map, so their relevance to individual development control decisions has always been much greater. Thus, while a structure plan would determine the projected number of new houses needed, the local plan would identify specific areas deemed capable of catering for such development.

The same basic approach is retained under the 2004 Act and its guidance. The local planning authority (the district authority or unitary authority) adopts local development plan documents, together with waste and minerals development plan documents produced by the county council or unitary authority. Somewhat confusingly, the local development scheme must specify which documents are to be local development documents and which documents are to be development plan documents—that is, which documents will form part of 'the development plan' (s. 15(2)). It must be presumed that any documents that are not formally part of the development plan, for the purposes of the presumption in favour of the plan (PCPA 2004, s. 38(6)) will nevertheless be 'material considerations' (and see further below).

In preparing a local development document, regard must be had to various sources—notably, central government policy and guidance, the RSS, and the community strategy prepared by the authority under s. 4 of the Local Government Act 2000 (PCPA 2004, s. 19(2)). All development plan documents must be submitted to the Secretary of State for independent examination and anyone making representations regarding changes has a right to be heard (s. 20); any development plan document must be in conformity with the RSS (the formal expression of the two-tier system). There are powers to modify and call in local development documents (the latter being a power that, under the previous legislation, was very rarely used). As with RSSs, there is no longer any specific legislative requirement to include certain environmental policies in local development plan documents. Local planning authorities no longer have the right to override an inspector's recommendations and propose modifications (s. 23). Notably, the same restriction does not apply to the Secretary of State in relation to the draft RSS, further illustrating the centralizing nature of the recent reforms.

Non-statutory plans and guidance

Local planning authorities frequently have other policies and drafts that have not gone through the statutory procedures. In practice, a large range of such 'non-statutory' material—ranging from draft local plans, to design briefs and technical specifications—is used by local planning authorities in making decisions. But there are obvious problems in this practice, because it may be seen to be subverting the statutory public participation requirements and thus the democratic legitimacy of the planning process.

In *Westminster City Council v. Great Portland Estates plc* [1985] AC 661, a distinction was drawn between different types of non-statutory guidance. The House of Lords required that all matters of *policy* should be included in the statutory plan and that only supplementary matters of detail, or those that relate to the implementation of these policies, should be put in non-statutory guidance. As long as this non-statutory material is not illegal—that is, it must relate to the character of the use of land—it is, however, a material consideration under s. 70(2) and must be considered alongside the statutory development plan, although perhaps not always accorded the same weight. The weight attached to it will depend on the circumstances in which it was produced.

What are now known as supplementary planning documents are not part of 'the development plan'—and so will not be tested by an independent examination—but will be part of the folder of documents making up the local development documents. Because the PCPA 2004 aims to keep the development plan components of local development documents more up to date than has been the case with adopted plans (or even first-draft revisions to plans), it may be that, in the future, less reliance will need to be placed in practice on supplementary planning documents. Nevertheless, it may still be tempting to put important policies into supplementary planning documents to avoid a formal examination in public; to a degree, this is checked by rules that require public participation in their making[26] and by guidance requiring rigorous procedures of community involvement, which also states that they must not be used to avoid policies and proposals that should be included in a development plan document being subjected to proper independent scrutiny.[27] At the moment, the courts have taken a fairly generous approach to this kind of guidance, while recognizing that it should not be used as a means to bypass public participation in plan making (*R (JA Pye (Oxford) Ltd and ors) v. Oxford City Council* [2002] EWCA Civ 1116).

Development plans—common issues and themes

(a) The role of the Secretary of State

As explained above, RSSs are an expression of central government policy. Accordingly, the Secretary of State has an important role in overseeing RSSs. In some ways, this is merely a continuation of his powers in relation to structure plans, although there are important differences. After 1991, structure plans did not have to be approved by the Secretary of State, although he retained a power to issue directions and, more significantly, to call a plan in, and was thus able to exercise ultimate control over policy. Although the power to call in was sparingly used, the threat was ever-present and the power to direct that a plan be modified was

---

26 Town and Country Planning (Local Development) (England) Regulations 2004, SI 2004/2204.
27 PPS 12, *Local Development Frameworks*, paras 2.42–2.44.

used on a number of occasions to force county councils to increase their housing provision (see Case 12.1).

CASE 12.1 Challenging a development plan—*West Sussex County Council v. Secretary of State for the Environment, Transport and the Regions* [1999] PLCR 365

Government policy is to meet projections in demand for housing by a significant expansion in numbers of new houses, especially in the south east of England. But doing so requires identifying how many houses each regional spatial strategy (RSS) is to promote and ensuring that local development documents provide for this. In this case, the Secretary of State directed the Council to modify its structure plan to provide for an extra 12,800 dwellings. The Council, whose structure plan already provided for 37,900 dwellings, challenged this decision on the grounds that insufficient regard had been given to regional policy guidance (RPG) for the south east, which required a consideration of broad planning objectives, economic needs, and the local environment.

The Court of Appeal held that the statutory provisions relating to development plans in the Town and Country Planning Act 1990 were drafted in wide terms, making it clear that the Secretary of State was pre-eminent on issues regarding plan modifications. If he thought that local proposals were unsatisfactory, he could direct their modification, regardless of any consultation and public appraisal processes in which the local authority had engaged, and regardless of government policy guidance (the RPG). The legislation made no provision to appeal such Ministerial decisions and so the only grounds of challenge were the usual grounds in judicial review. The direction was not wholly irrational and had lawfully been made.

This case illustrates where power lies in the planning system—but it also illustrates some of the tensions that were evident between central government and county councils over the allocation of land for house building, and a major driver behind the reforms in Pt I of the 2004 Act appears to have been an attempt to end the opposition of county councils to major house-building proposals.

In contrast, the 2004 Act once more *requires* the active involvement of the Secretary of State who, as noted above, must be sent draft revisions to the RSS. In all cases, it is the Secretary of State who publishes the final RSS, having considered any inspector's report and any further representations made. The intention, however, is that elected regional assemblies will take over reviewing, revising, and issuing RSSs.[28]

(b) Sustainability

Underpinning the shift towards spatial planning is a duty, in s. 39 of the 2004 Act, requiring all plan-making bodies to exercise their functions '*with the objective of contributing to the achievement of sustainable development*'. The extent to which this legal duty has any real content or value is debatable (see the similarly worded provision that applies to the Environment Agency in exercising its functions, discussed on p. 116). But its drafting indicates a clear desire to insulate individual planning applications from scrutiny through a sustainable development lens (the provision does not apply to Pt 4 of the Act dealing with development control). Whether central policy can really be used to *promote* environmentally sustainable developments remains something of a moot point, because there always remains local discretion about whether to permit such development (see, for example, the case of wind farms—p. 409), and policy guidance on environmentally desirable development is rarely as pro-development as it is with activities deemed to be economically crucial, such as 3G mobile phone masts.[29]

---

28 Office of the Deputy Prime Minister (2004) *Draft Regional Assemblies Bill: Policy Statement*, July, para. 50.
29 See PPG 8, *Telecommunications*.

Draft revisions to the RSS (s. 5(4)) and the preparation of local development documents (s. 19(5)) must both be subject to a 'sustainability appraisal'. It appears that this appraisal will include the requirements of the Regulations implementing the EC Strategic Environmental Assessment Directive (2001/42/EC)—the Assessment of Plans and Programmes Regulations 2004.[30] This is subject to guidance, rather than to further implementing regulations.[31] It is worth noting concerns that existing RPG has not been adequately appraised and, indeed, that the very process of sustainability appraisal has been criticized for marginalizing environmental considerations.[32] But the feasibility of meaningfully appraising development plan policies against the checklist mentioned in the SEA Directive has been questioned, the implication being that valuable resources may be channelled to this obligation at the expense of keeping plans up to date and using resources effectively.[33]

(c) Accountability

During the passage of the 2004 Act, a major concern with RSSs was the extent to which regional planning bodies might lack a democratic mandate, because there are, as yet, no elected regional assemblies in England and now, it seems, little prospect of them. This has been addressed, up to a point, by a requirement that at least 60 per cent of the membership of regional planning bodies must be drawn from elected representative planning authorities (district councils, county councils, metropolitan district councils, national park authorities, or the Broads Authority). Also, in keeping the RSS under review and monitoring its implementation, the regional planning body must 'seek the advice of'—that is, consult—any authority exercising 'county-level' planning functions (s. 4). The aim of this is to ensure a continuing involvement for county councils and unitary authorities, although the powers of county councils in development planning are clearly much reduced compared to their role in relation to structure plans. Local development documents remain the responsibility of elected local planning authorities.

(d) Consultation and participation

From the late 1990s, some regional planning guidance was made subject to formal scrutiny through an examination in public (a concept explained below). Whenever the RSS is revised, the regional planning body must publish a 'statement of community involvement' (s. 6). This rather open-ended provision is intended to give regional planning bodies some flexibility in consulting on revisions to the RSS, although it is a legal requirement that the statement is complied with and the draft Regulations require that the statement indicates who and how it has consulted, a summary of the main issues raised in the consultation, and how these have been addressed in the draft RSS. There are also requirements to consult with a wide range of interested bodies (including the various regulatory agencies with environmental responsibilities). Beyond this, much of the detail concerning public involvement—for example, the level of public involvement in the sustainability appraisal—is yet to be decided (although relevant in respect will be the Environmental Assessment of Plans and Programmes Regulations 2004[34]).

Once the draft RSS is submitted to the Secretary of State, there is further consultation. An examination in public into the draft RSS—a limited form of public inquiry at which there is no right to present a case unless invited to do so—*may* be arranged, which might be thought to mark a departure from the previous position under which, unless the Secretary of State directed otherwise, an examination in public had to be held (although, in practice, this was dispensed with in over half the cases). Guidance states, however, that only in the exceptional

30 SI 2004/1633.

31 ODPM (2004) *Sustainability Appraisal of Regional Spatial Strategies and Local Development Frameworks*, consultation paper.

32 RCEP 23rd Report (2002) *Environmental Planning*, paras 7.44–7.47.

33 S. Hockman [2003] JPL Supp 41.

34 SI 2004/1633.

circumstances of a minor revision will an examination in public be unnecessary, which, in effect, seems to retain something resembling current practice.[35]

For local development documents, the local development scheme must state that the local planning authority's statement of community involvement is part of the local development documents, alongside other components prescribed in regulations. But the statement of community involvement is not a development plan document—that is, it does not form part of 'the development plan' for the purposes of TCPA 1990, s. 70(2), and PCPA 2004, s. 38(6)—but, in some respects, it is treated as such—notably, in that it must be scrutinized by the Secretary of State.

Challenges to development plans

The law in relation to challenges to development plans remains basically unchanged following the 2004 Act. A challenge to a revised RSS, or to the adoption of a local development document, can be made by any 'person aggrieved' within six weeks of the decision under s. 287 (see PCPA 2004, s. 113). In the interests of speed, the aim is to limit legal challenges to this six-week 'window', but it is possible for a judicial review application to be made before this period if there has been some error of law, such as a breach of natural justice in the making of representations.[36]

Two grounds of appeal are provided: that the plan is outside the plan makers' powers, or that there has been some procedural error. In the latter case, any challenge must show that there has been substantial prejudice (which will not be the case if there has been a procedural error, but the adopted plan policies, notwithstanding the error, would not have been any different). In practice, the courts have held that these statutory grounds are to be equated with normal grounds for judicial review (see *Warren v. Uttlesford District Council* [1997] JPL 1130), and there is little difference in judicial review between a person aggrieved and someone with sufficient standing.

The leading case remains *Westminster City Council v. Great Portland Estates plc* [1985] AC 661. Among other things, this emphasizes the need to include *all* land use policies in plans, not least in the interests of public participation.[37] The courts have imposed a stricter duty on local planning authorities to give reasons when their development plan is being adopted than when planning permission is being refused (*Stirk v. Bridgnorth District Council* [1997] JPL 51). Because local planning authorities no longer have the right to override an inspector's recommendations and propose modifications, this may lead to fewer challenges being brought.

Developers or prospective developers bring most challenges to structure and local plans, while costs rules force amenity groups to prefer Ministerial lobbying. The same research also reveals the relative lack of challenges that are brought, bearing in mind the legal significance of the development plan after 1991. This may be explained by the fact that plans often simply legitimate national planning policies (which might suggest that we are unlikely to see a significant rise in the number of challenges being brought to the new-style development plans).[38]

Development plans—environmental critique

As far as incorporating environmental considerations is concerned, the record has been somewhat patchy. Despite government guidance,[39] many organizations raised concerns

---

35 PPS 11, *Regional Spatial Strategies*, para. 2.46.
36 See A. Robinson and J. Clement [2003] JPL 1384.
37 A case about supplementary planning guidance. On supplementary planning documents, see p. 389.
38 M. Purdue [1998] JPL 837.
39 Department of Environment (1991) *Policy Appraisal and the Environment*; Department of Environment (1993) *Environmental Appraisal of Development Plans: A Good Practice Guide*.

about development plan coverage and content, especially about the lack of mention of nature conservation issues.[40] More detailed research also indicates the priority attached to economic interests. Local authorities may view the environment either as a commodity or service, or in aesthetic terms, with ecological references being largely rhetorical. Integration of the environment with other key sectors such as transport may be lacking. Business interests and elected councillors anxious to create jobs exercise most power in determining development plan policies. This leads to an inevitable conclusion in those situations in which, as is sometimes the case, the development plan indicates that trade-offs between environmental and non-environmental assets will be handled *through the planning system itself* rather than through any other system of assessing public benefits.[41]

Having said that, recent years have seen considerable pressure for development plans to serve as vehicles for sustainable development. This was a major theme of PPG 12 (2000) *Development Plans*, which included guidance on sustainability appraisals of development plans, and on the integration of transport and land use policies. In its 2002 report on *Environmental Planning*, however, the RCEP commented, at para. 4.38, that '*Development plans may express admirable sentiments about issues such as energy conservation, but not in a form and context that are likely to change anything in the real world*'.

It has been held that policies in a development plan that restricted development leading to unacceptable levels of pollution could be used to justify refusing planning permission to an applicant with previous convictions for pollution offences (*Blake & Sons v. Secretary of State for the Environment and Colchester Borough Council* [1998] Env LR 309). This approach neatly sidesteps the normal rule that only issues to do with the proposed land use, not the proposed user, are material.

Development control—the meaning of 'development'

Section 57(1) of the 1990 Act states that '*Planning permission is required for the carrying out of any development of land*'. It is in relation to the system of development control that the town and country planning system has its greatest impact on environmental law. Planning permission is required for the carrying out of any development of land.

The general approach is to define development very widely, so that virtually everything is included initially,[42] and then to relax the need to apply for planning permission, either by:

- excluding activities from being 'development', which might include many activities with considerable environmental impacts, such as the use of land for agriculture (see p. 735);

- deeming planning permission to be granted under some kind of development order or similar provision (see p. 398).

This has the effect of shifting the focus in most practical situations from what is included to what is excluded.

The definition of development found in TCPA 1990, s. 55(1)—'*Development . . . means the carrying out of building, engineering, mining or other operations in, on, over or under land, or the making of any material change in the use of any buildings or other land*'—has effectively remained unchanged since 1947, so past decisions of the courts, which are the ultimate interpreters of the meaning of the Act, are relevant. Decisions of the Secretary of State on appeal are also of importance in understanding the definition. Although these are not binding as legal authority, in practice, they can have a prescriptive effect.

---

40 See, e.g., Campaign to Protect Rural England (1994) *Environmental Policy Omissions in Development Plans*.

41 S. Davoudi, A. Hull, and P. Healey (1996) 67 Town Planning Review 421.

42 For the avoidance of doubt, some things are specifically stated to constitute development—see s. 55(3)–(5).

The courts have decided that the existence of development is a question of 'fact and degree' in each particular case. It is for the local planning authority (or the Secretary of State on appeal) to apply the relevant law to the facts of each case to decide whether there has been development. The courts limit themselves to supervising and reviewing these decisions under normal judicial review grounds.

There are two limbs to 'development'—operational development and development by a material change of use.

Operational development

Operational development involves building, mining, or engineering operations. 'Other operations' is a little-discussed (or relied-on), catch-all category, apparently designed to ensure that matters such as waste disposal and drilling are covered.

- **Building operations**

   These are defined very widely in s. 336. 'Building' includes any structure or erection, and any part of a building as so defined, but does not include plant or machinery comprised in a building. 'Building operations' include rebuilding operations, structural alterations of or additions to buildings, demolition of buildings, and other operations normally undertaken by a person carrying on business as a builder.

   Any significant works are included, such as rebuilding works, works of alteration, the building of an extension, and the erection of such things as shop canopies, walls, advertising hoardings, and large sculptures. In one celebrated example, the erection of a model shark emerging from the roof of a house was held to amount to a building operation (although it ultimately received planning permission).[43] It is normally considered that very minor alterations, such as the installation of ordinary television aerials, are not significant enough to amount to development.

- **Engineering operations**

   The Act gives little guidance on the meaning of this term. The test used by the courts is whether they are *operations of the kind usually undertaken by engineers, that is, operations calling for the skills of an engineer*' (*Fayrewood Fish Farms v. Secretary of State for the Environment* [1984] JPL 267). There are many exceptions for public works in s. 55 and the General Permitted Development Order.

- **Mining operations**

   These include all forms of extractive operation, such as mining, quarrying, and the removal of materials from mineral deposits and waste tips (s. 55(4)). There are additional powers over minerals development, exercised by county planning authorities.

Development by material change of use of land or buildings

The power to control changes in the use of land is virtually exclusive to UK town and country planning, and makes it peculiarly able to exercise detailed control over land use. In the debates on the 1947 Act, Lord Reid—then an MP, but later a Law Lord—is reported to have said of material change of use: 'Nobody knows what that means.' And very little guidance is given in the Act on the meaning of this rather vague phrase. But, over the years, the judges have filled in any gaps by the creation of a number of important explanatory concepts.[44]

---

43 [1993] JPL 194.

44 Which might be said to run contrary to the notion that planning is based on a comprehensive legislative code—see p. 377. Some of these concepts are derived from policy guidance, e.g., the concept of the 'planning unit', illustrating the impact of policy.

Nevertheless, this remains a somewhat flexible phrase and flexibility is aided by decisions whether development has taken place in any particular case being a matter for the local planning authority, applying the law to the facts. What is important is that the change must be material in a planning sense—that is, that it must have:

- a physical impact on the land;

- a substantial impact;

- an impact that is relevant to town and country planning.

An example of a material change of use relating to environmental pollution would be changing the use of a quarry to a landfill. It is worth noting here that, in 1994, the RCEP recommended that the generation of 'appreciably higher levels of traffic' should always amount to a material land use change,[45] but this has never been adopted as a legal requirement (although planning policy on transport does require transport assessments alongside planning applications with significant transport implications—see PPG 13).

The unit of land to be considered when ascertaining whether there has been a change of use is called the 'planning unit'. This is normally the unit of occupation prior to the change and it is unusual to aggregate together more than one unit of occupation, or to subdivide one, unless *'two or more physically distinct areas are occupied for substantially different and unrelated purposes'* (*Burdle v. Secretary of State for the Environment* [1972] 1 WLR 1207). Thus a factory is usually treated as one unit, allowing some internal shifting of activities between parts of the site.

The courts have also laid down further tests. Thus, an ancillary use will not normally be of any planning concern (see Case 12.2). But if it becomes a dominant use, there has been a material change, such as when 44 dogs were kept in a dwelling house. In effect, the house had two main uses: residential and dog breeding (*Wallington v. Secretary of State for Wales* (1990) 62 P&CR 150). And an *intensification* of a use can also be a material change of use: the question that the courts often ask is whether the intensified use is so different in nature that it could be given a different name (see *Royal Borough of Kensington and Chelsea v. SSE* [1981] JPL 50). This might be the case if someone were to go from repairing her own car in her garage to mending several cars on a commercial basis.

CASE 12.2 **Changes of use and environmental protection—*Northavon District Council v. Secretary of State for the Environment* (1980) 40 P&CR 332**

In this case, a farmer wished to improve the drainage of his land and proposed stripping the topsoil, putting down a layer of filling including builder's rubble, and then replacing the topsoil. The Court of Appeal held that any deposit of waste would be incidental to the real purpose of the farmer's action, which was to raise the level of his land to improve its drainage. Hence the deposit of waste was not a material change of use. The Court was not swayed by the argument that this would lead to a 'fly-tipper's charter'.

This line of reasoning has important implications for various multifunctional activities having environmental impact—for example, a landfill site in which the waste gas is tapped off to generate heat. If the purpose of the site is to dispose of waste, then any generation of gas or heat may be only incidental and not a separate use of the land. But the two uses may be impossible to prioritize in this way: an example that the courts have given—in *R (Lowther) v. Durham County Council* [2002] Env LR 13, a case decided during the foot and mouth crisis—is the burning of slaughtered animals in power stations.

---

45 RCEP (1994) *Transport and the Environment*, Cm 2674, para. 9.66.

Quite where the dividing line is between these two kinds of cases, however, remains a little cloudy. In the *Lowther* case, the Court of Appeal upheld a decision that using secondary liquid fuels as a support fuel at a lime works that had previously only burnt petroleum coke (petcoke) was not a material change of use: the use remained primarily a lime works and the argument that any waste disposal or recovery operations would amount to a separate land use in planning terms was rejected.[46] One factor (stressed much more by Pill LJ than by Phillips MR) was the existence of extensive regulatory controls over disposal of hazardous waste and the public concern over this issue did not justify a finding that there was a separate planning use. This suggests that the degree of regulatory control over a use of land may be relevant in deciding whether there has been a material change of use—that is, controls on the *impacts* of the use may be relevant.

Exemption from the need to apply for planning permission

Activities that do not constitute development

The following operations and uses of land do not constitute development (ss. 55(2)(a)–(g)):

- maintenance, improvement, or alterations to a building affecting only its interior, or not materially affecting the external appearance;

- certain works carried out by highway authorities to maintain or improve roads;

- works by local authorities or statutory undertakers for the inspection, repair, or renewal of sewers, mains, etc., including breaking open streets;

- the use of any buildings or other land within the curtilage of a dwelling house for any purpose incidental to the enjoyment of the dwelling house as such;

- a change of use within the same class of the Use Classes Order;

- the use of land for the purposes of agriculture or forestry (including afforestation) and the use for any of those purposes of any building occupied together with land so used (see p. 735);

- the demolition of any description of building specified in a direction given by the Secretary of State to local planning authorities generally or to a particular local authority.

The Use Classes Order

The Use Classes Order is used as a way of avoiding the need for planning permission for what are considered to be changes between uses that have a reasonably similar land use impact. For example, the change of use from a post office to a funeral directors would not be development, because both are found in the same use class. The current Town and Country Planning (Use Classes) Order 1987[47] is significantly more liberal than previous Orders—a legacy of the deregulatory strategy followed in the 1980s. More recent widening of the general industrial class (B2) to include what were formerly grouped together as special industrial uses (under SI 1995/297) were justified on the basis that control could be exercised effectively by pollution control agencies. But given the different impacts on amenity that some authorized

---

46 The same process was challenged in *R v. Environment Agency, ex parte Gibson* [1999] Env LR 73.
47 SI 1987/764.

changes may give rise to—for example, change from an engineering use to a blood-boiling factory—this might be questioned.

Certain unusual uses (so-called *sui generis* uses) are not found in any class, and neither are concurrent uses in which the components are in different classes. Non-listed uses include petrol stations, scrapyards, and mineral storeyards, so a change to these uses always requires planning permission. Some uses of land, such as agricultural uses, are simply not mentioned in the Order, because the use of land for agriculture is not development.

Existing uses

Normally, there is a right to carry on the existing use of a site, unless it is in breach of planning control. This is roughly equivalent to a property right attaching to the land and has a distinct value. Of course, when the occupier of land voluntarily changes the use, the existing use right switches from the old to the new use.

Existing use rights may be abandoned by a lengthy period of disuse (*Hartley v. Minister of Housing and Local Government* [1970] 1 QB 413). It is also possible to lose their benefit by carrying out works or changes that effect a *radical change* to the site (*Jennings Motors Ltd v. Secretary of State for the Environment* [1982] QB 541). This applies whether planning permission is obtained or not. If there is a planning permission, any limitations in it will be operative; if there is no permission, then *any* use of the site will be in breach of planning control. Otherwise, an existing use right can only be removed by a discontinuance order (s. 102), or an order revoking planning permission (ss. 97–100). In both cases, compensation is payable.[48]

It is not possible to abandon a planning permission, because it is a public right attaching to the land, not the occupier. This is illustrated by *Pioneer Aggregates (UK) Ltd v. Secretary of State for the Environment* [1984] 3 WLR 32, in which a perpetual permission for quarrying was granted in 1950. Quarrying ceased in 1966 and, when it was recommenced in 1980, the local planning authority argued that the use had been abandoned. The House of Lords decided that the planning permission still applied to permit quarrying and any removal of that right would entail payment of compensation.

This position distinguishes planning control from most other areas of environmental control. As a matter of practice, the rules on compensation mean that there is little scope to vary a planning permission once it has been granted, even though variation and revocation are possible in theory (s. 97). Compensation must be paid even if the circumstances have changed radically in a way that was not foreseen at the time the permission was granted. This emphasizes that a grant of planning permission is an irrevocable event, effectively creating rights for the landowner in a way that a consent from a pollution control agency does not. (For an illustration of an environmentally harmful planning permission having to be purchased by Natural England to further nature conservation interests, see Box 19.4.)

In relation to minerals planning permissions, however, the position is rather different and awareness of the environmental harm that can be caused by permissions granted many decades previously means that old permissions can now have environmental protection conditions attached to them.[49]

---

48 For an example in which compensation was not payable, because of the interrelationship between planning and waste management controls, see *R v. Secretary of State for the Environment and Havering Borough Council, ex parte P F Ahern (London) Ltd* [1998] Env LR 189.

49 See Pt III of the Act, as amended by the 1991 Act, and generally D. Hughes, N. Parpworth, T. Jewell, P. de Prez, and J. Lowther (2002) *Environmental Law*, 4th edn, London: Butterworths, ch. 13.

'Development' activities for which planning permission is granted by statute

Certain activities are automatically granted planning permission under statute. Some use has always been made of a *general* development order. But the 1980s saw the use of new ways of deeming planning permission to be granted in *specific* areas, a departure from the previously uniform approach and a key deregulatory mechanism designed to effect the regeneration of the inner cities. PCPA 2004 provides further ways in which the need to apply for planning permission in the normal way is bypassed.

Development permitted under the General Permitted Development Order

The Town and Country Planning (General Permitted Development) Order 1995[50] (the GPDO), grants automatic planning permission for 33 classes of development, listed and defined in Sch. 1. These are called 'permitted development rights'.

The Town and Country Planning (General Development Procedure) Order 1995[51] (the GDPO), sets out various procedural requirements connected with both permitted development and normal planning applications. Three general types of activity are exempted:

- minor developments;
- developments carried out by a whole range of public services, such as drainage authorities and statutory undertakers;
- favoured activities, especially agriculture and forestry.

The GPDO often includes thresholds above which development consent will still be needed. In the case of certain permitted agricultural and forestry buildings, however, local planning authorities have certain powers over their siting and design, and prior notification now also extends to mobile phone masts. In some cases, permitted development rights are withdrawn for a number of developments, including those which require environmental assessment[52] or which are likely to have a significant impact upon certain areas of nature conservation value. Certain automatic rights are more restricted in national parks, areas of outstanding national beauty (AONBs) and conservation areas.

Under art. 4 of the GPDO, a local planning authority may restrict automatic rights by serving a direction withdrawing the automatic planning permission, in which case permission must be sought in the ordinary way. The direction may be general to a type of development or specific to a site. Such directions normally require the approval of the Secretary of State, must be made before the development is started, and involve the payment of compensation to owners and occupiers, because, effectively, they take away the right to develop.

Development permitted under a Special Development Order

A more specific version of permitted development is provided under s. 59. This process has been used for granting blanket permissions in, for example, new towns and enterprise zones.

---

50 SI 1995/418.

51 SI 1995/419.

52 See the Town and Country Planning (Environmental Assessment) (England and Wales) Regulations 1999, SI 1999/293.

The thermal oxide reprocessing plant (THORP) at Sellafield was also permitted in this way by the Town and Country Planning (Windscale and Calder Works) Special Development Order 1978.[53] In this case, the Order followed a public inquiry and a parliamentary debate, but neither is strictly required.

Development in an enterprise zone

The Local Government, Planning and Land Act 1980 also introduced enterprise zones to encourage business activity. The order establishing an enterprise zone, made by the Secretary of State after some limited publicity, grants automatic planning permission for categories of development specified in the enterprise zone scheme (1990 Act, s. 88), but the local authority draws up the scheme to cover those matters it wishes to permit. Thus, while the Secretary of State formally designates enterprise zones, local authorities decide what is to be permitted. They also remain the local planning authority for other development not covered by the scheme.

An enterprise zone normally lasts for ten years, and involves fiscal and administrative advantages for those in it, as well as the planning exemptions. Few new zones are now expected to be made, but development commenced before the expiry of the scheme retains the benefit of the automatic permission.

Development in a simplified planning zone

Simplified planning zones (SPZs) were introduced in the Housing and Planning Act 1986. As with an enterprise zone scheme, a simplified planning zone scheme grants automatic planning permission for the matters specified in it, but there are no non-planning effects (1990 Act, s. 82). Despite the streamlining of the designation in 1992 (SI 1992/2414), only a handful of SPZs have been made (ten in England).

PCPA 2004, s. 45, limits the discretion enjoyed by local planning authorities whether to make an SPZ and makes them more plan-led. Hence the provisions on SPZs only bite if the need for such a zone is identified in the RSS and must be in conformity with it. Local planning authorities only have a duty to consider whether to impose an SPZ, which they must do if they think that this would be desirable, but the Secretary of State may now, of his own volition, direct that an SPZ is made (as long as the RSS identifies the need for one). An SPZ lasts for up to ten years (which is more flexible than previously, when they had to be in place for a full ten-year period).

Government clearly envisages a small number of SPZs being used to facilitate the development of high-tech business clusters (such as the biotechnology developments around Cambridge). The value of SPZs remains unclear. It is not clear that planning acts as a drag on the economy (see p. 382), requiring the introduction of fast-track measures such as SPZs, and, in any case, the type of development that is anticipated for SPZs will often require environmental impact assessment (EIA), the need for which removes it from automatic permission under the SPZ. It is notable that business responses to the government Green Paper preceding the 2004 Act were 2:1 against the proposal for 'business planning zones', as then proposed.

National parks, AONBs, conservation areas, SSSIs, and designated green belt cannot be the subject of a scheme (s. 87). County matters are also excluded, as are matters covered by the need for an EIA.

---

53 SI 1978/523.

Developments authorized by a government department

If authorization from a government department is needed for a development to be carried out by bodies such as local authorities and statutory undertakers, then that authorization also acts as a deemed planning permission (s. 90). This prevents a duplication of effort, but does result in the decision being taken centrally rather than locally. For example, applications for the construction of projects such as major onshore wind farms would be dealt with like this, because permission is also required from the Department for Business, Enterprise and Regulatory Reform under the Electricity Act 1989 and operators are classed as statutory undertakers.

Local development orders

Section 40 of PCPA 2004 inserts new provisions into the main Act (as ss. 61A–C), which give local planning authorities the power, by a local development order (LDO), to grant planning permission either for a particular development or class of development specified in the order, and to do so for any or all of its area (even a specific site). The main restriction on the use of this enormously wide-ranging power is that orders must implement policies in the local development documents, and the major constraint is that the Secretary of State has a supervisory role in the making of LDOs and can rein in any excessive use of them. LDOs are essentially the converse of art. 4 directions (under the GPDO) and can be thought of as a form of local permitted development rights, but sharing similarities with the reformed simplified planning zones. Development affecting land protected by the EC Habitats Directive (92/43/EEC) and Sch. 1 developments under the EC EIA Directive (85/337/EEC) are excluded from the scope of LDOs.[54]

Special cases

Although not cases of 'deemed permission', streamlined procedures apply in the following cases.

- **Where local authorities grant themselves planning permission (s. 316 and the Town and Country Planning General Regulations 1992[55])**
  The intention to acquire planning permission must be publicized and representations taken into account. But any permission the authority resolves to grant itself is deemed to have been granted by the Secretary of State, so there is no right of appeal; it can be challenged only by judicial review. The possible conflicts of interest mean that the courts interpret the procedural requirements strictly (*Steeples v. Derbyshire County Council* [1985] 1 WLR 256).

- **Where use is made of private or hybrid Acts of Parliament**
  These avoid any of the planning procedures and effectively give the decision to a small parliamentary joint committee, with limited public scrutiny. An example with a significant environmental effect is the Channel Tunnel Act 1987. Nowadays, the Transport and Works Act 1992 tends to be used, principally for railways and tram projects. There will be a public inquiry and the Secretary of State can—and, in practice, will—consider granting deemed planning permission at the same time as any works order is determined.

---

54 See Communities and Local Government Circular 1/2006, *Guidance on Changes to the Development Control System*.
55 SI 1992/1492.

- **In relation to land owned by the Crown and government departments**

  Although immunity, for land owned by the Crown and government departments (but not nationalized industries), from the need to apply for planning permission has been removed under PCPA 2004, fast-track provisions allow a Crown body, for which development is required as a matter of urgent national importance, to apply directly to the Secretary of State for planning permission (who will treat it as if it has been 'called in').

Is planning permission required?

There is a fairly simple mechanism for ascertaining whether planning permission is required. Section 192 provides that anyone may apply to the district planning authority for a certificate of lawfulness of proposed use or development, specifying the proposed use or operation. A certificate must be granted if the authority is satisfied that the use or operation—which must be specific, rather than hypothetical—would be lawful if subsisting or carried out at the time of the application. This is then conclusive of the legality of the development, as long as circumstances do not change before the development takes place. In other words, a certificate is the equivalent of a planning permission for what it covers.

The exact procedures for an application are contained in the GDPO.

Applying for planning permission

Anyone can apply for planning permission. It is not necessary to be the owner or occupier of the property, or even a prospective occupier.

There are several types of permission that the applicant may seek, including full permission or retrospective permission (s. 63(2)), and an application for the renewal of planning permission. In addition, a developer may apply for 'outline permission' only (see s. 92 and GDPO, art. 3). This allows developers to 'test the water' with the local planning authority to see whether a general type of development would be acceptable. 'Reserved matters' include things such as appearance and landscaping; these need not be submitted at this stage, but must generally be approved within three years (GDPO, art. 4). Outline permission may also be sought if the nature of the development means that it is difficult to know what it will eventually contain, for example, retail parks (this has posed problems for developers where EIA is needed—see p. 445).

Recent changes to the regulations governing outline planning permission, motivated by a desire for more 'sustainable design' (designing in, from the outset, energy conservation measures, for example, such as passive solar heating) mean that design is excluded from being a reserved matter and local authorities are increasingly requiring, through supplementary planning documents, natural resource impact assessments for all but relatively minor developments. Hence, 'bare' outline permissions are effectively redundant and the nature of outline planning applications generally will certainly change because of the level of information required to satisfy the local authority about design and environmental impact.[56] This is also rather a good illustration of the way in which the nature of the planning system can be changed by a very small change to a regulation.

Applicants can also ask for a condition of a planning permission to be discharged without putting the rest of the permission at risk (s. 73). This is an important means of removing outdated restrictions and providing a measure of continuing control over development. Attempts to circumvent s. 73 through private negotiation or other means will be given hard scrutiny by the courts, because this jeopardizes the public's rights in the decision-making process (*Henry Boot Homes Ltd v. Bassetlaw District Council* [2002] EWCA Civ 983).

56 P Waddy [2006] JPL 4 (Dec. Supp.); R. Lewis and A. Goodman [2007] JPL 344; M. White [2006] JPL 1262.

Steps for the applicant to take

The applicant must apply on a standard form provided by the local planning authority. It must also notify owners and tenants of the land, and submit a certificate to the authority stating that it has done so. This enables these people to be aware of the application and to make representations that the authority must take into account. It is an offence knowingly to issue a false certificate.

In *Main v. Swansea City Council* (1984) 49 P&CR 26, the Court of Appeal decided that failure to carry out such procedures does not necessarily render a subsequent grant of planning permission void: it all depends on whether anyone with standing has been prejudiced as a result (and, of course, whether they bring any challenge without delay).

Fees are payable for all applications for planning permission and deemed applications in connection with an appeal against an enforcement notice. There are fixed charges for different types of application. At present, the fees do not cover the full administrative cost to the local planning authority of processing applications, but s. 53 of PCPA 2004 amends s. 303, TCPA 1990, and gives greater scope for charges or fees including allowing local planning authorities to set their own (not-for-profit) fees.

Steps for the local planning authority to take

On receipt of an application, the local planning authority will consult with a wide range of public bodies as required for specified situations by the GDPO 1995, art. 10. These include highways authorities, other local authorities, parish and community councils, the Environment Agency, the Department for Environment, Food and Rural Affairs (DEFRA), and the relevant nature conservancy council. There is a code of conduct governing this consultation procedure and those consulted have procedural rights in the event of an appeal. Any representations that are made are material considerations that must be taken into account by the local planning authority before it decides the application. But it must not slavishly follow the advice of another public body; otherwise, the decision will be challengeable for fettering of discretion. The obverse of this is that even where a body such as the Environment Agency has a total policy embargo on assenting to certain types of development that may lead to environmental harm, then granting a planning permission against this advice will not be unlawful (see, for example, *Ynys Mon Borough Council v. Secretary of State for Wales* [1993] JPL 225).[57]

The local planning authority must also publicize *all* applications (GDPO, arts 6–8) as is shown in Table 12.2.

Table 12.2 Publicity requirements for development			
	Local advert	Site notice	Notify neighbours
Major developments, e.g., developments on sites of more than 1 hectare, the building of ten or more houses, developments involving 1,000 m² or more of floor space, and mineral and waste applications	✓		Either/or
Applications requiring EIA, or which do not accord with the provisions of the development plan, or which affect a public right of way	✓	✓	
All other cases			Either/or

57 Discussed in W. Howarth (2001) 'Town and country planning and water quality planning' in C. Miller (ed.) *Planning and Environmental Protection*, Oxford: Hart.

In addition, the Town and Country Planning (Development Plans and Consultation) (Departure) Directions 1999 require that certain applications that do not accord with the provisions of the development plan should be referred to the Secretary of State so that a decision can be made whether to call them in.

A failure to comply with these procedures may invalidate a decision, but will not necessarily do so because of the discretionary nature of judicial review. For example, in one case, a local planning authority had, in error, failed to notify a neighbour of a planning application, but work had begun over two years later. Although the neighbour then promptly sought judicial review, the permission was not quashed despite the seriousness of the procedural error, because of the hardship to the developer (*R (Gavin) v. Haringey London Borough Council* [2003] EWHC 2591).

Determining the planning application

The Secretary of State

The Secretary of State has an unfettered power to call in any planning application for determination (s. 77) and, even as a matter of human rights law, does not need to give reasons for any decision not to call in an application (*R (Adlard) v. Secretary of State for Transport, Local Government and the Regions* [2002] EWCA Civ 735).[58] This immediately transfers jurisdiction from the local planning authority to the Secretary of State. This power is used sparingly—usually only for matters of national or regional importance or of local controversy, such as significant developments in the green belt.[59] There is a right to a public inquiry unless waived by the parties and the Secretary of State, and one is normally held. The procedures are virtually the same as those for appeals, suitably amended to provide for this being a first determination. There is no formal power to request the Secretary of State to call in an application: objectors should write to the Secretary of State putting their case for such an action. The Secretary of State also has related powers to make directions to local planning authorities—for example, to consult him before deciding an application (GDPO, art. 10(3)).

A further exception to the local planning authority being the decision maker is in relation to major infrastructure projects in England.[60] The context behind these specific proposals was concern at the length of time taken to conduct certain high-profile inquiries. Prior to the passage of PCPA 2004, the government originally proposed that Parliament make the decision in principle, leaving operational matters to a subsequent inquiry, but this was dropped (the issue has been returned to in the current Planning Reform Bill—see p. 426). Section 44 of PCPA 2004 makes comparatively modest reforms, inserting ss 76A and 76B into TCPA 1990. These give the Secretary of State a power to call in applications that are of national or regional importance. The difference between these new provisions and the existing call-in powers under s. 77 is that, in the interests of speed, the Secretary of State may appoint more than one inspector to hear different aspects of the inquiry. The presumption in favour of the development plan does not apply to such cases.

---

58 This decision has been criticized for being out of step with the more purposive approach to public participation and citizen rights in cases such as *Burkett* (see p. 318), which was decided one week after *Adlard* (see [2002] JPL 1379).

59 See ODPM (2005) *The Planning System: General Principles*, para. 26.

60 Originally, government proposed that Parliament should be given the power to decide in principle whether such developments should go ahead—a proposal that met with fierce criticism, but also serious practical problems in terms of parliamentary procedure.

The local planning authority

In the usual case, however, a local planning authority has eight weeks in which to decide the application (in accordance with the substantive rules outlined below), after which time, the applicant can appeal as if the application were refused (GDPO, art. 20).[61] This target is met in around 80 per cent of cases. The 'Best Value' reform target—under the Local Government Act 1999—is that authorities should delegate 90 per cent of decisions to officers.

Whether the application is first determined by the local planning authority or the Secretary of State, the decision maker may grant planning permission unconditionally, grant permission subject to conditions, or refuse permission. The decision must be in writing, and must include reasons for the decision and the imposition of any conditions. These are normally brief, but, in certain situations, a failure to provide reasons may make the decision void.[62] Public registers of all applications and decisions must be maintained (s. 69, and GDPO, art. 25). These, and the enforcement registers (see p. 306), are an invaluable guide to the planning history of a site, but increasing pressure to accommodate meaningful public participation means that the register now contains much more information on the application itself, including (up to a point) obligations from developers.

Summary of rights of third parties

Third parties or objectors have limited specific rights under the legislation, although statutory publicity is required for all applications and the Local Government (Access to Information) Act 1985 ensures the right to attend council meetings. Any representations made to the local planning authority must be considered as a material consideration. Furthermore, the local planning authority is now obliged to give a summary of reasons and relevant plan policies for *granting* planning permission: this is a human rights requirement, but has been formalized in the Town and Country Planning (General Development Procedure) (England) (Amendment) Order 2003 (amending art. 22 of the GDPO). Previously, all that was required was that reasons were given if permission was *refused*, because applicants would need to know this information to judge whether to appeal. Formally, developers are still treated more favourably, because clear and precise full reasons must be given when permission is refused or—as is invariably the case—conditions are imposed.) There is no right for third parties to address meetings of the local planning authority—although, in practice, most do allow very brief statements to be made—and no right to insist on a public hearing or inquiry.

In the UK, third parties have no right to appeal against a planning decision[63] and must apply for judicial review of any adverse decision. The expanded scope of the duty to give reasons when planning permission is granted may prove useful to third parties—developers are often successful in arguing that inadequate reasons have been given. But they still need standing, to act without delay, and be able to afford the large costs involved, and, in practice, have very little chance of success. Only local planning authority decisions can be subject to judicial review: decisions of the Secretary of State are immune from challenge except under s. 288 (see p. 421). If the applicant brings an appeal, third parties have wider procedural rights at that stage.

---

61 Even after this period, the local planning authority may reach a substantive decision, the intention being to prevent appeals going to the Secretary of State if this can be avoided: see PCPA 2004, s. 50, adding TCPA 1990, s. 78A.

62 *R (Wall) v. Brighton and Hove City Council* [2004] EWHC 2582 (Admin), discussed in D. Scharf [2005] JPL 747.

63 For criticism of this on human rights and Aarhus Convention grounds, see M. Grant [2000] JPL 1215, and see generally M. Purdue (2001) 2 Env LR 83. Both of these pre-dated the HL decision in *Alconbury* (see p. 380).

The local planning authority's discretion

In deciding whether or not to grant permission, the local planning authority *'shall have regard to the provisions of the development plan, so far as material to the application, and to any other material considerations'* (s. 70(2), TCPA 1990). Under PCPA 2004, s. 38(6):

If, in making any determination under the planning Acts, regard is to be had to the development plan, the determination shall be made in accordance with the development plan unless material considerations indicate otherwise.

The Secretary of State is subject to the same requirements in relation to decisions that the developer appeals (under s. 78) or which the Secretary of State himself calls in (under s. 77). It is central to an understanding of planning law to appreciate the scope of the above provisions:

- it gives the local planning authority a wide *discretion* whether or not to grant permission;

- this discretion must be exercised on grounds of *planning policy*, taking the development plan as the starting point.

(a) The role of the Secretary of State and the courts

The principal means of controlling this discretion is through the appeals system. The Secretary of State (usually through an inspector) considers afresh the whole application and can form his own opinion on what planning policy requires, effectively exercising a stranglehold over the appeals process. He can consider both legal grounds—for example, that the objections are not planning objections—and policy grounds—for example, that too much weight was attached to objections.

By contrast, the courts will only interfere if there has been some illegality in the decision-making process and ordinary principles of public law are applied. As long as the policies that are applied are lawful—that is, relevant to planning—the courts do not interfere with their content. This is effectively a principle of non-intervention in policy matters. Accordingly, the *weight* given to any policy is a matter for the decision maker, unless the decision is perverse. As Lord Hoffmann said in *Tesco Stores Ltd v. Secretary of State for the Environment and ors* [1995] 1 WLR 759, 780 (discussed in more detail in Case 12.4): *'If there is one principle of planning law more firmly settled than any other, it is that matters of planning judgment are within the exclusive province of the local planning authority or the Secretary of State.'*

But it is impermissible to have an absolute policy or to apply it rigidly, because this would constitute an unlawful fettering of discretion (*Stringer v. Minister of Housing and Local Government* [1970] 1 WLR 1281). The courts thus see their role as ensuring that decisions are made rationally in the light of all planning considerations. (This is ensured by the requirement that *reasons* must be given for decisions, which now extends to giving reasons for granting as well as refusing planning permission—see p. 404.) One difficulty, however, is in how the courts should approach cases in which the planning legislation states that particular weight should be given to one factor. This arises with the statutory presumption in favour of the development plan.

(b) The presumption in favour of the development plan

The Planning and Compensation Act 1991 introduced a presumption in favour of following the provisions of the development plan, because it replaced the existing duty to 'have regard to' the plan with a duty to act 'in accordance with' it. Thus, the period of 'market-led' or 'developer-led' planning was replaced by 'plan-led' planning. The presumption in favour of the plan is now contained in s. 38(6) of the 2004 Act.

In the leading case on this provision, the House of Lords held that the presumption in favour of the plan is neither a 'governing' nor a 'paramount' one (*City of Edinburgh Council v. Secretary of State for Scotland* [1998] JPL 224). Nor does a decision maker have to follow any particular procedure; the plan and the other considerations can, if preferred, be taken together, and the plan need not be considered first in time. The application of the *City of Edinburgh* case to England and Wales was confirmed in *R v. Leominster District Council, ex parte Pothecary* [1998] JPL 335, in which it was said that what is important is for how the decision maker has approached the duty to be apparent.

Thus, the planning system may be 'plan-led', but this is no guarantee that the plan will always be followed, because the weight to be accorded to the plan remains, ultimately, a matter for the decision maker. One point that has therefore acquired increased significance is the *interpretation* of development plans. In the past, it has often been assumed that this is a matter of law for the courts to decide. This is undoubtedly correct, but it does not solve the question of whether the courts will impose their own interpretation or will be content to adopt the less interventionist method of reviewing whether the decision maker's interpretation was a reasonable one. This is crucial to the extent to which the courts will interfere with decisions via s. 38(6) of the 2004 Act. Cases such as *Ex parte Pothecary*, as well as experience, suggest that the normal, non-interventionist approach will be used, thus reinforcing the view that the real change in planning that was envisaged in the 1990s will result from actual changes in policy rather than from anything the courts require. Or, as Lord Hope put it in *City of Edinburgh*: 'It would be a mistake to think that the effect of [the development plan presumption] *was to increase the power of the court to intervene in decisions about planning control.*'[64]

There is guidance on the basic approach that decision makers ought to employ in determining applications or appeals.[65] But this does little more than restate s. 38(6) and is notably short on fleshing out the policy strength to be given to the plan. For example, previous guidance from 1997 stipulated that, if the proposal was in conflict with the plan, then the developer would normally have to produce 'convincing reasons' to show why the plan should not have applied and that the weight to be given to the plan would be strengthened if the Secretary of State has not formally intervened at the plan-making stage. This change of wording may simply be a product of the government's desire that planning policy statements (PPSs) should be shorter documents. But an alternative view is that, despite the stated commitment to a plan-led system of development management, planning authorities and the Secretary of State will enjoy slightly greater flexibility in their planning decisions. This seems to be borne out by *R (on the application of the Council for National Parks Ltd) v. Pembrokeshire Coast National Park Authority and ors* [2005] EWCA Civ 888, a case in which a strong restraint policy, in the development plan, about development in the national park clashed with later policy guidance, which was more sympathetic to allowing development where local interests demanded. The Court of Appeal upheld the planning permission even though the policy guidance covered the same ground as the development plan. Some feel that this decision undercuts 'plan-led planning' if a material consideration can override a plan policy in this way. In this case, the courts seemed unprepared to allow the provisions of the development plan to prevail in the face of later, and less restrictive, policy guidance. In doing so, the courts are, in effect, not intervening on the decision maker's weighing of the changes in policy guidance set against the relative certainty created by the development plan.

(c) Other material considerations

The key point as to the meaning of 'other material considerations' is that the Act gives no guidance on this term, which has fallen to the courts to be interpreted. To be material, a consideration has to be material to planning and material to the application. Certain matters will always be taken into account: non-statutory plans, government planning guidance

---

64 At 226.
65 ODPM (2005) para. 10.

such as circulars and PPGs (*Pye Ltd v. West Oxfordshire District Council* [1982] JPL 577),[66] the results of consultations, and any representations made by third parties or objectors. Any representations made by a regulator such as the Environment Agency will be a material consideration that must be weighed alongside other material considerations (but not, as noted at p. 409, slavishly followed), although there are cases that suggest that good reasons must be given for not following such advice.[67] Other matters, such as impacts on amenity, on the local economy, transport and highways considerations, and the balance of land use in the area, will nearly always be material on the facts.

A range of other matters have also been held to be material in certain circumstances:

- the effect on private rights (*Stringer v. Minister of Housing and Local Government* [1970] 1 WLR 1281);

- the existing use of the site (*Clyde & Co. v. Secretary of State for the Environment* [1977] 1 WLR 926);

- the personal circumstances of the occupier (*Tameside Metropolitan Borough Council v. Secretary of State for the Environment* [1984] JPL 180);

- the precedent effect of a decision (*Collis Radio Ltd v. Secretary of State for the Environment* (1975) 29 P&CR 390);

- the availability of alternative sites (see Box 12.6).

BOX 12.6 **Alternatives**

The consideration of alternatives is increasingly central to environmental decision making. Examples include the substitution principle in chemicals regulation (see p. 56) and the status given to considering alternatives in environmental impact assessment (EIA) and strategic environmental assessment (SEA). In planning law, the general rule developed by the courts is that:

> the consideration of alternative *sites*[68] would only be relevant to a planning application in exceptional circumstances…such circumstances will particularly arise where the proposed development, although desirable in itself, involves on the site proposed such conspicuous adverse effects that the possibility of an alternative site lacking such drawbacks necessarily itself becomes, in the mind of a reasonable local authority, a relevant planning consideration upon the application in question.

(*R (Jones) v. North Warwickshire Borough Council* [2001] EWCA Civ 315, [30], emphasis added)

Examples that the courts have given include developments such as airports, petrochemical plants, and nuclear power stations—all of which, of course, require EIA—in relation to which, at most, only a very limited number of permissions are likely to be granted. But at the other end of the scale, in relation to which alternatives will not need to be considered, are development proposals under which the environmental impact is minimal and the planning objections are not especially strong.

In *Jodie Phillips v. First Secretary of State and ors* [2003] EWHC 2415, the siting of a 3G mobile phone mast was challenged. The development plan provided that, in cases in which there would be a conflict with environmental objectives, it would need to be demonstrated that there were no

---

66 Note that the meaning of words in policy guidance is a matter of law, but that the courts will only intervene if a planning authority's interpretation is perverse: *R v. Derbyshire County Council, ex parte Woods* [1998] Env LR 277.

67 See, e.g., *Goldfinch (Projects) Ltd v. National Assembly for Wales* [2002] EWHC 1275.

68 See further critique of the 'spatial fix' approach at p. 426.

possibility of sharing existing facilities, no satisfactory alternative sites, and no reasonable possibility of using existing structures, which is broadly the position in the relevant policy guidance (PPG8). Richards J held that the test in *Jones* was not exhaustive and that policy guidance may require alternatives to be considered even if, as here, there was no proven environmental harm: '… *the question, it seems to me, is not just "is this an acceptable location" but "is this the best location."*' This resulted in a different approach to that of *Jones*, which took, as the starting point, that alternatives would not have to be considered if the development proposed was acceptable in planning terms (an approach that emphasizes the rights of owners to develop their land, rather than the public interest in achieving, for example, the optimum environmental decision). The judge held that the Planning Inspector might have taken a different view on whether there was 'planning harm' if the alternative site put forward by the claimant had been given proper consideration. Put differently, the fears about the siting of the mast—in this case, near to a nursery school—might have been given more weight if the alternative site had been properly considered in the decision-making process.

The *Phillips* case illustrates the strength of policy guidance even over the development plan. The implication of this decision is likely to be felt in other areas of planning in which a 'sequential test' ranking sites according to their degree of desirability is used—for example, out-of-town retail development. The case is also a good example of how public concerns about environmental and health impacts will be material considerations, regardless of the degree to which they might be said to be objectively unjustified (see p. 425). But it also shows some difficulties with the concept of 'planning harm'—a concept that is being gradually eroded as planning tries to become more concerned with positive management than with negative controls.

The achievement of a separate planning objective of the local planning authority can also be material. Protecting the Royal Opera House by allowing it to raise funds by carrying out office development that would not otherwise have been permitted has been upheld (*R v. Westminster City Council, ex parte Monahan* [1988] JPL 557). This principle has been used to fund the conservation of wildlife sites, such as the London Wetland Centre, by allowing a limited amount of otherwise unacceptable development on the site.

It should be noted that emerging plans (*R v. City of London Corporation, ex parte Allan* (1980) 79 LGR 223) and whether the application is premature in the light of such plans (*Arlington Securities Ltd v. Secretary of State for the Environment* (1989) 57 P&CR 407) are not 'the development plan', but material considerations to be weighed in the balance. The closer a plan is to being adopted, the more weight it will carry. Equally, supplementary planning documents are not 'the plan', but material considerations. While the need for a development may also be material, it is not the job of the local authority to second-guess the financial viability of a scheme.[69]

Any human rights that are engaged by a planning decision will be a material consideration.[70] Following *Hatton v. United Kingdom* (2003) 37 EHRR 28 (see Case 11.1), it may be that acting lawfully under a planning permission would mean, for example, that there has been no 'domestic irregularity' so that substantive Convention rights would not have been breached. If this view were to prevail, it might suggest that decision makers should have an even greater onus to consider the human rights implications of their decisions.

---

69 In the future, the 'need' for certain developments may be decided centrally—see discussion of the current Planning Reform Bill at p.426.

70 For discussion of how decision makers should approach human rights concerns—in particular, Art. 8 (right to a home)—see the (divided) Court of Appeal in *First Secretary of State and ors v. Chichester District Council* [2004] EWCA Civ 1248.

Environmental considerations as material considerations

In relation to environmental matters, it is clear that planning permission may be refused on a number of grounds. An industrial development may be refused because of possible pollution or safety problems—for example, it is possible to prevent a plant handling dangerous substances, or a waste disposal site, from being sited near to a sensitive watercourse. A housing estate may be refused because of the inadequacy of the existing sewerage provision. The impact of noise or light on neighbouring properties will also be material. In a recent case, one of the reasons given by a local authority for refusing permission for development of an airport was climate change. Of course, environmental considerations will not necessarily point only one way. A good illustration is the Secretary of State's rejection of a bypass around Hastings. The South East Regional Assembly, and the county and district councils, unanimously supported the bypass, in part to alleviate air pollution problems caused by traffic congestion, but these were outweighed by strong conservation and countryside considerations.

There are also a number of situations in which EC obligations will be material considerations in planning decisions. Often the mechanism used for bringing these to planning authorities' attention is government guidance. For example, PPS 9 gives advice on the extent to which nature conservation interests protected under EC law should be taken into account.

But these are only some of the matters that must be taken into account. The final decision involves a balancing of all of the factors. A clear example of the discretion given to the local planning authority to decide that other factors outweigh environmental ones is *R v. Exeter City Council, ex parte JL Thomas & Co. Ltd* [1991] 1 QB 471, in which a decision to grant planning permission for a residential development that would be likely to lead to private nuisance claims by its future occupants was unchallengeable in public law.[71] That said, a planning permission cannot ignore external sources of pollution—for example, in determining a planning application for flats next to a nightclub (*R (O'Dwyer) v. Westminster City Council* [2006] EWHC 3016).

The extent to which environmental risks, 'genuine' or perceived, amount to material considerations is considered in more detail on p. 425.

The weight given to environmental considerations

The basic starting point is, as noted elsewhere, that the planning authority can give a material consideration any weight, or no weight at all (see p. 405). The weight given to environmental material considerations is illustrated in Case 12.3.

CASE 12.3 Weighting environmental material considerations—*West Coast Wind Farms Ltd v. Secretary of State for the Environment and North Devon DC* [1996] JPL 767

In this case, an application to construct two wind farms was refused. Although government planning advice at the time supported energy from wind, it also recognized the need to protect local environmental quality and this latter factor was accorded more weight. The Court of Appeal held that there was no policy presumption in favour of such developments, even if they were a policy aim. Although such sources might be 'needed' in a general sense, each application still had to be decided

---

71 Note that, following *Kane v. New Forest District Council (No. 1)* [2001] EWCA Civ 878, which was influenced in part by developments in human rights law, there is no general immunity for local planning authorities from claims in negligence (or, it is submitted, in nuisance) and, in principle, a local planning authority might be liable if it were to insist on a particular design feature that caused an actionable loss (see A. Samuels [2003] JPL 1514).

on its merits. In such situations, of course, refusals can be appealed and, if the policy is genuine, the Secretary of State can enforce it appropriately.

The case of wind farm development is interesting because, in 2004, the relevant policy guidance was revised because it was thought that too few developments were being granted permission (see HC Environmental Audit Committee, Session 2001–02, Fifth Report, paras 58–62). PPS 22 (2004) *Renewable Energy* now states (emphasis added):

> The wider environmental and economic benefits of all proposals for renewable energy projects, whatever their scale, are material considerations that should be given *significant weight* in determining whether proposals should be granted planning permission

Moreover, meeting one of the problems in the *West Coast* case: '*Planning authorities should not . . . reject planning applications simply because the level of output is small.*' The guidance also requires that regional spatial strategies (RSSs) should contain renewable energy targets and that the '*fact that a target has been reached should not be used in itself as a reason for refusing planning permission for further renewable energy projects*'. Under the revised guidance, therefore, decision makers must tilt the scales in favour of renewable energy projects.

A further point is worth making here. Toke[72] looks at the variables affecting onshore wind farm planning decisions—that is, planning officers' opinions, elected councillors' attitudes, the role played by NGOs such as the Campaign to Protect Rural England (CPRE), and central government policy. This research found a significant shift in the success of planning applications in the period 2001–03, because planning officers perceived central government policy to be moving in favour of wind farms (in large part because of the 2003 Energy White Paper). As noted above, the formal expression of this shift (at least in England, which is the area that Toke considers) did not take place until the relevant guidance was issued in 2004. This research shows the importance to decision making not only of formal planning policy documents, but also of more subtle influences—and the courts would undoubtedly consider this was a material consideration.

The more difficult situation is that in which an obviously harmful activity is consented to because each individual contribution to it is minor when looked at in isolation.

An especially difficult issue is how much weight should be given to statutory obligations, especially those emanating from EC environmental Directives.[73] In *R (Murray) v. Derbyshire County Council* [2002] Env LR 28, it was held that, while the waste management objectives in Art. 4 of the Waste Framework Directive (2006/12/EC) and its implementing regulations were clearly material considerations in deciding whether to grant planning permission for an extension to a landfill:

> an objective . . . is something different from a material consideration . . . An objective which is obligatory must always be kept in mind when making a decision even while the decision maker has regard to other material considerations.[74]

But the Court of Appeal did not favour creating a hierarchy of material considerations '*whereby the law would require decision makers to give different weight to different*

---

72 D. Toke (2005) 33(12) Energy Policy 1527.

73 For a somewhat dated, but still useful, overview, see M. Purdue (1997) 'The impact of EC environmental law on planning law in the United Kingdom' in J. Holder (ed.) *The Impact of EC Environmental Law in the United Kingdom*, Chichester: John Wiley. See also M. Tewdwr-Jones and R. Williams (2001) *The European Dimension of British Planning*, London: Routledge.

74 At [53].

considerations.[75] It did suggest that there may be cases in which it was apparent that the objective had been flagrantly disregarded, in which case the obligation would be breached. It is not clear, however, that this will necessarily be apparent at the time that the decision is made; courts generally place faith in decision makers and problems may only emerge with hindsight. There then arises the very tricky issue of whether, perhaps some years later, the granting of the permission will require re-examination.[76] (In relation to planning and pollution prevention obligations, see also *Blewett v. Derbyshire County Council* [2004] ECA Civ 1508, discussed in detail in Case 14.1.)

Planning conditions

Section 70(1) permits the local planning authority (and the Secretary of State on appeal) to impose such conditions 'as it thinks fit'. This wide discretionary power is limited by statutory guidance in ss 72 and 75, judicial control over what is permissible, and central government policy.

Statutory guidance is limited and relatively unimportant. Section 72 states that conditions attached to other land under the control of the applicant and conditions requiring commencement of the development within a specified time are permissible. It also allows for temporary permissions that can be used to grant planning permission on a trial basis, which can be especially valuable for innovative kinds of 'low-impact developments'.

What are of greater practical importance are the legal tests for the validity of conditions developed over the years by the courts. In contrast with the decisions on material considerations, these have produced some rather restrictive results, possibly because the cases were mainly decided earlier, when a more overt policy of protecting private property rights applied. In the leading case of *Newbury District Council v. Secretary of State for the Environment* [1981] AC 578, the House of Lords held that to be valid, conditions must:

(a) be imposed for a planning purpose and not for an ulterior motive;

(b) fairly and reasonably relate to the development permitted;

(c) not be perverse ('*so unreasonable that no reasonable authority could have imposed them*').

The courts have also held that a condition should not be 'hopelessly uncertain', although they have taken a broad view as to what this must entail, so that there may be considerable scope for saying that the terms of a condition are ascertainable (*Alderson v. Secretary of State for the Environment* (1984) 49 P&CR 307).

Ground (a) above goes to the nature and limits of planning itself. The courts have done this by concluding that certain matters of a social planning nature do not relate to town and country planning. For example, in *R v. Hillingdon London Borough Council, ex parte Royco Homes Ltd* [1974] 2 QB 720, a condition requiring that houses be occupied by people on the local authority housing list, who should then be granted ten years' security of tenure, was held to be illegal. The burden of housing people in need was placed by statute on the housing authority, not private developers. But the provision of affordable housing has been held to be for a planning purpose, in part because policy guidance has made it so, but also because the stress is on the type of housing, rather on the occupiers (*Mitchell v. Secretary of State for the Environment* [1994] JPL 916, and see PPS 3, *Housing*).[77]

75 Ibid.

76 Which raises very tricky issues about compensation for the developer and remedies for any affected individuals.

77 Should a developer be required to provide affordable housing when the proposed development would not cause planning harm without it? The answer now seems to be clear, because PPS1 moves away from notions of planning harm to a more positive vision of planning that includes, in the sustainable development equation, social exclusion; see also p. 382.

Such issues to do with the planning system and social exclusion make it arguable whether the nature and scope of the planning system today is the same as it was in 1974, not least because of the wider policy objectives of using the planning system to achieve sustainability (see PPS1), which necessarily involves going beyond issues of the mere use and character of land. In recent years, the courts have not been asked to rule on the nature of planning, which might be explained by the lack of anyone with sufficient practical interest to do so.

Ground (b) requires that conditions have some geographic and functional link to the site to which the application relates. So a condition requiring works to be carried out on land neither included in the application, nor under the control of the applicant, is illegal (*Ladbrokes Ltd v. Secretary of State* [1981] JPL 427). Thus, a requirement to screen a site by planting trees on neighbouring land will be illegal unless the land is under the applicant's control. But it is possible to make development conditional on the completion of work off-site, such as requiring infrastructure works (roads, sewers, etc.) to be satisfactory before development commences (*Grampian Regional Council v. Aberdeen District Council* (1983) 47 P&CR 633). These are consequently known as 'Grampian conditions'.

Finally, a condition can be struck down if it is perverse (ground (c)). This test has normally been used to prevent conditions undermining private property rights without compensation. A prime example is *Hall & Co. Ltd v. Shoreham-by-Sea Urban District Council* [1964] 1 WLR 240, in which a condition was attached to a permission for industrial development that required an access road to be built on the developer's land at its expense and dedicated to the public. The Court of Appeal held the condition illegal, even though it accepted that it was beneficial in planning terms because it created a usable access to otherwise inaccessible land. The position is no different if the developer suggests or accepts such an imposition (*Bradford Metropolitan Council v. Secretary of State for the Environment* (1987) 53 P&CR 55). This approach effectively frustrated the use of conditions to secure 'planning gain' for local communities, leading to the rise in the use of planning agreements and obligations for this purpose (see below).

Conditions and policy

On appeal, the Secretary of State can add, omit, or amend any conditions as part of the total rehearing of the issues. This can be done on legal, factual, or policy grounds, so an understanding of the Secretary of State's policy on conditions is essential.

Circular 11/95 requires conditions to be:

(a) necessary;

(b) relevant to planning;

(c) relevant to the development permitted;

(d) enforceable;

(e) precise;

(f) reasonable.

In addition, it lays down some very important general policy tests (at para. 15):

- '*As a matter of policy, a condition ought not to be imposed unless there is a definite need for it*';

- '*a condition should not be retained unless there are sound and clear cut reasons for doing so*';

- a condition '*requires special and precise justification*' if planning permission would not be refused if the condition were omitted.

The local planning authority should also consider whether the imposition of any conditions may render an otherwise objectionable development acceptable, so as to save the application from being refused.

These are not legal requirements, but a local planning authority ignores these tests at its peril because of the applicant's right of appeal. It also appears, from *Times Investments Ltd v. Secretary of State for the Environment* [1990] JPL 433, that a failure to have regard to these policies—for example, not to demonstrate the harm that would be caused by omitting a particular condition—may render the decision illegal for failure to have regard to a material consideration. Once again, therefore, the Secretary of State's guidance imposes significant restrictions on the decisions that may be reached.

Finally, note that current guidance refers to conditions being imposed if they are 'fair, reasonable and practicable' (para. 21), which seems to dispense with any necessity test.[78]

Planning conditions and environmental protection

Planning conditions can therefore be used to control a range of environmentally harmful activities, especially if these are not controlled by other regimes. An illustrative example is imposing conditions on new development limiting car parking spaces. Conditions may even be imposed in cases in which, as part of an enforcement appeal, it is thought better to grant retrospective permission if this will remedy existing environmental problems. This may still fairly and reasonably relate to the development, even though planning conditions are generally aimed at preventing future harm (*Cheshire County Council v. Secretary of State for the Environment* [1995] Env LR 316).

One particular issue relates to the use of planning conditions to achieve continuing environmental objectives—especially pollution control. There is a slender, but marked, distinction between the policy tests laid down in PPS 23 (*Planning and Pollution Control*), and the relevant circulars and the legal tests laid down in *Newbury District Council v. Secretary of State for the Environment* [1981] AC 578. One of the important differences is that the legal tests do not suggest that a condition will be unlawful if it duplicates other statutory controls. As long as the matter that is to be subject to the control sought has a planning purpose (a concept that seems to widen with the passing years), it is lawful.[79]

On the other hand, government policy in PPS 23 (echoing the RCEP Fifth Report) makes it clear that planning conditions should not be used to deal with difficulties that are the subject of controls under other legislation. The justification for this approach is that it prevents an unnecessary duplication of control or any argument over the nature of the conditions that are to be imposed. Whether it is desirable in policy terms is another matter and local planning authorities will always be wary of imposing conditions that duplicate other controls, because the Secretary of State will, more often than not, amend the condition on appeal.

The problems of overlapping conditions can be significant in pollution control. The Department of the Environment 1992 report, *Planning, Pollution and Waste Management*, found that there were two main circumstances under which planning conditions were used in the control of pollution. First, there were occasions on which the only—or, in some cases, the most straightforward—means of controlling pollution was by imposing planning conditions (for example, the control of groundwater pollution from direct or indirect sources, such as storage tanks).

---

78 ODPM (2005) para. 20.

79 If an aspect of the development is governed by another regulatory regime, then this might not be the subject of planning conditions, because the planning condition could require action over which the developer has no control—as with the planning condition regulating aircraft flight paths, which was unlawful, because this is governed by the Civil Aviation Authority under civil aviation legislation: *British Airports Authority v. Secretary of State for Scotland* [1980] JPL 260. This elevates the 'enforceability' test to a legal, rather than policy, test.

Secondly, conditions were used to override existing pollution control systems in circumstances in which it was argued that planning authorities had little confidence in the pollution control authorities and wished to maintain a degree of control to protect the amenities of the area. Examples included a condition to impose a release limit that would run with the land, rather than be associated with a licence to operate, and a condition to impose a release limit in a case in which the planning authority was concerned that the relevant pollution control authority would not enforce its own controls.

These types of condition were, and still are, clearly contrary to policy, but not unlawful. For example, an inspector imposed an overlapping condition on sulphur dioxide emissions in the planning appeal involving Ferro-Alloys and Metals Smelter in Glossop (see [1990] 2 LMELR 176). In that case, the planning authority was concerned about the enforcement record of Her Majesty's Inspectorate of Pollution (HMIP) and by its remarks that it might revise its condition downwards or not enforce it, and this was accepted by the inspector as good grounds for imposing the condition.

Although the powers (and resources) of the Environment Agency have improved since then, the legality of the determination still appears correct. This is because cases such as *Gateshead Metropolitan Borough Council v. Secretary of State for the Environment* [1995] JPL 432, *R v. Bolton Metropolitan Council, ex parte Kirkman* [1998] Env LR 719, and, most recently, *Hopkins Developments Ltd v. First Secretary of State and North Wiltshire District Council* [2007] Env LR 14 (see Case 14.8) go no further than to say that the existence of specialist (and effective) pollution control agencies is no more than a material consideration for the planning authority to weigh in the balance. Unless there are overriding obligations (in *Kirkman*, duties under the EC Waste Framework Directive were important), the courts will not say that the existence of such agencies means that the local planning authority cannot consider matters within their powers, because this would be unduly fettering discretion,[80] and the courts will not interfere, unless it is wholly unreasonable, with the planning decision maker's judgment about the risk of pollution.

The practical position therefore appears to be that, on the one hand, if a planning authority is generally in favour of a development, it may be content to leave a wide range of pollution control and environmental protection issues to specialist regulators, deflecting attention away from its own powers. On the other hand, if the development is less central to the local economy and of a kind that has caused concerns to residents, it may seek to impose conditions to prevent local environmental harm, knowing that such conditions may be overturned on appeal. This would allow it to enforce via, for example, a breach of condition notice, rather than to rely on enforcement by agencies less accountable to the local electorate.[81]

Planning obligations and contributions

The town and country planning legislation has always included powers under which a local planning authority could enter into an agreement relating to the development or use of land. For many years, little use was made of these powers, but, in the 1970s and 1980s, they came to be seen as a mechanism for the provision of some form of 'planning gain'—that is, some gain to the community that would not necessarily have been obtained without the agreement. But planning gain may take different forms (a useful model for thinking about the role of this mechanism is given in Box 12.7).

---

80 Not infrequently, planning controls on noise will be imposed on developments subject to IPPC (which includes noise emissions within the scope of control). See also *Blewett v. Derbyshire County Council* [2005] Env LR 15, regarding the role of the Environment Agency and local planning authorities as regards landfill.

81 For examples of the problems faced by local authorities when dealing with odour nuisances, see *Tameside Metropolitan Borough Council v. Smith Brothers (Hyde) Ltd* [1996] Env LR D4 and *R v. Secretary of State for the Environment, ex parte West Wiltshire District Council* [1996] Env LR 312.

BOX 12.7 **Models of environmental planning gain**[82]

Objective	Example	Comment notice
Securing implementation	Infrastructure improvements	Minimalist; facilitative
Meeting environmental costs	Habitat replacement	Compensatory
Advancing environmental needs	Securing net habitat gain	Environmentally redistributive

The increased importance of agreements—which might be positive or negative in character and which might require money to be paid to the local planning authority—illustrated the negotiative nature of modern town planning and showed that the concept of planning, as a strict system of regulation in which the regulator imposes restrictions on a developer, had become rather outdated. But it also gave rise to some concern: there was no need for approval of agreements by the Secretary of State, no provision for publicity or appeal, limited scrutiny of the content of agreements, and limited potential for a successful challenge by a third party. As a result, as the Nolan Committee (1997, Cm 3702) verified, cases arose in which local planning authorities 'sold' planning permission to the highest bidder or in which the developer effectively offered a bribe in return for favourable treatment.

When the Town and Country Planning Act was consolidated in 1990, the provisions on agreements were included as s. 106. Under the Planning and Compensation Act 1991, however, developers could give binding unilateral undertakings as well as to enter into agreements. 'Planning obligations' could therefore cover both agreements and undertakings. Although there was no wholesale use of unilateral undertakings as a 'developer's charter', they could be used effectively when the local planning authority was unwilling to agree terms. Their greatest advantage to developers was on appeal: a developer could offer an undertaking and the Secretary of State (subject to the tests detailed below) would have to take it into account in deciding whether to allow the appeal.[83]

The law will be further changed under the 2004 Act, the existing law being seen by government as *'opaque, slow, unfair, complex and reactive'*.[84] Although the government's original intention was to implement a tariff system—for example, paying a contribution based on the size of a development and with no element of negotiation—in the end, the 2004 Act will (probably in 2008 or 2009) repeal s. 106 and give the Secretary of State powers, through regulations, to make provision for what are termed 'planning contributions' (s. 46). Section 46 enables developers to pay the local planning authority—in money or quantified benefits in kind, or a combination of the two—according to scales that, most likely, will be set out in development plan documents. The central purpose behind planning contributions therefore is to allow developers to pay a predetermined charge for various services or facilities associated with development, rather than to have to negotiate these on a case-by-case basis. For example, contributions towards public transport might be made on this basis (in practice, this was often covered by supplementary planning guidance). Contributions are therefore intended to be less reactive by being plan-led.[85] But developers may depart from the predetermined scales of contribution if they wish and provision for negotiated agreements

82 Adapted from M. Loughlin (1981) OJLS 61, and P. Healey, M. Purdue, and F. Ennis (1995) *Negotiating Development, Rationales and Practice for Development Obligations and Planning Gain*, London: E & FN Spon.

83 And the local planning authority has limited discretion to avoid entering into an agreement subsequently: see *R v. Warwickshire County Council, ex parte Powergen plc* [1997] JPL 843, further stressing the influence of the Secretary of State.

84 ODPM (2004) *Contributing to Sustainable Communities: A New Approach To Planning Obligations.*

85 For an analysis of how planning obligations subverted the plan-led approach, see F. Cornford [2002] JPL 796.

(similar to what are now planning obligations) will almost certainly be retained (which, it is recognized, will probably be more relevant for mitigating environmental harms on specific development sites, in relation to which greater flexibility is generally needed).[86]

Planning obligations and contributions do not replace the need to seek planning permission in the normal way, but the existence of a valid obligation or contribution is definitely a material consideration that should be taken into account under s. 70(2). The local planning authority will normally link the permission and the obligation or contribution by imposing a condition on the permission that implementation depends on the acceptance of the obligation or contribution. Planning obligations or contributions can therefore enable the local planning authority and the developer to supplement a permission by achieving objectives that could not be achieved by planning conditions. Indeed, as the Court of Appeal in *Good v. Epping Forest District Council* [1994] JPL 372 remarked about planning obligations, why else would there be provision for them?

Section 46 provides a (very) bare legislative framework and most of the procedural detail remains to be fleshed out by regulations. For example, it is unclear whether developers will be able to offer unilateral contributions on appeal (although government has stated that the new provisions will not be any less flexible). Section 106 contained various rules: for example, that planning obligations could only be created by deed and by a person who has an interest in the relevant land, that they were enforceable against successors in title and were local land charges, and rules in relation to enforcement (this could either be by injunction, or by the local planning authority, after giving notice, entering the land, carrying out the appropriate operations and recovering its costs). It must be assumed that similar provisions will be made under the 2004 Act. Obligations made after the Contracts (Rights of Third Parties) Act 1999 came into force may be enforceable by the local residents in whose favour, in a sense, they are made.

As a matter of policy (Circular 05/2005), planning obligations are not to be used to obtain from developers any uplift in land value following the grant of planning permission, because the effect of this would amount to a form of betterment tax, although, as has been seen, it can be difficult in practice to differentiate these types of planning gain from other, more policy-acceptable, ones, such as contributions towards infrastructure. The present position is that government wishes to introduce a statutory planning charge called a 'community infrastructure levy', which will be used to extract from developers' associated infrastructure costs, while not scaling back the scope of planning obligations under s. 106.[87] The levy envisages developers paying for a share of infrastructure costs on a tariff basis. From a developer's point of view, concerns about paying twice over for infrastructure—for example, paying for a road junction under a planning obligation, but also paying for highways infrastructure through the levy—are unlikely to go away, while 'objectors' may wonder quite how transparent the system will be, or the basis on which infrastructure charges will be set (and how these will capture environmental costs not easily translated into money terms).

Old provisions continue to apply to agreements made before 25 October 1991; in terms of their variation and extinguishment, they are governed by the law on restrictive covenants under the Law of Property Act 1925, s. 84. The 2004 Act does not set out any transitional rules regarding planning obligations entered into before s. 46 comes into force; these must await the regulations.

86 The latest thinking is given in Department of Communities and Local Government (2006) *Changes to Planning Obligations*.

87 [2007] JPL Dec, B13, and, for comments [2008] JPL 245. The levy will be provided for under the Planning Reform Act. This now makes the Planning-Gain Supplement (Preparations) Act 2007 redundant.

Planning obligations—the case law

While there is obviously no case law yet on planning contributions, the lawful scope of planning obligations has caused difficulties, reflecting the tensions between *legal* tests and *policy* tests discussed above. In *R v. Plymouth City Council, ex parte Plymouth and South Devon Co-operative Society Ltd* (1993) 67 P&CR 78, the Court of Appeal had to examine the legality of the offer by two superstore developers of planning gain—including such things as construction of a tourist information centre, provision of a bird-watching hide, a contribution towards a 'Park and Ride' scheme, and up to £1m for infrastructure works at another site. The Court decided that community benefits could be material considerations even in cases in which they were not necessary to overcome or alleviate planning objections.

A planning obligation had to satisfy the three tests that applied to conditions:

(a) it must have a planning purpose;

(b) it must fairly and reasonably relate to the permitted development;

(c) it must not be perverse or grossly unreasonable.

The Court decided that the proposed benefits satisfied these tests.

The House of Lords subsequently refined this decision in the seminal *Tesco* case (Case 12.4).

CASE 12.4 *Tesco Stores Ltd v. Secretary of State for the Environment* [1995] 1 WLR 759

One superstore developer had entered into a planning obligation offering, in return for being granted planning permission, to fund a new road intended to relieve traffic congestion. The Inspector placed considerable weight on the offer and recommended permission be granted, but the Secretary of State disagreed and refused permission. In the House of Lords, it was argued that the offer of funding was a material consideration and that, because the Secretary of State failed to have regard to it, his decision was flawed. The House took a different approach from the Court of Appeal in *Plymouth*[88] and distinguished the tests for the legality of conditions and planning obligations. In particular, Lord Hoffmann, in an erudite judgment, held that a planning obligation could be valid even if it would not satisfy the second test set out in *Plymouth*, in the sense that the connection to the development had only to be more than *de minimis*. Thus, a planning obligation only has to satisfy tests (a) and (c) above. While it would be unlawful to take into account an obligation that had no connection *whatsoever* with the development, the weight to be attached to the obligation was entirely a matter for the decision maker (and different decision makers could take opposing views on the weight to attach to the same obligation). It was not necessary for the obligation to be proportional to the development, nor did it have to be necessary to allow the development to go ahead. All that was required was that the connection between the development and the obligation must be 'material'.

This key decision re-emphasizes that the earlier reported cases confused the *legal* question of the legitimacy of obligations with the *policy* test laid down in Circular 16/91 and its predecessors. In particular, the requirement that the development relates to a planning purpose merely reflects the legal requirement to take into account material considerations under s. 70(2), Town and Country Planning Act 1990. Moreover, the third test—that is, (c)—of general reasonableness equates with normal principles of administrative law.

The second test set out in *Plymouth* was, however, a test of policy that was specified in Circular 16/91 (and which finds its echo in Circular 05/2005, which says that obligations should be '*necessary*

---

88 *R v. Plymouth City Council, ex parte Plymouth and South Devon Co-operative Society Ltd* (1993) 67 P&CR 78.

to make the development acceptable in planning terms'). This guidance does not change the main thrust of the *Tesco* case. The government cautions that local authorities not be swayed by extra inducements, but it is difficult to see how a keen developer could be prevented from offering them, given the ever-widening scope of 'planning' and therefore of what is 'acceptable in planning terms', because it is difficult to envisage obligations that were not material—that is, which could not be linked to the development in some manner. The *Tesco* case itself, of course, involved the *rejection* of an excessively generous offer by a developer (the contribution of the superstore to traffic on the new road would have been minimal). But the House of Lords showed both sensitivity towards the great constraints on local government finance (legally, the offer could have been accepted) and a judicial deference to the use of negotiative planning.

Planning obligations—policy and practice

The legal tests are amplified by policy guidance on what is permissible by way of planning gain now set out in Circular 05/2005. Given that policy and practice have arguably been more important than law in this area, the terms of the circular are of special significance. They suggest that s. 106 should not be used to require a developer to provide more than that which is linked to the development in issue in terms of scale and kind. This appears to mean, for example, that a developer may be asked to provide more sewerage than is needed for the works applied for, but not sewerage for the whole general area. But this limitation seems unenforceable in many cases, because neither the developer nor the local planning author- ity will wish to challenge an arrangement that they have themselves reached. Indeed, such arrangements may be encouraged by the local plan, which was the situation in *Plymouth* (and see also *R v. South Northamptonshire District Council and ors, ex parte Crest Homes plc* [1995] JPL 200).

Moreover, other objectors may well lack either knowledge of the agreement or standing to challenge it. It is significant that the reported cases on planning obligations nearly all con- cern claims by one developer that a rival is being given preferential treatment as a result of an offer of planning gain that is questionable in terms of law or policy. The low visibility of planning obligations was one aspect of 'planning gain' criticized by the Nolan Committee (1997, Cm 3702).

Two cases illustrate some of the transparency problems, and how developers are treated more favourably than objectors. In *Daniel Davies and Co. v. London Borough of Southwark* [1994] JPL 1116, the Court of Appeal held that, if an agreement was merely 'regulatory', determining how premises would be used, then it was not necessary that objectors see the terms of the agreement before it was signed. There could, it was acknowledged, be extreme cases in which this rule would not apply, but the Court did not enlarge on what these might be. In *R (Lichfield Securities Ltd) v. Lichfield District Council* [2001] EWCA Civ 304, however, it was held that fairness demanded that *other developers* should be able to comment on the terms of planning obligations. This might be the case if major developments, such as large retail schemes, involved a range of developers or if, as in *Lichfield*, one developer was already contributing towards infrastructure on which a neighbouring development would also rely (because each party would need to know if their financial contribution was fair).

In part, such concerns about the openness of the system are addressed by the scale of charges for services being in the publicly available development plan. They have also been addressed by changes to art. 25 of the GDPO, which spells out what information must go on Part I of the planning register (which contains information about the application).[89] Copies

---

89 Town and Country Planning (General Development Procedure) (Amendment) (England) Order 2002, SI 2002/828.

of any planning obligation 'proposed or entered into in connection with the application' must be included. (Obligations *actually* entered into must also be placed on Part II of the register dealing with permissions granted.) One obvious practical difficulty, however, is in determining when an obligation has been 'proposed', because this is a negotiative process that might stretch out over many months or even years. (Government guidance is that agreed heads of terms should be recorded and any significant changes to these—that is, full drafts need not be made public.) Another point worth bearing in mind is that the obligation actually entered into need not contain the same commitments as earlier proposals: in other words, there are practical limitations to public involvement.

Nevertheless, it remains the case that, effectively, we now have two systems operating concerning planning obligations. In cases in which a planning obligation is being *required* of developers, the Secretary of State ought to apply his 'necessary to make the development acceptable in planning terms' policy on appeal (although this is not a legal test—see the *Tesco* case above). But in cases in which the obligation is being *offered* by developers, the decision makers are likely to give much more latitude to what developers put on the table and the courts will intervene only on legal, not policy, grounds. Whether this will remain the case is unclear—as things stand, the government seems to envisage planning obligations being used only to secure positive planning advantages in the specific case of affordable housing, but otherwise sees obligations as simply mitigating negative effects.

'Environmental planning gain'

The use of planning obligations to provide for environmental benefits, or at least to prevent net environmental losses, raises important questions about valuation of the environment—perhaps also about the Polluter Pays Principle and wider questions about sustainable development in planning. These cannot be explored in depth here. But research suggests that the idea of such 'environmental planning gain' has proved a powerful factor in allowing for greater development of rural land, allowing commodification of nature into a series of discrete environmental assets that might be traded in the interests of maintaining, or even enhancing, welfare and the environment.[90] Its significance may, however, rest more in its powerfulness as an idea rather than in practice.

There appears to have been rather limited use of environmental planning gain in practice, although, as has been pointed out, what there is tends to be compensatory rather than alleviating or preventing losses caused by the development[91]—for example, planning obligations are used to secure some of the compensation requirements under the Habitats Directive (92/43/EEC). A planning obligation might, however, be used as a means of cleaning up certain contaminated sites. For example, development of a greenfield site could be linked, through a planning obligation, to the clean-up of a brownfield site where, for example, the contaminated land was an 'orphan' site for which remediation would otherwise not be possible or paid out of public funds. They might also be used as a way of preventing the generation of additional traffic—for example, by requiring the developer of an urban housing development to agree that cars will not be allowed onto the land (although banning car *ownership* would be unlawful, because this would not relate to the land).

What is perhaps more important is that planning obligations will still allow decisions about what is in the public interest (including environmental objectives) to be decided in negotiations between developers and planning authorities. The 2004 Act reforms do very little to address this issue.

---

90 S. Whatmore and S. Boucher (1993) 18 Transactions of the Institute of British Geographers 166.

91 Healey et al. (1995). This approach is clearly sanctioned by *Tesco*.

Planning appeals

Section 78 provides a statutory right of appeal to the Secretary of State (in Wales, to the Planning Decision Committee of the Welsh Assembly) against refusals of permission or the imposition of any conditions, and in cases in which the local planning authority has failed to determine an application within eight weeks. Only the applicant, and not any third party, can appeal. An appeal amounts to a total rehearing of the application and the Secretary of State can make any decision originally open to the local planning authority.

An appeal is thus not primarily a contest, but a forum in which all relevant information may be produced and tested so that the inspector may make a rational decision. But it is clear that, over the years, appeals have come to resemble the confrontational model of court proceedings far more than was originally intended (and the process juridified, see below). There is clear evidence that the appeals process has been politicized, with the opportunity being taken to impose central government policy unless there are strong and clear local policies applicable (for example, in a local plan), or a clear restraint policy, such as the green belt, applies. In recent years, around 33 per cent of appeals are successful.

There is also a right to seek judicial review of local planning authority decisions, although, as a general principle of public law, either any alternative remedies must first be exhausted, or it must be shown that they would be inadequate if they were to be relied on (see *R v. Birmingham City Council, ex parte Ferrero Ltd* [1993] 1 All ER 530; see also *R v. Environment Agency, ex parte Petrus Oils Ltd* [1999] Env LR 732). In any event, an appeal to the Secretary of State will encompass policy matters and be cheaper. A decision to grant planning permission, or a refusal to allow an appeal, can only be challenged through judicial review. Such action requires the person initiating the challenge to have standing, which is fairly easily satisfied for those with some interest in the case (see *R v. Sheffield City Council, ex parte Mansfield* (1978) 37 P&CR 1).

Procedure on appeals

Either party (or the Secretary of State) has a right to a public hearing. In large cases, this will be a public inquiry under ss. 320 and 321. In an attempt to address some of the criticisms of the public inquiry system, there has been a shift towards the use of informal hearings to resolve planning disputes. Circular 05/00 makes it clear that it is central government policy to use hearings in all suitable cases and, to that end, the choice of the hearing procedure is made by the Planning Inspectorate, in consultation with the parties. In the vast majority of cases, however, an appeal is dealt with by way of written representations.[92] Only rarely will a decision be quashed because of inadequacies in the procedures actually adopted.

Apart from a very small number of matters of national importance, an inspector normally takes the decision. In the remaining cases, the inspector's report goes to the Secretary of State, who then makes the final decision in the light of the recommendations. Reasons must be given for the decision. This duty has been supplemented by the courts, which require the reasons to be adequate, intelligible, and not self-contradictory. Unlike normal civil litigation, in which the loser will usually pay all the costs of an action, parties to a planning appeal are normally expected to pay their own costs.

If an inquiry is held, it must be public and anyone is entitled to attend. In general, the procedure to be followed is at the discretion of the inspector. Rules are set out,[93] but because these are supplemented by the rules of natural justice and human rights protections—as,

---

92 Town and Country Planning (Appeals) (Written Representations) (England) Regulations 2000, SI 2000/1628.

93 In the Town and Country Planning (Inquiries Procedure) (England) Rules 2000, SI 2000/1624, and the Town and Country Planning (Determination by Inspectors) (Inquiries Procedure) Rules 2000, SI 2000/1625.

indeed, are the written representation procedures—an inspector normally permits anyone with anything new and relevant to say to put his or her case.

The Planning Inspectorate does not normally impose hearings in cases in which third-party evidence is expected, or there are disputed matters of fact, or complex matters of law or policy. As in any decision-making process, there is a balance to be struck between speed and informality, and procedural rigour. In *Dyason v. Secretary of State for the Environment and Chiltern District Council* [1998] JPL 778, it was stressed that 'a relaxed hearing is not necessarily a fair hearing', because some of the informality has been lost.

The courts have held that even the absence of an oral hearing will usually comply with Art. 6 of the European Convention on Human Rights (ECHR)—which provides for a 'fair and public hearing'—as long as there is nothing to suggest that the planning authority has acted unfairly or unreasonably (*R (Adlard) v. Secretary of State for the Environment, Transport and the Regions* [2002] EWCA Civ 735). The House of Lords has since held that this is so regardless of whether matters of fact-finding, rather than discretionary judgment, are at issue (*Begum v. London Borough of Tower Hamlets* [2003] UKHL 5). Arguably, this is a rather restrictive, and pragmatic, approach, based more on not causing chaos to administrative systems such as planning—and seeing Art. 6 rights not as self-standing, but as requiring some other human rights breach to be demonstrated as well[94]—rather than genuinely protecting the interests in particular of third parties.

Challenging the decision of the Secretary of State

The Secretary of State's decision can only be challenged under s. 288, owing to s. 284, which ousts all other challenges. Section 288 thus provides a statutory appeal; this must be distinguished from judicial review. About 150 cases under s. 288 are brought each year. These are the main source of decisions on planning law.

The s. 288 grounds approximate to judicial review grounds. A decision can be challenged either if it is not within the powers of the Act, or if substantial prejudice has been caused by a failure to comply with the relevant procedures (for example, the Inquiries Rules). These will cover bad faith, perverse decisions, failure to take account of relevant factors, taking into account irrelevant factors, mistakes of law, acting on no evidence, giving inadequate reasons, or a want of natural justice.

Under s. 288, the High Court is limited to quashing the decision of the Secretary of State and remitting the case. It cannot make the decision for the Secretary of State, but can make some fairly explicit directions as to the relevant law. Thus, even if an appeal under s. 288 is successful, there is no guarantee that the redetermination will be any more beneficial. The High Court also has a discretion whether to quash a decision and will refuse to do so if it considers that the defect made no difference to the eventual decision.

Any 'person aggrieved' by the decision can use s. 288. This includes all parties who appeared at the inquiry or made representations, as well as the appellant, the local planning authority, and owners and occupiers of the site (see *Turner v. Secretary of State for the Environment* (1973) 28 P&CR 123).

Enforcing planning law

Unlike most pollution control legislation, it is not in itself an offence to breach planning law. The offence consists of failing to comply with a notice served by the planning authority about unauthorized development or breach of a condition. The reason for this is that unauthorized development is not necessarily harmful; it would be wasteful to punish

94 See P. Craig [2003] Pub L 753.

activities that have some social, economic, or environmental benefit. Enforcement action is 'remedial rather than punitive' and consideration must be given to ways in which unlawful development could be made lawful, for example, by obvious mitigating measures or alternatives (*Tapecrown Ltd v. First Secretary of State* [2006] EWCA Civ 1744).

There are four types of notice used:

- planning contravention notices;
- breaches of condition notices;
- enforcement notices;
- stop notices.

Of these, planning contravention notices and enforcement notices are used most often (around 5,000 each a year), with around 1,150 breach of condition notices and 200 stop notices served annually. Injunctions can also be sought. All are discretionary mechanisms—in the case of enforcement notices and stop notices, it being explicitly provided that they 'may' be sought if the authority considers it 'expedient' to do so.[95] Further details about these can be found in the Online Resource Centre.

Finally, local planning authorities have wide powers to enter land at any reasonable time to ascertain whether there has been a breach of planning control and what remedial steps may be required (ss. 196A–C).

Immunity from enforcement under planning law

There are time limits for what is called 'taking enforcement action', which means serving an enforcement notice or breach of condition notice (s. 171A). These provide immunity from the service of such a notice in cases in which:

- four years have elapsed from the substantial completion of an operational development (s. 171B(1)), or from a change of use *to* a dwellinghouse (s. 171B(2));
- ten years have elapsed from any other breach of planning control (s. 171B(3)).

Immunity is also granted in cases in which there is a certificate of lawfulness of existing use or development, a certificate of lawfulness of proposed use or development, or an established use certificate granted under earlier legislation relating to the alleged breach (see ss. 191–94). These certificates are conclusive as to the lawfulness of the matters to which they relate (unless an enforcement notice is served and the uses covered by the certificate are not raised when the notice is appealed: *Staffordshire County Council v. Challinor* [2007] EWCA Civ 864). This is the case even if an existing use is in contravention of other environmental legislation—for example, if there are ongoing breaches of waste management law. This was the decision of the Court of Appeal in *R (Philcox) v. Epping Forest District Council* [2002] Env LR 2, which stressed that it is the legality of the use in *planning* terms that is at issue. The Court denied that this would allow waste operators, for example, to benefit from criminal activity.[96]

Appeals against notices

The Act has elaborate provisions for appeals to the Secretary of State against enforcement notices. Appeals suspend the enforcement notice until after the Secretary of State's decision.

---

95 But note the impact of human rights on this exercise of discretion—p. 424; note also that some instances of non-enforcement may result in a successful complaint being taken up with the Local Government Ombudsman.

96 For a view that this is misguided, see M. Cull (2002) 4 Env LR 117.

This allows the determined operator scope to delay the final operation of an enforcement notice for a considerable time, although there are provisions that seek to prevent this in blatant cases (see s. 289(4A), (4B), and (5C)).

There are seven grounds of appeal set out in s. 174(2):

(a) planning permission ought to be granted, or the relevant condition ought to be discharged;

(b) the alleged breach has not, in fact, taken place;

(c) the matters alleged in the enforcement notice do not in law constitute a breach of planning control;

(d) the matters alleged in the enforcement notice are immune from enforcement action;

(e) failures to carry out the correct procedures in serving the enforcement notice;

(f) the steps required to remedy the breach are excessive;

(g) the time allowed for compliance with the enforcement notice is unreasonably short.

These grounds are very wide, and cover both policy and legal grounds. Ground (a) is effectively an application for planning permission from the Secretary of State and the major 'policy' ground. Grounds (b)–(e) are collectively known as the 'legal' grounds, because they mix issues of fact and law. Ground (f) is also important. A local planning authority may not 'over-enforce'—that is, put the recipient of an enforcement notice in a worse position than that in which he or she was before the breach took place.

The procedure is similar to that for planning appeals. The Secretary of State may uphold an enforcement notice and refuse the appeal, quash it (often this involves granting retrospective planning permission), vary its terms, or amend it. Challenges beyond grounds (a)–(g) above must, however, be brought through judicial review—for example, if the notice is hopelessly uncertain or if some essential procedural requirement has not been met (see *Miller-Mead v. Minister of Housing and Local Government* [1963] 2 QB 196).

Because of the detailed appeal mechanisms, the validity of an enforcement notice may not be challenged in a prosecution for breach (*R v. Wicks* [1997] 2 All ER 801). By contrast, because there are no rights to appeal against a stop notice or a breach of condition notice, the courts have allowed challenges to their validity when prosecutions for ignoring them have been brought (see *R v. Jenner* [1983] 1 WLR 873 and *Dilieto v. Ealing Borough Council* [1998] 2 All ER 885, respectively).

Enforcement discretion

Only the local planning authority may serve a notice, although the Secretary of State has a reserve power to serve an enforcement notice (s. 182). A number of studies in the 1980s found that the enforcement of planning law was given a very low profile in many local planning authorities,[97] which tended to rely on complaints coming from the public rather than monitoring. Low fines hardly incentivized enforcement and informal negotiation was preferred. Concerns such as these prompted the Carnwath Report,[98] from which many of the changes to enforcement made under the Planning and Compensation Act 1991 stem. These provided a welcome broadening of the powers at planning authorities' disposal. The centrality of the planning authority's discretion, however, has largely remained unchecked by the national courts, although the European Court of Human Rights (ECtHR) has given a judgment

97 See, e.g., [1986] JPL 482.
98 DoE (1989) *Enforcing Planning Law.*

on this issue that may have significant implications for national enforcement practice (see Case 12.5).

CASE 12.5 *Antonetto v. Italy* (2003) 36 EHRR 10

A building was constructed on land adjacent to Antonetto's property, but the planning permission had been illegally granted and was quashed. Under Italian law, the planning authority was bound to order demolition, but failed to do so. A court then ordered the authority to demolish the building, but this too was ignored. The Strasbourg Court held that there had been a breach of Art. 6 of the European Convention on Human Rights (ECHR)—that is, the right to a fair trial—and also, because of the reduction in the value of Antonetto's land due to loss of light and loss of a view,[99] a breach of Art. 1 of the First Protocol (the right to peaceful enjoyment of possessions).

Although this case does not make 'underenforcement' unlawful—that is, not every aspect of the breach must be remedied—a failure to enforce may be challengeable if this leads to an unlawful interference with another's human rights and is not justified by some compelling public interest in the development remaining.[100] (There is some doubt about how strong this conclusion is, however, because of the discretionary nature of enforcement under the Town and Country Planning Act 1990 compared to Italian law, although the Strasbourg Court did find that the actions of the Italian planning authority were per se unlawful, and not only unlawful because it did not follow a national judicial order.) This provides a minimum baseline of protection from unlawful development that is environmentally harmful, but only in instances in which the ECHR provides limited protection for the natural environment as an incident of private property or 'home' rights. So it will be of limited use in cases in which, for example, there is unlawful development in the green belt not directly affecting any neighbouring property. And, in the case of human rights, note that even if neighbours are affected, there is a very high threshold to overcome, because it would have to be shown that any interference was both serious and not justified (see, for example, *Lough v. First Secretary of State* [2004] EWHC 23, a case about overshadowing from a high-rise development). In practice, only claims based on procedural grounds are ever likely to succeed

---

Under-enforcement is specifically approved of in official planning guidance on enforcement (although enforcement statistics show a rise over the last five years).[101] The extent to which economic considerations influence enforcement can be seen by survey evidence that enforcement is more common in south-east England than in depressed urban areas.[102] As part of its recent planning reforms, government mooted the possibility of removing local planning authorities' enforcement discretion (at least for major breaches) and making breaches of development control law a criminal offence, but these proposals have so far come to nothing.[103]

---

99 The loss of a view is not per se actionable in tort or property law: see, e.g., *Phipps v. Pears* [1965] 1 QB 76. The effect of *Antonetto* is probably very limited in relation to landscape conservation, because the focus is the deprivation of private property rights (see also S. Crow [2001] JPL 1349). Note also the similarities between *Antonetto* and the idea that the planning authority might be liable in tort for authorizing or continuing a nuisance—see p. 339.

100 For more detailed discussion of this case and its implications, see J.-J. Paradissis [2002] JPL 674.

101 Circular 10/97 *Enforcing Planning Controls.*

102 Enforcement may also be compromised by the fact that modern planning, especially for larger developments, is a collaborative process between private developers and planning authorities.

103 DTLR (2001) *Planning: Delivering a Fundamental Change*, para. 5.69; ODPM (2002) *Review of the Planning Enforcement System in England.*

Powers in cases in which there is no breach of planning law

There are some courses of action available to the local planning authority in cases in which there is no breach of the planning legislation. Normally, these require the payment of compensation for the loss of any rights that have been taken away, so they are little used. But they are of importance as reserve powers if there is something creating an environmental problem that may not be removed or controlled in any other way.

Under s. 102, a local planning authority may serve a discontinuance order, which may require that any use be discontinued or that any buildings or works be removed or altered. Under s. 97, a local planning authority may revoke or modify a planning permission that has already been granted. In both of these cases, there are provisions for a public local inquiry to be held and compensation to be paid. The Secretary of State must also confirm these orders before they have effect and has reserve powers to make either type. The local planning authority may also enter into a planning obligation in order to remove an existing building or use, although obviously the owner will require something of benefit in return.

Planning, the environment, and risk

The planning system clearly has an important role in protecting the environment, whether as a default for, as a supplement to, specialist controls. But it also plays a part in relation to general issues of environmental risk communication and regulation.

In relation to public fears, it is important to distinguish between risks and uncertainties—that is, between those matters that are feared because of some quantifiable risk, and those fears in relation to which the odds of something adverse happening are not even known. In relation to the former, there was an indication in *Gateshead Metropolitan Borough Council v. Secretary of State for the Environment* [1995] Env LR 37 that the courts would take a strict line, when Glidewell LJ stated that '*if in the end public concern is not justified, it cannot be conclusive*'.[104] But this view was disagreed with by the Court of Appeal in *Newport Borough Council v. Secretary of State for Wales and Browning Ferris Ltd* [1998] Env LR 174, which reaffirmed the view that public perception of risk, even if it were unsubstantiated, could be a material planning consideration—the approach that has been followed in more recent case law.[105] Of course, one reason why the Secretary of State has the final say in planning matters is precisely to override local opposition if this is deemed to be in the national interest.

What the courts may be more willing to do is hold that a planning authority has illegally ignored the odds in some way and intervene. This was the case in *Envirocor Waste Holdings Ltd v. Secretary of State for the Environment, ex parte Humberside County Council and British Cocoa Mills (Hull) Ltd* [1996] Env LR 49, a dispute about different calculations of the likely occurrence of a waste transfer station tainting the produce of a nearby factory. In that case, it was possible for the judge to overturn the inspector's decision, because there were various ways in which the inspector's calculation of risk could not be sustained. Another case in which the courts have overturned an inspector's risk assessment is *T Mobile (UK) Ltd v. First Secretary of State* [2005] Env LR 18, a challenge to the refusal to grant planning permission for a shared mobile phone mast near to three primary schools. In this case, government policy guidance (PPG8) set out how to calculate the odds in accordance with international standards. Although the emissions from the masts would fall within these limits, the inspector thought that insufficient reassurances had been given about material harm to living conditions. But

---

104 At 49.
105 *Trevett v. Secretary of State* [2002] EWHC 2696, and see also the *Jodie Phillips* case in Box 12.6.

the judge held that the policy guidance placed the emphasis on actual risk rather than per-ceived risk and that the inspector had erred in having regard to the latter.

A general difficulty remains, however, in that it may be difficult to distinguish between risk and uncertainty. There is often a gloss of certainty about some risk calculations and many assessments of risks are little better than glorified value judgments. Conversely, with some small-scale developments, it may be that what are better seen as quantifiable risks are, because of lack of available data, presented as uncertainties. In cases in which there is a regu-latory view about the assessment of risk, however, this view may carry considerable weight. Indeed, in *R v. Tandridge District Council, ex parte al Fayed* [1999] 1 PLR 104, the judge held that 'strong weight' should be given to any such assessment, especially in cases in which a particular issue of national policy was at stake, such that there was a need for a national con-sistency of approach to decision making. An appeal in this case was dismissed,[106] although, in the Court of Appeal, both sides agreed that objective unjustified fears could be material.

As regards the ultimate response of the planning system to issues of risk and uncertainty, there are essentially three options: ignore the fear, grant permission subject to appropri-ate conditions, or refuse the application. An uncertainty might conceivably be ignored, but ignoring a risk will make any decision liable to be overturned. The real issue therefore is whether the risks of environmental harm are managed or avoided. Arguably, PPG1 (1997) took the 'management' approach, advocating the prevention of harm through appropri-ate decisions about the siting of development and using the planning system to minimize impact.[107] Owens argues that this really combines the more traditional 'technical fix' attitude with a 'spatial fix' approach: if development goes in the least harmful place, it is acceptable.[108] This approach obviously runs counter to the notion of environmental carrying capacity in relation to natural environmental resources. It also contributes to the inadequacy of the planning system as an effective mechanism for reversing harmful environmental trends.[109]

Finally, the importance of taking a wider view on risk regulation cannot be avoided. In cases such as *Envirocor*, if the waste transfer station was not built, this posed serious regula-tory problems for waste management in the area. More broadly, in relation to house building, for example, environmental concerns are not exhausted by the location of the 3.8 million projected new households, but also include concerns about the impact of a doubling of aggregates extraction that may be needed to satisfy such a demand. Regulating this calls for strategic assessment—something that can only really be tackled at a level above that even of development plans.[110]

Future developments

A Planning Reform Bill was announced in the Queen's Speech in November 2007 and is cur-rently before Parliament. If you want to get a sense of what lies behind this, read the Barker Review of Land Use Planning (2006)[111] and the White Paper.[112] These are very much in favour of speeding up the planning system, emphasizing the market, and advocate a much more risk-based approach to planning within which the impact of development is to be stressed rather than its type. The Bill would also centralize certain aspects of decision making

---

106 See [2000] Env LR D23.

107 See S. Owens (1997) 68 TPR 293.

108 See also the discussion of alternatives when a planning application is being determined in Box 12.6.

109 A broadly similar approach is taken in PPS1. See also the discussion of the objectives of planning on p. 382.

110 On strategic environmental assessment—SEA—see p. 468.

111 See **www.barkerreviewofplanning.org.uk**. Another influential report is by R. Eddington (2006) *The Case for Action*, London: DfT, esp. Appendix 4A.

112 DCLG, DfT, DEFRA and DTI (2007) *Planning for a Sustainable Future*: *White Paper*.

over major developments—for example, the 'need' for new nuclear power stations would be decided in Parliament (where the government can expect to command a majority) and not discussed at inquiries,[113] which appears to be a way of reviving the government's original preferred approach to major infrastructure projects (see p. 403 above). This approach is criticized by environmental pressure groups as leading to a 'what colour would you like the gates of your nuclear plant?' style of decision making. There is a summary of the Barker Report and comment, at [2007] JPL 378, and the area will be considered further in the Online Resource Centre as and when legislation is enacted.

CHAPTER SUMMARY

The main features of town and country planning have been described at the start of this chapter. These are not repeated here and the following therefore highlights—and, in some cases, expands upon—some key themes of the chapter in relation to the nature of planning and its relevance to the environment.

1   Town and country planning law is not a specialized environmental protection regime, but it contributes to environmental protection in increasingly important ways. 'The environment' and, now, 'sustainable development' have become the dominant narratives of planning (even if this has not been translated into real-world environmental improvements through the planning system).

2   Planning law can control damaging activities that are not generally subject to specific environmental controls (such as noise and light pollution, or the destruction of habitat outside protected areas), or by acting in conjunction with specialist control regimes such as those that govern waste management or integrated pollution prevention control (IPPC). But if planning permission is given, it can also 'trump' other environmental controls.

3   Planning works mainly through anticipatory controls, although ongoing conditions can be imposed—and ongoing agreements entered into—for environmental reasons.

4   Some activities with potentially harmful environmental consequences are, for historic reasons and because of the complexity involved, not subject to planning controls (the main one being the use of land for agriculture).

5   Even under a plan-led system, planning remains a highly discretionary discipline within which individual applications are considered on their merits. This emphasis on discretion and the centrality of the Secretary of State are the two most striking features of the UK planning system.

6   All plan-making bodies must now exercise their functions 'with the objective of contributing to the achievement of sustainable development'. This duty does not apply to local planning authorities or to the Secretary of State when they determine individual planning applications. This is to focus issues about the sustainability of development onto the strategic level of decision making—for example, what are the waste management requirements for the county?—rather than on individual planning applications—for example, is this incinerator 'sustainable'?

7   Under the 1947 Act, planning had redistributive, as well as reconstructive, dreams. The former have all but disappeared, and private developers now generally pursue major development and redevelopment in conjunction with planning authorities.

8   The public interest is therefore served by facilitating the market rather than by constraining it. Hence, the planning system is always responding to decisions by developers about the most profitable sites at which to locate new development. The idea that the economy and its environmental consequences can be 'planned for' in advance is hopelessly optimistic.

---

113 See Department of Trade and Industry (2006) *Policy Framework for New Nuclear Build*, consultation document.

9 There is a constant tension in making planning decisions between speed and meaningful public participation. Recent legislative reforms have continued to emphasize the former, while the courts have shown some signs of protecting the latter.

10 Part of the reason why the courts have done so may be an increasing concern with procedural rights, born of a decade of increasingly purposive engagement with the law on environmental impact assessment.

11 As with other areas of environmental criminal law, enforcement tends to be selective, but the penalties that may be imposed can be severe (including the demolition of buildings built in breach of permission).

12 The 'rights culture' influences both the preceding points; it both provides a major context for upholding participatory rights and can also operate against strict enforcement of planning controls, because of the need to ensure that sanctions that potentially deprive people of their homes are proportionate to the ends being pursued (which may lead to environmental blight).

Q QUESTIONS

1 In your opinion, what are the objectives and values of modern town and country planning law?

2 When will a consideration be 'material' to deciding a planning decision? Are there any rules about the respective weight that should be given to particular factors and does the process ensure that proper weight is given to the environment in decision making? If not, what are the challenges in increasing the weight given to the environment in planning law?

3 Does land development law strike the right balance between private rights in property and the public interest in environmental protection? Is the 'possessive individualism' of human rights law a challenge to controlling and managing development in the public interest?

4 What is the legal scope for planning obligations and to what extent can 'planning gain' ensure that environmental damage is adequately prevented, mitigated, or compensated for?

5 Look at the Planning and Energy Bill (a private member's Bill introduced in parliamentary session 2007–08). Do you think that government has gone far enough to maximize the scope for planning law to address climate change?

6 There are proposals to place a mobile phone mast on the roof of a historic church. If possible, divide into groups advising the developer, the local planning authority, and nearby residents. What are the key planning issues? What further information would be needed?

7 To what extent might 'light pollution' be controlled by planning law? (You might find P. Jewkes [1998] JPL 10, and D. Hughes and M. Taylor (2004) 16 JEL 215 useful here, and note that the RCEP is, in 2008, undertaking a short study on problems associated with artificial lighting.)

8 It is likely that your university will be using your top-up fees to invest in capital works such as major building programmes. Try to get hold of the key documents relating to one such development, such as the planning permission, and any planning obligations entered into. Try also to get hold of relevant related documents, such as the development plans and key policy guidance, which would have influenced the permission. Think about how these have sought to prevent, mitigate, compensate, or trade off (against economic or social gains) any environmental harm, and whether more could have been done.

Planning policy

The high policy content of planning law makes planning policy texts more valuable than normal. An excellent general introductory text is B. Cullingworth and V. Nadin (2006) *Town and Country Planning in Britain*, 14th edn, London: Routledge, and environmental law students studying planning law in any depth will profit greatly from, at a minimum, chs 1 and 2. Y. Rydin (2003) *Urban and Environmental Planning in the UK*, 2nd edn, London: Macmillan, also provides a good overview. The extent of the changes to planning that have occurred since the 1947 Act are captured in B. Cullingworth (ed.) (1999) *British Planning: 50 Years of Urban and Regional Policy*, London: Athlone Press, with valuable chapters by Profs Grant and Purdue on compensation issues and the role of the courts, respectively. Sustainability issues are the theoretical focus of S. Owens and R. Cowell (2001) *Land and Limits*, London: Routledge. Both G. Monbiot (2000) *Captive State*, London: Macmillan, and R. Girling (2005) *Rubbish! Dirt on Our Hands and Crisis Ahead*, London: Transworld, contain chapters taking a journalistic, and often provocative, look at planning in action.

Planning law

All of the general texts on planning law take the 2004 Act into account. J. Cameron Blackhall (2005) *Planning Law and Practice*, 3rd edn, London: Cavendish, is a very readable introduction. V. Moore (2005) *A Practical Approach to Planning Law*, 9th edn, Oxford: Oxford University Press, also contains useful practical insights, but focuses more on the exposition of principle through case law, rather than on policy considerations. Among other texts, R. Duxbury (2006) *Telling and Duxbury's Planning Law and Procedure*, 13th edn, London: Butterworths, is readable, but relatively less comprehensive in coverage. On the 2004 Act, there is a Law Society guide (2005) *Planning and Compulsory Purchase Act 2004: A Guide to the New Law*, authored by the very strong team of Stephen Tromans, Martin Edwards, Richard Harwood, and Justine Thornton.

Still the most useful conceptual framework for thinking about planning law is P. McAuslan (1980) *Ideologies of Planning Law*, Oxford: Pergamon Press, especially chs 1 and 6. The incorporation of sustainable development concerns is discussed by M. Stallworthy (2002) *Sustainability, Land Use and the Environment*, London: Cavendish, especially chs 4, 6, and 7. Planning is a particular strength of J. Holder and M. Lee (2007) *Environmental Protection: Text and Materials*, Cambridge: Cambridge University Press—see especially chs 12, 13, and (for a case study on wind energy) 16. M. Purdue, 'An overview of the law on public participation in planning law and whether it complies with the Aarhus Convention' (2005) 17 ELM 107 is a useful bridge between Chapter 10 and Chapters 12 and 13, and is highly recommended.

For a complete and up-to-date account of the law, the looseleaf *Encyclopaedia of Planning Law*, London: Sweet and Maxwell, includes all of the relevant statutory and non-statutory material, and is updated monthly, with insightful annotations and analysis. The other pre-eminent source is the *Journal of Planning and Environment Law* (JPL), which contains information on legislative and policy developments, Ministerial decisions and case law analysis, as well as articles (often with a practice orientation).

Scotland

M. Poustie, 'Planning reforms in Scotland' [2007] JPL 489 looks at the Planning etc. (Scotland) Act 2006, which, among other things, uses the term 'development management' rather than 'development control' to signify that planning ought to have a less negative remit. The 2006 Act also provides the framework for a planning hierarchy distinguishing national, major, local, and minor (permitted) developments, an approach that may soon be proposed for the other UK countries.

Development planning

Changes to the nature of development planning, especially regional spatial strategies (RSSs) and the theoretical rationales for these, are discussed in M. Tewdwr-Jones, 'Spatial planning, practices and cultures' [2004] JPL 560. A report of some influence behind the emergence of RSSs is the 23rd Report of the Royal

Commission on Environmental Pollution (2002) *Environmental Planning*, ch. 10 of which discusses integrated spatial strategies. For more detail on the centrality of the Secretary of State in relation to development planning, see R Harwood (2005) 7(2) Env LR 124.

Development control, conditions, and obligations

P. Booth (2003) *Planning by Consent*, London: Routledge, traces the origins of development control back to early nuisance law and notions of property rights, and charts developments up to the present, putting into perspective concerns about delays in reaching planning decisions. A foundational article for thinking about the main mechanisms of development control is D Callies and M Grant, 'Paying for growth and planning gain: an Anglo–American comparison of development conditions, impact fees and development agreements' (1991) 23 Urban Lawyer 221. A. Samuels [2002] JPL 514 considers the legality of 'no car' planning obligations, but is valuable generally on the legality of development control measures to reduce environmental impacts.

On the moral dimension to planning agreements, see J. Alder [1990] JPL 880. R. Grove-White, 'Land use law and the environment' [1991] JLS 32 explains the importance of the planning system to shaping the debate on some of the 'first generation' of modern environmental controversies, such as nuclear plants. On planning and public perceptions of risks, N. Stanley, 'Public concern: the decision makers' dilemma' [1998] JPL 919, R. Kimball, 'Risk, jurisprudence and the environment' [2000] JPL 359, and C. Hilson, 'Planning law and public perceptions of risk' [2004] JPL 1638 are all recommended.

Planning and climate change

A valuable read in thinking about how planning law could better protect the environment, with reference to climate change, is the 26th Report of the Royal Commission on Environmental Pollution (2007) *The Urban Environment*. P. Waddy, 'Sustainable design and planning: the new policy imperative' [2006] JPL 4 (Dec supp) and S. Tromans, 'Climate change, energy and planning' [2007] JPL 357 consider some of the steps that are already being taken to reduce emissions, and the key challenges in making things such as zero carbon development a reality.

Planning and other sectoral issues

To varying degrees, planning is an important part of the law relating to other sectors covered in this book. This is very much the case with, for example, climate change and landscape, areas in which planning law plays a primary role in responding to the problems. In areas such as general pollution control, waste management, and nature conservation, planning generally plays a slightly different role, in the sense that there are laws in these areas dealing with these issues, but there is a degree of overlap with planning law. Each of the sectoral chapters considers the role that planning law plays. C. Miller (ed.) (2001) *Planning and Environmental Protection*, Oxford: Hart, is a valuable supplement to this book's sectoral coverage of planning law.

@ WEB LINKS

As well as providing the text of the key primary and secondary legislation (a source such as Westlaw, which includes the various amendments to the Town and Country Planning Act 1990, is essential) the Internet is the easiest way to access central government policy guidance and circulars. Familiarization with these—which are in the process of being revised and streamlined—is usually imperative. For England, see **www.communities.gov.uk**; for the devolved administrations, see **www.scotland.gov.uk**, **www.wales.gov.uk**, and **www.doeni.gov.uk**. A very useful portal is **www.planningportal.gov.uk**, which is managed by the Planning Inspectorate (**www.planning-inspectorate.gov.uk**) and which contains information on the planning system, links to online development plans (it is worth reading a development plan to get a feel for what they contain), and which allows planning appeals to be tracked.

13 Environmental assessment

→ **Overview**

In the last thirty years or so, environmental assessment has emerged as one of the key environmental law mechanisms. The essence of environmental assessment is that information about likely environmental impacts of things such as development projects, and now also plans and programmes, is properly considered before potentially harmful decisions are made. In this sense, it is a preventive ~~Not binding~~ tool. But, above all, it is a procedural technique, which means that damaging development can, in theory, still proceed. This chapter looks at the international, European, and national laws relating to environmental assessment, and the explosion of litigation that has occurred in the last few years.

In looking at environmental assessment, it may be useful to consider various issues and tensions—at which we looked in Chapters 4, 8, and 10—to inform your reading and understanding of environmental assessment. The first of these is the tension between adhering strictly to procedural rules and adopting a pragmatic approach to decisions that are considered sensible (and doing so in a reasonable time). Beyond this, you might think about the extent to which the value of environmental assessment lies in one or more of the following: (1) improving the quality of environmental decisions—for example, by preventing environmental harm and integrating the environment into decision making; (2) producing more legitimate environmental decisions; (3) raising public confidence in environmental decisions; and/or (4) giving individuals rights to participate in environmental decision making. You might also consider whether environmental assessment is used—by developers, decision makers or the public—in a defensive or a purposive way.

At the end of this chapter, you will be able to:

✔ understand what environmental assessment is and how it works;

✔ appreciate some of the key issues and challenges in using procedural law to protect the environment;

✔ evaluate how environmental assessment is used in practice;

✔ understand the implementation of one of the key EC environmental Directives.

What is 'environmental assessment'?

On a simple level, the legal mechanisms of environmental impact assessment (EIA) and strategic environmental assessment (SEA)—to which we refer together as 'environmental assessment'—are merely information-gathering exercises enabling decision makers to understand the environmental effects of certain projects (in the case of EIA) and plans or programmes (SEA) before deciding whether or not to grant consent or approval for that proposal. On this level, however, there is little to distinguish this concept from, for example, the normal planning process under which environmental effects are a material consideration in deciding whether or not to grant planning permission. Indeed, prior to specific legislation on environmental assessment, there were examples in which detailed assessments of the environmental effects of developments had been carried out—for example, in relation to power stations and motorways—and government has been advocating environmental policy appraisal since the early 1990s.

The innovation behind the formal EIA and SEA processes is the systematic use of the best objective sources of information and the emphasis on the use of the best techniques to gather that information. In recent years, the importance of allowing meaningful public participation in the decision-making process has also been stressed (see Chapter 10). Thus the ideal EIA, for example, would involve a totally bias-free collation of information about environmental impact, produced in a coherent, sound, and complete form, considering impact in an integrated manner. It should then allow the decision maker and members of the public to scrutinize the proposal, assess the weight of predicted effects, and suggest modifications or mitigation (or refusal) where appropriate.

Thus, environmental assessment is both a technique and a process. EIAs and SEAs are inanimate, rather than tangible. The key point is that, strictly, the 'assessment' is undertaken by the decision maker on the basis of *environmental information* with which it is supplied. This information consists, in part, of an 'environmental statement' prepared by the developer (or more likely, by hired consultants), which details at least the main environmental impacts of the project and any mitigating measures that are proposed to reduce the significance of those impacts. (With SEA, the equivalent document is termed the 'environmental report'.) But, just as importantly, the environmental information also includes other information supplied by various statutory consultees (for example, the Environment Agency, Natural England), independent third parties (such as local conservation and amenity groups), members of the public, and even the decision maker itself. So it is worth stressing that the developer does not produce an environmental assessment (a mistake that even some judges still make); the decision maker carries out the assessment on the basis of environmental information supplied.

BOX 13.1 **Key terms**

- **Environmental impact assessment (EIA)**
  A formal procedure through which decision makers gather environmental information about projects and take this information into account in decision making.

- **Strategic environmental assessment (SEA)**
  In EC law, the assessment of plans and programmes which, in certain sectors, set a framework for future development consent of projects subject to EIA, or which are required under the EC Habitats Directive. Arguably, a procedure of wider use.

- **Environmental statement (or environmental report)**
  A statement, prepared by the developer, of the main environmental impacts of the project and any proposed mitigating measures to reduce the significance of those impacts. For SEA, the equivalent term is environmental report.

- **Environmental information**
  Information from a range of sources about the environmental impact of the development. Includes the environmental statement or report, and information from statutory consultees and the public.

Environmental assessment should also begin as early as possible when projects are being planned, or plans and programmes mooted. A related point is that EIA and SEA should be *iterative* processes, in which information that comes to light is fed back into the decision-making process. This has two dimensions: first, a truly iterative process would ensure that the very *design* of the project, plan, or programme would be amended in the light of the information gathered; secondly, and also ideally, it would also involve some kind of monitoring of environmental impact after consent or approval has been given. It may be that, for certain activities, post-project monitoring is a requirement of international law, but in the EC neither of the main laws in this area—the 1985 EIA Directive (85/337/EEC) and the 2001 SEA Directive (2001/42/EC)—currently require this (although the latter does require an ongoing consideration of environmental information during plan making). But at present, as a matter of law, environmental assessment is wholly concerned with likely environmental impacts identified *before* consent or approval is given. (Whether some of the unspecific claims made in environmental statements could be monitored in practice is debatable, but, turning this around, we could say that statements should not contain claims that cannot be audited.)[1]

Crucially, EIA and SEA are inherently *procedural* mechanisms. Although they are intended to be preventive (and, some would argue, also precautionary), there is nothing that requires the decision maker to refuse a development project or amend a development plan because negative environmental impacts are highlighted by the environment assessment. Nor do EIA or SEA require conditions to be imposed on project consents, or plans to be amended, to mitigate or compensate for any such impact. There is therefore a marked contrast with other legal requirements to carry out assessments that sometimes provide for this. A good example is the duty to undertake an 'appropriate assessment' under Art. 6 of the EC Habitats Directive (92/43/EEC), which is coupled with a duty to take certain compensatory or mitigatory measures if this assessment reveals that harm to a protected species or habitat may occur (see p. 711). So, for example, following a valid EIA, it will only be by showing that a decision maker has erred as a matter of general administrative law—for example, by failing to consider significant impacts raised by the assessment process—that an authorization for a project might be reviewable. By formally imposing no constraints on decision makers as regards their eventual decisions,[2] therefore, environmental assessment is a particularly flexible tool of environmental law. Its importance lies in its ability to elevate attention to environmental impacts in decision making and induce reflection on the way in which impacts might be reduced. In this sense, environmental assessment is one manifestation of the turn towards more reflexive forms of environmental law (see p. 213). In trying to achieve these aims, however, environmental assessment imposes strict procedural requirements that contrast sharply with its formal lack of stipulation about eventual outcomes.

Environmental assessment in international law and practice

While most of this chapter is concerned with the environmental assessment regimes at EC and national levels, EIA-type requirements are now found in many international agreements, and a number of global and regional organizations—such as the World Bank—now bind themselves by EIA requirements (see Box 13.2). (SEA has recently been the subject of

---

1 For figures on the vagueness, or otherwise lack of auditability, of claims, see C. Wood (2002) *Environmental Impact Assessment: A Comparative Review*, 2nd edn, London: Pearson. This issue might be best dealt with not by a legal obligation on developers, but by institutional change, e.g., by an Environmental Assessment Commission scrutinizing the assessment process, as recommended by the Royal Commission on Environmental Pollution (RCEP) 23rd Report (2002) *Environmental Planning*, para. 7.35.

2 Notably, early advocacy of EIA, contained in the 1982 World Charter for Nature, did have this substantive edge.

an international convention—the 2003 Kiev Protocol.) EIA is also now firmly established in a wide range of national regimes, to the point where, taking international and national developments together, EIA has arguably reached the status either of a general principle of law or even a requirement of customary international law. Support for this view is found in the numerous references to EIA in Agenda 21 and the World Summit on Sustainable Development's Plan of Implementation, both as a general obligation on states and as a tool to be used in relation to many specific sectors. Perhaps more importantly Principle 17 of the Rio Declaration, in addition to its general advocacy for preventive and participatory measures, states, in vague but mandatory language, that:

Environmental impact assessment, as a national instrument, shall be undertaken for proposed activities that are likely to have a significant adverse impact on the environment and are subject to a decision of a competent national authority.[3]

BOX 13.2 The World Bank and environmental impact assessment (EIA)[4]

Any generally accepted international legal requirement for states to conduct an environmental assessment applies primarily to development projects with transboundary risks. But at international level, assessment standards can, in some cases, go beyond dealing with transboundary harms and apply to national development projects that do not generate cross-border risks—for example, the damming of an internal river for hydroelectric generation. A leading example of this is the way in which funding from the World Bank is now made subject to EIA. Since 1989, under its Operational Directive (now Operational Policy (OP) 4.01 (1999) *Environmental Assessment*), the World Bank has made the *consideration* of EIA a formal requirement for any of its operations. In particular, Category A projects—that is, those expected to have significant adverse environmental impacts that are sensitive, diverse, or unprecedented—must have a more comprehensive assessment, while Category B projects require less scrutiny, and projects below this threshold—that is, projects likely to have minimal or no adverse environmental impact—do not need to be assessed. Although the borrower undertakes the actual assessment, at least for Category A projects, independent experts must also be involved. Strictly, the Operational Directive is a set of guidelines for World Bank staff and an aim of this form of EIA is as much capacity building in environmental management in the host country as it is a normative standard.

Nevertheless, experience of this form of EIA shows some of the problems with procedural environmental law in a global setting. In many developing countries without traditions of pluralistic decision making, for example, expectations of public participation may be low and there may be limited scope for giving effective voice to those most affected. Indeed, a major criticism of the original 1989 rules was their silence on the provision of information to the public and guaranteed rights for the public to participate in the decision-making process. Now, discussions about the scope of any impact statement are, to encourage NGO involvement, often held in capital cities rather than 'on site'. Evidence suggests that participation requirements have often been overlooked or glossed over, in part because of a lack of receptiveness of World Bank staff to local customary norms, although the guidelines now place greater emphasis on NGO consultation for

---

3 On the status of this Declaration, see p. 147. Further support came at the 1997 UN General Assembly 'Rio+5' Summit, which declared the principle of EIA to be on a par with the Polluter Pays, Precautionary and 'common but differentiated responsibilities' Principles.

4 From K. R. Gray, 'International environmental impact assessment' (2000) Winter Colo J Intl Envtl L & Poly 83, and changes to the operational policy since then, to date.

all Category A or B projects. There is, however, a right to challenge World Bank decisions before an Inspection Panel and there are examples where the Panel has held that the Operational Directive was correctly followed. In one case, for example, funding was withdrawn because there had been a failure to complete an EIA before the project was appraised and negotiated, and because the project would commence before necessary institutional structures for monitoring the environmental impacts were in place.

Looking at the EIA of World Bank funding, therefore, shows some of the general challenges for EIA: selecting a means of deciding which projects require EIA (screening), deciding who will carry out the assessment—the proponent of the project? the decision maker? independent experts?—and ensuring that the assessment itself can be followed through into decision making and subsequent management, while establishing legal rules—about participation and access to justice—that are effective, but also sensitive to national legal and administrative traditions, and to cultural and political realities.

What 'adverse impact on the environment' means here is not specified, but it would appear to include not merely transboundary environmental harm, but also harm to the global environment (for example, climate change)[5] and to domestic environments (for example, a decision to damage a cherished landscape). In this sense, therefore, EIA may represent a sort of common environmental best practice standard in relation to the behaviour of states working towards agreed objectives, because the formulation in the Rio Declaration does not appear to be limited to cases of transboundary harm.[6]

Having said that, EIA in international law has developed primarily from the obligation on states to cooperate with each other, in good faith, in mitigating transboundary environmental risks—an obligation that rests on prior consultation based on adequate information. (Failure to carry out an EIA may also make it difficult for a state to show that it had exercised 'due diligence' in controlling or preventing foreseeable harm.) As Birnie and Boyle have noted:

Without prior assessment there can be no meaningful notification and consultation in most cases of environmental risk. The duty, in other words, is not merely to notify what is known but to know what needs to be notified.[7]

In response to this line of reasoning, the International Court of Justice (ICJ) has given qualified support for the entrenchment of EIA into international law, at least in relation to transboundary harm. In the *Nuclear Tests II* case,[8] Judge Weeramantry thought that transboundary EIA had '*reached the level of general recognition at which this Court should take notice of it*' and his dissenting opinion held that an EIA of French plans to resume underground nuclear tests in the Pacific was required.

An indication of the pace with which EIA has become part of international environmental law, however, can be seen from the *Danube Dam* case only two years later,[9] in which the majority of the ICJ interpreted the Treaty between Hungary and Slovakia as requiring the parties together to 'look afresh' at the environmental effects of the project. In Judge Weeramantry's concurring opinion, this places a duty on states of 'continuous environmental impact assessment'—continual assessment of environmental impact in the light of

5 Although the Climate Change Convention has a specific provision about environmental assessment: see Art. 4(1)(f).
6 See also Art. 14 of the 1992 Convention on Biological Diversity.
7 (2002) *International Law and the Environment*, 2nd edn, Oxford: Oxford University Press, p. 133.
8 *New Zealand v. France* [1995] ICJ Rep 288.
9 *Case concerning the Gabčíkovo-Nagymaros Project (Hungary/Slovakia)* 37 ILM (1998) 162—see Case 6.5.

modern knowledge—and that this is a component of states' procedural obligations in relation to sustainable development (his opinion having argued that sustainable development is a principle of customary international law).

This approach is notable because it goes beyond what is generally required when decisions about consenting harmful activities are being taken. For example, at national level, EIA only needs to be undertaken when application for consent is made (although SEA will require assessment of plans that, in their nature, are likely to be revised every few years) and does not require any post-project assessment. In international law, the 'good neighbourliness' duty is an ongoing one—hence EIA may also have to stretch beyond the original harmful development. So the *form* that EIA may take may depend on the legal *context* in which it is used. But it is also worth stressing that the ICJ seems to be conceiving of this duty on states to assess environmental impact as being a technical matter, rather than one that involves public participation and the right of the public to have their views taken into account. Whether international EIA law is simply a harmonization of existing state practice is considered in more depth in Box 13.3.

A further example of EIA being required under international law—this time, under a specific convention—is Art. 206 of the UN Convention on the Law of the Sea (UNCLOS), which provides that:

When states have reasonable grounds for believing that planned activities under their jurisdiction or control may cause substantial pollution of or significant and harmful changes to the marine environment, they shall, as far as practicable, assess the potential effects of such activities on the marine environment.

Again, this is quite a technical—rather than participatory—formulation of EIA. It has been the subject of a dispute between Ireland and the UK over the authorization of a plant to manufacture mixed oxide (MOX) fuel at the Sellafield nuclear complex, the radioactive discharge from which has proven controversial. Ireland argued that the UK had breached Art. 206, both because its 1993 assessment did not consider various potential impacts on the Irish Sea, and because the assessment had not been updated to take into account developments between 1993 and the authorization of the plant in 2001. When provisional measures were being decided, Judge Mensah (in a separate opinion) took a weak view of environmental assessment, seemingly holding that, if the UK had violated its procedural obligations, then these could be remedied even if the authorization was not halted in the interim. The minority judge took a stronger view of Art. 206, holding that more extensive provisional measures were justified because of the centrality of EIA to what he described as 'the international law of prevention' (see further Case 6.7 and Box 17.2).

What little international case law there is, therefore, indicates that EIA in international law is a procedural requirement that emerges, by inference, from substantive obligations owed between states (but see Box 13.3). But in cases in which it is required—and this is perhaps only in cases of transboundary risk to the environment of other states or in which it is provided for under specific treaties, as with harm to the marine environment—states may need to undertake a technical assessment (although not necessarily one that involves the wider public), and may have to revisit existing agreements in the light of new knowledge gained from an EIA-type process.

The major difficulty with international EIA law, however, comes in the detail. In specific environmental treaties, as the following example from Art. 14(1) of the Biodiversity Convention illustrates, the obligation to carry out EIA may be couched in (depending on one's point of view) either highly flexible or extraordinarily vague terms:

Each Contracting Party, as far as possible and as appropriate, shall: (a) Introduce appropriate procedures requiring environmental impact assessment of its proposed projects that are likely to have significant adverse effects on biological diversity with a view to avoiding or minimizing such effects and, where appropriate, allow for public participation in such procedures.

Formulations such as this mean that, as is often the case with customary international environmental law (see p. 142), it may be possible to identify an international principle, but pinning down what it actually requires in real-world situations is difficult.

Three problems in particular can be mentioned:

- determining which kinds of activities need to be assessed;
- determining the degree of environmental risk needed to trigger an EIA;
- determining the procedural requirements for an EIA.

The first of these has two distinct components. First, it might be thought desirable to establish, in advance, the kinds of activities that might be subject to EIA. The regional 1991 UNECE Convention on EIA in a Transboundary Context (the 'Espoo' Convention) does this by listing a range of activities that fall within its remit, such as power stations and nuclear installations. This is backed up by further provisions that allow for projects to fall within its remit if the parties agree and the Convention sets out criteria (based on size, location, and effects) to assist the parties in doing this. But most international environmental treaties, such as the Biodiversity Convention, tend not to be so specific, making their application to particular projects uncertain.

Secondly, international environmental law is only now embracing strategic environmental assessment (see the 2003 Kiev Protocol to the Espoo Convention), but is generally still wedded to assessing individual activities or projects. The degree of risk needed to trigger an EIA is especially problematic. The usual formulation, as seen above, is that there must be a likelihood of significant adverse effects on the environment (or some particular aspect of the environment).[10] An obvious difficulty—inherent, it must be said, to environmental assessment law generally—is that the assessment process is there to identify and respond to the risks, and their significance, so any attempt in advance to set thresholds for when EIA will be required will have a strong element of circularity to it. What is 'significant', therefore, is particularly open-ended and while instances such as the environmental impact caused by the unilateral damming of the Danube will be fairly clear-cut, in many cases, there may be uncertainty about how damaging the effects of projects or activities will be.

The actual procedural requirements of EIA in international law are also somewhat vague. For example, what level of information should be provided? And who should be consulted? Only in very limited instances has the type of information that should be generated been spelt out.[11] This has been criticized as falling some way behind accepted national practice,[12] but more telling is the criticism that any assessment process that excluded details of impacts, mitigation measures, and alternatives would simply fall short of what is required of states to cooperate in good faith on transboundary matters. There has been a tendency to limit consultation requirements to activities near state borders, which seems of limited utility for many projects (the Chernobyl nuclear plant, for example, is not near an international frontier). Consultation requirements in relation to common space such as the high seas can also be very limited.

There are, however, some signs of improvement: the Espoo Convention requires parties to consider '*more remote proposed activities which could give rise to significant transboundary effects far removed from the site of the development*'[13] and the latest proposals by the

---

10 Although note that the EC EIA Directive does not require the effects to be adverse—see p. 447.

11 The 1991 Espoo Convention, e.g., requires the state proposing the harmful activity to provide a description of the activity and its likely impact, mitigation measures and practical alternatives, as well as information about any uncertainties in the available knowledge. See also the United Nations Environment Programme (UNEP) (1987) *Goals and Principles of EIA*.

12 See, e.g., p. 456.

13 Appendix III, Espoo Convention. On transboundary effects, see the impact of the Convention on EC law, at p. 439.

International Law Commission on transboundary harm require consultation for all activities creating significant transboundary risk wherever situated.[14] The Espoo Convention regime also provides a specific mechanism for resolving any dispute that there might be as to whether EIA is required, by enabling any affected state to submit the issue to a compulsory inquiry commission.

BOX 13.3 '**The myth and reality of transboundary environmental impact assessment**'[15]

In this extract, Knox considers the rise of environmental impact assessment (EIA) in international treaties (mostly, in regional agreements such as the Espoo Convention, above) and questions why—given that the international law obligation is that one state should not cause harm to another—international EIA law has no substantive edge to it.

> The dominant story of transboundary environmental impact assessment in international law has the following elements: (1) customary international law prohibits transboundary pollution; (2) according to the classic version of this prohibition, contained in Principle 21 of the 1972 Stockholm Declaration, states must ensure that activities within their territory or under their control do not harm the environment beyond their territory; (3) to ensure that activities within their jurisdiction will not cause transboundary harm, states must assess the potential transboundary effects of the activities; and (4) to that end, states enter into international agreements requiring them to carry out transboundary environmental impact assessment (transboundary EIA) for activities that might cause transboundary harm. Despite its popularity, this story is not true...
>
> What, then, is going on? If transboundary EIA agreements are not designed to end transboundary pollution in accordance with Principle 21, what are they designed to do? One clue is that the agreements were not written on a clean slate. Most countries in North America and Western Europe have already enacted domestic EIA laws, which are limited in scope and lacking in substantive prohibitions but do contain detailed procedural obligations and provide important avenues for public participation. In large part, the regional EIA agreements reflect these domestic EIA laws. In fact, the main way that the agreements extend beyond the domestic laws is by ensuring that states apply EIA without extraterritorial discrimination—that they take extraterritorial effects into account just as they take domestic effects into account, and that they enable foreign residents to have access to the domestic EIA procedures to the same extent as local residents.

Knox therefore concludes that customary international EIA law is influenced more by what is known as the principle of non-discrimination, under which states should apply the same environmental protections to potential harm in other countries that they apply to such harm in their own:

> Examined closely, each regional transboundary EIA agreement is an application of the principle of nondiscrimination. The nondiscrimination principle has often been overlooked, cast into shadow by the glow surrounding Principle 21...

(On Principle 21 of the Stockholm Declaration and the later reformulation of this in Principle 2 of the Rio Declaration, see p. 146.)

---

14 Article 9, 2001 Draft Articles on the Prevention of Transboundary Harm from Hazardous Activities.
15 From J. Knox (2002) 96 AJIL 291.

A final consideration about EIA in an international context is whether an individual or group in one state—that is, not only the state itself—can challenge a decision to authorize a project in another state in which the adequacy of the EIA process is questioned. This dimension to legal standing has two aspects. The first is whether an individual in one state that might be affected by a development project in a neighbouring state has standing to review the EIA process (or lack of one) in the national courts of that neighbouring state—that is, whether national law provisions can give rights to non-nationals. Here, it is worth mentioning that, in a US case, Canadian nationals affected by oil developments in Alaska were given standing to challenge the adequacy of the EIA carried out under US national legislation (*Wilderness Society v. Morton* 463 F. 2d 1261 (1972)). In the UK, the most that is required, in the EC's EIA Directive (85/337/EEC), is to allow for consultation with neighbouring states (including the public of the neighbouring state) in relation to transboundary harm, while the provisions of the Espoo Convention apply to non-EC neighbours. But if the potentially affected state does not wish to get involved, it is unclear that any individual in that state would have any legal remedy.

The second issue is whether an individual in one state (with environmental assessment legislation) can challenge environmental assessment defects in relation to projects with impacts in other countries—that is, whether national environmental assessment law applies extraterritorially. Obviously, there would need to be some link between the action in the other country and the country with environmental assessment law—for example, if the country with environmental assessment law were to give development aid or export credit guarantees that allowed the overseas project to go ahead. Could a UK pressure group, for example, challenge inadequacies of EIA in relation to dam projects in other countries, if the construction work—to be underwritten by the UK government—was authorized in breach of that other country's EIA law? The answer would seem to be that this would not be enough, by itself, for a UK court to intervene: the UK court would only be concerned with whether the UK government had complied with its own legal duties—that is, whether it had followed its own rules and guidance on granting development assistance in the scenario described above.[16] But it is worth noting that there are—again, US—examples in which the courts have, under national law, allowed challenges to federal actions—such as spraying herbicide on marijuana plants in Mexico—to be brought in the US courts.

Environmental impact assessment in the EC

The EC EIA Directive

International legal developments show that EIA obligations (however vague) have stemmed from general duties of good neighbourliness between states. To some extent, the same is also the case with EC law and, as noted above, there are provisions giving potentially affected member States the right to be involved in decision making when projects have transboundary effects.[17] But the origins of Community EIA law lie mainly in two other rationales: one narrow; the other broader. The narrow justification is that Community laws on environmental assessment contribute to harmonizing the conditions of competition between member States. Put simply, the authorization process, for example, for a chemical installation in one member State should be as rigorous, procedurally, as that in any other member State.

16 As in *R v. Secretary of State for Foreign Affairs, ex parte World Development Movement* [1995] 1 All ER 611.

17 Article 7, EIA Directive, significantly amended by Directive 97/11/EC in the light of the Espoo Convention; implemented (eventually) by regs 27 and 28, 1999 Regulations. The potentially affected member State has the right to be notified, but then has a discretion whether to get involved in full consultation. This may rule out the possibility that individuals in neighbouring states have rights to be involved in the decision-making process in the other member States.

But this is too formalistic an explanation for the adoption of Community environmental assessment legislation. A broader rationale, and better explanation, is that the environment is a matter of common concern across the Community, such that the member States have collectively relinquished (or pooled) certain aspects of their sovereignty over development decisions that are likely to have significant effects on the environment, regardless of whether these effects (environmental or economic) are felt across Community frontiers. As Lord Hoffmann said in *R v. North Yorkshire County Council, ex parte Brown* [1998] Env LR 623 (see p. 445), '[The] *directive was adopted to protect the environment* throughout *the EU*' (emphasis added). In this crucial respect, therefore, EC law goes well beyond accepted international law and practice.

After many years of fierce negotiation,[18] Directive 85/337/EEC on the assessment of the effects of certain private and public projects on the environment (the EIA Directive) was adopted. The EIA Directive established the need to consider information about the effects of a development on the environment as a mandatory component of the decision-making process in relation to certain specified projects.

Directive 85/337/EEC, which was amended from 1999 by Directive 97/11/EC, requires member States to ensure that certain planning decisions that are likely to have significant environmental effects are taken only after a proper assessment of what those effects are likely to be (see Box 13.4). A distinction is made between projects listed in Annex I to the Directive (under which EIA is compulsory) and those listed in Annex II (under which EIA is only required if such significant effects are likely).

BOX 13.4 The EIA Directive—the general duty

Article 2(1) of the EIA Directive provides that:

> Member states shall adopt all measures necessary to ensure that, before consent is given, projects likely to have significant effects on the environment by virtue, inter alia, of their nature, size or location are made subject to a requirement for development consent and an assessment with regard to their effects.

The Directive sets out the detailed requirements for an assessment, which should include direct and indirect effects of a project on a variety of factors, including human beings, fauna, flora, the environment and material assets, and the cultural heritage. The developer must submit certain specified information relating to these impacts to the authority dealing with the application. There are also provisions for consultation with the authorities likely to be concerned with the project and with members of the general public, although the detailed arrangements for consultation are left to individual member States.

Two developments should also be mentioned here. First, the EC Directive on strategic environment assessment (SEA) (2001/42/EC) came into effect in 2004. This Directive extends the Community's involvement in environmental assessment beyond individual development projects, and takes in the assessment of certain plans and programmes (but not policies) that are prepared for a number of sectors, and which set a framework for future development consents of Annex I and II projects. (SEA is considered in more detail at the end of this chapter.)

---

18 On the negotiation of the EIA Directive (and the impact that strongly felt UK and Danish objections had), see N. Haigh (1987) JPL 4; J. Golub (1996) Environmental Politics 700; W. Sheate (1996) *Environmental Impact Assessment: Law and Policy-Making an Impact II*, London: Cameron May, pp. 18–22.

Secondly, further amendments to the EIA Directive have been made in order to align its provisions with those of the Aarhus Convention on access to information, public participation in decision-making, and access to justice in environmental matters.[19] The Aarhus Convention contains more specific provisions about public participation in decision making than the original EIA Directive and its implementation places certain limits on the scope for member States to determine their own procedures. These changes have been made by the Town and Country Planning (Environmental Impact Assessment) (Amendment) Regulations 2006.[20]

Implementing the EIA Directive in the UK

The original EIA Directive was adopted and implemented in England and Wales by regulations enacted under the European Communities Act 1972.[21] Since then, the Secretary of State has been granted power to make regulations extending, beyond the Directive, the categories of projects that can be subject to assessment.[22] This power has been used once, and only in a limited fashion, however, and the extension of the EIA regime to new projects has come about primarily through amendment to the EIA Directive. That said, in the implementation of Directive 97/11/EC, the core Town and Country Planning (Environmental Impact Assessment) (England and Wales) Regulations 1999 (the 1999 Regulations),[23] which cover projects requiring planning permission and which are listed in the Directive, were made both under the European Communities Act 1972 and under s. 71A of the Town and Country Planning Act 1990, so, in principle, EIA could be required for projects that are not listed in the Directive. But there is a reluctance to extend the scope of EIA beyond that required by EC law.

Projects that do not require planning permission because they are dealt with under separate consent procedures are governed by separate sets of regulations. These include proposals in areas such as afforestation and deforestation, highways, harbour works, marine fish farming, power stations and overhead power lines, and pipelines. These separate regulations all follow the framework of the general planning regulations, but the extraordinary delay in enacting some of these specialist regulations has been striking and not without environmental cost. For example, failure to implement EIA in relation to certain agricultural operations was considered a possible contributory factor in the serious floods of 2000.[24]

Is the project subject to EIA?

EIA law can be broken down into a number of discrete stages. The first stage is to determine whether or not the project falls within the criteria for the requirement of EIA. As we saw with EIA in international law, there is a central conundrum over which projects should be subject to EIA, because likely effects can really only be known after some kind of assessment. Logically, therefore, all projects would have to be assessed, but to require formal EIA in relation to every project proposal would be disproportionate to the objectives being sought. One way in which to address this might be to make a limited initial assessment—in effect, a

---

19 Directive 2003/35/EC. On the Aarhus Convention, see p. 294.

20 SI 2006/3295.

21 The main ones were the Town and Country Planning (Assessment of Environmental Effects) Regulations 1988, SI 1988/1199 (similar regulations applied to areas outside the planning system and in Scotland).

22 Planning and Compensation Act 1991, s. 15, which inserted s. 71A into the Town and Country Planning Act 1990.

23 SI 1999/293.

24 HC Environment, Transport and Regional Affairs Committee Second Report (Session 2000–01) *Development on, or Affecting, the Flood Plain*, para. 44.

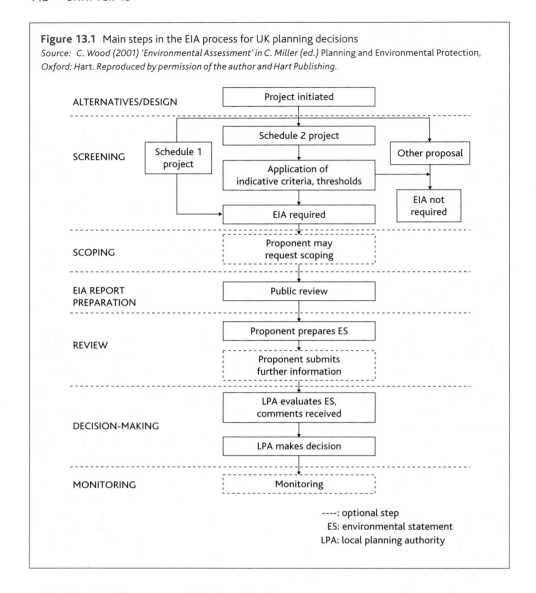

Figure 13.1 Main steps in the EIA process for UK planning decisions
Source: C. Wood (2001) 'Environmental Assessment' in C. Miller (ed.) Planning and Environmental Protection, Oxford: Hart. Reproduced by permission of the author and Hart Publishing.

'mini-EIA'—followed by a more detailed assessment if the potential for significant impact is revealed.[25] The EIA Directive, however, steers a pragmatic course by assuming that certain projects will give rise to likely effects (those projects listed in Annex I of the Directive) and then, in line with subsidiarity and flexibility, giving member States more discretion over which projects falling within Annex II of the Directive should be assessed.[26] By implication, therefore, under EC law, EIA is not required for any project that does not fall within one of the categories of projects listed in Annexes I or II of the Directive.

25 An example of this is the provision for initial environmental evaluations in the 1991 Antarctic Environmental Protocol, which are to determine if an activity will have more than a minor or transitory impact. Mini-EIA was recommended by the Commission in its first five-year review of the EIA Directive.

26 A logical consequence is that the decision regarding whether an EIA is needed for a Sch. 2 project must be made on the basis of less comprehensive information than would be generated by an EIA—see Case 13.4.

(It is worth noting here that the 1999 Regulations use the terms 'Schedule one' and 'Schedule two'—rather than Annex I and II—projects; we do the same, unless referring expressly to the EIA Directive.)

What is a 'project'?

EIA requires there to be a 'project' that is subject to a 'consent'. In the EIA Directive, the term 'project' is defined as the execution of construction works, or of other installations or schemes. This equates roughly with the concept of 'development' in English planning law. As noted above, however, many activities listed in the EIA Directive fall outside the range of activities classed as 'development' in planning law and hence specific regulations have had to be enacted in these areas—for example, the decommissioning of nuclear power stations. Whether demolition—which, as such, does not require planning permission—requires EIA remains an unsettled point.[27]

In some respects, however, whether something is a 'project' is a secondary consideration. Thus in *R (Edwards) v. Environment Agency (No. 2)* [2007] Env LR 9, a case about changing the fuel source at a cement works to waste tyres, the Court of Appeal could not find a category listed in the Directive into which this fell, so whether it was a 'project' was irrelevant (although it did stress that operations, as well as constructions, could be 'projects', which is in line with the interpretation given to 'projects' under EC nature conservation law— see p. 711).[28]

Two further issues relate to what the 'project' is that might require assessment. EIA might be avoided by breaking up a development project into several small projects, none of which individually require EIA (sometimes known as 'salami slicing'). More usually, however, the issue is whether decision makers must consider the cumulative impacts of development projects. In national guidance, local planning authorities are not only advised to have regard to possible cumulative effects, but where appropriate to consider together more than one application for development to determine whether or not EIA is required.[29] This follows national case law that has held it appropriate for a planning authority to look beyond what was being applied for if the reality was that the application was part of a more substantial development, because this would fall within what the likely effects of the project would be.[30]

An alternative approach, however, is to ask whether it makes sense to consider the individual project proposal in isolation. In Case C-227/01 *Commission v. Spain* [2005] Env LR 20, for example, a relatively short section of railway track was held to fall within the Annex I project category of 'construction of... lines for long-distance railway traffic', because it formed part of the Mediterranean Corridor linking Spain with the French border and, if one looked at each small stretch of the line in isolation, the Directive could be evaded.[31]

The European Court of Justice (ECJ) has yet to pronounce directly on the extent to which competent authorities may or must consider actual or likely projects beyond that under consideration, where the project forms part of a larger project. But the Advocate-General has, in one case, made reference to the inclusion of projects within 'current plans' (Case C-396/92 *Bund Naturschutz in Bayern and ors v. Freistaat Bayern* [1994] ECR I-3717). The ECJ has, however, pronounced on the issue of cumulative impacts (see Case 13.1).

27 *R (England) v. London Borough of Tower Hamlets* [2006] EWCA Civ 1742.

28 A similar case, bypassing 'project' by looking for an appropriate category, is *R (Mayor and Citizens of the City of Westminster, Preece and Adamson) v. The Mayor of London* [2002] EWHC 2440) (London congestion charge).

29 Circular 2/99, para. 46.

30 *R v. Swale Borough Council, ex parte RSPB* [1991] 1 PLR 6 (dredging did not require EIA, but ensuing development on land reclaimed as a consequence might require assessment). Cf *R (Candlish) v. Hastings Borough Council* [2005] EWHC 1539.

31 See also *R v. Secretary of State for Transport, ex parte Surrey County Council*, November 1993, unreported (widening of stretches of the M25 motorway).

CASE 13.1 Significant effects—the (ir)relevance of size—Case C-392/96 *Commission v. Ireland* [1999] ECR I-5901

Changing rural land uses can have significant environmental impact. Three such uses of land—changing uncultivated land or semi-natural areas to intensive agriculture, initial afforestation, and peat extraction—are Annex II projects. The European Court of Justice held that Ireland had incorrectly transposed the Environmental Impact Assessment (EIA) Directive, because very high size thresholds had been used, which meant that EIA was not required for every project likely to have significant effects on the environment. The Directive had also been breached because Ireland's transposing law only had regard to the size of projects and did not take into account their nature or location. For example, the rarity and sensitivity of active blanket bogs would, the Court suggested, mean that afforestation would have adverse impact regardless of the size of the planting.

The Court also considered whether the cumulative impacts of individual projects should fall within the scope of the Directive. For example, numerous initial afforestation projects could be undertaken in Ireland without EIA, provided that they were conducted by different developers, each of whom kept within the national threshold used (70ha). The ECJ held that:

> not taking account of the cumulative effect of projects means in practice that all projects of a certain type may escape the obligation to carry out an assessment when, taken together, they are likely to have significant effects on the environment.

This suggests that the cumulative impacts of projects may need to be assessed, but probably only in cases in which that particular type of project as a whole would otherwise be completely excluded from assessment—that is, the fact that one road, for example, falls below a national threshold will not mean that all road projects can be grouped together to take them above the threshold. Or, in other words, the obligation to assess cumulative impacts is different from that of strategic environmental assessment.

What is a 'consent'?

'Development consent' is defined as the decision of the competent authority that entitles the developer to proceed with the project. There is some difficulty with what 'proceeding with the project' means. This does not necessarily equate with planning permission, because other statutory consents could be required. Many developments—such as processes subject to integrated pollution prevention and control (IPPC), for example—may be built under a planning permission, but can only be operated with other licences.[32] And there are examples, such as with marine fish farms, in which EIA is required when consents are renewed, not only when there is new development. On one interpretation, therefore, it might be argued that the Directive requires the Environment Agency (for example) to request an EIA when considering an application from a landfill site for an environmental permit in relation to which the local planning authority had failed to require an assessment. Although this is not the case in UK law, we have long argued that it could be, because waste disposal installations are Annex II projects and the Directive has direct effect in some situations.[33] There is now some support for this. In *R (Gregan) v. Environment Agency* [2003] EWHC 3278, it was found

---

32 RCEP (2002) para. 5.24 called for there to be a common environmental statement when a large industrial plant is seeking both planning permission and an IPPC authorization. That is, narrow legalistic problems can be avoided by a more holistic approach to decision making.

33 For a more extreme example, see the case of offshore wind farms and the numerous consents needed: G. Plant [2003] JPL 939.

to be at least arguable that substantial modifications to a waste management licence could be a development consent for which EIA was required.

Another tricky issue has been the status of permitted development. Some activities are permitted development for which planning permission is deemed to be granted (see p. 398). These are usually minor developments, or developments in the public interest by statutory undertakers. Directive 97/11/EC, however, made clear that *all* such projects *must* obtain development consent—that is, that EIA also applies to projects for which consent is not needed because the project is not 'development' or the development is permitted by a development order.[34] Hence, all developments listed in Annexes I and II are subject to assessment, regardless of the national position in relation to automatic development consent.

Perhaps the most problematic issues with what the 'consent' is arise when the decision-making process is split into stages. Usually, this division is between an initial decision giving the go-ahead, in principle, for a project and a later decision fleshing out the details of the permission. For example, there is a particular difficulty in UK planning law deriving from outline planning permission being sought for development and then, if this permission is granted, 'reserved matters' being approved by the local planning authority at a later date. A further area that has given rise to difficulties has been the control of old mining permissions. The real issue is about what stage of the process the developer has to submit the environmental statement. Accordingly, in these cases, attention has so far focused on the sufficiency of information that developers are required to submit in their environmental statements at the outline stage (see Box 13.6). The leading cases are outlined in Case 13.2.

CASE 13.2 What is 'the consent'?

In *R v. Secretary of State for the Environment, ex parte Greenpeace Ltd* [1994] Env LR 401, a case that concerned the thermal oxide reprocessing plant (THORP) at Sellafield, Potts J rejected an argument that authorization under the Radioactive Substances Act 1993—without which the plant could not operate—was something for which separate development consent was required. The construction of the plant and its use for disposal of nuclear waste were all part of one project for which consent had been given before the Directive came into force.

By contrast, in *R v. North Yorkshire County Council, ex parte Brown* [1998] Env LR 623, the House of Lords had to consider whether environmental impact assessment was required when conditions were attached to an old mining permission, dating from 1947, under changes made by the Planning and Compensation Act 1991 (the 1991 Act sought to make such permissions more acceptable, especially in terms of their environmental impact). The House of Lords construed the EIA Regulations purposively in the light of the Directive and held that it was the decision on the new conditions that allowed the quarrying to proceed. The imposition of the conditions was a distinct event from, for example, the attaching of conditions to a planning permission.[35]

In the subsequent case *R (Wells) v. Secretary of State for Transport, Local Government and the Regions* [2004] Env LR 27, a case on similar facts to *Brown*, the European Court of Justice took a similar approach to that taken in *Brown*:

---

34 The rules on EIA and permitted development are now contained in the 1999 Regulations and in changes to the Town and Country Planning (General Permitted Development) Order 1995. Those developments that are permitted, but subject to separate control regimes, such as forestry operations, are covered by separate regulations.

35 For a similar case involving consent originally granted pre-1988 under a zoning plan, but for which a fresh consent procedure was initiated after 1988, see Case C-81/96 *Burgemeester en welthouders van Haarlemmerliede en Spaarnwoude and Others v. Gedeputeerde Staten van Noord-Holland* [1998] ECR I-3923.

> It would undermine the effectiveness of [the EIA Directive] to regard as mere modifications of an existing consent the adoption of decisions which…replace not only the terms but the very substance of a prior consent, such as an old mining permission.[36]

Wells also suggested that, with any type of multistage consent process, it would be unlawful to restrict EIA to the initial consent. In the main implementing regulations for EIA, however, it is the outline planning permission that is considered the 'consent', because, at the reserved matters stage, the local planning authority cannot raise objections to the principle of the development (although reserve matters must still be approved).

In Case C-508/03 *Commission v. UK* [2007] Env LR 1 and Case C-290/03 *R (Barker) v. Bromley London Borough Council* [2007] Env LR 2,[37] the ECJ, following *Wells*, has confirmed that EIA may be required at the stage of approving reserved matters. But this will only be the case if significant environmental effects emerge that have not been properly considered at the outline stage; this might be because of a failure to consider EIA at the outline stage, new evidence that emerges at the reserved matters stage, or a change of circumstances.[38] If the outline permission carefully sets the parameters for the reserved matters, a subsequent EIA should be rare.

Schedule 1 projects—mandatory EIA

Having considered what, in law, 'projects' and 'consents' are, which types of project do the EIA Directive and the 1999 Regulations cover? As might be expected, the projects falling within Sch. 1 to the 1999 Regulations, under which EIA is mandatory, include major projects such as crude oil refineries, thermal power stations, integrated chemical installations, motorways, and major roads. Following Directive 97/11/EC, the list now also includes such projects as pig and poultry units, and groundwater abstraction schemes. The ECJ has held that modifications to Annex I projects may, judged objectively, also fall within Annex I, if the modification itself exceeds the thresholds for Annex I projects (Case C-431/92 *Commission v. Germany* [1995] ECR I-2189).

It is worth noting that many of these types of project have always been subject to thorough scrutiny and are often considered at major public inquiries, involving many months of preparation and a vast range of documentation. But it is fair to say that, until the EIA Directive was implemented, the public was largely excluded from the technical debate unless it had the financial resources to instruct experts to act on its behalf. If the EIA process operates satisfactorily in disseminating information in intelligible terms, then the public may be able to play a more effective role in these inquiries.

For most projects falling within Sch. 1, the definition of the project is self-explanatory. For some kinds of project, however, thresholds are used to define the types of project to which mandatory EIA applies. For example, a thermal power station other than a nuclear power station is subject to mandatory EIA only if it has a heat output of 300 megawatts or more. If there is any degree of uncertainty over whether or not a project falls within Sch. 1, a ruling on the need for an assessment can be obtained from either the Secretary of State or the local planning authority (see p. 454). Exceptionally, it might be argued that an Annex I project will not, in fact, have significant environmental effects. The ECJ has held back from giving a clear ruling that this would not be relevant to whether EIA is required.[39] But it is submitted

---

36 At [46].

37 The final ruling is *R (Barker) v. Bromley London Borough Council* [2007] Env LR 20 (referral back to House of Lords).

38 Policy guidance on this may follow (interim guidance having been produced following the ECJ rulings).

39 Case C-227/01 *Commission v. Spain* [2005] Env LR 20.

that the answer is simply that, under Art. 4, all Annex I projects must be assessed unless one of the exemptions in Art. 2(3) applies and that, if a member State feels strongly that EIA is unnecessary, then it can, in advance, use Art. 2(3) (see p. 455).

BOX 13.5 EIA projects—matters of fact or matters of law?

For many years, the English courts took the view that whether a project is of a type that falls within Sch. 1 or Sch. 2—or indeed neither—was a matter of fact and degree for the planning authority, not a matter of law. This was always a questionable line of authority, which dated from a decision from the early years of implementing the Environmental Impact Assessment (EIA) Directive (*R v. Swale Borough Council, ex parte RSPB* [1991] 1 PLR 6 and strong criticism of this decision by Grant[40]). This has now been overturned and it is clear that the courts are sensitive to what the European Court of Justice has described as the 'wide scope and broad purpose' of the Directive (the *Kraaijeveld* case, see p. 448)—that is, that it should not be construed narrowly so that projects that might fall within Schs 1 or 2 are excluded even before their environmental impact is considered (*R (Goodman) v. Lewisham London Borough* [2003] Env LR 28).

That said, some of the categories of Sch. 2 in particular are potentially very wide—for example, an 'installation for the disposal of waste' could be anything from a compost bin to a landfill site—and decision makers appear to retain some discretion to decide whether, if looked at reasonably, an activity could be of the kind that is covered by EIA.

Schedule 2 projects—EIA only when significant environmental effects are likely

The projects within Sch. 2 to the 1999 Regulations are, by and large, the types of development that are less sensitive in nature. Examples include motorway service areas, food manufacture, holiday villages, golf courses, tanneries, paper manufacture, and urban development projects, such as retail parks. The list also includes Sch. 1 projects below their thresholds (for example, a thermal power station with a heat output of less than 300 megawatts), and modifications to Sch. 1 and Sch. 2 projects.[41] Notably, the significant effects need not be negative: as the judge in one case pointed out, '*benefit, like beauty, is in the eye of the beholder*',[42] and there may be disagreement about whether a development project is beneficial or harmful to the environment. A central purpose behind EIA is to give individuals the chance to express their views on such issues.[43] So a wastewater treatment plant, or an urban regeneration project specifically intended to improve the environment, might also need to be assessed.

That a project is of a kind mentioned in Sch. 2—which, as discussed above, is not a matter over which decision makers have much discretion—does not mean that EIA is necessarily required. EIA is only needed when the project is '*likely to have significant effects on the environment by virtue of factors such as its nature, size or location*' (EIA Directive, Art. 2(1)). Following important changes under Directive 97/11/EC, the 1999 Regulations contain

---

40 M. Grant [1991] JEL 135.

41 Although a modification to a Sch. 1 project may itself be a Sch. 1 project: see above.

42 *British Telecommunications plc v. Gloucester City Council* [2001] EWHC Admin 1001, [69].

43 *BT plc v. Gloucester City Council* [2001] EWHC 1001, [64]–[70]. See also *Berkeley (No. 1)* (Case 13.7), in which the trigger for the objection was environmental mitigation work (the river walkway). Note that the usual formulation in international agreements, discussed above, tends to require significant adverse environmental impacts, although there are exceptions (e.g., the Espoo Convention).

much more explicit guidance on when an EIA will be required. This is through selection (or 'screening') criteria to which the decision maker must have regard (Sch. 3), grouped together under general headings of:

- the characteristics of the development;
- the location of the development;
- the characteristics of the potential impact.

Under the first of these, the size of the development, its use of natural resources, and its waste production, for example, must all be considered. (These criteria are basically 'copied out' from Annex III of the Directive.)

Significant effects—the use of thresholds

The 1999 Regulations take advantage of the option under the Directive of using thresholds to 'screen out' from the need for EIA Sch. 2 projects that are unlikely to have significant environmental effects. Rather than determining every application on a case-by-case basis, therefore, relatively low-level 'exclusive' thresholds are used for many Sch. 2 developments, their use being to guide planning authorities and lighten the regulatory burden. These thresholds, however, need to be read alongside three general screening factors, contained in DETR Circular 2/99, *Environmental Impact Assessment* (WO 11/99):

- whether the project is of more than local importance in terms of its size and physical scale;
- the sensitivity of the location—for example, a site of special scientific interest (SSSI);
- whether it would give rise to unusually complex and potentially adverse environmental effects—for example, from a polluting discharge.

These factors flesh out the Secretary of State's interpretation of those situations in which the screening criteria will result in an EIA being needed. An Annex to Circular 2/99 also gives guidance on specific projects. For example, any motorway service area in a sensitive area, or above 0.5 hectares, must be screened, but government advice is that EIA is 'more likely' on greenfield sites and if the proposed development would be above 5 hectares. The guidance also gives further locational factors that might be relevant, such as a local biodiversity action plan, or the effect of the development on places such as air quality management areas and designated bathing waters. Small developments, and even minor modifications, may have major impacts, such as if a small airport runway is extended to accommodate much larger planes.

What limits have the courts placed on the discretion to rule out the need for EIA by the use of thresholds (and, by implication, on the question of 'significance')? The ECJ has held that thresholds cannot be so lax that a member State can, in advance, effectively exempt whole classes of projects listed in Annex II (Case C-133/94 *Commission v. Belgium* [1996] ECR I-2323). Thus in Case C-72/95 *Aanemersbedriff P K Kraaijeveld BV v. Gedeputeerde Staten van Zuid-Holland* [1996] ECR I-5403, the applicants challenged the modification of a zoning plan that dealt with the reinforcement of dykes. They argued that the works were subject to EIA under the terms of the Directive. The projects fell within Annex II, but the modification fell below the threshold set out in the domestic legislation. Trying to sidestep arguments that Annex II was not sufficiently precise to have direct effect (see p. 209), the ECJ held that the Dutch national court was able to consider whether a member State had exceeded the limits of its discretion in implementing the Directive.[44]

---

44 When the case went back to the Dutch Council of State, the decision not to require EIA for the specific dyke construction works was upheld, emphasizing that a reference to the ECJ simply clarifies a point of law.

Subsequently, in Case C-435/97 *World Wildlife Fund (WWF) and ors v. Autonome Provinz Bozen and ors* [2000] I CMLR 149, the ECJ was asked to consider a challenge to a decision not to require an EIA for redevelopment at Bolzano airport in Italy. The project would have changed the use of the airport from military to civilian and cargo flights, requiring some new development and intensifying effects from things such as noise. The Court followed the *Kraaijeveld* case in holding that the key test in relation to Annex II projects was whether such projects were likely to have significant environmental effects because of their size, nature, or location. If this was the case, then the relevant authorities had to ensure that the project in question was assessed.

In the *Kraaijeveld* and *Bozen* cases, therefore, what the ECJ has done is hold that the discretion given to the member States is limited by the overriding need to assess all projects in Annex II if they are likely to give rise to significant environmental effects because of their size, nature, or location.[45] On this basis, therefore, a member State cannot maintain that an Annex II project will never have significant environmental effects in its territory. Given that the sensitivity of the location is a key factor, this must surely be correct, because, for example, even an innocuous project might have a significant impact if sited in an important wildlife habitat.

Additionally, the ECJ has made it clear that *all* of the factors—size, nature, and location— must be taken into account in reaching decisions about the need for EIA and that relying exclusively on just one threshold factor (as Ireland did in relying on the size of various damaging rural activities—see Case 13.1) may breach the Directive. The UK approach avoids this pitfall by removing size thresholds in cases in which harmful projects are located in 'sensitive areas', which include SSSIs, European sites (under the Conservation (Natural Habitats etc.) Regulations 1994[46]), national parks, World Heritage sites and areas of outstanding natural beauty (AONBs). Case 13.3 considers the leading national case.

CASE 13.3 Minimum thresholds—*Berkeley v. Secretary of State for the Environment, Transport and the Regions (No. 3)* [2002] Env LR 14

Planning permission was granted for a block of flats by the River Thames. Environmental impact assessment had not been required, because the area of the proposed development, at 0.19 hectares, was below the 0.5 hectare threshold for urban development projects and because the development was not in a sensitive area. The Court of Appeal held that the decision not to require EIA was lawful. In effect, the Court upheld the threshold for such projects and decided that, as long as the threshold set by the Secretary of State took into account not only the size per se of the project, then it could lawfully be used to screen out the need for EIA for projects that fell beneath it.

The case, then, is a good example of the tension between formulating general rules and applying general principles. In the interests of subsidiarity and of efficient administration, the EIA Directive allows thresholds to be used and this must mean that projects below these thresholds are not examined on a detailed case-by-case basis. So the issue becomes whether the thresholds have been set reasonably and whether the individual project will actually have significant environmental effects is, at this point, irrelevant.

The UK approach has been criticized for relying heavily (outside sensitive areas) on size factors alone, as in *Berkeley (No. 3)*.[47] A slightly different example is *R (Horner) v. Lancashire*

---

45 That is, that the obligation in Art. 4 of the Directive is circumscribed by the general duty to assess projects with significant environmental effects found in Art. 2 of the Directive (see Case 13.1).

46 SI 1994/2716.

47 W. Upton, 'The continuing impact of the EIA regime' (2001) UKELA Yearbook.

County Council [2007] EWCA Civ 784, in which development was beneath the new floor-space area set as the threshold for Sch. 2 development at cement works. The court rejected the view that, given the nature of the development (a change to using animal waste-derived fuels in the kilns), there was an overriding duty to assess the project because, in effect, the threshold did not capture the nature of the environmental impact. But the court held that the threshold was not so low that, *Kraaijeveld*-like, it would defeat the purpose of the Directive; nor did the court think it completely inappropriate in the circumstances. The court noted that, exceptionally, the Secretary of State may still require EIA for projects falling below the relevant 'exclusive' threshold[48] and the court was simply not prepared to open this up for a case-by-case review.

The use of thresholds may also mean that a development well in excess of a threshold will not require EIA. For example, in *R (Kathro) v. Rhondda Cynon Taff Borough Council* [2002] Env LR 15, a community learning centre was proposed by the local authority, which, covering 11.5 hectares, was over 20 times in excess of the minimum threshold (0.5 hectares) for urban development projects. Following screening, however, no environmental assessment was required. The judge held that the local authority had given careful consideration to the likely effects of the development and that its decision was a 'conclusion reasonably open to it'.

Finally, by implication, factors other than size, nature, and location should not be taken into account in assessing the significance (or otherwise) of effects; simply because a development proposal is controversial or opposed at local or national level will not, per se, dictate whether there is an EIA (see Circular 02/99). Although the issue of other factors has not been ruled upon directly, the ECJ has held that the duty in the Habitats Directive (92/43/EEC) to subject projects 'likely to have significant effects' to 'appropriate assessment' does not allow member States to exempt projects from assessment because of their low cost or their purpose (Case C-256/98 *Commission v. France* [2000] ECR I-2487), and it must be likely that the Court would interpret the EIA Directive similarly.

Significant environmental effects—discretion beyond thresholds

From the above, it should be clear that thresholds never definitively determine whether EIA is required, at least in cases in which the threshold is exceeded. So a central question is the extent of discretion that planning authorities have in determining whether a Sch. 2 project needs EIA and the related question of what scope the courts have to overturn a decision that EIA is not required. Neither the Directive, nor the Regulations, explicitly define 'significant environmental effects', but guidance is found in the information that developers must supply in their environmental statements (see Box 13.6). Without repeating this information here, it is worth noting that this includes direct and indirect effects, and effects not only on component parts of the environment, such as air and water, but also environmental impacts more holistically.

The approach of the national courts has been to give planning authorities a fair degree of discretion in deciding whether a Sch. 2 project requires EIA, consistent with the approach taken to questions of discretion generally in planning law[49]—that is, the courts will only intervene if any decision is so unreasonable that no reasonable decision maker could have reached it. As was said in *R (Malster) v. Ipswich Borough Council and Ipswich Town Football*

---

48 If the Secretary of State directs: see reg. 4(8), 1999 Regs. This is a power to direct, not a duty: see *Berkeley v. Secretary of State for the Environment, Transport and the Regions (No. 3)* [2002] Env LR 14 (Case 13.3).

49 *R v. Swale Borough Council, ex parte RSPB* [1991] 1 PLR 6. See also *R v. Metropolitan Borough of Wirral and anor, ex parte Gray* [1998] Env LR D13. This contrasts with US law, in which a 'hard look' at the likely effects is required and in which the courts have, in effect, placed the onus on the proponent of the project to show that any impacts identified will be insignificant: R. Percival, A. Miller, C. Schroeder, and J. Leape (1996) *Environmental Regulation: Law, Science and Policy*, Little Brown, pp. 1050–59.

Club [2001] EWHC Admin 711, a case relating to redevelopment of the football ground (and see also *Berkeley (No. 3)*, Case 13.3):

A detailed knowledge of the locality and expertise in assessing the environmental effects of different kinds of development are both essential in answering the question [whether proposed developments will have significant environmental effects], which is pre-eminently a matter of judgement and degree rather than a question of fact. Unlike the local planning authority, the court does not possess such knowledge or expertise.[50]

But the courts have imposed a fairly low barrier on challengers to show that a project *might* have fallen within Sch. 2, in cases in which other procedural defects have been at stake. As Lord Hoffmann said in *Berkeley (No. 1)* (see Case 13.7):

It is arguable that the development was [a Sch. 2 development] and the conflicting evidence on the potential effect on the river is enough in itself to show that it was arguably likely to have significant effects on the environment. In those circumstances, individuals affected by the development had a directly enforceable right to have the need for an EIA considered before the grant of planning permission by the Secretary of State and not afterwards by a judge.[51]

This cautious approach can also be seen in relation to applications for outline planning permission. In cases in which outline permission is given for a development, and, for example, there is little more than an illustrative plan and nothing to restrict the eventual development to the size or nature indicated, then the courts seem prepared to quash the planning permission for lack of EIA. So in one case in which outline permission was sought for an accommodation centre for asylum applicants, the courts, in effect, said that the likely effects could not be regarded as insignificant because there was nothing in the application that limited the eventual size of the accommodation to a specific number of beds.[52] This, in effect, takes the test used in relation to the sufficiency of the environmental information contained in statements (see p. 457) and applies the same logic to the screening process.

The courts have offered sporadic guidance on the factors to which planning authorities need to have regard in determining whether there might be significant environmental effects. In *R v. St Edmundsbury Borough Council, ex parte Walton* [1999] JPL 805,[53] a planning officer had recommended that an application by the Greene King brewery be refused planning permission because of impact to, among other things, water meadows. But he had not required an environmental statement to be submitted. On this issue, the decision of the council not to require EIA was upheld and the case therefore suggests that the mere view that development should be refused on environmental grounds is not in itself enough to show 'significant' environmental impact such as to require EIA. In addition, in a similar way to the approach of the courts to cases about the planning–pollution interface, the significance of the impact must also be judged assuming that environmental regulators—but including here the action of planning authorities on things such as reserved matters—act reasonably competently.[54] This does not mean, however, that significance is to be judged only on the basis of the effects after such authorities have imposed conditions (a matter we consider in more detail below).

---

50 At [61].

51 At [36].

52 *R (Orchard) v. First Secretary of State* [2004] Env LR 12. See also *BT plc v. Gloucester City Council* [2001] EWHC 1001.

53 Note that the planning permission was quashed because of a procedural defect—see p. 454.

54 *R v. Rochdale Metropolitan Borough Council, ex parte Milne* [2001] Env LR 22 at [128]; *Smith v. Secretary of State for the Environment, Transport and the Regions* [2003] EWCA Civ 262, [51]. On the potential overlap between planning and pollution controls, see p. 504, and on mitigation, see p. 453.

It has also been held, in *R (Malster) v. Ipswich Borough Council and Ipswich Town Football Club* [2001] EWHC Admin 711, that because the Directive and the Regulations are concerned to protect the environment in the public interest, their purpose is not to protect the amenity of individuals: '*There may be a significant impact upon a particular dwelling or dwellings without there being any likely significant effect on the environment for the purposes of the Regulations.*'[55] This raises an important question of scale: within a locality, localized effects may be significant, but there is still the issue of the intensity of these effects. The *Ipswich* case points to looking at impacts through a wider lens, but neither the Directive nor the implementing Regulations define 'the environment', and a better view would be that consideration must be given both to the nature of the effects and the severity of the impact. (The case involved the shadow thrown by a new stand at the football ground and more intense localized impacts—for example, the landscape impact of a new football stadium—might perhaps have justified a finding of significance.) The *Ipswich* case also suggests that replacement with a development of similar environmental effects—such as replacing a football stand—will not lead to significant impact—that is, that, in certain cases, significance must be judged relative to the status quo.[56]

One possibility is that significance might be linked to the breach of substantive environmental law standards.[57] For example, a road scheme that would result in local air quality standards being exceeded, or even the breach of less formal standards such as World Health Organization (WHO) standards on noise, could be deemed for this reason alone to be likely to give rise to significant environmental effects. So far, there is no case law supporting this approach, although there is at least one case in which the possible breach of conservation law was sufficient for the courts to hold that a 'main effect' of the development project had not been sufficiently explored (see Case 13.4). Being guided by substantive standards, however, might be thought to go beyond what EC law envisages, because the Directive's screening criteria are expressed in general, qualitative terms—for example, 'pollution and nuisances', 'the extent of the impact', etc.—and could fairly easily have been linked to exceeding substantive legal standards if this was thought desirable. (It is worth mentioning in this context that, in practice, the most important factor in identifying impacts for the purposes of screening is professional judgment and experience, which ranks higher than using legal regulations and thresholds as a guide to impacts.[58])

Finally, there is the potentially tricky question about the factual basis on which it is argued that a development project is likely—or not—to have significant environmental effects. So far, the scope of the courts in resolving this sort of problem is not yet fully resolved (see Case 13.4).

CASE 13.4 *R (Jones) v. Mansfield DC* [2003] EWHC 7

Planning permission was granted, without environmental impact assessment (EIA), for an industrial estate in open countryside. There were concerns about the impact of the development on the golden plover, a bird safeguarded under EC conservation law. To allow for suitable mitigation in due course, the developer had undertaken to survey the site for a year before beginning construction. Richards J

---

55 At [73].

56 But note that modifications of projects may need to be assessed—see, e.g., p. 446.

57 J. Holder (2004) *Environmental Assessment*, Oxford: Oxford University Press.

58 J. Becker and G. Wood (2003) *Screening Decision-Making under the Town and Country Planning (EIA) (England and Wales) Regulations 1999 (2003), s 2.3*, Report to government, London: ODPM. It also appears that EIA is more likely to be required by those planning authorities least experienced in its use. It seems that this is due, in part, to more experienced authorities relying more on their own judgment of the significance of likely effects and placing less weight on thresholds, leading some commentators to question whether there is now a problem with some authorities being too formulaic and cautious in requiring EIA in cases in which it is not really needed.

held that this element of uncertainty as to the ecological value of the site—and, by implication, the nature of the impact of the development—was not a strong enough basis on which to say that the development would be likely to give rise to significant environmental effects and the planning authority's decision could not be overturned. In effect, the Court rejected the proposition that, at the stage of deciding whether significant effects would be likely, the decision maker should adopt a precautionary approach, stressing that the language used is 'would' give rise to such effects not 'could'.

The case is a good illustration of two things. First, it emphasizes that screening must be different from a full assessment (otherwise the practical effect would be that an EIA was needed to decide whether an EIA was needed, and the current two-schedule approach and two-stage process of screening followed by full EIA would be meaningless). Secondly, it shows that the absence of 'full information' is not the barrier at the screening stage that it will be at the stage at which an EIA is required: at the screening stage, the requirements for public involvement have yet to kick in; at the latter stage, they are fully engaged. (A useful case with which to contrast this case is *R v. Cornwall County Council, ex parte Hardy* [2001] Env LR 25—see Case 13.5.)

Significant effects and mitigating measures

Can mitigating measures be taken into consideration when deciding whether EIA is required? Because the environmental statement must describe any remedial and mitigation measures (see p. 456), a strict approach would suggest that they cannot, that mitigating measures could only be a secondary issue. But the main aim of EIA is to prevent environmental harm and if this can be designed out before the project is submitted for approval, then EIA can be said to have done its job.

The leading case is *Bellway Urban Renewal Southern v. Gillespie* [2003] Env LR 30,[59] a case involving construction on the contaminated site of an old gasworks. On the one hand, in principle, any Sch. 2-type project built on heavily contaminated land would require EIA, because the very act of development, or changing the use of the land, could lead to the risk of exposure to the contaminants. On the other hand, as we describe in Chapter 16, there are now relatively commonplace techniques used—for example, capping the site or removing the contaminated soil—that, if carried out correctly, will mitigate any likely environmental impacts caused by the contamination. The Court of Appeal in *Gillespie*, in effect, steers a course between these positions. According to Pill LJ, mitigation measures are not, in principle, to be ignored for the purposes of screening, because that would distort the reality of the project proposal. So a purposive construction of the Directive does not always require its provisions to be construed strictly so that EIA is more likely to be required.[60] But the fact that conditions can take the effects of the development below the threshold of significance is not enough to rule out the need for EIA. A matrix of factors need to be considered, including the nature of the remedial measures, their complexity and the degree of detail stipulated, and, in particular, the prospects that they will be successfully implemented.[61]

This approach is quite nuanced, but it still begs the question whether the EIA process ensures that the *best* advice about mitigating environmental impact emerges (which would be in line with the preventive and participatory nature of the Directive), not simply advice that is standard or sufficient. There are probably many cases in which likely significant effects can be mitigated using conventional techniques—for example, preventing noise and other disturbances from factories, clubs, or even football grounds[62] by regulating the permitted

---

59 See also *BT plc v. Gloucester City Council* [2001] EWHC 1001 and *R (Lebus) v. South Cambridgeshire District Council* [2003] Env LR 17.

60 Case C. *World Wildlife Fund (WWF) v. Autonome Provinz Bozen* [1999] ECR I-5613, [37] ('actual characteristics').

61 See *Bellway Urban Renewal Southern v. Gillespie* [2003] Env LR 30, *per* Pill LJ at [39]–[41].

62 On this example see *R (Catt) v. Brighton and Hove City Council* [2007] Env LR 32.

hours of operation. But as the more forthright judgment of Laws LJ in *Gillespie* suggests, mitigation measures that take a project below the EIA threshold will have to be ones in relation to which the *'nature, availability and effectiveness are already plainly established and plainly uncontroversial'*.[63] In effect, only mitigation measures like that will not require scrutiny and public consultation, as required by the Directive.

Screening procedures

With the subjectiveness of the indicative criteria for Sch. 2 projects and the uncertainty of interpreting the definition for Sch. 1 projects, there are a number of ways of establishing whether EIA is required—but these are open to applicants and not to third parties. Applicants can, at any time prior to making a planning application, seek an opinion from the local planning authority as to whether a proposed development falls within Schs 1 or 2, and whether it exceeds thresholds or is in any other way subject to EIA (a 'screening opinion'—see reg. 5(1), 1999 Regs). Without formal delegation,[64] or at least the involvement of officers with delegated powers,[65] screening opinions cannot be left to planning officers—a measure of the importance attached to EIA, because basic procedures can be delegated informally—and must be made in a publicly available formal statement (interested parties should not have to piece together the reasons why screening was or was not required, because this contravenes the principle of public participation that pervades the Directive).[66] If the local planning authority either fails to give an opinion within the short period required (three weeks), or finds that the project is subject to EIA, the developer may refer the matter to the Secretary of State for what is termed a 'screening direction' (in effect, an appeal of the screening opinion—reg. 5(6)). The Secretary of State can also make a screening direction without a request from a developer, in line with his power to require an environmental statement after an application has been called in or it has gone to appeal (regs 4(7) and 9).

The statutory time limit for any challenge to the failure to require EIA for the development starts to run with the grant of planning permission and not with the screening opinion (a screening opinion that does not require EIA does not necessarily mean that planning permission will be granted). In deciding whether an application has been made promptly, however, regard will be had to the period of time after the screening opinion was issued.[67] The public do not have rights to be involved in the screening process—that is, there is no obligation on the body doing the screening to publicize that it is going to screen a project and invite comment. For screening opinions, however, developers only need provide minimum information about the proposal, including at least a site plan, a description of the development and its nature and purpose, and its possible effects on the environment. It is therefore possible that, following a negative screening opinion, additional material might become available before planning permission is granted—possibly some considerable time later—which might take the development over the EIA threshold.

In *R (Fernback) v. Harrow Borough Council* [2002] Env LR 10, the applicant alleged that further information about the traffic impact of a housing development that came to light after a negative screening opinion meant that the local authority should overturn its earlier opinion. The High Court held that the Regulations did not make any provision for revisiting

---

63 At [46].

64 *R v. St Edmundsbury Borough Council, ex parte Walton* [1999] JPL 805 (no involvement of officers with delegated powers).

65 *R (Goodman) v. Lewisham London Borough* [2003] Env LR 28 (decision taken by officer without delegated powers, but with close involvement of a delegated officer).

66 *R (Lebus) v. South Cambridgeshire District Council* [2003] Env LR 17; cf the similar distaste for paper chases taken in relation to environmental statements in *Berkeley (No. 1)* (see Case 13.7).

67 *R (Catt) v. Brighton and Hove County Council* [2007] Env LR 32, following *Re Burkett* [2002] UKHL 23, discussed in Case 10.3.

a screening opinion if this had found that EIA was not required, unless the developer sought this. Hence, screening opinions, whether negative or positive, are determinative of whether the project requires EIA, subject to the powers of the Secretary of State to make a screening direction (either at the request of the developer or otherwise). This clearly provides developers with a fair degree of certainty as to whether EIA is required, while giving the Secretary of State a residual, and appellate, function in difficult cases. Although it was open to the local authority to decide, when considering the full planning application, that the proposed development required EIA, the problem in *Fernback* was that the three-week time period for doing so had long since elapsed. The remedy in such cases, it was suggested, was for the Secretary of State to be asked to issue a screening direction, not for the failure to require a further screening opinion to be challenged. It was clear, however, that the judge felt the additional impacts that were alleged were fairly minor and there is a suggestion in the decision that, had more substantial new information come to light such that the development would clearly have required EIA, a route might have been found requiring the council to revisit its original screening opinion.

Exemptions from EIA

In three defined situations, projects that would otherwise require EIA may be exempted from the normal procedural requirements (and being limitations to the general obligation, all of these will be interpreted narrowly).

1. Projects serving national defence purposes may be exempted, but only on a case-by-case basis.[68]

2. Member States may, in exceptional cases, exempt a specific project, in whole or in part, from the Directive's provisions, although they must notify the public of the exemption and the reasons for it, consider whether another form of assessment would be appropriate (and engage the public in this), and inform the Commission.[69] European Commission guidance suggests that 'exceptional cases' will be those in which there is:

   (i) an urgent and substantial need for the project;

   (ii) an inability to undertake the project earlier;

   (iii) an inability to meet the full requirements of the Directive.

   It advises that, even in cases in which an EIA of the whole project might not be required, those parts of the project that can nevertheless be assessed should be.[70]

3. The Directive does not apply to projects '*the details of which are adopted by a specific act of national legislation, since the objectives of* [the] *Directive, including that of supplying information, are achieved through the legislative process*'.[71]

This last, rather curiously worded, provision was discussed by the ECJ in relation to a motorway link between Luxembourg and Saarland in Germany (motorways being Annex I projects). The issue in Case C-287/98 *Luxembourg v. Linster* [2000] ECR I-6917 was whether the Luxembourg law that authorized compulsory purchase of land to enable construction

---

68 EIA Directive, Art. 1(4); 1999 Regs, reg. 4(a)(ii).

69 EIA Directive, Art. 2(3), as amended; TCPA EIA Regs 1999, reg. 4(4).

70 European Commission (2006) *Directive 85/337/EEC on the Assessment of the Effects of Certain Public and Private Projects on the Environment (EIA Directive), As Amended: Clarification of the Application of Article 2(3) of the EIA Directive*, available online at **ec.europa.eu/environment/eia/pdf/eia_art2_3.pdf**.

71 EIA Directive, Art. 1(5). Parliamentary standing orders have been amended in relation to private and hybrid Bills, but not to public general Acts.

of the motorway fell within this exemption. The ECJ held, in this case, that it did not. Although the law had been adopted after public parliamentary debate, the law itself left open various possible routes for the road and, because these had not been explored in the depth required by the Directive for prospective projects, the legislative process did not comply with the Directive.

What is notable about the judgment is how the Court interprets this provision to require the legislative process to comply with the purposes behind the Directive, rather than assuming that the legislative process is effectively EIA-compliant. This interpretation means that, even if projects are authorized by an Act of Parliament—and the present government has refound its desire to use Parliament to make the decision in principle on major infrastructure projects such as nuclear power stations (see p. 426)—those affected can raise challenges to the adequacy of the legislative process in EIA terms (which may be a unique example of parliamentary procedures being open to challenge in the courts).

The environmental statement

A key component of any EIA is the environmental statement. As Lord Bingham put it in *Berkeley (No. 1)*:[72] '[T]*he cornerstone of the regime established by the* [EIA] *Regulations is provision by the developer of an environmental statement.*'

The basic position is that any application that needs EIA must include an environmental statement. If it is not included, then the application is treated as if a screening opinion or direction is being sought (reg. 7). In cases in relation to which the local planning authority considers that the information given is insufficient to allow for proper consideration of the environmental effects of the development, further information can be requested (reg. 19). In those in which the process of consultation has been carried out properly, this should not arise.

There is no statutory provision as to the form of an environmental statement, but it *must* contain at least (reg. 2(1) and Pt II, Sch. 4):

- a description of the development comprising information on its site, design, and size;

- the data required to identify and assess the main effects that the development is likely to have on the environment;

- a description of the measures envisaged in order to avoid, reduce, and, if possible, remedy significant adverse effects;

- an outline of the main alternatives studied by the applicant or appellant and an indication of the main reasons for his or her choice, taking into account the environmental effects.

In addition, the environmental statement must include certain information as is reasonably required to assess the environmental effects of the development and which the applicant can, having regard in particular to current knowledge and methods of assessment, reasonably be required to compile. In some respects, this merely duplicates the categories mentioned above—for example, mitigation and remediation measures, and the main alternative studied—but, beyond this, more detailed information may need to be provided under such heads as mentioned in Box 13.6.

---

72 *Berkeley v. Secretary of State for the Environment, Transport and the Regions* [2001] Env LR 16, [4]—see Case 13.7.

BOX 13.6 **The required content of environment statements**[73]

(a) A description of the development, including its physical characteristics and the main characteristics of the production process, such as the nature and quantity of the materials used.

(b) An estimate, by type and quantity, of expected residues and emissions.

(c) A description of the aspects of the environment likely to be significantly affected by the development, including population, fauna, flora, soil, water, air, climatic factors, material assets, including the architectural and archaeological heritage, and landscape, and the interrelationship between these factors.

(d) A description of the likely significant environmental effects, covering the direct effects and any indirect, secondary, cumulative, short-, medium- and long-term, permanent and temporary, positive, and negative effects of the development, resulting from:
   • the existence of the development;
   • the use of natural resources;
   • the emission of pollutants, the creation of nuisances and the elimination of waste, together with a description of the forecasting methods used.

(e) An indication of any difficulties (technical deficiencies or lack of know-how) encountered by the developer in compiling the required information.

Reference to 'indirect effects' means that, for example, a developer of a brownfield site could refer to the saving of greenfield land. In theory, it would also be open to objectors to refer to negative indirect effects, such as effects on climate change, although the environmental statement is not supposed to be a document over which there is specific litigation.[74]

For all of this information, a non-technical summary of any information supplied must also be provided, enabling non-experts to understand its findings. It seems clear from recent case law that this document must not be overly complex for the general public to access and must genuinely engage meaningful public participation (see *Berkeley (No. 1)*, Case 13.7).

As to the content of statements, an important change made under the 1999 Regulations (following changes to the Directive) was to make much more information mandatory. This was to address concerns that information being supplied was, at worst, framed as little more than a piece of advocacy on behalf of the developer. There are still, however, legal limits on the amount of information that developers must provide in environmental statements. This is best illustrated by the issue, noted above, about the division between the grant of 'outline' planning permission and subsequent decisions on 'reserved matters', and the leading authorities on this are now the ECJ decisions in the *Commission v. UK* and *Barker* cases mentioned on p. 446. These cases demonstrate that, when permission is initially sought, there often cannot be 'full knowledge' of the likely effects (as the first Recital to the EIA Directive requires), but there are measures that can be taken to ensure that the developer uses its best endeavours to identify the project's significant effects and does not allow the project to develop in such a way that these give rise to significant effects that have not been considered when outline permission is granted.

Just how detailed or complete must a statement be? In *R (Blewett) v. Derbyshire County Council* [2004] Env LR 29, Sullivan J said that the key issue was, in effect, whether the

73 From reg. 2(1) and Pt I, Sch. 4.

74 Compare the USA. For a case in which the substance of an environmental statement has formed part of the dispute, see *R (Vetterlein) v. Hampshire County Council* [2002] Env LR 8.

document can be described as, in substance, an environmental statement:

It is important that decisions on EIA applications are made on the basis of "full information", but the Regulations are not based on the premise that the environmental statement will necessarily contain the full information.[75]

The process, he noted, allows for deficiencies in the environmental statement to be cured, for example, by the local planning authority asking for further information, and that the key is not the environmental statement per se, but the 'environmental information' of which the statement is only a part. In framing the Directive, the EC was keen to avoid litigation over the information provided by the developer (the Directive does not even use the term 'environmental statement') and *Blewett* is a good example of the reluctance of the courts to venture into this area. (For a more interventionist approach, see Case 13.3.)

The courts, therefore, only take a *Wednesbury* unreasonable approach to supervising the content of environmental statements. An example of this can be seen in *R (Kent) v. First Secretary of State* [2005] Env LR 30, in which the environmental statement contained an indicative list of wastes to be received at an old salt mine for landfilling hazardous wastes.[76] The claimant argued that, to identify the 'main effects', the environmental statement should have been more specific about the particular types of hazardous waste that would be land-filled and also that these should not have been left to the IPPC permit that would be required. The case therefore combines elements of the 'reserved matters' problem, as well as the issue of whether matters subject to other pollution control regimes have to be decided as part of the development consent process or can be left to specialist pollution controls (see Case 13.2 and p. 504). The Court rejected the claim that the IPPC permitting process was being used as a surrogate for a proper EIA. When the two issues were combined, as the judge put it:

the decision maker in the planning process must set the parameters within which the likely significant effects of the development can be assessed, but within those parameters he is entitled to take into account that there are matters which can properly be left for subsequent consideration and determination, whether it be by way of a planning condition or in the PPC permit process.... It follows that, provided that those parameters...are determined within which the future details can properly be worked out, reliance can be placed by the decision maker in the EIA process on the proper operation of those further controls.[77]

The judge therefore accepted the claimant's point that the IPPC process cannot be used to convert an unlawful environmental statement into a lawful one. But he held that this was not one of the 'few and far between' cases in which the environmental statement cannot reasonably be described as such. There was no manifest inadequacy in the environmental statement and the courts are reluctant to grant EIA any primacy over specialist control regimes. As Carnwath LJ put it in the *Jones* case,[78] the EIA process must be seen as '*an aid to efficient and inclusive decision-making in special cases, not an obstacle race*'.

A further limitation is the question of alternatives. Only alternatives studied by the developer need to be included in the environmental statement. In theory, therefore, only good practice requires alternatives to be studied as a matter of EIA law. Circular 2/99 states, however, that it would be open to a planning authority to decide that the absence of alternatives, or the known availability of better alternatives, was a material consideration that justified refusal. (These may be material even if the Circular did not mention it.) For example, if the proposal were to be for a nuclear power station, there would be a significant obligation to undertake a thorough search for the best available site. This would unquestionably involve a

75 At [68].
76 For the wider background, see R. Girling (2005) *Rubbish!*, London: Transworld, pp. 251–55.
77 At [78].
78 *R (Jones) v. Mansfield District Council* [2004] Env LR 21, at [58]—see Case 13.4.

national investigation. Whether it would require consideration of alternative forms of power generation, or even the scope for increases in energy conservation to offset the need for further power, is unclear (Circular 2/99 only refers to alternative *sites* for projects, not alternatives *to* projects, which is arguably a narrow understanding of what the Directive requires.) But if the proposal were to establish an intensive pig-rearing unit, then clearly there would not be the same degree of obligation. Notwithstanding this, if the unit were large enough, there would be an expectation that the site identified for the unit would be that giving rise to minimal environmental effects.

Scoping the statement—opinions, directions, and good practice

Following Directive 97/11/EC, the 1999 Regulations give developers the chance to ask the local planning authority, before submitting an application, for its opinion on the information to be provided in the environmental statement (see regs 10 and 11). These are known as 'scoping opinions', and must involve consultation bodies (see below) and must be given in writing to the developer, usually within five weeks (although a significant number of authorities appear not to do so). Public consultation on scoping opinions is not required; even if carried out (as is good practice), the direction of the scoping opinion rarely changes as a result. Screening and scoping opinions can be requested together. If the planning authority does not reply in time, there is a right to request a scoping direction from the Secretary of State. But, unlike screening opinions, there is no right to appeal a scoping opinion. This reflects the extent to which formal scoping is seen as less critical in the UK, which helps to explain why the UK has chosen not to require mandatory scoping, as it could under the Directive. Even where a scoping opinion or direction has been issued, the decision maker can still request further information at a later date.

Consulting on the environmental statement

As part of the scoping process, in gathering information, developers are not only expected to consult local planning authorities; they may also seek views from the statutory consultees and possibly non-statutory consultees.

Ordinarily, the developer will go to the local planning authority first to discuss the project. At that stage, the local planning authority may wish to identify the bodies with whom consultations should be undertaken. Such consultees must include, where appropriate, the Health and Safety Executive, the Highway Authority, English Heritage, Natural England, the Environment Agency, and any other appropriate statutory body (reg. 13). In practice, there was always likely to be wider consultation—for example, with local wildlife trusts—but to give effect to the proactive public participation requirements of the Aarhus Convention, there is now a legal duty to inform persons (which would include 'legal persons' such as pressure groups) that the planning authority knows has an interest in, or will be affected by, the development, and who might not otherwise be aware of the application. The 1999 Regulations have been amended in various places to ensure that such groups are informed of applications early in the process.

It is the developer's responsibility to approach the statutory consultees. Regulation 12 imposes a duty on the statutory consultees to make available, on request, any information in their possession that is relevant to the preparation of the environmental statement. This does not, however, require the public bodies to obtain information that they do not have or to disclose confidential information. The consultees can impose a reasonable charge for making such information available.

The information that it is envisaged would be made available would include specialized information, such as the results of ecological monitoring, which would help the identification and assessment of the environmental effects. Furthermore, there may be non-statutory consultees who could assist with this information. Developers can consult with these bodies if they offer some particular expertise or local insight. This type of non-statutory consultee might include such bodies as the Royal Society for the Protection of Birds (RSPB), the Campaign to Protect Rural England (CPRE), local nature groups, and members of the general public.

The (often extensive) consultation exercise forms the backbone of the whole EIA process and produces a number of advantages.

1. In development projects, some environmental issues are often obvious. The benefit of the consultation exercise, however, is that it identifies those issues that are perhaps not so evident.

2. A methodical, even approach to the objective analysis of environmental effects enables alterations to be made to a project at an early stage without great expense or inconvenience. These alterations can mitigate or eliminate adverse effects.

3. If a full and adequate consultation is carried out before a planning application is submitted, the amount of time taken by the local planning authority and other consultees to consider the application when submitted will be greatly reduced.

4. The consultation process affords the developer the opportunity of communicating with all parties who are likely to have an interest in the project. Misunderstandings can be cleared up on both sides. This then enables the developer and the local planning authority to concentrate on the relevant issues.

Criticism of environmental statements

Around 700 environmental statements are submitted every year in the UK, with around 75 per cent being made under the main planning regulations. This is nearly double the number of environmental statements submitted before the 1997 amending Directive was implemented—a rise that is accounted for predominantly by the change to the law (rather than by the high level of development in the late 1990s).

Considerable attention has focused on the quality of environmental statements submitted. Early research indicated considerable failings, with most academic studies finding fewer than half of all statements studied to be of acceptable quality. Most of these deficiencies were to be found in the assessment of the environmental impacts of the project. This was not helped by the lack of formal scoping and early research showed that as many as 50 per cent of local planning authorities were not consulted at the scoping stage.[79]

A related problem was that few planning officers had any experience of judging the adequacy of environmental statements and that developers (by using consultants who built up a greater experience of EIA) often possessed an information advantage over the authorities. To some extent, this problem is decreasing and many authorities now themselves engage consultants to review the adequacy of statements received. It is notable, however, that more than a quarter of local authorities have never issued a scoping opinion and that, because of lack of resources, those that have issued opinions spend far less time on them than developers spend on their scoping reports. The overall effect on the quality of environmental statements, however, is not clear. The issuing of central government guidance, both to developers and to decision makers,[80] emphasizing the need to differentiate between scientific calculation of impacts and the evaluation of the significance of the impact,[81] has probably helped to

79 Scoping has always formed part of good practice for EIA since the first guidance on EIA was issued in 1995.

80 See DoE (1994) *Evaluation of Environmental Information for Planning Projects*, and DoE (1995) *Preparation of Environmental Statements for Planning Projects that Require Environmental Assessment: A Good Practice Guide*.

81 For criticism of whether this really happens, see p. 70.

improve matters. Some of the worst statements—and worst excesses within environmental statements—seem to have gone, but problems remain with things such as predicting the likely impact of the project. The greater involvement of lawyers in the EIA process has been suggested as one factor in environmental statements being more conservative about these types of estimate.[82]

A problem was (and remains) that there are no agreed standards for environmental statements, although academic bodies have developed their own criteria. Calls from influential quarters for an independent 'Council for Environmental Assessment', which would be involved with scoping and quality review—along the lines of the EIA Commission in the Netherlands—have not been taken up in the UK.[83]

Many have argued that improving the quality of environmental statements is central to improving the quality of the EIA process as a whole. But it is at least arguable that too much attention has been paid to the adequacy of environmental statements at the expense of the overall treatment of environmental information. Research suggests that planning officers and consultees generally believe that the results of the consultation process have a more significant impact on planning decisions than the content of the environmental statement does.[84]

Determining EIA applications—considering environmental information

Once an environmental statement has been prepared and submitted, together with the planning application, there are further procedural steps that closely follow the standard procedure for planning applications, including the notification of statutory consultees. But the determination period for the application is extended to 16 weeks, there are increased publicity requirements,[85] and a reasonable number of copies should be made available to the public at a reasonable charge reflecting their printing and distribution costs.[86] The underlying purpose behind these enhanced procedural requirements is the requirement that the decision on the project takes 'environmental information' into account (reg. 3(2)), and that this information includes not only the environmental statement, but also the views of statutory consultees and any representations made by other persons about the environmental effects of the development (reg. 2(1)). Any grant of planning permission that does not take this environmental information into consideration is invalid.[87]

The importance of the legal right of the public meaningfully to participate in EIA has nowhere been more clearly expressed than by Lord Hoffmann in *Berkeley (No. 1)* (see Case 13.7):

The directly enforceable right of the citizen...is not merely a right to a fully informed decision on the substantive issue. It must have been adopted on an appropriate basis and that requires the inclusive and democratic procedure prescribed...in which the public, however misguided or wrongheaded its views may be, is given an opportunity to express its opinion on the environmental issues.[88]

---

82 (2003) ENDS Report 340, 29.

83 The RCEP appears to advocate mandatory scoping: see 23rd Report (2002) *Environmental Planning*, Cm. 5459, para. 7.31, but this has been rejected by government, which sees the existing powers of decision makers as adequate.

84 C. Wood and C. Jones (1997) 34(8) Urban Studies 1237.

85 1999 Regulations, reg. 32. The procedures for determining planning applications are described at p. 403.

86 1999 Regulations, regs 17 and 18. Note the difference in charging the public for an environmental statement and charging developers for information to be used in preparing the statement.

87 1999 Regulations, reg. 30.

88 At [38].

A central aim of EIA is to reduce the amount of uncertainty about decisions over environmentally harmful projects by the gathering, in advance, of environmental information. One issue that arises is the sufficiency of this information. Here, it is worth mentioning that the local planning authority may not invalidate an environmental statement because it considers the information supplied to be inadequate, but must instead use its powers to seek further information.[89] This provision emphasizes the need to gather information in advance of determining the application for the project.

A different side to this coin can be seen in Case 13.5.

CASE 13.5 *R v. Cornwall County Council, ex parte Hardy* [2001] Env LR 25

A planning application was submitted to extend an existing landfill site. The environmental statement raised a number of concerns, including possible impact on lesser horseshoe bats, a protected species under the EC Habitats Directive (92/43/EEC; see p. 706). Both English Nature (now Natural England) and local wildlife groups advised that the presence of bats needed further study, although they all thought that any likely impact could be dealt with after permission was granted—but before the development commenced—by appropriately worded planning conditions. The Council had accepted that advice on the basis that the bats or their resting places might be found in the area affected by the development, and were likely to be adversely affected by the development. But, in line with the advice of the conservation consultees, the Council only required, through planning conditions, that the applicant undertook further surveys and prepared appropriate mitigation measures.

On a challenge to the planning permission, the High Court held that it was for the local authority to judge the adequacy of the environmental information, subject only to *Wednesbury* irrationality. But Harrison J held that it was an 'inescapable conclusion'—because of the protected status of the bats and because the planning conditions effectively conceded that there could be adverse impacts—that this would amount to a 'significant adverse effect' and a 'main effect' of the development. Accordingly, the Council could not have concluded rationally that there were no significant nature conservation effects until it had the survey data. So the Council could not know whether it had the full environmental information it required (under reg. 3) before granting planning permission.

The case is also notable because the judge made it clear that leaving important issues until after the main decision had been taken would prevent the full involvement of consultees and meaningful public participation when this further information came to light, and hence would conflict with the underlying purpose behind the EIA Directive. The case is a good example of the importance of public involvement in EIA, because none of the conservation agencies and groups consulted argued for the strong and purposive approach ultimately taken by the Court. Indeed, during the case, the Council conceded that 'mitigating for' the impacts on the bats meant that they would have to go.

Following this case, the necessary survey work was undertaken, and a revised planning application submitted and approved—but the judgment fails to convey the extent to which environmental harm may arise: in seeking to overturn the initial grant of planning permission, counsel for the objector focused on one ground of challenge, to do with the bats and two other species, and other possible grounds were not pursued at that time. Sullivan J rejected a later challenge, raising some of these further grounds, partly because he thought these issues could and should have been raised earlier. One of these was that the site had not been studied for the presence of nightjar, a European protected species. Amazingly, when this was raised with the European Commission, the response seemed to

---

89 Under 1999 Regulations, reg. 19. In cases in which the developer fails to provide further information and the local planning authority decides to refuse planning permission, or fails to determine the application within the 16-week period, the developer has the usual right of appeal to the Secretary of State.

indicate that, as long as any development took place out of the season when nightjar would be at the site, there would not be significant environmental effects.

There is also the question of what obligations there are, if any, on the planning authority if granting planning permission following EIA. The defining characteristic of EIA, it is worth remembering, is its procedural nature. Hence, development projects with significant environmental effects can still proceed even if the EIA process reveals that environmental harm is likely. That said, there are some instances in which the hands of planning authorities will effectively be tied. An example is the obligation, in granting outline planning permission, to impose conditions ensuring that the process of evolution of the project keeps within the parameters applied for and assessed at the outline stage, so that the project, as it evolves with the benefit of approvals of reserved matters, remains the same as that which was assessed (see Case 13.2).

The duty to give reasons

Following Directive 97/11/EC, whether the outcome of an EIA application is to grant or refuse development consent, reasons must be given by the local planning authority to the Secretary of State and to the general public via a newspaper notice and through the planning register. Previously, such reasons were required only where the member States' legislation so provided. Thus the previous rule in the UK, that reasons need be given only in cases in which planning permission is refused, no longer applies if an EIA has been undertaken. Reasons are to include (reg. 21):

- the content of the decision and any conditions attached;

- the main reasons and considerations upon which it is based (on which see the judge's remarks in the *Hardy* case—Case 13.5), along with information about public participation;

- a description, where necessary, of the main preventive and mitigating measures employed.

These new provisions, however, do not provide a general duty to give reasons in relation to the *potential need* for EIA. There is, as we have seen, a duty to give clear, precise, and full reasons why EIA is required (reg. 4(6)), but information will often be sought about the reasons why no EIA was required in the first place. Until recently, the UK courts did not recognize any explicit duty to state both the reasons for the decision and the considerations upon which this is based, but this approach may have to be reconsidered in the light of a recent judgment of the ECJ (see Case 13.6).

CASE 13.6 **EIA—screening and reasons—***R v. Secretary of State for the Environment, Transport and the Regions and Parcelforce, ex parte Marson* [1998] JPL 869

Can a planning authority simply say that its planning committee has considered the need for environmental impact assessment (EIA), but has concluded that the development will not give rise to significant environmental effects and does not therefore require EIA? In a national case involving a Sch. 2 development, the Secretary of State did not think that it would give rise to significant environmental effects and so no EIA was required. No further reasons were given. The Court of Appeal held that there was nothing in national or EC law that required more information than that which had been provided. A concern was that the Court thought that reasons had been given, 'albeit in summary form', when all that the Secretary of State noted was the bare statement that there would not be likely significant effects. This is both a circular argument that does not give any explicit reason for its own conclusions and one that sits uneasily with the increased emphasis given to meaningful public participation in EIA. Indeed, this approach can be contrasted with recent steps to require certain utility regulators to publish reasons when they think that a proposal is important, but that an impact assessment of it is *not* required.[90]

Since then, the European Court of Justice has held that Italy breached the Directive because inadequate reasons were given when a ring road proposal was screened. In Case C-87/02 *Commission v. Italy* [2005] Env LR 3, the Court traced the decision-making process back to a single engineering report, on which, it was claimed, the decision had relied, but found that this did not look at the environmental effects of the project, only at whether, on hydraulic grounds, it was appropriate for the road to cross a river. 'Clear and precise reasons' for ruling out EIA had not therefore been given. Underlying this judgment is an obvious concern that the Directive could be a dead letter if the courts could not scrutinize the basis for screening decisions. Grey areas will, of course, remain and it is not clear whether the *Italy* case means only that screening will be inadequate in cases in which materials that could not possibly form the basis of a negative screening opinion have been relied on—that is, it is not clear how far any duty to give reasons stretches. Nevertheless, the decision does go some way towards giving the interests of 'the environment' a similar degree of procedural protection as those of developers.

What if environmental effects have been considered without EIA?

Even if the courts are prepared to intervene and hold that the development is of a kind for which an environmental statement *should* have been submitted, it does not automatically follow that an EIA will be required. There are two main components to this: the first is whether the procedures used amount to 'substantial compliance' with the Directive; the second is whether any national procedural rules—such as on standing or delay—might prevent EIA being required.

Substantial compliance

For many years, the answer to the first issue was that procedures that seemed to generate sufficient information about the project would suffice. In *R v. Poole Borough Council, ex parte Beebee* [1991] JPL 643, for example, the Council granted itself planning permission without considering whether or not an EIA was required.[91] Schiemann J took the view that the purpose of an EIA was to draw the decision maker's attention to any relevant information that would assist in reaching a decision. On the facts, he thought that the local planning authority had all the relevant information before it and that therefore an environmental statement would have been superfluous. All of the information that might have been gleaned from a formal statement had already emerged and ensured that the council had not arrived at an irrational decision.

Even on a narrow, technocentric basis, such an approach is questionable. Because a central purpose of EIA is to produce a systematic approach to the consideration of environmental effects using best practicable techniques and best available sources of information, it was bold to assert that the local planning authority had all of the necessary environmental

---

90 For example, s. 5A, Utilities Act 2000 (added by s. 6, Sustainable Energy Act 2003).

91 This is not per se incompatible with human rights legislation requiring determination of rights by an independent and impartial tribunal: see *R (Kathro) v. Rhondda Cynon Taff County Borough Council* [2002] Env LR 15.

information for an EIA. Indeed, the transcript of the case suggested that the officers' reports to the decision-making committee had a number of omissions, which would imply that there were deficiencies in the local authority's decision.

The problem with this approach is that the courts would have to prove negatives: that neither more, nor better, information would come to light if a formal EIA were carried out. It would also mean that the educative value of EIA as a process, and its inclusive, participatory nature, would be diminished. Fortunately, this approach has now been overruled by the House of Lords in a forthright ruling about the sufficiency of the EIA process.

CASE 13.7 *Berkeley v. Secretary of State for the Environment, Transport and the Regions* [2001] Env LR 16 (*Berkeley No. 1*)

Planning permission had been granted, without environmental impact assessment (EIA), for redevelopment of the ground of Fulham Football Club. As well as the ground redevelopment, the proposal involved the building of flats above a riverside walk and some encroachment onto the River Thames. Mitigation measures were proposed to compensate for potential damage to aquatic habitat caused by the walkway. These satisfied the (then) National Rivers Authority, but not the London Ecology Unit. The Secretary of State called in the application, but did not require an EIA and granted the planning permission, albeit subject to various conditions aimed at mitigating the environmental impact. The proposed redevelopment was opposed by a group of local residents.

In a case known as *Berkeley (No. 1)*, the issue was whether the planning permission was lawful, given the failure to undertake an EIA. In the Court of Appeal, the challenge failed because it was held that, even if a formal environmental statement had been submitted, this would have made no difference to the eventual decision. This was because the planning dispute had dragged on for years and the decision makers had an abundance of information before them from various sources, including the developer, statutory consultees, and local objectors. Before the House of Lords, however, the Secretary of State conceded that this approach was not lawful—the need for EIA could not simply be wished away—but argued instead that there had, in fact, been *substantial compliance* with the Directive and Regulations, because the Secretary of State had before him all of the documents needed to make his decision.[92]

Giving the Regulations and the Directive a very purposive interpretation, however, the House of Lords emphasized the extent to which EIA is a procedural mechanism involving the opportunity for informed public participation: it is not simply an information-gathering exercise.[93] Lord Hoffmann, in the leading judgment, held that the available documents provided a mere 'paper chase', which fell short of what was required of a proper environmental statement. It was not sufficient, for example, that interested parties had the opportunity to trace all of the relevant documents, if this would require 'a good deal of energy and persistence' on their part. Here, the developer had not provided an environmental statement in a single source and there was no non-technical summary, meaning that the rights of the public to be involved in the decision-making process were inevitably hindered. This was regardless of how much information was made available for the planning inquiry, of the objector's chance to comment on this and present her own information, and even, it seems, of whether the objector could point to any particular prejudice that she had suffered. The House of Lords stressed

---

92 Case C-431/92 *Commission v. Germany* [1995] ECR I-2189 suggested that, if the procedures in the Directive are otherwise complied with, something other than a formal environmental statement might suffice.

93 Even after *Berkeley (No. 1)*, the attitude that EIA is only about information gathering still persists. For an example in which a decision of a local authority not to require EIA was quashed because it had mistakenly thought that it already had enough information, see *R (Lebus) v. South Cambridgeshire District Council* [2003] Env LR 17.

that, when it came to errors of law—especially in cases related to EC law—the courts had little room for discretion.

A final point is that the legal proceedings were so lengthy that, by the time that the case reached the House of Lords, the specific proposal had, in fact, been shelved and this has been noted by judges in subsequent cases as a reason for limiting the strength of the procedural protections that were granted (see below and also p. 217). (A revised planning application, which was subjected to EIA, was also challenged unsuccessfully on other grounds.)[94]

EIA and national procedural rules

As discussed earlier (see p. 211), one of the problems in bringing cases based on alleged breaches of EC law is the discretion that national courts have to decide their own rules of procedure. These include, for example, rules on standing and on whether cases are brought with sufficient speed. When major development projects are at stake, the need to bring challenges quickly is particularly important, because, as time passes, the developer is likely to be incurring costs at the site and these costs will be a relevant factor for the court to consider if the case is not brought promptly. Third parties may also be making decisions—for example, entering into contracts, in reliance on what they think will happen in terms of planning. Set against this, however, is Art. 10 EC, which requires member States to take 'all appropriate measures' to ensure fulfilment of obligations arising under the EC Treaty.

In EIA cases, a key issue is whether the strictness of the legal duty to assess certain types of project means that national procedural rules must bend to accommodate this.[95] The starting point now for considering this issue is the decision of the House of Lords in *Berkeley (No. 1)* (Case 13.7). In that case, the House purposively stressed that breach of the EIA Directive is a serious matter in itself, and hence any discretion not to quash a planning permission on procedural grounds had to be confined to the 'narrowest possible bounds'. But the national courts have refused to accept that the decisions of the ECJ in *Kraaijeveld* and *Bozen* mean that they must set aside any national rule that would prevent the mandatory obligation to assess projects from being realized. Instead, the courts have had occasion to use legal rules and principles intended to foster good administration to defeat the need for EIA. In *R v. North West Leicestershire District Council and East Midlands International Airport Ltd, ex parte Moses (No. 2)* [2000] Env LR 443, a case concerning extension to a runway at the airport, there was a delay of several years in bringing the claim. The applicant invoked the EC principles of legal certainty and proportionality. But the Court of Appeal turned these principles around:

There comes a point, however, when these principles support the rejection rather than the admission of long delayed challenges where third parties have acted in reliance on apparently valid decisions. That point has long since been reached in this case.[96]

Despite the judgment in *Berkeley (No. 1)*, therefore, it appears that the matrix of considerations used by the courts to determine whether there has been undue delay in bringing judicial review apply equally in EIA cases. While non-compliance with the provisions of the

---

94 See *Adlard v. Secretary of State for the Environment, Transport and the Regions* [2002] EWHC 7 (Admin) (failed challenge to decision not to call in the application—and hence not to require a public inquiry—following a revised application; a material consideration seems to have been that, by this stage, a valid ES had been submitted and commented on). See further p. 403 and p. 421.

95 Generally, on the tension between procedural EC law and national procedural rules in EIA, see K-H. Ladeur and R. Prelle (2001) JEL 185.

96 At 455–56.

Directive will be an important factor in stretching the time for bringing the challenge, this is not the only factor and other considerations of what the courts deem to be good administration will also be taken into account.[97] One factor that will always be given weight, however, will be whether the developer is still actively pursuing the development. It is notable that in both *Berkeley (No. 1)* and *Barker* the House of Lords formally gave a remedy to the applicant when the project had long been abandoned, whereas in cases in which the project is still being pursued, there is far greater reluctance to find that a procedural error relating to EIA will mean that the permission must be quashed. In the *Barker* litigation (see p. 446), the ECJ held that the mere length of time after the original consent was given (several years) was not enough to override the obligations on the state under Art. 10 EC to ensure that EC law is given effect to. And, importantly, in *Wells* (see p. 445) the Court had previously held that Art. 10 EC might require a consent to be revoked or suspended. Indeed, the decision-making process in the *Wells* case is, in effect, being revisited and the Secretary of State has proposed a solution that, while not revoking the original consent (which would have led to a claim for compensation), attempts to subject the original minerals consent to the EIA process.[98]

But it is ultimately for the national court, taking these criteria into account, to decide the remedy and, as the ECJ noted in *Barker*, the principles of legal certainty and the protection of legitimate expectations require the withdrawal of an unlawful measure to occur within a 'reasonable time', and it would also be relevant how far the developer had relied on being able to develop lawfully.

Finally, in *Swan v. Secretary of State (No. 1)* [1998] Env LR 545, the Scottish courts did establish that a developer can still be required to submit an environmental statement, even though the development to which it relates has begun. In that case, the effects of the afforestation would be continuing, but an EIA was still possible. This decision has particular importance for projects that may not be carried out as soon as permission is granted—for example, mining and quarrying.

EIA—its impact on decision making

EIA is widely regarded as a central tool for environmental protection and the EIA Directive as the most important EC environmental Directive. In part, this is because it heralded the use of procedural law for environmental protection at EC level. But it is also because the Directive was the first to try to integrate environmental concerns into general decision making—a hallmark of sustainable development. That the Directive has been the subject of more complaints to the Commission about non-implementation than any other EC environmental measure is an indicator of its impact.

Initial fears about the costs to developers appear not to have been realized. Indeed, it is doubtful whether EIA is such a burden that developers should be particularly worried about it being required for their projects and concerns about costs seem to have receded over the years. As a research study examining the relative costs and benefits associated with implementation of the 1985 Directive in Greece, the Netherlands, Spain, and the UK found, costs in excess of 1 per cent of total capital expenditure were the exception. They also tended to occur in relation to particularly controversial projects in sensitive areas, or where good EIA practice had not been followed. Costs as a proportion of total capital expenditure may be as low as 0.2 per cent, with the EIA component being lowest for the largest projects.[99] Moreover,

---

97 *R v. Waveney District Council, ex parte Bell* [2001] Env LR 24 (five-week delay, no prejudice, arguments about delay rejected), and see further p. 217.

98 The option document is available online at **www.communities.gov.uk/documents/planningandbuilding/pdf/160466**.

99 European Commission (1996) *EIA in Europe: A Study on Costs and Benefits*.

the same research recorded a high percentage of respondents (which would appear to be developers and decision makers only) identifying a number of benefits to them or to the development proposal arising from the conduct of the assessment process. This included a finding that the environmental credibility of the developer had been enhanced in 61 per cent of cases. This is backed up by UK research that suggests that both planning officers (88 per cent) and developers or consultants (76 per cent) felt EIA to have been a net benefit in cases in which they had been involved.[100]

Such statistics may be seen as supporting the view of EIA as operating as a developers' charter, 'being used by developers to advance their projects in environmental terms'.[101] The views of consultees and third parties tend to receive less attention, although planning officers tend to take a more positive view of the quality of environmental statements than researchers, while consultees tend to take a more negative view.

As to substantive criticisms, the continued absence of any requirement for post-project monitoring continues to detract from the iterative nature of EIA, arguably detracting from EIA's learning role. And the lack of real powers to prevent biased, or overly cautious, statements still gives cause for concern. But if anything, the centrality of the environmental statement is diminishing and the assessment process is being elevated. Nowhere is this clearer than in the purposive judgments of the ECJ—and, at national level, the forceful opinion of the House of Lords in Berkeley (No. 1)—emphasizing that EIA gives those affected by development projects rights to be meaningfully involved in the decision-making process. To this extent, the national courts, in particular, have broken out of the confines of early judicial decisions that appeared to struggle with the underlying purpose behind the Directive. These decisions conceptualized EIA within existing parameters of national administrative law and legal traditions, and, in particular, seemed to be unduly influenced by deferential judicial approaches to national planning law.[102] The approach today is more informed by valuing participation in its own right.

Finally, it is notable that most planning officers feel that EIA probably makes no difference to the decision to permit or refuse any particular application.[103] Of course, on the one hand, this may be because greater attention is given to mitigating measures, either agreed early on, or eventually required under planning conditions or obligations. On the other hand, it might suggest that the boundaries within which individual decisions are taken leave relatively little scope for a significantly different resolution of the balancing of environmental and other objectives than would otherwise have occurred had environmental impact been considered as a material consideration in town and country planning law. As has been said: 'EIA can be "frozen out" from any real policy or institutional effectiveness if it is not sufficiently linked, formally and informally, to the ways problems are defined, structured and addressed.'[104] Whether formal strategic environmental assessment will sufficiently alter this wider picture remains to be seen.

The Strategic Environmental Assessment Directive

For some years, the limitations of project-based assessment have been apparent. Indeed, the National Environmental Protection Act 1969—the US law that inspired the 1985 Directive—covered all major federal actions and early drafts of the EIA Directive extended to wider

100 C. Jones, C. Wood, and B. Dipper (1998) 69 TPR 315.
101 S. Elworthy and J. Holder (1997) Environmental Protection: Text and Materials, London: Butterworths, p. 418.
102 J. Alder (1993) JEL 203.
103 Jones et al. (1998).
104 R. Bartlett (1990) 'Ecological reason in administration: environmental impact assessment and administrative theory' in R. Paehlke and D. Torgerson (eds) Managing Leviathan: Environmental Politics and the Administrative State, Peterborough: Broadview Press, p. 89.

strategic assessment. In 1991, proposals for a draft Directive on strategic environmental assessment (SEA) surfaced. Moves to adopt a Directive in this area were strengthened by a review of the EIA Directive in 1993, which found that the evaluation of many projects was taking place far too late in the development planning process (see Box 13.7).[105] Initially, the proposals for SEA extended to plans, *policies*, and programmes, but the inclusion of policy assessment in particular was strongly opposed by various member States. Accordingly, the Directive that was finally adopted, Directive 2001/42/EC, covers only the assessment of the effects of certain plans and programmes on the environment. The SEA Directive—which, like the EIA Directive, is procedural law—came into force in June 2004[106] and has been implemented by the Assessment of Plans and Programmes Regulations 2004.[107]

BOX 13.7 The limits of EIA and the need for SEA[108]

Fish farming in Scottish west coast waters expanded rapidly in the 1980s and again in the late 1990s, becoming an important sector of the rural economy, but also generating controversy over its environmental impact. Although a Sch. 2 project, during the early years of growth the thresholds were set so high that the sector was effectively excluded from EIA (in the light of subsequent case law on thresholds—a questionable approach at best). As one study made clear, however, even greater use of project EIA would fail to address the cumulative impacts of proliferation in important coastal habitats, the widespread disturbance to native wildlife caused by operational activities, impacts from the use of chemicals to control disease on fish farms, and impacts on wild fish stocks from escapees. Although the EIA Directive requires indirect and cumulative impacts to be included in the environmental statement, none of the impacts mentioned can really be captured by project-based EIA, for which a more strategic approach is needed. If used properly, EIA can address the sources of certain environmental harms, but not its symptoms, which, in the case of fish farming, include factors such as the feeding of wild fish to captive fish, something that is controversial in ecological terms, but which only some form of strategic or sustainability appraisal can really address.

The plans or programmes for which SEA is required are set out in Figure 13.2.

What is a 'plan' or a 'programme' is not defined either in the Directive or the implementing Regulations, but guidance from the European Commission[109] suggests that what something is called does not really matter and that it is the substance at which we must look. At UK level, Practical Guidance has been published[110] that gives an indicative (but not definitive) list of the types of plan and programme that will be covered. This includes not only the range of 'town and country planning' plans, but also, for example, the National Waste Strategy and local air quality action plans.

The plans or programmes must, however, be 'required by legislative, regulatory or administrative provisions'. This seems intended to limit SEA to public plans and programmes, but the breadth of this phrase is a little unclear. For example, planning policy guidance or statements (PPGs or PPSs) and circulars are not 'required' in this sense—they are not mentioned

---

105 Report from the Commission on the Implementation of Directive 85/337/EEC, COM(93)28 final.

106 There is also the Kiev Protocol to the UNECE Espoo Convention on Transboundary EIA, which covers SEA.

107 SI 2004/1633.

108 From S. Thompson, J. Treweek, and D. Thurling (1995) 45 Journal of Environmental Management 219.

109 *Implementation of Directive 2001/42/EC on the assessment of the effects of certain plans and programmes on the environment (2003).*

110 ODPM (2005) *A Practical Guide to the Strategic Environmental Assessment Directive.*

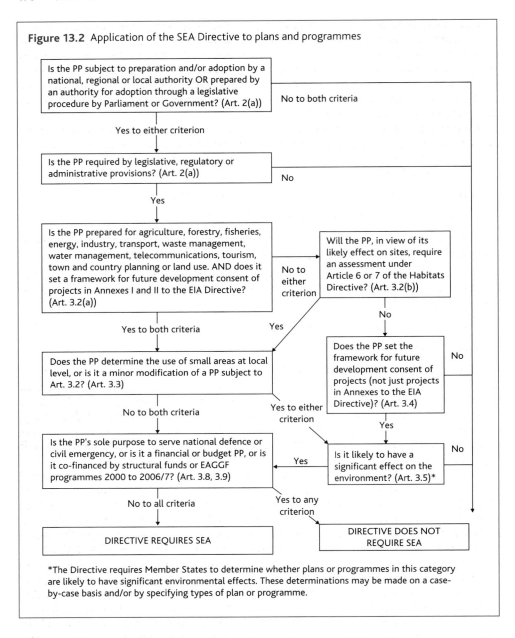

Figure 13.2 Application of the SEA Directive to plans and programmes

Is the PP subject to preparation and/or adoption by a national, regional or local authority OR prepared by an authority for adoption through a legislative procedure by Parliament or Government? (Art. 2(a))

No to both criteria

Yes to either criterion

Is the PP required by legislative, regulatory or administrative provisions? (Art. 2(a))

No

Yes

Is the PP prepared for agriculture, forestry, fisheries, energy, industry, transport, waste management, water management, telecommunications, tourism, town and country planning or land use. AND does it set a framework for future development consent of projects in Annexes I and II to the EIA Directive? (Art. 3.2(a))

No to either criterion

Will the PP, in view of its likely effect on sites, require an assessment under Article 6 or 7 of the Habitats Directive? (Art. 3.2(b))

No

Yes to both criteria

Yes

Does the PP determine the use of small areas at local level, or is it a minor modification of a PP subject to Art. 3.2? (Art. 3.3)

Does the PP set the framework for future development consent of projects (not just projects in Annexes to the EIA Directive)? (Art. 3.4)

No

No to both criteria

Yes to either criterion

Yes

Is the PP's sole purpose to serve national defence or civil emergency, or is it a financial or budget PP, or is it co-financed by structural funds or EAGGF programmes 2000 to 2006/7? (Art. 3.8, 3.9)

Yes

Is it likely to have a significant effect on the environment? (Art. 3.5)*

No

No to all criteria

Yes to any criterion

DIRECTIVE REQUIRES SEA

DIRECTIVE DOES NOT REQUIRE SEA

*The Directive requires Member States to determine whether plans or programmes in this category are likely to have significant environmental effects. These determinations may be made on a case-by-case basis and/or by specifying types of plan or programme.

in the planning legislation in the way that 'the development plan' is—but, as we saw in the previous chapter, they are absolutely central to how the whole planning system works. The Practical Guidance lists the planning policy statement on waste (PPS10) as requiring SEA, but, interestingly, does not list any other planning policy statement. This begs the question whether 'required' should be given a functional interpretation. If the case law of the ECJ on the EIA Directive is followed, then this, and a broad, functional reading of what is a 'plan' and a 'programme', is very likely.[111] Arguably, documents such as White Papers on airport or port development should be subject to SEA.

111 Compare the interpretation of 'projects' in the EIA Directive—see p. 443.

Deliberately linking SEA to EIA, as the SEA Directive does, might create problems because, for example, not all aspects of development plans or waste plans will relate to matters governed by EIA. In practice, it must be assumed that the EIA-related aspects of plans and programmes will not be looked at in isolation, and that, for convenience (and regulatory coherence), all aspects of these types of plan—for example, the whole of the National Waste Strategy under the Environment Act 1995 and perhaps also the Air Quality Strategy under the same Act—will be subject to SEA.

SEA operates in a similar way to project-based assessment. There is a requirement for the proponent to prepare an 'environmental report', setting out information on the assessment of the effects of implementing the plan or programme. This report must include information on, among other things:

- existing environmental problems relevant to the plan or programme;

- the environmental characteristics of the area affected;

- environmental obligations imposed to meet international, European, and national objectives, and how the plan or programme meets those objectives;

- the likely significant environmental effects that would be brought about by implementing the plan or programme, including consideration of things such as cumulative and synergistic effects, and both temporary and long-term effects;

- any envisaged mitigating measures (which must be as full as possible);

- a non-technical summary.

A key feature of the SEA Directive is the attention to the consideration of alternatives. Information about the plan or programme, or the area affected, will always also have to consider any 'reasonable alternatives', such as alternative types of development or alternative locations for it. There is a watered-down version of a requirement to describe the 'do nothing' alternative, and the authority must also provide both a statement of how the assessment was conducted and the reasons for not adopting alternatives considered. These clearly go well beyond the provisions relating to alternatives under project-based EIA.

Once the information is provided in an environmental report, there must be consultation with statutory consultees—including relevant environmental non-government organizations (NGOs)—and with the public in a similar way to EIA. Unlike EIA, however, public authorities have to consult the public on the scope and level of detail of information to be included in the report, effectively providing for mandatory scoping and giving the public two stages in the plan-making process to express their views. A further notable difference is that environmental information must be taken into consideration *during* the plan-making process, rather than simply before adoption; the public must be given an '*early and effective opportunity within appropriate time frames*' to comment, although precisely what this means is left to the member States and it is notable that, regarding participation, the Aarhus Convention requires '*early public involvement, when all options are open*' (emphasis added). Also, there must be measures for monitoring the implementation of the plan or programme. Both of these go some way towards making SEA a more iterative process than EIA—but the fact that the same body prepares the environmental report and the assessment may give rise to allegations of bias.

Finally, note that, just because an SEA has been conducted, this does not mean that EIA of projects that are in line with the strategically assessed plan or programme is not needed. And there is also the issue of whether consent for a development project might be withheld, or overturned, because a plan or programme that was taken into account in the decision-making process had not been lawfully subjected to SEA.

Developing environmental assessment

There are legal forms of environmental assessment that go beyond EIA and SEA. One example that we have already seen is sustainability appraisal, which is required for regional spatial strategies (RSSs—see p. 391). A sustainability appraisal is capable of meeting the legal requirements for an SEA, but goes further than this in attempting to integrate social and economic impacts. But to think, for example, of EIA as a tool that, in practice, is only concerned with environmental impacts would be to overlook the countless ways in which developers use environmental statements to communicate in some detail the economic and other benefits of their projects. The strict legal basis for this is arguably that an environmental statement is not restricted to negative effects and must include effects on population, but, more realistically, there would just be little point in challenging statements in an environmental statement about economic benefits, because this information would, in any case, be given by developers.

Of those assessment techniques beyond EIA and SEA, some are provided for in law and some are simply used as a matter of internal practice. Regulatory impact assessment, for example, is a tool used at national level, and elsewhere one can find health impact assessments, trade impact assessments, sustainability appraisals, and so on, all of which might touch on environmental issues. For example, although the EC has not extended SEA to its own plans and programmes, the European Commission must undertake 'regulatory impact assessments' when proposing legislation, and particularly important proposals are submitted to an extended impact assessment examining the economic, social, and environmental effects of the proposal before the proposal is submitted to the other lawmaking institutions. In 2005, more than fifty such assessments were made.

From an environmental perspective, common concerns about these forms of assessment include the absence of a required methodology, and a clear tendency so far, in general regulatory and sustainability assessments, to downplay environmental interests. As Krämer argues, such assessments lack a precise methodology, a means of holding the Commission even to its own internal guidelines, and simply lack the political will to be taken seriously in identifying, describing, and evaluating environmental impacts. Indeed, he goes further and argues that, while they never make any significant dent in legislative proposals in areas such as transport or energy, they actually serve to block or water down environmental proposals.[112]

CHAPTER SUMMARY

1   Assessing, in a formal, anticipatory, and structured manner, the impact of harmful human activities is increasingly a legal requirement in environmental decision making. This is taking place at all levels of environmental law, both international to national.

2   In international law, environmental impact assessment (EIA) duties are now contained in many specific treaties, but there is, as yet, no global EIA treaty. States must carry out an environmental assessment of particularly harmful activities, an obligation that many (but not all) consider flows from general duties to cooperate regarding transboundary harm, but the procedural requirements of this duty are vague.

3   At national level, the environmental impact of development projects has always been a material consideration in making planning decisions, but, for many projects, the process for assessing environmental impact has now been formalized under EC law.

112 L. Kramer (2007) 'The development of environmental assessments at the level of the European Union' in J. Holder and D. McGillivray (eds) *Taking Stock of Environmental Assessment: Law, Policy and Practice*, London: Routledge.

4   The two main measures are the 1985 EIA Directive (85/337/EEC) and the 2001 Strategic Environmental Assessment (SEA) Directive (2001/42/EC). The former is project-based, while the latter applies to certain plans and programmes. Both share certain common features.

5   Before consent is given, or a plan or programme is adopted, the proponent—for example, the developer or plan maker—prepares an environment statement (the term used for EIA) or environmental report (SEA). These documents detail the proposals, and their direct and indirect effects on the environment, along with any mitigating measures.

6   In both regimes, the public and regulatory agencies can comment on the proposals before the decision maker—who must have regard to all the environmental information (including the views of the public)—undertakes the final assessment.

7   EIA and SEA are essentially procedural tools: they require environmental information to be generated and taken into account by decision makers, but projects, plans, and programmes having adverse environmental impacts can still proceed.

8   EIA is mandatory for certain kinds of development project and discretionary for others, depending on whether there will be significant environmental effects due to their size, nature, or location. The types of project covered by EIA are spelt out in the Directive.

9   SEA applies to plans and programmes in certain sectors in relation to which these set a framework for future development consent of projects subject to EIA, or plans and programmes that require an assessment under the EC Habitats Directive (92/43/EEC). A significance threshold test also applies.

10 The EIA Directive is implemented by detailed Regulations that apply to projects requiring planning permission and by analogous Regulations covering activities falling outside the planning system. The SEA Directive has been transposed by a single set of Regulations in 2004.

11 With EIA, whether projects require assessment has often been contentious. This can take various forms, including whether something is a 'project' and which stage of its approval is the 'consent'. The latter has proved particularly problematic, because of the way in which planning permission is usually given for major development projects.

12 Other problem areas are whether projects will have 'significant' environmental effects, the use of legal thresholds, and whether a project should be assessed in isolation or in the light of wider proposals of which it forms a part. These problems may arise if there has not been an EIA, but can also arise in challenges to the adequacy of environmental statements. The SEA Directive goes some way towards considering development projects in their wider context.

13 Another controversial issue has been whether procedures will suffice if they fall short of formal EIA, but nevertheless appear to provide decision makers with environmental information. The courts have now held that, if they frustrate meaningful public participation, then they will not.

14 All of these areas of controversy are likely to find equivalents under the SEA Directive.

Q   QUESTIONS

1   If environmental impact assessment (EIA) is now part of customary international law, what is the exact nature of the obligations on states? And is EIA in international law a matter only for governments and government experts, or does it require public participation?

2   What difficulties are there in ensuring that projects with significant environmental effects are subjected to EIA? Are these legal problems, policy problems, or evidential problems?

3   Considering the Directive and the main implementing Regulations, is EIA required for either of the following?

    a Large-scale burning and burying of animal carcasses to combat disease.

    b Construction of an inland marina at an old gravel pit.

4 Consider whether, and if so, how, each of the following should be dealt with in the environmental state-ment, and what avenues are open to challenging any failure by the developer to provide this informa-tion or for the decision maker to require it from the developer.

    a Greenhouse emissions from construction of a plant for processing soyabeans.

    b Greenhouse emissions from construction of a new airport runway.

    c Alternative sites for a wind farm.

    Additionally, is it problematic that developers prepare environmental statements?

5 How useful a tool does environmental assessment seem to be? Should it have a more 'substantive' edge—that is, if potentially damaging environmental consequences are brought to light should, as a matter of law, the proposal be blocked? Or amended? Or should suitable conditions be applied? What other options might there be? (You might find it useful to compare environmental assessment with the provisions of Art. 6 of the EC Habitats Directive, discussed at p. 709.)

6 Bigbucks plc wants to develop the site of a disused steelworks into a multiplex cinema, retail park, and a hundred houses. It also proposes to set aside one third of the land as a wetland and actively to restore this area so that it can host locally rare species. The local planning authority does not require an envir-onmental statement and grants outline planning permission. After three weeks, the old steelworks has largely been demolished, but construction has not yet begun. A local amenity group asks you for advice concerning the lack of EIA. Advise the group. What further information would you need?

FURTHER READING

Anyone looking for a thoroughly engaging introduction to the basic issues involved in environmental impact assessment (EIA) and the initial scepticism with which these might be viewed by governments should look no further than the chapter by Chris Wood, a leading authority, in C. Miller (ed.) (2001) *Planning and Environmental Protection*, Oxford: Hart, complete with fictional *Yes, Minister*-type discussion. Other good introductory accounts of EIA are J. Glasson, R. Therivel, and A. Chadwick (2005) *Introduction to Environmental Impact Assessment*, 3rd edn, London: Routledge, and C. Wood (2002) *Environmental Impact Assessment: A Comparative Review*, 2nd edn, Harlow: Pearson. The journal *Impact Assessment and Project Appraisal* (formerly *Project Appraisal*) can also be recommended, although much of the good, policy-based research tends to be published together with the general planning literature.

EIA law—EC and national

Of the more legalistically focused literature, J. Alder, 'Environmental impact assessment: the inadequacies of English law' (1993) JEL 203, provides not only an excellent and accessible account of some of the early case law and implementation problems, but also an enduring framework through which to think about EIA law and its realization. P. Stookes, 'Getting to the real EIA' (2003) JEL 141 provides a good critical legal analysis of EIA as a whole—with a particular focus on public participation—and questions, in particular, the way in which 'significance' is defined in law and understood in practice. J. Holder (2004) *Environmental Assessment*, Oxford: Oxford University Press, provides a sophisticated legal analysis of environmental assessment, focusing on the contested areas of alternatives, prediction, and participation, while J. Holder and D. McGillivray (eds) (2007) *Taking Stock of Environmental Assessment*, London: Routledge-Cavendish, contains a number of essays that consider how EIA law might develop further. Particularly accessible are the chapter by Jones, Jay, Slinn, and Wood, which is an excellent survey of how this area has developed over the years, and the chapter by Krämer, which gives a critical, and sometimes cynical, view of EIA in the EC.

    The most comprehensive, practitioner-focused work is S. Tromans and K. Fuller (2003) *Environmental Impact Assessment: Law and Practice*, London: Butterworths. The case law is normally scrutinized in the

Journal of Planning and Environment Law (JPL), which usually includes an annual survey (by J. Pugh-Smith) of the leading cases.

Strategic environmental assessment

There is, as yet, no specific, book-length text on the law of strategic environmental assessment (SEA), although R. Therivel (2004) *Strategic Environmental Assessment in Action*, London: Earthscan, does consider the Directive and is good on practical examples. Useful articles include: W. Sheate, H. Byron, and S. Smith, 'Implementing the SEA Directive: sectoral challenges and opportunities for the UK and EU' (2003) 14 European Environment 73; I. Gilder, 'The impact of the SEA Directive' (2005) JPL (Occ Supp) 120; J. Robinson and D. Elvin, 'The assessment of plans and programmes' [2004] JPL 1028 (which provides excellent commentary on what some of the vague phrases in the SEA Directive might mean when applied to the UK).

Environmental assessment in international law

Useful coverage of the development and status of EIA in international law can be found in P. Birnie and A. Boyle (2002) *International Law and the Environment*, 2nd edn, Oxford: Oxford University Press, and in P. Sands (2003) *Principles of International Environmental Law*, 2nd edn, Cambridge: Cambridge University Press. Both consider the status of EIA as a binding norm of international environmental law in more depth than we can here and the latter also gives a nice account of early objections to EIA by developing countries at the time of the 1972 UN Conference at Stockholm, their concerns being that, if EIA were to require consultation with other states, then developed states might use it to block projects in developing countries.

@ **WEB LINKS**

At (English) national level, the main site is the Department for Communities and Local Government **www. communities.gov.uk**, which deals with both planning and environmental impact assessment (EIA). This contains links to the main guidance—which is essential reading for any evaluation of EIA going beyond the material in this chapter—together with fairly user-friendly overviews of EIA and strategic environmental assessment (SEA). The European Commission's EIA homepage **europa.eu.int/comm/environment/eia/ home.htm** has links to all EC legislation and guidance on EIA and SEA, together with useful reports on implementation. The UN Economic Commission for Europe **www.unece.org/env/eia** hosts information about the Espoo Convention on Transboundary EIA and its Kiev Protocol on SEA. Further information about the World Bank is at **www.worldbank.org**, while the work of the World Bank, including its Inspection Panel decisions, is tracked by the Centre for International Environmental Law www.ciel.org.

14 Environmental permitting and IPPC

→ **Overview**

This chapter deals with the latest in a long series of attempts to streamline or integrate various different industrial pollution control regimes—in this case, integrated pollution prevention and control (IPPC) and waste management licensing. The environmental permitting regime provides a broad, largely procedural, framework within which the substantive provisions of various European Directives are implemented across a range of industrial installations and waste management facilities. As such, the environmental permitting system introduces very few general changes of substance, merely reflecting, as many integrative measures have done, structural and administrative changes, and a reordering of what was already there.

The environmental permitting regime is designed to be a risk-based system that requires operators to apply for permits for some facilities or to register exemptions for others. The risk-based nature of the regime is reflected in the language of administrative efficiency that dominates the policy guidance. The substantive foundation of the regime is, however, an overriding duty upon regulators to achieve compliance with various EC Directives, thereby ensuring legal transposition—if not implementation—of a complex range of environmental standards.

Because the regime covers facilities that were previously regulated under the waste management licensing system and its exemptions, this chapter is directly linked to that on waste management (Chapter 18—non-permit aspects of waste management, such as the duty of care, still apply). Although this chapter sets out the details of the unified procedures, what is most interesting about the permitting regime is what it represents in terms of the ongoing development of the 'British' approach to environmental regulation. As such, there are indirect links to many other chapters, including those on sources of law (Chapter 4), EC environmental law (Chapter 7), and the regulation of environmental protection (Chapter 8). It also incorporates the substantive details of the transposition of the Integrated Pollution Prevention and Control (IPPC) Directive (2008/1/EC), which is perhaps the most complete and central example of the operation of the environmental permitting system.

At the end of this chapter, you will be able to:

✔ understand the main legal provisions dealing with the system of environmental permitting;

✔ appreciate the application of the permitting regime within the specific context of the Integrated Pollution Prevention and Control Directive as it applies to industrial installations;

✔ evaluate the benefits of an integrated system of pollution control;

✔ appreciate the different types of environmental standard within an applied context of industrial pollution control regulation.

Introduction—the development of integrated controls

The development of domestic pollution control regulation in the UK is underscored by themes of past fragmentation resulting from reactive regulation and more recent attempts to reintegrate controls through various legal and administrative changes.[1] Thus, the early evolution of pollution control legislation can be characterized as being reactive and piecemeal, responding to particular problems as and when they arose. As new environmental issues emerged, legislation was introduced, which often resulted in a number of disparate laws and regulatory agencies being responsible for discrete areas.[2] As a consequence, there was no unified concept of environmental protection. Each individual medium was seen as a separate area of control and no consideration was given to the possible consequences of imposing control on one sector in relation to others. For example, when strict controls are placed upon the levels of effluent discharge into water, a simple alteration to the production process may shift the disposal of the effluent to another sector, such as by incineration (air) or landfill. In addition, the large number of regulatory agencies often led to administrative inefficiency— that is, differing approaches to such things as enforcement or standard setting—and a general lack of transparency and accountability.

It was not until the 1960s that the idea that environmental problems required broader, more integrated solutions was first proposed.[3] Since that time, various attempts have been made to provide integrated solutions to pollution problems.[4] In 1976, the Royal Commission on Environmental Pollution (RCEP) recognized that the control of air pollution in isolation was likely to lead to a less-than-optimum solution of the total pollution control problems posed by industrial installations, because that approach failed to take account of the fact that the reduction of pollution in one form may well lead to an increase of pollution of other forms.[5] In particular, the RCEP argued that the existing standard of Best Practicable Means (BPM) be replaced by the use of the 'best practicable environmental option' (BPEO), which could be used to assess the aggregated pollution emitted by an industrial operation, and then to arrive at a balance in terms of disposals to land, emissions to air, and discharges to water. In addition, the RCEP suggested that, before integrated solutions could be attempted, a single unified regulatory agency was required. The move towards a unified regulatory agency was partially secured with the introduction of Her Majesty's Inspectorate of Pollution (HMIP) in 1987, although the division of responsibility for particular areas of pollution control continued beyond the creation of the National Rivers Authority (NRA) in 1989.

With the creation of HMIP in 1987, the way was open for the introduction of an integrated system of pollution control that took account of the requirements of assessing impacts upon the environment as a whole. The introduction of integrated pollution control (IPC) in Pt 1 of the Environmental Protection Act (EPA) 1990 established two systems of control, with one dealing with emissions to all media and the other, containing the same principal mechanisms of control, dealing with atmospheric emissions alone—thereby replacing antiquated provisions on air pollution under the Health and Safety at Work Act 1974 and the Alkali, &c. Works Regulations 1906.

---

1 See D. Robinson (1998) 'The Evolution of Regulatory Controls' in T. Jewell and J. Steele (eds) *Law and Environmental Decision Making*, Oxford: Oxford University Press.

2 See N. Haigh and F. Irwin (eds) (1990) *Integrated Pollution Control in Europe and North America*, Washington, DC: The Conservation Foundation and the Institute for European Environmental Policy.

3 L. Caldwell (1963) 23 Pub Adm R 138.

4 J. Krier and M Brownstein (1991) Environmental Law 119.

5 Fifth Report (1976) *Air Pollution Control: An Integrated Approach*, Cmnd 6731.

At the same time as the IPC provisions were being implemented in the UK, the European Commission was putting forward its proposals on 'integrated permitting' for industrial processes. This proposal developed into a Directive on integrated pollution control, which met considerable resistance from some member States, which objected to the concept of a single permit for all environmental releases.[6] Subsequently, the proposal metamorphosed into the Directive on integrated pollution prevention and control (96/61/EC), which placed an emphasis on the preventive nature of the control mechanism, rather than on the integration of the permitting system.

In many ways, the Directive echoed the existing IPC system in the UK, although there was a shift from control over environmental emissions to wider environmental impacts, and from isolated industrial processes to a wider definition of activities and installations. The UK was in the forefront of the argument in favour of bringing forward the requirements of this Directive for existing operations, primarily as a result of its experience with the system of IPC and the desire to ensure that the affected industrial sectors in other member States did not gain any competitive advantage during the implementation period. Thus the introduction of one of the first comprehensive systems of integrated pollution control in Pt 1 of EPA 1990 means that the UK is an acknowledged leader—at least in European terms—in this integrated approach.[7] But while these integrative efforts improved the patchwork of controls dating back to the Victorian era, continuing overlaps—especially between waste management and other controls—complicated the regulatory position.

Moves towards administrative integration—the environmental permitting regime

This short history of environmental integration illustrates the two different, but parallel, models of integration that have been developed over the last twenty or so years. The first model—*administrative integration*—reflects notions of efficiency, deregulation, and the streamlining of regulatory agencies. The second model is more substantive, and reflects an increased understanding of environmental systems and the inter-relationship of different aspects of the environment. This *substantive integration* can be seen on both a macro level, with large-scale strategic measures such as strategic environmental assessment (SEA)[8] and the Water Framework Directive,[9] but also an micro level, in initiatives on the assessment of individual projects through the Environmental Impact Assessment Directive (85/337/EEC) and of installations in the IPPC Directive.

Although there are questions about the extent to which pre-existing controls were effective from an *environmental* perspective, the call for a more *administratively efficient* system of pollution control regulation has led to the introduction of a streamlined permitting system under the Environmental Permitting (England and Wales) Regulations 2007,[10] which provide for a stand-alone system of environmental permits for specified 'regulated facilities' in England and Wales. The environmental permitting system combines the pre-existing waste management licensing system—along with its exemptions—with the pollution prevention and control (PPC) permitting system. The aim of administrative simplicity is underlined by the fact that, in general, the substantive nature of both systems remains largely unaltered (although there are detailed amendments). No additional regulatory 'burden' has therefore

---

6 M. Doppelhammer (2000) EELR 199.

7 J. Zottl (2000) 12(3) 281.

8 In its assessment of plans and programmes—see p. 468.

9 In relation to ecological standard setting and its approach to the management of water quality across broad geographical areas—see p. 593.

10 SI 2007/3538.

been created; thus, no new installations are regulated, nor have the standards that must be achieved changed.

This 'no change, but new rules' system operates by providing a single procedural framework that provides a broad outline for making applications and granting permits, as well as for monitoring and enforcement. This is coupled with a general duty upon regulators to '*exercise . . . relevant functions so as to achieve compliance with*' the specified Directives. These relevant functions include determining permit applications, setting conditions, and enforcing against breach including variation and revocation (reg. 9).

The Directives covered are as follows.

- Integrated Pollution Prevention and Control (2008/1/EC) (Sch. 7)

- Waste Framework (2006/12/EC) (Sch. 9)

- Landfill (1999/31/EC) (Sch. 10)

- End-of-Life Vehicles (2000/53/EC) (Sch. 11)

- Waste Electrical and Electronic Equipment (WEEE; 2002/96/EC) (Sch. 12)

- Waste Incineration (2000/76/EC) (Sch. 13)

- Solvents Emission (1999/13/EC) (Sch. 14)

- Large Combustion Plant (2001/80/EC) (Sch. 15)

- Asbestos (87/217/EEC) (Sch. 16)

- Titanium Dioxide (92/112/EEC) (Sch. 17)

- Petrol Vapour Recovery (94/63/EC) (Sch. 18)

In most cases, the Regulations simply transpose the main operative provisions of the Directive to the permitting regime. There are, however, other provisions of the Directive that are inapplicable within the permitting regime and still operate in self-standing systems. Most notably, the Waste Incineration, WEEE, and End-of-Life Vehicles Directives have other transposing and implementing regulations that apply the provisions of the relevant Directives outside the permitting regime.

The scope of environmental permitting

Regulated facilities

Only 'regulated facilities' require a permit under the Environmental Permitting (EP) Regulations. This definition includes (reg. 8):

- *installations*—namely, those activities that were controlled under the PPC regime. This covers the energy industry, metals industry, minerals industry, chemical industry, and other similar activities (Sch. 1);

- *waste operations*—namely, any disposal or recovery of waste, not carried out at an installation and which is not otherwise exempt or excluded (reg. 4);

- *mobile plant other than waste mobile plant*—namely, plant that is designed to move or be moved (reg. 2);

- *waste mobile plant*, unless exempt or excluded.[11]

---

11 An 'excluded waste operation' (reg. 4).

A single permit can cover more than one regulated facility, thus covering a site with more than one installation as listed in Sch. 1 of the EP Regulations (reg. 17). This avoids the need for many permits on a site carrying out different, but related, activities. In practice, this has raised questions as to the extent to which physically unrelated installations are part of the same 'site'.

CASE 14.1 *United Utilities v. Environment Agency* [2006] EWCA 633

United Utilities operated a number of sludge treatment facilities that connected to a single, distant facility for final treatment. Following this secondary treatment, the sludge was either sent for incineration or used as fertilizer on land.

One of the issues raised was the extent to which these facilities were on a single 'site' to which an IPPC permit would apply. The Court of Appeal discussed this issue in terms of the coherence of the 'site' in total. Proximity was a relevant consideration, but not conclusive, because there were many examples of industrial facilities that covered large areas that were clearly a single site.

On the facts of the case, however a 700–800m distance between the 'sites' was thought to be too far for a single site.

A single permit cannot cover regulated facilities with different regulators, nor for activities with more than one operator. Thus there is no single environmental permit for Pt B (local authority air pollution controlled) when combined with another category of regulated facility. The same is true for a mobile plant permit if these are combined with other categories of regulated facility. In these instances, two or more permits will be needed.

Excluded waste operations

Although the aim of the environmental permitting regime was to integrate consents, there is still a range of waste operations that are excluded from permitting, because they are covered under other regulatory regimes (reg. 4).

These exclusions cover operations that:

- are disposals at sea carried out under a permit under the Food and Environment Protection Act 1985;

- are discharges of liquid waste controlled under a discharge consent under the Water Resources Act 1991;

- involve the disposal of agricultural waste in, or on, land under a groundwater authorization;[12]

- involve the disposal or recovery of waste that is not treated as industrial or commercial waste.[13]

Exempt waste operations

Any waste operation that is exempt is not a regulated facility and therefore does not require an environmental permit (reg. 5). This covers waste operations that were exempt under the waste management licensing regime, mostly because they pose a low risk of environmental harm—within certain parameters. There are 52 exempted activities listed in Sch. 3.

---

12 Groundwater Regulations 1998, SI 1998/2746, reg. 18 and see p. 606.
13 Controlled Waste Regulations 1992, SI 1992/588, reg. 17(1).

The broad categories of activity that are covered are:

- the storage of waste at its place of production pending its treatment or disposal elsewhere (this will cover such things as storing waste in a skip—there is no time limit, as long as the producer can show that it is genuinely going to be collected);

- various activities relating to the recovery or reuse of waste, such as sorting waste at the place at which it is produced, baling it, shredding it, and compacting it;

- the storage or deposit of demolition or construction wastes for the purposes of construction work being undertaken on the land;

- the deposit of certain organic matter for the purposes of fertilizing or conditioning land;

- in order to encourage recycling, a great variety of recycling activities are exempted, although often subject to detailed restrictions on quantity (for example, the collection of paper and cardboard, aluminium and steel cans, plastics, glass and textiles for recycling, or the cleaning and washing of packaging or containers so that they can be reused).

Exempt waste operations must be consistent with the need to attain the waste objectives listed in the Waste Framework Directive (see p. 642), must be registered (Sch. 2, para. 3), and—unless specifically allowed for in the Regulations—an exemption cannot extend to hazardous waste (reg. 5(2) and Sch. 3).

The regulators

The primary responsibility for regulating the environmental permitting regime lies with the Environment Agency, although local authorities have residual responsibilities (reg. 32). The Environment Agency regulates Pt A(1) installations and mobile plant, as well as waste operations.[14] Local authorities regulate Pt A(2) and B installations, and mobile plant and waste operations that are associated with such installations.[15]

It is possible (but rare) for there to be a number of activities on site that make up more than one regulated facility—particularly if a waste operation is part of a Pt A(2) or B installation. In such circumstances, the Secretary of State has the power to issue a direction, or the operator has the power to make a written request for such a direction, so as to allocate regulatory responsibility to the regulator of the major activity of the site.[16] In such cases, there may be one regulator and more than one permit that applies to a single site.

The operator

Only the operator of a regulated facility can apply for and be granted an environmental permit.[17] The operator is defined by reference to 'control' over the regulated facility or mobile plant.[18] Operation and control are not necessarily active, because the operator may be subject to legal obligations in the pre- and post-operational phases of an installation.[19] The issue of 'control' is also closely linked to the authority and ability to comply with the conditions of the environmental permit.

---

14 Regulation 32(1) and Sch. 1, para. 2.
15 Regulation 32(2) and Sch. 2, para. 2.
16 Regulation 33.
17 Regulation 13. Indeed, the regulator must refuse to grant a permit if the applicant is not going to be the operator (see below).
18 Regulation 7.
19 Regulation 7(b).

This is a key issue when considering the day-to-day operation of a waste operation, such as a landfill site, which may be operated under an agreement with what was the holder of a waste management licence, such as a local authority. In such circumstances, control would not lie with the ex-holder of the licence, but with the actual operator of the facility in question.

A single permit cannot be granted to more than one operator. Thus, if two operators exist, either the control must be merged under one sole controller or more than one permit may be required.[20]

Transitional arrangements

All pre-existing waste management licences and PPC permits were automatically transformed into environmental permits on 6 April 2008.[21] Registered waste exemptions were also transferred automatically to exempt waste operations on that date.

All outstanding applications for waste management licences or PPC permits will become environmental permits on the day they are determined.[22] This includes all applications to vary, modify, or surrender an existing licence or permit.[23] Any other operator of a new regulated facility is required to obtain an environmental permit, or a waste exemption, before it can commence operations.[24]

Any appeals will be determined under the system in force at the date the appeal was lodged. Thus any appeals before April 2008 will be determined under the PPC/waste management licensing regime.[25]

Applications

All applications have to be submitted by the operator of the regulated facility (in contrast to a planning application, in relation to which anyone can be an applicant).[26] Applications are only considered if they are 'duly made'. This covers the supply of all of the information needed to make a determination. This would include submission on the correct form, with the correct fee, to the correct regulator.[27] The key point is that the time for considering an application runs only once the application is 'duly made', but ceases to run if further information is then required by notice.[28]

The time period for determining the application ranges from two months for an application to transfer, and three months for a surrender, variation, or standard permit (see below), to four months for the grant of a full environmental permit and to vary a permit in relation to which public consultation is required.[29]

There is a power for the Secretary of State to 'call in' applications if there are issues of 'substantial regional or national significance', or controversy, or issues of 'national security or foreign governments'.[30] Under this procedure, the regulator will undertake the normal

---

20 Regulation 17.

21 Regulations 69(1), (2), and 70.

22 Regulation 70.

23 Ibid.

24 Regulation 12.

25 Regulation 72(1)(c).

26 Schedule 5, para.2—the only exception is an application to transfer a permit, which must be made by the operator and proposed transferee.

27 Schedule 5.

28 Schedule 5, paras 4(1), 15(2), and 16.

29 Schedule 5.

30 Regulation 62 and see Department for Environment, Food and Rural Affairs (2008) *Environmental Permitting Core Guidance*, para. 5.45, available online at **www.defra.gov.uk/environment/epp/documents/core-guidance.pdf**.

consultation, but will send any representations directly to the Secretary of State, who will issue a direction in relation to the final decision.[31]

Consultation and public participation

There are extensive provisions for public participation in the application procedure.[32] Unlike previous pollution control regimes, there are no prescribed methods for public consultation, which—in theory, anyway—reflects a broader, more purposive approach to public participation. This is in keeping with changes brought about under the Aarhus Convention and also comments in case law on the need for proper consultation rather than paper exercises— particularly in highly technocratic decision-making processes.

CASE 14.2 Consultation and technocratic decision making—*Edwards v. Environment Agency (No. 2)* [2007] Env LR 9

The pollution prevention and control (PPC) regime is a classic example of technocratic decision making, in the sense that it involves technical questions that require expert interpretation. This raises fundamental questions over the extent to which it is possible to encourage public participation in any meaningful manner.

The Court of Appeal's decision in *Edwards v. EA* points towards a purposive approach to participation. In this case, Rugby Cement was granted a PPC permit to burn shredded and chipped tyres as a substitute fuel in its cement kilns on a trial basis. Although the requisite notice and advertisement requirements were complied with prior to the grant of the PPC permit, the applicant argued that there had been a procedural failure, in that the Environment Agency had failed to disclose a report on the impact of particulates emitted from the proposed installation. The Court of Appeal held that the failure to disclose the report was a breach of the common law duty of fairness to those objectors. But that was not the end of the matter: a finding on the evidence that the works would not cause environmental harm, and the fact that there were opportunities to review and modify the conditions of the permit, meant that it would be possible to undertake assessments on actual, as opposed to predicted, emissions. Accordingly, it would have been pointless to quash the permit simply to enable the public to be consulted on out-of-date data.

Overall, this case is a very good illustration of the tension between newer approaches to public participation involving full disclosure and quasi-deliberative processes, and the traditional 'top-down' technocratic decision-making process within which experts determine the technical parameters of the decision before and after consulting the public. On the one hand, the Court made it clear that there was a requirement to disclose all relevant material as part of any meaningful consultation exercise; on the other, the internal findings of the Environment Agency were left unchallenged.

Thus the regulations set down a general requirement to take steps to give 'public consultees' an opportunity to make representations on the application.[33] 'Public consultees' are considered to be all those who will, or are likely to be, affected by, or have an interest in, the application.[34] The general requirement does not apply to applications for mobile plant or standard Pt B applications. Substantial changes to Pt A installations must be consulted on

---

31 Regulation 62.

32 Schedule 5.

33 More detailed policies can be found in the formal Environment Agency's Public Participation Statement drawn up under reg. 59.

34 Schedule 5 para, 1.

in addition to any other variation applications in relation to which the regulator considers it necessary.[35]

BOX 14.1 Substantial changes, public participation and substitute liquid fuels (SLFs)

The question of what is a 'substantial change' to an installation is critical, because it triggers a requirement for a full application and detailed public involvement—as opposed to a non-public, partial application for a variation. 'Substantial change' is defined as meaning a change in the operation that may have significant negative effects on human beings or the environment.[36] The question of whether a change is 'significant' or not is assessed at the discretion of the regulator, with the aim of identifying whether there would be any justification for requiring the operator to submit proposals to consultation. Whether a change is substantial or not can have significant practical consequences in terms of the manner in which the change is publicized and monitored, and, most critically, whether it is subject to the rigours of the application procedure. Some of the problems in dealing with significant changes can be seen in the issue of burning substitute liquid fuels (SLFs, which can also be used to mean 'secondary liquid fuels') in cement kilns.

Cement manufacture is a prescribed installation under the IPPC legislation and was controlled under IPC authorizations prior to this. In the early 1990s, as a cost-saving exercise, the cement industry sought to use fuels other than the traditional coal to heat the kilns used in the manufacturing process. In 1992, Castle Cement, one of the main manufacturers of cement, introduced a new fuel, Cemfuel, at its Clitheroe works. Cemfuel was made up of waste-chlorinated solvents from processes such as paint manufacture and printing.

The local community surrounding the plant was concerned about the health effects of the burning of Cemfuel. At the outset, HM Inspectorate of Pollution (HMIP, as it then was) accepted that the change of fuel type from coal to Cemfuel did not constitute a 'substantial change' for the purposes of IPC. Cemfuel was used for over a year before Castle Cement applied for an IPC authorization. After substantial objections from members of the public and other criticisms, HMIP decided to vary the IPC authorization to limit the time to a trial period. By this time, other operators, such as Blue Circle, were conducting lengthy 'trial runs' of SLF as substitute fuels in cement kilns.

Subsequently, the Environment Agency (as it had become) was heavily criticized by the Environment Select Committee, which characterized the Agency's regulation of the cement industry as including a 'failure to command public confidence', a 'lack of openness', 'lax regulation', and 'inadequate monitoring'. The Report went on to recommend that further use of SLFs should not be allowed unless it was treated as a 'substantial change' under IPC, with all of the consequences in terms of public consultation and monitoring that this required.

The only requirements for public participation laid down are that the regulator must, within 30 working days of receiving a 'duly made' application:

- place the application on the public register;

- take steps to inform the public consultees of the application and where to see it on the public register;

- specify the address to, and the time period within which representations must be made.

---

35 Schedule 5 para. 5(2).
36 Schedule 5, para. 5(5).

There is also provision for transboundary consultation. In practice, this is unlikely to be a major factor, but, if the Secretary of State is 'aware' that an activity is likely to have significant negative effects on another member State, or if another member State requests information on an application, he is under a duty to notify that other member State of the application, so that 'consultation' may take place within a framework of bilateral relations.[37]

Commercial confidentiality and national security

In normal circumstances, the public is allowed free access to information regarding an application for a permit and associated matters.[38] There are, however, exceptions to this, on the grounds of commercial or industrial confidentiality and national security.[39] In the case of national security, the Secretary of State may direct the regulator to exclude the information or any person can give notice to the Secretary of State that the disclosure of such information would be contrary to the interests of national security.[40]

In relation to commercial or industrial confidentiality, the regulator must exclude such information if it concludes that it is confidential or if the Secretary of State directs that it be considered so. If an operator believes that any information contained within an application should be restricted, then an application may be made to exclude such information from the public registers.[41] This application is included along with the information relating to the permit and the regulator has to determine whether or not such information is commercially confidential.[42] The regulator has 20 working days (or such longer period as is agreed) in which to determine whether the information is not commercially confidential, if it is undetermined within that period it is deemed to be treated as such.[43] In cases in which the enforcing authority determines that the information is not commercially confidential, it must not enter such information on the register for 15 working days, so as to allow an applicant time to appeal against the decision to the Secretary of State.[44] Pending any appeal, the information is also excluded from the register.[45]

Determining the application

In determining a permit application, the regulator must either grant the permit (normally subject to conditions) or refuse the application.[46] The key objective that must be considered as part of the determination process is whether, in granting the permit, the requirements of any relevant EC Directive will be met and thus provide the required level of environmental protection. In keeping with the technical nature of the environmental permitting regime, the determination of an application requires an expert judgment with relatively few obvious policy considerations. As such, any decision to grant a permit is difficult to challenge.

CASE 14.3 *Levy v. Environment Agency* [2003] Env LR 11

Mr Levy lived near a cement works that was regulated under an IPC authorization. In August 2001, the Environment Agency granted a variation of the authorization to permit the permanent use of

---

37 Regulation 10.
38 Regulation 46.
39 Regulations 47–56.
40 Regulation 47(3).
41 Regulation 48.
42 Regulation 49.
43 Regulation 52(1).
44 Regulation 52(3).
45 Regulation 53(3).
46 Regulation 13.

scrap tyres as a substitute fuel for the works. Mr Levy applied for a judicial review of the decision to grant the variation. Among the different grounds for making the application, Mr Levy argued that the Environment Agency had approached the determination of the application in an unlawful manner by failing to require the use of Best Available Technique Not Entailing Excessive Cost (BATNEEC).

In holding that the Agency had approached the determination of application lawfully, Silber J effectively narrowed the potential for challenging determination processes involving technical questions such as in the case of IPPC applications. He held that the courts would be unlikely to intervene in the Environment Agency's discretion to determine technical questions (for example, the adequacy of pollution prevention techniques). He took the view that, in determining what was BATNEEC, the Agency had to 'use very sophisticated specialized scientific and environmental knowledge and expertise' and that this was only available to relatively few people. The technical nature of the decision meant that the courts should be 'very slow to interfere'. Accordingly, the Agency should be given a wider margin of appreciation than in other examples of administrative decision making.

Of course, this does not mean that such decisions are not capable of being challenged, because there may be procedural or substantive irregularities in the decision-making process. It does, however, mean that it is more likely that questions that are based upon technical matters—for example, the use of one technique as opposed to another—will fall under the sole decision of the Environment Agency. As Silber J put it: '[I]t is not for the court to second-guess the judgment of a specialized tribunal.'[47]

The regulator is under a *duty* to refuse an application if it considers that the applicant will not be the operator of the regulated facility or if it considers that the operator will not be able to operate the regulated facility in accordance with the environmental permit. This involves an assessment of whether the operator is competent.[48] Factors to be considered[49] include the adequacy of the operator's:

- management system, including accredited systems such as EMAS;[50]

- technical competence, which is normally assessed through management systems, but more formal certificates of technical competence may be developed;[51]

- history of compliance with previous regulatory requirements, including convictions for relevant offences;

- financial provision, although this is aimed at ensuring that there is sufficient funding to operate the environmental permit unless special circumstances apply, such as in the case of landfill sites.

Under IPC legislation, a similar provision has been interpreted as being a practical test of determining whether an applicant would be able to comply with all of the conditions that would be imposed on a permit. In asking this question, it would be relevant to consider the previous history of the applicant and the extent to which there had been compliance or non-compliance with conditions.

---

47 At [77], citing Sir Thomas Bingham MR in *R. v. Parole Board, ex parte Watson* [1996] 1 WLR 906, 917C.
48 Schedule 5, para. 13.
49 See DEFRA (2008) section 8.
50 See p. 246.
51 Schedule 5, para. 13.

> **CASE 14.4** *R v. Secretary of State for the Environment and RJ Compton and Sons, ex parte West Wiltshire District Council* [1996] Env LR 312
>
> RJ Compton and Sons operated an animal rendering business. There was evidence of operational failures, such as bad housekeeping, unauthorized emissions, and poor storage of waste, which suggested that significant operational improvements were required. RJ Compton applied for an authorization under Pt 1 of the Environmental Protection Act 1990. The local authority refused the application and the company appealed.
>
> One of the issues at the appeal was the track record of the company and whether it would be able to achieve the required environmental standards. The Inspector hearing the appeal thought that the company would not be able to comply with the Best Available Technique Not Entailing Excessive Cost (BATNEEC) standard and recommended that the appeal be dismissed. The Secretary of State disagreed and directed that the authorization be granted. The Secretary of State considered that the issue was whether it was *possible* that the applicant would carry on the operations in compliance with conditions. This was a theoretical approach, which is relatively easy to demonstrate. The Secretary of State justified this view on the basis that the regulator had enforcement options available for its use as and when the operator failed to comply with the conditions.
>
> The High Court disagreed with the Secretary of State's view, holding that he had failed to apply the test properly. The test should have been whether the applicant was *able* to comply with the conditions, which was a more *practical* test. On this basis, a history of non-compliance or environmental offences might be relevant in determining whether to refuse an application.

The regulator *may* refuse a permit if it is considered that the environmental impact would be unacceptable or that the requirements of the relevant EC Directives would not be met (see below).

Permit conditions

In granting an application, the regulator can attach any conditions to the permit that it sees fit. In particular, the regulator is under a statutory duty to ensure compliance with specified provisions of the relevant Directives. These requirements are summarized in Table 14.1, which is a brief summary of the requirements, but serves to show the contrast between the simplicity of the procedural framework and the complexity of the substantive requirements that cut across different industry sectors and apply in different ways in different applications.

A few preliminary points should be noted.

- The transposition is not absolutely comprehensive, in the sense that not all provisions are transposed. For example, if the Directive gives the member States a discretion to do something, then, if the decision is not to do so—that is, not to 'gold plate'—then these provisions of the Directives are to be ignored.

- It is only the specific obligations on regulators under the Directives that apply, primarily on the ground that not all of the obligations can be met by regulators exercising their statutory duty. For example, a provision in a Directive requiring the member State to report on progress will not be transposed via the Permitting Regulations.

- There is no attempt to translate the requirements into self-standing regulatory regimes. The obligation is simply to ensure compliance with the provisions within the Directives themselves, whether this is directly through the application of specific rules and principles at specific installations, or more indirectly, through the regulator acting in such a way as to seek to achieve the objectives of the Directive.

Table 14.1 Permit conditions

Directive	Relevant Directive provision(s)	Permitting Regulation(s)	Summary of objectives
Integrated Pollution Prevention and Control (2008/1/EC)	Articles 3, 6(1), 9, 10, 11, 12, 13, 14, and 15(1); Annexes II, III, IV, and V	Schedule 7	Prevention of accidents, pollution and waste production using Best Available Techniques (BAT)
			Energy efficiency
			Return of site to a satisfactory state post-operation
			Information in application
			Inclusion of emission limit values (ELVs) in permits
			Stricter permit conditions than BAT if environmental quality standards require
			Applications for changes to installations
			Ensuring the review and updating of permits where necessary
			Ensuring compliance with permit conditions, along with requirements for reporting incidents, inspections, and sampling information
			Ensure effective public participation
Waste Framework (2006/12/EC)	Articles 3(1), 4, 5, 9(1), 10, 11, 13, and 14	Regulations 5, 12, and 34; Schs 2, 3, 9, and 20	Establishing the waste hierarchy
			Preventing pollution and harm
			Establishing the waste disposal network
			Requiring a permit for waste disposal and recovery
			Allowing exemptions from the need for a permit
			Requiring periodic inspections of operations subject to permit or exemption
			Requiring record keeping

Directive	Articles	Schedule	Description
Landfill (1999/31/EC), as amended	Articles 1, 4, 5(3) and (4), 6, 7, 8, 9, 10, 11(1), 12, 13, and 14; Annexes	Schedule 10	Classifying and setting waste acceptance criteria and procedures for landfills Designating wastes that may be accepted at different classes of landfill Information in application Setting preconditions to the grant of a permit and commencement of landfill operations Imposing requirements in relation to permit conditions Ensuring charges for landfill cover operational costs Ensuring monitoring and control during operations Setting requirements for closure and after-care
End-of-Life Vehicles (2000/53/EC), as amended	Article 6(1) and (3); Annex I	Schedule 11	Setting minimum requirements for storage and treatment of waste motor vehicles
Waste Electrical and Electronic Equipment (2002/96/EC), as amended	Article 6(1), (3), and (4); Annex III	Schedule 12	Setting minimum requirements for treatment of waste electrical and electronic equipment
Waste Incineration (2000/76/EC)	Articles 4(2)–(5), 5, 6, 7(1)–(4), 8(1)–(7), 9, 10, 11, 12(2), and 13; Annexes II, III, IV, V, and VI	Schedule 13	Information in application Requirements relating to: grant of permit and conditions; waste delivery and reception; ELVs for air; other discharges and residues; operational control, monitoring, and reporting; abnormal operating conditions
Solvent Emissions (1999/13/EC), as amended	Articles 4(4), 5, 7(2), 8(1)–(4), 9, and 10; Annexes II and III	Schedule 14	Requirements relating to: substantial changes to installations; operational requirements; monitoring; compliance with minimum ELVs; reporting

Table 14.1 (Continued)

Directive	Relevant Directive provision(s)	Permitting Regulation(s)	Summary of objectives
Large Combustion Plant (2001/80/EC)	Articles 4(1)–(4), 5(1), 6–10, and 12–14; Annexes III–VIII(A)	Schedule 15	Ensuring compliance with, and reduction of, ELVs through participation in national emission reduction plan Consideration of combined heat and power generation Requirements relating to: ELVs; monitoring; method of discharge for waste gases; reporting of monitoring
Asbestos (87/217/EEC), as amended	Articles 3, 4(1), 5, 6(1) and (2), and 8; Annex	Schedule 16	Reduction and prevention of asbestos emissions to the environment and production of solid asbestos waste Limiting discharges of asbestos to air from use of asbestos Ensuring recycling of aqueous asbestos effluent Monitoring asbestos emissions
Titanium Dioxide (92/112/EEC)	Articles 4, 6, and 9–11; Annex	Schedule 17	Prohibition of discharges of certain wastes Imposing ELVs for other wastes Monitoring discharges Prevention, reuse, or safe disposal of waste
Petrol Vapour Recovery (94/63/EC)	Articles 3(1), 4(1)–(3), and 6(1); Annexes I, II, III, and IV	Schedule 18	Requirements relating to the design and operation of storage, and loading and unloading of equipment

- The Regulations represent a 'common platform' that can be extended internally (by incorporating other domestic regulatory systems) and externally (by facilitating the legal transposition of new European obligations in a streamlined fashion).

Notwithstanding the broad framework and application of the environmental permitting system, there are other existing consent or licensing systems that are not included. The most significant is the discharge consent system under the Water Resources Act 1991, which is specifically excluded. Others include the systems dealing with waste brokers and carriers, radioactive substances, and water abstraction. The future expansion of the environmental permitting regime to incorporate some of these systems has been explicitly acknowledged.[52]

Other than the duty to impose conditions in order to secure the objectives of the European Directives, a regulator can impose conditions that are necessary and enforceable. Necessity should be assessed in terms of environmental protection. An enforceable condition should clearly state an outcome that enables the operator to understand what needs to be done in order to comply.

Standard rules and permits

In keeping with the aim of administrative efficiency, the Secretary of State has the power to make standard rules for permits that apply across an industry sector.[53] The application of standard rules is voluntary—that is, it is the operator who decides whether to operate in accordance with standard rules or individually set permits. A standard permit is a permit with only one condition. That condition is adherence to a fixed package of rules designed for the standard permit holder.[54] Accordingly, there is no right of appeal against a standard permit.[55] The fundamental purpose of the standard rule is to provide a more efficient procedure for standardized operations. It will not be appropriate in complex installations. For the operator, it has the advantage of being cheaper, reflecting the lower amount of administrative effort required to process the application.

The standard rules are also simpler in terms of regulatory effect, in that they are concerned with overall outcomes, leaving the operator with a degree of flexibility as to how such outcomes may be achieved.[56] The application process is much simpler, because the exact nature of the permit will be available prior to an application being submitted—thus enabling operators to know what is to be imposed. The process is also simplified because there is a lower degree of public participation.

The transfer of permits

A permit is personal to an operator. It is, however, possible to transfer a permit from one operator to another.[57] Therefore, if a business has been sold, it is possible to transfer an existing permit to the new operator. An operator wishing to transfer a permit to someone else must make a joint application and pay a fee. There are provisions for partial transfer in cases in which part of the installation will remain within the control of the original operator. In determining whether to grant a transfer, the regulator is under a duty to achieve the requirements of the relevant Directives.

---

52 Full Regulatory Impact Assessment on Proposals for Creating a Streamlined Environmental Permitting and Compliance System, DEFRA (2007) paras 5.59 *et seq.*

53 Regulation 26.

54 Regulation 27(3).

55 Ibid.

56 Regulation 25(6).

57 Regulation 21.

There is a two-month time limit for determining a transfer.[58] If no determination has been made or if there has been no extension of the time period agreed between the parties, the permit is deemed to have been transferred. Otherwise, the transfer is effected on a date that is agreed between the parties.

The surrender of permits

An operator is not able to escape continuing obligations under a permit until the surrender of the permit. In general, the surrender or partial surrender of a permit is subject to prior regulatory approval,[59] but operators of Pt B installations, mobile plant, and certain Pt A(2) facilities for the incineration of non-hazardous waste can surrender by notification only.[60]

Because the environmental permitting regime regulates the clean-up of pollution that has been caused by permitted activities, there is a need to regulate the cessation of activities by the operator so that an assessment of the condition of the site can be made and remedial works undertaken. Indeed, the risks associated with surrender and other decommissioning of the installation must be taken into account when determining whether the installation meets the requirement of Best Available Techniques (BAT) at the design stage.[61]

It is presumed that the operator is responsible for any material difference between the condition of the site as contained in the original information that was submitted with the application and the conditions contained in any report submitted with an application for surrender. This presumption would appear to be irrefutable, because the regulator must be satisfied that there is no pollution risk and that no further steps need to be taken to return the site to a satisfactory state, irrespective of the cause of that pollution risk, before accepting the surrender of the permit.[62] Naturally, this emphasizes the importance of ensuring that the original information submitted with the application is as comprehensive as possible, so that pre-commencement liabilities that are attributable to other causes or parties do not appear in the pre-surrender report, because they will not be distinguishable from the contamination caused by the operation of the installation. In cases in which pollution is caused prior to cessation, the regulator has the power to serve an enforcement notice to remedy any harm caused.

The regulator must issue a notice of determination on the application for surrender within three months, or longer if agreed between the parties and if the regulator has requested further information from the applicant that has not been supplied.[63] If no determination is made within that period, the application is deemed to have been refused if the operator notifies the regulator of this in writing.

Reviewing permits

The regulator is under a duty to review permits periodically.[64] Such reviews are required to ensure that the permit conditions are up to date and capture changes in circumstances, such as environmental impacts, available techniques, or other relevant issues, such as Community-wide emission limit values (ELVs).[65] There is no prescribed period within which reviews must be undertaken[66] and the only guidance is that the Environment Agency will carry

---

58 Schedule 5.
59 Regulation 25.
60 Regulation 24.
61 Annex IV.
62 Schedule 5, para. 14.
63 Regulations 15 and 16.
64 Regulation 34.
65 DEFRA (2008) para. 10.32.

66 Although there is a requirement that permit conditions that reflect the requirements relating to groundwater are reviewed every four years—see ibid., para. 10.33.

out reviews *'having regard to its experience of regulating various sectors'.*[67] This review process is a key factor in ensuring the efficiency of a technology-forcing process standard such as BAT.[68]

Enforcement powers

There are a wide range of enforcement options with which to deal with operational breaches of permits, including the powers to serve enforcement notices (reg. 36), to suspend permitted activities (reg. 37), to revoke a permit (regs 22–23), and to vary the conditions of a permit (reg. 20). This flexibility ensures that the regulator has enforcement discretion when dealing with regulatory breaches.

As with all of the regulatory functions under the Regulations, the regulator must exercise these enforcement powers with the overriding aim of achieving the requirements of the European Directives. The mandatory nature of this duty means that, if breaches of permit are occurring or likely to occur, the regulator cannot ignore it. The duty means that necessary steps must be taken to ensure compliance with conditions.

In practice, a continuous breach of Directive requirements is very likely to be subject to formal enforcement action of some kind. The alternative would be open to review for failure to implement the Directive requirements. The regulators have a duty to carry out inspections of regulated facilities (reg. 34). There is, however, an emphasis on self-monitoring, and regulators often impose appropriate conditions requiring self-monitoring and reporting on breaches.[69] Failure to report a breach of a condition will normally constitute a further breach.

(a) Variation notices

The ability to vary a permit is not strictly an enforcement power when compared with, for example, enforcement, suspension, or revocation notices, because there is no explicit sanction for non-compliance (other than general powers for breach of condition). The effect of a variation may, however, be such that an operator would view it as having no practical distinction from an enforcement notice. The distinctive character of a variation notice relates more to a proactive approach to minimizing environmental impacts than that of punishing for breaches of existing conditions. A regulator may vary permit conditions at any time (reg. 20).

Normally, variation will be required as a result of a permit review, new considerations such as changes in materials or intensification of processes, or the introduction of new environmental quality standards. The variation procedure requires consultation and publicity both in cases in which the change is 'significant' and at the discretion of the regulator.[70]

(b) Revocation notices

The regulator has the power to revoke a permit, either in part or in whole, at any time by serving a revocation notice on the operator.[71] The power to revoke a permit is general in nature and is not restricted. It is something of an extreme measure and will normally only be appropriate when other enforcement options are inappropriate (for example, if activities on an installation have ceased and are not to be recommended) or have been exhausted. In such circumstances, revocation might apply to the activities on the site, while leaving the site closure conditions to be enforced against. A revocation notice can be withdrawn at any time before it

---

67 Ibid.
68 G. Lubbe-Wolff (2001) 13 JEL 84.
69 See, e.g., W. Howarth (1997) MLR 200.
70 Schedule 5, para. 5(2).
71 Regulation 22.

takes effect. In contrast to other enforcement powers, a revocation notice is suspended upon appeal and does not come into effect until the appeal is determined or withdrawn.[72]

Although the power to serve a revocation notice would appear to be draconian, it is subject to the right of appeal and subsequently to challenge by way of judicial review. The need to resolve any dispute by way of administrative appeal prior to any judicial review can be seen in the *Petrus Oils* case.

CASE 14.5 *R v. Environment Agency, ex parte Petrus Oils Ltd* [1999] Env LR 732

Petrus Oils operated a waste oil refinery that was controlled under an IPC authorization. There were many complaints from neighbours about the smells from the operation. The Agency issued a revocation notice. Petrus appealed against the revocation notice and applied for a judicial review of the Agency's decision to revoke the authorization.

The High Court held that Petrus should have pursued the revocation notice through the appeals process, rather than by arguing that it was unlawful. It was only in exceptional cases that a court would give leave to apply for judicial review if Parliament had provided for a statutory right of appeal against the decision that was sought to be challenged by way of judicial review. The real issue in dispute was whether the revocation was required in order to protect the environment. That involved questions of fact that were more appropriately dealt with by an inspector on appeal.

(c) Enforcement notices

If the regulator is of the opinion that the operator of an installation has contravened, is contravening, or is likely to contravene any condition of the permit, the regulator has a discretionary power to serve an enforcement notice.[73] The notice has to specify the steps required to remedy the problem and the timescale within which the steps must be taken.

(d) Suspension notices

If the regulator is of the opinion that the operation of an installation involves a risk of serious pollution, the regulator has a discretion to serve a suspension notice.[74] This discretion to serve a suspension notice is independent of any breach of a permit. The effect of a suspension notice is dramatic: any permit ceases to have effect either partially or totally. Guidance suggests that a suspension notice should allow activities to continue unless their cessation is necessary to address the risk of pollution.[75] In effect, the requirements of the suspension notice replace the permit. When the steps required in the notice have been taken, the notice can be withdrawn.

Offences and remedies

The EP Regulations provide a long list of further offences in relation to the environmental permitting system (reg. 38). The most serious of these relate to operational breaches, such as operating a regulated facility without a permit or in breach of a permit conditions, and to failing to comply with a statutory notice. Less serious offences are committed in relation to providing false information. All of these offences are punishable in the magistrates' court, with a maximum fine of £50,000 or imprisonment for a term of up to 12 months in the case of the most serious offences, and £5,000 or imprisonment up to a maximum of two years for

---

72 Regulation 31(9).
73 Regulation 36.
74 Regulation 37.
75 DEFRA (2008) para 10.13.

the lesser two categories. The more serious categories of offence are also triable in the Crown Court, with an unlimited fine and/or imprisonment for a term of up to five years.

It is open to any court, in sentencing an offender for failure to comply with an enforcement or suspension notice, to order that the effects of the offence be remedied (reg. 44). This allows for clean-up and compensation costs to come directly out of the offender's pocket. In many instances, these costs will far outstrip any reasonable fine that could be imposed.

There are further remedies available to the regulatory agency in the High Court. The regulator can seek an injunction in cases in which the enforcement of the criminal law is not securing adequate compliance (reg. 42). It must, however, exhaust other remedies before seeking an injunction.[76]

Defences

There is only one statutory defence in relation to permitted activities at regulated facilities: any acts that constituted the alleged breach must have been undertaken in an emergency in order to avoid danger to human health, reasonably practicable steps must have been taken to minimize pollution, and the particulars of the acts must have been supplied to the regulator as soon as reasonably practicable after their performance (reg. 40).

Appeals

There is a right of appeal against the refusal to grant or vary a permit, against revocation, variation, enforcement, and suspension notices, and against the imposition of unreasonable conditions upon a permit (reg. 31). Furthermore, there is a right of appeal in cases in which the regulatory agency has notified an operator that information contained within a permit, or application for permit, is not commercially confidential (reg. 53).

Generally, the time limit for appeals (see Sch. 6) is similar to that in the planning system, being six months from the date of refusal or deemed refusal to grant a permit. In cases in which there is an appeal against an enforcement, suspension, or variation notice, the time limit is two months from the date of the notice. If the regulatory agency is seeking to revoke a permit, the appeal must be made before the date on which the notice takes effect. Finally, in cases in which there is an appeal concerning commercial confidentiality, it must be submitted within 20 working days from the date of refusal.

A revocation notice will not take effect pending the hearing of an appeal (reg. 31(9)). In all other cases—that is, surrender, enforcement, suspension, or variation—there is no suspension of the notice pending an appeal (reg. 31(8)). Thus an operator cannot, if there is a rush order, gain an economic advantage by appealing against a notice so as to stop the enforcement process, continuing to pollute until the order is completed, and then stopping the process before the appeal is heard. An appeal must be made in writing to the Secretary of State. The appeal has to be accompanied by any relevant information, including any application, permit, correspondence, or decision, and a statement as to how the appellant wishes the appeal to be determined.[77]

An appeal can be heard in one of two ways: either by written representations or by a hearing. If either party to the appeal requests that it be heard by hearing, the Secretary of State must hold a hearing, although there is a discretion as to whether the hearing is held in public. The Secretary of State also has a power to direct that a hearing be held.[78]

---

76 See *Tameside Metropolitan Borough Council v. Smith Bros (Hyde) Ltd* [1996] Env LR 312.
77 See Sched. 6.
78 Schedule 6, para. 5.

Analysing the environmental permitting regime

The environmental permitting regime is an interesting example of the continuing development of the relationship between domestic and European environmental law. The overall impact of the regime might be said to be procedural rather than substantive, but the significance of the change should not be underestimated. The purported aim of the system is to introduce a risk-based approach to regulation that reduces rules, while targeting administrative effort on areas that require it. Fewer rules within a more coherent framework are intended to produce better outcomes in terms of environmental protection.

This typically 'British' rationale for deregulation only presents part of the picture. On the face of it, the system is complex: the EP Regulations stretch to some 130 pages, with 22 Schedules referring to the substantive provisions of a number of different European Directives and many amendments to existing legislation. As such, the Regulations take a new approach to the transposition and implementation of European environmental law.

The underlying themes of deregulation, administrative efficiency, and risk-based regulation have played a significant part in the rhetoric of domestic environmental regulation for many years. In addition, however, it is important to reflect upon the extent to which the regime represents a watershed in the 'Europeanization' of UK environmental law (although we offer some thoughts below on how the EP Regulations are part of a two-way process between the UK and the EC). The Regulations represent a recognition that a 'bare bones' or 'transmission belt' approach is arguably the best way of addressing the ever-increasing complexity and overlaps in European environmental law. This approach minimizes any difficulties in trying to ensure 'fit' as between existing domestic legal and administrative structures. As a consequence, there are benefits in terms of clarity of transposition, although implementation still presents a challenge for the regulators rather than legislators—with all of the flexibility that such an approach permits on a case-by-case basis.

We have seen that, historically, there has been a shift in approach towards the transposition and implementation of EC Directives, beginning with an administrative phase and culminating in an emphasis upon the 'copying out' into national legislation of obligations contained in EC environmental Directives.[79] There has also been a national antipathy towards 'gold plating'—that is, enacting measures going beyond that required by Directives—and, in this sense, the 'British' approach to EC environmental law has always been minimalist.[80]

Each of these approaches, however, has proven, in its way, to be unsatisfactory. The former approach was not consistent with judgments of the European Court, which stressed the need for transposition and implementation to be by binding legislative measures. But 'copy-out' has also proven problematic. One reason for this is that there is now much more guidance from the European Court on the interpretation of legal terms and concepts, which previously might have been transposed into national law in a more relative vacuum. One example is the extent to which the European Court has held that a number of key concepts found in environmental Directives are so-called 'autonomous concepts' for the purposes of EC law—i.e., concepts that must be given a consistent meaning in order to give proper effect to the Directive across the EC.[81] Another reason why copy-out is proving to be a less satisfactory approach is that many EC environmental Directives are now undergoing a period of consolidation and revision, which, in turn, requires national laws to be updated more frequently than before, sometimes because of relatively minor changes to the EC Directive.

79 See p. 216.
80 See p. 195 for a discussion of the adoption of higher environmental standards.
81 For example, the concept of 'project' for the purposes of the Environmental Impact Assessment Directive—see p. 443.

Recall that a Directive is 'binding, as to the result to be achieved, upon each member State', but leaves to the national authorities 'the choice of form and methods'.[82] In principle, therefore, member States are given choices about how they implement Directives, as long as these do not frustrate the overriding obligation to achieve the desired result. What we see with the environmental permitting regime, however, is what might be termed a 'conveyor belt' approach. What we mean by this is that the clarity or opacity of a Directive is directly imposed upon the enforcing authority, which is then put under a direct duty to fulfil the objectives of the Directive through the procedural mechanisms of the environmental permitting regime. Little or no attempt is made to clarify the meaning of terms that, by the nature of the European lawmaking process, might be deliberately or inevitably vague.

The transmission belt approach has certain advantages for example, certainty (in terms of lawful transposition) and flexibility (in terms of accommodating new legislative changes). Moreover, its use in the EP Regulations might reflect a degree of relative ease at the substantive content of the laws being implemented: for example, the extent to which there is already a degree of in-built flexibility to the standards required under the IPPC Directive, or the technical requirements for depositing waste in landfill in relation to which copy-out would be expected. Improvements in access to up-to-date versions of EC Directives may also be a factor. An alternative perspective, however, is that its use represents the ultimate triumph for the supremacy of EC law, or at least a recognition of the legal force of Directives. One other point is worth considering here: that the transmission belt is not necessarily one-way. The government has expressed its intention to use the permitting regime as a template with which to influence the shape of future European Directives—reflecting the possibility of the development of a European proceduralization with increasing integration of substance.

Whichever view one inclines towards, its use does beg questions relating to the ability of individuals to know how to challenge unlawful implementation when the nature of the duties are so vague and diffuse. What might be the consequences of the transmission belt approach? For the reasons given above, one might be that more attention will be paid to European case law. But another may be a greater role for national guidance in trying to interpret vague Directive terms. What we may be left with, then, is something with, arguably, the less legally attractive characteristics of both the initial, administrative phase and the deferential, copy-out phase.

Finally, while one could be forgiven for thinking that the EP Regulations mark a 'bowing down' before EC environmental law, there is an important sense in which they may mark a further stage not only in the Europeanization of domestic environmental law, but also in the policy of the UK towards making new EC environmental laws. It appears that the approach taken in the Permitting Regulations regime—in terms of bureaucratic simplification, taking a more risk-based and proportionate approach, and so on—will greatly shape the UK's negotiating position in relation to new EC environmental laws. In this sense, they illustrate both the taking and, perhaps in the future, the shaping of EC environmental law.

Applying the environmental permitting requirements in practice—the IPPC Directive

The listing of various provisions of the Integrated Pollution Prevention and Control (IPPC) Directive that must be complied with gives no real picture of how the regime works in practice. Although a number of Directives are listed and all have some relevance, the main Directives in terms of universal application are the Waste Framework Directive (in relation to waste operations and exemptions) and the IPPC Directive (in relation to installations).

82 Article 249 EC—see p. 204.

The former is covered in Chapter 18; the following provides some detailed context for the procedural framework of the environmental permitting regime.

The IPPC Directive forms part of a wider move towards the integration of environmental controls. In Europe, the notion of integrated controls was first put forward in the Fifth Environmental Action Programme (EAP), which identified IPPC as one of the priority areas for action. Subsequently, the European Commission drew heavily from the UK's experience with the system of integrated pollution control (IPC) established in the early 1990s when putting forward a proposal for an IPPC Directive. The proposed Directive relied upon meeting locally set environmental quality standards, rather than centrally set emission standards, thus reflecting the UK's approach to setting pollution control standards. This approach was the subject of criticism from some member States. In particular, Germany argued that uniform emission standards were vital in order to implement a harmonized system of integrated controls across all member States, to meet the Precautionary Principle and to avoid distortions of competition.[83] The concern was that, by allowing the setting of conditions that took into account local conditions, there would not be a 'level playing field' and standards would differ from member State to member State. Indeed, the Commission accepted that, although each member State would be controlled under the same regime, different countries and sectors might have different targets. These targets would be set by reference to varying factors, such as the quality of the local environment and economic viability of the installation.[84] There was, however, a degree of compromise in the final Directive that allowed for the setting of Community-wide emission standards if a 'need' for Community action could be identified (Art. 18).

In its final form, the IPPC Directive (2008/1/EC) reflects the newer, more flexible approach to environmental Directives adopted towards the end of the 1990s. It is less prescriptive than previous environmental Directives, with the main provisions being based upon the application of broad principles and procedures, rather than specified standards. The Directive sets out the types of installation that are covered in terms of thresholds and industry sectors (Art. 1 and Annex I), the obligations that apply to operators (Art. 3), the conditions that should be imposed in permits,[85] and various procedural matters in relation to the integrated permit system (Arts 4–9). Critically, in terms of environmental standards, it is silent in relation to specific environmental limits or even targets. This is in contrast to earlier pollution control Directives, which set out such limits explicitly.[86] The main coordination of Europe-wide standards comes through the exchange of information between the Commission and industry on BAT through the production of a BAT Reference (BREF) document for each of the industrial sectors covered under the Directive (Art. 16). Member States are required to take the BREF documents into account when setting permit conditions, but do not have to apply the guidance for every installation.

Another way in which the Directive provides for some consistency between member States is through the setting of Community-wide ELVs (Art. 19(1)). When a 'need' for Community action is identified—in particular through the information exchange and BREF process—standard ELVs can be set across all member States and individual permit conditions must reflect these. This combination of flexibility to set permit conditions by reference to local conditions, combined with 'back-stop' measures such as the information exchange and the ability to set Community-wide ELVs, ties in with the principle of subsidiarity, but with an institutional safeguard to prevent distortions as between member States.[87]

---

83 M. Doppelhammer (2000) EELR 199.

84 A. Gouldson and J. Murphy (1998) *Regulatory Realities: The Implementation and Impact of Industrial Environmental Regulation*, London: Earthscan, p. 47.

85 Critically, for the use of the BAT standard, and its interrelationship with emissions standards and environmental quality standards, see Arts 9 and 10.

86 For example, the Dangerous Substances in Water Directive (76/464/EEC; now 2006/11/EC).

87 Doppelhammer (2000).

In determining permits and considering conditions, regulators must impose ELVs in relation to specified polluting substances. Certain substances, listed in Annex III in respect of emissions to air and water, are considered to be suitable for stricter ELVs as a result of their impact on the receiving environment. The specific ELV will be set by reference to BAT, in addition to the individual circumstances of the installation and the local environment. This site-specific approach ensures that permitting is flexible, taking account of the techniques employed at the installation concerned, the local environment, and its location.

There are two exceptions to this general approach. The first is when general binding rules (GBRs) are applied for certain classes of installation (Art. 9(8)). These GBRs apply homogenous conditions across all installations that share similar characteristics, and are transposed in England and Wales with the introduction of standard permits (see below). The regulators have a discretion to ignore the application of GBRs if it is decided that they would be inappropriate—for example, if the site were to be situated near to a sensitive environmental receptor, such as a sensitive aquifer or a special area of conservation.

The second exception relates to areas in which Community-wide ELVs have been set. No Community-wide ELVs have yet been set, but the Commission has made it clear that, where ELVs are being set at a low level that is not based on BAT, such limits will be used.[88]

There are other general principles that must be taken into account when imposing conditions (Arts. 3 and 9). These include the need to achieve a high level of protection of the environment as a whole and to take all preventative measures against pollution, particularly through the application of BAT. BAT is a process standard that, in theory, is designed to prevent environmental emissions or, in the alternative, to reduce them to zero. How this is achieved is set out in guidance notes, by way of technological methods of achieving ELVs. These give guideline values against which can be established a level of performance that should be achieved for that particular installation.

The danger is that the setting out of ELVs in guidance notes can replace BAT as the real standard, causing regulators to focus on the achievement of ELVs to the exclusion of BAT. Such an approach was criticized in the case of *Thornby Farms Ltd v. Daventry District Council* [2002] Env LR 28 (Case 14.6). Although this decision concerned the application of Best Available Techniques Not Entailing Excessive Cost (BATNEEC) rather than BAT, it represents a relevant analysis of the question of what is meant by the application of the Preventative Principle in the context of industrial pollution control.

CASE 14.6 *Thornby Farms v. Daventry District Council* [2002] Env LR 28[89]

Thornby Farms (TF) owned farmland next to two pet incinerators. TF challenged the grant of an IPC authorization by Daventry District Council to operate the incinerators on the basis that the emission levels specified in the conditions were higher than could be achieved in practice. TF's primary concern was that the conditions had been set for ease of compliance, rather than the objective of preventing pollution. TF argued that the council had to apply the preventative principles laid down in the statute. These would not be met by conditions that permitted levels of emissions higher than the levels that the incinerator was capable of achieving.

The Court of Appeal dismissed the application, on the basis that the emission limit values (ELVs) did not represent Best Available Technique Not Entailing Excessive Cost (BATNEEC), and that the ELVs specified in the guidance were minimum levels that were not to be exceeded and not necessarily the best that could be achieved. The council had a discretion to decide the most appropriate method of

---

88 COM(2003) 354.
89 S. Bell (2003) 15 JEL 59.

achieving the pollution prevention objective, but that did not weaken the obligation to ensure that BATNEEC would be used.

The BAT standard under IPPC closely reflects the BATNEEC standard under IPC. The use of BAT is aimed at ensuring that environmental impacts from an installation as a whole are prevented or minimized. The decision in *Thornby Farms* indicates that BAT can only be translated as requiring the 'best that can be achieved', bearing in mind the general obligation to reduce emissions and environmental impacts.

Best Available Techniques (BAT)

At the heart of the IPPC system is the idea that operators must use the BAT standard in order to ensure a high level of protection of the environment when taken as a whole. The application of the BAT principle is made in the context of local conditions, which includes such things as the local environment and economic factors. Emissions limit values are then set by reference to both BAT and local conditions. Environmental quality standards (EQSs) are considered once the ELVs have been set. In circumstances under which an EQS set under European or national standards would be breached, it is possible to set conditions that are stricter than BAT or to refuse the permit (Art. 10). The achievement of these standards is achieved through the other Directives listed in the EP Regulations—such as the Waste Incineration Directive (2000/76/EC)—and other Directives with relevant EQSs, including those on water and air quality.[90] In this sense, EQSs represent a minimum threshold for the imposition of ELVs, with BAT meeting a higher standard of prevention and/or reduction over and above the EQS. The Court of Appeal expanded upon this relationship between BAT, EQSs, ELVs, and the imposition of conditions on an IPPC permit in the *Rockware Glass* case.

CASE 14.7 *R (Rockware Glass Ltd) v. Chester County Council* [2007] Env LR 3

Rockware (R) was the competitor of Quinn Glass Ltd (Q), which operated a glassworks that required a Pt B IPPC permit from the local authority, Chester City Council. Q was granted an IPPC permit that R claimed contained emission limits that were too low when considering Best Available Techniques (BAT) and the relevant environmental quality standard (EQS). R's underlying concern was that Q was allowed to install something other than BAT and that lower emission limits could be achieved through the use of BAT. The overall effect was that Q had a competitive advantage by installing cheaper abatement equipment. R won at first instance. Q appealed and argued that there was no duty to reduce emissions to a minimum; rather, the duty was simply to achieve emissions in relation to which a high level of protection was met, as required under Art. 9(1). Q also argued that meeting the EQS for air quality was sufficient to demonstrate that BAT had been achieved and there was no justification for imposing higher costs in terms of abatement equipment in order to meet lower emission standards. In these terms, the issue for the Court of Appeal was the exact nature of the interrelationship between emissions limit values (ELVs), EQS, and BAT. The Court of Appeal outlined the clear distinction between the general requirement of achieving EQS in terms of managing air quality, and the very specific requirements to prevent and reduce emissions from individual installations. The Court held that the specific requirement of the IPPC Directive was to reduce emissions

---

90 For discussion of the imposition of stricter conditions and/or refusal, see *R v. Secretary of State for the Environment and RJ Compton and Sons, ex parte West Wiltshire District Council* [1996] Env LR 312.

'as far as possible' and that the EQS only established minimum requirements for consideration in setting permit conditions. Thus emission limits 'trumped' EQS where lower ELVs could be set. Finally, BAT was a flexible concept and included alternative configurations that should be considered when determining what would be achievable.

Defining 'Best Available Techniques'

The phrase 'Best Available Techniques' is further broken down in the Directive (Art. 2(12)). It is a general concept that provides the basis for setting ELVs that are designed to prevent and, where prevention is not practicable, generally to reduce emissions and the impact on the environment as a whole. 'Best' is defined in relation to the effectiveness of the techniques in achieving a high level of protection of the environment as a whole. It is not an absolute term and there may be a number of different techniques that would fall within this definition.

'Available techniques', meanwhile, are those that have been developed on a scale that allows implementation by the relevant industrial sector under economically and technically viable conditions, taking into consideration the costs and advantages, whether or not the techniques are used or produced inside the UK, as long as they are accessible to the operator. This should exclude experimental techniques or techniques that have only been tested under conditions that are peculiar to other countries. 'Techniques' specifically includes both the technology used and the way in which the installation is designed, built, maintained, and decommissioned.

In relation to costs, any determination of BAT takes into account two broad criteria: the economic and environmental costs and benefits of particular techniques of pollution control, and the affordability of such techniques in the sector of industry concerned.

In addition to these specific definitions, there are various considerations listed in Annex IV of the Directive that should be taken into account when determining BAT. These are generic, but include:

- resource use, such as the reduction of hazardous substances and the consumption of raw materials;

- the reduction of waste, and the promotion of recovery and recycling;

- technical considerations, such as advances in technology and the availability of comparable processes that have been successfully run on an industrial scale;

- the time taken to introduce BAT;

- accident prevention.

The terms in the Directive are vague, which allows the regulatory agencies some discretion in determining applications on a case-by-case basis. There is, however, some supplementary guidance to be found in sector guidance notes and the BREF documents (see Box 14.2). The guidance notes are supposed to provide a coherent context in which decisions can be made in relation to permit conditions. The national statutory guidance notes are based upon the BREF documents. The IPPC notes are non-prescriptive, providing indicative standards for both new and existing installations, with clear timetables for upgrading in the case of existing plant. Each application is, however, considered individually and variations from the guidance note standard may be acceptable in certain circumstances.

BOX 14.2 The 'Sevilla process' and the production of BREF documents—technocratic, participatory standard setting

In practice, the determination of the Best Available Techniques (BAT) and emissions limit values (ELVs) that are to be used in IPPC permits are set by reference to European and national guidance. Article 17(2) of the IPPC Directive requires the European Commission to establish an exchange of information between member States and the industries that are controlled under IPPC in order to establish what is meant by 'BAT'. This exchange of information is often referred to as the 'Sevilla process', because the body responsible for coordinating the documents is based in Seville in Spain. The technical guidance is known as a BAT Reference (BREF) document and this is taken into account when determining BAT either for a sector or for an installation. Individual circumstances will also be taken into account and the BREF document will not set down uniform emission limits. While the BREF document is widely accepted across all of the member States, it may form the basis for sectoral daughter Directives to the main IPPC Directive.

The process of agreeing the BREF documents is a classic example of technocratic, participatory standard setting. In many cases, standards are set 'top-down' by government bodies or regulator. This type of technocratic standard setting is often a source of criticism of traditional command-and-control regulation. This criticism is that, in order to regulate effectively, the regulator needs to understand the workings of industrial sectors. Thus there is a 'clear imbalance' between the industrial participants and others involved in the standard-setting process.[91] The correction of this imbalance involves lengthy information-gathering exercises in order to establish the standard.

The Sevilla process seeks to address some of these problems by taking a more participatory approach to standard setting.[92] A technical working group has been set up for each BREF document. This group consists of industry representatives, regulators, research institutes, and NGOs. The Directive makes provision for most of these groups to participate. NGOs were not included, but were the special invitees of DG Environment in an attempt to widen participation. The working group then spends a considerable amount of time negotiating over the exact terms of BAT (experience suggests that between two and three years is the average).[93]

Empirical research showed that a wide range of factors was taken into account when setting standards, including political and legal issues. The establishment of BAT was as much concerned with pragmatism, as it was with technological and scientific matters.[94] Under the Directive, BAT was to be identified by reference to two criteria only: the costs and benefits of using particular techniques, and the effectiveness of the techniques in ensuring the protection of the environment as a whole. In the 'real world', however, the discussion of BAT was not necessarily as clear-cut as this, because there was little data available on cross-media impacts and there was no methodology by which to determine the trade-offs between environmental impacts across different media.

In addition to the imposition of ELVs shaped by the application of BAT, permits also must contain conditions relating to other environmental impacts of an activity. After an installation has closed, it must be returned to a satisfactory state and pollution risks arising as a result of the permitted activities should be avoided (Art. 3(1)(f)).

---

91 N. Gunningham and P. Grabosky (1998) *Smart Regulation: Designing Environment Policy*, Oxford: Clarendon Press, p. 44.

92 B. Lange (2002) ELJ 246.

93 COM(2003) 354.

94 Lange (2002).

How integrated is environmental permitting and IPPC?

Although the introduction of IPPC has seen a simplification of the administration and control of many environmental impacts from industrial processes, there is still a degree of overlap between different systems of pollution control. For example, while discharges of trade effluent to sewers will be considered in determining ELVs for particular pollutants, a trade effluent consent will still be required from the sewerage undertaker.[95] Another overlap relates to water pollution from Pt A(2) installations: these are controlled by local authorities, but, because these have no specialist expertise in relation to water pollution control, the Environment Agency, which has the greatest expertise in this area, has an overriding supervisory role in the setting of conditions for discharges to water for all Pt A(2) installations and may give notice to the relevant local authority specifying the minimum conditions controlling discharges to water.[96] Under s. 88 of the Water Resources Act (WRA) 1991, discharges made in accordance with an IPPC permit are not an offence under s. 85 of that Act—that is, causing or knowingly permitting the pollution of controlled waters. There are also issues about the overlap between IPPC, contaminated land, and statutory nuisance, but these are considered elsewhere.[97]

Unlike some of the other pollution control regimes, there is little legislative reference to any connection between the development control system and IPPC. One exception is that in the case of specified waste management activities, in relation to which one of the prerequisites for the grant of an environmental permit is that planning permission, if required, is in force. There is no obligation to obtain a planning permission for any development associated with a new or altered installation prior to obtaining a permit under the IPPC legislation (the reverse is also true). But, because a wide range of environmental impacts are material considerations in applications for permits, there is a practical link between environmental scrutiny under the planning regimes and under IPPC legislation.

Many of the installations that require a permit to operate will also be subject to the need for environmental assessment under the relevant legislation. In these cases, much of the information included within an environmental statement would form the basis of the information submitted with an IPPC application. The IPPC Directive and the Environmental Impact Assessment (EIA) Directive (97/11/EC) allow for information produced for the purposes of one Directive to be recycled for the purposes of the other. In practice, therefore, it would be appropriate to submit an environmental statement with both applications, although the IPPC application would need to concentrate on additional technical matters, such as ELVs and BAT. The EP Regulations, in relation to the grant or variation of a permit, provide that information obtained under EIA must be taken into account.[98]

Another important practical overlap is in the decision-making process. When dealing with a planning application, local authorities are advised to consider only the land-use implications of the development. This leads to inevitable questions about the nature of 'land-use' implications. The courts have examined the nature of the overlap between planning and pollution control in relation to the IPC system (which, for the purposes of the discussion, is the same as the IPPC system) in *Gateshead Metropolitan Borough Council v. Secretary of State for the Environment* [1995] Env LR 37.

---

95 Water Industry Act 1991, s. 118 and further the Online Resource Centre.
96 Regulation 58.
97 See, respectively, Chapter 16, and the Online Resource Centre.
98 Schedules 4 and 7.

CASE 14.8 Planning and pollution control—*Gateshead Metropolitan Borough Council v. Secretary of State for the Environment* [1995] Env LR 37[99]

The Secretary of State granted planning permission for a clinical waste incinerator in Gateshead. The inspector appointed to hear the appeal recommended that permission be refused. One of the issues that were taken into account by the inspector was the public fear that pollution from the site would be unacceptable. The Secretary of State concluded that the issue could be satisfactorily addressed as part of the IPC application and granted planning permission. That decision was challenged by the local planning authority, on the basis that the two systems were so closely interlinked that it was unreasonable to grant planning permission without knowing whether emissions could be adequately controlled under the IPC system.

In the High Court, Sullivan J decided that, although the two statutory regimes overlapped, the extent of the overlap would vary on each occasion. It was envisaged that there would be a range of cases, from those in which environmental considerations could be dealt with adequately under the pollution control system, to those in which environmental considerations could not be incorporated satisfactorily into an IPC authorization. The correct legal test was whether or not it was reasonable in the *Wednesbury* sense to arrive at the decision reached by the decision maker.

On appeal, the Court of Appeal affirmed this decision with only a slight variation of judgment. The issue of whether there was an unacceptable risk was, in the Court's view, a matter for the pollution control authority and the fact that the public had expressed concern about the issue was not conclusive. The Court went on to say, however, that the fact that planning permission had been granted should not have been viewed as a restriction on the pollution control authority's discretion to refuse the pollution control application if it thought it fit to do so.

Thus, there is no definite dividing line between planning and pollution control, and each decision maker is entitled to arrive at different conclusions if it exercises its discretion reasonably. Although this decision would apply to the overlap between IPPC and the planning system, the dividing line will be much more blurred, because the consideration of environmental impacts in each system will be largely similar. Therefore it would be unusual—but seemingly not unlawful—if one regulatory body were to arrive at a different conclusion from another even with the same information supporting the application (or, in the case of some installations, if the same regulatory body were to arrive at two different conclusions).

The planning–pollution interface is currently the subject of relevant planning policy statements (PPSs 10 and 23), which are in line with the *Gateshead* decision, but these precede the environmental permitting regime and, partly in response to permitting, there is, at the time of writing, a consultation process exploring further streamlining.[100]

Is IPPC a better way of approaching pollution?

All of the focus on the environmental permitting regime and its 'streamlined' approach to the 'proceduralization' of pollution control regulation deflects from more fundamental questions about the overall substantive approach to IPPC, which represents a significant departure from traditional forms of environmental regulation. In many ways, IPPC echoes the 'British' approach to pollution control: it is flexible, pragmatic, and tailored to individual

---

99 See also *R (on the application of Kent) v. First Secretary of State* [2005] Env LR 30.

100 See **www.defra.gov.uk/environment/waste/management/pdf/planning-pollution-control.pdf**.

circumstances; yet it is principled, progressive, and based upon pollution prevention. After some years of experience with transposing and implementing the requirements of the IPPC Directive, it is difficult to draw any real conclusions on the question of whether IPPC is actually a better way of dealing with pollution from industrial sources than previous techniques. In economic terms, the use of a standard that encourages technological innovation is more 'efficient' than the use of one that prescribes a uniform standard, because flexible standards allow operators to develop individual responses to meet the pollution prevention targets set for them. By contrast, uniform standards are perceived to be economically inefficient, because there may be no incentive to reduce pollution below the uniform standard even if it could be done at a lower cost.[101]

The use of process-based preventative standards also ties in with the ideas of ecological modernization and the weak view of sustainable development. The use of BAT adopts a positive view of pollution and suggests that technology can, and will, address environmental impacts. It identifies a move away from control technologies based around end-of-pipe abatement towards 'clean technologies' used in overall processes and based around integrated environmental solutions, such as energy efficiency, resource usage, and waste minimization. Perhaps most significantly, it indicates an emphasis on continual technological improvements and therefore enhanced environmental performance. This technocratic approach to pollution control is the dominating theme of European environmental regulation.

There are some weaknesses in the IPPC system. First, the scope of activities covered is still relatively narrow. Many major sources of pollutants (for example, greenhouse gas emissions from transport) are excluded. Secondly, the controls are aimed at the largest industrial operators, and therefore exclude many small and medium-sized enterprises (SMEs) that might benefit from pollution prevention technology. Thirdly, there is the problem of maintaining a 'level playing field'—that is, there is difficulty in benchmarking the achievement and performance of BAT in different member States. Although the information exchange is designed to address this potential problem, the process is too slow, the individual monitoring is too weak, and the enforcement is too lax to ensure that all member States are implementing the provisions in the same manner.

These potential disadvantages of IPPC reflect the negative side of ecological modernization—that is, that it is based around technical solutions proposed and agreed by technical people. The whole idea of 'sustainable production' is based around a model of economic growth that is unacceptable to some.[102] This technocratic approach—an approach that has been aided by judgments of the courts—has a knock-on effect that the public tends to be more excluded from the decision-making processes than it is in other areas (for example, planning), because of the technical nature of the debate. In addition, the parameters of the debate are often constrained by decisions made at European level as to appropriate BAT or ELVs that promote even less public involvement—at least on a general level. The idea that levels of public participation in the permitting system is low is reflected in the creation of extended rights for the public, as seen in the Aarhus Convention and the detailed public participation requirements of the IPPC Directive.[103]

Other initiatives to increase transparency and accountability include the establishment of the European Pollutant Release and Transfer Register (E-PRTR), which gathers together data on emissions to air and water from Annex I IPPC installations.

---

101 J. Simila (2002) 14 JEL 143; Gunningham and Grabosky (1999).

102 D. Wilkinson (2002) *Environment and Law*, London: Routledge, p. 249.

103 Articles 15 and 16.

1   There are two senses described here in which environmental regulation may be integrated. The first of these—substantive integration—aims to consider environmental impacts holistically. This can be at a very broad level—for example, forms of ecosystem management, or strategically assessing plans and programmes—or it can be at a more site-specific level, whereby, from any given installation, controls on emissions to individual media (air, water, land) are replaced with an integrated system of control over all environmental impacts. This latter approach to substantive integration is reflected in the system known as integrated pollution prevention and control (IPPC).

2   The second sense in which integration can be used is to describe processes through which the bureaucracy of environmental regulation is consolidated. This can involve institutional integration, such as the creation of relatively unified regulatory agencies such as the Environment Agency. This is usually justified on grounds of greater environmental coherence. But integration can also involve streamlining or unifying the rules that govern the control of harmful impacts; this sense of integration is prompted more by notions of 'better regulation', and includes the idea of easing the burden on the regulated through simplifying and standardizing the rules.

3   The Environmental Permitting (England and Wales) Regulations 2007 mark a decisive point in trying to integrate UK environmental law in this second sense. The Regulations aim to provide, as far as possible, a unified permitting system covering a number of areas in which EC environmental law must be given effect to, the main ones being IPPC and waste management. The Regulations make it possible to issue standard permits with 'off-the-shelf' conditions, as well as tailored permits in more complex cases. They mean that, in general, the same procedural rules (about applying, transferring, appealing, enforcing, public participation, etc.) apply across the board to all permits issued under the Regulations.

4   IPPC derives originally from European Directive 96/61/EC (with subsequent consolidation in 2008/1/EC), which, in turn, was based upon the UK system of integrated pollution control found in the Environmental Protection Act (EPA) 1990. The IPPC Directive takes a flexible approach to regulation, and is based upon member States applying broad principles and procedures, rather than specific numerical standards.

5   An environmental permit based upon IPPC utilizes the Best Available Techniques (BAT), a flexible process standard, which takes into account local circumstances and balances costs against environmental benefits. Emissions limit value (ELV) standards are then set by reference to the BAT for a particular installation. Environmental quality standards are taken into account in setting ELVs above those related to BAT if the quality standards represent national or European standards, or if local conditions require it.

6   IPPC applies only to activities carried out at the most polluting industrial installations. The vast majority of these installations are controlled by the Environment Agency, with a small residual number controlled by local authorities. IPPC applies to both new and existing installations.

7   The strengths of IPPC include the way in which it promotes technological innovation in an economically efficient manner, encourages the regulation of industrial sources by considering all environmental impacts as a whole, shifts the focus of industrial pollution control from end-of-pipe solutions to clean technology, and the practical workings of the idea of ecological modernization.

8   The weaknesses of IPPC might be said to include: the relatively small scope of application; the bias in favour of technological solutions that exclude greater public participation; the promotion of weaker forms of 'sustainable development' that do nothing to address underlying issues of resource depletion and over-consumption; and the lack of true integration of controls over all sources of pollution.

Q QUESTIONS

1 What are the advantages of taking an integrated approach to pollution problems, as seen in the integrated pollution prevention and control (IPPC) system under Directive 2008/1/EC and domestic law? Are there any disadvantages?

2 How 'integrated' is IPPC?

3 What is meant by the use of the environmental standard Best Available Techniques (BAT) to prevent or reduce pollution? Within IPPC, how does the use of BAT relate to the use of other environmental standards, such as emission and environmental quality standards?

4 Critically consider the Environmental Permitting (England and Wales) Regulations 2007 within the context of the development of the British approach to environmental regulation.

5 Megawaste operates a waste incineration business. It is presently trying to commence operations at a new site in Blackoldton. Waste incineration is a Pt A(1) installation under the Environmental Permitting (England and Wales) Regulations 2007. The Environment Agency rejects the application for an environmental permit on the ground that Megawaste cannot demonstrate the use of BAT. First, the Agency considers that other technologies are more suitable. In particular, microwaving waste should be preferred to incineration. There are no microwave waste disposal units operating in the UK, although they are used successfully in Denmark and the USA. Secondly, although the incinerator can meet the emissions limit values (ELVs) set out in the existing BAT Reference (BREF) document, it does not meet those set in a recently published European Directive on incineration, which sets much lower limits. The Directive, however, only requires these limits to be met within the next four years. Finally, the Agency argues that, even if the ELVs could be met, the aggregated effects of this plant would be harmful. The plant is situated in an area with a lot of motorways, and atmospheric conditions are already close to breaching European and national air quality standards for certain substances. Advise Megawaste on the legal validity of these grounds of refusal.

📖 FURTHER READING

Integrated pollution prevention and control (IPPC) is a relatively 'dry' topic that appears to be dominated by procedural and technical matters. One way of finding good relevant further reading in this area is to identify works that contextualize the detailed provisions in a general way. A. Gouldson and J. Murphy (1998) *Regulatory Realities*, London: Earthscan, puts a lot of the technical detail into context by examining the regulatory impacts of IPPC, IPC, and the voluntary system of environmental management standards under the EU's Eco-Management and Audit Scheme (EMAS). Written by non-lawyers, the book does not cover the detail of the law, but provides a good illustration of the use of different legal mechanisms used to bring about environmental improvement (see especially, chs 3 and 5).

On the IPPC Directive from a legal point of view, C. Backes and G. Betlem (eds) (1999) *Integrated Pollution Prevention and Control: The EEC Directive from a Comparative Legal and Economic Perspective*, The Hague: Kluwer, provides a comparative context by examining the position in three member States (Germany, the UK, and the Netherlands). Different perspectives on the IPPC Directive can be found in: N. Emmott and N. Haigh, 'Integrated pollution prevention and control: UK and EC approaches and possible next steps' [1996] JEL 301; M. Doppelhammer, 'More difficult than finding the way round Chinatown? The IPPC Directive and its implementation' (2000) EELR 199; M. Faure and J. Lefevre, 'The Draft Directive on Integrated Pollution Prevention and Control: an economic perspective' [1996] EELR 112; and M. Pallemaerts, 'The proposed IPPC Directive: re-regulations or de-regulation?' [1996] EELR 174. There is a study of the background to the Sevilla process and the writing of Best Available Techniques (BAT) Reference (BREF) documents in B. Lange, 'From boundary drawing to transitions: the creation of normativity under the EU Directive on Integrated Pollution Prevention and Control' (2002) 8(2) Eur LJ 246. And J. Scott, 'Flexibility in the Implementation of

EC Environmental Law' [2000] *Yearbook of European Environmental Law* 56 considers the IPPC Directive in terms of the wider 'proceduralization' of EC environmental law.

Background reading on the concept of integrating pollution controls can be found in J. Krier and M. Brownstein, 'On integrated pollution control' (1991) Environmental Law 119, and N. Haigh and F. Irwin (eds) (1990) *Integrated Pollution Control in Europe and North America*, Washington, DC: The Conservation Foundation.

For historical interest, there are a few articles on the system of IPC that are worth looking at. A. Mehta and K. Hawkins, 'IPC and its impact: perspectives from industry' (1998) 10 JEL 61 is an empirical study of the effect of the regime upon industry; a similar approach (although with a greater focus on enforcement practice) is taken in C. Lovat, 'Regulating IPC in Scotland' (2004) 16 JEL 48. M. Purdue, 'Integrated pollution control and the Environmental Protection Act 1990: a coming of age for environmental law?' [1991] 54 MLR 534 deals with the significance of the introduction of the IPC system, in terms of its impact upon environmental standard setting. A further source of some interest here is B. Pontin, 'Integrated pollution control in Victorian Britain: rethinking progress within the history of environmental law' (2007) 19(2) JEL 173, which puts the case that there was more integration then than is generally acknowledged.

There is, as yet, no secondary literature on environmental permitting, although there will undoubtedly be some that will emerge and the Online Resource Centre will mention the best. Works explaining the former pollution prevention and control regime—in so far as they discuss concepts such as BAT as found in the Directive—will still be of some use and a useful guide is J. Farthing, B. Marshall, and P. Kellett (2003) *Pollution Prevention and Control: The New Regime*, London: Lexis Nexis. The best place to start reading further about environmental permitting is the guidance that has been produced. There is 'core guidance' that explains the general procedures (available online at **www.defra.gov.uk/environment/epp/documents/core-guidance.pdf**) and specific, sectoral guidance (such as that on IPPC, available online at **www.defra.gov.uk/environment/epp/documents/ippc-parta-guidance.pdf**).

@ WEB LINKS

The starting point for any web-based research of IPPC should probably be the European Commission's web page at **europa.eu.int/comm/environment/ippc/index.htm**. The European IPPC Bureau's website at **eippcb.jrc.es** is a good source of technical information about the IPPC Directive and BREF documents. On a national level, the main source of information is DEFRA, online at **www.defra.gov.uk/environment/epp**, which links to the regulations and guidance, and will be the site via which any further developments to permitting will be consulted. The Environment Agency also has coverage of the Permitting Regulations via **www.environment-agency.gov.uk/business**.

15 Climate change and air quality

→ **Overview**

This chapter deals with legal controls to address global climate change and air quality. The complexity of these problems means that many different types of approach are necessary across a wide range of activities. This can be a little daunting at first, because many issues overlap. The chapter is, nevertheless, broadly divided, considering, first, the laws that seek to control climate change and, secondly, the laws that deal with air pollution and air quality. In each of these areas, there are laws at international, European, and national levels that need to be considered. It makes sense, however, to consider, first, some general issues, and also the international response to various forms of air and atmospheric pollution.

Coverage of certain major elements of domestic air pollution and air quality law, and also climate change, however, is necessarily incomplete in this chapter. For example, significant point source emissions of pollutants from many industrial sources fall within the system of integrated pollution prevention and control (see Chapter 14), more information on general controls at local level over smoke and fumes can be found in the Online Resource Centre, and climate change is now such a dominating concern across all areas of law and policy that reference to the subject can be found in every chapter of this book. Nevertheless, this chapter attempts to provide a degree of coherence by illustrating some of the underlying themes of this book, including consideration of the nature of regulatory impact, different types of environmental standard, technocratic approaches to regulatory standard setting, and the use of alternative environmental policy instruments, such as voluntary agreements and economic instruments.

At the end of this chapter, you should be able to:

✔ appreciate the main issues of addressing and managing the impact of global problems, such as climate change, through legal means;

✔ understand the nature of ground-level air pollution problems and some of the main ways in which they have been addressed at international, European, and national levels;

✔ assess the use of a mixed regulatory approach to the control of both of these concerns and evaluate the appropriateness of the legal response against the seriousness of the problems being addressed.

Air and atmospheric pollution

Air and atmospheric pollutants, and their sources

The range of problems affecting the atmosphere stretches across the full range of human activities, from highly toxic fumes emitted from a complicated industrial process, to such seemingly mundane activities as lighting a fire, driving a car, or using spray-on deodorant. Air pollutants come in many forms, with the main ones including the following.

- **Various gases produced from combustion processes**
  These include carbon monoxide (CO), carbon dioxide (CO_2) and oxides of nitrogen. Major sources include power stations, heating plants, industrial processes, and transportation. In terms of the amount emitted and the length of time it remains in the atmosphere, CO_2 is the most problematic greenhouse gas. The major source of nitrous oxides, however, is livestock production.[1]

- **Sulphur dioxide (SO_2)**
  This is released into the atmosphere as a result of burning fossil fuels that contain sulphur. It is an acidic gas, which combines with water vapour to produce acid rain. The most common sources of SO_2 are coal-fired power stations and other industrial sources, although recent research has shown a significant contribution from the burning of marine fuel on container ships and oil tankers.[2] A reduction of the use of coal as an energy source has seen ambient concentrations of SO_2 fall over the last fifty years.

- **Particulates of lead and other heavy metals**
  These arise from various activities, including combustion processes in motor vehicles, metal processing industries, and waste incineration (particularly waste batteries). The increasing use of unleaded petrol has seen concentrations of lead drop over recent years.

- **PM_{10}**
  These are very small airborne particulate matter, the particles of which are <10 μm. They arise from a variety of sources, and can vary in physical and chemical characteristics. The principal source of PM_{10} matter is emissions from diesel engines. Regulatory concern is now shifting to $PM_{2.5}$, which make up the majority of PM_{10} and which seem to be the most harmful elements of this kind of particulate matter.[3]

- **Various complex pollutants produced by the incomplete combustion of fuels**
  These are carcinogenic or highly toxic at very small levels and include: dioxins; furans; polyaromatic hydrocarbons (PAHs); polychlorinated biphenyls (PCBs).

- **Volatile organic compounds (VOCs)**
  VOCs are released in vehicle exhaust gases, either as unburned fuels or as combustion products, and are also emitted by the evaporation of solvents and motor fuels.

- **Chlorofluorocarbons (CFCs)**
  These have been used in aerosol sprays, solvents, and as refrigerants in fridges, freezers, and air-conditioning units. CFCs are inert in the lower atmosphere, then undergo a significant reaction in the upper atmosphere that destroys stratospheric ozone. This ozone absorbs ultraviolet radiation, which would otherwise be harmful to humans, animals, and plants.

- **Methane**
  This is emitted during the production and transport of coal, natural gas, and oil. Methane emissions also result from the decomposition of organic wastes in landfills and from herds of cattle.

---

1 H. Steinfeld, P. Gerber, T. Wassenaar, V. Castel, M. Rosales, and C. de Haan (2006) *Livestock's Long Shadow: Environmental Issues and Options*, Rome: UN Food and Agriculture Organization.

2 R. McKie, 'Ships sabotage war on acid rain' (2004) *The Observer*, 10 October.

3 2004/470/EC, Commission Decision of 29 April 2004 concerning guidance on a provisional reference method for the sampling and measurement of $PM_{2.5}$.

CASE 15.1 Carbon dioxide as a pollutant—*Massachusetts v. Environmental Protection Agency* (2007) 127 S Ct 1438

Carbon dioxide is inert, a vital food for plants, and is exhaled by humans. It carbonates drinks and can be perfectly harmless. But it is the most significant of the six major greenhouse gases, especially in terms of cumulative emissions (it remains in the atmosphere for a century). In the USA, the Environmental Protection Agency ruled that, for the purposes of the US Clean Air Act's provisions on motor vehicle emission standards, carbon dioxide was not a 'pollutant'. This decision was successfully challenged in the US Supreme Court (by a five–four majority).[4]

The case is interesting in the context of this chapter, because it shows how concerns about a global issue such as climate change do not necessarily fit within existing legal rules relating to air pollution. In the USA, the scope for federal action has had to be litigated and fought for; in contrast, the EC's competence to legislate over climate change has never seriously been questioned.

Most of these sources are man-made, but there are natural sources, including soil dust from large areas of land with little or no plant life, dust and sulphur dioxide from volcanic eruptions, smoke from wild fires, and methane gas from cattle. Indeed, for some air pollutants (for example, SO_2), these form the largest sources. It is also important to note that, as well as polluting *sources*, consideration also has to be given to the ways in which pollutants can be taken up without causing environmental harm. The best-known example is the role that forests and other land uses play, capturing CO_2 and, in effect, locking it away (at least in the short term). Hence, for example, CO_2 trading schemes calculate annual emissions by subtracting the amount of CO_2 soaked up in natural sinks from the amount emitted from industrial and other man-made processes.

The effects of air and atmospheric pollutants

As with other forms of pollution, the effect of different sources of pollution may differ, depending on such things as air temperature, wind speed, the height and velocity of discharge, and the presence of other pollutants, including any synergistic effects. The more serious effects are as follows.

- **Climate change**
  This is thought to be linked largely to the emission of six 'greenhouse gases'—namely, nitrous oxides, carbon dioxide, PFCs, methane, CFCs, and ground-level ozone. These gases trap the infrared radiation emitted by the Earth's surface, acting like a greenhouse, raising the air temperature to create a stable environment. An increase in that air temperature could have dramatic consequences. Some of the predicted changes include the flooding of low-lying land as the polar ice caps melt, while some things such as extreme weather events, changes in seasons, etc. are already being linked to climate change.

- **Acid rain**
  Acid rain arises when sulphur dioxide and nitrogen oxides mix with water vapour (and ammonia from agricultural sources) to form very weak sulphuric acid and nitric acid solutions in rainfall. Acid rain has been linked to the killing of fish, birds, and trees, and can cause damage to buildings. Acid rain can be carried for great distances on the wind, thereby displacing the source and effect of pollution.

---

4 *Massachusetts v. EPA* (2007) 127 S Ct 1438, see **www.supremecourtus.gov/opinions/06pdf/05–1120.pdf**.

- **Direct harm to human health**

  Many atmospheric pollutants have been linked to harm to human health. These can include respiratory problems (particulates, nitrous oxides, and sulphur dioxide), brain damage (lead), and cancer (dioxins). Official estimates suggest that up to 24,000 deaths are brought forward by short-term exposure to certain air pollutants from all sources, including traffic.[5]

Because such a wide range of activities affects the atmosphere, the range of environmental issues is also wide. On the one hand, there have always been difficulties with polluting activities affecting the locality in which they were situated. International difficulties have arisen with the creation of acid rain. In recent years, we have seen a realization among the international community that individual nations' actions can combine to create truly global difficulties. The destruction of the ozone layer and the issue of global warning have brought home the truly awesome consequences of the combined effect of certain human activities.

The history and development of early controls

The pollution of the local atmosphere from emissions has traditionally been easy to identify. Such problems date back to the early uses of coal in domestic fires. The production of fumes and particulates from fires caused pulmonary infections and related lung diseases. Thus, as far back as the thirteenth century, bans were placed on the burning of sea coal in parts of south London. With the advent of more complicated processes in the late eighteenth century, the problems of atmospheric pollution grew more severe. The Industrial Revolution increased the use of coal to drive new machinery and, more importantly, produced very acidic emissions as a consequence of the 'alkali works'. These works used the 'Leblanc' process to produce soda, but the by-product of the chemical process used meant that hydrochloric gas was emitted into the atmosphere that, when mixed with water, created acid rain.

The local effects of acid rain were severe, with industrialized areas of the country rendered desolate by very highly acidic moist air, burning trees, shrubs, and hedges. One of the centres for the alkali industry, St Helens in Lancashire, was reported as not having a single tree with any foliage on it. This concern led to the setting up of a Royal Commission to look into the problem of alkali pollution, which subsequently made the recommendations that led to the first Alkali Act, passed in 1863. Under this Act, a new Alkali Inspector was appointed, who regulated such alkali processes. Although the Act did not attempt to deal with smoke, it did introduce new stricter controls over the production of acidic emissions. It made the first attempts at restricting the composition of emissions, with the introduction of primitive emission standard requirements. Under the Act, there was a requirement that 95 per cent of all noxious emissions should be arrested within the plant, so that only 5 per cent of the previously emitted fumes were allowed into the atmosphere.

Neither of these Acts, nor a consolidation Act of 1906, dealt specifically with the control of smoke from either industrial or commercial premises. Attempts were made to control the emission of smoke through such Acts as the Public Health Act 1875, the Public Health (Smoke Abatement) Act 1926, and the Public Health Act 1936, but these dealt generally with smoke nuisances. These powers could not rid industrial cities of the problems of smoke pollution. The physical evidence of this pollution could be seen on blackened buildings and in the frequency of smog, which was prevalent from Victorian times. Such smog was caused by fog forming in winter months and combining with smoke particles to produce a compound of gases that could cut visibility to very low levels. Of more concern, however, was the effect that these smogs had upon the dispersion of pollution. With a heavy concentration of smog hanging over a city, the air was very still and convection was low. The onset of these

---

5 Committee on Medical Effects of Air Pollutants Annual Report (1997–98).

calm conditions made the dispersal of emissions much more difficult. The effects of these smogs were thought to be minimal—until December 1952, when a smog descended upon London that did not clear for five days. Nothing unusual was noticed until prize cattle at the Smithfield Show started to suffer from respiratory problems. The smog got everywhere, even inside the Sadler's Wells theatre, which resulted in the stoppage of a performance, because of the difficulty of seeing the stage. When the smog had lifted, it was estimated that at least four thousand people had lost their lives as a consequence of the smoke and other emissions.[6]

The government immediately responded by setting up the Beaver Committee to report on the difficulties surrounding smoke pollution. The recommendation of the Committee was to introduce legislation to eliminate particulate emissions, such as smoke, dust, and grit, so that such conditions would not arise again. With the introduction of the Clean Air Act 1956, later supplemented by the Clean Air Act 1968, controls were introduced for the first time to restrict the production of smoke, grit, and dust from all commercial and industrial activities not covered by the Alkali Acts, but also, more importantly, from domestic fires as well. The Acts introduced such concepts as smoke control areas and the complete prohibition on 'dark smoke' from chimneys.[7]

During the 1970s, the problems of the emission of smoke, dirt, dust, and grit lessened and, coupled with the new approach to industrial processes, a gradual improvement took place in the quality of the atmosphere in the UK. There was a move away from the use of coal as fuel to smokeless substances, such as coke and gas. Additionally, the gap left behind with the introduction of clean air zones was met by an increase in the use of electricity for power and heat. The main generator of electricity in the UK, the Central Electricity Generating Board, changed its practices in a direct reaction to the difficulties encountered with local pollution by replacing the short chimneys traditionally used in power stations with larger and taller stacks. The basis of this change was to disperse pollution at a higher level in the hope that any substances would be diluted over greater distances.[8] The consequence would be a reduction in the concentrations of pollutants in the nearby locality. Unfortunately, this reduction in the levels of local pollution only shifted the problems to a different location. While the pollution of the atmosphere declined nationally, the concern internationally rose. The change of policy from short to tall stacks for chimneys saw the creation of the first major transboundary pollution from acid rain. The effects of the transboundary acid rain could be seen not only in disparate parts of the UK, but also other countries within Europe, to which the prevailing winds carried such emissions. In particular, the Scandinavian countries received a large percentage of the 'export' of the UK's production of sulphur dioxide and acid rain. It was not until the 1980s that international and European efforts were made to address the problem through negotiated treaties and protocols.

BOX 15.1 **Regulatory impact**

One of the historic characteristics of the UK approach to environmental regulation has been that it is reactive, responding to known problems, rather than proactive, in trying to prevent new problems arising. Although there are defects with this approach, it has also proved to be an effective means of addressing certain types of environmental harm. The evidence of the history of domestic air quality legislation illustrates that, although there has been a recent preference for alternatives—for example, economic instruments and voluntary measures—the effectiveness of regulation as a mechanism to address environmental problems should not be underestimated.

---

6 See generally, D. Davis (2002) *When Smoke Ran Like Water*, New York: Basic Books, ch. 2.

7 These controls are now discussed in the Online Resource Centre.

8 C. Rose (1990) *The Dirty Man of Europe*, London: Simon and Schuster.

Regulation is a good way of addressing immediate problems and prohibitions on polluting substances or activities can have a dramatic effect. For example, the Alkali Act 1863 and its successors saw a remarkable reduction in the production of acidic emissions from almost 14,000 tonnes to about 45 tonnes. The Clean Air Act 1956 and its successors banned coal fires, and provided financial assistance to households to convert to smokeless fuel. As a result, sulphur dioxide levels in Manchester city centre fell from 481 µg/m^3 in 1960 to 58 µg/m^3 in 1990.

Even in international law, which is often characterized as being ineffective because of political constraints and the need to build consensus, there have been clear examples of the effectiveness of regulatory intervention. For example, the Montreal Protocol saw a large reduction in the total consumption of the main ozone-depleting substances. In 2002, the World Meteorological Organization concluded that the Protocol has been an effective mechanism and that depletion of the ozone layer will begin to ameliorate within the next ten years or so, and will reverse within a further fifty years.[9]

Although regulatory impact can be significant, there are also some obvious flaws in using reactive regulation. First, there is the issue of displacement. When serious problems must be addressed quickly, there is always the danger that regulatory measures do not remove the problem completely, but merely shift it elsewhere. The construction of tall chimneys to disperse sulphur dioxide simply causes the emissions to fall further away or may mean that the sulphur dioxide is released high enough into the atmosphere to create acid rain. A further example of displacement is that the Montreal Protocol led to a black market in illegal chlorofluorocarbons (CFCs).

Secondly, a reactive approach neither prevents pollution, nor sits easily with a precautionary approach. This is evidenced by a period of transition from the time at which a problem is acknowledged, and the implementation and practical effect of the new regulations.

Finally, reactive regulation often fails to recognize the complex interconnected nature of environmental problems, because it often only addresses one source. Thus, although the Clean Air Acts reduced the amount of sulphur dioxide in the atmosphere, it did not eradicate winter smog episodes completely. In the 1990s, various UK cities experienced dangerous smog levels. In London in December 1991, levels of nitrogen oxide rose to more than twice the safe level recommended by the World Health Organization and over 160 deaths were attributed to poor air quality. Although regulation had reduced smoke emissions, these had been replaced by similar emissions from the increase in the number of motor vehicles in urban areas.

Just as the problem of regional transboundary pollution was being addressed on the international stage in the 1980s, the focus of concern shifted to global threats brought about by air pollution. In the 1980s, scientific evidence started to link the release of CFCs and other chlorine-based substances with the destruction of the ozone layer. In addition, there was evidence that certain 'greenhouse gases' could cause a rise in the earth's temperature leading to climate change. The 'greenhouse effect', as it was referred to, has arisen because the production of various 'greenhouse' gases have increased in the past century with progressive industrialization. In the lower atmosphere, the production of emissions from power stations, car exhausts, and industrial plants have increased by almost 100 per cent. These emissions absorb radiated heat and it is now incontrovertible that the consequence of this is that exponentially higher ambient temperature levels are being created, which are already leading to demonstrable, and largely negative, climatic changes.

9 Even in the case of ozone-depleting substances, there is a case that more could have been done sooner, e.g., in relation to the HFCs that are used in place of CFCs and HCFCs, and which were known to have a considerable (x 117,000 greater than CO_2) greenhouse impact before their use as a substitute was expanded: see (2007) ENDS Report 393, 26–9.

BOX 15.2 **Knowledge of climate change**

The latest scientific report from 2007 of the Intergovernmental Panel on Climate Change (IPCC) finds that there is a 'very likely'—that is, greater than 90 per cent—chance that increases in global temperatures above natural background levels are man-made. There is an overwhelming global scientific consensus behind this view and the degree of confidence with which the IPCC has stated its views has increased over the last few years. But, for over a century, there has been scientific work on the link between man-made emissions of CO_2 and changes in global temperature.[10] Nationally, the Royal Commission on Environmental Pollution mentioned global warming in its first report in 1971.[11]

The degree and date of knowledge is particularly relevant to those who are exploring the scope for liability actions, because any legal action would probably require a finding that, as from a particular date, damage was foreseeable and reparation based on the emissions from that date.

Additionally, the amount of ozone in the upper atmosphere screens the earth from harmful UV-B radiation. This screen has deteriorated and there have been studies showing a 'hole' above Antarctica and beyond. This depletion of ozone has been linked to the use of CFCs. The creation of greenhouse gases and the depletion of the ozone layer are worldwide problems, the solution of which requires international cooperation. The use of international law as a mechanism for environmental protection is relatively unproven (with some notable exceptions, such as the Montreal Protocol described in Box 15.1) and there are some limitations to its usefulness. But the nature of the problems facing the world in terms of these two issues have led to significant steps being taken to prevent any further harm.

The regulatory challenge

Air, unlike other environmental media, is intangible and not capable of being owned. While it is a common resource, it is a transient medium that is uncontained and highly mobile. Emissions can diffuse quickly and the immediate impacts can be transferred away from the direct point of discharge. As a result, it has often been difficult to identify causal links between particular sources and effects of pollutants. Often, a problem has been identified and a regulatory solution proposed when the aggregation of many sources mean that the effects are difficult to reverse. This is true in respect of local, transboundary, and truly global problems.

These difficulties of establishing causal links also have the effect of raising the problem of uncertainty, risk, and the application of a precautionary approach. Issues such as the effects of acid rain and the existence of climate change have been the subject of intense disagreement between those who believe that a precautionary approach is essential and others who argue that harmful effects have not been sufficiently established, that the risks are tentative or unformed, and that the costs of taking preventative measures are too great.

Certain consequences of air pollution have a general impact, regardless of the source or how the consequences are created. In this sense, they are truly global problems, which require cooperation and joint commitment if they are to be solved. Thus political consensus about the nature of the problem, its causes, and its effects is essential before moving on to

---

10 For a useful summary, setting developments in wider contexts, see the 'Global Warming Timeline' available online at **www.aip.org/history/exhibits/climate/timeline.htm**.

11 RCEP First Report (1971) Cm 4585. The RCEP's Tenth Report (1984) *Tackling Pollution: Experience and Prospects*, Cmnd. 9149, also warned of the need for more research and possible international action on global warming.

consider the specific measures that should be adopted. The whole process can be undermined by countries failing to agree at either level.

A further challenge is that air pollution problems are complex in their causes and solutions. The range of polluters and the sources of pollutant are varied and diverse. Indeed, identifying 'the polluter' can depend on how the issue is looked at: in relation to climate change, is the polluter (to pose one example) the generator of electricity or the end user? Nationally, nearly one third of emissions are from the domestic sector—predominantly, space heating. There is no right answer to the question of whether this means tackling the source of demand (the user) or the source of supply (the generator), or a mixed approach.

This legal, scientific, and economic complexity means that no single regulatory mechanism will have more than a contributory effect. Accordingly, various types of mechanism must be used to deal with different facets of the same problem. Energy production and consumption, and different modes of transport, manufacturing, and agriculture all have a significant impact upon the atmosphere. Many of these sources are interconnected, in the sense that they are strongly associated with industrialization and economic development. Modifying energy production or transport usage raises significant problems for both developed industrialized nations, with established consumption patterns, and developing nations, who wish to encourage future industrialization and economic growth as an objective. This raises questions of fairness as between developed and developing nations, in relation to which the original cause of global problems (such as the depletion of the ozone layer or greenhouse gas emissions) is traced to the developed nations' historical pollution, while the developed nations seek to impose tighter current controls over those nations who wish to be able to develop in a similar fashion.

International law, and air and atmospheric pollution

The influence of international law on the regulation of air and atmospheric pollution has been significant. Perhaps in recognition of the fact that many of the problems caused by air pollution can have impacts across a large geographical area and, in certain circumstances, cause truly global effects, there have been a number of areas in which international law has helped to shape policies and rules on both continental and domestic levels. In addition, the level of cooperation on such issues is sometimes higher than in other areas, because there is a general acceptance that there is a mutual responsibility among the nation states of the world.

Transboundary pollution

As the description of the development of the controls over air pollution demonstrates, addressing local problems can often lead to a translocation of the impacts of pollutants over large distances. The problem of transboundary harm is not a recent phenomenon: air pollution from a Canadian smelter that destroyed crops and forest over the border in the USA, for example, led to the creation of a significant principle of customary international law.

CASE 15.2 Transboundary pollution and customary international law—*USA v. Canada* 3 RIAA 1907 (1941) (the *Trail Smelter* case)

A Canadian mining company operated a large zinc and lead smelter along the Columbia river at Trail, British Columbia. Sulphur dioxide emissions from two large 400-foot chimneys at the smelter had damaged crops (wheat and oats), trees used for logging, and pastures in the US State of Washington about ten miles south of the smelter. The US government objected to the Canadian government and the dispute went to arbitration on two occasions. The International Joint Commission by the USA and Canada awarded the US government some $428,000 to compensate for damage caused to forests and pastures, and imposed emission limits and monitoring requirements on the smelter. In doing so, it concluded that:

> no state has the right to use or permit the use of its territory in such a manner as to cause injury by fumes in or to the territory of another of the properties or persons therein, when the case is of serious consequence and the injury is established by clear and convincing evidence.[12]

Although the *Trail Smelter* arbitration establishes a clear principle of customary international law, in practice, it has been overtaken by negotiated treaties on transboundary air pollution. There are a number of reasons for this. First, there is the evidential difficulty of obtaining 'clear and convincing evidence' of the causal link between source and effects of long-range air pollution. The distance of 10 miles and the lack of alternative sources in the *Trail Smelter* case meant that this evidential burden was eased. The Programme for Monitoring and Evaluation of Long-Range Transmission of Air Pollutants in Europe (EMEP) has monitored transboundary pollution since its formation in 1977 and modern monitoring techniques can trace emissions with a degree of accuracy. In many cases, however, the causal link is not necessarily straightforward, because most countries 'export' as well as 'import' atmospheric pollution and the problem can be regional in nature, rather than bilateral, as in *Trail Smelter*.

Secondly, the principle is compensatory in nature, in that it seeks to pay for serious harm caused, rather than to prevent future harm. Preventative measures can only be imposed through international agreement on the standards to be employed. The failure to prevent harm is particularly problematic with transboundary pollution, in relation to which the consequences may not be appreciated until long after damage has been caused.

Thirdly, the requirement of 'serious consequences' is problematic, in that it is a flexible standard that may be dependent upon the nature of the receiving environment. For example, in the *Trail Smelter* case, the pollution caused serious damage to economic interests such as agriculture and forestry. If the damage had been caused to an 'unowned' wilderness area, it is unlikely that a claim would have been sustained.

Fourthly, the complex interconnected nature of transboundary pollution is not something that is easily justiciable in the context of the *Trail Smelter* principle. For example, the eventual negotiation of treaties on transboundary air pollution were slowed down by the reluctance of some countries to accept that there was even a problem.

Finally, in cases in which the principle is clearly breached, the relaxation of jurisdictional hurdles has increased the ability of private entities to seek redress through national courts.

The 1979 Geneva Convention on Long-Range Transboundary Air Pollution

The Geneva Convention on Long-Range Transboundary Air Pollution, agreed under the UN Economic Commission for Europe (UNECE) in 1979, was the first real attempt to set up a formal framework of controls over air pollution between nations. The Convention was purely preventative in nature and contained no liability provisions. The treaty came into force in 1983 and most of the major industrial European states are signatories, along with the USA and Canada.

The Convention is a classic example of a political compromise solution to an international problem. It is a framework treaty, which sets out various broad principles of cooperation and joint research into the problems of transboundary air pollution. The flexibility in the treaty is evidenced by the primary obligation, which is to endeavour to limit, and gradually to reduce and prevent, air pollution using best available technology where economically feasible (Arts 2 and 6). In this fashion, the treaty is more a statement of intent than a binding legal

12 3 RIAA 1907 (1941) at 1965.

instrument. In practice, the exchanging of information, coordinated research, and general collaboration on combating transboundary air pollution has led to further more specific measures in the shape of five Protocols relating to different types of air pollution.

The First Protocol on the reduction of sulphur dioxide was originally agreed in 1985 and was eventually replaced by a more prescriptive Protocol agreed in Oslo in 1994.[13] The original Protocol provided for a flat rate reduction of 30 per cent of sulphur dioxide emissions to be achieved by 1993. Three of the largest producers of sulphur dioxide, including the UK, declined to ratify the Protocol on the basis that the flat-rate reduction had not been allocated fairly and the timetable was unrealistic. The 1994 Oslo Protocol set different emissions reductions for each party set by reference to actual data on sulphur dioxide sources and effects. The UK signed and ratified the Oslo treaty, agreeing to reduce sulphur dioxide emissions to 20 per cent of 1980 levels by 2010. While the original Convention was a triumph of political expediency, the more rigorous Protocols that followed have seen sulphur dioxide levels fall. Implementation of the Convention's requirements have been possible as a result of the so-called 'dash for gas', which has seen polluting coal-fired power stations phased out and replaced with more efficient gas-fired stations, or fitted with expensive desulphurization abatement equipment.

The Second Protocol under the Geneva Convention deals with emissions of nitrous oxide (NOx) and was concluded in 1988 in Sofia. This Protocol required parties to stabilize NOx emissions at 1987 levels by 1994. In a similar fashion to the sulphur dioxide Protocol, it imposes a requirement to use the best available technology for national emissions standards. Further Protocols have been signed in relation to VOCs, air pollution from persistent organic pollutants, and heavy metals. These Protocols largely overlap with similar measures agreed within the European Community. Indeed, the EC is a signatory of these Protocols.

The 1985 Vienna Convention for the Protection of the Ozone Layer

Moves to protect the ozone layer were commenced in 1981 by the United Nations Environment Programme (UNEP). In 1985, the Vienna Convention for the Protection of the Ozone Layer was concluded. This four-year negotiation period reflected the difficulties in achieving a political consensus on the nature of the risks and the measures that were required.[14] Consensus was required, because the global impact of ozone depletion could only be addressed effectively through a large number of signatories to the Convention, along with deterrents to prevent the production and consumption of ozone-depleting materials by non-signatories. As in the case of the 1979 Geneva Convention on Transboundary Pollution, the Vienna Convention represented a pragmatic solution that sought to recognize the nature of the problem, but which took into account the need to ensure cooperation in achieving firm solutions. Thus the Convention was primarily a framework for future action requiring the assessment of the causes and effects of ozone depletion, with cooperation in relation to information and technology transfer. It imposed no specific binding obligations, although there was a requirement to take 'appropriate measures' to guard against activities that were modified or were likely to modify the ozone layer.

Notwithstanding the vagueness of the provisions of the Convention, it was notable for a number of reasons (see also Box 6.4).

1. It was the first example of international law addressing a *global* environmental problem.

2. It was one of the first Conventions that took an explicitly precautionary approach by acknowledging the need to take action against substances that were *likely* to have an impact on the ozone layer, even when some parties argued that the causal link between ozone depletion and environmental harm had not been proved.

---

13 See R. Churchill, G. Kutling, and L. Warren (1994) 6 JEL 169.
14 See R. Benedick (1998) *Ozone Diplomacy*, Cambridge, Mass: Harvard University Press.

3. The Convention saw a departure from traditional forms of protection against 'pollution' by referring to 'adverse effects', including climate change.

4. The fact that consensus could be achieved was significant, because it provided the platform for a more substantive response to the problem in the shape of the 1987 Montreal Protocol on Substances that Deplete the Ozone Layer.

The Montreal Protocol set concrete targets for the reduction, and eventual phasing out, of the production and consumption of substances that depleted the ozone layer. Further amendments in 1991 and 1992 added new substances, and brought forward the ban on CFCs and related substances to 1996. Various measures were incorporated into the Protocol to seek to balance the potential problem of the unfairness of phase-out on developing nations. These included a ten-year derogation from compliance with the phasing out and ban. Alternatively, a fund was established to help to smooth the progress of the adoption of alternatives to CFCs. The Protocol also addressed the problem of the production of ozone-depleting substances by non-signatories to the Convention by banning trade between parties and non-parties.

In order to ensure the effectiveness of the Protocol, there are formal non-compliance procedures, with various sanctions including loss of financial support from the alternative substances fund and funding from bodies such as the World Bank. The Protocol has proved to be responsive to cases of non-compliance (for example, Russian exports of CFCs). The evidence suggests that compliance levels are high even with the progressive widening of the controlled substances. The Montreal Protocol is a good example of the effectiveness of international law in addressing environmental problems when the global community is faced with a considerable risk, and a relatively straightforward regulatory task of the phasing out and banning of certain substances. It is also a good example of how an environmental law addressing one problem can impact positively on another: CFCs are potent greenhouse gases and the reductions in CFCs have so far made more of a contribution to curbing global warming than the measures agreed to in the Kyoto Protocol, discussed below.[15]

Climate change

Addressing the problem of climate change has proved to be a much greater challenge than achieving consensus on the problem of ozone depletion. Climate change is characterized by threats to the global environment that, while uncertain, are likely to be severe even if stringent action is taken today to curb emissions. It is also an issue that is not restricted to one sector of the economy: the global economy is currently built on a foundation of greenhouse gas emissions and action to change this threatens to destabilize economic development everywhere. Perhaps more worryingly, despite the scientific evidence[16] and the economic analysis, which strongly suggests that acting now will be more cost-effective than would be dealing with the problems in the future,[17] as a global community, we still seem to be in a state of collective denial about the severity of the problem, and the need for a rapid and wholesale response.[18] Responding to the potential threats of climate change demands a complex response, addressing areas as diverse as transportation, deforestation, power generation, control over natural resources, industrial and economic growth, and personal liberties, and hence the crossing of the usual sectoral boundaries.

15 G. Velders et al. (2007) 104(12) PNAS 4814, available online at **www.mnp.nl/bibliotheek/digitaaldepot/ Montreal_Protocol_PNAS_Mar2007.pdf**.

16 IPCC Working Group 1 Report (2007) *The Physical Science Base*, available online at **www.ipcc.ch/ipccreports/ ar4-wg1.htm**.

17 Stern Review (2006) *The Economics of Climate Change*, London: HM Treasury (the Stern Report).

18 G. Monbiot (2005) 17(2) ELM 57.

The 1992 Framework Convention on Climate Change

Recognizing the problem of potential global climate change, the World Meteorological Organization (WMO) and the UNEP established the Intergovernmental Panel on Climate Change (IPCC) in 1988. The IPPC's first report in 1990 provided an assessment of the problem and, in 1992, led to the adoption of the UN Framework Convention on Climate Change (UNFCCC) at the Rio Conference. The Convention was ratified by 50 countries (including the EC and the UK) and came into force in March 1994. The Convention is based around the concept of 'common but differentiated responsibility', recognizing the need for global action and the differing levels of obligation placed upon industrialized and developing countries. The Convention was very much a starting position, establishing a process for future action and a framework of principles and objectives that were to be guides to further implementation measures.

The main objective of the Convention was to stabilize greenhouse gas emissions at a level that would not interfere with the climate system or food production, but which would still allow sustainable economic development (Art. 2). The objective should be met within a time frame that would allow ecosystems to adapt to any changes. Thus the Convention recognizes the unavoidability of some changes in climate and seeks to achieve the possible by seeking to link it to the ability of nature to adapt to whatever changes occur. Article 3 of the Convention lays down certain guiding principles to follow in seeking to attain the Art. 2 objective. These include intergenerational equity, common but differentiated responsibility, the Precautionary Principle, the right to sustainable development, and the need to cooperate within a supportive and open international economic system. While this comprehensive set of principles does not create any binding obligations, it did set down a template for more specific emissions targets.

Article 4 of the Convention sets out the general commitments applicable to all parties (including the developing nations under Art. 4(1)) and more burdensome responsibilities only applicable to the parties listed in Annex I—that is, the developed nations and economies in transition from Eastern Europe under Art. 4(2) (see Box 15.3). These are general commitments to making national inventories of emissions, the integration of climate change issues across policymaking, and the adoption of measures to limit emissions of greenhouse gases. There is only one specific aim, applicable to the Annex I parties, of returning emissions to 1990 levels by 2000 (Art. 4(2)(a) and (b)), although the aim was largely superseded on the signing of the Kyoto Protocol.

The Kyoto Protocol

The need for stronger action was reflected in the setting of binding reduction targets for Annex I parties in the Kyoto Protocol, which was adopted in 1997 and entered into force in 2005. The Protocol was the subject of tough negotiations, primarily as a result of the political difficulties faced by the USA in setting significant reduction targets. The Protocol sets out specific reduction targets for different countries in relation to six gases: carbon dioxide; NOx; hydrofluorocarbons (HFCs); perfluorocarbons (PFCs); methane; ground-level ozone. The cuts average out at a 5.2 per cent reduction of 1990 levels of these gases at some time between 2008 and 2012. These different limits reflect the 'common but differentiated responsibility' approach, with some countries (for example, New Zealand and Russia) being required to stabilize emissions and others (for example, Australia and Norway) permitted an increase.

The Protocol is notable for the joint implementation mechanisms that allow the commitments to be shared among parties.

- **Aggregating emissions (Art. 4)**
  Two or more Annex I parties can aggregate their combined emissions and, provided that the overall limit assigned to the group as a whole is not exceeded, it does not matter that

individual parties have exceeded their own quota. This is useful for regional groupings, such as the EC, in giving flexibility over how to meet the overall target.

- **Joint implementation (Art. 6)**
  An Annex I party can receive credit for supporting projects that reduce another Annex I party's greenhouse gas emissions. This could include the energy efficiency measures or the transfer of clean technology.

- **Emissions trading systems (Arts 4 and 17)**
  These enable countries with a significant 'surplus' of emissions reduction as a result of exceeding targets either to sell that surplus to countries that have a 'deficit'—that is, those that are having difficulties in meeting their own target—or to 'stockpile' it as a safeguard against meeting future reduction targets.

- **The clean development mechanism (Art. 12)**
  Because the developing nations are not subjected to any reduction targets, there was some concern expressed that there was little incentive for them to adopt measures that would contribute to the overall achievement of the aims of the Climate Change Convention. Thus Annex I countries can gain credit for assisting the developing countries in the creation of projects that result in certified emission reductions. This might be in relation to sources of greenhouse gases, such as 'cleaner' power stations, or the overall reduction of emissions levels. Any reduction achieved can be offset against the Annex I country's own target (as long as the emission reductions achieved are 'additional' to those that would have occurred anyway).

One final notable feature is the use of carbon sinks. Four Articles of the Protocol allow for generation of carbon sink credits, which permit Annex I countries to reduce their obligation under the Protocol. For every tonne of carbon that is stored in a tree, an equivalent tonne of carbon from fossil fuels can be released into the atmosphere. Thus carbon credits are acquired through afforestation, reforestation, and forest management. The calculation of the actual extent of the reduction is a matter of some controversy, because the amount of the reduction in heavily forested countries could be significant in the overall total reduction (for example, it is estimated that Russia could claim over 25 per cent reduction of its overall target from the use of managed forests).

The progress on agreeing international action to address climate change and its causes has been slow, but the process has really only just begun. The Framework Convention and the Kyoto Protocol are the first attempts to set out principles and processes that will assist with the creation of long-term commitments to stabilize and adjust to changes in climate. The Convention takes a pragmatic political approach based upon cooperation, typically characterized by the various joint implementation mechanisms.

One development that should be mentioned is the steps taken in 2006 to establish a Compliance Committee for the Protocol.[19] This has two parts: an Enforcement Branch, with the power to determine consequences for parties that encounter problems with meeting their commitments; a Facilitative Branch, which is designed to provide advice and assistance to parties in order to promote compliance. Parties to the Protocol provide the UNFCCC Secretariat with annual reports of their greenhouse gas emissions, which then undergo a review process. The Secretariat also monitors the international carbon emission trading market and receives annual accounting reports from parties on carbon allowances that they have acquired or transferred to another party, or which result from project-level emission reductions. Compliance is then determined by comparing emissions to allowances.

19 Further details are available online at **unfccc.int/kyoto_mechanisms/compliance/items/3024.php** and the relevant text (from the Seventh Conference of the parties) is available online at **unfccc.int/resource/docs/cop7/13a03. pdf#page=64**.

The 'teeth' of the new procedure (in s. XV) tries to steer the parties into compliance through a range of mechanisms, some of which display 'reflexive law' characteristics. Thus there is provision requiring non-compliant states to submit plans, including an analysis of the causes of non-compliance, measures that the party intends to implement in order to remedy the non-compliance, a timetable for implementing enabling the assessment of progress, and regular reports thereafter. In addition, a non-compliant state may lose its entitlement to use joint implementation, clean development, and emissions trading mechanisms. There is also provision for a state, if it fails to meet its reduction targets, to lose 1.3 times this loss from the next round of emissions reductions commitments—that is, in the period from 2012. It should be stressed, however, that parties to the Protocol are not legally obliged to adhere to these compliance procedures.

It is difficult to give a definitive appraisal of the Convention and, in particular, of the Kyoto Protocol. The failure of the USA, the largest greenhouse gas emitter based on 1990 levels, to ratify the Protocol, and the general US hostility to the Protocol, at least in the early days of the second Bush administration, were widely seen as an obstacle.

The latest conference of the parties to the UNFCCC was in Bali, Indonesia, in December 2007. This was a crucial meeting, being the first since China, a non-Annex I country, became the largest[20] annual greenhouse gas emitter. Much attention was also focused on the position of the USA, which adopted a generally hostile approach in the negotiations, although it did ultimately agree, with all other states, to the Bali Action Plan,[21] which noted that climate change is unequivocal and recognized the need for 'deep cuts in global emissions'. The focus is on developed countries making emissions commitments, while developing countries take actions appropriate to their developmental needs and there was agreement that the role of forests as carbon sinks should be specifically recognized and deforestation in developing countries avoided (by making forests worth more standing than felled). But no timetabled targets were agreed and the conference, in effect, simply set in motion a process through which such targets might be forthcoming, possibly by 2009, when a post-Kyoto agreement is finally reached. The text is a masterclass in constructive ambiguity.

Climate change—other international law developments

Apart from the UNFCCC and the Kyoto process, there have been further developments in international law that have been motivated by a concern to address global climate change. One example relates to carbon capture and storage (CCS), a technique under which emissions are captured before entering the atmosphere and then stored—for example, in geological formations, such as exhausted oil-bearing strata. In principle, any project such as this, which leads to emissions reductions, can 'count' under the Clean Development Mechanism of the Kyoto Protocol. There is some uncertainty about the effectiveness of the technology, and the Protocol neither expressly prohibits, nor allows CCS in geological formations under the sea. But a 1996 Protocol to the 1972 Convention on the Prevention of Marine Pollution by Dumping of Wastes and Other Matters (the 'London Dumping Convention') has been amended so that 'CO_2 streams from CO_2 capture processes for sequestration' have now been added to the list of exceptions to the general ban on dumping waste at sea, which removed some potentially tricky legal problems relating to whether this would amount to dumping of waste at sea.[22] The UK appears to have taken a lead in seeking these, and related,

---

20 By state, not per capita.

21 See **unfccc.int/files/meetings/cop_13/application/pdf/cp_bali_action.pdf**.

22 For an overview, see R. Purdy (2006) 7(1) Sustainable Development Law and Policy 22; see also the Further Reading at the end of the chapter.

amendments,[23] which makes the lack of national action to adopt this technology somewhat perplexing.

Another example is the extent to which sites listed under the United Nations Educational, Scientific and Cultural Organization (UNESCO) World Heritage Convention may be affected by climate change and the extent to which a legal response is required.[24] Higher levels of atmospheric CO_2 are also thought to be leading to acidification of oceans, with detrimental effects. So far, there seems to be no action taken specifically to address this.

Europe and climate change

Concern about transboundary pollution and wider issues, such as climate change and ozone depletion, has seen the EC develop a significant role as a party to international negotiations on conventions and treaties. The EC has encouraged a number of worldwide initiatives by negotiating in its own right on issues that require global action. Thus, the EC is a signatory to the Vienna Convention for the Protection of the Ozone Layer. This, in turn, led to the implementation of Regulation 2037/2000, as amended, on substances that deplete the ozone layer—one of the few examples of a Europe-wide ban on specific substances.

The EC has taken a particular lead on climate change. The EC was a key supporter of binding targets and timetables for emissions reduction in the Kyoto Protocol, and was responsible for much of the momentum behind the negotiations towards the original Framework Convention. (Both the Convention and the Protocol have been ratified by the EC.) The EC was also highly influential in developing the idea of aggregated emissions quotas, which would allow member States to set unified targets. The EC agreed to an aggregated reduction target for greenhouse gases of 8 per cent of 1990 levels by 2008–12. Box 15.3 sets out the various allocations to the EU-15 member States under aggregated emissions quota. These were used as a basis for the setting of the National Allocation Plan for the purposes of the Emissions Trading Directive (2003/87/EC).[25]

Member States	Targets as a percentage of 1990 emissions levels (%)	Actual change 1990–98 (%)	Variance (%)
Belgium	−7.5	+6.5	+14
Denmark	−21	+9.5	+30.5
Germany	−21	−15.6	+5.4
Greece	+25	+18.1	−6.9
Spain	+15	+21.0	+6

BOX 15.3 Allocations of the Kyoto Protocol commitments among the EU-15[26]

23 For example, OSPAR Decision 2007/2 on the Storage of Carbon Dioxide Streams in Geological Formations. See now also COM(2008) 18, which proposes various amendments to EC laws to facilitate and control carbon capture and storage.

24 'UNESCO adopts climate change strategy for world heritage sites', available online at **www.ens-newswire.com/ens/jul2006/2006-07-11-01.asp**; see also S. Shearing (2007) 'Here today, gone tomorrow? Climate change and world heritage', available online at **ssrn.com/abstract=1021146**.

25 See Annex B of Decision 2002/358.

26 Of the remaining 12 member States in the EU, ten have individual emissions reduction targets under Kyoto and two (Malta and Cyprus) have no targets. The EU-15 are listed for illustrative purposes. See also COM(2008) 17 (the proposed effort-sharing decision).

Member States	Targets as a percentage of 1990 emissions levels (%)	Actual change 1990–98 (%)	Variance (%)
France	0	+0.9	+0.9
Ireland	+13	+19.1	+6.1
Italy	−6.5	+4.4	+10.9
Luxembourg	−28	−24	−4
Netherlands	−6	+8.4	+14.4
Austria	−13	+6.5	+19.5
Portugal	+27	+17.2	−9.8
Finland	0	+1.5	+1.5
Sweden	+4	+6.4	+2.4
United Kingdom	−12.5	−8.3	+4.2

© OECD/IEA, 2002, as modified by the authors. Reproduced with permission.

The EC's policy response to the Kyoto Protocol was to establish a European Climate Change Programme (ECCP), launched in 2000 and revised in 2005.[27] The approach of the ECCP has been broad and far-reaching, and is a good example of external integration of environmental considerations into other policy areas, because it involves initiatives across the energy, transport, and industrial sectors. After an initial planning phase, the ECCP has resulted in a broad range of initiatives including:

- a Directive setting up an emissions trading scheme (2003/87/EC), and a related Decision establishing guidelines for monitoring and reporting greenhouse gas emissions pursuant to this Directive (2004/156/EC, repealed by 2007/589/EC);

- a Directive allowing the use of joint implementation and clean development mechanism credits under the EU emissions trading scheme (2004/101/EC);

- a mechanism for monitoring EU greenhouse gas emissions and implementing the Kyoto Protocol (Decision 280/2004, implemented by Commission Decision 2005/166);[28]

- a Directive promoting cogeneration of heat and electricity (2004/8/EC);

- a Directive on the promotion of renewable energy (2001/77/EC), which promotes renewable energy sources, thus reducing reliance on fossil fuels, which produce greenhouse gases;[29]

- a Directive on the promotion of biofuels for transport (2003/30/EC), with the aim of making biofuels—that is, fuels made from biomass—5.75 per cent of the transport fuel market by 2011;[30]

27 See, generally, **ec.europa.eu/environment/climat/eccp.htm**.

28 These rules inter alia set the base lines from which allowable emissions per member State are calculated; these are presently calculated in Commission Decision 2006/944/EC.

29 Proposals to revise this Directive are in COM(2008) 19. These would require renewables to make a 20 per cent contribution to overall energy consumption in the EC by 2020, with individual member State targets.

30 There is political agreement at EU level for a 10 per cent contribution to road fuels by 2020, despite some uncertainty and disagreement about the overall beneficial impact of biofuels: COM(2008) 19 and (2008) ENDS Report, 17 January.

- a Directive on the energy performance of buildings (2002/91/EC), which sets minimum requirements for the energy performance and certification of energy efficiency for all new buildings;

- a revised Directive on energy end-use efficiency and energy services (2006/32/EC)—a demand management measure, setting EC-wide targets for greater energy efficiency.

Other pre-existing measures on air quality will also have an impact upon the reduction of greenhouse gas emissions. Some of these are considered below. Examples include the tightening of product standards for motor vehicles and the introduction of integrated pollution prevention and control (IPPC), including energy efficiency requirements. Overall, however, the policy approach seems to show a preference for measures to reduce emissions from existing sources—although, in 2007, political agreement was reached on a target of producing 20 per cent of energy from renewable sources by 2020 (it is unclear whether this is really a renewables or a non-fossil fuels target—the latter would allow nuclear power to count towards it).

Data on greenhouse gas emissions trends show that the EC has already met the commitment under the Framework Convention to stabilize its emissions at 1990 levels by 2000 and, in aggregate, it has achieved 50 per cent of the emissions target set under the Kyoto Protocol. As Box 15.3 shows, the EC is not complacent, because many countries are still some way behind the targets and most of the reductions that have been made have arisen as a result of industrial restructuring post-German reunification and the switch from coal to gas-fired power stations in the UK. The second ECCP report confirmed that, in both 2000 and 2001, greenhouse gas emissions rose, and that the Kyoto targets would be missed unless further policies and measures were adopted.

In 2007, political agreement was reached on a target of making an EU-wide reduction in greenhouse emissions of 20 per cent by 2020 and a 20 per cent target of renewable energy generation by this date. These are now the subject of more specific legislative proposals from the Commission (which will require some analysis in the Online Resource Centre when finally adopted).[31] A Directive banning traditional filament light bulbs, which are relatively energy-intensive to use, is expected in 2008. The renewables target will require negotiation between member States on how fairly to share this burden, because many accession states are heavily dependent on burning fossil fuels and have less developed renewables sectors. There is also an ambiguous reference to the role of nuclear power—this is obviously not a renewable resource, but neither, in terms of residues from generation, is it a major greenhouse gas-emitting source.

The European emissions trading system

The idea of a Europe-wide emissions trading system was first found in the Fifth EC Environmental Action Programme (EAP), as an example of a flexible, market-based mechanism to be a component of environmental policy. This initial idea was developed further in the response to the need for more flexible mechanisms to assist with the emissions reduction target in the Kyoto Protocol (see COM(1998) 353). The final version of the scheme in Directive 2003/87/EC forms a central element of the ECCP and is the first international emissions trading scheme in the world.

The Directive can be applied to the six greenhouse gases found in the Kyoto Protocol (listed in Annex II of the Directive) in relation to all combustion installations with a thermal input greater than 20MW, oil refineries, coke ovens, metal production such as iron or works, the pulp and paper industry, and minerals processes such as cement, glass, and brick production (Annex I). This covers over 12,000 installations across the enlarged EU, with over a thousand in the UK. The initial phase of the scheme ran from 2005–07, with a second phase

---

31 See COM(2008) 19 (revised Renewables Directive) and COM(2008) 17 (the 'effort-sharing' proposal).

from 2008–12 to link with the emissions reductions target under the Kyoto Protocol. Further five-year periods are expected subsequently.

Each installation subject to the Directive must be covered by a permit (Art. 4), which is subject to conditions covering monitoring and reporting of conditions (Arts 6 and 7). In most cases, this will be a permit issued under the IPPC legislation (Art. 8). In both the first and second phases of the scheme, however, only CO_2 emissions have been covered.

The scheme works on a 'cap and trade' basis. Member States must develop a national allocation plan (NAP), which sets a national emissions allowance for all installations covered by the scheme and specifies how each allowance will be apportioned to individual installations (Art. 9). The NAP is drawn up in consultation with industry and then submitted to the European Commission, which approves it.[32] During the operation of the trading scheme, installations that have emissions levels below their assigned pollution amounts may sell emissions rights to other entities that are in danger of exceeding their quotas. An installation must surrender any surplus allowance at the end of any period if it has not used or traded its allowance (Art. 6). Operators without enough allowances to cover their emissions must pay a fine for each excess tonne of CO_2 emitted (initially this was €40). The scheme is implemented in the UK through the Greenhouse Gas Emissions Trading Scheme Regulations 2005.[33] These Regulations provide the framework for a greenhouse gas emissions trading scheme by identifying those activities that are covered under the scheme (Annex I), making provision for a permitting system for the operation of an installation (permits cover all six greenhouse gases, not only CO_2), and the development of the NAP, or 'emissions bubble', upon which individual allowances will be based.

Phase I of the scheme, which ran from 2005 to 2007, got off to a difficult beginning, with challenges to the NAP at a European and domestic level.[34] The finally approved NAP for the UK covered approximately a thousand installations, giving rise to 45 per cent of CO_2 emissions and it is anticipated that emissions from these will be reduced by some 8 per cent.[35] Across the EU, however, Phase I of the scheme did not operate terribly well in practice. Some member States distorted the operation of the allowance market—partly by allocating excess allowances to shield existing industries—with the result that their allocations were greater than their actual emissions—that is, that supply was greater than demand. This was one factor that arguably led to early price volatility in the system in the spring of 2006, when this allocation pattern became evident (and the market price dropped from €30 to €9 in one week).[36] At it lowest—due, in part, to warm weather, meaning that less power was being generated and generators were selling emissions so as not to be left with an excess—the price reached €0.80.[37]

For the second phase of the scheme, the Commission has set a revised EU-wide CO_2 cap at 2.08bn tonnes. This figure represents a 10 per cent overall reduction in the amount of permits requested by member States, a move that reflects efforts by the Commission to tighten the system in order to prevent another carbon price collapse.[38]

---

32 The consultation allows the Members States to vary the Plan—see Case T-178/05 *United Kingdom v. Commission* [2006] Env LR 26.

33 SI 2005/925.

34 See Case T-178/05 *United Kingdom v. Commission* [2006] Env LR 26 and *Cemex UK Cement Ltd v. Department for Environment, Food and Rural Affairs* [2007] Env LR 21, respectively.

35 www.defra.gov.uk/environment/climatechange/trading/eu/index.htm.

36 On the general problem of states meddling in environmental trading markets, see J. Wiener (1999) 108 Yale LJ 677, Pt V. Intervention may be legitimately pursued to avoid hotspot problems, but hotspots do not really arise in CO_2 markets.

37 (2007) ENDS Report, 22 February.

38 A number of newer member States are challenging their national limits before the European courts.

One criterion, which was not in place for the 2005–07 trading period, requires NAPs to specify the maximum amount of joint implementation and clean development mechanism credits that may be used for compliance purposes by installations under the scheme.[39]

The scheme may be criticized for a lack of ambition, in the sense that member States that are on course to meet their Kyoto targets need not, in the second phase, reduce their permitted emissions beyond existing levels. Given that Kyoto reduction targets are woefully inadequate to restrain dangerous degrees of climate change, this is unsatisfactory, but it is a good example of the extent to which the EU carbon trading does not necessarily go beyond regulatory compliance, despite this being one of the major claims made for market-based economic instruments. The EU emissions trading scheme is also a good example of the extent to which economic tools can be highly bureaucratic affairs.

The UK and climate change

In recent years, the problem of climate change has become a central issue for environmental law and policy in the UK. Although the local and transboundary impacts of air pollutants continues to be subject to legal controls under pollution control and clean air legislation (as discussed below), the size and complexity of the challenge of climate change has accelerated the use of new instruments to try to regulate rising greenhouse gas emissions from a variety of sources.

The UK's Climate Change Programme was launched in 2000 and set out an ambitious programme of measures intended to help the UK to meet its commitment to reduce greenhouse gas emissions by 12.5 per cent on 1990 levels by 2012 and to meet a self-imposed goal of reducing carbon dioxide emissions by 20 per cent on 1990 levels by 2010.[40] The UK is one of the few countries in the world in which greenhouse gas emissions fell in the 1990s, thus complying with the commitments given in the UNFCCC. Carbon dioxide emissions fell by some 8.7 per cent between 1990 and 2002, and overall greenhouse gas emissions fell by 15.3 per cent over the same period. There is general recognition, however, that these cuts were 'one-off' gains, brought about from the switch from coal to gas, industrial modernization, and a greater reliance on nuclear energy.

The regulatory approach adopted in the first UK's Climate Change Programme was based upon:

- the reduction of industrial emissions of greenhouse gases through IPPC permits—this will implement reductions in some greenhouse gases required under the Large Combustion Plants (2001/80/EC) and Emissions Ceilings (2001/81/EC) Directives;

- energy efficiency measures, including alterations to the building regulations for new developments (these were revised in April 2006);

- the promotion of renewable sources of energy, including a target to double the UK's energy output from combined heat and power production, and a legal obligation to increase supplies of energy from renewable sources by 10.4 per cent by 2010 (see Utilities Act 2000, s. 62);

- investment in transport measures to reduce pollution caused by traffic congestion;

- the use of relatively blunt economic instruments to reduce the amount and impact of vehicle emissions. These include increases in fuel duties to reflect the environmental cost of vehicle use and to promote the benefits of fuel efficiency, the use of fuel duty differentials to encourage, for example, the use of ultra-low diesel fuel over normal diesel, the reform of company car taxation, and changes to the road tax;

---

39 This is achieved by means of the Linking Directive (2004/101/EC).

40 The 2000 Programme has been accused of a degree of 'optimism bias' in relation to its predications about the impact, on emissions, of its measures.

- the use of two main economic instruments—namely, the Climate Change Levy and a national emissions trading scheme—as a precursor to the Europe-wide scheme.

The Climate Change Programme was revised in 2006.[41] The new Programme continues most features of the original, but also includes:

- a commitment to produce annual reports to Parliament on emissions, future plans, and progress on domestic climate change (the first report was published in 2007);

- a commitment to plan for adaptation to climate change (it now being recognized that change is inevitable);[42]

- a renewable transport fuel obligation (from 2008).

Despite extensive consultation, some policy developments have not emerged from the Climate Change Programme. An example is the Department for Environment, Food and Rural Affairs (DEFRA) zero-carbon homes initiative, announced in the 2006 pre-Budget statement. Unlike its predecessor, the 2006 Programme extends beyond sectors such as energy production, manufacturing, transport, households, and the public sector, to agricultural and land use more generally (cattle wastes are a significant source of methane, which is a potent, if relatively short-lived, greenhouse gas). Much of the thinking contained in the 2006 Programme informs the Climate Change Bill that is presently before Parliament (see below).

It is important to stress that the UK approach has tended to focus on the supply side— that is, that it has mainly tried to limit emissions by energy producers. But emissions from sources such as transport and households are now significantly above 1990 levels, and emissions from aviation and shipping (which cannot readily be assigned to one state, but equally cannot be ignored altogether) are also rising fast. Many now argue that much more needs to be done in terms of reducing energy demand. This is a much more difficult issue politically, because it may involve restrictions on choice, liberty, and movement. One possible mechanism of tackling demand would be through personal or household carbon accounts, but—in the short term, at least—government has rejected these.[43]

Climate Change Levy

The Climate Change Levy (CCL) is a tax upon energy usage and is therefore levied upon users, as opposed to a carbon tax, which would be levied on the supply of fuel. It was introduced under s. 30 and Sch. 6 of the Finance Act 2000, and applies to all industrial and public sector users. Domestic use and small businesses that use energy at a 'domestic level' are excluded (paras 9 and 10). Certain fuels are also exempt, such as most renewable energy sources (para. 19), and approved combined heat-and-power schemes (paras 14 and 15).

The introduction of the tax was controversial, with many large industrial energy users complaining that it would affect competitiveness in the international marketplace. The CCL has therefore been designed to be revenue-neutral to the government, with the money accrued from the tax being used to pay for an across-the-board 0.3 per cent reduction of employers' National Insurance contributions. There is an additional incentive to invest in energy efficiency measures, with the companies able to reclaim 100 per cent of the capital allowances for energy-efficient products within the first year of expenditure. This also

---

41 (2006) *Climate Change: The UK Programme*, Cm 6764.

42 This is also the subject of the RCEP's ongoing study (see **www.rcep.org.uk**).

43 For an overview, see (2005) ENDS Report 366, 29–30. These kinds of personal carbon accounts (sometimes known as 'domestic tradeable quotas') have strong links with the 'contraction and convergence' proposal for a globally fair allocation of emission rights, under which states would, over time, have emission rights on a per-capita basis. See A. Mayer (2001) *Contraction and Convergence*, Dartington: Green Books.

reflects the shift of the burden of taxation from the 'goods' of wealth creation, employment, and investment, to the 'bads' of resource consumption and pollution.

Users from the most 'energy-intensive' sectors are able to obtain an 80 per cent discount from the CCL if they sign up to sectoral climate change agreements (CCAs) to reduce carbon emissions or to implement energy efficiency measures. An energy-intensive sector is defined as one that carries out activities that are listed under Pt A1 or A2 headings in Pt 1 of Sch. 1 to the Pollution Prevention and Control (England and Wales) Regulations 2000.[44] There are ten major energy-intensive sectors—aluminium; cement; ceramics; chemicals; food and drink; foundries; glass; non-ferrous metals; paper; steel—and over thirty smaller sectors. This includes many (but not all) of the major industrial sectors, and intensive pig and poultry units. Plans were announced in the 2004 Budget to extend the CCAs to sectors that passed an energy intensity threshold and a test based upon the effect of the CCL on international competitiveness.

The concluded CCAs set objectives and look at the ends, rather than the means, of securing reductions or energy efficiency gains. Thus they set reduction targets and monitoring requirements, and require the independent verification of compliance with the agreements. Failure to comply can result in the suspension or withdrawal of the discount. The first two years' operation of the CCL showed that the CCA was an effective mechanism for securing emissions reductions.[45]

Emissions trading

Emissions trading in the UK commenced, in 2002, as a voluntary economic instrument, which was aimed at reducing greenhouse gas emissions through a market-based approach that allows participants to buy and sell 'allowances' to produce emissions. The UK scheme took a 'cap and trade' approach, whereby participants agreed to specific reduction targets and received allowances based upon that 'cap'. The participant could then meet the target in three ways:

- by reducing emissions to the level of the cap;

- by making reductions to below the level of the cap, which allows them to bank the surplus or sell the allowance to participants;

- by meeting the reduction target through the purchase of surplus allowances from others.

The scheme ended in 2006, but it illustrated some of the flaws in emissions trading instruments. One of the fundamental problems was that any reduction of greenhouse gases achieved was not necessarily linked to the impact of the trading scheme. In other words, the economic rationale of emissions trading in rewarding companies who reduce emissions through efficiency or investment in new technology can be defeated by other factors. One of the most significant arguments is that many participants in the scheme bid for reduction allowances that they were already legally obliged to achieve as a result of pollution control authorization conditions. Other participants gained large reductions through a pre-planned fall in productivity or through loss of capacity as a result of greater competition.[46] The effect of many participants beating their reduction targets was that a large surplus of allowances became available to be banked against future increases or traded on the market. Basic economics dictates that when there is a large surplus of supply, prices will fall. Consequently, it became cheaper to buy allowances than to invest in abatement technology or energy efficiency measures in order to meet targets. In addition, there is the argument

44 SI 2000/1973.
45 (2003) ENDS Report 339, 23.
46 See (2002) ENDS Report 326, 25.

that large sums of public money have been spent in paying some participants to comply with the law.[47]

The introduction of the UK emissions trading scheme in 2002 was a precursor to the EU-wide scheme described above under Directive 2003/87/EC and transposed under the Greenhouse Gas Emissions Trading Scheme Regulations 2005[48] (see p. 525).

BOX 15.4 Economic instruments and atmospheric pollution—an assessment

The introduction of the Climate Change Levy and the emissions trading schemes is a significant departure from old-style command-and-control regulation in the field of atmospheric pollution law. As a basic taxation instrument, the Levy attempts to reflect the environmental cost of energy consumption, which should incentivize companies to reduce usage and invest in abatement measures. The ultimate aim is to achieve a particular environmental goal—namely, the reduction of the emission of greenhouse gases. Environmental taxes have the advantage of being predictable in terms of cost and they can be applied across broad categories of taxpayers. They also have disadvantages in that the aim is to secure an environmental goal, but there is a degree of uncertainty about whether this will be done. If a tax is set too low, it will not act as an incentive to change behaviour; if set too high, it may have a significant impact upon economic development and international competitiveness. Taxes can also be expensive to monitor and enforce. In terms of effectiveness, however, perhaps the biggest disadvantage of the Climate Change Levy is the exemption from the Levy for large sources of greenhouse gas emissions—namely, the domestic and transport sectors.

An emissions trading system has the advantage of being flexible, in the sense that it is akin to a performance standard that encourages technological improvement and fits in with the idea of ecological modernization. Such a scheme also provides a degree of certainty about the achievement of the environmental goal, because the limits are placed on the overall allowances, which can be traded. The schemes encourage compliance through efficiency and competitive advantage. It is even possible for there to be wider public participation in a trading system through the trading of non-target participants.

The actual evidence of the system demonstrates some of its disadvantages. Setting the cap is critical: if it is too high, the need for efficiency gains is reduced; too low and the goal becomes unachievable. In addition, care needs to be taken to ensure that reductions are triggered by more than legal obligations under pollution control legislation; reductions in capacity; or 'business as usual' projections.

Finally, emissions trading schemes are suitable when there are a relatively small number of participants with large sources of pollutants. If there are large numbers of small sources—for example, cars, households, or agriculture—an emissions trading scheme would probably be too cumbersome to operate unless there were operators who could be made responsible for aggregated emissions (for example, airline operators).[49]

---

47 See House of Commons, Committee of Public Accounts (2003–04) *The UK Emissions Trading Scheme: A New Way to Tackle Climate Change.*

48 SI 2005/925.

49 Although increasingly advocated, there is a current lack of government enthusiasm for domestic tradable carbon quotas—see p. 528.

The Climate Change and Sustainable Energy Act 2006

The Climate Change and Sustainable Energy Act 2006, introduced as a private member's Bill, focuses on boosting microgeneration and energy efficiency, and on tackling fuel poverty. It requires the government to report to Parliament annually on the UK's greenhouse gas emissions and to explain what it is doing to curb them. The government must also set targets for the number of microgeneration systems installed throughout England, Wales, and Scotland, although this requirement can be waived if the Secretary of State can demonstrate that the technology is flourishing. The Act also includes provisions to make energy companies pay a fair price for electricity from microgeneration and makes it easier for microrenewables to access the renewable obligation system. A 'carbon emissions reduction obligation' allows energy suppliers to use emissions reductions from microgeneration and other 'low emission sources or technologies' to meet their targets. The Act also strengthens the enforcement procedures for building regulations and requires local authorities to take more action to improve energy efficiency in their areas. It also includes measures to encourage community energy and renewable heating.

The Climate Change Bill

A Climate Change Bill was introduced in Parliament in November 2007 and legislation is expected by early summer 2008. This is likely to require emissions reduction targets for the UK and that the government sets a series of five-yearly carbon budgets designed to ensure that these targets are achieved. A target of 60 per cent emissions reductions by 2050 is likely to be the initial goal (with an interim target for 2020), although even this target would probably be inadequate in the light of the drastic reductions that appear to be needed if dangerous levels of atmospheric greenhouse gases are to be avoided. A mechanism may be established requiring a Committee on Climate Change, a statutory non-departmental body that will report to government, to determine by Autumn 2009 whether the target should be strengthened (the recommendations of this Committee are likely to influence any secondary legislation made under the Act).

Rather than comment on a Bill that is unlikely to reach the statute book unaltered, we will comment on any arising Climate Change Act in the Online Resource Centre. But a few general preliminary points may be made, including:

- the Bill is unique, in the sense that no other country has dedicated legislation, with reduction targets, on climate change;

- the Bill only covers CO_2 emissions (these are the predominant greenhouse gas emitted from the UK);

- the emissions covered are not from every sector of the UK economy—international shipping and aviation (which contribute ever-increasing amounts of emissions) are excluded;

- the five-yearly target budgets, and the ultimate target, are probably best seen as political aspirations, because it is unclear what the sanction (other than the sanctions imposed by nature itself) would be for any government that failed to meet them;[50]

- there will be issues as to whether targets and budgets can be met through overseas credits, such as those under the Kyoto Protocol's Clean Development Mechanism (some would like to see these excluded, but this would run contrary to international agreement so far and to the EC approach, which allows these up to a point);

- the Bill is not only about emissions reductions, but also about adapting to climate change, and a legally required climate change adaptation policy may be required;

---

50 P. McMaster (2008) JEL 113.

- the Bill contains enabling powers that could be used to introduce a carbon reduction commitment, a cap-and-trade scheme proposed for large, less energy-intensive organizations, such as supermarkets and universities;[51]

- although there is support in certain quarters for personal carbon accounts, DEFRA has said that the enabling powers in the Bill will not be used to introduce any personal carbon trading scheme.

Climate change compensation

So far, the legal response to climate change, at international, EU, and national levels, has been regulatory, focused mainly on reducing emissions through an array of flexible mechanisms. But consideration is also being given to using liability mechanisms to compensate for the adverse effects of climate change. There have already been a small number of test cases in the USA. One example is a public nuisance case brought by the Attorney-General of California against the six leading car manufacturers based in the USA, arguing that the defendants should compensate for damages to the State of California—that is, public land—brought about by things such as melting ice and coastal erosion. The case was dismissed on the grounds that it raises issues that are more political than judicial in nature, but is currently on appeal.[52]

As yet, no case has succeeded, and there are a number of difficulties with bringing actions like these. These include having to rely on relatively poorly defined areas of law, the fact that potential defendants have most likely been acting within the regulatory law at the time, issues of causation and foreseeability of damage (although see Box 15.2 above), and apportionment of liability. Of course, cases can raise public opinion and uncover documents that are embarrassing to defendants, without being successful. It is also undoubtedly the case that the threat of litigation has, if nothing else, made major emitters consider their potential liabilities. Domestic litigation may not be that far off.

Apart from traditional forms of damages actions, there may be other compensatory possibilities. One would be a global warming compensation fund, which would direct money from those developed economies that have benefited most from historic emissions (the USA, the EU, Japan, and Russia) to emerging and developing states. This money could be used, among other things, to pay for adaptation measures, which poorer economies are least able to afford. Another possibility might be to compensate those most affected by issuing them with allowances under an international emissions trading scheme (no such scheme as yet exists). This idea combines features of liability funds, such as currently operate for marine oil pollution (see Box 19.1), with some elements of the idea that one way in which to penalize polluters is, in effect, to force them to transfer shares in their companies to those they pollute.[53]

Europe and air pollution policy

The protection of the atmosphere was not seen as a priority by the EC until the mid-1980s. Indeed, relatively few proposals based purely on environmental protection (as opposed to market harmonization) were published before 1984. The reasons for this were twofold: first, a lack of political will; secondly, a genuine desire to move forward in other areas. As a

---

51 See (2007) ENDS Report 390, 41–3.

52 *People of the State of California (ex rel Lockyer) v. General Motors Corporation and ors* No. C06–05755 (ND Cal 20 Sept, 2006). Dismissed by District Court in September 2007: see **ag.ca.gov/globalwarming/litigation.php**.

53 D. Farber (2007) 155 U Pa L Rev 1605.

result of the effects of acid rain, however, the German government pressed for swift action in 1983 and the main framework Directive on emissions from industrial plant (84/360/EC) was introduced nearly ten years after the framework Directives for waste and water pollution.

In policy terms, air pollution and air quality are considered to be a short-term priority. The EC's Sixth Environment Action Programme identified air quality standards as falling within 'environment and health', one of the four main target areas for action until 2010. The EAP sets the objective of achieving levels of air quality that do not give rise to unacceptable impacts on, and risks to, human health and the environment. This is supplemented by a thematic strategy on air pollution, which outlines the environmental objectives for air quality and measures to be taken to achieve and meet these objectives.[54] This strategy is the culmination of the Clean Air for Europe (CAFE) programme,[55] which combined technical analysis and policy development in the area as a basis for a coherent long-term strategy—something that has not been evident in the earlier years of European air quality law and policy. The thematic strategy will be further developed with a new Air Quality Directive.[56]

European law on air quality

European law on air quality has developed significantly from the mid-1980s and now can be characterized as taking a mixed-regulation approach—that is, there are a variety of types of mechanism that are used to regulate air quality. These include the traditional use of environmental standards for environmental quality or emissions limit values (ELVs) for particular installations or substances, product standards (for example, for fuel or motor vehicles), prohibitions on the production, consumption, or use of substances (for example, CFCs), economic instruments, such as emissions trading, and information-based mechanisms, such as the Europe-wide pollutant inventory. A general summary of some of the more important air quality and air pollution Directives can be found in the summary Box 15.5.

One of the problems of this approach has been that there is a degree of overlap and a general lack of coherence, although, to a certain extent, this reflects the complex interrelated nature of problems and solutions.

BOX 15.5 Summary of main EC legislation on air quality and air pollution

Legislative instrument	Outline of relevant provisions
Directive 1994/63/EC on the control of volatile organic compound (VOC) emissions resulting from the storage of petrol and its distribution from terminals to service stations	Controls emissions of VOCs at petrol terminals and during distribution at service stations. Uses technical process standards to reduce evaporation of solvents during transport, etc.
Directive 1996/61/EC concerning integrated pollution prevention and control (IPPC)	Sets down use of Best Available Techniques (BAT) to prevent or minimize air pollution. Requires efficient use of energy by installations. Also provides basis for European Pollutant Emission Register.

---

54 COM(2005) 446.
55 See COM(2001) 245.
56 COM(2005) 447.

Legislative instrument	Outline of relevant provisions
Directive 1996/62/EC on ambient air quality assessment and management	Framework Directive with the aim of protecting public health and the environment from a range of specified air pollutants, particularly sulphur dioxide, nitrogen dioxide and oxides of nitrogen, and particulates. Daughter Directives followed for these pollutants.
Directive 1998/69/EC relating to measures to be taken against air pollution by emissions from motor vehicles	Latest in a long series of Directives dating back to 1970 restricting emissions of pollutants from light motor vehicles. Similar controls for heavy-duty vehicles are found in Directive 1999/86/EC.
Directive 1999/13/EC on the limitation of emissions of volatile organic compounds due to the use of organic solvents in certain activities and installations	Requires certain installations using organic solvents to take steps to reduce emissions of volatile organic compounds to air.
Directive 1999/32/EC relating to the reduction of the sulphur content of certain liquids fuels	Reduces sulphur content of petrol and diesel fuels.
Directive 2000/76/EC on the incineration of waste	Sets emission limit values for dust, SO_2, NOx, and heavy metals. Applies to all waste incinerators.
Directive 2001/80/EC on the limitation of emissions of certain pollutants into the air from large combustion plants	Controls emissions from large combustion plant to reduce emissions of sulphur dioxide, oxides of nitrogen, and particulates.
Directive 2001/81/EC on national emission ceilings for certain atmospheric pollutants	Sets national emission ceilings for pollutants causing acidification and eutrophication and for ozone precursors.

Environmental quality standards

A Framework Directive on Ambient Air Quality was formally agreed in 1996 (96/62/EC). (There are plans to amend this[57] and a new Ambient Air Quality and Cleaner Air for Europe Directive is likely to be adopted and in force by May 2008.)

The Framework Directive uses three types of quality objective: a limit value; a guide value; an alert threshold (which mirrors the approach taken under the national air quality strategy, discussed below). The Directive identifies 12 pollutants for each of which subsequent daughter Directives will set the numerical limit values or target. In addition to setting air quality limit and alert thresholds, the daughter Directives harmonize information requirements, such as monitoring and measuring methods, so that standards are comparable throughout the member States.

The Daughter Directives cover:

- NOx, SO_2, Pb and PM_{10} (99/30/EC);[58]

- benzene and carbon monoxide (2000/69/EC);

---

57 See COM(2005) 447.
58 The revised Directive—ibid.—will set specific standards for $PM_{2.5}$.

- ozone (2002/03/EC);

- arsenic, cadmium, mercury, nickel, and polycyclic aromatic hydrocarbons in ambient air (2004/107/EC).

Member States and their local authorities will need to monitor air quality, provide information to the public, and introduce improvement plans and programmes where air quality fails to meet the specified criteria. These are implemented in the UK through a combination of statutory air quality standards and the air quality management provisions of the Environment Act 1995.

National emissions ceilings

In 1997, the European Commission published a proposed acidification strategy, which was designed to reduce the emission of sulphur dioxide, oxides of nitrogen, and ammonia. Consequently, the National Emissions Ceilings Directive (2001/81/EC) sets upper limits for each member State for the total emissions in 2010 of those four pollutants, but generally leaves the method of implementation to each member State The Directive obliges member States to draw up national programmes in order to demonstrate how they are going to meet the national emissions ceilings by 2010, and to report, each year, their national emissions inventories and projections for 2010 to the European Commission and the European Environment Agency. These requirements have been implemented in the UK by the National Emission Ceiling Regulations 2002.[59]

Stationary source emissions limits

Various Directives make provision for the control of emissions from stationary point sources. The Large Combustion Plants Directive (2001/80/EC) sets out emissions limits for SO_2, NOx, and PM_{10} in the case of emissions from power stations with a thermal output of greater than 50 MW (this can also include large industrial power plants in refineries and steelworks). One of the significant aspects of the Directive is that it is retrospective applying to power stations established before the coming into force of the original Large Combustion Plants Directive in July 1987 (although there are derogations for the so-called enlargement states). Under the LCPD, 'new'—that is, post-Directive—plant must meet the specified emissions limit values for the four substances in the LCPD. For 'existing' plants—that is, those in operation pre-1987—member States have an option of complying with the limit values or operating within a 'national plan', which would set an annual 'emissions bubble' by aggregating a national level of emissions calculated by applying the ELV approach to existing plants.

Process standards

Certain Directives utilize process standards to prevent or minimize atmospheric emissions. For example, the IPPC Directive (96/61/EC) does not specify limit values for atmospheric emissions; it specifies general process standards for permitting of specified industrial installations (including some agricultural and waste installations), based on the application of Best Available Techniques (BAT), taking into account local conditions. Community-wide ELVs *can* be set if a 'need' for Community action is identified through the technical information exchange and the setting of technical guidance found in the BAT Reference (BREF) standards (see p. 502).

---

59 SI 2002/3118.

Emissions from motor vehicles

The regulation of transport poses significant challenges in terms of controlling air pollution. Emissions from passenger cars account for around half of all CO_2 emissions in the transport sector and almost 12 per cent of total CO_2 emissions in the EU. Product standards for vehicles and fuel have been used extensively in the regulation of air pollution. One of the main reasons for this is that, before the amendments to the EC Treaty, which permitted environmental protection measures, the introduction of such standards was seen to be justifiable in terms of market harmonization in areas in which environmental justifications were not accepted by every member State.

Vehicle emissions have been controlled under a number of increasingly complex amendments to the original controlling Directive 70/220/EEC. Generally, Directives have set product standards by fixing emission limits for carbon monoxide, hydrocarbons, nitrogen dioxide, and particulates. Various amendments have culminated in Directive 2001/100/EC, which sets out limits for cars and light vans. Emissions from larger vans and heavy-duty vehicles are controlled under a separate Directive (88/77/EC, as amended). In addition to the fixed emission limits, there have been a number of Directives controlling the roadworthiness of vehicles to ensure that the original product standards are being maintained. Directive 99/52/EC set out procedures for checking the roadworthiness of private cars; in addition to product standards for vehicles, Directive 98/70/EC (as amended by Directive 2003/17/EC) sets out environmental fuel quality specifications for petrol and diesel. These set specifications for the sulphur content of petrol and diesel, and the aromatics content of petrol, and are phased in over three stages from 2000 to 2008.

BOX 15.6 Voluntary instruments—car manufacturers and reducing CO$_2$ emissions

The use of voluntary agreements is becoming increasingly popular as part of a mixed regulation approach.[60] In the EC, the Fifth Environmental Action Programme promoted their use as a 'flexible mechanism'. Voluntary agreements are thought to offer certain advantages over traditional forms of regulation, including a faster, more streamlined process of reaching agreement when compared to making legislation, encouraging a responsible and proactive approach by industry, and allowing a flexible, cost-effective approach to environmental problems. There are potential weaknesses in a voluntary approach, including a lack of transparency or accountability, the setting of unambitious standards, the absence of technology-forcing mechanisms, the vague monitoring of compliance, and a lack of satisfactory enforcement mechanisms. The example of the first Europe-wide environmental agreements bears out some of these criticisms.

In 1996, the European Council of Ministers proposed a long-term strategy to reduce CO_2 emissions from passenger cars and improve fuel economy. The strategy aims at achieving an average CO_2 emission figure for new passenger cars of 120g CO_2/km by 2005—or by 2010 at the latest. One of three main elements of the strategy was voluntary environmental agreements made between the European Commission and the European, Japanese, and Korean car industry associations (ACEA, JAMA, and KAMA, respectively). Under these agreements, the car manufacturers made a commitment to reduce average CO_2 emissions from new cars to 140 g/km by 2008 (2009 in the case of JAMA and KAMA).

---

60 See further COM (1998) 495; COM (1999) 446; Recommendation 1999/125/EC OJ L 40, 13 February 1999, 49–50; G. Volpi and S. Singer (2000) *Will Voluntary Agreements at EU Level Deliver on Environmental Objectives? Lessons from the Agreement with the Automotive Industry*, WWF Discussion Paper.

The criticisms of the negotiation and final terms of the ACEA agreement were as follows.

- It took some four years to negotiate an agreement that will bite some ten years after it was concluded. This is hardly a swift alternative to the legislative process that would be expected to finalize a Directive, which could be transposed and implemented easily within that timetable.

- There was little wider public participation in the negotiation of the agreement, which was largely conducted between the Commission and the associations. In addition, compliance data will only be made public on a collective basis across the whole sector, meaning that individual manufacturer's performance will not be assessed.

- There were no enforcement mechanisms for non-compliance.

- The targets had become outdated by the foreseeable introduction of existing technologies. In effect, the targets represented a 'business as usual' model that would not necessarily stabilize CO_2 emissions from passenger cars at 1999 levels by 2010.

- The targets did not act as a sufficient incentive to develop alternative technologies.

Some of these criticisms go to the heart of the suitability of voluntary agreements as a mechanism to address serious environmental problems. The force of these criticisms was borne out when data suggested that, while good progress had been made, the agreement was ineffective in terms of reducing CO_2 levels from passenger vehicles.[61]

A new proposal to introduce a new strategy to achieve the desired reduction has now been published—some 11 years after the original.[62] This underlines one of the fundamental flaws of voluntary agreements. If it were proved to be ineffective, there would be little alternative other than to introduce legislative measures, which would arguably be akin to shutting the stable door after the horse had bolted.

The European Pollutant Release and Transfer Register

A further element in the broad mixed-regulation approach to air pollution is the establishment of accurate, publicly available information on air pollution from emissions. Various countries have established national pollutant inventories, such as the US Toxic Releases Inventory and the Environment Agency's Pollution Inventory. These registers, or inventories, aim to encourage transparency, accountability, and public participation, but can also act as a trigger for pollution prevention programmes.

The European Pollutant Release and Transfer Register (EPER) has its origins in the reporting requirement found in Art. 15(3) of the IPPC Directive (96/61/EC) and was finally established by Commission Decision 2000/479/EC. The European Commission and the European Environment Agency run it jointly. Under the EPER Decision, member States have to produce a three-yearly report on emissions to air and water at industrial installations, which are listed in Annex I of the IPPC Directive. The report covers 50 pollutants in total, of which 37 are atmospheric pollutants. These must be included if certain threshold values are exceeded. The aim of the EPER has been to allow direct comparisons of air emissions data across all member States. The information is available online at **www.eper.cec.eu.int** and can be searched by country, activity, pollutant, or facility. The website also has a map search function, with a summary of each industrial site and satellite photos. Some care should be taken with the data, however, because the figures may not necessarily represent an accurate picture of the

---

61 (2007) ENDS Report 392, 8–9.

62 COM(2007) 19. A draft regulation—COM(2007) 856—was published in December 2007; see (2008) ENDS Report 396, 45.

relative contributions of different member States. For example, the UK's experience with the setting up and reporting of data for the Pollutant Inventory may mean that it has access to better quality data than do other member States.

Under Regulation 166/2006, the European Pollutant Release and Transfer Register (E-PRTR) continues the development of a Europe-wide pollutant register.[63] The E-PRTR implements the obligations of the United Nations–Economic Commission for Europe Pollutant Release and Transfer Register (UN–ECE PRTR) Protocol. The obligations under the E-PRTR Regulation allow direct comparisons of environmental emissions (including non-atmospheric releases) across all member States. It will be an annual report—as opposed to that published every three years under EPER—and cover a wider range of facilities and substances than that covered under EPER. The first data to be released will be in 2009, relating to reporting year 2007.

Domestic air pollution and air quality law and policy

In the UK, the control of air pollution has been the classic example of the use of reactive legal controls to regulate specific problems as they arise. Policy approaches had hitherto been sparse and incoherent. In the mid-1990s, the approach was described as '*the fortuitous sum of a large number of unrelated regulatory decisions and individual choices*'.[64] Although the legal controls have been modernized and broadened, it was only recently that a coherent strategy was developed to deal with the problems of atmospheric pollution. It was not until the introduction of the air quality management system in the Environment Act 1995 that air pollution was addressed in a strategic manner.

The 1995 Act contained a number of framework provisions that enabled the development of various policies on air pollution. A number of factors led to this acceleration of policy and lawmaking. First, there was increasing evidence linking health problems with poor air quality, with the increase of the incidence of asthma and other diseases connected with a variety of atmospheric pollutants. There were a number of occasions (particularly in the summer months) when pollution levels rose to dangerous levels in cities.

Secondly, the quality of provision of information on air quality was improved, with an increase in the number of background monitoring stations. Although air quality standards (AQS) were introduced for a number of pollutants, any assessment of measuring improvement depended, to a large extent, upon the availability of long-term data. Most of England's major cities now have stations to monitor base data in order to assess compliance with standards for the main polluting emissions. It is anticipated that this will increase as the move towards established AQS grows.

Thirdly, the link between air pollution and transport—in particular, motor transport—had become much more pronounced. The Eighteenth Report of the Royal Commission on Environmental Pollution (RCEP), *Transport and the Environment*,[65] was published in October 1994. It concentrated on the environmental effects of vehicle emissions, proposing a number of objectives and targets for reducing the environmental impacts from transport as the basis for a transport policy for the UK, which will be sustainable well into the next century. It made wide-ranging recommendations about integrating transport policy and land use, increasing the use made of environmentally less damaging forms of transport for passengers and freight, and minimizing the adverse impact of road and rail transport.

Finally, and perhaps most importantly, in recent years, the most significant air pollution policy and law has been influenced heavily by the need to meet the greenhouse gas reduction

---

63 Decision 2000/479/EC.
64 Department of Environment (1994) *Improving Air Quality*, Consultation paper.
65 Cm 2674.

targets under the Kyoto Protocol, as well as the environmental quality standards laid down under various EC air quality Directives. This has seen a shift from the local controls under clean air legislation to a mixed regulatory approach, involving detailed national policies on air quality management, product standards, economic instruments, voluntary agreements, and public information tools.

National Air Quality Strategy

Central policy for maintaining and improving air quality is laid down in a National Air Quality Strategy. Under s. 80 of the Environment Act 1995, the Secretary of State is under a duty to prepare the Strategy, which will enable the UK to meet international and European commitments—most notably, on air quality standards and climate change. These standards and objectives provide the foundation for air quality policy, and set the context within which detailed legislation must be implemented and enforced. For example, the Environment Agency is to have regard to the Strategy when exercising its pollution control functions (s. 81). The Strategy sets a framework containing air quality standards for certain pollutants that are set centrally and provide overall targets that must not be exceeded. These targets are to be achieved through a variety of mechanisms, but, principally, under pollution control legislation through the setting of emissions limits.

The Strategy contains two standards for identified pollutants: a general target standard, which forms a long-term objective for policies and legislation; an alert threshold, which triggers the need for specific remedial action when exceeded. The current strategy, the Air Quality Strategy for England, Scotland, Wales and Northern Ireland, was published in 2007.[66] The Strategy covered ten main air pollutants: benzene; 1,3 butadiene; ammonia; carbon monoxide; lead; oxides of nitrogen; ozone; particulates; polycyclic aromatic hydrocarbons; sulphur dioxide.

The Strategy does not, however, have statutory force and imposes no direct obligations upon any regulatory body. Thus, the Environment Act 1995 provides a power to prescribe standards and/or objectives by way of regulation (ss. 87 and 91). These regulations, in turn, impose certain obligations upon local authorities. The 1995 Act provides for the creation of a system of local air quality management that obliges local authorities to undertake an assessment of air quality in their areas and to take action where statutory objectives are not being met. These statutory objectives have been incorporated into the Air Quality (England) Regulations 2000,[67] which set down the targets for air quality in each local area for a specified period. The Regulations establish air quality objectives for seven pollutants, including sulphur dioxide, nitrogen dioxide, benzene, and carbon monoxide. The standards are set in relation to the effect of the pollutant upon human health, although the effect upon the wider environment is also a material consideration.

Air Quality Standards Regulations 2007

The obligations under the Strategy and the 2000 Regulations are theoretically separate, and distinct from the requirements to transpose and implement the air quality limit values found in the Framework Directive on ambient air quality (96/62/EC) and the various daughter Directives made under this. The reason for this is that local authorities may have some powers to manage air quality within their areas, but this does not apply to all sources of pollutants. For example, most major point sources of air pollutants will be regulated and enforced by the Environment Agency under the IPPC regime. Thus, in some situations, local authorities will be powerless to ensure compliance with the European standards—a position that would clearly be an incomplete transposition of the Directive's obligations.

---

66 Cm 7169.
67 SI 2000/928 (as amended).

The strict legal position is that the EC standards are transposed and implemented through a stand-alone legal duty on the Secretary of State under the Air Quality Standards Regulations 2007.[68] These Regulations specify the various air quality standards laid down in EC legislation in terms of limit or target values (reg. 6, and Schs 1 and 2) and provide that the Secretary of State shall take the 'necessary measures' to ensure that European air quality standards are attained (reg. 7).[69] Other general duties apply, such as the maintenance of air quality standards (reg. 10) and a duty to assess and monitor air quality, as well as the release of public information in cases of breach (regs 24–25).

Meeting the National Air Quality Strategy's objectives

Where any of the statutory objectives are not likely to be met during the specified period, the relevant local authority must designate the area as an air quality management area (AQMA) and prepare an action plan indicating how it intends to meet the objectives. There are various powers that can be used to assist in meeting the objectives, as follows.

- **The use of smoke control powers under the Clean Air Act 1993**

  The control of smoke from industrial and domestic premises is an important part of the National Air Quality Strategy. Local authorities have the power to declare a smoke control area (which prohibits the emission of smoke from chimneys and the use of unauthorized fuels), in order to secure objectives contained in an action plan. In practice, however, most of the areas of the country in which smoke has been a problem have already been designated as smoke control areas.

- **The use of traffic management and planning powers**

  The ability of local authorities to tackle local hotspots of poor air quality, which result mainly from vehicles, has been enhanced with the introduction of local transport plans (LTPs). An LTP is designed to tackle the adverse effects of traffic, including any deterioration of air quality. Under the Transport Act 2000, each local transport authority must produce an LTP, which should set out policies for promoting public transport, and for charging for road users and parking. (In England, AQMA action plans can be incorporated into LTPs where local road transport emissions are the primary factor behind the AQMA and most local authorities have done so.) This might include such things as congestion charging and levies on car parking places.

  In addition to the strategic management of traffic through LTPs, there are statutory powers available to control traffic under a number of different statutes. The Road Traffic Reduction Act 1997 places a duty upon local authorities to review the levels of traffic on local roads and to produce targets for reducing numbers. This is supplemented nationally by the traffic reduction targets produced under the Road Traffic Reduction (National Targets) Act 1998. Under the Road Traffic Regulation Act 1984, local authorities have wide powers to regulate traffic under traffic regulation orders (TROs), which can be used to restrict traffic in certain areas (for example, pedestrianized areas of city centres) or even single roads. TROs can be made in order to achieve air quality objectives (s. 1(g) of the Road Traffic Regulation Act 1984). Further measures to reduce traffic and contribute to air quality improvements can be made by using traffic calming under the Highways (Traffic Calming) Regulations 1999,[70] which allow local authorities to create narrow 'gateways' into urban centres.

---

68 SI 2007/64.

69 In the case of target values, those measures should not entail 'disproportionate costs' or, in the case of PPC installations, anything other than Best Available Techniques Not Entailing Excessive Cost (BATNEEC).

70 SI 1999/1026.

- **The use of pollution control measures**

  This covers measures such as local authority powers under the pollution prevention and control (PPC) provisions and emissions from PPC installations, including controls over both point-source emissions and diffuse emissions, such as VOCs from the storage and distribution of petrol.

- **The control of land uses by way of planning controls**

  The link between land use planning and air pollution has been recognized explicitly in Planning Policy Statement 6 (*Planning and Town Centres*) and Planning Policy Guidance Note 13 (*Transport*). The impact of a development upon air quality in an AQMA would be a material consideration that would be taken into account when considering whether to grant planning permission. In addition, the designation of an AQMA would have to be taken into account when drawing up development plan policies in regional and local development plans.

The control of emissions from motor vehicles

The effect of transport on the environment is varied. There are obvious effects, such as emissions, noise, land-take for roads, and the use of raw materials (petrol, diesel, in addition to manufacturing materials). Emissions from vehicles are, however, probably the most significant issue that needs to be regulated and controlled.

The problems of pollution from motor vehicles were acknowledged as significant in the RCEP's First Report of 1971,[71] in which the Commission warned of the dangers of ignoring the environmental implications of traffic growth. With growth forecasts for road traffic of over 140 per cent between 1988 and 2025, the original warnings have taken on a repetitive nature. In particular, the RCEP Eighteenth Report (1994) *Transport and the Environment*[72] set out eight key objectives that were intended to make transport policy more sustainable. In relation to atmospheric pollution, this included targets for air quality and the reduction of carbon dioxide emissions.

The law in relation to the control of emissions from motor vehicles is under constant review and is too detailed to be covered here, other than in principle. Most controls target product standards in relation to vehicle-type approval, specified emissions limits from vehicles, the content of fuel, and maintenance tests. Most limits have their origin within EC legislation (see above).

When a new motor vehicle is produced, it must comply with all relevant standards, including EC emissions limits. The Motor Vehicles (Type Approval) (Great Britain) Regulations 1994[73] set out type-approval procedures, which are applied to specimen examples of vehicles prior to general sale. The Road Vehicle (Construction and Use) Regulations 2003,[74] meanwhile, set out requirements in relation to a variety of construction details, including catalytic convertors, the use of unleaded petrol, and emissions levels for vehicles in use. In particular, the annual Ministry of Transport (MOT) tests—and, more recently, roadside checks—have standards for smoke and carbon monoxide that must not be exceeded.

CHAPTER SUMMARY

1 Climate change and air pollution problems are complex, and require a range of different responses. This means that no single approach will be successful.

71 Cmnd 4585.
72 Cm 2674.
73 SI 1994/981.
74 SI 2003/2695.

2   Controls over air pollution have a long history, although the challenges have shifted from local controls, to regional issues (such as transboundary pollution), to global problems relating to atmospheric pollution (such as ozone depletion and climate change).

3   The international community has addressed international problems, such as transboundary pollution, climate change, and ozone depletion, through various negotiated agreements. The normal pattern for these has been based around an initial framework Convention that identifies the problem and calls for cooperation and research, followed by more detailed Protocols that contain specific measures to address the problem.

4   Climate change poses very serious challenges to the international community requiring the balancing of the interests of developed and developing nations. This has been addressed through the adoption of a 'common but differentiated responsibility' approach to the sharing of commitments to reduce greenhouse gas emissions, but overall very weak targets.

5   After a relatively slow start, the EC has taken a leading role in negotiating international conventions on behalf of its member States.

6   The UK and EC have adopted new policy instruments to help to reduce greenhouse gas emissions. These include economic instruments such as the UK Climate Change Levy and the EC Emissions Trading Scheme, and voluntary agreements in the form of climate change agreements. They also include legislation promoting the use of renewables and energy efficiency. A UK Climate Change Act is expected in 2008.

7   Product standards are used to address emissions from transport. These mostly consist of specification standards that are designed to reduced exhaust emissions or the content of fuel.

8   Increasing attention is being given to possible liabilities for causing adverse climate change. These include the use of common law torts and compensation funds.

9   The EC is increasingly the most important force in determining new air quality standards nationally. The main driver is a framework strategy on air quality, which is supplemented by daughter Directives that specify air quality limits for particular substances.

10   There is a range of further Directives that address emissions from different sources, such as industry, power stations, and transport.

11   The EC is adopting new, innovative policy instruments with which to address air pollution problems. The use of voluntary agreements with car manufacturers and EU-wide emissions trading schemes stand out as the first examples of these.

12   The legal duty to comply with European air quality standards rests with the Secretary of State for the Environment, Food and Rural Affairs, but, in practice, responsibility for air pollution rests with a combination of pollution control powers operated by the Environment Agency and local authorities, and air quality management powers held by local authorities.

13   Domestic air quality law is dominated by the National Air Quality Strategy and associated legislation. The Strategy contains two standards for identified pollutants: a general target standard, which forms a long-term objective for policies and legislation, and an alert threshold, which triggers the need for specific remedial action when exceeded.

14   The strategy is met through a system of local air quality management, which obliges local authorities to undertake an assessment of air quality in their areas and to take action where statutory objectives are not being achieved.

15   Local authorities also have control over the emissions of dark smoke and fumes under the clean air legislation.

Q QUESTIONS

1 What challenges do law and policymakers have to address when faced with the issue of climate change? What are the consequences of taking a 'common but differentiated responsibility' approach to the problem?

2 Provide a critical analysis of either the 2007 Bali climate change meeting or the passage of the UK Climate Change Bill.

3 What types of standard and regulatory instrument are used to control air quality and air pollution? Which do you think are most effective and why?

4 Albert lives in Acacia Avenue in a major urban area in the south of England. Acacia Avenue is used as a 'rat run' for cars travelling into the city centre. During hot periods of the summer, the levels of carbon monoxide, particulates, and sulphur dioxide in the air are much higher than those specified in the national air quality strategy. Albert suffers from bad asthma and has complained to his local authority about the situation. It says that these are peaks and that the standards are only breached during the summer months. The authority has also pointed out that Acacia Avenue has better air quality when compared to other urban areas in the same city, and that cars are becoming more efficient and less polluting, and has refused to take any further action. The whole area is in breach of standards laid down in EC Directive 96/62/EC on ambient air quality assessment and management, and the relevant standards laid down in various daughter Directives. Advise Albert on the legal obligations of the local authority and central government in relation to this poor air quality.

📖 FURTHER READING

Historical background

An interesting overview of the historical background to air pollution in the UK can be found in P. Brimblecombe (1987) *The Big Smoke: History of Air Pollution in London Since Mediaeval Times*, London: Routledge, which traces legislative developments in the context of social, industrial, and economic change.

Climate change—general and policy

There is seemingly no end of books on this subject, but we can recommend, in particular, G. Monbiot (2007) *Heat: How to Stop the Planet from Burning*, Cambridge, Mass: South End Press. P. Roberts (2004) *The End of Oil*, London: Bloomsbury, and R. Henson (2006) *The Rough Guide to Climate Change*, London: Rough Guides, are also accessible. In terms of shorter articles, read G. Monbiot, 'Climate change: a crisis of collective denial' (2005) ELM 57, and J. Lanchester, 'Warmer, warmer' (2007) 29(6) London Review of Books, which reviews the recent literature, such as by the IPCC and that by Monbiot, in a highly engaging way.

A. Meyer (2000) *Contraction and Convergence: The Global Solution to Climate Change*, Schumacher Briefing No. 5, Dartington: Green Books, sets out a theoretically neat and, in some respects, increasingly influential way of reducing emissions globally, converging ultimately on per capita quotas, which the author argues respect issues of fairness as between developed and developing states.

A good general source on policy, especially on economic policy and tools, is D. Helm (ed.) (2005) *Climate Change Policy*, Oxford: Oxford University Press. HM Treasury and Cabinet Office (2006) *The Economics of Climate Change* (the Stern Review) has been hugely influential not only in the UK, where it was commissioned, but globally. The full report, as well as summaries, is available online at **www.hm-treasury.gov.uk/ independent_reviews/stern_review_economics_climate_change/sternreview_index.cfm**.

A. Gore (2006) *An Inconvenient Truth*, Emmaus, Penn: Rodale, is the book that accompanies the influential film of the same name. Despite being, in places, over-the-top and self-promotional, it has arguably done more than any other contribution to the raising of awareness of this issue. As well as this film (Paramount, 2006), try to watch *Who Killed the Electric Car?* (Sony, 2007), a truly depressing tale of the power of the oil and automobile industries (in the USA, at least), which makes one wonder why the EC ever thought that these two sectors would voluntarily work together to drive fuel economy standards down.

International law and climate change

There is a lot of literature on this subject. R. Churchill and D. Freestone (eds) (1991) *International Law and Global Climate Change*, The Hague: Kluwer, is out of date, but it provides a good introduction to the agreement of the Climate Change Treaty. D. Freestone and C. Streck (eds) (2005) *Legal Aspects of Implementing the Kyoto Protocol Mechanisms: Making Kyoto Work*, Oxford: Oxford University Press, is reasonably up to date as far as developments in the Kyoto period (pre-2012) are concerned.

If you want to understand the complexity of negotiating an international agreement with insights of the role of governmental and non-governmental actors, you should read I. Mintzer and J. Leonard (eds) (2004) *Negotiating Climate Change: Inside Story of the Rio Convention*, Cambridge: Cambridge University Press. This book reveals the extent to which principles are traded and compromise attained. Sources on various aspects of climate change law at international level, going beyond consideration of how the regime is intended to work internally, include R. Purdy (2006) 'Geological carbon dioxide storage and the law' in S. Shackley and C. Gough (eds) *Carbon Capture and Its Storage: An Integrated Assessment*, Aldershot: Ashgate, which considers not only the international law obstacles, but also the compatibility of this technology with a range of EC and regional laws, and S. Charnovitz (2005) 'Trade and climate: potential conflicts and synergies' in Pew Center on Global Climate Change, *Beyond Kyoto: Advancing the International Effort Against Climate Change*, available online at **www.pewclimate.org/global-warming-in-depth/all_reports/beyond_kyoto**.

Climate change—EC and national sources

B. Richardson and K. Chanwai, 'The UK's Climate Change Levy: is it working?' (2003) JEL 39, M. Peeters, 'Emissions trading as a new dimension to European environmental law: the political agreement of the European Council on greenhouse gas allowance trading' (2003) ELR 82, and G. Volpi and S. Singer (2000) *Will Voluntary Agreements at EU Level Deliver on Environmental Objectives? Lessons from the Agreement with the Automotive Industry*, WWF Discussion Paper, available online at **www.uneptie.org/outreach/vi/reports/wwf.pdf**, provide a good starting point for further research. M. Stallworthy, 'Sustainability, coastal erosion and climate change: an environmental justice analysis' (2006) JEL 357 focuses attention on one of the main adaptation issues facing parts of the UK. L. Warren, 'Global climate change: a Stern response' (2007) Env L Rev 77 discusses both the 2006 Stern Report and recent IPCC findings, and sets these against an unsuccessful challenge to a coal-fired power station in Australia (see **www.lrt.qld.gov. au/LRT/PDF/Xstrata2_33.pdf**) in which the court demonstrated just how difficult it can be to make legal, and especially judicial, inroads on vast policy problems with seemingly infinite causes. (The case is a very sobering read.)

Climate litigation

There are a number of helpful analyses of the scope for litigation in this area. P. Cullet, 'Liability and redress for human-induced global warming: towards an international regime' (2007) 26A Stan Envtl LJ 99 is a good starting point, especially for liability in international law, while M. Kerr (2002) *Tort-Based Climate Change Litigation in Australia*, Melbourne: Australian Conservation Foundation, is a useful overview of possible causes of action, which should enable you to get a feel for their possible application (and tort law in Australia is very similar, although not identical, to English common law). Other articles include: D. A. Grossman, 'Warming up to a not so radical idea: tort-based climate change litigation' (2003) 28 Colum J Envtl L; K. J. Healy and J. Tapick, 'Climate change: it's not just a policy issue for corporate counsel—it's a legal problem' (2004) 29 Colum J Envtl L 89; K. L. Marburg, '2001 yearbook: air and atmosphere—combating the impacts of global warming: a novel legal strategy' (2001) Colo J Intl Envtl L & Poly 171; R. S. J. Tol and R. Verheyen, 'State responsibility and compensation for climate change damages' (2004) 32 Energy Policy 1109. All of these are really concerned with traditional reparation-type cases.

J. Gupta, 'Legal steps outside the climate convention: litigation as a tool to address climate change' (2007) 16(1) Review of EC and International Environmental Law 76 looks at a range of legal actions (not only those seeking reparation), while D. Farber, 'Basic compensation for the victims of climate change' (2007) 155 U Pa LR1605 has already been commented upon (p. 532).

International law, and other air and atmospheric problems

A good single chapter, which gives more depth than we can on the range of international law issues considered above, is I. Rowland (2007) 'Atmosphere and outer space' in D. Bodansky J. Brunnée, and E. Hey (eds) *The Oxford Handbook of International Environmental Law*, Oxford: Oxford University Press. O. Yoshida (2001) *The International Legal Regime for the Protection of the Stratospheric Ozone Layer*, The Hague: Kluwer, is a study of the effectiveness of international environmental law in circumstances under which there is sufficient political will to achieve specified objectives. P. Okowa (2000) *State Responsibility for Transboundary Air Pollution in International Law*, Oxford: Oxford University Press, provides a general overview of the topic. G. Roberts (2007) 'The holes in the ozone story' ENDS Report 393, 26–9 traces the development of this issue and the responses, and the interrelationship between the ozone and greenhouse problems (and see also the article by Sunstein, above, p. 168).

Air pollution—general

An introduction to the issues that also considers the challenges for the future is T. Williamson and L. Murley (eds) (2003) *The Clean Air Revolution: 1952–2052*, Brighton: NSCA. D. Hughes, N. Parpworth, and J. Upson (1998) *Air Pollution Law and Regulation*, Bristol: Jordans, is now very dated, but still useful background. Bang up to date is the coverage in Environmental Protection UK (2008) *Pollution Control Handbook 2008*. For a less legal and more policy-based approach, the latest Air Quality Strategy for England, Scotland, Wales and Northern Ireland (July 2007, Cm 7169) covers all of the issues in a reader-friendly fashion.

@ **WEB LINKS**

The best site for up-to-date information on the international aspects of climate change is the official United Nations site at **www.unfccc.int**. Here, you will find the full text of the Treaty and Kyoto Protocol, information on ratification and resources on the progress made post-ratification through the various meetings, Conferences of the Parties (CoPs), national reports and other technical information. The Inter-Governmental Panel on Climate Change also has a good selection of resources on its web page at **www.ipcc.ch**. A third potential source of information on climate change is available at **www.undp.org/energy/climate.htm**. Good campaigning sites are **www.climatelaw.org** and **www.ecoequity.org**. Sources on the Montreal Protocol can be found at **www.undp.org/chemicals/montrealprotocol.htm** and the Geneva Convention at **www.unece.org/env/lrtap/welcome.html**.

The Department for Environment, Food and Rural Affairs (DEFRA) links page offers access to a number of good sources of information on air pollutants, their sources, and relevant legislation. The main access point is **www.defra.gov.uk**, but there are further links to climate change and air quality pages. In the former—**www.defra.gov.uk/environment/climatechange/index.htm**—you will find the UK's Climate Change Programme and links to latest legislative developments; in the latter, there are links to the National Air Quality Archive (**www.airquality.co.uk**), which provides air quality statistics and 24-hour forecasts, and the National Atmospheric Emissions Inventory (**www.naei.org.uk**), which provides aggregated data on emissions from various sources including cars, power stations, and industrial plant.

The Royal Commission on Environmental Pollution (RCEP) site at **www.rcep.org.uk** has links to three recent reports that consider climate change. The 22nd Report, *Energy: The Changing Climate*, contains an in-depth study of the links between energy use and climate change. The special report on *The Environment Effects of Civil Aircraft in Flight* highlights a significant threat from a relatively unregulated source. And the 26th Report on *The Urban Environment* has much to say about domestic emissions from a range of sources, including new development and existing housing. Environmental Protection UK (formerly the

National Society for Clean Air) has a range of links and materials on its web page at **www.environmental-protection.org.uk**.

The European Commission site has detailed information on European legislation on different aspects of climate change (**europa.eu/scadplus/leg/en/s15012.htm**) and air pollution (**europa.eu.int/scadplus/leg/en/s15004.htm**). More general information on European policy initiatives on air quality, pollution, and climate change can be found through the relevant links at **ec.europa.eu/environment/air/index.htm** and **ec.europa.eu/environment/climat/home_en.htm** (the latter contains links to the annual reports on the EU's progress towards meeting its Kyoto targets, and is where developments in relation to the Commission's proposals on things like renewables targets and effort-sharing can be tracked). The home of the European Pollutant Emissions Register can be found at **www.eper.cec.eu.int**, although the new E-PRTR may when established have a different URL.

16 Contaminated land

> ### Overview
>
> The regulation of land or soil quality is the least developed of the pollution control systems dealing with environmental media. Soil quality is affected by many activities, but contamination from historical sources may present one of the most significant challenges. This chapter deals with the clean-up of contamination caused by historical sources. This presents a number of significant challenges, such as when should clean-up be required, to what level, and for what purposes? But probably the most significant of all of these issues is the identification of the party, or parties, who should pay for the consequences of historic pollution.
>
> Some pre-existing liability systems provide a partial answer to the problem. For example, private law mechanisms, such as nuisance and negligence, can impose liability for certain heads of damage (see Chapter 11); in other cases statutory schemes can be used to clean up certain sources of contamination. But the development of liability rules under private law principles has been discouraged, while other areas of pollution control regulation only address the problem of clean-up in a partial, and not wholly efficient, manner. As a result, we have a patchwork system of liability rules spread across a wide range of areas that address specific problems of contamination and clean-up.
>
> In this chapter, we will be considering the set of laws introduced to address the patchy nature of pre-existing regimes. Although the focus of this chapter is relatively narrow—that is, on the regulation of the clean-up of historically contaminated land—it is important always to bear in mind that the basic building blocks of statutory liability for cleaning up pollution can often be found in subject specific legislation that is addressed in different chapters in Part III.
>
> After studying this chapter, you should be able to:
>
> ✔ understand and evaluate a key example of statutory environmental liability within the UK;
>
> ✔ understand the basic framework of the allocation and apportionment of liability for historic contamination under the Environmental Protection Act 1990, Pt 2A;
>
> ✔ evaluate one example of the implementation of the Polluter Pays Principle (PPP);
>
> ✔ understand the definition of 'contaminated land' within the context of the Environmental Protection Act 1990, Pt 2A;
>
> ✔ analyse the impact of sustainable development upon the setting of environmental standards;
>
> ✔ assess the role of scientific standard setting in environmental liability regimes;
>
> ✔ distinguish between continuing controls and retrospective liability;
>
> ✔ assess the interaction of various sources of environmental law, including primary and secondary legislation, with policy and technical guidance.

Introduction

Why does this chapter deal with 'contaminated land' when it would seem consistent with other parts of this book to deal with the laws controlling 'land pollution' or 'land quality'? Unlike other areas of pollution control, in which there is a distinction between 'contamination' (which denotes the presence of a foreign substance) and 'pollution' (which is used to describe harm or threats of harm), *land* contamination and *land* pollution are generally considered to be synonymous. Moreover, there is a significant distinction that needs to be drawn between land pollution, which is created by existing activities and regulated under pollution control licences, and contamination that is the result of historic activity, which falls outside present-day controls. Finally, land pollution or contamination is only part of the challenge of maintaining soil quality: other threats are closely linked to patterns of land use, with significant issues arising in the context of the loss of soils arising from the growth of urbanization of 'greenfield' land, the erosion of soils, and the loss of nutrients caused by agricultural intensification.

In contrast to air and water quality, that of land and soil has been ignored over the last twenty years of growth in environmental regulation. Soil quality has had a relatively low profile, partly because it is not considered to be a matter of high public concern, leading the Royal Commission on Environmental Pollution (RCEP) to suggest that soil protection has been taken 'for granted'.[1] In addition to public apathy, there are technical characteristics that mean that it is much more difficult to come up with a coherent regulatory response to threats to soil. First, there is no clear standard to be met for 'good quality' soil. Different soils have different characteristics and what may be suitable for construction would be unsuitable for growing crops. Secondly, soil is not a common good (unlike air and water), but it can be owned, which means that there are issues of interference with private rights, and difficulties in terms of monitoring and enforcement. Finally, soil is non-renewable, and any damage to soil quantity is long term and difficult to reverse.

The presence of 'contamination' in land does not necessarily lead to harm, whether actual or potential, to the environment or human health. The existence of contamination needs, therefore, to be put into some form of context against which the need to intervene and require clean-up can be assessed. Relevant factors include the nature of the polluting substance, the presence and identity of a 'target' that is being affected by the contamination (for example, humans, nature conservation, or property interests), and the costs and benefits of carrying out clean-up works. It is in this sense that the definition of 'contamination' reflects some of the problems with the definition of 'pollution',[2] in that scientific, economic, and political factors need to be considered in deciding whether any regulatory control is required. In deciding to take action against contamination, the policymaker and the rule maker must identify the point at which contamination poses an unacceptable risk.

Contaminated land and environmental liability

Liability for environmental harm can take many forms. In some cases, the behaviour that causes contamination is a criminal offence; in others, civil liability might arise through nuisance or negligence if damage to a third party were to occur. In some of these situations, the law can require the clean-up and reinstatement of the environment, although the use of voluntary clean-up is widespread. Because of this reliance on voluntary action, many of the statutory clean-up powers are only used as a fallback position if mandatory action is required.

---

1 Royal Commission on Environmental Pollution 19th Report (1996) *Sustainable Use of Soil*, Cm 3165, para. 1.14.
2 See W. Howarth [1992] 56 MLR 171.

For example, in cases in which a criminal offence has been committed, the Environment Agency may negotiate with a polluter in respect of clean-up, with the threat of compulsory action if necessary. Liability for this type of clean-up and reinstatement of contaminated land is a good example of a class of liability that only covers *environmental* harm (as opposed to property damage).

This chapter provides a backdrop to some of the central issues of environmental liability. For example, it is clear that concepts such as the Polluter Pays Principle are not without some difficulty when they are translated into 'real world' rules. Just who is 'the polluter'? What if there is more than one 'polluter'? Should liability be shared equally, proportionately, or should one polluter be made to pay for all? What part should fault play in determining who pays for the consequences of pollution? Should 'polluters' avoid liability if they can demonstrate that they were using 'state of the art' pollution prevention systems or were complying with all relevant legislation when the pollution was caused? At what level should 'contamination' be deemed to become 'harmful' enough to require the intervention of law? Just as the decision about what action to take and when to take it is political (with a small 'p'), so is the decision about who should be made to pay for it. Although the Polluter Pays Principle is the foundation of most of the environmental liability systems that deal with land contamination, the characteristics that distinguish particular types of contamination clarify issues about the principle, such as whether it is based around fairness or blame.

Current contamination vs historical contamination

Overlapping controls

There are many powers available to prevent and remedy the effect of current contamination. In many cases, 'contamination' is synonymous with pollution and the relevant pollution control regimes apply. For example, when contaminating substances migrate into water, water pollution occurs, and the offences and powers of clean-up dealing with water pollution are applicable. Box 16.1 sets out the main statutory provisions that deal with contamination, which are controlled under existing pollution control regimes. The powers that deal with current contamination do not, however, deal with all forms of contamination. Historical contamination caused before the introduction of comprehensive pollution control regimes falls outside many of the continuing controls set out in Box 16.1 (although some can be used in certain circumstances).

These regimes create a web of liability mechanisms with which to deal with environmental harm caused by contamination arising out of current activities. These must be placed alongside instruments that create civil liabilities, and private law mechanisms such as nuisance and negligence. The breadth of these different mechanisms to deal with 'contamination' reflects one of the recurring themes of this book—that is, that there may be more than one available 'tool' with which to deal with an environmental problem, such as contamination, and that the key issue is the selection of the most appropriate tool to respond to any given set of circumstances. In some cases, there may be a combination of measures adopted.

The problems of overlapping controls

These overlaps present two different problems. The first is that there are difficulties of coordination when there are two concurrent powers available to two different regulators. For example, in cases in which pollution of controlled waters is being, or is likely to be, caused from contaminated land, the Environment Agency and the relevant local authority both possess powers to require clean-up—under the Water Resource Act (WRA) 1991, s. 161A and Pt 2A, respectively. There is a memorandum of understanding that governs

BOX 16.1 Powers to control current contamination

Overlapping power	Powers available to deal with contamination	Relevant statutory provisions	Who is responsible for clean-up?	Can a remediation notice be served?	Is contamination a criminal offence?	Other comments
Environmental Permitting	Remedy contamination or harm caused by a breach of an environmental permit related to activities carried on at 'regulated facilities' including installations and waste operations.	Environmental Permitting (England and Wales) Regulations 2007.	The holder of the permit	No (s. 78YB(1))	Yes, where contamination is caused by a breach of a condition of a permit or the implied BAT condition.	Additional powers available to vary, and enforce against conditions of permits, see regs 36, 37, and 42 EP Regs 2007
Unlawfully deposited waste	Require the removal of illegally deposited waste or to remove waste and remedy harm caused	EPA 1990, ss. 59 and 59ZA	The owner or occupier of the land on which waste is unlawfully deposited	No (s. 78YB(3))	Yes, because the waste will have been deposited without a waste management licence (see s. 33, EPA1990)	Arguably, this only applies to waste deposited after 1 April 1994 (i.e. the implementation of the waste management licensing regime) The decision in *Van de Walle* suggests that inadvertent deposits of material (e.g. from leaking pipes) is waste and should therefore be cleaned up under this power (see p. 651)

3 SI 2000/1973.

Overlapping power	Powers available to deal with contamination	Relevant statutory provisions	Who is responsible for clean-up?	Can a remediation notice be served?	Is contamination a criminal offence?	Other comments
Water pollution	Powers to serve a works notice to prevent or clean up contamination if there is or is likely to be pollution of controlled waters	WRA 1991, s. 161–161D	Any person who caused or knowingly permitted the pollution of the controlled waters	Yes	Yes, because it will be causing or knowingly permitting polluting matter to enter controlled waters (see s. 85, WRA 1991)	The powers to serve a works notice and a remediation notice are concurrent. Additional powers available to enforce against breaches of and vary existing discharge consents
Statutory nuisances	Power to abate a statutory nuisance as defined	EPA 1990, ss. 80–81	Any person responsible for the nuisance	Yes	No, only if abatement notice is not complied with within the time limit specified (see s. 80(4), EPA 1990)	If land is in a 'contaminated state', it is excluded from the definition of a statutory nuisance and thus an abatement notice cannot be served
Town and country planning	Power to impose planning conditions to clean up contamination prior to carrying out development. Also breach of condition notice	TCPA 1990, ss. 71(9), 187A	The person responsible for the breach	Yes	Yes, if there has been a breach of a planning condition (e.g. in relation to places of storage) Breach of condition is a criminal offence (see s. 187A, TCPA 1990)	The use of conditions to address contamination and the role of the planning system in helping to clean up contaminated sites is dealt with in Circular 2/2000 and PPS 23
Amenity notices	Power to require steps to be taken to remedy the condition of land that adversely affects the amenity of its area by serving an appropriate notice on the owner or occupier of the land	TCPA 1990, s. 215	Owner/occupier of the land	Yes	No, only if the amenity notice is not complied with (see s. 215, TCPA 1990)	Tends to be used in respect of visual disamenity

how the powers will be used.[3] In summary, in cases in which a site is identified as being contaminated land under Pt 2A, a remediation notice will normally be most appropriate, because it will be the most effective method of ensuring that the 'significant pollution linkage' no longer exists (see below). On the other hand, in those cases in which the source of pollution has completely entered the controlled waters, the works notice powers are likely to be more appropriate, because the site cannot be designated as contaminated land under Pt 2A.

The second problem is the overlap between the powers to clean up unlawfully deposited waste and the Pt 2A powers. The 'British' approach to the problem of contamination from different sources has been to have separate, but parallel, systems of control. In distinguishing between current and historical sources of contamination, the risk-based approach of Pt 2A is different from the strict approaches taken to breaches of licences or other pollution caused by current activities. The European Case C-1/03 *Van der Walle and ors v. Région de Bruxelles-Capitale* [2005] Env LR 24 (see Case 14.5) has, however, cast some doubt on this approach. In that case, the European Court of Justice (ECJ) held that waste oil and petrol that had leaked unintentionally from underground storage tanks in Belgium were waste for the purposes of the Waste Framework Directive (2006/12/EC).[4]

This poses the problem that, if accidental contamination is waste, a risk-based approach to clean-up is insufficient to transpose the requirements of the Waste Framework Directive. Under Pt 2A powers, remediation is only required when there is significant harm and only to the extent necessary to remove that significant harm. This is a much lower standard than that demanded by the Waste Framework Directive, which requires the general prevention of pollution and harm. On the other hand, clean-up powers under waste management legislation available under s. 59 of the Environmental Protection Act (EPA) 1990 are also inadequate, because this power only applies to active deposits or deposits that are knowingly caused or knowingly permitted. In the case of inadvertent leaks or spillages, the element of active participation or knowledge may be absent. Consequently, even with a seemingly complex system of overlapping powers to address both current and historical contamination from waste, there are apparent defects in the transposition of European waste law. It is worth noting that it is presumed that this gap would only apply to 'waste' deposited after 1 May 1994, when the European definition of waste was transposed into UK law under the Waste Management Licensing Regulations 1994.[5] Arguably, historical contamination before that date could be cleaned up under a risk-based approach.

Historical contamination and retrospective liability

One of the distinguishing features of historical contamination as compared to current contamination is the lawfulness of the actions that caused the presence of the contaminative substances. In all cases of current contamination, the actions of the polluter when causing the contamination are unlawful either of themselves or following the administrative action In cases in which contamination arises from acts that were committed lawfully many years ago, any current laws introduced that impose liability (criminal, civil, or statutory) upon the party who caused or permitted the contamination would be retrospective, or retroactive, in effect.

In many circumstances, 'retrospective' and 'retroactive' can, and are, used interchangeably. Occasionally, retroactive can be used in a specific sense to mean weakly retrospective.

---

3 See Local Government Association and Environment Agency (2003) *Working Better Together Protocol Series No 5: Land Contamination.*

4 See p. 651.

5 SI 1994/1056.

This would include liability rules that were in force at the time of the lawful act, but which can apply retrospectively, because there has been a change in the *standards* that trigger the liability. For example, there might be legislation that banned the presence of substance X in water at a certain level. At the time of the act that caused the presence of that substance, the level of the substance was below the statutory limit. In five years' time, the standard may have changed and the level of X may be above the statutory limit. The original legislation may not have had retrospective effect until the standards were changed. In this very specific sense, retroactive liability might be thought of as more legitimate than generally retrospective legislation, because the basis for liability existed before the act even if the trigger standard had evolved after the act.

Retrospective laws can be defined as laws that have effect on actions that took place before the law came into force, for example, by imposing sanctions upon conduct that was lawful when it occurred. There are many fundamental objections to the imposition of retrospective legislation. Morally, those that are subject to a law have a legitimate expectation that they will have some notice of the law, so that they can understand the consequences of their actions and exercise their own judgment about what they intend to do in order to comply with the law at any given time. Politically, retrospective legislation can be used as a tool to punish or reward selectively certain identifiable parties. While it is not unknown in modern environmental legislation,[6] there is still a requirement to have some strong justification for the imposition of retrospective liability.

By its very nature, historical contamination is the consequence of actions that occurred in the past—sometimes, many years distant. In the case of historically contaminated land, the unfairness of retrospective liability is arguably balanced by the need to address the long-term consequences of contamination and the implications for sustainable development should land be left to present environmental problems for many years into the future. The government has introduced a very complex system for allocating liability (or paying) for the clean-up of historically contaminated land. The complexity of the system reflects the government's attempts to balance the need to introduce a comprehensive and efficient system that is designed to clean up as many historically contaminated sites as possible as against the inherent unfairness of a retrospective liability and retroactive standards—that is, imposing trigger standards that have increased.

These 'balancing' features include:

- risk-based criteria for assessing whether land should be identified as 'contaminated';

- rules that give precedence to liability allocation arrangements between private parties;[7]

- exclusion for certain specified classes of parties;

- exclusion in cases in which the allocation of liability would cause hardship.

The European Commission has addressed the unfairness of introducing retrospective legislation by excluding historical contamination from the scope of the Environmental Liability Directive (2004/35/EC). Under Art. 17, all environmental damage caused by substances released into the environment, or actions carried out, before 30 June 2007 is excluded from the scope of liability under the Directive.

---

6 For example, both the End-of-Life Vehicles Directive (2000/53/EC) and the Waste Electrical and Electronic Equipment (WEEE) Directive (2002/96/EC) require producers to recover and recycle items that were put onto the market before the implementation of the Directive.

7 See further Box 16.5.

What is 'contaminated land'?

Although the phrase 'contaminated land' has become something of a term of art, it is far from being clear and precise.[8] Contaminated 'land' is often used as shorthand for contamination in land in relation to which the presence of that contamination may have a harmful impact on other environmental media, including water and even the atmosphere. The presence of contamination poses threats to humans, property, and the wider environment, in the form of explosions caused by the build-up of gases and toxic effects upon health, property, and the wider environment.[9] The key here is that in the absence of such threats, contamination—that is, the presence of alien substances in land—is less likely to be the subject of regulatory intervention.

depends on the harm.

On the one hand, the classification of land as 'contaminated' can have formal significance with legal sanctions; on the other hand, land contamination can have little consequence in terms of environmental harm. The juxtaposition of these two ideas is extremely important, because the use of the phrase 'contaminated land' needs to be assessed very carefully. When the phrase occurs, it requires some further investigation: is it being used in a formal sense to indicate a specific legal consequence, or is it merely being used as a shorthand for saying 'land in which there may be contamination that may or may not give rise to environmental harm or risk of environmental harm'?

The formal classification of land as 'contaminated' may have detrimental consequences in terms of the effective and productive use of resources. These consequences include the effects of blight and stigma that would cover loss in the value of the land and an inability to sell. These phrases can often be interchanged when used in the context of contamination. They are used here, however, to represent two different facets of the same issue. Where there are areas of land that have been subject to potentially contaminative uses, the risk of contamination is often associated with all of the land in that area, regardless of whether it is actually contaminated. This presumption of contamination can have a blighting effect, which can sterilize land that would otherwise be brought into effective use.[10]

There is a slightly different problem with land that has been identified as being contaminated, but which has been subjected to clean-up works. In such cases, the land may continue to be stigmatized with the label of 'contaminated', with the consequence that it, too, may be sterilized in terms of a productive future use.[11] The main issue here is whether such stigma leads to a recoverable loss or damage, for example, where the sale of land falls through because of past contamination that has subsequently been cleaned up.[12]

which wider value repercussions which might make this more likely to end.

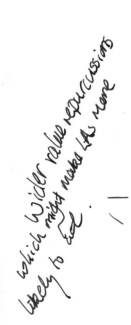

The regulation of historically contaminated land

The introduction of legislation to address the problems caused by historical contamination is relatively recent, reflecting the fact that, in contrast to other areas of pollution control, the problems of soil contamination are comparatively well concealed and the legal issues—particularly in respect of liability for historical contamination—arguably more complex and controversial. Indeed, it was not until the early 1990s that the growing concern about the

---

8 See, e.g., different definitions of the 'contaminated land' in EPA 1990, s. 78A(2) and the NATO Committee on Challenges to a Modern Society.

9 See the Loscoe disaster, as outlined in the Online Resource Centre.

10 See, e.g. M. Lee (1998) Environmental Liability 56.

11 For a good explanation of the problems with stigma damages, see J. Johnson (1996) 15 UCLA J Envtl L & Poly 185, 193.

12 See, e.g., *Blue Circle v. Ministry of Defence* [1999] Env LR 22.

extent and effects of historical contamination led to legislative intervention. Following a series of abortive policy and legislative initiatives, the final version of the legislation provides a complicated system for:

- defining and identifying historically contaminated land;
- prioritizing action to clean up sites that give rise to the greatest risks;
- identifying what works need to be undertaken to deal with those risks;
- allocating and apportioning the cost of carrying out the works among 'appropriate persons';
- for making those 'appropriate persons' carry out those works where necessary.

As such, it provides a very good example of a relatively self-contained system for environmental liability.

The statutory framework in Pt 2A of EPA 1990 sets out the structure of the system to deal with contaminated land. Pt 2A is concerned with:

- identifying land that needs cleaning up;
- deciding how to clean it up;
- determining who is going to do this (or pay for it being done by the regulators).

There is supplementary secondary legislation in the form of the Contaminated Land (England) Regulations 2006,[13] with corresponding regulations in the devolved countries (the references to 'Regulations' in the rest of this chapter refer to the English Regulations). These Regulations deal with certain aspects of the contaminated land regime, including the definition of 'special sites', the detailed arrangements for remediation notices (including content, service, and appeals), and public registers.

In practice, however, the most important elements of the new system are to be found in Circular 2/2006, *Part 2A of the Environmental Protection Act 1990: Contaminated Land*.[14] The circular sets out the context for the operation of the rest of the legislation and provides a general description of how the system operates. It provides detailed guidance on risk assessment, the allocation and apportionment of liability, and the correct approach to the strategic identification of sites.

The statutory definition of contaminated land

The definition of contaminated land is central to the operation of Pt 2A, because it is the trigger for all other procedures to commence. It also reflects the distinction in the liability imposed in relation to historical contamination as distinguished from current sources. Box 16.2 sets out the definition found in s. 78(2). The section distinguishes between contamination that is present in, on, or under land, and contamination that, although present in land, is entering, or likely to enter, into controlled waters. The two categories of contaminated land are defined to reflect the policy of requiring clean-up only when the contamination is causing unacceptable risks to the environment or to human health. Although this definition provides the trigger for the operation of Pt 2A, the statutory phrases are deliberately vague. It should therefore be noted that the statutory definition is meaningless without the backing of the statutory guidance. The importance of the guidance definition is emphasized by the fact that the enforcing authorities are to 'act in accordance with' the guidance on the definition of contaminated land (s. 78R(2)).

---

13 SI 2006/1380.
14 See www.defra.gov.uk/environment/land/contaminated/pdf/circular01–2006.pdf.

[Handwritten marginal note:] should / consider the possibility of cont entering controlled waters. ↳ Obtain plans of water holes or ground water tracks to assess liklihood of cont causing further harm.

> ### BOX 16.2 The definition of contaminated land
>
> 'Contaminated land' is defined by s. 78A(2), EPA 1990, as meaning:
>
> > …any land which appears to the local authority in whose area it is situated to be in such a condition, by reason of substances in, on or under the land, that:
> >
> > (a) significant harm is being caused or there is a significant possibility of such harm being caused; or
> >
> > (b) pollution of controlled waters is being, or is likely to be, caused;[15]
> >
> > and, in determining whether any land appears to be such land, a local authority shall…act in accordance with guidance issued by the Secretary of State…with respect to the manner in which that determination is to be made.
>
> Section 78(4) defines 'harm' as meaning:
>
> > harm to the health of living organisms or other interference with the ecological systems of which they form part and, in the case of man, includes harm to his property.

The definition can be broken down into smaller sub-definitions.

The existence of a pollutant linkage *Under what?*

The guidance fleshes out the statutory definition of 'significant harm and significant possibility' by introducing the concept of the 'pollutant linkage'. A pollutant linkage is formed when there is a linkage between a contaminant and a receptor, or target, such as humans or property, by means of a pathway. If any one aspect is missing, no linkage is formed. For example, if there is contamination, but it is self contained in the ground with no route into the wider environment, there is no pathway and the linkage cannot be formed. If such a linkage is present, it must be 'significant', forming what is known as a 'significant pollutant linkage' (SPL), for the land to come within the definition of 'contaminated land'. Significance is assessed in relation to the types of target that are being harmed by the contamination, the degree or nature of that harm, and the possibility of the harm being caused.

The types of receptor or target

The guidance narrowly defines the types of receptor or target that can form part of the SPL. These are:

- human beings;
- nature conservation sites (which includes all of the sites that are protected under nature conservation laws);
- buildings; — *with value to owners.*
- other property (which covers crops and animals that are subject to property rights, such as livestock).

Anything that is a target which falls outside of these categories—for example, wild animals, nature conservation sites that are not protected under nature conservation laws, or personal property, such as cars—does not fall within Pt 2A.

---

15 This definition is subject to an amendment under the Water Act 2003, which introduces a new second 'limb' to the definition of contaminated land for the purposes of Pt 2A as being where '*significant pollution of controlled waters is being caused or there is a significant possibility of such pollution being caused*': see Water Act, s.105(3)(5). At the time of writing, this amendment has not been brought into force.

The nature of the harm

The guidance provides that, in assessing the significance of the harm, the local authority needs to consider whether the harm caused to the specified receptors falls within specified categories in relation to each of those receptors. For example, in relation to humans, this includes serious injury, birth defects, and impairment of reproductive functions. In relation to nature conservation sites, it includes any harm that results in an irreversible or substantial adverse change to the functioning of the ecosystems that form a substantial part of the site. In relation to property, it includes substantial loss in crop value or substantial damage to buildings.

The possibility of significant harm being caused

In the absence of actual significant harm, the local authority must assess whether there is a significant *possibility* of significant harm being caused. The guidance explains that this should be based on an assessment of the risks involved with the contamination and, in particular, the 'magnitude or consequences' of the different types of significant harm being caused. This is a complicated exercise, which should take account of the nature and degree of the harm, such as an explosion of methane gas or toxic effects on the growth of crops, the susceptibility of the receptors—for example, a nearby school or a building with concrete foundations—and the timescale within which the harm might occur, ranging from imminent, to a period of a hundred years. Putting all of the factors together, the possibility of a methane gas explosion on a site next to a school that could occur imminently could have more significance than a site that is leaching corrosive chemical that might destroy the foundations of a building over a hundred-year period.

When considering the statistical assessment of the possibility of significant harm, the guidance provides that, in all cases other than harm to human health, this is assessed on the balance of probabilities—that is, is it more likely than not to cause significant harm? In cases of harm to human health, the relevant standard is that the risk must be medically 'unacceptable'.

Pollution of controlled waters

The second limb of the statutory definition of contaminated land covers situations in which the pollution of controlled waters is being caused, or is likely to be caused, by the condition of land by reason of substances present in, on, or under it. In such cases, that land is contaminated for the purposes of Pt 2A. 'Pollution of controlled waters' is defined simply as '*the entry into controlled waters of any poisonous, noxious or polluting matter or any solid waste matter*' (s. 78A(9)). The statutory guidance provides that the likelihood of the entry of the contaminant is to be assessed on the balance of probabilities. It should be noted that this definition excludes substances that have entered controlled waters at some time in the past, the entry of which has now ceased and is unlikely to recur (for example, contamination that is caused by past leaks from underground storage tanks, which are currently empty).

Unlike the other limb of 'contaminated land', the statutory definition was not originally risk-based, nor was it fleshed out in guidance, and there have been fears that potentially small amounts of contamination could have triggered the requirement for expensive and potentially disproportionate clean-up on a large number of sites. In order to clarify the situation, s. 86 of the Water Act 2003 amended the definition of 'contaminated land' by requiring that such water pollution was 'significant', with further guidance on what triggers this level of contamination. At the time of writing, this amendment had not been brought into force, with the government position being that time was needed to assess the implications of the implementation of the Water Framework Directive before enacting the amendment.[16]

---

16 Circular 1/2006, Annex 2, para.2.3.

In practice, however, given the small number of determinations of contaminated sites, it would appear as if the original definition has not given rise to the difficulties that had been envisaged.[17]

The identification of contaminated land

Local authorities are under a duty to inspect their areas from time to time for the purposes of identifying:

- contaminated land;
- special sites (s. 78B(1)).

In undertaking this duty, local authorities must 'act in accordance' with the statutory guidance in Circular 1/2006.[18] When identifying contaminated land, a local authority is entitled to take into account the cumulative impact of two or more separate sites when assessing whether there is 'significant harm' or 'pollution of controlled waters'. This will be important in cases in which the 'cocktail' effect of a number of contaminated sites causes significant harm, whereas any individual site will not give rise to any notable pollution (s. 78X(2)). In seeking to identify contaminated land, local authorities may rely upon information from a number of sources, including the owners or occupiers in question—who may have carried out a voluntary investigation of their own land. In cases in which pollution of controlled waters is being caused or the contamination is harming a nature conservation site, the local authority must consult the Environment Agency and Natural England, respectively, and have regard to any comments that they make before making the determination as to whether the land should be designated as 'contaminated land'. In cases in which this information is not sufficient to enable the local authority to identify the land as contaminated, it can carry out an inspection of the land if there is a 'reasonable possibility' that there is a pollutant linkage on the land. For the purposes of the identification duty, local authorities have the same powers of inspection and entry as the Environment Agency has under Environment Act 1995, s. 108.

Special sites

When contaminated land has been identified, local authorities must consider whether the site falls within one of the categories of 'special site' as defined under the Regulations.[19] Special sites are regulated directly by the Environment Agency. The general criteria for special sites are the seriousness of the harm or water pollution that would be, or is being, caused and whether the Environment Agency is more likely to have the expertise to act on those particular sites. For special sites to be designated, the local authority must, first, formally identify the land as contaminated for the purposes of Pt 2A. In practice, however, the Environment Agency has a role to play in the identification of special sites, either in conjunction with the local authority, by carrying out any investigation on behalf of the authority, or on its own account. In cases in which the authority considers that the land should be designated as a special site, it is under a duty to notify the Environment Agency (after seeking its advice), the owner/occupier, and any person who might be responsible for paying the costs of remediation (s. 78C(1)–(3)). The Agency has inspection and entry powers in relation to special sites (s. 78Q). It also has the power to terminate the designation of a special site if it appears to

---

17 See the statistics cited on p. 574.
18 Circular 1/2006, Annex 3, ch. B.
19 The classes of special site are listed in the 2006 Regulations, Sch. 1.

the Agency that it is no longer suitable for designation (s. 78Q(4)), although the land will continue to remain 'contaminated land' as identified by the local authority.

Notification and consultation

Once land has been identified as being contaminated, the local authority is under a duty to notify this fact to all owners, occupiers, people who appear to the local authority to be liable to pay the clean-up costs, and the Environment Agency (s. 78B(3)). In practice, many of those people will already be aware of the potential designation as a result of supplying information as part of the identification process. The notification to the Environment Agency enables it to consider whether the site should be designated as a special site and whether there is any need for site-specific guidance on the level or nature of the clean-up work.

After notification, there follows a period of consultation with the notified parties (s. 78H(1)). This duty does not apply in cases in which it appears to the authority that there is an imminent danger of serious harm or pollution of controlled waters (s. 78G(4) and 78H(4)). There is a minimum period of three months for consultation (before the service of a remediation notice), and the government has expressed the desire that this period be used, at best, to achieve agreement between the enforcing authorities and the persons who are carrying out the remediation, and, at worst, to narrow the areas of disagreement. Indeed, the emphasis on the voluntary nature of this process is formalized, with the preclusion of any further formal action, such as the service of a remediation notice, if a person has undertaken to carry out voluntary remediation works. In cases in which such agreement is reached, the person must describe the works in a 'remediation statement', which is published on the public register (s. 78H(7)).

The second main purpose of the consultation period is to discuss the works that are necessary and, in particular, whether they should be phased or whether a single action might deal with a number of SPLs. For example, digging out contaminated soil and disposing of it might deal with a number of different contaminants that have been caused by different people. Alternatively, the enforcing authority may consider that remediation would not be reasonable, bearing in mind the costs and the benefits—for example, where there were very low levels of water pollution. In such circumstances, the enforcing authority must publish a 'remediation declaration', explaining that no remediation is required notwithstanding the formal identification of the land as contaminated under Pt 2A (s. 78H(6)).

Remediation standards

The two clean-up levels that are most commonly adopted when cleaning up historical contamination refer to the use to which the land is put and the level of clean-up that is required to put the land to such a use without any of the risks associated with the original contamination. On the one hand, the so-called 'multifunctional' approach requires land to be cleaned up to a level so that it is fit for any possible use, including ecological uses; on the other hand, the 'suitable for use' standard is assessed against the current use or during the determination of any permission that is required for a future use. In such cases, the land is cleaned up prior to the commencement of development to a standard that is suitable for the future use. This approach ensures that the action is proportionate and does not have to address possible unknown future risks.

These standards that underpin the legal framework dealing with the clean-up of historically contaminated land need to be viewed in the wider context of the extensive impacts that such contamination has upon sustainable development. For example, identifying the appropriate level for clean-up standards for contaminated land involves questions of policy, science, and economics, which are closely linked to differing interpretations of sustainable development (see Box 16.3).

Although the 'suitable for use' approach is used to deal with historical contamination, there is an exception in situations in which contamination has been caused as a result of activities that are covered by an extant statutory authorization or licence. In those cases in which the relevant statutory provisions provide for a power to order clean-up, the requisite standard is to a reinstatement level—that is, to remove the contamination completely. Of course, in addition to these two general approaches to standard setting, there is the problem of setting the specific levels of contaminants that apply in particular cases.

BOX 16.3 Standard setting for contaminated land and sustainable development

---

In addition to the direct threats to the environment and human health caused by harmful contamination, there are significant consequences in terms of resource depletion. This arises out of the inability to reuse previously developed land and the supplementary increase in pressure to develop greenfield sites. This has to be balanced against the high cost of cleaning up contamination with its knock-on economic effects on an individual, local, regional, and even national scale. What standard should be adopted—multifunctional, 'suitable for use', or some other alternative?

The 'suitable for use' standard has been criticized mainly on the ground that it takes little account of the effect that any contaminants may have upon future development. In its 19th Report, the Royal Commission on Environmental Pollution (RCEP) took the view that the standard had 'serious limitations'—in particular, the way in which a 'cheap' clean-up of land so that it was suitable for open space could leave contaminants in the ground that might sterilize the land for other more sensitive uses and increase the pressure to develop greenfield sites.[20]

Under the 'multifunctional' approach, unnecessary work may be required, which can have significant financial consequences without any proportionate environmental benefits. This reflects some of the experience in the Netherlands, which introduced a multifunctional standard under its Soil Protection Act 1987. At the outset, it was estimated that there were two thousand sites that would need to be cleaned up at a cost of $500m—a target that was achievable within a generation. There were, however, approximately 100,000 contaminated sites, with an estimated total clean-up bill of $50bn. The Dutch government largely met the soaring cost of meeting the multifunctional standard. In the face of such cost, the multifunctional approach was abandoned in 1997.[21]

The RCEP suggested an alternative approach that would adopt the advantages of the two existing standards.[22] In considering both remediation standards and future use of the site, it was suggested that the test of the best practicable environmental option (BPEO) be adopted as a goal. Once established, the highest remediation standards that could be reached without excessive cost should be used, regardless of the use immediately intended after clean-up.

All of these standards reflect some of the central issues of sustainable development. On the one hand, the 'suitable for use' approach reflects a weak version of sustainable development: there is a trade-off between the recycling of 'brown land' as a sustainable resource and the level of costs required to recycle that resource. On the other hand, the multifunctional and BPEO approaches provide slightly 'stronger' versions of sustainable development, in the sense that they aim to maximize environmental improvement with costs being less of a factor. In the final analysis, however, all clean-up standards reflect a strongly anthropocentric version of sustainable development, with

---

20 See RCEP 19th Report (1996).
21 See 'Dutch in policy retreat on contaminated land' (1997) ENDS Report, 269, 46.
22 See RCEP 19th Report (1996).

the emphasis on economic development. For example, a survey of 367 remediation projects carried out between 1996 and 1999 revealed that the vast majority of sites were cleaned up because of the threat to human health and to enable redevelopment, as opposed to ecological reasons or simply to manage pollution.[23]

The nature of remediation works

When determining the most appropriate works required to meet the 'suitable for use' standard, the enforcing authority must apply the best practicable technique for the pollution linkage in question, both to the elimination of any significant pollution linkage and also to the remedying of any harm caused. If elimination is not possible, the standard becomes one of best practicable techniques of reducing the harm and remedying its impact, or at least minimizing its effect. The work may be spread over years to take into account technical or financial considerations. Indeed, it may be the case that a certain technological solution is impossible or unaffordable at the present time and can only be implemented at a later date.

The remediation methods will only be assessed as against the facts of any individual situation, but assessment and ongoing monitoring can be included as 'remediation' alongside preventative and restorative works. In comparing remediation methods, the costs and the benefits of each method must be assessed. This can include environmental, as well as financial, costs. Thus it would be appropriate to consider the environmental costs of dumping contaminated soils in a landfill site as against the financial cost of maintaining *in situ* remediation over a long period. Remediation can include assessment processes to establish the presence of a pollution linkage and actions to eliminate or minimize its impact by removing or treating the pollutant, interrupting the pathway, or protecting the receptor. It is necessary to measure the total costs against the benefits of intervention, and this, itself, involves weighing seriousness of harm or pollution and the remedial or minimizing effects of the works. Seriousness is judged by considering a number of factors relating mainly to the receptor. These include the size of the receptors, their nature and importance (taking into account their existing state), the impact upon them, and whether it would be lasting. Similar factors apply in cases in which the receptor is controlled waters.

Section 78E(4) requires action on the part of the enforcing authority to be reasonable and the guidance requires this also in relation to the cost of the remediation. The test for reasonableness of costs is that there is no alternative remediation scheme that would achieve the same standard for lower costs. Authorities must also take into account whether harm is already being caused (and, if not, its probability) and any wider environmental risks.

The duty to serve a remediation notice

Once land has been identified as contaminated, consultation has taken place between the enforcing authority and the relevant persons, and the relevant remediation works identified, the authority must serve a remediation notice (s. 78E). Although this duty is similar to the duty to serve an abatement notice under the statutory nuisance regime,[24] there are limits to the mandatory nature of the duty. There are a number of situations, however, in which an enforcing authority is precluded from serving a remediation notice.

23 See Environment Agency (2000) *Survey of Remedial Techniques for Land Contamination in England and Wales*, R&D Technical Report P401.

24 See *R v. Carrick District Council, ex parte Shelley* [1996] Env LR 273 and the Online Resource Centre.

BOX 16.4 When is a remediation notice not allowed to be served?

The enforcing authority is specifically precluded from serving a remediation notice in certain circumstances, which include the following.

- **There are other statutory powers that can be used to enforce a clean-up of the land (s. 78YB)**
  The justification for the primacy of these other statutory provisions is that the introduction of Pt 2A was not intended to add to the pre-existing regulatory burden; the policy aim was merely to clarify the law on contamination, rather than to introduce new liabilities.

- **Any requirement to carry out remediation would be unreasonable (s. 78H(5A))**
  This might be, for example, because the costs outweigh the benefits or because the statutory guidance suggests that particular works would be unreasonable. In such cases, a remediation declaration is required (s. 78H(6)).

- **The appropriate person has agreed to undertake voluntary remediation (s. 78H(5)(b))**

- **One of the persons who would be served with a remediation notice would suffer 'hardship' if required to pay for his or her share of any of the costs of remediation (s. 78N(3)(e))**
  'Hardship' is undefined in Pt 2A, and the guidance suggests that it should be determined on a case-by-case basis and having regard to the statutory guidance on the issue.[25] In such cases, the enforcing authority is precluded from serving the notice on *any* of the parties (in cases in which there is more than one party responsible) (s. 78H(5)(d)).

- **The enforcing authority is itself the appropriate person (s. 78H(5)(c))**
  For example, as a result of owning a contaminated site or by being the original polluter.

- **It is considered that there is imminent danger of serious harm or pollution (s. 78N(3)(a))**

- **There is pollution of controlled waters and the only appropriate persons who can be found are owners or occupiers (s. 78J)**

- **After reasonable inquiry, no appropriate person can be found (s. 78N(3)(f))**

If the enforcing authority is precluded from serving a remediation notice, it has a *power* to carry out the works itself and to seek to recover the costs of doing so (if that is possible) from the appropriate persons. The importance of these exceptions cannot be underestimated, because they are wide (particularly in the case of hardship) and shift the regulatory focus from mandatory duties to discretionary powers.

The remediation notice is to be served on the 'appropriate person' and is required to set out what must be done, along with the time period for carrying out the specified steps (s. 78E). In specifying the steps required under a remediation notice, the authority is under a duty to have regard to the statutory guidance and to balance the costs of carrying out the work with the seriousness of the harm or pollution caused (s. 78E(4)). The statutory guidance makes it clear that environmental benefits should be considered in addition to any financial benefits.

Remediation notices

Once the enforcing authority has allocated and apportioned liability, it must serve the remediation notice. Section 78E(1) and reg. 4 make provision for the details that must be included in the notice. The notice should give the recipients a clear picture of:

---

25 Chapter E of the Statutory Guidance.

- the nature of the work;

- who is required to carry it out;

- if there is more than one appropriate person, what proportion of the costs of the work must be borne by each of them;

- by when the work must be carried out;

- the identity of the other appropriate persons;

- the reasons for serving the notice;

- the rights of appeal;

- any other information that can help to clarify any uncertainty.

The allocation of liability—who is liable?

The 'appropriate person'

The issue of the identity of the 'appropriate person' on whom the remediation notice is served is, together with the definition of contaminated land, one of the central elements of Pt 2A.[26] In accordance with the Polluter Pays Principle, the appropriate person is defined as the person, or any of the persons, who caused or knowingly permitted the substances, or any of the substances, that have been the cause of the contamination to be in or under the land (s. 78F(2)). On some interpretations of this section, however, it might be argued that the Polluter Pays Principle is given a wide meaning that would cover a person who brought potentially polluting substances onto land, regardless of whether the substances polluted while under their control. In addition to contamination on the site in which it was originally present, the appropriate person can also be responsible for contamination that has escaped onto other land (s. 78K).

Within the statutory guidance, those appropriate persons who have caused or knowingly permitted the presence of the substances are known as 'Class A persons'. The phrase 'caused or knowingly permitted' is familiar in the context of environmental offences—particularly in relation to water pollution—but great care must be taken in extrapolating the principles in those cases and applying them in the contaminated land context.

BOX 16.5 Who is the polluter? The Polluter Pays Principle in action

Under the provisions concerning liabilities, responsibility for paying for remediation will, where feasible, follow the 'polluter pays' principle. In the first instance, any persons who caused or knowingly permitted the contaminating substances to be in, on or under the land will be the appropriate person(s) to undertake the remediation and meet its costs. However, if it is not possible to find any such person, responsibility will pass to the current owner or occupier of the land.

(Circular 1/2006, Annex 1, para. 37)

Who should pay for the clean-up of contaminated land? In accordance with accepted principles, the government suggests that, where 'feasible', it should be the 'polluter' who pays. But who is the 'polluter'?

---

26 For an excellent overview of the issues, see D. Lawrence and R. Lee (2003) 66 MLR 261.

Under Pt 2A, the assertion of the Polluter Pays Principle is nothing more than shorthand for a complex system of detailed regulatory tests. The principle is much wider than the idea that those with a direct responsibility for a polluting action should pay for the consequences of that pollution. It is a system designed to address the consequences of pollution through economic measures. Its basis lies within economic theory, which suggests that pollution is an unacknowledged cost—that is, the destruction of a collective good—which should be met by those who benefit from the fact that the cost has not been accounted for. This can be most easily understood by the idea of the 'unowned' environment, which is a good that is for the benefit of all. In legal terms, the corollary of the 'unowned' environment is that any harm caused is 'uncompensatable'. The Polluter Pays Principle seeks to attach a value to such common goods and to extract compensation for any harm caused.

When examining the concept by reference to the system of allocating liability for historical contamination, we see that the statutory definition of the 'polluter' found within Pt 2A and which is referred to above illustrates a number of points about the identity of the 'polluter'. First, the polluter is not defined narrowly by reference to intention, blame, or the reason behind the pollution. Generally, when identifying a 'polluter', we might look to direct links between intention and/or a direct link to the pollution. The guidance suggests that strict liability will apply. Going further, the test of 'knowing permission' may include the most peripheral of 'polluters'—for example, a landowner who has turned a blind eye to pollution caused by someone else. In addition, the identification of the 'polluter' is not linked to any explicit idea of punishment. There are criminal sanctions for illegally disposing of waste or of polluting groundwater, so why not simply punish the historical polluter? The Polluter Pays Principle is not concerned with explicit punishment. If this were the case, there would be many 'polluters' under the contaminated land regime who would justifiably feel hard done by, because their 'punishment' would arise out of retroactive legislation.

The key to the pure application of the Polluter Pays Principle is that it is fair and just to apply the principle when the pollution or contamination is a necessary consequence of an activity, even if it was not an intended goal. Thus intention, and even foreseeability, play no part in the application of the principle.

It should also be borne in mind that, in cases in which the principle breaks down—that is, if the actual polluter can no longer be found—the artificiality of the definition is revealed. In such circumstances, an innocent owner or occupier of the land becomes the 'polluter' for the purposes of allocating liability.

'Caused'

Whether a person has 'caused' the presence of contamination should be viewed as a question of fact in each case. Causation could be direct—that is, the person was responsible for placing pollutants in the ground—or indirect—that is, through leaks from equipment. In addition, more than one person could be said to have 'caused' the presence of the contaminant—for example, if a contractor were to dump the operator's waste contaminants on the operator's site, both parties would be appropriate persons. Following the existing case law, liability is strict such that fault, negligence, or knowledge are not required and there are a series of principles, as follows, that might be applied in determining whether causation is present.[27]

(a) Identify the activity that is linked to the presence of the contaminating substance—that is, what did the alleged appropriate person do to cause the presence of the substance?

27 Ibid.

This action and/or activity need not necessarily be linked directly to the immediate presence of the substances. Thus 'activities', such as the storage of materials and the maintenance of equipment, could amount to causation if the presence of the substance arose from leaking pipes or underground storage tanks.

(b) Was this action or activity a cause of the presence of the substance? This need not be the sole or direct cause, but simply part of a bigger picture of activities that have led to the presence of the contamination in the land. For example, if substances have been released as a result of vandalism to a storage tank, the activity of storage would be a cause, along with the vandalism.

(c) If an intervening act or event was directly connected to the causation of the presence of the substance in the land—that is, through the acts of a third party or natural event—was that act or event a normal fact of everyday life, or something extraordinary? Ordinary events will not break the causal chain between the appropriate person's activities and the presence of the substance, but whether something is extraordinary is a question of fact. Examples of ordinary activities or events have included vandalism and cracks in pipe work.[28]

[handwritten margin note: ← possible break in the chain of causation]

In practice, in most cases in which contamination is found on a site, there would be a rebuttable presumption—that is, it would be assumed unless the contrary could be proved—that the operator/occupier of the site at the time of the contamination had caused the presence of the pollutant. The presumption would be particularly strong in cases in which it could be demonstrated that the operator/occupier had generated or used the substances in question.

The preceding discussion is based upon the premise that the water pollution cases are a clear guide to the interpretation of 'causing' in the context of contaminated land cases. There might, however, be arguments that could be put forward to justify a distinction between the strictness of the liability for causing environmental criminal offences, in which the strictness is mitigated by varying the punishment to reflect the blameworthiness of the defendant, and that for causing historic contamination, in which the financial 'penalty' is fixed and potentially much more significant than any fine. The counter to these arguments would be that the statutory regime has other mechanisms for promoting fairness, such as the exclusion tests and the 'hardship' exemption, and that the policy aims behind the legislation would be defeated should 'innocent' parties be allowed to escape liability on the basis of their lack of fault.[29]

'Knowingly permitted'

The definition of 'knowingly permitted' raises more complex issues than under the 'caused' limb. Parliament has suggested, and the High Court has accepted, that 'knowing permission' requires both knowledge that the substances were in, on, or under the land and the existence of a power to prevent that presence.[30] Subsequent case law suggests that there must be direct evidence of actual knowledge of the presence of the substance; it is insufficient to infer such knowledge from the circumstances.[31] This is a restricted interpretation, suggesting that establishing actual knowledge requires direct evidence, which is not always obtainable.[32] But the severity of the requirement of actual knowledge is mitigated somewhat by the finding that it is knowledge of the presence of the substance that is required and not the knowledge of 'contamination'. For example, land could be transferred through a number of ownerships,

---

28 See pp. 610 and 611.

29 An argument reflected in the different decisions in the Court of Appeal and the House of Lords in *National Grid Gas Co. v. Environment Agency* (2006) Env LR 49 and (2007) 3 All ER 877, respectively.

30 Hansard, HL vol. 560, col. 1445.

31 *Circular Facilities v. Sevenoaks District Council* [2005] EWHC 865 and Case 16.1.

32 The severity of the consequences of the *Circular Facilities* case has been criticized as making the operation of Pt 2A potentially less effective: see V. Fogelman [2005] JPL 1269.

with each owner knowing that a substance had been stored on the land at some time in the past (for example, in underground storage tanks). The determining factor, in terms of knowledge, would be the presence of the substance, regardless of whether it was safely contained in the storage tank.

CASE 16.1 **The evidence required for 'knowledge'**—*Circular Facilities (London) Ltd v. Sevenoaks District Council* [2005] EWHC 865

Waste disposal of inert waste took place on land in Kent in the 1960s and 1970s. Subsequently planning permission to develop the land was granted in 1977. In 1978, the then owner commissioned a soil investigation report that identified certain contaminants in the land. In November 1978, the land was transferred to a small development company: Circular Facilities Ltd. Development of the land for residential purposes took place in 1980. As part of that development, Circular Facilities sent a copy of the soil investigation report to the local planning authority. All houses on the development were sold by the end of 1985. In 2002, the local authority identified the land as 'contaminated land' under Pt 2A. The authority served a remediation notice on Circular Facilities on the basis that it knowingly permitted the presence of the contaminants. This knowledge was to be inferred from the act of submitting the soil investigation report to the local planning authority in 1980.

Having lost the appeal against the remediation notice, Circular Facilities appealed to the High Court, arguing that the evidence did not support the allegation that it 'knew' of the presence of the contaminants. The High Court held that the mere existence of the soil investigation report on the planning register was insufficient to impute knowledge of the contents of the report to Circular Facilities. No attempt had been made to ascertain whether individuals such as the managing director of Circular Facilities (as the controlling mind) actually knew of the contamination. The absence of any direct evidence of knowledge was fatal. The case also suggests that a person need only have knowledge of a substance and need not be aware of the possibility that a chemical reaction or process could lead to the land being contaminated. Thus there did not have to be knowledge of the potential harm to which the presence of the substance in the soil could give rise.[33]

Although there is case law on the definition of 'permitting' in relation to regulatory matters, most of it relates to one-off incidents, such as permitting the entry of polluting matter into controlled waters. Permission in this context is generally a positive act, in the sense that involves some form of explicit or implied consent for the thing to be done. The *presence* of substances, on the other hand, is a continuing state of affairs within which permission may be assumed from a failure to address the presence of the pollutant. As in the example above, this could arise from ownership of land and knowledge of the presence of substances, regardless of a positive permission.

Owners and occupiers

In cases in which the owner or the occupier of the land is not a Class A person, he or she can only be the appropriate person if no Class A person can be 'found' after reasonable inquiry (s. 78F(4)). In these circumstances, owners and occupiers are known as 'Class B' persons for the purposes of the statutory guidance. 'Found' in this context would not include people who had died or companies that had ceased to exist. There are situations in which owners/occupiers could fall within both Class A and Class B, should they be responsible for the presence of some, but not all, of the substances on the land (as a Class A person) and if the parties who are responsible for the residual contamination cannot be found (as a Class B person). One

---

33 Compare the position in relation to waste deposits and constructive knowledge, see p. 659.

final important point to note is that Class B persons cannot be served with a remediation notice in respect of works relating to pollution of controlled waters or in respect of contamination that has escaped from other land onto their land, other than remediation in respect of land or water that they own or occupy (ss. 78J and 78K(3), (4), respectively).

'Owner' is defined in s. 78A as being the person entitled to receive a market rent (as opposed to a token, or 'peppercorn', rent) for the property. It specifically excludes mortgagees not in possession, which means that lenders can receive remediation notices if they are mortgagees in possession. Insolvency practitioners are also protected from personal liability unless the contamination is attributable to their own negligence (s. 78X(3)). 'Occupier' is not defined.

Contamination, successors in title, and statutory successors

The practical issues that arise as a result of long sequences of occupation and ownership of contaminated sites further complicate the interpretation of 'causing' and 'knowingly permitting'. These sequences may have involved transfers of ownership within company structures, changes of corporate identities, and companies that are in liquidation or have been wound up. Public bodies, such as local authorities, National Health Service (NHS) Trusts, or the utilities (water, gas, electricity) may have undertaken activities that caused contamination, but may have been reorganized, nationalized, or privatized—or, most likely, all three. Many of these companies are likely to have been involved in activities that could give rise to contamination. As an example, local authorities had historical operational responsibilities for waste disposal, which was largely unregulated.

Under company law, new, separate corporate entities are seen as different 'persons' with potentially different liabilities as 'appropriate persons' under Pt 2A. Thus, 'X Co.' in 1948 might be considered to be a different 'person' from 'Z Co.' in 2007. Moreover, it is quite common for *public* bodies to have schemes by which assets and liabilities are transferred between the old and new companies or bodies. One of the problems is that such schemes tended to transfer liabilities that existed at the date of transfer. As a consequence of the retrospective nature of Pt 2A, the liability for remediation question would not have existed. Thus, on normal principles, the liability would not transfer to the new body and because the original body had ceased to exist no party would be responsible for paying for remediation. On the other hand, the purposes of the legislation would be undermined if the creation of new 'persons' meant that the statutory successors avoided liability.

cf Crest Nicholson case

→ 85%.

15% split.

> CASE 16.2 **Protecting 'Sid'—the position of statutory successors—***R (on the application of National Grid Gas plc, formerly Transco plc) v. Environment Agency* [2008] Env LR 4

The Environment Agency sought to identify contaminated land on a housing development on a former gasworks site. National Grid was a statutory successor to a series of gas companies both public and private (including British Gas and Transco), and was considered to be a 'causer' of contamination on the basis of being a successor to the bodies that had caused the original contamination. National Grid argued that it was not a 'causer' and that, at the time that the liabilities were transferred between previous bodies, there had been no liability in existence. The High Court held that Pt 2A should be interpreted purposively. It had been Parliament's intention to allocate primary responsibility for the remediation of contaminated land on the original polluters in the form of causers and knowing permitters, rather than 'innocent' owners or the public purse. The only way of giving effect to this intention was to include statutory successors, as well as the original polluter, within Class A polluters.

National Grid appealed directly to the House of Lords, which accepted the appeal as being on a point of public importance. The Lords overturned the High Court decision, finding that it was impossible to construe the statutory definitions in a way that would make National Grid a 'polluter'. In doing so, the Lords took a very narrow interpretation of who was a 'causer or knowing permitter'. The underlying issue of the unfairness of retrospective liability seems to have played a part in the decision with the Lords. They held that very careful statutory language would be needed to impose any liability to clean up contaminated land on an 'innocent' company that had never owned nor had an interest in the land in question. The argument relied on by the Lords was that to make National Grid liable for the remediation would falsify the basis on which the investing public had been invited to subscribe for shares in British Gas plc—a statutory predecessor. The general public who had invested in British Gas—memorably advertised with the slogan 'If you see Sid, tell him'—was entitled to rely upon the fact that any liabilities of the new company were limited to those existing immediately before the date of transfer. The Lords considered that it was 'extraordinary' that a public body such as the Environment Agency should seek to impose a liability on a private company and thereby to reduce the value of the investment held by its shareholders.

This decision seems to ignore the obvious point that, in construing Pt 2A narrowly, there is no recognition of the fact that, in the absence of an original polluter, some 'innocent' party will pick up the cost of cleaning up, whether that be an owner/occupier or the general public. While it is restricted to the specific statutory liability transfer regime applicable to the gas industry, the rejection of a purposive, expansive construction of the identity of the polluter might be significant in other determinations.

Allocation of liability—other stages

The identification of the potential appropriate persons is an integral part of the notification of the identification of contaminated land under Pt 2A. This is, however, only one stage of the process of allocating liability for the clean-up of historically contaminated land. The other significant stages in the process include the following.

Forming liability groups

First, the enforcing authority must identify the number of different pollutants that are giving rise to significant harm, etc., via a pollutant linkage. This could be a single pollutant—with one SPL—or a number of different pollutants—with corresponding numbers of SPLs. The enforcing authorities must then identify those parties who caused or knowingly permitted the presence of the contaminant as Class A persons linked to each SPL. This group is referred to as the Class A liability group in relation to each SPL. Alternatively, in the absence of Class A persons in relation to any SPL, the owners/occupiers of the land form what is known as the Class B liability group in relation to that SPL. Thus, areas of contaminated land might have different substances that form different SPLs, in relation to which either some, or all, of the persons who caused or knowingly permitted the presence of the substance can be found—thereby forming Class A liability groups—or, in cases in which none of the Class A persons can be found, the owners and occupiers of the land on which the SPL is found form the Class B liability group.

Applying the exclusion tests

If a liability group has two or more members, the enforcing authority is obliged to apply a series of 'exclusion tests'. These tests exclude appropriate persons from liability and are applied in a specific order, and seek to exclude what might be perceived to be categories of appropriate persons who might appear to be less blameworthy. Thus, in cases in which there are large liability groups, the tests seek to differentiate between different causers and permitters. The rationale behind the exclusion tests would seem to be to mitigate any unfairness inherent in a system based upon strict and retrospective liability. The main flaw in this rationale is that the tests might, in certain circumstances, operate to increase the unfairness if liability groups are small.

There are six main tests for excluding Class A liability group members, which can be grouped under three headings.

- The first test excludes all of those persons who have Class A liability solely by reason of carrying out certain specified activities, including providing financial assistance, such as lending money, underwriting insurance, being a landlord in a case in which the tenant has caused the pollution, and providing technical, legal, or scientific advice.

- The second group of tests excludes parties who have transferred the responsibility for the contamination either by reducing the price of the land in question to reflect the condition of the land or by selling the land with information on the condition of the land, such that it is reasonable to expect that the purchaser of the land should pay for the clean-up of the land.

- The last group of tests excludes parties who are less blameworthy as a result of a change in circumstances from the date at which the substance was originally in, on, or under the land. These include harmful changes to the original substance brought about by the unforeseeable introduction of later substances, new activities that have caused the substances to escape from the original land, and the introduction of new developments that cause the creation of an SPL.[34]

The details of the exclusion tests are set out in Box 16.6.

Class B exclusion is much simpler, excluding only occupiers and tenants paying a market rent. These parties are excluded on the basis that they have no interest in the long-term value of the land and therefore will not benefit from any increase in the value should it be cleaned up.

There are a number of general rules that apply to all of the tests.

1. The rules cannot exclude parties if the result would be to exclude all of the liability group.

2. Exclusion is only referable to the specified liability group and not across all liability groups. Thus an appropriate person may be excluded from one group, but not necessarily from another.

3. The tests must be applied in numerical order.

4. If members of liability groups have reached a private agreement on the basis upon which liability should be allocated between them and a copy of the agreement has been provided to the enforcing authority, the authority must allocate and apportion any liability on the basis of that agreement, in relation to the parties to the agreement alone. For example, a buyer of land might agree to pay for any future liabilities that would be allocated to the seller of the land in return for a slightly reduced price. Any liabilities allocated to other appropriate persons would not fall within this agreement. A private agreement can be disregarded if it would have the effect of transferring liabilities to a person who would suffer hardship, on the basis that, in these circumstances, the enforcing authority would be precluded from serving a remediation notice and private agreements could be drafted as a liability avoidance mechanism.

5. The financial circumstances of the parties are disregarded when carrying out the exclusion tests. This avoids the problems of the so-called 'deep pockets' discrimination, under which the enforcing authority targets only those who can afford to pay.

6. If two or more of the persons within the liability group are part of the same group of companies, they are treated as a single person.

---

34 The *Circular Facilities* decision shows how the exclusion tests work in practice. The original polluter who had dumped the waste in the first place was excluded, on the basis that Circular Facilities had introduced a new receptor—namely, the housing development (see Case 16.1).

BOX 16.6 The exclusion tests

CLASS A PARTIES

Name	Who is excluded?	To what does the test apply?	Other comments
Test 1 'Excluded activities'	Person carrying out the 'excluded activity'	Excluded activities include: • lending to, insuring, advising, licensing, consenting to the activities of, or leasing land to another Class A party; • consigning waste to another person (whether or not that person can be found) if that other person took a contractual responsibility for disposing of the waste or the management of the site on which it was disposed; • being employed as a contractor if any actions or omissions that led to the presence of the contaminative substance were carried out in accordance with the contract.	Exclusion applies only if person caused or knowingly permitted the presence of the contaminative substance solely by reason of performing the excluded activity
Test 2 'Payments made for remediation'	Any person making a 'payment for remediation'	If a payment is made for remediation to be carried out and that remediation has not been carried out A payment can be made: • voluntarily in response to a claim for the costs of remediation; • to meet a contractual obligation to pay; • to settle a legal claim; • to meet a court order; • as part of a sale of land even if the 'payment' is a reduction of the price to reflect the cost of remediation, as long as the contract reflects this explicitly	Exclusion only applies if the excluded person has no further control over the land in question (e.g. by retaining a contractual right to supervise works or a reversion after the expiry of a long lease)
Test 3 'Sold with information'	Seller of land for which the buyer is made aware of any pollutant that forms a SPL	If: • it is prior to the sale becoming binding; • there is an 'arm's length' sale of land to another liability group member (the buyer);	Only applies to the sale of the freehold or long leases (>21 years) The seller must not retain any interest or rights over the land

Name	Who is excluded?	To what does the test apply?	Other comments
		• the buyer has sufficient information that would reason-ably allow that particular person to be aware of the 'broad measure' of a pollutant in any SPL; • the seller did nothing to misrepresent the implications of the presence.	Since 1990, if the buyer is a large commercial organization or public body, permission from seller to allow the buyer to undertake investigations is normally sufficient to indicate that the buyer has information
Test 4 'Changes to substances'	Class A person for whom the presence of the substance has only created an SPL because of interaction with another substance introduced by another person at a later date	If a substance has become 'significant' by reason of a change (physical, chemical, biological, or other) brought about by the introduction of a later substance	It was not reasonably foreseeable that the later substance would be introduced or that the change would occur, and that reasonable precautions were taken to prevent the introduction of the later substances Once the change has occurred, the Class A person must not: • allow any more of the original substance to enter the land; • do anything to contribute to the change; • fail to take reasonable steps to prevent the change happening.
Test 5 'Escaped substances'	Class A person for whom land has become contaminated as a result of the escape of substances from other land	If the escape is the responsibility of another liability group member	
Test 6 'Introduction of pathways or receptors'	Class A person for whom SPL is formed solely because of a subsequent introduction of a new pathway or receptor	If a substance is made into an SPL solely because of the effect of actions subsequent to the introduction of the substance that introduces new receptors or targets	Only applies to 'development' for the purposes of town and country planning legislation, or failure to take a step to prevent the creation of a receptor or pathway, or unreasonable failure to maintain or operate a risk management system used to prevent creation of new SPL

CLASS B PARTIES

Name	Who is excluded?	To what does the test apply?	Other comments
	Occupiers and tenants who pay a full market rent for the land		Excludes all of those who do not have a capital interest in the land in question, i.e. those who could not recover the costs of remediation in the enhanced value of the land on sale

BOX 16.7 The privatization of environmental liability

One of the interesting features of the exclusion tests is the way in which, by use of policy and statutory guidance, the government has effectively privatized large elements of environmental liability. Most statutory liability schemes identify clearly the polluter, who is liable to pay. Contractual provisions—known as indemnities—agreed between private parties, such as the buyer and seller of companies or land, can seek to allocate sums of money to pay for any environmental liabilities imposed by statute as between the parties. That agreement does not, however, affect the primary liability, because the statutory enforcing authority seeks to recover costs from the polluter identified within the statute.[35]

In the case of Pt 2A, the enforcing authority is obliged to give effect to private agreements and/or to exclude parties under various tests that are not necessarily clear or straightforward.[36] In effect, a private agreement made between a buyer and seller of contaminated land changes the definition of 'polluter' for the purposes of the statutory definition. The rationale for privatizing the liability system through giving effect to private agreements and applying exclusion tests is that it is allowing the market to negotiate the transfer of liability at a cost, normally reflected in the reduced value of contaminated land. This is designed to mitigate the inherent unfairness of the statutory scheme by allowing private parties to agree to allocate and apportion the liabilities between themselves. It is also designed to introduce a degree of certainty into the allocation of liability so that the parties may share out the potential risk within the transaction itself.

While such a system is interesting for lawyers and no doubt creates a vehicle for sharing liability so that the market can have a degree of confidence in the application of the liability model, it has the disadvantage of creating a system of 'rules within rules' that makes the whole system incredibly complex. Complex legislation is not, of itself, a bad thing: many of the issues that had to be addressed in Pt 2A are not without difficulty and simplistic regulation would merely have caused greater problems than those that it solved. Accordingly, the combination of a scheme that imposes retrospective liability for historical pollution needs to be carefully drafted in order to avoid injustice. In addition, the science and economics of land remediation are not necessarily straightforward, and no amount of legislative language can spell out the detail required to address these sorts of issue. But there are large parts of the statutory guidance that appear to have been drafted in order to complicate and obfuscate. While certainty in environmental legislation is always desirable, there are always going to be some 'unknowables', and the layering of complex rules, such as in the case of contaminated land legislation, merely serves to identify different and equally complicated issues.

Apportionment of liability

Once the exclusion tests have been carried out and the liability groups finalized, the enforcing authority must determine how much of the costs of carrying out the remedial works should be apportioned to each appropriate person. In general terms, the starting point is that liability should be apportioned on the basis of relative responsibility of each of the group members for creating or continuing the risk caused by the SPL. This might be related to the extent of time of occupation of the land or the use of a substance. In the absence of reasonable

---

35 For a good example of this, see *Eastern Counties Leather plc v. Eastern Counties Leather Group Ltd* [2003] Env LR 13.

36 For example, Tests 2 and 3 deal with transfers of liability as arranged by private organizations.

information upon which to base such an assessment of responsibility, the enforcing authority should apportion the costs equally between the group members.

Appeals

Any person who is the recipient of a remediation notice has the right of appeal to the Secretary of State within 21 days of the service of the notice (s. 78L(1)).[37] To put this apparently short time into context, the service of a remediation notice must be preceded by a three-month minimum consultation period, so the service of a notice should not come as a shock (s. 78H). As originally drafted, there was a division between appeals against remediation notices served by local authorities, which were heard by the local magistrates' court, and those served by the Environment Agency, which were heard by the Secretary of State. This distinction has been criticized as unjustifiable, and the single appeal route was introduced in the Clean Neighbourhoods and Environment Act 2005.[38]

Regulation 7 of the 2006 Regulations sets out the 19 main grounds of appeal. In summary, these cover such things as whether the land is 'contaminated land' for the purposes of Pt 2A, whether the appellant is an appropriate person, whether the appellant should have been excluded from the relevant liability group, whether the enforcing authority was precluded from serving a remediation notice, whether the requirements of the notice were reasonable, and whether the enforcing authority has acted in accordance with the statutory guidance.

An appeal suspends the operation of the notice until the determination or withdrawal of the appeal (reg. 12). First, the Secretary of State may hold a public inquiry (reg. 9(1)), at which third parties are able to make representations. Secondly, the Secretary of State may delegate the decision to the Planning Inspectorate. Inspectors appointed may be technically qualified and may be assisted by assessors with experience in contaminated land issues. Costs in relation to special site appeals will not be awarded in written representation appeals and in other cases—that is, in hearings and inquiries—except if there has been unreasonable behaviour on behalf of one of the parties, which has led to unnecessary expense.

Compliance with a remediation notice

After 21 days from the date of service of the notice, there are two possible outcomes. If the notice is complied with—the first possible outcome—it may be necessary to serve an additional remediation notice if it becomes clear, as a result of complying with the original notice, that further or different works are required.

Alternatively, the works may be sufficient to address the risks brought about by the SPL. Although there is no formal procedure for declassifying the land as 'contaminated', the enforcing authority must enter the details of the remediation carried out on the public register and it may confirm that no further enforcement action is anticipated.

Non-compliance with a remediation notice

The second possible outcome after the service of a remediation notice is that it is either not complied with, or is only partially complied with. It is an offence to fail to comply with a remediation notice without reasonable excuse (s. 78M). There are, however, only relatively minor penalties for this offence, which undermines the deterrence factor. The offence can only be tried in the magistrates' court. In cases in which the contaminated land is currently

---

37 NB This would not include someone who has been served a copy of the remediation notice (for example, the owner/occupier), whose only remedy would be by way of judicial review.

38 See Clean Neighbourhoods and Environment Act 2005, s. 104, and Contaminated Land (England) Regulations 2006, SI 2006/1380, reg. 2.

industrial, trade, or business premises, the maximum penalty is a fine of £20,000, with a further daily fine of up to £2,000 for every day before the enforcing authority has carried out any remediation (s. 78M(4)).

In cases of other contaminated land, the maximum fine is £5,000, with a maximum daily fine of £500 (s. 78M(3)).

The relevant authority has the power to carry out remediation works in cases in which the recipient of the remediation has failed to comply either with or without the appropriate person's agreement (s. 78N). The Agency has the power to recover all, or part, of its reasonable costs (s. 78P). In recovering costs, regard must be had to any hardship that the cost recovery might impose. In England and Wales, the relevant authority also has the power to serve a charging notice on the owner, which will constitute a charge on the premises that consists of, or includes, the contaminated land in question. The costs of any charge may be paid by instalments over a maximum 30-year period. A person served with the charging notice has a right of appeal, which must be made to the county court within 21 days of the receipt of the notice (s. 78P(8)).

Registers

Each enforcing authority is required to keep a public register of information in relation to Pt 2A (s. 78R). Schedule 3 to the Regulations sets out the details of the information that is to be kept on the register. These include particulars of remediation statements, remediation declarations, and remediation notices, appeals, convictions, notices in relation to special sites, and information about remediation work notified to the authority (although there is no official guarantee of compliance with remediation notices) (s. 78R3)).

Contaminated land and the market

In all of the complexity of Pt 2A, and the accompanying Regulations and guidance, it is sometimes easy to forget that the aim of the legislation is relatively simple to understand. In cases in which there are unacceptable risks to human health or the environment, there is an associated cost of clean-up that is required to minimize or remove that risk. That cost has to be met by somebody, whether that is the original polluter, the owner of the land, or the taxpayer. In the alternative, the cost is met by those living in close proximity to the land, and the habitats and resources that are affected by the contamination.

In many cases of contaminated land, the real focus is not on the operation of cumbersome rules of liability allocation and apportionment, but on creative ways of financing the cost of clean-up. The lengthy periods of consultation and, critically, the ban on the service of a remediation notice in cases in which voluntary action has been offered illustrate the point that the whole philosophy underpinning the new regime is that remedial action should generally be voluntary. In this sense, the role of the property market is paramount, because voluntary remediation is likely to take place if there are financial incentives, typically arising from the redevelopment of the land. Thus the planning system is to be at the forefront of tackling land contamination issues, with the Pt 2A powers kept in reserve for when the voluntary or development-led approach has failed.

Accordingly, the planning system is intended to complement the contaminated land regime under Pt 2A of EPA 1990. As stated above, Pt 2A only covers the existing use of land and so issues regarding contamination in relation to future uses of land will generally fall to the planning system to resolve, because the remediation of contaminated land will be promoted through the planning system, even if the site is identified as 'contaminated land' under Pt 2A. With regard to the operation of Pt 2A, the 'suitable for use' policy uses the development control context to set the boundaries for liability. The other side of this, of course, is that development unlocks new potential liabilities, by changing the context for the 'suitable for use' assessment. For example, any harm that may arise in respect of a site may be satisfactorily dealt with if the use is as a car park, but redevelopment for a residential use may introduce new pathways and receptors, so that new remediation requirements and liabilities may arise. Although planning conditions or obligations might deal with this, the new regime could operate to impose new liabilities on the original polluters and, even if not used directly, is likely to play a significant background role.

Finally, one aim of Pt 2A is to support the wider policy objective of recycling previously developed (although not necessarily contaminated) land—that is, the national target for 60 per cent of new development to take place on brownfield sites.

60% New development – Brownfield.

Part 2A in practice

Between April 2000 and July 2007, there were 538 determinations of contaminated land by local authorities and 29 special sites designated.[39] These figures are somewhat misleading, in that they include multiple determinations in relation to single sites. In truth, local authorities have only identified about 15 sites per annum. In total, only five remediation notices have been served.

Why has there been so little action? Like Pt 2A itself, the reasons are complex and overlapping. Is it possible that there is not as much contaminated land around as was first thought? There is an oft-quoted figure of 100,000 sites that are affected by contamination to some degree in England and Wales.[40] Of these, it is further estimated that between 5 and 20 per cent may require intervention to deal with the sort of harm that Pt 2A addresses. This would suggest that there is anything between 5,000 and 20,000 sites in England and Wales that are giving rise to unacceptable harm that requires regulatory intervention. But even this estimate is meaningless. One of the difficulties with the statutory definition of contaminated land found in Pt 2A is that, while it sets out very narrow parameters, the element of risk assessment involved in the formal determination is such that definitive figures are elusive. The more simplistic route of generic indicators of contamination through links with historic use of land was abandoned in the early 1990s, with the rejection of the ill-fated Register of Contaminative Uses under the now repealed s. 143 of EPA 1990. Individual assessment is lengthy and complicated, and we are unlikely ever to get a totally accurate figure for the amount of contaminated land in the UK.

There are, however, a number of inherent characteristics of the statutory regime that make it less likely that the provisions will be used in an effective manner—that is, to identify and clean up sites that pose a significant risk of harm. The key question to pose is whether Pt 2A is working—and the answer depends largely upon the context within which Pt 2A is framed. Just as the number of prosecutions under s. 85 of the WRA 1991 is not necessarily an indicator of water quality, regulatory action under Pt 2A is only part of the story. As this chapter tries to illustrate, Pt 2A is really the 'last-gasp' mechanism with which to deal with contamination. Continuing controls and the redevelopment of contaminated land are the most obvious mechanisms for dealing with contamination, and these are not reflected fully in the figures dealing with determinations and remediation notices.

39 See www.defra.gov.uk/environment/land/contaminated/faq.htm.
40 Environment Agency (2002) *The State of Contaminated Land.*

CHAPTER SUMMARY

1 Contamination is not synonymous with environmental harm. The key issues in designing laws to clean up contaminated land are the level at which 'contamination' is deemed to become harmful enough to require the intervention of law and who should be required to clean it up.

2 A distinction can be made between contamination arising out of current activities (regulated or otherwise) and historical activities. Care needs to be taken when regulating the latter type of contamination, because the imposition of retrospective legislation is inherently unfair.

3 Contaminated land has a very specific meaning in relation to historical activities. This is based around the presence of substances in, on, or under land that are giving rise to significant harm or the significant risk of significant harm.

4 The legislation dealing with the clean-up of historically contaminated land is found in Pt 2A of the Environmental Protection Act 1990. This, along with secondary legislation and statutory guidance, sets out how contaminated land is to be identified, how it will be cleaned up, and who will pay for that clean-up. The legislation is complex and evidence suggests that it has been used sparingly in practice.

5 The allocation of liability for historically contaminated land is said to be based upon the Polluter Pays Principle—that is, the person who caused or knowingly permitted the presence of the contaminating substances. In practice, however, the 'polluter' can be many different people, including the innocent owner or occupier of the land.

6 There are various methods by which the inherent unfairness of the retrospective liability of the contaminated land provisions is mitigated. The most significant of these is that voluntary action to clean up land will preclude the operation of the provisions. In addition, certain tests operate to exclude parties who are less blameworthy.

7 Voluntary remediation is most likely to take place where there are financial incentives, typically arising from the redevelopment of contaminated land. Thus the planning system plays an important role in addressing contamination, with the Pt 2A powers kept in reserve for cases in which the voluntary or development-led approach fails.

Q QUESTIONS

1 Do you think that the implementation of Pt 2A of the Environmental Protection Act 1990 was an effective method of dealing with historically contaminated land? What elements do you think are more effective and which are less?

2 What type of regulatory instrument(s) can be found under the system of liability under Pt 2A? What other regulatory instruments might be used?

3 How does the planning system operate as a market mechanism with which to deal with the costs of cleaning up contaminated land?

4 A site that has recently been designated as contaminated land under Pt 2A of the Environmental Protection Act 1990 was first developed as an engineering factory in the late 1950s. It was owned and operated by Hobblers Ltd until 1978. At that time, Acme Engineering bought Hobblers. In 1982, Acme went into liquidation and a receiver ran the site for a six-month period. Subsequently, the receiver sold the land to a chemical company called Truchem. In 1989, Truchem undertook a survey of the land prior to sale.

The site was eventually sold in 1994 to Polluto. When Truchem sold to Polluto, it did not say anything about the survey of the land carried out in 1989. It did, however, stress that the transaction was to be viewed as 'sold as seen' and reduced the price below the market value to reflect the fact that it was polluted to some extent. Polluto did not carry out any survey of the property. Polluto sold the site to Green Inc. six months ago. Subsequently, Polluto has got into financial trouble and is on the verge of closing its operations in the UK.

Recent investigations have revealed that chemicals have been leaking from faulty underground storage tanks that were negligently installed by Fix-It Ltd, employed as contractors in 1969. Each occupier of the site, up to and including Polluto, used these tanks. Green Inc. has not used the tanks.

Who can be served with a remediation notice?

 FURTHER READING

Contaminated land is a specialist area and this is reflected in the relative paucity of the academic writing on the subject. The starting point for any understanding of the contaminated land regime is the Department of the Environment Transport and the Regions (DETR) Circular 2/2000, which provides as clear a picture as possible (given the complexity of the provisions) of the way in which the law should work in practice. On wider issues related to contaminated land, there is one work that stands head and shoulders above the rest: S. Tromans and R. Turrell-Clarke (2008) *Contaminated Land*, 2nd edn, London: Sweet and Maxwell, provides a comprehensive coverage of the pre- and post-Pt 2A law, including precedents, and practical matters such as commercial and property considerations.

Other than these general works, the articles tend to concentrate on particular aspects of the contaminated land regime. There is an excellent overview of the problems of allocating liability for contaminated land in D. Lawrence and R. Lee, 'Permitting uncertainty: owners, occupiers and responsibility for remediation' (2003) 66 MLR 261. Other articles focus on other elements of the regime, ranging from the definition of contaminated land in risk assessment in R. Kimblin, 'Risk, jurisprudence and the environment' (2000) JPL 359, to a general overview in D. Woolley, 'Contaminated land: the real world' (2002) JPL 5. Although there is not much coverage of European initiatives on contaminated land in this chapter (for reasons that are spelt out in the relevant section), there are some moves towards developing European policy. A. Layard, 'The Europeanisation of contaminated land' (2004) Env LR 97 summarizes the position, while S. Christie and R. Teeuw, 'Policy and administration of contaminated land within the EU' (2000) Eur Env 24 gives a comparative perspective.

There have been a number of articles that discuss the impact of the rules on the practice of environmental law, and in the sale and purchase of contaminated land. This is a real issue, as can be seen in S. Payne, 'Clean-up and indemnity: a postscript to *Cambridge Water*' (2003) 15 JEL 202, which analyses a case dealing with the contractual allocation of liability for contamination arising out of the *Cambridge Water* decision. Other articles are a little specialist, dealing with the drafting of warranties and indemnities to transfer or limit liability post-sale. If that is what you are interested in, then have a look at any one of the following: B. Adams, 'Contaminated land: the new clean-up regime takes hold' (2000) 11 PLC 29; V. Fogelman, 'Transferring remediation liabilities in commercial transactions' (2001) 13 ELM 83; A. Thomson, 'Environmental indemnities: controlling exposure' (2002) 13 PLC 43.

For a stimulating examination of the problems of trying to regulate the clean-up of contaminated land while taking note of market effects (the stumbling block for the ill-fated Contaminative Uses Register), see J. Steele, 'Remedies and remediation: issues in environmental liability' (1995) 58 MLR 615.

If you are interested in a comparative approach, you may wish to analyse the operation of the Superfund legislation in the USA. This legislation has been the subject of much criticism, but it does illustrate a different way of approaching the problem. A good set of essays on the topic is found in R. Revesz and R. B. Stewart (eds) (1995) *Analyzing Superfund: Economics, Science and Law*, Washington, DC: Resources for the Future. There is also a lot of literature in US journals on the topic. A few that may be of interest and which can be sourced through one of the electronic databases (for example, Westlaw) are J. Lyons, 'Deep pockets and CERCLA: should Superfund be abolished?' (1987) Stan Envtl LJ 6, 271; C. Meyer, 'Does minimizing expenditures for CERCLA site remediation increase the future public abatement costs?' (1993) 9 J Nat Resources

& Envtl L 381; E. James, 'An American werewolf in London: applying the lessons of Superfund to Great Britain' (1994) 19 Yale J Intl L 349. Comparatively, another interesting source is T. Field, 'Liability to remedy asbestos pollution' (2006) JEL 479, which considers a case in which the South African High Court held that national environmental law did not extend to historical pollution, because this infringed the principle that law should not be retroactive (although, arguably, principles central to the environmental legislation, such as environmental justice principles, pointed the other way).

@ WEB LINKS

The recent development of the contaminated land regime means that there is good web-based access to many of the primary materials. The Department for Environment, Food and Rural Affairs (DEFRA) website at **www.defra.gov.uk/environment/land/index.htm** has links to the Regulations, and to relevant statutory and technical guidance on contaminated land, as well as material on soil protection. The Land Registration Network has extensive resources on contaminated land generally and Pt 2A in particular. The site can be found at **www.grc.cf.ac.uk/lrn/resources/land/index.php**. A good source of European materials, including a number of comparative studies of contaminated land legislation across the world, can be found at **europa.eu.int/comm/environment/liability/**. Finally, if you are interested in the technical aspects of contaminated land, have a look at **www.clarinet.at**, which provides an excellent database of materials and other resources dealing with the approaches taken across Europe to address contaminated land.

17 Water pollution and water quality

→ **Overview**

This chapter is about the quality of the water environment. This is a big topic, because there are well-developed bodies of law at national, European, and international levels, all covering different ground. In the interests of space, therefore, we focus on the control of pollution of inland and coastal waters, and do not cover in any detail wider issues about water resource management, such as land drainage or flood defence. The abstraction of water from the natural environment—which is becoming more tightly regulated (see, for example, Water Act 2003, Pt I)—is only discussed in so far as this has an impact on water quality. Discharges to sewers—which have as much in common with waste disposal as with water pollution and which have their own, more basic, regulatory system operated by sewerage undertakers—are dealt with in the Online Resource Centre.

Before reading this chapter, you will find it useful if you already have an appreciation of EC environmental law, particularly: the legal status of Directives, and their implementation and enforcement (see Chapter 7); the role of the Environment Agency (see Chapter 5); differing regulatory approaches and techniques, especially the contrast between emissions and target standards (see Chapter 8), and criminal and civil liability (see Chapters 9 and 11).

At the end of this chapter, you will be able to:

✔ appreciate the state of the water environment and the main sources of water pollution;

✔ understand in outline the regulation of the water industry and the role of the Environment Agency, and appreciate how improvements to water quality are funded;

✔ understand how 'water pollution' is defined and controlled, and understand standards for water quality;

✔ appreciate the scope of the main criminal offences for water pollution and the main responses to the challenge of diffuse water pollution;

✔ evaluate the importance of European law to the water environment;

✔ appreciate in outline the role played by international laws on water quality.

Water pollutants and their sources

Water pollutants come in many forms, including:

- deoxygenating materials, including sewage and other organic wastes, such as silage, farm wastes, and wastes from a number of heavily polluting industrial processes (for example, food processing and the production of smokeless fuel, textiles, paper, and dairy products);

- nutrient enrichment by such things as fertilizers, which may give rise to eutrophication, causing an accelerated growth of plants and algae, and leading to a decline in water quality;

- solids, such as silt, which may impede flows or block out light for growth;

- toxic materials—some materials, such as heavy metals, pesticides, or nitrate, are toxic to humans, animals, plants, or all three, often depending on the level of the dose received;

- materials that cause an impact on amenity, such as car tyres or shopping trolleys in rivers or canals;

- disease-carrying agents, such as bacteria;

- heat, which may affect biological conditions and which also deoxygenates water.

The effect of any potential pollutant varies according to the size, temperature, rate of flow, and oxygen content of the receiving waters, as well as the local geology and the presence of other pollutants and any resulting synergistic—that is, 'cocktail'—effects. The use made of a stream is also of enormous importance in deciding whether it can be said to be 'polluted', and this factor has a large impact on the attitude of the regulatory bodies towards the setting of standards and their enforcement. It is not sufficient to look only at the pollution of surface waters, because 30 per cent of the public water supply is taken from ground waters. As a result, the control of water pollution encompasses the control of liquid discharges to land, or from land such as landfill sites (see further p. 662).

The sources of pollution are also varied.

- There are around 105,000 discharges in relation to which there is in place a consent for discharge to waters. Many of these involve toxic materials or organic pollutants. Around half are for small private discharges.

- Many consents relate to sewage works, the organic content of which discharge makes it highly polluting. Sewage pollution currently gives rise to the highest number of serious water pollution incidents and regulating sewage pollution has been a central concern in the history of water pollution.

- Agricultural pollution is problematic, giving rise both to a significant number of pollution incidents annually, and to the more diffuse entry of pollutants from pesticide and fertilizer run-off. Groundwater contamination from pollutants such as sheep dips is also a major regulatory problem. The Policy Commission on the Future of Farming and Food noted in 2002 that '*Agriculture is the number one polluter of water in the country*' (as it appears to be across Europe).[1]

- Spills of oils and fuels are a frequent source of water pollution incident.

- Accidents often cause pollution, particularly from the storage and transport of hazardous substances.

- Leachate from waste sites, including those that are disused, are often highly contaminated.

Natural events can also influence water quality: heavy rainfall may lead to greater pollution from farm run-off, while drought—or overabstraction—will tend to concentrate pollutants. Also, the more the environment is already under some form of 'stress', the more severe pollution incidents will tend to be.

---

1 *Farming and Food: A Sustainable Future*, p. 68.

The state of the water environment

The general state of inland water quality is measured by the Environment Agency using the General Quality Assessment (GQA) scheme. This scheme has four separate elements, covering chemical and biological quality, nutrient status, and aesthetic quality. (The following statistics relate to England only.)

The GQA shows a marked improvement overall in 'chemical quality'. In 2006, 66 per cent of rivers were of good chemical quality (chemical quality being the indicator of general organic pollution). By also including 'biological assessment' (based on small water fauna), however, the GQA provides a better picture of the overall effect of all pollutants on the health of river ecosystems, although the grading of waters in this way is rather imprecise and biological quality depends on factors other than the quality of discharges. In 2006, 71 per cent of rivers were of good biological quality. Taking a baseline of 1990, the figures for both chemical and biological quality indicate a significant net improvement, which is largely attributed to better treatment of effluent by sewerage undertakers, following significant investment by the water industry after privatization in 1989. There has, however, been some levelling off in recent years, suggesting that some of the easier problems have now been addressed.

In 2006, 50 per cent of rivers had high concentrations of phosphate and 28 per cent of nitrate—these being the major factors affecting the 'nutrient status' of waters. Improvements in this area have been more modest than those in relation to organic pollutants, indicating the relative difficulty of controlling the input of pollutants such as fertilizers from diffuse sources. A survey of frequently visited sites in 2000 revealed that around two-thirds were of 'aesthetically' good or fair quality.

Taken together, the GQA and the Environment Agency's recording of water pollution incidents show some significant results in combating pollution from discrete discharge points (known as 'point sources'), but also the increasing challenge of combating diffuse sources of water pollution. Differences in quality between areas and regions still persist, however, and the quality of some stretches of river can still decline between surveys. What is undeniable, however, is that water quality is far removed from that in the nineteenth century, when a letter could be written with river water[2] and the lower reaches of the River Thames were little more than an open sewer.

The regulatory challenges

As the chapter title suggests, the central regulatory and environmental issue here is not simply preventing or controlling unwanted substances from entering the natural water environment. Indeed, the traditional 'British' approach to water quality regulation has been to defend the view that it makes no sense to start by asking 'what dangerous substances should we prevent from entering water?', because many substances can have a damaging impact on water quality in sufficient quantities. For example, there has been a successful water pollution prosecution following a spill of carbonated apple juice and milk has a polluting effect around 300 times that of sewage (see also Case 9.1). This illustrates that, in part, water quality regulation is about controlling the discharge of substances that are not inherently toxic or harmful, but which may have negative impacts depending on how much is discharged and where they are discharged.

The counterpart of this is that there is usually 'water pollution' only where waters are rendered unfit for some desirable use, such as drinking water supply or supporting

---

2 Royal Commission on Rivers Pollution Third Report (1871) *Pollution Arising from the Woollen Manufacture*, vol. 1, p. 12.

fish life.[3] The law therefore tends to aim to ensure a particular quality of water for various purposes, rather than only to prevent or minimize the entry of 'pollutants' (although some standards are clearly set to eliminate certain substances being present in certain waters, even where there is little evidence of actual harm being likely—the pesticides standards in the EC Directive on Drinking Water (98/83/EC) are fairly clear examples of this). This also allows for natural differences in the composition of water, and for things such as the rate and amount of flow to be taken into account.

In legal terms, this is reflected in a preference for target standards based on the character of the receiving environment, rather than the adoption of emission standards reducing certain harmful substances from the water environment. (This preferred approach has, with one or two notable exceptions, basically been followed in EC water Directives.) It is also reflected in the particular approach taken to regulating individual discharges, which is that official permission is not strictly needed before substances are discharged. Rather, the purpose of a discharge consent, issued by the Environment Agency, is to act as a defence to any charge of polluting water.

This peculiar legal nature of discharge consents has some important implications. Most notable is that, in the setting of consents, the adoption of process-based standards, such as Best Available Techniques (BAT), to minimize pollution has not generally been required.[4] In the context of quality standards, such an approach could lead to over-regulation and inefficiencies, although another way of looking at this is to emphasize that, as a result, discharge consents do not necessarily encourage a progressive tightening up of standards. But strict water quality objectives have never been favoured; instead, consents have tended to be set (and enforced) on an individualized basis, having general regard to the quality of the river and its catchment, and to particular things like the location of abstraction points for public supply.

Many of the more obvious and direct sources of pollution are being brought under control. The most important, and difficult, regulatory problem now is the increasing contribution of diffuse sources, such as agricultural run-off and pollution from urban development and vehicle emissions, to reductions in water quality. Such non-point sources of water pollution cannot really be controlled by consents, and instead need an imaginative mix of policy and legal mechanisms (see p. 616).

Two final issues relate to reaching fair decisions about who should pay for improving water quality and who should be given rights to pollute. The first of these is illustrated by looking at who pays for nitrate and pesticide removal. At present, this is mainly achieved by the water companies using expensive technology, which is ultimately paid for by water customers. But there is a strong argument for saying that farmers—the main users of these pollutants, which do not just affect water for drinking—should pay, with the cost filtering down to food consumers.

The second issue is that, as with certain air pollution limits, once it is decided that a certain overall level of pollution is to be tolerated, it must be decided how 'rights' to pollute are divided up and on what basis. This is something determined in the day-to-day setting and revision of consents, but it illustrates the more profound issues that the consent regime raises than simply protecting individual dischargers from criminal liability. The consent system, as well as other mechanisms to prevent or reduce water pollution, must be transparent, participatory, and accountable if it is to operate with any legitimacy.

---

3 Although the main water pollution offence of causing polluting matter to enter controlled waters does not require actual harm—see Case 17.3.

4 There was a defence for companies under the Rivers Pollution Prevention Act 1876 to use 'best practicable means'—see Box 2.2.

History of the water sector and controls on water quality

Over the years, the law on water pollution has tended to be the most developed of the systems of pollution control. It has also had the greatest degree of coherence, both in terms of the institutional arrangements and in terms of substantive law. These institutional arrangements have changed markedly over time and must be appreciated alongside changes to the structure of the water sector (see Box 17.1).

BOX 17.1 **The water sector and regulatory water pollution controls—timeline**	
Rivers Pollution Prevention Act 1876	Absolute prohibition on pollution, but broad defences for industry and almost totally unworkable
River Boards Act 1948	Previously water supply and sewage disposal functions exercised by municipal authorities
	Public health matters also dealt with on a local authority basis
	This Act created 32 river boards on a catchment-area basis, with certain regulatory functions
Rivers (Prevention of Pollution) Act 1951	River board consent required for new industrial or sewage discharges into most inland waters (controls extended to tidal and estuarial waters under the Clean Rivers (Estuaries and Tidal Waters) Act 1960)
Rivers (Prevention of Pollution) Act 1961	Existing discharges (pre-1951) brought under control
Water Resources Act 1963	Controls extended to discharges to certain underground waters
	River boards converted into 27 river authorities, with various regulatory functions, including pollution control and the new system of licensing water abstraction
	Water supply and sewage disposal remained essentially a local authority function (157 water supply undertakings and no fewer than 1,393 sewage authorities)
Water Act 1973	Ten regional water authorities established, responsible for all water-related functions within river basin areas, i.e. both operational and regulatory[5]
	System generally seen as ineffective, mainly because of underfunding for sewage treatment, and because the regional water authorities were both poacher and gamekeeper regarding water pollution
	A general decline in standards
Control of Pollution Act 1974	Pollution controls extended out to three miles offshore
	Limited public participation provisions (re)introduced (public registers, private prosecutions)
	Stronger preventive and remedial measures
	Main measures not brought into force until the mid-1980s because of cost concerns
	Certain provisions never implemented

---

5 The only real exception was the retention of 29 private water companies responsible for water supply in defined areas.

Water Act 1989	Water supply and sewerage functions privatized
	Water and sewerage companies subject to economic regulation under the Office of Water Trading (OFWAT) and environmental regulation under the National Rivers Authority (NRA)
	Operation/regulation split
	Provision for statutory water quality objectives
	Charging for trade and sewage discharges introduced
	Improvements to preventive and remedial powers
Environmental Protection Act 1990	Gave responsibility for discharges to water from the most polluting processes to HM Inspectorate of Pollution (HMIP)
Water Resources Act 1991	Consolidation of water law
	The Water Resources Act 1991 deals with quality and quantity; the Water Industry Act 1991 deals with the water and sewerage industries
Environment Act 1995	Creation of Environment Agency unites main enforcement bodies (NRA and HMIP)[6]
Water Framework Directive 2000 (2000/60/EC)	Partial consolidation and reorientation of EC water law
	Directive comes into force in stages between 2003–15
Water Act 2003	OFWAT becomes a regulation authority (a panel of regulators rather than a single director) from 2006

Note that, alongside these national-level changes, since the 1970s, there have been important EC Directives and international agreements that have greatly shaped national water pollution law.

As the timeline in Box 17.1 suggests, the water industry has historically been dominated by water collection, treatment, and supply, and the provision of sewers, sewage works, and sewage disposal. But, historically, the water industry also encompassed a range of additional concerns including:

- water pollution control;
- the regulation of bodies providing water services;
- fisheries;
- navigation;
- flood defence and land drainage;
- recreational activities;
- conservation responsibilities.

From this list, it is clear that, in reality, this is a set of activities, connected in the sense that they all relate to the water cycle, but separate in their objectives. Pollution control was only one function of the water industry prior to privatization in 1989, but its place in relation to these other activities needs to be understood.

---

6 Note that the Drinking Water Inspectorate remains outside the Environment Agency and that there are some areas of uncertainty about the role of local authorities in relation to discharges to water under the integrated permitting system in the Pollution Prevention and Control Act 1999.

Legal controls on water quality

Some of the difficulties of relying on the common law of nuisance or of riparian rights to control water pollution are expanded in Box 2.1, while the limitations of the Rivers Pollution Prevention Act 1876 are outlined in Box 2.2. Even with the advent in 1951 of the discharge consent regime, however, the emphasis was always on flexible standards, with most consents being set on an individualized basis by reference to the effect of a discharge on the receiving waters. Particular emphasis has been placed on biochemical oxygen demand (BOD) and the level of suspended solids, rather than on such things as metals and toxic substances, especially in relation to sewage discharges. In a sense, the setting of consents could almost be described as a 'rule of thumb' method. This approach is, however, changing in response to EC Directives and as a result of creating a more uniform system of control nationwide.

Water quality policy style and techniques

The establishment of the National Rivers Authority (NRA) in 1989 meant that the opportunity could be taken to establish a national policy on water quality—or at least one applicable to England and Wales. (Before then, there were, of course, general aims—for example, getting treatable wastes into the sewerage system, if possible, and cleaning up waters for economic reasons—and EC standards to which the UK had to adhere.) Key elements of this policy included increased attention to prevention of harm in such areas as farm pollution, a more rigorous enforcement policy involving greater use of prosecution, and a national strategy for reviewing all existing consents on a catchment-area basis. The general approach adopted by the NRA (and continued by the Environment Agency) was that river catchments should be managed on an integrated basis. This process is a good example of aspects of environmental policy being set by a body other than central government. The current government strategy dates from 2002, but is in the process of being revised, and is likely to be replaced in 2008 by a strategy that pays more attention than ever on mitigating and adapting to climate change (it being likely that, in the future, there will be both more floods and more droughts).

Scotland, Wales, and Northern Ireland

The position in the devolved administrations is slightly different. In Scotland, the water industry has not been privatized, and water supply and sewerage services are provided by Scottish Water—a public sector body accountable to the Scottish Parliament, but run on the lines of a private company. The Environment Act 1995 established the Scottish Environment Protection Agency (SEPA), which brought together all water pollution functions in one body (although SEPA does not have functions in relation to general water management such as flood control or fisheries). Following the Scotland Act 1998, water pollution is a matter for the Scottish Parliament, although, importantly, the negotiation of EC Directives remains with the UK government. In 2005, the Water Environment (Controlled Activities) (Scotland) Regulations 2005,[7] enacted under the Water Environment and Water Services Act (Scotland) 2003 (enacted in part to allow implementation of the EC Water Framework Directive 2000/60/EC), marked an important divergence of approach about how to consent polluting activities (at least until such time as the rest of the UK catches up). Three distinct levels of control are now provided for and are discussed in Box 17.2.

Under the Government of Wales Act 1998, responsibility for water pollution is a matter for the National Assembly for Wales, although the Assembly cannot amend primary legislation such as the Water Resources Act 1991, and matters concerning EC water law and policy remain the responsibility of central government. General references below to 'the

7 SSI 2005/348.

Secretary of State' or 'the Minister' should be read as including the Welsh Assembly where appropriate.

Water quality matters in Northern Ireland are the responsibility of the Environment and Heritage Service of the Department of the Environment (Northern Ireland). Water legislation was overhauled by the Water (Northern Ireland) Order 1999 (NI.6),[8] which brought the controls on discharge consents more into line with practice in England and gave more powers to the Department of Environment (NI) to make pollution prevention regulations.

International law and water quality

Marine pollution and the quality of the marine environment

Not surprisingly, international law has mostly been concerned with marine waters rather than with water quality at national level, although it is the nature of the water cycle that there is no clear divide between the two.

Roughly, it has been estimated that around 77 per cent of marine pollution globally results from discharges from land. Of this, around 60 per cent originates from run-off, either through direct discharges into coastal water or into freshwater passing into the sea through river estuaries, with the remainder coming via the atmosphere. Hence, much of the contamination entering the marine environment (around 56 per cent) is regulated at the point of origin of the contaminants by the regime that governs the quality of inland waters (described in detail below). It is worth stressing that much of the marine pollution that derives from atmospheric deposits is not regulated with specific regard to the eventual impact on the marine environment (for example, vehicle emissions).

International conventions—policy approaches

In international conventions on marine pollution, a target standard approach in the sense of using water quality objectives (binding or otherwise) is not generally taken. But, in some respects, the approach is difficult to classify as an emission control approach, because, apart from controlling things such as major oil spills, the objective is as much to do with preventing the release of oil and other substances per se regardless of impact. For example, most of the offences relating to discharging oil—which originate in international treaties—are committed even in the absence of any polluting impact.

The impact of international conventions

Compared with EC law, the impact of international conventions has been less dramatic, although there are instances in which EC standards and policy originate in hard and soft international law. One of the key provisions of the EC Water Framework Directive (2000/60/EC) has its origins in a regional marine convention (see Box 17.2).

BOX 17.2 International and EC law, and hazardous substances in the water environment

For what are intrinsically hazardous substances, the EC Water Framework Directive (2000/60/EC; see p. 593) requires measures that must be aimed at progressively reducing and, for priority

---

8 SI 1999/662.

hazardous substances, ceasing or phasing out discharges, emissions, and losses (Art. 16(1)). The background to this wording lies in a Declaration of the International North Sea Conference and the Hazardous Substances Strategy under the 1992 Oslo–Paris (OSPAR) Convention, under which parties are bound to make every endeavour to move towards the target of cessation of discharges, emissions, and losses of hazardous substances by 2020.

During the late stages of negotiating the Water Framework Directive, the European Parliament sought to incorporate the water quality strategy taken under the OSPAR Convention. Additionally, parties to the OSPAR Convention have agreed to achieve continuous reductions in releases of hazardous substances, with the ultimate aim of achieving concentrations in the environment near background levels for naturally occurring substances and close to zero for man-made synthetic substances. But the wording of the Framework Directive requires a progressive (rather than 'continuous') reduction in hazardous substances and only applies the phasing out obligation to 'priority hazardous substances'.[9] Nonetheless, the Directive also defines the 'close to zero' and 'background levels' requirements as part of what 'high ecological status' entails, and the baseline requirement to achieve 'good ecological status' (under Art. 4) does not therefore include these specific obligations, which are now the cornerstone of regional international marine pollution law under OSPAR.

Decisions taken by the International Conferences for the Protection of the North Sea have also influenced the development of the Precautionary Principle and, in line with this, banning the disposal of sewage sludge at sea, a measure now contained in the EC Urban Waste Water Treatment Directive (91/271/EEC). The impact of this on national disposal practices, such as greater spreading of sludge on land, as well as similar bans on the dumping and incineration of industrial waste, and on the coastal dumping of colliery spoil and power station ash, illustrates the way in which measures to protect the marine environment may have direct consequences at national level, to say nothing of the significant costs involved.

This impact of international law on national practices is also seen through the various international provisions aimed at preventing marine pollution from ships, notably the 1973–78 Marine Pollution (MARPOL) Convention,[10] which regulates deliberate, operational discharges of oil and, through Protocols, certain other substances (for example, noxious liquid substances and sewage) from vessels. These provisions must be enforced both by flag states and against foreign vessels by port states, and apply to the territorial sea as well as (in some situations) the exclusive economic zone. The Convention also regulates the design, construction, and maintenance standards for oil tankers, although it originally contained rather generous provisions for existing vessels, which, because of the life span of tankers, limited its effectiveness. This was addressed in amendments to the Convention adopted in 1992, which both strengthened the inspection procedures for older vessels and added a requirement to retrofit double hulls or an equivalent to tankers of 25 years of age and older.

The MARPOL Convention regime therefore takes a preventive approach to marine oil pollution. This is in contrast to other international agreements in this area, including the 1969 Intervention Convention, which allows for intervention on the high seas in the case of accidental oil spills from vessels in distress (introduced following the *Torrey Canyon* incident in 1967). They also include measures regulating liability and compensation for oil pollution damage under the 1992 Conventions on Civil Liability for Oil Pollution Damage and Establishment of an International Fund for Compensation for Oil Pollution Damage (discussed in more detail in Box 11.1).

---

9 Currently, 11 substances out of the initial 33 substances identified as hazardous.
10 International Convention for the Prevention of Pollution From Ships 1973, as modified.

By contrast with what are quite tightly defined obligations in relation to oil and other noxious substances, there are more general provisions in the 1982 UN Convention on the Law of the Sea (UNCLOS) on preventing, reducing, and controlling pollution of the marine environment from land-based sources (Art. 207), and similar obligations for pollution from things such as oil rigs and seabed mining (Art. 208). There are also rules about pollution from dumping (Art. 210), although, as with many provisions of UNCLOS in this area, states are encouraged to seek regional solutions and the 1992 Oslo–Paris (OSPAR) Convention dealing with the North Sea and North East Atlantic area is important, at least in relation to the development of policy. The parties also agreed to reduce to 'close to zero' by 2020 concentrations of artificial radioactive substances.

BOX 17.3 Sellafield and international water pollution law

Under Art. 206 of the United Nations Convention on Law of the Sea (UNCLOS):

> when states have reasonable grounds for believing that planned activities under their jurisdiction or control may cause substantial pollution of or significant and harmful changes to the marine environment, they shall, as far as practicable, assess the potential effects of such activities on the marine environment.

This obligation is similar to that imposed by EC and national law on environmental impact assessment.

In 2001, Ireland brought proceedings against the UK alleging that the UK had breached Art. 206 because it had authorized a mixed oxide (MOX) fuel plant at Sellafield, in reliance on an environmental impact statement from 1993 that had not considered the impact of the plant on the marine environment of the Irish Sea. The majority of the International Tribunal on the Law of the Sea (ITLOS) declined to suspend the plant's operation pending a full hearing on its merits. The Tribunal did, however, order the parties to cooperate and exchange information on possible environmental consequences of the plant being commissioned, and to devise measures to prevent pollution of the marine environment that might result from the plant's operation.

This ruling, which Sands[11] notes has 'a certain precautionary character', was based on considerations of 'prudence and caution'. It is worth noting, however, that part of Ireland's claim relates to the possible impact of the transportation of nuclear waste to Sellafield. Although this claim is made in the context of harm to the Irish Sea, any tightening of controls to which it may lead will probably have an indirect effect on parts of the marine environment that fall outside national jurisdiction.[12]

Taken together, these developments seem to mark a continuing move away from a 'dilute and disperse' approach in the waters around the UK. But the global ocean remains a dumping ground for land-based and atmospheric pollution, and, on the whole, international law has yet to find adequate, proactive ways of dealing with this.

---

11 P. Sands (2003) *Principles of International Environmental Law*, 2nd edn, Cambridge: Cambridge University Press, p. 276.

12 The issue of which court or tribunal should hear this kind of dispute is discussed in Box 7.2.

The EC and water quality

The EC has had an enormous impact on water pollution law and policy over the years. The First Environment Action Programme (EAP) in 1973 picked out water pollution as a priority matter and there has been a steady stream of Directives since. These have tackled such diverse topics as the reduction of pollution from dangerous substances, the improvement of the quality of bathing waters, nitrates in water, and the progressive introduction of adequate sewage treatment systems. The gradual implementation of the Water Framework Directive will mean that EC law will cover all pollutants in all waters.

EC water Directives follow three basic models as regards standard setting:

- those that adopt emission standards, which are mainly used for reducing dangerous substances;

- those that impose quality objectives on waters, which are mainly set according to the use that is to be made of those waters;

- those that regulate particular polluting processes.

There are also isolated cases in which Directives take different approaches to control, focusing on particular kinds of pollutants. Directive 73/404/EEC on detergents sets a product standard by prohibiting the marketing of detergents with average biodegradability of less than 90 per cent. Directive 78/176/EEC on titanium dioxide sets standards in relation to a specific industry (the paint industry).

Emission standard approaches

One of the first major water Directives was 76/464/EEC on dangerous substances in water (following various amendments, some of which are discussed below, the Directive is now consolidated as Directive 2006/11/EC). This is a framework Directive that aims to reduce or eliminate certain dangerous substances from water. It covers essentially the same waters as those controlled by the Environment Agency and has led to very tight controls over certain dangerous substances in discharge consents.

The Directive has always distinguished between two categories of substance: List I (the 'black list'), which contains the most hazardous substances; List II (the 'grey list'), for less dangerous substances. The agreed approach to 'grey list' substances was relatively uncontroversial, the Directive laying down a fairly general list—for example, metals such as zinc, copper, tin, nickel, and chromium; biocides; cyanides; fluorides; ammonia; nitrites—with the objective that pollution by these substances should be reduced. Accordingly, if any such substance has a harmful effect on the aquatic environment, member States must develop a national environmental quality standard and ensure that it is met in the receiving waters. These standards are set at a national, rather than at an EC, level. The member State must also introduce a reduction programme for grey list substances and must control discharges by setting standards in discharge consents that enable the environmental quality standards to be achieved (on the need for both of these, see Case 7.1).

The approach to black list substances has always been to seek the elimination of pollution by these substances, but agreeing the means of doing so was more contentious, and first demonstrated the differences between the UK and the rest of the EC over standard setting. The UK's system of a decentralized setting of non-uniform consents by reference to the quality of the receiving waters was seen to be directly contradictory to the desire of other member States for uniform—that is, minimum—centrally set emission standards for dangerous substances. After much argument, alternative approaches for black list substances was adopted, under which *either* an emission standard had to be set that did not exceed the appropriate EC limit value, *or* an emission standard set so that the EC environmental quality standard for the receiving waters was kept to at all times (this is known as the 'parallel' approach). Only the UK adopted the second approach.

Directive 76/464/EEC had an enormous impact on pollution control in the UK. Having claimed that it set its consents by reference to quality objectives for the receiving waters, the UK government was forced to introduce such a system on a formal basis and water quality objectives were introduced for the first time in the late 1970s, at first by administrative action. This was insufficient for compliance with EC law and sections relating to *statutory* water quality objectives were first introduced in the Water Act 1989. In general, significant discharges of black list and grey list substances are subject to integrated pollution prevention and control (IPPC). The rules providing for control by the Environment Agency of prescribed substances discharged to sewers (outlined in the Online Resource Centre) are also a result of this Directive. Under the Water Framework Directive, the black list has been replaced by the list of priority hazardous substances. In cases in which a daughter Directive is not agreed for a potential black list substance, the substance is treated as being on the grey list. A final point is that, although Directive 2006/11/EC is largely a consolidating Directive, the parallel approach has been dispensed with and only an emission standard approach may be used for List I substances. This reflects the fact that the modern EC water policy approach in relation to the most hazardous substances is one of elimination at source. The Directive will be fully repealed by the Water Framework Directive in 2013.

A similar story attaches to Directive 2006/118/EC on groundwater, except that, in this case, List I substances are to be prevented from entering ground waters, while discharges of List II substances should be limited, in both cases by a consent system.

One problem with the emission standards approach is that it does not work well for pollution from non-point—that is, diffuse—sources, nor if there are multiple polluters in one catchment area (see Box 17.5). Directive 86/280/EEC attempts to tackle this issue by requiring all *sources* of black list substances to be monitored.

CASE 17.1 The Dangerous Substances in Water Directive—Case C-282/02 *Commission v. Ireland* [2005] ECR I-4653

Ireland was alleged to be in breach of the 1976 Dangerous Substances Directive (76/464/EEC). Two aspects of the case illustrate the nature and scope of the Directive (and hence Directive 2006/11/EC as well). One is the extent to which the Directive applies to diffuse pollution, especially from agriculture. In relation to this, the European Court of Justice held that, as long as the source is fixed and the discharge is foreseeable, then a consent to comply with the Directive is required. This is in line with other judgments that, in effect, have held that the Directive may have to deal with what are effectively diffuse discharges. For example, in Case C-231/97 *Van Rooij* [1999] ECR I-6355, it was held that the Directive applied to discharges of polluted steam precipitating into watercourses. But what exactly a 'source' is here is uncertain.

Another is that Ireland tried to rely on a general pollution offence provision as being a 'more stringent measure' that it is allowed to take. On this, the ECJ held that while, in principle, a prohibitory regime can be an alternative to an authorization system, in this case, Ireland had failed to demonstrate that its general pollution offence could effectively replace the authorization system envisaged by the Directive. One reason for this was that, unlike the principal water pollution offence in England and Wales (s. 85(1), Water Resources Act 1991), the Irish offence has a defence of showing that all reasonable steps have been taken to avoid pollution. But other reasons were that the offence did not spell out which pollutants it covers and was not backed by a consent procedure that had regard to water quality objectives. Reasons such as these were instrumental in the changes to UK practice (and Ireland was really clutching at straws in arguing along these lines).

Quality objective approaches

For the quality approach, there are a number of stages.

1. Water with particular uses must first be identified (this is usually left to the discretion of the member States, but must be done on objective grounds).

2. The EC must establish a number of parameters, which are normally expressed either as imperative (I) values, to which member States must adhere, or guide (G) values, which member States must try to achieve.

3. Environmental quality objectives must be set for the waters, having regard to the parameters.

4. A competent national authority must be established for monitoring purposes and uniform sampling techniques are set by EC Directives.

5. Procedures are established for updating the I and G values in the light of new knowledge.

Directives that have adopted this approach include those on surface water for drinking (75/440/EEC), shellfish waters (2006/113/EC), water standards for freshwater fish (2006/44/EC), and bathing waters (2006/7/EC). The Drinking Water Directive (98/83/EC) also applies this approach, although, in this case, it is the quality of water at the tap that is regulated.

The water quality approach is illustrated by the Bathing Waters Directive. The original Directive, which dates from 1975 (Directive 76/160/EEC) was heavily criticized for being rather a crude piece of legislation, aiming at uniform standards for all bathing waters regardless of local conditions, and for not reflecting natural variability in quality between years. A revised Directive has now been passed (2006/11/EC) and new laws must be enacted by March 2008—but the quality objectives do not fall due until 2015, the aim being to synchronize the Bathing Water Directive with the Water Framework Directive.

The shift between the original and the revised Directives illustrates some of the key issues with Directives based on environmental quality standards and how these types of Directive have developed. Directive 2006/11/EC has a very narrow public health focus. Only two public health parameters need to be monitored, rather than the 19 parameters monitored previously (which included things such as pH and oil, which were never tested for anyway), although the required standards that need to be met for these are rather stricter than previously (and will require investment to achieve). The new Directive has four scoring categories—excellent, good, satisfactory, and poor—and greater information must be actively disseminated to the public about the quality of particular bathing waters.

A criticism of the old Directive was that a bad year's results could lead to a member State being in breach. The new Directive makes some very important changes to how compliance is measured. Certain samples taken during short-term pollution incidents can be disregarded and waters can, for example, still be 'satisfactory' even if the samples taken have fallen below this standard, as long as warning signs are noted and remedial action over the following year is taken. In addition, quality is to be determined on the basis of three- or four-year averages, rather than annually. Finally, bathing can be prohibited where it is judged to be uneconomical to bring waters up to the baseline satisfactory standard.

Putting all of these changes together, then, we see a clear emphasis on the target of the standard (bathers) and a much greater degree of flexibility in terms of demonstrating compliance. This is important because, as explained elsewhere, the European Court of Justice (ECJ) has held that the duty to comply with quality standards is generally an absolute one and that doing what is reasonably practicable is not enough (see Case 7.1)—an approach that, in an important ruling in the early 1990s, had led to the UK being found to have breached the original Directive (Case C-56/90 *Commission v. United Kingdom* [1993] ECR I-4109). Indeed, it might be said that the new rules make it virtually impossible for a member State to be fined for non-compliance, which is especially notable because, as this is a public health issue and one that can be difficult to remedy in the short term, fines could be very large.

Directives regulating particular polluting activities

Two important Directives regulate particular polluting activities. The Directive on Urban Waste Water Treatment (91/271/EEC) is potentially the most significant in terms of compliance costs. It lays down minimum standards for the treatment of urban waste waters—that is, domestic sewage and industrial waste waters. These treatment standards and the timescales within which they must be met, vary according to the population of the area concerned, but the basic idea is that some form of biological treatment ('secondary treatment') should be usual for domestic wastes. For example, a secondary or equivalent system of sewage treatment is required by the end of 2000 for a town with a population equivalent of more than 15,000. Stricter standards are required in sensitive areas and lower standards are permitted in less-sensitive areas. The Directive also required all member States to cease dumping sewage sludge at sea by the end of 1998. The Directive therefore grafts an emissions standard approach onto a quality standards framework and is fairly unusual in that water quality is not protected because of any immediate use value.

The Directive has had a particular impact on the UK—the only member State that carried out sewage sludge dumping and which traditionally employed a 'dilute and disperse' policy of discharging virtually untreated sewage into the sea via outfalls (see Box 2.8). The Directive was implemented by the Urban Waste Water Treatment (England and Wales) Regulations 1994.[13] It requires tighter standards in sensitive areas and allows less stringent standards in less sensitive areas (in the UK, termed 'high natural dispersion areas'). Classifying these has proven somewhat controversial legally—for example, a number of estuarial waters were classed as 'coastal' for the purposes of the Regulations, thus allowing lower levels of treatment to be applied.

CASE 17.2 *R v. Secretary of State for the Environment, ex parte Kingston upon Hull City Council* [1996] Env LR 248

The Secretary of State had drawn the boundaries of the estuary for the Humber and Severn rivers at the Humber and Severn road bridges, thus ensuring lower (and therefore cheaper) levels of treatment for treatment works alongside the rivers. His decision was successfully challenged on the grounds that costs should not have been taken into account, and that the correct way of drawing the boundaries was to carry out a genuine and rational assessment of what actually constituted the estuary. (Subsequently, the estuaries were redefined as a line between the two furthest points of land on each side of the river.)

The case illustrates the need for an objective approach to area designations (the ECJ has reached the same conclusion for a range of water quality and area-related Directives). But it is also a good example of a successful challenge to the implementation of an EC Directive and notable because issues of direct effect were not raised. It was enough that the local authorities could show that there had been an error in interpreting the Directive, without issues of individual rights being raised.

The Regulations have been a key driver behind increases to funding under which the amount of sewage outfalls receiving secondary treatment is now well above the 2 per cent level it stood at before the Directive.

---

13 SI 1994/2841.

The Agricultural Nitrates Directive (91/676/EEC) also regulates a particular polluting activity, requiring member States to designate 'nitrate vulnerable zones' (NVZs) and implement action programmes in these areas. The Directive therefore takes a largely quality objective approach, but, like Directive 91/271/EEC, is distinct in regulating water quality through the control of a particularly polluting activity. For more detail on the Directive and its implementation, see p. 619.

Summary of the impact of EC law

The EC has had a great impact on water pollution practice in the UK. While there have been many arguments about technical matters, such as the levels laid down for nitrate in drinking water and the need for a Bathing Waters Directive at all, most of the standards required have been introduced in one way or another, although normally belatedly. A formal system of water quality classifications and objectives, statutory regulations on drinking water quality, the introduction of specific standards for dangerous substances, and a dramatic shift in relation to the discharge of sewage effluent to the sea can all be attributed to EC initiatives. The general approach to pollution control has also been altered significantly.

Perhaps the greatest impact, however, has been the great publicity that has been engendered by having specific standards set at EC level against which government action can be measured. This has certainly contributed to the intensity of the debate over nitrate.

The Water Framework Directive

EC water pollution policy is presently undergoing fundamental change following the adoption of the Water Framework Directive (2000/60/EC), an ambitious attempt at comprehensively overhauling EC water policy. This followed a general recognition that much of the Community's existing water legislation was outdated and, in particular, insufficiently holistic in its approach to pollution control. The Directive is being phased in over a period of years and, by 2013, a number of existing Directives will have been repealed, because of the scope of the Framework Directive. The main ones to be repealed are the Dangerous Substances Directive (2006/11/EC), the Groundwater Directive (80/68/EEC), the Fish Waters Directive (2006/44/EC), and the Shellfish Water Directive (2006/113/EEC).[14]

Unlike previous water legislation, the Framework Directive covers surface water and groundwater together, as well as estuaries and coastal waters. Its main purposes are:

- to prevent further deterioration in, and to protect and enhance the status of, aquatic ecosystems;

- to promote sustainable water consumption, based on the long-term protection of available water resources;

- progressively to reduce discharges, emissions, and losses of priority substances;

- the cessation or phasing out of priority hazardous substances, with the ultimate aim that concentrations in the marine environment are near background levels for naturally occurring substances and close to zero for manmade synthetic substances;

- the progressive reduction of groundwater pollution and to prevent further pollution;

- to contribute to the provision of good quality surface and groundwaters needed for sustainable, balanced, and equitable water use.

14 It is worth noting that some key water Directives will not be repealed, the main ones being the Bathing Water Directive (2006/7/EC), the Drinking Water Quality Directive (98/83/EC), the Agricultural Nitrates Directive (91/676/EEC), and the Urban Waste Water Treatment Directive (91/271/EEC).

The Directive's overriding requirement is that member States 'aim to achieve' good surface water status (meaning both good chemical status and good ecological status), good ecological potential (for artificial or heavily modified waters), and good groundwater status in all waters by the end of 2015. For groundwater, good status is measured in terms of both quantity and chemical purity (i.e. abstractions and alterations to the natural rate of recharge are sustainable in the long term without leading to loss of ecological quality); for surface waters ecological quality is an additional criterion (i.e. in addition to ensuring that concentrations of certain 'black list' substances—now termed priority hazardous substances—do not exceed relevant environmental quality standards and other Community legislation setting such standards, 'good ecological status' means that a body of water which is demonstrated to be significantly influenced by human activity, nevertheless has a rich, balanced and sustainable ecosystem). Although the definition of good status is rudimentary, in many cases it will require member States to improve on the present situation.

One of the Framework Directive's innovations is that rivers and lakes must be managed by river basin—the natural hydrological unit—instead of according to administrative or political boundaries. In relation to each river basin, the Directive makes provision for the preparation of a strategic plan: a 'river basin management plan'. These must be published first by 2009 and updated every six years. The purpose of the plan will be to establish a programme of measures (the first is required by 2012) to ensure that all waters in the river basin achieve the objective of good water status. Although, institutionally, a catchment approach is taken in the UK, the programme of measures requires integrated catchment management, which the UK has yet to adopt (see, for example, the current approach to nutrients—seen as the most significant obstacle to achieving good status—which still tends to focus on water companies' removing nitrates and pesticides rather than requiring farmers to reduce their inputs). Indeed, the Directive is as much about land use generally as it is about water management. The Directive also requires that the public have the opportunity to be involved in the formulation of these plans, which marks a departure from the UK's approach which has been more technocratic.

The Directive avoids some of the problems of adopting a singular approach to environmental standards. Indeed, it recognizes the strengths of arguments in favour of both approaches that were put forward at the time of the 1976 Dangerous Substances Directive (76/464/EEC; see pp. 236 and 589). It takes a 'combined approach', requiring member States to set down in their programmes of measures both limit values to control emissions from individual point sources and environmental quality standards to limit the cumulative impact of such emissions. For listed hazardous substances, however, as noted above (see Box 17.2), the Directive requires that these be phased out.

The Framework Directive is also the first piece of EC water legislation to address the issue of water *quantity*, which is important, in part, because water quantity affects water quality. One consequence of this is that 'full cost recovery' pricing for water use is required by 2010. This will include costs of water use in terms of environmental damage, as well as adverse effects caused by overabstraction (although the details of this obligation are contested—for example, the water companies argue that it requires that the cost of removing diffuse pollutants from water are not subsidized by water consumers).

There is no doubting that the Framework Directive requires a fundamental change in existing law—both European and domestic. There remains, however, much uncertainty—and scepticism—about how the Directive will work in practice. First, for example, 'high ecological status' is defined in terms of what a pristine water environment would be and 'good ecological status' is defined in terms of a slight distortion or deviation from pristine conditions due to human activities. Because there are no truly pristine water environments in the UK, this means that defining 'good ecological status' means defining the legally required standard against a contestable baseline.[15]

15 On what this will require, see [2003] ENDS Report 347, 23. See also W. Howarth (2006) JEL 3.

Secondly, the Directive gives scope to member States to decide whether waters have been 'heavily modified' by human action. Effectively, this enables the human benefits of existing water uses (such as flood protection) to be taken into account, and the costs of improving the quality of these waters to be proportionate and not unduly expensive for the water quality improvements that might be made. Also, as an exception to the general aim of achieving good status, less stringent environmental objectives can be established where the natural condition of waters have been so affected by human activity that the necessary improvements would be unfeasible or disproportionately expensive and, in effect, the proposed improvement measures are the 'least worst' option for the water environment. In these and other cases, it is clear that the Directive marks a profound shift away from common standards that apply across the EC. Whereas, under most existing water Directives, the difficulty with, and cost of, implementation have traditionally been irrelevant,[16] under the Framework Directive, factors such as these are likely to be central. The idea of 'full cost recovery pricing' also begs a number of questions about the methodology of calculating the cost of 'environmental harm' (although, if some form of pricing can be agreed that is generally applicable, it may provide a firm basis for valuing the environment as a commodity in other areas).

Finally, perhaps the key issue is what 'the aim of achieving' good status actually means. The terminology used is clearly different from *requiring*, as an *objective*, good status (in the way that the ECJ has interpreted previous water Directives, such as the Bathing Water and Drinking Water Directives as requiring obligations of result—see p. 178). This may lead to difficulties for individuals or groups trying to enforce the Directive, although it might be possible to point to provisions of the Directive that list exceptional cases—in which failing to achieve good status will be condoned—as supporting the view that the good status requirement is an obligation of result and not just of means, and it might mean that legal challenges will be brought more about the process (for example, about the drawing up of programmes of measures) than about the quality standard. The uncertainties about what the Directive actually requires mean that estimating the cost of implementation is impossible, although it will undoubtedly run to billions of pounds.[17] What is easier to predict is that the inherently flexible nature of the Directive, and its regard to costs and notions of proportionality, will make enforcement much less straightforward and give to EC water law some of the less satisfactory qualities seen in the past in the UK.

The Framework Directive is to be supplemented by further Directives—for example, on what achieving good groundwater status entails. This is covered by Directive 2006/118/EC, which is interesting because—in relation to hazardous substances, at least—member States must take 'all measures necessary to prevent inputs into groundwater' (the obligation is not couched in terms of taking measures 'aiming to prevent' this, as the Council wanted). This backs up the point made above that, while the general 'aim to achieve' obligation under the Framework is potentially weak, this does not mean that the whole regime established under the Directive is also weak.

A final point about the Framework Directive is that all previous water Directives have been quite traditional 'command and control' laws, in the sense that standards have been laid down in the Directives themselves with relatively little scope for manoeuvre when it came to implementing, other than the discretion, under some of the Directives, to designate areas for greater or lesser degrees of control. While the Framework Directive is also 'command' legislation (and not premised on using economic tools), some elements of it exhibit a shift in approach to standard setting, illustrative of newer forms of EC environmental governance. The best example of this is the Common Implementation Strategy, under which there is ongoing dialogue at EC level to try to thrash out what some of the deliberately vague obligations under the Directive will entail in practice. This can be seen either as an abdication on

16 Although see the changes made to the Bathing Water Directive, noted on p. 591.

17 'Who will pay for the costs of water pollution' [2005] ENDS Report, 363, 25–8, provides a good analysis in particular of the state of play with implementing the Water Framework Directive and the high costs involved.

the part of the EC legislator to set specific standards or, more positively, as a recognition of the difficulties in doing so for an environmental medium such as water.

As regards national implementation, there are, as yet, only really framework implementing provisions (see the Water Environment (Water Framework Directive) (England and Wales) Regulations 2003,[18] various Directions to the Environment Agency, and for Scotland, see p. 585).

Water and sewerage financing

Since 1989, the public water supply and sewerage services have been provided by privatized undertakers under the regulatory oversight of what is now the Water Services Regulatory Authority (commonly, still referred to as OFWAT), along with the Secretary of State. These companies' overall charges for water and sewerage services are regulated by OFWAT under the Water Industry Act 1991. This is achieved by reference to a formula, known as 'RPI + K', under which the weighted average charge is allowed to increase by the retail price index (RPI) plus a company-specific factor (known as the 'K' factor). Water companies' costs, including the cost of 'environmental' improvements such as upgrading of sewage works and improvements in drinking water quality, must be taken into account when setting the K factor. Once the K factor is set, the water companies have to operate within it. This means that the trade-offs between environmental improvements by the water companies (for example, improved performance from sewage works, improved water quality from the public water supply, and reduced losses from leakage), improvements in levels of service, efficiency savings, and increased company profits and directors' pay are very clear.

K factors are set every five years in a process known as the 'asset management planning' or 'periodic review' (the next one is in 2009). It is clear that, in determining K, binding obligations under EC Directives cannot be avoided, despite the costs to consumers. This is not to say that price reviews have always ensured that compliance with mandatory standards have been achieved—for example, neither the 1989 or 1994 reviews aimed at ensuring sufficient compliance with the Bathing Water Directive. Where there is clear discretion is in the extent to which the water companies should finance desirable, but non-mandatory, environmental improvements, such as 'guide values' in EC water Directives or where river sites of special scientific interest (SSSIs) are affected. Given the increased levels of discretion that member States will have under the Water Framework Directive, it is likely that decisions of the economic regulator will become even more critical in determining both policy choices and legal obligations.[19]

The courts have considered these funding arrangements in contexts relevant to environmental protection. In *Marcic v. Thames Water Utilities plc* [2004] Env LR 25, the House of Lords held that a claim in nuisance or negligence and under the Human Rights Act 1998 for external sewage flooding could not succeed because the claimant was, in effect, asking the court to rewrite the sewerage undertaker's funding formula, as set by OFWAT, with one determined by the Court, and because s. 18 of the Water Industry Act 1991 provided a specific statutory mechanism for enforcing obligations by undertakers that should not be undermined by common law claims (see further Case 11.7). In *Ministry of Defence v. Thames Water Utilities Ltd* [2006] Env LR 37, however, it was held that a common law claim for negligence was not ruled out only because of the Water Industry Act enforcement mechanisms. *Marcic* was distinguished because, in *Ministry of Defence*, the Court held that the claimant, in trying to recover an overpayment of money for sewerage services, was not trying to cut

---

18 SI 2003/3242.

19 The views of a previous Director General of OFWAT on balancing environmental and economic interests are outlined in I. Byatt (1996) 3(4) JEPP 665.

across the statutory scheme, because the statutory scheme was not concerned with letting undertakers overcharge.[20]

Finally, in *Dobson v. Thames Water Utilities Ltd* [2007] EWHC 2021 (TCC), the Court had to consider claims in nuisance, negligence, and under the Human Rights Act relating to odours and mosquitoes from a sewerage works. The Court held that, following *Marcic*, these private law actions would be precluded if they were to undermine the statutory enforcement mechanisms. By failing or neglecting to press for capital funding from OFWAT to address the problem, however, Thames could be liable under the private law claims and it would be no defence to say that its ability to funds the necessary works would mean that it had to go beyond the existing funding arrangements and, in effect, 'dip into its own pockets' to do so.

There are some quite fine distinctions being made in the latter cases and some uncertainties, because, for example, a court might be asked to anticipate whether funding would have been provided if asked for. But these cases do show that the courts are prepared to find that remedies other than those under the WIA 1991—which might be considered generous to the undertakers—can be utilized. They also show that the financial certainty that the price review process provides is not the only consideration when dealing with wrongs that the water industry legislation has not reserved exclusively for OFWAT to deal with.

Drinking water quality

As far as the quality of the public water supply is concerned, under WIA 1991, s. 67, domestic water must be 'wholesome'. This term is defined in legislation in the Water Supply (Water Quality) Regulations 2000[21]—which implement the revised Drinking Water Quality Directive (98/83/EC)—which lay down a large number of specific criteria with which water must comply if supplied for domestic or food production purposes. The revised Directive demonstrates signs of the impact of the Subsidiarity Principle being applied, in that the number of parameters is reduced, and parameters without a health impact are set only for monitoring and remediation purposes. The Regulations require that information on water quality must be made available to the public.

Enforcement of s. 67 is through enforcement orders issued by the Secretary of State. The use of these has proven controversial and, although upheld by the domestic courts, has fallen foul of EC law and required changes to national legislation (on which, see Case 7.8).[22] There is, at present, no scope for direct criminal liability, but, under the Water Act 2003, the Secretary of State and the Drinking Water Inspectorate (DWI) will, probably from 2005, have the power to fine water companies for supplying water that is not wholesome.

In addition, it is an offence under WIA 1991, s. 70, to supply water that is 'unfit for human consumption', although prosecution for this offence may only be brought by the Secretary of State or the Director of Public Prosecutions. In practice, the Secretary of State has delegated enforcement powers to the DWI, with the Chief Inspector being given formal statutory recognition under s. 57 of the Water Act 2003.

In the last few years, the DWI has taken a number of successful prosecutions against water suppliers, mostly under s. 70 for supplying discoloured water. In *R v. Yorkshire Water Services Ltd* [2002] Env LR 18, it was held that there could be an offence even in cases in which there was only discolouration and no bacteriological contamination—water could be 'unfit' either if it would be likely to cause injury or if, due to its smell or appearance, a 'reasonable customer of firm character' would refuse to drink it or reject its use in preparing food.

---

20 A line of argument similar to that in *Allen v. Gulf Oil Refining Ltd* [1981] AC 1001—see Case 11.5.

21 SI 2000/3184.

22 The statutory mechanism of enforcement orders has also been central to determining whether there is civil liability for things like sewage flooding: see *Marcic v. Thames Water Utilities plc* [2004] Env LR 25 (see p. 596).

The Water Supply (Water Quality) Regulations 2000 (Amendment) Regulations 2007[23] now provide that supply companies use general risk assessment techniques to alert them to potential public health problems. Problems must be notified to the Secretary of State who can serve a notice requiring steps to be taken and failure to adhere to a notice is a criminal offence (although the penalty is very low). The enforcement approach remains largely cooperative. There is the possibility of an action at common law for breach of statutory duty or negligence (see *Read v. Croydon Corporation* [1938] 4 All ER 631, in which a ratepayer successfully sued in negligence for water supplied to his household, which caused his daughter to contract typhoid). Widespread incidents, such as at Camelford in 1988, may give rise to an action in public nuisance (*R v. South West Water Authority* [1991] LMELR 65).

The scope for an action in negligence and in contract was considered by the Privy Council in *Hamilton v. Papakura District Council* [2002] UKPC 57, a case brought by farmers in New Zealand who grew tomatoes hydroponically and whose water supply was contaminated with a herbicide that, while not affecting the quality of the water for normal drinking water purposes, affected their crop. The Privy Council unanimously rejected the claim in negligence, essentially because the farmers were not owed a duty of care to provide them with water of this exceptionally high quality. (Claims in nuisance and under the rule in *Rylands v. Fletcher* were rejected on the grounds of lack of foreseeability of damage.) The nature of supplying water to the public was central to this decision: if the water had to meet this high standard for the tomato growers, then, in practice, it would have to be of this quality for all of the council's water customers (which would put too onerous a burden on the council). The action in contract was more finely balanced, but was rejected by a 3–2 majority. Whether an action in contract for supplying poor quality water could get off the ground in the UK, however, is a matter of dispute: the traditional view is that the relationship between water companies and their customers is statutory, and that the respective rights and duties of the parties is contained in the water industry legislation.

Standard setting, water quality, and consents for the discharge of trade or sewage effluent

As noted previously, most pollution loading comes from discharges in relation to which there is a consent in order to avoid liability for a water pollution offence. It is therefore important to think of the consent system and of how consents are set within the context of the principal water pollution offences. Although water quality objectives are discussed at the end of this section, this does not mean that they are a final consideration for the Environment Agency when determining a consent application. Rather, because of the emphasis on environmental quality standards, they are likely to be central. But even in cases in which there are mandatory EC quality standards to be achieved, there will usually be some flexibility in the system when individual consents are set.

A consent[24] is required from the Environment Agency for:

- any discharge of trade or sewage effluent into 'controlled waters';

- any discharge of trade or sewage effluent through a pipe from land into the sea outside the limits of 'controlled waters';

- any discharge where a prohibition is in force.

---

23 SI 2007/2734.

24 It is worth noting that the discharge consent system has not been subsumed within the Environmental Permitting (England and Wales) Regulations 2007—although this is now being set in motion.

It is an offence under the Water Resources Act (WRA) 1991, s. 85, to 'cause or knowingly permit' such a discharge, although there is a defence if it is carried out in accordance with a consent. This means it is also an offence to breach any conditions attached to a consent—a point made explicit by s. 85(6). There is no need to show that the discharge has polluted the receiving waters, because the offence consists of discharging otherwise than in accordance with the consent.

'Trade effluent' is defined in s. 221 and includes any effluent from trade premises (these include agricultural, fish farming, and research establishments), other than domestic sewage or surface water. 'Sewage effluent', also defined in s. 221, includes any effluent, other than surface water, from a sewerage works. The discharge must be of effluent, so it seems that, if trade materials (such as fuel oil) escape, they are covered by the general pollution offence (see p. 607). But there is some doubt here, because effluent is defined in s. 221 to mean 'any liquid' and is not specifically limited to wastes.

A further problem relates to the interpretation of the word 'discharge'. This word is not defined in the Act. It is capable of carrying either an active meaning—that is, that the release of materials has to be part of a deliberate trade or sewage process—or a passive meaning—as in the discharge of blood from a wound. It is suggested that it carries an active meaning, because, otherwise, potential dischargers would be in the impossible position of having to apply for a consent for something that was not meant to happen. The effect of this reasoning is that accidental and non-routine emissions of trade or sewage effluent do not require a consent, and are covered by the general water pollution offence.

On the other hand, the ECJ has held that 'discharge' for the purposes of the Dangerous Substances in Water Directive (76/464/EEC, now 2006/11/EC) can include discharges of listed substances—polycyclic aromatic hydrocarbons (PAHs)—found in wood preservative with which wooden posts used for shoring up riverbanks had been treated (Case C-232/97 *Nederhoff* [1999] ECR I-6385) and discharges of polluted steam precipitating into water-courses (Case C-231/97 *Van Rooij* [1999] ECR I-6355). This is clearly a more expansive understanding of what 'discharge' means and, while it clearly applies to discharges regulated under this Directive, it remains to be seen whether the Environment Agency will insist on consents for similar discharges regulated solely as a matter of national law (and, if it does, how it will do so).

The prohibition is a device designed to cover those cases in which the type of discharge is not necessarily harmful and thus the blanket requirement of a consent is not justified. By prohibiting discharges on a selective basis, control can be exercised over just those situations in which it is required (see s. 86, WRA 1991).

There are three situations in which a prohibition may apply:

- the Environment Agency prohibits, by notice, a discharge of trade or sewage effluent from a building or fixed plant to any land or landlocked waters outside the definition of controlled waters—including such situations as soakaways from trade premises and some agricultural activities;

- the Agency prohibits a discharge of matter other than trade or sewage effluent from a drain or sewer—trade and sewage effluent are automatically covered by the need for a consent, so the intention here is to restrict such things as discharges of dangerous substances from a storm drain;

- any such discharges involving substances prescribed by regulations *automatically* invoke the prohibition.

In relation to the first two categories, the prohibition can only come into force three months after notice to the discharger, unless the Environment Agency is satisfied that there is an emergency.

Controlled waters

The discharge consent system and the water pollution offences apply to 'controlled waters'. 'Controlled waters' are defined in s. 104, and include virtually all inland and coastal waters. Controlled waters are made up of four subcategories:

- relevant territorial waters—that is, the sea within a line three miles out from the baselines from which the territorial sea is measured, despite the extension of the territorial limit to 12 miles in the Territorial Sea Act 1987;

- coastal waters—that is, the sea within those baselines up to the line of the highest tide and tidal waters up to the freshwater limit as defined by the Secretary of State on maps produced for that purpose;

- inland waters—that is, rivers, streams, underground streams, canals, lakes, and reservoirs, including those that are temporarily dry;

- groundwaters—that is, any waters contained in underground strata or in wells or boreholes.

In addition, the courts have held that a riverbed can form part of 'controlled waters' (see *National Rivers Authority v. Biffa Waste* [1996] Env LR 227), as can a man-made ditch, if it drains into controlled waters (*Environment Agency v. Brock plc* [1998] Env LR 607). Because s. 104 refers to 'waters *of* any watercourse' rather than waters *in* any watercourse, the definition extends to streams that have diverted from their normal course (*R v. Dovermoss Ltd* [1995] Env LR 258). Water supply mains and pipes, and sewers and drains (where separate controls on discharges apply), are excluded from the definition of controlled waters.

The consent system

The system for acquiring a consent is set out in WRA 1991, Sch. 10, and the Control of Pollution (Applications, Appeals and Registers) Regulations 1996,[25] and it involves a higher degree of public involvement than many other licensing-type systems.

Each discharge requires a consent, so, if a factory has three discharge pipes, it needs a consent for each one. The applicant applies to the Environment Agency, which has a discretion as to the details required. Normally, the applicant will have to state the place, nature, quantity, rate of flow, composition, and temperature of the proposed discharge. It is an offence under s. 206 to give incorrect information. There are publicity requirements, although these may be dispensed with if the Agency considers that the discharge will have 'no appreciable effect' on the receiving waters—a criterion that is fleshed out in guidance and which has been much relied on.

The Environment Agency must take into account timely written representations. It has the power to grant consent, either unconditionally or subject to conditions, or to refuse consent.

(a) Conditions

The Environment Agency may attach 'such conditions as it may think fit' and Sch. 10, para. 2(5) includes a non-exhaustive list. This includes such things as the quality, quantity, nature, composition, and temperature of the discharge, the siting and design of the outlet, the provision of meters for measuring these matters, the taking and recording of samples by the discharger, and the provision of information to the Agency. Frequently, the most significant conditions will relate to biochemical oxygen demand, levels of toxic or dangerous materials,

25 SI 1996/2971.

and suspended solids, although the Agency is presently considering the introduction of a more sophisticated test based on the toxicity of the discharge to aquatic life. For industrial discharges, it is normal to attach absolute numerical limits for the various parameters covered in the consent, with the result that any excess amounts to a breach of the consent.

Conditions requiring a specified treatment process are legal, but are not generally imposed, because, in the past, it has been government policy to require compliance with environmental standards while giving a discharger a choice of methods to achieve the standard. For some discharges, however, the effect of the Urban Waste Water Treatment Directive (91/271/EEC) may be that specific treatment methods are required (for example, biological treatment), although, generally, the Directive requires quality standards to be met. It is permissible for conditions to be staggered so that they get progressively stricter.

There is also a procedure for granting a retrospective consent, which enables the Environment Agency to formalize the legal position in relation to a discharge and also to attach conditions to an existing discharge.

(b) Sewage discharge consents

Sewage discharges have always caused regulatory problems, both because of their potent polluting power, and because of the previous conflict of interest between regulator and regulated when the water authorities were responsible for operating treatment works and policing discharges from such works (see p. 24). But the same conflict also existed when the local authorities ran the sewage works, because they also provided members for the river authorities and thus exercised an influence on their decisions.

Under WRA 1991, there is no conflict of interest. Sewerage undertakers are treated similarly to other dischargers in requiring a consent from the Environment Agency. One slight difference relates to the offences under s. 85: because sewerage undertakers treat wastes discharged by other people and thus have limited control over what is actually put into the sewers, they have a special defence under s. 87(2). This operates if the contravention of their discharge consent was due to an unconsented discharge made into the sewer by another person that they could not reasonably have prevented (see *National Rivers Authority v. Yorkshire Water Services Ltd* [1995] 1 AC 444, discussed at p. 610).

A more significant difference is that sewage works have, in the past, had their consents set on different terms from other dischargers. Before privatization, the relative lack of control over the quality of sewage effluent or its containment was comparatively unimportant, because the poacher–gamekeeper relationship meant that there was considerable scope for selective enforcement. With privatization pending, however, consents were relaxed so that, instead of containing absolute numerical limits, with the result that any breach of the limit amounted to a criminal offence, consents were set by reference to 'look-up' tables intended to ensure a 95 per cent compliance rate over a rolling 12-month period. Only in exceptional cases, in which a generous maximum (or 'upper tier') limit was exceeded, would there be liability for a one-off sewage pollution incident. These relaxations, which have been described as '*a sort of environmental betrayal*'[26] in order to reduce the undertakers' potential liabilities and make privatization more attractive, were not the first time that sewage discharge consents had been relaxed.[27]

Under, first, the NRA and, now, the Environment Agency, these 'percentile' consents are being replaced by absolute limits when consents come up for review. This has led to a significant rise in the number of prosecutions brought against sewerage undertakers, because only a single sample is now needed, rather than a series of samples from a 12-month period. It

---

26 D. Kinnersley (1994) *Coming Clean*, Harmondsworth: Penguin, p. 49.

27 In the late 1970s, the National Water Council commenced a review of consents that led to some relaxations, although the review was never completed and the results never published. Consents were also relaxed in the 1980s in anticipation of the availability of a right to bring private prosecutions (under the Control of Pollution Act 1974).

has also had a knock-on effect on trade effluent consents granted by the sewerage undertakers under WIA 1991. But the Secretary of State has decided that some leeway must still be given to take account of events beyond the control of the sewerage undertakers and revised consents give some protection to sewerage undertakers in cases in which they can show that they have operated the works reasonably practicably so as to minimize polluting effects—for example, if a sewage system overflows during heavy rainfall.[28]

A final issue is the impact of the Urban Waste Water Treatment Directive (91/271/EEC), discussed above. This imposes various restrictions on sewage discharges, although the general tenor of the Directive is purposive rather than standard setting—that is, it seeks to achieve specific goals depending on the area and population concerned, rather than to mandate that compliance with specific parameters or treatment methods should be met by all sewage works. Some new and revised consents require, in general terms, compliance with the Directive as a consent condition. Taken on its own, such a condition is probably meaningless and likely to be void for uncertainty.

(c) Revocation and variation

Under Sch. 10, para. 7, the Environment Agency has a discretion to review consents from time to time. A variation or a revocation can be made simply by notifying the discharger. Alternatively, the Secretary of State may direct that a variation take place (Sch. 10, para. 9). No compensation is payable except in one case considered below. There is no provision for public participation in relation to a variation or revocation. This power to make variations or revocations is a wide one that reflects the need to cater for new circumstances, such as a new polluter in the catchment area, or a newly perceived pollution threat, or a change in EC or international obligations. It also reasserts the position that no one has a right to pollute.

But there are limits on when a variation or revocation can be made. A period will be stipulated in the original consent, which cannot be less than four years, and a variation or revocation cannot take place within that period (measured from the setting of the original consent or the last variation), except with the permission of the discharger. In practice, there seems to be considerable variation between Environment Agency regions when it comes to reviewing consents after the four-year period. Exceptionally, the Secretary of State may direct a modification within the period in order to give effect to an EC or international obligation, or to protect public health, or flora and fauna dependent on an aquatic environment. There is no right to vary early solely because the discharger has been in breach of the consent,[29] or in order to cater for a new pollutant: both are situations in which such a right would be desirable. Arguably, this four-year period will lead to difficulties in taking a targeted approach to implementing the Water Framework Directive through revising consents. The Environment Agency will have to pay compensation to the discharger if a direction is made on grounds of public health or protection of flora and fauna within the period.

(d) Charges

A cost-recovery fee for the consent application is payable—that is, the fee is not linked to the polluting impact, but to the administrative costs of the consent system.[30] The charging system therefore only gives very limited effect to the Polluter Pays Principle. The possibility of going further and introducing charges reflecting the full environmental costs of discharges has been on the political agenda since 1990[31] and, in 1992, was taken further by the Royal

28 The key clauses are reproduced in S. Payne [1998] WL 13.

29 This may change if the Regulatory Enforcement and Sanctions Bill is enacted.

30 Environment Act 1995, ss. 41 and 42. Charging schemes must be approved by the Secretary of State and have Treasury consent.

31 HM Government (1990) *This Common Inheritance*, Cm 1200.

Commission on Environmental Pollution (RCEP).[32] The Labour Government consulted on this issue as part of a wider look at using economic instruments to control water pollution,[33] but appeared to conclude that the difficulties in full cost recovery outweighed any likely benefits. Part of the reason for this was no doubt because of the complex relationships between the various parties involved (dischargers and sewage undertakers) and the impact of extraneous factors, such as water flows, on pollution levels. In short, calculating the cost of water pollution per cubic metre of discharge is simply much harder than, for example, putting a price on the emission of a tonne of carbon dioxide. The 1997 consultation also looked at the possible use of tradable permits, but this has not been followed up (no doubt, in part, because there are very few stretches of river in which there are enough dischargers for there to be meaningful competition).

The role of the Secretary of State

The Secretary of State has a general, and very wide, power under s. 40 of the Environment Act 1995 to issue directions of a general or specific nature to the Environment Agency in relation to pollution control, among other matters. The supplementary powers of the Secretary of State to require information from the Agency in s. 202 should also be noted. The reason for the width of this power is the fact that large policymaking powers have effectively been delegated to the Agency, making some mechanism for central control desirable. The use of directions to achieve this should be compared with the use of circular guidance in other areas of environmental law, because they fulfil similar purposes. Directions are often used in relation to EC Directives, supplementing implementing regulations. At any stage, the Secretary of State may call in an application for decision (Sch. 10, para. 5). This is an unfettered discretion and ousts the jurisdiction of the Environment Agency to consider the consent—but it is rarely exercised.

Appeals

The applicant or discharger has a right to appeal to the Secretary of State against a refusal of consent, the attachment of unreasonable conditions, any adverse variation or revocation of a consent, or the setting of the period in which a consent cannot be varied (s. 91). The procedures for called-in applications and for appeals are set out in the Control of Pollution (Applications, Appeals, and Registers) Regulations 1996.[34] An appeal is a general rehearing of the matter in issue and the Secretary of State has the same powers as the Environment Agency originally had. As with planning appeals, in practice, appeals are heard by the Planning Inspectorate, although the Secretary of State retains the final decision in more important cases. Compared with the system of planning appeals, which accords enormous opportunities for argument on policy, this appeal right is far less commonly used. This may be because there is little perceived difference in policy between the Secretary of State and the Environment Agency.

How are consents set?

The Environment Agency, or the Secretary of State on appeal, has a wide discretion in setting the consent and it will be set by reference to a variety of factors. Although Sch. 10 is silent as to the factors that must be taken into account, applying ordinary public law principles, the

---

32 RCEP Sixteenth Report (1992) *Freshwater Quality*, Cm 1966.
33 Department for Environment, Transport and the Regions (1997) *Economic Instruments for Water Pollution*.
34 SI 1996/2971.

Agency must have regard to all material considerations. In addition, certain requirements appear from other sections of the Act, especially s. 84, and from EC law.

As stated before, it is important to grasp the individualized and flexible nature of these consents, although uniformity and consistency is now being sought by the Environment Agency. Relevant matters include:

- the water quality objectives and standards set for the receiving waters under s. 83 (see below), which emphasizes that one of the crucial elements in fixing a consent is the effect on the receiving waters—and this, in turn, depends on the use that is intended for those receiving waters;

- any other effects on the receiving waters, such as on a fishery or downstream user— particular regard being had to whether the waters are used for abstraction for water supply or irrigation;

- any relevant EC standards for the discharge concerned or for the quality of the receiving waters;

- any 'cocktail' effect of the discharge, in relation to which the Environment Agency will consider not only the immediate effect of the discharge, but also any impact that the discharge will have in combination with the current contents of the waters and any potential future discharges;

- the need to eliminate discharges of priority hazardous substances under Directive 2006/11/EC;

- the Agency's environmental duties laid out in the Environment Act 1995, ss. 4–7 (see p. 117), and duties that fall on it as a public body (for example, regarding SSSIs and biodiversity—see Chapter 19);

- any relevant objections and representations made, and the results of any consultation carried out;

- certain informal standard tests for particular types of discharge—for example, 'normal' standards for sewage works were suggested by the Eighth Report of the Royal Commission on Sewage Disposal in 1912 and these were applied for many years (the Environment Agency is now seeking to establish some uniformity of standards across the country for all types of discharge);

- any other material considerations.

There would be scope for having general binding rules applying across an industrial sector, but so far there appears to be little enthusiasm for these—in England, at least. In other member States, the regulators have criticized their use for making it harder to establish and maintain a cooperative relationship with dischargers,[35] but they have now been introduced in Scotland (see Box 17.4).

BOX 17.4 **A more risk-based approach to authorizations**

The Water Environment (Controlled Activities) (Scotland) Regulations 2005[36] provide for three levels of controls—collectively termed 'authorizations'—which are intended to serve as a more

---

35 See [1998] WL 195.
36 SSI 2005/348.

proportionate and risk-based regulatory regime for dealing with the effects on the water environment (not only on water pollution) from activities.

- **General binding rules (GBRs)**

  GBRs provide statutory controls over certain low-risk activities, including abstractions of less than 10m^3/day and the discharge of surface water run-off that does not cause water pollution. Any person undertaking an activity that falls within the scope of the GBR does not have to contact the regulator—that is, the Scottish Environment Protection Agency (SEPA)—to be registered, but must abide by any rule laid out in the Regulations that relates to that activity.[37]

- **Registration**

  Registration is intended to cover low-risk activities that cumulatively pose a risk to the water environment. It is expected that the majority of existing discharge consents will become registrations.

- **Water use licence**

  If site-specific controls are required and, in particular, if constraints upon the activity are to be imposed, then the activity will be authorized using a licence. Licences can cover sites, not only individual discharge points—for example, a single licence can cover a number of fish farm cages under the control of a single operator. A licence requires the identification of a 'responsible person' who, in SEPA's view, will secure compliance with the conditions of the licence. (This may be a company.) This is quite distinctive from the consenting regime in England and Wales, which does not have anything analogous to a 'fit and proper person' test. Licences are likely to be needed by the more major sewage and industrial discharges, abstractions, and impounding works.

SEPA can move the control over activities between registration and licences, and from GBR to registration or licences, as it considers necessary in order to protect the water environment (and can also move the level of control down from a licence to a registration, if this is appropriate).

Water quality objectives

Although the 'British' approach to the control of water pollution has tended, over the years, to concentrate on the environmental impact of pollutants, *statutory* water quality objectives developed as a response primarily to the EC, to Directives such as the Dangerous Substances in Water Directive, and to the need to show that consents were not set on an informal, ad hoc basis, but by reference to binding legal obligations to meet quality standards for the receiving environment. The legal framework for these objectives is contained in ss. 82–84 of the Water Resources Act 1991. Classification regulations set the standards that waters must reach in order to come within a certain classification (s. 82). The Secretary of State then establishes (under s. 83) a water quality *objective* for each stretch of controlled waters. This sets specified classifications as an objective and, accordingly, incorporates the relevant water quality *standards*. These then act as explicit policy goals for the Environment Agency, which is under a legal duty under s. 84 to exercise its functions, including the granting of discharge consents, so as to achieve and maintain the statutory water quality objective at all times, at

---

37 The most recent list of GBRs are contained in the Water Environment (Controlled Activities) (Scotland) Amendment Regulations 2007, SSI 2007/219.

least as far as it is practicable to do so. These processes have been used on a number of occasions to implement EC water quality Directives.

A central feature of water quality objectives is that, as stated above, under s. 84, the Environment Agency and Secretary of State must exercise their powers under the Act so as to achieve statutory water quality objectives at all times, so far as it is practicable to do so. It does not follow that the Agency is in breach of s. 84 simply by failing to achieve the appropriate standards—but it does mean that its powers in relation to the setting and variation of consents, remedial and enforcement action, and preventive controls should be exercised to achieve the standards if practicable, because a judicial review action could conceivably be brought to ensure the enforcement of the duty (although a more fruitful avenue would probably be to press the Secretary of State to use his powers under s. 40 to issue a direction to the Environment Agency). Under the Environmental Protection Act (EPA) 1990, s. 7(2) (c), a similar duty is placed on the Environment Agency to try to achieve statutory water quality objectives when considering authorizations for IPPC. Stricter emission limits values must also be met if these are required by an environmental quality standard, although only if the standard is under an EC Directive (under Sch 1, para. 3 of the Pollution Prevention and Control Act 1999, the Minister can direct that national quality objectives are adhered to). These must be used regardless of whether they are 'available' (and so cost considerations seem to be irrelevant).[38]

Although statutory water quality objectives continue to be used to implement existing EC water quality Directives, there is no prospect that they will be used beyond this. For practical purposes, therefore, the system is in effect in abeyance. A major reason is that attention is now focused on the quality objectives required under the EC Water Framework Directive and the specific mechanisms that the Directive envisages—river basin management plans and programmes of measures—to aim to achieve these objectives. Although ss. 82–84 might be used to give effect to the Framework Directive, a separate mechanism could also be used. There is some commonality of approach, however, between the Framework Directive and statutory water quality objectives, in the sense that both ultimately hinge on public authorities aiming at securing these objectives via prescribed mechanisms, rather than on the objectives being objectively binding standards. A key difference is that the Water Framework Directive will provide for legal targets for general ecological water quality and at some considerable cost (see p. 595); by contrast, government has generally disliked the prospect of using statutory water quality objectives, because of the costs involved.

Groundwater pollution

Different provisions apply to certain activities that may lead to black or grey list substances contaminating groundwater. Particularly risky activities here include manufacturing leaks and spills, the disposal of agricultural pesticides including sheep dips, and underground storage tanks.

The Groundwater Regulations 1998[39] belatedly implemented the 1980 EC Groundwater Directive (80/68/EEC) (although the Directive's provisions were, up to a point, implemented in relation to waste disposal by the Waste Management Licensing Regulations 1994).[40] The Regulations require the discharge consent system to prevent the entry of black list substances

---

38 Environmental Permitting (England and Wales) Regulations 2007, SI 2007/3538, Sch. 7, and see p. 488.
39 SI 1998/2746.
40 SI 1994/1056.

and pollution from grey list substances.[41] But the Regulations also use consent-type provisions to regulate indirect discharges, such as those that might arise from the disposal and tipping of listed substances.[42] They also provide for a 'notice' provision similar to prohibition notices in relation to activities on or in the ground (such as underground storage tanks), although only if pollution might arise (reg. 19). The Environment Agency has discretion whether to serve such a notice and must take account of any code of practice issued. There are very limited publicity requirements for these authorizations and notices. In practice, notices seem to be used as a last resort, in cases in which negotiation and persuasion have failed.

A significant difference is that the Groundwater Regulations 1998 also create a specific offence of discharging listed substances if there is a *risk* of *indirect* groundwater pollution, by amending the wording of s. 85 of WRA 1991 specifically to cover this situation. What is unique about this is not that the risk of pollution is covered (see below), but that what amounts to a pollution offence is defined in WRA 1991 and that no actual entry or discharge into water is required.

Water pollution offences

Turning from the consent system, it is important to remember that, from the discharger's perspective, a key purpose of this system is to guard against criminal liability for polluting controlled waters.[43] The water pollution offences in WRA 1991 that are described below[44] are therefore important in that they provide the context for the consent system (it should be stressed again that the discharge consent system does not require dischargers to be 'licensed' or to meet general process-based standards, as is the case, for example, with industrial operators under the IPPC systems, although, in practice, the difference is not that great). But the water pollution offences are also the key means of imposing criminal liability on those who discharge without a consent—for example, in cases in which substances are illicitly dumped into a river or there is a pollution spill after an incident. The offences below are in addition to the offence of breaching any condition of a discharge consent, which, of course, only applies to consent holders (s. 85(6)).

General pollution offence

There is a general offence under s. 85(1) of causing or knowingly permitting any poisonous, noxious, or polluting matter or any waste to enter controlled waters. As is common within the flexible definitions of 'pollution control' in the UK, the words 'poisonous, noxious or polluting' are not defined—but the wording is very wide (see Case 17.3).

CASE 17.3 'Poisonous, noxious or polluting'—*R v. Dovermoss Ltd* [1995] Env LR 258

Slurry had been spread on farmland. A stream had become blocked and changed its course so that it ran over the field, causing the slurry to contaminate spring water with levels of ammonia in excess

---

41 On the meaning of 'prevent' in this context, see *R (Lewis) v. Environment Agency* [2006] Env LR 10, a landfill liner would 'prevent' pollution, though it might deteriorate within a century.

42 Groundwater Regulations 1998, reg. 18. The Waste Management (England and Wales) Regulations 2006 brought waste management licensing fully within the scope of the Groundwater Regulations 1998.

43 Waste in this context is now specifically defined as under the EC Waste Framework Directive (2006/12/EC)— see s. 85(7)—and hence excludes waste waters (except for waste in liquid form)—see p. 673.

44 Less commonly used offences are contained inter alia in the Salmon and Freshwater Fisheries Act 1975, s. 4 (relating only to waters containing fish) and in specific regulatory provisions prohibiting the supply of certain polluting substances, e.g., anglers' lead weights, PCBs, and tri-organotin compounds.

of the levels prescribed under EC drinking water legislation. The Court of Appeal held that 'polluting' requires simply that a likelihood or *capability* of causing harm to animals, plants, or those who use the water could be demonstrated; *actual* harm is not necessary. Even mere discolouration may be sufficient, at least for the matter to be 'polluting'.[45]

The case illustrates how the main water pollution offences are not focused on pollution, but rather on the discharge or entry of polluting matter. One reason for this is because the actual effect of the polluting matter may depend on subsequent factors. As was held in an earlier case:[46] '*If the act would be criminal in fair weather when a river was low, it does not become innocent because rainfall causes a flood.*' It also illustrates how, despite increasing attention being paid to ecological effects, the law also protects more mundane human interests, such as the aesthetic look of a river.[47]

This general offence complements the more specific offence of discharging trade or sewage effluent without consent (s. 85(3)). Obviously, it covers any entry of polluting matter that is not trade or sewage effluent. But an illegal discharge of trade or sewage effluent also amounts to an offence under the general offence if it causes pollution.

The general offence also covers accidental and non-routine escapes of trade or sewage effluent, because, while the specific offence requires a 'discharge', the general offence only requires an entry. In addition, non-point discharges, such as agricultural run-off, are potentially covered by the general offence.

There is a further offence in s. 85(5) of substantially aggravating pollution by impeding the proper flow of inland, non-tidal waters.

Defences

A number of defences to these water pollution offences are set out in s. 88. A discharge or entry made in accordance with any of the following is a defence:

- a discharge consent from the Environment Agency (or earlier equivalents);

- an IPPC permit (see Chapter 14);

- an environmental permit (unless it authorizes a Part B activity);[48]

- a 'dumping at sea' licence granted by the Department for Environment, Food and Rural Affairs (DEFRA) under the Food and Environment Protection Act 1985;

- an Act of Parliament;

- any statutory order (such as a drought order).

Among a miscellany of other defences, s. 89 provides a defence if the entry or discharge was made in an emergency in order to avoid danger to life or health. In such a case, the discharger must inform the Environment Agency as soon as reasonably practicable and take reasonable steps to minimize any pollution. This defence was successfully relied on in *Express Ltd (t/a Express Dairies Distribution) v. Environment Agency* [2003] Env LR 29, in which, following a tyre blowout, the driver of a milk tanker pulled over onto the hard shoulder of a motorway and the milk entered a brook via roadside drains. The Court accepted that the

---

45 See also *Express Ltd v. Environment Agency* [2005] Env LR 7. For discussion of this issue, see W. Howarth (1993) MLR 171.

46 *R v. Justices of Antrim* (1906) 2 IR 298.

47 For another case on this same issue in a different context (the EC Agricultural Nitrates Directive), see the broad interpretation given to 'eutrophication', as including visual disamenity as well as adverse ecological effects, in Case C-280/02 *Commission v. France* [2004] ECR I-8573.

48 Under the Environmental Permitting (England and Wales) Regulations 2007, SI 2007/3538, Sch. 3, para. 4.

defence applied, even though it also held that the chain of causation in relation to the water pollution offence had not been broken (see below). What mattered was not that the operation that caused the polluting matter to enter the controlled water was done in an emergency, but rather that the entry was caused in order to avoid danger to life or health. It appears that only a danger to human life or health would suffice.

There are some complex provisions in s. 87 relating to responsibility for discharges from sewerage works. In addition to the impact of the wide interpretation given to the concept of 'causing' on sewerage undertakers (see below), s. 87(1) deems sewerage undertakers to have caused a discharge of sewage effluent if they were bound to receive into the sewer or works matter included in the discharge. In other words, they are responsible for all discharges from sewers or works unless the pollution is caused by an illegal—that is, unconsented—discharge into the sewer. Section 87(2) does, however, provide a defence in cases in which a contravention of s. 85 is attributable to an unconsented discharge into the sewerage system by a third party that the sewerage undertaker could not reasonably have been expected to prevent. In *National Rivers Authority v. Yorkshire Water Services Ltd* [1995] 1 AC 444, the House of Lords decided that, notwithstanding the precise wording of s. 87(2), the defence applies to all the offences in s. 85. It should be noted that the defence covers the situation in which the sewerage undertaker could not reasonably have prevented the discharge *into* the sewer, rather than *from* the sewer, but that the original discharger into the sewer can be prosecuted under s. 85 for causing pollution of controlled waters as well as under WIA 1991, s. 118, for the illegal discharge to the sewer.[49]

Although farmers no longer have a defence of acting in accordance with good agricultural practice, there is non-binding guidance (The Water Code Revised 1998, issued under SI 1998/3084) that will affect any decision whether to prosecute and the level of any fine imposed. Conformity may also influence any decision about whether the actions of a farmer are judged reasonable for the purposes of a nuisance action (see *Savage v. Fairclough* [2000] Env LR 183).

The meaning of 'cause or knowingly permit'

The offences under s. 85 require that the defendant 'cause or knowingly permit' the relevant discharge or entry. It is clear that there are two separate offences, 'causing' and 'knowingly permitting', and that the former lays down an offence of strict liability because it is not conditioned by any requirement of knowledge.

Until recently, the leading case in this area was the *Alphacell* case, in which the House of Lords provided reasonably clear guidance as to what 'causing' required (see Case 17.4).

CASE 17.4 *Alphacell Ltd v. Woodward* [1972] AC 824

Settling tanks at a paper factory overflowed into a river. The biochemical oxygen demand (BOD) of the discharge was well above the level permitted in the consent. Although the magistrates did not find that the firm had been negligent (a strange decision because pumps that should have stopped the flow were blocked by brambles and ferns), the House of Lords held that there was no need to prove negligence or fault. Alphacell was guilty of the general offence of causing pollution simply by carrying on the activity that gave rise to the pollution. As long as its activities were themselves intentional, all that needed to be shown was a causal link between the activities and the discharge. The directness of the entry was also irrelevant: in this case, the entry was via a channel into a river.[50]

---

49 The specific rules about discharges to sewers are covered in the Online Resource Centre.
50 For further discussion of strict liability in environmental crime, see p. 260.

This test was reiterated in many cases. For example, in *National Rivers Authority v. Yorkshire Water Services Ltd* [1995] 1 AC 444, an industrial solvent had been discharged illegally into the sewers by an unidentified industrial firm. The solvent had travelled through the sewers and, as a result of the design of the sewage works, into controlled waters, in a virtually undiluted condition. The House of Lords, reaffirming *Alphacell*, stated that there was ample evidence on which to find that the sewerage undertaker had caused the discharge from the sewage works (although, in fact, the conviction was quashed because the undertaker could take advantage of the special defence in s. 87(2)—see above).

Two further cases illustrate the scope of liability. In *CPC (UK) Ltd v. National Rivers Authority* [1995] Env LR 131, a factory operator was held to have caused polluting matter to enter controlled waters when a pipe carrying cleaning fluid fractured, allowing the fluid to flow into a river via a storm drain. The conviction was upheld even though the cause of the fracture was defective work carried out by subcontractors for the previous owner, a defect that a rigorous environmental audit of the premises before the current owners bought it had failed to detect. The current owners caused the pollution because they were operating it at the time of the polluting incident: this was enough to satisfy the test laid down by Lord Wilberforce in *Alphacell* that causing 'must involve some active operation or chain of operations involving as a result the pollution of the stream'.[51] And in *Attorney-General's Reference (No. 1 of 1994)* [1995] 1 WLR 599, a sewerage undertaker was held to have caused a water pollution incident by running a sewerage system in an unmaintained state. Although it was argued that this was an omission, the Court reformulated the issue by pointing out that the active operation was running a sewage disposal system in an unmaintained state. The Court also added that it was possible for more than one person to be liable for causing one pollution incident—the offence simply required that the defendant caused the discharge or entry, not that it was the sole, or even the principal, cause. (Thus in the *CPC* case, an action could also have been brought against the subcontractors, or in the *Yorkshire Water Services* case also against the original discharger into the sewer, had they been identified. Indeed, in one case involving pollution from a landfill site, three separate parties—the landfill operator, the contractor, and a firm of consultants brought in to advise on certain works—were successfully prosecuted.)[52]

There was a line of cases, however, in which the courts held that the defendant had been passive rather than active, and therefore not liable for causing pollution. These began with *Price v. Cromack* [1975] 1 WLR 988, in which a farmer had a contract permitting an animal firm to discharge waste into lagoons on his land. One lagoon wall failed and the resulting escape severely polluted a river. The farmer was acquitted of causing pollution on the ground that he had only permitted the accumulation and had not caused the pollution. *Price v. Cromack* was followed in *Wychavon District Council v. National Rivers Authority* [1993] 1 WLR 125 and *National Rivers Authority v. Welsh Development Agency* [1993] Env LR 407. In the *Wychavon* case, raw sewage escaped from a sewer under the control of the council acting as agent of the water company in maintaining and repairing the sewerage system. The immediate cause was a blockage in the sewer. The Divisional Court held that the council was not guilty of the causing offence, because it had merely remained inactive. In the *Welsh Development Agency* case, the Court decided that the landlord of an industrial estate did not cause a discharge of trade effluent from the estate's surface water drains when the effluent originated from one of the units on the estate. These two cases both purported to follow *Alphacell*, but appeared to ignore that, in *Alphacell*, it was the underlying operation, not the immediate cause of the pollution, that must be active. (In *Alphacell*, the active operation was identified as a complex one that involved the carrying on of a paper factory with an effluent treatment plant situated

---

51 At 834.

52 See (2001) ENDS Report 319, 53.

next to a river and which had an overflow channel that led directly to a river: it was inevitable that, if something went wrong, polluting matter would enter the river.)

In its decision in the *Empress Car* case, however, the House of Lords reviewed this suspect line of cases (see Case 17.5).

CASE 17.5 *Empress Car Company (Abertillery) Ltd v. National Rivers Authority* [1998] Env LR 396

An oil tank had a protective bund, but, to make it easier to use the oil, the tank was connected via a pipe to a smaller drum outside the bund. The outlet from the tank had an unlocked tap, which was vandalized. The drum overfilled, leading to pollution of a river via a storm drain. Following *Alphacell*,[53] Lord Hoffmann held that the defendant must have 'done something', but this something need not be the immediate act that led to the pollution. Maintaining a diesel tank was 'doing something'; so was maintaining lagoons or operating sewerage systems. The *Wychavon*[54] and *Welsh Development Authority*[55] cases were therefore strongly disapproved of as being too restrictive, and an attempt was made to restore the meaning of 'active operation' laid down in *Alphacell*.

This case continues the purposive approach to interpreting 'cause' in water pollution offences, without which it is generally considered that the legislation would be ineffective.

A further point here is that WRA 1991, s. 217(3), makes it an offence if a breach of any of the water pollution offences is due to the act or default of some other person. If this is the case, then that person can be charged with an offence regardless of whether proceedings are taken against the person who was directly responsible. This provision of concurrent liability was probably intended to apply in cases in which, for example, someone who caused pollution was 'acting under orders'. Because, as noted above, more than one person can cause water pollution under s. 85, it is not clear that this provision is of much practical use. But it has been successfully relied on, in *Express Ltd v. Environment Agency* [2005] Env LR 7, to prosecute a dairy owner who allowed its premises to be used to transfer cream from an outside supplier to one of its customers, during which some of the cream ended up, via surface drains, in a brook. The Divisional Court held that the method of transferring the cream was unsafe and had not been subject to an adequate risk assessment, which would have been required if the dairy owner was to be immune from liability under s. 217(3).

Third parties, natural forces, and other intervening 'causes'

Despite the apparent strictness of *Alphacell*, there was a line of cases in which the courts imposed limits to the wide interpretation of the concept of 'causing pollution' in relation to which a third party or other intervening act was thought to interrupt the chain of causation. In *Impress (Worcester) Ltd v. Rees* [1971] 2 All ER 357, fuel oil from a tank was released into the River Severn. The defendant successfully pleaded that this was the act of a trespasser. In *National Rivers Authority v. Wright Engineering Co. Ltd* [1994] 4 All ER 281, vandals had interfered with an oil storage tank, which then leaked into controlled waters. Once again, the company was held not to have caused the polluting entry, although it was accepted that the forseeability of the vandalism would be a relevant factor in deciding who caused the pollution incident. In *Alphacell*, however, the presence of leaves and other debris that blocked the overflow channel were to be expected in autumn. Similarly, in *Southern Water Authority*

---

53 *Alphacell Ltd v. Woodward* [1972] AC 824.
54 *Wychavon District Council v. National Rivers Authority* [1993] 1 WLR 125.
55 *National Rivers Authority v. Welsh Development Agency* [1993] Env LR 407.

v. Pegrum (1989) 153 JP 581, the heavy rain that filled up slurry lagoons so that they over-flowed and polluted a river was not so out of the ordinary as to break the chain of causation.

In *Empress Car*, Lord Hoffmann reaffirmed what had really already been laid down in *Alphacell* concerning causation—namely, that, once it was established that something had been done to cause pollution, the only question that needs to be asked is whether the defendant caused the pollution. But he then stated a general test as to when the chain of causation will be broken. He did so by trying to avoid questions of whether the specific intervention was foreseeable (the approach that had been taken in *Wright Engineering*).

The true common sense distinction is, in my view, between acts and events which, although necessarily foreseeable in the particular case, are in the generality a normal and familiar fact of life, and acts or events which are abnormal and extraordinary.[56]

In his view, vandalism is foreseeable, whereas a terrorist attack is not. This approach may make it easier for magistrates to determine whether or not the defendant caused the pollution, but does not wholly remove scope for argument. For example, on the one hand, terrorist attacks may be extraordinary, but water companies plan against them; on the other hand, incidents of vandalism may be rare in some rural settings. Ultimately, however, the new test does leave some room for arguments that, in individual cases, an event is extraordinary. In *Environment Agency v. Brock plc* [1998] Env LR 607, a case involving pollution following a fracture to a pipe with a latent defect, however, the Divisional Court seemed to imply that any such defect would always be an 'ordinary fact of life', suggesting that this was a matter of law rather than fact.

The ambit of this approach to causation was further explored in *Express Dairies* (see p. 608). The tanker owners argued that the series of events, from the tyre blowout to the milk entering the brook (the blown-out tyre damaged the mud flap, which then dislodged the side under-run protection rail, which then became detached and sheered the outlet valve for the milk), was so extraordinary, being unheard of to them, that the chain of causation had been broken. But this was rejected on the grounds that blowouts are ordinary events and nothing extraordinary, in the sense of an action by a third party or natural event, had happened between the blowout and the eventual spill. This confirms the strict approach to criminal liability that will be taken by the courts under s. 85, but might be considered to lead to harsh consequences in cases in which a quite unforeseeable chain of events not involving ultroneous causes follows an initially ordinary event.

'Knowingly permitting'

The offence of 'knowingly permitting' has given rise to fewer cases and is clearly more limited than the 'causing' offence because of the knowledge requirement. But it may be of use in situations in which a person is passive even after knowing of the polluting incident. For example, in *Price v. Cromack*, the judge suggested that the farmer could well have been charged with knowingly permitting the pollution and, in the *Wychavon* case, it is fairly clear that the local authority could have been charged with knowingly permitting the pollution once it had been drawn to its attention (on the facts, it had delayed for some time before taking steps to remedy the situation).[57]

One issue of great importance to the 'knowingly permitting' offence is the level of knowledge required. In *Schulmans Incorporated Ltd v. National Rivers Authority* [1993] Env LR D1, the judge held that constructive knowledge was sufficient, although he did not go on to elaborate the point.[58]

---

56 *Empress Car Company (Abertillery) Ltd v. National Rivers Authority* [1998] Env LR 396, 408.

57 For discussion about the position of contractors working on behalf of the party that originally caused the pollution, see *Environment Agency v. Biffa Waste Services Ltd* [2006] EWHC 1102 (Admin).

58 See, for discussion, D. Wilkinson [1993] WL 25.

Liability of companies and consent holders

Two final cases are of importance for the s. 85 offences. In *Taylor Woodrow Property Management Ltd v. National Rivers Authority* (1994) 158 JP 1101, a property company held a discharge consent relating to an outfall from an industrial estate. Even though it did not itself actually make any discharge, it was held liable under s. 85(6) for contravening the conditions of the consent. It thus appears that the holder of a consent is always capable of being prosecuted for breach of positive conditions attached to the consent. It can also be noted that this is a very neat way of avoiding any argument concerning whether the defendant has carried out an active operation, but only in cases in which there is a consent.

Company directors and other senior managers can be guilty of a water pollution offence in addition to any charge brought against the company, if there is consent or connivance on that person's part, or some form of neglect (s. 217(1)), although this has never been used. And in *National Rivers Authority v. Alfred McAlpine Homes East Ltd* [1994] 4 All ER 286, the company was held to be vicariously liable for acts of its employees, irrespective of whether those employees exercised 'the controlling mind' of the company. This appears to be a straightforward application of the principle of vicarious liability, but it does illustrate the need for companies to establish proper environmental management systems.

The Strict interpretation of water pollution offences—implications

It is quite clear, from comments in the cases referred to above, that the judges have been prepared to adopt a fairly purposive view of the legislation in order to further the aim of environmental protection. One result has been that the s. 85 offences have been given a very wide interpretation. This has had a number of implications.

1. A wide range of accidental occurrences are offences.

2. Any excess over the requirements of a numerical consent amounts to a criminal offence, no matter how small it is.

3. Firms are given a clear incentive to adopt an appropriate environmental management system so that accidents and breaches of consent do not occur.

4. When a prosecution is brought, there is a very high success rate (it is currently around 95 per cent). But the Environment Agency has a discretion whether to prosecute and has adopted a policy that means that a prosecution will not be brought in every case (see p. 278).

The courts also have a discretion in sentencing, which may mitigate perceived injustices: in the *CPC* case, the defendants were eventually given an absolute discharge. This discretion on prosecuting and on sentencing, however, means that it would be dangerous for the courts to import the interpretation of 'causing' given in *Empress Car* into other provisions, such as those in relation to contaminated land (see p. 555) or water pollution clean-up powers (see p. 616), in which cases there is less discretion to mitigate the strictness of liability.

Sampling and enforcement powers

Environment Agency officers have wide rights of entry to property under s. 108 of the Environment Act 1995. These include a right to take samples of water or effluent, or to install monitoring equipment. In practice, some form of monitoring requirement—typically, self-monitoring—is now included in most discharge consents and s. 111 states simply that information provided or obtained as a result of a licence condition is admissible, including where it is provided by means of an apparatus—that is, some form of measuring device. There is a rebuttable presumption that such an apparatus is accurate. Hence the results of self-monitoring can be used for enforcement purposes, at least if required under a consent. In practice, most consents that require self-monitoring will also make it a condition to pass on information gathered, so that failure to do will also be an offence.

There is also a potential problem relating to the admissibility of the public registers, because it is fairly clearly hearsay evidence. It appears that samples taken by the Environment Agency are admissible under the Criminal Justice Act 1988, s. 24. This section also seems to avoid any problem relating to self-incrimination in cases in which the discharger's own voluntarily taken data is used, because that data will count as a confession (see the Police and Criminal Evidence Act 1984, ss. 76 and 82). Although it is arguable that the decision in *Saunders v. United Kingdom* (1997) 23 EHRR 313 changes this, the decision in *R v. Hertfordshire County Council, ex parte Green Environmental Industries Ltd* [2000] 1 All ER 773 indicates that information placed on the registers can be relied on, because it is not sought as part of a specific criminal investigation. In the unlikely event that information supplied under self-monitoring was held by the courts to be inadmissible, the Environment Agency might have to use remote monitoring (a costly option that might be thought excessive). But it is worth stressing that there would remain sound regulatory reasons to require self-monitoring: good environmental management practice demands that firms gather information about their environmental impact and use this to improve performance over time.

Enforcement policy and penalties

A central issue relating to water pollution—and, indeed, of this whole book—is whether the rules are actually enforced by the regulators. The NRA established a national prosecution policy and it became clear that the traditional recipe of a conciliatory approach to enforcement with very low prosecution rates was rapidly reformulated.

Prosecution policy is governed by the Environment Agency's revised Enforcement and Prosecution Policy and associated Functional Guidelines (see p. 278). Statistics on water pollution incidents are given in annual reports by the Environment Agency (although finding statistics on prosecutions is increasingly difficult, because the Agency now prefers to highlight the worst offenders on a sector-by-sector basis). As Figure 17.1 illustrates, the

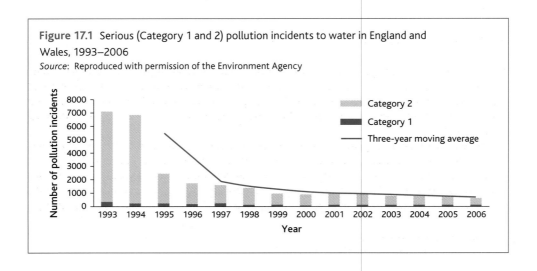

Figure 17.1 Serious (Category 1 and 2) pollution incidents to water in England and Wales, 1993–2006
Source: Reproduced with permission of the Environment Agency

long-term steady decrease in incidents since the mid-1990s has begun to level off. Under the Environment Agency's policy, the Category 1 incidents are likely to result in prosecution, making around a hundred water pollution prosecutions a year.

One difficulty with the annually published statistics is that they do not include breaches of discharge consents and it remains the case that most prosecutions are for accidental or other unusual incidents, rather than for consistent breaches of consent. This has led to complaints from environmental groups that the NRA (and now the Environment Agency) has not taken action against persistent polluters with significant rigour. This seems to be borne out by compliance statistics, which indicate that only around a dozen or so prosecutions are taken annually for breach of consent conditions.

These statistics also show, however, that *monitoring* of consents for breaches is very variable: on average, only two-thirds of consents are monitored annually and those regions in which monitoring is lowest have (perhaps unsurprisingly) the lowest levels of prosecutions for consent breaches.[59] Following the Legislative and Regulatory Reform Act 2006 and the need to embed the 'Hampton principles' about better regulation (see p. 269), the Environment Agency is presently consulting on more targeted, risk-based monitoring, although it seems to have ruled out wholesale reliance on operator self-monitoring.

The scope to bring a private prosecution under WRA 1991 is important. While little used, its availability remains a threat to dischargers—particularly in the light of the information on the public registers—and it may also be used by environmental groups as a means of registering their disquiet over official inaction over certain discharges. The threat of a private prosecution following the *Sea Empress* spill may have galvanized the Environment Agency into prosecuting (see p. 271; see also the use of a private prosecution in Box 9.13).

Owing to the strict liability nature of water pollution offences, most prosecutions (over 90 per cent) are successful. The Agency is also increasingly willing to bring prosecutions in the Crown Court, where fines may be unlimited. The *Anglian Water* case (discussed in Box 9.13) is a good recent example of what the courts consider to be aggravating and mitigating factors, and appropriate fine levels.[60] In general terms, however, the courts do seem to regard water pollution as a serious environmental offence and that industry ought to have preventive systems in place when accidents occur, but they are mindful of a range of further factors.

In contrast to waste management offences, scant use has been made of custodial sentences (a magistrates' court can impose a three-month sentence and a Crown Court, a two-year sentence): so far, only one two-month sentence has been imposed for a water pollution offence following an agricultural oil pollution incident (see [1998] WL 66).

Access to information

Public registers of a range of environmental information relating to water pollution date back to the Control of Pollution Act 1974, although these provisions were not implemented until 1985. Prior to that, the system tended to be operated with a fair degree of secrecy about consents and samples taken. The relevant provisions are repeated in WRA 1991, with some amendments.

Under s. 190, a public register must be kept by the Environment Agency of all applications for consent, consents actually granted, any conditions attached to a consent, and notices of water quality objectives made under s. 83. Prescribed details of authorizations granted for the purposes of IPPC must also be recorded on the water registers. In addition, the results of *any* samples of the receiving waters or of effluent (which includes samples taken by a

---

59 See (2001) 321 ENDS Report 37.

60 And see also *R. v. Cemex Cement Ltd* [2008] Env LR 6.

discharger as a condition of consent) and any information produced by their analysis must be registered.

Registers must be open for inspection by any member of the public free of charge at all reasonable times, with reasonable facilities for taking copies afforded on payment of a reasonable fee. The Control of Pollution (Applications, Appeals and Registers) Regulations 1996[61] specify the detailed shape of the registers. Details of any sample must be entered on the register within two months of the date of the sample.

The public register provides an invaluable database for groups and individuals wishing to monitor water quality. It can be used to mount a private prosecution (as in *Wales v. Thames Water Authority* (1987) 1(3) Environmental Law 3, in which the water authority was successfully prosecuted for pollution from a sewage works in reliance on the information that it had itself recorded on the register), or to provide evidence for a civil claim, but its use in providing general information on the state of the water environment is rather limited. The admissibility of the registers as evidence seems quite clear now that they are kept by the Environment Agency.

Preventative and remedial powers, and diffuse pollution

In common with other areas of pollution control, the regulatory system that controls water pollution has a range of powers in relation to the prevention of harm. The exercise of these powers is undoubtedly aided by the presence of water quality objectives against which action may be judged. These powers can be used both for consented discharges (in which cases 'enforcement notices' are used) and for activities that are unconsented, but in relation to which water pollution may need to be prevented (if the Environment Agency can either recover the costs of preventing or remedying harm, or serve a notice on the responsible person to do so).

Anti-pollution works and enforcement notices

Under s. 161 of WRA 1991, the Environment Agency has widely drafted powers to prevent pollution incidents in relation to which there is a threat of water pollution, to clean up after them, and to carry out remedial or restorative works. For example, s. 161 covers such things as diverting a potential pollutant spilt in an accident in order to prevent it from entering a watercourse, cleaning up the effects of a spillage, restocking a river with fish, and investigations into pollution incidents. Section 161 requires the Agency itself to undertake works or operations before recovering the costs. Under ss. 161A–D, however, the Agency can serve a works notice on the appropriate responsible person requiring that person to prevent or clean up pollution. Only in cases in which it is necessary for the Environment Agency to carry out works 'forthwith' or if the polluter cannot be found, can the Agency act.

Failure to comply with a works notice is an offence.[62] If the Environment Agency has acted, it can recover the costs incurred in these works, operations, or investigations from anyone who has caused or knowingly permitted the pollutant to be present in controlled waters, or who has caused or knowingly permitted the pollutant to be a threat to controlled waters. The one exception is that these powers cannot be exercised so as to impede or prevent the making of a discharge in pursuance of a consent. In this case, the Agency is limited to considering whether the consent should be varied, although there is no power to override the period of immunity against variation merely on the grounds that a discharger has committed a breach or an act of pollution.[63]

---

61 SI 1996/2971.

62 Procedural issues are dealt with in the Anti-Pollution Works Regulations 1999, SI 1999/1006.

63 This may change if the Regulatory Enforcement and Sanctions Bill is enacted.

There is a degree of overlap between these powers and the power to clean up contaminated sites. There is published guidance on the manner in which each of these powers should be exercised (see p. 548), although, in general terms, Pt 2A of EPA 1990 should be used, because this is a mandatory provision. (This also has the benefit that the contaminated land provisions ought to remediate harm caused to other parts of the environment.)

Section 161 is now routinely used by the Environment Agency for recovering both investigation and remediation costs following significant pollution incidents. It is now also used *before* prosecution is brought, and, indeed, there may be circumstances in which *only* the powers in s. 161 are used and there is no prosecution (the legality of this can be seen in *Bruton v. Clarke* [1994] WL 145). This suggests that environmental restoration is no longer seen as a supplement to prosecution, but an important regulatory device in its own right (and is a good example of the Environment Agency prioritizing environmental quality over sanctioning criminal acts and of what might be termed a restorative approach to enforcing environmental law—see p. 287). Section 161 is particularly useful, because the potential cost may act as a greater deterrent than the threat of prosecution. In most cases, the costs of a clean-up operation are likely to be higher than the potential fine.

Where there has been, or is likely to be, a breach of a discharge consent condition, the Environment Agency may serve an 'enforcement notice' under WRA 1991, s. 90B. This must identify the breach (or likely breach), the steps required to remedy the breach, and the time within which these must be carried out. Failure to comply with an enforcement notice is an offence and there are the normal rights of appeal. Enforcement notices give the Agency another option other than prosecution when faced with a pollution incident. They are also useful in preventing pollution from non-accidental sources and in requiring improvements in situations in which there is an 'accident waiting to happen'.

Other preventive tools

There are also other mechanisms that can be used against activities that cannot be consented because they do not generally 'discharge' (for example, slurry tanks) and which do not necessarily give rise to an immediate risk of harm, but in relation to which preventive measures are appropriate.

(a) Precautions against pollution

Under s. 92, the Secretary of State may make regulations concerning precautions to be taken in relation to any poisonous, noxious, or polluting matter to prevent it from entering controlled waters. (Section 92 uses the language of precaution, but these are better seen as preventive powers.) Such regulations may prevent anyone having custody or control of poisonous, noxious, or polluting matter, unless the steps required in the regulations or specified by the Environment Agency are carried out. These regulations may create additional criminal offences and administrative remedies in relation to breaches, although these may not have penalties higher than for the pollution offences under s. 85.

The Control of Pollution (Silage, Slurry and Agricultural Fuel Oil) Regulations 1991[64] were the first Regulations made under s. 92. They introduced precautionary controls over the design and operation of some potentially very polluting activities, by imposing specific controls over silage-making operations, slurry stores, and agricultural fuel oil stores. All new or substantially altered facilities are covered (many of which are performance standards, rather than strict design requirements), although it is possible for the Environment Agency to bring existing activities under control if it is satisfied that there is a significant risk of pollution to controlled waters. These Regulations complement the planning system in preventing pollution problems arising—but control is exercisable over operational details in a more specific

---

64 SI 1991/324, as amended by SI 1997/547.

way than is possible through the planning system: oversight and monitoring is carried out by a more specialist body, and the controls relate to agricultural matters not normally covered by planning powers. The legislative approach, however, is clearly limited to the adequacy of containment facilities and has been criticized for not addressing the eventual disposal of farm wastes more generally—for example, through farm waste management plans.

Further regulations govern industrial fuel oil stores more generally, although not yet in Wales. The Control of Pollution (Oil Storage) (England) Regulations 2001[65] aim to tackle the fact that oil spills are one of the most common sources of pollution incident. As with the earlier Regulations, they require preventive measures, such as adequate bunds around oil tanks, and failure to adhere to these requirements is a criminal offence. The Regulations do not, in practice, extend to single private dwellings, nor do they apply to underground tanks (which are covered by the Groundwater Regulations 1998),[66] although they do apply to all kinds of oil (except waste oils), not only fuel oil. For existing tanks, the Regulations are effective from 1 September 2005, although the Environment Agency may serve a notice before then if there is a significant risk of pollution.

(b) Water protection zones

Under s. 93, the Secretary of State may designate water protection zones. Such an order may effectively establish a system of local law within the zone with regard to water pollution. Orders under this section may either prohibit or restrict specified activities within the designated zone, with a view to preventing or controlling the entry of poisonous, noxious, or polluting matter into controlled waters, or may provide for a system whereby the Environment Agency determines prohibited or restricted activities. It is not possible to require the carrying out of positive works. An order may also include provisions relating to procedures for obtaining consent for such restricted activities from the Agency, with criminal sanctions being available for breaches.

The first, and only, water protection zone was designated in 1999, covering most of the River Dee catchment. The Water Protection Zone (River Dee Catchment) Designation Order 1999[67] effectively provides for a specialist consent regime within the zone to regulate the storage and use of certain controlled substances by industrial and other processes, although construction sites, retail premises, farms, and sites covered by IPPC are excluded. Consents are determined following a risk assessment, and Best Available Techniques Not Entailing Excessive Cost (BATNEEC) principles apply when there is an appreciable risk of pollution.[68] It is thought that there will be such a risk in relation to about a hundred of the 300–500 sites affected. Undertaking activities without a consent or in breach of its conditions is an offence, although, in contrast with the strictness of the main water pollution offences, there is a 'due diligence' defence and there are also rather generous defences of showing genuine lack of knowledge that the activity was being carried on or that an excessive amount of substances being kept or used. While generous in places to industry, these provisions should contribute to protecting the catchment from accidental and diffuse discharges, at least cost overall. They also make explicit provision for precautionary consent conditions to apply. It is notable that water protection zones have only been used as a response to industrial point-source hotspots rather than, for example, diffuse pollution from agriculture.

One limitation in s. 93(3) is that a water protection zone should not concern itself with nitrate from agricultural sources. This is because agricultural nitrate was separately provided for in terms of protection, through s. 94 (which provided for nitrate sensitive areas),

---

65 SI 2001/2954.

66 SI 1998/2746.

67 SI 1999/915.

68 See the Water Protection Zone (River Dee Catchment) (Procedural and Other Provisions) Regulations 1999, SI 1999/916.

although this has now been superseded by provisions that give effect to an EC Directive on agricultural nitrates (see below).

(c) Nitrate vulnerable zones (NVZs)

The Agricultural Nitrates Directive (91/676/EEC) is one of two key water quality Directives that are focused on polluting processes. The Directive requires that nitrate vulnerable zones (NVZs) are designated in specific areas where there are excessive levels of nitrate pollution from agricultural sources. Action plans for each NVZ must then be drawn up, which are designed to reduce and prevent water pollution from nitrates and agricultural sources.[69] These plans include fairly detailed rules about things such as when fertilizers can be applied and the amount that can be applied. Implementation is through the Protection of Water against Agricultural and Nitrate Pollution (England and Wales) Regulations 1996.[70]

Unlike nitrate sensitive areas, NVZs are always mandatory and there is no prospect of compensation payments for farmers in NVZs. This helps to explain the concerns raised by many farmers to the designations, which culminated in a legal challenge brought by two farmers, supported by the National Farmers Union (NFU). In Case C-293/97 *R v. Secretary of State for the Environment and Minister of Agriculture, Fisheries and Food, ex parte Standley* [1999] Env LR 801, the main ground of challenge was that the UK government, when drawing up its initial list of NVZs, had failed to consider whether the excessive nitrate levels were caused by non-agricultural sources. The farmers argued that this failure discriminated against agricultural users in the NVZ, because the cost of reducing the nitrate concentrations to an acceptable level was to be borne wholly by the farmers when there were other users that may have been responsible for the nitrate pollution. The case was referred to the ECJ, which upheld the approach of the government in identifying waters in which agricultural sources made a 'sufficient contribution' to excessive nitrate levels, in line with a purposive interpretation of the Directive. Indeed, the Court hinted that something rather less than a significant contribution might have been enough, showing the amount of freedom that member States enjoy. This flexibility is also seen in the Court's rejection of an argument that the UK violated the Polluter Pays Principle (see now Art. 174(2) EC), because the Directive had sufficient room to ensure that action programmes targeted the contribution of farmers proportionate to those of other polluters.

The Directive says little about how such other sources are to be regulated, although other sources such as sewage treatment works will probably be subject to duties to reduce nitrate pollution under measures such as the Urban Waste Water Treatment Directive (91/271/EEC), under which a small number of sensitive areas were designated in 1997, and again in 2002, because of risks from nitrate.

One danger with flexibility here, however, is the danger of implementing the Directive too minimally. Originally, 68 NVZs were designated, on the basis that nitrate levels in surface or groundwater used for drinking water abstraction were above the Drinking Water Directive limit of 50 mg/l. But in Case C-69/99 *Commission v. United Kingdom* [2000] ECR I-10979, the government conceded that it ought also to have designated *all* surface water and groundwater in areas in which nitrate levels exceeded this limit—that is, it should not have interpreted the Agricultural Nitrates Directive as a Directive concerned only with improving drinking water quality. As a result of this decision, around 55 per cent of land area in England is now covered by NVZ designations. By contrast, the whole of the Netherlands, Denmark, and Germany have been designated.

---

69 See the Action Programmes for Nitrate Vulnerable Zones (England and Wales) Regulations 1998, SI 1998/1202.

70 SI 1996/888, as amended by SI 2006/1289, to provide for public participation in the making of individual action programmes.

BOX 17.5 Diffuse water pollution and the law

The increasing need to tackle water pollution from diffuse sources, such as agriculture and urban run-off, has already been noted. Cases such as *Standley*[71] illustrate some of the difficulties that the law faces. Whereas point sources are under the control of dischargers, diffuse pollutants may accumulate as they are washed from one area of land to another, making it difficult to attribute the input of pollutants such as nitrates and phosphates to particular individuals.

Pollution is also caused by seemingly innocuous activities: phosphorous may be lost by ploughing or even overgrazing, and by tractor tramlines compacting the soil and making pollutants run off the land. And some pollutants may take several years before they eventually contaminate a river or a borehole, so there is a problem of regulating a moving target and apportioning the costs of diffuse pollution fairly—potentially over decades. All of this requires a mix of legal and other responses designed to change things such as agricultural land management practices to prevent or minimize inputs, for example, by controlling inputs of fertilizers (perhaps through voluntary action, or by some form of taxation—see below), or by using mechanisms such as cross-compliance, under which farmers will only receive support payments if their land is kept in good agricultural and environmental condition (which seems to have proven successful—see Box 20.6).

The scope for traditional 'thou shalt not' forms of law is very limited, but there are examples of its use—for example, in addition to the action programme rules for nitrate vulnerable zones (NVZs), there is a notice provision under the Groundwater Regulations 1998[72] under which the Environment Agency can effectively put restrictions on the use of sheep dips and petrol stations. It is not clear that there exists the political desire to micromanage activities such as agriculture through the use of command-style regulation, with the criminal or administrative responsibilities that would attach to this, and it is arguably poor policy to attempt to do so (although, in Scotland, consideration is being given to the use of general binding rules to cover a range of minor activities—see Box 17.4).

As Gunningham and Sinclair point out,[73] it is likely to be more effective to use a mix of tools such as

(i) farm management standards—that is, process standards requiring farmers to become more aware of their impacts and to plan, systematically, to reduce these, and by influencing access to polluting inputs such as fertilizers, or perhaps better, by encouraging greater use of less polluting fertilizers, because, in practice, demand for fertilizers is fairly inelastic and does not respond very well to price changes;

(ii) landscape changes—for example, buffer zones between intensively farmed fields and watercourses (something that it now provided for under EC agri-environmental law—see p. 746);

(iii) greater attention to the wider picture of land uses—for example, by using land use planning laws to influence the location, within a catchment, of potentially polluting behaviour, or through tools such as NVZs, which (unlike town and country planning laws) control not only new, but also existing sources.

The land use approach, through catchment planning, is central to the Water Framework Directive's approach to reaching 'good status' (see p. 594).

---

71 Case C-293/97 *R v. Secretary of State for the Environment and Minister of Agriculture, Fisheries and Food, ex parte Standley* [1999] Env LR 801.

72 SI 1998/2746.

73 N. Gunningham and D. Sinclair (2005) JEL 51

(d) Economic instruments

Finally, mention should be made of the use of economic tools to combat water pollution. There is some evidence that suggests that 'upstream' taxes and charges are most effective in meeting targets under the Urban Waste Water Treatment Directive (91/271/EEC). (It is estimated that 50 per cent of all money spent on complying with EC environmental law is spent on complying with this Directive.) A study by the European Environment Agency found that the costs of implementing the Directive in Denmark, which relies heavily on downstream sewage treatment plant, compares unfavourably with that in the Netherlands, where the emphasis has been on giving polluters incentives to reduce pollution at source (and where a significant part of the reduction in sewage-related pollution took place via levies before the Urban Waste Water Treatment Directive came into force).[74]

At national level, it has been suggested that point-source dischargers could be made to pay a charge reflecting either the value of improved water quality or the marginal cost of pollution abatement.[75] These proposals, however, received little support, not least because they appeared to envisage that pollution charges could reduce administrative regulation (something that the RCEP had rejected as being unrealistic in its 1992 report on *Freshwater Quality*). Other than potential problems with 'hotspots' in which pollution might become concentrated (which would clearly be a problem in complying with statutory or EC-driven water quality objectives), the proposals have so far come to nothing. This is because the existing consent systems already, to some extent, take environmental impact into account when charges for trade effluent consents and discharge consents are set, because the Environment Agency must already take costs and benefits into account when determining consents, and because it is not clear why a discharger should be required to improve the quality of effluent if it is not harmful to the environment (a point that goes back to one of the general themes of this chapter about the nature of water pollution). Point-source dischargers might also object that they should not be required to pay charges if those who pollute more diffusely are not.

Although new forms of environmental charges may have limited utility in relation to point sources, the need for innovative regulatory approaches to combat diffuse water pollution means that there is more likelihood that we will see developments in this area. One particular proposal has been the introduction of a pesticide tax, which might go some way to reducing the UK's relatively high usage of pesticides compared to other EC countries. This was first mooted in 1998, but rejected by government in 2000, when, in the midst of a crisis, the farming industry put forward alternative proposals of a voluntary nature to reduce pesticide use. This appears to be the present government's preferred approach, although it is keeping a pesticide tax under review.

Overlapping controls

Land use planning and environmental assessment

Local planning authorities have the ability to make important decisions relating to water pollution through the town and country planning system. But it is clearly recommended in central government guidance, such as Circular 11/95 on planning conditions and Planning Policy Statement 23, *Planning and Pollution Control*, that planning powers should be used mainly for locational and siting decisions, and that matters about the regulation of pollution should be left to the specialist regulators to control through the specialist consent systems. It is clear that potential water pollution arising from a proposed development is a material

---

74 European Environment Agency (2005) *Effectiveness of Urban Wastewater Treatment Policies in Selected Countries: An EEA Pilot Study*, available online at **reports.eea.europa.eu/eea_report_2005_2/en**.

75 DETR (1998) *Economic Instruments for Water Pollution*, Consultation paper.

consideration in any planning decision and the Environment Agency is a statutory consultee under the General Development Procedure Order 1995[76] in relation to many applications for planning permission. In the past, this has been of great importance in relation to ground-waters, because the Environment Agency could be notified of potentially harmful activities that it could then seek to control using its own powers.[77] In addition, planning permission may be refused because of inadequate sewerage in the area.

The Environment Agency will also have an important role to play at a more strategic level in the making of development plans and the river basin management plans required under the Water Framework Directive are as much land use plans as anything (and need to be fed into the process of making regional spatial strategies).

It is notable that there are specific regulations governing certain abstractions of water that may have significantly harmful environmental effects and that, for these, the Environment Agency is the competent authority (these were made under the revised Environmental Impact Assessment Directive). But there is nothing comparable as regards water quality, with the result that, in relation to environmental impact assessment (EIA) and water quality matters, the Enviroment Agency is only ever a consultee in the assessment process.

Pollution prevention and control, and waste management

There are separate controls for those processes for which an environmental permit is now required. Acting in accordance with an environmental permit will be a defence to the water pollution offences under s. 85 of WRA 1991.

Some of the overlaps, and gaps, between environmental permitting (as it applies to waste management) and water pollution controls are discussed at p. 673.

Radioactive discharges

Under the Control of Pollution (Radioactive Waste) Regulations 1989,[78] the radioactivity of a discharge is to be ignored for the purposes of WRA 1991. In other words, the non-radioactive elements of a discharge or entry are dealt with under WRA1991 and the radioactive elements under the Radioactive Substances Act 1993 by the Environment Agency.

Statutory nuisances

In addition to the statutory nuisances listed in Pt III of EPA 1990, two further statutory nuisances are provided for in the Public Health Act 1936. Section 259(1)(a) provides that any pool, pond, ditch, gutter, or watercourse that is in a state that is prejudicial to health or a nuisance is a statutory nuisance. This will cover small ponds and ditches, which are not within the consent system, as well as controlled waters, although not estuarial or coastal waters (*R v. Falmouth and Truro Port Health Authority, ex parte South West Water Ltd* [2000] NPC 36). Section 259(1)(b) covers any watercourse that is silted up or choked so as to obstruct the proper flow of water, thus causing a nuisance or which is prejudicial to health. This is limited to watercourses that are not normally navigated.

The normal procedures for statutory nuisance apply to these situations, thus creating an alternative course of action for a local authority or individual wishing to clean up a grossly polluted watercourse.

---

76 SI 1995/419.

77 Although it is now clear that the scope of obligations under the Groundwater Directive means that reliance should not be placed on a body that can only influence decision making by representations and obligations under the Directive are imposed on any consenting authority.

78 SI 1989/1158.

Nature conservation

Under the EC Habitats Directive (92/43/EEC), discharge consents can only be granted and must be reviewed in light of their potential impact upon European sites (see p. 716). The Environment Agency is also under biodiversity and conservation duties (see pp. 688 and 117).

Contaminated land

Historically contaminated land may be contaminating controlled waters, or pose the risk of such contamination. In such cases, Pt 2A of EPA 1990 will apply. It is worth noting that the inconsistency caused by defining contaminated land by reference to significant environmental harm or to the pollution of controlled waters—that is, any pollution, not only significant pollution—was addressed in s. 86 of the Water Act 2003, which requires there to be 'significant' pollution of controlled waters (hence disapplying Pt 2A in cases of minor water pollution). This change has yet to be brought into force, however, and government is resisting doing so until implications of Water Framework Directive implementation are addressed (see p. 555).

Water pollution and private law controls

Private law controls still play a significant role in the control of water pollution. Indeed, for various technical reasons, they are probably of greater use for water pollution than for other forms of pollution and may be used to produce, directly or indirectly, environmental improvements (although they have, at best, a limited strategic role).

One right that has already been mentioned is the right of private prosecution for breaches of the criminal law. This has been available for many water pollution offences since 1985, as a result of the removal by the Control of Pollution Act 1974 of the restrictions on it. More significant, however, are the various civil law claims that may be brought. For example, the Anglers' Conservation Association is estimated to have been involved in over a thousand cases involving water pollution since the Second World War. The two main remedies available are damages to compensate an owner of the riverbed, the river banks, or a fishery for any losses caused, and an injunction to restrain future breaches of the law.

It is important to note that acting within the terms of a discharge consent does not act as a defence to a civil action, because the private law system operates separately from the public regulatory mechanisms. This is made explicit in WRA 1991, s. 100(b), but it can also be implied from cases such as *Blackburn v. ARC Ltd* [1998] Env LR 469, which decided that environmental authorizations should not, in principle, license what are otherwise a nuisance (see p. 359).

There are a number of reasons why water pollution cases—at least, those relating to pollution from point sources—have proven easier to bring than, for example, air pollution cases:

- causation is easier to show, because of the defined channels in which water normally flows;

- apart from tidal waters, water only flows one way, so there is not the same 'give and take' involved between the polluter and the polluted—hence the substantive legal rules tend to be more protective of the polluted;

- many rural landowners have the money to bring an action—indeed, pollution to fisheries will often justify an action in commercial terms;

- there are a number of campaigning and amenity bodies concerned with water problems, far more than are concerned with air (or noise) pollution;

- acquiring evidence is more straightforward, particularly since the advent of the public registers, which may provide evidence relating to the quality of the receiving waters before and after an incident and also relating to discharges.

Riparian rights

The usefulness of the civil law in this area stems mainly from the nature of riparian rights. Owners of land adjoining a watercourse (including estuaries), termed 'riparian owners', normally own the riverbed, but not the water itself. As a natural incident of the soil itself, however, they have the right to receive the water in its natural state, subject only to reasonable usage by an upstream owner for ordinary purposes (*Chasemore v. Richards* (1859) 7 HL Cas 349). Owners of other property rights, such as fisheries, have the same right.

The most authoritative statement of this principle was given by Lord Macnaghten in *John Young & Co. v. Bankier Distillery Co.* [1893] AC 691, 698:

A riparian proprietor is entitled to have the water of the stream, on the bank of which his property lies, flow down as it has been accustomed to flow down to his property, subject to the ordinary use of the flowing water by upper proprietors, and to such further use, if any, on their part in connection with their property as may be reasonable in the circumstances. Every riparian owner is thus entitled to the water of his stream, in its natural flow, without sensible diminution or increase, and without sensible alteration in its character or quality.[79]

This means that any unreasonable interference with the natural quantity or quality of the water is an actionable nuisance. The strictness of this test was shown in this case. An upstream mineowner discharged water into a stream from a mine. This altered the chemistry of the water from soft to hard and thus altered the quality of the downstream distillery's whisky. The water had not been made impure, but the distillery obtained an injunction, because the nature of the water had been changed. The case illustrates the relative nature of the definition of water pollution and, indeed, emphasizes that the common law does not lay down any absolute standards in relation to water quality. It is worth noting, however, that this test only applies in cases in which the upstream usage is not ordinary—a good example of the balancing process that the law of nuisance tries to carry out.

Some of the technical difficulties relating to the law of nuisance, such as the causation question and the locality doctrine, have been neatly answered in the water pollution cases. It appears from the reasoning in *Bankier Distillery Co.* that an invasion of the natural right to water is treated as equivalent to damage to land, thus circumventing the locality doctrine. It is also clear that actual harm need not be shown; merely, a 'sensible alteration'—a position that is supported by *Nicholls v. Ely Beet Sugar Factory Ltd* [1936] Ch 343, in which the claim of interference with riparian rights was held to be analogous to trespass. It follows that an action can be brought against any upstream polluter, even if only one of many and responsible for only a part of the whole pollution. All that needs to be shown is that the polluter is contributing to the pollution (*Crossley and Sons Ltd v. Lightowler* (1867) LR 2 Ch App 478).

As can be seen, however, many of the leading cases on riparian rights are of some antiquity, and it is an open question whether a court would give the same strict level of protection today. For example, the rise of extensive regulatory controls over the twentieth century and the general trend of incorporating negligence considerations such as foreseeability into the land torts might justify the higher courts in diluting the strictness of protection that the law on riparian rights affords (it is worth pointing out, however, that, by requiring the actions of the upstream owner to be 'unreasonable', there is a certain element of built-in flexibility to the law here).

Pollution of groundwater

Liability may also arise in nuisance for polluting percolating groundwaters, as long as causation can be shown. This was first established in *Ballard v. Tomlinson* (1885) 29 ChD 115, in which a brewery successfully sued for the contamination of its well caused by a neighbour who used his own well for the disposal of sewage. The extent of this liability was clarified in *Cambridge Water Co. v. Eastern Counties Leather plc* [1994] 2 AC 264, a case discussed in

79 At 698.

Cases 11.3. As explained there, the House of Lords took the opportunity to move the law of nuisance and the law under the rule in *Rylands v. Fletcher* towards negligence, by requiring the defendant to show that the type of damage that occurred was foreseeable. *Ballard v. Tomlinson*, in which foreseeability did not arise, was distinguished. This decision satisfied those whose primary concern was with avoiding the prospect of retrospective civil liability, but disappointed those commentators who argued for the primacy of strict liability in the civil law of water pollution as a reflection of the Polluter Pays Principle.

The decision also casts great doubt on whether there is anything particularly strict about liability for groundwater pollution law any more, at least as far as liability for past activities is concerned. But it does not necessarily restrict the recovery of damages, or the imposition of an injunction, in cases in which polluting activities currently cause damage to groundwaters, or, indeed, those in which the cause of the pollution was recent. It must be pointed out that liability in nuisance is personal in the sense that, even if the original polluter is liable for pollution damage, it does not follow that a subsequent purchaser of the site would also be liable. But purchasers of potentially contaminated land must bear in mind the possible implications of cases such as *Goldman v. Hargrave* [1967] 1 AC 645, which establish that there is liability for 'adopting' a natural nuisance in certain circumstances (see p. 344).

Other claims

Other common law claims may also be available. In *Jones v. Llanrwst Urban District Council* [1911] 1 Ch 393, the owner of a riverbed claimed successfully in trespass for deposits of solid wastes. In restricted cases, a claim in negligence might also be upheld. Following the Camelford aluminium poisoning incident in 1988, a successful criminal action in public nuisance was also taken: see *R v. South West Water Authority* [1991] 3 LMELR 65,[80] and private claims were settled out of court on the basis of an admitted breach of the statutory duty to supply wholesome water.

In the context of water pollution, the High Court has struck out a claim under breach of statutory duty following damage to shellfish beds that the claimant alleged was attributed to unlawful acts of a sewerage undertaker, holding that such claims had to be pursued in public law (*Bowden v. South West Water Services Ltd* [1998] Env LR 445). In a follow-up to this case ([1999] Env LR 438), however, the Court of Appeal allowed the claimant to pursue a claim based on liability against the state (a *Francovich* claim—see p. 210), because of the extent to which the Directive on Shellfish Waters (79/923/EEC) might be said to confer rights on individual shellfishermen. Similar claims under the Urban Waste Treatment Waters Directive (91/271/EEC) and the Bathing Waters Directive (76/160/EEC) were rejected, however, because the claimant could not say that he derived individual rights under them. This decision gives a good indication of the extent to which the need to prove an individual right to take a state liability claim may, in practice, mean showing that an individual economic interest might be infringed, rather than appealing to any wider environmental interests, limiting such claims to quite narrow classes of claimants.

Lastly, it is often stated that a prescriptive right to acquire an easement to pollute can be acquired. While this remains true as a matter of principle, such an occurrence will be rare, because it is not possible to acquire a prescriptive right in cases in which the act relied upon to gain the right is illegal. In most water pollution cases, the polluting activity will be illegal.

Remedies

Damages will be recoverable for any loss to the person whose rights have been infringed. This will include such things as any clean-up costs, the cost of restocking the water with fish,

---

80 As a criminal matter, this would now be dealt with under WIA 1991, s. 70—see p. 597.

any loss of profits from subscriptions for such things as fishing rights, and, in some circumstances, loss of amenity (see *Bruton v. Clarke* [1994] WL 145).

Injunctions are also available for water pollution, although they will normally be suspended to allow the defendants time to correct matters. For example, in *Pride of Derby and Derbyshire Angling Association Ltd v. British Celanese Ltd and ors* [1953] Ch 149, injunctions and damages were obtained against British Celanese Ltd (for industrial effluent), Derby Corporation (for untreated sewage), and the British Electricity Authority (for thermal pollution from a power station), but suspended for two years.

CHAPTER SUMMARY

1   Water pollution law is the most developed of the systems of pollution control. It has also had the greatest degree of institutional and legal coherence.

2   The body with general responsibility for water quality in England and Wales is the Environment Agency, usually acting under the Water Resources Act 1991.

3   There is no overall statutory national strategy comparable to those found in the air quality and waste management sectors. For England, DEFRA published *Directing the Flow: Priorities for Future Water Policy* in 2002, but this is not a document that required public participation and consultation before adoption. A fresh strategy document—*Future Water* (Cm 7319)—was published in 2008.

4   The addition of any substance into inland or coastal waters is not generally prejudged as being harmful. It is only considered harmful if it interferes with some desirable use for the water.

5   Accordingly, environmental quality standards are generally preferred, although for the more hazardous polluting substances, which may not break down quickly or which bioaccumulate, emission standards are used.

6   This policy approach does not mean that precedence is given to binding objectives for water quality. At national level, such objectives tend to be non-binding, although the impact of EC Directives has changed this in relation to certain waters, such as bathing waters. Otherwise, quality objectives act to guide the Environment Agency in setting discharge consents.

7   EC law is increasingly the most important force in determining new water quality standards and in driving up the costs of compliance. The introduction of more precise standards has also contributed enormously to raising public debate about water quality and increased the scope for legal challenges to poor water quality.

8   For the future, the EC Water Framework Directive will have a significant impact on all aspects of water pollution control and water quality management. But some of the key legal requirements in the Directive, such as 'good ecological status' and the aim of achieving good status of waters, remain vague.

9   Under national law, it is an offence to 'cause or knowingly permit' the discharge or entry of polluting matter, but acting in accordance with a discharge consent acts as a defence.

10   What amounts to 'polluting matter' is very wide, extending to substances capable of causing harm to humans or the water environment, rather than only those that cause actual harm.

11   Accordingly, much of the focus of case law has been on what will amount to 'causing' water pollution. The courts have interpreted this very purposively.

12   Only the most serious incidents are likely to result in prosecution by the Environment Agency. Selective enforcement and sensitive sentencing generally temper the wide interpretation given to causing water pollution. Monitoring is likely to become more selective on a risk-based basis.

13   The Agency has powers to require polluters to clean up water pollution or, as a last resort, to undertake works itself and charge the polluter. Clean-up costs often exceed fines.

14   Pollution from diffuse sources such as agricultural run-off is not consented, because there are no specific discharge points that can be monitored. Pollution from these types of source must therefore be controlled using other methods and integrative solutions.

15   The methods most commonly used to control diffuse discharges are specification standards, such as apply to the storage of oil or farm slurry, or area-based controls over sites designated because of, for example, high nitrate levels. A programmatic approach to reduction may also be taken, such as under the EC Agricultural Nitrates Directive, and wider land use controls are really needed to tackle water quality problems in an integrated way, as under the Water Framework Directive.

16   Economic tools, with the exception of cross-compliance, have not been extensively used. The charges levied by the Environment Agency for discharge consents, however, go some way towards making the polluter pay, while subsidies are sometimes (controversially) used to encourage farmers in certain areas to reduce their nitrate loading. There is some evidence that 'upstream' taxes can be particularly cost-effective in reducing pollution loading.

17   International law has tended to affect national standard setting only indirectly. In recent years, the international treaty regime concerning the North Sea has become more influential.

Q QUESTIONS

1   Alfie stores silage in a store that has recently been constructed for him by a reputable contractor. Following exceptionally unseasonable weather, the local river bursts its banks and, because of a latent defect, the store is flooded. Silage ends up in the river, where fish and wildlife are harmed. The Environment Agency is alerted, and incurs costs in removing the silage and restocking the river. Advise Alfie about any legal action that might be taken by the Environment Agency and by the local angling club, which claims that it has been adversely affected, and how he should respond.

2   What are the main approaches used by the EC in relation to water quality? What are their strengths and weaknesses? What legal issues arise in particular with each of them? Analyse at least one case in relation to each approach.

3   What legal difficulties might there be in implementing and enforcing the Water Framework Directive? (You might want to treat this as a research question, because, over the coming years, the shape of the implementing measures will become clearer.)

4   Consider the current system in England and Wales for granting discharge consents. How might this be modernized to take account of policy and regulatory developments of the kinds discussed in Chapters 8 and 14? Are the Scottish Controlled Activities Regulations 2005 (see p. 604) a good model to follow?

5   What legal measures might be passed to combat diffuse water pollution? What practical, policy, and legal difficulties might there be?

6   Do we use the right blend of tools to address poor water quality? What improvements would you suggest?

📖 FURTHER READING

Water policy

Good starting points for understanding water quality regulation and the modern development of policy are D. Kinnersley (1994) *Coming Clean: The Politics of Water and the Environment*, Harmondsworth: Penguin, a refreshingly polemical account, and, more academically and historically, W. Maloney and J. Richardson

(1995) *Managing Policy Change in Britain: The Politics of Water*, Edinburgh: Edinburgh University Press. In February 2008, a revised policy document—*Future Water* (Cm 7319)—was published by DEFRA, and replaces *Directing the Flow* (2002).

Water law

Comprehensive surveys of the law relating to water quality, including EC and international law, are J. H. Bates (looseleaf, updated) *Water and Drainage Law*, London: Sweet and Maxwell, and W. Howarth and D. McGillivray (2001) *Water Pollution and Water Quality Law*, Crayford: Shaw and Sons. The latter is a little out of date in places, but has chapter-by-chapter bibliographies that may serve as a useful springboard to further research. The *Journal of Water Law* (WL; Lawtext) is the specialist periodical, and contains both current awareness of UK and EC developments, and articles (many of which relate to developments globally). Another excellent general source, both on policy and law, is, as ever, N. Haigh (looseleaf, updated) *Manual of European Environmental Policy*, Leeds: Maney, which considers all of the Directives mentioned here and their implementation.

International law

D. Freestone and S. Salman (2007) 'Ocean and freshwater resources' in D. Bodansky, J. Brunnee and E. Hey (eds) *Oxford Handbook of International Environmental Law*, Oxford: Oxford University Press, is an excellent starting point for exploring this further. More comprehensive treatment can be found in R. Barnes, D. Freestone and D. Ong (eds) (2006) *The Law of the Sea: Progress and Prospects*, Oxford: Oxford University Press, a collection that goes well beyond the relatively narrow range of international law issues that we cover, and in the relevant chapters of Birnie and Boyle, and of Sands (see further reading to Chapter 6).

EC law

More detail on the specific Directives can be found in the general works mentioned above and those works on EC environmental law mentioned at the end of Chapter 7. Some of the policy issues in the negotiation of the 'second generation' of EC water Directives are discussed in A. Jordan, 'European Community water policy standards: locked in or watered down?' (1999) 37(1) JCMS 13. J. Scott and J. Holder (2006) 'Law and new environmental governance in the European Union' in G. de Burca and J. Scott (eds) *New Governance and Constitutionalism in Europe and the United States*, Oxford: Hart, considers the role of the common implementation strategy under the Water Framework Directive as a case study in new forms of environmental governance in the EC and gives a very good sense of how the detail of EC water law is arrived at.

Command regulation

A number of articles, the titles of which are reasonably self-explanatory, will help with further research: W. Howarth, 'Poisonous, noxious or polluting' [1993] MLR 171 explores the laws reluctance to define water pollution; W. Howarth, 'Self-monitoring, self-policing, self-incrimination and pollution law' [1997] MLR 200; C. Ryan, 'Unforeseeable but not unusual: the validity of the *Empress* test' [1998] JEL 345; N. Stanley, 'The *Empress* decision and causing water pollution' [1999] WL 37; D. Wilkinson, 'Definition of a break in the chain of causation' [2003] WL 96. S. Bell and L. Etherington, 'Out of sight, out of mind: a study of the transposition and implementation of the Groundwater Directive in the United Kingdom and Gibraltar' (2007) 1 Env LR 6 looks, in particular, at the challenge of controlling indirect discharges to groundwater and also considers how Directive 2006/118/EC changes the law in this area.

Diffuse pollution

S. Elworthy, 'Finding the causes of events or preventing a "state of affairs"? Designation of nitrate vulnerable zones' [1998] JEL 92 is an excellent analysis of the problems of regulating pollution from diffuse sources and of what making the water polluter pays means. N. Gunningham and D. Sinclair, 'Policy instrument choice and diffuse source pollution' (2005) 17 JEL 51 provides a good overview of how to tackle diffuse water pollution, which is of particular relevance to this chapter (see further comment on this in Chapter 8).

@ WEB LINKS

The Environment Agency **www.environment-agency.gov.uk** has the latest facts and figures about river quality and pollution incidents, although little prosecution and sentencing data. The Department for Environment, Food and Rural Affairs (DEFRA) and its devolved counterparts hold useful information, especially on current policy reforms and on the implementation of EC Directives, and the ongoing implementation of the Water Framework Directive with which you should keep up to date (see, for example, **www. defra.gov.uk/environment/water/quality/index.htm**). The websites of the Office of Water Services **www.ofwat.gov.uk** and the Drinking Water Inspectorate **www.dwi.gov.uk** are usefully browsed when looking at water supply and financing issues. On EC water quality law and policy, see **ec.europa.eu/ environment/water/index_en.htm**. Relating to the international agreements considered above, see the OSPAR Convention **www.ospar.org**, the latest International North Sea Conference **www.sweden.gov.se/ sb/d/6363**, and the International Tribunal for the Law of the Sea **www.itlos.org**.

18 Waste management

→ **Overview**

This chapter deals with the legal control of waste. Waste management law is a good example of mixed regulation, because a wide range of mechanisms is used to address not only the problems of pollution caused by waste disposal, but also positive mechanisms, such as producer responsibility, which attempt to address the causes of waste production. This chapter concentrates on the regulation of the waste chain, from initial production, to final disposal. This includes the coverage of the difficult question of the definition of 'waste' and a brief explanation of the application of the environmental permitting system that now covers waste management. The details of the permitting system can be found in Chapter 14. In addition, there is some discussion of the growing number of policies and laws that seek to encourage waste minimization, recycling, and recovery. There is brief coverage of relevant economic instruments, such as taxation and tradable permits. In general, the chapter looks at national law, although the important contribution of European law and the purposive approach to regulation is also considered. The regulation of international trade in the import and export of hazardous waste is also discussed briefly.

At the end of this chapter, you should be able to:

✔ understand the nature and scale of the problems of managing the production and disposal of waste, and some of the main ways in which they have been addressed at international, European, and national levels;

✔ appreciate the challenge of regulating the management and disposal of waste;

✔ understand the historical development of waste management law and policy, particularly at national and European levels;

✔ understand the frameworks of international and European waste management law;

✔ appreciate some of the main difficulties of defining 'waste', as reflected in the major case law on the topic;

✔ identify the general definition of 'waste';

✔ understand in outline the environmental permitting system as it applies to waste;

✔ appreciate some of the different approaches to managing waste production, including producer responsibility legislation and measures to encourage recycling;

✔ understand the role of economic instruments in waste management.

The nature and scale of the problem

Managing the production and disposal of waste is one of the most significant environmental challenges that the UK faces over the next twenty years. In 2004, around 335 million tonnes of waste was produced in the UK.[1] Of this, about 100 million tonnes comes from households, industry, and commercial sources, with the remainder originating from construction and demolition sites, farms, and spoil from mining and quarrying. At present, large proportions of waste from these latter categories are recycled or reused. For example, inert demolition rubble is often reused in new construction projects or road building. Perhaps more critically, much of the waste from these categories falls outside present legal controls, because it is either not 'waste' for the purposes of waste legislation or it is classified as exempt from many of the controls. Accordingly, most legal controls have been directed at dealing with municipal, industrial, and commercial wastes. The amount of municipal waste is growing at around 0.5 per cent per year. The trend in growth has slowed over recent years, but there are still significant challenges in order to reduce waste production.[2]

Historically, most of the waste disposed of in the UK was landfilled. Almost 80 per cent of municipal waste was disposed of in landfill sites, with low levels of recovery and recycling.[3] By comparison, on average, other EU member States have had much lower rates of landfill (45 per cent) and higher levels of recycling (26 per cent). There were a variety of reasons for the comparatively poor performance of the UK in comparison to other countries. Much of the reliance on landfill as the preferred option for waste disposal reflected the availability of suitable landfill sites with relatively stable geological conditions. The reliance on landfill, in turn, led to the lack of development of other recycling and recovery options. This abundance of cheap landfill sites has also contributed to inertia in terms of new laws and policies that would have encouraged alternative waste recycling and recovery options or waste minimization. This position is in sharp contrast to other European countries, which made greater use of legal and economic instruments, such as bans on the landfilling of certain wastes, extended producer responsibility for waste recycling and recovery, high taxes on landfill, and direct charging for the disposal of household waste. A combination of these measures provided incentives to minimize waste production and develop alternative facilities to sort, recover, and recycle waste.

The position in the UK is in the process of changing, with many new initiatives and policies.[4] Partly, this is because many existing landfill sites are reaching their full capacity and because the supply of suitable new locations for landfill sites is very limited indeed. In some areas, the problem is acute, leading to the need to transport waste long distances. Another driver is the need to implement European legislation that sets waste reduction, recycling, and recovery targets. The main consequence is that, although waste production is set to rise, the amount of waste going to landfill is falling and will continue to fall over the next 15 years.[5] On the assumption that this reduction is not met through waste minimization initiatives, there will have to be a huge increase in alternative disposal, recovery, and recycling routes. Principally, this will be met through an increase in waste incineration capacity, with the recovery of the

---

1 See http://www.defra.gov.uk/environment/statistics/waste/kf/wrkf02.htm.

2 See www.defra.gov.uk/environment/statistics/wastats/archive.htm. Historical data shows municipal waste arisings were growing at between 3–4 per cent in the late 1990s—one of the fastest growth rates in Europe.

3 Recycling rates have been low. In the early 1980s, the recycling rate for household waste was less than 1 per cent, with rates rising to approximately 12 per cent by 2001 and 26 per cent by 2005–06: see www.defra.gov.uk/environment/statistics.

4 Comprehensive coverage of the current and historical position can be found in the National Waste Strategy 2007.

5 Ibid., p. 11.

energy produced.[6] Other waste management methods, such as composting and recycling, will also have to be increased.[7]

The challenge of regulating waste management

Waste management provides some different, if not unique, challenges in comparison with other areas of pollution control. First, the central issue of *what* is controlled—that is, the definition of waste—is not clear. Most of the problems associated with defining 'waste' adequately stem from the fact that it is not necessarily synonymous with actual pollution or harm. The threat to the environment may arise as a result of the risk of pollution or harm in circumstances under which the waste is mishandled or abandoned. There is therefore a need to regulate the whole waste cycle, from the production of the waste, through the handling, storing, transportation, and treatment of waste, up to and including the final disposal, independently of whether there is any actual pollution or harm caused. Consequently, there are many 'grey areas' that can lead to uncertainty and confusion. These include such things as:

- whether something which can be reused, but is discarded, should be classified as waste—for example, electrical equipment that is placed into a dustbin, but which functions perfectly;

- whether something that is not wanted by one person—and is therefore 'got rid of'—but is valued by another—evidenced by the fact that they will 'buy' it—can be waste;

- whether a residue or a by-product from an industrial process, which can be used as a replacement for a raw material such as a fuel, should be classified as waste.

Secondly, there is the problem of trying to blend different types of legal measure to encourage waste minimization and reuse. There is an inevitable requirement to replace those things that have been discarded and, consequently, there are issues of resource depletion that can only be tackled through the minimization, reuse, and recovery of waste. Traditional forms of regulation are useful when addressing the control of environmental risks from the *disposal* of waste, but in doing so, they can often fail to address this issue. In this sense, legislative controls over the management of waste have proved to be inadequate as positive mechanisms for environmental improvement. Traditionally, 'command and control' mechanisms have focused on the regulation of activities after the production of the waste. For example, a system that licenses the treatment or disposal of waste is not necessarily efficient when it comes to promoting the reduction of the production of waste or encouraging recycling and recovery.

Finally, and linked closely to the second point, there is the difficult challenge of sustainable waste management. Ultimately, the main indicator of sustainability would be a continuous reduction in the volume of waste arisings. Up until recently, there have been few legal measures introduced to meet this goal. A lack of sufficient information on waste arisings, the use of 'predict and provide' methods that base future growth in waste facilities on extrapolated historic figures, and a lack of coordinated waste policies on a national basis have contributed to the failure to address sustainability issues. As with so many other areas, the picture is being changed as a result of European legislation that sets binding targets for the recycling, recovery, and reduction of waste.[8] For example, in contrast to the regulation of waste disposal, the introduction of positive instruments such as producer responsibility requirements makes producers responsible for products throughout their life cycle, including designing

---

6 Ibid. There is a target of 75 per cent recovery of municipal waste by 2020.
7 Ibid. There is a recycling target of 50 per cent of household waste by 2020.
8 For example, through the Landfill Directive 99/31/EC.

products for ease of recycling and recovery, imposing an obligation to take back used products, and meeting certain recycling and recovery targets for proportions of products placed on the market.[9]

The history of domestic waste law and policy

Early domestic laws were not primarily environmental in nature, being aimed at preventing accumulations of waste that might cause public health problems.[10] In addition, the controls were not used to prevent harm, but were used to clean up existing problems. Preventative controls were only introduced with the planning system in 1947. This continues to the present day, with the existence of some form of planning permission being a pre-requisite for an environmental permit for waste operations. The planning system, however, is not suited to controlling technical or post-operational activities on a waste management site, such as controlling technical specifications of liners or dealing with long-term aftercare of a landfill site.

These weaknesses were only addressed in the 1970s, with a phase that can be characterized as concentrating on the regulation of waste disposal. This involved continuing controls over waste disposal under licensing systems for hazardous waste under the Deposit of Poisonous Wastes Act 1972 and then, more generally, for most non-hazardous wastes in Pt I of the Control of Pollution Act (COPA) 1974. COPA 1974 introduced a comprehensive system in which a waste disposal licence was required before 'controlled waste' could be finally disposed of either in a landfill site or by incineration. Although the system was not without its flaws, it provided a framework that was adopted by other countries and, in particular, for the first major European legislation on waste, the Framework Directive.[11]

Following the implementation of COPA 1974, it became increasingly clear that there were still problems dealing with the management of waste—as distinct from its final disposal—and that the scope of the Act was too narrow.

BOX 18.1 The defects of the Control of Pollution Act 1974

In 1989, after some 15 years of operation, COPA 1974 was the subject of 'consistent and universal criticism' as part of a House of Commons Environment Committee investigation.[12] The identified defects illustrate some of the challenges of waste regulation and foreshadow some of the changes brought in under Environmental Protection Act (EPA) 1990.

- COPA sought to control the final deposit of waste rather than its management. Problems arose with the storage, treatment, and transportation of waste. For example, where waste had been fly-tipped, it was only possible to prosecute the person who had actually caused or knowingly permitted the deposit of the waste, leaving others further up the chain of waste management free from control, notwithstanding the fact that these others may have had a significant degree of responsibility for what had happened.

- There were problems with enforcement. For example, there was no offence of failing to comply with a licence condition. A decision in *Leigh Land Reclamation Ltd v. Walsall Metropolitan*

---

9 For example, see, in relation to vehicles, the End-of-Life Vehicles Directive 2000/53/EC.

10 Although more traditional waste problems such as fly-tipping were an issue: see, e.g., E. Cockayne (2007) *Hubbub: Filth, Noise and Stench in England*, New Haven: Yale University Press, pp.188–89.

11 75/442/EEC.

12 House of Commons Environment Select Committee Second Report (Session 1988–89) *Toxic Waste*.

> *Borough Council* (1991) 155 JP 547 meant that, as long as the deposit of waste was in accordance with the licence conditions, it was irrelevant if other conditions relating to the site were not being complied with. This had the effect of ensuring that many operational and administrative licence conditions were practically unenforceable.

- Once planning permission had been granted for waste disposal operations, there were limited grounds on which to refuse a grant of a waste disposal licence or to refuse a transfer, or to vary or revoke a licence.
- Licence holders had the right to surrender a disposal licence at any time, in which case, any conditions attached to it would automatically cease to have any effect. In practice, this meant that an operator could abandon a site and relinquish any future responsibility for its supervision.
- There was a lack of strategic guidance on waste management. This failure was at both national and local levels. Only 23 out of a possible 79 waste disposal plans were produced by local waste disposal authorities.[13] National guidance on the application of waste policies in the form of waste management papers were produced very slowly and patchily.
- There was a significant overlap in regulatory and operational responsibilities. The regulatory authorities created by COPA 1974 were also the main operators of waste disposal sites. The inherent conflict between these two roles led to an undermining of public confidence in the ability of the regulator to control its own activities.

Many of these defects were addressed with the introduction of Pt II of the Environmental Protection Act (EPA) 1990, which introduced a phase of a greater emphasis on waste *management*. This involved the control of the whole of the waste cycle 'from cradle to grave'. In particular, EPA 1990 increased controls over waste producers and carriers, and restructured the administration of waste regulation. The implementation of Pt II (and accompanying secondary legislation) was piecemeal, mainly as a result of some of the difficult issues it covered. Although some of the provisions were brought into force on 1 April 1992, the main bulk of Pt 2 was brought into operation on 1 May 1994, along with the Waste Management Licensing Regulations,[14] which transposed the requirements of the amended Waste Framework Directive and provided the first comprehensive system of waste *management* (as opposed to disposal) licensing provisions.

More recently, the diversity of waste law has broadened in an attempt to address the subtler, but no less important, defects in previous legislation. These include the lack of a consistent approach to strategic waste planning, and the failure of command-and-control regulation to tackle issues of waste prevention, minimization, and recycling. Thus the Environment Act 1995 provided for the production of a National Waste Strategy to articulate specific objectives for waste management. In relation to the encouragement of waste minimization, the 1995 Act also contained powers to make producer responsibility schemes and the Finance Act 1996 introduced a tax on landfill that was designed to reflect the full cost of waste disposal. More recently, the Landfill Regulations 2002[15] contained specific binding targets for reducing the amount of waste going to landfill and specific technical requirements for landfill sites.

The continuing development of waste management legislation is reflected in the introduction under the Environmental Permitting (England and Wales) Regulations 2007[16] of

---

13 Ibid.
14 SI 1994/1056.
15 SI 2002/1559.
16 SI 2007/3538, as amended by SI 2008/9.

a simplified 'permitting' system in 2008. This system has been designed to simplify and streamline the overlapping nature of much waste regulation and other pollution control systems. At the same time, the system is more flexible and able to deal with low-risk activities higher up the waste hierarchy—such as low-level recycling facilities—in a different, less intrusive fashion, as compared to high-risk, intensive waste disposal activities such as landfill and incineration.

International law and waste management

Generally, waste regulation has been concerned with controlling the management of waste within the domestic context. There are three main areas in which international environmental law has played a significant part. First, the Organisation for Economic Co-operation and Development (OECD) has played a significant part in harmonizing international definitions of waste, which, in turn, is reflected in the European List of Wastes (see below).

Secondly, international law has had a major impact on preventing the dumping of waste at sea. The United Nations Convention on the Law of the Sea (UNCLOS) provides a general obligation to prevent marine pollution, which covers dumping.[17] More particularly, the 1972 London Convention on the Prevention of Marine Pollution by Dumping of Wastes and Other Matter provides a global framework for the control of the deliberate disposal at sea of wastes or other matter, with various regional agreements—such as the 1998 Oslo–Paris (OSPAR) Convention for the Protection of the Marine Environment of the North East Atlantic—applying to specific geographical areas.[18]

Thirdly, as waste regulation became tighter in some countries, the costs of disposal rose and it became common practice to export hazardous wastes to developing countries in which it could be disposed of at a lower cost—mainly as a result of lower environmental standards. The control of transboundary movement of hazardous waste is governed at the international level by the Basel Convention on the Control of Transboundary Movements of Hazardous Waste and their Disposal. The Convention entered into force in May 1992 and was ratified by the UK on 7 February 1994. The Convention establishes a system whereby the exporter of waste must obtain the consent of the regulatory authorities in the importing country prior to shipping that waste. That consent must include a written confirmation that the importer of the waste will deal with the waste in an environmentally sound manner. In cases in which the consignment of waste cannot take place—for example, in circumstances under which it would not be handled in an 'environmentally sound manner'—the exporter of the waste is bound to take back the waste within 90 days.

While the Basel Convention has attempted to regularize the position in relation to the export of hazardous waste to developing countries, it has been argued that the Convention legitimates the trade in hazardous waste, which is open to abuse through the use of vague subjective standards, such as managing the transfer in an 'environmentally sound manner', and the lack of effective monitoring and control.[19] The result is that there is a risk that waste is still imported into developing countries either illegally or without proper regard to the risks associated with its recovery.

The EC Regulation on the Supervision and Control of Shipments of Waste within, into and out of the Community, gives effect to the Basel Convention throughout the EC.[20] The Regulation subjects the transfer of all waste (not only that which is hazardous) between

17 Articles 192–94.

18 W. Howarth and D. McGillivray (2001) *Water Pollution and Water Quality Law*, Crayford: Shaw, p. 898.

19 P. Birnie and A. Boyle (2003) *International Law and the Environment*, 2nd edn, Oxford: Oxford University Press, p. 436.

20 See Regulation 1013/2006.

countries to a system of 'prior informed consent' of the regulatory agencies in the two respective countries. The Regulation has direct effect, but the UK subsequently ratified the Basel Convention in 1994[21] and its requirements are now implemented under the Transfrontier Shipment of Waste Regulations 2007[22] and the UK Management Plan for the Imports and Exports of Waste. This management plan sets out the policy behind the Regulations. It is advisory and non-binding (although it gains its force through the Regulations).

The type of notification that must be given differs depending upon the nature of the waste that is shipped, whether the waste is destined for recovery or disposal, and whether the waste is transferred between two member States or out of the EC. Waste that is being transported for disposal is relatively straightforward and must comply with the requirements of the Basel Convention. In the UK, the Management Plan for the Imports and Exports of Waste bans all exports of waste for disposal and bans most imports for disposal, other than in exceptional cases in which wider environmental considerations apply.

Waste transported for recovery is controlled under a more complicated system. The EC Regulation adopts two processes:

- a prior written notification and consent process, which is used for hazardous and semi-hazardous waste intended for recovery;

- an information-based procedure in which shipments are accompanied by certain information, which is used for non-hazardous waste intended for recovery.

The procedures are linked to two lists of wastes.

- 'Green list' waste listed in Annex III of the Regulation is covered by the the information-based procedure. Shipments of 'green list' waste need to be accompanied by a contract between the parties involved in the transport, basic information, such as a description of the waste, quantity shipped, the name and address of the person to whom the waste is consigned, and a description of the recovery operation involved. In addition, such shipments are only allowed if the waste is dealt with in an environmentally sound manner throughout its movement and it is treated using techniques that are broadly equivalent to those used within the EU—that is, under the Waste Framework Directive. Finally, the person shipping the waste and the consignee must keep a copy of the completed documentation for three years.

- 'Amber list' wastes can be found in Annex IV to the Regulation. Shipments of 'amber' waste must be subject to the notification procedures found in the Basel Convention. Under the notification procedure, the notifier (shipper of the waste) must submit the notification to the 'home' regulatory authority, which then sends it on to the regulatory authorities at the destination and in any transit countries. The regulatory authorities have 30 days in which to give their consent (with or without conditions) or to object. If a shipment cannot be completed, the notifier must take the waste back.

BOX 18.2 **The defects of the transfrontier shipment legislation**

The importance of effective transfrontier shipment legislation increases as domestic waste disposal costs rise; the availability of cheaper disposal routes abroad becomes attractive—particularly if credit for recycling and recovery can be gained within domestic regimes.[23] In 2005 and

---

21 As required under Council Decision 93/98/EEC.

22 SI 2007/1711.

23 For example, packaging waste that is recovered or recycled abroad is eligible for packaging waste export recovery notes (PERNs), which can be used as evidence of compliance with the relevant producer responsibility legislation.

2006, over 50 per cent of shipments were identified to be non-compliant with the requirements of the Transfrontier Shipment of Waste Regulations.[24] Most of the breaches related to mixtures of wastes collected from municipal waste streams. The inspections demonstrated that they were being exported as 'green list' or 'non-notifiable' wastes, whereas the true legal position was that they should have been notified to the Environment Agency. Other illegal shipments were being exported to countries that did not wish to accept. Thus one of the key changes in the amended Regulations is to impose stricter controls over the movement of 'green list' wastes. This applies for the first time to movements of waste outside the EU. In addition, there is now an obligation to ensure the 'environmentally sound' management of *all* waste throughout the shipment, and during its recovery and disposal.

Other defects related to the import of hazardous wastes as demonstrated by the saga of the import of the so-called *US Ghost Ships*. The US Maritime administration (MARAD) owned 130 old warships that needed dismantling. The ships were hazardous, because of small quantities of hazardous wastes, such as PCBs and asbestos, within the structures. MARAD approached a UK company to carry out the work on 13 of the ships in a dock at Hartlepool. MARAD applied for transfrontier shipment (TFS) consent in June 2003. Under the Regulation, the Environment Agency was only allowed 30 days within which consent had to be given or consent was deemed to be granted. Once granted, the TFS approval could not be revoked.

The Environment Agency issued its consent in July 2003. Subsequently, it became clear that there were a number of problems with the proposed recovery processes that were to be carried out on the ships. The planning permission for the site was invalid and the existing waste management licence needed to be modified to cover the proposed recovery operations. As a consequence, the US ships could not be dismantled, because the necessary authorizations were not in place. The ships had, however, already set sail for the UK. The Agency's attempt to modify the waste management licence breached the Habitats Directive as a result of the failure to assess the potential impact of the dismantling on a nearby nature conservation site. Friends of the Earth overturned the modification in the High Court (see further *R (Friends of the Earth) v. Environment Agency* [2004] Env LR 31).

The saga of the *Ghost Ships* demonstrated that, as in other areas of environmental regulation, the many overlapping powers and responsibilities need to be clearly coordinated. The importation of hazardous waste requires a number of related consents or authorizations in addition to the requirement for TFS approval. The 30-day period for consent is too short to allow for proper consideration of the overall consequences of importation and there is no formal process of consultation with statutory bodies or the public.

European waste management law and policy

European policy on waste management is based largely upon broad objectives centred around a 'waste hierarchy'. One of the weaknesses of the EC's previous Environment Action Programmes (EAPs) however, has, been the vagueness of the specific methods of promoting the waste hierarchy. The Sixth EAP, *Environment 2010: Our Future, Our Choice*, identified waste and resources as one of the four priority areas for action. The Programme generally follows the waste hierarchy in the setting of objectives in terms of prevention, recycling,

24 Department for Environment, Food and Rural Affairs (2006) *Consultation on Transfrontier Shipments of Waste: Review of the Transfrontier Shipment of Waste Regulations 1994 and the UK Management Plan for Exports and Imports of Waste*, para. 3.4.

and reuse. Various waste streams are identified for specific action and the idea of integrated product policy in reducing waste is emphasized. The general objectives found in the Sixth EAP are supplemented by a more specific thematic strategy on waste prevention and recycling, which sets out plans to identify priority wastes, measures to ensure their recycling and collection, and instruments to encourage the creation of markets for recycled materials.[25]

BOX 18.3 The waste hierarchy

The cornerstone of all waste law is the aim of meeting, as far as possible, a hierarchy of waste with policies and laws designed to promote measures as high up the hierarchy as possible. The hierarchy is as follows.

1 Prevention

The primary aim is to prevent the creation of waste at source through the proper design of products and processes. This is linked with such initiatives as the development of integrated product policy, clean technology, eco-labelling, and product life cycle analysis.

2 Recycling and reuse

A second aim is to recycle or to reuse waste that is produced, with particular emphasis to be placed on the use of waste as a source of energy, for example, through combined heat and power schemes linked to waste incinerators. An obvious example of the EC's role in this area is its development of the producer responsibility obligation, covering such waste streams as packaging waste, end-of-life vehicles, batteries, and electrical and electronic waste.

3 Proper management and disposal

A third aim is that waste should be disposed of safely, preferably by incineration, with landfill only used as a last resort.

European law on waste management is based around Directives that lay down general principles, such as the setting up of licensing and inspection systems to ensure that the management of waste does not harm human health and the environment. These general principles can be found in broad framework Directives on waste (2006/12/EC) and hazardous waste (91/689/EC). These general principles are complemented by more detailed legislation. These cover two main areas. First, there are a number of important Directives that address methods of waste treatment, including Directives on landfill (99/31/EC), incineration (2000/76/EC), and integrated pollution prevention and control (IPPC) (2008/1/EC). These Directives lay down standards for waste treatment—such as emissions of dioxins from incinerators and the type of liner for landfills—and ban the disposal of certain products in landfills—for example, liquid wastes and tyres.

Secondly, there is a group of waste Directives that are more concerned with the management of particular types of waste. Some of these Directives address particularly hazardous wastes,[26] whereas others seek to reduce the amount of wastes arising in certain waste streams.[27]

---

25 COM (2005) 666.

26 For example, Directives dealing with waste PCBs (96/59/EC) and batteries (91/157/EEC).

27 For example, packaging, electrical equipment, and vehicles.

The broad framework Directives

The Framework Directive on Waste

The original Waste Framework Directive (75/442/EEC) was aimed largely at establishing a common set of principles dealing with the strategic planning and authorization of waste disposal. It was amended in 1991 (by Directive 91/156/EEC) and replaced by a new codified version in 2006 (2006/12/EC). The Framework Directive, along with all other relevant waste Directives, is directly transposed into English law through the Environmental Permitting (England and Wales) Regulations 2007.[28]

BOX 18.4 The key provisions of the Waste Framework Directive

Article 1 sets out the definition of waste as '*any substance or objects in the categories set out in Annex I which the holder discards or intends or is required to discard*'.

Article 2 excludes certain wastes from the scope of the Directive. Gaseous effluents are excluded entirely whereas other classes, including 'waste waters', waste from mines and quarries, and certain classes of agricultural waste, are excluded if they are '*already covered by other legislation*'.

Article 3 establishes the waste hierarchy, by requiring appropriate measures to encourage the prevention or reduction of waste and the recovery of waste by recycling, reuse, or reclamation, including the conversion of waste to energy through incineration.

Article 4 sets out the 'objectives' for safe waste management, requiring member States to '*take the necessary measures to ensure that waste is recovered or disposed of without endangering human health and without using processes or methods which could harm the environment*'.

Article 5 sets out a goal of self-sufficiency of waste disposal capacity within the EC, with the establishment of a network of disposal installations to deal with waste produced.

Article 7 provides for the need for waste management plans to be drawn up by national authorities (represented in the UK by the National Waste Strategies and other plans).

Article 8 imposes a duty to ensure that only authorized operators handle waste.

Articles 9 and 10 provide for the licensing of waste disposal and waste recovery operations (transposed by the Environmental Permitting (England and Wales) Regulations 2007).

Article 14 provides for the keeping of records of the nature of waste, its transport, and its treatment (transposed under the transfer note system under the duty of care).

Annex I sets out 16 categories of waste from Q1 to Q16, with Q16 being a catch-all category of '*any materials, substances or products which are not contained in the above categories*'.

Annex IIA lists 15 waste disposal operations and Annex IIB lists 13 waste recovery operations.

The European List of Wastes

While the Framework Directive sets out objectives and controls over waste generally, there are more specific obligations in relation to categorizing waste. Article 2 of the Framework Directive, along with Art. 1(4) of the Hazardous Waste Directive, require the drawing up of a list of wastes. Initially, this was found in the European Waste Catalogue,[29] which classified

---

28 SI 2007/3538.
29 Decision 94/3/EC.

waste into one of 20 main groups. The Waste Catalogue was subsequently amended by the European List of Wastes.[30]

The Hazardous Waste Directive

The Hazardous Waste Directive makes provision for the management of certain wastes that are specifically regulated because of their hazardous or toxic properties. Hazardous wastes are subject to the requirements of the Framework Directive in addition to the stricter requirements of the Hazardous Waste Directive. The annexes to the Directive set out the properties that bring wastes within the definition of 'hazardous'. The European List of Wastes has the effect of determining the classes of waste that fall within the definition of 'hazardous'.[31]

Waste Treatment Directives

In addition to the general principles laid down in the Framework Directive and in the Hazardous Waste Directive, the second group of European Directives addresses methods of waste treatment. For example, the Integrated Pollution Prevention and Control (IPPC) Directive regulates waste treatment and encourages waste minimization as part of many significant industrial installations, including landfill sites and incinerators. There is an overlap between this Directive and two other important waste treatment Directives on landfill and waste incineration. These latter Directives introduce specific standards for waste treatment (for example, emission and performance standards), whereas the former Directive applies a general framework of standards and objectives to the waste installation as a whole. The extent of these overlaps has been ameliorated by the incorporation of the main substantive provisions into the environmental permitting regime.

The Waste Incineration Directive

The Waste Incineration Directive 2000/76/EC replaced and extended two previous Directives on the incineration of municipal and hazardous waste.[32] The Directive has a general application to both normal incinerators and those plants in which the incineration of waste is used primarily as fuel to produce energy or other products (known as 'co-incineration') (Art. 1). This would include waste to energy plants and such things as cement kilns. All incinerators are required to be subject to authorization[33] and the authorizations, or permits, must have conditions listing the type and quantities of hazardous and non-hazardous waste that may be treated, the plant's incineration or co-incineration capacity, and the sampling and measurement procedures that are to be used (Art. 4). The Directive lays down minimum time and temperatures for waste combustion in order to guarantee complete waste combustion (Art. 5) and there are emission limit values (ELVs) set down for atmospheric emissions of certain substances, such as heavy metals, dioxins and furans, and greenhouse gases (Annexes II and V).

The Landfill Directive

The Landfill Directive has the main objectives of harmonizing waste disposal standards across member States, with particular emphasis on standards of design, operation, and after-care for landfill sites. It is also intended to act as the first major stimulant to the recovery

---

30 Decision 2000/532/EC as amended. This List is used as a way of classifying wastes in many European waste Directives and is transposed under the List of Wastes (England) Regulations 2005, SI 2005/895.

31 There are additional provisions in the Directive dealing with licensing, exemptions, and the keeping of records in relation to hazardous waste. These requirements have been transposed and are implemented under the Hazardous Waste Regulations 2005, SI 2005/894.

32 89/369/EEC and 89/429/EEC (municipal waste) and 94/67/EC (hazardous waste).

33 In England and Wales, under the Environmental Permitting (England and Wales) Regulations 2007.

and recycling of waste.[34] The main part of the Directive sets out targets for the reduction of the amount of biodegradable municipal waste[35] put into landfills and thereby reduce the amount of methane produced. Thus Art. 5 of the Directive requires the amount of bio-degradable municipal waste that is disposed of in landfills to be reduced in three stages: by 25 per cent, 50 per cent, and 65 per cent of the 1995 levels by 2006, 2009, and 2016, respectively. Even these deadlines can be extended in cases in which, as in that of the UK, more than 80 per cent of biodegradable municipal waste was disposed of in landfills in 1995 (making the deadlines 2010, 2013, and 2020, respectively). In addition to these waste reduction targets the Directive:

- defines different categories of waste (municipal waste, hazardous waste, non-hazardous waste, and inert waste) and landfills (landfills for hazardous waste, for non-hazardous waste, and landfills for inert waste) (Arts 2 and 4);

- bans the co-disposal of hazardous, non-hazardous, and inert wastes in the same land-fill, and completely bans the landfill of certain hazardous waste, liquid wastes, and tyres (Arts 5 and 6);

- introduces waste acceptance criteria at all sites in order to reduce risks and requires that all waste must be pretreated before disposal, which includes sorting and compaction of wastes (Art. 6);

- requires that an operator makes adequate financial provision for maintenance and after-care (Art. 10);

- lays down general standards for all landfills, including such things as leachate collection and control, and controls over gas and leachate produced at landfill sites (Annex I). In particular, all landfill gases must be either used to produce energy or flared off; only a minor-ity of current sites do this.

The significance of the Landfill Directive can be assessed against the background of dis-agreement between member States that postponed the adoption of the Directive for approxi-mately nine years. The Directive has already had a major impact upon current policies and practice, and the introduction of landfill quotas, bans on co-disposal, and waste acceptance criteria should see a move away from the historical reliance upon landfill in the UK.[36]

Subject-specific waste Directives

The third group of Directives cover a range of specific waste streams. These include the following.

- **A series of Directives imposing producer responsibility for certain wastes**
  These Directives aim to prevent the production of particular types of waste, and to encour-age its recycling, reuse, and recovery. The first of these was a Directive on packaging and packaging waste (94/62/EC), and this has been followed by Directives on the management of end-of-life vehicles (2000/53/EC) and on waste electrical and electronic equipment (WEEE) (2002/96/EC). Typically, these Directives encourage the redesign of products—cars; white goods—to ease recovery and recycling, while requiring the establishment of waste collection systems; and the setting of recovery and recycling targets as percentages of the waste produced.

---

34 See, generally, H. Cameron (1999) Env LR 266.

35 That is, household or similar waste that is capable of decomposition.

36 The Directive is transposed by the Environmental Permitting (England and Wales) Regulations 2007, SI 2007/3538, reg. 35(d) and Sch. 10.

- **Directives on wastes that needs regulating in particular ways**
These include waste oils (75/439/EEC), batteries and accumulators (91/157/EEC), titanium dioxide (78/176/EEC), and PCBs and polychlorinated triphenyls (96/59/EC). Although the Directives deal with these materials specifically, the transposition of the Directives' requirements is generally through the environmental permitting system concerning waste—with slight variations for batteries and PCBs.[37]

Domestic waste policy

For many years, the development of waste policy mirrored that of the law, in that the primary aim was to address the environmental risks involved in the disposal of waste. The first steps towards a wider policy base were made with the introduction of the Framework Directive, which required member States not only to control the disposal of waste, but also to encourage the prevention, recycling, and reuse of waste. The concept of the waste hierarchy was explicitly adopted in the UK in 1990[38] and, although these principles provided a good foundation upon which to build waste policy, the growth of detailed policies was largely unstructured, with the effect that the overall objectives were often difficult to discern. In addition, the implementation of waste disposal plans and waste local plans, dealing with strategic waste management and planning respectively, had been patchy, leading to inconsistent local guidance.

In the light of the amendments to the Framework Directive in 1991,[39] proposals were made to develop a National Waste Strategy. In 1995, a non-statutory waste strategy was published.[40] In the same year, the strategy was given statutory underpinning after the Environment Act 1995 inserted a requirement to produce a National Waste Strategy under s. 44A of EPA 1990. This gives the Secretary of State power to prepare a statement containing policies in relation to the recovery and disposal of waste.

The process of producing the 'National' Waste Strategy was slow and protracted, with the final version being produced in May 2000.[41] The English Strategy—there are now separate strategies for each of the home countries—was updated in 2007 to take into account changes over the intervening period.[42] It constitutes the waste management plan for the purposes of Art. 7 of the Waste Framework Directive, the Hazardous Waste Directive, the Packaging Waste Directive, and the Landfill Directive. The cumulative impact of the Strategy and the legal instruments associated with it is clear, particularly when coupled with the developments in relation to discharges to sewers and controls over incineration. Waste minimization is to be encouraged, because the costs of disposal, by whatever route, are likely to increase significantly as the national Strategy is implemented.

The statutory objectives

The objectives set out in Arts 3–7 of the Waste Framework Directive are transposed into UK law in the Environmental Permitting Regulations, Schs 9 and 20, and through the requirement to incorporate the objectives in the National Waste Strategy under Sch. 2A of EPA 1990. Although the European Court of Justice (ECJ) has held that these objectives do

---

37 See Chapter 14.
38 (1990) *This Common Inheritance*, Cm 1200.
39 In particular, the requirement of waste management plans—see Art. 7.
40 (1995) *Making Waste Work: A Strategy for Sustainable Waste Management in England and Wales*, Cm 3040.
41 *Waste Strategy 2000 for England and Wales*, Cm 4693.
42 *Waste Strategy for England 2007*, Cm 7086.

not have 'direct effect',[43] the Court of Appeal has held[44] that they create a separate self-standing duty upon regulatory authorities to ensure that waste is recovered or disposed of without endangering human health or the environment.[45] This duty applies to waste regulatory authorities, such as the Environment Agency, and local planning authorities exercising waste-related functions.[46]

In addition to the application to planning authorities, the objectives also apply to the consideration of any waste-related applications.

BOX 18.5 The statutory objectives

The statutory objectives are found by reference to Arts 4 and 5 of the Waste Framework Directive, and the duties in the Environmental Permitting Regulations placed on the Agency, Ministers, and planning authorities. The most relevant elements are as follows.

- **Article 4**

  1. Member States shall take the necessary measures to ensure that waste is recovered or disposed of without endangering human health and without using processes or methods which could harm the environment, and in particular:

     (a) without risk to water, air or soil, or to plants or animals;

     (b) without causing a nuisance through noise or odours;

     (c) without adversely affecting the countryside or places of special interest.

  2. Member States shall take the necessary measures to prohibit the abandonment, dumping or uncontrolled disposal of waste.

- **Article 5**

  1. Member States shall take appropriate measures to establish an integrated and adequate network of disposal installations, taking account of the best available technology not involving excessive costs. The network must enable the Community as a whole to become self-sufficient in waste disposal and the Member States to move towards that aim individually, taking into account geographical circumstances or the need for specialised installations for certain types of waste.

  2. The network referred to in paragraph 1 must enable waste to be disposed of in one of the nearest appropriate installations, by means of the most appropriate methods and technologies in order to ensure a high level of protection for the environment and public health.

Transposition of the objectives has been relatively simple, first by copy-out and now, in the Environmental Permitting Regulations, by reference to the Framework Directive itself. Implementation, however, has proved to be more of a problem. The objectives are inconsistent, with some aimed at 'ensuring' risk-free waste disposal, while others are concerned with a high level of environmental protection. 'Ensuring' the avoidance of risk to human health or the prevention of pollution of the environment is a practical impossibility: most—if not all—waste recovery or disposal operations cause, or at least risk, some pollution of the environment. If the 'objectives' in Art. 4 were to be interpreted literally in this way, they would never be met.

---

43 See *Comitato di Coordianmento per la Difesa della Cava and ors v. Regione Lombardia and ors* [1994] Env LR 281.
44 In the context of the former Waste Management Licensing Regulations 1994.
45 *R v. Bolton Metropolitan Borough Council, ex parte Kirkman* [1998] Env LR 719.
46 Environmental Permitting Regulations 2007, Sch. 9, paras 3 and 4, and Sch. 20, paras 3 and 4.

What, then, do the objectives require? The courts have interpreted the consideration of the objectives in a number of ways.[47] They are mandatory, in the sense that they must be considered. Thus, in *R v. Environment Agency, ex parte Sellars and Petty* [1999] Env LR 73, the Environment Agency's failure to consider the objectives at all was found to be unlawful. In *R v. Bolton Metropolitan Borough Council, ex parte Kirkman* [1998] Env LR 719, the Court of Appeal considered that the objectives were material considerations that were to be taken into account when determining decisions. This view was adopted in *R v. Leicester County Council, Hepworth Building Products Ltd and Onyx (UK) Ltd, ex parte Blackfordby and Boothcorpe Action Group Ltd* [2001] Env LR 2, in which the High Court held that, to meet the objectives, a decision maker must consider whether the aim of ensuring that waste is disposed of or recovered without endangering human health or harming the environment would be achieved.

The Court of Appeal further clarified the nature of the obligation in *R v. Daventry District Council, ex parte Thornby Farms Ltd; R (Murray) v. Derbyshire County Council* [2002] Env LR 28, in which Pill LJ said:

An objective … is something different from a material consideration … it is an end at which to aim, a goal … A material consideration is a factor to be taken into account when making a decision, and the objective to be attained will be such a consideration, but it is more than that. An objective which is obligatory must always be kept in mind when making a decision even while the decision maker has regard to other material considerations.[48]

In practical terms, this means that a decision maker must state that the objectives have been kept in mind, identify the material considerations that have been taken into account and the extent to which they move towards or away from the aim of the objectives.[49] The decision maker's discretion is not unlimited, however, and the Court of Appeal made it clear that there would be circumstances under which the considerations produce a result that involves so plain and flagrant a disregard for the objective that there is a breach of legal obligation. This idea that the objectives are important, but not overriding, was adopted by the Court of Appeal in *R (on the application of Blewett) v. Derbyshire County Council* [2005] Env LR 15.

What is 'waste'?

The definition of 'waste' is multifaceted. There are general issues, such as whether something has the basic characteristic of waste—namely, being discarded. Furthermore, there are certain categories of waste that are linked to either the properties of the waste itself—such as hazardous or inert waste—or the identity of the producer—such as household, commercial, or industrial waste—that are used for classification purposes in relation to waste licensing schemes.

The concept of waste has proved to be particularly difficult to define with any certainty. There are a number of reasons for this.[50] First, there is no inherent physical characteristic that can be used to define waste. Unlike other areas of pollution control, the idea of waste is not necessarily associated with pollution—although all pollution is associated with waste. The link between waste and environmental harm is that, unless waste is managed properly and therefore regulated accordingly, there is a *potential* for pollution.

---

47 These judgments have related to earlier implementing legislation, but, in principle, these decisions are equally relevant under the Environmental Permitting Regulations.

48 At [53].

49 *R (Horner) v. Lancashire County Council* [2005] EWHC 2273 (Admin) and S. Bell (2003) 15 JEL 59.

50 I. Cheyne and M. Purdue (1995) 7 JEL 149.

Secondly, there is the subjective nature of the view that one can take when considering whether the material is waste. In particular, one person's waste can be another person's raw material. This can be closely linked to the third reason, which is that there is an implicit connection between the concept of waste and a lack of value or worth of an object. Implicitly, something can only be waste if it is not wanted. There are, however, some categories of objects that have been discarded by the original holder, but which have a value, because they can be used either for their original or another purpose. In the latter case, there may be some sort of treatment required prior to reuse.

Fourthly, the waste management hierarchy emphasizes the reuse and recycling of material. In such circumstances, on the one hand, there is no sense in over-regulating by drawing up a very wide definition of waste, because this would discourage environmentally beneficial activities that would reduce the amount of raw materials required and consequently the waste produced. On the other hand, many recycling and reclamation processes have the capability of causing harm if left unregulated. In drawing up any definition, the rule maker must seek to strike a balance between these two competing considerations.

BOX 18.6 Purposive rules vs detailed categories

One of the characteristics of environmental laws is that there is a tendency to combine wide purposive definitions with detailed categories. This approach aims to balance flexibility with certainty. The legislation on the definition of waste is a very good example of this. Note the very wide general definition of waste and contrast this with the detailed categories of waste. The general definition ensures a high level of environmental protection by making the definition of waste contextual—that is, by basing it on the intention of the holder—while the detailed categories provide a degree of detail that clarifies the general definition.

One of the main challenges of adopting such an approach is that the purposes of the legislation need to be transparent and straightforward, otherwise there is confusion in the manner in which the legislation should be applied and a tendency towards over- or under-regulation. One of the fundamental tensions within waste legislation is the way in which it promotes the *prevention* of waste as well as the *regulation* of waste after it is produced. As the cases on the definition of waste demonstrate, the courts have struggled to balance out these competing purposes. By taking a broad purposive interpretation of the definition of waste in order to ensure comprehensive regulation, prevention is given a lower priority and the purposes of the waste hierarchy are frustrated.

Under domestic law, the definition of 'waste' and 'waste management activities' is very complex. There are two broad principles that apply.

1. The only waste that is regulated under EPA 1990 is known as 'Directive waste', to reflect the description of waste as found in the Directive.

2. The activities that are subject to the requirements contained in the Environmental Permitting Regulations 2007 are known as 'Directive disposal' and 'Directive recovery'.

Directive waste

The general definition of 'Directive waste' is to be found in Art. 1(a) of the Framework Directive, which provides that it is '*any substance or object in the categories set out in Annex I* [to the Framework Directive] *which the holder discards or intends or is required to discard*'. The Environmental Permitting (England and Wales) Regulations adopt an identical definition (reg. 2), which means that all of the elements of the definition of waste—such as the meaning of 'discard', as this has been interpreted by the ECJ—are of direct relevance.

The starting point for the definition of waste is, therefore, the list of 'categories' that can be found in Annex I of the Directive.[51] There are 16 categories—Q1–Q16—covering a range of descriptions of production residues and contaminated or adulterated materials. While these descriptions are helpful in determining whether something is waste, on closer examination, it becomes clear that the description of various categories of waste is illustrative, rather than determinative. The first thing to note is that the list sets out substances or objects that are waste *only* when they are discarded. For example, animal slurry, which is specifically listed in the Annex, was held not to be a waste if it was used as a fertilizer as part of a lawful practice of spreading on clearly identified parcels and if its storage was limited to the needs of those spreading operations.[52] In these circumstances, the slurry was not 'discarded'. Thus, a substance or object in one of the categories in the list will not necessarily be waste unless it can be demonstrated that it falls within the general definition in Art. 1(a).

Secondly, there is a totally inclusive category, Q16, which covers all 'materials, substances or products' that are not contained in any of the other categories. This would cover everything that could conceivably exist. The inclusion of this general category suggests that there is a specific purpose in setting out other, more detailed, categories—otherwise, the all-inclusive category would render the others superfluous.

It is clear from the descriptions of the categories that they cover substances or objects that may be presumed to be discarded, or will be discarded in the near future. At best, this could set up a rebuttable presumption, which could be contradicted by specific evidence of an absence to discard.

In addition to these general categories of waste, there is an extensive list of wastes prepared by the European Commission.[53] In common with the Annex I list, this is merely illustrative, because its main purpose is to ensure uniformity in the classification of wastes across member States and is not conclusive in determining whether any of the listed substances is actually waste. The practical effect of the general category of waste means that there is a two-stage test that applies to the question of whether a substance, material, or product is Directive waste.

BOX 18.7 The two-stage test for determining whether something is Directive waste

1. Is it a substance, material, or product, and does it therefore come within any of the categories set out in the specific definitions in Annex I?

If the answer is 'yes'—and, for practical purposes, that will almost certainly be the case—

2. Has the substance, material, or product been discarded by its holder, or is there an intention or requirement to discard it?

It is the second of these two questions that gives the key to the definition of Directive waste. As we shall see, the case law on the definition of waste suggests that material is not waste merely because it falls within a class set out in Annex I, but that the critical question is whether it has been discarded.

---

51 Waste Management Licensing Regulations 1994, Sch. 4, Pt II.
52 Case C-416/02 *Commission v. Spain* [2005] ECR I-7487.
53 Decision 2000/532/EC.

In many cases, the question of whether something is waste or not will be straightforward. If I throw away perfectly useable topsoil by putting it in a skip, for example, my intention to discard it is clear. This is so notwithstanding that the soil might have a commercial value or a useful purpose for a passer-by, who might dig it out and then reuse it for landscaping.[54] There are, however, other situations in which the intention to discard is not as clear and it is in these cases that the courts have wrestled with the elusive definition of waste. One of the important factors is whether the substance has been consigned to a waste recovery or disposal operation.[55] The definition of 'disposal operations' is relatively straightforward. Annex IIA of the Framework Directive lists a series of operations that are standard ways of finally disposing of waste, including varieties of incineration and landfill.[56] By definition, when a substance is consigned to a disposal operation such as landfill or incineration, it is clear that there is an intention to discard, because the mere fact of final disposal means that it cannot be reused. One point that should be made, however, is that the list is not exhaustive and that there are other types of disposal that are not included, particularly in relation to such things as deliberate discharges of pollutants into the atmosphere, where they are controlled under separate legislation.

The situation with substances consigned to recovery operations is not necessarily clear, because many recovery operations that use waste principally as a fuel are not easily distinguished from industrial processes. In such cases, the recovery process is part and parcel of a bigger industrial process.[57] In Case C-304/94 *Euro Tombesi* [1998] Env LR 59, the Advocate-General suggested that the mere consignment of a material to a recovery process listed in Annex IIB of the Framework Directive was sufficient to amount to discarding and therefore identify the substance as waste. This reasoning became known as the '*Tombesi* bypass',[58] because it neatly 'bypassed' the question of whether something had been discarded by turning the definition on its head—something consigned to a recovery process has been discarded. The full judgment of the ECJ did not go as far as the Advocate-General, preferring instead to conclude that the consignment of a substance to a recovery process could amount to discarding, which would indicate that the substance was a waste.

The general approach taken in *Tombesi* was followed by the ECJ in Case C-126/96 *Inter-Environnement Wallonie v. Regione Wallone* [1998] Env LR 625, when the Court concluded that, although there was a distinction between industrial processes and recovery operations, it would normally be the case that substances subjected to a recovery process would be waste. This reasoning was also adopted in the English courts in *Mayer Parry Recycling Ltd v. Environment Agency* [1999] Env LR 489, in which it was held that scrap metal that could be reused without being subjected to any recovery operation was not waste.

Problems arise with the *Tombesi* bypass approach when a substance is consigned to a recovery process that can also be a normal industrial process. Consider, for example, the situation in which an industrial by-product is used to fuel partially a cement kiln. This is a recovery operation—the energy 'recovered' from the fuel is used to make cement; it is, however, also a normal industrial process that uses raw materials for fuel (for example, coal). The decisions in *Tombesi* and *Inter-Environnement Wallonie* did nothing to clarify this distinction. They simply shifted the question from 'has the substance been discarded?' to 'has the substance been consigned to a recovery process?'

---

54 For example, see *Kent County Council v. Queenborough Rolling Mill Co. Ltd* (1990) 89 LGR 306, Joined Cases C-206/88 and C-207/88 *Vessoso and Zanetti* [1990] ECR I-1461 and I-1509.

55 As listed in Annex IIA and IIB of the Directive.

56 Listed in the Environmental Permitting Regulations in Sch. 1.

57 This problem also is evident in comparing the use of a product (coal) and waste (substitute liquid fuels, or SLFs): L. Kramer (2003) 11(1) Env Liab 3.

58 G. Van Calster [1997] Eur Bus LR 137.

One way of differentiating between recovery operations and industrial processes has been the adoption of a separate concept of the 'specialized recovery operation'. There is no specific legislative definition of this phrase, but it is described in Circular 11/94 as being intended to cover operations that either reuse substances or objects that are waste because they have fallen out of normal use, or recycle them in a way that eliminates or diminishes sufficiently the threat posed by their original production as waste and produces a raw material that can be used in the same way as raw material or a non-waste compound.[59] In cases in which substances are consigned to a specialized recovery operation, they will always be waste. Although this approach has been viewed favourably by the ECJ[60] and the High Court,[61] it is still not a legal test and, in the light of subsequent decisions discussed below, it would seem that it is still a helpful, as opposed to determinative, way of determining whether a substance is consigned to a recovery process.

In Case C-418/97 *ARCO Chemie Nederland Ltd v. Minister van Volkshuivesting and EPON* [2003] Env LR 40, the ECJ rejected the interpretation of the Advocate-General's opinion in *Tombesi*, concluding that consigning something to a recovery operation did not necessarily mean that it was waste. The only appropriate test was whether the substance had been 'discarded'. This was something that could only be assessed in the light of the circumstances of the case. The Court rejected any notion of conclusive tests such as the *Tombesi* bypass, but concluded that the term 'discard' had to be interpreted generously in the light of the aims of the Waste Framework Directive. Consequently, the decision in *Mayer Parry* that materials that could be reused without undergoing a recovery operation were not waste was overturned.

CASE 18.1 The closing of the *Tombesi* bypass—*Attorney-General's Reference (No. 5 of 2000)* [2002] Env LR 5

The operators of an animal rendering plant produced a by-product that was collected and spread on farmland. The operators were prosecuted for a breach of the duty of care under s. 34 of the EPA 1990 for failing to prevent the unlawful disposal of waste (the by-product) on land. At the trial, the operators argued that, following the decision in *Mayer Parry*, the by-product was not waste, because it was capable of being reused without being subjected to a recovery process. The trial judge agreed and the operators were acquitted.

The Attorney General referred the matter to the Court of Appeal. The decision in *ARCO* had postdated the decision in *Mayer Parry* and had therefore been doubted in subsequent decisions.[62] The Court of Appeal rejected the decision in *Mayer Parry* and its reliance on the Advocate-General's opinion in *Tombesi*. The Court concluded that the by-product was capable of being waste, notwithstanding that it had not been subjected to a waste recovery process.[63]

One of the problems with the European case law on the definition of waste is that the ECJ appeared to be very reluctant to lay down specific tests to determine whether something was 'discarded', preferring to emphasize the purposive nature of the Directive and then to leave the judgment of such matters to the national courts. In various cases,[64] certain factors have

---

59 See Circular 11/94, para. 2.25.

60 Case C-304/94 *Euro Tombesi* [1998] Env LR 59.

61 Case C-444/00 *Mayer Parry Recycling Ltd v. Environment Agency* [1999] Env LR 489.

62 For example, see the judgment of Stanley Burnton J in *Castle Cement v. Environment Agency and Lowther* [2001] Env LR 45.

63 J. Pike (2002) 14 JEL 197.

64 For example, Case C-126/96 *Inter-Environnement Wallonie v. Regione Wallone* [1998] Env LR 625, Case C-418/97 *ARCO Chemie Nederland Ltd v. Minister van Volkshuivesting and EPON* [2003] Env LR 40, and Case C-9/00 *Palin Granit Oy v. Vehmassaion kansanterveystyon kuntayhtyman hallitus* [2002] Env LR 35.

been identified that might assist in determining whether something has been discarded. These include:

- meeting the broad aims of the Waste Framework Directive (for example, to prevent the dangerous disposal of waste);
- whether the substance has been consigned to a disposal or recovery operation;
- whether the substance is a production residue, rather than a product with a subsequent use;
- whether the substance is normally regarded as a waste;
- whether there is any other use for the substance that might be envisaged other than disposal or recovery;
- what was the degree of likelihood that the substance would be reused without any further reprocessing prior to that use;
- whether there was some financial advantage to the holder in reusing the substance;
- whether any special precautions had to be taken when the substance was reused.

Irrelevant factors have included:

- how and where the substance was stored;
- its composition;
- whether it posed any real risk to human health or the environment.

It should be noted that these are *indicative*, not conclusive, factors.

CASE 18.2 A broad definition of waste—Case C-9/00 *Palin Granit Oy v. Vehmassaion kansanterveystyon kuntayhtyman hallitus* [2002] Env LR 35

This is a good example of the broad flexible approach to the definition of waste. Palin Granit stored leftover stone at a granite quarry in Finland. The Finnish waste authorities considered the leftover stone to be waste for the purposes of Finnish law and that its storage site was a landfill. PG argued that the leftover stone was stored for short periods for subsequent use without the need for any recovery measures and did not pose any risk to human health or the environment. The Finnish waste authority argued that the leftover stone should have been regarded as waste as long as evidence of reuse of the stone had not been provided. The Finnish Court referred to the European Court of Justice the question of whether the leftover stone produced from stone quarrying was capable of being regarded as 'waste'. The ECJ discussed the various factors that had been identified in previous cases and, in applying those factors, concluded that the leftover stone from quarrying was not the product primarily sought by the operator of a granite quarry. It could more properly be described as a 'production residue' and therefore as waste. The reuse of the granite was uncertain and only foreseeable in the longer term.

The extensive case law on the definition of waste indicates the complexity of trying to interpret a broad purposive definition within the context of many different factual contexts. The ECJ has, after a tentative start, produced successive judgments that have widened the definition of waste considerably. The Court appears to want to avoid trying to produce conclusive principles by pursuing influential, but non-determinative, factors that point towards something being discarded.

This 'piecemeal' and iterative process of defining waste on a case-by-case basis by the ECJ has been criticized implicitly by the Court of Appeal, which accused the ECJ of paying 'lip service' to the 'discarding' test while, in practice, subordinating the subjective question implicit in that definition to a series of objective indicators that were clearly derived from a vague purposive approach to interpreting the Directive's provisions.[65] These tests were not truly workable and the implication was that the 'discarding' test was inapplicable in certain cases—such as those in which the waste holder was an end-user, whose only subjective intention was to use, not to get rid of, the materials in issue. In such circumstances, it was a nonsense to talk of 'discarding'—certainly within the normal meaning of the word. In some ways, this dismissal of the ECJ's decisions underplays the significance that is consistently attached to whether the broad aims of the Waste Framework Directive are being met. This promotes a very broad purposive definition of waste that has the advantage of capturing more waste disposal or recovery operations, which may give rise to environmental risks. There are, however, limits to such a broad purposive interpretation.

CASE 18.3 When does waste cease to be waste? *OSS Group Ltd v. Environment Agency* [2008] Env LR 8

OSS collected and treated waste oil, and resold it as a fuel. The central issue was whether the treated oil ceased to be waste following treatment and prior to sale. The Environment Agency argued that the oil only ceased to be waste after it was burned as a fuel. The Court of Appeal acknowledged the difficulties in making a judgment on the imprecise definition of waste found in Art. 1(a) of the Directive, but held that the oil was not being 'discarded' in any ordinary sense of the term. It was necessary to make a balanced, purposive judgment on the facts of the case to see whether the oil was still waste when burned.[66] The key factors were that OSS had converted the waste oil into a distinct, marketable product, which could be used in exactly the same way as an ordinary fuel and with no worse environmental effects.

This purposive approach highlights the fact that the definition of waste is not something that is determined in isolation. It is inherently linked to the management of waste and other objectives of the Waste Framework Directive. In seeking to define waste, the courts have in mind the requirement that holders of waste must manage the waste substances in accordance with the requirements of the Framework Directive. These include ensuring that waste should be recovered or disposed of without endangering human health, or in ways that could harm the environment, and that there should be a prohibition on the abandonment, dumping, and uncontrolled disposal of waste.

Many of the cases brought before the courts have not really been concerned with the inherent nature of the substances or materials themselves. What was at the heart of many of these disputes was the exact framework under which particular activities should be controlled. Thus *Palin Granit* (Case 18.2) was primarily concerned with the question of whether a quarry had to be licensed as a landfill site and *Castle Cement v. Environment Agency and Lowther* [2001] Env LR 45 was concerned with the question of whether a cement kiln was regulated as part of an industrial installation or as a separate hazardous waste incinerator. What matters is not whether something is waste, but how it is controlled. This has given rise to the ECJ seeking to expand the definition of waste to include accidental releases of contaminants into soil and groundwater.

---

65 *OSS Group Ltd v Environment Agency* [2008] Env LR 8.
66 Relying upon the decision in *Scottish Power Generation Ltd v. Scottish Environment Protection Agency* 2005 SLT 98.

CASE 18.4 Extending the concept of 'discarding'—Case C-1/03 *Van de Walle and ors* [2005] Env LR 24

The European Court of Justice was asked to consider the question of whether petrol leaking from underground storage tanks at a Texaco filling station was waste. As with the previous case law, the key question was whether it could be said that the petrol had been discarded. The ECJ held that accidental leaks and spillages of petrol were substances that the holder did not intend to produce and which were 'discarded', albeit involuntarily, at the time of production or distribution. The ECJ also ruled that soils contaminated by the hydrocarbons were waste even where they had not been excavated, because the soil could not be recovered or disposed of without some decontamination works. Finally, the ECJ considered that Texaco, as the petrol supplier, was the producer (and therefore holder) of the waste for the purposes of the Framework Directive in instances in which the leak was caused—even if only in part—by a 'disregard of contractual obligations' to service and maintain the tanks on the part of Texaco.

In the UK, accidental spillages or leakages of substances have not necessarily been considered to be waste[67] and there are consequently questions about the extent to which the UK has transposed the requirements of the Waste Framework Directive. The central problem created by the *Van de Walle* decision is that the ECJ has expanded the concept of waste and the application of the Framework Directive into new areas. While that may be necessary to respond to a set of facts in Belgium, the decision cuts across long-established statutory controls in other member States. For example, there are controls to prevent such leaks and to remedy the consequences under various pieces of legislation dealing with, for example, water pollution[68] and historic pollution.[69] It also begs the question about the role and purpose of other EC legislation, such as the Water Framework Directive and Environmental Liability Directive, which purportedly address such problems.

The *OSS* decision (Case 18.3) represents a shift away from a seemingly all-encompassing approach to defining waste. This represents a positive move, because a broad definition of waste is a relatively blunt instrument with which to achieve the purposes of the Waste Framework Directive. There is a danger that this approach may lead to over-regulation, under which relatively low-risk sites are subject to onerous waste licensing regulation. In the UK, where the waste licensing system has been aimed at dealing with landfill sites, the application of similar systems of regulation to many recycling sites can act as a disincentive to investment in much-needed recycling and recovery operations. One aim of the Environmental Permitting Regulations 2007 is, in theory, to provide less of a regulatory burden on such sites through a unified permit and a more flexible approach to regulating exemptions under the permitting system (see Chapter 14).

Secondly, the danger with a broad definition of waste is that there is so much uncertainty that it is difficult to carry out activities with materials that might be waste without reference to the Environment Agency. The absence of any formal mechanism for determining the question means that the resolution of any disputes is complicated and normally only available through judicial review or the criminal courts on a prosecution. Although this vagueness of the definition of waste is a practical problem, the courts have held that the definition is sufficiently clear to enable those who are affected to regulate their conduct and that therefore there is no breach of Art. 7 of the European Convention of Human Rights.

---

67 This included leaks of sewage, which the ECJ has also held to be 'discarded' as waste: see Case C-252/05 R (*Thames Water Utilities) v. Bromley Magistrates' Court* [2008] Env LR 3.

68 For example, s. 161A, Water Resources Act 1991, and the Groundwater Regulations 1998.

69 EPA 1990, Pt 2A.

CASE 18.5 The uncertainty of defining 'waste'—*R (Rackham) v. Swaffham Magistrates Court and the Environment Agency* [2004] EWHC17

The owner of a farm (R) mixed municipal waste with compost and other green waste to make a product. He took the view that the mixed material was not waste. The Environment Agency disagreed and prosecuted. R sought to challenge the prosecution. One of the grounds of challenge was that the definition of waste (as derived from the *ARCO Chemie* decision)[70] could not be defined with sufficient certainty to enable R to know what to do to comply with the law. As such, the prosecution was a breach of the right not to be punished without law under Art. 7 of the European Convention on Human Rights. The High Court dismissed the application, holding that, although the decision in *ARCO* required the exercise of judgment, it was not so uncertain as to amount to a breach of Art. 7.

Controlled waste

The environmental permitting system relating to waste applies to 'controlled waste', which is defined as 'household, industrial or commercial waste or any such waste'.[71] 'Any such waste' does not extend beyond the general categories.[72] Directive waste and controlled waste are effectively synonymous, because any substance that is not Directive waste cannot be controlled waste.[73] The categories of household, industrial, or commercial waste are still important, however, because the extent of the controls under the environmental permitting system differs depending upon within which class waste falls.

Hazardous waste

There are additional controls over hazardous waste, which, for many years, was called 'special waste' in the UK. The Hazardous Waste (England and Wales) Regulations 2005[74] came into force over three years after the deadline date for the transposition of the Hazardous Waste Directive.

The Hazardous Waste Regulations (reg. 6) define hazardous waste as any waste:

- listed as hazardous in the List of Wastes (England) Regulations 2005;
- that is exceptionally classified as hazardous by the Secretary of State or any of the national executives;
- that is declared hazardous by virtue of any regulations under s. 62 of EPA 1990.

There are about two hundred types of 'newly hazardous' waste in relation to which the Regulations have redefined certain wastes as 'hazardous', including televisions and fluorescent light bulbs. While 'domestic' waste may be defined as 'hazardous' if it has hazardous properties, it is excluded from the requirement of the Regulations (reg. 12(2)). Although there is no definition of 'domestic waste' in the Regulations, the Department for Environment, Food and Rural Affairs (DEFRA) has indicated that it comprises waste from accommodation used purely for living purposes (and without commercial gain) and which is disposed of via the normal mixed domestic refuse collection. Asbestos waste and any hazardous waste that is collected separately is not classified as 'domestic waste', regardless of origin. Regulation 19

---

70 C-418/97 *ARCO Chemie Nederland Ltd v. Minister van Volkshuivesting and EPON* [2003] Env LR 40.
71 EPA 1990, s. 75(4).
72 *Thanet District Council v. Kent County Council* [1993] Env LR 391.
73 Controlled Waste Regulations 1992, reg. 7A.
74 SI 2005/894 and the List of Wastes (England) Regulations 2005, SI 2005/895.

bans the mixing of hazardous waste with any other non-hazardous wastes or any different category of hazardous wastes, unless it is mixed under a waste management licence or IPPC permit. Regulation 20 imposes a duty to separate different categories of hazardous waste where technically feasible.

Notification requirements

Regulation 21 requires all premises at which hazardous waste is produced or removed to be notified to the Environment Agency by the producer of the waste or the person who arranges for the removal of the waste (the consignor). The notification requirement is annual—that is, it lasts for 12 months—and notification is accompanied by an annual fee. It is an offence to remove hazardous waste from premises that have not been notified, unless they are exempt premises (reg. 22) or the waste has been fly-tipped onto the premises (reg. 23). The exemptions include a range of residential commercial, educational, and medical premises. The exemptions only apply if the premises produce no more than 200 kg of hazardous waste in a year. Other than these exemptions, no premises producing hazardous waste, however small the quantity, is exempt from the obligation to notify.

Consignment notes

The Regulations provide for a system in which movements of hazardous waste must be 'consigned' before transfer (regs 35–38). Before any hazardous waste can be removed from premises, a consignment note must be completed and, when collected by a registered waste carrier, copies of the note must accompany the load to the place of final disposal or recovery. In many ways, the consignment note mirrors the duty of care transfer note system, because it records the nature of the waste and the identities of the producer, the carrier, and the person responsible for final disposal or recovery. A consignment note is required for every movement of hazardous waste, even when the waste is produced from premises that are exempt from the requirement to notify.

Record keeping

The Regulations require producers, holders, carriers, consignors, and consignees to keep records of consignment notes (regs 49–51). These must be kept in the form of a register for a minimum of three years, except in the case of carriers, for whom the period is 12 months (regs 49–50). Consignees are required to provide the Environment Agency with a quarterly return, setting out the consignments that they have received during that period (reg. 53). Consignees are required to send a return to producers or holders who sent waste to them (reg. 54). In addition, anyone who deposits hazardous waste in or on any land, or who recovers hazardous waste, is required to record the location of each deposit or the nature of the recovery in the form of site records (regs 47–48). Such records are to be cross-referenced to the register of consignment notes.

Offences

Regulation 65 makes it an offence to fail to comply with the different requirements of the Regulations. For example, it would be an offence to fail to notify premises, or to remove hazardous waste without a consignment note, or to fill out consignment notes incorrectly. It is a defence to prove that the failure to comply was as a result of a grave danger or emergency, and that all reasonable steps were taken to minimize any threats to the public and environment, and to rectify the failure as soon as reasonably practicable. In non-emergency situations, a due diligence defence is available (reg. 66).

The penalties for each offence are a fine of up to £5,000 on summary conviction—that is, in a magistrates' court—or an unlimited fine and/or up to two years in prison on conviction on indictment—that is, in the Crown Court. In addition, there are offences of knowingly or recklessly making statements that are false or misleading, or intentionally making a false entry in records. In relation to these latter offences, the Environment Agency may issue fixed penalty notices of £300, instead of seeking conviction in relation to such offences.

Waste authorities

The administration of waste management is divided into three and the main functions are set out in Table 18.1. EPA 1990 separated out the operational functions from the regulatory and the Environment Act 1995 centralized the regulatory function within the Environment Agency. Thus, the main responsibilities fall to the Environment Agency as the main regulatory agency, with differing operational functions carried out by waste collection authorities and waste disposal authorities. As the names suggest, collection authorities are responsible for arranging for waste collection, whereas disposal authorities must make arrangements for waste disposal in conjunction with private waste disposal contractors.

Table 18.1 Waste authorities

Authority	Functions	Main statutory operational provisions
Environment Agency	Waste regulation authority	EPA 1990, s. 30
	Supervision, monitoring, and enforcement of permitted activities and waste disposal sites	Environmental Permitting (England and Wales) Regulations 2007
	Enforcement of duty of care	EPA 1990, s. 34
	Registration of exempt waste operations	Environmental Permitting (England and Wales) Regulations 2007, Sch. 2
	Registration of waste carriers	Control of Pollution (Amendment) Act 1989
Waste collection authorities (district councils and London boroughs)	Collecting household waste in their areas Collecting commercial waste where requested and payment made Collecting industrial waste (with consent of waste disposal authority and payment)	EPA 1990, s. 45
	Preparing waste recycling plans	EPA 1990, s. 49
	Making arrangements for the provision of waste bins for household and commercial waste	EPA 1990, ss. 46–7
	Preparing joint municipal waste strategies with responsibility for meeting waste reduction targets	Waste and Emissions Trading Act 2003, s. 32

TABLE 18.1 (Continued)

Authority	Functions	Main statutory operational provisions
Waste disposal authorities (county councils, metropolitan authorities, and joint boards)	Duty to dispose of controlled waste by means of arrangements with private waste disposal contractors	EPA 1990, s. 51
	Duty to provide civic amenity sites at which residents can dispose of household rubbish without charge	EPA 1990, s. 51
	Preparing joint municipal waste strategies with responsibility for measures in relation to waste minimization and recycling	Waste and Emissions Trading Act 2003, s. 32

In addition, 'arrangements' must be made between waste disposal authorities and private waste disposal contractors. Originally formed from the operational 'arm' of waste disposal authorities, these private companies provide a competitive market for the provision of waste disposal. *→ a step away from the poacher-gamekeeper conundrum.*

Recycling

Although there are administrative and legislative provisions dealing with the promotion of waste recycling, the current emphasis is on voluntary and economic instruments rather than compulsory regulation. As a result, UK legislation does not include many formal duties to recycle—with the notable exception of the producer responsibility obligations. This also explains the historical opposition to the introduction of such targets and the difficulties that have been experienced in achieving the targets or in setting up regulatory systems to implement the European legislation.

The authority with the most important role in relation to recycling is the waste collection authority, because it collects most domestic and commercial waste, and is able to separate recyclable wastes at an early stage. The authority may require separate receptacles to be used for household wastes that are to be recycled and those that are not (EPA 1990, s. 46(2)). It may buy or acquire waste with a view to recycling it (s. 55) and, if it makes arrangements for recycling waste, it does not have to deliver the waste to the waste disposal authority, as it would otherwise have to do under s. 48. It is also under a duty to draw up a waste recycling plan for its area, which involves publicizing the arrangements it intends to make to facilitate recycling (s. 49).

Perhaps most significantly, in the light of government policy on economic instruments, the waste collection authority is entitled to a recycling credit from the waste disposal authority under s. 52 when it recycles waste. The idea behind this provision is that it acts as an incentive to recycle waste by getting the waste disposal authority to pay the waste collection authority the amount of money it saves by not having to dispose of the waste. The amount payable is based on the net saving that the waste disposal authority makes as a result of the recycling activities. At present, the rate is fixed at half the average cost saving to the waste disposal authority, but the government has announced that this is to rise to the full amount. The waste disposal authority *may* also make such a payment to anyone else who recycles waste and thus removes it from the waste stream (s. 52(3)).

All of these different incentives provide a framework within which waste authorities *may* undertake recycling. Unfortunately, the UK record on recycling was so poor that further measures were required, particularly in light of the statutory obligation to reduce the amount of waste going to landfill required under the Landfill Directive. The introduction of performance standards, along with related measures, has seen a dramatic increase in municipal waste recycling rates.[75] In addition to these performance standards, the Household Waste Recycling Act 2003 requires all English local authorities to provide kerbside collections for all householders for a minimum of two materials by 2010. The only exceptions to this general duty are where the costs of collection would be 'unreasonably high' (for example, in rural areas) or where 'alternative arrangements' are made (for example, aggregated collection points in relation to blocks of flats).

Environmental permitting

Historically, the regulation of waste management—namely, the deposit, treating, keeping, or disposing of controlled waste took place through the waste management licensing system found in Pt 2 of EPA 1990. There were significant overlaps here when the IPPC Directive introduced two parallel systems of control, with certain waste installations, such as large landfill sites and waste incineration plants, being regulated under the IPPC system. In addition, there were a large range of waste activities that fell outside the IPPC regime either because they fell below the threshold for inclusion or because they were not listed as prescribed installations. These activities were controlled under the waste management licensing regime.

These layers of complexity were removed with the creation of the single, streamlined system of environmental permitting under the Environmental Permitting (England and Wales) Regulations 2007. Under this system, the IPPC regime and waste licensing operate under a single procedural framework with different substantive provisions being linked directly to relevant European obligations under various Directives (this procedural framework is covered in Chapter 14).

The creation of the permitting system does not, however, remove all complexity from waste management. In addition to the procedural framework of permitting, there are a range of substantive provisions that apply to non-permitted waste activities, such as collection and transport, as well as broader general duties relating to the safe management of waste.

An environmental permit is required for a waste operation or certain waste mobile plant. Along with installations, these are collectively known as 'regulated facilities'. A waste operation is any operation involving the Directive disposal or Directive recovery of waste (reg. 2). Thus any recovery or disposal operation requires an environmental permit unless otherwise excluded or exempt.[76] There is a detailed list of exemptions in Sch. 3. In addition, an exempt activity must meet the waste framework objectives and be registered.

BOX 18.8 The main features of waste management and environmental permitting

- **Waste management functions**
  These are split between regulatory and operational functions. The Environment Agency has the vast majority of regulatory control over waste management through the permitting system

---

75 A series of annual orders set a general minimum standard for recycling. These standards are enforced through s. 15 of the Local Government Act 1999, which allows the Secretary of State to intervene directly if local authorities are not meeting the 'Best Value' performance indicators. For example, see the Local Government (Best Value) Performance Indicators and Performance Standards (England) Order 2007, SI 2007/585.

76 See p. 479.

(there are residual elements under the control of local authorities), while operational functions are split between the waste collection authorities, waste disposal authorities, and the private sector waste disposal companies.

- **A criminal duty of care**
  This applies to all who deal with waste and ensures that waste is properly handled throughout the process, from production, through to final disposal.

- **An all-embracing criminal offence of treating, keeping, or disposing of waste in a manner that is likely to cause pollution of the environment or harm to human health**
  This operates independently of the permitting system and effectively imposes minimum standards for the handling of all wastes.

- **A comprehensive system of environmental permitting dealing with all aspects of waste management**
  In particular, there are expanded powers to refuse permits on the ground that the applicant is not competent to hold a permit, sophisticated powers of enforcement, and increased maximum penalties in the event of breach.

The broad procedural framework covers applications for, and grant of, permits, monitoring and enforcement, appeals and registers. The detail is set out in Chapter 14.

There are certain variations that are only applicable to waste operations:

- a regulator cannot grant a permit in the absence of a planning permission if the use of a site requires it (Sch. 9);

- in exercising any statutory function, such as granting or enforcing a permit, the regulator must do so with the aim of implementing the Waste Framework Directive objectives (discussed above at p. 642) and must keep relevant records.

Other than these broad differences, the detailed arrangements for granting permits for waste activities are to be found in the operative provisions of the Landfill Directive (see below), Waste Incineration Directive, End-of Life Vehicles Directive, and the Waste Electrical and Electronic Equipment Directive. In this sense, other than these very specific obligations, the regulator has a broad discretion to impose conditions that are designed to ensure that waste is recovered or disposed of without endangering human health and without using processes or methods that could harm the environment.

Offences

There are offences that apply to permitted activities at regulated facilities and more general offences that apply to any activity. Section 33(1) of EPA 1990 makes it a criminal offence to:

- deposit controlled waste in or on land, unless it is in accordance with an environment permit—this applies to any deposit, whether temporary or permanent, and is not restricted to Directive disposal and recovery operations;

- submit controlled waste to any listed operation (other than a disposal operation mentioned above) unless it is under and in accordance with an environmental permit—this offence can be committed either in or on land, or by means of mobile plant. 'Listed operation' here means anything falling within the categories of disposal and recovery operations listed in Annexes IIA and IIB of the Framework Directive;

[handwritten margin notes: "general offence. S.33(1)(c)"]

[handwritten top margin: "standard of proof. cause/permit → knowingly."]

- knowingly cause or knowingly permit either of the above;
- treat, keep, or dispose of controlled waste in a manner that is likely to cause pollution of the environment or harm to human health.[77]

These offences are not limited to deposits, but extend to keeping, treating, or disposing of controlled waste. The offences do not, however, apply to most of the categories of excluded waste operations[78] and certain temporary storage activities are also excluded.[79] It is clear that offences in the first two categories and the last category above are ones of strict liability, but it should be noted that the third category interposes 'knowingly' in front of both 'cause' and 'permit'.

BOX 18.9 The meaning of 'deposit'

The definition of 'deposit' is central to s. 33(1)(a) of the Environmental Protection Act 1990 and the courts have adopted a relatively wide definition. Initially, in *Leigh Land Reclamation Ltd v. Walsall Metropolitan Borough Council* (1991) 155 JP 547, it was held that waste was deposited at a land-fill site only when there was no realistic prospect of further examination or inspection, and it had reached its final resting place. This decision caused enormous practical problems for waste regu-lation authorities, because it became difficult to prove that waste had definitely reached its final resting place when defendants argued it was going to be moved on a future occasion.

The decision in *Leigh* was overturned by the Divisional Court in *R v. Metropolitan Stipendiary Magistrate, ex parte London Waste Regulation Authority* [1993] All ER 113, in which it was held that 'deposit' applied to temporary deposits as well as to permanent ones, which seems to reflect both common sense and the wider scope of EPA 1990 in dealing with waste *management* rather than *disposal*.

This definition was widened once again in *Thames Waste Management Ltd v. Surrey County Council* [1997] Env LR 148, in which it was held that 'deposit' could cover continuing activities if the context of the waste management licence would suggest that it was appropriate to do so. Thus a deposit can continue over a significant period, while other activities are carried out.

There was some uncertainty over the exact number of offences that could be committed under s. 33: is the treating, keeping, or disposing of Directive waste a single offence commit-ted in the alternative, or are there three separate offences? The practical difficulty that arises as a result of this uncertainty is that, if the latter position is correct, any indictment alleging all three in one charge would be duplicitous. In *R v. Leighton and Town and Country Refuse Collections Ltd* [1997] Env LR 411, the court considered the specific question of whether there are a number of alternative ways of committing the same offence. The court found that, although each relevant paragraph of s. 33(1) created a separate offence, each of those offences could be committed in any of the ways specified within the paragraph. For example, it was possible to bring a charge of disposing or treating or keeping of controlled waste in a man-ner that is likely to cause pollution of the environment or harm to human health contrary to s. 33(1)(c) of EPA 1990. This eases the evidential burden on the prosecution when framing an indictment.

---

77 Discussed below—see p. 661.
78 With the exception of wastes excluded by reg. 7(1) Controlled Waste Regulations 1992.
79 Environmental Permitting Regulations, reg. 68.

The courts have interpreted the phrase 'knowingly' very strictly. In *Shanks and McEwan (Teesside) Ltd v. Environment Agency* [1997] Env LR 305, the defendant was charged with knowingly permitting the deposit of controlled waste in contravention of a licence condition. It was argued that, although the defendant knew of the deposit of the waste, it did not know it was in breach of condition. The court followed the previous decision in *Ashcroft v. Cambro Waste Products Ltd* [1981] 1 WLR 1349 in taking a very strict view of the phrase. The prosecution need prove only knowledge of the deposit of the waste material; it is not necessary to demonstrate knowledge of the breach of the licence condition that gives rise to the offence. Thus, once the prosecution demonstrate that waste had been knowingly permitted to be deposited, the burden then falls on the defence to establish that the deposit was made in accordance with the conditions of the environmental permit.

It is also possible to infer knowledge. In *Kent County Council v. Beaney* [1993] Env LR 225, it was held that knowing permission may be inferred from the facts of a case in which the deposit of waste was obvious from surrounding events. This concept of constructive knowledge was developed further in the *Shanks and McEwan (Teesside)* decision. In that case, Mance J took the view that it was sufficient that the defendant company (including its senior management) knowingly operated and held out its site for the reception and deposit of controlled waste. Once this was established, it was not necessary to demonstrate that there was any knowledge of the specific breach of the licence condition. This approach broadens the offence considerably and, in effect, places the operators of landfill sites under a strict liability for breaches of environmental permit conditions.

As far as the concept of causation is concerned, this has been discussed on a number of occasions in relation to the similar offences under the Water Resources Act 1991. But analogies with these cases should be made with care, because they do not consider the situation in which 'knowingly' is inserted in front of 'cause'. This appears to suggest that someone who orders another to deposit waste will be guilty under this section only if it is shown that he or she knew that the deposit was to take place unlawfully. One subsection that may help here is s. 33(5), which states that, if controlled waste is deposited from a motor vehicle, the person who controls the vehicle, or who is in a position to control its use, will be treated as knowingly causing the deposit.

CASE 18.6 Vehicle ownership and waste offences—*Environment Agency v. Melland* [2002] Env LR 29

The defendant (M) was prosecuted for offences of fly-tipping waste on an industrial estate. The evidence was that M was the owner of the vehicle that had been seen at the site, although M was not the driver. M was acquitted of the offence on the basis that, although he owned the vehicle, the element of control required under s. 33(5) of EPA 1990 was not present. On appeal, the High Court held that evidence of ownership of a vehicle was capable of amounting to evidence of control. This is a presumptive test and there will be other occasions on which ownership would not indicate control (for example, if the owner was a hire company).

The maximum penalty for these offences is, on conviction in the magistrates' court, 12 months' imprisonment and/or a fine of £50,000 or, on conviction in the Crown Court, five years' imprisonment and/or an unlimited fine (s. 33(8)). In the case of householders, the penalties for breaching s. 33(1)(c) are a £5,000 or unlimited fine (s. 33(9)). An injunction may also be sought in appropriate cases.[80]

---

80 See Environmental Permitting (England and Wales) Regulations 2007, reg. 42.

The range of remedies available to a sentencing court is not only restricted to traditional sanctions. There are also powers to order compensation in the form of clean-up costs to the Environment Agency, waste collection authority, or occupier of the land on which the illegal deposit has taken place (s. 33B). This can pay for the removal of waste and other steps to minimize the environmental harm. In addition, there is a power to confiscate any vehicles used in the commission of an offence (s. 33C). These remedies also apply in cases in which a condition of an environmental permit relating to waste has been breached, but note that the Environmental Permitting Regulations 2007 also have stand-alone offences and restorative remedies (see p. 494).

Any director, manager, secretary, or other similar officer of a corporate body can be prosecuted personally if the offence is committed with his or her consent or connivance, or is attributable to his or her neglect (reg. 41). A 'manager' only covers someone who is part of the 'controlling mind' of the company. This liability is additional to the individual liability of the person who carried out, or knowingly caused or knowingly permitted, the deposit. Waste management is one area of environmental law in which sentences of imprisonment have actually been imposed, although they have been reserved for serious offences and for those cases in which an offender offends repeatedly.

Defences

Once again, there is one defence that applies only for permitted activities and others that apply more generally. The specific defence to permitted activities is found in reg. 40 relating to acts carried out in an emergency in order to avoid danger to the public (although not danger to the environment). The onus of proof establishing whether or not an emergency exists rests with the defendant upon the balance of probabilities. In *Waste Incineration Services Ltd v. Dudley Metropolitan Borough Council* [1993] Env LR 29, the court viewed the phrase 'emergency' (as used in a condition of a waste disposal licence) objectively and without reference to how the licence holder perceived a given set of facts.

There is a defence to any unpermitted activity under s. 33(7)(a) if the defendant took all reasonable precautions and exercised all due diligence to avoid the commission of the offence. This is a familiar defence that is included in many pieces of regulatory legislation. Essentially, it involves the defendant showing either that it took the appropriate steps on the facts of the case, or that it set up an adequate system. In many ways, the requirements are similar to those laid down by the duty of care. For example, the defence is of great use for receivers of waste—that is, carriers and waste disposal site operators—who may inadvertently deal with it in an illegal fashion if misled by the consignor. But it does impose quite a high standard on them to take steps to ensure that the consignment contains what it is meant to contain. It is arguable that this defence introduces an element of self-policing into the waste disposal chain, in the sense that very specific checks are required to rely on the defence.

CASE 18.7 **The due diligence defence—***Durham County Council v. Peter Connors Industrial Services Ltd* [1993] Env LR 197 and *Environment Agency v. Short* [1998] Env LR 300

The nature of the due diligence defence is illustrated in two cases. In *Durham County Council v. Peter Connors Industrial Services Ltd* [1993] Env LR 197, a system of operation that relied upon the person disposing of waste regularly collecting a skip that had been filled with waste by another without checking on the contents of the skip every time was not sufficient to come within an analogous defence under s. 3(4) of the Control of Pollution Act 1974. It was held that the collector of waste had to take care to inform itself on each occasion that it collected the waste as to the nature of the contents of the skip. The defence required a specific inquiry to be made of any person who knew what the waste was and whether or not the future deposit of that waste would involve a breach of the Act.

In *Environment Agency v. Short* [1998] Env LR 300, the defendant (S) left waste timber at a construction site to be burnt after being told incorrectly by the site owner that the site did not require a waste management licence because it was exempt. The High Court held that the onus was on S to make specific inquiries as to whether the exemption extended to the timber.

Dangerous disposal of waste

There is a very important further offence created by s. 33(1)(c): it is an offence to treat, keep, or dispose of controlled waste in a manner that is likely to cause pollution of the environment or harm to human health. The importance of this offence is that it applies irrespective of the need for an environmental permit. In other words, activities that are exempted from the need for a permit are still governed by what is, in effect, a general requirement to act safely. The paragraph might also be said to supplement the permitting system by acting as a form of residual condition attached to a permit, because, in theory, it applies even when a permit is being complied with. The offence is drafted remarkably widely, because 'pollution of the environment' is defined in s. 29 by reference to harm to *any* living organism. 'Harm' in this context means any harm to the health of living organisms or interference with the ecological systems of which they form a part.

The paragraph is mainly targeted at providing a straightforward offence that can be used in relation to fly-tipping and other forms of irresponsible waste disposal, but it also covers such things as storage of wastes on the production site—the harm to human health could be a harm to employees. This offence also covers householders who treat, keep, or deposit waste within the curtilage of a dwelling house. The maximum penalty for breach of s. 33(1)(c) is the same as for offences relating to a waste management licence—other than in the case of householders (s. 33(9)). The section does not, however, apply to activities that are under regulations made under s. 33(3). This has only been done in the cases of activities that are adequately controlled under regimes other than waste management.

Clean-up powers

Section 59 gives the Environment Agency and waste collection authorities powers to require the removal of controlled waste. These apply whenever controlled waste has been deposited on land in contravention of s. 33(1)—that is, the deposit was not in accordance with an environmental permit or it breached s. 33(1)(c).

The initial responsibility falls on the occupier of the land, although there are supplementary powers in relation to the owners of land (s. 59ZA). The Environment Agency may serve a notice on the occupier requiring the waste to be removed or requiring steps to be taken to mitigate the consequences of the deposit. The notice must specify a period within which this action should be taken, although it cannot be less than 21 days. There is a right to appeal to the magistrates' court during the 21-day period. Such an appeal must be allowed if the court is satisfied that the appellant neither deposited nor knowingly caused or knowingly permitted the deposit, or if there is a material defect in the notice (s. 59(3)). An appeal suspends the operation of the notice until it is determined (s. 59(4)). It is a summary offence, with a maximum fine of £5,000 to fail to comply with a notice served under s. 59 (s. 59(5)). This offence is a continuing one and a further fine of up to £1,000 can be imposed for every day on which the failure to comply continues after conviction. Ultimately, the Environment Agency has default powers to carry out the steps specified in the notice itself and to recover any expenses reasonably incurred from the person on whom it was served (s. 59(6)).

If the occupier did not make or knowingly permit the unlawful deposit, or there is no occupier, the Environment Agency may remove the waste or take mitigating steps immediately. This course of action is also available if these steps were immediately necessary to remove or prevent pollution or harm to human health (s. 59(7)). The Agency may then recover its costs from any person who deposited the waste, or knowingly caused or knowingly permitted its deposit, unless that person can show that the cost was incurred unnecessarily (s. 59(8)). Ultimate responsibility for unlawfully deposited waste therefore falls on the person who deposited it, rather than on the occupier—but it may not be possible to trace the person responsible, or they may have no money to pay the Agency's costs, in which case the position is, in practice, that the Environment Agency has a choice whether to leave the waste where it is or pick up the bill itself. Nevertheless, this is an important power that can be used in addition to a prosecution under s. 33, because it tackles directly the problem that faces the Environment Agency. The Agency's powers under the Water Resources Act 1991, s. 161, should also be considered in this context, because they may be used to deal with deposits of waste that threaten controlled waters.

Landfills

Until recently, major landfill sites were controlled under a separate and additional system of control to that governing waste management, with the Landfill (England and Wales) Regulations 2002[81] implementing the requirements of the Landfill Directive 1999/31/EC. The Regulations were a dramatic departure from the discretionary, flexible approach to standards set under the then waste management licensing system. The implementation of the operational aspects of the Regulations was then carried out under the IPPC regime.

In bringing together requirements concerning both IPPC and waste disposal generally, the Environmental Permitting Regulations 2007, in principle, simplify the law in this area (and, as a result, the 2002 Regulations are revoked). For landfills, the 'transmission belt' approach to transposition is at its starkest and, in the main, the relevant rules in the Regulations—reg. 35(d) and Sch. 10—simply require the Environment Agency to give effect to the provisions of the Landfill Directive, in the sense of (as appropriate) complying with, or having regard to, the provisions of the Directive (or acting so that the UK complies with its obligations). Landfills are, however, still a Part A(1) operation and are therefore also subject to those aspects of the Environmental Permitting Regulations that give effect to the IPPC Directive.[82]

The main operational provisions relating to landfills provide for the following.

- The ending of the UK practice of the co-disposal of hazardous and non-hazardous waste, with the classification of landfills into three types—for hazardous, non-hazardous, or inert waste. Waste from outside the designated class is not permitted to be disposed of at classified landfills (Art. 6, Landfill Directive).

- Complete bans on the disposal of certain wastes going to landfill, including all liquid wastes, infectious clinical and hospital wastes, tyres, and waste that, in the conditions of landfill, is explosive, corrosive, oxidizing, flammable, or highly flammable (Art. 5(3)).

- Detailed technical requirements for all landfills (Annexes I and III). This includes pollution prevention measures and monitoring requirements. This is the first time that detailed standards have been laid down in waste legislation. These standards are prescriptive and apply to all relevant landfills. Landfill operators were required to submit so-called 'conditioning plans' to the Environment Agency that set out how they would meet the relevant standards; failure to do so meant that the site would be closed (Art. 14). The tightening of standards for hazardous waste sites meant that many operators were forced to undertake significant improvements on certain sites or simply 'switch' to a less onerous class of

81 SI 2002/1559.
82 See Environmental Permitting (England and Wales) Regulations 2007, Sch. 1 Part 5.

landfill. It is feared that this might lead to a shortage in the number of sites that are able to accept hazardous waste.

- The requirement to treat most wastes before landfill (Art. 6(a)).

- Introduction of waste acceptance criteria, which comprise a set of procedures for the characterization of waste and compliance testing, together with a set of leaching and other criteria to define which wastes may be accepted at inert, non-hazardous, and hazardous landfills (Annex II).

- Powers to close landfill sites by means of a 'closure notice' procedure, with the ability to enforce continuing aftercare conditions (Art. 13).

- The formal introduction of the 'List of Wastes' descriptions. The Regulations amend the Environmental Protection (Duty of Care) Regulations 1991[83] to require that a duty of care transfer note identify the waste to which it relates by reference to the appropriate codes in the List.

- The setting of waste reduction targets for municipal biodegradable waste (Art. 5(2)).

In the long term, the Directive is likely to have a dramatic impact on disposal costs, particularly in the case of hazardous wastes. This will result from increased transport costs to fewer sites, and an increase in costs arising from pre-treatment and complying with the waste acceptance criteria. In addition, increased emphasis will be placed on alternatives to landfill, including different recovery, treatment, and disposal operations, as well as incentives to minimize waste production.

CASE 18.8 **What is a landfill?** *Blackland Park Exploration Ltd v. Environment Agency* [2004] Env LR 33

The Permitting Regulations only apply to waste that is disposed of at landfills. A 'landfill' is defined as meaning '*a waste disposal site for the deposit of waste onto or into land*'. This includes any permanent site that is used to store waste for more than one year prior to final disposal, but does not include a permanent storage site at which waste is stored for a period of less than three years prior to *recovery*.

In this case, the Court of Appeal had to consider whether the re-injection of contaminated liquids into groundwater at an onshore oil production facility was the deposit of waste in a landfill for the purposes of the 2002 Landfill Regulations (which used the same definition). If it were a deposit in a landfill, the ban on the disposal of liquid wastes at landfill sites would apply, thereby prohibiting the operation at the site. The operator argued that the re-injection was a discharge to groundwater, which should be controlled by means of a discharge consent under the Water Resources Act 1991. The Court of Appeal held that the Directive and the Regulations should be interpreted widely. What was most persuasive to the Court of Appeal was that, once the waste was deposited in the groundwater, it did not dissipate beyond the site. It was naturally buoyant and constrained by an upper layer of clay. Accordingly, the waste was deposited in land and the fact that there was a lot of water present was no different, in principle, from the presence of water at the bottom of a disused mine. If this reasoning were followed more generally, many other discharges into 'static' waters would be considered to be deposits in landfill.

---

83 SI 1991/2839.

The duty of care

One of the key indicators that the introduction of EPA 1990 saw a switch from waste disposal to waste management was the introduction of the duty of care.[84] Section 34 provides that the duty of care applies to any person who produces, imports, carries, keeps, treats, or disposes of controlled waste, or who, as a broker, has control of it. A restricted duty even applies to occupiers of domestic premises, in relation to household waste produced on the property (s. 34(2)).[85] The duty applies only to controlled waste (and therefore does not include such things as agricultural or mining waste). It applies in addition to controls through environmental permitting.

Any person subject to the duty has to take reasonable steps to do the following.

1. **Prevent any other person contravening s. 33—that is, the law relating to the unauthorized deposit, keeping, treatment, or disposal of controlled waste**
   This requires steps to be taken to check that others deal with waste properly further down the waste disposal chain. For example, a transferor of waste should know where the waste is going before parting with it, which, in turn, involves checking that the site to which the waste is to be taken is licensed to take it and that the carrier is actually taking it there. The standard of reasonableness is objective, in the sense that holders of waste ought to act on signs that something is amiss. But the standard is also related to the resources and knowledge of the individual, with the result that large firms may be expected to carry out more rigorous investigations than small ones.

2. **Prevent any other person contravening an environmental permit**
   This is a broad requirement and applies not only to waste operations, but also to installations.

3. **Prevent the escape of waste**
   This requires proper storage and packaging of waste, taking into account any hazardous characteristics. The escape of waste does not include deliberate deposits, which would fall within the s. 33 offences.

4. **Ensure that the waste is transferred only to an authorized person**
   This would include a waste collection authority, waste management licence holder, or registered waste carrier.

5. **Ensure that an adequate written description of the waste is given to anyone to whom the waste is transferred**
   The Environmental Protection (Duty of Care) Regulations 1991[86] require that, when controlled waste is transferred, there must be a transfer note, although this does not actually have to travel with the waste. The transfer note must identify the waste and state its quantity, the kind of container it is in, the time and place of transfer, and the name, address, and other relevant details of the transferor and transferee. The Regulations also require that the transferor and transferee sign the transfer note, and that the transfer note and the written description be kept for at least two years from the date of transfer. It is permissible for multiple consignments of waste up to one year to be covered by one transfer note, as long as the description of the waste, the identity of the parties, and all other details remain the same for each consignment.

---

84 See **www.defra.gov.uk**. A description of the policy background to this change can be found in the RCEP 11th Report (1985) *Managing Waste: The Duty of Care*, Cmnd. 9675.

85 The duty is restricted, in the sense that a householder is only required to ensure that the waste is transferred to an authorized person. No other aspect of the duty applies.

86 As amended.

There is also a Code of Practice on the Duty of Care, produced by the Secretary of State.[87] The Code sets down a guide for what would amount to reasonable steps taken in seeking to fulfil the duty. This is a statutory code, made under s. 34(7). Contravention of its provisions is not of itself a criminal offence, but it could be said that contravention gives rise to a presumption that the duty has been breached, because s. 34(10) states that it should be taken into account in deciding whether the duty has been complied with. The Code may also be used as evidence in civil cases and in prosecutions under s. 33.

CASE 18.9 Definition of escape—*Gateway Professional Services (Management) Ltd v. Kingston Upon Hull City Council* [2004] Env LR 42

The defendant company deposited a number of black bags containing commercial office waste on land adjoining its site. The company was convicted of the offence of failing to take all reasonable measures to prevent the escape of waste contrary to the duty of care. On appeal, the High Court held that a deliberate deposit of waste was not the same as an 'escape'. The deliberate dumping of waste was covered by EPA 1990, s. 33(1)(a).

Everyone in the waste chain is subject to the duty of care. The system should therefore have an element of self-policing. For example, a producer of waste would be well advised not to transfer it to someone it suspects of being a 'cowboy', because, if the waste is fly-tipped, that could lead the Environment Agency to prosecute the producer for breach of the duty of care and also give rise to possible criminal actions for knowingly permitting the deposit, and to potential liability in civil law (under s. 73, see p. 673), or under clean-up powers (under s. 59, see p. 661). Equally, a waste carrier should not accept improperly labelled or packaged waste, and should make periodic checks on the waste it receives, because it will have responsibility under the duty of care if there is something wrong.

Breach of the duty of care is a criminal offence (s. 34(6)). The maximum penalty is, on conviction in the magistrates' court, a £5,000 fine or, on conviction in the Crown Court, an unlimited fine. In cases in which no documents have been presented, which are necessary to comply with the duty, there is the option to issue a fixed penalty notice (s. 34A).[88] It should be noted that the duty of care is broken irrespective of whether harm is caused: it is the failure to take reasonable steps that is the criminal offence, not any damage that results from it. This creates a position in which offences will be committed frequently.

The main function of the duty of care is to encourage responsible behaviour, and the development of appropriate management systems for the storage, transfer, and monitoring of waste, rather than to punish wrongdoing. Because of the documentation procedures, it also makes waste consignments easier to trace. Some of the reported prosecutions for breaches of the duty illustrate these points. For example, in one case, a demolition contractor was fined £800 for failing to ensure that a skip contained only materials described in the transfer note—the infringement came about because employees had not been given sufficient instruction that only certain materials could be put in the skip. When it comes to sentencing for the offence, however, many of the breaches, such as failing to make out a transfer note, are seen by the courts as technical in nature and thus only small fines are imposed—hence the introduction of fixed penalty notices. This seems to underplay the importance of this type of management-based control.

---

87 (1996) *Waste Management: The Duty of Care—A Code of Practice*, London: HMSO.
88 The fixed penalty currently stands at £300.

Carriage of waste

Intimately connected with the duty of care is the requirement that all carriers of waste are registered with the Environment Agency. The requirements in this respect arise out of the Control of Pollution (Amendment) Act 1989. This was a private member's Bill (although it did ultimately have government support) that sought to deal with the growing problem of fly-tipping by providing some powers over carriers. The Act is supplemented by the Controlled Waste (Registration of Carriers and Seizure of Vehicles) Regulations 1991.[89] It is an offence under the 1989 Act, s. 1(1), to carry controlled waste without being registered with the Environment Agency. The offence is a summary one only, with a maximum fine of £5,000. The defences are very similar to those available for offences under EPA 1990, s. 33. (It should be remembered that it is normally a separate offence under the duty of care to deal with an unregistered carrier.)

Certain bodies, such as local authorities, charities, and voluntary groups, are specifically exempt from the requirement to register by virtue of reg. 2, which also states that a producer may carry its own wastes without having to seek registration, as long as the waste is not demolition or construction waste. In addition, s. 1(1) refers only to carrying waste in the course of a business or with a view to profit, meaning that such things as carrying waste to a local authority waste site on behalf of a neighbour are not covered.

An application for registration must be made to the regional office of the Environment Agency where the carrier has its principal place of business (reg. 4). There is only one substantive ground for refusal of registration, which is that the applicant is not a desirable carrier. This fulfils a similar function to the 'competence' requirement in environmental permitting, although it is rather more specific. It has two elements:

1. that the carrier, or someone closely connected with the carrier's business, has been convicted of one of the relevant offences listed in Sch. 1 to the Regulations;

2. that the Environment Agency considers it undesirable for the carrier to be authorized to carry controlled waste (reg. 5).

There is a power to revoke a registration on these grounds (reg. 10). But the impact of these provisions is limited somewhat by the Rehabilitation of Offenders Act 1974, which, effectively, will allow most convictions to become spent after five years. In addition, there is a right to appeal to the Secretary of State against refusal or revocation and, in accordance with the advice in Circular 11/91, a refusal to register was overturned even though the applicant had been convicted of seven waste offences in the past.[90] Unless revoked, a registration lasts for three years, when it must be renewed, although the carrier may surrender a registration at any time. A fee is payable for an application or a renewal (reg. 4(9)). The Environment Agency must keep a public register, to be open for inspection free of charge, of firms that are registered in its area (reg. 3).

Enforcement of the Act is mainly in the hands of the Environment Agency. Appointed officers (and also police officers) are given powers to stop and search vehicles, as long as they have reasonable grounds for believing that controlled waste has, is or is about to be carried by an unregistered carrier (s. 5(1)). They may also require the carrier to produce its certificate of registration. It is a summary offence intentionally to obstruct an officer exercising these powers, with a maximum penalty of £5,000. There are powers to seize vehicles used in the commission of an offence (s. 5(2)(d)) and to issue fixed penalty notices (s. 5B–C). Environment Agency officers also have the powers provided under EPA 1990, s. 71, and the Environment Act 1995, ss. 108 and 109.

---

89 SI 1991/1624, as amended by SI 1998/605.
90 See (1993) 217 ENDS Report 13.

Waste brokers

There is a growing business in arranging for the disposal or movement of other people's wastes. These people may not require a waste management licence, because they never actually handle the waste themselves. The Waste Management Licensing Regulations 1994 control such brokers or dealers in waste. Regulation 20 makes it an offence for any establishment or undertaking to arrange, as a dealer or broker, for the disposal or recovery of Directive waste on behalf of another person unless it is registered with the Environment Agency. Exemptions apply to those with an environmental permit, or other statutory consents (for example, a discharge consent), charitable or voluntary registered waste carriers, and bodies with statutory responsibilities for waste management (for example, waste collection and disposal authorities).

Schedule 5 to the Regulations sets out the procedure for registration. Perhaps the most important consideration in determining whether an establishment or undertaking is to be registered is the number of 'relevant offences' committed by the applicant or connected persons. Generally, the considerations are the same as the test for 'technical competence' in relation to applications for a permit. A fee is payable on application for registration and the entry in the register is available to the general public. The entry in the register lasts for a maximum of three years unless it is renewed.

Economic instruments and waste management

The use of economic instruments is more common in relation to waste management than in other areas of pollution control. Arguably, this is because it is one of the best ways of reflecting the true environmental cost of managing and disposing of waste, and can help to provide an incentive to minimize production. The three main instruments (other than the recovery of administration costs through charging schemes) are provisions that encourage producer responsibility for particular wastes, a tax on wastes that are disposed of in landfill sites, and a scheme that allows waste disposal authorities to trade in landfill allowances.

The landfill tax

The landfill tax was introduced under the Finance Act 1996. There are various secondary regulations and guidance notes that flesh out the main statutory provisions, including the Landfill Tax Regulations 1996,[91] the Landfill Tax (Qualifying Materials) Order 1996,[92] and the Landfill Tax (Contaminated Land) Order 1996.[93] The provisions came into force in October 1996 and have the effect that the vast majority of waste disposed of in landfill sites is subject to a tax at the point of disposal. There are three classes of material:

- the main class, which is subject to the highest rate of tax;

- a second group of specific 'inactive' materials, which is subject to a lower rate of tax;

- a third class of waste, which is exempt from the tax.

In 2008, the highest rate of tax was set at £24 per tonne. The intention is to increase this standard rate by £8 per tonne per year so that, by 2010–11, it is doubled to £48 per tonne.

---

91 SI 1996/1527, as amended.
92 SI 1996/1528.
93 SI 1996/1529.

The definition of 'waste' for the purposes of the tax is found in the Finance Act 1996 s. 64. Although it is similar to the general definition of waste under EPA 1990 and the Waste Framework Directive, it must be borne in mind that the landfill tax legislation has a different statutory purpose as compared to the Directive. Accordingly, what might be considered to be waste under the Directive may not be waste for the purposes of landfill tax legislation.

BOX 18.10 The definition of 'waste' under the landfill tax

A purposive approach to defining waste can work in more than one way. Although the landfill tax is applied to the disposal of 'waste', this is interpreted in a different way to the definition of waste under the Waste Framework Directive. The aim of the landfill tax is to promote recycling and reduce the amount of waste going to landfill. Thus, a purposive approach to the definition is not necessarily constrained by the purposes of the Directive.

Landfill tax is only payable on taxable disposals. This includes a disposal of material as waste at a landfill site.[94] In *Parkwood Landfill v. Customs and Excise Commissioners* [2003] Env LR 19, the Court of Appeal held that materials that had been deposited at a landfill site, but which had been subsequently recycled and reused to construct a road and landscaping at the site, were not waste for the purposes of determining whether a taxable disposal had been made. Taking a purposive approach to the landfill tax legislation, the Court held that it would be contrary to the promotion of recycling if the use of recycled material at landfill sites would be made subject to the tax. Such material would still, however, be 'waste' for the purposes of the Waste Framework Directive.

The operators of the landfill sites pay the tax to HM Revenue and Customs (HMRC) on a quarterly basis, although it is envisaged that this cost will be passed on to the disposers of the waste (and then, theoretically, to the producers of the waste). Although the main purpose of the tax was to ensure that environmental costs of waste disposal were acknowledged, it is also a source of revenue for central government. Some of the income raised by the tax is used to reduce employers' National Insurance contributions.

At the time that the tax was introduced, there was some criticism of the failure to use the revenue for environmental purposes.[95] The Landfill Tax Credit Scheme (LTCS) was introduced to address these concerns. Under the scheme, landfill operators who are subject to the tax can claim a credit against any payment of tax for any contribution that is made to an approved environmental body to pay for a project that is approved under the Landfill Tax Regulations. These cover a wide range of environmental projects, including the reclamation and restoration of contaminated land (as long as it does not benefit the original polluter), the creation of public amenity space or a wildlife habitat, and maintaining historic buildings and churches within the vicinity of a landfill site.

Evidence suggests that the tax has not had a significant impact upon the amount of waste arising.[96] This is largely the result of relatively low rates of tax that were levied at the introduction of the tax. In addition, there is some evidence that tax avoidance schemes have exploited loopholes in the waste management legislation, such as using inert waste for landscaping purposes—which is exempt from environmental permitting—and that fly-tipping of waste has increased. Although these concerns reflect more than insignificant problems, the landfill tax is becoming an accepted regulatory tool that is to be used in conjunction with

---

94 Finance Act 1996, s. 40.

95 J. Morris and P. Phillips (2000) Env LR 150.

96 HC Environment Select Committee (1999) *The Operation of the Landfill Tax*; HM Customs and Excise (1998) *Review of Landfill Tax*; Coopers and Lybrand (1997) *Landfill Tax: Is it Working?*, Cardiff: Coopers and Lybrand.

other mechanisms to assist in reducing waste arisings, and encouraging reuse, recycling, and recovery. It is this combined impact of significant rate increases, recycling initiatives, and the impact of the requirements of the Landfill Directive that reflects a mixed-regulation approach to controlling waste production.

Producer responsibility

Section 93 of the Environment Act 1995 provides for the introduction of regulations to impose obligations on the producers of materials, or products to recycle, recover, or reuse those products or materials. Three products have been the subject to the legislation on producer responsibility, packaging and packaging waste,[97] end-of-life vehicles, and waste electrical and electronic equipment.

Packaging and packaging waste

The first producer responsibility legislation introduced an obligation to recover and recycle packaging waste in 1997. The Producer Responsibility Obligations (Packaging Waste) Regulations 2007[98] transpose the requirements of the EC Directive on packaging and packaging waste.[99] A key feature of the Regulations is the shared approach, which spreads the responsibility for meeting the recovery and recycling targets right along the packaging chain, from production, through to retail.

Packaging 'producers' (reg. 4) who manufacture raw materials for packaging, convert those raw materials into packaging, fill that packaging with goods, or sell the packaging to the final consumer are subject to the three obligations: to register with and supply data on annual packaging handled (regs 6–7 and Sch. 3, Pt 1); to recover and recycle certain specified percentages of packaging handled in the previous year (Sch. 2); to complete a certificate of compliance that verifies that the company has met the recovery and recycling obligation for the preceding year (regs 20–22 and Sch. 4). An obligated company can choose to meet its obligations individually or join a 'compliance scheme', which takes on the legal responsibility for complying with the Regulations on behalf of its members (regs 6 and 14–18). If companies join a compliance scheme, they fall outside the operation of the Regulations (although, in practice, the compliance scheme passes on the requirements under the terms of membership). In these cases, the compliance scheme is subject to the Regulations, with the consequent need to comply with the obligations on an aggregate basis on behalf of its members.

What is most interesting about the scheme of the Regulations is the way in which a variety of different mechanisms are used to secure the overall objective. The system operates, in practice, by compelling obligated businesses to purchase evidence of compliance from reprocessors who recover and recycle packaging materials in the form of packaging recovery notes (PRNs) or packaging waste export recovery notes (PERNS) (reg. 4(5)). Thus the Regulations mix the use of the market in these PRNs (which will fluctuate in price under the normal principles of supply and demand) with the prospect of criminal sanctions for non-compliance to encourage businesses to consider the amount of packaging that they use.[100]

End-of-life vehicles

The End-of-Life Vehicles (Producer Responsibility) Regulations 2005[101] transposed the requirements of the End-of-Life Vehicles Directive (2000/53/EC). The Regulations are

---

97 See, generally, P. Bailey (1999) *Packaging Law Europe*, Aldershot: Ashgate.
98 SI 2007/871.
99 94/62/EC, as amended by Regulation 1882/2003, Directive 2004/12/EC, and Directive 2005/20/EC.
100 K. Kroepelian (2000) 9(2) RECIEL 165.
101 SI 2005/263.

intended to promote the recycling and recovery of such vehicles, but do so in a broader fashion than the packaging waste regime.[102] The Directive was transposed over one year late, which reflects the complexity and controversy of the proposals. Once again, there are requirements of producer registration (reg. 7) and a system of collection of end-of-life vehicles (regs 10–12). The historic rate of recycling of the vehicles is about 75 per cent, but the Directive imposed a requirement to recycle 80 per cent of end-of-life vehicles by weight by 2006, with a further recycling target of 85 per cent by 2015 (reg. 18). Manufacturers of vehicles are responsible for the costs of collecting and treating vehicles put on the market after July 2002 when they have a negative value (some such vehicles will have a positive value).

Waste electrical and electronic equipment (WEEE)

The Waste Electrical and Electronic Equipment Regulations 2006[103] implement the requirements of the Waste Electrical and Electronic Equipment Directive (2002/96/EC). WEEE encourages and sets criteria for the collection, treatment, recycling, and recovery of all forms of electrical equipment. The Directive adopts the broader approach to producer responsibility taken in the End-of-Life Vehicle Directive, with some focus on the design and manufacture of electrical products to facilitate recycling and recovery. To this end, there is a 'sister' Directive that bans the use of certain hazardous substances in electrical equipment.[104] The Regulations apply to all battery- or mains-operated electrical and electronic equipment falling into one of ten categories set out in the Directive (Schs 1 and 2). Under the Regulations, *retailers* of electrical equipment must take back consumer WEEE free of charge. *Producers* of electrical equipment will have a number of obligations including:

– joining a compliance scheme (reg. 10);

– providing data on the volumes and types of electrical and electronic equipment placed on the UK market, and exported to EU countries, and on recycling and recovery of WEEE (regs 8 and 12 and Sch. 5);

– labelling products with prescribed labels, making it clear that products are not to be disposed of in bins (reg. 15 and Sch. 4);

– paying for recycling and recovery (regs 8–9).

– The waste facilities that recover and recycle WEEE must use the Best Available Treatment Recovery and Recycling Techniques (BATRRT). Such facilities are also subject to a detailed permitting procedure. The aim is to give priority to the reuse of whole appliances, and then components, sub-assemblies, and consumables.

The development of producer responsibility

These brief descriptions of the producer responsibility schemes illustrate that producer responsibility legislation has developed, over time, from a bare requirement to recover and recycle into a more sophisticated approach, which uses various methods to facilitate reuse and recycling. This includes banning substances that are difficult to reuse, and requiring the use of 'eco-design' principles and increased information on how to recycle waste products as a means of facilitating reuse, recovery, and recycling. At the other end of the life cycle, there are specific controls over the reuse and recycling of waste products. This approach of trying to influence each stage of the product's life links into the idea of integrated product policy, under which the whole life cycle of a product is examined in order to minimize environmental impacts.[105]

102 M. Lee (2002) 11(4) EELR 114.

103 SI 2006/3289.

104 Restriction on Hazardous Substances Directive 2002/95/EC.

105 M. Townsend and J. Parry (2002) 10(4) Env Liab 153.

Waste disposal, and town and country planning

The disposal of waste on land presents some difficult questions of a land use nature—indeed, the Town and Country Planning Acts were the primary control over waste before COPA 1974 was enacted. The development of land for waste management purposes is controlled under an additional and complementary layer of regulations that has remained largely unchanged through the introduction of waste management licensing legislation.

The deposit of waste in land is deemed to be development that requires planning permission (see below). Furthermore, the use of land for waste management purposes other than disposal may require planning permission if it amounts to a material change of use. In most cases, the storage of waste on land will be incidental to the main use (for example, in the case of an unrelated industrial use), although there may be cases, such as the change of fuel in a cement kiln from conventional fuels to waste-derived fuels, in which the boundary is not clearly distinguishable.

The administration of waste planning

The main responsibility for waste planning falls to waste planning authorities (normally at a county, metropolitan, or unitary level). Waste planning is addressed at the regional level through the regional spatial strategies (RSS). Under the Planning and Compulsory Purchase Act 2004, regional planning bodies are responsible for drawing up an RSS that will address regional waste policies and provide a spatial framework for local development frameworks.

Development plans

Waste planning policies have traditionally been considered separately from other policies. Prior to the introduction of the Planning and Compulsory Purchase Act 2004, waste policies were found in regional planning guidance at the regional level and, at a more local level, in the unitary development plan, or a combination of the structure plan and the waste local plan or minerals and waste local plan. Under the 2004 Act, the RSS will replace current regional planning guidance. All other development plans will be replaced with a minerals and waste development framework (MWDF).

The MWDF is a collection of various local development documents, which collectively provide the spatial planning strategy and planning policies for waste. Within the MWDF, there are development plan documents that have statutory development status for the purposes of determining planning applications. These include: the minerals and waste development scheme, which sets out the policy framework; the waste core strategy, which sets out the strategic policies and objectives; a site-specific allocation map. In addition, non-statutory guidance can form part of the MWDF as supplementary plan documents (SPDs).

Development control

Section 55(3)(b) of the Town and Country Planning Act 1990 provides that the deposit of refuse or waste materials on land involves the material change in the use of that land if the area of the deposit is extended or if the height of the deposit is extended above the original ground level. In addition, depending upon the facts of the case, tipping can amount to an engineering operation (if it involves technical supervision, for example) or may even fall within the catch-all definition of an 'other operation'.

A planning application for the use of land, or for the carrying out of operations in or on land, for the deposit of refuse or waste materials and/or the erection of any building, plant, or machinery designed to be used wholly or mainly for the purposes of treating, storing, processing, or disposing of refuse or waste materials is a county matter (see Town and Country Planning Act 1990, Sch. 1). The application is made direct to the county planning authority, which is then under a duty to notify the district authority within 14 days as part of the consultation procedure (under Art. 12 of the Town and Country Planning (General Development Procedure) Order 1995).

The wider context is worth recalling here: an environmental permit relating to a waste operation must not be granted if use of the site for carrying on that operation requires planning permission and no such permission is in force.[106]

Planning conditions and obligations

The difficulties with using planning conditions to control environmentally sensitive developments have been covered elsewhere. Planning permissions for waste disposal operations require special consideration. The main criterion for conditions on a planning permission for waste disposal is that they be for a planning purpose. Examples of matters that would normally be dealt with by way of conditions on the planning permission include: phasing of operations; the extent of tipping; access to and from the site; the *general* nature of the waste; restoration plans, including site contours, minimum depth of topsoil, etc.; aftercare for a short-term period.

To avoid duplicating environmental controls, there are certain areas that should not normally be covered, because they are more properly dealt with under the waste management regime. These include: the duration of activity; the supervision of activities (including site offices and other administrative responsibilities); the specific types of waste to be covered; the keeping of records; associated works. Although it is advisable to separate the two areas of control, it is not unlawful to impose conditions that overlap.

Other overlapping controls

Contaminated land

The deposit or discharge of waste (whether knowingly or otherwise) is a significant cause of contamination, and there is a good deal of interaction between the environmental permitting regime and the provisions dealing with the clean-up of contaminated land. First, in cases in which contamination arises as a result of the illegal deposit of controlled waste, the right to serve a remediation notice under Pt 2A is removed (s. 78(YB)(3)). This is because there is an equivalent power to remove such waste under EPA 1990, s. 59. Prior to the decision in Case C-1/04 *Van de Walle* (Case 18.4), this would have covered a situation in which there was an active deposit of waste—that is, in the case of an unlicensed landfill—rather than passive leakage of substances—for example, seeping from an underground tank. The latter would have been controlled under the contaminated land provisions in EPA 1990, Pt 2A. Following *Van de Walle,* however, the risk-based approach of Pt 2A would not be sufficient to implement the provisions of the Waste Framework Directive.

Secondly, if contamination arises because of activities regulated under an environmental permit, and enforcement action can be taken under the permit, then no remediation notice can be served (s. 78(YB)(1)).

Finally, in cases in which clean-up operations are required under a remediation notice, such operations will require an environmental permit as a disposal or recovery operation.

---

106 Environmental Permitting Regulations, Sch. 9, para. 2.

Water pollution

The treatment of liquid effluent prior to discharge into sewer or into controlled waters is, arguably, the treatment of waste and there has been some confusion about the extent to which effluent treatment plant fell under the waste management licensing regime. Under the Framework Directive, the physico-chemical or biological treatment of 'waste' is defined as a disposal operation that would be subject to the requirement for licensing. But the Department of Environment determined, in 1996, that such treatment was excepted from the waste licensing system, because it was 'waste in liquid form', which was controlled under other legislation—namely, the Urban Waste Water Treatment Directive (91/271/EEC), and the corresponding domestic legislation, the Urban Waste Water Treatment (England and Wales) Regulations 1994[107] and/or the Water Resources Act 1991. This interpretation as to what 'waste in liquid form' means has now been rejected by the House of Lords.

CASE 18.10 *United Utilities v. Environment Agency* [2007] UKHL 41

In this case, the House of Lords had to examine the position of sewage works. A sewerage undertaker operated an intermediate facility for treating sewage sludge, before it was sent for final treatment. The issue was whether this intermediate activity was a waste disposal operation in which the final product was discarded. If it was such, it would be covered by the Pollution Prevention and Control Regulations (the same issue applies in relation to the Environmental Permitting Regulations, because both give effect to terms of the IPPC Directive). The Directive distinguished treatment prior to recovery and treatment prior to disposal. The Lords held that the scheme, as a whole, would make no sense if these kinds of intermediate facility—which produced material that would ultimately be disposed of—were not included within the system of control under IPPC.

Whatever the merits of this interpretation, it has now largely been superseded by the fact that the environmental permitting regime covers various installations activities relating to sewage treatment.

The landfilling of waste, in particular, can provide a threat to groundwater quality. In order to implement the Groundwater Directive (80/68/EEC), therefore, an environmental permit is treated as an authorization for the purposes of the Groundwater Regulations 1998.[108] Accordingly, a permit can only be granted if there are adequate measures for preventing groundwater pollution by substances listed in List I and II in the Directive.

Civil liability for the unlawful disposal of waste

Civil liability is provided for in s. 73(6) of EPA 1990. This subsection applies to cases in which any damage is caused by a deposit of controlled waste in contravention of ss. 33(1) or 63(2)—that is, if the deposit was not in accordance with an environmental permit, or if it breached s. 33(1)(c), or if it breached the provision on unlawful disposal of non-controlled waste. Any person who deposited the waste is liable to pay damages for any personal injury or property damage that was caused, except if it was due wholly to the fault of the person who suffered it, or if he or she voluntarily accepted the risk of the damage. Liability also attaches to any

---

107 SI 1994/2841.
108 SI 1998/2746.

person who knowingly caused or knowingly permitted such waste to be deposited, with the result that anyone who orders an unlawful deposit, or who stands by in the knowledge that it is happening, will also be liable.

Because liability is linked to the commission of an offence under ss. 33 or 63(2), it is strict and fault need not be shown, although the defences available under those sections will also apply. As a result, it is likely that an action under s. 73(6) will be preferable, because it avoids many of the problems associated with proving environmental claims in tort. Thus an action under s. 73(6) can be brought in addition to a claim in negligence.

Section 73(6) provides an alternative to the common law causes of action, which are explained in Chapter 11. The leading case on waste sites is the Canadian case of *Gertsen v. Municipality of Toronto* (1973) 41 DLR (3d) 646, in which an occupier of land successfully claimed damages for personal injury. His injuries were the result of an explosion caused by the spark from his car engine when he started it up in his garage, which had filled with high levels of methane escaping from the disused landfill site on which it was built. The action was successful under the rule in *Rylands v. Fletcher*, nuisance, and negligence, although it must be doubted whether, on the current state of the law, all of these causes of action would have succeeded in an English court. Section 73(6) will avoid some of the difficulties associated with the common law actions in cases in which there has been an unlawful deposit.

CASE 18.11 Civil liability for dangerous waste management—*C v. Imperial Design* [2001] Env LR 33

In practice, s. 73(6) of EPA 1990 appears to be relatively underused. One of the few reported decisions on the issue illustrates some of the overlap between different types of liability for dangerous waste management.[109] The claimant C, aged 13 years old, found a drum containing waste solvent belonging to the defendant while playing on land near the defendant's factory. C set fire to the solvent and the drum exploded, causing severe burns. C brought an action in negligence and breach of the duty in s. 73(6). The trial judge found the defendant liable under that section and, in doing so, sought to rely upon a breach of the duty of care under EPA 1990, s. 34. He considered that, by allowing the waste to escape from the factory, the defendant had breached the duty of care and was therefore liable under s. 73(6).

The Court of Appeal disagreed, pointing out that liability under s. 73(6) is dependent upon an offence under EPA 1990, ss. 33 or 62. Indeed, if an offence has been committed under s. 34, it would almost certainly lead to a finding of negligence or vice versa, and there would be no reason to create the sort of no-fault liability imposed under s. 73(6). On the facts of the case, no criminal conviction had occurred and the trial judge had given no finding of fact on whether a criminal offence had been committed. In some cases, that would have been fatal to C's claim; instead the Court relied upon the finding of negligence in relation to the defendant's activities—that is, that the defendant had failed to take 'reasonable precautions' or 'measures...reasonable in the circumstances' to ensure safe waste management. This finding meant that the Court could ignore the statutory claim under s. 73(6). This illustrates the point that the only time at which it should be necessary to use s. 73(6) will be in situations within which the strictness of the liability is critical—that is, when no negligence can be demonstrated.

---

109 The case is discussed in detail in M. Lee (2002) 14 JEL 74.

Future directions—integrated product policy

The existing framework of waste management legislation has been criticized at domestic, European, and international levels.[110] One element of these criticisms is that most waste legislation has been aimed at the last part of a product's life cycle, as 'end-of-pipe' solutions— that is, ensuring that, when a product is no longer wanted, it is disposed of safely. Although other environmental controls address 'middle-of-the-pipe' impacts typically arising in the production process (for example, pollution prevention and waste minimization), there has been little emphasis on the 'front-of-pipe' impacts—that is, the research, development, and design of products to minimize their overall environmental effects. One response to this dissatisfaction with current approaches has been to consider and reduce environmental impacts over the full life cycle of a product, from production of raw materials, through production, distribution, and use to final disposal. There are echoes of this approach in the producer responsibility legislation, which promotes reuse and recycling through the use of less hazardous substances in the manufacturing process, and through designing products for ease of recycling.

This full life cycle approach has been developed by the European Commission in its integrated product policy (IPP). This started in 2001 with the production of a Green Paper on IPP, which outlined the rationale for developing product-related environmental policies and suggested some possible mechanisms that might be used.[111] Consequently, IPP was identified as one of the primary elements of the Sixth EAP.[112] These ideas were developed further in 2003, with the European Commission's adoption of a Communication on IPP.[113] The Communication is rather heavy on aspirations and light on specific commitments, preferring flexibility and stakeholder involvement to prescriptive legislation. It suggests a variety of legal and policy measures that might be used in an IPP, depending upon the particular product.

To implement its IPP strategy, the Commission has two priorities. First, it must establish a basic policy framework that identifies effective instruments to be used across different products. This might include the basis for such things as economic instruments, product or specification standards, eco-labelling, voluntary agreements, green procurement criteria, or standardized life cycle analysis databases. Secondly, it must apply the framework to specific products, starting with those products that are considered to be most environmentally damaging.

One of the challenges of IPP is determining the optimal level of regulation. With so many different instruments that might be used within an IPP, the difficulty is ensuring that the most effective blend of instruments is selected. Given the direct impact that IPP has upon manufacturers, the effectiveness of any new measures will probably be in proportion to their controversy.

CHAPTER SUMMARY

1   Managing the production and disposal of waste is one of the most significant environmental challenges that the UK faces over the next twenty years.

2   The amount of waste being produced in the UK is increasing. Sustainable waste management should see waste arising falling, which would mean reversing current rising rates of consumption.

110   See S. Tromans (2001) 13 JEL 13 and E. Tufet-Opi (2002) 14 JEL 3 generally, on the inadequacies of waste law and the response of IPP.
111   U. Schleissner (2001) EELR 86.
112   (2002) *Environment 2010: Our Future, Our Choice.*
113   *Integrated Product Policy: Building on Environmental Life-Cycle Thinking*, COM(2003) 302.

3   Traditionally, waste management regulation in the UK has concentrated on controlling the disposal of waste in large landfill sites. This is changing partly as a result of dwindling capacity in existing landfill sites, and partly because of pressure under European legislation to increase recycling and recovery.

4   Regulating waste is difficult, because the concept of 'waste' is difficult to define with any degree of certainty.

5   International waste law is largely aimed at controlling transboundary movements of waste and agreeing on the categorization of different waste.

6   European waste law is based around a central Waste Framework Directive that lays down a definition of waste, broad objectives for the management of waste, and a system of waste regulation.

7   There are other European Directives that address particular waste treatment methods—for example, incineration and landfill—and particular waste streams—for example, packaging and batteries.

8   Domestic waste policy is dominated by a national waste strategy, which sets out the policy framework and goals for waste regulation. The Secretary of State formulates this with full public consultation. The strategy sets out targets for waste management, including reduction, recycling, and recovery. The strategy is not legally binding, but influences national and local decision making on waste facilities and licensing.

9   The concept of 'waste' is broadly defined by reference to whether something has been 'discarded'. This covers the disposal, recycling, and recovery of materials, although there is a difficult distinction that must be drawn between the use of raw materials in industrial processes—for example, the use of something as a fuel—and the recovery of waste. Within this broad definition, there are classes of waste—for example, household, industrial, and commercial—that are relevant, for example, when considering waste licensing or targets for reduction.

10   Certain wastes known as 'hazardous wastes' are subject to extra controls. Categories of hazardous wastes can be found in detailed lists or the term is defined by reference to general hazardous properties.

11   The management of waste (which includes keeping, treating, or disposing) requires an environmental permit from the Environment Agency. Certain activities are exempt from the need for a permit subject to specified limits—for example, time and quantity limits for the storage of particular wastes.

12   There is a general 'duty of care' that applies to all of those who are involved in the waste chain, from production, to final disposal. Breach of the duty is a criminal offence. Compliance with the duty requires reasonable steps to be taken to ensure that an authorized person handles waste safely and that an offence is not committed. There is a code of practice that gives some guidance on the type of steps that would be considered to be reasonable.

13   An environmental permit in respect of waste can only be granted if there is a planning permission in force (if planning permission is required), if the applicant is deemed to be competent, if there has been an adequate investigation of whether the activities will lead to the pollution of groundwater, and if there will be no pollution of the environment or harm to human health.

14   The basic framework of rules governing environmental permits for waste (including those relating to public participation) are the same as those for environmental permits generally.

15   Permit conditions can relate to any activities that the permit authorizes and can cover matters after the authorized activities have ceased (for example, monitoring and other aftercare matters) or off-site controls (for example, leachate management).

16   The Environment Agency has a duty to monitor and review permitted activities and can exercise wide powers, including the variation, suspension, or revocation of existing licences.

17   There are, within domestic legislation, controls over the transportation of waste, involving the registration of waste carriers.

18   There are economic instruments, such as the landfill tax and the producer responsibility legislation, that encourage waste minimization and recycling.

19   Integrated product policy will make producers consider all of the environmental impacts of a product, from the design stage, to final disposal. It is intended that this will reduce waste production.

Q   QUESTIONS

1   In what ways does the law seek to meet the waste hierarchy of the prevention of production of waste, encouraging reuse and recycling, and promoting safe management and disposal?

2   Walter is the inventor of the Inklene ink cleaning and solvent recovery unit. This is a unit that attaches to printing presses and operates a closed-loop cleaning system. It cleans the used ink from the presses with non-hazardous solvents. Then, with various filters, it cleans the solvents and separates the ink, which are then both pumped back to the printing press for reuse on the presses. The unit is connected for 24 hours and then removed elsewhere. At present, the printing press owners throw both the used solvent and ink away. The unit will cut down solvent and ink usage by over 95 per cent. The local Environment Agency officer has advised Walter that the Inklene unit requires an environmental permit to operate. Advise Walter on whether the officer is correct and, if so, on what steps he must take to obtain a permit.

3   Fred is the owner of a factory. His rubbish is collected once a week from a skip that is placed just inside the factory gates. One week, the waste collection company fails to collect the waste and the skip fills up to overflowing. Fred places his waste in cardboard boxes by the skip. Local youths break into the factory yard at night and play football with the boxes. One of the boxes breaks, releasing toxic material that causes severe injuries to one of the youths. The next morning, Fred contacts one of his mates and asks him to dispose of the waste. The waste is subsequently found on a nearby playing field. Advise Fred on the offences that he may have committed and the liabilities that he may have incurred.

📖   FURTHER READING

General texts

The introduction of the Environmental Permitting regime has rendered many texts—particularly those that discuss waste management licensing—as out of date. Even before the introduction of the permitting regime, the changes in waste management law over the last ten years have been rapid and dramatic. Thus sourcing the most up-to-date text as possible is critical, because anything before 2000 will fail to cover many of the recent developments in such things as the Landfill Regulations, the definition of waste, and new producer responsibility legislation. R. Hawkins and H. Shaw (2004) *The Practical Guide to Waste Management Law*, London: Thomas Telford, is a superb introduction to the topic. It has the advantage of being relatively up to date, but it is also highly accessible, with tables and illustrative examples. Be warned however: the commentary is opinionated, controversial, and humorous—this is not a dry academic work. Another recommended text is D. Lawrence (2000) *Waste Regulation Law*, London: Butterworths: although this is now very out of date, it is comprehensive in its coverage, and is detailed in its evaluation and analysis.

A good introduction to some of the problems of European waste legislation can be found in S. Tromans, 'EC waste law: a complete mess?' [2001] 13 JEL 13. As the title suggests, this is an extensive (and devastating) critique of all aspects of European waste management law, and covers areas such as the trade in waste, which are not covered in this chapter.

Waste policy

The starting point for any research on waste is the *Waste Strategy for England 2007* (Cm 7086). This sets the framework for waste management, and sets out both the problems and some potential solutions. To see how far we have come, readers could usefully look at the 11th Report of the Royal Commission on Environmental Pollution (1985) *Managing Waste: The Duty of Care*, Cm 9675. This report not only deals with the historical context of waste management law and practice, but also provides a damning indictment of past practices.

The definition of waste

There are many articles examining the case law and issues surrounding the definition of waste. Some care should be taken, because pre-2000 articles do not necessarily represent the law as it stands today. Some of the older articles are still useful, however, because they discuss some of the problems of coming up with a workable definition of 'waste'. The best articles include: M. Purdue, 'Defining waste' (1990) 2 JEL 250; J. Smith, 'The challenges of environmentally sound and efficient regulation of waste' (1993) 3 JEL 91; J. Fluck, 'The term "waste" in EU law' [1994] EELR 79; I. Cheyne and M. Purdue, 'Fitting definition to purpose: the search for a satisfactory definition of waste' (1995) 7 JEL 149; M. Purdue and A. van Rossem, 'The distinction between using secondary raw materials and the recovery of waste: the Directive definition of waste' (1998) 10 JEL 116; G. Van Calster, 'The EC definition of waste: the Euro *Tombesi* bypass and the Basel relief routes' (1997) EBLR 137; I. Cheyne, 'The definition of waste in EC law' (2002) 14 JEL 61; J. Pike, 'Waste not, want not: an (even) wider definition of waste' (2002) 14 JEL 197; L. Kramer 'The distinction between product and waste in Community law' (2003) 11(1) ELLR 3.

Other waste topics

The breadth of this chapter means that there are many other sources that could provide further reading on specialist topics. Works of direct relevance are footnoted. Those listed here are only a selection.

We are in a period during which the impact of waste reduction and recycling targets is becoming more prevalent. The implications of this are discussed in D. Pocklington, 'The role of mandatory targets in mandatory waste management legislation' (2003) 15(5) ELM 285. There are some areas that have not been covered in this chapter, primarily on grounds of space. One of these is the interrelationship between different waste Directives. For example, the relationship between recycling in the Packaging Waste Directive and the Waste Framework Directive is covered in S. Tromans, 'Defining recycling' (2004) 16 JEL 80 and M. Lee, 'Resources, recycling and waste' (2004) Env LR 49. An overview of the operational problems in the initial years of the landfill tax can be found in J. Morris and P. Phillips, 'The UK landfill tax: an evaluation of the first three years' (2000) Env LR 150.

On the question of insolvency and waste management licences, see A. Keay and P. de Prez, 'Insolvency and environmental principles: a case study in a conflict of public interests' (2001) 3(2) Env LR 90, C. Shelbourn, 'Can the insolvent polluter pay? Environmental licences and the insolvent company' (2000) 12 JEL 207, and J. Armour, 'Who pays when polluters go bust?' (2000) LQR 200.

F. Nunan, 'Barriers to the use of voluntary agreements: a case study of the development of the packaging waste regulations in the UK' (1999) 9(6) Euro Env 238 provides a good introduction to producer responsibility legislation as compared to alternative methods of addressing the problem. Other articles on producer responsibility include M. Lee, 'New generation regulation? The case of end-of-life vehicles' (2002) 11(4) EELR 114 and K. Kroepelian, 'Extended producer responsibility: new legal structures for improved ecological self-organisation in Europe' (2000) 9(2) RECIEL 165.

Integrated product policy is a relatively new initiative, but there is some literature that provides the background. Have a look at I. Rose and G. Knighton, 'IPP: a new approach to environmental regulations' (1999) 8(10) EELR 266 and U. Schleissner, 'Integrated product policy: where is the EU heading?' (2001) 10(3) EELR 86.

The Internet provides many good information sources for waste. A great gateway into other sites (as well as a site that provides a lot of up-to-date information) is that of the Land Regeneration Network **www. grc.cf.ac.uk/lrn/resources/waste**. A lot of effort has been put into keeping the page up to date and there are links to case law, legislation, and technical briefing notes on waste-related topics. As with other areas, DEFRA's site provides some good resources. At **www.defra.gov.uk/environment/waste/intro.htm**, you will find the National Waste Strategy and other policy documents. European resources can be found at **europa.eu.int/comm/environment/waste/index.htm**.

There is a lot of information on recycling. **www.letsrecycle.com** and **www.wastewatch.org.uk** provide a lot of information about practical measures that have been taken to increase recovery and recycling. The Waste and Resources Action Programme can be found at **www.wrap.org.uk**. This non-profit-making organization was set up to help deliver the targets in the Waste Strategy. It will play an increasingly important role in waste management over the long term.

For the industry view, the Environmental Services Association is the trade body for the Waste Industry and provides publications on many waste issues online at **www.esauk.org/work/briefings**.

On producer responsibility, Valpak, the largest compliance scheme, can be found at **www.valpak.co.uk**.

19 The conservation of nature

> **Overview**
>
> This chapter looks at the laws that aim specifically to protect plants, animals, and natural habitats. This has become a popular subject in recent years, for a variety of reasons that include increasing interest in all things connected with wildlife and alarm at the appalling rate of decline in, and loss of, the natural environment. Using the law to conserve nature, however, involves finding solutions to some complex policy issues. Finding space for species and habitats to be conserved often clashes with other legitimate social interests, such as economic development and respect for private property. These tensions—which mean that nature conservation law can be a controversial policy area[1]—are the central theme of this chapter.
>
> In looking at laws that have as their primary focus the conservation of species and their habitats, we distinguish between laws that are justified as a matter of straight wildlife conservation, and those that relate to matters of amenity and landscape (which are dealt with in the following chapter). In many ways, however, the law now pursues both these objectives together. This is especially true of the use of economic instruments in furthering nature conservation, landscape, and recreational interests in an integrated way, and, as we will see, a major challenge is the integration of nature conservation into general decision making—for example, in relation to agriculture or the control of development. But little coverage is given to international conservation law and, in relation to this, you should refer to the works mentioned at the end of the chapter. Partly, this is because international laws are often effectively subsumed within more enforceable regimes at national level (this is basically the case with the protection given to sites designated under the 1971 Ramsar Convention on Wetlands); largely, it is because the central themes of this chapter can be more than adequately explored by looking at national and EC law.[2]
>
> Finally, it must be stressed that the effective conservation of species and habitats depends as much on the responses to other environmental threats—especially climate change,[3] pollution, and inappropriate land uses—as it does on the specific methods of protecting species and habitats mentioned here, which would undoubtedly be useless if applied in isolation.
>
> Before reading this chapter, you may find it useful to have looked at competing perspectives on how the natural environment can be valued and how wildlife interests are treated from a sustainable development perspective (see Chapter 3), the legal status of EC Directives (there are two key Directives in this area), and the use of a range of regulatory approaches, especially economic tools.

---

1 For example, the contentious passage of the Wildlife and Countryside Act (WCA) 1981, described in P. Lowe, G. Cox, M. MacEwan, T. O'Riordan, and M. Winter (1986) *Countryside Conflicts*, London: Gower, ch. 6.

2 This means that certain mechanisms to secure the sustainable and equitable use of the components of biodiversity—such as intellectual property rights, farmers' rights, and differentiated responsibilities as between 'northern' and 'southern' countries—are not covered.

3 Climate change may not, of course, be a threat to some habitats and species, which may prosper, yet, even in the medium term, some habitats and species may be lost completely from the UK.

At the end of this chapter, you will be able to:

✔ appreciate a range of reasons for conserving nature;

✔ understand the main regulatory challenges in nature conservation, especially the drawbacks of using a negative approach to conserving habitats and finding the right balance in the costs of nature conservation falling on landowners or the general public;

✔ evaluate how the law weighs conservation interests against other valued interests, such as economic development;

✔ assess some of the approaches to, and challenges of, integrating nature conservation into decision making.

Why conserve?

Conscious of the intrinsic value of biological diversity and of the ecological, genetic, social, economic, scientific, educational, cultural, recreational and aesthetic values of biological diversity and its components

Conscious also of the importance of biological diversity for evolution and for maintaining life sustaining systems of the biosphere

(Preamble, 1992 Convention on Biological Diversity)

There are many reasons why species and habitats are valued. One reason for conserving nature is scientific study. The seminal 1947 Huxley Report advocated designating protected areas for their educative value as 'living laboratories'[4] and it is notable that the main national habitat designation dating from this period is the site of special *scientific* interest (SSSI). Nature might also be conserved on aesthetic or cultural, or even spiritual, grounds. An example of this is the Convention on the International Trade in Endangered Species, Appendix III of which restricts the trade in species that are not strictly endangered, but which nevertheless have a special place in the life of a country—for example, as emblematic of the nation.

Of course, species may be valued for the economic and social benefits that they now provide, such as food, and early hunting laws essentially protected game species to ensure their continued exploitation. Nature can also be valued for the benefits that it might provide in the future—for example, new strains of crops or new pharmaceutical products—for which a diversity of genetic material is probably needed, while diversity may also be needed to maintain the functioning of resilient biological systems upon which all humans and animals depend—for example, by protecting against events such as pest infestation or disease, which might reduce the diversity of species. Nature can also be seen as having considerable economic value, although this value is not always appreciated sufficiently by decision makers, because it is often not very well captured in the marketplace. Addressing the unprecedented rate of species extinctions by conserving biological diversity (or 'biodiversity')—that is, the richness of life on earth—can be justified as a form of long-term insurance for human health and welfare.

In practice, however, most protected areas in the UK are designated on the basis of the rarity of relatively large and well-known organisms, such as birds, plants, and larger invertebrates such as molluscs. It is difficult to say, therefore, that the laws considered in this chapter have as their focus the conservation of biological diversity in the sense that this is defined, in Art. 2 of the Biodiversity Convention, as including diversity within species, between species, and of ecosystems.

---

4 Wildlife Conservation Special Committee (the 'Huxley Committee') (1947) *Conservation of Nature in England and Wales*, Cmd 7122.

As well as some of the temporal considerations mentioned above—for example, the rights or interests of future generations—there are also spatial dimensions to valuing nature that influence conservation policy. Although there are obviously examples of distant species being highly valued (for example, whales), the greatest value placed on plants, animals, and habitats is generally at the local level.[5] But similarly, the value of potentially damaging activities such as economic development or agricultural improvements are also of greatest importance locally. In different ways, therefore, often the value of plants and animals, *and* the potential economic benefits from developing their habitats, are felt most strongly at the local level, while the wider public benefits (either for economic and social development or for biodiversity conservation) are either more abstract or more diffusely appreciated.

The reasons for valuing nature conservation outlined above are utilitarian and essentially anthropocentric. Even statutes aimed at protecting wild animals from cruelty can be justified on the grounds of civilizing human behaviour. There have been some soft law moves in the direction of justifying conservation laws on the basis that, as the UN World Charter for Nature (1982) put it *'all life warrants respect regardless of its usefulness to Man'*—and the current overarching UK policy document also justifies action on the ground that we ought not to *'treat nature as if it had been designed for our convenience and abuse'*[6]—but binding legal texts tend to retreat from this point of view. Thus, despite the 1992 Convention on Biological Diversity speaking of the 'intrinsic value' of biodiversity, its real focus is the sustainable use of nature—that is, making biodiversity pay its way.

Three final points are worth making here. The first is that there are obviously values that compete with those of nature conservation. These, of course, may include development, which can only be achieved at the expense of wildlife and habitat. But it can also include other values. For example, in *R (Greenpeace) v. Secretary of State for the Environment, Food and Rural Affairs* [2003] Env LR 9, a case involving an import of Brazilian mahogany, the majority of the Court of Appeal stressed that exporters should be able to rely on documents that, on their face, authorized the shipment. In doing so, the Court placed greater value on the importance of commercial certainty than it did on nature conservation, which (as Laws LJ in the minority clearly wished) could have been more highly valued if the circumstances surrounding the grant of the export permit were given more weight.

Secondly, as many of the above justifications show, there are good reasons to take a precautionary approach to conservation. Yet there is a considerable degree of uncertainty about what to conserve: the most species? Higher taxonomic categories? The breadth of these categories? Or the evolutionary distance between species?[7] This is something about which there is no real consensus. There is also the key issue of how damaging or destroying natural assets is conceived in terms of pursuing sustainable development, in particular whether 'strong' or 'weak' formulations of this concept—which (partly for reasons of risk perception) place different emphases on the substitutability of natural resources such as species and habitats—should be taken (see p. 61). In law, this is often played out in the resolution of disputes between conservation and other land-use interests—for example, what degree of damage to a particular habitat or habitat type can be authorized, and the form of compensatory measures (if any) that should be taken.

The history and development of controls

A brief history of nature conservation helps explain the current structure of the law. Until the nineteenth century, the need to protect wildlife was normally perceived solely in human terms, such as the desirability of preserving game and quarry species, and protected areas

5 Which, in practice, often influences how resources are devoted, when compared to losses at higher spatial scales.

6 UK Biodiversity Partnership (2007) *Conserving Biodiversity: The UK Approach*, London: DEFRA.

7 See C. Stone (1995) 68 S Cal LR 577, 614.

in which to hunt them. There is little doubt that an incidental benefit of this human-centred approach was the protection of other animals and plants, and the preservation of whole areas in a fairly undeveloped state (for example, the New Forest), but there were few laws designed specifically to protect wildlife.

Early controls

From Victorian times, the tendency was to enact legislation outlawing unwelcome activities in response to particular problems as they were identified. The rationale for this piecemeal intervention was as much based on concern about cruelty as it was based on any positive desire to conserve nature for its own sake. Some good examples are the Sea Birds Protection Acts of 1869, 1872, and 1880, passed to combat the slaughter of birds at places such as Flamborough Head, and various pieces of legislation intended to restrict the international trade in feathers for clothing and hats. But there was no grand design underlying these restrictions. The weight of conservation fell on voluntary organizations—indeed, the UK had the world's first developed conservation movement—and no official bodies were established to monitor or enforce the legislation that did exist.

These voluntary organizations gradually developed a strategy that became, and remains, the typical approach to nature conservation—that is, the designation of selected areas or sites that are specially protected. The first modern uses of this technique related to the protection of common lands for recreational purposes, but it was soon used for the development of nature reserves, even though, at this time, they were seen as a somewhat peripheral interest of the nature conservation movement. For example, the National Trust acquired parts of Wicken Fen in 1899, the Norfolk Naturalists Trust was founded to buy Cley Marshes in 1926, and the Royal Society for the Protection of Birds (RSPB) bought its first nature reserve (on Romney Marsh) in 1929. But in the absence of any legislative protection for such sites, their safety lay in the exercise of ordinary property rights. After all, the property owner's freedom to exclude others and to use the land for any purposes is one mechanism for controlling land use in limited areas. But the limitations of this approach are well illustrated by the RSPB's first reserve, which had to be abandoned when drainage activities on neighbouring land destroyed its natural interest.

The post-war period

After 1945, the site designation approach was adopted as a matter of national policy. The beginning of the modern age of nature conservation can be traced to that time and the publication of two influential reports, the Huxley and Ritchie Reports,[8] many of the recommendations of which were accepted and acted upon.

A specialist national nature conservation body—the Nature Conservancy—was established and one of its main roles was to create a series of protected sites across the nation, rather than the somewhat random series produced by private acquisition. The two main habitat protection measures—the national nature reserve (NNR) and the SSSI—both date from this period. The scientific basis of nature conservation was emphasized, and it was linked firmly to education and research on the natural environment. Nature conservation was also split from amenity, recreation, and landscape matters, which were given their own separate institutions and laws, and it is worth reflecting that the powers for nature conservation at that time were both stronger and met with far less opposition than those for recreation in the countryside. But nature conservation law was intimately bound up with two key Acts from this period dealing with the promotion of agriculture (the Agriculture Act 1947) and

8 The 'Huxley Committee' (1947); Scottish Wild Life Conservation Committee (the 'Ritchie Committee') (1947) *National Parks and the Conservation of Nature in Scotland*, Cmd 7235.

with development control (the Town and Country Planning Act 1947, which excluded agricultural land use from the meaning of 'development'—see p. 734). Together, they reflected the view that the main threat to nature was from urbanization, rather than from changing agricultural practices, and set the scene for the decades ahead.

Current policy

Many of the features of this structure remain, but the climate in which they operate has changed radically, with the result that many of the similarities that the current system has with that structure are illusory. There have been devastating changes in both the urban and rural environments, and these have altered the role of site designation dramatically from an educational to a safeguarding one. One result has been the expansion of the NNR and SSSI system way beyond that envisaged—or, indeed, considered necessary—by the Huxley and Ritchie Committees, in order to ensure that at least a basic pool of key sites is protected. Conceiving of nature conservation interests as a 'common heritage' or 'common concern' among states has also emerged, and so, for many sites and species, the main body of rules now stem from the implementation of EC Directives or international conventions.

Another result is that general environmental awareness has now shifted the focus of policy away from the designation and protection of certain key sites towards the protection of the wider countryside. It is now accepted that there is little future in having isolated areas of protected wildlife in an otherwise barren landscape and so nature conservation is increasingly seen as a factor to weigh in the balance when considering policy everywhere. This adds to the political dimension that nature conservation has rapidly acquired. It also leads nature conservation law into a potential head-on collision with traditional views of property and personal rights, and the clash of values that this entails.

In addition, the enjoyment of nature has emerged as a major leisure pursuit, blurring the distinction in the public mind and in policy between nature conservation as a scientifically justified discipline and as a recreation. There has been an undreamt-of increase in voluntary activity in relation to the countryside, resulting in large numbers of reserves and sites protected by voluntary bodies and non-statutory designations.

Future directions and challenges

There is now a greater appreciation of the dynamic qualities of nature and of the major challenges to conservation that climate change in particular will bring. Nature conservation interests cannot be frozen in time, because they are constantly evolving and adapting to changing environmental circumstances. This sits uneasily with the current approach to conservation, which looks to preserve existing species and habitats for the future. Instead of trying only to preserve the best of what we presently have, we may need more imaginative thinking about the sort of natural heritage we want, or need, to meet future circumstances. This may involve the promotion of much larger protected areas (which are more robust in conservation terms) than we have at present, and taking a more relaxed view of things such as non-native species (for example, the UK may need to host species struggling to maintain a presence in their original habitat). And, as we become more aware of the biodiversity richness of the marine environment, this is increasingly calling for action.

Types of legal protection and the conservation law toolbox

From this brief survey, it can be seen that the protections and safeguards offered by the law can be divided into four rough categories, in each of which different legal mechanisms tend to be relied upon.[9]

Habitat conservation by designating key sites

The conservation of habitats through their designation as key sites has been a favoured technique and a bewildering array of legislative designations has built up, with special rules and protections differing for each one.[10] There is quite a degree of overlap here and many designations are cumulative. The main issue in site designation is whether, because of its conservation importance, a statutory conservation agency (or a sympathetic wildlife organization) already owns the land. If it does, then designation empowers those seeking to conserve the site; if it does not, then designation may clash with the way in which the landowner wishes to see the land used. The main point to stress is that straight criminal offences are rarely invoked to protect natural habitats from damage or destruction, and other methods have traditionally been preferred. These have involved, for example, getting local authorities to recognize the value of conservation interests when making land-use planning decisions, or giving landowners financial incentives to manage their land in ways that are sympathetic to nature conservation. Recent reforms, however, have heralded a greater willingness to criminalize behaviour that damages valued habitats (see, for example, p. 695).

Protecting individual animals and plants

While protecting animals and plants within their natural habitats is central to nature conservation, certain species are also protected regardless of whether they are within designated areas. This type of protection is achieved on a somewhat ad hoc basis, although a degree of coherence is provided by the Wildlife and Countryside Act 1981 and laws implementing key EC Directives, both of which contain various criminal offences and licensing regimes. Nature conservation is not the only aim being pursued: there is still a large element of protection against cruelty, and there are important exceptions relating to game and quarry species. Criminal offences and licensing are also the main legal tools used to control (with varying degrees of success) potentially harmful movements of animals and plants, whether through wildlife trafficking, in relation to which import and export permits are used—as under the measures implementing the 1973 Convention on International Trade in Endangered Species of Wild Fauna and Flora (CITES)—or, more problematic ecologically, the import of invasive non-native species (see WCA 1981, s. 14 and Sch. 9). (Space prevents further discussion of these topics here.)

Integrating nature conservation

The realization that the protection of species and of isolated sites is insufficient, both in scientific terms and in terms of the expectations of people who are interested in nature, has led to the search for general policies that are conducive to nature conservation, especially as part

---

9 Because biodiversity is a public good, in some measure, its component species have a value that cannot be captured by markets.

10 Strictly, habitat protection is a narrower category than site protection, because the former relates to protecting habitats of valued species or valued habitat types per se, whereas the latter may be used to protect and conserve a wider range of interests, but the terms are used synonymously here.

of agriculture and forestry policy (see p. 745). Grants and incentives are often used to meet these policy objectives. This is all part of the general trend towards integrating environmental considerations into decision making—for example, by placing conservation duties on public bodies, through impact assessment or by requiring decision makers to act in ways that achieve conservation objectives.

Incidental protection

It remains clear that nature conservation interests are often served by taking advantage of legal powers that were not designed with nature conservation in mind. The best example is the purchase of private nature reserves by voluntary bodies, thus taking advantage of ordinary property rights, but another good example is the nature conservation value of the large tracts of land used for Ministry of Defence training grounds.

The conservation law toolbox—conclusions

A striking feature of nature conservation law is that very little 'do not'-type regulation is used, certainly when compared to many other areas of environmental law. There are three main explanations for this, one of which lies in the importance of human influence for nature conservation. Many bird species, for example, prosper in areas of lowland heath kept free from the invasion of scrub and trees, while the interest of chalk downland depends on grazing. Indeed, safeguarding most species and habitats requires active land management—grazing, harvesting, water-level management, etc.—rather than restrictions designed to prevent things happening. This is reflected in recent reforms, under which there are now enforceable powers to compel landowners to manage their land in the interests of conservation.

A second, related, reason is that habitats and species are subject to certain population dynamics (reflected, for example, in how they respond to changing pressures), which means that containing them within designated parcels of land requires a greater degree of active land management than would allowing habitats or populations of species to move around in response to natural environmental changes. In other words, the very nature of protected area controls, especially in small areas such as those designated in the UK, requires more interventionist management.

A third reason is that nature conservation laws may conflict with the core private law right of landowners to determine the use of their property. Although much circumscribed in practice, the *idea* of this right has always exercised a powerful influence over nature conservation law. Respect for private property rights lies at the heart of the historic approach of the law in prioritizing the pro-development planning system over nature conservation interests, and in seeking voluntary agreement with landowners (through financial incentives or compensation) rather than imposing prescriptive regulatory controls.

The nature conservation agencies

The administration of nature conservation, which was once the responsibility of the Nature Conservancy Council (NCC)—a UK-wide body—is presently divided among the following national agencies:

- Natural England;
- the Countryside Council for Wales (CCW);
- Scottish Natural Heritage.

All of these bodies' statutory remits cover both nature conservation and amenity, and recreational matters—the Environmental Protection Act (EPA) 1990, s. 130; the Natural Heritage (Scotland) Act 1991; Natural Environment and Rural Communities (NERC) Act 2006, s. 2—although, between 1991 and 2006, the institutional structure in England was different and responsibility was divided between English Nature (which had a nature conservation remit), and the Countryside Commission (latterly, the Countryside Agency), which had a more landscape orientation. Because the law in Scotland changed in 2004 and in England in 2006, it is getting increasingly difficult to make general statements about the functions, powers, and constitutions of these bodies. For ease of explanation, therefore, we tend to discuss Natural England and give pointers to the position in the other jurisdictions in areas in which there are significant or notable differences. We use the term 'nature conservancy council' and 'NCC' throughout this book to refer generically to the relevant national body in its own area. (In Northern Ireland, nature conservation is a matter for the Environment and Heritage Service of the Department of the Environment.)

Each of the three national bodies, however, is established on a broadly similar basis. Council members are appointed by government and they are the government's statutory advisers on nature conservation issues, with specific responsibilities for advising on species and habitat protection, the dissemination of knowledge about nature conservation, the support and conduct of research into nature conservation, and the safeguarding of protected sites. In particular, they are responsible for selecting and managing NNRs, and for the designation and oversight of SSSIs. They are also statutory consultees in relation to a large number of decisions made by other public bodies, including decisions on applications for planning permission and for pollution consents.

In one sense, therefore, the three bodies are classic quangos and could be said to be largely unaccountable for many of their decisions. But they could also be said to be accountable to the interests of wildlife and ecology. Like the Environment Agency, there has been a debate over whether this extends merely to implementing and enforcing the law as it is, or extends beyond this, to 'championing' the cause of nature conservation.[11] It now seems that this is to be resolved by recognizing, for example, that Natural England ought to be a champion within its field of responsibility, but that this role is to be constrained by Ministerial direction where appropriate—that is, that it should champion what government wants it to. It is notable that there is nothing in NERC 2006, for example, which requires Natural England to prioritize conservation interests over other interests that fall within its remit.

Since the break-up of the NCC in 1991, there has been an umbrella organization: the Joint Nature Conservation Committee (JNCC). This has few executive functions, but carries out important roles in relation to matters spanning the national NCCs, such as the retention of common standards (for example, common criteria for the designation of SSSIs). Under s. 31, NERC 2006, the remit of the JNCC was formally extended to the UK—that is, to include Northern Ireland—which is sensible, given the JNCC's role in helping the UK meet its wider obligations (for example, under the Ramsar Convention on Wetlands and other international agreements, and EC Directives).

Under NERC 2006, Natural England may enter into an agreement either with another conservation body or with any other body. This would allow Natural England to delegate certain of its functions to bodies better placed to deliver. For example, it might delegate some of its monitoring functions to research centres or even to specialist non-government organizations (NGOs). These provisions are a measure of how expertise in conservation is quite diffusely spread out and perhaps also of how many of the main NGOs have much more of an 'insider' status in this area than, for example, in relation to pollution control.

11 HC Environment, Transport and Regional Affairs Committee (1998) *English Nature.*

General biodiversity duties

Despite specialist nature conservation agencies, a final point of note mirrors those made above about integrating conservation into all aspects of policy. It is important that all bodies whose activities impact on the natural environment should have to consider the impact of their decisions on nature conservation. At least in England and Wales, the law has edged forward cautiously here, first by placing a general duty on all public bodies to further and enhance nature conservation (although only in relation to certain designated sites—see pp. 702 and 717) and, more recently, by placing a general duty on all public bodies to have regard to conserving biodiversity—a duty that is not tied to protected areas (this has been the case in Scotland since 2004, but south of the border it only applied to Ministers, government departments, and the Welsh Assembly). In addition, Ministers and government departments must have particular regard to the Biodiversity Convention 1992, although public bodies and statutory undertakers need not (NERC 2006, s. 40).

The general biodiversity duty does not, therefore, require that conservation is 'furthered', because of concerns that this would lead to legal challenges to individual decisions that the duty had not been complied with because conservation had not been furthered.[12] In practice, however, the process of integrating conservation policies into environmental decision making can prove to be challenging. The Environment Agency, which, within certain, constraints has a duty to further conservation, has been criticized for insufficiently integrating nature conservation concerns into its core functions.[13]

Habitat conservation—national law

Although there is a rapidly growing number of protective designations for areas of habitat, the main domestic ones remain the interrelated categories of NNR and SSSI.[14] The increasingly important EC designations are discussed later in this chapter. Both NNRs and SSSIs were originally introduced in the National Parks and Access to the Countryside Act 1949 on the recommendation of the Huxley and Ritchie Committees. The NNR powers remain essentially those enacted in 1949, but the SSSI provisions have been significantly altered and strengthened, first by Pt II of the Wildlife and Countryside Act (WCA) 1981, and more recently by amendments in England and Wales to the 1981 Act made under Pt III of the Countryside and Rights of Way Act (CROWA) 2000. (In Scotland, the 1981 Act has been strengthened, along broadly similar lines, by the Nature Conservation (Scotland) Act 2004.)[15]

The difference between NNRs and SSSIs can best be explained by saying that NNRs are actively controlled and managed by the NCC, whereas, in SSSIs, the occupier of the land retains control, subject to a number of restrictions on use decided by the NCC. Because all NNRs are notified as SSSIs and benefit from the restrictions on them, however, it is more useful if the legal protections for SSSIs are explained in detail. Focusing on SSSIs also makes practical sense, because, generally, the nature conservation interest has to coexist with other land uses, such as agricultural or economic development. By contrast, the intention in the Huxley Report (p. 683) was that NNRs should be selected where the land was '*for one reason*

---

12 See the discussion on p. 117 about the general hesitancy in placing statutory duties to 'further' environmental objectives.

13 HC Environment, Transport and the Regions Committee (2000) *The Environment Agency*, paras 137–39.

14 There is also separate provision for limestone pavements: see WCA 1981, s. 34. Most, if not all, significant areas of this unique habitat (and geological feature) are covered by limestone pavement orders. Limestone pavements are also listed in Annex I of the EC Habitats Directive.

15 But greater emphasis is placed on involving a wider range of bodies, and the public, in site designation and management, albeit in the context of sites still being designated on scientific grounds.

or another beyond the margin of economic development' and, because the study and conservation of nature is the predominant use of the land, the conservation condition of NNRs is generally much better than that of SSSIs.

National nature reserves (NNRs)

NNRs are areas managed for study or research into flora, fauna, or geological or physiographical interest, or for preserving such features that are of special interest. Since NERC 2006, an NNR can be designated not only for these conservation purposes, but also for recreational purposes, if managing the land for the recreational purpose does not compromise its management for the conservation purpose.[16] There were 356 NNRs in the UK as at September 2006, covering over 226,000 hectares.

Designation is simple: the NCC merely declares that an area is an NNR. But to do this, it has to have control of the site so that it can manage it. Control is achieved either by buying the land, leasing it, or entering into a nature reserve agreement with the owner, so NNRs are not necessarily the very best sites and private property rights are central to their conservation. About a third of NNRs are now declared on nationally important land managed by an approved body (for example, a wildlife trust),[17] which is a useful device that has allowed the NCC to expand the number of NNRs without incurring the costs associated with acquiring land. Because by-laws can now be made for any SSSI, however, there are now no additional statutory restrictions on the use of an NNR other than those imposed on all SSSIs.

There are no NNRs in Northern Ireland, although there are 47 nature reserves, declared by government, of equivalent status.

BOX 19.1 Marine nature reserves (MNRs) and marine nature conservation

Marine nature reserves (MNRs) are the counterparts to national nature reserves (NNRs) in tidal and coastal waters, and may be designated for any area of land or water from the high-tide mark to a line three miles from the baselines established for measuring the territorial sea.[18] They may be designated on the same grounds of conservation and study as NNRs (Wildlife and Countryside Act 1981, s. 36), and are actively managed by the relevant nature conservancy council (NCC).

MNRs feature a number of differences from NNRs. Some stem from the absence of property rights over most of the potential area of MNRs; others are a consequence of the limited vision of MNRs in the 1981 Act. Designation is by the Secretary of State on the application of the NCC, but there are significant obstacles: the procedure is lengthy (WCA 1981, Sch. 12) and the main control is the power for the NCC to make by-laws that cannot restrict any lawful right of passage by vessels other than pleasure boats (WCA 1981, s. 37). Only three small MNRs have ever been designated. There are a few voluntary marine reserves and, in Scotland, a number of non-statutory marine consultation areas have been designated (mostly on the west coast), as a flag to other decision makers about the quality and sensitivity of the marine environment.

The inadequate conservation of the marine environment has long been a source of concern. In 2004, a major *Review of Marine Nature Conservation* by the Department for Environment, Food

---

16 National Parks and Access to the Countryside Act (NPACA) 1949, s. 15, amended by NERC 2006, s. 105(1) and Sch. 11, para. 12. At local level, local authorities may designate and manage local nature reserves along broadly similar lines: see NPACA 1949, s. 21. Mostly, they have been designated to promote conservation education in urban areas.

17 WCA 1981, s. 35. Strictly, only these latter sites are NNRs; those designated under s. 15 of the 1949 Act are strictly 'nature reserves', but they have always been referred to as national nature reserves.

18 See the Territorial Sea Act 1987.

and Rural Affairs (DEFRA) confirmed the need for significant, integrated reforms. Following many years of lobbying and various failed private Bills, the government has now taken up the issue and a commitment was made in the 2005 Queen's Speech to enact legislation by 2007. The 2007 Queen's Speech eventually announced a government-sponsored draft Marine Bill. The Bill is intended to go much further than simply tweaking nature conservation laws—for example, by extending marine planning and the streamlining of consents to develop or operate in the marine environment (obviously very important for things such as offshore renewables). New institutional arrangements are likely, as is some integration of conservation and fisheries policy.[19]

Sites of special scientific interest (SSSIs)

SSSIs are a representative sample of British habitats, each site being seen as '*an integral part of a national series*' established with the aim of '*maintaining the present diversity of wild animals and plants in Great Britain*'.[20] Site selection is on scientific grounds rather than to enhance amenity or provide recreation. For biological sites, the best examples of various habitat types (including natural, semi-natural, and man-made landscapes) are chosen, determined on the basis of 'naturalness, diversity, typicalness and size', along with sites catering for rare habitats and species. A geographical spread is ensured by selecting typical sites within sub-regional areas. Geological SSSIs are treated differently, the intention being to '*conserve those localities essential to the continued conduct of research and education in the earth sciences*',[21] again in the context of a national representative series.

By the end of March 2003 (May 2003 for Wales), throughout the UK there were 6,581 SSSIs notified under the 1981 Act (4,112 in England, 1,018 in Wales, and 1,451 in Scotland). Together they covered 2,322,737 hectares—over 7 per cent of the land area—although the proportion is far higher in some areas, notably Scotland (12.8 per cent). The largest SSSI is The Wash, covering 622,054 hectares; the smallest SSSI in England is a 7m^2 barn in Gloucestershire, notified because it hosts a large breeding colony of lesser horseshoe bats. Also included are a number of linear sites, such as rivers.

Conservation law and policy, and SSSIs

A few preliminary points need to be made about the evolution of the law relating to SSSIs. These require an appreciation both of changing threats to SSSIs since 1949, as well as significant, even radical, changes to law and policy.

Under the 1949 Act, the idea was that the main focus of the NCC's work would centre on the acquisition and management of NNRs. By contrast, SSSIs were to be protected only through notification to local planning authorities, which, under their newly acquired planning functions, were to include SSSIs in development plans and hence protect them from (mainly urban) development through planning controls. Consistent with this approach—but remarkable nonetheless—there was no duty to notify landowners of SSSIs. Hence, the NCC played a fairly limited role in relation to SSSIs and, at best, an information-based approach was preferred. With the advent of new pressures on nature conservation, however, the limitations of this approach became clear—evidenced, for example, by NCC statistics released at the time that the 1981 Act was being debated showing that between 10 and 15 per cent of

19 A useful source to read in this connection is the 2004 report of the Royal Commission on Environmental Protection (RCEP) on the *Environmental Effects of Marine Fisheries*, available online at **www.rcep.org.uk/fisheries.htm**.

20 See, in general, NCC (1989) *Guidelines for Selection of Biological SSSIs*.

21 *Geological Conservation Review*, NCC 43 (Volume series from 1977 onwards).

SSSIs had suffered significant damage or loss in 1980 alone, the majority of which was caused by agriculture rather than urban development.

The 1981 Act, however, took only very limited strides towards overcoming the shortcomings in relation to SSSIs, which, by then, had become the dominant site designation. Despite some strengthening, there was a continued preference for a policy of voluntariness (which might have been expected from the Conservative Government of the day). This is the view that compulsory controls should only be used as a last resort, because they will only serve to antagonize landowners, who are seen as having the main responsibility for site protection. Pursuant to this policy, the favoured mechanism of control was the management agreement: many damaging activities were either unregulated or could proceed with planning permission, and so the Act forced the NCC into seeking to enter into agreements with landowners to protect the site, with compensation being paid for losses incurred by owners. To do this, many of the legal requirements focused on a duty to notify the NCC of threats to sites.

Despite an ever-increasing number of management agreements, by the late 1990s, a momentum had built up for further reform. Figures from a 1994 study by the National Audit Office reported that over one-fifth of SSSIs in England suffered loss and damage between 1987 and 1993.[22] And the annual reports of English Nature between 1996–97 and 2000–01 charted a significant decline in the percentage of sites the condition of which was favourable or improving, and corresponding increases in those identified as unfavourable, declining, or destroyed. These official reports also highlighted the changing threats to SSSIs—a point reinforced by a number of independent analyses.[23] Some threats, such as those arising from agriculture or development, had always been deliberately excluded from control. But other damaging activities were of more recent origin: these included the neglect of land (which creates difficult issues of management and control), activities by statutory undertakers, and recreational activities, such as quad biking.

In England and Wales, CROWA 2000 has addressed some of these problems and, in doing so, has shifted the policy of the law from voluntarism towards regulated site management.[24] As explained below, the NCC now has much greater powers to ban adverse activities and to require positive management, and, for this reason, the whole process of safeguarding SSSIs is more regulatory and increasingly legalistic. But the policy of the law has not shifted to one of 'command and control'. What lies behind the new law is a model, as the Department of Environment, Food and Rural Affairs (DEFRA) guidance puts it, of 'constructive dialogue and partnership'—albeit a partnership within which the bargaining position of the NCC has been significantly strengthened.

Government has imposed a public service agreement (PSA) target that, by 2010, 95 per cent of all land in SSSIs should either be in favourable condition or, if unfavourable, recovering. By October 2007, 76 per cent of land in SSSIs in England had met this target. (The comparable figure for English NNRs is 84 per cent.)

Notifying SSSIs

Where the Nature Conservancy Council are of the opinion that any area of land is of special interest by reason of any of its flora, fauna, or geological or physiographical features, it shall be the duty of the Council to notify that fact—

---

22 National Audit Office (1994) *Protecting and Managing Sites of Special Scientific Interest.*

23 T. Rowell (1991) *SSSIs: A Health Check*, London: Wildlife Link; WWF-UK (1997) *A Muzzled Watchdog? Is English Nature Protecting Wildlife?* The position in Scotland may be even worse.

24 See the guidance in Department for Environment, Food and Rural Affairs (2003) *SSSIs: Encouraging Positive Partnerships.*

(a) to the local planning authority in whose area the land is situated;

(b) to every owner and occupier of any of that land;[25] and

(c) to the Secretary of State.[26]

(Wildlife and Countryside Act 1981, s. 28(1))

As can be seen, the NCC is given a wide discretion both to formulate reasonable criteria for notification and to carry out the task of individual selection.

An important feature of WCA 1981, s. 28(1), is that the NCC has a *duty* to notify the people and bodies listed.[27] With the stronger regulatory measures introduced under CROWA 2000, the consequences of notification are that much greater—arguably, making the largely unaccountable nature of the notifying agencies more problematic (on which, see Box 19.2). Notifications must specify the special features of the site and must also list operations that the NCC considers likely to damage the site (see Box 19.3). Because a valid criticism of the 1981 Act was that landowners perceived notification as negative in nature, in line with the recognized need for active site management, CROWA 2000 now requires that notifications also contain a statement of the NCC's views about the management of the land, including any views about the conservation and enhancement of flora or fauna, or other notified features (s. 28(4)). Management statements for all existing SSSIs had to be made by the end of January 2006. Since NERC 2006 only reasonable steps need now be taken to serve a notification (and to serve a range of other notices etc.—see s. 70B, WCA 1981). This is an important change, because one reason why land has not been notified, or notified quickly enough, has been delays in tracking down all of the owners (a particular problem in relation to, for example, common land).

The nature of the duty to notify was discussed in *R v. Nature Conservancy Council, ex parte London Brick Co. Ltd* [1996] Env LR 1, which concerned a challenge to the notification of an SSSI relating to old clay pits on a brickworks in Peterborough. May J discussed the procedures for establishing an SSSI and decided that there were, in fact, two steps involved.

1. Under s. 28(1), a *duty* is imposed on the NCC to notify a site that fulfils the appropriate scientific criteria. This notification has provisional effect, but a period of three months is provided during which representations or objections can be made.

2. The NCC must consider these representations or objections and then has a *discretion* whether to confirm the notification (with or without modifications). If confirmation is not made within nine months of the date on which the notification was served, the notification lapses.[28]

In *Fisher v. English Nature* [2004] Env LR 7, however, Lightman J took a different approach. Although s. 28 states that the site 'may' be confirmed, the judge noted that, if the NCC continues to believe that the criteria for listing are satisfied, then it can only exercise its discretion one way—that is, to confirm. If it were not to do so, then even if the site were not confirmed as an SSSI, it would still satisfy the criteria for notification and the NCC would have to notify again; Lightman J clearly thought that it would absurd if this were required. Hence (at para. 18): '*Section 28(1) affords scope for judgement; it affords no scope for discretion.*' This approach was essentially approved of by the Court of Appeal ([2005] Env LR 10), although the court stressed that confirmation '*is to be exercised in accordance with the conclusion reached as a*

---

25 Including commoners—see DEFRA (2003) para. 15 (a provision originally in the Bill). See also the discussion of public bodies' duties at p. 702.

26 Since CROWA 2000, the general public is now also notified through advertising—see p. 703. The Nature Conservation (Scotland) Act 2004 requires a much wider range of bodies and interested parties to be notified.

27 Notably, the Secretary of State has no power of direction over the NCC regarding SSSI notifications: see EPA 1990, ss. 131(4) and 132(1)(a).

28 Under WCA 1981, s. 28(4A), now WCA 1981, s. 28(5) (as amended by CROWA 2000).

result of the outcome of a genuine, open-minded consultation/investigation process' (para. 135) between notification and confirmation.

In *London Brick*, May J accepted that English Nature's policy normally to confirm a notification unless the site is unavoidably going to be destroyed[29] is a reasonable policy and he upheld the confirmation. And in *Fisher*, Lightman J held that the NCC could not refuse to confirm simply because the species or habitat might be better conserved through other means—for example, voluntary agreements, or even under EC conservation law![30] In the interests of natural justice, however, confirmation must be on the same basis as notification[31] and, following CROWA 2000, a confirmation cannot add to the list of potentially damaging operations or extend the area to which the designation applies (s. 28(7)).

The implications of the decisions in *London Brick* and in *Fisher* are significant, because they both strongly suggest that it would be illegal for the NCC to refuse to notify on political or tactical grounds (although it must exercise its 'opinion', not rigidly apply rules, and it could arguably refuse to confirm a notification if, as a matter of expert judgment, the conservation interest on the site was doomed). So it may well be possible for an environmental group to succeed in an action to compel the NCC to notify—and, if *Fisher* is followed, confirm—a site.[32] Conversely, it will be difficult to mount a successful challenge against an unwelcome notification in cases in which, in the NCC's opinion, the requisite special interest can be shown. Thus, in *R (on the application of Western Power Distribution Investments Ltd) v. Countryside Council for Wales* [2007] Env LR 25, in which there was conflicting ecological evidence submitted by both parties, the Court thought it was acceptable for CCW to prefer its own evidence and did not venture into trying to assess which side's evidence was 'better'.

A further effect of this definition is that the list is not unchanging. New SSSIs will be notified as new information about sites—or about species ecology—is acquired and as the importance of safeguarding certain habitats increases.[33] It must also be understood that, in an age when sites are being damaged and destroyed, one site may become of greater importance simply because of the loss of another site. The NCC now has formal power to denotify a site, or part of a site, that is not of special interest,[34] although, in doing so, the Environment Agency and certain statutory undertakers—as well as the original parties notified—are effectively given up to nine months to make representations before the denotification is confirmed. This breathing space mirrors the two-stage process to notification in s. 28(1) and (5).

BOX 19.2 **Notifying sites of special scientific interest (SSSIs) and human rights law**

In many ways, the legal rules under which sites are notified as SSSIs seem outdated in modern regulatory terms. Officers of the relevant nature conservancy council (NCC) normally make the notification and there is no scope formally for the landowner or the general public to comment until the start of the nine-month confirmation period (in practice, there is dialogue with the landowner before notification takes place). Thereafter, the eventual decision to confirm is taken by the NCC Council—a classic quango—from which there is no right to appeal (in practice, the Council

---

29 But see comment on the *Aggregate Industries* case in Box 19.2.

30 *Fisher v. English Nature* [2004] Env LR 7, [20].

31 *R v. Nature Conservancy Council, ex parte Bolton Metropolitan Borough Council* [1995] Env LR 237.

32 In *R (on the application of Western Power Distribution Investments Ltd) v. Countryside Council for Wales* [2007] Env LR 25, the policy of CCW only to notify sites under some kind of threat was held to be lawful; what mattered was whether the site met the criteria for notification.

33 See, on this, *R (Aggregate Industries Ltd) v. English Nature* [2003] Env LR 3, [110]–[118].

34 Although there was no express power to do so, between 1981 and 1991, 579 SSSIs (around 15 per cent of the total) were denotified because they had lost the features making them 'special'.

makes its decision in open session, following any representations).[35] This procedure reflects the extent to which identifying SSSIs has always been presented as a process within which experts make judgments and take decisions on the basis of specialist knowledge.

R (Aggregate Industries Ltd) v. English Nature [2003] Env LR 3, the facts of which are mentioned below, raised the compatibility of this process with the 'due process' protections under Art. 6 of the European Convention on Human Rights (see p. 380). It was argued that, because the Council of English Nature confirms decisions made by its officers, this could not be done independently and impartially.[36] The High Court held that, because of the impact on landowners' rights to use their land, SSSI designation did involve Art. 6 rights.[37] But while the dispute was effectively between English Nature's officers and the landowner, the role of the Council of English Nature in confirming the SSSI notification was human rights-compliant. This was because of various procedural safeguards for landowners, such as the right to make informed representations, to appeal a refusal to consent to an activity, and to ask for the notification to be varied or revoked. But the position of English Nature as an expert conservation body, exercising its judgment on difficult questions of scientific policy, was also important. In cases in which such expert bodies take decisions, then the ordinary right to seek judicial review may be enough for the process as a whole to conform to human rights law.[38]

What is notable from this decision, then, is that the human rights issues are being decided in the light of the entire body of rules governing the designation and control of SSSIs. But the decision also confirms the status of the NCC as an expert agency whose decisions about the conservation value of land will only rarely be challengeable in the courts. In this case, s. 28 was not challenged as violating the right to property contained in Art. 1 of the First Protocol to the Convention. This has been raised in subsequent cases,[39] but so far this argument has been rejected.

It is up to the NCC to define the exact boundaries of the SSSI. In the *Aggregate Industries* case (see Box 19.2), it was held that the whole of a large tract of afforested land could be notified, even though the rotational plantation and management of the site meant that, at any one time, only certain areas would, in fact, provide suitable habitat (a mix of open and overgrown land) for the bird species that the NCC was aiming to conserve (especially woodlark and nightjar). This is a variant of the principle that emerged from *Sweet v. Secretary of State and Nature Conservancy Council* [1989] JEL 245, in which it appeared permissible for land of lesser intrinsic scientific interest to be notified if it is part of the same environmental unit as land that is of interest, but it avoids any doubt (s. 28B). The new provision, however, makes no mention of what might be described as surrounding 'buffer lands' and it must now be doubted whether they may be notified.[40] One geographical limitation, however, is that while inland waters are included within the definition of 'land' in the Act, SSSIs cannot be

---

35 In Scotland, there is an independent review body that advises Scottish Natural Heritage when the scientific basis for notification is challenged.

36 A second challenge under Art. 6 was that the procedures under the 1981 Act were not fair and public, but, since 2001, meetings of the Council are held in public and landowners are given the chance to make written and oral representations, and this argument was rejected. Note that the same grounds had been successfully argued in *William Sinclair Holdings Ltd v. English Nature* [2002] Env LR 4, but not on the basis of a full hearing and fully argued determination.

37 *Oerlemans v. The Netherlands* (1991) 15 EHRR 561.

38 See now *Runa Begum v. Tower Hamlets London Borough Council* [2003] UKHL 5.

39 See *Fisher v. English Nature* [2005] Env LR 10 and *Trailer and Marina (Leven) Ltd v. Secretary of State for the Environment, Food and Rural Affairs* [2004] EWCA Civ 1580 (see p. 701).

40 The NCC now has a power to designate 'extra land' (WCA 1981, s. 28B), but this can only be done after notification of the SSSI and is probably a provision intended to allow the boundaries of large SSSIs to be corrected

notified for waters below the low-water mark (thus excluding many estuaries). In the absence of effective specialist designations for the marine environment, marine nature conservation therefore continues to be afforded secondary legal status at national level (see further Box 19.1).

There is also the question of whether land should be notified where the species it hosts are only there temporarily. The Act does not say anything about this, but it is Natural England's policy to notify sites even if they are only of temporary significance for internationally important species (this might be the case where, as in the SSSI at the centre of the *Aggregate Industries* case, afforested land only provides suitable habitat until the tree crop closes over).[41] It is not clear whether, in practice, the NCC will also apply this policy to SSSIs that are only of national importance, but it would appear to be defendable because the presence of any species on a site is, to some extent, temporary, and the more temporary the occupation, the less that there will be any adverse consequences to the landowner in the longer term (because the site can be denotified).

A final point of note here is that, until CROWA 2000, the NCC had no power to enter land to decide whether it should be notified as an SSSI. This absurd situation has now been corrected and the NCC may enter any land to determine whether it should be designated. (These powers of entry also extend to entering land to check its condition and to investigate whether any criminal offences have been committed—a necessary power in light of the strengthening to the law discussed below.)

Duties on owners and occupiers

Once SSSIs have been notified, the previous position was that owners and occupiers were placed under a reciprocal duty. They had to notify the NCC in writing before carrying out any operation likely to damage an SSSI (see Box 19.3). But four months after this notification, or earlier if the written consent of the NCC was obtained, the operation could go ahead unimpeded—unless it required and failed to get planning permission. It was an offence 'without reasonable excuse' to carry out a potentially damaging operation either without notifying the NCC, or within the four-month period, but the maximum penalty was only a £2,500 fine.

Until CROWA 2000, then, the restrictive effect of designation as an SSSI was therefore only to impose a four-month ban on potentially damaging operations. These provisions illustrate the voluntary mechanism that, until recently, was the favoured policy approach. The whole purpose of the law was to give the NCC an opportunity to persuade the owner or occupier not to act in a harmful manner—if necessary, by negotiating a management agreement. As the figures mentioned above about the declining condition of SSSIs showed, however, this approach left a lot to be desired.

As Lord Mustill observed in *Southern Water Authority v. Nature Conservancy Council* [1992] 1 WLR 775:

It needs only a moment to see that this regime is toothless, for it demands no more from the owner or occupier of an SSSI than a little patience…In truth the Act does no more in the great majority of cases than give the council a breathing space within which to apply moral pressure, with a view to persuading the owner or occupier to make a voluntary agreement.[42]

---

without having to renotify the whole site, rather than to allow for buffer land to be designated (although S. Payne [2001] ELM 239 takes a different view). The 'subheading' in the legislation speaks of 'enlargement'.

41 See also *Fisher v. English Nature* [2004] Env LR 7, in which the confirmation as an SSSI of a large tract of cultivated land was upheld despite the migratory stone curlews only occupying the habitat from March to October and changing their sites annually with the rotation of the crops (upheld [2005] Env LR 10).

42 At 778.

Under s. 29 of WCA 1981, slightly stronger powers were available for areas subject to a nature conservation order. These were mainly used to protect sites imminently threatened with destruction and, for awkward landowners, provided a longer period to agree a management agreement and carried with it the threat of compulsory purchase. But these powers were sparingly used; there was no duty to make orders—only about forty were ever made—and the NCC never used these compulsory purchase powers as a result of a dispute over conservation.

Following CROWA 2000, the ability to impose obligations on landowners and occupiers has increased significantly, with the result that nature conservation orders have been abolished (because all SSSIs now receive greater protection than sites designated under WCA 1981, s. 29). A dual approach is taken, depending on whether the threat to the SSSI is prospective or ongoing.

(a) Prospective threats

If a potentially damaging operation is to be carried out, the NCC must still be notified, but the major change is that it may now refuse consent indefinitely (s. 28E). Failure to respond to the request for consent is taken to be a deemed refusal, closing completely the former 'waiting period' approach. Harmful activities can only be carried out, therefore, if the NCC consents, or if the work is carried out under a management agreement or management scheme (see below), and it is an offence, subject to a fine of up to £20,000 in the magistrates' court or an unlimited fine in the Crown Court, to cause or permit a potentially damaging operation to be carried out (s. 28P(1)). In setting fine levels, courts must have regard to any actual or potential financial benefit that accrues to the offender (s. 28P(9)). When compared to other environmental law offences, however, and especially to species conservation offences (see p. 725), the absence of even limited custodial sanctions for this and other offences relating to habitat conservation is remarkable.

BOX 19.3 Operations likely to damage SSSIs

Where the threat to a site of special scientific interest (SSSI) is from future activities, the relevant nature conservancy council (NCC) must specify the features of the land that are of special interest (see above), but must also specify any operations that are likely to damage those features. What, then, are 'operations likely to damage' (often referred to as a 'potentially damaging operations')?

The courts have made it clear that 'operation' can include virtually anything that has an impact on the site, and 'operations' is not limited to its meaning under town and country planning legislation. In *Sweet v. Secretary of State and Nature Conservancy Council* [1989] JEL 245, it was held to include:

cultivation, including ploughing, rotavation, harrowing and reseeding; grazing; mowing or other methods of cutting vegetation; application of manure, fertilisers and lime; burning; the release into the site of any wild feral or domestic animal, reptile, amphibian, bird, fish or invertebrate, or any plant or seed; the storage of materials; the use of materials; the use of vehicles or craft likely to damage or disturb features of interest.

Such things as drainage, building operations, and the application of pesticides are clearly covered. Because it is impossible to predict all the threats to an SSSI or the amount of damage that a particular activity will do, the listed activities on any SSSI—which are modified from a national template—is necessarily lengthy and general. One consequence of this is that the vast majority of requests for consent to undertake a potentially damaging operation are granted, because they will relate to listed activities at the innocuous end of the spectrum (for example, taking down a dangerous tree on an SSSI in relation to which tree management is a listed operation).

One thing that is not an 'operation', however, is doing nothing and, on many sites, neglect will be as detrimental as wilful damage to the conservation interest. A good example of this is the species of water beetle threatened in *R v. Nature Conservancy Council, ex parte London Brick Co. Ltd* [1996] Env LR 1 following the decision to stop pumping out the pits. For this reason, the Countryside and Rights of Way Act 2000 uses a different mechanism—the management scheme—to combat this type of conservation problem.

Finally, what does 'likely' mean? In the Scottish case of *North Uist Fisheries Ltd v. Secretary of State for Scotland* 1992 SLT 333, the judge suggested that 'likely' required any potential damage to be probable rather than a bare possibility. This interpretation was obiter and it is unlikely to be followed today, not least because, as the case law on EC conservation law shows, the courts are much more inclined to give terms like this a precautionary interpretation (see p. 711).

Consents may be made subject to conditions and may be time-limited. Consents can also be modified or withdrawn at any time, although only if the NCC compensates for losses incurred (s. 28M). In practice, most consents are granted. Figures for 2002–03 show that, out of 1,836 requests to carry out a potentially damaging operation, English Nature refused nine and made 138 subject to conditions.

To balance the restrictions imposed by this new approach, however, in cases of conflict, landowners and occupiers may appeal to the Secretary of State or Welsh Assembly. A hearing or public inquiry must be held if this is requested either by the landowner or occupier or the NCC, and, in effect, the Secretary of State determines the request for consent afresh (s. 28F). The right to appeal is a significant factor in the courts' holding the notification process to be human rights-compliant (see Box 19.2), but there is little scope for other interested parties to voice their opinions, not least because landowners need only notify the NCC of their proposals, the NCC need not publicize these, and hearings may be held in private. Guidance recommends the use of mediation.

As things stand, under CROWA 2000, the only legal criteria against which the NCC must decide whether to allow or refuse a potentially damaging operation, or which guide the Minister when hearing an appeal, is the general duty that both have (along with all other public bodies) to further the conservation and enhancement of the features that justified notification of the land as an SSSI (see p. 702). Unlike other public bodies, however, which will usually be subject to conflicting duties (for example, the Forestry Commission's duty to provide timber), it may be possible to bring an action in judicial review against the NCC if it were to consent to activities that did not further an SSSI's conservation and enhancement.[43] It is notable that, in Scotland, there is a right to appeal to the Scottish Land Court on the merits, not simply to seek a judicial review of the legality of the restriction.[44]

(b) Ongoing problems

In the case of ongoing problems with an SSSI, such as might arise from neglect or poor management, positive regulation can be required. The NCC may propose a 'management scheme' (s. 28J) for the conservation or restoration of an SSSI and must, after at least three months' consultation, serve this on every owner and occupier. From the time that the proposals are first served, the NCC has nine months in which to decide whether the scheme will take effect.

---

43 Although, under s. 37 of the Countryside Act 1968, the NCC must also have due regard to the needs of agriculture and forestry, and to the economic and social interests of rural areas.

44 It had been proposed that this appeal would have to consider whether Scottish National Heritage acted reasonably and proportionately, an alternative course of action would not damage the SSSI, and social or economic benefits of national importance outweigh the adverse effects on the SSSI. These steps have some similarities with those required in relation to 'European sites' under EC law (see p. 709), but also some important differences. For example, there is no mention of a requirement to undertake action to compensate for damage that is consented.

Modifications to the scheme can be made, but not if the final scheme would be more oner-ous on the landowner or occupier. In effect, therefore, the consultation period may only be used to ameliorate the strictness of any obligations being proposed (although it is open to the NCC at any time to propose a new management scheme with more stringent conditions).

A twin-track approach is taken to securing compliance with management schemes. First, the NCC must try to agree a reasonable management agreement with the landowner, so this remains the preferred policy approach. But if it cannot reach agreement, management schemes can be enforced by serving 'management notices' (s. 28K). Management notices allow the NCC to require reasonable measures to ensure that the land is managed in accord-ance with the management scheme. For example, in order to conserve bird habitat, the NCC might serve a management notice that scrub be cleared. If the notice is not complied with, the NCC can enter the site and carry out the works itself, including restoration works, char-ging to the owner or occupier any reasonable costs incurred. There may be cases, however, in which it will simply not be feasible for the NCC to undertake the work itself (for example, if the problem is undergrazing, the NCC might be reluctant to add extra livestock itself). In these situations, the only available sanction will be to seek a fine against the landowner for not complying with the management notice.

Management notices may be appealed along similar lines to appeals relating to consents. One notable difference, however, is that landowners can appeal on the grounds that another owner or occupier of the SSSI is responsible for its conservation or restoration. This might apply, for example, in cases in which there are multiple owners and occupiers of an SSSI (as might be the case, for example, with common land) and there is a dispute about where responsibility for the site's inadequate conservation or restoration lies. In this situation, the Secretary of State must engage in a balancing exercise, deciding, as between the various landowners and occupiers, on whose shoulders responsibility under the management notice should lie. This is done according to a matrix of factors that try to ensure that responsibility is imposed equitably: the relative interests of landowners and occupiers in the land, their relative responsibility for the unfavourable state of the SSSI, and the relative degree of benefit to be derived from carrying out the requirements of the management notice.

The provision for management notices is a considerable advance from the old law, under which restoration of an SSSI could only be required if a nature conservation order was breached. Because of the requirement to try to agree a reasonable management agreement, however—and because policy guidance suggests that notices will only be used in exceptional circumstances—these new measures may only go a limited way towards shifting the finan-cial burden of addressing environmental damage or degradation from the public purse to the landowner (although they should strengthen the hand of the NCC in negotiating man-agement agreements).

Defences

Taken together, these new obligations on landowners and occupiers clearly strike at the heart of the voluntary principle—but they do not completely circumscribe landowners' and occupiers' control of their land. This is because CROWA 2000 continues the previous policy of the law in, first, exempting operations carried out in an emergency, but also, and much more importantly, making it a reasonable excuse to carry out a potentially damaging opera-tion if the local planning authority has granted planning permission. This does not include an automatic planning permission,[45] but it does mean that a planning permission consid-ered on its merits still trumps any controls that the NCC may impose on an SSSI (see further below).

A further defence arises when an activity has been carried out in accordance with a con-sent from any public body (for example, a drainage authority). This new provision is in line

---

45 That is, one granted by the General Permitted Development Order: see WCA 1981, s. 28P(4).

with changes made under CROWA 2000, under which public bodies must engage in a dialogue with the NCC before granting authorizations (see p. 703).

Planning permission

In addition to any controls specific to SSSIs, planning permission is required for operations and material changes of use that fall within the definition of 'development' (see p. 393). If the application relates to an SSSI or is likely to affect an SSSI, or relates to development within a 2-km 'consultation area' around an SSSI, the local planning authority must consult with the NCC before making a decision.[46] The objective is the familiar one of informing the NCC in advance of a potential threat to the site, so that it may give advice or offer a management agreement. Prior to the 1981 Act, this was the *only* legal protection for SSSIs.

These requirements are very limited in practice. Many activities likely to damage SSSIs, such as those relating to agriculture, forestry, and works carried out by statutory undertakers, are not covered by the need for planning permission, either because they are not development or because they are granted exemption. In any case, the local planning authority is not bound by the NCC's advice—it is only one material consideration to be taken into account. The economic and other arguments in favour of the development may well outweigh the need to protect the SSSI. For example, in 1990, Havering District Council granted outline planning permission for a large theme park on Rainham Marshes, the largest SSSI in Greater London. The Secretary of State refused to call the application in, even though this would have been the largest ever loss of SSSI land to a development with planning permission. In another example, Poole Borough Council granted itself planning permission for housing on Canford Heath, an SSSI within the town's boundaries. After an unsuccessful High Court challenge (*R v. Poole Borough Council, ex parte Beebee* [1991] JPL 643), the Secretary of State took the almost unprecedented step of revoking the planning permission.

English policy on planning and nature conservation is currently set out in Planning Policy Statement 9 (2005) *Biodiversity and Geological Conservation*. As well as explaining the various statutory and international protections, PPS 9 emphasizes that the nature conservation interest of a site, and the importance of the site in national and international terms, is clearly a material consideration when it comes to a decision whether to grant planning permission. But it goes further than this and seems to suggest that, if negative impacts cannot be avoided, mitigated, or compensated for, then harmful development should not go ahead.[47] PPS 9 is also notable for giving Ramsar sites the same weight in planning decision making as sites designated under EC Directives.

If planning permission is granted for development, then, as noted above, it acts as a defence to a prosecution for damaging an SSSI (s. 28(8)). This does not only apply to new permissions; it also exempts existing mineral and peat extraction permissions over SSSIs from the 1981 Act. These relate to sites that tend not to have been identified as of importance when the permission was originally granted. The NCC's options are limited and all involve the payment of potentially large sums of money, because:

- revocation of the planning permission entails a liability to pay compensation;

- a management agreement would probably have to compensate for lost profits;

- compulsory purchase will normally be at the market price (see Box 19.4).

---

46 Town and Country Planning (General Development Procedure) Order 1995, art. 10.

47 And see also Office of the Deputy Prime Minister (2005) Circular 06/2005; DEFRA (2005) Circular 01/2005. On this sequential approach, see further p. 383.

BOX 19.4 **Buying out conservation interests**

The raised mires at Thorne and Hatfield Moors in Yorkshire are important for their species richness, and as a paleo-environmental resource. For these reasons, some of the Moors is owned and managed by Natural England as a national nature reserve (NNR), while this and other areas are sites of special scientific interest (SSSIs). But the Moors are also a rich source of peat extracted under long-standing planning permissions. These, of course, 'trump' the SSSI designations (see above). The Moors became something of a conservation *cause célèbre* in the 1990s when English Nature suggested that they might be denotified (although, in the end, SSSI status was maintained). For many, the visible removal of much of the conservation interest by lawful peat stripping seemed to embody key inadequacies of the Wildlife and Countryside Act 1981 and peat-winning machinery at Thorne Moor was damaged by the protest group EarthFirst.

The identification of much of this land—and land at Wedholme Flow in Cumbria—as a proposed special area of conservation under the EC Habitats Directive (92/43/EEC), however, meant that these planning permissions needed to be reviewed for their compatibility with EC conservation law (see p. 716). This led the main stakeholders—the peat extractors (Scotts), English Nature, and the government—to review the sites' prospects. The outcome was that, for over £18m, English Nature essentially bought Scott's freehold or leasehold interests in the land, as well as its interests in the peat itself. Although, in time, Natural England will manage the sites, it also paid Scotts to undertake initial restoration work.[48]

The buy-out of these peat moors is a good illustration of the continuing need, despite the shift in approach taken by the Countryside and Rights of Way Act 2000, to pay certain landowners not to damage conservation interests. When the damaging activity has planning permission, the only real course of action for the relevant nature conservancy council (NCC) is to compensate the owner for the loss of the income that the permission would have generated. In other words, the planning permission gives the landowner a legitimate expectation about future profits that, if it is to be lost, the law must compensate (see below). But compare farming: this does not require planning permission, so there is nothing equivalent that the state has given and hence nothing to be compensated. At best, farmers receive public money to encourage particular activities and—as recent changes indicate—this can be redirected towards different objectives (or, in theory, simply removed—see Chapter 20).

A final point is to consider the impact of a new SSSI designation on land such as peat moors. As long as the peat removal is carried out under a valid planning permission, the extractor will not suffer any loss directly from the designation; in principle, removal can continue. But the extractor may suffer losses because of pressure on consumers not to buy peat taken from designated conservation areas. If so, the law will not compensate for the loss of market share, because this arises not because of any taking of rights by the state, but because of the actions of retailers and individual consumers.

Management agreements

Management agreements are effectively contracts in which owners or occupiers of land agree to manage it in the interests of nature conservation in return for payment from the NCC.[49]

---

48 A more detailed summary of the agreement can be found via Natural England's website.

49 A contractual approach also lies behind the use of planning obligations to secure nature conservation gain—see p. 414 above. Land of outstanding scientific interest may also qualify for tax relief—see English Nature (1992) *Capital Taxation and Nature Conservation.*

In England, at least, the law on management agreements was overhauled under NERC 2006 and there are now very general powers for Natural England to enter into 'SSSI agreements' for a wide range of purposes (see s. 7, NERC 2006). (In Wales and in Scotland, restrictions still limit agreements to SSSI land or adjacent land, and only restrictive agreements will bind successors in title under the Countryside Act 1968, s. 15.) This is in line with the current policy preference for securing agreements that are, above all, based on ecological coherence (and—in England, at least—it is a good example of how the environmental imperative of managing land for conservation is now seen as being more important than a traditional property law restriction protecting third parties). As will already be clear, the possibility of a management agreement underpinned the voluntary approach to nature conservation favoured by successive administrations until CROWA 2000 (although they were little used before WCA 1981 and, even after 1981, the great majority of potentially damaging operations notices were resolved without using agreements).

Historically, a valid criticism of management agreements was that—because, as a matter of government policy, they were based on assessing the net profits foregone or the difference in capital values with or without the restriction, which includes such things as lost agricultural grants or lost revenues had the land been converted to a more profitable use[50]—they compensated landowners for *not* doing something desirable (in this case, positive management), which is both inefficient and poor conservation policy.[51] There was even the suggestion that, in order to claim for 'lost profits', some enterprising landowners threatened works they never really intended to undertake, putting the NCC in the invidious position of having to decide whether to call the landowners' bluff.[52] Even prior to CROWA 2000, however, such compensatory agreements were, in practice, being replaced by agreements under which positive management was encouraged[53] and it is these types of payment that now predominate.

The changes to management agreement policy that were already taking place have now been formalized in guidance that makes it clear that, for *new* operations, payment will not be made unless there is some positive conservation benefit.[54] As Ouseley J said in *Trailer and Marina (Leven) Ltd v. Secretary of State for the Environment, Food and Rural Affairs* [2004] EWHC 153 (Admin), an unsuccessful challenge that the decision not to continue compensating a canal owner for lost profits breached his or her property rights under Art. 1 of the First Protocol to the European Convention on Human Rights: '*The restriction on compensation reflects a changing view over time as to the relationship between an owner's rights and the public interest, the importance of which has grown significantly.*'[55]

But agreements will still compensate for income foregone (although this will be assessed in the light of payments received for positive land management), and payment is *required* if an existing consent is modified or withdrawn and the owner or occupier suffers loss, or if a stop notice is issued (CROWA 2000, s. 28M(1), and Sch. 11, paras 9 and 17, respectively). It is not merely the guidance that has changed: the whole context within which management agreements were once negotiated has now changed and, unless a potentially damaging

---

50 See the Appendix to Department of Environment Circular 4/83.

51 Probably the worst example of how the former guidelines worked is *Cameron v. Nature Conservancy Council* 1991 SLT (Lands Tribunal) 85. The system was nicely captured in the unofficial acronym CUCO—that is, 'cough up and clear off'.

52 In most cases, proprietors brought forward proposals that they had only tentatively been thinking about—see L. Livingstone, J. Rowan-Robinson, and R. Cunningham (1990) *Management Agreements for Nature Conservation in Scotland*, Aberdeen: University of Aberdeen.

53 In England, the Wildlife Enhancement Scheme; in Wales, Tir Gofal (the latter being a 'whole farm' scheme, which has always extended beyond land notified as an SSSI and which integrates environmentally sensitive area payments). See C. Rodgers and J. Bishop (1998) *Management Agreements for Nature Conservation*, London: RICS.

54 Department of Environment, Transport and the Regions (2001) *Guidelines on Management Agreement Payments and Other Related Matters.*

55 At [94]. Upheld on appeal—see [2004] EWCA Civ 1580.

operation will be undertaken under a planning permission (see, for example, Box 19.3), the NCC's bargaining position has been strengthened considerably. Even in areas in which seeking a management agreement remains the policy of the law, as with management schemes, the context is different, because although the law requires the NCC to enter into 'reasonable' agreements, management notices (that government guidance indicates are to be used exceptionally) still exist as a theoretical further tier of controls. And there are also revised powers to compulsorily purchase sites in relation to which either the NCC:

- cannot conclude, on reasonable terms, a management agreement; or

- has entered into an agreement, but it is being breached in such a way that the land is not being managed satisfactorily.[56]

As with the pre-CROWA position, however, it must be unlikely that these powers will be greatly used, because of the expense involved and because it is rarely an effective use of the NCC's resources.[57]

Duties on public bodies

A further limitation of the original 1981 Act was that, while criminal liability for carrying out a potentially damaging operation within the four-month 'waiting' period was strict, it could only be committed by owners and occupiers of the SSSI. (Owners and occupiers know about the designation of a site, either because they are notified, or because it is a local land charge—s. 28(9).)

This restriction was given a narrow meaning by the courts. In *Southern Water Authority v. Nature Conservancy Council* [1992] 1 WLR 775, the House of Lords decided that, for the purposes of s. 28, someone is an occupier if they have some form of stable relationship with the land. As a result, a water authority that carried out drainage works while temporarily on an SSSI did not commit an offence under s. 28, even though it knew that these were potentially damaging operations and that they would cause significant harm to the SSSI (pointedly, the House of Lords referred to the authority's actions as 'ecological vandalism').

CROWA 2000 strengthened the law in relation to a wide range of public bodies and privatized utilities (superseding specific duties on water and sewerage undertakers, and on the Environment Agency), although it is significant that it has done so essentially using a beefed-up version of the advice-based approach described above. New duties are now imposed on all public bodies, including:

- government Ministers and departments, and the National Assembly for Wales;

- local authorities—for example, local planning authorities;

- statutory undertakers, including private utilities.

These public bodies are placed under a duty—similar to the general conservation duties on the Environment Agency other than in relation to its pollution control functions (see p. 117)—to take reasonable steps, consistent with the proper exercise of their functions, to further the conservation and enhancement of the features that justified notification of the land as an SSSI. For environmental law, this is quite a strongly worded provision, although it is probably enforceable (by judicial review) in only the most flagrant of cases. Public bodies must also give at least 28 days' notice of any operations that are likely to harm any feature of special interest within an SSSI. This duty applies regardless of whether the operations are

---

56 WCA 1981, s. 28N, and see also CROWA 2000, s. 75(4).

57 An interesting contrast is Danish law, under which compensation is provided 'in kind' by the state buying good farming land and exchanging it for high nature conservation land held by farmers. The NCC cannot do this, because it has no power to purchase land that is not designated as an SSSI, unless it is subject to a management agreement: CROWA 2000, ss. 28N and 75(4).

to take place within the SSSI. After notice is given, the NCC can either assent to the works (with or without conditions) or it may refuse to assent. If no assent is given, or if it is made conditional, then the public authority must not carry out the works without giving written notice of how it has taken into account the NCC's advice and giving at least a further 28 days' notice. Unless there is a reasonable excuse for 'jumping the gun', if it does so, the authority will commit an offence.

These provisions, then, are not intended to prevent harmful activities using licensing-type powers, but, in line with the general policy approach, try to create a dialogue between the public authority and the NCC, and guidance requires the advice of the NCC to be given due weight and less damaging alternatives to be considered.[58] They mean, however, that an undertaker that is also an owner or occupier is subject to less stringent duties than other owners and occupiers, which, as a matter of principle, does not seem justified.[59] CROWA 2000 does, however, also require public authorities to minimize damage caused by their operations and, as far as is reasonably practicable, to restore any damaged features, which provides a regulatory 'bottom line' to this advice-focused approach. Breach of these provisions makes a public authority liable to a fine, in the magistrates' court, of up to £20,000 or, in the Crown Court, an unlimited fine, and, as with offences carried out by owners and occupiers, fines must be set with regard to any benefit accruing.

Similar provisions to these apply to works that, although not undertaken by public authorities, are authorized by them (see p. 698). These provisions would apply, for example, to impacts on an SSSI such as increased run-off from a housing development granted planning permission by a local planning authority. But there is no criminal sanction against any public authority that authorizes works in breach of the Act (although the matter might be referred to Ministers and there is the option of judicial review).

Duties on the general public

A further implication of the restriction in WCA 1981 to activities by owners and occupiers was that members of the general public were not placed under any legal obligations in relation to SSSIs.[60] This was understandable in policy terms when the main threats were seen as coming from development and adverse land management, but became increasingly untenable the more that new threats to SSSIs emerged from activities carried out by outsiders (for example, bait digging or off-road motorcycling).

CROWA 2000 made it an offence for *any* person intentionally or recklessly to destroy or damage an SSSI, or intentionally or recklessly to disturb a site's fauna. The person must, however, know that what is destroyed, damaged, or disturbed is within an SSSI (which explains why notifications must now also be advertised). The offence only extends to the special interest of the land and does not extend to *any* damage to an SSSI. But it is clear that the extent of knowledge that needs to be shown is only that the land is an SSSI; members of the public need not know of the specific conservation importance and management requirements of the features of the site that are damaged. NERC 2006 stretched criminal liability even further by adding a further offence of intentional or reckless destruction or damage to the listed features, or disturbing the listed fauna, of an SSSI even in the absence of such knowledge, although the proposed fine is much less (a maximum of £2,500).

The penalties are similar to those on public bodies—but an exception is made in cases in which the damaging activity occurs under planning permission (and other statutory

---

58 DEFRA (2003) *Sites of Special Scientific Interest: Encouraging Positive Partnerships*, para. 75. On reflexive environmental regulation, see Chapter 8.

59 That is, CROWA 2000 has not reversed the *Southern Water Authority* case by deeming undertakers to be 'occupiers'. A pragmatic factor behind this may be the difficulty of notifying undertakers qua occupiers.

60 Anyone could commit an offence on a site where a nature conservation order had been made under WCA 1981, s. 29, a position justified by the publicity given to such orders. These were little used.

consent, if this is needed and validly obtained), or occurs in an emergency. One implication of this is that an offence will be committed if a non-owner or occupier does something that a public body has consented but where the public body has not itself complied with the Act (although it must be doubted whether the NCC would ever prosecute in such circumstances).

National habitat law—conclusions

It is wise not to overstate the reforms to the law on SSSIs initiated under CROWA 2000. It is true that the policy of the law is no longer voluntaristic and that there is an ever more legalistic, and punitive, edge to the legislative scheme, but, following CROWA 2000, the main mechanism remains the use of financial incentives, rather than negative controls. The main difference is probably that, in reaching agreements, the hand of the NCC has been strengthened by its power to refuse to give its consent to activities, whereas previously its ultimate sanction was compulsory purchase and the whole context of the law was hostile to this approach. CROWA 2000 has therefore responded to some of the specific, day-to-day problems encountered under the previous legislation and, for the first time, actually seems intended—and able—to protect sites. But it does not appear to herald a radical change in realigning the balance between the interests of private landowners and of the public in conserving nature.

Habitat conservation—EC law

In terms of their direct impact on UK conservation law, two EC Directives have had the greatest influence and will continue to be of paramount importance in the future:

- Directive 79/409/EC on the Conservation of Wild Birds (the 1979 Wild Birds Directive);
- Directive 92/43/EC on the Conservation of Natural Habitats and of Wild Fauna and Flora (the 1992 Habitats Directive).

Together, these contain some important provisions on the protection of individual animals and plants (which we discuss below), but arguably their greatest impact is in relation to habitat conservation. As with sites protected under national law, the key to understanding the law in this area is to keep a clear distinction between the law relating to the designation of sites and the laws governing the level of protection of these sites.[61] As with SSSIs, the latter are usually weaker and more flexible than the former, especially when it comes to taking economic interests into account.

EC habitat conservation law and policy

A central aim of EC law is to designate a Community-wide network of sites (known as 'Natura 2000') that are important for their conservation importance. These sites are designated, and conserved, under Community law and the legal tool used is the Directive, giving member States such as the UK a certain flexibility about the way in which the Directives' binding obligations are achieved.

The UK approach to implementation—and some of the shortcomings of this—is discussed below, but at this point, it is worth emphasizing that habitat conservation law is

---

61 The Habitats Directive also includes some more general duties, including a requirement that member States monitor the conservation status of all habitats and species (Art. 11) and a general duty relating to the management of certain important landscape features (Art. 10).

one of the more contentious areas of Community environmental law.[62] For example, the Habitats Directive was only adopted after many years of argument within the EC and has been beset by implementation problems. A central reason for this is that, as with environmental impact assessment (EIA), EC habitat conservation laws necessarily restrict the extent to which member States can determine how parts of their territory are used—e.g., for development—which is a central aspect of state sovereignty. Weighed against this, however, is the view, found in the Habitats Directive, that *'the threatened habitats and species form part of the Community's natural heritage'*[63]—a perspective that justifies both a common degree of restraint among the member States and common responsibilities,[64] in the interests of nature conservation in the EC.

Designating Natura 2000 sites

A central feature of the Habitats Directive is that it provides for the creation of a coherent ecological network known as Natura 2000. The network will consist of special areas of conservation (SACs)—that is, sites containing the natural habitat types listed in Annex I of the Directive (for example, raised bogs) and sites containing the habitats of the species listed in Annex II of the Directive. It will also incorporate, however, the special protection areas (SPAs) classified under the Wild Birds Directive. Hence, Natura 2000 is made up of sites designated under two separate Directives with different rules about designation.

Special protection areas

Under the Wild Birds Directive, member States are required in general terms to take measures, including the creation of protected areas, to maintain a sufficient diversity of habitats for *all* European bird species (Arts 1, 2, and 3). They must also take special conservation measures to conserve the habitats of the rare or vulnerable species listed in Annex I and of all regularly occurring migratory species (Art. 4). These special measures should include the designation of SPAs for such birds.

In Case C-355/90 *Commission v. Spain* [1993] ECR I-4221, the European Court of Justice (ECJ) held that the Spanish government was in breach of Art. 4 by failing to designate an important wetland area, the Marismas de Santoña (or 'Santoña Marshes'), as an SPA. The case established that a member State is effectively under a duty to designate an area as an SPA (and thus to protect it) if it fulfils the objective ornithological criteria laid down in the Directive.

Subsequent decisions of the ECJ have followed this strict approach to the duty of member States to designate SPAs (see Case 19.1).[65]

62 For example, over 50 per cent of EC environmental infringement cases in 1992–2002 related to the Wild Birds and Habitats Directives (see H. Neal (2002) 'Enforcing biodiversity: a UK and EU perspective' in J. Boswell and R. Lee (eds) *Economics, Ethics and the Environment*, London: Cavendish, p. 56), while, historically, conservation law has generated more ECJ case law than any other area of environmental law (see, e.g., W. Wils [1994] JEL 222).

63 Preamble. See also Case C-44/95 *R v. Secretary of State for the Environment, ex parte Royal Society for the Protection of Birds* [1997] QB 206, [23] and Case C-339/87 *Commission v. Netherlands* [1990] ECR I-851, in which the Court speaks of 'common heritage' in relation to the Wild Birds Directive.

64 Common responsibility is seen in relation to the most endangered, or 'priority', habitats and species, in relation to which, because they are unevenly distributed and are often numerous in less economically wealthy states, the Directive provides for EC co-financing as an exception to the Polluter Pays Principle.

65 Other factors that the ECJ has rejected for not designating SPAs include the effect of the Common Agriculture Policy (Case C-96/98 *Commission v. France* [2000] 2 CMLR 681), waiting for public consultation, and the fact that the land is state-owned (Case C-166/97 *Commission v. France* [1999] Env LR 781).

CASE 19.1 Case C-44/95 *R v. Secretary of State for the Environment, ex parte Royal Society for the Protection of Birds* [1997] QB 206 (the *Lappel Bank* case)

The Royal Society for the Protection of Birds (RSPB) challenged the failure of the government to include an area known as 'Lappel Bank' from a special protection area (SPA) on the Medway Estuary and Marshes in Kent. The area did not itself host Annex I or migratory species, but its loss would likely affect the overall integrity of the ecosystem.[66] The UK government argued that economic considerations were relevant, because these are mentioned in the Directive's Preamble, and that the reason for not designating the area was to allow for economic development of the Port of Sheerness. The RSPB relied on the decision of the European Court of Justice in the *Santoña Marshes* case[67] to argue that, at the designation stage, only ornithological criteria were relevant. The ECJ essentially took the latter view of the Directive, holding that the duty to designate sites was an obligation on Member States that was unaffected by economic considerations. Regrettably, however, the House of Lords had refused interim relief pending the ECJ's decision (see [1997] Env LR 431) and the RSPB was unable to make the necessary financial undertaking to the developers (essentially setting compensation money aside) should the ECJ have decided differently. Consequently, the habitat was destroyed by the building of a 22-hectare car park.

In 2006, sea defences on Wallasea Island in Essex were breached in order to create new habitat to compensate for the loss of Lappel Bank and another similarly destroyed site.

In Case C-3/96 *Commission v. Netherlands* [1999] Env LR 147, the issue for the ECJ was not the failure to designate a particular site, or part of a site, but rather whether the Netherlands had breached its obligations under the Directive by not designating a *sufficient* number (and total area) of sites. A study in 1989 for the Commission (the 'IBA' study) had suggested that 70 sites (covering 797,920 hectares) should have been designated, but, in fact, only 23 sites (covering 327,602 hectares) had been designated. In finding against the Netherlands, the Court held that the member States' discretion extended only to the application of objective ornithological criteria in identifying the most suitable territories for the conservation of Annex I species. The Netherlands had not put forward any evidence to suggest that the 1989 study was not a valid indication of how many sites should have been designated, nor could it argue that other conservation methods were being used on undesignated sites. But in cases in which there is evidence that the 1989 study is no longer authoritative, any listing of a site in it cannot be determinative (*Bown v. Secretary of State for Transport* [2004] Env LR 26).

Special areas of conservation

Under the Habitats Directive, the procedure for producing the list of SACs is more prescriptive. Member States must send the Commission a list of candidate sites, drawn up by reference to the criteria laid down in Annex III (Stage 1) of the Directive (for example, representivity and area). The Commission must then draw up a draft list of 'sites of Community importance' (SCIs), taking account of the criteria set out in Annex III (Stage 2). The Commission adopts a final list thereafter in the light of scientific advice from a committee of independent experts. The Commission produces a separate list of those sites that host one or more of the *priority* habitat types or species that are identified in Annexes I and II (termed 'priority sites'). There are provisions for a bilateral consultation process between the Commission and a member State if the Commission considers that a priority site has been left off a member

---

66 By holding that the area should have been designated, therefore, the case is a good example of the ECJ, in practice, taking a precautionary approach to adjudication.

67 Case C-355/90 *Commission v. Spain* [1993] ECR I-4221.

State's list, with ultimate recourse to the EC Council (Art. 5). Once the Commission has adopted the list of SCIs, member States are under a duty to designate any site on the list as an SAC. In practice, the timetable for implementing each of these stages ran well behind schedule, due mainly to member States' tardiness in submitting adequate lists of candidate SACs, but SACs have now been designated at national level.

While case law had made clear that only ornithological criteria were relevant in designating SPAs under the Wild Birds Directive, the Habitats Directive contains a general provision stating that '*measures taken pursuant to* [the] *Directive shall take account of economic, social and cultural requirements and regional and local characteristics*' (Art. 2(3)). Whether this allowed economic considerations to influence the designation of candidate SACs was the subject of a referral from the English High Court to the ECJ (see Case 19.2).

In a subsequent case—mirroring its approach to SPAs under the Wild Birds Directive—the ECJ has held that a member State can breach its obligations under the Habitats Directive if it submits a list of candidate SACs that is manifestly inadequate (Case C-71/99 *Commission v. Germany* [2001] ECR I-5811). From an enforcement perspective, taking action against a member State on these grounds is clearly preferable to taking numerous separate actions, but the Court has not spelt out with any clarity the parameters of 'manifest inadequacy' and important evidential issues remain.

CASE 19.2 Economic considerations and special areas of conservation—Case C-371/98
R v. Secretary of State for the Environment, Transport and the Regions, ex parte First Corporate Shipping Ltd [2001] ECR I-9235

First Corporate Shipping Ltd (FCS) is the statutory port authority at Bristol. The Secretary of State was minded to propose the Severn Estuary as a candidate special area of conservation (SAC). FCS judicially reviewed this decision and the High Court referred the matter to the European Court of Justice to decide whether, as FCS argued, economic and other non-ecological considerations mentioned in Art. 2(3) of the Habitats Directive were relevant to the designation of candidate SACs. The ECJ held, however, that member States may not take economic considerations into account when submitting candidate SACs. The selection criteria laid down in the Directive were exclusively ecological. Moreover, taking non-ecological criteria into account at this stage would frustrate the scheme of the Directive, because it would prevent the Commission from drawing up the draft list of sites of Community importance (SCIs) solely on the basis of sites' ecological importance.

Although this was the only point that the ECJ was asked to rule on, the Advocate-General also considered subsequent stages of the designation process. He noted that, under guidance issued in 1996, the Commission must also be sent information about '*impacts and activities in and around the site*', which '*may have an influence, either positive or negative, on the conservation and management of the site*'. The guidance suggests that, for habitat types, relevant factors '*may include the human activities, both in the site or in its neighbouring areas, that are likely to influence the conservation status of the habitat type, the ownership of the land, the existing legal status of the site*'. This might suggest, for example, that land owned by a conservation NGO might be preferred to land in multiple profit-making ownership. But the central point should, in principle, be that such activities are material to the designation process only because they are likely to influence the conservation status of the habitat type, not because the activity per se justifies the exclusion of sites *merely because of the economic impact of including them.*[68]

The difficulty with the Advocate-General's approach is that he refers to economic 'requirements'. This seems to suggest that it is economic *needs*, rather than *effects*, that are relevant. The ECJ has

---

68 For a comparison, see p. 693 on the non-notification of SSSIs where the conservation interest is 'doomed'.

yet to pronounce on this guidance; if it were to follow the Advocate-General's approach on this issue, the danger would be that important sites would not be designated because of economic needs, which seems to contradict other provisions of the Directive that require existing consents, etc., that affect European sites to be reviewed.

A further issue is the geographical extent of SPAs and SACs. Although the view of the UK government was that the Habitats Directive, which applies to the 'European territory of the member States', did not extend beyond the 12-mile territorial limit, the High Court has held that the Directive applies as far as the continental shelf. In a purposive decision in *R v. Secretary of State for Trade and Industry, ex parte Greenpeace (No. 2)* [2000] Env LR 221, a challenge to the awarding of oil exploration licences, the Court took into account, among other things, that some distant water species are listed in the Directive.[69] The ECJ has taken the same view, which is now provided for in the Offshore Marine Conservation (Natural Habitats, &c.) Regulations 2007.[70]

UK law and policy on site designation

By August 2007, 253 SPAs covering 1,583,928 hectares had been designated in the UK[71] and there are only a handful of proposed SPAs (mostly in Scotland).

The designation of candidate SACs has been more problematic. By June 1999, 340 sites in the UK had been submitted to the Commission, with the government indicating that this marked the end of this stage. Just before a meeting that year with the Commission and with other member States in the Atlantic bioregion of the EC, however, the UK agreed to review its selection of SACs and, by July 2002, 571 sites covering 2,389,228 hectares had been submitted.[72] Further candidate SACs have been designated since then (there are now 611), but more sites will eventually be selected, not least in the marine environment beyond territorial waters, for the reasons noted above, although there is a practical difficulty in designating candidate SACs for species such as seals, dolphins, and porpoises, which range widely. All 611 sites are now full SACs—that is, they have been approved by the Commission and become part of Natura 2000.

The following cases illustrate the discretion that the national courts have afforded to the NCC when selecting sites. In *World Wildlife Fund-UK Ltd and Royal Society for the Protection of Birds v. Secretary of State for Scotland and ors* [1999] Env 632, WWF and RSPB sought judicial review in the Scottish courts of various decisions connected with the exclusion of areas of Cairngorm from a candidate SAC. The area excluded was to be used for a funicular railway to take skiers up the mountain, but it was held that, although choosing sites and drawing boundaries was all part of one exercise, there was room for discretion in the drawing of boundaries as long as the discretion was exercised only on ornithological grounds. These did not need to be so objective that a court could rule on them. The Scottish Office and its advisers had taken one view; the objectors had taken another. It was not for the judge to say that the official line was wrong. An interesting feature of the case, however, is that the area was excluded from the candidate site partly because it was already developed. This begs questions about the extent to which the presence of existing development can justify not designating areas of otherwise important sites.

---

69 A view criticized by J. Jans (2000) JEL 385. See now the Offshore Petroleum Activities (Conservation of Habitats) Regulations 2001, SI 2001/1754.

70 SI 2007/1842, which transpose the Wild Birds and Habitats Directive generally beyond the UK's territorial waters out to the 200-nautical-mile limit.

71 The selection guidelines are available at **www.jncc.gov.uk**.

72 On selection criteria and implementation, see JNCC (2007) *The Habitats Directive: Selection of Special Areas of Conservation in the UK*, available online at **www.jncc.gov.uk/SACselection**.

In *R (on the application of Newsum and others) v. Welsh Assembly (No. 2)* [2006] Env LR 1, by contrast, the legal challenge was *to* designation as a candidate SAC. The area in question, which hosted a rare grassland and great crested newts, was not on the original list of sites submitted by the UK, but was subsequently added following the events of 1999 when, in effect, the Commission asked the UK to think again and nominate more sites. Newsum alleged that the decision to include its land, which included a quarry with an extant minerals planning permission, was 'quota-driven', partly because sites in Wales were under-represented. This was dismissed—the Directive requires that member States select sites that reflect their whole territory, so, in this sense, having a certain proportion of Welsh sites was not unreasonable. It was also claimed that the planning permission should have been taken into account as a factor in not designating the site. This was also dismissed, following *First Corporate Shipping* (see Case 19.2). Indeed, the judge accepted that development pressures such as this would trigger a review of the relevant consent once a site was an SAC and that their presence was all the more reason to act. The Court also held that the whole site was lawfully proposed, even though the grassland and newts occupied only a small proportion of it. This was because it was acceptable to have a management regime that covered the whole of the area.

As with selecting SSSIs, therefore, the practical implication of these cases is that decisions on site selection and boundaries are matters of expert opinion, are not merely reviewable matters of fact, and that, unless they are wholly irrational, they are unlikely to be interfered with by the courts.

Conserving and managing Natura 2000 sites

As originally adopted in 1979, under the Wild Birds Directive, once an SPA has been designated, member States had to take appropriate steps to avoid significant pollution or deterioration of the habitat or disturbance of the birds within it (Art. 4(4)). The meaning of this rather curtly worded provision was considered by the ECJ in Case C-57/89 *Commission v. Germany* [1991] ECR I-883, a case about an area known as the 'Leybucht Dykes'. This established that reducing the area of an SPA was only justified on very limited grounds, such as where the works were necessary for reasons of public health or public safety (which was actually the situation in the case itself), and that works could not be permitted for economic or recreational reasons, thus creating a strong presumption against development in such an area. This point was reinforced by the *Santoña Marshes* case (see p. 705), which applied the same test to the deterioration of a site as a result of pollution or other works.

The effect of these rulings, however, was very quickly mitigated by the Habitats Directive. As far as maintaining the conservation status of sites is concerned, this brought the Wild Birds Directive into line with a new regime laid down in Art. 6 of the Habitats Directive.[73] (As a matter of national law, the UK also applies these tests to candidate SACs and, as a matter of policy, to proposed SPAs—see below.) The details of the new regime are set out in Box 19.5.

BOX 19.5 Conservation of Natura 2000 sites—Art. 6 of the Habitats Directive

The protection provided by the Habitats Directive divides between general measures that apply at all times and measures that apply to specific, future activities.

---

73 A curious effect is that sites that should have been designated as SPAs continue to be subject to the old provisions of Art. 4(4), because the less restrictive provisions of the Habitats Directive only apply to areas actually classified as SPAs: see Case C-374/98 *Commission v. France* [2000] ECR I-10799 (the *Basses Corbières* case). Because, as discussed below, Art. 4(4) has been held to be directly effective, this gives member States a certain incentive to designate SPAs.

Provision	Application
General	
Adopt 'necessary conservation measures' such as management plans, and 'appropriate statutory, administrative or contractual measures' (Art. 6(1)—i.e. the focus is proactive)	SACs only (the only provision that does not apply to SPAs, but there are analogous provisions in Art. 4(1) and (2) of the Wild Birds Directive)
Take appropriate steps to avoid the deterioration of the sites and significant disturbance of the species for which the areas have been designated (Art. 6(2))[74]	SACs Sites of Community Importance (SCIs) SPAs Sites subject to the Art. 5 consultation procedure
Specific provisions regarding specific plans and projects	
Subject any plan or project not directly connected with the management of the site, but which is likely to have a significant effect on it, to an 'appropriate assessment' of the implications The competent national authorities can then agree to the plan or project only if it will not 'adversely affect the integrity of the site concerned' (Art. 6(3))	SACs SCIs SPAs
If there is no alternative solution, a plan or project may be carried out if there are *imperative reasons of overriding public interest, including those of a social or economic nature*' (Art. 6(4). A more restrictive test applies to 'priority sites'.) But the member State must take compensatory measures to ensure the overall coherence of Natura 2000	SACs SCIs SPAs

Deterioration and significant disturbance

In *Royal Society for the Protection of Birds v. Secretary of State for Scotland* [2001] Env LR 19, the granting of licences to shoot barnacle geese, to prevent crop damage, was held to breach Art. 6(2) of the Directive. The shooting was to be on an SPA on Islay designated for the conservation of the geese. But, on appeal, the court held that the Directive's obligation to avoid significant disturbance to the species meant assessing this in relation to the individual Natura 2000 site in question and not, as had been done, to its whole area of distribution in the EC.

This important decision illustrates a key feature of nature conservation: that the cumulative impact of decisions with relatively minor impact is as significant as more major interventions and must be judged accordingly. The prospect of a species or habitat 'dying by a thousand cuts' is thereby reduced. Nevertheless, there are still tricky questions of scale to be considered and it is not clear that the impact on individual sites will always be determinative. Consider the example of 'managed retreat'—that is, the policy of not defending the whole coastline from the sea, but, in certain areas, allowing nature to take its course. This policy will mean that, in some areas, saltmarsh and mudflat habitats (Annex I habitats) will be lost, but that, overall, there may, in fact, be a net gain of these habitats. Reasoning from the *Islay*

---

74 Member States must therefore adopt conservation plans and ensure that they are implemented. So, in Case C-117/00 *Commission v. Ireland* [2002] ECR I-5335, the ECJ held that Ireland had, in fact, to ensure that sheep densities were reduced on heath and bog land to conserve the red grouse.

Geese case above, implementing this policy would be difficult, because it might be arguable that each area of habitat lost would violate Art. 6(2).[75] In so far as Art. 6(2) is directed at general conservation policy rather than consented activities on specific sites, however, a distinction might be drawn if the overall purposes of the Directive are achieved. In Case C-6/04 *Commission v. United Kingdom* [2005] ECR I-9017, the ECJ held that Art. 6(2), in prohibiting the deterioration of habitat, covered 'natural' disturbances as much as 'non-natural' ones—that is, it covered things such as the invasion of scrub as much as overgrazing.

The need for appropriate assessment, and for no adverse effect

Articles 6(3) and (4) apply prospectively to a 'plan or project'. 'Project' is a particularly unspecific term to use in law and its interpretation is likely to depend on the wider context within which it appears. In Case C-127/02 *Landelijke Vereniging tot Behoud van de Waddenzee, Nederlandse Vereniging tot Bescherming van Vogels v. Staatssecretaris van Landbouw, Natuurbeheer en Visserij* [2005] Env LR 14, the issue was whether licences to harvest cockles in the Waddenzee was a 'project'. The Court held that it was, relying on the broad interpretation of 'project' in the Environmental Impact Assessment (EIA) Directive (85/337/EEC; see p. 443). Nationally, there has been uncertainty about the breadth of what a 'project' is—for example, whether 'project' covered plant cutting in the Broads. In Case C-6/04 *Commission v. United Kingdom* [2005] ECR I-9017, the ECJ held that 'plan or project' applied to land use plans under town and country planning law. (This would seem obvious, but the UK had not implemented in this way, and has had to amend the 1994 Regulations.)[76]

In the *Waddenzee* case, on whether a plan or project is 'likely to have a significant effect', the ECJ gave a very precautionary ruling, interpreting this as meaning that any significant effect would have to be ruled out on the basis of objective information—that is, that there must be 'no reasonable scientific doubt' remaining about the absence of such effects; otherwise, the procedure in Art. 6(4) applies.[77] The Court does not, however, go on to explain what a significant effect is; it refers only to actions that will 'undermine' the site's conservation objectives. It must be presumed that it means 'significant' in relation to the favourable conservation status of the site in question.

'Appropriate assessment' is not an EIA under the EIA Directive, but it does share some similarities. In principle, an appropriate assessment is a technocratic assessment focusing on the integrity of the site, unlike an EIA, which is a much wider procedure involving mandatory public consultation. But a properly conducted EIA should suffice. One thing worth noting is that appropriate assessment is not only a procedural tool, but also works to uphold a standard of ensuring the integrity of sites. By contrast, EIA has no such baseline.

Alternatives

As with other areas of environmental law, there is provision in the Habitats Directive for justifying harmful activities on the grounds that there is no alternative. Commission guidance suggests that this might involve alternative locations (or, in the case of linear developments, different routes), different scales or designs of development, or alternative processes, while the alternative of doing nothing should also be considered (see Box 19.3). It is also conceivable that a court might demand that the proponent of a project show that the development proposed is the only way to create jobs in an area and that the expansion of other sectors might not achieve this (it is notable that the Directive does not refer to 'reasonable alternatives').

---

75 Because the law offers no protection to property owners from the consequences of managed retreat (i.e. the law does not require decision makers to avoid losses to property or property values), this example is often held up by the anti-conservation lobby to illustrate how law favours the interests of 'nature' over human interests. Colloquially, it is said here that the 'rights' of nature take precedence over human rights.

76 Conservation (Natural Habitats etc.) (Amendment) Regulations 2007, SI 2007/1843, reg. 5(55) and Sch. 1.

77 On the importance of this case in relation to the Precautionary Principle, see p. 77.

The main issue, however, probably lies in the quality and quantity of evidence that a decision maker should have in reaching decisions on alternatives. In a case in which, on safety grounds, a proposal to reroute a road through a candidate SAC was at stake, the German courts held that, first, the authorities should have shown that it was impossible to make the existing road safer (for example, by road junctions or adjusted speed limits), and secondly, that the authorities should have presented evidence that the new road would, in fact, lead to fewer casualties.[78] A challenge to the exclusion from consideration of expansion at Gatwick airport—in 1979, the government had concluded an agreement with West Sussex County Council that no further runways would be constructed there before 2019—was successful, however, because the effect of this would mean that a proposal to construct a runway at an SPA in Kent could not consider expansion at Gatwick as an alternative solution and therefore whether the site in Kent was needed, because of imperative reasons of overriding public interest (*R (Medway Council) v. Secretary of State for Transport* [2002] EWHC 2516). (The 2003 White Paper on *Aviation*, however, concluded that the 1979 agreement should not be overturned.)

The leading case now is Case C-239/04 *Commission v. Portugal* [2006] ECR I-10183, in which the ECJ held that, by not being able to show evidence that it had considered routes for a motorway that did not go through an SPA, Portugal had failed to show that there was no alternative solution. It was immaterial whether, in fact, the route chosen was or was not likely to be the least harmful; what mattered was the lack of evidence.

Compensatory measures

Even if imperative economic or social reasons justify developing a European site, compensatory measures must be taken to ensure the overall coherence of Natura 2000. But what does 'compensatory' mean in this context? Some examples given by the Commission that might amount to valid compensatory measures are:[79]

- recreating a habitat on a new or enlarged site, to be incorporated into Natura 2000;

- improving a habitat on part of the site or on another Natura 2000 site, proportional to the loss due to the project;

- in exceptional cases, proposing a new site under the Habitats Directive (this is clearly problematic, because the total stock of possible sites will have been diminished).

In principle, the result of compensatory measures must normally be operational at the time at which the damage occurs on the Natura 2000 site—that is, there should be no 'time gap'. In *Humber Sea Terminals v. Secretary of State for Transport* [2006] Env LR 4, however, the High Court held that the compensation measures did not have to be in place on the ground at the time that consent for the development was given. When consent was given was the time at which the arising duty on the Secretary of State to secure the coherence of Natura 2000 was triggered and this became a continuing duty thereafter. Quite what the precise nature of this duty is remains a little uncertain, not least because what the 'coherence' of Natura 2000 entails is not precisely defined. For example, the Commission has consented to new habitat that does not exactly replicate the habitat functions that have been lost (see the Cardiff Bay case, in Box 19.6). But what is clear is that the compensation must be ecological; other things that might improve human welfare, such as health care or recreational facilities, will not compensate for conservation interests.[80]

---

78 Federal Administrative Court [2000] 22 Natur und Recht 8, 448–53.

79 European Commission (2000) *Managing Natura 2000 Sites: The Provisions of Article 6 of the 'Habitats' Directive 92/43/EEC*.

80 Under Electricity Act 1989, Sch. 9, reasonable mitigation measures must be provided for, which is obviously a weaker formulation of an ecological compensation duty.

BOX 19.6 The Cardiff Bay Barrage

To promote development, a barrage across the mouth of the Taff and Ely rivers in Cardiff was proposed to create a large 'freshwater' lake. The barrage, however, would destroy intertidal mudflats that hosted internationally important numbers of wintering dunlin and redshank. On economic grounds, the government excluded the area from the Lower Severn special protection area (SPA).[81] But it was recognized that, under the Habitats Directive, there was a need to compensate for the area lost and eventually a new wetland reserve on the Gwent Levels was constructed. This, however, was as part of a wider compensation package, a noticeable feature of which was that it did not directly compensate for the loss of habitat for the dunlin and redshank. Instead, two species of duck were selected for achieving nationally important numbers on the new site, while compensation for the dunlin and redshank took the form of general UK monitoring of their population and undertaking an accelerated programme of designating large numbers of significant estuarial sites for their conservation.

Because the habitat loss will be permanent, there is also the problem of ensuring that the compensatory measures can, through adequate funding, continue in perpetuity. It is important to emphasize that the compensatory measures were never subject to judicial scrutiny.[82] Nevertheless, as one commentator put it:[83]

> the detailed involvement of the EC added weight to the requirement for environmental compensation but also facilitated the negotiation of loss, by allowing nature to be constructed in substitutable terms, in which 'coherence' and site 'integrity' became defined in terms of what is quantifiable, manageable and creatable.

Balanced against this, however, is the reality that the new site is actively managed for conservation, unlike the site that was lost.

BOX 19.7 Dibden Bay

Associated British Ports sought permission for a deep-water container port at Dibden Bay on Southampton Water. The proposed development would have harmed a special protection area (SPA) and two candidate special areas of conservation (SACs). At the public inquiry, English Nature advised that the proposed compensatory measures would not be adequate to offset the detriment to these sites. The Secretary of State for Transport agreed and permission was refused. The Secretary of State also followed the Commission's guidance on alternatives in deciding that these had to go beyond simply considering alternative local sites for the development and might extend to considering alternative solutions located in other regions, or even other countries.[84]

In other jurisdictions, compensatory measures have included the creation of habitat and species 'banks'. For example, under the 1973 US Endangered Species Act, if a landowner hosts specimens of a species in excess of a determined minimum, then these can be banked and either used to offset damaging development on other parts of their land, or even 'sold' to

---

81 In the light of subsequent case law, this was clearly unlawful—see p. 705.
82 Although a public inquiry was held in relation to the compulsory purchase of the farmland.
83 R. Cowell [2000] J Env Planning and Management 689.
84 See further G. Machin (2005) 2 Law, Science and Policy 285.

other landowners to offset their requirements. One reason behind this is that, at the margins, it is more economic for an existing landowner to conserve than to require, for example, a landowner who hosts a small number of rare species to establish new habitat for them. As such, it is a good example of the use of economic instruments in nature conservation, although there are obviously some differences from, for example, carbon trading, because the environmental effects of 1 tonne of carbon being emitted are not locationally specific, whereas the ecological value of 1 hectare of habitat may vary enormously.

Priority sites

When compared with the position set out in the *Leybucht Dykes* case (see p. 709), the exception in Art. 6(4) lessens the protection that is offered. For priority sites, however, Art. 6(4) limits the exception to considerations relating to human health or public safety, situations in which the impact is beneficial to the environment, and those in which the Commission has accepted that there are reasons of overriding public interest. It is relevant, therefore, that there are no priority bird species and thus the stronger controls applicable to priority sites cannot apply to SPAs designated under the Wild Birds Directive.

It was originally thought that the effect of this was to retain the *Leybucht Dykes* position for priority sites. From the opinions that the Commission has given, however, all that it seems to do is use the criteria that apply to non-priority sites—Are there alternatives? Is the ecological compensation appropriate?—and apply these, albeit rigorously. In other words, economic considerations are reintroduced into the derogations procedure.[85]

Article 6 and direct effect

Does Art. 6 apply to a site that is not part of the Natura 2000 network? This raises the issues of whether its provisions are directly effective in national courts (on direct effect, see p. 209). Paragraphs (2)–(4) of Art. 6 of the Habitats Directive lay down clear requirements, so it is arguable that they are directly effective. A potential difficulty, however, is that the process of designating SACs involves the Commission in making a judgment, on the basis of the lists submitted, about which sites to select as SCIs, which involves discretion. On this basis, the provisions for designating SACs would be insufficiently precise and unconditional for direct effect.

The ECJ has, in a sense, used this discretion as a reason *for* applying a certain degree of protection to candidate SACs and sites on the draft list of SCIs. Because the Commission selects the final list of SCIs on the basis of information about the state of candidate SACs, then these sites have to be conserved, otherwise the selection process would not be based on up-to-date information (Case C-244/05 *Bund Naturschutz in Bayern eV v. Freistaat Bayern* [2006] ECR I-8445). Hence, member States must take appropriate protective measures to maintain the ecological characteristics of such sites and must not authorize anything that poses a risk of seriously compromising these characteristics. It seems clear that these duties on member States can be enforced through legal challenges in the national courts, although they only extend to candidate sites that have been proposed by the member State and not to any site that, it is argued, should have been proposed (on which, see the cases mentioned on p. 706).

What about SPAs? Their designation is a matter primarily for the member States, subject to review by the courts. In the *Santoña Marshes* case (see p. 705), the ECJ suggested that Art. 4(4) of the Wild Birds Directive had direct effect, so the scheme for conserving SPAs would apply to sites that should have been designated. And as the *Commission v. Netherlands* case (see p. 706) shows, the important bird area (IBA) list can be used as an evidence base to show that a site should be classified as an SPA (although this is, at best, only a rebuttable presumption). Moreover, Art. 10 of the EC Treaty requires member States to abstain from measures that could jeopardize the attainment of the objectives of the EC Treaty and this has

---

85 A. Nollkaemper (1997) JEL 271; J. Lowther (2003) Env Liability 155.

been relied on by the courts to justify upholding protective measures on sites that have not yet been designated as SACs.[86]

A final point that can be made here is that an individual or organization might be able to assert that a species, rather than habitat, protection provision of the Wild Birds or Habitats Directives has been breached. These are described below, but essentially, for certain species, they provide a level of protection against disturbance, and deterioration, of breeding and resting places regardless of whether these areas have been designated (see p. 721). This line of argument would avoid having to show that a particular site should, in law, have been designated.

UK implementation

In the UK, the preferred approach to implementing both the Wild Birds and Habitats Directives was initially to provide protection through the town planning and SSSI systems. But there are problems with this approach: first, this did not impose any additional domestic requirements on owners or occupiers to those applicable to all SSSIs; secondly, parts of many SPAs (and also many Ramsar sites) are below low-water mark—where SSSIs cannot be notified—and many estuarine and, more recently, marine areas are now recognized as SCIs. In the light of the *Leybucht Dykes* and *Santoña Marshes* cases, it became clear that this approach would be inadequate in legal terms, especially to implement the more detailed requirements of the Habitats Directive. As a result, the Conservation (Natural Habitats etc.) Regulations 1994[87] were enacted. The Habitats Regulations apply to 'European sites' and it is important to note what is covered by this definition (see Box 19.8). But it should also be borne in mind that government has accepted, as a matter of planning policy, that all sites that meet the criteria for designation as an SPA (termed 'potential SPAs') should be treated as if they had been formally designated. This policy, which extends to possible SACs—that is, to sites being considered as candidate SACs, but not yet submitted to the Commission—is now enshrined in planning guidance.[88]

BOX 19.8 European sites

The 1994 Habitats Regulations apply additional protections to 'European sites', which are defined as:

- special areas of conservation (SACs, once finally designated by government);
- sites adopted by the Commission as sites of Community importance (SCIs);
- special protection areas (SPAs) designated under the Wild Birds Directive;
- sites subject to consultation under Art. 5 of the Habitats Directive (although the protection is limited in relation to these, as under the Directive, to the obligations under Art. 6(2));
- candidate SACs submitted to the Commission (until such sites are either adopted as SACs or fail to make the final list).[89]

The Secretary of State draws up a public register of European sites (reg. 11) and notifies them to the NCC (reg. 12), which then notifies local planning authorities, owners and occupiers, and anyone else the Secretary of State may direct (reg. 13).

---

86 *Korenburgerveen* [2002] 29 Milieu en Recht 3, 95–9.

87 SI 1994/2716.

88 PPS9 (2005) *Biodiversity and Geological Conservation*; Scottish Executive (2000) *Habitats and Birds Directive*.

89 Added by SI 2000/192, which gives legal force to the policy (since 1994) of treating candidate SACs as European sites.

In enacting the Habitats Regulations, rather than remodel the law on nature conservation entirely, a minimalist approach was adopted, and the Regulations simply grafted onto the existing SSSI and town planning mechanisms the additional protections required by the Directive, and then only where absolutely necessary.[90]

The central features of the Habitats Regulations are as follows.

- If it appears to the NCC that a plan or project is likely to have a significant effect on the site, it must carry out an appropriate assessment and may only give consent for a potentially damaging operation if the plan or project will not affect the site's integrity. Legislation has been enacted to make clear that this duty extends to land use plans.[91]

- If the NCC considers that there is a risk that the operation will be carried out without consent, it must notify the Secretary of State, who has the power to make a special nature conservation order. In cases in which such an order is in force, the NCC must carry out an appropriate assessment and *must* refuse consent, unless it is satisfied that the plan or project will not affect the integrity of the site. The owner or occupier may refer the refusal to the Secretary of State, who is given a power to direct the NCC to grant consent. But this power of direction can be used only if:

  (i) there is no alternative solution;

  (ii) the plan or project must be carried out 'for imperative reasons of overriding public interest' (which is defined as in Art. 6(4) of the Directive and includes the more restrictive test for priority sites).[92]

If consent is granted, appropriate compensatory measures must be carried out.

- Existing consents must be reviewed by the NCC and may be withdrawn or modified without compensation.

- By-laws may be made for terrestrial European sites (and over surrounding or adjoining sites) as if they were NNRs.

It is notable that the position in the UK is that whether there are 'imperative reasons of overriding public importance' will depend on the following guiding principles:

- a need to address a serious risk to human health and public safety;

- the interests of national security and defence;

- provision of a clear and demonstrable direct environmental benefit on a national or international scale;

- a vital contribution to strategic economic development or regeneration;

- whether failure to proceed would have unacceptable social and/or economic consequences.[93]

It is also stated that issues of scale will be important in any calculation—that is, that nationally important projects are more likely to pass the threshold than projects of local significance.[94]

---

90 See S. Ball (1996) 'Reforming the law of habitat protection' in C. Rodgers (ed.) *Nature Conservation and Countryside Law*, Cardiff: University of Wales Press; C. Rodgers [2001] JPL 265.

91 Schedule 1, Conservation (Natural Habitats, &c) (Amendment) (England and Wales) Regulations 2006, inserting a new Pt IVA into the Conservation (Habitats, &c.) Regulations 1994. See also p. 711.

92 The UK hosts a number of priority habitat types (such as Caledonian Scots pine forests and limestone pavements), but only one priority plant species—the liverwort Western rustwort.

93 See **www.defra.gov.uk/wildlife-countryside/ewd** and see Scottish Executive (2000).

94 On the 'overriding public interest' test, see also p. 714.

The power to make a special nature conservation order is the central feature of the Habitats Regulations, because it provides a form of absolute protection by introducing a mechanism through which a damaging activity may be prevented permanently. But the success of the whole Regulations—at least in terms of whether the Directive is properly implemented in practice—depends on the willingness of the Secretary of State to make such orders and then to refuse consent where appropriate. Only a handful of orders have been made, however, and it is clear from the whole scheme of protection that the government envisaged special nature conservation orders as instruments of last resort to be used only when absolutely necessary. As with SSSIs, the main mechanism that has been used is the management agreement and around half of all sums paid out by the NCC have been in relation to European sites. Set against that, reg. 3(2) requires the Secretary of State and the nature conservation bodies to exercise their nature conservation functions 'so as to secure compliance' with the Directive.

The ability to impose permanent bans on operations was a radical departure for UK nature conservation law. With the changes to the law made under CROWA 2000, however, similar powers are now available for all SSSIs and the same is also true of many of the other provisions that were once specific to European sites (for example, the power to make by-laws). Moreover, in certain respects, the protection given to nationally important sites is now greater than that enjoyed by European sites and, at the time of writing, there are proposals to strengthen the Habitats Regulations in line with the level of protection given to all SSSIs. Among other things, these would remove the power to make special nature conservation orders, because, in effect, these would now be redundant.

Some differences would still remain. As noted above, when it comes to considering plans or projects that might harm sites, the law on SSSIs is still not structured in the staged, risk assessment way that the law governing European sites is and there are no specific legislative objectives that guide decision making in the way that the concept of 'favourable conservation status' is central to the Habitats Regulations. Also, designation of sites will remain with Ministers rather than the NCC.

European sites, public bodies, and other regulatory systems

A feature of the Habitats Directive is that, because it places a general obligation on member States to secure the favourable conservation status of Natura 2000 sites and European protected species, the Habitats Regulations:

- place general duties on all public bodies to have regard to the Directive's requirements;

- (more strongly) specifically require environment and agriculture Ministers and the NCC to exercise their nature conservation functions so as to secure compliance with the Directive;

- also make important amendments to a number of other regulatory systems.

Hence, in cases in which a plan or project is likely to have a significant effect on a European site, before granting such things as planning permission or a pollution authorization, the relevant regulatory agency must consult with the NCC and carry out an appropriate assessment of the implications of the plan or project for the site (reg. 48). The agency must agree to the plan or project only if it will not adversely affect the integrity of the site, unless the provisions of regs. 49 and 53 are satisfied (these repeat the exceptions laid down in Art. 6(4) of the Directive). A particularly controversial illustration of the strength of these duties is the current ban on virtually all residential development in an area around the Thames Heath Basin SPA, designated in 2005. The main ground is that more residents will mean more cats and dogs and, unless new open space is provided for them, it cannot be ruled out that these will not cause harm to the SPA.[95]

95 See www.surreyheath.gov.uk/planning/PlanningPolicyandConservation/ThamesBasinSPA.htm.

The Secretary of State is also given powers to prohibit the plan or project, either temporarily or permanently. In addition, *existing* permissions, consents, and authorizations must be reviewed as soon as reasonably practicable (reg. 50), which may be one situation in which the Regulations go beyond what is required under the Directive. If the integrity of the site is adversely affected, the agency should use its normal powers of revocation or modification, paying compensation if that would be the usual position. By way of example, the Environment Agency has issued detailed policy guidance on how it will comply with these duties when making decisions on new or existing Agency permissions (such as discharge consents). It is notable that the timetable agreed between the Environment Agency and central government for reviewing existing consents envisages that the review process will be completed by 2010, although there will be prioritization within this period.[96]

A final point to note is that the ECJ has held that the general duties on public bodies, etc. mentioned above cannot substitute for proper implementation of specific provisions of the Directive (Case C-6/04 *Commission v. United Kingdom* [2005] ECR I-9017). So, for example, the UK could not successfully argue that these duties were sufficient to show that it was implementing the Directive in territorial waters, or monitoring correctly, because the Directive lays down detailed rules about things such as this.

European marine sites

As we have just seen, the wording of the Habitats Regulations was initially unsatisfactory, in part because it relied on placing general duties on public bodies having functions relevant to marine conservation to exercise these so as to secure compliance with the requirements of the Directive. In addition to these, however, more specific powers and duties were also laid down, but were very brief, and gave decision makers too much discretion, for example, to make management schemes, directions, and so on. Having said that, marine habitats and species are poorly represented in the Directive itself, which has an almost exclusive focus on territorial and coastal habitats. This may be one reason why greater attention was given to terrestrial habitats and species, although the principal reason is probably the relative lack of visibility of marine biodiversity. The law in this area has been completely reshaped by the Offshore Marine Conservation (Natural Habitats etc.) Regulations 2007,[97] which set out a completely new set of rules, rather than trying to 'tweak' the 1994 Regulations to apply to marine conservation. Further discussion of these Regulations is beyond the scope of this book.

EC habitat law—conclusions

In many ways, EC law has provided a more rigorous legislative scheme for conserving valued sites and habitats than that which previously existed. By requiring staged risk assessment when potentially damaging plans or projects are proposed, and by doing so against specific conservation objectives (site integrity, favourable conservation status, etc.), it has undoubtedly raised the status of conservation interests beyond simply being a 'material consideration' in decision making that can be trumped by competing interests such as economic development. This is not to say, however, that nature conservation is elevated above other interests and the overturning of the *Leybucht* decision by the Habitats Directive is testimony to the Community's desire for a flexible conservation law that will not completely emasculate important national interests—especially, economic interests.

---

96 The guidance, which is divided between a number of documents, is available online at www. environment-agency.gov.uk/business.

97 SI 2007/1842.

As a final point about habitat conservation (which applies equally to SSSIs), one commentator has advanced four priorities, which can be summarized as:

1. protect the best;

2. restore the rest;

3. recreate some of what we have lost;

4. create new habitats for new circumstances.[98]

Together with the reforms to the law on SSSIs, EC law has formally strengthened the first of these—protecting the existing 'jewels in the crown' of nature conservation—but comparable legal strides have not been taken in the other areas that need action, in particular to plan ahead to meet future challenges such as the effects of climate change. In reality, the challenge of going beyond 'freezing in time' the present pattern of habitat and species distribution is probably beyond the reach of regulatory legal rules, and demands more facilitative responses.

The protection of individual animals and plants

The common law is generally unsympathetic to wild creatures, according them no rights of their own. But property rights may usefully be exercised in order to protect them. Wild animals are subject to the qualified ownership of the landowner whose land they are on, while, in property law terms, wild plants are part of the land itself. As a result, wild animals and plants have no common law protection against the landowner. But anyone else who kills or injures a wild animal, or picks a wild plant, commits the torts of trespass and interference with property. While the normal remedy would be damages for the value of the item taken (and thus is of little practical use), it would be possible to seek an injunction to restrain continued breaches. An owner of a nature reserve could, in theory, use these property rights to protect against threats to the wildlife on it. In addition, a person who uproots plants may commit the crimes of theft and criminal damage, although there is an exception in the Theft Act 1968, s. 4(3), for picking flowers, fruit, foliage, and fungi.

As a consequence of the limitations of the common law, the main protection for wild creatures is statutory. Part I of WCA 1981 contains the bulk of the law in this area, although the Habitat Regulations 1994 have made some important changes to ensure compliance with the species conservation provisions of the Habitats Directive.[99] Some important changes to Pt I of the 1981 Act have been made in England and Wales by CROWA 2000, and in Scotland, by the Nature Conservation (Scotland) Act 2004.

Furthering conservation or preventing cruelty?

The main national legislation—WCA 1981—combines nature conservation and welfare-oriented provisions with provisions outlawing collecting. But other wildlife statutes, while in various respects furthering conservation, are better seen as primarily concerned with preventing cruelty or unnecessary suffering.[100] The EC, on the other hand, has an ambiguous attitude to adopting legislation aimed at protecting wildlife from cruelty. While there

98 M. Avery (2001) ECOS 3.

99 See Arts 12–16, Habitats Directive. There are also numerous pieces of legislation relating to hunted species, such as deer, game birds, wildfowl, rabbits, and, of course, fish, although in all of these Acts, protection of individual animals is incidental. Reference to specialist books is recommended.

100 See many provisions of the Conservation of Seals Act 1970, the Protection of Badgers Act 1992, and the Wild Mammals (Protection) Act 1996.

is legislation relating to cruelty to non-Community species, such as seal pups,[101] the EC has generally been unsympathetic to adopting welfare-based legislation for wild species within the Community (see Box 19.9), although it has signed up to certain international agreements that contain significant welfare obligations.[102]

BOX 19.9 The EC and wildlife cruelty—the case of zoo animals

EC proposals dating back to the early 1990s advocated a Directive alleviating cruelty to wild animals in zoos. In 1999, however, the Directive eventually adopted—after a complete change of position by the UK—was concerned with the contribution of zoos to public education about biodiversity conservation, implementing in part the 1992 Biodiversity Convention. This is in line with the 1997 Amsterdam Treaty, which—under Protocol 33 and Declaration No. 24—limits the EU's regard to animal welfare to agriculture policy, transport, internal market, and research. The exclusion of EC environmental policy indicates that this provision applies only to farm, not wild, animals. Thus, while many of the provisions of EC wildlife law may, in practice, prevent suffering to endangered species, it is clear that, as things stand, preventing animal cruelty is only an incidental consequence of EC conservation law.

Do you think it is right that the EC should consider certain species part of a common European heritage (see p. 705), but not legislate to protect these from cruelty?

Species conservation offences—national law

Although they have differing or overlapping rationales, the chosen method of control under statute for both conservation and cruelty-based provisions has traditionally been to establish criminal offences of interfering with specified wildlife.

- **Wild birds**

  The strongest provisions relate to wild birds (a legacy of the historical influence of the voluntary bodies, but also a result of the Wild Birds Directive, which requires certain legislative protections), in the sense that they are reverse listed—that is, the 1981 Act applies unless the birds are exempted in the Schedules covering pest and quarry species. Specifically, it is an offence (under s. 1(1) and (2)):

  – intentionally to kill, injure, or take any wild bird;

  – intentionally to take, damage, or destroy a nest while it is in use or being built (or, for certain species such as golden eagles, which return to the same nest, to damage or destroy the nest at any time);

  – intentionally to take or destroy eggs;

  – to be in possession of a wild bird or egg (live or dead).

  There are also offences—both for reasons of avoiding cruelty and preventing overexploitation—relating to indiscriminate methods of killing or taking wild birds and to the sale or advertising for sale of wild birds (ss. 5 and 6). For these purposes, a bird is presumed to be wild unless proved otherwise. It is notable that birds are divided into two categories,

---

101 See, e.g., a number of relatively early measures relating to things such as restricting the import of pelts from animals caught by leghold traps (EEC Regulation 3254/91), and banning certain imports of seal skins (Directive 83/129/EEC) and whale products (EEC Regulation 348/81).

102 For example, the 1973 CITES Treaty and agreements in relation to fur traps, discussed in Nollkaemper (1996) JEL 237; S. Harrop and D. Bowles [1998] JIWLP 64; S. Harrop (2000) JEL 333.

with rarer birds being listed in Sch. 1 to the Act and receiving slightly greater protection. Thus, intentionally or recklessly disturbing a Sch. 1 bird on or near its nest, or disturbing its dependent young, is an offence (WCA 1981, s. 1(5), as amended by CROWA 2000, s. 81, Sch. 12, para. 1).

- **Animals and plants**
  These, on the other hand, are covered only if specifically listed in other Schedules. Regarding animals, Sch. 5 to the 1981 Act includes all bats, reptiles, and amphibians, but only the rarest mammals (for example, otters and red squirrels), fish, butterflies, and other forms of life. For those animals that are protected, there is a range of offences similar to those for wild birds. It is an offence intentionally to kill, injure, or take any scheduled wild animal, or to possess any such animal, live or dead, or any part of one. Additional offences relate to the sale or advertisement for sale of wild animals, illegal methods of killing or taking any wild animal, and illegal methods of killing or taking those animals listed in Sch. 6 (see, respectively WCA 1981, ss. 9(1), (2), and 5, and 11(1) and (2)). There is also an offence of intentionally or recklessly damaging, destroying, or obstructing any structure or place used for shelter or protection by a Sch. 5 animal, or disturbing such an animal while it is occupying such a structure (s. 9(4)). For species that habitually return to the same breeding site, such as bats, this criminalizes damage or destruction even if the site is not presently occupied. For dolphins, whales, and basking sharks, which do not have a 'shelter' as such, CROWA 2000 now makes their intentional or reckless disturbance an offence, the intention being that this will apply to inappropriate use of things such as motorboats and jet skis (s. 9(4A); see Box 19.10).

- **Plants**
  It is an offence for anyone other than the owner, occupier, or other authorized person intentionally to uproot any wild plant. In addition, it is an offence for anyone—that is, including the landowner—intentionally (but not, it must be noted, recklessly) to pick, uproot, or destroy any of the numerous species of rare wild plant listed in Sch. 8. The sale or advertisement for sale of Sch. 8 plants is also an offence (s. 13). In some cases, a plant can be subject only to these latter provisions on sale rather than the full protection of Sch. 8 listing; a current example is the bluebell.

Species conservation offences—EC law

In addition to the above, the Habitats Regulations create some further offences in relation to the animals and plants defined as 'European protected species', which are listed in Schs 2 and 4 to the Regulations, respectively. The number of species listed is quite small, and includes the common otter, dolphins, and great crested newts.

To ensure compliance with the EC Habitats Directive, the government chose to set out the requirements of the Directive more or less in full, rather than to amend the existing legislation. The result is that the Regulations cover similar ground to WCA 1981, but with some occasional subtle changes in wording to make the offences wider than normal.

The key provisions make it an offence:

- deliberately to capture, injure, or kill any wild animal of a European protected species;

- deliberately to disturb any such animal, if this disturbance would be significant;

- deliberately to take or destroy eggs from such an animal;

- to damage or destroy a breeding site or resting place of such an animal;[103]

103 The Directive refers to 'deterioration or destruction' (Art. 12(1)(d)). There are draft proposals to add the carrying out of an act that results in the deterioration of these places.

- deliberately to pick, collect, cut, uproot, or destroy a wild plant of a European protected species;

- to keep, transport, or sell (or offer to sell) such a plant, or animal, whether live or dead.

Compared with WCA 1981, some features of the Habitats Regulations are worth highlighting, including the general preference for prohibiting 'deliberate' rather than 'intentional' acts, which may mean that criminal intent—that is, *mens rea*—need not be shown. In the context of the offence relating to deliberately capturing or killing a European protected species, in a case in which it was alleged that snares used for foxes could also catch otters, the ECJ has held that '*it must be proven that the author of the act intended the capture or killing of a specimen belonging to a protected animal species or, at the very least, accepted the possibility of such capture or killing*' (Case C-221/04 *Commission v. Spain* [2006] ECR I-4515, [71]). Like the interpretation given to deliberate disturbance (see Box 19.10), this is a broad, and precautionary, one and suggests that 'deliberately' in any of the offences mentioned above should be given this interpretation.

There is also much greater protection given to breeding and resting sites, because, subject to any licence that is given (on which, see below), the prohibition in the Habitats Regulations is not qualified and is therefore a strict liability provision, whereas in WCA 1981, any interference with a place of shelter or protection must be intentional or reckless for it to be unlawful. Also, the only prohibition relating to species habitats in Pt I, WCA 1981, that does not need the action to be 'intentional' or 'reckless' relates to disturbing a listed animal species while it is *occupying* a place of structure or protection, whereas the Habitats Regulations cover damage or destruction of breeding or resting places *at any time*.

BOX 19.10 'Do not disturb'

Birds, animals, and plants can be harmed in many ways, from the accidental, to the intentional. One of the offences that is commonly provided for covers disturbing a species, whether intentionally, deliberately, recklessly, or simply without qualification. For example, bats roosting in typical places such as attics and outbuildings cannot be disturbed by rebuilding or timber treatment unless a licence is granted.[104] But laws often provide defences to these offences if the harm that is caused is incidental to some other lawful activity. What, then, is 'unlawful disturbance'?

In Case C-103/00 *Commission v. Hellenic Republic* [2002] ECR I-1147, Greece was held to have failed to prevent deliberate disturbance to the endangered loggerhead turtle. The breach was both a failure to enact suitable legislation and a breach in fact. Although areas had been designated for strict protection, mopeds, pedalos, and small boats were being used on, or close to, key breeding beaches. Clearly, any disturbance to the turtles was unintentional, but incidental to tourist activity. Nonetheless, the European Court of Justice held that Greece had failed to prevent acts of deliberate disturbance, although only because they were prohibited and because there were notices at the beaches referring to the area being protected. So, if these actions had been lawful— for example, authorized development rather than the illegal buildings on some of the beaches (which was found to breach the Directive's provisions on deterioration and destruction of breeding sites, which do not need to be done deliberately)—the Court may not have held that the disturbance was deliberate. The Court also seemed to stress that Greece had failed to prevent *repeated*

---

104 See Case C-6/04 *Commission v. United Kingdom* [2005] ECR I-9017 and Conservation (Natural Habitats &c) Regulations 1994, SI 1994/2716, reg. 39, as amended by Conservation (Natural Habitats etc) (Amendment) Regulations 2007, SI 2007/1843, reg. 13. In WCA 1981, ss. 10 and 16, there are similar provisions relating to defences and licences to those available for wild birds.

breaches of its rules, suggesting that a one-off incident might not amount to disturbance. That the number of loggerhead turtle nests had not decreased over the previous 15 years was irrelevant to these findings, a good example of how securing implementation involves attention to long-term legal and institutional structures as well as to results. This case is also an excellent example of the shortcomings of international conservation law. Since its inception, the parties to the 1979 Berne Wildlife Convention had discussed this problem, but moral pressure had failed and the file was eventually closed when the European Commission took action under the Habitats Directive.

In Case C-6/04 *Commission v. United Kingdom* [2005] ECR I-9017, the ECJ ruled against the UK's use of the defence of damage being the 'incidental result of a lawful action' and, as a result, the Habitats Regulations[105] have been amended to exclude this defence. Hence, in principle, disturbing a Habitats Directive species is a strict liability offence with no defence and the only way to exclude criminal liability is through licensing. This puts a very clear onus on, for example, developers to survey areas that they think might contain listed species before they begin operations and obtain a licence if necessary. But to limit the reach of the criminal law, the UK has done two things: first, it has defined 'disturbance' so that it excludes anything deemed to be insignificant; secondly, it has amended the Habitats Regulations, so that a person will not do something 'deliberately' only because the action had the result that he did the thing in question, and he intended those actions and knew that they might have that result (reg. 14). It is clear from reg. 15 that this provision is intended to cover sea fishing—for example, where a protected species is, despite reasonable steps, accidentally caught in a net; it is unclear whether it applies more generally. The main issue is whether it is an acceptable way of implementing the Directive because, other than in relation to sea fishing, it is not qualified in any way by reference to taking reasonable avoidance action. This example neatly illustrates some of the difficulties in laying down laws that strike the right balance between conserving wildlife and allowing normal activities to continue without being overly burdened.

Two further points are worth making. First, 'disturbing' a species is not controlled only by species conservation offences, but also by habitat conservation provisions (see p. 710), hence there may be more than one way to address harmful disturbance. Secondly, in ecological terms, species disturbance—in the sense that species are exposed to stresses that induce evolutionary responses—is seen as an important factor in population dynamics, so while the law prevents unlawful *human* disturbance, there may be value in 'natural' disturbances, such as forest fires.

Exceptions, defences, and licensing

A feature of species conservation offences is the numerous exceptions and defences for acceptable activities, many of which require permission or a licence from an official body. For example, game birds—that is, pheasant, partridge, grouse, and ptarmigan—are excluded from the protection provided by WCA 1981, apart from anti-cruelty measures relating to illegal methods of killing or taking them (s. 27). A long list of further exceptions also applies if a licence has been obtained from the appropriate official authority. It includes such things as the carrying out of research, educational activities, conservation work, and ringing of birds (s. 16), and most licences are granted for these relatively uncontentious activities, which are aimed at benefiting species conservation.

The most problematic issue, however, is the extent to which species may be killed or harmed if this is done to further some legitimate social objective such as agriculture or development (or even the conservation of other species). In this area, implementation of the EC Directives initially followed some of the approaches traditionally taken at national level, but, as a result of judgments of the ECJ, there has had to be some tightening of the defences. Two examples illustrate this point.

(a) Species licensing

The first relates to those situations in which a licence is sought from the appropriate authority either to control a so-called 'pest' species or to facilitate development. Historically, the law has always allowed for the destruction of species considered to be pests and, in early times, even *required* landowners to do so (for example, in Scotland, the law required wolf hunts, which clearly proved successful). Under WCA 1981, it is a defence for any owner or occupier, or other authorized person to show that killing or injuring is necessary for things such as crop protection, disease prevention, or the protection of public health and safety, and prior permission is not needed (s. 4, in relation to birds; s. 10(4), in relation to animals listed in Sch. 5). For listed animal species, however, the defence does not apply if, beforehand, it was apparent that the harmful action would be necessary and a licence was not applied for or had yet to be determined.[106]

This policy preference for licensing—and away from blanket criminal offences and defences—is typical of the recent approach of the law, in part as a response to the Wild Birds and Habitats Directives. Hence WCA 1981 no longer lists any bird species that owners, occupiers, or authorized persons may, without further permission, kill or from which they may take or destroy their nests or eggs (s. 2(2) and Sch. 2, Pt II). Instead, listed pest species of birds may be interfered with under general licences issued by environment and agriculture Ministers, but only for the reasons given in the licence (for example, public health, crop protection, etc.).[107] The policy approach, therefore, is a more administrative one. Indeed, virtually any prohibited activity affecting wild birds may be licensed, but only if there is no other satisfactory solution (s. 1A(a)).

For European protected species, a licence can be granted for preventing serious damage to crops, etc., from such species and, more generally, can also be granted for imperative reasons of overriding public interest, including those of a social or economic nature (Habitats Regulations, reg. 44).[108] But it must be shown that there is no satisfactory alternative and that the authorized action will not be detrimental to maintaining the favourable conservation status of the species in its natural range. This is an important legal baseline that is notable by its absence in WCA 1981, but exactly what it means is unclear (the Commission interprets it as meaning that status has not got worse since the Habitats Directive came into force in 1994). Until 1999, in cases in which development impacted on a European protected species, the practice was to issue licences under reg. 44(2)(c)—that is, 'conservation' licences—thus allowing for development to go ahead if the species was in some way conserved (for example, translocated off-site, an approach that is often used where great crested newts are found on development sites).

Since 2000, following a reasoned opinion from the Commission, the 'overriding public interest' derogation must now be used. Because of the policy judgments to be made in situations involving development, central government is now the licensing authority (although the NCC advises on the impact on favourable conservation status).[109] This way of proceeding was challenged by the European Commission in an action against the UK on the grounds that the practice for potentially harmful development—under which the decision to grant

---

106 A circuitous way of saying, in effect, that these general defences are obsolete.

107 *RSPCA v. Cundey* [2002] Env LR 17 (a good example of a voluntary body prosecuting wildlife crime).

108 See *Newsum v. Welsh Assembly* [2004] EWHC 50, and analysis by J. Holder (2004) 16 JEL 377. See now *Newsum v. Welsh Assembly* [2005] Env LR 16 (CA).

109 In Scotland, licensing had always been handled by central government.

planning permission is taken first, followed by the application for a licence being considered by government—suggested that:

licences seem to be issued as a formality after development consent for a construction or infrastructure project has already been given, and do not appear to involve a careful weighing of the arguments for and against allowing damage to occur.

In Case C-434/01 *Commission v. United Kingdom* [2003] ECR I-13239, however, the ECJ rejected the Commission's complaint, on the basis that the licence issuing authority is formally required to consider strictly the conditions contained in reg. 44 and that this was sufficient performance of the Directive's provisions. The mere suggestion that licences were being issued with, in effect, one hand tied behind the decision maker's back, was not enough (a good example of law looking to matters of form over substance).

Nevertheless, guidance in Scotland and Wales seeks to tighten this by requiring planning authorities to consider the derogations in Art. 16 of the Directive—that is, coupling the decisions on planning permissions and on licensing (which will put an added strain on local authority resources)—but, formally, the position in England is as yet unchanged.

(b) 'Incidental result of a lawful operation'

The second main dimension to the conflict between species conservation and other activities is that, under WCA 1981, it is a defence that the action was an '*incidental result of a lawful operation and could not reasonably have been avoided*'.[110] This type of defence would clearly apply to such events as unavoidable road accidents (a serious problem for otter conservation), but its application to activities in relation to which damage to a species is knowable in advance and yet still authorized is more problematic. This is because the defence does not require that harmful activities are reasonably avoided, but simply that, in carrying out any lawful operation, the *consequence* is one that cannot reasonably be avoided. This, obviously, is a rather different matter, but if, for example, bats were discovered on a site after planning permission had been granted, but the NCC was not consulted, there would be a strong case to say that the developer was not protected by this defence (unless it could be shown that the NCC's advice could not have prevented the bats from inevitable harm). Controversially, the defence found its way into the Habitats Regulations in relation to European protected species, but—up to a point—has now been removed, although it still applies to species protected only under national law.

Enforcing wildlife crime

As the above indicates, the piecemeal approach to species conservation in Pt I of WCA 1981 and the relevant provisions in the Habitats Regulations contain numerous criminal offences. The specific penalties for these cannot be covered exhaustively, but some general observations may be made. First, the previous distinction that WCA 1981 made between ordinary penalties and 'special' penalties in relation to offences involving Sch. 1 bird species has largely been removed, with the higher penalties applying to most offences.

Secondly, following CROWA 2000, most of the offences in Pt I, WCA 1981, can now be punished both by fines (of up to £5,000) and by the possibility of six months' imprisonment.[111] This brings WCA 1981 into line with other conservation and cruelty laws, such as the Protection of Badgers Act 1992 and the Wild Mammals (Protection) Act 1996, which have always been enforceable through custodial sentences. It also moves species conservation law

---

110 WCA 1981, ss. 4(2)(c) (in relation to birds), 10(3)(c) (Sch. 5 animals), and 13(2) (plants). Similarly, see Protection of Badgers Act 1992, s. 6(c).

111 Recent cases are available online at **www.defra.gov.uk/paw/prosecutions**.

into line with other conservation and environmental crimes, although maximum fines relating to habitat conservation laws are significantly higher.

Thirdly, however, there have, as yet, been no changes to the penalty provisions of the Habitats Regulations, with the paradoxical result that offences involving European protected species presently attract lesser penalties than under WCA 1981. (There is greater consistency in relation to sentencing powers, and higher fines generally, in Scotland.)

Increasing the penalties for species offences goes some way to elevating the status of these sorts of crimes. Changes under s. 12 of NERC 2006 to give Natural England the right to bring its own prosecutions (both for species and habitats offences) also indicate an increasing attention to law enforcement. But there are many practical and legal problems with enforcing wildlife crime: many offences are simply very difficult to detect, especially if they take place in remote locations. In addition, despite most police forces having wildlife liaison officers, wildlife crimes are not recordable crimes. This means that solving them will not appear in the headline crime statistics, so police forces may be disinclined to devote appropriate resources to tackling them. For this and other reasons, the favoured policy approach is to try to share the burden of enforcing wildlife crime between the police, the NCC, and organizations such as the RSPB and the Royal Society for the Prevention of Cruelty to Animals (RSPCA), showing a continuing reliance being placed on voluntary bodies in species conservation (see also Box 9.6).

Integrative approaches

At one level, current policy tends to isolate conservation from the pressures of the wider economy, without doing anything to lessen the forces creating those pressures. This is reflected in the conservation 'stamp collecting' approach of designating protected sites. Yet the most apparent trend in modern conservation law and policy has been integration. This is reflected in provisions such as Art. 10 of the 1992 Biological Diversity Convention, which requires the integration of biodiversity conservation into national decision making. While this is a largely exhortatory provision, there are a number of ways in which an integrative approach to nature conservation can be taken—for example, integrating nature conservation objectives into other fields, such as agriculture policy, through financial incentive schemes, which is hugely important and which we discuss elsewhere (see p. 745). Even the limited approach of placing obligations on a wide range of public decision makers (see pp. 702 and 717) can be considered a (limited) integrative measure.

Biodiversity action plans

The 1992 Convention on Biological Diversity aims to conserve biological diversity through a variety of means, including species and habitat conservation. Under Art. 6 of the Convention, the contracting parties must, in accordance with their particular conditions and capabilities, develop or adapt national strategies, plans, and programmes for biodiversity conservation, and integrate the conservation and sustainable use of biological diversity into relevant sectoral or cross-sectoral plans, programmes, and policies. This is one of the few provisions of the Convention that does not require action only 'as far as possible and as appropriate'—a general feature of the Convention that clearly weakens its effectiveness. Nevertheless, it goes beyond a protected area approach to conservation and, in the UK, has given considerable impetus to the development of wider conservation initiatives.

Under Art. 6, the UK Biodiversity Action Plan 1994 was produced—an important document guiding subsequent policy in this area. This, in turn, has led to the development of action plans. In 2007, the number of such plans was increased dramatically, especially for species, and there are now plans for 1,149 species of plants and animals, and 65 habitats. The scheme is intended to increase public awareness and involvement, but also to develop costed targets for key species and integration between public sector agencies. An important tool used is to seek 'champions' for species, especially from the voluntary and private sectors, as well as government funding, but in those cases in which these have come forward, they have tended, understandably, to be interested in sponsoring 'charismatic' species, such as otters and butterflies. Alongside the changes to SSSI law in CROWA 2000, these plans are the most important development in national conservation policy since the 1981 Act, although they are not immune to charges of being overly bureaucratic and species-centred (and continuing declines in numbers of species are one factor behind more plans being needed, as the figures mentioned above indicate).

Biodiversity action plans were first given legal recognition under CROWA 2000. Section 41 of NERC 2006 now contains the provisions that require the Secretary of State to list species and habitats of principal importance for biodiversity conservation—for example, the red squirrel, the otter, and the corncrake—and to take reasonably practicable steps to further their conservation or to promote this by others. This gives biodiversity action plans a legal underpinning, but does not confer statutory status on the plans themselves. Moreover, it is not obvious how such a general obligation on the Secretary of State will be enforced, if at all—but its very existence may alleviate some of the funding problems that the NCC experienced in implementing biodiversity action plans.

Future developments

The main development relating to this chapter is likely to be whether a Marine Act is enacted in the next year or so. Another thing worth keeping an eye on is the next report of the Royal Commission on Environmental Pollution, which will look at adapting to climate change: this is one of the big topics in conservation policy and may require a different approach to the use of the legal tools we now have—perhaps along with some new tools.

CHAPTER SUMMARY

1   Nature is valued for a wide range of reasons, but a central policy choice lies in deciding which species and habitats should be conserved, and at what cost.

2   The administration of nature conservation law is primarily the responsibility of specialist agencies with a scientific focus. These bodies have greater legitimacy in identifying species and habitats for special protection than they do in making trade-offs between conservation and other socially valued interests, which has more of a political dimension.

3   Nature conservation laws often divide into the use of criminal offences to conserve protected species, and administrative and fiscal controls to conserve habitats. In both respects, however, licensing regimes are increasingly subject to overriding conservation objectives.

4   There are species conservation offences not only about direct interference (for example, unlawful killing), but also about disturbing habitat, so it is difficult to draw a bright line between laws about conserving species and conserving their habitats. Often, both will apply to an activity, such as potentially damaging development.

5   The most important protected area designations are found at national and EC level. At national level, the law governing sites of special scientific interest (SSSIs) has recently been strengthened under the Countryside and Rights of Way Act (CROWA) 2000, shifting policy from voluntarism to regulated site management, backed by binding prohibitions. But there remains an emphasis on voluntary agreement

being reached between the relevant NCC and landowners, facilitated by the use of financial incentives for positive conservation benefits.

6   There remains no overarching objective for the legislation on SSSIs. By contrast, EC law is directed towards maintaining or restoring important habitat types and habitats of species at a favourable status. This requires stability of a species' or habitat's range over the long term, but adverse affects on individual sites cannot be marginalized because of lack of harm to a species' conservation as a whole.

7   At national level, there is a lot of flexibility in striking the balance between conservation and other interests. When activities damaging to a species are being licensed, there is a modest requirement that no other satisfactory solution exists. Habitat damage can be consented by the relevant NCC, subject only to its general statutory duties, but if planning permission is required, then damage may be authorized subject to government guidance. This requires conservation impact to be a material planning consideration, but falls some way short of a strong presumption against development.

8   Under the Habitats Directive, striking the balance on Natura 2000 sites between nature and other interests is a more tightly defined process, based on a staged risk assessment and the provision of (environmental) compensation. For the most endangered species and habitats, economic reasons cannot justify damaging activities.

9   A key challenge for nature conservation law and policy is integration. This can range from long-standing practices, such as notifying planning authorities of SSSIs in their area, to more modern approaches, such as placing general conservation obligations on public bodies or requiring action plans for key species and habitats to be drawn up.

Q   QUESTIONS

1   What should be the objective of what we call nature conservation law? To protect animals, plants, and habitats? To conserve them? To restore them? To enhance them? What are the implications (for regulators, landowners, and others) of taking each of these approaches?

2   Of the main UK conservation designations, only national nature reserves (NNRs) are included in a globally recognized categorization of protected areas (available online at **www.unep-wcmc.org/protected_areas/categories/index.html**). Sites of special scientific interest (SSSIs) are not included. Is this fair?

3   Who should pay for conserving nature? Is the Polluter Pays Principle applicable to nature conservation?

4   Does the law on SSSIs now steer the right course between seeking cooperation with landowners through financial incentives and preventing damaging activities?

5   Compare and contrast the law relating to terrestrial SSSIs and European sites. You might consider here any of the following:

    a   any legal purposes or objectives (or otherwise);

    b   the designation of sites;

    c   conserving such sites.

    Does either regime strike the right balance between nature conservation and economic interests? (You may find that competing theories of sustainable development—see p. 61—provide a useful framework here.)

6   A ferry operator is planning to expand operations. On the land to be developed—which is in an area of regionally high unemployment—there are a number of otter holts. Some of the land is an SSSI (although not because of the otters), but none of the land has been designated as a European site. The

local planning authority grants planning permission for the development, subject to a condition requiring artificial otter holts to be built on another site and the otters translocated. A local wildlife organization seeks to review the grant of planning permission on the grounds that, under the EC Habitats Directive:

a the land should have been designated as a European site;

b the planning authority should not have authorized development that would adversely affect the otter holts on the site;

c the 'compensation' measures fell short of what was required, because the general state of the habitat surrounding the new holts was not as favourable for otters;

d the planning authority did not have regard to the otter being a priority species.

Advise the wildlife organization. What further information would you need?

 FURTHER READING

There are many more provisions aimed at conserving species and habitats, at national, EC, and international levels, than the illustrative selections in this chapter. For these, C. Reid (2002) *Nature Conservation Law*, 2nd edn, Edinburgh: W. Green, provides the best (and most up-to-date) overview, but it must be handled with care, because it covers neither the Nature Conservation (Scotland) Act 2004 nor the Natural Environment and Rural Communities Act 2006. On the latter, see K. Cook, 'The Natural Environment and Rural Communities Act 2006 (legislative comment)' (2006) 8(4) Env LR 292.

Other useful articles about national law include: K. Last, 'The Wildlife and Countryside Act 1981: has it made a difference?' (1999) JEL 15; D. Brock, 'Is nature taking over?' [2003] JPL Supp 50 (which questions whether the balance in the legal protection of conservation interests has now tipped too far towards 'nature' at the expense of humans); and R. N. Lawton, 'Ecological compensation within the UK planning system' (2007) 18(2) WL 47.

For EC conservation law, the European Commission has published a compendium of leading cases and article-by-article analysis of these in its (2006) *Nature and Biodiversity Cases: Ruling of the European Court of Justice*, available online at **ec.europa.eu/environment/nature/info/pubs/docs/others/ecj_rulings_en.pdf**. Two articles by N. de Sadeleer—'Habitats conservation in EC Law: from nature sanctuaries to ecological networks' (2005) 5 Yearbook of European Environmental Law 215, and 'The Birds, Habitats, and Environmental Liability Directives to the rescue of wildlife under threat' (2007) 7 Yearbook of European Environmental Law 36—both offer in-depth analysis and wider context. A really excellent article that critiques wildlife law for focusing too much on what are really welfare concerns at the expense of more ecological approaches, and which criticizes the failure to conserve the 'commonplace' in biodiversity, is S. Harrop, 'Conservation regulation: a backward step for biodiversity?' (1999) 8 Biodiversity and Conservation 679. B. Martin 'To control or not to control? The need to control some alien species, the effectiveness of legislation and possible future developments in the law' (2007) 27(3) Liv LR 259 is a comprehensive analysis of the law in an important area that we do not cover here.

International conservation law

Our omission of international conservation law can be rectified by the relevant chapters of P. W. Birnie and A. E. Boyle (2002) *International Law and the Environment*, 2nd edn, Oxford: Oxford University Press, which also contains a useful account of the development of scientific thinking and policy at international level (and how the law has often lagged far behind these), or P. Sands (2003) *Principles of International Environmental Law*, 2nd edn, Cambridge: Cambridge University Press. A useful source is L. Guruswamy and J. McNeely (eds) (1998) *Protection of Global Biodiversity: Converging Strategies*, Durham: Duke University Press, which contains an excellent essay by M. Sagoff, arguing that intrinsic worth is the most compelling reason to value nature. The wide-ranging Convention on Biological Diversity is very clearly explained, article by article, in the Secretariat of the Convention on Biological Diversity (ed.) (2001) *Handbook on the Convention on Biological Diversity*, London: Earthscan, which also comments on further agreements between the contracting parties. There is also a special 2002 issue of the *Review of EC and International Environmental Law*—11(1)—concerned with biodiversity.

Conservation policy

There are two key places to start in relation to this subject. Nationally, there is the UK Biodiversity Partnership's (2007) *Conserving Biodiversity: The UK Approach*, available online at **www.defra.gov.uk/ wildlife-countryside/pdfs/biodiversity/ConBioUK-Oct2007.pdf**. At EC level, there is the Communication from the Commission (2006) *Halting the Loss of Biodiversity by 2010—and Beyond: Sustaining Ecosystem Services for Human Well-Being*, COM/2006/0216/Final, available online at **eur-lex.europa.eu**. Both are up-to-date and concise statements of the underlying problems, and of the policy objectives and approaches that will be pursued. These are forward-thinking and a good accompanying read is W. M. Adams (2003) *Future Nature*, revd edn, London: Earthscan, a hugely engaging attempt to think critically about what conservation means in a modern world in which everything has been affected by man. P. Marren (2002) *Nature Conservation: A Review of the Conservation of Wildlife in Britain, 1950–2001*, London: HarperCollins, is a forthright book, written by a key insider, which gives colour to most of the legal provisions and many of the legal cases considered here.

There are many other valuable texts, but most of these are now rather dated. If you want to pursue how policy has developed, see the further reading in previous editions of this book.

@ **WEB LINKS**

Law and guidance at national level can be found via the Department for Environment, Food and Rural Affairs (DEFRA) at **www.defra.gov.uk**—particularly the pages of the wildlife and countryside division—and its devolved counterparts. Information on nature conservation policy and some of the differences across the UK can be found through the websites of the national agencies—**www.naturalengland.org.uk**, **www. ccw.gov.uk**, **www.snh.org.uk**, and **www.ehsni.gov.uk**—and of the Joint Nature Conservation Committee at **www.jncc.gov.uk**, which has a lot of information about how sites of special scientific interest (SSSIs) and Natura 2000 sites are selected in the UK, and reports on progress on implementation of the Habitats Directive. Natural England's website now has very full information about individual SSSIs, including why they have been designated, the operations likely to damage the site, and the current status of the site. The European Commission maintains a site that has both the main Directives and key policy guidance, such as on implementation of the Habitats Directive, at **ec.europa.eu/environment/nature/index_en.htm**.

20 Landscape management

→ **Overview**

This chapter looks at the legal protection and management of various features of the UK country-side—that is, its landscape, trees, forests, and hedgerows. (We do not consider the specific protections of human artefacts, such as archaeological sites.) This involves applying some controls at which you have already looked: in particular, town and country planning law. Sometimes, this gives added levels of protection, but many of the activities that shape the countryside are not covered by planning law. Nature conservation designations are also important in this area, because what humans see as landscape features may also be the habitat of protected species of plants and animals. But effective landscape management relies heavily on using economic instruments, especially grants and subsidies to landowners.

For all of these reasons, you will get most from this chapter if you have already looked at Chapters 8, 12, and 19, and if you bear in mind that this topic demands that you think about the full scope of the regulatory toolbox.

At the end of this chapter, you will be able to:

✔ appreciate the particular legal challenges in managing natural landscapes;

✔ understand the main landscape designations and how they work in practice;

✔ understand the main ways in which positive assistance is given to promote landscape management;

✔ appreciate how traditional legal approaches are used to protect forests, trees, and hedgerows in the UK.

Introduction

Effective landscape management involves a number of different things. In relation to landscape, there is the restriction of urban expansion and urban development in the countryside, the preservation of the particular rural character of an area, and the protection of distinctive landscapes or landscape types. With trees, forests, and hedgerows, the focus is generally on smaller, sometimes individual, environmental features, the key problem for the law being in grappling with two familiar and related difficulties—controlling destructive, rather than constructive, acts and establishing adequate control over natural things. In both cases, however, protection and management pose some difficult problems. The two main reasons are that, first, the shape of most of what is to be protected is the result of hundreds of years of human intervention. Secondly, landscape management is inherently subjective, which makes it difficult to decide exactly what to preserve and why (see Box 20.1).

Some of the difficulties in this respect can be seen in the statement of the (then) Countryside Commission that future generations must be passed a national inheritance '*with all its richness intact*'.[1] However obscure this objective, it must surely be preferable to the view, expressed by 90 per cent of respondents to a survey in 2003 by the Countryside Agency, that it is important '*to keep the English countryside the way it is now*', which fails to recognize the changing nature and perception of the countryside, and changing priorities. Landscape plays a role in constructing cultural identity and this is a key motivation behind the Council of Europe European Landscape Convention. This might form one part of a more 'bioregional' approach to decision making, in which nature conservation would also play an important part. As discussed briefly in Chapter 19, nature conservation and landscape issues are increasingly being integrated, following many decades of relative isolation.

BOX 20.1 Landscape, values, and communities—the case of wind farms

Wind farms are an increasingly common feature of the countryside. They are often located in exposed areas of high landscape value. This has led to conflict between those who stress the contribution of wind energy in reducing greenhouse emissions and those who place greater weight on the importance of not 'spoiling' the landscape. But this clash of opinion is complicated by various factors. Wind farms are a further change to land continuously altered by humans over the centuries and it is a subjective judgment to say that a wind turbine is less appropriate in a national park, or less beautiful than, for example, a poorly insulated 'chocolate box' cottage. Also, those who object to wind turbines may do so on grounds that are unrelated to landscape—for example, that energy efficiency or reduced demand for electricity would be preferable, or even that the need to address climate change is so acute that only more drastic steps such as a revival of nuclear energy will be effective.

We saw in Chapter 3 the role that values play in this kind of decision making, and, in particular, how possible clashes between individual and collective perspectives ('not in my back yard', or 'NIMBY'-ism) may colour attitudes to polluting or obtrusive development. There is survey evidence, however, indicating that local residents view wind farms in a relatively positive light. In a 2003 poll of residents near to the larger wind farms in Scotland,[2] 20 per cent of respondents said that their local wind farm had a broadly positive impact on the area, compared with 7 per cent who said it had a negative impact, while most respondents said that the impact was neutral. Those living closest to the wind farms were even more positive about their impact. And while 27 per cent thought that there *would* be landscape problems, only 12 per cent said that the landscape had *actually* been spoiled. A majority of respondents (54 per cent) and an even higher percentage of those living closest supported significant expansion of the wind farm. This is a good illustration of the extent to which environmental values are not static, but change, not only as a result of debate, but also through experience. Note that, partly for planning reasons, most development is likely to take place offshore.

Regulatory mechanisms

Three main methods of control are used:

- relying on the town and country planning legislation to control developments in the countryside in the same way that they are controlled in towns;

1 Countryside Commission (1998) *Protecting Our Finest Countryside: Advice to Government.*
2 MORI Scotland (2003) *Public Attitude to Windfarms*, Scottish Executive Social Research.

- imposing special protections in designated areas, or in relation to designated features such as hedgerows (in practice, these added protections often tend to stem from the town and country planning system as well, although there are some that do not);

- utilizing grants and other incentives to ensure the proper care of the countryside or natural features, again with special schemes available in selected areas. Economic tools are widely used in the promotion of desirable objectives, such as tree planting and hedge laying.

A particular feature of the third mechanism is the reliance on voluntary controls, rather than on compulsion. Because most countryside land is privately owned, it is perhaps inevitable that positive action, as much as restrictive controls, will be used.

The international and EC dimensions

Compared with most other topics covered in this book, international and EC law has had relatively little direct impact on national law and policy relating to landscape management. This is undoubtedly because of the often local and subjective nature of this topic, although some conventions have, in recent years, included landscape features within a general definition of 'the environment' (as is the case with the 1991 Espoo Convention on Environmental Impact Assessment in a Transboundary Context and the 1992 Transboundary Watercourses Convention). Attempts to conclude a global convention on forests have so far been unsuccessful and only a Non-binding Statement of Forest Principles was agreed at the Earth Summit in 1992, although there are emerging signs that a global treaty may now be more acceptable to countries such as Indonesia, which strongly resisted such a development at Rio, and, in 2000, the United Nations Forum on Forests was created.

The 1972 World Heritage Convention, however, is a notable example of an attempt to use international law to protect national features of global significance. As well as cultural treasures, the treaty aims to protect natural heritage of 'outstanding universal value' for aesthetic or scientific reasons. The treaty is unusual, because states are obliged not only to protect sites that are eventually accepted onto a 'World Heritage List', but are also under general obligations to protect any areas worthy of inclusion on such a list. States must keep under review heritage covered by the treaty and protect it even if it is not accepted on to the list, although it is unlikely that any decision about an area forming part of the world heritage would be reviewable by the courts (for an Australian example, see *Queensland v. Commonwealth* (1989) 167 CLR 232). The added protection of being listed is that sites are eligible for assistance from the World Heritage Fund, run by the United Nations Educational, Scientific and Cultural Organization (UNESCO). The list is currently biased in favour of cultural heritage and the 29 sites for which the UK is responsible are also mostly built heritage—for example, Canterbury Cathedral.

CASE 20.1 *Coal Contractors v. Secretary of State for the Environment* [1995] JPL 421

Planning permission was applied for for an open cast coalmine very near to Hadrian's Wall, a world heritage site (WHS). Although there was no planning policy on WHSs, there was a Ministerial statement to the effect that inappropriate development should be avoided at such sites. Applying his own policy, the Minister decided that to grant planning permission would adversely affect the wider setting of the WHS, even though the effect on the landscape was—for topographical reasons—not adverse. Permission was therefore refused. WHS designation can therefore provide extended landscape protection in and around such sites, but, notably, WHS designation added an extra dimension to the decision beyond only the landscape impact of the development.

Note also that the Secretary of State found that there 'was no complete embargo on any particular form of development within a WHS'. Ultimately, it was a matter of political judgment and discretion whether the development was approved, and, had the decision been to grant planning permission, this decision, while it might have been politically (and even diplomatically) unpopular, would almost certainly have been unchallengeable. In 2007, a White Paper proposed that a planning circular would be published strengthening the level of protection from development and that significant development-affected WHSs would be subject to call-in by the Minister (on call-in powers—see p. 403).[3]

At the European level, there is no EC legislation relating directly to landscape. The Environmental Impact Assessment Directive (85/337/EEC) does require information about the effects of projects on landscape and cultural heritage to be assessed, but the impact of the EC is most closely felt through the Common Agricultural Policy (CAP)[4] and from EC regulations aimed at integrating agricultural and environmental objectives (see below). Under the Habitats Directive (92/43/EEC), member States must encourage in their land-use planning and development policies the conservation of linear landscape features, such as hedgerows, which play an important part in biodiversity conservation. This obligation marks an important break from a pure protected areas approach to conservation (on which, see generally Chapter 19), and emphasizes the links between nature conservation and landscape management that are increasingly being made.

In 2004, a Council of Europe European Landscape Convention entered into force. This has more general application than the World Heritage Convention, going beyond protecting the 'jewels in the crown', but, depending on one's perspective, either puts rather too general, or too wide-ranging, obligations on the parties. The UK, which took a lead in negotiating the Convention, signed and ratified in 2006, and it became binding on the UK in March 2007. The Convention does not seem to require any specific legal changes.

Town and country planning

The starting point for protecting the countryside has always been the development control system. But it has never proved particularly successful because, despite its name, it has always had an urban bias. There have been very few adaptations of the basic structure to cope with countryside matters. Indeed, it is commonly referred to as the 'town planning' system, the countryside aspect being forgotten.

There are a number of reasons for this. A major one is the history of the system, which had a consequent effect on the nature of the legal mechanisms that were adopted. The town and country planning system developed in 1947 was specifically designed to meet predominantly urban problems, such as community layout and design, industrial location, post-war reconstruction, public health and overcrowding, and transportation changes. As far as the rural environment was concerned, the main policy was the protection of the countryside against urban creep and expansion. The legal mechanisms that were adopted were thus mainly negative, such as the need for planning permission, and did not reflect the need for positive management in the countryside.

In addition, in 1947, there was perceived to be little need to control developments in the countryside, because it was generally considered that landowners and farmers had done a good job in shaping the landscape, and, in any case, agriculture itself required protection after the rural depression of the 1930s and the Atlantic Blockade of the Second World War.

---

3 Department for Culture, Media and Sport/Welsh Assembly Government (2007) *Heritage Protection for the Twenty-First Century*, Cm 7057, p. 28.

4 Note that forestry is not included in this.

Agriculture and forestry—the two main activities likely to have an impact on the landscape—were granted generous exemptions in the legislation that, despite some minor changes, still remains today.

As a result, there are distinct limitations on the use of development control in the countryside, and its most important role is in controlling new buildings and structures.

- Many rural activities that have a significant impact on the landscape do not constitute development. For example, afforestation or deforestation, the removal of hedgerows or stone walls, ploughing, and the cultivation of new crops (such as oilseed rape) are all entirely excluded from the development control system.

- The Town and Country Planning Act 1990, s. 55(2)(e), provides that a change of use to agriculture or forestry is not development. While it is obvious that this covers a change from an urban to a rural use, in landscape terms, it is more significant that this paragraph excludes from development control a change from unused land (often of high nature conservation or landscape value) to agriculture or forestry, or from agriculture to forestry, or from forestry to agriculture, or from one type of agriculture or forestry to another. 'Agriculture' is defined very widely in the Town and Country Planning Act 1990, s. 336, to include such diverse things as intensive livestock production, fish farming, horticulture, and extensive grazing.

- Further exemptions are set out in the Town and Country Planning (General Permitted Development) Order 1995[5] (the GPDO), Sch. 2, under which blanket automatic planning permissions (permitted development rights) are granted. For example, the GPDO exempts the construction of fences and walls up to 2 metres in height, and some temporary uses up to 28 days per year.

- The GPDO, Sch. 2, paras 6 and 7, provide permitted development rights for a wide range of agricultural and forestry operations, such as new roads, buildings, drainage works, and excavations, subject to some generous limitations on size and height (for example, each building may be up to 465 square metres in area and 12 metres in height). There are other, more technical limitations, such as that the erection or alteration of structures for the accommodation of livestock, or for storing slurry or sewage sludge, within 400 metres of non-agricultural dwellings or other buildings is not permitted under the GPDO.

- A final limitation on the usefulness of the development control system in the countryside is that this is a political system. Decisions are made by local planning authorities, and are likely to reflect the economic needs and policy preferences of local residents, although reference must always be made to Planning Policy Statement 7, *Sustainable Development in Rural Areas*, which sets out general government planning policies towards the countryside. Local authorities may also underestimate the importance of a local area in national terms.[6]

BOX 20.2 Landscape and spatial planning

As noted in Chapter 12, a central aim of the reforms under the Planning and Compulsory Purchase Act 2004 was to make planning more integrative. In relation to landscape, some steps towards this aim were already provided for by placing statutory duties on public bodies to have regard to the

---

5 SI 1995/418.

6 These same limitations explain why the network of SSSIs is not protected properly by controls dependent on the town and country planning system—see p. 699.

main landscape designations (see pp. 739 and 743). This is fleshed out by planning guidance under which, in the revision of regional spatial strategies, regional planning bodies are expected to demonstrate how they have taken the statutory purposes of the national parks and areas of outstanding natural beauty (AONBs) into account, including significant indirect effect on a national park or the Broads (but not AONBs) on the landscape setting (PPS11, para. 2.9). Regional spatial strategies should also take into account agriculture (but not, for some reason, forestry—see PPS11, para. 1.3). The 2004 Act does not therefore bring agriculture and forestry within the planning system in the sense of requiring planning permission, but it does go some way towards integrating them into the wider planning of development. Whether these concerns will be integrated in practice remains to be seen; in its 23rd Report on *Environmental Planning* (2002, Cm 5459), the Royal Commission on Environmental Pollution was critical of how effective local planning authorities have been in doing so.

Extra protections under planning law

In some circumstances, there are extra protections provided by the town and country planning system in the countryside.

- The extent of development permitted under the GPDO is limited in national parks, the Norfolk and Suffolk Broads, areas of outstanding natural beauty (AONBs), conservation areas, and any area specified by the Department for Environment, Food and Rural Affairs (DEFRA) under the Wildlife and Countryside Act (WCA) 1981, s. 41(3). (Collectively these areas are known as 'Art. 1(5) land'.)[7] While the limitations are not great, this does mean that stricter controls apply to such things as extensions to houses and other buildings.

- A system of prior notification applies to farm or forestry developments otherwise permitted by the GPDO, Sch. 2, paras 6 and 7. This means that 28 days' prior notification of the proposed development must be submitted to the local planning authority, which may then impose conditions relating to the siting, design, and external appearance of the development in the light of the likely effects on the surroundings. Since 1999, prior notification procedures now also apply to mobile phone masts, although only ground-based masts (as opposed to antenna and masts on buildings) require publicity, which—along with the sums of money offered—helped to explain the preference for masts on buildings such as schools and churches (until the Stewart Report in 2000 stressed the need for caution in relation to the impacts on children, from which point no new masts have been erected on schools).

- As a matter of policy, the local planning authority may impose restrictive conditions on activities requiring permission. For example, specific design criteria are commonly imposed where there is a local style. It may also make non-statutory designations of such things as sites of high landscape value in its development plan.

- An Art. 4 direction may be imposed under the GPDO, requiring planning permission to be sought for something that would otherwise be granted automatic permission (see p. 398). Because Art. 4 directions entail the payment of compensation by the local planning authority if planning permission is then refused, their use is rare (even though the cost is sometimes grant-aided by central government agencies).

7 There are proposals to extend this list of designations to include world heritage sites: see Department for Culture, Media and Sport/Welsh Assembly Government (2007).

It is important to note that green belts—creatures of planning policy, but never planning law—are primarily intended to act as a brake on suburban growth. There is a policy presumption against major development in green belts, unless 'very special circumstances' dictate otherwise,[8] which, around many urban areas, entrenches the divide between urban and rural. While green belts are not designated on nature conservation or landscape grounds, they undoubtedly contribute indirectly to these objectives. There is currently a debate as to whether 'belts' of land around towns and cities should be superseded by other approaches to green infrastructure. Development tends to leapfrog over the greenbelt and can end up being sited in more vulnerable parts of the natural environment. There is a case that things such as green wedges, corridors, etc., might have greater ecological value, although the shift of approach is seen by some as motivated primarily to opening the green belt up to accommodate the current government's extensive house-building targets.

Natural England

In England, landscape matters were, for many years, the responsibility of the Countryside Commission, originally created in 1949 as the 'National Parks Commission'. In April 1999, a new Countryside Agency was formed by changing the name of the Countryside Commission to the 'Countryside Agency', and then transferring certain functions of the Rural Development Commission (RDC) to the new Agency.[9] These bodies had functions in relation to natural beauty and recreation only. In 2007, a new body—Natural England—was established under the Natural Environment and Rural Communities Act (NERC) 2006, bringing together English Nature, certain functions (mainly related to landscape conservation) of the Countryside Agency, and most of the functions of the Rural Development Service. The rest of the Countryside Agency became the Commission for Rural Communities, which has more of a rural advocacy function. Similarly integrated institutions with equivalent responsibilities to those of Natural England are Scottish Natural Heritage and the Countryside Council for Wales (CCW).

We comment on the constitution and general powers Natural England on p. 113, but it is worth noting again that its general purpose is *'to ensure that the natural environment is conserved, enhanced and managed for the benefit of present and future generations, thereby contributing to sustainable development'*, and that this purpose includes conserving and enhancing the landscape (NERC 2006, s. 2). In addition, all the landscape agencies, and all Ministers, government departments, and public bodies, must have regard to the desirability of conserving the 'natural beauty and amenity'[10] of the countryside (Countryside Act 1968, s. 11). These are broad-ranging duties, applying to the functions of these bodies under any enactment, but their usefulness is limited by the weakness of their formulation.

Landscape designations

Apart from the limited protection accorded to landscapes by planning law, there are a number of designations of land that may be made. Ultimately, however, these depend either on the town planning system or on voluntary powers. There are few, if any, compulsory powers to support landscape protection.

In line with this voluntary philosophy, there is a power for any local planning authority to enter into a management agreement with any owner of land for conserving or enhancing its

---

8 Planning Policy Guidance Note 2 (1995) *Green Belts.*

9 See SI 1999/416.

10 In Scotland, the 'natural heritage'—see Countryside (Scotland) Act 1967, s. 66.

natural beauty or amenity, or for promoting its enjoyment by the public (WCA 1981, s. 39). Since the Countryside and Rights of Way Act (CROWA) 2000, a wider range of bodies also have powers under this section to enter into management agreements, including a conservation board for an AONB in its area (WCA 1981, s. 39(5), as amended). Natural England has general powers to enter into management agreements (NERC 2006, s. 7) that would be used.

BOX 20.3 Countryside designations—benefit or burden?

A feature of key landscape designations is that they may actually *increase* pressure on the land designated. Particularly with national parks, it is at least debatable whether the designation increases some of the adverse effects associated with high tourist demand or simply reflects already existing demands, but what is clear is that many visitors are drawn to areas, at least in part, *because* of their designation. There is a clear contrast here with nature conservation designations, which generally do not have this potentially damaging 'honey pot' effect.

Nature conservation designations, meanwhile, tend to depress the value of land, whereas land values inside national parks tend to be higher than those immediately outside the park. One historical consequence of the depressed land value of nature conservation sites was, paradoxically, to expose them to particular development pressures. A designation, such as a site of special scientific interest (SSSI), could prevent planning permission being granted to the landowner for a profitable development, but this would not prevent permission being granted by local or central government for public developments such as infrastructure projects. In these cases, the public interest would weigh more heavily and designated land would have the advantage that the cost of compensating affected landowners was relatively low (because landowners would only receive compensation for the value of their land in its undeveloped state).

National parks

National parks in the UK do not equate to the concept of a 'national park' used in most other countries. Instead of being wilderness areas with few, if any, inhabitants, they contain land on which large numbers of people live. They are effectively working environments. The aim of national park designation is to plan and manage the area so as to create a balance between recreation, amenity, wildlife, and economic development. Land ownership is unaffected by designation, although various public bodies are given powers to purchase land and, in practice, much of some parks is in the ownership of a public body, or of the National Trust.

General objectives and duties

National parks were first provided for in the National Parks and Access to the Countryside Act 1949. This Act still provides the basic structure of the legislation on national parks, although it has been much amended, especially by the Countryside Act 1968, the Environment Act 1995, Pt III, and Pt V of NERC 2006. The purposes of national parks were originally stated in the Hobhouse Report,[11] and set out in the National Parks and Access to the Countryside Act 1949, s. 5, in terms of two general objectives: the preservation and enhancement of the natural beauty of the areas, and the promotion of their enjoyment by the public. In recognition of the way that attitudes towards the national parks have changed since 1949, the

---

11 National Parks Committee (1947) *National Parks in England and Wales*.

Environment Act 1995, s. 61 substituted a new s. 5, which set out somewhat wider purposes:

(a) conserving and enhancing the natural beauty, wildlife and cultural heritage of the areas..., and

(b) ...promoting opportunities for the understanding and enjoyment of the special qualities of those areas by the public.

NERC 2006 did not change these basic purposes, but it did expand the interpretation given to some of these terms (see Box 20.4).

BOX 20.4 **The separation (and integration?) of landscape**

The historian T. C. Smout[12] has written that:

> Every age constructs nature in a different way. In the seventeenth century, use and delight were very difficult to separate. By the end of the eighteenth, they occupied different spheres in the mind. By the twentieth, they were in frequent conflict.

This nicely captures the way in which, historically, landscape (and nature conservation) emerged as discrete concerns. This came from a separation in how the countryside was seen from, initially, a place within which work and leisure were inextricably bound together, to a position in which the aesthetic and leisure interests of one section of society often clashed with the economic interests of other groups. In thinking about the objectives of national parks (and also areas of outstanding natural beauty—AONBs—see below) and how these are prioritized, it is worth reflecting on this historical development.

Since the 1995 Act, s. 11A(2) of the 1949 Act also gives statutory effect to the so-called 'Sandford principle', which is that, in cases in which there is a conflict between purposes (a) and (b), then greater weight should be attached to purpose (a). The balance between environmental, amenity, and economic factors is also made explicit in s. 11A(1), which requires national park authorities to seek to foster the economic and social well-being of local communities within the national park, albeit in the context of pursuing the purposes set out in s. 5. NERC 2006 removed the restriction that prevented significant money from being spent in pursuing this.

The impact of the changed purposes was reinforced by s. 11A(2), which also requires all public bodies and statutory undertakers to have regard to the new purposes when exercising or performing any functions affecting land in a national park. A review in 2002 by DEFRA of national park authorities, however, suggested that these provisions were not adequately applied in practice, because of a lack of awareness, understanding, and compliance, both on the ground and at departmental level.[13]

The criteria for designation mirror the twin statutory objectives (but see Box 20.4). Responsibility for proposing and designating a national park originally lay with the National Parks Commission, which designated the first ten parks in the 1950s. This responsibility has now devolved to Natural England and CCW.

Currently, there are 11 fairly sizeable national parks in England and Wales. The parks are the Peak District, the Lake District, the Yorkshire Dales, the North York Moors,

---

12 T. C. Smout (2000) *Nature Contested*, Edinburgh: Edinburgh University Press, p. 18.

13 Department for Environment, Food and Rural Affairs (2002) *Review of English National Park Authorities*, para. 18; see [2002] JPL 1334. To address this, guidance was published: see DEFRA (2005) *Duties on Relevant Authorities to Have Regard to the Purposes of National Parks, Areas of Outstanding Natural Beauty (AONBs) and the Norfolk and Suffolk Broads: Guidance Note*. This will need to be updated following NERC 2006.

Northumberland, Snowdonia, the Brecon Beacons, the Pembrokeshire Coast, Exmoor, Dartmoor, and the New Forest. In addition, the Broads Authority was established by the Norfolk and Suffolk Broads Act 1988. This has a similar constitution and powers to the national parks, with the inclusion of powers over navigation and water space. For the purposes of most legal protections, it is treated as a national park, although it is notable that the Sandford principle does not apply.[14]

Latterly, the Countryside Commission/Agency had taken the view that further designations of national parks in England would devalue the concept (although, in 1998, it eventually supported designation of the New Forest). In September 1999, the government announced that it was asking the Countryside Agency to consider designating national parks in the South Downs and the New Forest. The latter is now a national park; designation of the former is at an advanced stage (but see Case 20.2). What is interesting about the recent development is that, despite responsibility for proposing and designating parks resting with (now) Natural England, central government (the confirmation and funding of which is needed) was able to initiate the designation process by political direction. The rationale for these new parks appears to be slightly different from that of the existing parks. For example, there was already a New Forest heritage area in which, as a matter of government policy, the same planning principles that govern development in national parks were applied.

CASE 20.2 National parks, natural beauty, and the NERC Act 2006—*Meyrick Estate Management Ltd v. Secretary of State for the Environment, Food and Rural Affairs* [2007] Env LR 26

A landowner challenged the inclusion of its estate (which included a Grade 1 listed building) in the proposed New Forest national park. Following a public inquiry, the Inspector concluded that the estate should be included because of its natural beauty and the opportunities it afforded for open-air recreation (the statutory tests in s. 5(2), National Parks and Access to the Countryside Act 1949). Both of these grounds were successfully challenged in the High Court.[15] The Secretary of State appealed, but, before the appeal hearing, the Natural Environment and Rural Communities (NERC) Act 2006 (which DEFRA promoted) amended the 1949 Act in various ways. First, a new s. 5(2A) was introduced that

(i) included cultural heritage in the matters capable of being taken into account in determining 'natural beauty';

(ii) allowed the extent to which it was possible to promote opportunities for the understanding and enjoyment of the area's special qualities by the public to be taken into account.

Secondly, s. 99 of the 2006 Act provided that, if an area consisted of, or included, land, the flora, fauna, or physiological features of which were partly the product of human intervention in the landscape, this did not prevent it from being treated as an area of natural beauty. This provision was intended to make clear that agricultural land could be deemed to be 'natural'—large agricultural estates such as Chatsworth in the Peak District have always been included in national parks.

It is worth reading the debates, in both Houses of Parliament, on these amendments because they reveal quite sharp differences between the government and the opposition on the value of parks.[16]

---

14 Some of the practical consequences of this—in particular, the tensions between biodiversity conservation and navigation on the Broads—are discussed in L. Ledoux, S. Crooks, A. Jordan, and K. Turner (2003) *Implementing EU Biodiversity Policy: A UK Case Study*, CSERGE Working Paper, GEC 2000–03.

15 [2006] Env LR D6.

16 See, e.g., House of Commons debates, 29 March 2006, and House of Lords Debates, 20 March 2006.

The Court of Appeal held that, because the estate was not, in fact, open to public access, the test used by the Inspector—that is, of *potential* opportunities for open-air recreation—was the wrong one and dismissed the appeal without considering the issue of 'natural beauty'. On this, it is worth noting that the High Court had distinguished between the criteria for designation (in s. 5(2) of NPACA 1949) and those relating to the statutory purposes behind parks (in s. 5(1)). The difference is interesting because the designation criteria were—until NERC 2006 anyway—narrower than the general purpose and management provisions. Usually, in nature conservation law, it is the other way around, so that sites are designated using strict criteria, but can then be interefered with to take economic and social criteria into account. Meyrick's case was decided under the old law and, although an order varying the faulty designation order could have been applied for—which would have been subject to the new NERC Act rules and probably would have succeeded—this was not done, so Meyrick's land remains outside the national park.

Until recently, there were no national parks in Scotland, although there were designations with a roughly similar impact. This changed with the National Parks (Scotland) Act 2000, which enables the Scottish Parliament to propose and designate national parks.[17] The procedure for designation is somewhat different. In addition to being satisfied about the outstanding national importance of the area's natural heritage, or natural and cultural heritage combined, Ministers must be satisfied that the area has a distinctive character and coherent identity, and that designation would meet the special needs of the area and would be the best means of ensuring that the aims of the national park are achieved in a coordinated way. (Proposing a national park is a power, not a duty.)

The statutory objectives of Scottish national parks are similar to those of parks in England and Wales in that they include conservation of the natural and cultural heritage, and the promotion of public understanding, enjoyment, and recreation. But they also include the promotion of the sustainable use of the natural resources of the area, and the promotion of sustainable social and economic development of the communities of the area. As with the 1949 Act, there is a version of the 'Sandford principle' in that, in cases in which there is a conflict of aims, it is the conservation aim that must be given greater weight. So far, Loch Lomond and the Trossachs, and the Cairngorms, have been designated, following advice from Scottish Natural Heritage.

Administrative responsibilities

The national parks are the only areas in which a new institutional structure has been created in an attempt to protect the countryside, but control remains essentially local, because Natural England and CCW have no executive functions. Under s. 63 of the Environment Act 1995, the Secretary of State has power to establish by order a national park authority in the form set out in Sch. 7. This has altered the previous arrangements whereby each national park was administered by an authority run by a committee of the relevant county council or a separate, autonomous board. This has had the effect of creating autonomous local authorities for national parks, with primary responsibility for planning functions.

The national park authorities were formally established on 1 April 1997. Schedule 7 provides that a national park authority is subject to most legislative provisions affecting local authorities, including those on access to meetings and the jurisdiction of the Commissioner for Local Administration (the ombudsman). For national parks in England, a majority of members are to come from a combination of those appointed by district, county, or unitary authorities in the area, and from those appointed by the Secretary of State, but appointed to

---

17 Notably, DEFRA (2002) contains many proposals that would adapt policy and governance in line with the approach taken in Scotland.

represent parish councils. The remaining minority ('national members') are appointed by the Secretary of State. (In Wales, the National Assembly appoints half of the members, after consultation with CCW, and half are appointed by the constituent local authorities.) The authority then elects its own chair and deputy chair.

The position in Scotland is slightly different: there is an equal division between appointees nominated by the Scottish Parliament and the relevant local authorities, but only after at least 20 per cent of each governing board has been directly elected at local level.

In England and Wales, under s. 66 of the Environment Act 1995, national park authorities must prepare a national park management plan, although they may adopt existing management plans (made under the Local Government Act 1972). There are provisions for regular review. The management plan performs a different strategic function from the purely planning-based development plan, covering wider management policy issues.

In Scotland, there is a similar duty on national park authorities to produce plans that, following consultation, are approved by Ministers (National Parks (Scotland) Act 2000, s. 12). Unlike in England and Wales, a more explicitly integrative approach is taken, and a plan must set out and coordinate *the functions of other public bodies and office-holders so far as affecting the National Park*' (s. 11), and all public bodies must have regard to these plans in exercising their functions as these affect national parks (s. 14). This puts on public bodies a more specific obligation than the general duty on public bodies in s. 11A(2) of the 1949 Act.

There are powers to provide funding for the national park authorities. Under the Environment Act 1995, s. 72, the relevant Secretary of State has a wide discretion to make grants to a national park authority, while s. 71 empowers the authorities to issue levies to the constituent local authorities. Seventy-five per cent of funding comes from central government. Grants from Natural England and CCW for works and schemes are normally payable at a higher rate in a national park than they are outside.

Controls on development

Protection of the parks has always been strongly tied to the town and country planning system. The national park authority is designated the sole local planning authority for its area. One exception concerns tree preservation orders (TPOs), in relation to which the district council retains concurrent jurisdiction with the national park authority. Strategic planning in national parks centres around the national park development plan that was first required by the Planning and Compensation Act 1991. (As with all plan making in national parks, this requires consultation with Natural England or CCW.)

In Scotland, planning functions are not automatically transferred to national park authorities and decisions are taken on a park-by-park basis. In Loch Lomond and the Trossachs, all development planning and development control functions (and TPO functions) have been transferred to the national park authority, with the exception of structure plan functions. For these functions, responsibility continues to be exercised by local authorities, in consultation with the national park authority. In the Cairngorms, however, the major difference is that development control functions have not been transferred, although the national park authority has the power to call in, for its own determination, planning applications that raise a planning issue of general significance to the national park aims. In both parks, however, where responsibilities have been transferred to a national park authority, these are exercised by a committee, which must have a majority of members who are either directly elected or who are members of a local authority. These provisions are aimed at addressing concerns—voiced in England and Wales—that planning functions in national parks lack a sufficient local democratic mandate, and a consequential tension between local authorities and national park authorities.

As far as the substantive detail of planning law is concerned, apart from the limited restrictions referred to above, the main protection lies in the formulation and application of sensitive policies for the protection of the park through the planning process. But national parks are certainly not inviolable, as the siting of Fylingdales' early warning station, Milford Haven's oil terminal, and numerous quarries in the Peak District illustrate.

BOX 20.5 Planning policy, national parks, and areas of outstanding natural beauty (AONBs), and low-impact living

Until recently, policy guidance stated that '*major development should not take place in the National Parks . . . save in exceptional circumstances*' and that such development must demonstrably be in the public interest. The public interest was to be assessed by considering the national need for the development, the impact on the local economy of permitting or refusing consent, the cost of alternatives, and detrimental environmental effects (PPG 7, para. 4.5).

An illustration of exceptional circumstances justifying development is *Dartmoor National Park Authority v. Secretary of State for Transport, Local Government and the Regions* [2003] EWHC 236. The national park authority opposed a planning application for what the applicants described as 'low-impact sustainable development'. This involved the erection in woodland of a number of 'benders', mostly for living in. The Inspector thought the proposed development would seriously harm the character of the woodland, contrary to the development plan, but strong material considerations amounting to exceptional circumstances justified granting temporary planning permission for five years. Key factors were the experimental and temporary nature of the development—'*The principles of sustainability behind the experiment are central to Government policy and it is therefore of importance that they are tried and tested in a practical way*', the need to live in the woodland—which is normally resisted—being central to the applicants' philosophy, and the positive management of the wood that would result (including replacing non-native species with indigenous trees, to make the woodland more in keeping in landscape terms). A challenge to this decision in the High Court was rejected. (As we have noted elsewhere, temporary planning permissions are a well-established example of an adaptive form of regulation—see p. 228—because, at the end of the temporary period, there is complete flexibility as to whether the permission is renewed and the terms on which this might be done.)

Since 2000, following an answer to a parliamentary question, the same guidance was applied to major developments in AONBs (and is now found in PPS 7 (2004), para. 22, which repeats the tests mentioned above), another example of the many and varied ways in which rules of environmental law emerge.

Areas of outstanding natural beauty (AONBs)

AONBs, first provided for under the 1949 Act, are now designated, under CROWA 2000, s. 82, solely for their natural beauty, with the objective of conserving and enhancing these features. Even though, in landscape terms, they are meant to be the equivalent of national parks, by comparison with the parks, they are little known and understood. Unlike national parks, there is no duty to consider their designation and many of the powers available within them are optional for the local planning authority. Indeed, writing in 1980, Marion Shoard described them as the '*Cinderellas of the landscape designation system*'.[18]

AONBs have a number of similarities with national parks and, since the changes made under CROWA 2000, the similarities in regulatory approach are even stronger. For example, there are now general duties on all public bodies as there are with national parks (s. 85).

---

18 M. Shoard (1980) *The Theft of the Countryside*, London: Temple Smith, p. 144.

AONBs tend to be extensive areas: 41 have been designated, covering over 14 per cent of England and Wales. (The designation does not extend to Scotland, where there are instead 'national scenic areas'.) They are designated in the same way as national parks—that is, the Natural England/CCW makes a proposal for designation, which requires confirmation by the Secretary of State, normally after extensive consultation (in only one case has there also been a public inquiry). They rely on town planning procedures for their legal protection and the town planning powers are essentially the same as in national parks, including the duty to consult with Natural England/CCW over the making of development plans. Since CROWA 2000, there are also duties to prepare management plans for all AONBs and to keep these under review (s. 89), and relevant authorities—that is, public bodies—must have regard to the statutory purposes of AONBs (s. 85). This duty to prepare management plans falls either on local authorities in the area or, if one has been established by the Secretary of State (under s. 86 and Sch. 13), a conservation board. Conservation boards build on non-statutory part-nerships between local authorities and other key actors in AONBs, which were encouraged in the 1990s and proved to be generally successful. In practice, conservation boards are likely to be established only for larger AONBs.

But there are significant differences too: AONBs do not have a statutory role as far as recre-ation is concerned (although, under s. 87(1), conservation boards (only) must have regard to protecting beauty *and* its enjoyment); nor is extra finance specifically provided for AONBs, although the establishment of the Countryside Agency brought with it some increased fund-ing (and power to make grants to conservation boards—s. 91). But perhaps the major differ-ence from national parks is that the local planning authority generally remains unchanged. This is the case even if a conservation board has been established. Although certain planning functions may be transferred to conservation boards, this does not extend to functions relat-ing to development planning, development control, or planning enforcement.

Other landscape protections

A further type of designation is 'heritage coast'. Areas are selected by Natural England and the local planning authority acting together, and are subject to protective policies within the planning process. Forty-four areas covering 1,493 km of coast have been designated, although there have been no new designations since 1991. It should also be noted that a fairly strong Planning Policy Guidance Note 20, *Coastal Planning*, establishes a number of restraint policies on coastal development. Balanced against this, however, is the general pol-icy of 'managed retreat', meaning that, in certain cases, coastal land is allowed to erode nat-urally, because stemming the erosion would not be useful.

There is a power for a national park authority to make moorland conservation orders by statutory instrument (WCA 1981, s. 42). These orders impose a notification requirement similar to that applied to sites of special scientific interest (SSSIs), with the intention that the national park authority may offer a management agreement. It is accordingly a crim-inal offence to plough or convert any moor or heath subject to an order that has not been agricultural land within the preceding 20 years, unless the national park authority has been notified in advance. This section is distinctly limited. Orders can only be made in a national park and only provide for a temporary ban on operations, and works can go ahead after 12 months even if the national park authority refuses consent for them. It does not appear that any such orders have ever been made. With the strengthening of the law on the protec-tion of SSSIs under CROWA 2000 (see Chapter 19), the policy approach now appears out-moded and, even as a procedural protection, such orders have been superseded by the Town and Country Planning (Environmental Impact Assessment) Regulations 1999[19] covering

19 SI 1999/293.

primary conversion of uncultivated land and semi-natural areas, which are not limited to national parks, but apply to all such land (see p. 747).

The House of Commons Select Committee on the Environment recommended landscape protection orders in 1985. Despite support from the Countryside Commission, this proposal produced a very limited response from the government, which envisaged their use only as a stopgap power pending the making of a management agreement, and the proposals have never been acted upon.

Finally, there is a conditional exemption from inheritance tax if owners agree to maintain land, preserve its character, and provide reasonable public access to it. This is an economic instrument that plays a role in conserving landscapes, albeit on a haphazard basis. If these measures are not undertaken, then the exemption is removed and tax is payable.

Agriculture, landscape, and nature conservation

There is insufficient space in this book to trace the history of agricultural grants and their relationship with damage to the countryside, but, in the past, their availability has often been held responsible for a great number of damaging changes (see, for example, the works by Shoard and Harvey listed in the Further Reading at the end of this chapter). The nature of agricultural grants and, indeed, of the whole shape of agriculture has changed dramatic-ally in recent years, as farm incomes have fallen, the EC has sought to reform the CAP, and farmers are increasingly paid to produce landscapes and habitats. More than 50 per cent of agricultural land in the UK is now in an agri-environmental scheme and, in the last decade or so, the sums of money paid under these schemes has increased ten-fold, and now stands at around £300m, accounting for around 20 per cent of total spending on agriculture.

BOX 20.6 The changing nature of agricultural support

One of the main criticisms levelled against the EC's Common Agriculture Policy (CAP) is that, historically, it subsidized farmers according to their productivity, giving farmers incentives to intensify production, bring marginal land into productivity, and to put excessive numbers of farm animals on their land. Some of the downsides of these payments include the removal of hedge-rows and overgrazing, which is a problem both for nature conservation reasons and landscape management (and contributes to other problems, such as flooding). Recent reforms[20] have sought to change this, so that farmers are subsidized according to how much land they farm ('area pay-ments' or 'single payments') and, since 2005, there has been a 'decoupling' between production and subsidy. One factor behind decoupling is to move agricultural support into what is known as the 'Green Box' for World Trade Organization purposes, which would signify that it has minimal or non-trade distorting impact, rather than the present CAP which is more trade-distorting (and categorized in the 'Amber Box').

The impacts of decoupling may be mixed: pressures on soils, air, and water resources may reduce, but impacts on landscape and biodiversity could be damaging. To counter this, single payments will be linked to requirements to meet specific EC legislation on the environment—for example, the Wild Birds (79/409/EEC), Habitats (92/43/EEC), and Nitrates (91/676/EEC) Directives[21]—and to keep farmland in good agricultural and environmental condition. This is known as 'cross-compliance':

---

20 Under, in particular, EC Regulation 1782/2003.
21 For an example of cross-compliance being used to implement the Nitrates Directive, see Case 20.3.

farmers must comply with these obligations or lose their entitlement to payments.[22] Member States have a certain amount of discretion to determine what, for example, 'good environmental condition' entails, but the member State fleshes this out—for example, the 2 m uncultivated buffer zones that are now seen next to many hedges and watercourses derive from this obligation. For EC laws, there must be compliance with the implementing measures—that is, those obligations that are addressed to individuals and not to the member State. Cross-compliance is used to support the enforcement of various landscape and conservation protections. The new support arrangements ought to make agri-environmental schemes (see below) more attractive, because they are not competing with much higher payments based on productivity.

There are various protective procedures that have an important impact on the protection of the landscape and deserve greater attention. Alongside these, it should be noted that, under the Environment Act 1995, s. 98, DEFRA and the Welsh Assembly may make grants for any purposes conducive to the conservation or enhancement of the natural beauty or amenity of the countryside (including its flora and fauna), or the promotion of the enjoyment of the countryside by the public.

Prior notification

Since 1980, there has been a scheme in which farmers in national parks and the Broads should give advance notification to the national park authority of their intention to seek agricultural grants. (A similar scheme applies in relation to SSSIs, requiring prior notification of the relevant nature conservancy council.) The scheme is non-statutory and therefore is not backed up by any legal sanctions, but it has had a high success rate in preventing objectionable proposals from being carried out.[23]

Environmentally sensitive areas (ESAs) and countryside stewardship/Tir Gofal

Environmentally sensitive areas (ESAs) formally dated from EEC Regulation 797/85 on improving the efficiency of agricultural structures, which permitted member States to give special aid to farmers in environmentally sensitive areas. Effect was given to the EC Regulation in the UK by the Agriculture Act 1986, s. 18, which allowed what is now DEFRA to designate an ESA after consultation with Natural England or with CCW, with the aim of conserving landscape and wildlife. Twenty-two ESAs covering 1.1 million hectares were designated in England, and six in Wales (covering 165,000 hectares). A distinctive feature of ESAs, in terms of policy, was that, while each was differently managed, they marked the start of standard rates of payment for standard agri-environmental practices, rather than negotiating agreements individually.

By contrast to ESAs, the countryside stewardship scheme (which dated from 1991) operated outside of ESAs and was not restricted to farm businesses. The scheme aimed to protect, restore, and recreate targeted landscapes, their wildlife habitats, and historical features—that is, it pursued both nature conservation and landscape management objectives. As with ESAs, the scheme was entirely voluntary on both sides and applicants entered into agreements, usually for ten years, to undertake specified works. At its peak, over 500,000 hectares

22 Only with intentional non-compliance is there likely to be scope for full withholding of payment; negligent non-compliance is treated differently. See the Common Agricultural Policy Single Payment and Support Schemes Regulations 2005, SI 2005/219.

23 Countryside Commission (1987) *Farm Grant Notifications in National Parks*.

were included. Both ESAs and countryside stewardship are now closed to new applicants (see below).

In Wales, the pilot Tir Cymen scheme was replaced by Tir Gofal, which incorporates features not merely of ESAs and countryside stewardship, but also incorporates nature conservation management agreements. As with countryside stewardship, the scheme extends to whole farms and has no explicit statutory basis. Unlike the other schemes, however, it remains open.

The Environmental Stewardship Scheme

The reason that both ESAs and countryside stewardship are now closed to new applicants is that, from 2005, a new scheme in England—the Environmental Stewardship Scheme (ESS)—was established, the twin aims of which are to broaden the scope of using positive assistance and to provide for more targeted payments where these are needed. A two-tier payment scheme has therefore been established. The main innovation lies in the lower tier—the Entry Level Scheme (ELS)[24]—which is not restricted to specific features, habitats, or landscape types, making it open to most farmers. Modest support for limited commitments from landowners is available, but it does seek to incentivize landscape and nature conservation into wider countryside management, and to move beyond an 'enclave' approach.

The higher tier is more targeted, and more akin to that in ESAs and under country stewardship (existing agreements under these schemes are transferred). In 2005, 1,354,000 hectares (significantly more than ESAs and country stewardship combined) came within ESS.

Since 2007, all schemes are subject to cross-compliance.

The EC Rural Development Regulation

As an adjunct to the CAP, there has been an EC Rural Development Regulation since 1999 (see now Regulation 1698/2005), which provides that financial support may be given for *'improving the environment and the countryside by supporting land management'*.[25] Farmers have to commit for at least five years, although the member States are given a lot of room to decide what practices must be undertaken (or avoided) to get the money. Countryside stewardship was one way in which the Rural Development Regulation was implemented and the ESS is another. As the name suggests, the main aim of the Regulation is in keeping farmers on the land, especially in more marginal areas, although a surprisingly high percentage of farms participate in the scheme. Council Regulation 1698/2005 covers the period 2008–13, and is supported through cross-compliance. Regulation 1698/2005 will also require that at least a quarter of each member State's rural development spending is spent on measures to improve the environment and countryside (Art. 17).

Agriculture, landscape, and environmental impact assessment

Projects for the use of uncultivated land or semi-natural areas for intensive agricultural purposes have always been listed in Annex II of the EC Environmental Impact Assessment (EIA) Directive (85/337/EEC). But their inclusion in Sch. 2 to the general implementing regulations covering town and country planning was always meaningless, because these activities fall outside the town and country planning system. This gap was (very belatedly) plugged by the Environmental Impact Assessment (Uncultivated Land and Semi-Natural Areas) (England) Regulations 2001,[26] but came under challenge in the *Alford* case (Case 20.3).

---

24 There is also an Organic Entry Level Scheme (OELS).
25 Regulation 1698/2005, Art. 4(1)(b).
26 SI 2001/3966.

CASE 20.3 *DEFRA v. Alford* [2005] EWHC 808[27]

A farmer was convicted of spreading modest amounts of manure and seaweed on her land. This improved the grassland, but adversely affected various acid-loving flora. The High Court overturned the original conviction, on the ground that this had not been done for an intensive agricultural purpose. In particular, the Court found that bringing land back to a normal level of agricultural productivity (albeit after many years) could not amount to an 'intensive' agricultural purpose. The Court favoured the definition of 'intensive' as meaning the use of 'artificial' aids to increasing productivity over a definition of 'intensive' as meaning any practice that aimed at increasing productivity for a given area of land—that is, as being the opposite of 'extensive', under which, for example, yields are increased by extending the acreage under the plough. This may be a correct reading of the dictionary meaning of 'intensive' in this context, but it does beg the question whether it makes sense for the law to intervene because of *how* environmental harm is caused rather than *whether* it is caused. Perhaps the real root of the problem is that the concept of intensiveness is one that might ordinarily be thought of as admitting of degrees, whereas the difficulty here is that 'intensive' is being used in an absolute way (an agricultural purpose being either intensive or not). It is notable that the Environmental Impact Assessment (Agriculture) (England) (No. 2) Regulations 2006[28] cover projects to increase the agricultural productivity of uncultivated land even in cases in which this is 'below the norm'—a change justified on the grounds that the *Alford* decision *'did not enable the UK to meet the aims of the EIA Directive'*.

The 2006 Regulations mean that certain agricultural projects must be screened by Natural England for the significance of their environmental impact and, if they are likely to give rise to significant environmental effects, then an environmental statement must be submitted to Natural England. Various features of these Regulations are especially notable. One is that they provide for criminal liability if uncultivated land is brought into more intensive production without EIA. The second is that EIA is not linked to any consent procedure (as it usually is in other areas). Because there is no consent procedure, there is no real monitoring and, while there have been successful prosecutions,[29] these have tended to follow tip-offs from the public. It is also notable that no environmental statement has ever been required, because, when there has been screening, ways have been found to bring the proposed project beneath the significance threshold. The thresholds in the 2006 Regulations are generous and, although they can be disapplied in sensitive areas, it is unlikely that many projects will require a full EIA.

Trees, woodland, and hedgerows

The rest of this chapter looks at the protection afforded to trees, woodlands, and hedgerows. What we see is a development from early, mainly negative, controls, such as the use of tree preservation orders (TPOs), which have existed in town and country planning law since 1932, towards a more varied approach, encompassing the use of economic instruments and consumer information. We also see a slight shift in emphasis from pure amenity considerations (which have always been to the fore with TPOs) towards wider environmental considerations. A good example of these are the limited environmental duties to which the

---

27 For more detailed analysis, see D. McGillivray (2005) 17 JEL 395.

28 SI 2006/2522.

29 See (2004) ENDS Report 353, 162.

Forestry Commission is subject when granting felling licences, although the primary focus of forestry legislation with trees as commercial items means that this general area is covered only briefly. The conservation of some trees can, of course, be safeguarded through protective designations or agreements of the kind discussed in Chapter 19.

In theory, the use of negative restrictions is particularly unsuitable for the proper management of natural resources, such as trees, that require positive management. Although some lessons have been learnt, the Hedgerows Regulations 1997[30] are arguably a throwback to 'command and control' measures, a central weakness of which is the inability to address mismanagement or neglect, now the major threat to hedgerow conservation. But there are also environmental consequences from tree or hedge *planting*.[31] For larger projects, this is dealt with through environmental impact assessment.[32]

Tree planting on a smaller scale is unlikely to be legally regulated, falling outside the town and country planning system, and being unlikely to give rise to any private law remedy, because there is neither a general right to a view (*Hunter v. Canary Wharf* [1997] 2 WLR 684, and see Case 11.4), nor to light (other than light to buildings). Under Pt VIII of the Anti-Social Behaviour Act 2003, local authorities now have obligations to deal with complaints about high evergreen hedges and powers to reduce such hedges to a reasonable height. These provisions, however, are best seen as a measure to tackle neighbour disputes; they apply when the reasonable enjoyment of a neighbour's property is affected and are not a landscape conservation provision in any wider sense. They are considered in more detail in the Online Resource Centre.

Trees and planning permission

Ordinary town planning rules have a limited impact on tree protection. Planning permission is not required for the planting or cutting down of trees or woodland, because trees, being natural, are not structures or buildings for the purposes of the development control system. Section 55(2)(e) also excludes from the definition of 'development' any change of use of land to forestry or woodland. But specific protective measures are found in ss 197–214 of the Town and Country Planning Act 1990, which deal with TPOs. All references to section numbers in relation to TPOs refer to this Act.

Section 197 imposes a general duty on local planning authorities to make adequate provision for trees when planning permission is granted. This may involve attaching conditions relating to trees to the permission—for example, that certain trees should be retained or replaced by others, or that new trees should be planted as part of the landscaping of the site. It also involves considering whether to impose a TPO on any existing trees. A further possibility is to refuse permission on the grounds that existing trees or woodland should be retained. Full advice on trees and the planning system is given in the Department of the Environment, Transport and the Regions (2000) *Tree Preservation Orders: A Guide to the Law and Good Practice*.

Tree preservation orders (TPOs)

A TPO is a means by which individual trees, groups of trees, or woodlands may be protected against damage. A woodland TPO is arguably the most restrictive, because it includes trees that take root after the order is made. A TPO may be imposed on specified trees '*if it appears to a local planning authority that it is expedient in the interests of amenity*' (s. 198). Because

---

30 SI 1997/1160.

31 See, e.g., the concerns raised in *Kincardine and Deeside District Council v. Forestry Commissioners* [1993] Env LR 151.

32 See the Environmental Impact Assessment (Forestry) (England and Wales) Regulations 1999, SI 1999/2228.

the section refers explicitly to amenity, it does not seem that a tree could be protected for nature conservation purposes.

Most TPOs are made in urban areas, although rural woodland may also be protected. The DETR Guidance suggests that TPOs will not normally be made on trees under good arboricultural or silvicultural management.

TPO offences

Any person who, in contravention of a TPO

(a) cuts down, uproots or wilfully destroys a tree, or

(b) wilfully damages, tops or lops a tree in such a manner as to be likely to destroy it

commits an offence, unless consent has been obtained from the local planning authority (s. 210(1)). On summary conviction, the maximum fine is £20,000; on conviction on indictment, the level of the fine is unlimited. In determining the amount of any fine, the court must have regard to the financial benefit accruing, or likely to accrue, to the convicted person in consequence of the offence. This is a significant provision, because many offences against TPOs are committed by developers who stand to make a substantial gain on the development value of their land (see, for example, the £50,000 fine imposed on a property company for deliberately felling 25 trees after designation, reported at [1991] JPL 101). There is a further offence of contravening the provisions of a TPO (s. 210(4)), for which the maximum fine is £2,500. This will cover such things as ignoring conditions imposed on works permitted by a TPO. If no other enforcement action works, an injunction to stop contravention of a TPO is available (s. 214A), although courts will be reluctant to exercise their discretion to issue an injunction except in clear cases. One notorious persistent offender (a Kent farmer) was, however, imprisoned for failing to comply with the terms of an injunction.

These offences may be committed by any person, not only the owner or occupier of the property. They are offences of strict liability[33] and thus, in *Maidstone Borough Council v. Mortimer* [1980] 3 All ER 552, a contractor was guilty of an offence even though the owner of the site had assured him that consent for the works had been given. (It seems that the owner would also commit an offence in such a situation, because the contractor is acting as an agent.) This strict position is justified by the fact that a TPO is a public document (it is a local land charge), so anyone can check the position before carrying out works.[34]

Part of the offence requires that it be committed 'wilfully'. This has been interpreted to mean that it is the act of damaging or destroying the tree that must be wilful—that is, deliberate—not the contravention of the TPO. *Barnet London Borough Council v. Eastern Electricity Board* [1973] 1 WLR 430 illustrates that this may include a negligent act. In that case, contractors negligently damaged the roots of six trees subject to a TPO, shortening their life expectancy. The Divisional Court held that this amounted to a wilful destruction. The case also illustrates that the concept of destruction includes something less than immediate death to the tree, for example, ring barking.

Making a TPO

The local planning authority has responsibility for making TPOs. This normally means the district planning authority, or the national park authority in a national park.[35] The authority that imposes the TPO is then the relevant local authority for all procedures for consent and for enforcement purposes. The Secretary of State has a reserve power to make a TPO under s, 202, although this is unlikely to be used much.

33 On strict liability offences, see p. 260.

34 Compare the justifications for the strictness of felling licences (see Case 20.7).

35 A county planning authority has jurisdiction over its own land and where it grants planning permission (e.g. on waste disposal or minerals applications).

The procedures for making a TPO are set out in the Town and Country Planning (Trees) Regulations 1999.[36] The local planning authority produces a draft TPO, which is placed on public deposit, and all owners, occupiers, and those with felling rights are notified. At least 28 days are then allowed for objections, which must be considered before the local planning authority itself confirms the TPO (prior to 1980, a TPO required confirmation by the Secretary of State). There is no appeal against the making of a TPO, although there is a right to challenge its validity in the High Court under s. 288. In practice, arguments about the desirability of protecting the tree are considered at the stage of seeking consent to fell.

Normally, a TPO does not have effect until it is confirmed. But under s. 201, a provisional (or interim) TPO may be made by the local planning authority. This is done simply by stating that s. 201 applies and the TPO will then have immediate effect, although it will lapse if not confirmed within six months. Such a provisional TPO is of obvious use in cases in which there is an imminent threat of felling.

Each TPO is separately drafted and accompanied by a map. This position allows for flexibility—for example, conditions specific to that TPO may be attached, or permitted woodland management operations may be established for a coppiced woodland—but it does make the making of a TPO quite a cumbersome process—certainly more cumbersome than those protective designations for which all that is required is that standard rules or restrictions apply to the designated land. But there is a standard form, which is set out in the Schedule to the 1999 Regulations, and most TPOs will be substantially in the form set out in the Schedule. The normal position is therefore that TPOs include a list of permitted operations and of prohibited operations, some of which are especially tailored for that site.

CASE 20.4 What is a tree? *Kent County Council v. Batchelor* (1976) 33 P & CR 185 and *Bullock v. Secretary of State for the Environment* (1980) 40 P & CR 246

In the first of these two cases, Lord Denning MR somewhat arbitrarily suggested that a diameter of 7–8 inches at least was needed before something could be said to be a tree. This was expressly not accepted by Phillips J in the second of the two cases, who thought that anything ordinarily called a 'tree' could be covered by a tree preservation order (TPO). He accepted expressly that a coppiced woodland could be covered—a position that seems sensible, because, from an ecological point of view, a coppice is effectively a single entity and not a collection of unconnected trees.

Phillips J's view is to be preferred and is supported by s. 206(4), Town and Country Planning Act 1990. This states that a TPO will attach to any tree planted as a replacement for one subject to a TPO. Such a replacement will often be a sapling or smaller tree. Although the dividing line is imprecise, some things cannot, however, be the subject of a TPO—for example, hedges, bushes, and shrubs. It appears to be accepted that a stump of a tree is capable of remaining a tree if it is still alive. So a TPO can continue to apply to felled trees, but not uprooted trees.

A further issue relates to whether local authorities actually have the resources to make TPOs. It appears that a number of local authorities have adopted a policy of not making any further TPOs because of the time and expense involved. The legality of such a policy must be questioned, because it appears to amount to an effective fettering of discretion.

Defences to TPO offences

There are a number of exceptions to these offences.

- Some works are permitted in the TPO itself. For example, the standard form of TPO exempts works on cultivated fruit trees and, now, also any pruning of a fruit tree if this is

---

36 SI 1999/1892.

in accordance with 'good horticultural practice'. Also exempt are the 'cutting down, topping, lopping or uprooting of a tree' if this is needed to implement a planning permission. There has, however, been some narrowing in relation to development permitted under the GPDO. This is only exempted if carried out by a statutory undertaker or body such as the Environment Agency.

- It is possible to seek consent from the local planning authority (see below).

- It is an exception to cut down, uproot, top, or lop trees that are dead, dying or dangerous, or 'so far as may be necessary for the prevention or abatement of a nuisance' (s. 198(6)). The nuisance exception relates to the position in which a tree is a civil nuisance. It is potentially a very wide exception, because it may be a civil nuisance for a tree to affect a neighbour's foundations or access,[37] but if measures to the tree short of cutting down or uprooting it could abate the nuisance, then the exception will not apply to more drastic action—that is, any measure must be proportional (and it is also worth mentioning here that *removing* trees can cause problems to neighbouring land, through land 'heave').

  This was one part of the decision in *Perrin v. Northamptonshire Borough Council* [2007] Env LR 12. The judge also held that, for the purposes of s. 198(6), 'nuisance' should be construed narrowly as covering only actual damage caused (or which is imminent), and not simply a mere encroachment. This was because the exception goes beyond what the common law of nuisance allows, which, in relation to encroachments, is only to remove the things that have encroached, but it also makes sense in prioritizing the public amenity importance over the mere invasion of a legal right without harm. It was also held that whether action is 'necessary' cannot be determined according to factors such as whether damage could be prevented in some other way—for example, by underpinning the neighbouring property—because these could always be done, chopping down the tree could never be 'necessary'.

  Some interesting issues arise from this case. It suggests that TPOs should not shift the burden of addressing the nuisance from the tree owner to the person affected, especially if the remedial action that the person affected could undertake would cost much more than it would to remove the tree. But because the person affected can, to protect damage to their property, cut down the tree without consulting the local authority, nothing might be done to see whether a reasonable solution could be found that preserves the tree and prevents harm. In other words, as *Perrin* indicates, s. 198(6) does not take into account how valuable the tree is in amenity terms. It is, however, not a nuisance to deprive a neighbour of the right to a view or the right to light to his land (see p. 749), so this section would not justify interference with protected trees on these grounds (although the 'high hedges' provisions of the Anti-Social Behaviour Act 2003 might be used—see the Online Resource Centre).

- There are further exceptions in cases in which the Forestry Commission is already effectively controlling forestry activities on the land through a forestry dedication covenant, or a grant or loan made under the Forestry Acts (s. 200).

CASE 20.5 *Elliott v. Islington London Borough Council* [1991] 1 EGLR 167

This case illustrates the potential for conflict between public and private rights when dealing with private nuisance. Mr Elliott obtained a mandatory injunction against Islington London Borough Council requiring that a horse chestnut tree, which was in an adjoining park and was damaging his garden wall, be removed. (The tree was not actually subject to a tree preservation order, because it was the

---

37 On which, see the important decision in *Delaware Mansions v. Westminster City Council* [2001] UKHL 55.

council's practice not to designate trees on its own land, but this does not affect the point being made.) It is believed that the injunction was, in fact, never enforced following a later compromise agreed between the parties, but, in the Court of Appeal, Lord Donaldson MR showed the primacy accorded to private rights over the public interest when he stated:

> It is not generally appropriate to refuse to enforce specific private rights on the basis that that would cause hardship to the public: the court would be legislating to deprive people of their rights.

Consent

It is possible to apply to the local planning authority for consent to carry out any works that are prohibited by a TPO. Any consent that is granted may be subject to conditions, such as the planting of replacement trees. There are no publicity requirements for an application for consent, although Circular 36/78 encourages it, and the notification of neighbours and the placing of site notices are common. There is an appeal to the Secretary of State[38] against a refusal of consent, and the procedures and powers on an appeal are similar to those for an appeal against refusal of planning permission, although they give effect to recent proposals on streamlining (see p. 420). There are now powers to vary or revoke a TPO (reg. 9), which would fulfil the same purpose.

CASE 20.6 *Robinson v. East Riding of Yorkshire Council* [2003] JPL 894

Robinson wanted to use some of his extensive grounds for touring caravans, which would involve felling a number of trees. As a matter of urgency and following a brief inspection, the council made a tree preservation order covering all of the grounds (including areas without trees). The court observed that, depending on the circumstances, protecting landowners' rights might mean that more specific orders rather than one 'blanket' TPO may be needed, at least in the long run. But the law relating to TPOs was inevitably anticipatory in character and there are safeguards to protect landowners' interests. Although a TPO cannot be appealed, the same result is achieved by seeking consent from the local authority to carry out works on a tree and an appeal to the Secretary of State thereafter (see above). Hence: '*The making of a tree preservation order is . . . the beginning of the road and not the end of it.*' The appeal was dismissed.

Replacement trees

The replacement of trees covered by a TPO may be required by the terms of the TPO itself (for example, in return for permitted works), by a condition attached to a planning permission, by the terms of a consent, or by s. 206. Section 206 provides that, if a tree is removed or destroyed in contravention of a TPO, or because it was dead, dying, or dangerous, a replacement tree of appropriate size and species must be planted at the same place as soon as reasonably possible. The owner may ask the local planning authority for this requirement to be lifted. The TPO attaches to the replacement tree.

Special provisions apply to woodlands. There is no need to replace a dead, dying, or dangerous tree, and the obligation is to replace the same number of trees on or near those

---

38 Inevitably, inspectors who will visit the site will hear appeals. The scope for the Secretary of State, on the basis of papers and photographs only, to reach a different decision to the inspector will be limited: see *Richmond upon Thames London Borough Council v. Secretary of State for the Environment, Transport and the Regions (Tree Preservation Order)* [2002] JPL 33.

removed, or as agreed by the local planning authority. Flexibility has been provided in such a case, because it will often be impossible to determine exactly how many trees were removed and from where (reg. 8).

Enforcement notices

Because contravening a TPO is itself a criminal offence, there is less need for an enforcement notice requirement than for ordinary breaches of development control. But there is a power for the local planning authority to serve an enforcement notice if a replanting obligation is not complied with. Such a notice must be served within four years of the failure and may require such replanting as is specified by the authority (s. 207). There is a right of appeal against an enforcement notice to the Secretary of State, who may uphold, modify, or quash it (s. 208).

Failure to comply with an enforcement notice is not a criminal offence, but the local planning authority may enter the relevant land, carry out the replanting as required, and recover the cost from the owner (s. 209).

Trees and conservation areas

All trees in a designated conservation area are subject to a statutory restriction (effectively, a statutory TPO), which prohibits the cutting down, lopping, topping, uprooting, wilful damage, or wilful destruction of the tree (s. 211). This is more limited than most individual TPOs. In addition, regulations may be made by the Secretary of State that exempt specified works (s. 212).

There is one crucial difference between these statutory TPOs and ordinary ones: prohibited acts may go ahead six weeks after notification of an intention to do them has been given to the local planning authority. The purpose of this section is to enable the local planning authority to have prior notification of potentially damaging works to trees in conservation areas.[39] The local authority then has six weeks in which to decide whether to impose a TPO: if it does not, the works may go ahead. It is an offence to do any of the prohibited acts without notifying the local planning authority and waiting six weeks, unless consent is given earlier. The penalties for this offence, and the replanting and enforcement provisions, are the same as for ordinary TPOs.

Compensation for a TPO

No compensation is payable for the imposition of a TPO, but it is payable in cases in which loss or damage is caused by a refusal of consent (including revocation or modification) or by a conditional consent (s. 203).

Originally, it was thought that this compensation was payable to compensate for the value of cut timber forgone, but this assumption was shown to be unwarranted by *Bell v. Canterbury City Council* [1989] 1 JEL 90. In this case, the Court of Appeal confirmed that the level of compensation payable was for the loss in value of the land. Accordingly, it awarded compensation at £1,000 per acre to a farmer who was prevented from converting a coppiced woodland to beef or sheep farming. Such large amounts of compensation would obviously limit the use of TPOs by local authorities, especially on woodlands that may have potential for agricultural or urban development.

An immediate response was to alter the existing Regulations—namely, the TPO Regulations 1969.[40] It had always been possible for the local planning authority to certify that refusal was in the interests of good forestry or that the trees were of outstanding or

---

39 A similar form of control is applied for the protection of SSSIs—see p. 692.
40 SI **1969**/17.

special amenity value; in such a case, no compensation would be payable. This certificate was originally available for individual trees, but the 1969 Regulations were amended (by SI 1988/963) to apply the procedure to woodlands.

A more significant response, however, was to alter the practice of the Forestry Commission in relation to woodland TPOs. In woodland, the volume of timber being cut will normally require a felling licence from the Forestry Commission (see below). Normally, the Commission would refer any application relating to trees subject to a TPO to the local planning authority, but a change of practice consequent to *Bell v. Canterbury City Council* was that the Commission agreed to refuse a felling licence if TPO consent would be refused. The effect is that the Commission pays compensation, but at the level set out in the Forestry Act 1967, which relates to the value of the timber. The 1999 Regulations give statutory effect to this position by limiting compensation to loss in value of the timber and then applying this valuation method to trees covered by felling licences. Losses under £500 cannot be recovered.

TPOs—proposals for change

The 1999 Regulations give effect to some of the changes suggested as far back as 1990, when the then Conservative Government issued a consultation paper entitled *Review of Tree Preservation Policies and Legislation*, and later in a further review of the legislation in 1994. Many of the proposals made in that review, however, would require primary legislation, including amending s. 201 so that all TPOs have immediate effect and proposals to give local authorities positive powers to demand works on protected trees. This has not been forthcoming.

Ancient woodlands

There is now quite stringent policy guidance concerning 'ancient woodland'. Local planning authorities are instructed to:

identify any areas of ancient woodland in their areas that do not have statutory protection (e.g. as an SSSI) and...not grant planning permission for any development that would result in its loss or deterioration unless the need for, and benefits of, the development in that location outweigh the loss of the woodland habitat.

(PPS 9 (2005) para. 10)

The guidance also encourages conservation of individual, 'veteran' trees.

Forests

There are legal controls on afforestation and deforestation, involving economic incentives and other voluntary schemes, licensing powers, and the utilization of private property rights.

BOX 20.7 Forests—lessons from history, satellites, and trade

The word 'forest' has legal origins, originally being used to mark out land for deer—and not necessarily for trees—and delineating land in relation to which specific forest law and forest courts operated. The legal forest was nearly always much wider than the physical forest, to cover deer when they strayed beyond the trees. This, as Oliver Rackham notes,[41] led scholars to make the double error of assuming that land described as forest represented physical forest and that all of these areas were wooded: 'Hence the pseudo-historical belief that medieval England was very wooded.'

Today, there are twice as many trees as there were a century ago—probably more than at any time since the Middle Ages—a resurgence that is almost entirely due to planting. Much of this planting, however—which, until recently, tended to be monocultures of fast-growing spruce—has been considered unfavourable, both in landscape and nature conservation terms. And notably, despite this increase, the UK is one of the world's largest importers of wood products, importing around 85 per cent of its timber needs.

Afforestation

Outside of any requirement for EIA, the main tool used to regulate afforestation is incentive payments. In the early 1990s, two main schemes were put in place: the Woodland Grant Scheme and the Farm Woodland Premium Scheme. These marked a clear departure from the previous overriding policy objective of timber production (which was supported by generous tax breaks and which led, by 1984, to 98 per cent of Forestry Commission plantings being non-native conifers—mainly the much-despised Sitka spruce). These schemes are closed to new applicants and the replacement scheme (in England) is the English Woodland Grant Scheme, which began in 2005 and which gives grants for a broad range of purposes, including:

- increasing and maintaining the area of woodland under certified sustainable forest management and approved management schemes;

- expanding the area of woodland with public access;

- bringing woodland SSSIs into favourable condition;

- assisting delivery of priority habitat and species action plans for woodlands;

- improving the environment of disadvantaged urban communities;

- woodland creation.

Felling licences

By contrast with the minimal legal controls over afforestation, under s. 9(2) of the Forestry Act 1967, a felling licence is required from the Forestry Commission for the felling of trees over 8 cm in diameter (15 cm in coppices), measured 1.3m from the ground, unless in a garden, etc., or part of a hedge. It is an offence to fell without a licence, which again may be committed by anyone (see *Forestry Commission v. Frost* (1989) 154 JP 14). Fines either of up to £2,500 or twice the value of the trees when they were felled can be imposed, but, in practice, the development value of the land without the trees may far exceed this. That the sanctions are so low and non-custodial does, however, have a bearing on whether criminal liability can be imposed without *mens rea*—that is, whether the Act gives rise to strict liability criminal offences (see Case 20.7).

41 O. Rackham (1996) *Trees and Woodlands in the British Landscape*, Abingdon: Routledge, p. 166.

CASE 20.7 *R (Grundy & Co. Excavations Ltd) v. Halton Division Magistrates Court* [2003] EWHC Admin 272

How do the courts view tree-felling offences? In this case, the claimants had felled 86 trees without a licence, but they had done so in agreement with the landowner. Clearly, the landowner was guilty of an offence, but were the contractors?

This is obviously an important practical issue, because landowners will rarely undertake large-scale felling personally. The answer turned on whether the offence was one of strict liability or whether *mens rea* (criminal intent) was needed. With environmental crimes like water pollution offences, we have seen that the courts have dispensed with the need for *mens rea* because the regulatory system would otherwise be unworkable, although the price of doing so has been to label such crimes as quasi-criminal and not 'true' crimes (see p. 262). The Court of Appeal consequently thought that the offence of unlicensed tree felling was:

> plainly on the 'quasi-criminal' and not the 'truly criminal' side of the line.... The offence involves only a monetary penalty and carries no real social disgrace or infamy and no moral stigma or obloquy. It is a classic regulatory offence designed not... to protect segments of the public such as employees, common consumers and motorists, but to protect the nation's trees... comparatively little weight should be attached to the presumption that *mens rea* is required before a person can be held guilty of a criminal offence and that the presumption is displaced here because it was clearly or by necessary implication the intention of the statute. The statute is concerned with an issue of public concern, namely the preservation of the country's natural heritage and, to my mind the creation of strict liability is likely to promote these objects.

Felling controls are based on commercial factors, rather than on amenity factors. But the Forestry Commission is under a duty to endeavour to achieve a balance between the management of forests, and the conservation of landscape and nature (Forestry Act 1967, s. 1(3A), inserted by the Wildlife and Countryside (Amendment) Act 1985, s. 4). A felling licence is not required for fruit trees, trees in gardens, orchards, churchyards, or public open space, topping or lopping of trees, operations under a forestry dedication scheme, thinning trees less than 10cm in diameter, or harvesting less than 5 cubic metres of timber per quarter. Nor is a licence required if felling is immediately required for development authorized under the town and country planning system, or if the felling is necessary for preventing danger or preventing or abating a nuisance. The onus is on the defendant to prove that he or she can rely on one of these exceptions. Because, for example, the defendant is best placed to say what the diameter of a tree was and the licensing system would otherwise be unworkable, this onus is not incompatible with human rights law (see *Grundy*, Case 20.7).

To avoid duplication of effort, if a felling licence is required and there is a TPO in force, the following procedure applies. The application goes to the Forestry Commission, which has three choices:

- it may refer the matter to the local planning authority, in which case, the TPO legislation applies;

- it may refuse the licence, in which case it will pay compensation under the Forestry Act 1967;

- it may grant a licence.

A felling licence is the equivalent of a TPO consent, but, before the Commission grants a licence, it must consult with the local planning authority. If the authority objects to a proposed grant of a licence, the matter is referred to the Secretary of State for decision. If a licence is granted, there is an obligation to restock the land, unless the Commission waives it (see the Forestry Act 1986).

Consultation on felling and afforestation

There are no formal requirements for the Forestry Commission (or, in the case of the Farm Woodland Premium Scheme, DEFRA) to consult on applications for felling licences or grant applications. It is, however, Forestry Commission policy to consult local authorities, and bodies such as Natural England, about grant applications and all applications for new planting are placed on a public register. In both cases, there is an appeal—ultimately, to the Minister.

Community forests and the National Forest

There is a 'Forests for the Community' programme run as a joint venture between Natural England and the Forestry Commission, together with local authorities. The aim is to promote the creation, regeneration, and multipurpose use of well-wooded landscapes around major towns and cities. Community forests are non-statutory designations, and their establishment is facilitated in part through planning policy guidance under which development plans should play a facilitative role and provide that any development proposals within them respect the woodland setting. Their establishment therefore relies heavily on the exercise of private rights by the Forestry Commission. To date, there are 12 community forest areas in England, together with the National Forest in the Midlands, the establishment of which is being facilitated in a similar way.

Consumer information and certification schemes

One consequence to emerge from the Forest Principles and from Agenda 21, both agreed at the 1992 Rio Earth Summit (see p. 147), was the emergence of forest management certification and eco-labelling as a preferred policy approach both of producers and of wider civil society (such as environmental NGOs). At national level, we now have the UK Woodland Assurance Scheme,[42] which aims to assure purchasers of wood products in the scheme that the timber has come from sustainably managed sources. The voluntary scheme is notable for being a partnership between the public and private sectors, and environmental organizations, and operates through a combination of auditing of producers by a certification body and subsequent use of an eco-label.

Hedgerows

There was an enormous loss of hedgerows between 1945 and 1990, mainly as a result of agricultural intensification. Hedges have never had the same protection as trees, however, because the definition of a 'tree' means that the TPO legislation does not apply to hedges (although it is capable of applying to trees in hedgerows). Numerous promises were made in relation to hedgerow protection until, finally, the Environment Act 1995, s. 97, made provision for the protection of special categories of hedgerows (but only in England and Wales). Under this section, the Secretary of State has the power to make regulations prohibiting the removal, damage, or destruction of 'important hedgerows'. The Hedgerows Regulations 1997[43] generally apply to a wide class of hedgerows (in particular, to hedgerows that are 20 metres or more long, or which meet another hedgerow at each end and which, in each case, are on, or adjacent to, land used for certain specified purposes). Domestic hedgerows are excluded.

---

42 And now also the Forest Stewardship Council (FSC) UK Standard.
43 SI 1997/1160.

The protection is basic, to say the least. An owner (or, in certain cases, a relevant utility operator) must notify the local planning authority before removing any hedgerow, or stretch of hedgerow. The local planning authority has 42 days in which to serve a retention notice, failing which, consent is deemed to have been given. Consent can only be refused if the hedgerow is important. The 'unimportant' hedgerows can be removed after that period. To qualify as an important hedgerow, the hedge must be not less than 30 years old and must comply with certain detailed criteria laid down within the Regulations, relating to such matters as the number and type of species contained in the hedgerow. Thus, the range of hedgerows that can actually be protected is relatively narrow.

The accompanying guidance emphasizes cooperation with farmers rather than confrontation, thus continuing the tradition of voluntariness found in other areas pre-CROWA 2000. In cases in which an offence is committed, however, fines can be imposed on defaulters (as with TPOs, the courts are directed to take account of any financial benefit accruing from the removal) and the courts can also order replanting.

CASE 20.8 *Conwy County Borough Council v. Lloyd* [2003] Env LR 264

A landowner served a removal notice on the local authority, but, before the 42-day period expired, he removed the whole hedgerow. He was prosecuted, but successfully argued that what he had done was permitted under the Regulations as being for the 'proper management of the hedgerow' (reg. 6(1)(j)), because it was claimed the hedge was at risk of collapse and dangerous to livestock and machinery. On appeal, the local authority argued that proper management could not mean the removal of the whole hedgerow, particularly a hedgerow of some 100 metres' length. But the Court held that the 'very structure of the Regulations themselves... contemplate the possibility of removal without notice'. Whether removal constituted 'proper management' was a question of fact.

While this approach may be correct in law, the danger is that unscrupulous landowners may be encouraged to remove a hedgerow—on 'proper management' grounds—in order to make it harder for the local authority to determine whether the hedge was important. The position is not helped by the absence of any requirement to replant hedges that have been removed for management reasons (a requirement that would seem to be justified in cases such as this, in which it is the *condition* of the hedge that was the alleged problem).

The Hedgerow Regulations have been criticized for placing too much emphasis on the need for objectively verifiable indicators of importance and thus restricting their ambit to a small category of hedges (around 20 per cent) of historic importance. For Holder,[44] this is a consequence of seeing the importance of hedgerows as '*little more than the sum of their parts*', rather than trying to give weight to matters of cultural and local importance. This is also evidenced in the absence of public consultation built into the Regulations. A government review of the Hedgerow Regulations in 1998 placed priority on consistency and commercial certainty, over giving greater powers to local authorities to determine locally important factors. Nowadays, neglect is as much a threat to hedgerows as uprooting—this is not covered in the Regulations, but is addressed through agri-environmental payments.

In the absence of control under the Regulations, other legal remedies may be possible. These include individual enforcement of the provisions of enclosure Acts, such as in *Seymour v. Flamborough Parish Council*, The Times, 3 January 1997, in which Cracknell J ordered the council to preserve what was an '*undistinguished, badly maintained, straggly and unkempt*' hawthorn hedge, because it was still bound by the Flamborough Enclosure Act 1765, which

---

44 [1999] MLR 100.

required the parish council to maintain the hedge forever—a somewhat ironic note on which to end a book on twenty-first-century environmental regulation.

CHAPTER SUMMARY

1 Landscape management ranges from the protection of wide areas of land for their scenic value, down to much smaller objects such as trees and hedgerows.

2 The challenge for the law is that this often involves controlling destructive, rather than constructive, acts and establishing adequate control over natural things. What is a valued landscape, tree, etc. is a subjective judgment.

3 Protecting the most prized areas for their landscape value involves land designations, but, on designated land, the controls applied involve either slightly stronger planning laws than would normally apply or the use of positive assistance.

4 Prized landscapes do not have the same kind or degree of legal protection that important habitats enjoy. They remain working environments, rather than wildlife havens, and are not immune from development.

5 Increasingly, nature conservation and landscape management goals are pursued together—for example, through management planning or financial incentives—and also institutionally.

6 In the wider countryside, economic instruments are the policy tools of choice, because the aim is positive protection of the countryside. Traditional legal tools are almost never used.

7 Financial assistance can be given by a countryside agency under an agreement, or it can be given as a condition of an agricultural subsidy (cross-compliance). There is a clear shift towards paying farmers to conserve or establish landscape and wildlife.

8 Local authorities can require tree planting when planning permission is granted, but otherwise town and country planning law does not generally cover tree planting and felling.

9 The main exception to this is when a local planning authority makes a tree preservation order (TPO). These can protect from destruction anything from an individual tree to an area of woodland.

10 Commercial afforestation is generally steered by the use of grants, which now encourage the planting of native trees, and with much greater emphasis on landscape and conservation.

11 Commercial tree felling must be done under licence.

12 Local authorities can conserve important hedgerows by serving retention notices, but this power is quite limited in scope.

QUESTIONS

1 Are there 'standards' for landscape conservation?

2 Sam and Tina flee the rat race and buy a small farm in a national park. They aim to farm the land as an experiment in sustainable agriculture. This will involve reroofing their house with photovoltaic cells and setting up a mini 'Eden Project' in a natural dip in the land. To help them to pay the bills, they intend to allow paying visitors into the glasshouses. Some local residents are concerned about the impact of the project, including the loss of a stand of trees and a section of hedgerow if the development goes ahead. Advise the local authority.

3 Refer back to Chapter 19. How do the legal controls on landscape differ from those that are used to conserve nature? Think about the following.

a Any different policy issues.

b The legal force of their respective objectives.

c The tools used to achieve these objectives.

Does the level of protection for landscape and landscape features seem adequate?

4 The author (and president of the Campaign to Protect Rural England) Bill Bryson has asked (slightly rhetorically), '*Why you don't make the whole of England a National Park?*' How would you answer this question?

5 Do you think that agri-environmental schemes are compatible with the Polluter Pays Principle? Does it matter if they are not?

FURTHER READING

Greater detail than we can provide here can be found in B. Jones, J. Palmer, and A. Sydenham (2004) *Countryside Law*, 4th edn, Crayford: Shaw and Sons, J. Rowan-Robinson and D. McKenzie Skene (eds) (2000) *Countryside Law in Scotland*, Edinburgh: T and T Clark, and—in relation to the latter sections of this chapter—C. Mynors (2002) *The Law of Trees, Forests and Hedgerows*, London: Sweet and Maxwell. Many books on planning law include a brief chapter on tree preservation.

C. Willmore, 'What's in a name? The role of "national park" designation' [2002] JPL 1325 looks at whether national parks really live up to expectations about their level of protection, while F. Cheever, 'British national parks for North Americans' (2007) 26 Stan Envtl LJ 247 asks what the USA (where national parks have wilderness connotations) can learn from the UK experience. J. Holder, 'Law and landscape: the legal construction and protection of hedgerows' [1999] MLR 100 considers the Hedgerows Regulations 1997 against a backdrop of reflections on legal constructions of landscape. B. Jack 'The European Community and biodiversity loss: missing the target?' (2006) 15(3) RECIEL 304 is a helpful overview of the development of agri-environmental law and of some of its surprising shortcomings in delivering conservation benefits (and is an equally valuable source for Chapter 19).

On policy questions, M. Shoard (1980) *The Theft of the Countryside*, London: Temple Smith, puts the case for extending planning controls to agriculture and forestry, while G. Harvey (1997) *The Killing of the Countryside*, London: Jonathan Cape, focuses on the negative effects of the Common Agricultural Policy (CAP). A more optimistic version of conservation (and landscape amenity) in the wider countryside is B. Green (1996) *Countryside Conservation*, London: E. and F. N. Spon, which examines the range of policy options in this area—in particular, whether to make agriculture generally less extensive, or to allow further intensification on the best farmland, and use the remaining land primarily for its amenity and conservation value.

Beyond the legal literature, we must mention some outstanding works that give a rounded appreciation of nature and landscape, especially Oliver Rackham's superlative works (2000) *The History of the Countryside*, London: Orion, and (1996) *Trees and Woodlands in the British Landscape*, Abingdon: Routledge, and K. Thomas (1984) *Man and the Natural World*, London: Penguin. More recently, the role that values and perceptions play in our understanding of the countryside, and the conflicts that arise, has been the subject of two outstanding and engaging works: T. Smout (2000) *Nature Contested*, Edinburgh: Edinburgh University Press, and P. Macnaghten and J. Urry (1998) *Contested Natures*, London: Sage.

WEB LINKS

An excellent general starting point for web research is **www.naturenet.net**, which has comprehensive links to numerous official (and unofficial) sites, as well as brief information about countryside law. In terms of official policy and information, the main starting points are the national countryside agencies— Natural England (**www.naturalengland.org.uk**), the Countryside Council for Wales (**www.ccw.gov.uk**), and Scottish Natural Heritage (**www.snh.org.uk**)—and central government: **www.defra.gov.uk**; **www. scotland.gov.uk**; **www.wales.gov.uk**. The websites of the national agencies usually contain reports to government on the state of the countryside and now have postcode searching to establish whether land is within an agri-environmental scheme, etc. The Association of National Parks at **www.nationalparks.gov. uk** and the National Association of Areas of Outstanding Natural Beauty (AONBs) at **www.aonb.org.uk** provide helpful information about these areas. For forestry issues, start with the Forestry Commission at **www.forestry.gov.uk**.

INDEX

A

Aarhus Convention
  access to environmental justice
    provisions 313
  access to information
    provisions 298
  public participation, and 311
  three pillars 294
administrative regulation
  coherent system of control,
    as 217
  generally 222–3
  meaning 223
  rules, setting 223
advisory bodies
  examples 112
  nature 112
Agenda 21 57, 61, 135, 147, 434, 758
  Earth Summit, signed at 57
  sustainable development, as
    blueprint for 57
Agreement on Sanitary and
  Phytosanitary Measures (SPS
  Agreement)
  scope of 161
  trade-environment disputes,
    relevance to 161
Agreement on Technical Barriers
  to Trade (TBT Agreement)
  GATT, relationship with 161–2
  trade-environment disputes,
    relevance to 161
agriculture
  EC Rural Development
    Regulation 747
  environmental impact
    assessment 748
  Environmental
    Stewardship 747
  environmentally sensitive
    areas 746–7
  farm development, prior
    notification of 735
  grants
    intention to seek, prior
      notification of 746
    system 745
  promotion of 683
  support, changing nature
    of 745–6
  water pollution, as major
    source of 580

Agriculture and Biotechnology
  Commission
  public participation and 312
air pollution
  clean air zones 513
  consequences of 515
  control measures, use of 541
  controls, history of 512–15
  domestic law and policy 527,
    538–9
  economic instruments, impact
    of 530
  emissions trading
    scheme 529–32
  enforcement of system,
    inconsistency 280
  European Community
    initiatives 523–7
  European law 523–7, 533–4
  European Pollutant Emission
    Register 538
  international law 516
  local authorities, role of 122
  monitoring 539–41
  motor vehicles, emissions
    from 536–7, 541
  National Emissions
    Ceilings 527, 535
  ozone monitoring 541
  pollutants
    acid rain 511
    climate change 511
    direct harm to health,
      causing 512
    effects of 511–12
    range of 516
  process standards 535
  regulatory challenge 515–16
  regulatory impact 513–14
  smoke see smoke
  source 509–10
  transboundary
    climate change see climate
      change
    customary international law,
      principle of 516–17
    Geneva Convention 517–18
    NOx emissions 518
    problem of 516–17
    Programme for Monitoring
      and Evaluation 517
    sulphur dioxide, reduction
      of 518

  Vienna Convention for the
    Protection of the Ozone
    Layer 518–19
air quality
  ambient, Framework
    Directive 534
  domestic law and policy 527,
    538–9
  European law 523–7, 533–4
  land uses, control of 6541
  National Air Quality
    Strategy 539–41
  National Strategy
    objectives, meeting 540–1
    standards 539–41
  objectives 238
  pollution control measures, use
    of 541
  Regulations 539–40
  standards 214
  traffic management and
    planning powers 540
air travel
  government responsibility
    for 107–8
Alkali Inspectorate
  establishment of 19
alkali works
  statutory provisions 19–20
animals
  cruelty, protection against
    685
  harmful movements, control
    of 685
  nature conservation see nature
    conservation
  protection, relevance to
    environmental problems 8
  species conservation offences
    defences 723–4
    EC law, in 721
    exceptions 723–5
    lawful operations, incidental
      results of 725
    licensing 723–5
    national law, in 720–1
    penalties 725–6
  zoo, in 720
appeals
  contaminated land 573
  environmental 95
  environmental permitting
    regime 495

areas of outstanding natural
beauty
conservation board 736
designation 743–4
development in 736
number of 744

B

Basel Convention
waste management 635–6
batteries and accumulators
waste management 642
biodiversity
action plans 726–7
conservation, integration
into national decision-
making 726
Biological Diversity Treaty
Cartagena Biosafety
Protocol 157
compliance, securing 157
disappointment, as 157
birds
Natura 2000 sites 705–6
Natura 2000 sites *see* Natura
2000 sites
species conservation offences
defences 723–4
EC law, in 720–1
exceptions 723–5
lawful operations, incidental
results of 725
licensing 723–5
national law, in 720–1
penalties 725–6
breach of statutory duty
civil remedy, availability of 348
damages, remedy in 348–9

C

climate change
Bill 531–2
carbon capture and storage 522
Climate Change and
Sustainable Energy Act 2006
531
compensation 532–3
domestic law and policy 527,
538–9
emissions trading
scheme 529–32
European Climate Change
programme 524
European Community
initiatives 523–7
European Emissions Trading
System 525–7
Framework Convention
adoption of 520

aggregating emissions 520–1
carbon sinks, use of 521
clean development
mechanism 521
compliance, securing 156
emissions trading
system 521
general commitments 520
joint implementation
mechanisms 521
Kyoto Protocol 142, 520–2
main objective 520
specific reduction
targets 520
global environment, threat to 519
greenhouse gases 511, 515
European emissions 525–7
Intergovernmental Panel 520
levy 528–9
London Dumping
Convention 522
policy 25
UK Climate Change
Programme 527–8
UNESCO World Heritage
Sites 523
coast
heritage 744
common heritage
concept of 137
company
environmental crime, liability
for 264–7
compliance
costs of 37–8
conservation areas
development in 736
trees in 754
consumer protection
environmental problems,
relevant to 8
contaminated land
accidents 52
appeals 573
classification as, effects 554
clean up costs 559
clean up works, subject to 554
consultation 559
contamination, causing 564–5
controlled waters, pollution
of 557–8
current contamination
controls 549–52
historic, overlapping control
of 549–52
definition 555–6, 555–7
environmental liability 548–9
European law 552
explosions, causing 544
harm

nature of 557
whether leading to 548
historic contamination
controls, main features
of 554–5
current, overlapping control
of 549–52
development of law dealing
with 554–7
package of rules 555
retrospective liability
for 552–3
identification of 558–61
land pollution, and 548
liability, allocation of
apportionment 572–3
appropriate person 563–4
causing
contamination 564–5
exclusion tests 568–72
knowingly permitting
contamination 565–6
liability groups 568
owners and occupiers,
between 566–7
privatization of liability 572
local authorities, role of 122
meaning 554
notification requirements 559
patchwork system of rules 547
paying for 34
pollutant linkage, existence
of 556
polluter pays principle 564
practical issues 575
property, toxic effects on 554
receptor/target, types of 556
regime for 554–5
register of information 574
remediation
cost of 561
methods, assessing 561
standards 559–61
works, nature of 561
remediation notice
appeal against 563
appeals 573
appropriate person, service
on 563–4
compliance with 573
duty to serve 561–2
non-compliance with
573–4
service of 562
significant harm, possibility
of 557
special sites 558–9
standard setting 559–61
statutory definition 555–6
statutory successors 567–8

successors in title 567–8
sustainable development
    560–1
terminology 554
threat posed by 555
toxic environmental
    effects 554
toxic health effects 554
waste, contamination by 554
waste management 672
water pollution, overlapping
    controls 623
controlled waste
    waste management 652
Convention on the International
    Trade in Endangered Species
    (CITES)
    compliance, securing 156–7
    International Union for the
        Conservation of Nature, role
        of 149
    TRAFFIC, role of 150
Council of Europe
    European Landscape
        Convention 732
countryside
    regulatory agencies 120–1
Countryside Agency
    Natural England,
        becoming 737
Countryside Commission
    Countryside Agency,
        becoming 737
Countryside Council for Wales
    general role of 113, 121
    national parks, and 739
    nature conservation, and 686
courts
    appellate function 126
    EC environmental law,
        approach to 216–17
    environmental administration,
        role in 126–7
    environmental cases in 126
    environmental law, approach
        to 35–6
    planning, role in 377, 380–1
cultural heritage
    environmental problems,
        relevant to 8

D

damages
    actual damage, for 350
    future loss, for 352
    punitive 352
    remedy of 351–2
    water pollution, for 625–6
Danube, River
    damming 151–2

Department of Business Enterprise
    and Regulatory Reform
    responsibilities 103, 104
Department of Communities and
    Local Government
    responsibilities 103, 104
Department of the Environment,
    Food and Rural Affairs
    Environmental Agency, grants
        to 119–20
    environmental matters, control
        of 106
    policies, imposition of 108
    predecessor, role of 106
    role of 103
    Secretary of State, powers of 108
Department for Transport
    responsibilities 103, 104
development
    activities not constituting 396
    areas of outstanding natural
        beauty, in 736
    building operations 394
    conservation areas, in 736
    countryside, control in 734–6
    engineering operations 394
    enterprise zones, in 398–9
    fact and degree, existence as
        question of 394
    farm or forestry, prior
        notification of 736
    General Development
        Orders 378, 398
    government department,
        authorized by 400
    material change of use of land
        or buildings, by 394–6
    meaning 393–6
    mining operations 394
    National Parks, in 736, 742–3
    Norfolk and Suffolk Broads,
        in 736
    operational 394
    simplified planning zone,
        in 399
    Special Development
        Orders 398–9
    waste management 671
director
    environmental crime, liability
        for 266–7
    persons being 267
duty of care
    waste management 609–11,
        664–5

E

eco-labelling
    European system 308, 309
ecosystem

global, value of 51
electrical and electronic
    equipment
    waste management 641, 670
emissions
    air pollution from see air
        pollution
    climate change see climate
        change
    European Emissions Trading
        System 525–7
    European Pollutant Emission
        Register 538
    motor vehicles, from 525, 541
    national ceilings 527, 535
    process standards 533, 535
    standards 214
        see also standards
    statutory source limits 535
    trading scheme 529–321
    water, into see water pollution;
        water quality
end-of-life vehicles
    waste management 641, 669–70
energy
    consumption, information to
        consumer 309–10
    new standards, adaptation to 31
enforcement of environmental law
    access to information,
        importance of 26
    administrative 272
    approach to 270–1
    British approach to 275–8
    capture theory 275
    compliance, securing 272
    cost of 281
    differing levels of,
        geographically 278
    discretion in 235
    Enforcement Concordat 280
    hierarchy of mechanisms 277
    inconsistent 280
    informal 272
    Northern Ireland, in 276
    optimal 287–8
    practices 272–3
    purposes of 273
    Pyramid 274, 281
    restorative enforcement 287
    Scotland, in 276
    specific policies, development
        of 278–9
    styles of
        compliance approach 273
        conciliatory approach 273
        cooperative approach 273
        different, using 274–5
        practice, in 278
        responsive regulation 273–4
        sanctioning 273

enterprise zone
    development in 398–9
environment
    definition
        difficulty of 7
        European Commission,
            by 8
        general 8
        social and cultural
            influences 8
        specific 7
        statutory 7
    importance of 3
    layers of 8
    relational concept, as 7
Environment Agency
    aims, duties and
        objectives 116–19
    breaches of law, investigation
        of 270
    Common Incident
        Classification Scheme 279
    cost-benefit duty 119
    creation 102
    creation of 23, 115
    Department of the
        Environment, Food and
        Rural Affairs, grants
        from 119–20
    enforcement policy 278–81
    financial arrangements
        119–20
    functions 115–16
    funding 269
    history of 115
    information, power to
        require 270
    inspection, entry and
        enforcement powers 270–1
    number of prosecutions by
        277
    practical significance of
        duties 118–19
    responsibilities of 113
    role of 115–16
    structure 115
    sustainable development,
        objective of 28
    waste management functions
        licences see waste
            management
        public registers of
            information 601
        supervision 598
environmental administration
    bodies involved, identification
        of 98–9
    bodies involved in 124
    central government, by 98,
        103–12

    see also government
    courts, role of 126–7
    devolution, impact of 101
    diversity of bodies, by 98
    institutional arrangements,
        importance of 98
    integration 99
    local authorities, role of see
        local authorities
    non-governmental
        organizations, by 98
        roles of 123–5
    Northern Ireland, in 99–101
    quasi-governmental bodies,
        by 98
    regions, in 99–101
    regulatory agencies, by 98
    Scotland, in 99–101
    Wales, in 99–101
environmental agencies
    activities, studies of 277
    capture theory 275
    enforcement
        historical background 268–9
        regulatory 268–71
    enforcement styles adopted
        by 278
    inspection, entry and
        enforcement powers 270–1
    operational and regulatory
        functions, overlap 268
    prosecutions by 272
    resources of 269–70
environmental assessment
    beginning 432
    duty to undertake 432–3
    environmental report
        meaning 432
        preparation of 471
    impact see environmental
        impact assessment
    information gathering
        by 431–2
    international law and practice,
        in 433–9
    meaning 431–2
    permitted development subject
        to 445
    strategic see strategic
        environmental assessment
    technique and process, as 432
environmental asset
    market price of 330
Environmental Audit Committee
    introduction 102
Environmental Court
    proposals for 323–5
environmental crime
    Common Incident
        Classification Scheme 279

corporate liability for 264–7
corporate offenders 264–7
defences
    due diligence, proposal
        for 263–4
    emergency situations 263
    reasonable excuse 264
    statutory consent, acting in
        accordance with 263
definitions of 254–5
direct sanctions 247
directors' liability for 266–7
enforcement see enforcement of
    environmental law
enforcement agencies
    arm's length relationship 68
    historical background 238–9
    inspection, entry
        and enforcement
        powers 270–1
    regulatory 268–71
    resources of 269–70
geographical limitations 254
groupings of offences 257–8
harm, nature and extent of 259
individual offenders 264–7
industrial operators,
    commission by 259
information, power to
    require 270
jurisdictional limitations 254
legal approaches to
    defining 254
list of 257–8
meaning 254
moral dimension 258–60
outer boundaries of 254
private prosecutions 271
prosecutions
    company, against 268
    decision, factors in 279–81
    internal guidelines 279–80
    Northern Ireland, in 276
    policies 278–81
    private 271
    Scotland, in 276
    statistics 269
real crimes distinguished 259
regulatory body, ignoring
    dictates of 248
regulatory nature of 259
sanctions
    administrative 281
    alternative 285–7
    civil penalties 286
    compensation and
        confiscation orders 285
    criminal 281–3
    custodial sentences 283
    fines 281–2

naming and shaming 285–6
tariff, rejection of 284
Scotland, prosecutions in 276
sentencing 34, 284–5
strict liability, imposing
arguments for 261–3
defence, without 263
deterrence, for 261–2
due diligence defence,
proposal for 263–4
efficiency and ease of
prosecution 262–3
negligence or fault, not need
to prove 260
polluter pays principle,
according with 263
public interest, goal of 261
risk management,
encouraging 261–2
uniformity, lack of 258
use of criminal law,
devaluing 262
white collar nature of 265
wide range of activities as 256
wildlife 269
environmental disputes
causes of 11
complexity of 11
frequency of 4
resolution, law assisting in 11
environmental harm
definition 12
liability for 548–9
prevention of 29–30
environmental impact assessment
activities subject to 436–7
adequacy, challenging 438
adverse impact, meaning 435
applications, consideration of
further information,
obtaining 461–4
period for 461
procedural steps 461
public participation 459–60,
461
reasons, duty to give 463–4
consideration of effects
without 464–6
decision-making, impact
on 467–8
degree of risk triggering 436
developers, burden for 467–8
development 472
environmental statement
alternatives in 459
consultation 457–8
content of 456–9
criticism of 460–1
form of 456
indirect effects 457

key component, as 456
meaning 432
non-technical summary of
information in 457
scoping opinions 459
Espoo Convention 437
European Community, in
cumulative impacts of
several projects 444
development consent,
meaning 444–6
Directive 26, 439–41
general duty 439
implementation of
Directive 441
mandatory 446–7
origins of law 439
project, meaning 443–4
project subject to,
determining 441–3
Schedule 1 projects 446–7
Schedule 2 projects 447–54
exemptions from 455–6
failure to consider impact 433
grant of permission following,
obligations on 463
individual in one state
challenging in another 439
information gathering by 432
international agreements,
requirements in 433–4
international case law 436
international law and practice,
in 433–9
landscape, effect of projects
on 734
limits of 469
mandatory 446–7
meaning 431–2
national procedural
rules 466–7
procedural mechanism, as 433
rural land uses, change of 444
Schedule 1 projects 446–7
Schedule 2 projects 447–54
significant environmental
effects likely, where
all factors, taking into
account 449
amenity of individuals, not
protecting 452
challenge to failure to
require 454
courts, guidance
from 450–1
discretion beyond
thresholds 450–3
examples of 447–54
factual basis 452–3
mitigating measures 453–4

outline permission,
application for 451
Schedule 2 projects 447–54
screening criteria 447
screening practice 454–5
screening procedures 454–5
substantive environmental
law standards, breach
of 452
thresholds, use of 448–50
technical formulation 436
transboundary harm, as to 435
transboundary, myth and
reality of 438
uncertainty over decisions,
reduction of 462
UNCLOS, under 436
uncultivated land or semi-
natural areas 748
waste management licence, on
application for 445
World Bank
requirement 434–5
environmental impacts
global nature of 9
local 11
environmental information
Aarhus Convention, provisions
of 298
access to
arguments for 295
Britain, in 310–11
broadening of 310
consistency and
transparency 298
Directive 90/313 300–1
Environmental Information
Regulations 301–6
European institutions, held
by 298–9
European
legislation 299–301
exemptions 302
Freedom of Information
Act 302
history of 298
human rights provisions 298
increase in 296
international approaches
to 298
rationale for 296–7
refusal notice 303
right, importance of 298
Transparency Treaty 299
United Kingdom, in 301–6
classes of 333
consumer, to
eco-labelling 309
energy consumption, as
to 309–10

environmental information
(*cont.*)
  green claims 309
  product certification 309–10
  products, on 308–9
  definition 299–300, 303
  exceptions to duty to
    disclose 304
  exempt, classes of 304
  full public disclosure,
    objections to 297
  making available 247
  meaning 432
  obligation to provide 326
  public authorities, obligation to
    disclose 298, 303
  public interest, disclosure
    in 326
  public registers of
    appeal, rights of 305
    availability of
      information 305
    exceptions from
      disclosure 305
    main, list of 305–6
    nature of information in 305
  reporting 307–8
  sustainable development, link
    with 295
  voluntary disclosure, system
    of 307–8
  water pollution, relating
    to 615–16
environmental justice
  access to 313
  judicial review *see* judicial
    review
environmental law
  ad hoc nature of 19
  administration *see*
    environmental
    administration
  administrative sanctions 38
  balancing values 47
  book on, reasons for 3–4
  borrowed concepts in 32
  change in emphasis 20–1
  changing styles of
    regulation 25
  civil liability 38
  clean-up costs 38
  competing interests,
    balancing 47
  conceptual apparatus 5
  consolidation 22–3
  courts, approach of 35–6,
    216–17
  decriminalization 34
  definitions, importance of 6

development, responsibility
  for 34–5
direction of 22–3
directives, transposing 216
EC *see* European Community
  law
enforcement *see* enforcement of
  environmental law
environmental principles as
  legal principles 214
flexible mechanisms of
  control 12
formal EC standards, effect
  of 214–16
framework for behaviour 10
future prospects 32–6
guidance as 9
history of 17–18
identifiable subject of 4
integrative 24
internationalization 27
landmarks 21–2
legislation *see* environmental
  legislation
legitimacy 46
local 18
main statutes 23
management of environment,
  central to 4
meaning 4–6
modern age of 20–9
national 84
nature of liability imposed 35
negative and positive tools
  of 10
non-compliance, criminal
  offences 38
peripheral topics 5
policy, integration with 99
political nature of 11–13, 225
principles of *see* environmental
  principles
private and common property,
  protection of 17
protection of environment,
  for 9
public participation *see* public
  participation
publicity, adverse 38
reflections on 32–6
remedies, providing 11
rights, and 13–15
risk, and 47–8
rules, as 9
science, relationship with 47
sources *see* sources of
  environmental law
standards 214–16, 229
  see also standards

substantive 5
tensions, resolving 37
themes 10–13
UK, influence of EC
  law 213–17
values *see* values
vastness and complexity of 4
environmental legislation
  characteristics of 89–92
  context 94
  definitions 89–90
  delayed commencement of 89
  discretions in 91
  gradualism 93
  practice, in 92–4
  primary 85
  purposive and listing
    approaches 90
  scientific evidence, reliance
    on 93
  secondary 86–7
  tertiary 87–9
  tiers of rules 89
environmental liability
  contaminated land, for *see*
    contaminated land
  private law, and *see* private law
  privatization of 572
environmental permitting regime
  administrative
    integration 478–9
  analysis of regime 496–7
  appeals 495
  applications 482–3
  conditions 487–91
  confidentiality 485
  consultation 483–4
  decision-making 483–4
  defences 495
  deregulation 496
  determining application 485–7
  Directives 479
  enforcement
    enforcement notices 494
    powers 493
    revocation notices 493–4
    suspension notices 494
    variation notices 493
  enforcement notices 494
  excluded waste operations 480
  exempt waste operations 480–1
  IPPC Directive 497–505
  national security 485
  no change, but new rules
    approach 479
  offences 494–5
  operator 481–2
  permit conditions 487–91
  public participation 483–4

refusal of application 486–7
regulated facilities 479–80
regulators 481
remedies 494–5
reviewing permits 492–3
revocation notices 493–4
scope 479–81
sludge treatment 480
standard rules 491
substitute liquid fuels 484
surrender of permits 492
suspension notices 494
transfer of permits 491–2
transitional arrangements 482
variation notices 493
waste management 656–7
environmental permitting regime
substitute liquid fuels 484
environmental policy
administration *see*
environmental
administration
climate change 25–6
diffuse pollution, tackling 31
governance 32
harm, preventing 29–30
law, integration with 99
law, of 11–13
public participation *see* public
participation
second generation 29–32
shared responsibility 31–2
targets, setting 30–1
environmental principles
definitions 53–4
formulation of 53–4
integration 56
interrelationship of 54
polluter pays 54, 55
precautionary 54, 55, 64–71
see also precautionary
principle
preventative 54, 55
proximity 56
public participation 56
substantive 54
substitution 56
summary of 54
sustainable development 54, 55
see also sustainable
development
environmental protection
administrative
centralization 24–5
administrative discretion,
exercise of 35
challenge of 3–4
common law as mechanism
for 356

complexity of problems 37,
41–2
court or tribunal dealing
with 35
criminal cases 38
criminal and civil law, role
of 248–9
history of 18
increase in litigation 36
institutional coherence 24
integrative laws 24
international law, importance
of 134
international
responsibilities 27
judicial attitudes, change
in 43–4
national strategies 23–4
planning system, emphasis
in 383
private law, utility of
costs of 355–6
fault-based system, as 354
future of 356–7
imprecise of unduly
absolute standards, based
on 353–4
private interests, relating
to 352–3
proof, problems of 354
reactive controls 355
right to bring claim 353
self-regulation
changing behaviour, relevant
factors 245
information based
mechanisms 247
management
standards 245–6
meaning 245
private agreements 247–8
triggers for action 245
standards, setting 37
statutory nuisance *see* statutory
nuisance
statutory regimes, effect
of 360–1
theoretical issues 49
voluntary bodies 19
environmental regulation
administrative 223–8
anticipatory controls 227
approach to, changes in 238–9
British approach to 236–7
centralization 235–6
context, importance of 238
continuing controls 227–8
criminal and civil law, role
of 248–9

decentralization 235–6
decision-making, process
of 224–8
deregulation 238–9
discretion in 235
economic tools
administrative cost of
operating system, charges
for 240–1
civil law remedies 241–2
cost recovery
charging 240–1
deposit or refund
schemes 243
environmental or pollution
control measures, charges
to finance 241
free market, opposite to 240
full environmental cost,
charges reflecting 241
future use of 243–4
instruments, categories
of 240
polluting materials or
processes, charges levied
on 242
pollution credits, market
in 243
subsidies and grants 243
use of 239–40
enforcement of standards and
permissions 225
feedback mechanisms 226–7
general policies, establishment
of 224–5
individual situations,
application of standards and
policies to 225
information, provision of 226
local decisions 235
market mechanisms 239–40
new formalism 239
offences 248–9
see also environmental crime
optimal 249
permissions and consents 227
planning and prevention 227
pragmatic and flexible
approach 223
public bodies, by 223
reactive approach to 513–14
specific policies 225
standards *see* standards
summary of process 224
environmental risk
environmental values, *see*
values
regulation, role of planning
law 425–6

European Community
  activities of 173
  British environmental
    protection law, as source
    of 170, 172–3
  Commission
    Directorates-General 174
    non-compliance,
      enforcement 206–8
    role of 174
  Council of Ministers 174–5
    making of environmental
      law, role in 181
    voting in 181–2
  Court of Justice see European
    Court of Justice
  Directive on Environmental
    Liability 363–5
  economic basis of 183–4
  enlargement 174
  environmental law
    international law
      developments, flowing
      from 137
    key developments 171–2
  environmental policy
    acceptance of need for 184
    Action Programmes 184,
      190–2
    basis of 198
    Britain, influence in 213–17
    constitutional basis of 185–7
    correct legal basis 187–8
    draft Constitution
      provisions 186
    drawing up 184
    enlargement, effect of 199
    key developments 171–2
    little or no legislation on 194
    Maastricht Treaty, provisions
      of 186
    rationale 183–4
    shared responsibility 190
    Single European Act,
      provisions of 185–6
    support for 185
    Sustainable Development
      Strategy 185
    Treaty of Amsterdam,
      provisions of 186
    Treaty of Lisbon
      provisions 186–7
  European Parliament 175
    making of environmental
      law, role in 181–2
  European Reform Treaty 174
  European Union, as 80
  external matters, division of
    competence on 136–7

free movement of goods
  arbitrary discrimination,
    prohibition 202
  country's own nationals,
    discrimination in favour
    of 202
  EC legislation, action not
    covered by 203
  environmental protection,
    overriding for 201–4
  higher national standards,
    effect of adoption
    of 201–4
  provisional measures,
    permitted 202
  waste imports, ban on 202
institutions 174–7
law see European Community
  law
linked Communities 173
Member States
  loss of sovereignty 82
  number of 80
multilateral environmental
  treaties, signing 136
national environmental
  protection standards, effect
  of 203
nature of 173–4
Treaties 173–4
European Community law
  adoption of, voting
    procedure 187
  challenging 182–3
  Commission, enforcement
    by 206–8
  competence for 187–8
  compliance by member
    state 204–6
  direct effect, doctrine of 209
  Directives 82
    compliance with 204–6
    implementation, means
      of 205
  environmental 80–2
    attribution 187
    Britain, influence in 213–17
    Cardiff process 171
    challenging 182–3
    competence for 187–8
    constitutional basis of 185–7
    context of 195
    correct legal basis 187–8
    Council, role of 181–2
    court decisions 180
    courts, approach of 216–17
    dangerous substances,
      on 184
    decisions 179–80

Directives 178
  range of 192–4
disproportionate costs,
  alleviation of 199
draft Constitution
  provisions 186
emissions, control of 198–9
enlargement, effect of 199
flexibility 197
free trade, and 201–4
harmonization, move away
  from 200
harmonizing 188
higher national standards,
  adoption of 188, 195–6
internal market
  legislation 195–6, 197–8
key Directives 26
laws implementing, breach
  of 205
Maastricht Treaty, provisions
  of 186
making 181–2
national provisions, approval
  or rejection of 295
new directions 200–4
objectives, policy and
  principle 188–9
opinions 179–80
Parliament, role of 181–2
pollution reduction
  obligations 206
pollution reduction
  programmes, compliance
  with 204–6
practical compliance
  targets 178
proportionality 180,
  197–200
purposive character of 81
purposive interpretation 217
purposive and literal
  interpretations 81
qualified majority voting,
  effect of 214
quality standards,
  compliance with 178
rationale 183–4
recommendations 179–80
Regulations 178
rise of 26
scope of 188–92
Single European Act,
  provisions of 185–6
sources of 177–81
specific justification for 188
subsidiarity 197–200
top-down, move away
  from 200

Treaty of Amsterdam,
provisions of 186
treaty base 187
Treaty of Lisbon
provisions 186–7
treaty provisions 177–8
uniformity or
flexibility 194–204
explicit treaty base, need
for 186
national litigation, challenge
in 183
non-compliance with
Commission, enforcement
by 206–8
direct effect, doctrine of 209
future prospects 213
individual remedies 209–13
infringement
proceedings 207
national procedural rules
and remedies 211–12
new approaches to 213
penalty payments 207–8
state liability for 210–11
useful effect, concept
of 209–13
vertical and horizontal
effect 210
public procurement 204
Regulations 82
relevance of 9
specific nature of 80
supremacy of 177
useful effect, concept of 177,
209
vertical and horizontal
effect 210
European Court of Human Rights
judgments and opinions, courts
having regard to 331–2
victim test 338
European Court of Justice
environmental cases, referral
of 175–6
environmental law,
interpretation of 175
judges of 175
matters referred to 175
non-compliance with
EC law, infringement
proceedings 207
European Environment Agency
enforcement or policing powers
lack of 177
European information, source
of 299
European Pollutant Emissions
Register 176

reports 176
role of 176
European Environment
Information and Observation
Network
national information
organizations, linking 299

F

fisheries
International Court of Justice,
jurisdiction of 152–3
overexploitation 139
forestry
afforestation 756
consultation 758
incentive payments 756
Community forests 758
consumer information 758
development, prior notification
of 736
felling
consultation 758
licences 756–7
offences 757
forest management
certification 758
forest, meaning 755–6
legal controls 755–6
National Forest 758
Woodland Assurance
Scheme 758
Woodland Grant Scheme 756
Forestry Commission
felling licences, grant of 749,
756–7

G

General Agreement on Tariffs and
Trade
action pursuant to
environmental treaties,
defence of 162–3
Agreement on Technical
Barriers to Trade (TBT
Agreement), relationship
with 161–2
Asbestos case 162–3
General Agreement on Trade in
Services (GATS)
financial services market,
greening 161
genetically modified organisms
environmental problems,
relevant to 8
global commons
activities affecting 137–8
damage to, prevention of 139

global common heritage,
and 137–8
overexploitation 138–9
tragedy of, thesis 138–9
globalization
crises, of 27
environment, impact on 139
governance
environmental 32
meaning 32
government
air travel, responsibility
for 107–8
Department for Business
Enterprise and Regulatory
Reform 103, 105
Department of Communities
and Local Government 103,
104
Department of the
Environment, Food and
Rural Affairs 106, 106–10
Department of Local
Government, Transport and
the Regions 106
Department for Transport 103,
105
departments, areas of
responsibility 103–6
environmental matters, policy
and rule-making powers 103
fragmentation of
responsibilities 103–5
general environmental
duties 109
House of Commons
Environmental Audit Select
Committee 106
lack of coordination 107
non-departmental public
bodies 112
Office of the Deputy Prime
Minister 110
Parliamentary Select
Committees 109–10
scrutiny of 109–10
sustainable development
in 106
Treasury 103, 105

H

hazardous substances
bringing onto land 343
consent 425–6
water environment, in
586–7
health and safety
environmental problems,
relevant to 8

hedgerows
  loss of 758–9
  protection scheme 758–9
  regulations 749
HM Inspectorate of Pollution
  integrated powers 24
human rights
  collective remedies 72
  determination of planning
    application, considerations
    in 408
  environmental 71–3
  environmental protection, as
    tool for 14–15
  environmental values,
    and 72–3
  European Convention 72–3
    incorporation into domestic
    legislation 298
  judicial review, overlap of
    remedies 314
  margin of appreciation 72
  polluting activity, judging
    reasonableness of 334
  poor levels of environmental
    protection, based on 331
  private and family life, right to
    respect for
    environmental pollution,
    effect of 330–2
    fair balance between
    individual rights and
    interests of community,
    striking 359
  private law claims, role relating
    to 330–2
  right to bring case 317
  victim, action by 317
hunting
  ban 43

I

injunction
  planning enforcement, for 422
  remedy of 350
  water pollution, against 623,
    626
Integrated Pollution Prevention
  and Control
  water pollution, overlapping
    controls 621–3
international agreements
  high-level effect 135
  national law, becoming part
    of 134
International Court of Justice
  case load 151
  compulsory jurisdiction, states
    accepting 151

environmental case
  before 151–2
Environmental Chamber 151
limits to jurisdiction 152–3
international dispute settlement
  bodies 151
International Court of Justice
  see International Court of
  Justice
international courts and
  tribunals, by 150, 153–4
international trade and
  environmental law, conflict
  of 163
litigation, problems of 153
non-legal routes 151
tribunals, range of 154
international environmental law
  activities having impact
    between states, as to 147
  activities within states, as
    to 137
  customary, development of 146
  development, role of UK in 136
  direct application 134–5
  duty-centred approaches 166
  European Community, of see
    European Community
  existing agreements, making
    more effective 148
  future directions 164–6
  GATT-incompatibility 163
  indirect application 135
  institutional
    organizations 149–50
  institutional reform 166
  key players 149–50
  liability rules 165–6
  maturing of 148
  policy development 145–6
  policy, impact on 135–6
  post-Rio developments 148–9
  procedural rights 165
  rights-based approached 164–5
  scope of 79–80
  sudden shocks, impact of 148
international law
  enforcement 154
  environmental see international
    environmental law
  environmental problems,
    approach to 145
  environmental protection,
    importance for 134
  implementation and
    monitoring 155
  key features 133
  nation states, law of 137
  non-compliance, cross-
    checking 156

non-state actors,
  involving 156–7
parties to 154–5
policy development 145–6
positive assistance 155–6
private 133
sources of
  custom 142
  declarations 143
  generally recognized
    principles of law 143
  hard law 139–42
  international jurists, work
    of 143
  judicial decisions 153
  principles 143–4
  recommendations 144
  soft law 143–5
  standards 144–5
  treaties 140–2
  see also treaties
states, governing relations
  between 80
UK, relationship with 134–6
waste management 635–7
International Law Commission
  development of law, role in 149
  drafting of treaties, role in 149
international trade
  environment, effect on 158–64
  international environmental
    law, precedence of 163–4
  national measures
    hindering 158
  process controls 158
  regulation of 158
  Shrimp/Turtle dispute 160–1
  Tuna/Dolphin dispute 159–60
International Union for the
  Conservation of Nature
  influence of 149
  members and status 149
Irish Sea
  Sellafield, discharges
    from 153–4

J

judicial review
  access to justice, enhancing 314
  alternative remedies 319–20
  collateral challenge 319–20
  costs 320–1
  delay in bringing case 317–19
  grounds of 313–14
  human rights remedy, overlap
    with 314
  merits of case, no consideration
    of 322
  planning decisions, of 420

prejudice, showing 322
prompt action for relief 317–19
public bodies, accountability
  of 313
standing
  Attorney General, of 317
  basis of law 314–15
  environment, interest in 315
  general environmental
    interest groups, of 316–17
  proximity 315
  public interest 315
  representational 316–17
  sufficient interest 315
statutory right of appeal,
  adequacy of 320
time, running of 318
usefulness of 320–1
justice
environmental, access to 313
Environmental Court,
  proposals for 323–5

L

landfill
Directive 607, 640–1
landfill tax 667–9
meaning 609
regulations 607–8
sites
  control of 607
  power to close 608
tax 242
  introduction of 613
  waste, definition 613–14
waste acceptance criteria 608
waste management 631, 662–3
landscape management
designations 737–8
effective, components of 731
Environmental Stewardship
  scheme 747
European dimension 733–4
green belts 737
heritage coast 744
international dimension 733–4
moorland 744
Natural England 737
planning system 734–6
protection orders 745
regulatory mechanisms 732–3
subjective nature of 731
urban expansion and
  development, restriction of 731
wind farms 732
law
core subjects 5
different areas, tools in
  environmental context 34

nature of 11–12
rules, as 9
value and culture, affected by 9
litter
environmental problems,
  relevant to 8
local authorities
London, in 121
metropolitan districts, in 121
non-metropolitan areas, in 121
responsibilities of
  air pollution 122
  contaminated land 122
  noise control 122
  public health 122
  sustainable
    development 122–3
  town and country
    planning 121
  waste collection and
    disposal 122
restructuring 121
unitary 121

M

margin of appreciation
human rights, in 72
use of 14
marine pollution
international law 586
MARPOL Convention 587
UNCLOS regime 588
migratory species
protection 139
moorland
management of 744
motor vehicles
emissions form 541
emissions from 536–7
waste management
  offences 604–5

N

National Parks
administrative responsibilities
  for 741–2
authorities 741–2
designation 739–40
development, control of 742–3
development in 736
farms in, prior notification of
  intention to seek grants 746
funding 742
general objectives and
  duties 738–41
management plan 742
number of 739–40
planning authorities 384

provision for 738
responsibility for 739
Sandford principle 739
Scotland, in 741
working environments, as 738
National Parks Commission
Countryside Agency,
  becoming 737
National Rivers Authority
creation 102
enforcement by 268
enforcement policy 278
Environmental Agency,
  integration in 115
national security
environmental permitting
  regime 485
Natura 2000 sites
alternatives 711–12
boundaries 708
conserving 709–18
designation of 705–9
  UK law and policy 708–9
direct effect of
  provisions 714–15
failure to designate, breach of
  obligations 706
favourable conservation
  status 717
management of 709–18
overall coherence,
  compensatory
  measures 712–14
priority sites 714
significant disturbance
  of 710–11
special areas of
  conservation 706–8
  exclusion of area from,
    judicial review of
    decisions 708
  UK law and policy 708–9
special protection areas
  705–6
UK implementation of
  provisions 715–17
Natural England
landscape designations 737–8
responsibility of 737
role of 113, 120–1
statutory remit 687
natural resources
proper management of 749
Nature Conservancy Council
pollution control authorities,
  separation from 24–5
splitting up 686–7
nature conservation
agencies 686–7

nature conservation (*cont.*)
  biodiversity duties, general 688
  commercial certainty,
    importance of 682
  cumulative impact of
    decisions 710–11
  current policy 684
  early controls 683
  European marine sites 718
  future developments 727
  future directions and
    challenges 684
  habitats
    Directive 704
    EC law 704–19
    European sites 717–18
    key sites, designation of 685
    national law 688–704
    Natura 2000 *see*
      Natura 2000 sites
    permanent ban on
      operations 717
    priorities for 719
    regulations 717–18
    UK implementation of
      provisions 715–17
  history of 682–4
  human influence 685
  incidental protection 686
  individual animals and plants,
    protection of 685
    common law, limitations
      of 719
    conservation,
      furthering 719–20
    cruelty, prevention
      of 719–20
    statutory 719–20
    wildlife crime,
      enforcing 725–6
  integration 685–6
  integrative approaches 726–7
  interests, buying out 700
  landowners' rights, conflict
    with 686
  management
    agreements 700–2
  Marine Nature
    Reserves 689–90
  National Nature Reserves
    designation 689
    meaning 689
    Sites of Special Scientific
      Interest compared 688
  Nature Conservancy body 683
  Planning Policy Guidance
    Note 9
  Planning Policy Statement 699
  population dynamics 686

post-war period, in 683–4
precautionary approach 682
reasons for 681–2
reorganisation of
  organisations 686–7
scientific study, for 681
Sites of Special Scientific
  Interest *see* Sites of Special
  Scientific Interest
soft law moves 682
spatial dimensions 682
species conservation offences
  defences 723–4
  EC law, in 721–3
  exceptions 723–5
  lawful operations, incidental
    results of 725
  licensing 723–5
  national law, in 720–1
  penalties 725–6
value of species 681
voluntary organisations 683
water pollution, overlapping
  controls 623
nature reserves
  voluntary bodies 19
negligence
  damage, causing 343
  environmental damage, failure
    to warn 343–4
  fault-based, being 343
  material contribution to
    damage 354
  pollution, use to control 343
  principles of 343
  time limit for claim 343
noise
  local authorities, role of 122
non-compliance
  costs of 38–9
non-departmental public bodies
  role of 112
non-governmental organizations
  compliance, role as to 149–50
  diversity of 123
  environmental administration,
    role in 98, 123–5
  environmental, list of 124
  environmental and other
    interests, representing 149
  implementation and
    enforcement of law, role
    in 125
  law, influence on 125
Norfolk and Suffolk Broads
  development in 736
North Sea
  International Conferences for
    Protection of 587

international environmental
  regulation, requiring 139
Northern Ireland
  environmental
    administration 99–101
  environmental enforcement
    in 276
  planning authorities 384–5
  regulatory agencies 115
  water quality 585–6
nuclear installations
  statutory civil liability 361
nuclear tests
  attempts to stop 138
nuisance
  development of law of 19
  natural 344–5
  planning permission, effect of
    defence of statutory
      authority, equivalent
      to 388–9
    public law challenge to 358
    public nuisance following
      grant 358
  private
    balancing factors 333–7
    basis for claim 332–3
    claimant coming to 338–9
    claimant, person
      being 337–8
    claimant's use of land,
      relevance of 334–5
    concern of 332
    damage to and interference
      with enjoyment of
      property 333–4
    defences to claim 338–40
    fault, relevance of 335–6
    isolated incidents 334
    locality doctrine 333–4
    nature, duration and
      intensity of 334
    persons liable for 337–8
    prescription 338
    proprietary rights,
      protection of 332
    public benefit of
      activity 336–7
    statutory authority, defence
      of 339
    victim test 338
  proprietary interest, claim
    requiring 355
  public 340–1
    planning permission,
      following grant of 358
  sewage flooding, repeated
    incidents of 345
  statutory *see* statutory nuisance

unnatural 375–7 *see also*
Rylands v Fletcher, rule in

O

obligations *erga omnes*
  meaning 138
Office of the Deputy Prime
  Minister
  role of 110
oil pollution
  compensation for 361–2
  MARPOL Convention 587
  spills, cleaning up 33
  statutory civil liability 361–2
Ombudsman
  complaint to 322
ozone layer
  Vienna Convention 518–19

P

packaging waste
  waste management 641, 669
Parliamentary Commissioner for
  Administration
  complaint to 322
PCBs
  waste management 642
planning *see* town and country
  planning
planning application
  appeals process 405
  applicant
    person being 401
    steps taken by 402
  consultations 402
  courts, role of 405
  determination of
    alternatives, consideration
      of 407–8
    development plan,
      presumption in favour
      of 405–6
    environmental
      considerations 409
    human rights
      considerations 408
    material
      considerations 406–8
    separate planning objective,
      achievement of 409
  discretion, control of 405
  fees for 402
  form 401
  local planning authority
    decision by 404
    steps taken by 402
  major infrastructure projects,
    for 403

publicity 402–3
publicity for 402
regional assemblies, role of 403
Secretary of State
  calling in 403
  role of 405–6
third parties, rights of 404
planning permission
  appeals
    procedure 420–1
    public hearing, right
      to 420–1
    rehearing, as 420–1
    right of 420
  application for *see* planning
    application
  Article 4 direction 736
  automatic grant of 378
  conditional, grant of 404
  conditions
    application for discharge
      of 472
    breach of condition
      notice 421–2
    discretion as to 410
    environmental protection,
      for 413–14
    fair and reasonable 411
    geographic and function link
      to application site 411,
      412
    imposition of 411
    overlapping 413
    perverse 412
    policy on 412–13
    pollution control,
      significance for 413–14
    ulterior motive, for 411
    uncertain 411
    validity of 411–12
    waste management 672
  defence of statutory authority,
    equivalent to 358–9
  design criteria 736
  development of land, required
    for 393
    see also development
  environmental impact
    assessment *see*
    environmental impact
    assessment
  environmental planning
    gain 414, 419
  exemption from need to apply
    for
    activities not constituting
      development 396
    existing uses, carrying
      on 397

Use Classes Order 396–7
future developments 426–7
General Development
  Orders 378, 398
grant of 405
judicial review of decisions 420
local authorities granting to
  themselves 400
mineral extraction, for 445–6
modification 425
outline 403
planning obligations and
  contributions
  case law 417–18
  environmental 414–16, 419
  existing building or use,
    removal of 425
  lawful scope of 417–18
  material consideration,
    as 416
  policy and practice 418–19
  positive or negative 415
  power to enter into 414–15
  statutory provisions 415–16
  systems concerning 418
  waste management 672
public law challenge to 358–9
relaxation of need for 393
reserved matters, challenge at
  stage of 463
Secretary of State's decision,
  challenging 421
Sites of Special Scientific
  Interest, for operations
  on 699–700
statute, granted by
  automatic 398
  Crown and government
    departments, land of 401
  enterprise zones,
    development in 398–9
  General Development
    Orders 378, 398
  government department,
    development authorized
    by 400
  Local Development
    Orders 400
  private or hybrid Acts 400
  simplified planning zone,
    in 399
  special cases 400–1
  Special Development
    Orders 398–9
temporary 411
trees, provision for 749
types of 403
whether required,
  ascertaining 402

plants
  harmful movements, control
    of 685
  nature conservation *see* nature
    conservation
  species conservation offences
    defences 723–4
    EC law, in 721–3
    exceptions 723–5
    lawful operations, incidental
      results of 725
    licensing 723–5
    national law, in 721
    penalties 725–6
pollution
  air, *see* air pollution
  claimant's use of land,
    relevance of 334–5
  context, importance of 238
  control
    command and control,
      features of 25, 34
    focus of law 22
    gradualism 222
    information, availability
      of 337
    institutional coherence 24
    standards 235
  corporate liability for 265–6
  credits, market in 243
  definition 12
  diffuse, tackling 31
  early controls, legacy of 20
  EC reduction obligations 206
  EC reduction programmes,
    compliance with 204–6
  enforcement of law
    approach to 272
    licences and authorizations,
      variation or revocation
      of 272
  integrated control *see*
    Integrated Pollution
    Prevention and Control
  integrative laws 24
  judicial attitudes, change
    in 43–4
  level of 12
  material change of use of land
    or buildings as 394–6
  materials or processes, charges
    levied on 242
  medieval statutes 17
  negligence, claims in 342–3
  new standards, adaptation
    to 32
  nuisance, claim in
    private 332
    see also nuisance

public 340–1
offences 248–9
  fines 282
  naming and shaming
    offenders 285–6
  see also environmental crime
oil *see* oil pollution
planning conditions,
  significance of 413–14
polluter pays principle 55,
    244–5
  contaminated land 564
  strict liability, according
    with 263
right to respect for private and
  family life, effect on 330–2
rivers, of, Royal
  Commission 17–18
second generation policy 29
shared responsibility 31–2
transboundary, impact on
  other state 139
trespass, action in 341–2
waste, as 29
water *see* water pollution
polychlorinated triphenyls
  waste management 642
precautionary principle
  application in practice 70–1
  assessment of risks, reliance on
    science 71
  basis of 54
  conventions interpreting 65
  European law, in 67–9
  generally 54
  individual decision-making,
    impact on 70
  international disputes, in 65–7
  international law, in 65–7
  interpretations of 64
  public controversy, areas of 65
  rules involving 70
  standards 71
  UK law, in 69–70
  weak form of 69
principles
  actions and decisions,
    guiding 80
  characteristics of 80
  environmental *see*
    environmental principles
  environmental problems,
    addressing 81
private law claims
  breach of statutory duty 348–9
  civil law remedies
    common law 349
    damages 351–2
    effective 349

injunctions 350
positive and negative
  features 349
contractual agreements,
  under 349
EC developments 363–5
environmental liability,
  overlapping and competing
  functions 329–30
environmental protection, for
  costs of 355–6
fault-based system, as 354
future of 356–7
imprecise of unduly
  absolute standards, based
  on 353–4
private interests, protection
  of 352–3
proof, problems of 354
reactive controls 355
right to bring claim 353
human rights law, role
  of 330–2
liability provisions,
  overlapping and competing
  functions 329–30
limitation of controls 359–60
negligence 342–3
nuisance, in
  natural 344–5
  private 332
  see also nuisance
  public 340–1
  unnatural 375–7 *see also*
    Rylands v Fletcher, rule in
property ownership, stemming
  from 348–9
public law controls,
  co-existence with 357–60
public regulation, conflict
  with 357–60
riparian rights, protection
  of 348
statutory civil liability
  nuclear installations 361
  oil spills 361–2
trespass 341–2
product liability
  environmental problems,
    relevant to 8
property
  environmental problems,
    reduction of 33
property law
  environmental ends, use for 10
  private law claims 348–9
public health
  early laws 18
  local authorities, role of 122

public participation
    Aarhus Convention 311
    Agriculture and Biotechnology
        Commission 312
    arguments for 294
    basic principle, development
        of 294
    benefits of 294–5
    decision-making, in 337–8
    deliberative 312
    development plans, in 391–2
    EIA Directive 313
    environmental impact
        assessment, in 460
    influence on law, policies
        and individual decisions,
        attempting 312
    information see environmental
        information
    legal force, degrees of 312
    nature of 294–5
    pluralistic 311
    procedural framework 313
    public understanding, need
        for 294
    quality of 313
    Rio Declaration, recognition of
        importance in 294
    stakeholder 312
    types of 311–13

R

radioactive discharges
    water pollution, overlapping
        controls 622
radioactivity
    environmental problems,
        relevant to 8
recycling
    waste management 655–6
Regional Development Agencies
    creation of 101
regulatory agencies
    amalgamation 115
    enforcement by 268–71
    main, list of 113–14
    Northern Ireland, in 115
    Scotland, in 114
rights
    actions and decisions,
        guiding 81
    broad strands of 14
    environment, of 14
    environmental law, in 13–15
    environmental problems,
        addressing 81
    human interests,
        protecting 14–15
    language of 13

meaning 13
riparian rights
    nature of 624
    protection of 348, 624
    unreasonable interference
        with 624
risk
    acceptable level of 68
    environment and health, to 47–8
    environmental, approach
        to 47–8
Risk Society
    development of 295
rivers
    management of 594
    phosphate levels 581
    pollution, Royal
        Commission 17–18
    regulation catchment
        approach 18–19
    riparian rights 348, 624
    Rivers Pollution Prevention
        Act 19
road traffic
    management and planning
        powers 540
Royal Commission on
    Environmental Pollution
    remit 110–11
    reports 111–12
    standing Commission, as 110
Rylands v Fletcher, rule in
    dangerousness of activity 347
    defences 348
    escape, meaning 347
    establishment of 345–6
    extraordinary use of
        land 346–7
    interest in land, claimant
        having 347
    non-natural use of land 346–7
    principle 345–6

S

science
    environmental law, relationship
        with 47
Scotland
    environmental
        administration 99–101
    environmental enforcement
        in 276
    National Parks 741
    planning authorities 384
    regulatory agencies 114
    Scottish Environment
        Protection Agency 585
    Scottish Natural Heritage 121,
        686

waste exemptions 100
    water quality 585
Scottish Enterprise
    remit 101
Scottish Environment Protection
    Agency 102, 276, 585
sewage
    disposal
        cost of 37
        trade effluent see trade effluent
    flooding, repeated incidents
        of 345
    industrial towns, removal
        from 18
    rivers, in 18
    sludge, marine disposal of 27
    works, discharges from 609
sewerage
    discharges to sewers, charges
        for 241
sewerage services
    charges for 596–7
    discharge consents 601–2
sewerage undertakers
    role of 120
    trade effluent consents see trade
        effluent
simplified planning zone
    development in 399
Sites of Special Scientific Interest
    boundaries, defining 694
    conservation interests, buying
        out 70
    designation 688
        restrictive effect of 695
    destruction or damage, offence
        of 703
    evolution of law 690–1
    general public, duties to 703–4
    geological 690
    human rights law, and 693
    loss and damage, suffering 691
    management notices 697–8
    management schemes, securing
        compliance with 697–8
    National Nature Reserves
        compared 688
    national series of 690
    notifying 891–5
    number of 89
    ongoing problems with 697–8
    operations on
        consents, time-limited 696
        defences 698–9
        harmful activities,
            prevention of 702
        likely to cause damage 696
        permanent ban on 717
        planning permission
            for 699–700

Sites of Special Scientific Interest
(*cont.*)
    public bodies, duties
        of 702–3
    statutory undertakers,
        by 699, 702
    owners and occupiers, duties
        of 695–6
    peat moors, designation 700
    policy of law 704
    prospective threats to 696–7
    public bodies, duties of 702–3
    temporary, species being 695
smog
    controls 20
smoke
    abatement, bodies 19
    Beaver Commission 513
    control of 513
        powers, use of 540
sources of environmental law
    administrative appeals 95
    case law 94–5
    characteristics and
        functions 80
    diversity of 223
    European Community 177–81
    European law 80–2
    growth in 26
    international
        custom 142
        declarations 143
        generally recognized
            principles of law 143
        hard law 139–42
        international jurists, work
            of 143
        judicial decisions 143
        principles 143–4
        recommendations 144
        soft law 143–5
        standards 144–5
        treaties 140–2
        see also treaties
    international law 79–80
    layers of 82–3
    legislation
        characteristics of 89–92
        primary 85
        secondary 86–7
        tertiary 87–9
    national law 84, 84–5
    quasi-judicial decisions 95
    regulations 86
        detailed categories 86
        European obligations,
            transposing 87
        procedural 86
        standards, types of 87

rules and guidance
    consistency and
        transparency in decision-
        making, structuring 88
    discretion, structuring 88
    formal legislation,
        supplementing 88
    informal 87
    persuasive status 89
    procedure or technical
        matters, on 88
    statements of regulatory
        policy and practice 87–8
    statutory provisions,
        interpretation of 87
    uncertainty and confusion
        as to 88
standards
    ambient 229–30
    breach of 452
    Britain and EC, differences
        in 250–1
    characteristics of 233
    contaminated land, for 560–1
    emission 214
        definition 230
        examples 231
        locally set 234
        strengths and weaknesses
            of 233–5
        uniform, centrally set 234
        variable 234
        Water Framework
            Directive 236
    enforcement 225
    environmental quality
        definition 229–30
        effect of target, concentrating
            on 229
        examples 230
        imprecise and precise 229
        limitations 234
        objectives, as 234
        parameters 229
        strengths and weaknesses
            of 233–5
    European wide 236
    flexible, move away from 239
    individual situations,
        application to 226
    interrelationship of 232–3
    law, in 229–32
    maintenance of 260
    management 245–6
    pollution control, for 236, 237
    practical application 252
    process
        examples of 231
        imposition of 231

        strengths and weaknesses
            of 234
    product
        definition 231
        examples 232
        strengths and weaknesses
            of 235
    setting 225
    strengths and weaknesses
        of 233–5
    target 229–30
    use, examples of 232
statutory nuisance
    control of 360
    development of 360
    history of 360
    inspection of areas for 360
    noise *see* noise
    retention of law of 20
    water pollution, overlapping
        controls 622
strategic environmental
    assessment
    alternatives, consideration
        of 471
    development 472
    Directive 440
        adoption of 469
        regulations
            implementing 469
    environmental impact
        assessment, link with 471
    environmental report 471
    extent of proposals 469
    information gathering by 432
    meaning 432
    need for 468–72
    plan or programme for which
        required 469–71
    procedural mechanism, as 433
strict liability
    environmental crime, for
        arguments for 261–3
        defence, without 263
        deterrence, for 261–2
        due diligence defence,
            proposal for 263, 263–4
        efficiency and ease of
            prosecution 262–3
        negligence or fault, not need
            to prove 260
        polluter pays principle,
            according with 263
        public interest, goal of 261
        risk management,
            encouraging 261–2
sustainable development
    achieving in practice 61–3
    central concept of 27–8

Commission 61
concept of 56–7
contaminated land, standards
    for 560–1
economic growth, commitment
    to 29
environmental principle, as 54,
    55
EU Strategy 185
European law and policy,
    in 58–9
fairness, assessment of 63
goal of 57
government, in 106
intergenerational equity 63
international law, in 57–8
legal and policy instrument,
    as 57–61
local authorities, duties
    of 122–3
meaning 56–7
Ministerial Sub-Committee on
    Sustainable Development in
    Government 106
needs, definition of 61–2
origin 57
precautionary principle
    compared 69
priorities for action 60
provision of environmental
    information, link with 295
solution or sham, as 28–9
technology, role of 62–3
UK law, in 28
UK law and policy, in 59–61
weak v strong versions of 61
World Summit on Sustainable
    Development (Johannesburg
    Summit) 148–9
World Trade Organization,
    promotion by 158

T

titanium dioxide
    waste management 642
town and country planning
    anticipatory control
        system 227
    application, see planning
        application
    breach of law 421–2
    building controls, and 375
    centralization of system 380
    control, history of 18
    countryside, development
        control in 734–6
    courts, role of 377, 380–1
    decentralization 380

decisions, legalistic nature
    of 381
development see development
development plans
    accountability 391
    challenging 390, 392
    changes in system 385–6
    consultation and
        participation 391–2
    environmental
        critique 392–3
    forward planning by 385–93
    permissive, being 385
    Planning and Compulsory
        Purchase Act 2004,
        changes under 386–92
    purpose of 385
    Secretary of State, role
        of 389–90
    starting point for decisions,
        as 384
    status of 386
    sustainability 390–1
    tiers of 386–7
    zoning ordinances, and 385
discontinuance order 425
enforcement
    appeals 422–3
    breach of condition
        notice 421–2
    discretion 423–4
    enforcement notice 422
    immunity from 422
    injunctions 422
    notices 421–2
    planning contravention
        notice 422
    stop notice 422
    time limits 422
    under enforcement 424
environmental policy, as tool
    of 374–5
environmental projects 228
environmental protection,
    and 376
    emphasis on 382
environmental risk regulation,
    role in 425–6
future developments 426–7
hazardous substances, control
    of 425–6
history of system 377–8, 734
ideologies of 378
land use, control of air
    pollution by 541
landscape management,
    provision for 734–6
legislation 377–8
    discretion in 225

local authorities, role of 121
Local Development Documents
    accountability 391
    basic approach 388
    consultation and
        participation 391–2
    guidance 388
    Local Development Scheme,
        under 388
    non-statutory 389
    preparation of 388–9
    sustainability 390–1
local planning authority, remit
    of 227
main features 373–4
major infrastructure projects,
    decisions on 381–2, 403
meaning 378–82
negotiative process, as 375
no breach of law, powers
    on 425
obligations, nature of 349
permission see planning
    permission
planning authorities
    local authorities 384
    national parks, in 384
    Northern Ireland, in 384–5
    Scotland, in 384
    Wales, in 384
Planning and Compulsory
    Purchase Act 2004, changes
    under 381–2, 386–92
policy
    centrality of 380
    Secretary of State, role
        of 380
political decision-making
    system, as 376
positive management, shift
    to 381
private agreements 247–8
private law, shortcomings
    of 376
public law nature of 381
regional spatial strategies
    national policy, giving effect
        to 388
    requirement of 388
    Secretary of State, role
        of 388, 390
    upper tier of development
        planning, as 386
scope of law 375
scope of 378
Secretary of State, role of 380
Supplementary Planning
    Documents 489
waste management

town and country planning (*cont.*)
administration of waste
planning 671
development control 671–2
development plans 671
issues 671
planning conditions ad
obligations 672
water pollution, overlapping
controls 621–2
trade effluent
water pollution from 598–9
Treasury
responsibilities 103, 105
treaties
coming into force 141–2
conformity of national law
with 136
effective, making 154–8
enforcement 149
environment, relating to 140
financial aspects,
administration of 155
implementation and
monitoring 155
implementing legislation,
relationship with 136
individual states, advocated
by 149
International Law Commission,
role of 149
national law, becoming part
of 135
non-compliance, cross-
checking 156
non-compliant states, trade
restrictions against 157–8
non-state actors,
involving 156–7
parties to 154–5
positive assistance 155
ratification 142
success of 142
terminology 140
Vienna Convention, basic rules
in 140
tree preservation orders
change, proposals for 755
consent for works 753
considerations 749–50
enforcement notices 754
felling licences 756–7
interim 751
making, responsibility
for 750–1
meaning 749–50
offences 750
defences 751–3
provisional 751

refusal of consent,
compensation for 754–5
replacement of trees covered
by 753–4
responsibility for 742
specified trees, on 750
tree, meaning 751
works permitted in 751–2
trees 749, 751, 754
see also forestry; tree
preservation orders
trespass
air-borne pollution, by 341
deer hunting, use of law to
hamper 341
direct interference with
land 342
injunction, basis for 342
intentional 342
justified 342
meaning 341
negligent 342–4

U

UN Conference on the
Environment and Development
(Rio Conference)
legal texts emerging from 147
Rio Declaration 147–8
UN Conference on the Human
Environment (Stockholm
Conference)
Action Plan following 146
Stockholm Declaration 146,
147
UN Environment Programme
establishment of 146
role of 149
treaty-making, approach
to 149

V

values
balancing 47
bodies regulated,
influencing 45–6
characterization of 36
definition 42–3
environmental issues,
perspectives on
economic 50, 50–1, 52
environmental 49–50, 52
meaning 49
practice, in 52–3
rule-making 49
scientific 52, 53
social and cultural 51–2, 53
ethics 43

ethics, and 36
human rights, and 71–2
individual decision-making,
influencing 45
interaction with law 43–6
interpretation and enforcement
of law, influencing 44
legitimacy of laws, assisting
with 46
meaning 36
moral judgements 42
new policy and law,
triggering 43
shifts in 46

W

Wales
Countryside Council for
Wales 121, 686
environmental
administration 99–101
planning authorities 384
Tir Gofal scheme 747
water quality 585
waste
brokers 612–13
carriage of 611–12
clean-up powers 607
collection and disposal 122
controlled
carriage of 611–12
keeping, treating or disposal
of 603–4
removal, power to
require 607
dangerous disposal of 606
definition
landfill tax, for 613–14
waste management 644–5
duty of care 609–11
fly-tipping 606
imports, ban on 202
land, contaminating 554
land, spreading on 597–8
landfill *see* landfill
management *see* waste
management
minimization 30
offences, custodial
sentences 283
recycling credits 243
watercourses, in 18
waste management
Amber list waste 636
appeals 602
Basel Convention 635–6
batteries and accumulators 642
brokers, waste 667
carriage of waste 666

challenges facing 632–3
civil liability for unlawful
disposal 673–4
clean-up powers 661–2
contaminated land 672
Control of Pollution Act 1974
633–4
controlled waste 652
dangerous disposal of
waste 661
defences 660–1
Directive waste 645–52
diversity of law 634
domestic policy 642–4
duty of care 609–11, 664–5
economic instruments 667–70
electrical and electronic
equipment 641, 670
end-of-life vehicles 641,
669–70
enforcement powers 598–602
environmental permitting
regime 634–5, 656–7
European law
basis 637, 638
batteries and
accumulators 642
electrical and electronic
equipment 641
end-of-life vehicles 641
Framework Directive on
Waste 639–40
Hazardous Waste
Directive 640
Landfill Directive 640–1
list of wastes 639–40
oils, waste 642
packaging waste 641
PCBs 642
policy 637–9
polychlorinated
triphenyls 642
producer responsibility 641
titanium dioxide 642
Waste Framework
Directive 639
waste hierarchy 637–8
Waste Incineration
Directive 640
Framework Directive on
Waste 639–40
future developments 675
greater emphasis on 634
Green list waste 636
hazardous waste 652–3
consignment notes 653
notification 653
offences 653–4
record keeping 653

Hazardous Waste
Directive 640
history of regulation 633–5
integrated controls,
development of 477–8
integrated product policy 675
international law 635–7
landfill 631, 662–3
Landfill Directive 640–1
landfill tax 667–9
licence
appeals 602
condition, contravening 605
fees and charges 600–1
modification 599
revocation 600
supervision 598
suspension 599–600
meaning of waste 644–5
methods 631–2
nature of problem 631–2
offences 657–60
controlled waste, keeping,
treating or disposal
of 603–4
custodial sentences 615
dangerous disposal of
waste 606
defences 605–6
deposits, as to 603
licence, contravening
condition of 605
number of 603–4
penalty for 605
vehicle ownership, relating
to 604–5
oils, waste 642
packaging waste 641, 669
PCBs 642
planning conditions ad
obligations 672
policy 633–5
polychlorinated triphenyls 642
preventative controls 633
producer responsibility 641
background 669
development 670
electrical and electronic
equipment 670
end-of-life vehicles 669–70
packaging waste 669
public registers of
information 601
recycling 655–6
scale of problem 631–2
Secretary of State, powers
of 601
special waste 652
statutory objectives 642–4

titanium dioxide 642
town and country planning
administration of waste
planning 671
development control 671–2
development plans 671
issues 671
planning conditions ad
obligations 672
transfrontier shipment 635–7
UNCLOS 635
waste authorities 654–5
Waste Incineration
Directive 640
water pollution 673
water pollution, overlapping
controls 621
waste management
environmental permitting
regime 634–5
water
contamination 33
controlled 600
drinking
contaminated 18
legislation 215, 216, 217
litigation on 216–17
quality of 597–8
good status, aim of 31
industry, concerns of 584
pollution see water pollution
quantity, EC legislation
addressing 594
riparian rights, protection
of 348
sector, history of 583–6
Urban Waste Water Treatment
Directive 587
water industry
environmental improvement
schemes 596
finance 596–7
privatization of 214
water pollution
access to information 615–16
accidents 580
agricultural 580
anti-pollution works 616–17
Britain and EC, differing
standards in 236–7
causing or knowingly
permitting, meaning 609–12
common law claims 625
companies, liability of 611–12
contaminated land, from 555,
557–8
control, history of 18
controlled waters 600
damages for 625–6

water pollution (*cont.*)
  diffuse sources, from 619–20
  discharge consents
    appeals 603
    application for 600
    charges 602–3
    conditions 600–1
    holders, liability of 613
    individualized and flexible
      nature of 604
    requirement 600
    revocation 602
    setting 603–4
    sewage, for 601–2
    system 600–3
    variation 602
  discharges
    causing or knowingly
      permitting 599
    controlled waters, into 600
    meaning 599
    selective prohibition 599
  early controls, legacy of 20
  enforcement
    enforcement notices 616–17
    penalties 614–16
    policy 614–16
    powers 616
  European Community law
    Action Programme 589
    Bathing Waters
      Directive 589
    directives 589
    emission standard
      approaches 589–90
    full cost recovery
      pricing 594
    fundamental change in 593
    impact, summary of 593
    particular polluting
      activities, Directives
      regulating 592–3
    quality objective
      approaches 591–2
    rivers and lakes,
      management of 594
    Water Framework
      Directive 593–6
  General Quality Assessment
    (GQA) 581
  groundwater, of 606–7, 624–5
  hazardous substances 586–7
  incidents, recording 581
  information, access to 615–16
  injunctions against 623, 626
  intervening causes 611–12
  knowingly permitting 612
  management agreements 34
  natural forces, effect of 611–12

nitrate vulnerable zones 593,
  619–20
offences
  act or default of another, due
    to 611
  aggravating 608
  causing 258
  causing or knowingly
    permitting,
    meaning 609–12
  companies, liability of
    613
  consent holders, liability
    of 613
  consent system, context
    for 607
  defences 608–9
  general 607–8
  judicial attitudes, summary
    of 7613
  knowingly permitting 612
  poisonous, noxious or
    polluting matter, allowing
    to enter controlled
    waters 607–8
  private prosecutions 615–16,
    623
  prosecution policy 614
  scope of liability 610
  sentencing 614–15
  strict liability 615
oil storage requirements 618
overlapping controls
  contaminated land 623
  integrated pollution
    control 621–2
  land use planning
    controls 621–2
  nature conservation 7623
  radioactive discharges 623
  statutory nuisance 622
  waste management 622
particular polluting activities,
  Directives regulating 592
passive causing of 610
paying for 602–3
point sources 581
pollutants
  effect of 580
  forms of 580
  sources of 579–80
precautions against 617–18
preventative powers
  anti-pollution works 616–17
  economic instruments, use
    of 621
  enforcement notices 616–17
  nitrate vulnerable
    zones 619–20

precautionary tools 616–21
  use of 616
  water protection
    zones 618–19
private law controls
  common law claims 625
  groundwater
    pollution 624–5
  private prosecutions 623
  remedies 625–6
  riparian rights 624
  role of 623
registers 615–16
regulatory challenges 581–3
rights, dividing up 584
Rivers Pollution Prevention
  Act 18–19
sampling powers 613–14
Secretary of State, role of 603
Sellafield, from 588
statistics 615
third parties causing 611–12
timeline 583–4
trade effluent, from 598–9
waste management 673
Water Framework
  Directive 236, 237
water protection zones
  618–19
water quality
  biological assessment 581
  classification
    effects of 605–6
    individual waters, of 606
  devolved administrations,
    in 585–6
  drinking water 597–8
  environment, state of 581
  historical assessment 581
  improvement, charges for
    621
  international law 586
  legal controls 585
  measurement 703
  objectives 605–6
  particular purposes, for 582
  policy, style and
    techniques 585
water supply
  charges for 596–7
  clean, provision of 595
watercourse
  dumping of waste in 18
  riparian rights 624
Welsh Development Agency
  remit 101
wildlife
  crime
    custodial sentences 283

enforcing 725–6
responsibility for 269
individual animals and plants,
protection of *see* nature
conservation
trade in *see* Convention on
the International Trade in
Endangered Species
(CITES)
trafficking 685
wind farms

landscape management,
and 732
World Bank
environmental role 150
World Commission on
Environment and Development
(Brundtland Commission)
Brundtland Report ('Our
Common Future') 28, 146–7
sustainable development, idea
of 28–9

World Summit on Sustainable
Development (Johannesburg
Summit)
focus of 148–9
World Trade Organization
Appellate Body 153
Committee on Trade and the
Environment 158
environmental role 150
international trade, regulation
of 158